Literacy for the 21ST Century

A Balanced Approach

Gail E. Tompkins

Custom Edition

Taken from:
Literacy for the 21st Century: A Balanced Approach, Fifth Edition
by Gail E. Tompkins

Custom Publishing

New York   Boston   San Francisco
London   Toronto   Sydney   Tokyo   Singapore   Madrid
Mexico City   Munich   Paris   Cape Town   Hong Kong   Montreal

Images courtesy of PhotoDisc/Getty Images.

Taken from:

Literacy for the 21st Century: A Balanced Approach, Fifth Edition
by Gail E. Tompkins
Copyright © 2010, 2006, 2003, 2001, 1997 by Pearson Education, Inc.
Published by Allyn & Bacon
Boston, MA 02116

This special edition published in cooperation with Pearson Custom Publishing.

10 9 8 7 6 5 4 3

2009220018

DC

**Pearson
Custom Publishing**
is a division of

www.pearsonhighered.com

ISBN 10: 0-558-17236-9
ISBN 13: 978-0-558-17236-7

About the Author

Gail E. Tompkins is Professor *Emerita* at California State University, Fresno. She regularly works with teachers in their kindergarten through eighth-grade classrooms and leads staff-development programs on reading and writing. Dr. Tompkins was inducted into the California Reading Association's Reading Hall of Fame in recognition of her publications and other accomplishments in the field of reading, and she has received the prestigious Provost's Award for Excellence in Teaching at California State University, Fresno. Previously, Dr. Tompkins taught at the University of Oklahoma in Norman, where she received the Regents' Award for Superior Teaching, and at Miami University in Ohio, where she taught at the McGuffey Laboratory School and worked with preservice teachers. She was also an elementary teacher in Virginia for eight years.

Dr. Tompkins is the author of six other books published by Merrill and Allyn & Bacon, imprints of Pearson Education: *Language Arts: Patterns of Practice*, 7th ed. (2009), *Language Arts Essentials* (2006), *Teaching Writing: Balancing Process and Product*, 5th ed. (2008), *50 Literacy Strategies*, 3rd ed. (2009), and two grade-level-specific versions of this text: *Literacy for the 21st Century: Teaching Reading and Writing in Pre-Kindergarten Through Grade 4*, 2nd ed. (2007), and *Literacy for the 21st Century: Teaching Reading and Writing in Grades 4 Through 8* (2004).

During the last three decades, Dr. Tompkins has also worked with kindergarten through college-level writing teachers at two National Writing Project sites. She directed the Oklahoma Writing Project when she taught at the University of Oklahoma, and more recently she was the director of the San Joaquin Valley Writing Project in California, where she initiated a program to encourage teachers to write for publication. Merrill and Allyn & Bacon, imprints of Pearson Education, have published three collections of classroom-tested teaching strategies and lessons written by teachers in the San Joaquin Valley Writing Project: *Teaching Vocabulary: 50 Creative Strategies, Grades 6-12*, 2nd ed. (2008), edited by Gail E. Tompkins and Cathy L. Blanchfield; *50 Ways to Develop Strategic Writers* (2005), also edited by Gail E. Tompkins and Cathy L. Blanchfield; and *Sharing the Pen: Interactive Writing With Young Children* (2004), edited by Gail E. Tompkins and Stephanie Collom.

Brief CONTENTS

CONTENTS

Part 1

Literacy in the 21st Century 1

Chapter 1

Becoming an Effective Teacher of Reading 4

Chapter 2

Teaching the Reading and Writing Processes 38

Part 2

Components of Literacy Development   103

Chapter 5

Cracking the Alphabetic Code   142

Chapter 6

Developing Fluent Readers and Writers   184

Chapter 7

Expanding Students' Knowledge of Words   220

Part 3

Organizing for Literacy Instruction   317

Chapter 10

Organizing for Instruction   320

Part 4

Compendium of Instructional Procedures   426

SPECIAL FEATURES

Assessment Tools

Literacy Portraits: VIEWING GUIDE

MiniLesson

New Literacies

Be Strategic!

Teaching Struggling Readers and Writers

PREFACE

Welcome to *Literacy for the 21st Century: A Balanced Approach*! I invite you to step into my vision for reading and writing instruction in kindergarten through eighth-grade classrooms. In this model school, diverse groups of students meet grade-level standards while becoming confident and thoughtful readers and writers. New technologies are certainly changing what it means to read and write. And today, effective literacy instruction is based on scientific research and classroom-tested approaches. It must also include a focus on developing strategic readers and writers, an increased understanding of how to scaffold English learners, and attention to new literacies that support students' use of technology. Teachers create a classroom climate where literacy flourishes, and differentiate instruction by adjusting their lessons and providing multiple options for learning so that every student can be successful.

My Goals

First and foremost, I've written this text for you. *Literacy for the 21st Century* is meant to serve as a valuable resource that you can take into the classroom with you. As I address the topic of each chapter, I've linked theory and research with classroom practice so that you'll understand what's important to teach, why it's important, and how to teach it effectively. I've featured real teachers throughout the text so you can envision yourself using the classroom practices I recommend. Also, I've compiled step-by-step directions for 40 of the best instructional and assessment activities—including guided reading, K-W-L charts, and running records—in the Compendium of Instructional Procedures, placed at the end of the text for easy access.

With this new edition, I've tried to answer all the questions you might have about teaching reading and writing—about instructional approaches, about English learners, about students who struggle, about using technology to teach reading and writing—and in doing that, to create the most relevant and valuable teacher resource possible. The text continues to balance this presentation of information with authentic classroom vignettes, student artifacts, and new video footage that shows students learning phonics, fluency, vocabulary, comprehension, and writing to help you understand what effective literacy learning in the 21st century really looks like.

Strategic Readers and Writers. You'll notice an increased emphasis on developing strategic readers and writers in this edition. I highlight research findings that can really improve the quality of literacy instruction because I believe that teaching students about reading and writing strategies is that important.

The word *strategies* has two meanings. First, teachers develop a repertoire of instructional procedures called *teaching strategies* that guide students to decode and comprehend what they're reading and to draft and refine their writing; many of them appear in the Compendium of Instructional Procedures at the end of this text. Teachers also teach their students to use *learning strategies* to actively direct their thinking. So, in this edition, I present the strategies that capable readers and writers use to identify unfamiliar words, learn the meanings of vocabulary words, comprehend what they're reading, write compositions, and prepare for high-stakes standardized tests, for example. With this information, you'll be prepared to help your students become capable readers and writers.

Look for features that emphasize and strengthen my goals for developing readers and writers.

 ◆ **Be Strategic!** This feature helps you identify and teach the cognitive and metacognitive strategies that successful readers and writers use.

 ◆ **Nurturing English Learners.** Expanded chapter sections focus on ways to scaffold students who are learning to read and write at the same time they're learning to speak English.

 ◆ **Teaching Struggling Readers and Writers.** Using recommendations drawn from research, this expanded feature explains how to assist students who don't meet grade-level standards.

 ◆ **Chapter 11, Differentiating Instruction.** A new chapter helps you understand how to vary instruction without sacrificing grade-level expectations and provide interventions so that all students can be successful.

> **Be Strategic!**
>
> **Phonemic Awareness Strategies**
>
> As students manipulate sounds orally, they learn to use these two strategies:
> ▶ Blend
> ▶ Segment
>
> Students apply these oral strategies to written language for decoding and spelling words.

Balance

Balance is the key to teaching reading and writing: balancing reading and writing, balancing explicit instruction with genuine application, and balancing assessment and instruction.

Balancing Reading and Writing. This text is unique because it links reading with writing in every chapter. You'll learn that reading and writing are related processes of constructing meaning, and that writing has a dynamic impact on students' reading achievement. These text features highlight this balance:

◆ **Chapter-Opening Vignettes.** As the signature feature of this text, these classroom stories illustrate how effective teachers integrate reading and writing to maximize students' literacy learning.

◆ **Book Lists.** These recommendations simplify your job of locating books to use when teaching about genre, as mentor texts, and as models for writing activities.

◆ **Teaching Struggling Readers and Writers.** This expanded feature provides pivotal information on topics such as fluency, revising, the difficulty of vowels, vocabulary in content-area texts, and comprehension to help students who struggle make real progress in developing literacy competency.

 ◆ **New Literacies.** This new feature describes ways to prepare students for the reading and writing demands of the 21st century's digital information and communication technologies.

New Literacies
Online Games

Students practice phonics and spelling concepts they're learning as they play online games. These interactive games provide opportunities for students to match letters to pictures of objects illustrating their sounds, identify rhymes, sort words according to vowel pattern, and spell words, for example. They provide engaging practice opportunities because the colorful screen displays, sound effects, fast-paced action, and feedback about game performance grab students' attention, maintain their enthusiasm, and scaffold their learning (Chamberlain, 2005; Kinzer, 2005).

Teachers choose games based on concepts they're teaching and students' achievement levels. Teachers preview the games and bookmark those they want to use, and then students use the bookmarks to quickly access the game they'll play at the computer center. They play the games individually or with partners. Because most young children are experienced gameplayers and because many games have tutorial features, teachers don't have to spend much time introducing them, but it's helpful to have a parent-volunteer or older student available to assist when there are problems.

Here are some suggested websites with phonics and spelling games:

Game Goo: Learning That Sticks
www.earobics.com/gamegoo
Visit the Game Goo website to
recognition ph

PBS Kids
www.pbsk
Play games
"Between t
"Word Worl
bet, rhyming

RIF's Readi
www.rif.org/re
Join the Readi
website to play
games at the Ga
Zone and Expres
books and learn r

Scholastic Kids
www.scholastic.co
Check Scholastic's
a word, word scrab
the Big Red Dog a
Homework Hub to cr
using students' spelli

Sesa

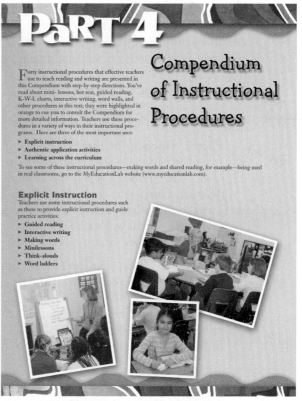

Balancing Explicit Instruction With Authentic Application. The most effective literacy instruction involves a combination of explicit instruction with opportunities to apply what students are learning in genuine reading and writing activities. These text features highlight this balance:

- ◆ **Minilessons.** This popular feature presents clear, concise strategy and skill instruction, ready for you to take right into your classroom.

- ◆ **Compendium of Instructional Procedures.** This valuable resource at the end of the text provides a bank of step-by-step, evidence-based teaching procedures. Look for orange terms in the chapter text that point you to procedures described step-by-step in the Compendium.

- ◆ **New!** **Chapter 10, Organizing for Instruction.** This new chapter condenses the information on basal reader programs, literature focus units, literature circles, and reading and writing workshop that appeared in separate chapters in previous editions. This arrangement makes it easier for you to compare and contrast the four most popular instructional approaches.

- ◆ **Overview of Instructional Approaches.** A special feature in Chapter 10, Organizing for Instruction, highlights the characteristics of basal reader programs, literature focus units, literature circles, and reading and writing workshop.

Balancing Assessment and Instruction. Assessment must drive instruction, a principle I examine in depth in this new edition. You'll learn how to determine students' reading levels and use informal assessment tools and classroom tests to screen students at the beginning of the school year, monitor their progress, diagnose reading difficulties, and document students' learning. These text features highlight this balance:

- ◆ **New!** **Chapter 3, Assessing Students' Literacy Development.** This chapter, placed early in the text, lays the groundwork for assessing students' achievement and for using the results to inform instruction. This chapter also provides critical information about preparing students' for high-stakes achievement tests.

- ◆ **Assessment Tools.** This feature found throughout the text recommends informal classroom tools and specific tests to screen, diagnose, monitor, and document students' progress in reading and writing.

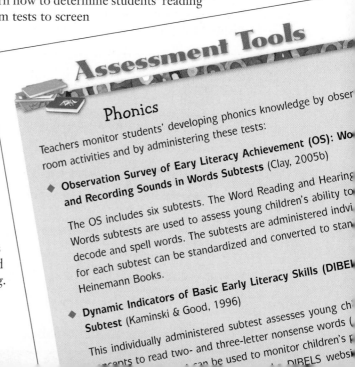

Examine Students' Literacy Development

I want this text to provide you with authentic experiences, grounded in today's multiethnic and multilingual classrooms. I've always incorporated what I've learned throughout the text—in vignettes, student samples, book lists, minilessons, and other features—but for this edition, I've added something special. :You'll see what a year of literacy teaching and learning looks like in a second-grade classroom through features in the text and online. Check these features to learn more about this yearlong documentation of students' literacy learning, and watch the footage on MyEducationLab:

 ◆ **Part 1 Opener.** In the Part 1 opening photo spread on pages 1–3, you'll meet Ms. Janusz, a remarkable second-grade teacher at Worthington Estates Elementary School, outside Columbus, OH, and see how she implements a balanced approach to literacy instruction.

 ◆ **Part 2 Opener.** In the Part 2 opening photo spread on pages, 103–105, you'll meet five students from Ms. Janusz's class—Rhiannon, Rakie, Michael, Curt'Lynn, and Jimmy—who are featured in the online Literacy Portraits that track their reading and writing achievement through their second-grade year.

 ◆ **Literacy Portraits.** The five Literacy Portraits are video case studies with footage showing each student involved in reading and writing activities along with teacher commentary and related work samples. They're available online at MyEducationLab.

 ◆ **Literacy Portraits:** Viewing Guide. You'll find this feature in the text to draw your attention to specific video clips that best illustrate what I'm presenting in a chapter—phonics, fluency, comprehension, and more—as Ms. Janusz nurtures her students' reading and writing development.

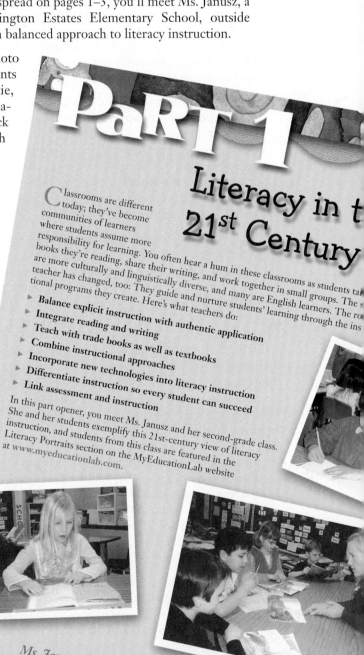

PaRT 1

Literacy in t
21st Century

Classrooms are different today; they've become communities of learners where students assume more responsibility for learning. You often hear a hum in these classrooms as students ta books they're reading, share their writing, and work together in small groups. The s are more culturally and linguistically diverse, and many are English learners. The ro teacher has changed, too: They guide and nurture students' learning through the ins tional programs they create. Here's what teachers do:

▸ Balance explicit instruction with authentic application
▸ Integrate reading and writing
▸ Teach with trade books as well as textbooks
▸ Combine instructional approaches
▸ Incorporate new technologies into literacy instruction
▸ Differentiate instruction so every student can succeed
▸ Link assessment and instruction

In this part opener, you meet Ms. Janusz and her second-grade class. She and her students exemplify this 21st-century view of literacy instruction, and students from this class are featured in the Literacy Portraits section on the MyEducationLab website at www.myeducationlab.com.

Ms. Janusz works to develop her students' abilities to read and rite fluently. She's teaching them to decode and spell words strategies, and focus on meaning when they

---

Literacy Portraits:VIEWING GUIDE

Ms. Janusz's classroom is filled with stories and informational books. She uses these books for instructional purposes, and plenty of books are available for students to read independently. These second graders know about genres. They can identify books representing each genre and talk about the differences between them. Ms. Janusz teaches minilessons on genres and points out the genre of books she's reading aloud. She doesn't call all books "stories." Go to the Literacy Profiles section of the MyEducationLab website and click on Rhiannon's Student Interview to watch her compare fiction and nonfiction. As you listen to Rhiannon, think about the information provided in this chapter. What conclusions can you draw about what Ms. Janusz has taught about text factors? Also, look at other video clips of Rhiannon to see how she applies her knowledge about genres in both reading and writing.

myeducationlab

YOUR Learning Network

The fifth edition of *Literacy for the 21st Century* is more than a textbook; it's one part of a learning network that's been carefully developed to enhance your learning experience. In each chapter, you'll find the theory, research, and classroom practice to prepare you for a lifetime of teaching students to read and write, and you'll also learn the tools to equip you for the job, plus ideas, examples, and mentoring to inspire your own teaching. The second part is MyEducationLab, which provides online resources to further your learning.

Visit MyEducationLab. MyEducationLab, at **www.myeducationlab.com**, is the online part of the learning network designed specifically for this text. This robust website contains video footage, homework and activities, modules for building teaching skills, the Literacy Portraits, and much more! Look for these reminders in each chapter to help you make the most of this valuable online resource:

> **Literacy Portraits: VIEWING GUIDE**
>
> Ms. Janusz uses flexible groups—whole class, small groups, buddies, and individuals—for instruction. Go to the Literacy Profiles section of MyEducationLab and watch these four video clips: Click on Michael's November button to see him reading a poem to the class; Rakie's December button to watch her participate in a guided reading group; Rhiannon's December button to view her reading individually with the teacher; and Curt'Lynn's March button to watch her read with a classmate. As you view these video segments, think about why Ms. Janusz grouped the students as she did. It's not enough to use varied grouping patterns; what matters most is that when students participate in a group, their learning is enhanced. When they set up groups, teachers consider their instructional goal, the activitiy, and group membership. How do you think Ms. Janusz's grouping patterns benefited these students' learning?
>
> **myeducationlab**

- ◆ **Literacy Portraits: Viewing Guide.** This feature throughout the text directs you to video footage on the five students that demonstrates how they're growing as readers and writers.

- ◆ **Margin Notes.** This reminder directs you to Building Teaching Skills and Dispositions activities that help you refine your knowledge and prepare to assess students' reading and writing development.

- ◆ **End-of-Chapter Element.** This feature outlines all the resources on MyEducationLab for you to explore to deepen your understanding of the topics you've been reading about.

Instructor Resource Center. The Instructor Resource Center at www.pearsonhighered.com has a variety of print and media resources available in downloadable, digital format—all in one location. As a registered faculty member, you can access and download pass code-protected resource files, course-management content, and other premium online content directly to your computer.

Digital resources available for *Literacy for the 21st Century: A Balanced Approach*, 5e include the following:

◆ A test bank of multiple choice and essay tests.

◆ PowerPoint presentations specifically designed for each chapter.

◆ Chapter-by-chapter materials, including objectives, suggested readings, discussion questions, and in-class activities, and guidance on how to use the vignettes meaningfully in your instruction.

◆ A MyEducationLab guide to help you make the best use of MyEducationLab in your classes.

To access these items online, go to **www.pearsonhighered.com** and click on the Instructor option. You'll find an Instructor Resource Center option in the top navigation bar. There you will be able to log in or complete a one-time registration for a user name and password. If you have any questions regarding this process or the materials available online, please contact your local Pearson sales representative.

TestGen.   A completely revised test bank also accompanies the text. These multiple-choice and essay questions can be used to assess students' understanding of chapter concepts and their ability to apply what they've read. A computerized version of the test bank (TestGen) is available, along with assessment software, allowing instructors to create and customize exams and track student progress.

ACKNOWLEDGMENTS

Many people helped and encouraged me as I developed and revised this text. My heartfelt thanks go to each of them. First, I want to thank my students over the years at California State University, Fresno, the University of Oklahoma, and Miami University, who taught me while I taught them, and the teacher-consultants in the San Joaquin Valley Writing Project and the Oklahoma Writing Project, who shared their expertise with me. Their insightful questions challenged and broadened my thinking. Thanks, too, go to the teachers who welcomed me into their classrooms, showed me how they created a balanced literacy program, and allowed me to learn from them and their students. In particular, I want to express my appreciation to the teachers and students who appear in the part openers, vignettes, and video clips on MyEducationLab: Rich Abrams, Washington Intermediate School; Eileen Boland, Tenaya Middle School; Whitney Donnelly, Williams Ranch School; Stacy Firpo, Aynesworth Elementary School; Laurie Goodman, Pioneer Middle School; Susanne Hagen, Phoenix Learning Center; Sally Mast, Thomas Elementary School; Susan McCloskey, Greenberg Elementary School; Kristi McNeal, Copper Hills Elementary School; Nicki Paniccia McNeal, Century Elementary School; Jennifer Miller-McColm, Roosevelt Elementary School; Gay Ockey, Hildago Elementary School; Kacey Sanom, John Muir Elementary School; Leah Scheitrum, Jackson Elementary School; Stacy Shasky, Fairmead School; Darcy Williams, Aynesworth Elementary School; and Susan Zumwalt, Jackson Elementary School.

In addition, special thanks to Lisa Janusz, who welcomed us into her second-grade classroom every month while we videotaped her literacy instruction, collected writing samples, and interviewed students. She's a remarkable teacher who uses her knowledge of how children learn to propel her second graders toward high levels of achievement.

I also want to thank the professors and teaching professionals who reviewed my text for their insightful comments that informed my development of this text and this revision: Bonnie Armbruster, University of Illinois at Urbana; Jean Casey, California State University, Long Beach; Beth Cavanaugh, McGraw IB World School; Rosemary Fessinger, University of New Mexico; Kristen Gehsman, St. Michael's College; Amanda Grotting, Sun Valley Elementary; Helen Hoffner, Holy Family University; Leslie Hopping, Columbus Academy; Carolyn Jaynes, California State University, Sacramento; Laura Pardo, Hope College; Kimberly Penn, Dos Rios Elementary School; Molly Sperling, Devonshire Alternative; Dr. Preston Van Loon, Iowa Wesleyan College; and Janet Wicker, McKendree College.

Finally, I want to recognize Jeff Johnston and his remarkable team at Merrill in Columbus, Ohio who have produced so many high-quality publications. I've been honored to be a Merrill author for more than 20 years. Now that Merrill and Allyn and Bacon have been reorganized, I've become an Allyn and Bacon author, and I look forward to many years of working with Paul Smith and his team. Linda Bishop continues to be the guiding force behind my work, and Hope Madden is my cheerleader, encouraging me every step of the way and spurring me toward impossible deadlines. A special thank you to Linda for her inspired idea that led to the Literacy Profiles project in Lisa Janusz's classroom and to Hope for her year-long supervision of the project and expert editing of the video clips. I know it will be an important resource for students and professors at the MyEducationLab website. I want to express my sincere appreciation to Janet Domingo, my most accommodating production editor who has skillfully supervised the production of this book and deftly juggled the last-minute details, and to Melissa Gruzs, who expertly copy-edited my manuscript, addressed my memory lapses and inconsistencies, and proofread my pages. It's because of the entire team's dedication that the text is so good. Thank you!

PART 1

Literacy in the 21st Century

Classrooms are different today; they've become communities of learners where students assume more responsibility for learning. You often hear a hum in these classrooms as students talk about books they're reading, share their writing, and work together in small groups. The students are more culturally and linguistically diverse, and many are English learners. The role of teachers has changed, too: They guide and nurture students' learning through the instructional programs they create. Here's what teachers do:

▶ **Balance explicit instruction with authentic application**

▶ **Integrate reading and writing**

▶ **Teach with trade books as well as textbooks**

▶ **Combine instructional approaches**

▶ **Incorporate new technologies into literacy instruction**

▶ **Differentiate instruction so every student can succeed**

▶ **Link assessment and instruction**

In this part opener, you meet Ms. Janusz and her second-grade class. She and her students exemplify this 21st-century view of literacy instruction, and students from this class are featured in the Literacy Portraits section on the MyEducationLab website at **www.myeducationlab.com**.

Ms. Janusz works to develop her students' abilities to read and write fluently. She's teaching them to decode and spell words, use literacy strategies, and focus on meaning when they're reading and writing.

Students read leveled books with Ms. Janusz in guided reading groups, and she assesses their progress by listening to them read aloud.

The second graders practice the phonics skills that Ms. Janusz is teaching as they do word sorts.

After she shares a trade book, Ms. Janusz often uses it to teach a mini-lesson on a reading or writing strategy or skill.

Visualizing

WIZ GR 00

I make pictures in my mind when I read.

Because the students' reading levels range from first- to fourth-grade, and some students are English learners, Ms. Janusz differentiates instruction. She varies grouping patterns and instructional materials.

During reading workshop, students read "just right" books independently and with buddies.

Ms. Janusz balances explicit instruction with authentic reading and writing in her literacy program. Guided reading is the teaching component and reading and writing workshop are the application activities.

During writing workshop, the second graders draft, conference with Ms. Janusz, and revise and edit their writing with classmates. Later, they publish their books, sometimes using word processing so their writing will look professional.

ChapTer 1

Becoming an Effective Teacher of Reading

Literacy is the ability to use reading and writing for a variety of tasks at school and outside of school. Let's begin with two definitions. *Reading* is a complex process of understanding written text. Readers interpret meaning in a way that's appropriate to the type of text they're reading and their purpose. Similarly, *writing* is a complex process of producing text. Writers create meaning in a way that's appropriate to the type of text and their purpose. Peter Afflerbach (2007) describes reading as a dynamic, strategic, and goal-oriented process. The same is true of writing. *Dynamic* means that readers and writers are actively involved in reading and writing. *Strategic* means that readers and writers consciously monitor their learning. *Goal-oriented* means that reading and writing are purposeful; readers and writers have a plan in mind.

Our concept of what it means to be literate is changing. Traditional definitions of literacy focused on the ability to read words, but now literacy is considered a tool, a means to participate more fully in the technological society of the 21st century. In addition, Kress (2003) and Kist (2005) talk about *new literacies*—sophisticated technological ways to read and write multimodal texts incorporating words, images, and sounds—which provide opportunities for students to create innovative spaces for making meaning, exploring their world, and voicing their lives. These texts often combine varied forms of representation, including computer graphics, video clips, and digital photos.

Students read and write them differently than they do traditional books (Karchmer, Mallette, Kara-Soteriou, & Leu, 2005).

Gambrell, Malloy, and Mazzoni (2007) recommend that teachers develop a vision of what they hope to achieve with the students they teach and then work to accomplish their plans. The goal of literacy instruction is to ensure that all students achieve their full literacy potential, and in that light, this chapter introduces eight principles of balanced literacy instruction. These principles are stated in terms of what effective teachers do, and they provide the foundation for the chapters that follow.

PRINCIPLE 1: EFFECTIVE TEACHERS UNDERSTAND HOW STUDENTS LEARN

Understanding how students learn, and particularly how they learn to read and write, influences the instructional approaches that teachers use. Until the 1960s, behaviorism, a teacher-centered theory, was the dominant view of learning; since then, student-centered theories have become more influential, and literacy instruction has changed to reflect these theories. In the last few years, however, behaviorism has begun a resurgence as evidenced by the federal No Child Left Behind Act, renewed popularity of basal reading programs, current emphasis on curriculum standards, and mandated high-stakes testing. Tracey and Morrow (2006) argue that multiple theoretical perspectives improve the quality of literacy instruction, and the stance presented in this text is that instruction should represent a balance between teacher-centered and student-centered theories. Figure 1–1 presents an overview of the learning theories.

Behaviorism

Behaviorists focus on the observable and measurable aspects of students' behavior. They believe that behavior can be learned or unlearned, and that learning is the result of stimulus-and-response actions (O'Donohue & Kitchener, 1998). Reading is viewed as a conditioned response. This theory is described as teacher centered because it focuses on the teacher's active role as a dispenser of knowledge. Skinner (1974) explained that students learn to read by learning a series of discrete skills and subskills. Teachers use explicit instruction to teach skills in a planned, sequential order. Information is presented in small steps and reinforced through practice activities until students master it because each step is built on the previous one. Students practice skills they're learning by completing fill-in-the-blank worksheets. They usually work individually, not in small groups or with partners. Behavior modification is another key feature: Behaviorists believe that teachers control and motivate students through a combination of rewards and punishments.

Constructivism

The constructivist theory describes students as active and engaged learners who construct their own knowledge. Learning isn't observable because it involves mental

Figure 1–1 ◆ Overview of the Learning Theories

Orientation	Theory	Characteristics	Applications
Teacher-Centered	Behaviorism	• Focuses on observable changes in behavior • Views the teacher's role as providing information and supervising practice • Describes learning as the result of stimulus-response actions • Uses incentives and rewards for motivation	• Basal readers • Minilessons • Repeated readings
Student-Centered	Constructivism	• Describes learning as the active construction of knowledge • Recognizes the importance of background knowledge • Views learners as innately curious • Advocates collaboration, not competition • Suggests ways to engage students so they can be successful	• Literature focus units • K-W-L charts • Reading logs • Thematic units • Word sorts
	Sociolinguistics	• Emphasizes the importance of language and social interaction on learning • Views reading and writing as social and cultural activities • Explains that students learn best through authentic activities • Describes the teacher's role as scaffolding students' learning • Advocates culturally responsive teaching • Challenges students to confront injustices and inequities in society	• Literature circles • Shared reading • Buddy reading • Reading and writing workshop • Author's chair
	Cognitive/Information Processing	• Compares the mind to a computer • Recommends integrating reading and writing • Views reading and writing as meaning-making processes • Explains that readers' interpretations are individualized • Describes students as strategic readers and writers	• Guided reading • Graphic organizers • Grand conversations • Interactive writing • Reciprocal questioning

processes. It occurs when students integrate new knowledge with their existing knowledge. Constructivists believe that learning is what the brain does naturally (Smith, 1971). This theory is student centered. It differs substantially from the behaviorist theory and requires a reexamination of the teacher's role: Instead of being dispensers of knowledge, teachers engage students with experiences so that they construct their own knowledge. This theory has been widely applied to literacy instruction; here are the applications for teaching students to read and write:

◆ Students relate what they know to what they're learning.
◆ Students create their own knowledge.
◆ Motivated students are more successful.

New Literacies
The Internet

The Internet is rapidly changing what it means to be literate. Students are increasingly becoming involved in on-line activities such as these:

- Reading electronic storybooks
- Playing interactive phonics and spelling games
- Crafting multimodal stories
- Posting book reviews
- E-mailing messages
- Researching informational topics
- Exploring the websites of favorite authors
- Participating in virtual book clubs
- Collaborating with students in other schools on projects

These students are excited about literacy because the World Wide Web fosters their motivation and engagement with reading and writing.

Some students learn to surf the Web, locate and read infor-mation, and communicate using e-mail and instant messaging outside of school. Others, however, haven't had as many experi-ences or aren't as successful when they experiment with new technologies. Teaching students how to read and write online has become a priority so that they can become fully literate in today's digital world (Henry, 2006).

Internet texts are different than books (Castek, Bevans-Mangelson, & Goldstone, 2006). Whereas print materials are linear and sequential, online texts are a unique genre with these characteristics:

Nonlinearity. Hypertext lacks the familiar linear organization of books; instead, it's dynamic and can be used in a variety of ways. Readers impose a structure that fits their needs and reconfigure the organization, when necessary.

Multiple Modalities. Online texts are multimodal, inte-grating words, images, and sound to create meaning. Readers need to know how to interpret each mode and how it contributes to the overall meaning.

Intertextuality. Many related texts are available on the Internet, and they influence and shape each other. As students read these texts, they prioritize, evaluate, and synthesize the information being presented.

Interactivity. Webpages often include interactive fea-tures that engage readers and allow them to customize their searches, link to other websites, play games, listen to video clips, and send e-mails.

Because of these features, reading and writing on the Internet require students to become proficient in new ways of accessing, comprehending, and communicating information, which are re-ferred to as *new literacies*. Four Internet reading strategies are navigating, coauthoring, evaluating, and synthesizing: Students navigate the Internet to search for and locate information; coau-thor online texts as they impose an organization on the informa-tion they're reading; evaluate the accuracy, relevance, and quality of information on webpages; and synthesize information from multiple texts (Castek, Bevans-Mangelson, & Goldstone, 2006; Leu, Kinzer, Coiro, & Cammack, 2004).

Writing online differs from using paper and pencil, too. It's more informal, although messages should be grammatically acceptable and use conventional spelling like other types of writing. Immediacy is another difference: Within seconds, writ-ers post their writing or send brief messages back and forth. Third, writers create multimodal messages by adding photos, video clips, and website links. The fourth difference is audience: Writers send e-mail messages to people in distant locations, in-cluding military parents serving in Iraq, and their postings can be read by people worldwide.

The Internet requires students to develop new ways of read-ing and writing. Literacy in the 21st century involves more than teaching students to read books and write using paper and pencil; it's essential that teachers prepare their students to use the Internet and other information communication technologies successfully (Karchmer, Mallette, Kara-Soteriou, & Leu, 2005).

Students Relate What They Know to What They're Learning. Students' knowledge is organized into cognitive structures called *schemas*, and schema theory describes the processes students use to learn. Jean Piaget (1969) explained that learning is the modification of students' schemas as they actively interact with their environment. Imagine that the brain is a mental filing cabinet, and that new information is organized with existing knowledge in the filing system. When students already know something about a topic, the new information is added to that mental file, or schema, in a revision process Piaget called *assimilation*, and when students begin learning about a completely new topic, they create a mental file and place the new information in it. Piaget called this more difficult construction process *accommodation*. Everyone's cognitive structure is different, reflecting existing knowledge and prior experiences, so when students read a novel set in India or revise a rough draft, some students are likely to be more successful than others. The more students already know about a topic, the easier it is for them to assimilate new information.

Students Create Their Own Knowledge. John Dewey, one of the first American constructivists, advocated an inquiry approach to develop citizens who could participate fully in our democracy (Tracey & Morrow, 2006). He believed that students are innately curious and actively create their own knowledge. Collaboration, not competition, is more conducive to learning, according to Dewey. Through the inquiry process, students collaborate to conduct investigations in which they ask questions, seek information, create new knowledge to solve problems, and reflect on their learning.

Motivated Students Are More Successful. Engagement theory examines students' motivation and interest in reading and writing to suggest ways to nurture students' engagement, because students who are engaged are intrinsically motivated, do more reading and writing, enjoy these activities, and have higher achievement (Guthrie & Wigfield, 2000). Engaged students have self-efficacy, the belief in their capability to succeed and reach their goals (Bandura, 1997). They have high aspirations and are more likely to be successful, and each success builds their feelings of self-efficacy. Students with high self-efficacy are resilient and persistent, despite obstacles and challenges that get in the way of success. These theorists report that students are more engaged when they participate in authentic reading and writing activities and when they collaborate with classmates in a nurturing community of learners.

Sociolinguistics

As the theory's name suggests, sociolinguists recognize the importance of language and social interaction in learning. They believe that oral language provides the foundation for learning to read and write (Snow, Burns, & Griffin, 1998). Probably the best-known sociolinguist is Lev Vygotsky (1978, 1986), who theorized that language helps to organize thought and that students use language to learn as well as to communicate and share experiences with others. Understanding that students use language for social purposes allows teachers to plan instructional activities that incorporate a social component, such as having students work in small groups, talk about books they're reading, and share their writing with classmates.

Social interaction enhances learning in two other ways: scaffolding and the zone of proximal development (Dixon-Krauss, 1996). Scaffolding is a support mechanism that teachers use as they teach. Vygotsky suggested that students can accomplish more difficult tasks in collaboration with adults than on their own. For example, when teachers assist students in reading a book they couldn't read independently or help students revise a piece of writing, they are scaffolding. Vygotsky also suggested that students learn very little when they perform tasks that they can already do independently; he recommended the zone of proximal development, the range of tasks between students' actual developmental level and their potential development. More-challenging tasks done with the teacher's scaffolding are more conducive to learning. As students learn, teachers gradually withdraw their support so that students eventually perform the task independently. Then the cycle begins again. Sociolinguistic theory is applied in these ways for reading and writing instruction:

- ◆ Culturally responsive teaching empowers students.
- ◆ Students learn through authentic literacy activities.
- ◆ Students use literacy to challenge injustices and inequities.

Culturally Responsive Teaching Empowers Students. The sociocultural theory adds a cultural dimension to our understanding of how students learn: These theorists view reading and writing as social activities that reflect the culture and community in which students live, and they explain that students from different cultures have different expectations about literacy learning and preferred ways of learning (Heath, 1983; Moll & Gonzales, 2004). Teachers apply the sociocultural theory as they create culturally responsive classrooms that empower all students, including those from marginalized groups, to become more successful readers and writers (Gay, 2000). Teachers are respectful of all students and confident in their ability to learn to read and write. Culturally responsive teaching acknowledges the legitimacy of all students' cultures and social customs and teaches students to appreciate their classmates' cultural heritages. Teachers often use books of multicultural literature to develop students' cross-cultural awareness, including *Goin' Somewhere Special* (McKissack, 2001) and *Feathers* (Woodson, 2007), stories describing the African American experience; *Esperanza Rising* (Ryan, 2002) and *The Circuit* (Jiménez, 1999), stories about the Mexican American experience; and *Happy Birthday Mr. Kang* (Roth, 2001) and *Project Mulberry* (Park, 2007), stories portraying the Korean American experience.

In addition, teachers who appreciate the contribution of culture and community to learning are often much more successful in building bridges between home and school. Becoming culturally responsive involves teachers' willingness to examine their instructional practices if they aren't working and to make changes so that all students can be successful (Banks, Cochran-Smith, Moll, Richert, Zeichner, LePage, Darling-Hammond, & Duffy, 2005).

Students Learn Through Authentic Literacy Activities. Situated learning explains that learning is a function of the activity, context, and culture in which it occurs or is situated; it's an extension of the sociocultural theory. Lave and Wenger (1991) contend that learning is contextual, or embedded in the social and physical environment. Two important tenets are that knowledge must be presented in an authentic way and that learning requires social interaction and collaboration. This theory rejects the notion of separating learning to do something and actually doing it and emphasizes the idea of apprenticeship (Brown, Collins, & Duguid, 1989). In an apprenticeship, beginners move from the edge of a learning community to its center as they learn and become more involved within the culture. Eventually the learners reach the center of the community as they become experts. For example, if you want to become a cook, you could go to a cooking school or learn as you work in a restaurant; situated learning suggests that working in a restaurant is more effective.

When applied to literacy, situated learning theory emphasizes that students learn to read and write through authentic reading and writing activities. They join a community of learners in the classroom and become readers and writers through social interaction with classmates. The teacher serves as an expert model, much like a chef does in a restaurant.

Students Use Literacy to Challenge Injustices and Inequities. Pablo Freire (2000) called for a sweeping transformation in education so that students ask fundamental questions about justice and equity. Critical literacy theorists believe that language is a means for social action and advocate that teachers do more than teach students to read and write; students should become agents of social change (McDaniel, 2004; Wink, 2005). This application of sociolinguistics has a political agenda: The increasing social and cultural diversity in American society adds urgency to resolving inequities and injustices.

Luke and Freebody's (1997) model of reading includes critical literacy as the fourth and highest level. I've adapted their model to incorporate both reading and writing:

Code Breakers. Students become code breakers as they learn phonics, word-identification strategies, and high-frequency words that help them learn to read and write fluently.

Text Participants. Students become text participants as they learn about text structures and genres in order to comprehend what they read and as they learn to develop coherent ideas in the texts they write.

Text Users. Students become text users as they read and write multigenre texts and compare the effect of genre and purpose on texts.

Text Critics. Students become text critics as they examine the issues raised in books and other texts they read and write.

One way that teachers help students examine social justice issues is to read and discuss books such as *The Breadwinner* (Ellis, 2000), the story of a girl in Taliban-controlled Afghanistan who pretends to be a boy to support her family; *Pink and Say* (Polacco, 1994), a story about two Civil War soldiers, one white and the other African American, and the heart-wrenching indignities that the African American soldier and his family suffer; and *Homeless Bird* (Whelan, 2000), the story of an Indian girl who has no future when she is widowed. These stories and others listed in Figure 1–2 describe injustices that students can understand and discuss (Lewison, Leland, & Harste, 2008; McLaughlin & De Voogd, 2004). In fact, teachers report that their students are often more engaged in reading about social issues than other books and that their interaction patterns change after reading these stories.

Critical literacy emphasizes students' potential to become thoughtful, active citizens. The reason injustice persists in society, Shannon (1995) hypothesizes, is

---

Figure 1–2 ◆ Books That Foster Critical Literacy

Avi. (1993). *Nothing but the truth*. New York: Avon. (U)
Bunting, E. (1997). *A day's work*. New York: Clarion Books. (P)
Bunting, E. (1999). *Smoky night*. San Diego: Voyager. (P–M)
Curtis, C. P. (2000). *The Watsons go to Birmingham—1963*. New York: Laurel Leaf. (M–U)
Fleischman, P. (2004). *Seedfolks*. New York: Harper-Trophy. (M)
Golenbock, P. (1992). *Teammates*. San Diego: Voyager. (M)
Hesse, K. (2001). *Witness*. New York: Scholastic. (U)

Hiaasen, C. (2006). *Hoot*. New York: Yearling. (M–U)
Hiaasen, C. (2007). *Flush*. New York: Knopf. (M–U)
Lowry, L. (2006). *The giver*. New York: Delacorte. (U)
Ringgold, F. (2003). *If a bus could talk: The story of Rosa Parks*. New York: Aladdin Books. (P–M)
Ryan, P. M. (2002). *Esperanza rising*. New York: Blue Sky Press. (M)
Uchida, Y. (1996). *The bracelet*. New York: Putnam. (P)
Winter, J. (2008). *Wangari's trees of peace: A true story from Africa*. San Diego: Harcourt. (P–M)
Woodson, J. (2001). *The other side*. New York: Putnam. (P)

P = primary grades (K–2); M = middle grades (3–5); U = upper grades (6–8)

because people don't "ask why things are the way they are, who benefits from these conditions, and how can we make them more equitable" (p. 123). Through critical literacy, students become empowered to transform their world (Bomer & Bomer, 2001). They learn social justice concepts, read literature that reflects diverse voices, notice injustices in the world, and use writing to take action for social change.

Cognitive/Information Processing

Two closely aligned theories of learning are cognitive processing and information processing: These theories attempt to explain unobservable mental processes, including reading and writing (Tracey & Morrow, 2006). Readers and writers are described as active learners who use knowledge and strategies to solve problems. These theorists believe that the mind functions like a computer, and they hypothesize that information moves through a series of processing units—sensory register, short-term memory, and long-term memory—as it's processed and stored (Flavell, 1979). There's a control mechanism, too, that oversees learning.

Cognitive/information processing theorists create models of the reading and writing processes, often relying on flow charts to describe the complicated and interactive workings of the mind (Hayes, 2004; Kintsch, 2004; Rumelhart, 2004). They believe in an integrated approach to reading and writing, and their models describe a two-way flow of information between what readers and writers know and the letters and words written on the page. Here are other ways these theories guide literacy instruction:

◆ Reading and writing are meaning-making processes.
◆ Readers' interpretations are individualized.
◆ Readers and writers are strategic.

Reading and Writing Are Meaning-Making Processes. Models of the reading process describe what readers do as they read, and they emphasize that readers focus on comprehension as they read (Ruddell & Unrau, 2004; Rumelhart, 2004; Stanovich, 2000). Readers construct meaning using a combination of text-based information (information from the text) and reader-based information (information from students' background knowledge). In the past, theorists argued over whether students' attention during reading moves from noticing the letters on the page and grouping them into words to making meaning in the brain, or the other way around, from activating background knowledge in the brain to examining letters and words on the page, but they now agree that the two processes take place interactively and simultaneously. The interactive model of reading includes an executive monitor that manages the construction of meaning (Ruddell & Unrau, 2004). This control mechanism monitors students' attention, determines whether what they are reading makes sense, and takes action when problems arise.

Hayes's (2004) model of writing describes what writers do as they write. It emphasizes that writing is a meaning-making process. Students don't write one-shot compositions; instead, they move through a series of stages as they plan, draft, revise, and edit their writing to ensure that readers will understand what they've written. Writers use the same control mechanism that readers do to make plans, select strategies, and solve problems. Writing is a social activity, too, and students turn to classmates and the teacher to share their writing and to get feedback on how well they're communicating.

Readers' Interpretations Are Individualized. Louise Rosenblatt's transactive theory (2004) explains how students create meaning as they read. She describes comprehension, which she calls *interpretation*, as the result of a two-way transaction between readers and the text. Students don't try to figure out the author's meaning as they read; instead, they negotiate an interpretation that makes sense to them based on the text they're reading and their knowledge about literature and the world. Their interpretations are individualized because students bring different background knowledge and experiences to the reading event. Even though interpretations vary, they can always be substantiated by the text.

There are two overarching purposes for reading: When readers read for enjoyment or pleasure, they assume an aesthetic stance, and when they read to locate and remember information, they use an efferent stance (Rosenblatt, 2005). This doesn't mean that students read stories and poems aesthetically and informational books and content-area textbooks efferently. Instead, these stances represent the ends of a continuum, and readers often use a combination of the two stances when they read, whether they're reading stories, informational books, or poems. But, when teachers emphasize that students should read to remember specific information from the story they're reading, they're forcing students to read efferently. Teachers need to consider the purposes they set for students because when students read stories efferently rather than aesthetically, they don't develop a love of reading and are less likely to become lifelong readers.

Readers and Writers Are Strategic. Students use both cognitive and metacognitive strategies to direct their thinking. Cognitive strategies are goal-directed mental operations that students use to manage their reading and writing and solve problems that arise (Dean, 2006; Pressley, 2002). Visualizing, drawing inferences, and evaluating are cognitive strategies that readers use to construct meaning, and organizing, revising, and proofreading are cognitive strategies that writers use to compose meaning in texts they're writing.

Metacognitive strategies, such as monitoring, repairing, and evaluating, regulate students' thinking and their use of cognitive strategies. The word *metacognition* is often defined as "thinking about your own thinking," but more accurately, it refers to a sophisticated level of thinking that students use to actively control their thinking (Baker, 2002; Flavell, 1979). Metacognition is a control mechanism; it involves both students' awareness about their thinking and their active control of thinking.

You've read about behaviorism, constructivism, sociolinguistics, and cognitive/information processing, and as you continue reading, you'll see each of these theories of learning reflected in the balanced approach to literacy instruction presented in this textbook.

PRINCIPLE 2: EFFECTIVE TEACHERS SUPPORT STUDENTS' USE OF THE CUEING SYSTEMS

Language is a complex system for creating meaning through socially shared conventions (Halliday, 1978). English, like other languages, involves four cueing systems:

◆ The phonological, or sound, system
◆ The syntactic, or structural, system
◆ The semantic, or meaning, system
◆ The pragmatic, or social and cultural use, system

Together, these systems make communication possible; children and adults use all four systems simultaneously as they read, write, listen, and talk. The priority people place on various cueing systems can vary; however, the phonological system is especially important for beginning readers and writers as they apply phonics skills to decode and spell words. Information about the four cueing systems is summarized in Figure 1–3.

Figure 1–3 ◆ Relationships Among the Four Cueing Systems

System	Terms	Applications
Phonological System The sound system of English with approximately 44 sounds and more than 500 ways to spell them	• Phoneme (the smallest unit of sound) • Grapheme (the written representation of a phoneme using one or more letters) • Phonological awareness (knowledge about the sound structure of words, at the phoneme, onset-rime, and syllable levels) • Phonemic awareness (the ability to orally manipulate phonemes in words) • Phonics (instruction about phoneme-grapheme correspondences and spelling rules)	• Pronouncing words • Detecting regional and other dialects • Decoding words when reading • Using invented spelling • Reading and writing alliterations and onomatopoeia • Noticing rhyming words • Dividing words into syllables
Syntactic System The structural system of English that governs how words are combined into sentences.	• Syntax (the structure or grammar of a sentence) • Morpheme (the smallest meaningful unit of language) • Free morpheme (a morpheme that can stand alone as a word) • Bound morpheme (a morpheme that must be attached to a free morpheme)	• Adding inflectional endings to words • Combining words to form compound words • Adding prefixes and suffixes to root words • Using capitalization and punctuation to indicate beginnings and ends of sentences • Writing simple, compound, and complex sentences • Combining sentences
Semantic System The meaning system of English that focuses on vocabulary	• Semantics (meaning) • Synonyms (words that mean the same or nearly the same thing) • Antonyms (opposites) • Homonyms (words that sound alike but are spelled differently)	• Learning the meanings of words • Discovering that many words have multiple meanings • Using context clues to figure out an unfamiliar word • Studying synonyms, antonyms, and homonyms • Using a dictionary and a thesaurus
Pragmatic System The system of English that varies language according to social and cultural uses	• Function (the purpose for which a person uses language) • Standard English (the form of English used in textbooks and by television newscasters) • Nonstandard English (other forms of English)	• Varying language to fit specific purposes • Reading and writing dialogue in dialects • Comparing standard and nonstandard forms of English

The Phonological System

There are approximately 44 speech sounds in English. Students learn to pronounce these sounds as they learn to talk, and they learn to associate the sounds with letters as they learn to read and write. Sounds are called *phonemes*, and they are represented in print with diagonal lines to differentiate them from graphemes (letters or letter combinations). Thus, the first grapheme in *mother* is *m*, and the phoneme is /m/. The phoneme in *soap* that is represented by the grapheme *oa* is called "long o" and is written /ō/.

The phonological system is important for both oral and written language. Regional differences exist in the way people pronounce phonemes; for example, New Yorkers pronounce sounds differently from Georgians. Students learning English as a second language learn to pronounce the sounds in English, and not surprisingly, they have more difficulty learning sounds that are different from those in their native language. For example, because Spanish doesn't have /th/, native Spanish speakers have difficulty pronouncing this sound, often substituting /d/ for /th/ because the sounds are articulated in similar ways. Younger children usually learn to pronounce the difficult sounds more easily than older children and adults.

This system plays a crucial role in reading instruction during the primary grades. In a purely phonetic language, there would be a one-to-one correspondence between letters and sounds, and teaching students to decode words would be simple. But English is not a purely phonetic language because there are 26 letters and 44 sounds and many ways to combine the letters to spell some of the sounds, especially vowels. Consider these ways to spell long *e*: *sea*, *green*, *Pete*, *me*, and *people*. And the patterns used to spell long *e* don't always work—*head* and *great* are exceptions. Phonics, which describes the phoneme-grapheme correspondences and related spelling rules, is an important component of reading instruction. Students use phonics to decode words, but it isn't a complete reading program because many common words can't be decoded easily and because reading involves more than just decoding.

The Syntactic System

The syntactic system is the structural organization of English. This system is the grammar that regulates how words are combined into sentences; the word *grammar* here means the rules governing how words are combined in sentences, not parts of speech. Students use the syntactic system as they combine words to form sentences. Word order is important in English, and English speakers must arrange words into a sequence that makes sense. Young Spanish speakers who are learning English, for example, learn to say "This is my red sweater," not "This is my sweater red," the literal translation from Spanish.

Students use their knowledge of the syntactic system as they read: They expect that the words they're reading have been strung together into sentences. When they come to an unfamiliar word, they recognize its role in the sentence even if they don't know the terms for parts of speech. In the sentence "The horses galloped through the gate and out into the field," students may not know the word *through*, but they can easily substitute a reasonable word or phrase, such as *out of* or *past*.

Another component of syntax is word forms. Words such as *dog* and *play* are morphemes, the smallest meaningful units in language. Word parts that change the meaning of a word are also morphemes; when the plural marker *-s* is added to *dog* to make *dogs*, for instance, or the past-tense marker *-ed* is added to *play* to make *played*, these words now have two morphemes because the inflectional endings change the meaning of the words. The words *dog* and *play* are free morphemes because they convey meaning while standing alone; the endings -*s* and -*ed* are bound morphemes because they must be attached to free morphemes to convey meaning. Compound words are two or more morphemes combined to create a new word: *Birthday*, for example, is a compound word made up of two free morphemes.

The Semantic System

The semantic system focuses on meaning. Vocabulary is the key component of this system: Researchers estimate that children have a vocabulary of 5,000 words by the time they enter school, and they continue to acquire 3,000 to 4,000 words each year; by the time they graduate from high school, their vocabularies reach 50,000 words (Stahl & Nagy, 2005)! Students learn some words through instruction, but they learn many more words informally through reading and through social studies and science units. Students' depth of knowledge about words increases, too, from knowing one meaning for a word to knowing how to use it in many different ways. Think about the word *fire*, which has more than a dozen meanings; the most common are related to combustion, but others deal with an intense feeling, discharging a gun, or dismissing someone. To *light a fire under* someone and being *under fire* are idiomatic expressions, and compound words using *fire* include *firearm*, *fire extinguisher*, *firefly*, *fireproof*, and *fireworks*.

The Pragmatic System

Pragmatics deals with the social aspects of language use. People use language for many purposes; how they talk and write varies according to their purpose and audience. Language use also varies among social classes, ethnic groups, and geographic regions; these varieties are known as *dialects*. School is one cultural community, and the language of school is Standard English. This dialect is formal—the one used in textbooks, newspapers, and magazines and by television newscasters. Other forms, including those spoken in urban ghettos or in Appalachia, are generally classified as nonstandard English. These nonstandard forms of English are alternatives in which the phonology, syntax, and semantics differ from those of Standard English. They're neither inferior nor substandard; instead, they reflect the communities of the speakers, and the speakers communicate as effectively as those who use Standard English. The goal is for students to add Standard English to their repertoire of language registers, not to replace their home dialect with Standard English.

Teachers understand that students use all four cueing systems as they read and write. For example, when students read the sentence "Jimmy is playing ball with his father" correctly, they are probably using information from all four systems. When a child substitutes *dad* for *father* and reads "Jimmy is playing ball with his dad," he might be focusing on the semantic or pragmatic system rather than on the phonological system. When a child substitutes *basketball* for *ball* and reads "Jimmy is playing basketball with his father," he might be relying on an illustration or his own experience playing basketball. Or, because both *basketball* and *ball* begin with *b*, he might have used the beginning sound as an aid in decoding, but he apparently didn't consider how long the word *basketball* is compared with the word *ball*. When the child changes the syntax, as in "Jimmy, he play ball with his father," he may speak a nonstandard dialect. Sometimes a child reads the sentence as "Jump is play boat with his father," so that it doesn't make sense: The child chooses words with the correct beginning sound and uses appropriate parts of speech for at least some of the words, but there's no comprehension. This is a serious problem because the child doesn't seem to understand that what he reads must make sense.

PRINCIPLE 3: EFFECTIVE TEACHERS CREATE A COMMUNITY OF LEARNERS

Classrooms are social settings. Together, students and their teacher create their classroom community, and the type of community they create strongly influences the learning that takes place (Angelillo, 2008). The classroom community should feel safe and respectful so students are motivated to learn and actively involved in reading and writing activities. Perhaps the most striking quality is the partnership that the teacher and students create: They become a "family" in which all the members respect one another and support each other's learning. Students value culturally and linguistically diverse classmates and recognize that all students make important contributions to the classroom (Wells & Chang-Wells, 1992).

The teacher and the students work together for their common good. Consider the differences between renting and owning a home. In a classroom community, students and the teacher are joint "owners" of the classroom. Students assume responsibility for their own behavior and learning, work collaboratively with classmates, complete assignments, and care for the classroom. In traditional classrooms, in contrast, the classroom belongs to the teacher, and students are "renters" for the school year. This doesn't mean that in a classroom community, teachers abdicate their leadership responsibilities; on the contrary, teachers retain all of their roles as guide, instructor, monitor, coach, mentor, and grader. Sometimes these roles are shared with students, but the ultimate responsibility remains with the teacher.

Literacy Portraits: VIEWING GUIDE

Ms. Janusz spent the first month of the school year creating a community of learners in her classroom. She taught the second graders how to participate in reading and writing workshop, including procedures for choosing books, reading with a buddy, and keeping a writer's notebook. They learned to work cooperatively, take responsibility for their work and behavior, and show respect to their classmates. Ms. Janusz continues to build on this foundation that she laid in September so that the classroom functions effectively, and everyone is a contributing member of the class. View Curt'Lynn's March video clip in the Literacy Portraits section of MyEducationLab to see her buddy read with a classmate, and Jimmy's October video clip to watch him participate in a writing conference with Michael. Which of the characteristics of a community of learners described in Figure 1–4 do you notice in the video clips?

myeducationlab

Characteristics of a Classroom Community

A classroom community has specific, identifiable characteristics that are conducive to learning:

Responsibility. Students are valued members of the classroom community who are responsible for their learning, their behavior, and the contributions they make.

Opportunities. Students have opportunities to read authentic texts and write for real audiences—their classmates, their parents, and community members.

Engagement. Students are motivated to learn and actively involved in reading and writing activities, often choosing the books they'll read and their topics for writing.

Demonstration. Teachers provide demonstrations of literacy strategies and skills using think-alouds, and they encourage children also to demonstrate how they use strategies and skills.

Risk Taking. Students are encouraged to explore topics, make guesses, and take risks.

Instruction. Teachers provide instruction through minilessons and guided practice.

Check the Compendium of Instructional Procedures, which follows Chapter 12, for more information on the highlighted terms.

Response. Students share responses after reading and get feedback from classmates about their writing.

Choice. Students often make choices about the books they read and the writing they do within the parameters set by the teacher.

Time. Students need large chunks of time to pursue reading and writing activities; 2 to 3 hours of uninterrupted time each day for literacy instruction is recommended.

Assessment. Teachers and students work together to establish guidelines for assessment so that they can monitor their own work and participate in evaluating its quality. (Cambourne & Turbill, 1987)

Figure 1–4 lays out the teacher's and students' roles in a classroom community.

Figure 1–4 ◆ Characteristics of a Community of Learners		
Characteristic	**Teacher's Role**	**Students' Role**
Responsibility	Teachers set guidelines and expect students to be responsible. They also model responsible behavior.	Students assume responsibility for their learning and behavior in the classroom.
Opportunities	Teachers provide opportunities for students to read and write in genuine and meaningful activities.	Students actively participate in activities, for example, reading independently and sharing their writing with classmates.
Engagement	Teachers nurture students' engagement through authentic activities and opportunities to work with classmates.	Students become more engaged in literacy activities and spend more time reading and writing.
Demonstration	Teachers model what good readers and writers do using think-alouds to explain their thinking.	Students carefully observe teachers' demonstrations and then practice by modeling their thinking for classmates.
Risk Taking	Teachers encourage students to take risks while exploring a new idea and de-emphasize the need to always get things "right."	Students understand that learning is a process of taking risks and exploring ideas.
Instruction	Teachers provide explicit instruction through minilessons and provide opportunities for guided practice.	Students participate in minilessons and apply what they're learning in literacy activities.
Response	Teachers provide opportunities for students to respond to books they're reading and to classmates' writing.	Students respond to books in reading logs and grand conversations and listen attentively to classmates share their writing.
Choice	Teachers offer choices because they understand that students are more motivated when they can make choices.	Students make choices about some books they read, projects they create, and compositions they write.
Time	Teachers organize the schedule with large chunks of time for reading and writing.	Students understand the classroom schedule and complete assignments when they're due.
Assessment	Teachers monitor students' learning and set guidelines about how students will be graded.	Students understand how they will be assessed and often participate in self-assessment.

How to Create a Classroom Community

Teachers are more successful when they take the first 2 weeks of the school year to establish the classroom environment; it's unrealistic to assume that students will instinctively be cooperative, responsible, and respectful of classmates. Teachers explicitly explain classroom routines, such as how to get supplies out and put them away and how to work with classmates in a cooperative group, and they set the expectation that students will adhere to the routines. They demonstrate literacy procedures, including how to choose a book, how to provide feedback about a classmate's writing, and how to participate in a grand conversation. Third, teachers model ways of interacting with students, respecting classmates, and assisting them with reading and writing projects.

Teachers are the classroom managers: They set expectations and clearly explain to students what's expected of them and what's valued in the classroom. The classroom rules are specific and consistent, and teachers also set limits. Students might be allowed to talk quietly with classmates when they're working, for example, but they're not allowed to shout across the classroom or talk when the teacher's talking or when classmates are presenting to the class. Teachers also model classroom rules themselves as they interact with students. This process of socialization at the beginning of the school year is crucial to the success of the literacy program.

Not everything can be accomplished during the first 2 weeks, however; teachers continue to reinforce classroom routines and literacy procedures. One way is to have student leaders model the desired routines and behaviors; this way, other students are likely to follow the lead. Teachers also continue to teach additional literacy procedures as students become involved in new types of activities. The classroom community evolves during the school year, but the foundation is laid during the first 2 weeks.

The classroom environment is predictable with familiar routines and literacy procedures. Students feel comfortable, safe, and more willing to take risks in a predictable classroom environment. This is especially true for students from varied cultures, English learners, and students who struggle (Fay & Whaley, 2004).

The classroom community also extends beyond the walls of the classroom to include the entire school and the wider community. Within the school, students become "buddies" with students in other classes and get together to read and write in pairs (Friedland & Truesdell, 2004). When parents and other community members come into the school, they demonstrate the value they place on education by working as tutors and aides, sharing their cultures, and demonstrating other types of expertise.

PRINCIPLE 4: EFFECTIVE TEACHERS ADOPT A BALANCED APPROACH TO INSTRUCTION

The balanced approach to instruction is based on a comprehensive view of literacy that combines explicit instruction, guided practice, collaborative learning, and independent reading and writing. It's grown out of the so-called "reading wars" of the late 20th century in which teachers and researchers argued for either teacher-centered or student-centered instruction. Cunningham and Allington (2007) compare the balanced approach to a multivitamin, suggesting that it brings together the best of teacher- and student-centered learning theories. Even though balanced programs vary, they usually embody these characteristics:

- Literacy involves both reading and writing.
- Oral language is integrated with reading and writing.
- Reading instruction includes phonemic awareness, phonics, fluency, vocabulary, and comprehension.
- Writing instruction includes the writing process, the qualities of good writing to communicate ideas effectively, and conventional spelling, grammar, and punctuation to make those ideas more readable.
- Reading and writing are used as tools for content-area learning.
- Strategies and skills are taught explicitly, with a gradual release of responsibility to students.
- Students often work collaboratively and talk with classmates.
- Students are more motivated and engaged when they participate in authentic literacy activities.

Pearson, Raphael, Benson, and Madda (2007) explain that "achieving balance is a complex process that requires flexibility and artful orchestration of literacy's various contextual and conceptual aspects" (p. 33).

The characteristics of the balanced approach are embodied in an instructional program that includes these components:

- Reading
- Phonics and other literacy skills
- Reading and writing strategies
- Vocabulary
- Comprehension
- Literature
- Content-area study
- Oral language
- Writing
- Spelling

Each component is described in Figure 1–5, and as you continue reading this textbook, you'll understand what an instructional program that incorporates these components looks like. Creating a balance is important, according to Juel, Biancarosa, Coker, and Deffes (2003), because when one component is over- or underemphasized, the development of the others suffers.

A balanced literacy program integrating these components is recommended for all students, including students in high-poverty urban schools, struggling readers, and English learners (Braunger & Lewis, 2006; Duffy-Hester, 1999). What matters most is that teachers know their students well so they can adapt the components in their instructional program to ensure that all students succeed.

Teaching Struggling Readers and Writers

More Reading and Writing

Struggling students need to spend more time reading and writing.

Struggling students need to increase their volume of reading and writing. Allington (2006) recommends that teachers dramatically increase the amount of time struggling readers spend reading each day so that they can become more capable and confident readers and develop greater interest in reading. Reading volume matters; better readers typically read three times as much as struggling readers do. This recommendation for increased volume is for writing, too: Struggling writers need to spend more time writing.

In addition to explicit instruction and guided practice, students need large blocks of uninterrupted time for authentic reading and writing, and reading and writing workshop is one of the best ways to provide this opportunity. During reading workshop, students read self-selected books at their own reading level, and during writing workshop, they draft and refine compositions on self-selected topics. Practice is just as important for reading and writing as it is when you're learning to ride a bike or play the piano.

How much classroom time should students spend reading and writing? Although there's no hard-and-fast rule, Allington (2006) recommends that each day students spend at least 90 minutes reading and 45 minutes writing. Researchers have found that the most effective teachers provide more time for reading and writing than less effective teachers do (Allington & Johnston, 2002). It's often difficult for struggling students to sustain reading and writing activities for as long as their classmates do, but with teacher support, they can increase the time they spend reading and writing.

Figure 1–5 ◆ Components of the Balanced Literacy Approach

Component	Description
Reading	Students participate in modeled, shared, interactive, guided, and independent reading experiences using picture-book stories and novels, informational books, books of poetry, basal textbooks, content-area reading textbooks, and Internet materials.
Phonics and Other Literacy Skills	Students learn to use automatic actions called *skills* in reading and writing, including phonics to decode and spell words.
Reading and Writing Strategies	Students learn to use problem-solving and monitoring behaviors called *strategies* as they read and write, including predicting, drawing inferences, revising, and repairing.
Vocabulary	Students learn the meaning of words through wide reading, listening to books read aloud, and content-area study, and they apply word-learning strategies, including using context clues, to figure out the meaning of unfamiliar words.
Comprehension	Students learn to use reader factors, including comprehension strategies, and text factors, including text structures, to understand what they're reading.
Literature	Students become engaged readers who enjoy literature through reading and responding to books and learning about genres, text structures, and literary features.
Content-Area Study	Students use reading and writing as tools to learn about social studies and science topics in thematic units.
Oral Language	Students use talk and listening as they work with classmates, participate in grand conversations, give oral presentations, and listen to the teacher read aloud.
Writing	Students learn to use the writing process to draft and refine stories, poems, reports, essays, and other compositions.
Spelling	Students apply what they're learning about English orthography to spell words, and their spellings gradually become conventional.

PRINCIPLE 5: EFFECTIVE TEACHERS SCAFFOLD STUDENTS' READING AND WRITING

Teachers scaffold students' reading and writing as they demonstrate, guide, and teach, and they vary the amount of support they provide according to the instructional purpose and students' needs. Sometimes teachers model how experienced readers read or record children's dictation when the writing's too difficult for them to do on their own. At other times, they guide students as they read a leveled book or proofread their writing. Teachers use five levels of support, moving from more to less as students assume responsibility (Fountas & Pinnell, 1996). Figure 1–6 summarizes these five levels of support—modeled, shared, interactive, guided, and independent—for reading and writing activities.

Teachers working with kindergartners through eighth graders use all five levels. When teachers introduce a reading strategy, for instance, they model how to use it. And,

Figure 1–6 ◆ A Continuum of Literacy Instruction

Level of Support		Reading	Writing
High ↑	*Modeled*	Teacher reads aloud, modeling how good readers read fluently and with expression. Books too difficult for students to read themselves are used. Examples: interactive read-alouds and listening centers.	Teacher writes in front of students, creating the text, doing the writing, and thinking aloud about writing strategies and skills. Example: demonstrations.
	Shared	Teacher and students read books together, with students following as the teacher reads and then repeating familiar refrains. Books students can't read by themselves are used. Examples: big books, buddy reading.	Teacher and students create the text together; then the teacher does the actual writing. Students may assist by spelling familiar or high-frequency words. Example: Language Experience Approach.
	Interactive	Teacher and students read together and take turns doing the reading. The teacher helps students read fluently and with expression. Instructional-level books are used. Examples: choral reading and readers theatre.	Teacher and students create the text and share the pen to do the writing. Teacher and students talk about writing conventions. Example: interactive writing.
	Guided	Teacher plans and teaches reading lessons to small, homogeneous groups using instructional-level books. Focus is on supporting and observing students' use of strategies. Example: guided reading lessons.	Teacher plans and teaches lesson on a writing procedure, strategy, or skill, and students participate in supervised practice activities. Example: class collaborations.
↓ **Low**	*Independent*	Students choose and read self-selected books independently. Teacher conferences with students to monitor their progress. Examples: reading workshop and reading centers.	Students use the writing process to write stories, informational books, and other compositions. Teacher monitors students' progress. Examples: writing workshop and writing centers.

when teachers want students to practice a strategy they've already introduced, they guide students through a reading activity, slowly releasing more responsibility to them. Once students can apply the strategy easily, they're encouraged to use it independently. The purpose of the activity, not the activity itself, determines the level of support. Teachers are less actively involved during independent reading and writing, but the quality of instruction that students have received is clearest because they're applying what they've learned.

Modeled Reading and Writing

Teachers provide the greatest amount of support when they model how expert readers read and expert writers write. When teachers read aloud, they're modeling: They read fluently and with expression, and they talk about their thoughts and the strategies they're using. When they model writing, teachers write a composition on chart paper or an interactive white board so that everyone can see what the teacher does and how it's being written. Teachers use this support level to demonstrate procedures, such as choosing a book to read or doing a word sort, and to introduce new writing genres, such as writing a poem. Teachers often do a think-aloud to share what they're thinking as they read or write and the decisions they make and the strategies they use. Teachers use modeling for these purposes:

- Demonstrate fluent reading and writing
- Explain how to use reading and writing strategies, such as predicting, using context clues, and revising
- Teach the procedure for a literacy activity
- Show how reading and writing conventions and other skills work

Shared Reading and Writing

Teachers "share" reading and writing tasks with students at this level. Probably the best-known shared activity is shared reading, which teachers use to read big books with young children. The teacher does most of the reading, but children join in to read familiar and predictable words and phrases. Teachers who work with older students can also use shared reading (Allen, 2002). When a novel is too difficult for students to read independently, for example, teachers often read it aloud while students follow along, reading silently when they can.

Teachers use shared writing in a variety of ways. Primary-grade teachers often use the Language Experience Approach to write children's dictation on paintings and brainstorm lists of words on the chalkboard, for example, and teachers of older students use shared writing when they make K-W-L charts, draw graphic organizers, and write collaborative books.

Sharing differs from modeling in that students actually participate in the activity rather than simply observing the teacher. In shared reading, students follow along as the teacher reads, and in shared writing, they suggest the words and sentences that the teacher writes. Teachers use shared reading and writing for these purposes:

- Involve students in literacy activities they can't do independently
- Create opportunities for students to experience success in reading and writing
- Provide practice before students read and write independently

Interactive Reading and Writing

Students assume an increasingly important role in interactive reading and writing. They no longer observe the teacher reading or writing, repeat familiar words, or suggest words that the teacher writes; instead, they're more actively involved in reading and writing. They support their classmates by sharing the reading and writing responsibilities, and their teacher provides assistance when needed. Choral reading and readers theatre are two examples of interactive reading. In choral reading, students take turns reading lines of a poem, and in readers theatre, they assume the roles of characters and read lines in a script. In these activities, the students support each other by actively participating and sharing the work.

In interactive writing, students and the teacher create a text and write a message (Button, Johnson, & Furgerson, 1996; Tompkins & Collom, 2004). The text is composed by the group, and the teacher assists as students write the text word by word on chart paper. Students take turns writing known letters and familiar words, adding punctuation marks, and marking spaces between words. The teacher helps them to spell all words correctly and use written language conventions so that the text can be read easily. Everyone participates in creating and writing the text on chart paper, and they also write the text on small dry-erase boards. After writing, students read and reread the text using shared and independent reading. Teachers use interactive reading and writing for these purposes:

◆ Practice reading and writing high-frequency words
◆ Apply phonics and spelling skills
◆ Read and write texts that students can't do independently
◆ Have students share their literacy expertise with classmates

Guided Reading and Writing

Teachers continue to support students during guided reading and writing, but at this level, students do the actual reading and writing themselves. In guided reading, small, homogeneous groups of students meet with the teacher to read a book at their instructional level. The teacher introduces the book and guides students as they begin reading. Then students continue reading on their own while the teacher supervises. Afterward, they discuss the book, review vocabulary words, and practice skills. Later, students reread the book independently.

Minilessons are another type of guided reading and writing. As teachers teach about strategies, skills, and genres and other text factors, they support students as they learn. They also provide practice activities and supervise as students apply what they're learning.

In guided writing, teachers plan structured writing activities and then supervise students as they write. For example, when students make pages for a collaborative book, it's guided writing because the teacher organizes the activity and supervises students as they work. Teachers also provide guidance as they conference with students about their writing.

Teachers use guided reading and writing to provide instruction and assistance as students are actually reading and writing. Teachers use guided reading and writing for these purposes:

◆ Support students' reading in appropriate instructional-level materials
◆ Teach literacy strategies and skills
◆ Involve students in collaborative writing projects
◆ Teach students to use the writing process—in particular, how to revise and edit

Independent Reading and Writing

Students do the reading and writing themselves at the independent level. They apply the strategies and skills they've learned in authentic literacy activities. During independent reading, students usually choose their own books and work at their own pace as they read and respond to books. Similarly, during independent writing, students usually choose their own topics and move at their own pace as they develop and refine their writing. It would be wrong to suggest, however, that teachers play no role in independent-level activities. They continue to monitor students, but they provide much less guidance at this level.

Through independent reading, students learn how pleasurable reading is and, teachers hope, become lifelong readers. In addition, as they write, students come to view themselves as authors. Teachers use independent reading and writing for these purposes:

◆ Create opportunities for students to practice the reading and writing strategies and skills they've learned
◆ Provide authentic literacy experiences in which students choose their own topics, purposes, and materials
◆ Develop lifelong readers and writers

PRINCIPLE 6: EFFECTIVE TEACHERS ORGANIZE FOR LITERACY INSTRUCTION

There's no one instructional program that best represents the balanced approach to literacy; instead, teachers organize for instruction by creating their own program that fits their students' needs and their school's standards and curricular guidelines. Instructional programs should reflect these principles:

◆ Teachers create a community of learners in their classroom.
◆ Teachers implement the components of the balanced approach.
◆ Teachers scaffold students' reading and writing experiences.

Teachers choose among a variety of instructional programs, combine parts of two or more programs, alternate programs, or add other components to meet their students' needs. Four of the most popular programs are basal reading programs, literature focus units, literature circles, and reading and writing workshop. Figure 1–7 presents a comparison of these four instructional programs.

Figure 1–7 ◆ Instructional Programs

	Basal Reading Programs	Literature Focus Units
Description	Students read textbooks containing stories, informational articles, and poems that are sequenced according to grade level. Teachers follow directions in the teacher's guide to teach word identification, vocabulary, comprehension, grammar, and writing lessons. Directions are also provided for working with English learners and struggling students.	Teachers and students read and respond to a book together as a class. They choose high-quality literature that is appropriate for the grade level and students' interests. The book may be too difficult for some students to read on their own, so teachers read it aloud or use shared reading. After reading, students usually create projects.
Strengths	• Textbooks are aligned with grade-level standards. • Students read selections at their grade level. • Teachers teach strategies and skills and provide structured practice opportunities. • Teachers are available to reteach strategies and skills as needed. • The teacher's guide provides detailed instructions. • Assessment materials are included in the program.	• Teachers choose picture-book stories, novels, or informational books for units. • Teachers scaffold reading instruction as they read with the whole class or small groups. • Teachers teach minilessons on reading strategies and skills. • Students study vocabulary. • Students develop projects to extend their reading.
Limitations	• Selections may be too difficult for some students. • Selections may lack the authenticity of good literature. • Programs include many worksheets. • Most of the instruction is presented to the whole class.	• Students all read the same book whether or not they like it and whether or not it's at their reading level. • Many of the activities are teacher directed.

Basal Reading Programs

Commercially produced reading programs are known as *basal readers*. These programs feature a textbook containing reading selections with accompanying workbooks, supplemental books, and related instructional materials at each grade level. Phonics, vocabulary, comprehension, grammar, and spelling instruction is coordinated with the reading selections and aligned with grade-level standards. The teacher's guide provides detailed procedures for teaching the selections and related skills and strategies. Instruction is typically presented to the whole class, with reteaching to small groups of struggling students. Testing materials are also included so that teachers can monitor students' progress. Publishers tout basal readers as a complete literacy program, but effective teachers realize that they aren't.

Literature Focus Units

Teachers create literature focus units featuring high-quality picture-book stories and novels. The books are usually included in a district- or state-approved list of award-winning books that all students are expected to read at a particular grade level. These

Literature Circles	Reading and Writing Workshop
Teachers choose five or six books and collect multiple copies of each one. Students each choose the book they want to read and form circles or "book clubs" to read and respond to the book. They develop a reading and discussion schedule and assume roles for the discussion. Teachers sometimes participate in the discussions.	Students choose books and read and respond to them independently during reading workshop and write books on self-selected topics during writing workshop. Teachers monitor students' work through conferences. During a sharing period, students share with classmates the books they read and the books they write. Teachers also teach minilessons on reading and writing strategies and skills.
• Teachers differentiate instruction by providing books at varied reading levels. • Students are more strongly motivated because they choose the books they read. • Students work with their classmates. • Students participate in authentic literacy experiences using trade books. • Activities are student directed. • Teachers may participate in discussions to help students think more deeply about the book.	• Students read books appropriate for their reading levels. • Students are more engaged because they choose the books they read. • Students work through the stages of the writing process during writing workshop. • Activities are student directed, and students work at their own pace. • Teachers have opportunities to work individually with students during conferences.
• Teachers often feel a loss of control because students are reading different books. • To be successful, students must learn to be task oriented and to use time wisely. • Sometimes students choose books that are too difficult or too easy for them.	• Teachers often feel a loss of control because students are reading different books and working at different stages of the writing process. • To be successful, students must learn to be task oriented and to use time wisely.

books include classics such as *The Very Hungry Caterpillar* (Carle, 1994) and *Charlotte's Web* (White, 2006) and award winners such as *Officer Buckle and Gloria* (Rathmann, 1995) and *Holes* (Sachar, 2003). Everyone in the class reads and responds to the same book, and the teacher supports students' learning through a combination of explicit instruction and reading and writing activities. Through these units, teachers teach students about literary genres and authors, and they develop students' interest in literature.

Literature Circles

Small groups of students get together in literature circles or book clubs to read a story or other book. To begin, teachers select five or six books at varying reading levels to meet the needs of all students in the class. Often, the books are related in some way—representing the same theme or written by the same author, for instance. They collect multiple copies of each book and give a book talk to introduce them. Then students choose a book to read and form a group to read and respond to the book. They set a reading and discussion schedule and work independently, although teachers sometimes sit in on the discussions. Through the experience of reading and discussing a book together, students develop responsibility for completing assignments and learn more about how to respond to books.

Reading and Writing Workshop

In reading workshop, students select books, read independently at their own pace, and conference with the teacher about their reading. Similarly, in writing workshop, students write books on topics that they choose and the teacher conferences with them about their writing. Teachers set aside a time for reading and writing workshop, and all students read and write while the teacher conferences with small groups. Teachers also teach minilessons on reading and writing strategies and skills and read books aloud to the whole class. In a workshop program, students read and write more like adults do, making choices, working independently, and developing responsibility. Many teachers report that reading and writing workshop are more motivational than other literacy programs and that fourth through eighth graders particularly value the opportunity to make choices and work independently.

These approaches are used at all grade levels, and teachers generally combine them because students learn best through a variety of reading and writing experiences. Sometimes the books that students read are more difficult or teachers are introducing a new writing genre that requires more teacher support and guidance. Some teachers alternate literature focus units or literature circles with reading and writing workshop and basal readers, whereas others use some components from each approach throughout the school year.

Nurturing English Learners

Go to the Building Teaching Skills and Dispositions section of Chapter 1 on **MyEducationLab.com** to learn how Ms. Janusz supports Rakie, an English learner.

English learners (ELs) benefit from participating in the same instructional programs that mainstream students do, but teachers adapt these programs to create classroom learning contexts that respect minority students and meet their needs (Brock & Raphael, 2005; Peregoy & Boyle, 2009; Shanahan & Beck, 2006). Learning to read and write is more challenging for English learners because they're learning to speak English at the same time they're developing literacy. Here are some ways that teachers scaffold English learners' oral language acquisition and literacy development:

Literature Circles
These eighth graders are participating in a discussion during a literature circle featuring Rodman Philbrick's *Freak the Mighty* (1993), the memorable story of two unlikely friends. The students talk about events in the story, returning to the book to read sentences aloud. They also check the meaning of several words in a dictionary that one student keeps on his desk. They've read half of the book so far, and their conversation focuses on the friendship Max and Kevin have formed. They talk about their own friends and what it means to be a friend, and they make predictions about how the story will end.

Explicit Instruction. Teachers present additional instruction on literacy strategies and skills because ELs are more at-risk than other students (Genesee & Riches, 2006). They also spend more time teaching unfamiliar academic vocabulary related to reading and writing (e.g., *vowel, homonym, paragraph, index, quotation marks, predict, revise, summarize*).

Oral Language. Teachers provide many opportunities each day for students to practice speaking English comfortably and informally with partners and in small groups. Through these conversations, ELs develop both conversational and academic language, which supports their reading and writing development (Rothenberg & Fisher, 2007).

Small-Group Work. Teachers provide opportunities for students to work in small groups because classmates' social interaction supports their learning (Genesee & Riches, 2006). English learners talk with classmates as they read and write, and at the same time, they're learning the culture of literacy.

Reading Aloud to Students. Teachers read aloud a variety of stories, informational books, and books of poetry, including some that represent students' home cultures (Rothenberg & Fisher, 2007). As they read, teachers model fluent reading, and students become more familiar with English sounds, vocabulary, and written language structures.

Background Knowledge. Teachers organize instruction into themes to build students' world knowledge about grade-level-appropriate concepts, and they develop ELs' literary knowledge through minilessons and a variety of reading and writing activities (Braunger & Lewis, 2006).

Authentic Literacy Activities. Teachers provide daily opportunities for students to apply the strategies and skills they're learning as they read and write for authentic, real-life purposes (Akhavan, 2006). English learners participate in meaningful literacy activities through literature circles and reading and writing workshop.

These recommendations promote English learners' academic success.

Teachers' attitudes about minority students and knowledge about how they learn a second language play a critical role in the effectiveness of instruction (Gay, 2000). It's important that teachers understand that English learners have different cultural and linguistic backgrounds and plan instructional programs accordingly. Most classrooms reflect the European American middle-class culture, which differs significantly from minority students' backgrounds. Brock and Raphael (2005) point out that "mismatches between teachers' and students' cultural and linguistic backgrounds matter because such mismatches can impact negatively on students' opportunities for academic success" (p. 5). Teachers and students use language in different ways. For example, some students are reluctant to volunteer answers to teachers' questions, and others may not answer if the questions are different than those their parents ask (Peregoy & Boyle, 2009). Teachers who learn about their students' home language and culture and embed them into their instruction are likely to be more successful.

PRINCIPLE 7: EFFECTIVE TEACHERS LINK INSTRUCTION AND ASSESSMENT

Assessment is an integral and ongoing part of both learning and teaching (Mariotti & Homan, 2005). Sometimes teachers equate standardized high-stakes achievement tests with assessment, but classroom assessment is much more than a once-a-year test. It's a daily part of classroom life: Teachers use a variety of informal procedures and commercial tests to monitor students' reading and writing progress and ensure that they're meeting district and state standards. Cunningham and Allington (2007) describe assessment as "collecting and analyzing data to make decisions about how children are performing and growing" (p. 202).

Purposes of Classroom Assessment

Teachers assess students' learning for these purposes:

Determining Students' Reading Levels. Because students within a classroom normally read at a wide range of levels, it's essential that teachers determine students' reading levels so that they can plan appropriate instruction.

Monitoring Students' Progress. Teachers regularly assess students to ensure that they're making expected progress in reading and writing, and when they're not progressing, teachers take action to get students back on track.

Diagnosing Students' Strengths and Weaknesses. Teachers examine students' progress in specific literacy components, including phonics, fluency, comprehension, writing, and spelling, to identify their strengths and weaknesses. Diagnosis is especially important when students are struggling or aren't making expected progress.

Documenting Students' Learning. Teachers use test results and collections of students' work to provide evidence of their accomplishments. Students' work samples are often collected in portfolios.

Assessment is linked to instruction; teachers use assessment results to inform their teaching (Snow, Griffin, & Burns, 2005). As they plan, teachers use their knowledge about students' reading levels, their background knowledge, and their strategy and skill competencies to plan appropriate instruction that's neither too easy nor too difficult. Teachers monitor instruction that's in progress as they observe students, conference with them, and check their work to ensure that their instruction is effective, and they make modifications, including reteaching when necessary, to improve the quality of their instruction and meet students' needs. Teachers also judge the effectiveness of their instruction after it's completed. It's easy to blame students when learning isn't occurring, but teachers need to consider how they can improve their teaching so that their students will be more successful.

Classroom Assessment Tools

Teachers use a variety of informal assessment tools that they create themselves and classroom tests that are commercially available. Informal assessment tools include the following:

◆ Observation of students as they participate in instructional activities
◆ **Running records** of students' oral reading to analyze their ability to solve reading problems
◆ Examination of students' work
◆ Conferences to talk with students about their reading and writing
◆ Checklists to monitor students' learning
◆ **Rubrics** to assess students' writing and other activities

These assessment tools support instruction, and teachers choose which tool to use according to the kind of information they need. Teachers administer commercial tests to individual students or the entire class to determine their overall reading achievement or their proficiency in a particular component—phonics, spelling, fluency, or comprehension, for example. In upcoming chapters, you'll learn how to assess students' reading and writing and which assessment tools to use.

The results of yearly, high-stakes standardized tests also provide evidence of students' literacy achievement. The usefulness of these data is limited, however, because the tests are usually administered in the spring and the results aren't released until after the school year ends. At the beginning of the next school year, teachers do examine the data and use what they learn in planning for their new class, but the impact isn't as great as it would be for the teachers who worked with those students during the previous year. Another way the results are used is in measuring the effectiveness of teachers' instruction by examining how much students grew since the previous year's test and whether students met grade-level standards.

PRINCIPLE 8: EFFECTIVE TEACHERS BECOME PARTNERS WITH PARENTS

Parents play a crucial role in helping children become successful readers and writers. They support their children's learning by actively participating in literacy activities, such as reading aloud and modeling literate behaviors. Researchers have concluded again and again that home-literacy activities profoundly influence children's academic success (Bus, van Ijzendoorn, & Pellegrini, 1995): They score higher on standardized achievement tests, have better school attendance, and exhibit higher-level thinking when parents are involved in their education.

Most teachers recognize the importance of home-literacy activities and want to become partners with their students' parents. In some communities, parents respond enthusiastically when teachers ask them to listen to their children read aloud or monitor their independent reading, or when teachers invite them to participate in a home–school writing event, for example, but in other communities, there's little or no response. When partnership attempts are unsuccessful, teachers feel frustrated and conclude that they can't expect much support from their students' parents.

Teachers' expectations of parent involvement have been based on middle-class parents who typically see themselves as partners with teachers, reading to and with their children, playing educational games, going to the public library to check out books, and helping with homework. Other parents view their role in educating their school-age children differently (Edwards, 2004). Some are willing to attend teacher–parent conferences and support school projects such as bake sales and carnivals, but they expect teachers to do the teaching. Others feel inadequate when it comes to helping their children. Their own unsuccessful school experiences, cultural differences, or limited ability to read and write in English contribute to these feelings.

Lareau (2000) explained that parents' viewpoints reflect their culture and socioeconomic status: Middle-class parents usually work with teachers to support their children's literacy development; working-class parents believe that teachers are better qualified to teach their children; and poor, minority, and immigrant parents often feel powerless to help their children learn to read and write. Parents' involvement is also related to educational level: Parents who didn't graduate from high school are less likely to get involved in their children's literacy learning (Paratore, 2001). Educational level also correlates with parents' personal and parental reading habits: Parents who are high school graduates are more likely to read newspapers and books, read to their children, and take them to the public library.

Ways to Work With Parents

Not all parents understand the crucial role they play in their children's literacy development and academic success. It's up to teachers to establish collaborative relationships with parents so that they can work together and meet children's needs more effectively. Edwards (2004) explains that parent–teacher collaborations "involve rethinking the relationship between home and school such that students' opportunities to learn are expanded" (p. xvii). Teachers begin by accepting that parents view their role in different ways and by becoming more knowledgeable about cultural diversity and how it affects parent–teacher relationships.

Respect the Literacy Activities of Families. Nearly all families incorporate reading and writing activities into their daily routines, but these activities may differ from school-based literacy activities that teachers value. In middle-class families, for example, parents read the newspaper, write messages using magnetic letters on the refrigerator, search for information on the Internet, and read bedtime stories to children, and in other families, they read the Bible and magazines, write letters, pay bills, and do crossword puzzles. Teachers often overlook the importance of literacy activities that differ from those they value. Because culture and learning are closely linked, some children are at risk of failing because they aren't familiar with the literacy activities and language patterns that teachers use (Gay, 2000; Purcell-Gates, 2000). Nieto (2002) urges teachers to recognize the value of parents' literacy activities, even though they may not match teachers' expectations, and use them in developing a literacy program that's culturally responsive.

Reach Out to Families in New Ways. Because their attempts to form partnerships with parents haven't been successful, teachers are striving to find better ways to foster parent–teacher communication and involvement. Based on her work in establishing effective partnerships, Edwards (2004) recommends that teachers work together to create schoolwide programs that begin in September with a yearlong schedule of activities that address particular literacy goals at each grade level. Effective communication is essential: When teachers demonstrate that they want to listen to parents, giving them opportunities to share insights about their children and to ask questions about how children learn to read and write, parents become more willing to give of their time to work with teachers and support their children's learning.

Build Parents' Knowledge of Literacy Procedures. Too often, teachers assume that parents know how to support their children's literacy learning, but many parents don't know how to read aloud, respond to their children's writing, or use other literacy procedures. Researchers have found that when teachers offer specific suggestions and provide clear directions, parents are more likely to be successful (Edwards, 2004).

Because today's classrooms are culturally diverse, it's essential that teachers examine their personal biases and critique the effectiveness of their instructional practices. Once they understand the role of culture in learning, teachers can create an empowering classroom culture and improve communication with parents. When teachers have faith in their students' ability to learn and commit themselves to ensuring that their students are successful, their efforts to involve parents will be more successful.

Home-Literacy Activities

Many parent-involvement programs focus on preschoolers, but parents continue to play an important role in supporting their children's reading and writing development through elementary and high school. Parents implement home-literacy activities as well as support their children's in-school literacy development through activities such as these:

- Reading aloud to children
- Listening to children read aloud and reading along with them
- Making time for children to read books independently a priority
- Providing books and other reading materials in the home
- Talking with children about books they're reading
- Asking children what they're learning at school
- Providing the materials and opportunities for children to write at home
- Taking children to the library to check out books and multimedia materials
- Giving books and magazine subscriptions as gifts
- Monitoring children as they complete homework assignments
- Emphasizing the value of literacy and the importance of school success

Teachers who work with older students expand parent–teacher partnerships by showing parents how to talk with their children about books they're reading, respond to their writing, and monitor their completion of homework assignments.

Teachers have developed a variety of innovative home-literacy activities for K–8 students that involve opportunities for parents and their children to read and write together. Here's a list of seven recommended activities:

    Interactive Read-Alouds. Teachers not only encourage parents to read aloud to their children every day, but they also demonstrate how to read aloud effectively using interactive read-alouds (Enz, 2003). They teach parents how to choose appropriate books and use techniques to boost their children's engagement with the book, such as making predictions, asking questions, and talking about illustrations. Teachers also explain the benefit of rereading books and suggest that parents promote children's response after reading through role-playing, using puppets to retell the story, drawing pictures, and other activities.

Traveling Book Bags. Teachers put together traveling bags of books that beginning readers take home to read with their parents (Vukelich, Christie, & Enz, 2001). For each bag, they collect three or four books, usually on a single topic; a stuffed animal, puppet, or artifact; and a response journal. If parents have low-level literacy or don't speak English, teachers also include cassette-tape recordings of the books and a small tape player so that the whole family can enjoy the books. Children take the book bags home and spend a week reading and talking about the books and writing responses in the journal. Then they exchange the book bags for new ones. Teachers who work with older students make more sophisticated book bags, loaded with maps, brochures, charts and diagrams, magazines, lists of related website addresses, and books related to a thematic unit, for students to take home and explore.

Family Book Clubs. Parents and their children read and discuss books together, and sometimes they invite other families to join the book club. Parents and children choose a book that interests them (and is appropriate for the children's age and reading level) that everyone will read and discuss. After parents and children finish reading, everyone gets together to talk about the book. This activity, based on the book club popularized in *The Mother-Daughter Book Club: How Ten Busy Mothers and Daughters Came Together to Talk, Laugh, and Learn Through Their Love of Reading* (Dodson, 2007), is a great way for parents to foster their children's love of reading.

Online Reading and Writing. Computers are rapidly becoming part of everyday life, and parents and children can use computers together to search the Internet for information, read articles posted on websites, play literacy games, and use e-mail and instant messaging to stay in touch with relatives and friends (Rasinski & Padak, 2008).

Family Journals. Children and their parents write back and forth in special family journals (Wollman-Bonilla, 2000). At school, children write entries, explaining what's going on in their classroom and what they're learning, and then they take their journals home to share with their parents. Next, parents write back, commenting on children's entries, asking questions, and offering praise and encouragement.

Family Reading/Writing Nights. Parents and their children come to school for a special evening of reading or writing books together (Hutchins, Greenfeld, & Epstein, 2008). Individual teachers, a grade-level group of teachers, or an entire school can organize these programs. At a family reading night, children and parents read books together and participate in reading-related presentations and activities. Sometimes children dress up as book characters, perform a readers theatre script, or give book talks about favorite books. Teachers also give away books that children add to their home library. At a family writing night, children and parents write books together, usually about family events. Teachers also have opportunities at these events to share tips with parents about ways to support their children's literacy development.

Family Literacy Portfolios. Parents save samples of their children's reading and writing and collect them in large folders or portfolios, and then they share the portfolios with teachers during parent–teacher conferences (Krol-Sinclair, Hindin, Emig, & McClure, 2003). Samples of children's reading and writing can include drawings with captions, notes, stories and poems, handmade birthday cards, craft projects, lists of books read, and photocopies of the covers of favorite books. Parents also include observation notes about the ways their children use literacy. When parents bring portfolios to parent–teacher conferences, they assume a more active role in talking about their children's literacy development, and teachers gain valuable insights about their students' home-literacy activities.

These home-literacy activities are effective because teachers set specific goals, provide clear directions, and value parents' collaboration.

Working With Non-English-Speaking and Low-Literacy Parents

Many parents can't actively support their children's literacy through reading and writing because they don't read or write well themselves, or can't read or write in the same language their children do. However, all parents can support their children's literacy by telling stories, discussing current events, sharing cultural information and practices, and encouraging children to talk about what they're learning at school. In addition, there's a way that non-English-speaking and low-literacy parents can share a literacy activity with their children: They can "read" wordless picture books where the story is told entirely through illustrations. A list of recommended wordless picture books, including some that appeal to older students, is presented in Figure 1–8. One of the

Figure 1–8 ◆ Wordless Picture Books

Banyai, I. (1998). *Zoom.* New York: Puffin Books. (U)

Banyai, I. (2005). *The other side.* San Francisco: Chronicle Books. (U)

Faller, R. (2006). *The adventures of Polo.* New York: Roaring Brook Press. (P)

Faller, R. (2007). Polo: *The runaway book.* New York: Roaring Brook Press. (P)

Franson, S. E. (2007). *Un-brella.* New York: Roaring Brook Press. (P)

Geisert, A. (2006). *Oops.* Boston: Houghton Mifflin. (P–M)

Heuer, C. (2006). *Lola & Fred.* New York: 4N Publishing. (M)

Heuer, C. (2007). *Lola & Fred & Tom.* New York: 4N Publishing. (P–M)

Jenkins, S. (2003). *Looking down.* Boston: Houghton Mifflin. (P)

Khing, T. T. (2007) *Where is the cake?* New York: Abrams. (P)

Lehman, B. (2004). *The red book.* Boston: Houghton Mifflin. (P–M)

Lehman B. (2006). *Museum trip.* Boston: Houghton Mifflin. (P–M)

Lehman B. (2007). *Rainstorm.* Boston: Houghton Mifflin. (P)

Lehman, B. (2008). *Trainstop.* Boston: Houghton Mifflin. (P)

Mayer, M. (2003). *Frog, where are you?* New York: Dial Books. (M)

Newgarden, M., & Cash, M. M. (2007). *Bow-wow bugs a bug.* San Diego: Harcourt. (p)

Rogers, G. (2007). *Midsummer knight.* New York: Roaring Brook Press. (P–M)

Schories, J. (2006). *Jack and the night visitors.* Honesdale, PA: Front Street. (P)

Tan, S. (2007). *The arrival.* New York: Scholastic. (U)

Turkle, B. (1992). *Deep in the forest.* New York: Puffin Books. (P)

Van Ommen, S. (2007). *The surprise.* Honesdale, PA: Front Street. (P)

Varon, S. (2006). *Chicken and cat.* New York: Scholastic. (P)

Wiesner, D. (1995). *June 29, 1999.* New York: Clarion Books. (M–U)

Wiesner, D. (1997). *Tuesday.* New York: Clarion Books. (M–U)

Wiesner, D. (2006). *Flotsam.* New York: Clarion Books. (M–U)

most sophisticated books on the list is Shaun Tan's *The Arrival* (2007), which depicts the journey of an immigrant who leaves his family and comes to a bizarre new world. The book illustrates the displacement and awe with which immigrants respond to their new surroundings. Parents and children read these books by examining the illustrations and creating a story based on them. It's not as easy as it sounds; usually parents and children read a wordless book several times to thoroughly comprehend it. In the first reading, the focus is on grasping the story line, and then with successive readings, they notice new details in the illustrations, make inferences, and elaborate the story.

Teachers must establish two-way communication with parents and learn from parents about their children's strengths and needs and home-literacy practices. Creating a partnership means more than turning parents into homework monitors; instead, teachers can help parents develop the tools to support their children's literacy learning, and teachers can build on the knowledge and experiences that families bring to their children's education.

Chapter 1 Review

How Effective Teachers Teach Reading and Writing

▶ Teachers apply learning theories as they teach reading and writing.

▶ Teachers create a community of learners in their classrooms.

▶ Teachers adopt the balanced approach to literacy instruction that reflects teacher-centered and student-centered learning theories.

▶ Teachers scaffold students' reading and writing and then gradually withdraw their support as students become proficient.

▶ Teachers link instruction and assessment.

PEARSON
myeducationlab
Where the Classroom Comes to Life

Go to MyEducationLab at www.myeducationlab.com to deepen your understanding of the concepts presented in this chapter:

▶ Judge the importance of community in Ms. Janusz's second-grade classroom by viewing video segments in the Literacy Portraits.
▶ Check your understanding of chapter concepts with the multiple-choice and essay quizzes in the Study Plan.
▶ Apply some of the main ideas discussed in the chapter in the Activities and Applications section of the website.
▶ Practice what you've learned in this chapter in Building Teaching Skills and Dispositions before applying the ideas in your own classroom.

PROFESSIONAL REFERENCES

Afflerbach, P. (2007). *Understanding and using reading assessment, K–12*. Newark, DE: International Reading Association.

Akhavan, N. (2006). *Help! My kids don't all speak English: How to set up a language workshop in your linguistically diverse classroom*. Portsmouth, NH: Heinemann.

Allen, J. (2002). *On the same page: Shared reading beyond the primary grades*. Portland, ME: Stenhouse.

Allington, R. L. (2006). *What really matters for struggling readers: Designing research-based programs* (2nd ed.). Boston: Allyn & Bacon/Pearson.

Allington, R. L., & Johnston, P. H. (Eds.). (2002). *Reading to learn: Lessons from exemplary fourth-grade classrooms*. New York: Guilford Press.

Angelillo, J. (2008). *Whole-class teaching*. Portsmouth, NH: Heinemann.

Baker, L. (2002). Metacognition in comprehension instruction. In C. C. Block & M. Pressley (Eds.), *Comprehension instruction: Research-based best practices* (pp. 77–95). New York: Guilford Press.

Bandura, A. (1997). *Self-efficacy: The exercise of control*. New York: W. H. Freeman.

Banks, J., Cochran-Smith, M., Moll, L., Richert, A., Zeichner, K., LePage, P., Darling-Hammond, L., & Duffy, H. (2005). Teaching diverse learners. In L. Darling-Hammond & J. Bransford (Eds.), *Preparing teachers for a changing world* (pp. 232–274). San Francisco: Jossey-Bass.

Bomer, R., & Bomer, K. (2001). *For a better world: Reading and writing for social action*. Portsmouth, NH: Heinemann.

Braunger, J., & Lewis, J. P. (2006). *Building a knowledge base in reading* (2nd ed.). Newark, DE: International Reading Association/National Council of Teachers of English.

Brock, C. H., & Raphael, T. E. (2005). *Windows to language, literacy, and culture: Insights from an English-language learner*. Newark, DE: International Reading Association.

Brown, J. S., Collins, A., & Duguid, S. (1989). Situated cognition and the culture of learning. *Educational Researcher, 18*(1), 32–42.

Bus, A. G., van Ijzendoorn, M. H., & Pellegrini, A. D. (1995). Joint book reading makes for success in learning to read: A meta-analysis on intergenerational transmission of literacy. *Review of Educational Research, 65*, 1–21.

Button, K., Johnson, M. J., & Furgerson, P. (1996). Interactive writing in a primary classroom. *The Reading Teacher, 49*, 446–454.

Cambourne, B., & Turbill, J. (1987). *Coping with chaos*. Rozelle, New South Wales, Australia: Primary English Teaching Association.

Castek, J., Bevans-Mangelson, J., & Goldstone, B. (2006). Reading adventures online: Five ways to introduce the new literacies of the Internet through children's literature. *The Reading Teacher, 59*, 714–728.

Cunningham, P. M., & Allington, R. L. (2007). *Classrooms that work: They can all read and write*. Boston: Allyn & Bacon.

Dean, D. (2005). *Strategic writing: The writing process and beyond in the secondary English classroom*. Urbana, IL: National Council of Teachers of English.

Dixon-Krauss, L. (1996). *Vygotsky in the classroom*. White Plains, NY: Longman.

Dodson, S. (2007). *The mother-daughter book club: How ten busy mothers and daughters came together to talk, laugh, and learn through their love of reading* (rev. ed.). New York: HarperCollins.

Duffy-Hester, A. (1999). Teaching struggling readers in elementary school classrooms: A review of classroom reading programs and principles for instruction. *The Reading Teacher, 52*, 480–495.

Edwards, P. A. (2004). *Children's literacy development: Making it happen through school, family, and community involvement*. Boston: Allyn & Bacon/Pearson.

Enz, B. J. (2003). The ABCs of family literacy. In A. DeBruin-Parecki & B. Krol-Sinclair (Eds.), *Family literacy: From theory to practice* (pp. 50–67). Newark, DE: International Reading Association.

Fay, K., & Whaley, S. (2004). *Becoming one community: Reading and writing with English language learners*. Portland, ME: Stenhouse.

Flavell, J. H. (1979). Metacognition and cognitive monitoring: A new area of cognitive-developmental inquiry. *American Psychologist, 34*, 906–911.

Fountas, I. C., & Pinnell, G. S. (1996). *Guided reading: Good first teaching for all children*. Portsmouth, NH: Heinemann.

Freire, P. (2000). *Pedagogy of the oppressed* (30th anniversary ed.). New York: Continuum.

Friedland, E. S., & Truesdell, K. S. (2004). Kids reading together: Ensuring the success of a buddy reading program. *The Reading Teacher, 58*, 76–83.

Gambrell, L. B., Malloy, J. A., & Mazzoni, S. A. (2007). Evidence-based best practices for comprehensive literacy instruction. In L. B. Gambrell, L. M. Morrow, & M. Pressley (Eds.), *Best practices in literacy instruction* (3rd ed., pp. 11–29). New York: Guilford Press.

Gay, G. (2000). *Culturally responsive teaching: Theory, research, and practice*. New York: Teachers College Press.

Genesee, F., & Riches, C. (2006). Literacy: Instructional issues. In F. Genesee, K. Lindholm-Leary, W. M. Saunders, & D. Christian (Eds.), *Educating English language learners: A synthesis of research evidence* (pp. 109–175). New York: Cambridge University Press.

Guthrie, J. T., & Wigfield, A. (2000). Engagement and motivation in reading. In M. L. Kamil, P. B. Mosenthal, P. D. Pearson, & R. Barr (Eds.), *Handbook of reading research* (Vol. 3, pp. 403–422). New York: Erlbaum.

Halliday, M. A. K. (1978). *Language as social semiotic: The social interpretation of language and meaning*. Baltimore: University Park Press.

Hayes, J. R. (2004). A new framework for understanding cognition and affect in writing. In R. B. Ruddell & N. J. Unrau (Eds.), *Theoretical models and processes of reading* (5th ed., pp. 1399–1430). Newark, DE: International Reading Association.

Heath, S. B. (1983). Research currents: A lot of talk about nothing. *Language Arts, 60,* 999–1007.

Henry, L. A. (2006). SEARCHing for an answer: The critical role of new literacies while reading on the Internet. *The Reading Teacher, 59,* 614–627.

Hutchins, D., Greenfeld, M., & Epstein, J. (2008). *Family reading night*. Larchmont, NY: Eye on Education.

Juel, C., Biancarosa, G., Coker, D., & Deffes, R. (2003). Walking with Rosie: A cautionary tale of early reading instruction. *Educational Leadership, 60,* 12–18.

Karchmer, R. A., Mallette, M. H., Kara-Soteriou, J., & Leu, D. (Eds.). (2005). *Innovative approaches to literacy education: Using the Internet to support new literacies*. Newark, DE: International Reading Association.

Kintsch, W. (2004). The construction-integration model and its implications for instruction. In R. B. Ruddell & N. J. Unrau (Eds.), *Theoretical models and processes of reading* (5th ed., pp. 1270–1328). Newark, DE: International Reading Association.

Kist, W. (2005). *New literacies in action: Teaching and learning in multiple media*. New York: Teachers College Press.

Kress, G. (2003). *Literacy in the new media age*. London: Routledge.

Krol-Sinclair, B., Hindin, A., Emig, J. M., & McClure, K. A. (2003). Using family literacy portfolios as context for parent-teacher communication. In A. DeBruin-Parecki & B. Krol-Sinclair (Eds.), *Family literacy: From theory to practice* (pp. 266–281). Newark, DE: International Reading Association.

Lareau, A. (2000). *Home advantage: Social class and parental intervention in elementary education* (2nd ed.). Lanham, MD: Rowman & Littlefield.

Lave, J., & Wenger, E. (1991). *Situated learning: Legitimate peripheral participation*. Cambridge, UK: Cambridge University Press.

Leu, D. J., Jr., Kinzer, C. K., Coiro, J., & Cammack, D. W. (2004). Toward a theory of new literacies emerging from the Internet and other communication technologies. In R. B. Ruddell & N. J. Unrau (Eds.), *Theoretical models and processes of reading* (5th ed., pp. 1570–1613). Newark, DE: International Reading Association.

Lewison, M., Leland, C., & Harste, J. C. (2008). *Creating critical classrooms: K–8 reading and writing with an edge*. New York: Erlbaum.

Luke, A., & Freebody, P. (1997). Shaping the social practices of reading. In S. Muspratt, A. Luke, & P. Freebody (Eds.), *Constructing critical literacies* (pp. 185–225). Cresskill, NJ: Hampton.

Mariotti, A. S., & Homan, S. P. (2005). *Linking reading assessment to instruction*. London: Routledge.

McDaniel, C. (2004). Critical literacy: A questioning stance and the possibility for change. *The Reading Teacher, 57,* 472–481.

McLaughlin, M., & De Voogd, G. L. (2004). *Critical literacy: Enhancing students' comprehension of text*. New York: Scholastic.

Moll, L. C., & Gonzales, N. (2004). Engaging life: A funds of knowledge approach to multicultural education. In J. A. Banks & C. A. M. Banks (Eds.), *Handbook of research on multicultural education* (2nd ed., pp. 699–715). San Francisco: Jossey-Bass.

Nieto, S. (2002). *Language, culture, and teaching: Critical perspectives for a new century*. Mahwah, NJ: Erlbaum.

O'Donohue, W., & Kitchener, R. F. (Eds.). (1998). *Handbook of behaviorism*. New York: Academic Press.

Paratore, J. R. (2001). *Opening doors, opening opportunities: Family literacy in an urban community*. Boston: Allyn & Bacon.

Pearson, P. D., Raphael, T. E., Benson, V. L., & Madda, C. L. (2007). Balance in comprehensive literacy instruction: Then and now. In L. B. Gambrell, L. M. Morrow, & M. Pressley (Eds.), *Best practices in literacy instruction* (3rd ed., pp. 31–54). New York: Guilford Press.

Peregoy, S. F., & Boyle, O. F. (2009). *Reading, writing, and learning in ESL: A resource book for teaching K–12 English learners* (5th ed.). Boston: Allyn & Bacon/ Pearson.

Piaget, J. (1969). *The psychology of intelligence*. Paterson, NJ: Littlefield, Adams.

Pressley, M. (2002). Comprehension strategies instruction. In C. C. Block & M. Pressley (Eds.), *Comprehension instruction: Research-based best practices* (pp. 11–27). New York: Guilford Press.

Purcell-Gates, V. (2000). Family literacy. In M. L. Kamil, P. B. Mosenthal, P. D. Pearson, & R. Barr (Eds.), *Handbook of reading research* (Vol. 3, pp. 853–870). Mahwah, NJ: Erlbaum.

Rasinski, T., & Padak, N. (2008). Beyond stories. *The Reading Teacher, 61,* 582–584.

Rosenblatt, L. M. (2004). The transactional theory of reading and writing. In R. B. Ruddell & N. J. Unrau (Eds.), *Theoretical models and processes of reading* (5th ed., pp. 1363–1398). Newark, DE: International Reading Association.

Rosenblatt, L. (2005). *Making meaning with text: Selected essays*. Portsmouth, NH: Heinemann.

Rothenberg, C., & Fisher, D. (2007). *Teaching English language learners: A differentiated approach*. Upper Saddle River, NJ: Merrill/Prentice Hall.

Ruddell, R. B., & Unrau, N. J. (2004). Reading as a meaning-construction process: The reader, the text, and the teacher.

In R. B. Ruddell & N. J. Unrau (Eds.), *Theoretical models and processes of reading* (5th ed., pp. 1462–1521). Newark, DE: International Reading Association.

Rumelhart, D. E. (2004). Toward an interactive model of reading. In R. B. Ruddell & N. J. Unrau (Eds.), *Theoretical models and processes of reading* (5th ed., pp. 1149–1179). Newark, DE: International Reading Association.

Shanahan, T., & Beck, I. (2006). Effective literacy teaching for English-language learners. In D. August & T. Shanahan (Eds.), *Developing literacy in second-language learners: Report of the National Literacy Panel on Language-Minority Children and Youth* (pp. 415–488). Mahwah, NJ: Erlbaum.

Shannon, P. (1995). *Text, lies, & videotape: Stories about life, literacy, & learning*. Portsmouth, NH: Heinemann.

Skinner, B. F. (1974). *About behaviorism*. New York: Random House.

Smith, F. (1971). *Understanding reading: A psycholinguistic analysis of reading and learning to read*. New York: Holt, Rinehart and Winston.

Snow, C., Burns, M. S., & Griffin, P. (1998). *Preventing reading difficulties in young children*. Washington, DC: National Academy Press.

Snow, C. E., Griffin, P., & Burns, M. S. (Eds.). (2005). *Knowledge to support the teaching of reading: Preparing teachers for a changing world*. San Francisco: Jossey-Bass.

Stahl, S. A., & Nagy, W. E. (2005). *Teaching word meanings*. Mahwah, NJ: Erlbaum.

Stanovich, K. E. (2000). *Progress in understanding reading: Scientific foundations and new frontiers*. New York: Guilford Press.

Tompkins, G. E., & Collom, S. (Eds.). (2004). *Sharing the pen: Interactive writing with young children*. Upper Saddle River, NJ: Merrill/Prentice Hall.

Tracey, D. H., & Morrow, L. M. (2006). *Lenses on reading: An introduction to theories and models*. New York: Guilford Press.

Vukelich, C., Christie, J., & Enz, B. (2001). *Helping young children learn language and literacy*. Boston: Allyn & Bacon.

Vygotsky, L. S. (1978). *Mind in society*. Cambridge, MA: Harvard University Press.

Vygotsky, L. S. (1986). *Thought and language*. Cambridge, MA: MIT Press.

Wells, G., & Chang-Wells, G. L. (1992). *Constructing knowledge together: Classrooms as centers of inquiry and literacy*. Portsmouth, NH: Heinemann.

Wink, J. (2005). *Critical pedagogy: Notes from the real world* (3rd ed.). Boston: Allyn & Bacon/Pearson.

Wollman-Bonilla, J. (2000). *Family message journals: Teaching writing through family involvement*. Urbana, IL: National Council of Teachers of English.

CHILDREN'S BOOK REFERENCES

Carle, E. (1994). *The very hungry caterpillar*. New York: Scholastic.

Ellis, D. (2000). *The breadwinner*. Toronto: Groundwood Books.

Jiménez, F. (1999). *The circuit*. Boston: Houghton Mifflin.

McKissack, P. (2001). *Goin' somewhere special*. New York: Atheneum.

Park, L. S. (2007). *Project mulberry*. New York: Yearling.

Philbrick, R. (1993). *Freak the mighty*. New York: Blue Sky Press.

Polacco, P. (1994). *Pink and Say*. New York: Philomel.

Rathmann, P. (1995). *Officer Buckle and Gloria*. New York: Putnam.

Roth, S. (2001). *Happy birthday Mr. Kang*. Washington, DC: National Geographic Children's Books.

Ryan, P. M. (2002). *Esperanza rising*. New York: Scholastic/Blue Sky Press.

Sachar, L. (2003). *Holes*. New York: Yearling.

Tan, S. (2007). *The arrival*. New York: Scholastic.

Whelan, G. (2000). *Homeless bird*. New York: Scholastic.

White, E. B. (2006). *Charlotte's web*. New York: HarperCollins.

Woodson, J. (2007). *Feathers*. New York: Putnam.

CHAPTER 2

Teaching the Reading and Writing Processes

Mrs. Goodman's Seventh Graders Read The Giver

The seventh graders in Mrs. Goodman's class are reading the Newbery Medal winner *The Giver* (Lowry, 2006b). In this futuristic story, 12-year-old Jonas is selected to become the next Keeper of the Memories, and he discovers the terrible truth about his community. Mrs. Goodman has a class set of paperback copies of the book, and her students use the reading process as they read and explore it.

To introduce the book, Mrs. Goodman asks her students to get into small groups to brainstorm lists of all the things they would change about life if they could. Their lists, written on butcher paper, include no more homework, no AIDS, no crime, no gangs, no parents, no taking out the garbage, and being allowed to drive cars at age 10. The groups hang their lists on the chalkboard and share them. Mrs. Goodman puts checkmarks by many of the items, seeming to agree with the points. Next she explains that the class is going to read a story about life in the future. She explains that *The Giver* takes place in a planned utopian, or "perfect," society with the qualities that she checked on students' lists.

She passes out copies of the book and uses shared reading to read the first chapter aloud as students follow along in their books. Then the class talks about the first chapter in a grand conversation, asking a lot of questions: Why were there so many rules? Doesn't anyone drive a car? What does *released* mean? Why are children called a "Seven" or a "Four"? What does it mean that people are "given" spouses—don't they fall in love and get married? Why does Jonas have to tell his feelings? Classmates share their ideas and are eager to continue reading. Mrs. Goodman's reading aloud of the first chapter and the questions that the students raised generate interest in the story. The power of this story grabs them all.

They set a schedule for reading and discussion. Every 3 days, they'll come together to talk about the chapters they've read, and over 2 weeks, the class will complete the book. They'll also write in reading logs after reading the first chapter and then five more times as they're reading. In these logs, students write reactions to the story. Maria wrote this journal entry after finishing the book:

> Jonas had to do it. He had to save Gabriel's life because the next day Jonas's father was going to release (kill) him. He had it all planned out. That was important. He was very brave to leave his parents and his home. But I guess they weren't his parents really and his home wasn't all that good. I don't know if I could have done it but he did the right thing. He had to get out. He saved himself and he saved little Gabe. I'm glad he took Gabriel. That community was supposed to be safe but it really was dangerous. It was weird to not have colors. I guess that things that at first seem to be good are really bad.

Ron explored some of the themes of the story:

> Starving. He has memories of food. He's still hungry. But he's free. Food is safe. Freedom is surprises. Never saw a bird before. Same-same-same. Before he was starved for colors, memories and choice. Choice. To do what you want. To be who you can be. He won't starve.

Alicia thought about a lesson her mother taught her as she wrote:

> As Jonas fled from the community he lost his memories so that they would go back to the people there. Would they learn from them? Would they remember them? Or would life go on just the same? I think you have to do it yourself if you are going to learn. That's what my mom says. Somebody else can't do it for you. But Jonas did it. He got out with Gabe.

Tomas wrote about the Christmas connection at the end of the story:

> Jonas and Gabe came to the town at Christmas. Why did Lois Lowry do that? Gabe is like the baby Jesus, I think. It is like a rebirth—being born again. Jonas and his old community didn't go to church. Maybe they didn't believe in God. Now Jonas will be a Christian and the people in the church will welcome them. Gabe won't be released. I think Gabe is like Jesus because people tried to release Jesus.

During their grand conversations, students talk about many of the same points they raise in their journal entries. The story fascinates them—at first they think about how simple and safe life would be, but then they think about all the things they take for granted that they'd have to give up to live in Jonas's ordered society. They talk

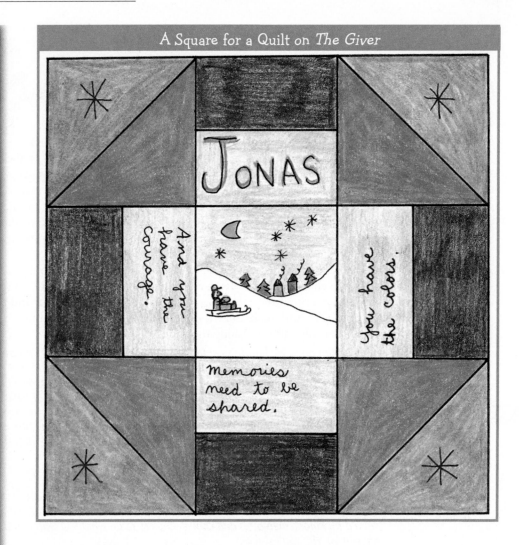

A Square for a Quilt on *The Giver*

about bravery and making choices, and they applaud Jonas's decision to flee with Gabriel. They also wonder if Jonas and Gabe survive.

The students collect "important" words from the story for the word wall. After reading Chapters 4, 5, and 6, they add these words to the word wall posted in the classroom:

relinquish	bikeports	regulated	infraction
invariably	gravitating	rehabilitation	stirrings
serene	chastisement	assignment	reprieve

Sometimes students choose unfamiliar or long words, but they also choose words such as *assignment* that are important to the story. Students refer to the word wall for words and their spellings when they're writing. Later during the unit, Mrs. Goodman teaches a minilesson about root words using some of these words.

As students read the book, Mrs. Goodman teaches a series of minilessons about reading strategies. After students read about colors in the story, for example, she teaches a minilesson on visualizing. She begins by rereading excerpts about Jonas being selected to be the next Receiver and asks students to draw a picture of the scene in their minds. She asks them to focus on the sights, sounds, smells, and feelings, and she talks about how important it is for readers to bring a story to life in their minds. Then students draw pictures of their visualizations and share them in small groups.

Another minilesson is about literary opposites. Mrs. Goodman explains that authors often introduce conflict and develop themes using contrasts or opposites. She asks students to think of opposites in *The Giver*; one example she suggests is *safe* and *free*. Other opposites that the students suggest include the following:

alive—released	families—family units
choice—no choice	memories—no memories
color—black and white	rules—anarchy
conform—do your own thing	stirrings—the pill

Mrs. Goodman asks students to think about how the opposites relate to the story and how Lois Lowry made them explicit in *The Giver*. Students talk about how the community seemed safe at the beginning of the story, but chapter by chapter, Lowry uncovered the community's shortcomings. They also talk about themes of the story reflected in these opposites.

After they finish reading the book, the students have a read-around in which they select and read aloud favorite passages to the class. Then students make a quilt to probe the themes in the story: Each student prepares a paper quilt square with an illustration and several sentences of text. One quilt square is shown on the preceding page. The students decide to use white, gray, and black to represent the sameness of Jonas's community, red for the first color Jonas saw, and colors in the center to represent Elsewhere.

Students also choose projects to work on individually or in small groups. One student makes a book box with objects related to the story, and two others read *Hailstones and Halibut Bones* (O'Neill, 1990), a collection of color poetry, and write their own color poems. One student makes an open-mind portrait of Jonas to show his thoughts the night he decided to escape with Gabe. Some students form literature circles to read *Gathering Blue* (2006a) and *The Messenger* (2006c), two related books by Lois Lowry. Others write about their own memories. They use the writing process to draft, refine, and publish their writing, and they share their published pieces as a culminating activity at the end of the unit.

The reading process that Mrs. Goodman uses represents a significant shift in thinking about what students do as they read. Mrs. Goodman understands that readers construct meaning as they negotiate the texts they're reading, and that they use their background experiences and knowledge of written language as they read. She knows that it's quite common for two students to read the same book and come away with different interpretations because meaning doesn't exist on the pages of a book; instead, comprehension is created through the interaction between readers and the texts they're reading. This individualized view of readers' interpretations reflects Rosenblatt's transactive theory (2004).

The reading process involves a series of stages during which readers comprehend the text. The term *text* refers to all reading materials—stories, maps, newspapers, cereal boxes, textbooks, e-mail, and so on; it's not limited to basal reading textbooks. The writing process is a similar recursive process involving a variety of activities as students gather and organize ideas, draft their compositions, revise and edit the drafts, and, finally, publish their writings. Students learn to use the writing process to craft and refine their compositions—autobiographies, stories, reports, poems, and essays.

THE READING PROCESS

Reading is a constructive process of creating meaning that involves the reader, the text, and the purpose within social and cultural contexts. The goal is comprehension, understanding the text and being able to use it for the intended purpose. Readers don't simply look at the words on a page and grasp the meaning; rather, it's a complex process involving these essential components:

Phonemic Awareness and Phonics. Students use their knowledge about the phonological system, including how to manipulate sounds in spoken words and apply phoneme-grapheme correspondences and phonics rules, as they read. They develop these abilities through phonemic awareness and phonics instruction in the primary grades.

Word Identification. Students recognize common or high-frequency words automatically and use their knowledge of phonics and word parts to decode unfamiliar words. Until students can recognize most of the words they're reading, they're slow, word-by-word readers.

Fluency. Students become fluent readers once they recognize most words automatically and read quickly and with expression. This is a milestone because students have limited cognitive resources to devote to reading, and beginning readers use most of this energy to decode words. Fluent readers, in contrast, devote most of their cognitive resources to comprehension.

Vocabulary. Students think about the meaning of words they're reading, choosing appropriate meanings, recognizing figurative uses, and relating them to their background knowledge. Knowing the meaning of words influences comprehension because it's difficult to understand when the words being read don't make sense.

Comprehension. Students use a combination of reader and text factors to understand what they're reading. They predict, connect, monitor, repair, and use other comprehension strategies as well as their knowledge of genres, organizational patterns, and literary devices to create meaning.

These components are supported by scientifically based reading research (National Reading Panel, 2000). As you continue reading this text, you'll learn how teachers teach and assess each of these components.

Teachers use the reading process to involve students in activities to teach, practice, and apply these components. The reading process is organized into five stages: prereading, reading, responding, exploring, and applying. This process is used, no matter which instructional program teachers have chosen, even though some of the activities at each stage differ. Figure 2–1 presents an overview of the reading process.

Stage 1: Prereading

The reading process begins before readers open a book. The first stage, prereading, occurs as readers prepare to read. In the vignette, Mrs. Goodman built her students' background knowledge and stimulated their interest in *The Giver* as they talked about how wonderful life would be in a "perfect" world. As readers get ready to read, they activate background knowledge, set purposes, and make plans for reading.

Activating Background Knowledge. Students have both general and specific background knowledge (Braunger & Lewis, 2006). General knowledge is world knowledge, what students have acquired through life experiences and learning in their home

Figure 2–1 ◆ Key Features of the Reading Process

Stage 1: Prereading
- Activate or build background knowledge and related vocabulary.
- Set purposes.
- Introduce key vocabulary words.
- Make predictions.
- Preview the text.

Stage 2: Reading
- Read independently, with a buddy, or using shared or guided reading, or listen to the text read aloud.
- Apply reading strategies and skills.
- Examine illustrations, charts, and diagrams.
- Read the text from beginning to end.
- Read one or more sections of text to learn specific information.
- Take notes.

Stage 3: Responding
- Write in reading logs.
- Participate in grand conversations or other discussions.

Stage 4: Exploring
- Reread all or part of the text.
- Learn new vocabulary words.
- Participate in minilessons on reading strategies and skills.
- Examine the author's craft.
- Identify memorable quotes.

Stage 5: Applying
- Construct projects.
- Read related books.
- Use information in thematic units.
- Evaluate the reading experience.

communities and at school, and specific knowledge is literary knowledge, what students need to read and comprehend a text. Literary knowledge includes information about reading, genres, and text structures. Students activate their world and literary background knowledge in this stage. They think about the title of a book, look at the book cover and inside illustrations, and read the first paragraph to trigger this activation.

When students don't have enough background knowledge to read a text, teachers build their knowledge base. They build knowledge about reading by teaching reading strategies and skills, knowledge about genres by examining the structure of the genre and explaining how reading varies according to genre, knowledge about a topic by providing a text set of books for students to read, engaging students in discussions, sharing artifacts, and introducing key vocabulary words. It's not enough just to build students' knowledge about the topic; literary knowledge is also essential!

Setting Purposes. The purpose guides students' reading. It provides motivation and direction for reading, as well as a mechanism for students to monitor their reading to see if they're fulfilling their purpose. Sustaining a single purpose while students read the text is more effective than presenting students with a series of purposes (Blanton, Wood, & Moorman, 1990). Sometimes teachers set purposes for reading, and sometimes students set their own purposes. In literature focus units and basal reading textbooks, teachers usually explain how students are expected to read and what they'll do after reading. In contrast, students set their own purposes for reading during literature circles and reading workshop; they choose texts that are intrinsically interesting or that explain something they want to learn more about. As students develop as readers, they become more effective at choosing books and setting their own purposes.

Planning for Reading. Once students activate their background knowledge and identify their purpose for reading, they take their first look at the text and plan for reading. Students vary how they make plans according to the type of selection they're preparing to read. For stories, they make predictions about the characters and events in the story. They often base their predictions on the book's title or the cover illustration. If they've read other stories by the same author or in the same genre, students also use this information in making their predictions. Sometimes students share their predictions orally, and at other times, they write predictions in their reading logs.

Check the Compendium of Instructional Procedures, which follows Chapter 12, for more information on the highlighted terms.

When students are preparing to read informational books and content-area textbook chapters, they preview the selection by flipping through the pages and noting section headings, illustrations, and diagrams. Sometimes they examine the table of contents to see how the book is organized, or they consult the index to locate specific information they want to read. They also notice highlighted terminology that's unfamiliar to them. To help students plan, teachers often use anticipation guides and prereading plans.

Stage 2: Reading

Students read the book or other selection in the reading stage. Outside of school, most people usually read silently and independently, but in the classroom, teachers and students use five types of reading:

- Independent reading
- Buddy reading
- Guided reading
- Shared reading
- Reading aloud to students

These types of reading vary in the amount of teacher scaffolding: Teachers provide very little support during independent reading, and the most support as they read aloud to students. As they decide which type of reading to use, teachers consider the purpose for reading, students' reading levels, and the number of available copies of the text.

Independent Reading. When students read independently, they read silently by themselves, for their own purposes, and at their own pace. It's essential that the books students select are at their reading level. Primary-grade students often read the featured selection independently during literature focus units, but this is often after they've already read the selection once or twice with the teacher's assistance. In the upper grades, many students read chapter books independently, but less capable readers may not be able to read the featured book independently. Students also independently read related books from the text set as part of these units.

During reading workshop, students read independently; even first graders can participate by rereading familiar books as well as new books at their reading level. Because students choose the books they want to read, they need to learn how to choose books at an appropriate level of difficulty.

Independent reading is an important part of a balanced reading program because it's the most authentic type of reading. It's the way students develop a love of reading and come to think of themselves as readers. The reading selection, however, must be at an appropriate level of difficulty so that students can read it independently. Otherwise, teachers use another type of reading to scaffold students and make it possible for them to be successful.

Buddy Reading. Students read or reread a selection with a classmate or sometimes with an older student (Friedland & Truesdell, 2004). Buddy reading is an enjoyable social activity, and students can often read selections together that neither one could read individually. Buddy reading is a good alternative to independent reading, and by working together, students are often able to figure out unfamiliar words and talk out comprehension problems.

As teachers introduce buddy reading, they show students how to read with buddies and how to support each other as they read. Students take turns reading aloud to each other or read in unison. They often stop and help each other identify an unfamiliar word or take a minute or two at the end of each page to talk about what they've read. Buddy reading is a valuable way of providing the practice that beginning readers need

Go to the Building Teaching Skills and Dispositions section of Chapter 2 on **MyEducationLab.com** to watch second graders Rakie and Audri participate in buddy reading.

to become fluent; it's also an effective way to work with students with special learning needs and students who are learning English. However, unless the teacher has explained the technique and taught students how to work collaboratively, buddy reading often deteriorates into the stronger of the two buddies reading aloud to the other student, but that isn't the intention of the technique.

Guided Reading. Teachers use guided reading to work with groups of four or five students who are reading at the same level. They select a book that students can read at their instructional level, with approximately 90–94% accuracy. Teachers support students' reading and their use of reading strategies during guided reading (Fountas & Pinnell, 1996). Students do the actual reading themselves, although the teacher may read aloud to get them started on the first page or two. Young children often murmur the words softly as they read, which helps the teacher keep track of students' reading and the strategies they're using. Older, more fluent readers usually read silently during guided reading.

Guided reading lessons usually last 25 to 30 minutes. When the students arrive for the small-group lesson, they often reread, either individually or with a buddy, familiar books used in previous lessons. For the new guided reading lesson, students read books that they haven't read before. Beginning readers usually read small picture books at one sitting, but older students who are reading longer chapter books take several days to a week or two to read their books (Allen, 2000).

Teachers observe students as they read during guided reading lessons. They spend a few minutes observing each reader, sitting either in front of or beside the student. They watch for evidence of strategy use and confirm the student's attempts to identify words and solve reading problems. Teachers take notes about their observations and use the information to decide which minilessons to teach and which books to choose for students to read.

Shared Reading. Teachers use shared reading to read aloud books and other texts that children can't read independently (Holdaway, 1979). Often primary-grade teachers use big books so that both small groups and whole-class groups can see the text and read along. Teachers model what fluent readers do as they involve students in enjoyable reading activities (Fountas & Pinnell, 1996). After reading the text several times, teachers use it to teach phonics concepts and high-frequency words. Students can also read small versions of the book independently or with buddies and use the text's pattern or structure for writing activities.

Shared reading is best known as part of a balanced literacy program in the primary grades. Teachers read aloud books that are appropriate for children's interest level but too difficult for them to read themselves. As an instructional procedure, shared reading differs from reading aloud because children see the text as the teacher reads. Children often join in the reading of predictable refrains and rhyming words, and after listening to the text read several times, they often remember enough of it to read along with the teacher.

Shared reading is also used to read novels with older students when the books are too difficult for them to read independently (Allen, 2002). Teachers distribute copies of the book to all students, and students follow along as the teacher reads aloud. Sometimes students take turns reading sections aloud, but the goal is not for everyone to have a turn reading. Students who want to read and are fluent enough to keep the reading meaningful volunteer to read. Often the teacher begins reading, and when a student wants to take over the reading, he or she begins reading aloud with the teacher; then the teacher drops off and the student continues reading. After a paragraph or a page, another student joins in and the first student drops off. Many teachers call this technique "popcorn reading."

Reading Aloud to Students. Teachers use the interactive read-aloud procedure as they read aloud books that are developmentally appropriate but written above students' reading levels (Fisher, Flood, Lapp, & Frey, 2004). As they read, teachers engage students in activities rather than postponing student involvement until after reading. Students become active participants, for example, as they make predictions, repeat refrains, ask questions, identify big ideas, and make connections. In addition, when teachers read aloud, they model what good readers do and how good readers use reading strategies (Cappellini, 2005). Reading aloud also provides an opportunity for teachers to think aloud about their use of reading strategies.

Read-alouds are an important component of literacy instruction at all grade levels, not just for young children who can't read many books on their own (Allen, 2000). Teachers read books aloud during literature focus units, reading and writing workshop, and thematic units. There are many benefits of reading aloud: introducing vocabulary, modeling comprehension strategies, and increasing students' motivation (Rasinski, 2003).

The types of reading are compared in Figure 2–2. In the vignette at the beginning of this chapter, Mrs. Goodman used a combination of these approaches. She used shared reading as she read the first chapter aloud, with students following in their own copies of *The Giver*. Later, students read together in small groups, with a buddy, or

Figure 2–2 ◆ Types of Reading

Type	Strengths	Limitations
Independent Reading Students read a text on their own without teacher scaffolding.	• Students develop responsibility. • Students learn to select texts. • Experience is authentic.	• Students may not choose texts that they can read independently. • Teacher has little involvement or control.
Buddy Reading Two students take turns as they read a text together.	• Students collaborate and assist each other. • Students become more fluent readers. • Students talk to develop comprehension.	• One student may simply read to the other. • Teacher has little involvement or control.
Guided Reading Teacher supports students as they apply reading strategies and skills to read a text.	• Teacher teaches reading strategies and skills. • Teacher provides scaffolding. • Teacher monitors students' reading.	• Multiple copies of texts at the appropriate reading level are needed. • Teacher controls the reading experience.
Shared Reading Teacher reads aloud while students follow along using a big book or individual copies.	• Teacher teaches concepts about print. • Teacher models fluent reading and reading strategies. • Students become a community of readers.	• Big books or a class set of books are needed. • Text may not be appropriate for all students.
Reading Aloud to Students Teacher reads aloud and provides opportunities for students to be actively involved in the experience.	• Students have access to books they can't read themselves. • Teacher models fluent reading and reading strategies. • Students build background knowledge and vocabulary.	• Students have no opportunity to read. • Students may not be interested in the text.

independently. As teachers plan their instructional programs, they include reading aloud to students, teacher-led student reading, and independent reading each day.

Stage 3: Responding

Students respond to what they've read and continue to negotiate the meaning after reading. This stage reflects Rosenblatt's (2005) transactive theory. Two ways that students make tentative and exploratory comments immediately after reading are by writing in reading logs and participating in grand conversations or other discussions.

Writing in Reading Logs. Students write and draw their thoughts and feelings about what they have read in reading logs. As students write about what they have read, they unravel their thinking and, at the same time, elaborate on and clarify their responses. Students usually write in reading logs when they're reading stories and poems; sometimes they also write in reading logs when they're reading informational books, but during thematic units, they make notes of important information or draw charts and diagrams in learning logs.

Students usually make reading logs by stapling together 10 to 12 sheets of paper. They decorate the covers, keeping with the theme of the book, and write entries after reading. Sometimes students choose topics for their entries, and sometimes teachers pose questions to guide students' thinking about their reading. Teachers monitor students' entries, reading and often responding to them. Because these journals are learning tools, teachers rarely correct students' spellings; they focus their responses on the ideas, but they expect students to spell the title of the book, the names of characters, and high-frequency words accurately. At the end of the unit, teachers review students' work and often grade the reading logs based on whether students completed all the entries and on the quality of the ideas expressed in their entries.

Participating in Discussions. Students also talk about the text with classmates in grand conversations about stories and poems and discussions about informational books and chapters in content-area textbooks. Peterson and Eeds (2007) explain that in grand conversations, students share their personal responses and tell what they liked about the text. After sharing personal reactions, they shift the focus to "puzzle over what the author has written and . . . share what it is they find revealed" (p. 61). Often students make connections between the text and their own lives or between the text and other literature they have read. If they're reading a chapter book, they also make predictions about what might happen in the next chapter.

Teachers often share their ideas in grand conversations, but they act as interested participants, not leaders. The talk is primarily among the students, but teachers ask questions regarding things they are genuinely interested in learning more about and share information in response to questions that students ask. In the past, many discussions have been "gentle inquisitions" during which students recited answers to factual questions that teachers asked to determine whether students read and understood an assignment. Although teachers can still judge whether students have read the assignment, the focus in grand conversations is on clarifying and deepening students' understanding of the story they've read.

Teachers and students also have discussions after reading informational books and chapters in content-area textbooks. Students talk about what interested them and what they learned about the topic, but teachers also focus students' attention on the big ideas, ask clarifying questions, share information, and reread brief excerpts to explore an idea.

These discussions can be held with the whole class or with small groups. Young children usually meet as a class, whereas older students often prefer to talk in small groups. When students meet as a class, there's a feeling of community, and the teacher can be part of the group. When students meet in small groups, they have more opportunities to share their interpretations, but fewer viewpoints are expressed in each group and teachers must move around, spending only a few minutes with each group. Teachers often compromise by having students begin their discussions in small groups and then come together as a class so that the groups can share what they discussed.

Stage 4: Exploring

Students go back into the text to examine it more analytically. This stage is more teacher directed than the others; it reflects the teacher-centered theory. Students reread the selection or excerpts from it, examine the author's craft, and focus on words and sentences from the selection. Teachers also teach minilessons on strategies and skills.

Rereading the Selection. As students reread the selection or excerpts from it, they think again about what they've read. Each time they reread a selection, students benefit in specific ways (Yaden, 1988): They deepen their comprehension as they move beyond their initial focus on the events of a story or the big ideas in an informational book to understanding the theme of the story or the relationships among the big ideas in a nonfiction text.

Examining the Author's Craft. Teachers plan exploring activities to focus students' attention on the genres, text structures, and literary devices that authors use. Students use story boards to sequence the events in the story, and make graphic organizers to highlight the plot, characters, and other elements of story structure. Another way students learn about the structure of stories is by writing books based on the selection they have read. In sequels, students tell what happens to the characters after the story ends.

Teachers share information about the author of the featured selection and introduce other books by the same author. Sometimes students read several books by the same author and make comparisons among them. To focus on literary devices, students often reread excerpts to locate examples of onomatopoeia, similes and metaphors, and other types of figurative language and wordplay.

Focusing on Words and Sentences. Teachers and students add "important" words to the word wall posted in the classroom. Students refer to it when they write and use the words for word-study activities, including drawing word clusters and posters to highlight particular words, doing word sorts to categorize words, and completing semantic feature analysis charts.

Students also locate "important" sentences in books they read; these sentences are worthy of examination because they contain figurative language, employ an interesting sentence structure, express a theme, or illustrate a character trait. Students often copy the sentences onto sentence strips to display in the classroom. Sometimes students copy the sentences in their reading logs and use them to begin their entries.

Teaching Minilessons. Teachers present minilessons on procedures, concepts, strategies, and skills (Angelillo, 2008). They introduce the topic and make connections between the topic and examples in the featured selection students have read. In the vignette, Mrs. Goodman presented minilessons on visualizing and root words and affixes using examples from *The Giver*.

Stage 5: Applying

Readers extend their comprehension, reflect on their understanding, and value the reading experience in this final stage. Often they create projects to apply what they've learned, and these projects take many forms, including open-mind portraits, essays, readers theatre performances, and PowerPoint presentations. A list of projects is presented in Figure 2–3. Usually students choose which project they want to do and work independently, with a classmate, or in a small group, but sometimes the class decides to work together on a project. In Mrs. Goodman's class, for example, some students wrote color poems while classmates read other books by Lois Lowry or wrote about memories.

Figure 2–3 ◆ Application Projects

Visual Projects
- Design a graphic organizer or model about a book.
- Create a collage to represent the theme or big ideas in a book.
- Prepare illustrations of a story's events to make clothesline props to use in retelling the story.
- Make a book box and fill it with objects and pictures representing the book.
- Construct a paper quilt about a book.
- Create an open-mind portrait to probe the thoughts of one character.

Writing Projects
- Rewrite a story from a different point of view.
- Write another episode or a sequel for a book.
- Write simulated letters from one character to another.
- Create a found poem using words and phrases from a book.
- Write a poem on a topic related to a book.
- Keep a simulated journal from one character's viewpoint.
- Write an essay to examine the book's theme or a controversial issue.
- Create a multigenre project about a book.

Reading Projects
- Read other books from the text set.
- Read another book by the same author.
- Collect several poems that complement the book.

Talk and Drama Projects
- Give a readers theatre presentation of an excerpt from a book.
- Create a choral reading using an excerpt from a book and have classmates read it.
- Write a script and present a play based on a book.
- Dress as a book character and sit on the "hot seat" to answer classmates' questions.
- Present a rap, song, or poem about a book.

Internet Projects
- Write a book review and post it online.
- Investigate an author's website and share information from it with classmates.
- Create a multimodal project about the book using text, images, and sounds.
- Search the Web for information on a topic related to the book and share the results with classmates.
- Create a PowerPoint presentation about the book.

Social Action Projects
- Write a letter to the editor of the local newspaper on a topic related to a book.
- Get involved in a community project related to a book.

Reading Strategies and Skills

Reading is a complex process involving both strategies and skills. Strategies represent the thinking that readers do as they read, whereas skills are quick, automatic behaviors that don't require any thought. For example, readers use the connecting strategy to compare the story they're reading to their own lives, the world around them, and other books they've read. They're actively thinking as they make connections. In contrast, noticing quotation marks that signal a character's dialogue is a skill; students don't have to think about what these punctuation marks are signaling because they recognize their meaning automatically. The terms *strategy* and *skill* can be confusing; sometimes they're considered synonyms, but they're not. It's important to clarify the distinctions between the two.

Strategies are deliberate, goal-directed actions (Afflerbach, Pearson, & Paris, 2008). Readers exercise control in choosing appropriate strategies, using them flexibly, and monitoring their effectiveness. Strategies are linked with motivation. Afflerbach and his colleagues explain that "strategic readers feel confident that they can monitor and improve their own reading so they have both knowledge and motivation to succeed" (p. 370). Strategies reflect the cognitive/information processing theory. In contrast, skills are automatic actions that occur without deliberate control or conscious awareness. The emphasis is on their effortless and accurate use. Skills reflect the behavioral theory, and they're used in the same way, no matter the reading situation. It's crucial that students become both strategic and skilled readers.

Types of Strategies and Skills. Comprehension strategies are probably the best-known type, but readers use strategies throughout the reading process:

Decoding Strategies. Students use strategies, such as using phonic and morphemic analysis, to identify unfamiliar words.

Word-Learning Strategies. Students apply strategies, such as analyzing word parts, to figure out the meaning of unfamiliar words.

Comprehension Strategies. Students use strategies, such as predicting, drawing inferences, and visualizing, to understand what they're reading.

Study Strategies. Students apply strategies, such as taking notes and questioning, to learn information when they're reading content-area textbooks.

You'll learn more about these types of strategies in upcoming chapters.

Students also learn skills that they use when they're reading. Phonics skills are probably the best known, but, like strategies, they're used throughout the reading process. They can be grouped into the same categories as reading strategies:

Decoding Skills. Students use their knowledge of sound-symbol correspondences and phonics rules to decode words.

Word-Learning Skills. Students identify synonyms, recognize metaphors, notice capital letters signaling proper nouns and adjectives, and use other word-learning skills.

Comprehension Skills. Students recognize details and connect them to main ideas, separate fact and opinion, and use other comprehension skills.

Study Skills. Students use skills, including consulting an index and noticing boldface terms in the text, to help them locate and remember information.

Students often use these skills in connection with strategies; the big difference is that strategies are used thoughtfully and skills are automatic.

Guidelines
for Strategy Instruction

▸ Teach strategies in minilessons using explanations, demonstrations, think-alouds, and practice activities.

▸ Provide step-by-step explanations and modeling so that students understand what the strategy does, and how and when to use it.

▸ Provide both guided and independent practice opportunities so that students can apply the strategy in new situations.

▸ Have students apply the strategy in content-area activities as well as in literacy activities.

▸ Teach groups of strategies in routines so that students learn to orchestrate the use of multiple strategies.

▸ Ask students to reflect on their use of single strategies and strategy routines.

▸ Hang charts of strategies and strategy routines students are learning in the classroom, and encourage students to refer to them when reading and writing.

▸ Differentiate between strategies and skills so that students understand that strategies are problem-solving tactics and skills are automatic behaviors.

Minilessons. Students need explicit instruction about reading strategies because they don't acquire the knowledge through reading (Dowhower, 1999; Pressley, 2000). Teachers need to provide three types of information about a strategy for students to learn to use it:

◆ Declarative knowledge—what the strategy does
◆ Procedural knowledge—how to use the strategy
◆ Conditional knowledge—when to use the strategy (Baker & Brown, 1984)

Let's examine the declarative, procedural, and conditional knowledge for the questioning strategy, which is a comprehension strategy that students use to ask themselves questions while they're reading. They use it direct their reading, monitor whether they're understanding, and construct meaning (declarative knowledge). They ask themselves questions such as "What's going to happen next?" "How does this relate to what I know about ____?" and "Does this make sense?" (procedural knowledge). Students use this strategy again and again while they're reading (conditional knowledge).

Teachers use minilessons to teach students about strategies. They explain the strategy and model its use, and then students practice using it with teacher guidance and supervision before using it independently. Through this instruction, students develop metacognitive awareness, their ability to think about their strategy use (Paris, Wasik, & Turner, 1991). The feature on this page presents a list of guidelines for strategy instruction.

Teachers demonstrate the thought processes readers use as they read by using think-alouds (Wilhelm, 2001). Teachers think aloud or explain what they're thinking while they're reading so that students become more aware of how capable readers think; in the process, students also learn to think aloud about their use of strategies. They set a purpose for reading, predict what will happen next, make connections, ask questions, summarize what's happened so far, draw inferences, evaluate the text, and make other comments that reflect their thinking. Think-alouds are valuable both when teachers model them for students and when students engage in them themselves. When students use think-alouds, they become more thoughtful, strategic readers and improve their ability to monitor their comprehension.

Students can record their strategy use with small self-stick notes. Teachers distribute pads of notes and explain how to use them. Students can focus on their use of a single strategy or a group of strategies. They write comments about the strategies on the self-stick notes while they're reading and place them in the margin of the pages so they can locate them when the book is closed. Afterward, students share their notes and talk about the strategies they used in a discussion with classmates or in a conference with the teacher.

THE WRITING PROCESS

The writing process is a series of five stages that describe what students think and do as they write; the stages are prewriting, drafting, revising, editing, and publishing. The labeling of the stages doesn't mean that the writing process is a linear series of neatly packaged categories; rather, research has shown that the process involves recurring cycles, and labeling is simply an aid to identifying writing activities. In the classroom, the stages merge and recur as students write. The key features of each stage are shown in Figure 2–4.

Stage 1: Prewriting

Prewriting is the "getting ready to write" stage. The traditional notion that writers have a topic completely thought out and ready to flow onto the page is ridiculous: If writers wait for ideas to fully develop, they may wait forever. Instead, writers begin tentatively—talking, reading, brainstorming—to see what they know and in what direction they want to go. Prewriting has probably been the most neglected stage in the writing process; however, it's as crucial to writers as a warm-up is to athletes. Murray (1982) believes that at least 70% of writing time should be spent in prewriting. During prewriting, students choose a topic, consider purpose and form, and gather and organize ideas for writing.

Figure 2–4 ◆ Key Features of the Writing Process

Stage 1: Prewriting

- Choose a topic.
- Consider the purpose for writing.
- Identify the genre the writing will take.
- Engage in rehearsal activities to gather ideas.
- Use a graphic organizer to organize ideas.

Stage 2: Drafting

- Write a rough draft.
- Emphasize ideas rather than mechanical correctness.

Stage 3: Revising

- Reread the rough draft.
- Share writing in writing groups.

- Make substantive changes that reflect classmates' comments.
- Conference with the teacher.

Stage 4: Editing

- Proofread the revised rough draft.
- Identify and correct spelling, capitalization, punctuation, and grammar errors.
- Conference with the teacher.

Stage 5: Publishing

- Make the final copy.
- Share the finished writing with an appropriate audience.

Choosing a Topic. Students should choose their own topics for writing—topics that they're interested in and know about—so that they'll be more engaged, but that isn't always possible. Sometimes teachers provide the topics, especially in connection with literature focus units and content-area units. It's best when teacher-selected topics are broad so students can narrow them in the way that's best for them.

Considering Purpose and Form. As students prepare to write, they need to think about the purpose of their writing: Are they writing to entertain? to inform? to persuade? Setting the purpose for writing is just as important as setting the purpose for reading, because purpose influences decisions students make about form.

One of the most important considerations is the genre or form the writing will take: a story? a letter? a poem? an essay? A writing activity could be handled in any one of these ways. Students learn to use a variety of writing genres; six are described in Figure 2–5. Through reading and writing, students become knowledgeable about these genres and how they're structured (Donovan & Smolkin, 2002). Langer (1985) found that by third grade, students respond in distinctly different ways to story- and report-writing assignments; they organize the writing differently and include varied kinds of information and elaboration. Because students are learning the distinctions between various genres, it's important that teachers use the correct terminology and not label all writing as "stories."

Gathering and Organizing Ideas. Students engage in activities to gather and organize ideas for writing during the prewriting stage. Graves (1983) calls what writers do to prepare for writing "rehearsal" activities. To gather ideas, they draw pictures, brainstorm lists of words, read books, do Internet research, and talk about ideas with classmates. Students make graphic organizers to visually display the arrangement of their ideas. Their choice of graphic organizer varies with the writing genre: For stories, they often use a three-part diagram to emphasize the beginning-middle-end structure of stories, and to write persuasive essays, they use a cluster with one ray to develop the ideas for each argument.

Stage 2: Drafting

Students get their ideas down on paper and write a first draft of their compositions in this stage. Because they don't begin writing with their pieces already composed in their minds, students begin tentatively with the ideas they've developed through prewriting activities. Their drafts are usually messy, reflecting the outpouring of ideas with cross-outs, lines, and arrows as they think of

Teaching Struggling Readers and Writers

The Writing Process

Struggling writers need to use the writing process.

Many struggling writers don't like to write, and they avoid writing whenever possible because they don't know what to do (Christenson, 2002). One of the best ways to review the writing process with struggling writers is to use interactive writing, a procedure normally used with young children, to demonstrate the writing process and the strategies writers use, including organizing and revising. Because it's a group activity, students are more willing to participate.

Once they're familiar with the stages in the writing process, students apply what they've learned to write collaborative compositions. Each student drafts a paragraph or short section and then moves through the writing process; this way, the workload is manageable for both students and their teachers. Once students have learned to use the writing process and have developed a repertoire of writing strategies, they're better prepared to write independently.

Struggling writers who don't understand the writing process often break the process as soon as they write a first draft, thinking their work is finished; they don't realize that they need to revise and edit their writing to communicate more effectively. The key to enticing struggling writers to revise and edit is to help them develop a sense of audience. Many novice writers write primarily for themselves, but when they want their classmates or another audience to understand their message, they begin to recognize the importance of refining their writing. Teachers emphasize audience by encouraging students to share their writing from the author's chair. Lots of writing and sharing are necessary before students learn to appreciate the writing process.

Figure 2–5 ◆ Writing Genres

Genre	Purpose	Activities
Descriptive Writing	Students observe carefully and choose precise language. They take notice of sensory details and create comparisons (metaphors and similes) to make their writing more powerful.	Character sketches Comparisons Descriptive essays Descriptive sentences Found poems
Expository Writing	Students collect and synthesize information. This writing is objective; reports are the most common type. Students use expository writing to give directions, sequence steps, compare one thing to another, explain causes and effects, or describe problems and solutions.	Alphabet books Autobiographies Directions Essays Posters Reports Summaries
Journals and Letters	Students write to themselves and to specific, known audiences. Their writing is personal and often less formal than other genres. They share news, explore new ideas, and record notes. Students learn the special formatting that letters and envelopes require.	Business letters Courtesy letters Double-entry journals E-mail messages Friendly letters Learning logs Personal journals
Narrative Writing	Students retell familiar stories, develop sequels for stories they have read, write stories about events in their own lives, and create original stories. They include a beginning, middle, and end in the narratives to develop the plot and characters.	Original short stories Personal narratives Retellings of stories Sequels to stories Story scripts
Persuasive Writing	Persuasion is winning someone to your viewpoint or cause using appeals to logic, moral character, and emotion. Students present their position clearly and support it with examples and evidence.	Advertisements Book and movie reviews Letters to the editor Persuasive essays Persuasive letters
Poetry Writing	Students create word pictures and play with rhyme and other stylistic devices as they create poems. Through their wordplay, students learn that poetic language is vivid and powerful but concise and that poems can be arranged in different ways on a page.	Acrostic poems Color poems Free verse Haiku "I Am" poems Poems for two voices

better ways to express ideas. Students write quickly, with little concern about legible handwriting, spelling correctness, and careful use of capitalization and punctuation.

When they write rough drafts, students skip every other line to leave space for revisions. They use arrows to move sections of text, cross-outs to delete sections, and scissors and tape to cut apart and rearrange text, just as adult writers do. They write only on one side of a sheet of paper so it can be cut apart or rearranged. Wide spacing between lines is crucial. At first, teachers make small x's on every other line of students' papers as a reminder to skip lines during drafting, but once they understand the importance of leaving space, students skip lines automatically.

Students label their drafts by writing *rough draft* in ink at the top or by using a ROUGH DRAFT stamp. This label indicates to the writer, other students, parents, and administrators that the composition is a draft in which the emphasis is on content, not mechanics; it also explains why the teacher hasn't graded the paper.

Instead of writing drafts by hand, many students, even those in kindergarten through third grade, use computers to compose rough drafts, polish their writing, and print out final copies. There are many benefits of using computers for word processing. Students are often more motivated to write, and they tend to write longer pieces. Their writing looks neater, and they use spell-check programs to identify and correct misspelled words.

Stage 3: Revising

During the revising stage, writers refine ideas in their compositions. Students often break the writing process cycle as soon as they complete a rough draft, believing that once they have jotted down their ideas, the writing task is complete. Experienced writers, however, know they must turn to others for reactions and revise on the basis of these comments. Revision is not just polishing; it is meeting the needs of readers by adding, substituting, deleting, and rearranging material. *Revision* means "seeing again," and in this stage, writers see their compositions again with the help of classmates and the teacher. Revising consists of three activities: rereading the rough draft, sharing the rough draft in a writing group, and revising on the basis of feedback.

Rereading the Rough Draft. After finishing the rough draft, writers need to distance themselves from it for a day or two, then reread it from a fresh perspective, as a reader might. As they reread, students make changes—adding, substituting, deleting, and moving—and place question marks by sections that need work; it is these trouble spots that students ask for help with in their writing groups.

Sharing in Writing Groups. Students meet in writing groups to share their compositions with classmates. They respond to the writer's rough draft and suggest possible revisions. Writing groups provide a scaffold in which teachers and classmates talk about plans and strategies for writing and revising (Applebee & Langer, 1983; Calkins, 1983).

Writing groups can form spontaneously when several students have completed drafts and are ready to share their compositions, or they can be formal groupings with identified leaders. In some classrooms, writing groups form when four or five students finish writing their rough drafts; students gather around a conference table or in a corner of the classroom and take turns reading their rough drafts aloud. Classmates in the group listen and respond, offering compliments and suggestions for revision. Sometimes the teacher joins the writing group, but if the teacher is involved in something else, students work independently.

In other classrooms, the writing groups are assigned; students get together when all students in the group have completed their rough drafts and are ready to share their writing. Sometimes the teacher participates in these groups, providing feedback along with the students. Or, the writing groups can function independently: Each is made up of four or five students, and a list of groups and their members is posted in the classroom. The teacher puts a star

Literacy Portraits: VIEWING GUIDE

Michael and his classmates are confident writers who willingly share their rough drafts and revise their writing. Watch Michael share his rough draft with Ben in his May video clip. Next, view Michael's February video clip where Ms. Janusz teaches a minilesson on writing effective endings and then conferences with Michael about how he plans to end the story he's writing. You might also check Rhiannon's April video clip of her writing conference with Ms. Janusz. Because Rhiannon's writing is a challenge to read, Ms. Janusz usually combines revising and editing when she works with her. Ideas are born so quickly in Rhiannon's imagination that she forgets about inserting punctuation when she writes, and her abbreviated phonetic spellings are difficult to decipher. Getting students to revise isn't easy. What do you notice in these video clips to suggest why these second graders are so successful?

myeducationlab

by one student's name, and that student serves as a group leader. The leader changes every quarter.

Making Revisions. Students make four types of changes to their rough drafts: additions, substitutions, deletions, and moves (Faigley & Witte, 1981). As they revise, students might add words, substitute sentences, delete paragraphs, and move phrases. Students often use a blue or red pen to cross out, draw arrows, and write in the space left between the double-spaced lines of their rough drafts so that revisions will show clearly; that way, teachers can see the types of revisions students make by examining their revised rough drafts. Revisions are another gauge of students' growth as writers.

Revising Centers. Many teachers set up revising centers to give students revision options: They can talk about the ideas in their rough draft with a classmate, examine the organization of their writing, consider their word choice, or check that they have included all required components in the composition. A list of revising centers is shown in Figure 2–6. Teachers introduce these centers as they teach their students

Figure 2–6 ◆ Revising and Editing Centers

Type	Center	Activities
Revising	Rereading	Students reread their rough drafts with a partner and the partner offers compliments and asks questions.
	Word Choice	Students choose 5–10 words in their rough drafts and look for more specific or more powerful synonyms using a thesaurus, word walls in the classroom, or suggestions from classmates.
	Graphic Organizer	Students draw a chart or diagram to illustrate the organization of their compositions, and they revise their rough drafts if the organization isn't effective or the writing isn't complete.
	Highlighting	Students use highlighter pens to mark their rough drafts according to the teacher's direction. Depending on the skills being taught, students may mark topic sentences, descriptive language, or sensory details.
	Sentence Combining	Students choose a section of their rough drafts with too many short sentences (often signaled by overuse of *and*) and use sentence combining to improve the flow of the writing.
Editing	Spelling	Students work with a partner to proofread their writing. They locate misspelled words and use a dictionary to correct them. Students may also check for specific errors in their use of recently taught skills.
	Homophones	Students check their rough drafts for homophone errors (e.g., *there–their–they're*), and consulting a chart posted in the center, they correct the errors.
	Punctuation	Students proofread their writing to check for punctuation marks. They make corrections as needed, and then highlight the punctuation marks in their compositions.
	Capitalization	Students check that each sentence begins with a capital letter, the word *I* is capitalized, and proper nouns and adjectives are capitalized. After the errors are corrected, students highlight all capitalized letters in the compositions.
	Sentences	Students analyze the sentences in their rough drafts and categorize them as simple, compound, complex, or fragment on a chart. Then they make any necessary changes.

about the writing process and the qualities of good writing, and then students work at these centers before or after participating in a writing group. Teachers usually provide a checklist of center options that students put in their writing folders, and then they check off the centers that they complete. Through these center activities, students develop a repertoire of revising strategies and personalize their writing process.

Stage 4: Editing

Editing is putting the piece of writing into its final form. Until this stage, the focus has been primarily on the content of students' writing. Once the focus changes to mechanics, students polish their writing by correcting spelling mistakes and other mechanical errors. Mechanics are the commonly accepted conventions of written Standard English; they consist of capitalization, punctuation, spelling, sentence structure, usage, and formatting considerations specific to poems, scripts, letters, and other writing genres. The use of these commonly accepted conventions is a courtesy to those who will read the composition.

Students are more efficient editors if they set the composition aside for a few days before beginning to edit. After working so closely with a piece of writing during drafting and revising, they're too familiar with it to notice many mechanical errors. With the distance gained by waiting a few days, students are better able to approach editing with a fresh perspective and gather the enthusiasm necessary to finish the writing process. Then students move through two activities in the editing stage: proofreading to locate errors and correcting the ones they find.

Proofreading. Students proofread their compositions to locate and mark possible errors. Proofreading is a unique type of reading in which students read word by word, hunting for errors rather than reading for meaning. Concentrating on mechanics is difficult because of our natural inclination to read for meaning; even experienced proofreaders often find themselves focusing on comprehension and thus overlooking errors that don't inhibit meaning. It's important, therefore, to take time to explain proofreading to students and to demonstrate how it differs from regular reading.

To demonstrate proofreading, teachers copy a piece of writing on the chalkboard or display it on an overhead projector. The teacher reads it several times, each time hunting for a particular type of error. During each reading, the teacher reads the composition slowly, softly pronouncing each word and touching it with a pencil or pen to focus attention on it. The teacher marks possible errors as they are located.

Editing checklists help students focus on particular types of errors. Teachers can develop checklists with two to six items appropriate for the grade level. A first-grade checklist, for example, might have only two items—perhaps one about capital letters at the beginning of sentences and a second about periods at the end of sentences. In contrast, a middle-grade checklist might contain items such as using commas in a series, indenting paragraphs, capitalizing proper nouns and adjectives, and spelling homonyms correctly. Teachers revise the checklist during the school year to focus attention on skills that have recently been taught.

A third-grade editing checklist is presented in the Assessment Tools feature on page 58. The writer and a classmate work as partners to edit their compositions. First, students proofread their own compositions, searching for errors in each category on the checklist, and, after proofreading, check off each item. After completing the checklist, students sign their names and trade checklists and compositions: Now they become editors and complete each other's checklist. Having both writer and editor sign the checklist helps them to take the activity seriously.

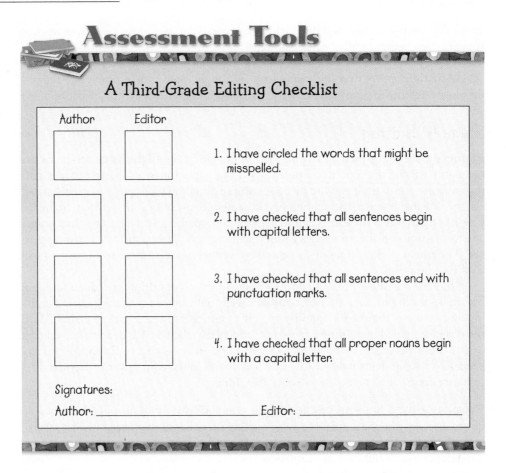

Assessment Tools

A Third-Grade Editing Checklist

Author	Editor	
		1. I have circled the words that might be misspelled.
		2. I have checked that all sentences begin with capital letters.
		3. I have checked that all sentences end with punctuation marks.
		4. I have checked that all proper nouns begin with a capital letter.

Signatures:

Author: _____   Editor: _____

Correcting Errors. After students proofread their compositions and locate as many errors as they can, they use red pens to correct the errors independently or with an editor's assistance. Some errors are easy to correct, some require use of a dictionary, and others involve instruction from the teacher. It is unrealistic to expect students to locate and correct every mechanical error in their compositions; not even published books are always error-free! Once in a while, students may change a correct spelling or punctuation mark and make it incorrect, but they correct far more errors than they create.

Students also work at editing centers to check for and correct specific types of errors. A list of editing centers is also shown in Figure 2–6. Teachers often vary the activities at the center to reflect the types of errors students are making. Students who continue to misspell common words can check for these words on a chart posted in the center. Or, after a series of lessons on contractions or punctuation marks, for example, one or more centers will focus on applying the newly taught skill.

Editing can end after students and their editors correct as many mechanical errors as possible, or after students meet with the teacher for a final editing conference. When mechanical correctness is crucial, this conference is important. Teachers proofread the composition with the student, and they identify and make the remaining corrections together, or the teacher makes checkmarks in the margin to note errors for the student to correct independently.

Stage 5: Publishing

In this stage, students bring their compositions to life by writing final copies and by sharing them orally with an appropriate audience. When they share their writing with real audiences of classmates, other students, parents, and the community, students come to think of themselves as authors. Publication is powerful: Students are motivated not only to continue writing but also to improve the quality of their writing through revising and editing (Weber, 2002).

Making Books. One of the most popular ways for students to publish their writing is by making books. Simple booklets can be made by folding a sheet of paper into quarters, like a greeting card. Students write the title on the front and use the three remaining sides for their composition. They can also construct booklets by stapling sheets of writing paper together and adding covers made out of construction paper. Sheets of wallpaper cut from old sample books also make sturdy covers. These stapled booklets can be cut into various shapes, too. Students can make more sophisticated books by covering cardboard covers with contact paper, wallpaper samples, or cloth. Pages are sewn or stapled together, and the first and last pages (endpapers) are glued to the cardboard covers to hold the book together.

Sharing Writing. One of the best ways for students to share their writing is to sit in a special chair in the classroom called the *author's chair* and read their writing aloud to classmates. Afterward, classmates ask questions, offer compliments, and celebrate the completion of the writing project. Sharing writing is a social activity that helps writers develop sensitivity to audiences and confidence in themselves as authors. Beyond just providing the opportunity for students to share writing, teachers need to teach students how to make appropriate comments as they respond to their classmates' writing. Teachers also serve as a model for responding to students' writing without dominating the sharing.

Here are some other ways for students to share their writing:

◆ Read it to parents and siblings
◆ Share it at a back-to-school event
◆ Place it in the class or school library
◆ Read it to students in other classes
◆ Display it as a mobile or on a poster
◆ Contribute it to a class anthology
◆ Post it on the class website
◆ Submit it to the school's literary magazine
◆ Display it at a school or community event
◆ Send it to a children's literary magazine
◆ Submit it to an e-zine (online literary magazine)

The best literary magazines for students are *Stone Soup* and *Skipping Stones*. *Stone Soup* is a magazine of children's writing and artwork for children ages 8–13. This prestigious magazine seeks children's stories and poems. At its website (www.stonesoup. com), students can download a sample issue and listen to authors reading their own writing. Subscription information is available there as well as directions for submitting students' writing. *Skipping Stones* is an international magazine for children ages 8–16 that accepts stories, articles, photos, cartoons, letters, and drawings. This award-winning publication focuses on global interdependence, celebrates cultural and environmental richness, and provides a forum for children from around the world to share ideas and experiences. To read excerpts from the current issue and to get information about subscribing and submitting writing to *Skipping Stones*, go to the magazine's

Author's Chair
These fifth graders take turns sitting in the special author's chair to read their published writings aloud to classmates. It's a celebratory activity, and after reading, students take turns asking questions and offering compliments. These students have learned to show interest in their classmates' writing and to think about the writing so that they can participate in the discussion that follows the reading. Afterward, another student is cho-sen to share, and the pro-cess is repeated. As students sharing their writing from the author's chair, they learn to think of themselves as authors and consider their audience more carefully when they write.

website at www.skippingstones.org. Many teachers subscribe to these magazines and use the writings as models when they're teaching writing. Other literary magazines worth considering are *Magic Dragon* (www.magicdragonmagazine.com) and *New Moon: The Magazine for Girls and Their Dreams* (www.newmoon.org). Too often, literary magazines are labors of love rather than viable financial ventures, so even highly esteemed and popular magazines go out of business. Students should always check that a literary magazine is still accepting submissions before sending their writing.

Writing Strategies and Skills

Writing strategies are like reading strategies; they're tools students use deliberately to craft effective compositions. Students apply many of the same strategies for both reading and writing, such as activating background knowledge, questioning, repairing, and evaluating, and they also use some specific writing strategies. Dean (2006) explains that using the writing process makes writers more strategic, and writers use a variety of strategies at each stage:

Prewriting Strategies. Students use prewriting strategies, including organizing, to develop ideas before beginning to write. Examples: generating ideas and organizing ideas.

Drafting Strategies. Students apply drafting strategies to focus on ideas while writing the first draft. Examples: narrowing the topic and providing examples.

Revising Strategies. Students use revising strategies to communicate their ideas more effectively. Examples: rereading, detecting problems, elaborating ideas, combining sentences, and choosing precise words.

New Literacies
Online Publication Sites

The Internet offers unlimited opportunities for students to display their writing online, share it with a global audience, and receive authentic feedback from readers (McNabb, 2006). When students create multimodal projects that incorporate audio, video, animation, or graphics into their writing, electronic publication is essential so that readers can fully experience what students are communicating. Students are learning to use new literacies when they express their ideas with multimodal features and engage in online communication (Labbo, 2005).

Here's a list of five of the best online publication sites for students:

Cyber Kids

www.cyberkids.com
This site publishes original writing, mostly stories and poetry, written by 7- to 16-year-olds. The multimodal stories are especially interesting.

Kids' Space

www.kids-space.org
This website posts children's art, writing, and music pieces from around the world. In the writing category, stories, play scripts, and poems written by 5- to 16-year-olds are invited.

KidsWWwrite

www.kalwriters.com/kidswwwrite
Students' stories and poems are published in this e-zine that's divided into areas for 5- to 8-year-olds, 9- to 12-year-olds, and 13- to 16-year-olds.

Poetry Zone

www.poetryzone.ndirect.co.uk
This British website posts students' poetry in the Poetry Gallery and provides other poetry resources for teachers.

Stories From the Web

www.storiesfromtheweb.org
This website, divided into preschool–grade 1, grades 2–5, and grades 6–8 areas, accepts submissions of students' stories, play scripts, poems, raps, and songs.

Students can also use Internet search engines to locate new e-zines. It's inevitable that some online publication websites will shut down, but others will spring up to take their place.

Each electronic magazine posts its own guidelines for contributors and submission information that students should read and follow. Most e-zines specify that students' submissions must be original, and that writing that deals with violent or offensive topics or that employs inappropriate language won't be published. Students usually aren't paid for their writing. Submissions must be ready for posting; it's naïve to assume that an editor will format students' writing or correct misspellings and other mechanical errors. Students usually complete an on-line information sheet and e-mail their writing to the e-zine's website, and parents are required to submit a statement giving permission for their child's writing to be posted online.

Students can also display their writing on the class website for others to read and respond to in guest books, blogs, and e-mail messages (Weber, 2002). Even first graders can access and read the writing posted on their class website (McGowan, 2005)! If the teacher doesn't have a class website, students can work with their teacher to create one and post their writing there.

Editing Strategies. Students apply strategies to identify and correct spelling and other mechanical errors. Example: proofreading.

Publishing Strategies. Students use strategies to prepare the final drafts of their compositions and share them with classmates and other authentic audiences. Examples: designing the layout and reading expressively.

Students use these writing strategies purposefully as they draft and refine their writing.

Writing skills are knowledge-based, automatic actions that students learn to apply during the writing process. Here are five types of skills that writers use:

Content Skills. Students apply skills, including topic sentences, to arrange information into paragraphs. These skills are most important during the drafting and revising stages.

Word Skills. Students use skills, including synonyms and metaphors, during drafting and revising to make their writing clearer.

Sentence Skills. Students apply skills, including types of sentences, to make their writing more interesting to read. They use these skills during drafting and revising.

Grammar Skills. Students use skills, including verb tenses and subject-verb agreement, to correct any nonstandard English errors during editing.

Mechanical Skills. Students apply spelling, capitalization, and punctuation skills to make their compositions more readable, especially during the editing stage.

Teachers use minilessons with demonstrations and think-alouds to teach writing strategies and skills, and then students apply what they're learning during guided practice and independent writing projects. These strategies and skills are often reflected in rubrics that teachers and students use to assess students' writing.

Qualities of Good Writing

Students learn about the qualities of good writing through minilessons and apply what they're learning as they use the writing process. Spandel (2005) has identified these six qualities, which she calls *traits*:

Ideas. The ideas are the essence of a composition. Students choose an interesting idea and then narrow and develop it using main ideas and details. They choose an idea during prewriting and develop it as they draft and revise their writing.

Organization. The organization is the skeleton of the composition. Students hook the reader in the beginning, identify the purpose, present ideas logically, provide transitions between ideas, and end with a satisfying conclusion so that the important questions are answered. Students organize their writing during prewriting and follow their plans as they draft.

Voice. The writer's distinctive style is voice; it's what breathes life into a piece of writing. Culham (2003) calls voice "the writer's music coming out through the words" (p. 102). During the drafting and revising stages, students create voice in their writing through the words they use, the sentences they craft, and the tone they adopt.

Word Choice. Careful word choice makes the meaning clear and the composition more interesting to read. Students learn to choose lively verbs and specific nouns, adjectives, and adverbs; create word pictures; and use idiomatic expressions as they craft their pieces. They focus on word choice as they draft and revise their writing.

Sentence Fluency. Sentence fluency is the rhythm and flow of language. Students vary the length and structure of their writing so that it has a natural cadence and is easy to read aloud. They develop sentence fluency as they draft, revise, and edit their writing.

Mechanics. The mechanics are spelling, capitalization, punctuation, and grammar. In the editing stage, students proofread their compositions and correct spelling and grammar errors to make the writing easier to read.

Teachers teach series of lessons about each quality. They explain the quality, show examples from children's literature and students' own writing, involve students in activities to investigate and experiment with the quality, and encourage students to apply what they've learned in their own writing as they move through the writing process. Figure 2–7 presents a list of books and activities that teachers can use in teaching the qualities of good writing.

Figure 2–7 ◆ Teaching the Qualities of Good Writing

Quality	Books	Ways to Teach
Ideas	Baylor, B. (1995). *I'm in charge of celebrations*. New York: Aladdin Books. (P–M–U) Moss, T. (1998). *I want to be*. New York: Puffin Books. (P–M) Van Allsburg, C. (1996). *The mysteries of Harris Burdick*. Boston: Houghton Mifflin. (M–U) Wyeth, S. D. (2002). *Something beautiful*. New York: Dragonfly. (P–M–U)	• Read aloud books with well-developed ideas. • Choose photos, pictures, or objects to write about. • Quickwrite to narrow and develop an idea. • Make graphic organizers to develop an idea.
Organization	Brown, M. W. (2006). *Another important book*. New York: HarperTrophy. (P–M) Fanelli, S. (2007). *My map book*. New York: Walker. (P–M) Fleischman, P. (2004). *Seedfolks*. New York: HarperTrophy. (M–U) Ryan, P. M. (2001). *Mice and beans*. New York: Scholastic. (P–M)	• Analyze the structure of a book using a graphic organizer. • Collect effective leads from books. • Find examples of effective transitions in books. • Collect effective endings from books.
Voice	Browne, A. (2001). *Voices in the park*. New York: Dorling Kindersley. (P–M) Hesse, K. (2001). *Witness*. New York: Scholastic. (U) Ives, D. (2005). *Scrib*. New York: HarperCollins. (M–U) Raschka, C. (2007). *Yo! Yes?* New York: Scholastic. (P)	• Read aloud books with strong voices. • Have students describe the voice in a text. • Personalize a story by telling it from one character's viewpoint. • Add emotion to a voiceless piece of writing.
Word Choice	Barrett, J. (2001). *Things that are the most in the world*. New York: Aladdin Books. (P–M) Leedy, L., & Street, P. (2003). *There's a frog in my throat! 440 animal sayings a little bird told me*. New York: Holiday House. (P–M–U) Scieszka, J. (2001). *Baloney (Henry P.)* New York: Viking. (M) Shannon, G. (1999). *Tomorrow's alphabet*. New York: HarperTrophy. (P–M)	• Read aloud books with good word choice. • Collect lively and precise words. • Learn to use a thesaurus. • Craft metaphors and similes.
Sentence Fluency	Aylesworth, J. (1995). *Old black fly*. New York: Henry Holt. (P) Grimes, N. (2002). *My man blue*. New York: Puffin Books. (M) Grossman, B. (1998). *My little sister ate one hare*. New York: Dragonfly. (P–M) Locker, T. (2003). *Cloud dance*. San Diego: Voyager. (M)	• Do choral readings of books with sentence fluency. • Collect favorite sentences on sentence strips. • Practice writing alliterative sentences. • Reread favorite books.
Mechanics	Holm, J. L. (2007). *Middle school is worse than meatloaf: A year told through stuff*. New York: Atheneum. (U) Pattison, D. (2003). *The journey of Oliver K. Woodman*. San Diego: Harcourt Brace. (M) Pulver, R. (2003). *Punctuation takes a vacation*. New York: Holiday House. (P–M–U) Truss, L. (2006). *Eats, shoots & leaves: Why commas really do make a difference!* New York: Putnam. (M)	• Proofread excerpts from books to find mechanical errors that have been added. • Add capital letters to excerpts that have had them removed. • Add punctuation marks to excerpts that have had them removed. • Correct grammar errors that have been added to excerpts from books.

Adapted from Culham (2003); Spandel (2001, 2005).
P = primary grades (K–2); M = middle grades (3–5); U = upper grades (6–8)

As students study the six qualities, they internalize what good writers do. They learn to recognize good writing, develop a vocabulary for talking about writing, become better able to evaluate their own writing, and acquire strategies for improving the quality of their writing.

Assessment Tools

Writing

Teachers use rubrics to assess the quality of students' compositions. Some rubrics are general and can be used for almost any writing assignment, whereas others are designed for a specific writing assignment. Sometimes teachers use rubrics developed by school districts; at other times, they develop their own rubrics to assess the specific components and qualities they have stressed. Rubrics should have 4 to 6 achievement levels and address ideas, organization, language, and mechanics. Teachers often search the Internet for writing rubrics they can adapt and use. Many rubrics are available that have been developed by teachers, school districts, state departments of education, and publishers of educational materials.

Second-Grade Rubric for Stories	
5	Writing has an original title. Story shows originality, sense of humor, or cleverness. Writer uses paragraphs to organize ideas. Writing contains few spelling, capitalization, or punctuation errors. Writer varies sentence structure and word choice. Writer shows a sense of audience.
4	Writing has an appropriate title. Beginning, middle, and end of the story are well developed. A problem or goal is identified in the story. Writing includes details that support plot, characters, and setting. Writing is organized into paragraphs. Writing contains few capitalization and punctuation errors. Writer spells most high-frequency words correctly.
3	Writing may have a title. Writing has at least two of the three parts of a story (beginning-middle-end). Writing shows a sequence of events. Writing is not organized into paragraphs. Spelling, grammar, capitalization, or punctuation errors may interfere with meaning.
2	Writing has at least one of the three parts of a story (beginning-middle-end). Writing shows a partial sequence of events. Writing is brief and underdeveloped. Spelling, grammar, capitalization, and punctuation errors interfere with meaning.
1	Writing lacks a sense of story. Illustrations suggest a story. Writing is brief. Some words are recognizable, but the writing is difficult to read.

Assessing Students' Writing

Teachers assess both the process students use as they write and the quality of their compositions. They observe as students use the writing process to develop their compositions and conference with students as they revise and edit their writing. Teachers notice, for example, whether students use writing strategies to organize ideas for writing and whether they take into account feedback from classmates when they revise. So that students can document their writing process activities, teachers also have them keep all drafts of their compositions in writing folders.

Teachers develop rubrics, or scoring guides, to assess the quality of students' writing (Farr & Tone, 1994). Rubrics make the analysis of writing simpler and the assessment process more reliable and consistent. They may have 4, 5, or 6 levels, with descriptors related to ideas, organization, language, and mechanics at each level. Some rubrics are general and are appropriate for almost any writing assignment, whereas others are designed for a specific writing assignment. The Assessment Tools feature on the preceding page presents a second-grade rubric.

Teachers use rubrics to assess writing. They read the composition and highlight words and phrases in the rubric that best describe it. Usually sentences in more than one level are marked, so the score is determined by examining the highlighted sentences and noting which level is marked most often.

Students, too, can learn to create rubrics to assess the quality of their writing. To be successful, they need to analyze examples of other students' writing and determine the qualities that demonstrate strong, average, and weak papers; teachers need to model how to address the qualities at each level in the rubric. Skillings and Ferrell (2000) taught second and third graders to develop the criteria for evaluating their writing, and the students moved from using the rubrics their teachers prepared to creating their own 3-point rubrics, which they labeled as the "very best" level, the "okay" level, and the "not so good" level. Perhaps the most important outcome of teaching students to create rubrics, according to Skillings and Ferrell, is that students develop metacognitive strategies and the ability to think about themselves as writers.

READING AND WRITING ARE RECIPROCAL PROCESSES

Reading and writing are reciprocal; they're both constructive, meaning-making processes. Researchers have found that reading leads to better writing, and writing has the same effect on reading (Spivey, 1997). Not surprisingly, they've also learned that integrating instruction improves both reading and writing (Tierney & Shanahan, 1991). It's possible that students use the same type of thinking for both reading and writing (Braunger & Lewis, 2006).

Comparing the Two Processes

The reading and writing processes have comparable activities at each stage (Butler & Turbill, 1984). A comparison of the two processes is shown in Figure 2–8. For example, notice the similarities between the activities in the third stage of reading and writing—responding and revising, respectively. Fitzgerald (1989) analyzed these two activities and concluded that they draw on similar author-reader-text interactions. Similar analyses can be made for other stages as well.

Figure 2–8 ◆ A Comparison of the Reading and Writing Processes

	What Readers Do	What Writers Do
Stage 1	**Prereading** Readers use knowledge about • the topic • reading • genres • cueing systems	**Prewriting** Writers use knowledge about • the topic • writing • genres • cueing systems
Stage 2	**Reading** Readers • use word-identification strategies • use comprehension strategies • monitor reading • create meaning	**Drafting** Writers • use transcription strategies • use meaning-making strategies • monitor writing • create meaning
Stage 3	**Responding** Readers • respond to the text • deepen meaning • clarify misunderstandings • expand ideas	**Revising** Writers • respond to the text • deepen meaning • clarify misunderstandings • expand ideas
Stage 4	**Exploring** Readers • examine the impact of words and literary language • explore structural elements • compare the text to others	**Editing** Writers • identify and correct mechanical errors • review paragraph and sentence structure
Stage 5	**Applying** Readers • create projects • share projects with classmates • reflect on the reading process • feel success • want to read again	**Publishing** Writers • make the final copy of their compositions • share their compositions with genuine audiences • reflect on the writing process • feel success • want to write again

Tierney (1983) explains that reading and writing involve concurrent, complex transactions between writers as readers and readers as writers. It seems natural that writers read other authors' books for ideas and to learn about organizing their writing, and they also read and reread their own writing as they revise to communicate more effectively. The quality of these reading experiences seems closely tied to success in writing. Thinking of readers as writers may be more difficult, but readers participate in many of the same activities that writers use—activating background knowledge, setting purposes, determining importance, monitoring, repairing, and evaluating.

Classroom Connections

Many classroom activities involve both reading and writing. Making connections between reading and writing is a natural part of classroom life. Students read and then write or write and then read: They write reading log entries after reading to deepen their understanding of what they've read, for example, or they make graphic organizers to organize the information they're reading in a content-area textbook or informational book. Similarly, they read rough drafts aloud to make sure they flow and then read them to classmates to get feedback on how well they're communicating, or they use a structural pattern from a poem they've read in one they're writing. Shanahan (1988) outlined these guidelines for connecting reading and writing so that students develop a clearer understanding of literacy:

◆ Involve students in daily reading and writing experiences.
◆ Introduce the reading and writing processes in kindergarten.
◆ Plan instruction that reflects the developmental nature of reading and writing.
◆ Make the reading-writing connection explicit to students.
◆ Emphasize both the processes and the products of reading and writing.
◆ Set clear purposes for reading and writing.
◆ Teach reading and writing through authentic literacy experiences.

It's not enough, however, for students to see themselves as readers and writers; they need to grasp the relationships between the two roles and move flexibly between them. Readers think like writers to understand the author's purpose and viewpoint, for instance, and writers assume alternative viewpoints as potential readers.

Chapter 2
Review

How Effective Teachers Teach the Reading and Writing Processes

▶ Teachers use the reading process—prereading, reading, responding, exploring, and applying—to ensure that students comprehend books they read.

▶ Teachers use independent reading, buddy reading, guided reading, shared reading, and interactive read-alouds to share books with students.

▶ Teachers teach students how to use the writing process—prewriting, drafting, revising, editing, and publishing—to write and refine their compositions.

▶ Teachers teach students about the qualities of good writing—ideas, organization, voice, word choice, sentence fluency, and conventions.

▶ Teachers understand that reading and writing are reciprocal meaning-making processes.

PEARSON
myeducationlab
Where the Classroom Comes to Life

Go to MyEducationLab at www.myeducationlab.com to deepen your understanding of the concepts presented in this chapter:

▶ Examine how the second graders in Ms. Janusz's classroom revise their writing by viewing video segments in the Literacy Portraits.
▶ Check your understanding of chapter concepts with the multiple-choice and essay quizzes in the Study Plan.
▶ Apply some of the main ideas discussed in the chapter in the Activities and Applications section of the website.
▶ Practice what you've learned in this chapter in Building Teaching Skills and Dispositions before applying the ideas in your own classroom.

PROFESSIONAL REFERENCES

Afflerbach, P., Pearson, P. D., & Paris, S. G. (2008). Clarifying differences between reading skills and reading strategies. *The Reading Teacher, 61*, 364–373.

Allen, J. (2000). *Yellow brick road: Shared and guided paths to independent reading, 4–12.* Portland, ME: Stenhouse.

Allen, J. (2002). *On the same page: Shared reading beyond the primary grades.* Portland, ME: Stenhouse.

Angelillo, J. (2008). *Whole-class teaching: Minilessons and more.* Portsmouth, NH: Heinemann.

Applebee, A. N., & Langer, J. A. (1983). Instructional scaffolding: Reading and writing and natural language activities. *Language Arts, 60*, 168–175.

Baker, L., & Brown, A. (1984). Metacognitive skills of reading. In P. D. Pearson, M. Kamil, P. Mosenthal, & R. Barr (Eds.), *Handbook of reading research* (pp. 353–394). New York: Longman.

Blanton, W. E., Wood, K. D., & Moorman, G. B. (1990). The role of purpose in reading instruction. *The Reading Teacher, 43*, 486–493.

Braunger, J., & Lewis, J. P. (2006). *Building a knowledge base in reading* (2nd ed.). Newark, DE: International Reading Association/National Council of Teachers of English.

Butler, A., & Turbill, J. (1984). *Towards a reading-writing classroom.* Portsmouth, NH: Heinemann.

Calkins, L. M. (1983). *Lessons from a child: On the teaching and learning of writing.* Portsmouth, NH: Heinemann.

Cappellini, M. (2005). *Balancing reading and language learning: A resource for teaching English language learners, K–5.* York, ME: Stenhouse.

Christenson, T. A. (2002). *Supporting struggling writers in the elementary classroom.* Newark, DE: International Reading Association.

Culham, R. (2003). *6 + 1 traits of writing.* New York: Scholastic.

Dean, D. (2006). *Strategic writing.* Urbana, IL: National Council of Teachers of English.

Donovan, C. A., & Smolkin, L. B. (2002). Children's genre knowledge: An examination of K–5 students' performance on multiple tasks providing differing levels of scaffolding. *Reading Research Quarterly, 37*, 428–465.

Dowhower, S. L. (1999). Supporting a strategic stance in the classroom: A comprehension framework for helping teachers help students to be strategic. *The Reading Teacher, 52*, 672–688.

Faigley, L., & Witte, S. (1981). Analyzing revision. *College Composition and Communication, 32*, 400–410.

Farr, R., & Tone, B. (1994). *Portfolio and performance assessment.* Orlando: Harcourt Brace.

Fisher, D., Flood, J., Lapp, D., & Frey, N. (2004). Interactive read-alouds: Is there a common set of implementation practices? *The Reading Teacher, 58*, 8–17.

Fitzgerald, J. (1989). Enhancing two related thought processes: Revision in writing and critical thinking. *The Reading Teacher, 43*, 42–48.

Fountas, I. C., & Pinnell, G. S. (1996). *Guided reading: Good first teaching for all children.* Portsmouth, NH: Heinemann.

Friedland, E. S., & Truesdell, K. S. (2004). Kids reading together. *The Reading Teacher, 58*, 76–83.

Graves, D. H. (1983). *Writing: Teachers and children at work.* Exeter, NH: Heinemann.

Holdaway, D. (1979). *The foundations of literacy.* Portsmouth, NH: Heinemann.

Labbo, L. D. (2005). Fundamental qualities of effective Internet literacy instruction: An exploration of worthwhile classroom practices. In R. A. Karchmer, M. H. Mallette, J. Kara-Soteriou, & D. J. Leu, Jr. (Eds.), *Innovative approaches to literacy education: Using the Internet to support new literacies* (pp. 165–179). Newark, DE: International Reading Association.

Langer, J. A. (1985). Children's sense of genre. *Written Communication, 2*, 157–187.

McGowan, M. (2005). My Internet projects and other online resources for the literacy classroom. In R. A. Karchmer, M. H. Mallette, J. Kara-Soteriou, & D. J. Leu, Jr. (Eds.), *Innovative approaches to literacy education: Using the Internet to support new literacies* (pp. 85–102). Newark, DE: International Reading Association.

McNabb, M. L. (2006). *Literacy learning in networked classrooms: Using the Internet with middle-level students.* Newark, DE: International Reading Association.

Murray, D. H. (1982). *Learning by teaching.* Montclair, NJ: Boynton/Cook.

National Reading Panel. (2000). *Teaching children to read: An evidence-based assessment of the scientific research literature on reading and its implications for reading instruction.* Washington, DC: National Institute of Child Health and Human Development.

Paris, S. G., Wasik, D. A., & Turner, J. C. (1991). The development of strategic readers. In R. Barr, M. L. Kamil, P. B. Mosenthal, & P. D. Pearson (Eds.), *Handbook of reading research* (Vol. 2, pp. 609–640). New York: Longman.

Peterson. R., & Eeds, M. (2007). *Grand conversations: Literature groups in action* (updated ed). New York: Scholastic.

Pressley, M. (2000). What should comprehension instruction be instruction of? In M. L. Kamil, P. B. Mosenthal, P. D. Pearson, & R. Barr (Eds.), *Handbook of reading research* (Vol. 3, pp. 545–561). Mahwah, NJ: Erlbaum.

Rasinski, T. V. (2003). *The fluent reader.* New York: Scholastic.

Rosenblatt, L. M. (2004). The transactive theory of reading and writing. In R. B. Ruddell & N. J. Unrau (Eds.), *Theoretical models and processes of reading* (5th ed., pp. 1363–1398). Newark, DE: International Reading Association.

Rosenblatt, L. (2005). *Making meaning with texts: Selected essays*. Portsmouth, NH: Heinemann.

Shanahan, T. (1988). The reading-writing relationship: Seven instructional principles. *The Reading Teacher, 41*, 636–647.

Skillings, M. J., & Ferrell, R. (2000). Student-generated rubrics: Bringing students into the assessment process. *The Reading Teacher, 53*, 452–455.

Spandel, V. (2001). *Books, lessons, ideas for teaching the six traits*. Wilmington, MA: Great Source.

Spandel, V. (2005). *Creating writers through 6-trait writing assessment and instruction* (4th ed.). Boston: Allyn & Bacon.

Spivey, N. (1997). *The constructivist metaphor: Reading, writing, and the making of meaning*. New York: Academic Press.

Tierney, R. J. (1983). Writer-reader transactions: Defining the dimensions of negotiation. In P. L. Stock (Ed.), *Forum: Essays on theory and practice in the teaching of writing* (pp. 147–151). Upper Montclair, NJ: Boynton/Cook.

Tierney, R. J., & Shanahan, T. (1991). Research on the reading-writing relationship: Interactions, transactions, and outcomes. In R. Barr, M. L. Kamil, P. B. Mosenthal, & P. D. Pearson (Eds.), *Handbook of reading research* (Vol. 2, pp. 246–280). Mahwah, NJ: Erlbaum.

Weber, C. (2002). *Publishing with students: A comprehensive guide*. Portsmouth, NH: Heinemann.

Wilhelm, J. D. (2001). *Improving comprehension with think-aloud strategies*. New York: Scholastic.

Yaden, D. B., Jr. (1988). Understanding stories through repeated read-alouds: How many does it take? *The Reading Teacher, 41*, 556–560.

CHILDREN'S BOOK REFERENCES

Lowry, L. (2006a). *Gathering blue*. New York: Delacorte.

Lowry, L. (2006b). *The giver*. New York: Delacorte.

Lowry, L. (2006c). *The messenger*. New York: Delacorte.

O'Neill, M. (1990). *Hailstones and halibut bones*. New York: Doubleday.

CHAPTER 3

Assessing Students' Literacy Development

Mrs. McNeal Conducts Second-Quarter Assessments

The end of the second quarter is approaching, and Mrs. McNeal is assessing her first-grade students. She collects four types of assessment data about her students' reading, writing, and spelling development. Then she uses the information to document children's achievement, verify that they're meeting state and district standards, determine report card grades, and make instructional plans for the next quarter.

Today, Mrs. McNeal assesses Seth, who is 6½ years old. He's a quiet, well-behaved child who regularly completes his work. She has a collection of Seth's writing and other papers he's done, but she wants to assess his current reading level. At the beginning of the school year, Mrs. McNeal considered him an average student, but in the past month, his reading progress has accelerated. She's anxious to see how much progress he's made.

Assessment 1: Determining Seth's Instructional Reading Level. Mrs. McNeal regularly takes running records as she listens to children reread familiar books in order to monitor their ability to recognize familiar and high-frequency words, decode unfamiliar words, and use reading strategies. In addition, Mrs. McNeal assesses each child's instructional reading level at the beginning of the school year and at the end of each quarter. She uses the *Developmental Reading Assessment* (DRA) (Beaver, 2006), an assessment kit designed for kindergarten through third grade, which includes 44 small paperback books arranged from kindergarten to fifth-grade reading levels.

To determine a child's instructional reading level, Mrs. McNeal chooses a book that the child hasn't read before and introduces it by reading the title, examining the picture on the cover, and talking about the story. The child does a picture walk, looking through the book and talking about what's happening on each page, using the illustrations as a guide. Next, the child reads the book aloud as Mrs. McNeal takes a running record, checking the words the child reads correctly and noting those read incorrectly. Then the child retells the story and the teacher assesses his or her understanding, prompting with questions, if necessary. Afterward, Mrs. McNeal scores the running record to determine the child's instructional reading level.

At the beginning of the school year, most of Mrs. McNeal's first graders were reading at level 4; by midyear, they should be reading at level 8; and by the end of the school year, they're expected to reach level 18 to 20. Seth was reading at level 4 in August, like many of his classmates, and at the end of the first quarter, he was reading at level 8. Now Mrs. McNeal decides to test him at level 16 because he's reading a level-16 book in his guided reading group.

Seth reads *The Pot of Gold* (2001), a level-16 book in the DRA assessment kit. The book recounts an Irish folktale about a man named Grumble who makes an elf show him where his pot of gold is hidden. Grumble marks the spot by tying a scarf around a nearby tree branch and goes to get a shovel with which to dig up the gold. Grumble admonishes the elf not to move the scarf, and he doesn't. Instead he ties many other scarves on nearby trees so that Grumble can't find the elf's gold. Mrs. McNeal takes a running record while Seth reads; it's shown on page 72.

As indicated on the running record sheet, there are 266 words in the book. Seth makes 17 errors but self-corrects 5 of them; his accuracy rate is 95%. Mrs. McNeal analyzes Seth's errors and concludes that he overdepends on visual (or phonological) cues while ignoring semantic ones. Of the 12 errors, only one—*Grumply* for *Grumble*—makes sense in the sentence. When Seth retells the story, he shows that he understands the big idea, but his retelling isn't especially strong: He retells the beginning and the end of the story but leaves out important details in the middle. However, he does make interesting connections between the story and his own life. Mrs. McNeal concludes that level 16 is his instructional level and that his ability to read words is stronger than his comprehension.

Mrs. McNeal makes notes about Seth's instructional priorities for the next quarter. Comprehension will be her focus for Seth. She'll teach him more about the structure of stories, including plot and setting, and help him use semantic cues to support the visual ones. She'll encourage him to structure his oral and written retellings in three parts—beginning, middle, and end—and to include more details in his retellings. She also decides

A Running Record Scoring Sheet

Name __Seth__ Date __Jan. 18__

Level __16__ Title __The Pot of Gold__ Easy (Instructional) Hard

Running Record		E	SC	E	SC
2	✓✓✓✓✓✓✓✓ ✓ ✓ grumply| ✓ ✓ ✓ ✓ ✓ ✓ Grumble|T ✓ ✓ ✓ always|T A|T ✓✓✓✓✓✓✓ ✓✓✓✓✓✓✓✓✓✓	1 1		m s (v)	
3	✓✓✓✓✓✓✓✓✓ ✓✓✓✓✓✓ did not| ✓ ✓✓ didn't| ✓✓✓✓✓✓✓✓ ✓✓✓✓✓✓✓✓ ✓✓✓✓✓✓✓	1		(m)(s)v	
4	✓✓✓✓✓✓✓✓✓ ✓✓✓✓✓✓✓✓✓ ✓✓✓✓✓				
5	✓✓✓✓✓✓✓ ✓ ✓✓✓✓✓✓ I| make| ✓✓ I'll| move| ✓✓✓✓✓✓✓✓✓✓ safr| ✓✓✓✓✓✓ or| ✓✓ scarf| of|	1 1 1 1		(m)(s)(v) m s (v) m s (v) m s (v)	
6	✓✓✓✓✓ ✓ me|sc self| ✓✓✓ my| scarf| ✓✓✓✓✓✓✓ ✓✓✓✓✓✓✓	1	1	m s (v) m s (v)	(m)(s)(v)
7	✓✓✓✓✓✓✓ ✓✓✓✓✓✓ ✓ ✓✓✓✓✓✓✓				
8	✓✓✓✓✓✓✓✓✓ ✓✓✓✓✓✓✓✓✓ ✓✓				
9	✓✓✓ take| ✓ scafer| ✓✓✓ taken| scarf| ✓✓✓✓✓✓✓	1 1		(m)s(v) m s (v)	
10	✓✓✓✓✓✓✓✓ ✓✓✓ they|sc R ✓✓✓✓✓✓ that| ✓ ✓✓✓✓ maybe| sit| ✓✓ may| still|	1 1	1	m s (v) m s (v) m s (v)	(m)(s)(v)

Scoring	Picture Walk
12/266 95% accuracy	Gets gist of story

Types of Errors: M S (V)	Oral Reading
Overdependent on V cues	Reads fluently

Self-correction Rate	Retelling/Questions
1:5	Tells BME but middle is brief

to introduce Seth to easy chapter books, such as Cynthia Rylant's Henry and Mudge series about the adventures of a boy named Henry and his dog, Mudge (e.g., *Henry and Mudge and the Big Sleepover*, 2007).

Assessment 2: Testing Seth's Knowledge of High-Frequency Words.

Mrs. McNeal's goal for her first graders is to recognize at least 75 of the 100 high-frequency words by the end of the school year. In August, most children could read at least 12 words; Seth read 16 correctly. Today, Mrs. McNeal asks Seth again to read the list of 100 high-frequency words, which is arranged in order of difficulty. She expects that he'll be able to read 50 to 60 of the words and when he misses 5 in a row, she'll stop, but Seth surprises her and reads the entire list! He misses only these 6 words: *don't, how, there, very, were,* and *would*. Seth's high score reinforces his results on the running record: He's a very good word reader.

Assessment 3: Checking Seth's Ability to Write and Spell Words.

Several days ago, Mrs. McNeal administered the "Words I Know" Test to the class: She asked the children to write as many words as they could in 10 minutes without copying from classroom charts. In August, most children could spell 15 to 20 words correctly; Mrs. McNeal's goal is that they be able to write 50 words by the end of the school year. Seth wrote 22 words in August, and on the recent test, he wrote 50 correctly spelled words. Seth's "Words I Know" test is shown here.

Seth's "Words I Know" Test

Mrs. McNeal reviews the list of words that Seth wrote and notices that most are one-syllable words with short vowels, such as *cat* and *fin*, but he's beginning to write words with more-complex spellings, such as *what, come,* and *night*, words with inflectional endings, such as *going*, and two-syllable words, such as *cowboys*. She concludes that Seth is making very good progress, both in terms of the number of words he can write and the complexity of the spelling patterns he's using.

Assessment 4: Scoring Seth's Compositions. Mrs. McNeal looks through Seth's journal and chooses several representative samples written in the past 3 weeks to score; one of the samples is shown below. Here is the text with conventional spelling and punctuation:

> *Last night I kept waking up. My dad slept with me. Then I fell fast asleep. Then dad went to bed.*

Using the school district's 6-point rubric, Mrs. McNeal scores the composition as a 4. A score of 5 is considered grade-level at the end of the school year, and Mrs. McNeal believes that Seth will reach that level before then. She notes that he's writing several sentences in an entry, even though he often omits punctuation at the ends of sentences. Seth writes fluently but sometimes omits a word or two. Mrs. McNeal plans to talk to him about the importance of rereading his writing to catch any omissions, add punctuation marks, and correct misspelled words.

Seth's Journal Entry

Seth correctly spells more than two thirds of the words he writes, and he uses invented spelling that generally represents beginning, middle, or ending sounds. In this entry, Seth wrote 21 words, spelling 13 of them correctly; this means that Seth spelled 71% correctly. He reversed the order of letters in three words (*lats* for *last, fli* for *fell, ot* for *to*) but didn't make any letter-order reversals in the other two samples that Mrs. McNeal evaluated. She recognizes that many first graders form letters backward and make letter-order reversals and isn't concerned about Seth's reversals because she thinks that he'll outgrow them.

Assessment 5: Measuring Seth's Phonics and Spelling Knowledge. Each week, the first graders craft two sentences for a dictation test. On Monday, they create the sentences and write them on chart paper that's displayed in the classroom. During the week, they practice writing the sentences on small dry-erase boards, and Mrs. McNeal uses the text for **minilessons** during which she draws children's attention to high-frequency words they've studied, the phonetic features of various words, and capitalization and punctuation rules applied in the sentences. Last week's sentences focused on the solar system and *The Magic School Bus Lost in the Solar System* (Cole, 1993), a book Mrs. McNeal read aloud to the class:

> *Their bus turned into a rocket ship. They wanted to visit all of the planets.*

After practicing the sentences all week, Mrs. McNeal dictates them for the students to write on Friday. She tells them to try to spell words correctly and to write all the sounds they hear in the words they don't know how to spell. Seth wrote:

> *The bus turd into a rocket ship they wande to vist all of the planis.*

Seth spelled 10 of the 15 words correctly and included 46 of 51 sounds in his writing. In addition, he omitted the period at the end of the first sentence and didn't capitalize the first word in the second sentence.

Mrs. McNeal uses this test to check students' phonics knowledge and ability to spell high-frequency words. Seth spelled most of the high-frequency words correctly, except that he wrote *the* for *their*. Seth's other errors involved the second syllable of the word or an inflectional ending. Mrs. McNeal concludes that Seth is making good progress in learning to spell high-frequency words and that he's ready to learn more about two-syllable words and inflectional endings.

Grading Seth's Reading, Writing, and Spelling Achievement. Having collected these data, Mrs. McNeal is ready to complete Seth's report card. Seth and his classmates receive separate number grades in reading, writing, and spelling: The grades range from 1, not meeting grade-level standards, to 4, exceeding standards. Seth will receive a 3 in reading, writing, and spelling. A score of 3 means that Seth is meeting grade-level standards in all three areas. Even though his reading level is higher than average, his dependence on visual cues when decoding unfamiliar words and his weakness in comprehension keep him at level 3 in reading.

Assessment has become a priority in 21st-century schools. School districts and state and federal education agencies have increased their demands for accountability, and today, most students take annual high-stakes tests to judge their achievement. Teachers are collecting more assessment data now, and doing it more frequently than in the past. They're using the information to make instructional decisions, as Mrs. McNeal demonstrated in the vignette. Researchers explain that "a system of frequent assessment, coupled with strong content standards and effective reading instruction, helps ensure that teachers' . . . approaches are appropriate to each student's needs" (Kame'enui, Simmons, & Cornachione, 2000, p. 1). By linking assessment and instruction, teachers improve students' learning and their teaching.

As you continue reading, you'll notice that the term *assessment* is used much more often than *evaluation*. These terms are often considered interchangeable, but they're not. Assessment is formative; it's ongoing and provides immediate feedback to improve teaching and learning. It's usually authentic, based on the literacy activities in which students are engaged. Observations, conferences, and student work samples are examples of authentic assessment. In contrast, evaluation is summative; it's final, generally administered at the end of a unit or a school year, and used to judge quality. Tests are the most common type of evaluation, and they're used to compare one student's achievement against that of other students or against grade-level standards.

CLASSROOM-BASED READING ASSESSMENT

The purpose of classroom assessment is to collect meaningful information about what students know and do, and it takes many forms (Afflerbach, 2007a). Teachers use these four types of assessment to monitor and examine students' learning:

◆ Kits of leveled books to determine students' reading levels

◆ Informal procedures, such as observations and conferences, to monitor student progress

◆ Tests to diagnose students' strengths and weaknesses in specific components of reading and writing

◆ Collections of work samples to document students' learning

Each type of assessment serves a different purpose, so it's important that teachers choose assessment tools carefully. Researchers recommend that teachers use a combination of informal and formal assessment tools to improve the fairness and effectiveness of classroom literacy assessment (Kuhs, Johnson, Agruso, & Monrad, 2001).

Teaching Struggling Readers and Writers

"Just Right" Books

Struggling readers need books they can read.

Too often, struggling readers pick up books that are too difficult, and when they attempt to read them, they give up in frustration. What students need are "just right" books that they can read fluently and can comprehend (Allington, 2006). When students read interesting books at their independent reading level, they're more successful. The "three-finger rule" is a quick way to determine whether a book is a good match for a student: Have the student turn to any page in the book, read it aloud, and raise a finger whenever there's an unknown word. If the student knows every word, it's too easy, but if there's one or two difficult words on a page, the book is probably an appropriate choice. If there are three or more difficult words on a page, the book's too difficult for independent reading.

Determining Students' Reading Levels

Teachers match students with books at appropriate levels of difficulty because students are more likely to be successful when they're reading books that aren't too easy or too difficult. Books that are too easy don't provide enough challenge, and books that are too difficult frustrate students. Researchers have identified three reading levels that take into account students' ability to recognize words automatically, read fluently, and comprehend what they're reading:

Independent Reading Level. Students can read books at this level comfortably, on their own. They recognize almost all words; their accuracy rate is 95–100%. Their reading is fluent, and they comprehend what they're reading. Books at this level are only slightly easier than those at their instructional level, and they still engage students' interest.

Instructional Reading Level. Students can read and understand books at this level with support, but not on their own. They recognize most words; their accuracy rate is 90–94%. Their reading may be fluent, but sometimes it isn't. With support from the teacher or classmates, students comprehend what they're reading, but if they're reading independently, their understanding is limited. This level reflects Vygotsky's zone of proximal development, discussed in Chapter 1.

Frustration Reading Level. Books at this level are too difficult for students to read successfully, even with assistance. Students don't recognize enough words automatically; their accuracy is less than 90%. Students' reading is choppy and word by word, and it often doesn't make sense. In addition, students show little understanding of what's been read.

Students should be assessed regularly to determine their reading levels and monitor their progress.

These reading levels have important implications for instruction. Students read independent-level books when they're reading for pleasure and instructional-level books when they're participating in guided reading or another instructional activity. They shouldn't be expected to read books at their frustration level; when it's essential that struggling students experience grade-appropriate literature or learn content-area information, teachers should read the text aloud to students.

> Check the Compendium of Instructional Procedures, which follows Chapter 12, for more information on the highlighted terms.

Readability Formulas. For nearly a century, readability formulas have been used to estimate the ease with which reading materials, both trade books and textbooks, can be read. Readability scores serve as rough gauges of text difficulty and are traditionally reported as grade-level scores. If a book has a readability score of fifth grade, for example, teachers assume that average fifth graders will be able to read it. Sometimes readability scores are marked with *RL* and a grade level, such as *RL 5*, on books.

Readability scores are determined by correlating semantic and syntactic features in a text. Several passages from a text are identified for analysis, and then vocabulary sophistication is measured by counting the number of syllables in each word, and sentence complexity by the number of words in each sentence. The syllable counts and the word counts from each passage are averaged, and the readability score is calculated by plotting the averages on a graph. It seems reasonable to expect that texts with shorter words and sentences would be easier to read than others with longer words and sentences; however, readability formulas take into account only two text factors; they can't account for reader factors, including the experience and knowledge that readers bring to reading, their cognitive and linguistic backgrounds, or their motivation for reading.

One fairly quick and simple readability formula is the Fry Readability Graph, developed by Edward Fry (1968); it's presented in the Assessment Tools feature on page 78. This graph is used to predict the grade-level score for texts, ranging from first grade through college level. Teachers use a readability formula as an aid in evaluating textbook and trade-book selections for classroom use; however, they can't assume that materials rated as appropriate for a particular level will be appropriate for all students because students within a class typically vary three grade levels or more in their reading levels.

Just looking at a book isn't enough to determine its readability, because books that seem quite different sometimes score at the same level. For example, *Sarah, Plain and Tall* (MacLachlan, 2004), *Tales of a Fourth Grade Nothing* (Blume, 2007), *Bunnicula: A Rabbit-Tale of Mystery* (Howe & Howe, 2006), and *The Hundred Penny Box* (Mathis, 2006) are four novels that score at the third-grade reading level according to Fry's Readability Graph, even though their topics, use of illustrations, font sizes, and page length differ significantly.

Literacy Portraits: VIEWING GUIDE

Ms. Janusz regularly monitors the second graders' reading achievement. Working one-on-one, she introduces a leveled book and asks the student to read the first part aloud while she takes a running record on a separate sheet of paper. Then the student reads the rest of the book silently. She also asks questions after the student finishes reading orally and again after the student reaches the end of the book. Go to the Literacy Portraits section of MyEducationLab to watch Ms. Janusz assess Jimmy's reading in his October video clip and again in his March video clip. As you watch the videos, think about how Jimmy grew as a reader during the school year. Does he decode unfamiliar words, read fluently, and comprehend what he's read orally and silently? Next, reflect on how Ms. Janusz linked instruction and assessment when she took advantage of teachable moments while she assessed his reading.

myeducationlab

Assessment Tools

The Fry Readability Graph

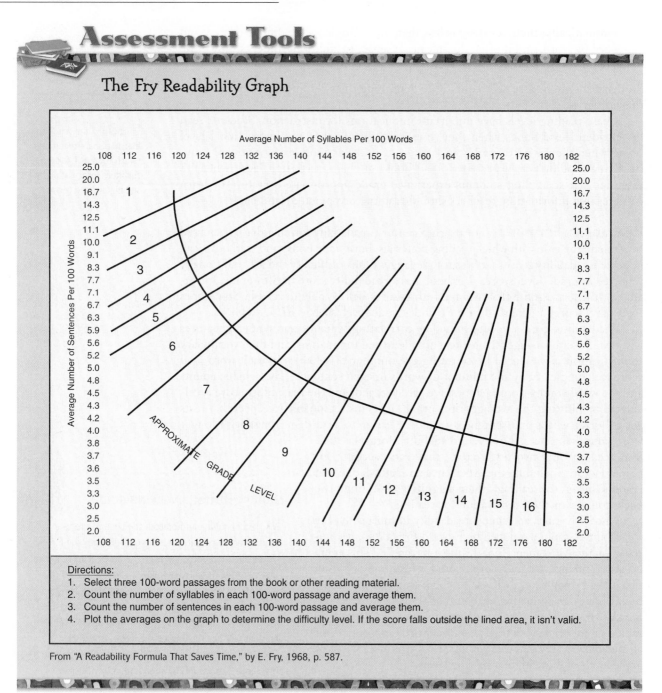

Directions:
1. Select three 100-word passages from the book or other reading material.
2. Count the number of syllables in each 100-word passage and average them.
3. Count the number of sentences in each 100-word passage and average them.
4. Plot the averages on the graph to determine the difficulty level. If the score falls outside the lined area, it isn't valid.

From "A Readability Formula That Saves Time," by E. Fry, 1968, p. 587.

Leveled Books. Basal readers have traditionally been leveled according to grade levels, but grade-level designations, especially in kindergarten and first grade, are too broad. Fountas and Pinnell (2006b) developed a text gradient, or classification system that arranges books along a continuum from easiest to hardest, to match students to books in grades K–8. Their system is based on these 10 variables that influence reading difficulty:

◆ Genre and format of the book
◆ Organization and use of text structures

♦ Familiarity with and interest level of the content
♦ Complexity of ideas and themes
♦ Language and literary features
♦ Sentence length and complexity
♦ Sophistication of the vocabulary
♦ Word length and ease of decoding
♦ Relationship of illustrations to the text
♦ Length of the book, its layout, and other print features

Fountas and Pinnell used these criteria to identify 26 levels, labeled A through Z, for their text gradient, which teachers also can use to level books in their classrooms. More than 18,000 books have been leveled according to this text gradient. A sample trade book for each level is shown in Figure 3–1; other leveled books are listed in *The Fountas and Pinnell Leveled Book List, K–8* (Fountas & Pinnell, 2006a) and online at www.fountasandpinnellleveledbooks.com.

Figure 3–1 ♦ Books Leveled Using Fountas and Pinnell's Text Gradient

Level	Grade	Book
A	K	Burningham, J. (1985). *Colors*. New York: Crown.
B	K–1	Carle, E. (1997). *Have you seen my cat?* New York: Aladdin Books.
C	K–1	Martin, B., Jr. (2008). *Brown bear, brown bear, what do you see?* New York: Henry Holt.
D	1	Peek, M. (2006). *Mary wore her red dress*. New York: Clarion Books.
E	1	Hill, E. (2005). *Where's Spot?* New York: Putnam.
F	1	Hutchins, P. (2005). *Rosie's walk*. New York: Aladdin Books.
G	1	Shaw, N. (2006). *Sheep in a jeep*. Boston: Houghton Mifflin.
H	1–2	Kraus, R. (2005). *Whose mouse are you?* New York: Aladdin Books.
I	1–2	Wood, A. (2005). *The napping house*. San Diego: Harcourt.
J	2	Rylant, C. (1996). *Henry and Mudge and the bedtime thumps*. New York: Simon & Schuster.
K	2	Heller, R. (1999). *Chickens aren't the only ones*. New York: Putnam.
L	2–3	Marshall, J. (2000). *The three little pigs*. New York: Grosset & Dunlap.
M	2–3	Park, B. (2007). *Junie B. Jones and the stupid smelly bus*. New York: Random House.
N	3	Danziger, P. (2006). *Amber Brown is not a crayon*. New York: Puffin Books.
O	3–4	Cleary, B. (1992). *Ramona Quimby, age 8*. New York: HarperTrophy.
P	3–4	Mathis, S. B. (2006). *The hundred penny box*. New York: Puffin Books.
Q	4	Howe, D., & Howe, J. (2006). *Bunnicula: A rabbit-tale of mystery*. New York: Aladdin Books.
R	4	Paulsen, G. (2007). *Hatchet*. New York: Simon & Schuster.
S	4–5	Norton, M. (2003). *The borrowers*. San Diego: Odyssey Classics.
T	4–5	Curtis, C. P. (2004). *Bud, not Buddy*. New York: Laurel Leaf.
U	5	Lowry, L. (1998). *Number the stars*. New York: Yearling.
V	5–6	Sachar, L. (2003). *Holes*. New York: Yearling.
W	5–6	Choi, S. N. (1993). *Year of impossible goodbyes*. New York: Yearling.
X	6–8	Hesse, K. (1999). *Out of the dust*. New York: Scholastic.
Y	6–8	Lowry, L. (2006). *The giver*. New York: Delacorte.
Z	7–8	Hinton, S. E. (2006). *The outsiders*. New York: Puffin Books.

Fountas & Pinnell, 2006a.

The Lexile Framework. The newest approach to matching books to readers is the Lexile Framework, developed by MetaMetrics. This approach is different because it's used to measure both students' reading levels and the difficulty level of books. Word familiarity and sentence complexity are the two factors used to determine the difficulty level of books. Lexile scores range from 100 to 1300, representing kindergarten through 12th-grade reading levels. Figure 3–2 presents a list of books ranked according to the Lexile Framework.

Students' results on high-stakes tests are often linked to the Lexile Framework. Standardized achievement tests, including the Iowa Test of Basic Skills and the Stanford Achievement Test, report test results as Lexile scores, and a number of standards-based state reading tests, including the California English-Language Arts Standards Test, the North Carolina End-of-Grade Tests, and the Texas Assessment of Knowledge and Skills, do the same. With this information, students, parents, and teachers can match students to books by searching the online Lexile database to locate books at the student's reading level.

The Lexile Framework is a promising program, because the wide range of scores allows teachers to more closely match students and books. The availability of the on-line database with more than 44,000 leveled books that students, parents, and teachers can access makes it a very useful assessment tool; however, matching students to books is more complicated than determining a numerical score!

Figure 3–2 ◆ Books Ranked According to the Lexile Framework

Level	Grade	Book
100–149	K	Willems, M. (2003). *Don't let the pigeon drive the bus!* New York: Hyperion Books.
150–199	K–1	Marshall, E. (1999). *Fox all week.* New York: Puffin Books.
200–249	1	Bridwell, N. (2002). *Clifford the big red dog.* New York: Scholastic.
250–299	1	Kellogg, S. (2002). *Pinkerton, behave!* New York: Dial Books.
300–349	1–2	Allard, H. (1985). *Miss Nelson is missing!* Boston: Houghton Mifflin.
350–399	2	Bourgeois, P. (1997). *Franklin's bad day.* New York: Scholastic.
400–449	2	Coerr, E. (1989). *The Josefina story quilt.* New York: HarperTrophy.
450–499	2–3	Bunting, E. (1998). *Going home.* New York: HarperTrophy.
500–549	3	Rathmann, P. (1995). *Officer Buckle and Gloria.* New York: Putnam.
550–599	3–4	Sobol, D. (2008). *Encyclopedia Brown saves the day.* New York: Puffin Books.
600–649	3–4	Cole, J. (1994). *The magic school bus on the ocean floor.* New York: Scholastic.
650–699	4	Lowry, L. (1998). *Number the stars.* New York: Yearling.
700–749	4	Howe, D., & Howe, J. (2006). *Bunnicula: A rabbit-tale of mystery.* New York: Aladdin Books.
750–799	4–5	Creech, S. (2005). *Walk two moons.* New York: HarperTrophy.
800–849	5	Dahl, R. (2007). *Charlie and the chocolate factory.* New York: Puffin Books.
850–899	5–6	Naylor, P. (2000). *Shiloh.* New York: Aladdin Books.
900–949	6–7	Lewis, C. S. (2005). *The lion, the witch and the wardrobe.* New York: HarperCollins.
950–999	7	O'Dell, S. (2006). *The black pearl.* Boston: Houghton Mifflin.
1000–1049	8	Philbrick, R. (2001). *Freak the mighty.* New York: Scholastic.
1050–1099	9–10	Tolkien, J. R. R. (2007). *The hobbit.* Boston: Houghton Mifflin.
1100–1149	10–11	Freedman, R. (2006). *Freedom walkers: The story of the Montgomery bus boycott.* New York: Holiday House.
1150–1199	11–12	Brooks, B. (1995). *The moves make the man.* New York: HarperTrophy.
1200–1300	12	Alcott, L. M. (2004). *Little women.* New York: Signet Classics.

Assessment Tools

Determining Students' Reading Levels

Teachers use screening assessments to determine students' instructional reading levels, monitor their progress, and document student achievement through a school year and across grade levels. Here are three screening assessments:

◆ **Developmental Reading Assessment (DRA)** (Beaver, 2006)

The DRA is available as two kits, one for grades K–3 and the other for grades 4–8, to assess students' reading performance using leveled fiction and nonfiction books. The K–3 kit also includes an individualized diagnostic instrument to assess students' phonemic awareness and phonics knowledge. Teachers use an online system to manage students' scores and group students for instruction.

◆ **Fountas and Pinnell Benchmark Assessment System** (Fountas & Pinnell, 2007)

The Fountas and Pinnell Benchmark Assessment System is sold as two kits, one for grades K–2 and the other for grades 3–8. Each kit contains 30 leveled fiction and nonfiction books written specifically for the kit and CDs with assessment forms to manage students' scores. Teachers use the books in the kit to match students' reading levels to the Fountas and Pinnell 26-level text gradient.

For both of these assessments, teachers test students individually. The teacher selects an appropriate book for the student to read, and then introduces it; the student reads the book, and the teacher takes a running record of the student's reading. Then the student retells the text and answers comprehension questions. The teacher scores and analyzes the results, and testing continues until the teacher determines the student's instructional level.

◆ **Scholastic Reading Inventory (SRI)**

The SRI is a unique computer-adaptive assessment program for grades 1–12 that reports students' reading levels using Lexile scores. Students take this 20-minute computerized test individually. The student reads a narrative or informational passage on the computer screen and answers multiple-choice comprehension questions. This test is computer-adaptive because if the student answers a question correctly, the next one will be more difficult, and if the answer is wrong, the next one will be easier. Students read passages and answer questions until their reading level is determined. Students receive a customized take-home letter with their Lexile score and a personalized list of recommended books.

These assessments are usually administered at the beginning of the school year and periodically during the year to monitor students' progress. The results are also used to group students for guided reading and to identify students who need diagnostic testing.

Monitoring Students' Progress

Monitoring is vital to student success (Braunger & Lewis, 2006). Teachers monitor students' learning every day and use the results to make instructional decisions (Winograd & Arrington, 1999). As they monitor students' progress, teachers learn about their students, about themselves as teachers, and about the impact of their instructional program. Teachers use these informal, formative procedures to monitor students' progress:

Observations. Effective teachers are "kid watchers," a term Yetta Goodman (1978) coined to describe the "direct and informal observation of students" (p. 37). To be effective kid watchers, teachers must understand how children learn to read and write. The focus is on what students do as they read or write, not on whether they're behaving properly or working quietly. Of course, little learning can occur in disruptive situations, but during these observations, the focus is on literacy, not behavior. Observations should be planned. Teachers usually observe a specific group of students each day so that over the course of a week, they watch everyone in the class.

Anecdotal Notes. Teachers write brief notes in notebooks or on self-stick notes as they observe students (Boyd-Batstone, 2004). The most useful notes describe specific events, report rather than evaluate, and relate the events to other information about the student. Teachers make notes about students' reading and writing activities, the questions students ask, and the strategies and skills they use fluently and those they don't understand. These records monitor and document students' growth and pinpoint problem areas to address in future minilessons or conferences. A teacher's anecdotal notes about sixth-grade students participating in a literature circle on *Bunnicula: A Rabbit-Tale of Mystery* (Howe & Howe, 2006) appear in Figure 3–3.

Figure 3–3 ◆ Anecdotal Notes About a Literature Circle

March 7
Met with the *Bunnicula* literature circle as they started reading the book. They have their reading, writing, and discussion schedule set. Sari questioned how a dog could write the book. We reread the Editor's Note. She asked if Harold really wrote the book. She's the only one confused in the group. Is she always so literal? Mario pointed out that you have to know that Harold supposedly wrote the book to understand the first-person viewpoint of the book. Talked to Sari about fantasy. Told her she'll be laughing out loud as she reads this book. She doubts it.

March 8
Returned to *Bunnicula* literature circle for first grand conversation, especially to check on Sari. Annie, Mario, Ted, Rod, Laurie, and Belinda talked about their pets and imagined them taking over their homes. Sari is not getting into the book. She doesn't have any pets and can't imagine the pets doing these things. I asked if she wanted to change groups. Perhaps a realistic book would be better. She says no. Is that because Ted is in the group?

March 10
The group is reading chapters 4 and 5 today. Laurie asks questions about white vegetables and vampires. Rod goes to get an encyclopedia to find out about vampires. Mario asks about DDT. Everyone—even Sari—involved in reading.

March 13
During a grand conversation, students compare the characters Harold and Chester. The group plans to make a Venn diagram comparing the characters for the sharing on Friday. Students decide that character is the most important element, but Ted argues that humor is the most important element in the story. Other students say humor isn't an element. I asked what humor is a reaction to—characters or plot? I checked journals and all are up to date.

March 15
The group has finished reading the book. I share sequels from the class library. Sari grabs one to read. She's glad she stayed with the book. Ted wants to write his own sequel in writing workshop. Mario plans to write a letter to James Howe.

March 17
Ted and Sari talk about *Bunnicula* and share related books. Rod and Mario share the Venn diagram of characters. Annie reads her favorite part, and Laurie shows her collection of rabbits. Belinda hangs back. I wonder if she has been involved. I need to talk to her.

Conferences. Teachers talk with students to monitor their progress in reading and writing activities as well as to set goals and help them solve problems. Here are six types of conferences that teachers have with students:

On-the-Spot Conferences. The teacher visits with students at their desks to monitor some aspect of the students' work or to check on progress. These conferences are brief, with the teacher often spending less than a minute with each student.

Planning Conferences. The teacher and the student make plans for reading or writing at the conference. At a prereading conference, they may talk about information related to the book, difficult concepts or vocabulary words related to the book, or the reading log the student will keep. At a prewriting conference, they may discuss possible writing topics or how to narrow a broad topic.

Revising Conferences. A small group of students meets with the teacher to share their rough drafts and get specific suggestions about how to revise them.

Book Discussion Conferences. Students meet with the teacher to discuss the book they've read. They may share reading log entries, discuss plot or characters, or compare the story to others they've read.

Editing Conferences. The teacher reviews students' proofread compositions and helps them correct spelling, punctuation, capitalization, and other mechanical errors.

Evaluation Conferences. The teacher meets with students after they've completed an assignment or project to talk about their growth as readers and writers. Students reflect on their accomplishments and set goals.

Often these conferences are brief and impromptu, held at students' desks as the teacher moves around the classroom; however, at other times, the conferences are planned, and students meet with the teacher at a designated conference table.

Checklists. Checklists simplify assessment and enhance students' learning (Kuhs, Johnson, Agruso, & Monrad, 2001). Teachers identify the evaluation criteria in advance so students understand what's expected of them before they begin working. Grading is easier because teachers have already set the evaluation criteria, and it's

Assessment Tools

Book Talk Checklist

Name Jaime   Date November 12

Title Cockroach Cooties

Author Laurence Yep

- ✓ Hold up the book to show to classmates.
- ✓ State the title and author's name.
- ✓ Interest classmates in the book by asking a question, reading an excerpt, or sharing some information.
- ___ Summarize the book, without giving away the ending.
- ✓ Talk loud enough for everyone to hear you.
- ✓ Look at the audience.
- ___ Limit the book talk to 3 minutes.

fairer, too, because teachers use the same criteria to grade all students' work. The Assessment Tools feature on page 83 shows a fourth-grade checklist for giving book talks. At the beginning of the school year, the teacher introduced book talks, modeled how to do one, and developed the checklist with the students. Students use the checklist whenever they're preparing to give a book talk, and the teacher uses it as a rating scale to evaluate the effectiveness of their book talks.

Rubrics. Rubrics are scoring guides that evaluate student performance in reading and writing according to specific criteria and levels of achievement (Afflerbach, 2007b). They're similar to checklists because they specify what students are expected to be able to do, but they go beyond checklists because they describe levels of achievement. A 4-level rubric for assessing sixth graders' independent reading during reading workshop is shown in the Assessment Tools feature below. Students complete the rubric at the end of each quarter. The quality levels, ranging from Outstanding (highest) to Beginning (lowest), are shown in the column on the far left, and the achievement categories are listed across the top row: number of books read during the quarter, reading level of the books, genres represented by the books, and students' interpretations. The Interpretation category assesses students' comprehension.

Assessment Tools

Independent Reading Rubric

Level	Books Read	Difficulty Level	Genres	Interpretation
Outstanding	Finishes 5 or more books	Reads "just right" books and tries "too hard" books sometimes	Reads books from three or more genres	Makes insightful interpretation with evidence from the book, author's style, and genre
Proficient	Finishes 3 or 4 books	Reads mostly "just right" books	Reads books from two genres	Shares accurate interpretation using a summary, inferences, and story structure
Developing	Finishes 2 or 3 books	Reads mostly "too easy" books	Tries a different genre once in a while	Provides literal interpretation by summarizing events and making personal connections
Beginning	Finishes 1 book	Always reads "too easy" books	Sticks with one genre	Offers incomplete or inaccurate response

Students' Work Samples. Teachers have students collect their work in folders to document their learning. Work samples might include reading logs, audiotapes of students' reading, photos of projects, videotapes of puppet shows and oral presentations, and books students have written. Students often choose some of these work samples to place in their portfolios.

Assessment Tools

Diagnostic Reading and Writing Assessments

Component	Test (With Recommended Grade Levels)	Where to Learn More
Concepts About Print	Observation Survey of Early Literacy Achievement (K–2)	Chapter 4, Working With the Youngest Readers and Writers, p. 113
Phonemic Awareness	Dynamic Indicators of Basic Early Literacy Skills (K–3) Phonological Awareness Literacy Screening (K–3) Yopp-Singer Test of Phonemic Segmentation (K)	Chapter 5, Cracking the Alphabetic Code, p. 154
Phonics	Dynamic Indicators of Basic Early Literacy Skills (K–3) The Names Test (3–8) Observation Survey of Early Literacy Achievement (K–2) The Tile Test (K–2)	Chapter 5, Cracking the Alphabetic Code, p. 166
Word Recognition	High-frequency word lists (K–3) Observation Survey of Early Literacy Achievement (K–2) Writing samples (K–3)	Chapter 6, Developing Fluent Readers and Writers, p. 196
Word Identification	Developmental Reading Assessment (K–8) The Names Test (3–8) Phonological Awareness Literacy Screening (K–3) Running records (K–8)	Chapter 6, Developing Fluent Readers and Writers, p. 207
Fluency	Dynamic Indicators of Basic Early Literacy Skills (K–3) Fluency checks (1–8) Informal reading inventories (2–8) Running records (K–8)	Chapter 6, Developing Fluent Readers and Writers, p. 216
Vocabulary	Expressive Vocabulary Test (K–8) Informal reading inventories (2–8) Peabody Picture Vocabulary Test (K–8)	Chapter 7, Expanding Students' Knowledge of Words, p. 248
Comprehension	Comprehension Thinking Strategies Assessment (1–8) Developmental Reading Assessment (K–8) Informal reading inventories (2–8)	Chapter 8, Facilitating Students' Comprehension: Reader Factors, p. 276
Writing	Rubrics (K–8)	Chapter 2, Teaching the Reading and Writing Processes, p. 64
Spelling	Developmental Spelling Analysis (K–8) Phonological Awareness Literacy Screening (K–3) Qualitative Spelling Inventory (K–8)	Chapter 5, Cracking the Alphabetic Code, p. 180

Diagnosing Students' Strengths and Weaknesses

Teachers use diagnostic reading assessments to identify students' strengths and weaknesses, examine any area of difficulty in more detail, and decide how to modify instruction to meet students' needs. They use a variety of diagnostic tests to examine students' achievement in phonemic awareness, phonics, fluency, vocabulary, comprehension, and other components of reading and writing. The Assessment Tools feature on page 85 lists the diagnostic tests recommended in this text and directs you to the chapter where you can learn more about how to use them.

Two of the assessments that teachers commonly use are running records and informal reading inventories. They're used to determine students' reading levels as well as to diagnose difficulties in word identification, fluency, and comprehension and to monitor students' growth as readers. Mrs. McNeal used running records in the vignette at the beginning of this chapter, and as you continue reading this text, you'll notice that they're referred to again and again.

Go to the Building Teaching Skills and Dispositions section of Chapter 3 on **MyEducationLab.com** to watch as Ms. Janusz conducts an assessment.

Running Records. Teachers often take running records of students' oral reading to assess their word identification and reading fluency (Clay, 2006). With a running record, teachers calculate the percentage of words the student reads correctly and then analyze the miscues or errors. They make a series of checkmarks on a sheet of paper as the student reads words correctly and use other marks to indicate words that the student substitutes, repeats, mispronounces, or doesn't know, as Mrs. McNeal did in the vignette. Although teachers can take the running record on a blank sheet of paper, it's much easier to make a copy of the page or pages the student will read and take the running record next to or on top of the actual text. Using a copy of the text is especially important when assessing older students who read more-complex texts and read them more quickly than younger children do.

After identifying the words the student misread, teachers calculate the percentage of words the student read correctly. They use this percentage to determine whether the book or other reading material is too easy, too difficult, or appropriate for the student at this time. If the student reads 95% or more of the words correctly, the book is easy, or at the independent reading level for that student. If the student reads 90–94% of the words correctly, the book is at his or her instructional level. If the student reads fewer than 90% of the words correctly, the book is too difficult: It's at the student's frustration level.

Teachers can categorize miscues according to the semantic, graphophonic, and syntactic cueing systems in order to examine what word-identification strategies students are using. As they categorize the miscues, teachers should ask themselves these questions:

- ◆ Does the reader self-correct the miscue?
- ◆ Does the miscue change the meaning of the sentence?
- ◆ Is the miscue phonologically similar to the word in the text?
- ◆ Is the miscue acceptable within the syntax (or structure) of the sentence?

The miscues that interfere with meaning and those that are syntactically unacceptable are the most serious because the student doesn't realize that reading should make sense. Miscues can be classified and charted; the Assessment Tools feature on the next page shows the analysis of Seth's miscues on the running record in the vignette at the beginning of the chapter. Only words that students mispronounce or substitute can be analyzed; repetitions and omissions are not calculated.

Mary Shea (2006) developed a modified procedure for using running records with fifth- through eighth-grade struggling readers. Instead of having these students read a complete text as younger children do, she recommends using a 1-minute probe: The student reads aloud for 1 minute from a text that's being used in class, and the teacher marks a copy of the text as the student reads. Afterward, the student retells what he or she has just read, and the teacher prompts the student about any ideas that aren't mentioned. Shea also suggests making an audio- or videotape of the student's reading and reviewing it to gain additional insights.

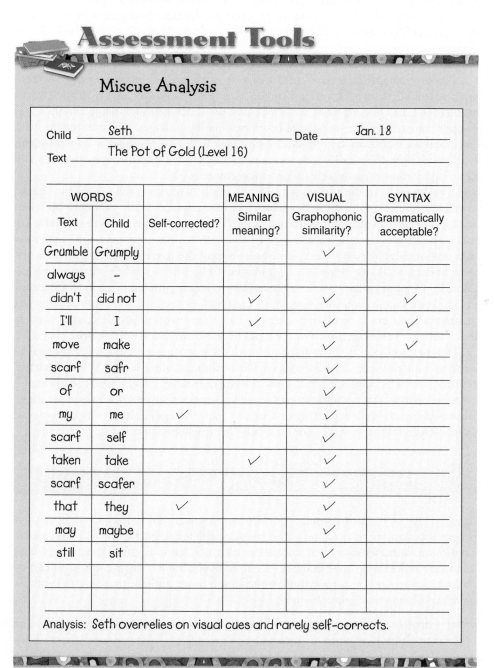

Assessment Tools

Miscue Analysis

Child _____ Seth _____ Date _____ Jan. 18 _____

Text _____ The Pot of Gold (Level 16) _____

WORDS			MEANING	VISUAL	SYNTAX
Text	Child	Self-corrected?	Similar meaning?	Graphophonic similarity?	Grammatically acceptable?
Grumble	Grumply			✓	
always	–				
didn't	did not		✓	✓	✓
I'll	I		✓	✓	✓
move	make			✓	✓
scarf	safr			✓	
of	or			✓	
my	me	✓		✓	
scarf	self			✓	
taken	take		✓	✓	
scarf	scafer			✓	
that	they	✓		✓	
may	maybe			✓	
still	sit			✓	

Analysis: Seth overrelies on visual cues and rarely self-corrects.

Running records are an effective assessment tool because they are authentic (Shea, 2000). Students demonstrate how they read using their regular reading materials as teachers make a detailed account of their ability to read a book. Teachers collect valuable information about the strategies and skills students use to decode words and construct meaning.

Informal Reading Inventories. Teachers use commercial tests called *informal reading inventories* (IRIs) to evaluate students' reading performance. They can be used in first- through eighth-grade levels, but first-grade teachers often find that IRIs don't provide as much useful information about beginning readers as running records do. These popular reading tests are often used as a screening instrument to determine whether students are reading at grade level, but they're also a valuable diagnostic tool (Nilsson, 2008). Teachers can use IRIs to identify struggling students' instructional needs, particularly in the areas of word identification, oral reading fluency, and comprehension.

These individualized tests consist of two parts: graded word lists and passages ranging from first- to at least eighth-grade level. The word lists contain 10 to 20 words at each level, and students read the words until they become too difficult; this indicates an approximate level for students to begin reading the passages. Because students who can't read the words on their grade-level list may have a word-identification problem, teachers analyze the words students read incorrectly, looking for error patterns and deciding whether students rely on one cueing system.

The graded reading passages include both narrative and expository texts, presented in order of difficulty. Students read these passages orally or silently and then answer a series of comprehension questions. Three types of questions generally are used: They ask students to recall specific information, draw inferences, or explain the meaning of vocabulary words. When students read the passage orally, teachers assess their fluency. Students beyond third grade should be able to read the passages at their grade level fluently; if they can't, they may have a fluency problem. Teachers also examine students' comprehension. If students can't answer the questions after reading the passage at their grade level, they may have a comprehension problem, and teachers check to see if there's a pattern to the types of questions that students miss.

Teachers use scoring sheets to record students' performance data, and they calculate students' independent, instructional, and frustration reading levels. When students' reading level is below their grade-level placement, teachers also check their listening capacity; that is, their ability to understand passages that are read aloud to them. Knowing whether students can understand and learn from grade-level texts that are read aloud is crucial because that's a common way that teachers support struggling readers.

Nurturing English Learners

Teachers assess English learners' developing language proficiency as well as their progress in learning to read and write. It's more challenging to assess ELs than native English speakers, because when students aren't proficient in English, their scores don't accurately reflect what they know (Peregoy & Boyle, 2008). Their cultural and experiential backgrounds also contribute to making it more difficult to assure that assessment tools being used aren't biased.

Oral Language Assessment. Teachers assess students who speak a language other than English at home to determine their English language proficiency. They typically use commercial oral language tests to determine if students are proficient in English. If they're not, teachers place them in appropriate English language development programs and monitor their progress toward English language proficiency. Two widely used tests are the Language Assessment Scales, published by CTB/McGraw-Hill, and the IDEA Language Proficiency Test, published by Ballard and Tighe; both tests assess K–12 students' oral and written language (listening, speaking, reading, and writing) proficiency in English. Individual states have developed language assessments that are aligned with their English language proficiency standards; for example, the New York State English as a Second Language Achievement Test and the California English Language Development Test.

An authentic assessment tool that many teachers use is the Student Oral Language Observation Matrix (SOLOM), developed by the San Jose (CA) Area Bilingual Consortium. It's not a test per se; rather, the SOLOM is a rating scale that teachers use to assess students' command of English as they observe them talking and listening in real, day-to-day classroom activities. The SOLOM addresses five components of oral language:

- ◆ **Listening.** Teachers score students along a continuum from unable to comprehend simple statements to understanding everyday conversations.
- ◆ **Fluency.** Teachers score students along a continuum from halting, fragmentary speech to fluent speech, approximating that of native speakers.
- ◆ **Vocabulary.** Teachers score students along a continuum from extremely limited word knowledge to using words and idioms skillfully.
- ◆ **Pronunciation.** Teachers score students along a continuum from virtually unintelligible speech to using pronunciation and intonation proficiently, similar to native speakers.
- ◆ **Grammar.** Teachers score students along a continuum from excessive errors that make speech unintelligible to applying word order, grammar, and usage rules effectively.

Each component has a five-point range that's scored 1 to 5; the total score on the matrix is 25, and a score of 20 or higher indicates that students are fluent speakers of English. The SOLOM is available free of charge online at www.cal.org, at other websites, and in many professional books.

Reading Assessment. English learners face two challenges: They're learning to speak English at the same time they're learning to read. They learn to read the same way that native English speakers do, but they face additional challenges because their knowledge of English phonology, semantics, syntax, and pragmatics is limited and their background knowledge is different (Peregoy & Boyle, 2008). Some English learners are fluent readers in their home language (Garcia, 2000). These students already have substantial funds of knowledge about how written language works and about the reading process that they build on as they learn to read in English (Moll, 1994). Having this knowledge gives them a head start, but students also have to learn what transfers to English reading and what doesn't.

Teachers use the same assessments that they use for native English speakers to identify English learners' reading levels, monitor their growth, and document their learning. Peregoy and Boyle (2008) recommend using data from running records or informal reading inventories along with classroom-based informal assessments, such as observing and conferencing with students.

Because many English learners have less background knowledge about topics in books they're reading, it's important that teachers assess ELs' background knowledge before instruction so they can modify their teaching to meet students' needs. One of the best ways to accomplish this is with a K-W-L chart. As they work with students to complete the first two sections of the chart, teachers learn what students know about a topic and have an opportunity to build additional background knowledge and introduce related vocabulary. Later, when students complete the K-W-L chart, teachers get a clear picture of what they've learned and which vocabulary words they can use.

Another way teachers learn about ELs' development is by asking them to assess themselves as readers (Peregoy & Boyle, 2008). Teachers ask students, for example, what they do when they come to an unfamiliar word, what differences they've noticed between narrative and expository texts, which reading strategies they use, and what types of books they prefer. These quick assessments, commonly done during conferences at the end of a grading period, shed light on students' growth in a way that other assessments can't.

Writing Assessment. English learners' writing develops as their oral language grows and as they become more-fluent readers (Riches & Genesee, 2006). For beginning writers, fluency is the first priority. They move from writing strings of familiar words to grouping words into short sentences that often follow a pattern, much like young native English speakers do. As they develop some writing fluency, ELs begin to stick to a single focus, often repeating words and sentences to make their writing longer. Once they become fluent writers, ELs are usually able to organize their ideas more effectively and group them into paragraphs. They incorporate more-specific vocabulary and expand the length and variety of sentences. Their mechanical errors become less serious, and their writing is much easier to read. At this point, teachers begin teaching the qualities of good writing and choosing writing strategies and skills to teach based on the errors that students make.

Peregoy and Boyle (2008) explain that ELs' writing involves fluency, form, and correctness, and that teachers' assessment of students' writing should reflect these components:

- ◆ Teachers monitor students' ability to write quickly, easily, and comfortably.
- ◆ Teachers assess students' ability to apply writing genres, develop their topic, organize the presentation of ideas, and use sophisticated vocabulary and a variety of sentence structures.
- ◆ Teachers check that students control standard English grammar and usage, spell most words correctly, and use capitalization and punctuation conventions appropriately.

Teachers use rubrics to assess ELs' writing, and the rubrics address fluency, form, and correctness as well as the qualities of good writing that teachers have taught. They also conference with students about their writing and provide quick minilessons, as needed. To learn about students as writers, teachers observe them as they write, noticing how they move through the writing process, interact in writing groups, and share their writing from the author's chair. In addition, students document writing development by placing their best writing in portfolios.

Alternative Assessments. Because of the difficulties inherent in assessing English learners, it's important to use varied types of assessment that involve different language and literacy tasks and ways of demonstrating proficiency (Huerta-Macias, 1995). In addition to commercial tests, O'Malley and Pierce (1996) urge teachers to use authentic assessment tools, including oral performances, story retellings, oral interviews with students, writing samples, illustrations, diagrams, posters, and projects.

Assessment is especially important for students who are learning to speak English at the same time they're learning to read and write in English. Teachers use many of the same assessment tools that they use for their native English speakers but they also depend on alternative, more-authentic assessments because it's difficult to accurately measure these students' growth. Assessment results must be valid because teachers use them to make placement decisions, modify instruction, and document learning.

Documenting Students' Learning

Teachers routinely collect students' work samples, including cassette tapes of them reading aloud, lists of books they've read, reading logs, writing samples with rubrics, and photos of projects. They also keep students' test results and the anecdotal notes they make as they observe students and meet with them in conferences. Teachers use these data to document students' progress toward meeting grade-level standards as well as to evaluate their own teaching effectiveness. Students also collect their best work in portfolios to document their own learning and accomplishments.

PORTFOLIO ASSESSMENT

 Portfolios are systematic and meaningful collections of artifacts documenting students' literacy development over a period of time (Hebert, 2001). These collections are dynamic and reflect students' day-to-day reading and writing activities as well as content-area activities. Students' work samples provide "windows" on the strategies they use as readers and writers. Not only do students select pieces to be placed in their portfolios, they also learn to establish criteria for their selections. Because of students' involvement in selecting pieces for their portfolios and reflecting on them, portfolio assessment respects students and their abilities. Portfolios help students, teachers, and parents see patterns of growth from one literacy milestone to another in ways that are not possible with other types of assessment.

Collecting Work in Portfolios

Portfolios are folders, large envelopes, or boxes that hold students' work. Teachers often have students label and decorate large folders and then store them in plastic crates or cardboard boxes. Students date and label items as they place them in their portfolios, and they often attach notes to the items to explain the context for the activity and why they selected a particular item. Students' portfolios should be stored in the classroom in a place where they are readily accessible; students like to review their portfolios periodically and add new pieces to them.

Students usually choose the items to place in their portfolios within the guidelines the teacher provides. Some students submit the original piece of work; others want to keep the original, so they place a copy in the portfolio instead. In addition to the reading and writing samples that go directly into portfolios, students can record oral language and drama samples on audiotapes and videotapes to place in their portfolios. Large-size art and writing projects can be photographed, and the photographs can be placed in the portfolio. Student work might include books, choral readings on audiotapes, reading logs and learning logs, graphic organizers, multigenre projects, lists of books read, and compositions. This variety of work samples reflects the students' literacy programs. Samples from literature focus units, literature circles, reading and writing workshop, basal reading programs, and content-area units can be included.

New Literacies
E-Portfolios

Instead of collecting papers with their writing samples, cassette tapes with their oral reading samples, photos of projects, and other artifacts in bulky folders that take up lots of space, students can create electronic portfolios to showcase their best work and document their learning. Their artwork and writing samples are scanned, reading samples are recorded, and artifacts are photographed using a digital camera. In addition, collaborative books and projects can be saved in each student's portfolio. Students add text boxes or video clips to provide context for the samples, reflect on their learning, and explain how their work demonstrates that they've met grade-level standards. They also insert hyperlinks to connect sections and enhance their e-portfolios by adding music and graphics.

Teachers create a template that lays out the design, including a title, table of contents, and collections of artifacts. Sometimes rubrics are included to show how the artifacts were assessed. Collections from each grade are saved in separate files within students' portfolios. Teachers can browse electronic portfolios that have been posted on the Web to get ideas about how to design and organize their students' collections of work samples.

E-portfolios are versatile assessment tools: They allow for the flexible input of a variety of multimodal items, incorporate a hierarchical organization, make searching for and retrieving items easy to do, and can be displayed for various audiences to view. Electronic portfolios are practical, too, especially if teachers and students know how to use computers, software, and related equipment, and if they're willing to devote the time needed to start up the portfolio system. They're quick and easy to access because they're stored on CD-ROMs or at the school's website. Web-based portfolios are sometimes called *webfolios*.

Even primary-grade students can assist in developing these technology-based collections, and older students who are more familiar with using computers, scanning writing samples, importing digital photos, and adding video clips can do more of the work themselves. Parent volunteers and cross-age tech buddies can teach students how to get started and provide support when they're adding work samples.

An exciting new online tool for creating portfolios is the KEEP Toolkit, developed by the Carnegie Foundation for the Advancement of Teaching. Its purpose is to provide an economical and accessible tool that teachers and students can use to create compact and engaging Web-based representations of teaching and learning that can be shared with others. Tools in the KEEP Toolkit are used to enter information, upload files, and create snapshots, single webpages or a linked series of webpages created using a template. These presentations can be added to or revised at any time. There's no charge to use this password-protected website. The files are stored on a server at the Carnegie Foundation and given a URL so others can access them. A collection of electronic portfolios created by elementary and secondary teachers and their students is displayed in the Gallery of Teaching and Learning section of the Carnegie Foundation's website (www.cfkeep.org).

Because the 21st century has a knowledge economy, students need to be able to express their knowledge. When teachers introduce e-portfolios in the primary grades and students are encouraged to use them effectively throughout their schooling, they're likely to continue using them in adult life to document and showcase their accomplishments.

Many teachers collect students' work in folders, and they assume that portfolios are basically the same as work folders; however, the two types of collections differ in several important ways. Perhaps the most important difference is that portfolios are student oriented, whereas work folders are usually teachers' collections—students choose which samples will be placed in portfolios, but teachers often place all completed assignments in work folders. Next, portfolios focus on students' strengths, not their weaknesses. Because students choose items for portfolios, they choose samples that best represent their literacy development. Another difference is that portfolios involve reflection (D'Aoust, 1992); through reflection, students pause and become aware of their strengths as readers and writers. They also use their work samples to identify the literacy procedures, strategies, and skills they already know and the ones they need to focus on.

Involving Students in Self-Assessment

Portfolios are a tool for engaging students in self-assessment and goal setting. Students learn to reflect on and assess their own reading and writing activities and their development as readers and writers (Stires, 1991). Teachers begin by asking students to think about their reading and writing in terms of contrasts. For reading, students identify the books they've read that they liked most and least, and they ask themselves what these choices suggest about themselves as readers. They also identify what they do well in reading and what they need to improve. In writing, students make similar contrasts: They identify their best compositions and others that weren't as good, and they think about what they do well when they write and what to improve. By making these comparisons, students begin to reflect on their literacy development.

Teachers use *minilessons* and conferences to teach about the characteristics of good readers and writers. In particular, they discuss these topics:

◆ What fluent reading is
◆ Which reading strategies and skills students use
◆ How students demonstrate their comprehension
◆ How students value books they've read
◆ What makes a good project to apply reading knowledge
◆ What makes an effective piece of writing
◆ Which writing strategies are most effective
◆ How to use writing rubrics
◆ How proofreading and correcting mechanical errors are a courtesy to readers

As students learn about what it means to be effective readers and writers, they acquire the tools they need to reflect on and evaluate their own reading and writing. They

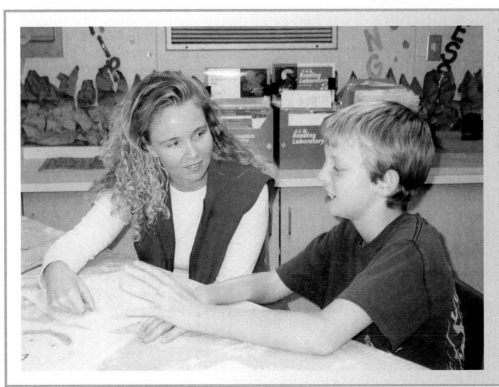

Conferences
This fourth grader meets with his teacher for 15 to 20 minutes to talk about his achievement at the end of the second grading period. Even though it's time-consuming, this teacher meets with each student at the end of every grading period to talk about the student's progress, identify standards-based accomplishments, select pieces to add to the portfolio, determine grades, and set goals for the next quarter. Through this process, teachers involve students in assessment, and students become more responsible for their own learning as they self-assess their progress and set goals for themselves.

learn how to think about themselves as readers and writers and acquire the vocabulary to use in their reflections, such as *goal*, *strategy*, and *rubric*.

Students write notes on items they choose to put into their portfolios. In these self-assessments, students explain the reasons for their choices and identify strengths and accomplishments in their work. In some classrooms, students write their reflections and other comments on index cards, and in other classrooms, they design special comment sheets that they attach to the items in their portfolios.

Teachers usually collect baseline reading and writing samples at the beginning of the school year and then conduct portfolio review conferences with students at the end of each grading period. At these conferences, the teacher and the student talk about the items being placed in the portfolio and the student's self-assessments. Students also talk about what they want to improve or what they want to accomplish during the next grading period, and these points become their goals for the next grading period.

Self-assessment can also be used for an assessment at the end of the school year. Coughlan (1988) asked his seventh-grade students to "show me what you have learned about writing this year" and to "explain how you have grown as a written language user, comparing what you knew in September to what you know now" (p. 375). These upper-grade students used a process approach to develop and refine their compositions, and they submitted all drafts with their final copies. Coughlan examined both the content of students' compositions and the strategies they used in thinking through the assignment and writing their responses. He found this "test" to be a very worthwhile project because it "forced the students to look within themselves . . . realize just how much they had learned" (p. 378). Moreover, students' compositions verified what they had learned about writing and that they could articulate their learning.

Showcasing Students' Portfolios

At the end of the school year, many teachers organize "Portfolio Share Days" to celebrate students' accomplishments and to provide an opportunity for students to share their portfolios with classmates and the wider community (Porter & Cleland, 1995). Often family members, local businesspeople, school administrators, local politicians, college students, and others are invited to attend. Students and community members form small groups, and students share their portfolios, pointing out their accomplishments and strengths. This activity is especially useful in involving community members in the school and showing them the types of literacy activities in which students are involved as well as how students are becoming effective readers and writers.

These sharing days also help students accept responsibility for their own learning—especially those students who have not been as motivated as their classmates. When less motivated students listen to their classmates talk about their work and how they have grown as readers and writers, they often decide to work harder the next year.

Why Are Portfolios Worthwhile?

Portfolios are used to document students' work, evaluate their progress, and showcase their best work (Afflerbach, 2007b). Collections of work samples add context to students' learning, and students become more reflective about the quality of their reading and writing. There are other benefits, too:

◆ Students feel ownership of their work.
◆ Students become more responsible about their work.
◆ Students set goals and are motivated to work toward accomplishing them.
◆ Students make connections between learning and assessing.

- Students' self-esteem is enhanced.
- Portfolios eliminate the need to grade all student work.
- Portfolios are used in student and parent conferences.
- Portfolios complement the information provided on report cards.

In schools where portfolios are used schoolwide, students overwhelmingly report that by using portfolios, they're better able to show their parents what they're learning and also better able to set goals for themselves (Kuhs, Johnson, Agruso, & Monrad, 2001). Teachers also find that portfolios enable them to assess their students more thoroughly, and students are better able to see their own progress.

HIGH-STAKES TESTING

Annual high-stakes testing is emphasized in American schools with the goal of improving the quality of reading instruction. These tests are designed to objectively measure students' knowledge according to grade-level standards. The current emphasis on testing and state-level standards are reform efforts that began in response to The National Commission on Education report *A Nation at Risk* (1983), which argued that American schools were failing miserably. The report stated that American students' test scores were dropping, comparing unfavorably with students' scores in other industrialized countries, and it concluded that the United States was in jeopardy of losing its global superiority. The No Child Left Behind Act, which promoted an increased focus on reading instruction to improve students' reading performance and narrow the racial and ethnic gaps in achievement, reinforced the call for annual standardized testing.

Researchers have repeatedly refuted these arguments (Bracey, 2004; McQuillan, 1998). Allington (2006) explained that average test scores have remained stable for 30 years despite the dramatic increases in federal funding over the past decade. He goes on to explain that reporting average scores obscures important findings, and it's necessary to examine subgroup data to discover that most students from middle-class families read well even though many students from low-income families lag behind. Despite a gap, he also notes that significant progress has been made in closing the achievement gap between white and minority students at the same time the number of minority students has grown tremendously. Finally, he points out that grade-level standards of achievement have increased in the last 50 years so that what was considered fifth-grade level is now fourth-grade level, and older readability formulas have been renormed to reflect today's higher grade-level standards. Nonetheless, the public's perception that schools are failing persists.

High-stakes testing is different than classroom assessment. The test scores typically provide little information for making day-to-day instructional decisions, but students, teachers, administrators, and schools are judged and held accountable by the results. The scores are used to make important educational decisions for students—to determine school placement and high school graduation, for example. These scores influence administrators' evaluations of teachers' effectiveness and even their salaries in some states, and they reward or sanction administrators, schools, and school districts.

Standardized tests are comprehensive with batteries of subtests, covering decoding, vocabulary, comprehension, writing mechanics, and spelling. Figure 3–4 presents an overview of the most commonly used tests. Most tests use multiple-choice test items, although a few are introducing open-ended questions that require students to write responses. Beginning in second grade, classroom teachers administer the tests to their students, typically in the spring. Most require multiple testing periods to administer all of the subtests.

Figure 3–4 ◆ Standardized Achievement Tests

Test	Purpose	Components	Special Features	Publisher
Iowa Test of Basic Skills (ITBS)	The ITBS provides information to improve instruction at grades K–8.	Phonics Vocabulary Comprehension Oral language Mechanics Spelling	The ITBS is the oldest statewide assessment program. It can be administered at the beginning of the school year to better inform instruction.	Iowa schools are served by the Iowa Testing Program; outside Iowa, the ITBS is available from the Riverside Publishing Company.
Metropolitan Achievement Test (MAT)	The MAT measures K–8 students using real-world content. Some items are multiple choice; others are performance-based tasks.	Emergent literacy Vocabulary Comprehension Mechanics Writing Spelling	Test items are aligned with the IRA/NCTE Language Arts Standards. The MAT also provides a Lexile measure of students' reading levels.	The MAT can be ordered from Pearson.
Stanford Achievement Test (SAT)	The SAT measures K–8 students' progress toward meeting the challenges set forth by the NCLB Act and state standards.	Phonemic awareness Phonics Vocabulary Comprehension Mechanics Writing Spelling	The SAT also provides a Lexile measure of students' reading levels.	The SAT is published by Pearson.
TerraNova Test (TNT)	The TNT is a standardized test that uses both multiple-choice and constructed-response items that allow students to write responses.	Word analysis Vocabulary Comprehension Mechanics Spelling	Lexile scores are reported so teachers can match students to books. Also, one version of the TNT is available as an online test.	The TNT is published by CTB/McGraw-Hill.

Problems With High-Stakes Testing

A number of problems are associated with high-stakes testing (IRA, 1999). Students feel the pressure of these tests, and researchers have confirmed what many teachers have noticed: Students don't try harder because of them (Hoffman, Assaf, & Paris, 2005). Struggling students, in particular, get discouraged and feel defeated, and over time, test pressure destroys their motivation and actually harms their achievement. In addition, student dropout rates are rising.

Teachers complain that they feel compelled to improve students' test scores at any price, and they lose valuable instructional time for test-taking and practice sessions (Hollingworth, 2007). Overemphasizing the test often leads teachers to abandon a balanced approach to instruction: Sometimes students spend more time completing practice tests than reading books and writing compositions. One of the most insidious side effects is that teachers are often directed to focus on certain groups of students, especially those scoring just below a cutoff point, in hopes of improving test scores.

Preparing for Standardized Tests

Standardized tests are a unique text genre, and they require readers and writers to do different things than they would normally, so teachers can't assume that students already know how to take reading tests. It's essential that teachers prepare students to take high-stakes tests without abandoning a balanced approach to instruction that's aligned to state standards (Calkins, Montgomery, & Santman, 1998). Greene and Melton (2007) agree; they maintain that teachers must prepare students for high-stakes tests without sacrificing their instructional program. Unfortunately, with the pressure to raise test scores, some teachers are having students take more multiple-choice tests while writing fewer essays and creating fewer projects.

Hollingworth (2007) recommends these five ways to prepare students for high-stakes tests without sacrificing the instructional program:

◆ Teachers check that their state's curriculum standards align with their instructional program and make any needed adjustments to ensure that they're teaching what's going to be on the test.
◆ Teachers set goals with students and use informal assessments to regularly monitor their progress.
◆ Teachers actively engage students in authentic literacy activities so that they become capable readers and writers.
◆ Teachers explain the purpose of the tests and how the results will be used, without making students anxious.
◆ Teachers stick with a balanced approach that combines explicit instruction and authentic application.

Other researchers advise that in addition to these recommendations, teachers prepare students to take standardized tests by teaching them how to read and answer test items and having them take practice tests to hone their test-taking strategies (McCabe, 2003). Preparing for tests involves explaining their purpose, examining the genre and format of multiple-choice tests, teaching the formal language of tests and test-taking strategies, and providing opportunities for students to take practice tests; and these lessons should be folded into the existing instructional program, not replace it. Greene and Melton (2007) organized test preparation into minilessons that they taught as part of reading workshop.

The Genre of Standardized Tests. Students need opportunities to examine old test forms to learn about the genre of standardized tests and how test questions are formatted. They'll notice that tests look different than other texts they've read; they're typically printed in black and white, the text is dense, and few illustrations are included. Sometimes words, phrases, and lines in the text are numbered, bolded, or underlined. Through this exploration, students begin to think about what makes one type of text harder to read than others, and with practice, they get used to how tests are formatted so that they're better able to read them.

The Language of Testing. Standardized reading tests use formal language that's unfamiliar to many students. For example, some tests use the word *passage* instead of *text* and *author's intent* instead of *main idea*. Test makers also use *locate, except, theme, reveal, inform, reason, in order to, provide suspense,* and other words that students may not understand. Greene and Melton (2007) call the language of testing "test talk" and explain that "students are helpless on standardized reading tests if they can't decipher test talk" (p. 8). Students need help understanding test talk so that high-stakes tests really measure what they know.

Test-Taking Strategies. Students vary the test-taking strategies they use according to the type of test they're taking. Most standardized tests employ multiple-choice questions. Here's a list of test-taking strategies that students use to answer multiple-choice questions:

Read the entire question first. Students read the entire question first to make sure they understand what it's asking. For questions about a reading passage, students read the questions first to guide their reading.

Look for key words in the question. Students identify key words in the question, such as *compare*, *except*, and *author's intent*, that will guide them to choose the correct answer.

Read all answer choices before choosing the correct answer. After students read the question, they stop and think about the answer before reading all the possible answers. Then they eliminate the unlikely answer choices and identify the correct answer.

Answer easier questions first. Students answer the questions they know, skipping the difficult ones, and then they go back and answer the questions they skipped.

Make smart guesses. When students don't know the answer to a question, they make a smart guess, unless there's a penalty for guessing. To make a smart guess, students eliminate the answer choices they're sure are wrong, think about what they know about the topic, and then pick the best remaining answer choice. The correct answer is often the longest one.

Stick with your first answer. Students shouldn't second-guess themselves; their first answer is probably right. They shouldn't change answers unless they're certain that their first answer was wrong.

Pace yourself. Students budget their time wisely so they'll be able to finish the test. They don't spend too much time on any one question.

Check your work carefully. Students check that they've answered every question, if they finish early.

Students use these test-taking strategies along with reading strategies, including determining importance, questioning, and rereading, when they're taking standardized tests. Teaching students about question-answer-relationships helps them to understand that sometimes answers to test questions can be found in a passage they've just read, or they have to use their own knowledge.

Preparing for tests should be embedded in literacy activities and not take up a great deal of instructional time. Teachers often teach test-taking strategies through minilessons where they explain the strategy, model its use, and provide opportunities for guided practice and discussion. Greene and Melton (2007) recommend teaching minilessons on test-taking strategies as well as the genre of tests, test formats, and the language of tests as part of reading workshop. They reported that their students, many of whom are English learners and struggling readers and writers, became more confident and empowered test-takers through test-preparation minilessons, and their test scores improved.

Practice Tests. Teachers design practice tests with the same types of items used on the standardized tests students will take. They use easy-to read materials for practice tests so students can focus on practicing test-taking strategies without being challenged by the difficulty level of the text or the questions. They include a combination of unrelated narrative, poetic, and expository passages on the tests because all three types of texts are used on high-stakes tests. Teachers also provide answer sheets similar to those used on the standardized test so that students gain experience using them. So that students will be familiar with the testing conditions, teachers simulate them in the classroom or take students to where the test will be administered for practice sessions. Through these practice tests, students develop both confidence in their test-taking abilities and the stamina to persist through long tests.

Preparation for reading tests is especially important because when students aren't familiar with multiple-choice tests, they'll score lower than they otherwise would. Don't confuse test preparation with teaching to the test: Preparing for a test involves teaching students how to take a test, whereas teaching to the test is the unethical practice of drilling students on actual questions from old tests. The term "teaching to the test" is also used in a less pejorative way to describe when teachers tailor instruction to meet state-mandated standards.

Be Strategic!

Test-Taking Strategies

Students use these test-taking strategies to answer multiple-choice questions on standardized tests:

► Read the entire question first
► Look for key words in the question
► Read all answer choices before choosing the correct one
► Answer easier questions first
► Make smart guesses
► Stick with your first answer
► Pace yourself
► Check your work carefully

Students learn to use these strategies through test-prep lessons and practice tests.

Nurturing English Learners

Researchers question the use of standardized achievement tests with English learners because these tests are often invalid, underestimating students' achievement (Peregoy & Boyle, 2008). It seems obvious that when students have limited English proficiency, their test performance would be affected; however, even students who do well in the classroom often score poorly on standardized achievement tests (Lindholm-Leary & Borsato, 2006). There are several reasons for this dichotomy. First, test-taking procedures are less familiar whereas classroom routines are more predictable and comfortable, and it's likely that ELs are more stressed by their unfamiliarity than native English speakers are. A second reason is that the language used in directions and test items is often complex, making comprehension more difficult for ELs. Another reason is cultural differences: English learners often lack background knowledge about the topics addressed in the reading passages and test questions.

Researchers believe that the best way to assess English learners more fairly is to provide accommodations, by modifying either the test or the testing procedure (Lindholm-Leary & Borsato, 2006). They've experimented with modifying tests by simplifying the language, translating the test into students' home language, or adding visual supports, and modifying the testing procedure by providing additional time, allowing students to use bilingual dictionaries, or translating or explaining the directions. Unfortunately, data are inconclusive about the effectiveness of these accommodations. Currently, there's renewed interest in rewriting test questions on high-stakes tests to avoid unnecessarily complex English syntactic structures and academic vocabulary so that ELs can actually demonstrate their knowledge.

Probably the best way to ameliorate the effects of ELs' potentially invalid test results is to use multiple measures, including some authentic assessments, to document English learners' language proficiency and literacy achievement. This accommodation, however, is unlikely to be implemented in today's educational climate where both students and teachers are being held accountable using the results from a single test.

The Politics of High-Stakes Testing

The debate over high-stakes testing is a politically charged issue (Casbarro, 2005). Test scores are being used as a means to reform schools, and although improving the quality of instruction and ensuring that all students have equal access to educational opportunities are essential, there are unwanted consequences for both students and teachers. Does high-stakes testing work? Proponents claim that schools are being reformed; however, although some gains in test scores for minority groups have been reported, many teachers feel that the improvement is the result of "teaching to the test." So far, no results indicate that students have actually become better readers and writers because of standardized achievement tests.

The goal of the No Child Left Behind Act is admirable, but test experts have argued that a single evaluation shouldn't be used to judge either students' learning or teachers' effectiveness. Braunger and Lewis (2006) point out that "ironically, the national focus on accountability . . . may leave little room for assessment linked to instruction that could actually improve literacy outcomes for students who are being left behind" (p. 130).

Chapter 3
Review

How Effective Teachers Assess Students' Literacy Development

▶ Teachers determine students' independent, instructional, and frustration reading levels.

▶ Teachers informally monitor students' progress in reading and writing.

▶ Teachers use diagnostic assessments to identify students' strengths and weaknesses and then provide instruction to address problem areas.

▶ Teachers have students document their learning in portfolios.

▶ Teachers prepare students for high-stakes tests without sacrificing their instructional programs.

Go to MyEducationLab at www.myeducationlab.com to deepen your understanding of the concepts presented in this chapter:

▶ Expand your knowledge about assessing students' instructional reading levels by viewing video segments in the Literacy Portraits.

▶ Check your understanding of chapter concepts with the multiple-choice and essay quizzes in the Study Plan.

▶ Apply some of the main ideas discussed in the chapter in the Activities and Applications section of the website.

▶ Practice what you've learned in this chapter in Building Teaching Skills and Dispositions before applying the ideas in your own classroom.

PROFESSIONAL REFERENCES

Afflerbach, P. (2007a). Best practices in literacy assessment. In L. B. Gambrell, L. M. Morrow, & M. Pressley (Eds.), *Best practices in literacy instruction* (3rd ed., pp. 264–282). New York: Guilford Press.

Afflerbach, P. (2007b). *Understanding and using reading assessment, K–12.* Newark, DE: International Reading Association.

Allington, R. L. (2006). *What really matters for struggling readers: Designing research-based programs* (2nd ed.). Boston: Allyn & Bacon/Pearson.

Beaver, J. (2006). *Developmental reading assessment* (2nd ed.). Upper Saddle River, NJ: Celebration Press/Pearson.

Boyd-Batstone, P. (2004). Focused anecdotal records assessment: A tool for standards-based, authentic assessment. *The Reading Teacher, 58,* 230–239.

Bracey, G. W. (2004). *Setting the record straight: Responses to misconceptions about public education in the United States.* Portsmouth, NH: Heinemann.

Braunger, J., & Lewis, J. P. (2006). *Building a knowledge base in reading* (2nd ed.). Newark, DE: International Reading Association/National Council of Teachers of English.

Calkins, L., Montgomery, K., & Santman, D. (1998). *A teacher's guide to standardized reading tests: Knowledge is power.* Portsmouth, NH: Heinemann.

Casbarro, J. (2005, February). The politics of high-stakes testing. *Education Digest, 70*(6), 20–23.

Clay, M. M. (2006). *An observation survey of early literacy assessment* (2nd ed.). Portsmouth, NH: Heinemann.

Coughlan, M. (1988). Let the students show us what they know. *Language Arts, 65,* 375–378.

D'Aoust, C. (1992). Portfolios: Process for students and teachers. In K. B. Yancy (Ed.), *Portfolios in the writing classroom* (pp. 39–48). Urbana, IL: National Council of Teachers of English.

Fountas, I. C., & Pinnell, G. S. (2006a). *The Fountas and Pinnell leveled book list, K–8* (2006–2008 ed.). Portsmouth, NH: Heinemann.

Fountas, I. C., & Pinnell, G. S. (2006b). *Leveled books, K–8: Matching texts to readers for effective teaching.* Portsmouth, NH: Heinemann.

Fountas, I. C., & Pinnell, G. S. (2007). *The Fountas and Pinnell benchmark assessment system.* Portsmouth, NH: Heinemann.

Fry, E. (1968). A readability formula that saves time. *Journal of Reading, 11,* 587.

Garcia, G. E. (2000). Bilingual children's reading. In M. Kamil, P. Mosenthal, P. D. Pearson, & R. Barr (Eds.), *Handbook of reading research* (Vol. 3, pp. 813–834). Newark, DE: International Reading Association.

Goodman, Y. M. (1978). Kid watching: An alternative to testing. *The National Elementary Principal, 57,* 41–45.

Greene, A. H., & Melton, G. D. (2007). *Test talk: Integrating test preparation into reading workshop.* Portsmouth, ME: Stenhouse.

Hebert, E. A. (2001). *The power of portfolios: What children can teach us about learning and assessment.* San Francisco: Jossey-Bass.

Hoffman, J. V., Assaf, L. C., & Paris, S. G. (2005). High-stakes testing in reading: Today in Texas, tomorrow? In S. J. Barrentine & S. M. Stokes (Eds.), *Reading assessment: Principles and practices for elementary teachers* (2nd ed., pp. 108–120). Newark, DE: International Reading Association.

Hollingworth, L. (2007). Five ways to prepare for standardized tests without sacrificing best practice. *The Reading Teacher, 61,* 339–342.

Huerta-Macias, A. (1995). Alternative assessment: Responses to commonly asked questions. *TESOL Journal, 5,* 8–10.

International Reading Association (IRA). (1999). *High-stakes assessments in reading: A position statement.* Newark, DE: Author.

Kame'enui, E., Simmons, D., & Cornachione, C. (2000). *A practical guide to reading assessments.* Newark, DE: International Reading Association.

Kuhs, T. M., Johnson, R. L., Agruso, S. A., & Monrad, D. M. (2001). *Put to the test: Tools and techniques for classroom assessment.* Portsmouth, NH: Heinemann.

Lindholm-Leary, K., & Borsato, G. (2006). Academic achievement. In F. Genesee, K. Lindholm-Leary, W. M. Saunders, & D. Christian (Eds.), *Educating English language learners: A synthesis of research evidence* (pp. 176–222). New York: Cambridge University Press.

McCabe, P. P. (2003). Enhancing self-efficacy for high-stakes reading tests. *The Reading Teacher, 57,* 12–20.

McQuillan, J. (1998). *The literacy crisis: False claims, real solutions.* Portsmouth, NH: Heinemann.

Moll, L. (1994). Literacy research in community and classrooms: A sociocultural approach. In R. R. Ruddell, M. R. Ruddell, & H. Singer (Eds.), *Theoretical models and processes of reading* (4th ed., pp. 197–207). Newark, DE: International Reading Association.

National Commission on Excellence in Education. (1983). *A nation at risk: The imperative for educational reform.* Washington, DC: U.S. Government Printing Office.

Nilsson, N. L. (2008). A critical analysis of eight informal reading inventories. *The Reading Teacher, 61,* 526–536.

O'Malley, J. M., & Pierce, L. V. (1996). *Authentic assessment for English language learners: Practical approaches for teachers.* Boston: Addison-Wesley.

Peregoy, S. F., & Boyle, O. F. (2008). *Reading, writing, and learning in ESL: A resource book for teaching K–12 English learners* (5th ed.). Boston: Allyn & Bacon/Pearson.

Peterson, B. (2001). *Literary pathways: Selecting books to support new readers.* Portsmouth, NH: Heinemann.

Porter, C., & Cleland, J. (1995). *The portfolio as a learning strategy.* Portsmouth, NH: Heinemann.

Riches, C., & Genesee, F. (2006). Literacy: Crosslinguistic and crossmodal issues. In F. Genesee, K. Lindholm-Leary, W. M. Saunders, & D. Christian (Eds.), *Educating English language learners: A synthesis of research evidence* (pp. 64–108). New York: Cambridge University Press.

Shea, M. (2000). *Taking running records.* New York: Scholastic.

Shea, M. (2006). *Where's the glitch? How to use running records with older readers, grades 5–8.* Portsmouth, NH: Heinemann.

Stires, S. (1991). Thinking through the process: Self-evaluation in writing. In B. M. Power & R. Hubbard (Eds.), *The Heinemann reader: Literacy in process* (pp. 295–310). Portsmouth, NH: Heinemann.

Winograd, P., & Arrington, H. J. (1999). Best practices in literacy assessment. In L. B. Gambrell, L. M. Morrow, S. B. Neuman, & M. Pressley (Eds.), *Best practices in literacy instruction* (pp. 210–241). New York: Guilford Press.

CHILDREN'S BOOK REFERENCES

Blume, J. (2007). *Tales of a fourth grade nothing.* New York: Puffin Books.

Cole, J. (1993). *The magic school bus lost in the solar system.* New York: Scholastic.

Howe, D., & Howe, J. (2006). *Bunnicula: A rabbit-tale of mystery.* New York: Aladdin Books.

MacLachlan, P. (2004). *Sarah, plain and tall.* New York: HarperTrophy.

Mathis, S. B. (2006). *The hundred penny box.* New York: Puffin Books.

Rylant, C. (2007). *Henry and Mudge and the big sleepover.* New York: Aladdin Books.

The pot of gold (an Irish folk tale). (2001). Upper Saddle River, NJ: Celebration Press/Pearson.

PaRT 2

Components of Literacy Development

Researchers have identified these components of literacy development that students need to learn to become effective readers and writers:

▶ **Alphabetic Code**
Students learn phonemic awareness, phonics, and spelling to understand our sound-symbol system.

▶ **Fluency**
Students learn to read fluently so that they have cognitive resources available for comprehension.

▶ **Vocabulary**
Students acquire a wide vocabulary and learn how to unlock the meaning of new words.

▶ **Comprehension**
Students learn to use strategies to direct their comprehension.

In this part opener, I'd like to introduce you to five students in Ms. Janusz's second-grade class. You'll learn about them and how they develop as readers and writers in their online Literacy Portraits—case study video clips and writing samples—located at the MyEducationLab website (www.myeducationlab.com). There you can track these students' development in phonics, fluency, vocabulary and comprehension. Four of them began second grade not meeting grade-level expectations, but the fifth student, Jimmy, exemplifies second-grade standards. I've included Jimmy's Literacy Portrait for a grade-level comparison. All five students have shown tremendous growth during second grade as they've become more-capable readers and writers.

Rakie's favorite color is pink, and she loves her cat, JoJo. She came to America from Africa when she was very young, and she's currently enrolled in the school's pull-out ESL program. Rakie enjoys reading books with her friends in the library area. Her favorite book is Doreen Cronin's *Click Clack Moo: Cows That Type* because she appreciates that troublesome duck. Rakie's a fluent reader, but she has difficulty understanding what she reads, mainly because of unfamiliar vocabulary, a common problem for English learners. Rakie's bright, and Ms. Janusz is pleased that she's making great strides!

A minte leter
I opened the door
and JoJo was foze
in a ice cobe.

Michael

Beep beep beep beep it was 9:00 am. I new I had to wacke up. I toock my first Step, Slip the flors were frozen Solid.

Michael is gregarious and loves fun in any size or shape. He takes karate lessons, and his Xbox video gaming system is a prized possession. In September, Michael, who is bilingual, was reading below grade level and couldn't stay on task, but after Ms. Janusz encouraged him to choose books that he wanted to read and to identify topics for writing, his motivation began to grow. Now, he's making rapid progress! He's not crazy about reading except for The Magic Tree House series of chapter books, but he really enjoys writing. He says that his stories are good because he uses wordplay effectively.

Rhiannon

Rhiannon, the youngest in Ms. Janusz's class, is a charmer. Her gusto for life is contagious! In September, she held books upside down, but she's made tremendous progress since then. Mo Willems is her favorite author; she loves his stories, including *Don't Let the Pigeon Drive the Bus!* She struggles to decode unfamiliar words, usually depending on the sound-it-out strategy. Rhiannon's passionate about writing. She creates inventive stories about her dogs, Taco and Tequila, and gets very animated when sharing them with classmates, but abbreviated spellings make her writing difficult to read.

I SODit to my DaD. B U D uP! So I pot Logr cLos onanD Pas anD soD It to my DaD. B U D u P!

TRANSLATION:

I showed it to my Dad.
BUNDLE UP!
So I put longer clothes on and
pants and showed it to my Dad.
BUNDLE UP!

Curt'Lynn

Curt'Lynn enjoys playing with her buddies Leah and Audri at recess and spending time with her Granny. Her reading was at early-first-grade level at the beginning of second grade. She often "read" books to herself, telling the story through the illustrations. Now Curt'Lynn loves to read Dr. Seuss books because they're funny. Her focus is on decoding words, but she's beginning to think about whether the words she's reading make sense. Curt'Lynn recognizes that her reading has been improving this year because, as she explains, it's becoming easier to get the words right.

When I was just 4 years old, I was a CherLeedre Because I rill wueted to be a cherLeedre.

It was a haunted house! The door creKed opin. "BOO!" said a ghost. And Lady was gone! "AAAA!" said Jim.

Jimmy

Jimmy's a big sports fan—he likes the Cleveland Indians and the Ohio State Buckeyes, in particular—but his real passion is World War II. He likes to play Army with his best friend, Sam. Jimmy often chooses nonfiction books on varied topics to read; recently, he read a biography about rock-and-roll idol Elvis Presley. Jimmy's a bright student who achieves at or above grade level in all subjects. He's eager to please and worries about making a mistake when he's sharing his writing or reading aloud. In September, Jimmy had trouble with comprehension, but now he's a confident, strategic reader.

To learn more about these students, go to the Literacy Portraits section of the MyEducationLab website and click on the Teacher Interviews to view Gail Tompkins's conversations with Ms. Janusz.

ChapTer 4

Working With the Youngest Readers and Writers

Ms. McCloskey's Students Become Readers and Writers

Kindergarten through third-grade students sit together on the carpet for a shared reading lesson. They watch and listen intently as Ms. McCloskey prepares to read *Make Way for Ducklings* (McCloskey, 2001), the big-book version of an award-winning story about the dangers facing a family of ducks living in the city of Boston. She reads the title and the author's name, and some children recognize that the author's last name is the same as hers, but she points out that they aren't related. She reads the first page and asks the class to make predictions about what will happen in the story. During this first reading, Ms. McCloskey reads each page expressively and tracks the text, word by word, with a pointer as she reads. She clarifies the meaning as she talks about the illustrations on each page. A child helps balance the book on the easel and turn the pages for her. After she finishes, they talk about the story. Some of the English learners are initially hesitant, but others eagerly relate their own experiences to the story and ask questions to learn more.

The next day, Ms. McCloskey rereads *Make Way for Ducklings*. She begins by asking for volunteers to retell the story. Children take turns retelling each page, using the illustrations as clues. Ms. McCloskey includes this oral language activity because many of her students are English learners. The class is multilingual and multicultural: Approximately 45% of the children are Asian Americans who speak Hmong, Khmer, or Lao; 45% are Hispanics who speak Spanish or English at home; and the remaining 10% are African Americans and whites who speak English.

Next, Ms. McCloskey rereads the story, stopping several times to ask the class to think about the characters, draw inferences, and reflect on the theme. Her questions include: Why did the police officer help the ducks? What would have happened to the ducks if the police officer didn't help? Do you think that animals should live in cities? What was Robert McCloskey trying to say to us in this story? On the third day, Ms. McCloskey reads the story again, and the children take turns using the pointer to track the text and join in reading familiar words. After they finish, the children clap because rereading the now familiar story provides a sense of accomplishment.

Ms. McCloskey understands that her students are moving through three developmental stages—emergent, beginning, and fluent—as they learn to read and write. She monitors each child's development to provide instruction that meets his or her needs. As she reads the big book aloud, she uses a pointer to show the direction of print, from left to right and top to bottom on the page. She also moves the pointer across the lines of text, word by word, to demonstrate the relationship between the words on the page and the words she's reading aloud. These are concepts that many of the youngest, emergent-stage readers are learning.

Others are beginning readers who are learning to recognize high-frequency words and decode phonetically regular words. One day after rereading the story, Ms. McCloskey turns to one of the pages and asks the children to identify familiar high-frequency words (e.g., *don't, make*) and decode other CVC words (e.g., *run, big*). She also asks children to isolate individual sentences on the page and note the capital letter at the beginning and the punctuation that marks the end of the sentence.

The third group are fluent readers. Ms. McCloskey addresses their needs, too, as she rereads a page from the story: She asks several children to identify adjectives and notice inflectional endings on verbs. She also rereads the last sentence on the page and asks a child to explain why commas are used in it.

Ms. McCloskey draws the children's attention to the text as a natural part of shared reading. She demonstrates concepts; points out letters, words, and punctuation marks; models strategies; and asks questions about concepts of print. As they watch Ms. McCloskey and listen to their classmates, the children think about letters, words, and sentences and learn more about literacy.

Ms. McCloskey and her teaching partner, Mrs. Papaleo, share a large classroom and 38 students; despite the number of children present, the room feels spacious. Children's desks are arranged in clusters around the large, open area in the middle where children meet for whole-class activities. An easel to display big books is placed next to the teacher's chair. Several chart racks stand nearby; one rack holds Ms. McCloskey's morning messages and interactive writing texts that children have written, a second one holds charts with poems that the children use for choral reading, and a third rack holds a pocket chart with word cards and sentence strips.

On one side of the classroom is the library with books arranged in crates by topic. One crate has frog books, and others have books about the ocean, plants, and the five senses. Other crates contain books by authors who have been featured in author studies, including Eric Carle, Kevin Henkes, and Paula Danziger. Picture books and chapter books are neatly arranged in the crates; children take turns keeping the area neat. Sets of leveled books are arranged on a shelf above the children's reach for the teachers to use in guided reading lessons. A child-size sofa, a table and chairs, pillows, and rugs make the library area cozy and inviting. A listening center is set up at a nearby table with a tape player and headphones that accommodate six children at a time.

A word wall with high-frequency words fills a partition separating instructional areas. It's divided into sections for each letter of the alphabet. Arranged on it are nearly 100 words written on small cards cut into the shape of the words. The teachers introduce new words each week and post them on the word wall. The children often practice reading and writing the words as a center activity, and they refer to the word wall to spell words when they're writing.

A bank of computers with a printer are located on another side of the classroom. Everyone uses them, even the youngest children. Those who have stronger computer skills assist their classmates. They use word processing to publish their writing during writing workshop and monitor their independent reading practice on the computer using the Accelerated Reader® program. At other times, they search the Internet to find information related to topics they're studying in science and social studies, and use software programs to learn typing skills.

Literacy center materials are stored in another area. Clear plastic boxes hold sets of magnetic letters, puppets and other props, dry-erase boards and pens, puzzles and games, flash cards, and other manipulatives. The teachers choose materials to use during minilessons, and they also set boxes of materials out for children to use during center time.

Ms. McCloskey spends the morning teaching reading and writing using a variety of teacher-directed and student-choice activities. Her daily schedule is shown in the box on page 109. After shared reading and a minilesson, the children participate in reading and writing workshop.

The children write books during writing workshop. They pick up their writing folders and write independently at their desks. While most of them are working, Ms. McCloskey brings together a small group for a special activity: She conducts interactive writing lessons with emergent writers and teaches the writing process and revision strategies to more fluent writers. Today she's conferencing with six children who are beginning writers. Because they're writing longer compositions, Ms. McCloskey has decided to introduce revising. After each child reads his or her rough draft aloud to the group, classmates ask questions and offer compliments, and Ms. McCloskey encourages them to make a change in their writing so that their readers will understand it better. Anthony reads aloud a story about his soccer game, and after a classmate asks a question, he realizes that he needs to add more about how

Ms. McCloskey's Schedule		
Time	Activity	Description
8:10–8:20	Class Meeting	Children participate in opening activities, read the morning message from their teachers, and talk about plans for the day.
8:20–8:45	Shared Reading	The teachers read big books and poems written on charts; this activity often serves as a lead-in to the minilesson.
8:45–9:00	Minilesson	The teachers teach minilessons on literacy procedures, concepts, strategies, and skills.
9:00–9:45	Writing Workshop	Children write books while the teachers confer with individual children and small groups. They also do interactive writing activities.
9:45–10:00	Recess	
10:00–11:15	Reading Workshop	Children read self-selected books independently while the teachers do guided reading lessons with small groups.
11:15–11:30	Class Meeting	Children share their writing from the author's chair, and they review the morning's activities.
11:30–12:10	Lunch	
12:10–12:30	Read-Aloud	Teachers read aloud picture books and chapter books, and children discuss them in grand conversations.

he scored a goal. He moves back to his desk to revise. The group continues with children sharing their writing and beginning to make revisions. At the end of writing workshop, the children come together for author's chair. Each day, three children take turns sitting in the author's chair to read their writing to classmates.

During reading workshop, children read independently or with a buddy while Ms. McCloskey and her teaching partner conduct guided reading lessons. The children have access to a wide variety of books in the classroom library, including predictable books for emergent readers, decodable books for beginning readers, and easy-to-read chapter books for fluent readers. The children know how to choose books that they can read successfully so they're able to spend their time really reading. The children keep lists of the books they read in their workshop folders so that their teachers can monitor their progress.

Ms. McCloskey is working with a group of four emergent readers, and today they'll read *Playing* (Prince, 1999), a seven-page predictable book with one line of text on each page that uses the pattern "I like to ____." She begins by asking children what they like to do when they're playing. Der says, "I like to play with my brother, " and Ms. McCloskey writes that on a strip of paper. Some children say only a word or two, and she expands the words into a sentence for the child to repeat; then she writes the expanded sentence and reads it with the child. Next, she introduces the book and reads the title and the author's name. Ms. McCloskey does a picture walk, talking about the picture on each page and naming the activity the child is doing—running, jumping, sliding, and so on. She reviews the "I like to ____" pattern, and then the children read the book independently while Ms. McCloskey supervises and provides assistance as needed. The children eagerly reread the book several times, becoming more confident and excited with each reading.

Literacy Centers

Center	Description
Bag a Story	Children use objects in a paper bag to create a story. They draw pictures or write sentences to tell the story they've created.
Clip Boards	Children search the classroom for words beginning with a particular letter or featuring a spelling pattern and write them on paper attached to clip boards.
Games	Children play alphabet, phonics, and other literacy card and board games with classmates.
Library	Children read books related to a thematic unit and write or draw about the books in reading logs.
Listening	Children listen to a tape of a story or informational book while they follow along in a copy of the book.
Making Words	Children practice a making words activity that they've previously done together as a class with teacher guidance.
Messages	Children write notes to classmates and the teachers and post them on a special "Message Center" bulletin board.
Poetry Frames	Children arrange word cards on a chart-sized poetry frame to create a poem and then practice reading it.
Reading the Room	Children use pointers to point to and reread big books, charts, signs, and other texts posted in the classroom.
Research	Children use the Internet, informational books, photos, and realia to learn more about topics in literature focus units and thematic units.
Story Reenactment	Children use small props, finger puppets, or flannel board figures to reenact familiar stories with classmates.
Word Sort	Children categorize high-frequency or thematic word cards displayed in a pocket chart.

Ms. McCloskey reviews the high-frequency words *I*, *like*, and *to*, and the children point them out on the classroom word wall. They use magnetic letters to spell the words and then write sentences that begin with *I like to* . . . on dry-erase boards. Then Ms. McCloskey cuts apart their sentence strips for them to sequence; afterward the children put their sentences into envelopes to practice another day. At the end of the lesson, the teacher suggests that the children might want to write "I like to _____" books during writing workshop the next day.

During the last 30 minutes before lunch, the children work at literacy centers. Ms. McCloskey and Mrs. Papaleo have set out 12 centers, and the children are free to work at any one they choose. They're familiar with the routine and know what's expected of them at each center. The two teachers circulate around the classroom, monitoring children's work and taking advantage of teachable moments to clarify misunderstandings, reinforce previous lessons, and extend children's learning. A list of the literacy centers is presented in the box above.

After lunch, Ms. McCloskey reads aloud picture books and easy-to-read chapter books. Sometimes she reads books by a particular author, but at other times, she reads books related to a thematic unit. She uses these read-alouds to teach predicting, visualizing, and other reading strategies. This week, she's reading award-winning books, and today she reads aloud *The Stray Dog* (Simont, 2001), the story of a homeless dog that's taken in by a loving family. She uses the interactive read-aloud procedure to involve children in the book as she reads, and afterward they talk about it in a **grand conversation**. Ms. McCloskey asks them to share their connections to the story, and the teachers record them on a chart divided into three sections. Most comments are text-to-self connections, but several children make other types of connections. Rosario says, "I am thinking of a movie. It was 101 Dalmatians. It was about dogs, too." That's a text-to-text connection. Angelo offers a text-to-world connection: "You got to stay away from stray dogs. They can bite you, and they might have this bad disease called rabies—it can kill you."

L iteracy is a process that begins in infancy and continues into adulthood, if not throughout life. It used to be that 5-year-old children came to kindergarten to be "readied" for reading and writing instruction, which formally began in first grade. The implication was that there's a point in children's development when it's time to teach them to read and write. For those not ready, a variety of "readiness" activities would prepare them. Since the 1970s, this view has been discredited because preschoolers have demonstrated that they could recognize signs and other environmental print, retell stories, scribble letters, invent printlike writing, and listen to stories read aloud (Morrow & Tracey, 2007). Some young children even teach themselves to read!

This perspective on how children become literate—that is, how they learn to read and write—is known as *emergent literacy*, a term that New Zealand educator Marie Clay coined. Studies from 1966 on have shaped the current outlook (McGee & Richgels, 2003; Morrow & Tracey, 2007). Now, researchers are looking at literacy learning from the child's point of view. Literacy development has been broadened to incorporate the cultural and social aspects of language learning, and children's experiences with and understandings about written language—both reading and writing —are included as part of emergent literacy.

FOSTERING AN INTEREST IN LITERACY

Young children's introduction to written language begins before they come to school. Parents and other caregivers read to them, and they learn to read signs and other environmental print in their community. They experiment with writing and have their parents write messages for them; they also observe adults writing. When young children come to school, their knowledge about written language expands quickly as they learn concepts about print and participate in meaningful experiences with reading and writing.

Concepts About Print

Through experiences in their homes and communities, young children learn that print carries meaning and that reading and writing are used for a variety of purposes (Clay, 2000a). They notice menus in restaurants, write and receive postcards and letters to communicate with friends and relatives, and listen to stories read aloud for enjoyment. Children also observe parents and teachers using written language for all these reasons.

Children's understanding about the purposes of reading and writing reflects how written language is used in their community. Although reading and writing are part of daily life for almost every family, families use written language for different purposes in different communities (Heath, 1983). Young children have a wide range of literacy experiences in both middle-class and working-class families, even though those experiences might not be the same (Taylor & Dorsey-Gaines, 1987). In some communities, written language is used mainly as a tool for practical purposes such as paying bills, whereas in others, reading and writing are also used for leisure-time activities. In still other communities, written language serves even wider functions, such as debating social and political issues.

Preschool and kindergarten teachers demonstrate the purposes of written language and provide opportunities for children to experiment with reading and writing in many ways:

Posting signs in the classroom

Making a list of classroom rules

Using reading and writing materials in literacy play centers

Exchanging messages with classmates

Reading and writing stories

Labeling classroom items

Drawing and writing in journals

Writing notes to parents

Young children learn other concepts about print through these activities, too: They learn book-orientation concepts, including how to hold a book and turn pages, and that the text, not the illustrations, carries the message. Children also learn directionality concepts—that print is written and read from left to right and from top to bottom on a page. They match voice to print, pointing word by word to the text as it is read aloud. Children also notice punctuation marks and learn their names and their purposes.

Check the Compendium of Instructional Procedures, which follows Chapter 12, for more information on the highlighted terms.

Assessing Children's Concepts About Print. Teachers observe children as they look at books and reread familiar ones. They also watch as children do pretend writing and write their names and other familiar words and phrases. They notice which concepts children understand and which ones they need to continue to talk about and demonstrate during shared reading.

Teachers use Marie Clay's Concepts About Print (CAP) Test (2006) to assess young children's understanding of these written language concepts, and it's explained in the Assessment Tools box on the next page. Teachers also create their own versions of the test to use with any story they're reading with a child. As they read aloud any big book or small book, teachers ask the child to point out book-orientation concepts, directionality concepts, and letter and word concepts. They can use the CAP Test scoring sheet shown in this same Assessment Tools feature or develop one of their own to monitor children's growing understanding of these concepts.

Assessment Tools

Concepts About Print

Teachers monitor children's growing awareness of the concepts about print as they observe them during shared reading and other reading and writing activities. The most widely used assessment is Marie Clay's Concepts About Print Test:

◆ **Concepts About Print (CAP) Test** (Clay, 2006)

The CAP Test assesses young children's understanding of three types of concepts about print: book-orientation concepts, directionality concepts, and letter and word concepts. The test has 24 items and is administered individually in about 10 minutes. The teacher reads a short book aloud while a child looks on. The child is asked to open the book, turn pages, and point out particular print features as the text is read. Four forms of the CAP Test booklet are available: *Sand* (Clay, 2007b), *Stones* (Clay, 2007c), *Follow Me, Moon* (Clay, 2000b), and *No Shoes* (Clay, 2007a), as well as a Spanish version. Teachers carefully observe children as they respond, and then mark their responses on a scoring sheet. The test is available for purchase from Heinemann Books.

Instead of using the test booklets, teachers can also administer the test using other books available in the classroom.

CAP Test Scoring Sheet

Name _____   Date _____

Title of Book _____

Check the items that the child demonstrates.

1. Book-Orientation Concepts
   - ☐ Shows the front of a book.
   - ☐ Turns to the first page of the story.
   - ☐ Shows where to start reading on a page.

2. Directionality Concepts
   - ☐ Shows the direction of print across a line of text.
   - ☐ Shows the direction of print on a page with more than one line of print.
   - ☐ Points to track words as the teacher reads.

3. Letter and Word Concepts
   - ☐ Points to any letter on a page.
   - ☐ Points to a particular letter on a page.
   - ☐ Puts fingers around any word on a page.
   - ☐ Puts fingers around a particular word on a page.
   - ☐ Puts fingers around any sentence on a page.
   - ☐ Points to the first and last letters of a word.
   - ☐ Points to a period or other punctuation mark.
   - ☐ Points to a capital letter.

Summary Comments:

Concepts About Words

At first, young children have only vague notions of literacy terms, such as *word, letter, sound,* and *sentence,* that teachers use in talking about reading and writing, but children develop an increasingly sophisticated understanding of these terms. Papandropoulou and Sinclair (1974) identified four stages of word consciousness. At first, young children don't differentiate between words and things. At the next level, they describe words as labels for things; children consider words that stand for objects as words, but they don't classify articles and prepositions as words because words such as *the* and *with* can't be represented with objects. At the third level, children understand that words carry meaning and that stories are built from words. Finally, more-fluent readers and writers describe words as autonomous elements having meanings of their own with definite semantic and syntactic relationships. Children might say, "You make words with letters." Also, children understand that words have different appearances: They can be spoken, listened to, read, and written. Invernizzi (2003) explains the importance of reaching the fourth level this way: "A concept of word allows children to hold onto the printed word in their mind's eye and scan it from left to right, noting every sound in the beginning, middle, and end" (p. 152).

Children develop concepts about words through active participation in literacy activities. They watch as teachers point to words in big books during shared reading, and they mimic the teacher and point to words as they reread familiar texts. After many, many shared reading experiences, children notice that word boundaries are marked with spaces, and they pick out familiar words. With experience, children's pointing becomes more exact, and they become more proficient at picking out specific words in the text, noticing that words at the beginning of sentences are marked with capital letters and words at the end of sentences are followed with punctuation marks.

Environmental Print. Young children begin reading by recognizing logos on fast-food restaurants, department stores, grocery stores, and commonly used household items within familiar contexts (Harste, Woodward, & Burke, 1984). They recognize the golden arches of McDonald's and say "McDonald's," but when they're shown the word *McDonald's* written on a sheet of paper without the familiar sign and restaurant setting, they can't read the word. At first, young children depend on context to read familiar words and memorized texts, but slowly, they develop relationships linking form and meaning as they gain more reading and writing experience.

Writing. As children begin to experiment with writing, they use scribbles and letter-like forms to represent words (Schickedanz & Casbergue, 2004). As they learn about letter names and phoneme-grapheme (sound-letter) correspondences, they use one, two, or three letters to stand for words. At first, they run their writing together, but they slowly learn to mark word boundaries by segmenting writing into words and leaving spaces between words. They sometimes add dots or lines as markers between words or draw circles around words. They also move from capitalizing words randomly to using capital letters at the beginning of sentences and marking proper nouns and adjectives. Similarly, children move from using a period at the end of each line of writing to marking the ends of sentences with periods.

Literacy Play Centers. Young children learn about the purposes of reading and writing as they use written language in their play: As they construct block buildings, children write signs and tape them on the buildings; as they play doctor, children

Writing Center

These first graders write in journals, make books, and compose notes to class-mates at the writing center. This center is stocked with writing supplies, a word wall with high-frequency words is displayed on a dry-erase board, and a message center (shown in the upper right-hand part of the photo) is available for children to post their notes. They keep their writing projects in folders stored nearby. Children work at this center while the teacher works with guided reading groups. Through this center activity, young children develop the independence they need for writing workshop.

write prescriptions on slips of paper; and as they play teacher, children read stories aloud to stuffed animal "students" (McGee, 2007). Young children use these activities to reenact familiar, everyday activities and to pretend to be someone else. Through these literacy play activities, children use reading and writing for a variety of purposes.

Kindergarten teachers add literacy materials to play centers to enhance their value for literacy learning. Housekeeping centers are probably the most common play centers, and they can easily be transformed into a grocery store, a post office, or a medical center by changing the props. They become literacy play centers when materials for reading and writing are included: Food packages, price stickers, and play money are props in grocery store centers; letters, stamps, and mailboxes are props in post office centers; and appointment books, prescription pads, and folders for patient records are props in medical centers. A variety of literacy play centers can be set up in classrooms and coordinated with literature focus units and thematic units.

Concepts About the Alphabet

Young children also develop concepts about the alphabet and how letters are used to represent phonemes. Pinnell and Fountas (1998) identified these components of letter knowledge:

◆ The letter's name
◆ The formation of the letter in upper- and lowercase manuscript handwriting
◆ The features of the letter that distinguish it from other letters
◆ The direction the letter must be turned to distinguish it from other letters (e.g., *b* and *d*)
◆ The use of the letter in known words (e.g., names and common words)

- The sound the letter represents in isolation
- The sound the letter represents in combination with others (e.g., *ch*, *th*)
- The sound the letter represents in the context of a word (e.g., the *c* sounds in *cat*, *city*, and *chair*)

Children use this knowledge to decode unfamiliar words as they read and to create spellings for words as they write.

The most basic information children learn about the alphabet is how to identify and form the letters in handwriting. They notice letters in environmental print and learn to sing the ABC song. By the time children enter kindergarten, they usually recognize some letters, especially those in their own names, in names of family members and pets, and in common words in their homes and communities. Children also write some of these familiar letters.

Research suggests that children don't learn alphabet letter names in any particular order or by isolating letters from meaningful written language in skill-and-drill activities. McGee and Richgels (2008) conclude that learning letters of the alphabet requires many, many experiences with meaningful written language and recommend that teachers take these steps to encourage children's alphabet learning:

Capitalize on children's interests. Teachers provide letter activities that children enjoy, and they talk about letters when children are interested in talking about them. Teachers know what features to comment on because they observe children during reading and writing activities to find out which letters or features of letters children are exploring.

Talk about the role of letters in reading and writing. Teachers talk about how letters represent sounds and how letters combine to spell words and point out capital letters and lowercase letters. Teachers often talk about the role of letters as they write with children.

Provide a variety of opportunities for alphabet learning. Teachers use children's names and environmental print in literacy activities, do interactive writing, encourage children to use invented spelling, share alphabet books, and play letter games.

Teachers begin teaching letters of the alphabet using two sources of words—children's own names and environmental print. They teach the ABC song to provide children with a strategy for identifying the name of an unknown letter. Children learn to sing this song and point to each letter on an alphabet chart until they reach the unfamiliar one; this is a very useful strategy because it gives them a real sense of independence in identifying letters. Teachers also provide routines, activities, and games for talking about and manipulating letters. During these familiar, predictable activities, teachers and children say letter names, manipulate magnetic letters, and write letters on dry-erase boards. At first, the teacher structures and guides the activities, but with experience, the children internalize the routine and do it independently, often at a literacy center. Figure 4–1 presents 10 routines to teach the letters of the alphabet.

Being able to name the letters of the alphabet is a good predictor of beginning reading achievement, even though knowing the names of the letters doesn't directly affect a child's ability to read (Adams, 1990; Snow, Burns, & Griffin, 1998). A more likely explanation for this relationship between letter knowledge and reading is that children who have been actively involved in reading and writing activities before entering first grade know the names of the letters, and they're more likely to begin reading quickly. Simply teaching children to name the letters without the accompanying reading and writing experiences doesn't have this effect.

Figure 4–1 ◆ Routines to Teach the Letters of the Alphabet

Environmental Print
Children sort food labels, toy traffic signs, and other environmental print to find examples of a letter being studied.

Alphabet Books
Teachers read aloud alphabet books to build vocabulary, and later, children reread the books to find words when making books about a letter.

Magnetic Letters
Children pick all examples of one letter from a collection of magnetic letters or match upper- and lowercase letterforms of magnetic letters. They also arrange the letters in alphabetical order and use them to spell familiar words.

Letter Stamps
Children use letter stamps and ink pads to print letters on paper or in booklets. They also use letter-shaped sponges to paint letters and letter-shaped cookie cutters to cut out clay letters.

Alphabet Chart
Children point to letters and pictures on the alphabet chart as they recite the alphabet and the name of the picture, such as "A-airplane, B-baby, C-cat," and so on.

Letter Containers
Teachers collect coffee cans or shoe boxes, one for each letter, and place several familiar objects that represent the letter in each container. Teachers use these containers to introduce the letters, and children use them for sorting and matching activities.

Letter Frames
Teachers make circle-shaped letter frames from tagboard, collect large plastic bracelets, or shape pipe cleaners or Wikki-Stix (pipe cleaners covered in wax) into circles for students to use to highlight particular letters on charts or in big books.

Letter Books and Posters
Children make letter books with pictures of objects beginning with a particular letter on each page. They add letter stamps, stickers, or pictures cut from magazines. For posters, the teacher draws a large letterform on a chart and children add pictures, stickers, and letter stamps.

Letter Sorts
Children sort objects and pictures representing two or more letters and place them in containers marked with the specific letters.

Dry-Erase Boards
Children practice writing upper- and lowercase forms of a letter and familiar words on dry-erase boards.

OW CHILDREN DEVELOP AS READERS AND WRITERS

Young children move through three stages as they learn to read and write: emergent, beginning, and fluent (Juel, 1991). During the emergent stage, young children gain an understanding of the communicative purpose of print, and they move from pretend reading to reading predictable books and from using scribbles to simulate writing to writing patterned sentences, such as *I see a bird. I see a tree. I see a car*. The focus of the second stage, beginning reading and writing, is on children's growing ability to use phonics to "crack the alphabetic code" in order to decode and spell words. Children also learn to read and write many high-frequency words and write several sentences to develop a story or other composition. In the fluent stage, children are automatic, fluent readers, and in writing, they develop good handwriting skills, spell many high-frequency words correctly, and organize their writing into multiple-paragraph compositions. Figure 4–2 summarizes children's accomplishments in reading and writing development at each stage.

Figure 4–2 ◆ Young Children's Literacy Development

Stage	Reading	Writing
Emergent	Children: • notice environmental print • show interest in books • pretend to read • use picture cues and predictable patterns in books to retell the story • reread familiar books with predictable patterns • identify some letter names • recognize 5–20 familiar or high-frequency words	Children: • distinguish between writing and drawing • write letters and letterlike forms or scribble randomly on the page • develop an understanding of directionality • show interest in writing • write their first and last names • write 5–20 familiar or high-frequency words • use sentence frames to write a sentence
Beginning	Children: • identify letter names and sounds • match spoken words to written words • recognize 20–100 high-frequency words • use beginning, middle, and ending sounds to decode words • apply knowledge of the cueing systems to monitor reading • self-correct while reading • read slowly, word by word • read orally • point to words when reading • make reasonable predictions	Children: • write from left to right • print the upper- and lowercase letters • write one or more sentences • add a title • spell many words phonetically • spell 20–50 high-frequency words correctly • write single-draft compositions • use capital letters to begin sentences • use periods, question marks, and exclamation points to mark the end of sentences • can reread their writing
Fluent	Children: • identify most words automatically • read with expression • read at a rate of 100 words per minute or more • prefer to read silently • identify unfamiliar words using the cueing systems • recognize 100–300 high-frequency words • use a variety of strategies effectively • often read independently • use knowledge of text structure and genre to support comprehension • make inferences	Children: • use the writing process to write drafts and final copies • write compositions with one or more paragraphs • indent paragraphs • spell most of the 100 high-frequency words • use sophisticated and technical vocabulary • apply vowel patterns to spell words • add inflectional endings on words • apply capitalization rules • use commas, quotation marks, and other punctuation marks

Stage 1: Emergent Reading and Writing

Children gain an understanding of the communicative purpose of print and develop an interest in reading and writing during the emergent stage. They notice environmental print in the world around them and develop concepts about print as teachers read and write with them. As children dictate stories for the teacher to record, for example, they learn that their speech can be written down, and they observe how teachers write from left to right and top to bottom.

During the emergent stage, children accomplish the following:

◆ Develop an interest in reading and writing
◆ Acquire concepts about print

- Develop book-handling skills
- Learn to identify the letters of the alphabet
- Develop handwriting skills
- Learn to read and write some high-frequency words

Children are usually emergent readers and writers in kindergarten, but some children whose parents have read to them every day and provided a variety of literacy experiences do learn how to read before they come to school. Caroline, a 5-year-old emergent reader and writer in Ms. McCloskey's classroom, is presented in the spotlight feature on pages 120–121.

Young children make scribbles to represent writing. These scribbles may appear randomly on a page at first, but with experience, children line up the letters or scribbles from left to right on a line and from top to bottom on a page. Children also begin to "read," or tell what their writing says (Schickedanz & Casbergue, 2004). At first, they can reread their writing only immediately after writing, but with experience, they learn to remember what their writing says, and as their writing becomes more conventional, they're able to read it more easily.

Emergent readers and writers participate in a variety of literacy activities ranging from modeled and shared reading and writing, during which they watch as teachers read and write, to independent reading and writing that they do themselves. Ms. McCloskey's students, for example, listened to her read aloud books and read big books using shared reading, and they also participated in reading and writing workshop. When working with children at the emergent stage, however, teachers often use modeled and shared reading and writing activities because they are demonstrating what readers and writers do and teaching concepts about print.

Stage 2: Beginning Reading and Writing

This stage marks children's growing awareness of the alphabetic principle. Children learn about phoneme-grapheme correspondences, phonics rules in words such as *run, hand, this, make, day,* and *road,* and word families, including *-ill* (*fill, hill, will*) and *-ake* (*bake, make, take*). They also apply (and misapply) their developing phonics knowledge to spell words. For example, they spell *night* as *NIT* and *train* as *TRANE.* At the same time, they're learning to read and write high-frequency words, many of which can't be sounded out, such as *what, are,* and *there.*

During the beginning stage of reading and writing development, children accomplish the following:

- Learn phonics skills
- Recognize 20–100 high-frequency words
- Apply reading strategies, including cross-checking, predicting, and repairing
- Write five or more sentences, sometimes organized into a paragraph
- Spell phonetically
- Spell 20–50 high-frequency words
- Use capital letters to begin sentences
- Use punctuation marks to indicate the ends of sentences
- Reread their writing

Most first and second graders are beginning readers and writers, and with instruction in literacy strategies and skills and daily opportunities to read and write, children move through this stage to reach the fluent stage. Anthony, a 6-year-old beginning reader and writer in Ms. McCloskey's classroom, is presented in the spotlight feature on pages 122–123.

Spotlight on . . .

An Emergent Reader and Writer

Five-year-old Caroline is a friendly, eager child who is learning to speak English as she learns to read and write. Caroline's grandparents emigrated from Thailand to the United States; her family speaks Hmong at home, and she speaks English only at school. When her Hmong-speaking classmates start to talk in their native language, she admonishes them to speak English because "we learn English school."

When she came to kindergarten, Caroline didn't know any letters of the alphabet and had never held a pencil. She had not listened to stories read aloud and had no book-handling experience. She spoke barely a few words of English. The classroom culture and language were very different than those of her home, but Caroline was eager to learn. For the first few days, she stood back, observing her classmates; then she said "I do" and joined them.

Caroline has made remarkable growth in 5 months. She has been reading books with repetitive sentences on each page, but now at level 3, she is beginning to use phonics to sound out unfamiliar words. She knows the names of most letters and the sounds that the letters represent. She can read about 20 high-frequency words. She has developed good book-handling skills and follows the line of words on a page. She reads word by word and points at the text as she reads. She is learning consonant and vowel sounds, but because of her pronunciation of English sounds and lack of vocabulary, she has difficulty decoding words.

Caroline demonstrates that she understands the books she reads, and she makes text-to-self connections. Recently, she was reading a book about a child having a birthday, and she pointed to the picture of a young, blond mother wrapping a child's birthday present. She looked up at Ms. McCloskey and said,

Emergent Reader and Writer Characteristics That Caroline Exemplifies

Reading	Writing
• Shows great interest in reading	• Shows great interest in writing
• Has developed book-handling skills	• Writes from left to right and top to bottom on a page
• Identifies most of the letters of the alphabet	• Prints most of the letters of the alphabet
• Knows some letter sounds	• Writes 20 high-frequency words
• Sounds out a few CVC words	• Leaves spaces between words
• Reads 20 high-frequency words	• Writes sentences
• Uses predictable patterns in text to reread familiar books	• Begins sentences with a capital letter
• Makes text-to-self connections	• Puts periods at the ends of sentences
	• Rereads what she has written immediately afterward

"She no mom, she sister. This wrong." The woman in the picture looks nothing like her mother.

Caroline began participating in writing workshop on the first day of school, and for several weeks, she scribbled. Within a month, she learned how to print some letters because she wanted her writing to look like her classmates'. Soon she wrote her own name, copied classmates' names, and wrote words she saw posted in the classroom.

A month ago, Ms. McCloskey gave Caroline a ring for key words. Every few days, Caroline chooses a new word to add to her ring. Ms. McCloskey writes the word on a word card that is added to Caroline's ring. Caroline has 31 words now, including *you* and *birthday*. She flips through the cards to practice reading, and she uses the words when she writes sentences.

After 4 months of instruction, Caroline began writing sentences. Ms. McCloskey introduced the frame "I see a _____" and Caroline wrote sentences using familiar words, including some from her key words ring. Then, to make her writing longer, she wrote the same sentence over and over, as shown in the "Apple" writing sample.

Next, she began reading and writing color words, and she expanded her writing to two sentences. Her two-sentence writing sample, "Zebras," also is shown here. Most of the words that Caroline writes are spelled correctly because she uses key words and words she locates in a picture dictionary. Notice that Caroline puts a period at the end of each sentence; but recently she has noticed that some of her classmates put a period at the end of each line so she added periods at the end of each line in the "Zebra" sample, too. When she draws a picture to accompany a sentence, Caroline can usually read her writing immediately after she has written it, but by the next day, she often doesn't remember what she has written.

Caroline has one of the thickest writing folders in the classroom, and she's very proud of her writing. Nearly 100 pages of writing are stuffed into the folder, tracing her development as a writer since the beginning of the school year.

In the 5 months she has been in kindergarten, Caroline has made excellent progress in learning to read and write. She is an emergent-stage reader and writer. She can read books with repetitive patterns and is learning phonics and high-frequency words. She can write words and craft sentences. A list of the emergent-stage characteristics that Caroline exemplifies is shown in the chart.

Spotlight on . . .

A Beginning Reader and Writer

Anthony, a first grader with a ready smile, is a beginning reader and writer. He's 6 years old, and he says that he likes to read and write. His best friend, Angel, is also in Ms. McCloskey's classroom, and they often sit together to read and write. (The photo shows Anthony, on the right, buddy-reading with his friend Angel.) The boys eat together in the lunchroom and always play together outside, too.

Anthony is a well-behaved child who is extremely competitive. He knows he's reading at level 12 now, and he announced to Ms. McCloskey that he wants to be reading at level 15. She explained that to do that, he needs to practice reading each night at home with his mom, and he's been taking several books home each night to practice. Ms. McCloskey predicts that Anthony will be reading at level 18 by the end of the year; level 18 is the school's benchmark for the end of first grade.

According to Ms. McCloskey's assessment of Anthony's reading at the end of the second quarter, he recognizes 80 of the 100 high-frequency words taught in first grade, and he can decode most one-syllable words with short and long vowel sounds, including words with consonant blends and digraphs, such as *shock*, *chest*, and *spike*. He's beginning to try to sound out some of the more-complex vowel digraphs and diphthongs (e.g., *loud*, *boil*, *soon*) and *r*-controlled vowels (e.g., *chart*, *snore*), and in the past month, Ms. McCloskey has noticed that his ability to decode words is growing and that about two thirds of the time, he can identify these words with more-complex vowel sounds in the context of a sentence. He also is decoding some two- and three-syllable words, such as *dinner*, *parents*, and *hospital*, in books he's reading.

Beginning Reader and Writer Characteristics That Anthony Exemplifies

Reading

- Likes to read
- Reads orally
- Points to words when he reads challenging texts
- Recognizes 80 high-frequency words
- Uses phonics knowledge to decode unfamiliar words
- Makes good predictions
- Uses the cross-checking strategy
- Retells what he reads
- Makes text-to-self and text-to-world connections

Writing

- Likes to write
- Writes single-draft compositions
- Adds a title
- Writes organized compositions on a single topic
- Writes more than five sentences in a composition
- Has a beginning, middle, and end in his story
- Refers to the word wall to spell high-frequency words
- Uses his knowledge of phonics to spell words
- Uses capital letters to mark the beginnings of sentences
- Uses periods to mark the ends of sentences
- Reads his writing to classmates

Anthony reads orally and points only when he reads challenging texts. He's beginning to chunk words into phrases as he reads, and he notices when something he is reading doesn't make sense. He uses the cross-checking strategy to make corrections and get back on track.

Anthony has read 17 books this month, according to his reading workshop log. He is increasingly choosing easy-to-read chapter books to read, including Syd Hoff's *Sammy the Seal* (2000b) and *Oliver* (2000a). After he reads, he often shares his books with his friend Angel, and they reread them together and talk about their favorite parts. He regularly uses the connecting strategy and shares his text-to-self and text-to-world connections with Angel and Ms. McCloskey. When he reads two or more books by the same author, he shares text-to-text comparisons and can explain to his teacher how these comparisons make him a better reader: "Now I think and read at the same time," he explains.

Anthony likes to write during writing workshop. He identified his "Being Sick" story as the very best one he's written, and Ms. McCloskey agrees. Anthony tells an interesting and complete story with a beginning, middle, and end. And, you can hear his voice clearly in the story. Anthony's story is shown in the box, and here is a translation of it:

Being Sick

Sometimes I go outside with no! jacket on and the air went in my ear. I went inside and stayed in the house. My ear started to hurt because I had pain. I went to see if Mom was there. I found her. I told her I have an ear ache. My mom put some ear ache stuff in my ear and it made it better.

Anthony's spelling errors are characteristic of phonetic spellers. He sounds out the spelling of many words, such as *sum tims* (sometimes) and *hrt* (hurt), and he's experimenting with final *e* markers at the end of *tolde* and *pane*, but ignores them on other words. He uses the word wall in the classroom and spells many high-frequency words correctly (e.g., *with*, *went*, *have*).

Anthony writes single-draft compositions in paragraph form, and he creates a title for his stories. He writes in sentences and includes simple, compound, and complex sentences in his writing. He uses capital letters to mark the beginnings of sentences and periods to mark the ends of sentences well, but he continues to randomly put capital letters at the beginnings of words.

Anthony is at the beginning stage of reading and writing development. He reads word by word, uses his finger to track text while reading, and stops to decode unfamiliar words. He's applying what he's learning about phonics to decode words when reading and to spell words when writing. He writes multisentence compositions with good sentence structure, but his phonetic spelling makes his writing difficult to read.

Being Sick
Sum tims I go autsid With No! JaKit on and the err went in my ere. I went insid and stad in the house. My ere Strdit to hrt becuase I had pane. I went to see if Mom Was ther. I fand her. I tolde her I have A Eer Fea. My Mom put Sum Ear Fea Stuf in My Ear. And it Mad it Betr.

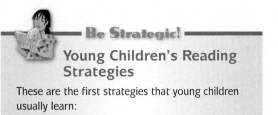

Children usually read aloud slowly, in a word-by-word fashion, stopping often to sound out unfamiliar words. They point at each word as they read, but by the end of this stage, their reading becomes smoother and more fluent, and they point at words only when the text is especially challenging.

Although the emphasis in this stage is on decoding and recognizing words, children also learn that reading involves comprehension. They make predictions to guide their thinking about events in stories they read, and they make connections between what they're reading and their own lives and the world around them as they personalize the reading experience. They monitor their reading to recognize when it doesn't make sense, cross-check using phonological, semantic, syntactic, and pragmatic information in the text to figure out the problem, and repair or self-correct it (Fountas & Pinnell, 1996). They also learn about story structure, particularly that stories have a beginning, middle, and end, and use this knowledge to guide their reading and retelling.

Children move from writing one or two sentences to developing longer compositions, with five, eight, or more sentences organized into paragraphs, by the end of this stage. Their writing is better developed, too, because they're acquiring a sense of audience, and they want their classmates to like what they've written. Children continue to write single-draft compositions but begin to make a few revisions and editing corrections as they learn about the writing process toward the end of the stage.

Children apply what they're learning about phonics in their spelling, and they correctly spell many of the high-frequency words that they've learned to read. They know how to spell some high-frequency words and can locate others on word walls posted in the classroom. They learn to use capital letters to mark the beginnings of sentences and punctuation to mark the ends of sentences. Children are more adept at rereading their writing, both immediately afterward and days later, because they're able to read many of the words they've written.

Teachers plan activities for children at the beginning stage that range from modeled to independent reading and writing activities, but the emphasis is on interactive and guided activities. Through interactive writing, choral reading, and guided reading, teachers scaffold children as they read and write and use minilessons to provide strategy and skill instruction. For example, Ms. McCloskey's students were divided into small, homogeneous groups for guided reading lessons. The children met to read books at their reading levels, and Ms. McCloskey introduced new vocabulary words, taught reading strategies and skills, and assessed their comprehension.

Teachers introduce the writing process to beginning-stage writers once they develop a sense of audience and want to make their writing better so their classmates will like it. Children don't immediately begin writing rough drafts and final copies or doing both revising and editing: They often begin the writing process by rereading their compositions and adding a word or two, correcting a misspelled word, or capitalizing a lowercase letter. These changes are cosmetic, but the idea that the writing process doesn't end after the first draft is established. Next, children show interest in making a final copy that really looks good. They either recopy the composition by hand or use word processing and print out the final copy. Once children understand that writing involves a rough draft and a final copy, they're ready to learn more about revising and editing, and they usually reach this point at about the same time they become fluent writers.

Stage 3: Fluent Reading and Writing

The third stage marks children's move into fluent reading and writing. Fluent readers recognize hundreds and hundreds of words automatically and have the tools to identify unfamiliar words when reading. Fluent writers use the writing process to draft, revise, and publish their writing and participate in writing groups. They're familiar with a variety of genres and know how to organize their writing. They use conventional spelling and other written language conventions, including capital letters and punctuation marks.

Fluent readers and writers accomplish the following:

♦ Read fluently and with expression
♦ Recognize most one-syllable words automatically and can decode other words efficiently
♦ Use decoding and comprehension strategies effectively
♦ Write well-developed, multiparagraph compositions
♦ Use the writing process to draft and refine their writing
♦ Write stories, reports, letters, and other genres
♦ Spell most high-frequency and other one-syllable words correctly
♦ Use capital letters and punctuation marks correctly most of the time

Some second graders reach this stage, and all children should be fluent readers and writers by the end of third grade. Reaching this stage is an important milestone because it indicates that children are ready for the increased literacy demands of fourth grade, when they're expected to read longer chapter-book stories, use writing to respond to literature, read content-area textbooks, and write essays and reports. Jazmen, an 8-year-old fluent reader and writer in Ms. McCloskey's classroom, is profiled in the spotlight feature on pages 126–127.

The distinguishing characteristic of fluent readers is that they read words accurately, rapidly, and expressively. Fluent readers automatically recognize many words and can decode unfamiliar words efficiently. Their reading rate has increased to 100 words or more per minute; in addition, they can vary their speed according to the demands of the text they're reading.

Most fluent readers prefer to read silently because they can read more quickly than when they read orally. No longer do they point at words as they read. Children can read many books independently, actively making predictions, visualizing, monitoring their understanding, and making repairs when necessary. They have a range of strategies available and use them enhance their comprehension.

Fluent readers' comprehension is stronger, and they think more deeply about their reading than emergent and beginning readers do. It's likely that children's comprehension improves at this stage because they have more cognitive energy available for comprehension now; in contrast, beginning readers use much more cognitive energy to decode words. So, as children become fluent, they use less energy for word identification and have more cognitive resources available for comprehending what they read.

During this stage, children read longer, more sophisticated picture books and chapter books, but they generally prefer chapter books because they enjoy really getting into a story or digging deeply in an informational book. They learn more about the literary genres, their structural patterns, and literary devices, such as alliteration, personification, and symbolism. They participate in literature focus units featuring an author, genre, or book, in small-group literature circles where children read and discuss a book together, and in author studies where they read and compare several books

Spotlight on . . .

A Fluent Reader and Writer

Jazmen is a confident and articulate African American third grader. She's 8 years old, and she celebrated her birthday last fall with a family trip to the Magic Mountain amusement park in Southern California. She smiles easily and likes to shake her head so that her braided, beaded hair swirls around her head. Jazmen is a pro at using computers, and she often provides assistance to her classmates. When asked about her favorite school activity, Jazmen says that she likes using the computer best of all. In fact, she is interested in learning more about careers that involve computers because she knows that she always wants to work with them.

Ms. McCloskey identified Jazmen for this feature because she's made such remarkable progress this year. This is the second year that Jazmen has been in Ms. McCloskey's class. Last year, she seemed stuck in the beginning stage, not making too much progress, according to Ms. McCloskey, "but this year, it's like a light-bulb has been turned on!" She's now a fluent reader and writer.

Jazmen likes to read, and she reports that she has a lot of books at home. According to the Accelerated Reader® program, she is reading at 3.8 (third grade, eighth month) level, which means she is reading at or slightly above grade level. She enjoys reading the Marvin Redpost (e.g., *Marvin Redpost: A Magic Crystal?*, by Louis Sachar, 2000) and Zack Files (e.g., *Never Trust a Cat Who Wears Earrings*, by Dan Greenburg, 1997) series of easy-to-read paperback chapter books. She says that she enjoys these books because they're funny.

Currently she's reading Paula Danziger's series of chapter-book stories about a third grader named Amber Brown who deals with the realities of contemporary life, including adjusting to her parents' divorce. The first book in the series is *Amber Brown Is Not a Crayon* (2006), about Amber and her best friend, Justin, who moves away at the end of the book; other chapter books in the series are *Amber Brown Goes Fourth* (2007),

Fluent Reader and Writer Characteristics That Jazmen Exemplifies

Reading	Writing
• Recognizes most words automatically • Reads with expression • Reads more than 100 words per minute • Reads independently • Uses a variety of strategies • Makes connections when reading • Thinks inferentially • Applies knowledge of story structure and genre when reading	• Uses the writing process • Has a sense of audience and purpose • Writes a complete story with a beginning, middle, and end • Writes in paragraphs • Indents paragraphs • Uses sophisticated language • Spells most words correctly • Uses capital letters and punctuation to mark sentence boundaries

Amber Brown Is Feeling Blue (1999), *Amber Brown Sees Red* (1998), and *Amber Brown Is Green With Envy* (2004).

Jazmen reads well. She recognizes words automatically and reads with expression. She says that when you're reading to someone, you have to be interesting and that's why she reads the way she does. Her most outstanding achievement, according to Ms. McCloskey, is that she thinks inferentially about stories. She can juggle thinking about plot, characters, setting, and theme in order to make thoughtful connections and interpretations. She knows about various genres and literary elements, and she uses this knowledge as she reflects on her reading.

Jazmen likes to write. She gets her ideas for stories from television programs. She explains, "When I'm watching TV, I get these ideas and I draw pictures of them and that's how I think of a story." She's currently working on a story entitled "Lucky and the Color Purple," about a princess named Lucky who possesses magical qualities. Why are her stories interesting? Jazmen says, "Most important is that they are creative." She shares her stories with her classmates, and they agree that Jazmen is a good writer.

Jazmen is particularly pleased with her story "The Super Hero With the Long Hair," which is shown here. The story has a strong voice. Jazmen wanted her story to sound interesting, so she substituted *whined* and *grouched* for *said*. Ms. McCloskey explained that she likes the story because it's complete with a beginning, middle, and end, and because Jazmen uses dialogue (and quotation marks) effectively. The errors remaining on the final draft of the paper also suggest direction for future instruction. Jazmen spelled 95% of the words in her composition correctly. In particular, Jazmen appears ready to learn more about plurals and possessives and using commas within sentences.

During her third-grade year, Jazmen has become a fluent reader and writer, and she exemplifies the characteristics listed in the chart. In fact, her classmates look to her for leadership when they're working on reading and writing projects. They ask her assistance in choosing books and decoding difficult words. Jazmen's writing has become more polished this year, too. She's become a thoughtful writer, and she uses the writing process to draft and refine her writing. Her classmates ask her to respond to their writing, and they're eager to listen to her read her new stories from the author's chair.

The Super Hero With the Long Hair

One beutiful day Nancy woke up. When she realized her hair was more beutiful than ever. She started pumping n the bed.

After that she started brushing her hair. She kept on brushing and brushing and brushing. The finally her sister's got so jealous they got mad.

Then they asked, "Can we brush you're hair and give you a little S...T...Y...L...E?" "Sure," said Nancy. They brushed and brushed.

All of a sudden they started cutting her hair. "What kind of S...T...Y...L...E are you doing?" "A pretty hair style." "Of course pretty. Is it really really pretty?"

"Yes yes it's really really pretty." Kelly said in a diskusting way. Then Kelly was done—Nancy went to go look in the bathroom miror. She started to cry. Her sister's started to laugh.

Then the light started to glow on the phone. Niky answered it. It was the mayor. "Hello mayor yes we'll be right on our way. The mayor said townsvill's in trouble. There's a monster outside and he's distroying all of townsvill!" shouted Niky.

"Go without me," whined Nancy. "What?" ""We can't go without you. You're the leader." "Just go without me!" Grouched Nancy.

They left. She started to talk to her dad. She made up her mind about going. She also made up some joke's. She flew to the monster and told her joke's to him and he laughed so hard he flew all the way to Jupiter.

Her sister's said, "Are we even?" The she lazorbeeded her sister's hair and said, "Now were even."

They lived happily everafter.

by the same author and examine that author's writing style. They're able to explain why they liked a particular book and make recommendations to classmates.

Fluent writers understand that writing is a process, and they use the writing process stages—prewriting, drafting, revising, editing, and publishing. They make plans for writing and write both rough drafts and final copies. They reread their rough drafts and make revisions and editing changes that reflect their understanding of writing forms and their purpose for writing. They increasingly share their rough drafts with classmates and turn to them for advice on how to make their writing better.

Children get ideas for writing from books they've read and from television programs and movies they've viewed. They organize their writing into paragraphs, indent paragraphs, and focus on a single idea in each paragraph. They develop ideas more completely and use more-sophisticated vocabulary to express their ideas.

Fluent writers are aware of writing genres and organize their writing into stories, reports, letters, and poems. Their stories have a beginning, middle, and end, and the reports they write are structured using sequence, comparison, or cause-and-effect structures. Their letters reflect an understanding of the parts of a letter and how they're arranged on a page. Their poems incorporate alliteration, symbolism, rhyme, or other poetic devices to create vivid impressions.

Children's writing looks more conventional. They spell most of the 100 high-frequency words correctly and use phonics to spell other one-syllable words correctly. They add inflectional endings (e.g., *-s, -ed, -ing*) and experiment with spelling two-syllable and longer words. They've learned to capitalize the first word in sentences and names and to use punctuation marks correctly at the ends of sentences, although they're still experimenting with punctuation marks within sentences.

A list of instructional recommendations for each of the three stages of reading and writing development is presented in Figure 4–3.

INSTRUCTIONAL PRACTICES

Teachers who work with young readers and writers use many of the same instructional practices used with older students, such as reading aloud to children, doing guided reading with leveled books, teaching from basal reading textbooks, and providing opportunities for independent reading and writing in reading and writing workshop. Teachers adapt these approaches to provide enough scaffolding so that young children are successful. Other instructional practices have been developed specifically for young children and other novice readers and writers.

Morning Message

Morning message is a daily literacy routine that teachers use to teach literacy concepts, strategies, and skills (Payne & Schulman, 1999). Before the children arrive, teachers write a brief message on chart paper, usually in the form of a friendly letter, about what will happen that day; then the message is read at the beginning of the school day. Afterward, children reread it and count the letters, words, and sentences in the message. They also pick out familiar letters and words, words following a particular phonics pattern, high-frequency words, or capital letters and punctuation marks, depending on children's level of literacy development.

Figure 4–3 ◆ Instructional Recommendations for the Three Stages of Reading and Writing

Stage	Reading	Writing
Emergent	• Use environmental print. • Include literacy materials in play centers. • Read aloud to children. • Read big books and poems on charts using shared reading. • Introduce the title and author of books before reading. • Teach directionality and letter and word concepts using big books. • Encourage children to make predictions and text-to-self connections. • Have children retell and dramatize stories. • Have children respond to literature through talk and drawing. • Have children manipulate sounds using phonemic awareness activities. • Use alphabet-learning routines. • Take children's dictation using the Language Experience Approach. • Teach 20–24 high-frequency words. • Post words on a word wall.	• Have children use crayons for drawing and pencils for writing. • Encourage children to use scribble writing or write random letters if they can't do more conventional writing. • Teach handwriting skills. • Use interactive writing for whole-class and small-group writing projects. • Have children write their names on sign-in sheets each day. • Have children write their own names and names of classmates. • Have children inventory or make lists of words they know how to write. • Have children "write the classroom" by making lists of familiar words they find in the classroom. • Have children use frames such as "I like _____" and "I see a _____" to write sentences. • Encourage children to remember what they write so they can read it.
Beginning	• Read charts of poems and songs using choral reading. • Read leveled books using guided reading. • Provide daily opportunities to read and reread books independently. • Teach phonics concepts and rules. • Teach children to cross-check using the cueing systems. • Teach the 100 high-frequency words. • Point out whether texts are stories, informational books, or poems. • Teach predicting, connecting, cross-checking, and other strategies. • Teach the elements of story structure, particularly beginning, middle, and end. • Have children write in reading logs and participate in grand conversations. • Have children take books home to read with parents.	• Use interactive writing to teach concepts about print and spelling rules. • Provide daily opportunities to write for a variety of purposes and using different genres. • Introduce the writing process. • Teach children to develop a single idea in their compositions. • Teach children to proofread their compositions. • Teach children to spell the 100 high-frequency words. • Teach contractions. • Teach capitalization and punctuation skills. • Have children use computers to publish their writing. • Have children share their writing from the author's chair.
Fluent	• Have children participate in literature circles. • Have children participate in reading workshop. • Teach about genres and literary features. • Involve children in author studies. • Teach children to make text-to-self, text-to-world, and text-to-text connections. • Have children respond to literature through talk and writing.	• Have children participate in writing workshop. • Teach children to use the writing process. • Teach children to revise and edit their writing. • Teach paragraphing skills. • Teach spelling rules. • Teach homophones. • Teach synonyms. • Teach root words and affixes. • Teach children to use a dictionary and a thesaurus.

Teachers usually follow a predictable pattern in their messages each day to make it easier for children to read, as these two morning messages show:

Dear Kindergartners,   *Dear Kindergartners,*
Today is Monday.   *Today is Thursday.*
We will plant seeds.   *We will measure the plants.*
We will make books   *We will write about how*
about plants.   *plants grow.*
            Love,   *Love,*
            Ms. Thao   *Ms. Thao*

The morning messages that teachers write for first and second graders become gradually more complex, as this second-grade teacher's message demonstrates:

Good Morning!
Today is Monday, February 4, 2008.
New literature circles begin on Wednesday.
I'll tell you about the new book choices this
morning, and then you can sign up for your
favorite book. Who remembers what a
synonym is? Can you give an example?
            Love,
            Ms. Salazar

Teachers usually choose children to take the messages home to share with their families, either day by day or at the end of each week.

Teachers have adapted the morning message routine in a variety of ways to support their literacy programs. Here are three variations:

Fill-in-the-blank morning message. The teacher writes the morning message, omitting some words for children to fill in. The teacher reads the entire message once, and then during the second reading, children identify the missing words and write them in the blanks. Sometimes teachers write the missing words on cards and display them in a pocket chart to simplify the activity. Here's a first-grade class's morning message:

              Mr. Diaz's Morning Message
Today is _____, October 15, 2008.
It is the _____ day of school. We love to _____
The Cat in the Hat by Dr. _____. We can read
words that rhyme with cat: _____, _____,
and _____.

The missing words are *Wednesday, 37th, read, Seuss, bat, hat,* and *rat.* After completing the chart, the children reread the message, count the sentences, circle high-frequency words they've learned, and think of additional rhyming words.

One child dictates a message to share with classmates. The children take turns creating a message to share personal news with classmates. The teacher writes the child's dictation on chart paper. Children usually read their own messages aloud to classmates, pointing to each word as they read, just like their teacher does. In this example, Ivan shares some big news:

Ivan's News
I have a new baby sister. Her name is
Ava. She sleeps all the time, and I have
to be very quiet so I won't wake her up.

After reading and rereading the message and examining individual words and punctuation marks, the children decide to write a welcome message to Ivan's sister at the bottom of the chart paper. They dictate it for the teacher to record and sign their names; then Ivan takes the chart paper home to share with his family.

New Literacies
Interactive Books

Technology is transforming literacy instruction, even for the youngest readers. Interactive books are one example of how young children can use technology as they learn concepts about print, read high-frequency words, develop reading fluency, expand vocabulary knowledge, and practice comprehension strategies. These electronic books have text and illustrations similar to traditional picture books, but they incorporate computer technology to enhance children's reading experience (Lefever-Davis & Pearman, 2005): They feature audio renditions of the entire text as children read along, pronunciations of individual words when children highlight them, and hotspots that children click to produce sound effects and graphic animations where characters talk and settings spring to life.

Many interactive books, based on high-quality books of children's literature, are available on CD-ROM. Here are some of the best ones:

- Dr. Seuss's rhyming stories *The Cat in the Hat* and *Green Eggs and Ham*, from the Learning Company
- H. A. Rey's *Curious George* stories about a hilarious little monkey, from Simon and Schuster
- Norman Bridwell's *Clifford* stories about a big red dog named Clifford, from Scholastic
- Stan and Jan Berenstain's adventures about a bear family in *Berenstain Bears*, from Broderbund
- Marc Brown's series about an aardvark named Arthur and his friends, from the Learning Company
- Janell Cannon's *Stellaluna*, a charming story about a bat named Stellaluna, from Living Books
- Mercer Mayer's *Just Grandma and Me*, a story about a little critter who takes a trip to the beach with his grandmother, from the Learning Company

Other interactive books for K–5 students are available from LeapFrog SchoolHouse: The Leveled Reading Series provides interactive books for independent reading practice, and the Language First! Program includes books for English learners at four levels of English proficiency with native-language audio support in Spanish, Vietnamese, Cantonese, Haitian Creole, and Hmong.

In addition to interactive books on CD-ROM, others are available at these websites:

Book Pals

www.storylineonline.net

Streaming video programs featuring Screen Actors Guild members reading popular children's books, including Mem Fox's *Wilfred Gordon McDonald Partridge*.

Dora the Explorer

www.nickjr.com

Interactive stories featuring Dora the Explorer from her Nickelodeon cable network series.

PBS Kids

www.pbskids.org

Interactive books from the Between the Lions PBS series, and stories featuring Arthur and Curious George.

Storytime Online

www.kennedy-center.org/multimedia/storytimeonline/

Streaming media presentations of Judith Viorst's *Alexander and the Terrible, Horrible, No Good, Very Bad Day* and other stories.

Tumble Books

www.tumblebooks.com

A collection of animated talking picture books for children, available by subscription.

Children appreciate the control they have in choosing how much support the interactive book provides while they're reading, and researchers have documented that children's word knowledge and comprehension are enhanced by these reading experiences (Lefever-Davis & Pearman, 2005). There's a potential drawback, however: Children can become dependent on the electronic support in decoding words that interactive books provide.

Children create a message collaboratively. Some teachers write class news at the end of the school day instead of morning messages. They discuss the day's activities and decide together what to write. Teachers use interactive writing so that children can do most of the writing. Here's an example of a first-grade class's news:

> *Room 3 News*
> *We are studying insects. Today we*
> *read Diary of a Fly by Doreen Cronin.*
> *It's a totally hilarious book! We learned*
> *that flies walk on walls, and they eat*
> *regurgitated food. That's so yucky!*

Through these adaptations, children learn about the format of friendly letters and other writing genres and the relationships between reading and writing. The writing is authentic, and children learn how to use writing to share information with others.

Shared Reading

Teachers use shared reading to read aloud books that are appropriate for children's interest level but too difficult for them to read for themselves (Parkes, 2000). Teachers use the five stages of the reading process in shared reading, as Ms. McCloskey did in the vignette at the beginning of the chapter. The steps in shared reading are presented in Figure 4–4, showing how the activities fit into the five stages of the reading process. Through the reading process, teachers model what fluent readers do as they involve children in enjoyable reading activities (Fountas & Pinnell, 1996). After the text is read several times, teachers use it to teach phonics and high-frequency words. Children also read small versions of the book with partners or independently, and the pattern or structure found in the text can be used for writing activities.

The books chosen for shared reading are available as big books and are close to children's reading level, but still beyond their ability to read independently. As an instructional strategy, shared reading differs from interactive read-alouds because they see the text as the teacher reads. Also, children often join in the reading of predictable refrains and rhyming words, and after listening to the teacher read the text several times, children often remember enough of the text to read along with the teacher. Through shared reading, teachers also demonstrate how print works, provide opportunities for children to make predictions, and increase children's confidence in their ability to read.

Big books are greatly enlarged picture books that teachers use in shared reading, most commonly with primary-grade students. In this technique, developed in New Zealand, teachers place an enlarged picture book on an easel or chart stand where all children can see it. They read it aloud, pointing to every word. Before long, children join in the reading, especially in repeating the refrain. Then teachers reread the book, inviting children to help with the reading. The next time the book is read, teachers read to the point that the text becomes predictable, such as the beginning of a refrain, and children supply the missing text; having them supply the missing words is important because it leads to independent reading. Once children are familiar with the text, they're invited to read the big book independently (Parkes, 2000).

Predictable Books. The stories and other books that teachers use for shared reading with young children often have repeated sentences, rhyme, or other patterns; books that incorporate these patterns are called *predictable books*. These are the four most common patterns:

Figure 4–4 ◆ How a Shared Reading Lesson Fits Into the Reading Process

1. **Prereading**
   - Activate or build background knowledge on a topic related to the book.
   - Show the cover of the book and read the title.
   - Talk about the author and the illustrator.
   - Have students make predictions.

2. **Reading**
   - Use a big book or text printed on a chart.
   - Use a pointer to track during reading.
   - Read expressively with very few stops during the first reading.
   - Highlight vocabulary and repetitive patterns.
   - Reread the book once or twice, and encourage students to join in the reading.

3. **Responding**
   - Discuss the book in a grand conversation.
   - Ask inferential and higher-level questions, such as "What would happen if . . .?" and "What did this book make you think of?"
   - Share the pen to write a sentence interactively about the book.
   - Have students draw and write in reading logs.

4. **Exploring**
   - Reread the book using small books.
   - Add important words to the word wall.
   - Teach minilessons on strategies and skills.
   - Present more information about the author and the illustrator.
   - Provide a text set with other books by the author or on the same topic.

5. **Applying**
   - Have students write a collaborative book to retell the story.
   - Have students write an innovation imitating the pattern used in the book.
   - Have students dramatize the story or use puppets to retell it.

Repetition. Authors repeat sentences to create a predictable pattern in many picture books. In *Barnyard Banter* (Fleming, 1997), for example, a white goose chases an elusive butterfly around a farm as the cows, roosters, and other animals call out their greetings using a predictable pattern.

Cumulative Sequence. Sentences are repeated and expanded in each episode in these books. For example, in *The Gingerbread Boy* (Galdone, 2008), the cookie repeats and expands his boast as he meets each character on his run away from the Little Old Man and the Little Old Woman.

Rhyme and Rhythm. Rhyme and rhythm are two poetic devices that authors use to add a musical quality to their writing. Many of the popular Dr. Seuss books, such as *Fox in Socks* (1965), use rhyme and rhythm. The sentences have a strong beat, and rhyme is used at the end of lines. Other books that incorporate rhyme and rhythm include familiar songs, such as *Shoo Fly!* (Trapani, 2000), and booklong verses, such as *Pattern Fish* (Harris, 2000).

Sequential Patterns. Some authors use a familiar sequence—such as the months of the year, days of the week, numbers 1 to 10, or letters of the alphabet—to structure their books. For example, in *The Very Hungry Caterpillar* (Carle, 2002), the author uses number and day-of-the-week sequences as the caterpillar eats through an amazing array of foods.

Figure 4–5 lists predictable books representing each category. These books are valuable for emergent readers because the repeated sentences, patterns, and sequences make it easier for children to predict the next sentence or episode (Tompkins & Webeler, 1983).

Language Experience Approach

The Language Experience Approach (LEA) is based on children's language and experiences (Ashton-Warner, 1986). In this approach, teachers do shared writing: Children dictate words and sentences about their experiences, and the teacher writes down what the children say; the text they develop becomes the reading material. Because the language comes from the children themselves and because the content is based on their experiences, they're usually able to read the text easily. Reading and writing are connected, because children are actively involved in reading what they've written.

Using this approach, children create individual booklets. They draw pictures on each page or cut pictures from magazines to glue on each page, and then they dictate the text that the teacher writes beside each illustration. Children can also make collaborative books, where each child creates one page to be added to a class book. For example, as part of the unit on "The Three Bears," a kindergarten class made a collaborative book on bears. Children each chose a fact about bears for their page; they drew an illustration and dictated the text for their teacher to record. One page from this class book is shown in Figure 4–6. The teacher took the children's dictation rather than having them write the book themselves because she wanted it to be written in conventional spelling so everyone in the classroom could read and reread the book.

When taking dictation, it's a great temptation to change the child's language to the teacher's own, in either word choice or grammar, but editing should be kept to a minimum

Figure 4–5 ◆ Predictable Books for Young Children

Repetition

Carle, E. (1997). *Have you seen my cat?* New York: Aladdin Books.

Guarino, D. (2004). *Is your mama a llama?* New York: Scholastic.

Martin, B., Jr. (2007). *Baby bear, baby bear, what do you see?* New York: Henry Holt.

Rathmann, P. (2000). *Good night, gorilla.* New York: Puffin Books.

Rosen, M. (2004). *We're going on a bear hunt.* New York: Candlewick Press.

Cumulative Sequence

Aylesworth, J. (1996). *The gingerbread man.* New York: Scholastic.

Fleming, D. (2006). *The cow who clucked.* New York: Henry Holt.

Pinkney, J. (2006). *The little red hen.* New York: Dial Books.

Taback, S. (2004). *The house that Jack built.* New York: Puffin Books.

Wood, A. (2007). *Silly Sally.* San Diego: Harcourt.

Rhyme and Rhythm

Fleming, D. (1995). *In the tall, tall grass.* New York: Henry Holt.

Hoberman, M. A. (2003). *Miss Mary Mack: A hand-clapping rhyme.* Boston: Little, Brown.

Hoberman, M. A. (2004). *The eensy-weensy spider.* Boston: Little, Brown.

Martin, B., Jr., & Archambault, J. (2000). *Chicka chicka boom boom.* New York: Aladdin Books.

Shaw, N. (2006). *Sheep in a jeep.* Boston: Houghton Mifflin.

Sequential Patterns

Baker, K. (2007). *Hickory dickory dock.* San Diego: Harcourt.

Carle, E. (1997). *Today is Monday.* New York: Putnam.

Carle, E. (2005). *A house for hermit crab.* New York: Aladdin Books.

Christelow, E. (2006). *Five little monkeys jumping on the bed.* New York: Clarion Books.

Wood, A. (2004). *Ten little fish.* New York: Blue Sky Press/Scholastic.

Figure 4–6 ◆ One Page From a Class Book About Bears

Polar bears live in
ice and snow.

Jesse

so that children don't get the impression that their language is inferior or inadequate. Also, as children become familiar with dictating to the teacher, they learn to pace their dictation to the teacher's writing speed. At first, children dictate as they think of ideas, but with experience, they watch as the teacher writes and supply the text word by word. This change also provides evidence of children's developing concepts about print.

Interactive Writing

In **interactive writing**, children and the teacher create a text together and "share the pen" as they write the text on chart paper (Button, Johnson, & Furgerson, 1996; McCarrier, Pinnell, & Fountas, 2000). The children compose the message together, and then the teacher guides them as they write it word by word on chart paper. Children take turns writing known letters and familiar words, adding punctuation marks, and leaving spaces between words. All children participate in creating and writing the text on chart paper, and they also write the text on small dry-erase boards or on paper as it is written on the chart paper. Afterward, children read and reread the text together with classmates and on their own.

Children use interactive writing to write class news, predictions before reading, retellings of stories, thank-you letters, reports, math story problems, and many other types of group writings (Tompkins & Collom, 2004). Two interactive writing samples are shown in Figure 4–7; the top sample was written by a kindergarten class during a health unit, and the second one is a story problem written by a first-grade class during math. After writing this story problem, children wrote other subtraction problems individually. The boxes drawn around some of the letters and words represent correction tape that was used to correct misspellings or poorly formed letters. In the kindergarten sample, children took turns writing individual letters; in the first-grade sample, children took turns writing entire words.

Go to the Building Teaching Skills and Dispositions section of Chapter 4 on **MyEducationLab.com** to see students participating in interactive writing.

Figure 4–7 ◆ Two Samples of Interactive Writing

Wash your hands with soap to kill germs.

Luis had 5 pieces of candy but he ate 3 of them. Then he gave 1 to his friend Mario. How many does he have now?

Through interactive writing, children learn concepts about print, letter-sound relationships and spelling patterns, handwriting concepts, and capitalization and punctuation skills. Teachers model correct spelling and use of conventions of print, and children practice segmenting the sounds in words and spelling familiar words.

Teachers help children spell all words conventionally. They teach high-frequency words such as *the* and *of*, assist children in segmenting sounds and syllables in other words, point out unusual spelling patterns such as *pieces* and *germs*, and teach other conventions of print. Whenever children misspell a word or form a letter incorrectly, teachers use correction tape to cover the mistake and help them make the correction. For example, when a child wrote the numeral *8* to spell *ate* in the second sample in Figure 4–7, the teacher explained the *eight–ate* homophone, covered the numeral with correction tape, and helped the child spell the word, including the silent *e*. Teachers emphasize the importance of using conventional spelling as a courtesy to readers, not that a child made a mistake. In contrast to the emphasis on conventional spelling in interactive writing, children are encouraged to use invented spelling and other spelling strategies when writing independently. They learn to look for familiar words posted on classroom word walls or in books they have read, think about spelling patterns, or ask a classmate for help. Teachers also talk about purpose and explain that in personal writing and rough drafts, children do use invented spelling. Increasingly, however, children want to use conventional spelling and even ask to use the correction tape to fix errors they make as they write.

Manuscript Handwriting

Children enter kindergarten with different backgrounds of handwriting experience. Some 5-year-olds have never held a pencil, but many others have written cursivelike scribbles or manuscript letterlike lines and circles. Some have learned to print their names and even a few other letters. Handwriting instruction in kindergarten typically includes developing children's ability to hold pencils, refining their fine-motor control, and focusing on letter formation. Some people might argue that kindergartners are too young to learn handwriting skills, but young children should be encouraged to write from the first day of school. They write letters and words on labels, draw and write stories, keep journals, and write other types of messages. The more they write, the greater their need becomes for instruction in handwriting. Instruction is necessary so that children don't learn bad habits that later must be broken.

To teach children how to form letters, many kindergarten and first-grade teachers create brief directions for forming letters that they sing to a familiar tune; for example, to form a lowercase letter *a*, try "All around and make a tail" sung to the tune of "Row, Row, Row Your Boat." As teachers sing the directions, they model the formation of the letter in the air or on the chalkboard using large arm motions. Then children sing along and practice forming the letter in the air. Later, they practice writing letters using sponge paintbrushes dipped in water at the chalkboard or pens on dry-erase boards as well as in authentic paper-and-pencil writing activities.

Handwriting research suggests that moving models are much more effective than still models, which suggests that worksheets on the letters aren't very useful because children often don't form the letters correctly. Researchers recommend that children watch teachers to see how letters are formed and then practice forming them themselves. Also, teachers supervise children as they write so that they can correct those who form letters incorrectly. It's important that children write circles counterclockwise, starting from 1:00, and form most lines from top to bottom and left to right across the page. When children follow these guidelines, they're less likely to tear the paper they're writing on, and they'll have an easier transition to cursive handwriting.

Writing Centers

Writing centers are set up in kindergarten and first-grade classrooms so that children have a special place where they can go to write. The center should be located at a table with chairs, and a box of supplies, including pencils, crayons, a date stamp, different kinds of paper, journal notebooks, a stapler, blank books, notepaper, and envelopes, should be stored nearby. The alphabet, printed in upper- and lowercase letters, should be available on the table for children to refer to as they write. In addition, there should be a crate where children can file their work. When children come to the writing center, they draw and write in journals, compile books, and write messages to classmates (Tunks & Giles, 2007). Teachers assist children and provide information about letters, words, and sentences as needed, or aides, parent-volunteers, or older students can assist.

Figure 4–8 presents two reading log entries created by kindergartners and first graders at the writing center. The top piece shows a kindergartner's response to *If You Give a Mouse a Cookie* (Numeroff, 2000). The child's writing says, "I love chocolate chip cookies." The bottom piece was written by a first grader after reading *Are You My Mother?* (Eastman, 2005). The child wrote, "The bird said, 'Are you my mother, you big ole Snort?'" After children shared their log entries during a grand conversation, this child added, "The mommy said, 'Here is a worm. I am

Figure 4–8 ◆ Two Children's Reading Log Entries

here. I'm here.'" Notice that the part the mother says is written as though it were coming out of the bird's mouth and going up into the air.

Young children also make books at the writing center based on the books they have read. For example, they can use the same patterns as in *Baby Bear, Baby Bear, What Do You See?* (Martin, 2007), *If You Give a Mouse a Cookie* (Numeroff, 2000), and *Lunch* (Fleming, 1996) to create innovations, or new versions of familiar stories. A first grader's four-page book about a mouse named Jerry, written after reading *If You Give a Mouse a Cookie*, is shown in Figure 4–9. In these writing projects, children often use invented spelling, but they're encouraged to spell familiar words and words from the story correctly.

Children also write notes and letters to classmates at the writing center. They learn about the format of friendly letters and how to phrase the greeting and the closing. Then they apply what they're learning as they write to classmates to say hello, offer a compliment, share news, trade telephone numbers, and offer birthday wishes. As they write messages, the children practice writing their names, their classmates' names, and the words they're learning to read and spell. The classmates who receive the messages also gain practice reading the messages. Teachers participate, too, by regularly writing brief messages to children. Through their activities, they model how to write messages and how to read and respond to the messages they

Figure 4–9 ◆ A First Grader's Four-Page Innovation for *If You Give a Mouse a Cookie*

receive. To facilitate the sharing of these messages, teachers often set up a message bulletin board or individual mailboxes made from milk cartons or shoe boxes. This activity is especially valuable because children discover the social purposes of reading and writing as they write and receive notes and letters.

Chapter 4 Review

How Effective Teachers Support the Youngest Children's Literacy Development

▶ Teachers foster young children's interest in literacy and teach concepts about written language.

▶ Teachers understand that children move through the emergent, beginning, and fluent stages of literacy development.

▶ Teachers match instructional activities to children's stage of reading and writing development.

▶ Teachers monitor children's literacy development to ensure that they're moving through the three stages, and they intervene when children aren't making expected progress.

PEARSON
myeducationlab
Where the Classroom Comes to Life

Go to MyEducationLab at www.myeducationlab.com to deepen your understanding of the concepts presented in this chapter:

▶ Check your understanding of chapter concepts with the multiple-choice and essay quizzes in the Study Plan.
▶ Apply some of the main ideas discussed in the chapter in the Activities and Applications section of the website.
▶ Practice what you've learned in this chapter in Building Teaching Skills and Dispositions before applying the ideas in your own classroom.

PROFESSIONAL REFERENCES

Adams, M. J. (1990). *Beginning to read: Thinking and learning about print.* Cambridge, MA: MIT Press.

Ashton-Warner, S. (1986). *Teacher.* New York: Simon & Schuster.

Button, K., Johnson, M. J., & Furgerson, P. (1996). Interactive writing in a primary classroom. *The Reading Teacher, 49,* 446–454.

Clay, M. M. (2000a). *Concepts about print: What have children learned about the way we print language?* Portsmouth, NH: Heinemann.

Clay, M. M. (2000b). *Follow me, moon.* Portsmouth, NH: Heinemann.

Clay, M. M. (2006). *An observation survey of early literacy achievement* (2nd ed.). Portsmouth, NH: Heinemann.

Clay, M. M. (2007a). *No shoes.* Portsmouth, NH: Heinemann.

Clay, M. M. (2007b). *Sand.* Portsmouth, NH: Heinemann.

Clay, M. M. (2007c). *Stones.* Portsmouth, NH: Heinemann.

Fountas, I. C., & Pinnell, G. S. (1996). *Guided reading: Good first teaching for all children.* Portsmouth, NH: Heinemann.

Harste, J., Woodward, V., & Burke, C. (1984). *Language stories and literacy lessons*. Portsmouth, NH: Heinemann.

Heath, S. B. (1983). *Ways with words*. New York: Oxford University Press.

Invernizzi, M. (2003). Concepts, sounds, and the ABCs: A diet for a very young reader. In D. M. Barone & L. M. Morrow (Eds.), *Literacy and young children: Research-based practices* (pp. 140–156). New York: Guilford Press.

Juel, C. (1991). Beginning reading. In R. Barr, M. L. Kamil, P. Mosenthal, & P. D. Pearson (Eds.), *Handbook of reading research* (Vol. 2, pp. 759–788). New York: Longman.

Lefever-Davis, S., & Pearman, C. (2005). Early readers and electronic texts: CD-ROM storybook features that influence reading behaviors. *The Reading Teacher, 58*, 446–454.

McCarrier, A., Pinnell, G. S., & Fountas, I. C. (2000). *Interactive writing: How language and literacy come together, K–2*. Portsmouth, NH: Heinemann.

McGee, L. M. (2007). *Transforming literacy practices in preschool: Research-based practices that give all children the opportunity to reach their potential as learners*. New York: Scholastic.

McGee, L. M., & Richgels, D. J. (2003). *Designing early literacy programs: Strategies for at-risk preschool and kindergarten children*. New York: Guilford Press.

McGee, L. M., & Richgels, D. J. (2008). *Literacy's beginnings: Supporting young readers and writers* (5th ed.). Boston: Allyn & Bacon.

Morrow, L. M., & Tracey, D. H. (2007). Best practices in early literacy development in preschool, kindergarten, and first grade. In L. B. Gambrell, L. M. Morrow, & M.

Pressley (Eds.), *Best practices in literacy instruction* (3rd ed., pp. 57–82). New York: Guilford Press.

Papandropoulou, I., & Sinclair, H. (1974). What is a word? Experimental study of children's ideas on grammar. *Human Development, 17*, 241–258.

Parkes, B. (2000). *Read it again! Revisting shared reading*. Portland, ME: Stenhouse.

Payne, C. D., & Schulman, M. B. (1999). *Getting the most out of morning messages and other shared writing lessons*. New York: Scholastic.

Pinnell, G. S., & Fountas, I. C. (1998). *Word matters: Teaching phonics and spelling in the reading/writing classroom*. Portsmouth, NH: Heinemann.

Schickedanz, J., & Casbergue, R. (2004). *Writing in preschool: Learning to orchestrate meaning and marks*. Newark, DE: International Reading Association.

Snow, C. E., Burns, M. S., & Griffin, P. (Eds.). (1998). *Preventing reading difficulties in young children*. Washington, DC: National Academy Press.

Taylor, D., & Dorsey-Gaines, C. (1987). *Growing up literate: Learning from inner-city families*. Portsmouth, NH: Heinemann.

Tompkins, G. E., & Collom, S. (2004). *Sharing the pen: Interactive writing with young children*. Upper Saddle River, NJ: Merrill/Prentice Hall.

Tompkins, G. E., & Webeler, M. (1983). What will happen next? Using predictable books with young children. *The Reading Teacher, 36*, 498–502.

Tunks, K. W., & Giles, K. M. (2007). *Write now! Publishing with young authors, preK–grade 2*. Portsmouth, NH: Heinemann.

CHILDREN'S BOOK REFERENCES

Carle, E. (2002). *The very hungry caterpillar*. New York: Puffin Books.

Cronin, D. (2007). *Diary of a fly*. New York: HarperCollins.

Danziger, P. (1998). *Amber Brown sees red*. New York: Scholastic.

Danziger, P. (1999). *Amber Brown is feeling blue*. New York: Scholastic.

Danziger, P. (2004). *Amber Brown is green with envy*. New York: Scholastic.

Danziger, P. (2006). *Amber Brown is not a crayon*. New York: Scholastic.

Danziger, P. (2007). *Amber Brown goes fourth*. New York: Puffin Books.

Eastman, P. D. (2005). *Are you my mother?* New York: HarperCollins.

Fleming, D. (1996). *Lunch*. New York: Henry Holt.

Fleming, D. (1997). *Barnyard banter*. New York: Henry Holt.

Galdone, P. (2008). *The gingerbread boy*. New York: Clarion Books.

Greenburg, D. (1997). *Never trust a cat who wears earrings*. New York: Grosset & Dunlap.

Harris, T. (2000). *Pattern fish*. Brookfield, CT: Millbrook Press.

Hoff, S. (2000a). *Oliver*. New York: HarperTrophy.

Hoff, S. (2000b). *Sammy the seal*. New York: HarperTrophy.

Martin, B., Jr. (2007). *Baby bear, baby bear, what do you see?* New York: Henry Holt.

McCloskey, R. (2001). *Make way for ducklings*. New York: Viking.

Most, B. (1984). *If the dinosaurs came back*. San Diego: Harcourt Brace.

Numeroff, L. J. (2000). *If you give a mouse a cookie*. New York: HarperCollins.

Prince, S. (1999). *Playing*. Littleton, MA: Sundance.

Sachar, L. (2000). *Marvin Redpost: A magic crystal?* New York: Random House.

Seuss, Dr. (1965). *Fox in socks*. New York: Random House.

Simont, M. (2001). *The stray dog*. New York: HarperCollins.

Trapani, I. (2000). *Shoo fly!* Watertown, MA: Charlesbridge.

CHAPTER 5

Cracking the Alphabetic Code

Mrs. Firpo Teaches Phonics Using a Basal Reading Program

It's 8:10 on Thursday morning, and the 19 first graders in Mrs. Firpo's classroom are gathered on the carpet for their phonics lesson that the teacher calls "word work." This week's topic is the long *i* and long *e* sounds for *y*: For example, in *my* and *multiply*, the *y* is pronounced as long *i*, and in *baby* and *sunny*, the *y* is pronounced as long *e*. She shows pictures representing words that end with *y*: *fly*, *baby*, *jelly*, *bunny*, and *sky*. The children identify each object and say its name slowly to isolate the final sound. Saleena goes first. She picks up the picture of a fly and says, "It's a fly: /f/ /l/ /ī/. It ends with the ī sound." Vincent is confused when it's his turn to identify the long *e* sound at the end of *bunny* so Mrs. Firpo demonstrates how to segment the sounds in the word: /b/ /ŭ/ /n/ /ē/. Then Vincent recognizes the long *e* sound at the end of the word. Next, the first graders sort the picture cards according to the final sound and place them in two columns in a nearby pocket chart. They add labels to the columns: *y* = ī and *y* = ē.

Mrs. Firpo begins her phonics lessons with an oral activity because she knows it's important to integrate phonemic awareness with phonics. In the oral activities, children focus on orally segmenting and blending the sounds they hear in words—

without worrying about phoneme-grapheme correspondences. Next, she introduces a set of cards with words ending in *y* for the children to read and classify. They take turns using phonics to sound out these words: *funny, my, try, happy, why, fussy, very, sticky, shy,* and *cry*. They add the word cards to the columns on the pocket chart. Then the teacher asks the children to suggest other words that end in *y*; Fernando names *yucky*, Crystal says *crunchy*, and Joel adds *dry*. Mrs. Firpo writes these words on small cards, too, and adds them to the pocket chart. Then Austin uses the pointer to point to each card in the pocket chart for the class to read aloud.

At the end of this 15-minute lesson, the children return to their desks and get out their dry-erase boards for spelling practice. This week's spelling words end in *y* pronounced as long *i*. Mrs. Firpo calls out each word, and the children practice writing it three times on their small dry-erase boards. If they need help spelling the word, they check the list of spelling words on the Focus Wall. As they write, Mrs. Firpo circulates around the classroom, modeling how to form letters, reminding Jordan and Kendra to leave a "two-finger" space between words, and checking that their spellings are correct.

Mrs. Firpo's Focus Wall is shown in the box on page 144. Each week, Mrs. Firpo posts the strategies and skills she'll be teaching, and the vocabulary words and spelling words are listed there, too. The vocabulary words are written on cards and displayed in a pocket chart attached to the Focus Wall so that they can be rearranged and used for various activities. Mrs. Firpo uses *Houghton Mifflin Reading* (Cooper & Pikulski, 2003), a basal reading textbook series; each week's topics are identified for her in the teacher's edition of the textbook. The reason why she posts these topics is to emphasize what she's teaching and what children are learning. In addition, Mrs. Firpo has her state's reading and writing standards for first grade listed on a chart next to the wall.

Next, Mrs. Firpo guides children as they complete several pages in the workbook that accompanies the basal reader. Some pages reinforce phonics and spelling concepts, and others focus on comprehension, vocabulary, grammar, and writing. Today, they begin on page 201. First the children examine the illustration at the top of the page, and then they write two sentences about the silly things they see in the picture on the lines at the bottom of the page. They talk about the illustration, identifying the silly things they see. Felicia says, "I see a bunny reading a book, and I think that's silly." Mrs. Firpo gives Felicia a "thumbs up" to compliment her. And Fernando comments, "I see something else. It's a bear up in a balloon." "Is the balloon up in the sky?" Mrs. Firpo asks because she wants to emphasize the phonics pattern of the week. Fernando agrees that it is, and he repeats, "I see a bear up in a balloon in the sky." He, too, gets a "thumbs up."

After children identify five or six silly things, they get ready to write. Mrs. Firpo reminds them to begin their sentences with capital letters and end them with periods. As they write their sentences, Alicia notices that she has written *bunny*—a word that ends in *y* and has an ē sound. Mrs. Firpo congratulates her and encourages other children to point out when they write words that end in *y*. Joel waves his hand in the air, eager to report that he has written *sky*—a word that ends in *y* and has an ī sound.

Then the children move on to page 202. On this page, there's a word bank with words that end in *y* and represent the ī sound at the top and sentences with blanks at the

Mrs. Firpo's Focus Wall

Theme 9: Special Friends   Week: 1   Reading Level: 1.5

PHONICS FOCUS: Long i and long e sounds for y

WORD PATTERN: -ay

say	day	way	bay	stay	gray
pay	may	lay	ray	pray	spray

SPELLING CONCEPT: Long i sound at the end of a
word spelled with y

COMPREHENSION STRATEGY: Monitoring

COMPREHENSION SKILL: Noting Details

GRAMMAR CONCEPT: is/are

WRITING GENRE: Friendly Letters

VOCABULARY WORDS

ocean	though	by
dance	talk	my
open	else	cry
ever	around	any
	Grandaddy	

SPELLING WORDS

1. by   5. cry
2. my   6. why
3. fly   7. pry
4. try   8. multiply

bottom. The children practice reading the words in the word bank. After reading the words several times, Vincent volunteers, "I get it! Look at these words: They all have *y* and they say ī." Mrs. Firpo is pleased and gives him a "thumbs up." Next, the teacher reads aloud the sentences at the bottom of the page and asks children to supply the missing words. Then they work independently to reread the sentences and complete them by filling in the missing words. Mrs. Firpo moves from one group of desks to the next as the children work, monitoring their work and providing assistance as needed.

Each week, the children receive take-home books that Mrs. Firpo has duplicated and stapled together; these books reinforce the week's phonics lesson and the vocabulary introduced in the reading textbook. The first graders read the books at school and use them for a phonics activity; then they take them home to practice reading with their families. Today's book is *I Spy*: It's eight pages long, with illustrations and text on each page. Mrs. Firpo introduces the book and reads it aloud once while the children follow along in their copies. They keep their books at their desks to use for a seatwork activity, and later they put the books in book bags that they take home each day. Already they've collected more than 75 books!

During the last 40 minutes of the reading period, Mrs. Firpo conducts guided reading groups. Her students' reading levels range from beginning first grade to the middle of second grade, with about half of them reading at grade level. She has grouped the first graders into four guided reading groups, and she meets with two groups each day. Children reading below grade level read leveled books, and those reading at and above grade level read easy-to-read chapter books, including Barbara Park's series of funny stories about a girl named Junie B. Jones (e.g., *Junie B., First Grader: Boss of Lunch* [2003]) and Mary Pope Osborne's Magic Tree House series of adventure stories (e.g., *High Tide in Hawaii* [2003]). Mrs. Firpo calls this period *differentiated instruction* because children participate in a variety of activities, based on their reading levels.

While Mrs. Firpo does guided reading with one group, the others are involved in seatwork and center activities. For the seatwork activity, children read their take-home book and highlight all the words in it ending in *y* pronounced as ī; they don't highlight *bunny, play,* and other words where the *y* is not pronounced as ī. They also work in small groups to cut out pictures and words that end in *y*, sort into *y* = ē, *y* = ī, and *y* = *other* categories, and paste them on a sheet of paper. The pictures and words for the activity include *puppy, city, they, buy, pretty, play, funny, dry, party, fifty, boy, sky, fly, today,* and *yummy.*

The first graders practice their spelling words using magnetic letters at the spelling center, practice the phonics focus and word pattern using letter cards and flip books at the phonics center, make books at the writing center, listen to the take-home books read aloud at the listening center, and read electronic books interactively at the computer center. The centers are arranged around the perimeter of the classroom; children know how to work at centers and understand what they're expected to do at each one.

After a 15-minute recess, children spend the last 55 minutes of literacy instruction in writing workshop. Each week, the class focuses on the genre specified in the basal reading program; this week's focus is on writing personal letters. First, Mrs. Firpo teaches a **minilesson** and guides children as they complete more pages in their workbooks. Today, she reviews how to use commas in a friendly letter. The children examine several letters hanging in the classroom that the class wrote earlier in the school year using **interactive writing**. After the class rereads each letter, Mrs. Firpo asks the children to mark the commas used in the letters with Vis-à-Vis pens (so their marks can be cleaned off afterward). Crystal points out that commas are used in the date, Saleena notices that a comma is used at the end of the greeting, and Luis marks the comma used after the closing. Next, children practice adding commas in the sample friendly letters on page 208 in their workbooks.

Then children spend the remaining 35 minutes of writing workshop working on the letters they're writing to their families this week. Mrs. Firpo works with five children on their letters while the others work independently. At the end of the writing time, Joel and Angelica sit in the author's chair to read their letters aloud to their classmates. Angelica's letter to her grandmother is shown in the box below.

Mrs. Firpo's students spend 3½ hours each morning involved in literacy instruction. Most of the goals, activities, and instructional materials come from the basal reading program, but Mrs. Firpo adapts some activities to meet her students' varied instructional needs. Through these phonemic awareness, phonics, and spelling activities, these first graders are learning to crack the alphabetic code.

Angelica's Letter to Her Grandmother

April 29, 2008

Dear Nanna Isabel,

I am writting you a letter. My birthday is in 35 days! Did you no that? I wud like to get a present. I want you to come to my party.
It will be very funny.

Love,

Angelica

nglish is an alphabetic language, and children crack this code as they learn about phonemes (sounds), graphemes (letters), and graphophonemic (letter-sound) relationships. They learn about phonemes as they notice rhyming words, segment words into individual sounds, and invent silly words by playing with sounds, much like Dr. Seuss did. They learn about letters as they sing the ABC song, name the letters of the alphabet, and spell their own names. They learn graphophonemic relationships as they match letters and letter combinations to sounds, blend sounds to form words, and decode and spell vowel patterns. By third grade, most students have figured out the alphabetic code, and in fourth through eighth grades, students apply what they've learned to decode and spell multisyllabic words. You may think of all of this as phonics, but children actually develop three separate but related abilities about the alphabetic code:

- ◆ **Phonemic Awareness.** Children learn to notice and manipulate the sounds of oral language. Those who are phonemically aware understand that spoken words are made up of sounds, and they can segment and blend sounds in spoken words.
- ◆ **Phonics.** Children learn to convert letters into sounds and blend them to recognize words. Those who can apply phonics concepts understand that there are predictable sound-symbol correspondences in English, and they can use decoding strategies to figure out unfamiliar written words.
- ◆ **Spelling.** Children learn to segment spoken words into sounds and convert the sounds into letters to spell words. Those who have learned to spell conventionally understand English sound-symbol correspondences and spelling patterns, and they can use spelling strategies to spell unfamiliar words.

In the vignette, Mrs. Firpo incorporated all three components into her literacy program. She began the word work lesson on the long *e* and long *i* sounds of *y* with an oral phonemic awareness activity; next, she moved to a phonics activity where children read words that ended in *y* and categorized them on a pocket chart. Later, they practiced spelling words that ended with *y* on dry-erase boards. Teaching these graphophonemic relationships is not a complete reading program, but phonemic awareness, phonics, and spelling are integral to effective literacy instruction, especially for young children (National Reading Panel, 2000).

Go to the Building Teaching Skills and Dispositions section of Chapter 5 on **MyEducationLab.com** to see a kindergarten teacher and a speech therapist help children distinguish sounds.

PHONEMIC AWARENESS

Phonemic awareness is children's basic understanding that speech is composed of a series of individual sounds, and it provides the foundation for phonics and spelling (Armbruster, Lehr, & Osborn, 2001). When children can choose a duck as the animal whose name begins with /d/ from a collection of toy animals, identify *duck* and *luck* as rhyming words in a song, or blend the sounds /d/ /ŭ/ /k/ to pronounce *duck*, they are phonemically aware. Cunningham and Allington (2007) describe phonemic awareness as children's ability to "take words apart, put them back together again, and change them" (p. 37). The emphasis is on the sounds of spoken words, not on reading letters or pronouncing letter names. Developing phonemic awareness enables children to use sound-symbol correspondences to read and spell words (Gillon, 2004).

Phonemes are the smallest units of speech, and they're written as graphemes, or letters of the alphabet. In this book, phonemes are marked using diagonal lines (e.g., /d/) and graphemes are italicized (e.g., *d*). Sometimes phonemes (e.g., /k/ in *duck*) are spelled with two graphemes (*ck*).

Understanding that words are composed of smaller units—phonemes—is a significant achievement for young children because phonemes are abstract language units.

Phonemes carry no meaning, and children think of words according to their meanings, not their linguistic characteristics (Griffith & Olson, 1992). When children think about ducks, for example, they think of feathered animals that swim in ponds, fly through the air, and make noises we describe as "quacks"; they don't think of "duck" as a word with three phonemes or four graphemes, or as a word beginning with /d/ and rhyming with *luck*. Phonemic awareness requires that children treat speech as an object and that they shift their attention away from the meaning of words to the linguistic features of speech. This focus on phonemes is even more complicated because phonemes are not discrete units in speech: Often they are slurred or clipped in speech—think about the blended initial sound in *tree* and the ending sound in *eating*.

Be Strategic!

Phonemic Awareness Strategies

As students manipulate sounds orally, they learn to use these two strategies:

- ▶ Blend
- ▶ Segment

Students apply these oral strategies to written language for decoding and spelling words.

Phonemic Awareness Strategies

Children become phonemically aware by manipulating spoken language in these ways:

Identifying Sounds in Words. Children learn to identify a word that begins or ends with a particular sound. For example, when shown a brush, a car, and a doll, they can identify *doll* as the word that ends with /l/.

Categorizing Sounds in Words. Children learn to recognize the "odd" word in a set of three words; for example, when the teacher says *ring, rabbit*, and *sun*, they recognize that *sun* doesn't belong.

Substituting Sounds to Make New Words. Children learn to remove a sound from a word and substitute a different sound. Sometimes they substitute the beginning sound, changing *bar* to *car*, for example. Or, they change the middle sound, making *tip* from *top*, or substitute the ending sound, changing *gate* to *game*.

Blending Sounds to Form Words. Children learn to blend two, three, or four individual sounds to form a word; the teacher says /b/ /ĭ/ /g/, for example, and the children repeat the sounds, blending them to form the word *big*.

Segmenting a Word Into Sounds. Children learn to break a word into its beginning, middle, and ending sounds. For example, children segment the word *feet* into /f/ /ē/ /t/ and *go* into /g/ /ō/.

Children use these strategies, especially blending and segmenting, to decode and spell words. When children use phonics to sound out a word, for example, they say the sounds represented by each letter and blend them to read the word. Similarly, to spell a word, children say the word slowly to themselves, segmenting the sounds.

Teaching Phonemic Awareness

Teachers nurture children's phonemic awareness through the language-rich environments they create in the classroom. As they sing songs, chant rhymes, read aloud word-play books, and play games, children have many opportunities to orally match, isolate, blend, and substitute sounds and to segment words into sounds (Griffith & Olson, 1992). Teachers often incorporate phonemic awareness into other oral language and literacy activities, but it's also important to teach lessons that focus specifically on the phonemic awareness strategies.

Phonemic awareness instruction should meet three criteria. First, the activities should be appropriate for 4-, 5-, and 6-year-old children. Activities involving songs, nursery rhymes, riddles, and wordplay books are good choices because they encourage children's playful experimentation with oral language. Second, the instruction should be planned and purposeful, not just incidental. Teachers need to choose instructional materials and plan activities that focus children's attention on the sound structure of oral language. Third, phonemic awareness activities should be integrated with other components of a balanced literacy program. It's crucial that children perceive the connection between oral and written language (Yopp & Yopp, 2000).

Many wordplay books are available for young children. A list of books is presented in Figure 5–1. Books such as *Cock-a-Doodle-Moo!* (Most, 1996) and *Rattletrap Car* (Root, 2004) stimulate children to experiment with sounds and to create nonsense words. Teachers often read wordplay books aloud more than once. During the first reading, children focus on comprehension or what interests them in the book. During a second reading, however, children's attention shifts to the wordplay elements, and teachers direct their attention to the way the author manipulated words and sounds by making comments and asking questions—"Did you notice how _____ and _____ rhyme?"—and encourage children to make similar comments themselves.

Teachers often incorporate wordplay books, songs, and games into the minilessons they teach. The feature on the next page presents a kindergarten teacher's minilesson on blending sounds into a word. The teacher reread Dr. Seuss's *Fox in Socks* (1965) and then asked children to identify words from the book that she pronounced sound by sound. This book is rich in wordplay: rhyming (e.g., *do, you, goo, chew*), initial consonant substitution (e.g., *trick, quick, slick*), vowel substitution (e.g., *blabber, blibber, blubber*), and alliteration (e.g., *Luke Luck likes lakes*).

Figure 5–1 ◆ Wordplay Books to Develop Phonemic Awareness

Crebbin, J. (1998). *Cows in the kitchen*. Cambridge, MA: Candlewick Press.

Degan, B. (1985). *Jamberry*. New York: HarperTrophy.

Deming, A. G. (1994). *Who is tapping at my window?* New York: Penguin.

Downey, L. (2000). *The flea's sneeze*. New York: Henry Holt.

Ehlert, L. (1993). *Eating the alphabet: Fruits and vegetables from A to Z*. San Diego: Voyager.

Gollub, M. (2000). *The jazz fly*. Santa Rosa, CA: Tortuga Press.

Hillenbrand, W. (2002). *Fiddle-I-fee*. San Diego: Gulliver Books.

Hoberman, M. A. (1998). *Miss Mary Mack*. Boston: Little, Brown.

Hoberman, M. A. (2003). *The lady with the alligator purse*. Boston: Little, Brown.

Hoberman, M. A. (2004). *The eensy-weensy spider*. Boston: Little, Brown.

Hutchins, P. (2002). *Don't forget the bacon!* New York: Red Fox Books.

Martin, B., Jr., & Archambault, J. (2000). *Chicka chicka boom boom*. New York: Aladdin Books.

Most, B. (1991). *A dinosaur named after me*. San Diego: Harcourt Brace.

Most, B. (1996). *Cock-a-doodle-moo!* San Diego: Harcourt Brace.

Most, B. (2003). *The cow that went oink*. San Diego: Voyager.

Prelutsky, J. (1989). *The baby uggs are hatching*. New York: Mulberry Books.

Raffi. (1988). *Down by the bay*. New York: Crown.

Raffi. (1990). *The wheels on the bus*. New York: Crown.

Root, P. (2003). *One duck stuck*. Cambridge, MA: Candlewick Press.

Seuss, Dr. (1963). *Hop on pop*. New York: Random House.

Shaw, N. (2006). *Sheep in a jeep*. Boston: Houghton Mifflin.

Slate, J. (1996). *Miss Bindergarten gets ready for kindergarten*. New York: Dutton.

Slepian, J., & Seidler, A. (2001). *The hungry thing*. New York: Scholastic.

Taback, S. (1997). *There was an old lady who swallowed a fly*. New York: Viking.

Taback, S. (2004). *This is the house that Jack built*. New York: Puffin Books.

Westcott, N. B. (2003). *I know an old lady who swallowed a fly*. Boston: Little, Brown.

Wilson, K. (2003). *A frog in a bag*. New York: McElderry.

Minilesson

TOPIC: Blending Sounds Into Words
GRADE: Kindergarten
TIME: One 20-minute period

Ms. Lewis regularly includes a 20-minute lesson on phonemic awareness in her literacy block. She usually rereads a familiar wordplay book and plays a phonemic awareness game with the kindergartners that empha-sizes one of the phonemic awareness strategies.

1 Introduce the Topic

Ms. Lewis brings her 19 kindergartners together on the rug and explains that she's going to reread Dr. Seuss's *Fox in Socks* (1965). It's one of their favorite books, and they clap their pleasure. She explains that after reading, they're going to play a word game.

2 Share Examples

Ms. Lewis reads aloud *Fox in Socks*, showing the pictures on each page as she reads. She encourages the chil-dren to read along. Sometimes she stops and invites the children to fill in the last rhyming word in a sentence or to echo read (repeating after her like an echo) the alliterative sentences. After they finish reading, she asks what they like best about the book. Pearl replies, "It's just a really funny book. That's why it is so good." "What makes it funny?" Ms. Lewis asks. Teri explains, "The words are funny. They make my tongue laugh. You know—*fox–socks–box–Knox*. That's funny on my tongue!" "Oh," Ms. Lewis clarifies, "your tongue likes to say rhyming words. I like to say them, too." Other children recall other rhyming words in the book: *clocks–tocks–blocks–box, noodle–poodle*, and *new–do–blue–goo*.

3 Provide Information

"Let me tell you about our game," Ms. Lewis explains. "I'm going to say some of the words from the book, but I'm going to say them sound by sound, and I want you to blend the sounds together and guess the word." "Are they rhyming words?" Teri asks. "Sure," the teacher agrees. "I'll say two words that rhyme, sound by sound, for you to guess." She says the sounds /f/ /ŏ/ /x/ and /b/ /ŏ/ /x/ and the children correctly blend the sounds and say the words *fox* and *box*. She repeats the procedure for *clock–tock, come–dumb, big–pig, new–blue, rose–hose, game–lame*, and *slow–crow*. Ms. Lewis stops and talks about how to "bump" or blend the sounds to figure out the words. She models how she blends the sounds to form the word. "Make the words harder," several children say, and Ms. Lewis offers several more-difficult pairs of rhyming words, including *chick–trick* and *beetle–tweedle*.

4 Guide Practice

Ms. Lewis continues playing the guessing game, but now she segments individual words. As each child correctly identifies a word, that child leaves the group and goes to work with the aide. Finally, six children remain who need additional practice. They continue blending *do, new*, and other two-sound words and some of the easier three-sound words, including *box, come*, and *like*.

5 Assess Learning

Through the guided practice part of the lesson, Ms. Lewis informally checks to see which children need more practice blending sounds into words and provides additional practice for them.

Sound-Matching Activities. In sound matching, children choose one of several words beginning with a particular sound or say a word that begins with a particular sound (Yopp, 1992). For these games, teachers use familiar objects (e.g., feather, toothbrush, book) and toys (e.g., small plastic animals, toy trucks, artificial fruits and vegetables), as well as pictures of familiar objects.

Teachers can play a sound-matching guessing game (Lewkowicz, 1994). For this game, teachers collect two boxes and pairs of objects to place in the boxes (e.g., forks, mittens, erasers, combs, and books); one item from each pair is placed in each box. After the teacher shows children the objects in the boxes and they name them together, two children play the game. One child selects an object, holds it, and pronounces the initial (or medial or final) sound. The second child chooses the same object from the second box and holds it up. Classmates check to see if the two players are holding the same object.

Children also identify rhyming words as part of sound-matching activities: They name a word that rhymes with a given word and identify rhyming words from familiar songs and stories. As children listen to parents and teachers read Dr. Seuss books, such as *Fox in Socks* (1965) and *Hop on Pop* (1963), and other wordplay books, they refine their understanding of rhyme.

Sound-Isolation Activities. Teachers say a word and then children identify the sounds at the beginning, middle, or end of the word, or teachers and children isolate sounds as they sing familiar songs. Yopp (1992) created these new verses to the tune of "Old MacDonald Had a Farm":

> What's the sound that starts these words:
> Chicken, chin, and cheek?
> (wait for response)
>
> /ch/ is the sound that starts these words:
> Chicken, chin, and cheek.
> With a /ch/, /ch/ here, and a /ch/, /ch/ there,
> Here a /ch/, there a /ch/, everywhere a /ch/, /ch/.
>
> /ch/ is the sound that starts these words:
> Chicken, chin, and cheek. (p. 700)

Teachers change the question at the beginning of the verse to focus on medial and final sounds. For example:

> What's the sound in the middle of these words?
> Whale, game, and rain. (p. 700)

And for final sounds:

> What's the sound at the end of these words?
> Leaf, cough, and beef. (p. 700)

Teachers also set out trays of objects and ask children to choose the one object that doesn't belong because it begins with a different sound. For example, from a tray with a toy pig, a puppet, a teddy bear, and a pen, the teddy bear doesn't belong.

Sound-Blending Activities. Children blend sounds in order to combine them to form a word. For example, children blend the sounds /d/ /ŭ/ /k/ to form the word *duck*. Teachers play the "What am I thinking of?" guessing game with children by identifying several characteristics of the item and then saying its name, articulating each of the sounds slowly and separately (Yopp, 1992). Then children blend the sounds and identify the word, using the phonological and semantic information that the teacher provided. For example:

I'm thinking of a small animal that lives in the pond when it is young. When it is an adult, it lives on land and it is called a /f/ /r/ /ō/ /g/. What is it?

The children blend the sounds to pronounce the word *frog*. Then the teacher can move into phonics and spelling by setting out magnetic letters for children to arrange to spell *frog*. In this example, the teacher connects the game with a thematic unit, thereby making the game more meaningful for children.

Sound-Addition and -Substitution Activities.

Children play with words and create nonsense words as they add or substitute sounds in words in songs they sing or in books that are read aloud to them. Teachers read wordplay books such as Pat Hutchins's *Don't Forget the Bacon!* (1989), in which a boy leaves for the store with a mental list of four items to buy. As he walks, he repeats his list, substituting words each time: "A cake for tea" changes to "a cape for me" and then to "a rake for leaves." Children suggest other substitutions, such as "a game for a bee."

Students substitute sounds in refrains of songs (Yopp, 1992). For example, students can change the "Ee-igh, ee-igh, oh!" refrain in "Old MacDonald Had a Farm" to "Bee-bigh, bee-bigh, boh!" to focus on the initial /b/ sound. Teachers can choose one sound, such as /sh/, and have children substitute it for the beginning sound in their names and in words for items in the classroom. For example, *Jimmy* becomes *Shimmy*, *José* becomes *Shosé*, and *clock* becomes *shock*.

Sound-Segmentation Activities.

One of the more difficult phonemic awareness activities is segmentation, in which children isolate the sounds in a spoken word (Yopp, 1988). An introductory segmentation activity is to draw out the beginning sound in words. Children enjoy exaggerating the initial sound in their own names and other familiar words. For example, a pet guinea pig named Popsicle lives in Mrs. Firpo's classroom, and the children exaggerate the beginning sound of her name so that it is pronounced as "P-P-P-Popsicle." Children can also pick up objects or pictures of objects and identify the initial sound; a child who picks up a toy tiger says, "This is a truck and it starts with /t/."

From that beginning, children move to identifying all the sounds in a word. Using a toy truck again, the child would say, "This is a truck, /t/ /r/ /ŭ/ /k/." Yopp (1992) suggests singing a song to the tune of "Twinkle, Twinkle, Little Star" in which children segment entire words. Here is one example:

> Listen, listen
> To my word
> Then tell me all the sounds you heard: coat
> (slowly)
> /k/ is one sound
> /o–/ is two
> /t/ is last in coat
> It's true. (p. 702)

After several repetitions of the verse segmenting other words, the song ends this way:

> Thanks for listening
> To my words
> And telling all the sounds you heard! (p. 702)

Teachers also use Elkonin boxes to teach students to segment words; this activity comes from the work of Russian psychologist D. B. Elkonin (Clay, 2005a). As seen in Figure 5–2, the teacher shows an object or a picture of an object and draws a row of boxes, with one box for each sound in the name of the object or picture. Then the teacher or a child moves a marker into each box as the sound is pronounced. Children can move small markers onto cards on their desks, or the teacher can draw the boxes on

Figure 5–2 ◆ Ways to Use Elkonin Boxes

Type	Goal	Steps in the Activity
Phonemic Awareness	Segmenting sounds in a one-syllable word	1. Show children an object or a picture of an object with a one-syllable name, such as a duck, game, bee, or cup. 2. Prepare a diagram with a row of boxes, side-by-side, corresponding to the number of sounds heard in the name of the object. Draw the row of boxes on the chalkboard or on a small dry-erase board. For example, draw two boxes to represent the two sounds in *bee* or three boxes for the three sounds in *duck*. 3. Distribute coins or other small items to use as markers. 4. Say the name of the object slowly and move a marker into each box as the sound is pronounced. Then have children repeat the procedure. *(diagram of a row of three boxes with a marker in the first box and two markers with arrows pointing to the second and third boxes)*
	Segmenting syllables in a multisyllabic word	1. Show children an object or a picture of an object with a multisyllabic name, such as a butterfly, alligator, cowboy, or umbrella. 2. Prepare a diagram with a row of boxes, corresponding to the number of syllables in the name of the object. For example, draw four boxes to represent the four syllables in *alligator*. 3. Distribute markers. 4. Say the name of the object slowly and move a marker into each box as the syllable is pronounced. Then have children repeat the procedure.
Spelling	Representing sounds with letters	1. Draw a row of boxes corresponding to the number of sounds heard in a word. For example, draw two boxes for *go*, three boxes for *ship*, and four boxes for *frog*. 2. Pronounce the word, pointing to each box as the corresponding sound is pronounced. 3. Have the child write the letter or letters representing the sound in each box.
	Applying spelling patterns	1. Draw a row of boxes corresponding to the number of sounds heard in a word. For example, draw three boxes for the word *duck, game,* or *light*. 2. Pronounce the word, pointing to each box as the corresponding sound is pronounced. 3. Have the child write the letter or letters representing the sound in each box. 4. Pronounce the word again and examine how each sound is spelled. Insert additional unpronounced letters to complete the spelling patterns. *(diagram of three boxes containing the handwritten letters "d", "u", "ck")*

the chalkboard and use tape or small magnets to hold the larger markers in place. Elkonin boxes can also be used for spelling activities: When a child is trying to spell a word, such as *duck*, the teacher can draw three boxes, do the segmentation activity, and then have the child write the letters representing each sound in the boxes.

Children are experimenting with oral language in these activities. They stimulate children's interest in language and provide valuable experiences with books and words. Effective teachers recognize the importance of building this foundation as children are beginning to read and write. Guidelines for phonemic awareness activities are reviewed here.

Guidelines
for Teaching Phonemic Awareness

► Begin with oral activities using objects and pictures, but after children learn to identify the letters of the alphabet, add reading and writing components.

► Emphasize experimentation as children sing songs and play word games because these activities are intended to be fun.

► Read and reread wordplay books, and encourage children to experiment with rhyming words, alliteration, and other wordplay activities.

► Teach minilessons on manipulating words, moving from easier to more-complex levels.

► Emphasize blending and segmenting because children need these two strategies for phonics and spelling.

► Use small-group activities so children can be more actively involved in manipulating language.

► Teach phonemic awareness in the context of authentic reading and writing activities.

► Spend 20 hours teaching phonemic awareness strategies, but recognize that children develop phonemic awareness at different rates and that some children will need more or less instruction.

Nurturing English Learners

It's more difficult to develop English learners' phonemic awareness than native English speakers' because they're just learning to speak English; however, this training is worthwhile for English learners as long as familiar and meaningful words are used (Riches & Genesee, 2006). Teachers create a rich literacy environment and begin by reading books and poems aloud and singing songs so children can learn to recognize and pronounce English sound patterns.

To plan effective phonemic awareness instruction, teachers need to be familiar with English learners' home languages and understand how they differ from English (Peregoy & Boyle, 2008). Instruction should begin with sounds that children can pronounce easily and that don't conflict with those in their home language. Sounds that aren't present in children's home language or those that they don't perceive as unique, such as /ch/–/sh/ or /ĕ/–/ĭ/ for Spanish speakers, are more difficult. Children may need more time to practice producing and manipulating these difficult sounds.

Researchers recommend explicit instruction on phonemic awareness and practice opportunities for English learners (Snow, Burns, & Griffin, 1998). They sing familiar songs and play language games like native speakers do, but teachers also draw ELs' attention to pronouncing English sounds and words. Teachers often integrate phonemic awareness training, vocabulary instruction, and reading and writing activities to show how oral language sounds are represented by letters in written words (Peregoy & Boyle, 2008).

Phonemic awareness is a common underlying linguistic ability that transfers from one language to another (Riches & Genesee, 2006). Children who have learned to read in their home language are phonemically aware, and this knowledge supports their reading and writing development in English.

Assessing Children's Phonemic Awareness

Through phonemic awareness instruction, children learn strategies for segmenting, blending, and substituting sounds in words. Teachers often monitor their learning as

Assessment Tools

Phonemic Awareness

Kindergarten and first-grade teachers monitor children's learning by observing them during classroom activities, and they screen, monitor, diagnose, and document their growing phonemic awareness by administering these tests:

◆ **Dynamic Indicators of Basic Early Literacy Skills (DIBELS): Phoneme Segmentation Fluency Subtest** (Kaminski & Good, 1996)

This individually administered subtest assesses children's ability to segment words with two and three phonemes. Multiple forms are available so that this test can be used periodically to monitor children's progress. The test is available free of charge on the DIBELS website, but there is a charge for analyzing and reporting the test results.

◆ **Phonological Awareness Literacy Screening (PALS) System: Rhyme Awareness and Beginning Sound Subtests** (Invernizzi, Meier, & Juel, 2003)

The kindergarten level of PALS includes brief subtests to assess young children's phonemic awareness. Children look at pictures and supply rhyming words or produce the beginning sounds for picture names. The grades 1–3 tests also include phonemic awareness subtests for children who score below grade level on other tests. PALS is available from the University of Virginia; it's free for Virginia teachers, but teachers in other states pay for it.

◆ **Test of Phonological Awareness (TPA)** (Torgesen & Bryant, 2004)

This group test designed for children ages 5–8 measures their ability to isolate individual sounds in spoken words and understand the relationship between letters and phonemes. It takes 40 minutes. The TPA is available from LinguiSystems.

◆ **Yopp-Singer Test of Phonemic Segmentation** (Yopp, 1995)

This individually administered oral test for kindergartners measures their ability to accurately segment the phonemes in words; it contains 22 items and is administered in less than 10 minutes. The test is free; it can be found in the September 1995 issue of *The Reading Teacher* or online. A Spanish version is also available.

Information gained from classroom observations and these assessments is used to identify students who aren't yet phonemically aware, plan appropriate instruction, and monitor their progress.

they participate in phonemic awareness activities: When children sort picture cards according to beginning sounds or identify rhyming words in a familiar song, they're demonstrating their ability to manipulate sounds. Teachers also administer one of several readily available phonemic awareness tests to screen children's ability to use phonemic awareness strategies, monitor their progress, and document their learning. Four phonemic-awareness tests are described in the Assessment Tools feature on the preceding page.

Why Is Phonemic Awareness Important?

A clear connection exists between phonemic awareness and learning to read; researchers have concluded that phonemic awareness is a prerequisite for learning to read. As they become phonemically aware, children recognize that speech can be segmented into smaller units; this knowledge is very useful as they learn about sound-symbol correspondences and spelling patterns (Cunningham, 2007).

Children can be explicitly taught to segment and blend speech, and those who receive approximately 20 hours of training in phonemic awareness do better in both reading and spelling (Juel, Griffith, & Gough, 1986). Phonemic awareness is also nurtured in spontaneous ways by providing children with language-rich environments and emphasizing wordplay as teachers read books aloud and engage children in singing songs, chanting poems, and telling riddles.

Moreover, phonemic awareness has been shown to be the most powerful predictor of later reading achievement. Klesius, Griffith, and Zielonka (1991) found that children who began first grade with strong phonemic awareness did well regardless of the kind of reading instruction they received, and no one type of instruction was better for children who were low in phonemic awareness at the beginning of first grade.

PHONICS

Phonics is the set of relationships between phonology (the sounds in speech) and orthography (the spelling patterns of written language). The emphasis is on spelling patterns, not individual letters, because there isn't a one-to-one correspondence between phonemes and graphemes in English. Sounds are spelled in different ways. There are several reasons for this variety. One reason is that sounds, especially vowels, vary according to their location in a word (e.g., *go–got*). Adjacent letters often influence how letters are pronounced (e.g., *bed–bead*), as do vowel markers such as the final *e* (e.g., *bit–bite*) (Shefelbine, 1995).

Language origin, or etymology, of words also influences their pronunciation. For example, the *ch* digraph is pronounced in several ways; the three most common are /ch/ as in *chain* (English), /sh/ as in *chauffeur* (French), and /k/ as in *chaos* (Greek). Neither the location of the digraph within the word nor adjacent letters account for these pronunciation differences: In all three words, the *ch* digraph is at the beginning of the word and is followed by two vowels, the first of which is *a*. Some letters in words aren't pronounced, either. In words such as *write*, the *w* isn't pronounced, even though it probably was at one time. The same is true for the *k* in *knight*, *know*, and *knee*. "Silent" letters in words such as *sign* and *bomb* reflect their parent words, *signature* and *bombard*, and have been retained for semantic, not phonological, reasons (Venezky, 1999).

New Literacies
Online Games

Students practice phonics and spelling concepts they're learning as they play online games. These interactive games provide opportunities for students to match letters to pictures of objects illustrating their sounds, identify rhymes, sort words according to vowel pattern, and spell words, for example. They provide engaging practice opportunities because the colorful screen displays, sound effects, fast-paced action, and feedback about game performance grab students' attention, maintain their enthusiasm, and scaffold their learning (Chamberlain, 2005; Kinzer, 2005).

Teachers choose games based on concepts they're teaching and students' achievement levels. Teachers preview the games and bookmark those they want to use, and then students use the bookmarks to quickly access the game they'll play at the computer center. They play the games individually or with partners. Because most young children are experienced game-players and because many games have tutorial features, teachers don't have to spend much time introducing them, but it's helpful to have a parent-volunteer or older student available to assist when there are problems.

Here are some suggested websites with phonics and spelling games:

Game Goo: Learning That Sticks

www.earobics.com/gamegoo
Visit the Game Goo website to play games to practice letter recognition, phonics, synonym, antonym, and spelling concepts. The fast-action games are divided into three levels of difficulty.

Gamequarium

www.gamequarium.com
Check this mega-website with links to alphabet, phonics, and spelling games at other websites. Although hundreds of literacy-related games can be accessed through this site, Gamequarium is only a portal, so the quality of the games and computer requirements vary.

PBS Kids

www.pbskids.org
Play games and view video clips from the popular PBS series "Between the Lions," "Sesame Street," Reading Rainbow," "Word World," and "Super Why!" to learn letters of the alphabet, rhyming words, phonics, and spelling concepts.

RIF's Reading Planet Club

www.rif.org/readingplanet/
Join the Reading Planet Club at the Reading Is Fundamental website to play a variety of phonics, word-study, and spelling games at the Game Station, and be sure to check out the Book Zone and Express Yourself to read about featured authors and books and learn more about writing.

Scholastic Kids

www.scholastic.com
Check Scholastic's Learning Arcade to play concentration, make a word, word scrabble, and word find games featuring Clifford the Big Red Dog and other book characters. Also, visit the Homework Hub to create spelling scrambles and word searches using students' spelling words (up to 10 words).

Sesame Workshop

www.sesameworkshop.org
Try these interactive games about letters, consonant sounds, and rhyming words featuring Big Bird, Elmo, Grover, and the other familiar Sesame Street characters. These easy-to-play games engage young children without overwhelming them.

All of the games are free, but advertisements pop up at some sites.

When primary-grade teachers incorporate technology, such as interactive phonics and spelling games, into their literacy program, children are enhancing their traditional reading and writing competencies as well as their new 21st-century literacy.

Phonics Concepts

Phonics explains the relationships between phonemes and graphemes. There are 44 phonemes in English, and they are represented by the 26 letters. The alphabetic principle suggests that there should be a one-to-one correspondence between phonemes and graphemes, so that each sound is consistently represented by one letter. English, however, is an imperfect phonetic language, and there are more than 500 ways to represent the 44 phonemes using single letters or combinations of letters. Consider the word *day*: The two phonemes, /d/ and /ā/, are represented by three letters. The letter *d* is a consonant, and *a* and *y* are vowels. Interestingly, *y* isn't always a vowel; it's a consonant at the beginning of a word and a vowel at the end. When two vowels are side by side at the end of a word, they represent a long vowel sound. In *day*, the vowel sound is long *a*. Primary-grade students learn these phonics concepts to decode unfamiliar words.

Consonants. Phonemes are classified as either consonants or vowels. The consonants are *b, c, d, f, g, h, j, k, l, m, n, p, q, r, s, t, v, w, x, y*, and *z*. Most consonants represent a single sound consistently, but there are some exceptions. *C*, for example, doesn't represent a sound of its own: When it's followed by *a, o*, or *u*, it is pronounced /k/ (e.g., *castle, coffee, cut*), and when it's followed by *e, i*, or *y*, it is pronounced /s/ (e.g., *cell, city, cycle*). *G* represents two sounds, as the word *garbage* illustrates: It's usually pronounced /g/ (e.g., *glass, go, green, guppy*), but when *g* is followed by *e, i*, or *y*, it's pronounced /j/, as in *giant*. *X* is also pronounced differently according to its location in a word. At the beginning of a word, it's often pronounced /z/, as in *xylophone*, but sometimes the letter name is used, as in *x-ray*. At the end of a word, *x* is pronounced /ks/, as in *box*. The letters *w* and *y* are particularly interesting: At the beginning of a word or a syllable, they're consonants (e.g., *wind, yard*), but when they're in the middle or at the end, they are vowels (e.g., *saw, flown, day, by*).

Two kinds of combination consonants are blends and digraphs. Consonant blends occur when two or three consonants appear next to each other in words and their individual sounds are "blended" together, as in *grass, belt*, and *spring*. Consonant digraphs are letter combinations representing single sounds that aren't represented by either letter; the four most common are *ch* as in *chair* and *each*, *sh* as in *shell* and *wish*, *th* as in *father* and *both*, and *wh* as in *whale*. Another consonant digraph is *ph*, as in *photo* and *graph*.

Vowels. The remaining five letters—*a, e, i, o*, and *u*—represent vowels, and *w* and *y* are vowels when used in the middle and at the end of syllables and words. Vowels often represent several sounds. The two most common are short (marked with the symbol ˘, called a *breve*) and long sounds (marked with the symbol ¯, called a *macron*). The short vowel sounds are /ă/ as in *cat*, /ĕ/ as in *bed*, /ĭ/ as in *win*, /ŏ/ as in *hot*, and /ŭ/ as in *cup*. The long vowel sounds—/ā/, /ē/, /ī/, /ō/, and /ū/—are the same as the letter names, and they are illustrated in the words *make, feet, bike, coal*, and *rule*. Long vowel sounds are usually spelled with two vowels, except when the long vowel is at the end of a one-syllable word or a syllable, as in *she* or *secret* and *try* or *tribal*. When *y* is a vowel by itself at the end of a word, it's pronounced as long *e* or long *i*, depending on the length of the word. In one-syllable words such as *by* and *cry*, the *y* is pronounced as long *i*, but in longer words such as *baby* and *happy*, the *y* is usually pronounced as long *e*.

Vowel sounds are more complicated than consonant sounds, and there are many vowel combinations representing long vowels and other vowel sounds. Consider these combinations:

ai as in *nail*	*oa* as in *soap*
au as in *laugh* and *caught*	*oi* as in *oil*

aw as in *saw*　　　　　　　　*oo* as in *cook* and *moon*
ea as in *peach* and *bread*　　*ou* as in *house* and *through*
ew as in *sew* and *few*　　　　*ow* as in *now* and *snow*
ia as in *dial*　　　　　　　　*oy* as in *toy*
ie as in *cookie*

Most vowel combinations are vowel digraphs or diphthongs: When two vowels represent a single sound, the combination is a vowel digraph (e.g., *nail*, *snow*), and when the two vowels represent a glide from one sound to another, the combination is a diphthong. Two vowel combinations that are consistently diphthongs are *oi* and *oy*, but other combinations, such as *ou* as in *house* (but not in *through*) and *ow* as in *now* (but not in *snow*), are diphthongs when they represent a glided sound. In *through*, the *ou* represents the /ū/ sound as in *moon*, and in *snow*, the *ow* represents the /ō/ sound.

When one or more vowels in a word are followed by an *r*, it's called an *r-controlled vowel* because the *r* influences the pronunciation of the vowel sound. For example, read these words aloud: *start, award, nerve, squirt, horse, word, surf, square, stairs, pearl, beard, cheer, where, here, pier, wire, board, floor, scored, fourth,* and *cure*. Some words have a single vowel plus *r* and others have two vowels plus *r*, or the *r* is in between the vowels. Single vowels with *r* are more predictable than the other types. The most consistent *r*-controlled vowels are *ar* as in *car* and *shark* and *or* as in *fork* and *born*. The remaining single vowel + *r* combinations, *er, ir,* and *ur*, are difficult to spell because they're often pronounced /ûr/ in words, including *herd, father, girls, first, burn,* and *nurse*.

Three-letter spellings of *r*-controlled vowels are more complicated; they include *-are* (*care*), *-ear* (*fear*), *-ere* (*here*), *-oar* (*roar*), and *-our* (*your*). Consider these *-ear* words: *bears, beard, cleared, early, earth, hear, heard, heart, learner, pear, pearls, spear, wearing, yearly,* and *yearn*. The vowel sound is pronounced in four ways. The most common pronunciation for *ear* is /ûr/, as in *earth, learner,* and *pearls*; this pronunciation is used when *ear* is followed by a consonant, except in *heart* and *beard*. The next most common pronunciation is found in *cleared* and *spear*, where the vowel sounds like the word *ear*. In several words, including *bear* and *wearing*, the vowel sound is pronounced as in the word *air*. Finally, in *heart*, *ear* is pronounced as in *car*. Teachers usually introduce the more-predictable ways to decode *r*-controlled vowels, but students learn words with less common pronunciations, including *award, courage, flour, heart, here, very,* and *work*, in other ways.

The vowels in the unaccented syllables of multisyllabic words are often softened and pronounced "uh," as in the first syllable of *about* and *machine*, and the final syllable of *pencil, tunnel, zebra,* and *selection*. This vowel sound is called *schwa* and is represented in dictionaries with ə, which looks like an inverted *e*.

Blending Into Words. Readers blend or combine sounds in order to decode words. Even though children may identify each sound, one by one, they must also be able to blend them into a word. For example, to read the short-vowel word *best*, children identify /b/ /ě/ /s/ /t/ and then combine them to form the word. For long-vowel words, children must identify the vowel pattern as well as the surrounding letters. In *pancake*, for example, children identify /p/ /ă/ /n/ /k/ /ā/ /k/ and recognize that the *e* at the end of the word is silent and marks the preceding vowel as long. Shefelbine (1995) emphasizes the importance of blending and explains that students who have difficulty decoding words usually know the sound-symbol correspondences but can't blend the sounds into recognizable words. The ability to blend sounds into words is part of phonemic awareness, and students who haven't had practice blending speech sounds into words are likely to have trouble blending sounds into words in order to decode unfamiliar words.

Phonograms. One-syllable words and syllables in longer words can be divided into two parts, the onset and the rime: The onset is the consonant sound, if any, that precedes the vowel, and the rime is the vowel and any consonant sounds that follow it. For example, in *show*, *sh* is the onset and *ow* is the rime, and in *ball*, *b* is the onset and *all* is the rime. For *at* and *up*, there is no onset; the entire word is the rime. Research has shown that children make more errors decoding and spelling the rime than the onset and more errors on vowels than on consonants (Caldwell & Leslie, 2005). In fact, rimes may provide an important key to word identification.

Wylie and Durrell (1970) identified 37 rimes, including *-ay*, *-ing*, *-oke*, and *-ump*, that are found in nearly 500 common words; these rimes and some words using each one are presented in Figure 5–3. Knowing these rimes and recognizing common words made from them are very helpful for beginning readers because they can use the words to decode other words (Cunningham, 2009). For example, when children know the *-ay* rime and recognize *say*, they use this knowledge to pronounce *clay*: They identify the *-ay* rime and blend *cl* with *ay* to decode the word. This strategy is called *decoding by analogy*, and you'll read more about it in Chapter 6, "Developing Students' Reading and Writing Fluency."

Teachers refer to rimes as *phonograms* or *word families* when they teach them, even though *phonogram* is a misnomer; by definition, a *phonogram* is a letter or group of letters that represent a single sound. Two of the rimes, *-aw* and *-ay*, represent single sounds, but the other 35 don't.

Beginning readers often read and write words using each phonogram. First and second graders can read and write these words made using *-ain*: *brain, chain, drain, grain, main, pain, plain, rain, sprain, stain,* and *train*. Students must be familiar with consonant blends and digraphs to read and spell these words. Teachers often post these word lists on a word families word wall, as shown in Figure 5–4. Each phonogram and the words made using it are listed in a separate section of the word wall. Teachers use the words on the word wall for a variety of phonics activities, and students refer to it to spell words when they're writing.

Check the Compendium of Instructional Procedures, which follows Chapter 12, for more information on the highlighted terms.

Figure 5–3 ◆ The 37 Rimes and Common Words Using Them

Rime	Examples	Rime	Examples
-ack	black, pack, quack, stack	-ide	bride, hide, ride, side
-ail	mail, nail, sail, tail	-ight	bright, fight, light, might
-ain	brain, chain, plain, rain	-ill	fill, hill, kill, will
-ake	cake, shake, take, wake	-in	chin, grin, pin, win
-ale	male, sale, tale, whale	-ine	fine, line, mine, nine
-ame	came, flame, game, name	-ing	king, sing, thing, wing
-an	can, man, pan, than	-ink	pink, sink, think, wink
-ank	bank, drank, sank, thank	-ip	drip, hip, lip, ship
-ap	cap, clap, map, slap	-it	bit, flit, quit, sit
-ash	cash, dash, flash, trash	-ock	block, clock, knock, sock
-at	bat, cat, rat, that	-oke	choke, joke, poke, woke
-ate	gate, hate, late, plate	-op	chop, drop, hop, shop
-aw	claw, draw, jaw, saw	-ore	chore, more, shore, store
-ay	day, play, say, way	-ot	dot, got, knot, trot
-eat	beat, heat, meat, wheat	-uck	duck, luck, suck, truck
-ell	bell, sell, shell, well	-ug	bug, drug, hug, rug
-est	best, chest, nest, west	-ump	bump, dump, hump, lump
-ice	mice, nice, rice, slice	-unk	bunk, dunk, junk, sunk
-ick	brick, pick, sick, thick		

Figure 5-4 ◆ Excerpt From a Word Wall of Phonograms

-ock		-oke		-old	
block	lock	broke	poke	bold	hold
clock	rock	Coke	smoke	cold	sold
dock	sock	choke	woke	fold	told
flock		joke		gold	
		*soak			

-op		-ore		-ot	
cop	pop	more	store	dot	lot
chop	plop	sore	tore	got	not
drop	shop	shore	wore	hot	shot
hop	stop	snore		knot	spot
mop	top				
		*door *pour *soar			
		*floor *your *war			

* = exceptions

Phonics Rules. Because English doesn't have a one-to-one correspondence between sounds and letters, linguists have created rules to clarify English spelling patterns. One rule is that *q* is followed by *u* and pronounced /kw/, as in *queen, quick,* and *earthquake; Iraq, Qantas,* and other names are exceptions. Another rule that has few exceptions relates to *r*-controlled vowels: *r* influences the preceding vowels so that they're neither long nor short. Examples are *car, wear,* and *four.* There are exceptions, however; one is *fire.*

Many rules aren't very useful because there are more exceptions than words that conform (Clymer, 1963). A good example is this long-vowel rule: When there are two adjacent vowels, the long vowel sound of the first one is pronounced and the second is silent; teachers sometimes call this the "when two vowels go walking, the first one does the talking" rule. Examples of conforming words are *meat, soap,* and *each.* There are many more exceptions, however, including *food, said, head, chief, bread, look, soup, does, too,* and *again.*

Only a few phonics rules have a high degree of utility for readers. Students should learn the ones that work most of the time because they're the most useful (Adams, 1990). Eight useful rules are listed in Figure 5–5. Even though they're fairly reliable, very few of them approach 100% utility. The rule about *r*-controlled vowels just mentioned has been calculated to be useful in 78% of words in which the letter *r* follows the vowel (Adams, 1990). Other commonly taught, useful rules have even lower percentages of utility. The CVC pattern rule—which says that when a one-syllable word has only one vowel and the vowel comes between two consonants, it is usually short, as in *bat, land,* and *cup*—is estimated to work only 62% of the time. Exceptions include *told, fall, fork,* and *birth.* The CVCe pattern rule—which says that when there are two vowels in a one-syllable word and one vowel is an *e* at the end of the word, the first vowel is long and the final *e* is silent—is estimated to work in 63% of CVCe words. Examples of conforming words are *came, hole,* and *pipe;* but three very common words—*have, come,* and *love*—are exceptions.

Figure 5–5 ◆ The Most Useful Phonics Rules

Pattern	Description	Examples	
Two sounds of *c*	The letter *c* can be pronounced as /k/ or /s/. When *c* is followed by *a*, *o*, or *u*, it's pronounced /k/—the hard *c* sound. When *c* is followed by *e*, *i*, or *y*, it's pronounced /s/—the soft *c* sound.	cat cough cut	cent city cycle
Two sounds of *g*	The sound associated with the letter *g* depends on the letter following it. When *g* is followed by *a*, *o*, or *u*, it's pronounced as /g/—the hard *g* sound. When *g* is followed by *e*, *i*, or *y*, it's usually pronounced /j/—the soft *g* sound. Exceptions include *get* and *give*.	gate go guess	gentle giant gypsy
CVC pattern	When a one-syllable word has only one vowel and the vowel comes between two consonants, it is usually short. One exception is *told*.	bat cup land	
Final *e* or CVCe pattern	When there are two vowels in a one-syllable word and one of them is an *e* at the end of the word, the first vowel is long and the final *e* is silent. Three exceptions are *have*, *come*, and *love*.	home safe cute	
CV pattern	When a vowel follows a consonant in a one-syllable word, the vowel is long. Exceptions include *the*, *to*, and *do*.	go be	
r-controlled vowels	Vowels that are followed by the letter *r* are overpowered and are neither short nor long. One exception is *fire*.	car dear	birth pair
-*igh*	When *gh* follows *i*, the *i* is long and the *gh* is silent. One exception is *neighbor*.	high night	
kn- and *wr*-	In words beginning with *kn*- and *wr*-, the first letter is not pronounced.	knee write	

Adapted from Clymer, 1963.

Teaching Phonics

The best way to teach phonics is through a combination of explicit instruction and authentic application activities. The National Reading Panel (2000) reviewed the research about phonics instruction and concluded that the most effective programs were systematic; that is, the most useful phonics skills are taught in a predetermined sequence. Most teachers begin with consonants and then introduce the short vowels so that children can read and spell consonant-vowel-consonant or CVC-pattern words, such as *dig* and *cup*. Then children learn about consonant blends and diagraphs and long vowels so that they can read and spell consonant-vowel-consonant-*e* or CVCe-pattern words, such as *broke* and *white*, and consonant-vowel-vowel-consonant or CVVC-pattern words, such as *clean*, *wheel*, and *snail*. Finally, children learn about the less common vowel diagraphs and diphthongs, such as *claw*, *bought*, *shook*, and *boil*, and *r*-controlled vowels, including *square*, *hard*, *four*, and *year*. Figure 5–6 details this sequence of phonics skills.

Children also learn strategies to use in identifying unfamiliar words (Mesmer & Griffith, 2005). Three of the most useful strategies are sounding out words, decoding by analogy, and applying phonics rules. When children sound out words, they convert letters and patterns of letters into sounds and blend them to pronounce the word; it's most effective when children are reading phonetically regular one-syllable words. In the second strategy, decoding by analogy, children apply their knowledge of phonograms to analyze the structure of an unfamiliar word (White, 2005). They use known words to recognize unfamiliar ones. For example, if children are familiar with will, they can use it to identify *grill*. They also apply phonics rules to identify unfamiliar words, such as *while* and *clean*. These strategies are especially useful when children don't recognize many words, but they become less important as readers gain more experience and can recognize most words automatically.

The second component of phonics instruction is daily opportunities for children to apply the phonics strategies and skills they're learning in authentic reading and writing activities (National Reading Panel, 2000). Cunningham and Cunningham (2002) estimate that the ratio of time spent on real reading and writing to time spent on phonics instruction should be 3 to 1. Without this meaningful application of what they are learning, phonics instruction is often ineffective (Dahl, Scharer, Lawson, & Grogan, 2001).

Phonics instruction begins in kindergarten when children learn to connect consonant and short vowel sounds to the letters, and it's completed by third grade because older students rarely benefit from it (Ivey & Baker, 2004; National Reading Panel, 2000). Guidelines for teaching phonics are presented here.

Be Strategic!

Phonics Strategies

Students apply their phonics knowledge to decode words when they use these strategies:

▶ Sound it out
▶ Decode by analogy
▶ Apply phonics rules

These strategies are most effective for decoding phonetically regular one-syllable words.

Guidelines

for Teaching Phonics

▶ Teach high-utility phonics concepts that are most useful for reading unfamiliar words.

▶ Follow a developmental continuum for systematic phonics instruction, beginning with rhyming and ending with phonics rules.

▶ Provide explicit instruction to teach phonics strategies and skills.

▶ Provide opportunities for students to apply what they are learning about phonics through word sorts, making words, interactive writing, and other literacy activities.

▶ Take advantage of teachable moments to clarify misunderstandings and infuse phonics instruction into literacy activities.

▶ Use oral activities to reinforce phonemic awareness strategies as students blend and segment written words during phonics and spelling instruction.

▶ Review phonics as part of spelling, when necessary, in the upper grades.

Figure 5–6 ◆ Sequence of Phonics Instruction

Grade	Skill	Description	Examples
K	More common consonants	Children identify consonant sounds, match sounds to letters, and substitute sounds in words.	/b/, /d/, /f/, /m/, /n/, /p/, /s/, /t/
K–1	Less common consonants	Children identify consonant sounds, match sounds to letters, and substitute sounds in words.	/g/, /h/, /j/, /k/, /l/, /q/, /v/, /w/, /x/, /y/, /z/
	Short vowels	Children identify the five short vowel sounds and match them to letters.	/ă/ = cat, /ĕ/ = bed, /ĭ/ = pig, /ŏ/ = hot, /ŭ/ = cut
	CVC pattern	Children read and spell CVC-pattern words.	dad, men, sit, hop, but
1	Consonant blends	Children identify and blend consonant sounds at the beginning and end of words.	/pl/ = plant /str/ = string
	Phonograms	Children break CVC words into onsets and rimes and use phonograms to form new words.	not: dot, shot, spot will: still, fill, drill
	Consonant digraphs	Children identify consonant diagraphs, match sounds to letters, and read and spell words with consonant digraphs.	/ch/ = chop /sh/ = dash /th/ = with /wh/ = when
	Long vowel sounds	Children identify the five long vowel sounds and match them to letters.	/ā/ = name, /ē/ = bee, /ī/ = ice, /ō/ = soap, /ū/ = tune
	CVCe pattern	Children read and spell CVCe-pattern words.	game, ride, stone
	Common long vowel digraphs	Children identify the vowel sound represented by common long vowel digraphs and read and spell words using them.	/ā/ = ai (rain), ay (day) /ē/ = ea (reach), ee (sweet) /ō/ = oa (soap), ow (know)
1–2	*w* and *y*	Children recognize when *w* and *y* are consonants and when they're vowels, and identify the sounds they represent.	window, yesterday y = /ī/ (by) y = /ē/ (baby)
	Phonograms	Children divide long-vowel words into onsets and rimes and use phonograms to form new words.	woke: joke, broke, smoke day: gray, day, stay
	Hard and soft consonant sounds	Children identify the hard and soft sounds represented by *c* and *g*, and read and spell words using them.	g = girl (hard), gem (soft) c = cat (hard), city (soft)
2–3	Less common vowel digraphs	Children identify the sounds of less common vowel digraphs and read and spell words using them.	/ô/ = al (walk), au (caught), aw (saw), ou (bought) /ā/ = ei (weigh) /ē/ = ey (key), ie (chief) /ī/ = ie (pie) /o͝o/ = oo (good), ou (could) /ū/ = oo (moon), ew (new), ue (blue), ui (fruit)
	Vowel diphthongs	Children identify the vowel diphthongs and read and write words using them.	/oi/ = oi (boil), oy (toy) /ou/ = ou (cloud), ow (down)
	Less common consonant digraphs	Children identify the sounds of less common consonant digraphs and read and write words using them.	ph = phone ng = sing gh = laugh tch = match
	r-controlled vowels	Children identify *r*-controlled vowel patterns and read and spell words using them.	/âr/ = hair, care, bear, there, their /ar/ = heart, star /er/ = clear, deer, here /or/ = born, more, warm /ûr/ = learn, first, work, burn

Explicit Instruction. Teachers present minilessons on phonics concepts to the whole class or to small groups of students, depending on the their instructional needs. They follow the minilesson format, explicitly presenting information about a phonics strategy or skill, demonstrating how to use it, and presenting words for students to use in guided practice, as Mrs. Firpo did in the vignette at the beginning of the chapter. During the minilesson, teachers use these activities to provide guided practice opportunities for students to manipulate sounds and read and write words:

◆ Sort objects, pictures, and word cards according to a phonics concept.
◆ Write letters or words on small dry-erase boards.
◆ Arrange magnetic letters or letter cards to spell words.
◆ Make class charts of words representing phonics concepts, such as the two sounds of *g* or the *-ore* phonogram.
◆ Make a poster or book of words representing a phonics concept.
◆ Locate other words exemplifying the spelling pattern in books students are reading.

The minilesson feature on the next page shows how a first-grade teacher teaches a minilesson on reading and spelling CVC-pattern words using final consonant blends.

Application Activities. Children apply the phonics concepts they're learning as they read and write and participate in teacher-directed activities. In interactive writing, for example, children segment words into sounds and take turns writing letters and sometimes whole words on the chart (McCarrier, Pinnell, & Fountas, 2000; Tompkins & Collom, 2004). Teachers help children correct any errors, and they take advantage of teachable moments to review consonant and vowel sounds and spelling patterns, as well as handwriting skills and rules for capitalization and punctuation. Making words, word ladders, and word sorts are other activities that children do to apply what they're learning about phoneme-grapheme correspondences, word families, and phonics rules.

Assessing Students' Phonics Knowledge

Primary teachers assess children's developing phonics knowledge using a combination of tests, observation, and reading and writing samples. They often use a test to screen children at the beginning of the school year, monitor their progress at midyear, and document their achievement at the end of the year. When children aren't making expected progress, teachers administer a test to diagnose the problem and plan for instruction. Four tests that assess children's phonics knowledge, including one designed for older, struggling readers, are described in the Assessment Tools feature on page 166.

Teaching Struggling Readers and Writers

Phonics

Struggling readers need to learn to decode words.

Phonics is a very useful tool for identifying unfamiliar words, and struggling readers need to learn to decode words. Most struggling students already know letter-sound relationships, but they guess at words based on the first letter or they sound out the letters, one by one, without blending the sounds or considering spelling patterns.

Instruction for students who can't decode words includes two components (Cunningham, 2009; McKenna, 2002): First, review word families, create a word wall divided into sections for words representing each phonogram, and teach students to decode by analogy. Second, teach spelling patterns and have students practice them using word sorts. Some teachers have students read decodable texts to practice particular phonics patterns. For example, this passage emphasizes /ă/ and the CVC pattern:

The cat sat on a mat. The cat was black. He sat and sat.
The black cat was sad. Too bad!

Even though publishers of these texts often tout their research base, Allington (2006) found no research to support their claims. Trade books at students' independent reading levels are more effective for decoding practice.

Sometimes teachers skip phonics instruction because they feel that struggling readers have been taught phonics without much benefit, but McKenna (2002) counters: "Unfortunately, there is no way to . . . bypass the decoding stage of reading development" (p. 9). Here's the reasoning: If students can't decode words, they won't become fluent readers; if they can't read fluently, they won't comprehend what they're reading; and if they can't comprehend, they won't become successful readers.

Minilesson

TOPIC: Decoding CVC Words With Final Consonant Blends
GRADE: First Grade
TIME: One 30-minute period

Mrs. Nazir is teaching her first graders about consonant blends. She introduced initial consonant blends to the class, and children practiced reading and spelling words, such as *club, drop*, and *swim*, that were chosen from the selection they were reading in their basal readers. Then, in small groups, they completed workbook pages and made words using plastic tiles with onsets and rimes printed on them. For example, using the *-ip* phonogram, they made *clip, drip, flip, skip*, and *trip*. This is the fifth whole-class lesson in the series. Today, Mrs. Nazir is introducing final consonant blends.

1 Introduce the Topic

Mrs. Nazir explains that blends are also used at the end of words. She writes these words on the chalkboard: *best, rang, hand, pink*, and *bump*. Together the children sound them out: They pronounce the initial consonant sound, the short vowel sound, and the final consonants. They blend the final consonants, then they blend the entire word and say it aloud. Children use the words in sentences to ensure that everyone understands them, and Dillon, T.J., Pauline, Cody, and Brittany circle the blends in the words on the chalkboard. The teacher points out that *st* is a familiar blend also used at the beginning of words, but that the other blends are used only at the end of words.

2 Share Examples

Mrs. Nazir says these words: *must, wing, test, band, hang, sink, bend*, and *bump*. The first graders repeat each word, isolate the blend, and identify it. Carson says, "The word is *must*—/m/ /ŭ/ /s/ /t/—and the blend is *st* at the end." Bryan points out that Ng is his last name, and everyone claps because his name is so special. Several children volunteer additional words: Dillon suggests *blast*, and Henry adds *dump* and *string*. Then the teacher passes out word cards and children read the words, including *just, lamp, went*, and *hang*. They sound out each word carefully, pronouncing the initial consonant, the short vowel, and the final consonant blend. Then they blend the sounds and say the word.

3 Provide Information

Mrs. Nazir posts a piece of chart paper, and labels it "The *-ink* Word Family." The children brainstorm these words with the *-ink* phonogram: *blink, sink, pink, rink, mink, stink*, and *wink*, and they take turns writing the words on the chart. They also suggest *twinkle* and *wrinkle*, and Mrs. Nazir adds them to the chart.

4 Guide Practice

Children create other word family charts using *-and, -ang, -ank, -end, -ent, -est, -ing, -ump*, and *-ust*. Each group brainstorms at least five words and writes them on the chart. Mrs. Nazir monitors children's work and helps them think of additional words and correct spelling errors. Then children post their word family charts and share them with the class.

5 Assess Learning

Mrs. Nazir observes the first graders as they brainstorm words, blend sounds, and spell the words. She notices several children who need more practice and will call them together for a follow-up lesson.

Assessment Tools

Phonics

Teachers monitor students' developing phonics knowledge by observing them during classroom activities and by administering these tests:

◆ **Observation Survey of Early Literacy Achievement (OS): Word Reading and Hearing and Recording Sounds in Words Subtests** (Clay, 2005b)

The OS includes six subtests. The Word Reading and Hearing and Recording Sounds in Words subtests are used to assess young children's ability to apply phonics concepts to decode and spell words. The subtests are administered individually, and children's scores for each subtest can be standardized and converted to stanines. The OS is published by Heinemann Books.

◆ **Dynamic Indicators of Basic Early Literacy Skills (DIBELS): Nonsense Word Fluency Subtest** (Kaminski & Good, 1996)

This individually administered subtest assesses young children's ability to apply phonics concepts to read two- and three-letter nonsense words (e.g., *ap, jid*). Multiple forms are available, so this test can be used to monitor children's progress during kindergarten and first grade. The test is available at the DIBELS website free of charge, but there's a charge for scoring tests and for reporting scores.

◆ **The Tile Test** (Norman & Calfee, 2004)

This individually administered test assesses K–2 students' knowledge of phonics. Children manipulate letter tiles to make words, and teachers also arrange tiles to spell words for them to read. The Tile Test can easily be administered in 10 to 15 minutes. It's available online, free of charge.

◆ **The Names Test: A Quick Assessment of Decoding Ability** (Cunningham, 1990; Duffelmeyer et al., 1994; Mather, Sammons, & Schwartz, 2006)

The Names Test measures older students' (grades 3–8) ability to decode words. The test is a list of names that illustrate phoneme-grapheme correspondences and phonics rules. As students read the names, teachers mark which ones they read correctly and which they mispronounce. Then teachers analyze the errors to determine which phonics concepts students haven't learned. This free assessment is available online.

These tests are useful assessment tools that teachers use to screen, monitor, diagnose, and document children's phonics knowledge and to make instructional decisions.

Teachers observe children as they participate in phonics activities and when they're reading and writing to see how they're applying the phonics strategies and skills they're learning. When children use magnetic letters to write words with the *-at* phonogram, such as *bat, cat, hat, mat, rat*, and *sat*, for example, they're demonstrating their phonics knowledge. They also show what they've learned during interactive writing, making words, and word sort activities. Similarly, as teachers listen to children read aloud or read children's writing, they analyze their errors to determine which phonics concepts children are confusing or those they don't yet understand.

What's the Role of Phonics in a Balanced Literacy Program?

Phonics is a controversial topic. Some parents and politicians, as well as even a few teachers, believe that most of our educational ills could be solved if children were taught to read using phonics. A few people still argue that phonics is a complete reading program, but that view ignores what we know about the interrelatedness of the four cueing systems. Reading is a complex process, and the phonological system works in conjunction with the semantic, syntactic, and pragmatic systems, not in isolation.

The controversy now centers on the best way to teach phonics. Marilyn Adams (1990), in her landmark review of the research on phonics instruction, recommends that phonics be taught within a balanced approach that integrates instruction in reading strategies and skills with meaningful opportunities for reading and writing. She emphasizes that phonics instruction should focus on the most useful information for identifying words, that it should be systematic and intensive, and that it should be completed by third grade.

SPELLING

Learning to spell is also part of "cracking the code." As children learn about phonics, they apply what they're learning through both reading and writing. Children's early spellings reflect what they know about phoneme-grapheme relationships, phonics rules, and spelling patterns. As their knowledge grows, their spelling increasingly approximates conventional spelling.

Students need to learn to spell words conventionally so that they can communicate effectively through writing. Learning phonics during the primary grades is part of spelling instruction, but students also need to learn other strategies and information about English orthography. In the past, weekly spelling tests were the main instructional approach; now, they're only one part of a comprehensive spelling program. Guidelines for spelling instruction are presented here.

Guidelines
for Teaching Spelling

▶ Analyze the errors in students' writing to provide appropriate spelling instruction based on their stage of development.

▶ Connect phonemic awareness, phonics, and spelling during minilessons by having students manipulate words orally and read and spell them.

▶ Guide students to use strategies to spell unfamiliar words.

▶ Teach students to spell high-frequency words before less common ones.

▶ Post words on word walls and use them for a variety of spelling activities.

▶ Involve students in making words, word ladders, word sorts, and other hands-on spelling activities.

▶ Consider spelling tests as only one part of an instructional program.

▶ Involve students in daily authentic reading and writing activities to apply their spelling knowledge.

Stages of Spelling Development

As young children begin to write, they create unique spellings, called *invented spelling*, based on their knowledge of phonology (Read, 1975). The children in Read's studies used letter names to spell words, such as *U* (*you*) and *R* (*are*), and they used consonant sounds rather consistently: *GRL* (*girl*), *TIGR* (*tiger*), and *NIT* (*night*). They used several unusual but phonetically based spelling patterns to represent affricates; for example, they replaced *tr* with *chr* (e.g., *CHRIBLES* for *troubles*) and *dr* with *jr* (e.g., *JRAGIN* for *dragon*). Words with long vowels were spelled using letter names: *MI* (*my*), *LADE* (*lady*), and *FEL* (*feel*). The children used several ingenious strategies to spell words with short vowels: The preschoolers selected letters to represent short vowels on the basis of place of articulation in the mouth. Short *i* was represented with *e*, as in *FES* (*fish*), short *e* with *a*, as in *LAFFT* (*left*), and short *o* with *i*, as in *CLIK* (*clock*). These spellings may seem odd to adults, but they are based on phonetic relationships.

Based on examinations of children's spellings, researchers have identified five stages that students move through on their way to becoming conventional spellers: emergent spelling, letter name-alphabetic spelling, within-word pattern spelling, syllables and affixes spelling, and derivational relations spelling (Bear, Invernizzi, Templeton, & Johnston, 2008). At each stage, students use different strategies and focus on particular aspects of spelling. The characteristics of the five stages are summarized in Figure 5–7.

Stage 1: Emergent Spelling. Children string scribbles, letters, and letterlike forms together, but they don't associate the marks they make with any specific phonemes. Spelling at this stage represents a natural, early expression of the alphabet and other written-language concepts. Children may write from left to right, right to left, top to bottom, or randomly across the page, but by the end of the stage, they have an understanding of directionality. Some emergent spellers have a large repertoire of letterforms to use in writing, whereas others repeat a small number of letters over and over. They use both upper- and lowercase letters but show a distinct preference for uppercase letters. Toward the end of the stage, children are beginning to discover how spelling works and that letters represent sounds in words. This stage is typical of 3- to 5-year-olds. During the emergent stage, children learn these concepts:

- The distinction between drawing and writing
- How to make letters
- The direction of writing on a page
- Some letter-sound matches

Stage 2: Letter Name-Alphabetic Spelling. Children learn to represent phonemes in words with letters. They develop an understanding of the alphabetic principle, that a link exists between letters and sounds. At first, the spellings are quite abbreviated and represent only the most prominent features in words. Children use only several letters of the alphabet to represent an entire word. Examples of early Stage 2 spelling are *D* (*dog*) and *KE* (*cookie*), and children may still be writing mainly with capital letters. Children slowly pronounce the word they want to spell, listening for familiar letter names and sounds.

In the middle of the letter name-alphabetic stage, children use most beginning and ending consonants and include a vowel in most syllables; they spell *like* as *lik* and *bed* as *bad*. By the end of the stage, they use consonant blends and digraphs and short-vowel patterns to spell *hat*, *get*, and *win*, but some still spell *ship* as *sep*. They can also spell

Figure 5–7 ◆ Stages of Spelling Development

Stage 1: Emergent Spelling
Children string scribbles, letters, and letterlike forms together, but they don't associate the marks they make with any specific phonemes. This stage is typical of 3- to 5-year-olds. Children learn these concepts:

- The distinction between drawing and writing
- How to make letters
- The direction of writing on a page
- Some letter-sound matches

Stage 2: Letter Name-Alphabetic Spelling
Children learn to represent phonemes in words with letters. At first, their spellings are quite abbreviated, but they learn to use consonant blends and digraphs and short-vowel patterns to spell many short-vowel words. Spellers are 5- to 7-year-olds. Children learn these concepts:

- The alphabetic principle
- Consonant sounds
- Short vowel sounds
- Consonant blends and digraphs

Stage 3: Within-Word Pattern Spelling
Students learn long-vowel patterns and *r*-controlled vowels, but they may confuse spelling patterns and spell *meet* as *mete*, and they reverse the order of letters, such as *form* for *from* and *gril* for *girl*. Spellers are 7- to 9-year-olds, and they learn these concepts:

- Long-vowel spelling patterns
- *r*-controlled vowels
- More-complex consonant patterns
- Diphthongs and other less common vowel patterns

Stage 4: Syllables and Affixes Spelling
Students apply what they have learned about one-syllable words to spell longer words, and they learn to break words into syllables. They also learn to add inflectional endings (e.g., *-es*, *-ed*, *-ing*) and to differentiate between homophones, such as *your–you're*. Spellers are often 9- to 11-year-olds, and they learn these concepts:

- Inflectional endings
- Rules for adding inflectional endings
- Syllabication
- Homophones

Stage 5: Derivational Relations Spelling
Students explore the relationship between spelling and meaning and learn that words with related meanings are often related in spelling despite changes in sound (e.g., *wise–wisdom*, *sign–signal*, *nation–national*). They also learn about Latin and Greek root words and derivational affixes (e.g., *amphi-*, *pre-*, *-able*, *-tion*). Spellers are 11- to 14-year-olds. Students learn these concepts:

- Consonant alternations
- Vowel alternations
- Latin affixes and root words
- Greek affixes and root words
- Etymologies

Adapted from Bear, Invernizzi, Templeton, & Johnston, 2008.

some CVCe words such as *name* correctly. Spellers at this stage are usually 5- to 7-year-olds. During the letter-name stage, children learn these concepts:

♦ The alphabetic principle
♦ Consonant sounds
♦ Short vowel sounds
♦ Consonant blends and digraphs

Stage 3: Within-Word Pattern Spelling. Students begin the within-word pattern stage when they can spell most one-syllable short-vowel words, and during this stage, they learn to spell long-vowel patterns and *r*-controlled vowels. They experiment with long-vowel patterns and learn that words such as *come* and *bread* are exceptions that don't fit the vowel patterns. Students may confuse spelling patterns and spell *meet* as *mete*, and they reverse the order of letters, such as *form* for *from* and *gril* for *girl*. They also learn about complex consonant sounds, including *-tch* (*match*) and *-dge* (*judge*), and less frequent vowel patterns, such as *oi/oy* (*boy*), *au* (*caught*), *aw* (*saw*), *ew* (*sew, few*), *ou* (*house*), and *ow* (*cow*). Students also become aware of homophones and compare long- and short-vowel combinations (*hope–hop*) as they experiment with vowel patterns. Students at this stage are 7- to 9-year-olds, and they learn these spelling concepts:

♦ Long-vowel spelling patterns
♦ *r*-controlled vowels
♦ More-complex consonant patterns
♦ Diphthongs and other less common vowel patterns

Stage 4: Syllables and Affixes Spelling. Students focus on syllables in this stage and apply what they've learned about one-syllable words to longer, multisyllabic words. They learn about inflectional endings (*-s, -es, -ed,* and *-ing*) and rules about consonant doubling, changing the final *y* to *i*, or dropping the final *e* before adding an inflectional suffix. They also learn about homophones and compound words and are introduced to some of the more-common prefixes and suffixes. Spellers in this stage are generally 9- to 11-year-olds. Students learn these concepts during the syllables and affixes stage of spelling development:

♦ Inflectional endings (*-s, -es, -ed, -ing*)
♦ Rules for adding inflectional endings
♦ Syllabication
♦ Homophones

Stage 5: Derivational Relations Spelling. Students explore the relationship between spelling and meaning during the derivational relations stage, and they learn that words with related meanings are often related in spelling despite changes in vowel and consonant sounds (e.g., *wise–wisdom, sign–signal, nation–national*). The focus in this stage is on morphemes, and students learn about Greek and Latin root words and affixes. They also begin to examine etymologies and the role of history in shaping how words are spelled. They learn about eponyms (words from people's names), such as *maverick* and *sandwich*. Spellers at this stage are 11- to 14-year-olds. Students learn these concepts at this stage of spelling development:

♦ Consonant alternations (e.g., *soft–soften, magic–magician*)
♦ Vowel alternations (e.g., *please–pleasant, define–definition, explain–explanation*)
♦ Greek and Latin affixes and root words
♦ Etymologies

Children's spelling provides evidence of their growing understanding of English orthography. The words they spell correctly show which phonics concepts, spelling patterns, and other language features they've learned to apply, and the words they invent and misspell show what they're still learning to use and those features of spelling that they haven't noticed or learned about. Invented spelling is sometimes criticized because it appears that students are learning bad habits by misspelling words, but researchers have confirmed that students grow more quickly in phonemic awareness, phonics, and spelling when they use invented spelling as long as they are also receiving spelling instruction (Snow, Burns, & Griffin, 1998). As students learn more about spelling, their invented spellings become more sophisticated to reflect their new knowledge, even if the words are still spelled incorrectly, and increasingly students spell more and more words correctly as they move through the stages of spelling development.

Nurturing English Learners

English learners move through the same five developmental stages that native English speakers do, but they move more slowly because they're less familiar with the letter-sound correspondences, spelling patterns, and grammar of English (Bear, Helman, Invernizzi, Templeton, & Johnston, 2007). Students' spelling development reflects their reading achievement, but it lags behind reading: When ELs learn a word, they begin by learning its meaning and how to pronounce it. Almost immediately, they're introduced to the word's written form, and with practice, they learn to recognize and read it. Soon they're writing the word, too. At first their spellings reflect what they know about the English spelling system, but with spelling instruction and reading and writing practice, they learn to spell words correctly. Because spelling is more demanding than reading, it's not surprising that students' knowledge about spelling grows this way.

It's essential that teachers learn about English learners' home language, especially about the ways it differs from English, and then they need to explicitly teach students about the contrasts because they're harder to learn than the similarities (Bear, Helman, Invernizzi, Templeton, & Johnston, 2007). Consider these written language differences, for example: Chinese uses syllable-length characters instead of letters; Arabic is written from right to left, and the way letters are formed varies according to their location within a word; and vowels aren't used in Croatian and Czech. Some languages, including Arabic, Spanish, Kiswahili (Swahili), and Russian, are more phonetically consistent than English; students who speak these languages are often confused by the number of ways a sound can be spelled in English. There are phonological differences, too: Many languages, including Korean, don't have the /th/ sound; there's no /p/ in Arabic, so Arabic speakers often substitute /b/ in English; and /l/ and /r/ sound alike to speakers of Asian languages. Vowels are particularly difficult for English learners because they're often pronounced differently in their home language. For example, Russian speakers don't differentiate between short and long vowels, and Spanish speakers often substitute /ĕ/ for /ā/ and /ŏ/ for /ŏ/. Many African and Asian languages, including Kiswahili, Punjabi, Chinese, and Thai, as well as Navajo, a Native American language, are tonal; in these languages, pitch, not spelling differences, is used to distinguish between words. In addition, there are syntactic differences that affect spelling: Hmong speakers don't add plural markers to nouns; Korean speakers add grammatical information to the end of verbs instead of using auxiliary verbs; and Chinese speakers aren't familiar with prefixes or suffixes because they're not used in their language.

Teachers base their instruction on English learners' stage of spelling development, and they emphasize the contrasts between students' home languages and English. At each developmental stage, teachers focus their instruction on concepts that confuse English learners, according to Bear and his colleagues (2007):

Emergent Stage. Students learn English letters, sounds, and words, and they learn that English is written from left to right and top to bottom, with spaces between words. Developing this awareness is more difficult for students whose home languages are not alphabetic.

Letter Name-Alphabetic Stage. Students learn that letters represent sounds, and the sounds that are the same in ELs' home languages and English are the easiest to learn. They learn both consonant and vowel sounds. Those consonant sounds that are more difficult include /d/, /j/, /r/, /sh/, and /th/. English learners often have difficulty pronouncing and spelling final consonant blends (e.g., *-st* as in *fast*, *-ng* as in *king*, *-mp* as in *stomp*, and *-rd* as in *board*). Long and short vowel sounds are especially hard because they're often pronounced differently than in students' home languages.

Within-Word Pattern Stage. Students move from representing individual sounds in words to using spelling patterns. They practice CVCe and CVVC spelling patterns and words that are exceptions to these rules; *r*-controlled vowels are especially tricky because they're found in common words, and sound often doesn't predict spelling (e.g., *bear/care/hair, bird/heard/fern/burst*). English learners also learn to spell homophones (e.g., *wear–where, to–too–two*) and contractions during this stage.

Syllables and Affixes Stage. Students learn spelling and grammar concepts together as they investigate verb forms (e.g., *talk–talked, take–took–taken, think–thought*), change adjectives to adverbs (e.g., *quick–quickly*), and add inflectional endings (e.g., *walks–walked–walking*) and comparatives and superlatives (e.g., *sunny–sunnier–sunniest*). They also learn to pronounce accented and unaccented syllables differently and to use the schwa sound in unaccented syllables.

Derivational Relations Stage. Students learn about Latin and Greek root words and vowel alternations in related words (e.g., *define–definition*). Some ELs use tonal changes to signal these relationships in their home languages, but they must learn that related words in English are signaled by similar spelling and changes in how the vowels are pronounced.

Spelling instruction for English learners is similar to that for native speakers: Teachers use a combination of explicit instruction, word sorts and other practice activities, and authentic reading and writing activities. The biggest difference is that ELs need more instruction on the English spelling concepts that confuse them, often because these features aren't used in their home languages.

Teaching Spelling

Perhaps the best-known way to teach spelling is through weekly spelling tests, but tests should never be considered a complete spelling program. To become good spellers, students need to learn about the English orthographic system and move through the stages of spelling development. They develop strategies to use in spelling unknown words and gain experience in using dictionaries and other resources. A complete spelling program includes the following components:

◆ Teaching spelling strategies
◆ Matching instruction to students' stage of spelling development
◆ Providing daily reading and writing opportunities
◆ Teaching students to learn to spell high-frequency words

Students learn spelling strategies that they can use to figure out the spelling of unfamiliar words. As students move through the stages of spelling development, they

Word Sorts
This second grader is participating in a phonics word sort: She's arranging letter cards to spell long *e* words that use the CVVC vowel pattern, including *mean*, *beat*, *peach*, *read*, and *cream*. Her teacher began the lesson by identifying specific words for the students to spell using small paper letter cards, and now they're rearranging them to spell other long e words that follow the CVVC pattern. Some students, including this girl, work independently while others collaborate with classmates for this spelling lesson. Afterward, the teacher will place several sets of these letter cards in a literacy center for students who need extra practice spelling long *e* words. Later, they'll examine other spelling patterns using word sorts.

become increasingly more sophisticated in their use of phonological, semantic, and historical knowledge to spell words; that is, they become more strategic. Important spelling strategies include the following:

◆ Segmenting the word and spelling each sound, often called *sound it out*
◆ Spelling unknown words by analogy to familiar words
◆ Applying affixes to root words
◆ Proofreading to locate spelling errors in a rough draft
◆ Locating the spelling of unfamiliar words in a dictionary

Teachers often give the traditional *sound it out* advice when young children ask how to spell an unfamiliar word, but teachers provide more useful information when they suggest that students use a strategic *think it out* approach. This advice reminds students that spelling involves more than phonological information and encourages them to think about spelling patterns, root words and affixes, and what the word looks like.

Two of the most important ways that students learn to spell are through daily reading and writing activities. Students who are good readers tend to be good spellers, too: As they read, students visualize words—the shape of the word and the configuration of letters within it—and they use this knowledge to spell many words correctly and to recognize when a word they've written doesn't look right. Through writing, of course, students gain valuable practice using the strategies they have learned to spell words. And, as teachers work with students to proofread and edit their writing, they learn more about spelling and other writing conventions.

In addition to reading and writing activities, students learn about the English orthographic system through minilessons about phonics, high-frequency words,

MiniLesson

TOPIC: Spelling -at Family Words
GRADE: First Grade
TIME: One 10-minute period

Mr. Cheng teaches phonics skills during guided reading lessons. He introduces, practices, and reviews phonics concepts using words from selections his first graders are reading. The children decode and spell words using letter and word cards, magnetic letters, and small dry-erase boards and pens.

1 Introduce the Topic

Mr. Cheng holds up a copy of *At Home*, the small paperback level E book the children read yesterday, and asks them to reread the title. Then he asks the children to identify the first word, *at*. After they read the word, he hands a card with the word *at* written on it to each of the six children in the guided reading group. "Who can read this word?" he asks. Several children recognize it immediately, and others carefully sound out the two-letter word.

2 Share Examples

Mr. Cheng asks children to think about rhyming words: "Who knows what rhyming words are?" Mike answers that rhyming words sound alike at the end—for example, *Mike, bike*, and *like*. The teacher explains that there are many words in English that rhyme, and that today, they are going to read and write words that rhyme with *at*. "One rhyming word is *cat*," he explains. Children name rhyming words, including *hat, fat*, and *bat*. Mr. Cheng helps each child in the group to name at least three rhyming words.

3 Provide Information

Mr. Cheng explains that children can spell these *at* words by adding a consonant in front of *at*. For example, he places the foam letter *c* in front of his *at* card, and the children blend *c* to *at* to decode *cat*. Then he repeats the procedure by substituting other foam letters for the *c* to spell *bat, fat, hat, mat, pat, rat*, and *sat*. He continues the activity until every child successfully decodes one of the words.

4 Guide Practice

Mr. Cheng passes out small plastic trays with foam letters to each child and asks them to add one of the letters to their *at* cards to spell the words as he pronounces them. He continues the activity until children have had several opportunities to spell each word, and they can quickly choose the correct initial consonant to spell it. Then Mr. Cheng collects the *at* cards and trays with foam letters.

5 Assess Learning

Mr. Cheng passes out small dry-erase boards and pens. He asks the first graders to write the words as he says each one aloud: *cat, hat, mat, pat, rat, sat, bat, fat*. He carefully observes as each child segments the onset and rime to spell the word. The children hold up their boards to show him their spellings. Afterward, children erase the word and repeat the process, writing the next word. After children write all eight words, Mr. Cheng quickly jots a note about which children need additional practice with the -at word family before continuing with the guided reading lesson.

spelling rules, and spelling strategies. The minilesson feature on the preceding page shows how Mr. Cheng teaches his first graders to spell *-at* family words. Then in the following sections, you'll read about a number of spelling activities that expand students' spelling knowledge and help them move through the stages of spelling development.

Word Walls. Teachers use two types of word walls in their classrooms. One word wall features "important" words from books students are reading or thematic units. Words may be written on a large sheet of paper hanging in the classroom or on word cards and placed in a large pocket chart. Then students refer to these word walls when they're writing. Seeing the words posted on word walls and other charts in the classroom and using them in their writing help students learn to spell the words.

The second type of word wall displays high-frequency words. Researchers have identified the most commonly used words and recommend that students learn to spell 100 of these words because of their usefulness. The most frequently used words represent more than 50% of all the words children and adults write! Figure 5–8 lists the 100 most frequently used words.

Be Strategic!

Spelling Strategies

Students use these strategies to spell words and to verify that words they've written are spelled correctly:

► Sound it out
► Spell by analogy
► Apply affixes
► Proofread
► Check a dictionary

Sounding out spellings works best for spelling phonetically regular words in first and second grade; later, students learn more-effective strategies to think out correct spellings for longer words.

Figure 5–8 ◆ The 100 Most Frequently Used Words

A		B	C	D E	
a	and	back	came	day	do
about	are	be	can	did	don't
after	around	because	could	didn't	down
all	as	but			
am	at	by			
an					

F G		H		I J		K L	
for		had	his	I	is	know	
from		have	home	if	it	like	
get		he	house	in	just	little	
got		her	how	into			
		him					

M N		O		P Q R		S	
man	no	of	our	people		said	she
me	not	on	out	put		saw	so
mother	now	one	over			school	some
my		or				see	

T		U V	W X		Y Z
that	think	up	was	when	you
the	this	us	we	who	your
them	time	very	well	will	
then	to		went	with	
there	too		were	would	
they	two		what		
things					

Making Words. Teachers choose a five- to eight-letter word (or longer words for older students) and prepare sets of letter cards for a making words activity (Cunningham & Cunningham, 1992). Then students use the cards to practice spelling words and to review spelling patterns and rules. They arrange and rearrange the cards to spell one-letter words, two-letter words, three-letter words, and so forth, until they use all the letters to spell the original word. Second graders, for example, can create these words using the letters in *weather: a, at, we, he, the, are, art, ear, eat, hat, her, hear, here, hate, heart, wheat, there,* and *where.*

Word Sorts. Students use word sorts to explore, compare, and contrast word features as they sort a pack of word cards. Teachers prepare word cards for students to sort into two or more categories according to their spelling patterns or other criteria (Bear et al., 2008). Sometimes teachers tell students what categories to use, which makes the sort a closed sort; when students determine the categories themselves, the sort is an open sort. Students can sort word cards and then return them to an envelope for future use, or they can glue the cards onto a sheet of paper.

Interactive Writing. Teachers use interactive writing to teach spelling concepts as well as other concepts about written language. Because correct spelling and legible handwriting are courtesies for readers, they emphasize correct spelling as students take turns to collaboratively write a message. It is likely that students will misspell a few words as they write, so teachers take advantage of these "teachable moments" to clarify students' misunderstandings. Through interactive writing, students learn to use a variety of resources to correct misspelled words, including classroom word walls, books, classmates, and the dictionary.

Proofreading. Proofreading is a special kind of reading that students use to locate misspelled words and other mechanical errors in rough drafts. As students learn about the writing process, they are introduced to proofreading in the editing stage. More in-depth instruction about how to use proofreading to locate spelling errors and then correct these misspelled words is part of spelling instruction (Cramer, 1998). Through a series of minilessons, students can learn to proofread sample student papers and mark misspelled words. Then, working in pairs, students can correct the misspelled words.

Proofreading should be introduced in the primary grades. Young children and their teachers proofread collaborative books and dictated stories together, and students can be encouraged to read over their own compositions and make necessary corrections soon after they begin writing. This way, students accept proofreading as a natural part of writing. Proofreading activities are more valuable for teaching spelling than are dictation activities, in which teachers dictate sentences for students to write and correctly capitalize and punctuate. Few people use dictation in their daily lives, but we use proofreading skills every time we polish a piece of writing.

Dictionary Use. Students need to learn to locate the spelling of unfamiliar words in the dictionary. Although it is relatively easy to find a "known" word in the dictionary, it is hard to locate unfamiliar words, and students need to learn what to do when they don't know how to spell a word. One approach is to predict possible spellings for unknown words, then check the most probable spellings in a dictionary.

Students should be encouraged to check the spelling of words in a dictionary as well as to use a dictionary to check multiple meanings or etymology. Too often, students view consulting a dictionary as punishment; teachers must work to change this view. One way to do this is to appoint several students as dictionary checkers: These students keep dictionaries on their desks, and they're consulted whenever questions about spelling, a word's meaning, or word usage arise.

Spelling Options. In English, alternate spellings occur for many sounds because so many words borrowed from other languages retain their native spellings. There are many more options for vowel sounds than for consonants. Spelling options sometimes vary according to the letter's position in the word. For example, *ff* is found in the middle and at the end of words but not at the beginning (e.g., *muffin, cuff*), and *gh* represents /f/ only at the end of a syllable or word (e.g., *cough, laughter*).

Teachers point out spelling options as they write words on word walls and when students ask about the spelling of a word. They also can teach upper-grade students about these options in a series of minilessons. During each lesson, students can focus on one phoneme, such as /ō/ or /k/, and as a class or small group they can develop a list of the various ways the sound is spelled, giving examples of each spelling.

Weekly Spelling Tests

Many teachers question the usefulness of spelling tests, because research on invented spelling suggests that spelling is best learned through reading and writing (Gentry & Gillet, 1993). In addition, teachers complain that lists of spelling words are unrelated to the words students are reading and writing and that the 30 minutes of valuable instructional time spent each day in completing spelling activities is excessive. Even so, parents and school board members value spelling tests as evidence that spelling is being taught. Weekly spelling tests, when they are used, should be individualized so that students learn to spell the words they need for writing.

In the individualized approach to spelling instruction, students choose the words they'll study, many of which are words they use in their writing projects. Students study 5 to 10 specific words during the week using a study strategy; this approach places more responsibility on students for their own learning. Teachers develop a weekly word list of 20 or more words of varying difficulty from which students select words to study. Words for the master list include high-frequency words, words from the word wall related to literature focus units and thematic units, and words students needed for their writing projects during the previous week. Words from spelling programs can also be added to the list.

On Monday, the teacher administers a pretest using the master list of words, and students spell as many of the words as they can. Students correct their own pretests, and from the words they misspell they create individual spelling lists. They make two copies of their study list, using the numbers on the master list to make it easier to take the final test on Friday. Students use one copy of the list for study activities, and the teacher keeps the second copy.

Students spend approximately 5 to 10 minutes studying the words on their study lists each day during the week. Research shows that instead of "busy-work" activities such as using their spelling words in sentences or gluing yarn in the shape of the words, it's more effective for students to use this study strategy:

1. Look at the word and say it to yourself.
2. Say each letter in the word to yourself.
3. Close your eyes and spell the word to yourself.
4. Write the word, and check that you spelled it correctly.
5. Write the word again, and check that you spelled it correctly.

This strategy focuses on the whole word rather than on breaking the word apart into sounds or syllables. Teachers explain how to use the strategy during a minilesson at the beginning of the school year and then post a copy of it in the classroom. In addition, students often trade word lists on Wednesday to give each other a practice test.

A final test is administered on Friday. The teacher reads the master list, and students write only those words they've practiced during the week. To make the test easier to administer, students first list the numbers of the words they've practiced from their study lists on their test papers. Any words that students misspell should be included on their lists the following week.

Assessing Students' Spelling

The choices students make as they spell words are important indicators of their knowledge of both phonics and spelling. For example, a student who spells phonetically might spell *money* as *mune*, and others who are experimenting with long vowels might spell the word as *monye* or *monie*. Teachers classify and analyze the words students misspell in their writing to gauge their level of spelling development and to plan for instruction. The steps in determining a student's stage of spelling development are explained in this Assessment Tools feature. An analysis of a first grader's spelling development is shown in the Assessment Tools feature on the next page.

Teachers analyze the errors in students' compositions, analyze their errors on weekly spelling tests, and administer diagnostic tests. The Assessment Tools feature on page 180 lists tests that teachers use to determine their students' stage of spelling development.

Assessment Tools

How to Determine a Student's Stage of Spelling Development

1. **Choose a Writing Sample**
   Teachers choose a student's writing sample to analyze. In the primary grades, the sample should total at least 50 words, in the middle grades 100 words, and in the upper grades 200 words. Teachers must be able to decipher most words in the sample to analyze it.

2. **Identify Spelling Errors**
   Teachers read the writing sample to note the errors and identify the words the student was trying to spell. If necessary, teachers check with the writer to determine the intended word.

3. **Make a Spelling Analysis Chart**
   Teachers draw a chart with five columns, one for each stage of spelling development.

4. **Categorize the Spelling Errors**
   Teachers classify the student's spelling errors according to the stage of development. They list each error in one of the stages, ignoring proper nouns, capitalization errors, and grammar errors. Teachers ignore poorly formed letters or reversed letterforms in kindergarten and first grade, but these are significant errors when older students make them. To simplify the analysis, teachers write both the student's error and the correct spelling in parentheses.

5. **Tally the Errors**
   Teachers count the errors in each column, and the one with the most errors indicates the student's current stage of development.

6. **Identify Topics for Instruction**
   Teachers examine the student's errors to identify topics for instruction.

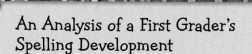

Assessment Tools

An Analysis of a First Grader's Spelling Development

Writing Sample

> To bay a perezun at home kob
> uz anb seb that a bome wuz in
> or skuwl anb mab uz go at zib
> anb makbe uz wat a haf uf
> a awr anb it mab uz wazt or
> time on loren ee ing.
>
>   THE eNb

Translation

Today a person at home called us and said that a bomb was in our school and made us go outside and made us wait a half of an hour and it made us waste our time on learning. The end.

Spelling Analysis Chart

Emergent	Letter Name-Alphabetic	Within-Word Patterns	Syllables and Affixes	Derivational Relations
	kod (called)	bome (bomb)	peresun (person)	
	sed (said)	or (our)	loreneeing (learning)	
	wus (was)	skuwl (school)		
	mad (made)	makde (made)		
	at (out)	uf (of)		
	sid (side)	awr (hour)		
	wat (wait)	or (our)		
	haf (half)			
	mad (made)			
	wazt (waste)			

Conclusion

The student spelled 56% of the words correctly, and most of his spelling errors were in the Letter Name-Alphabetic and Within-Word Patterns stages, which is typical of first graders' spelling.

Topics for instruction

high-frequency words
CVCe vowel pattern
-ed inflectional ending

Assessment Tools

Spelling

Teachers assess students' spelling development by examining misspelled words in the compositions that students write. They classify students' spelling errors according to the stages of spelling development and plan instruction based on their analysis. Teachers also examine students' misspellings on weekly spelling tests and diagnostic tests. Here are three tests designed for classroom teachers to screen, monitor, diagnose, and document students' spelling development:

◆ **Developmental Spelling Analysis (DSA)** (Ganske, 2000)

The DSA is a dictated spelling inventory with two components: a Screening Inventory for determining students' stage of spelling development, and Feature Inventories to highlight students' knowledge of specific spelling concepts. The DSA with detailed guidelines is available in Ganske's book, *Word Journeys: Assessment-Guided Phonics, Spelling, and Vocabulary Instruction* (2000).

◆ **Phonological Awareness Literacy Screening (PALS) System: Spelling Subtest** (Invernizzi, Meier, & Juel, 2003)

The kindergarten-level battery of tests includes a brief spelling subtest in which children write the sounds they hear in CVC words. In the grades 1–3 tests, the spelling subtest includes words that exemplify phonics features that are appropriate for that grade level. Children receive credit for spelling the specific feature correctly and additional points for spelling the word correctly. The PALS test is available free for Virginia teachers from the University of Virginia, and it can be purchased by teachers in other states.

◆ **Qualitative Spelling Inventory (QSI)** (Bear et al., 2008)

The QSI has two forms, one for grades K–6 and another for grades 6–8. These tests each include 20 or 25 spelling words listed according to difficulty and can easily be administered to small groups or whole classes. The QSI is available in *Words Their Way: Word Study for Phonics, Vocabulary, and Spelling Instruction* (Bear et al., 2008).

Through these tests, teachers identify students' stage of spelling development and use this information to monitor their progress and plan for instruction.

What's the Controversy About Spelling Instruction?

The press and concerned parent groups periodically raise questions about invented spelling and the importance of weekly spelling tests. There is a misplaced public perception that today's children can't spell: Researchers who have examined the types of errors students make have noted that the number of misspellings increases in grades 1 through 4, as students write longer compositions, but that the percentage of errors decreases. The percentage continues to decline in the upper grades, although some students continue to make errors.

Chapter 5
Review

How Effective Teachers Assist Students in "Cracking the Code"

▶ Teachers teach students to "crack the code" through phonemic awareness, phonics, and spelling instruction.

▶ Teachers understand that phonemic awareness is the foundation for phonics instruction.

▶ Teachers teach high-utility phonics concepts, rules, phonograms, and spelling patterns.

▶ Teachers recognize that students' spelling errors are a measure of their understanding of phonics.

PEARSON
myeducationlab
Where the Classroom Comes to Life

Go to MyEducationLab at www.myeducationlab.com to deepen your understanding of the concepts presented in this chapter:

▶ Analyze how second graders apply phonics knowledge in reading and spelling by viewing video segments in the Literacy Portraits.
▶ Check your understanding of chapter concepts with the multiple-choice and essay quizzes in the Study Plan.
▶ Apply some of the main ideas discussed in the chapter in the Activities and Applications section of the website.
▶ Practice what you've learned in this chapter in Building Teaching Skills and Dispositions before applying the ideas in your own classroom.

PROFESSIONAL REFERENCES

Adams, M. J. (1990). *Beginning to read: Thinking and learning about print.* Cambridge, MA: MIT Press.

Allington, R. L. (2006). *What really matters for struggling readers: Designing research-based programs* (2nd ed.). Boston: Allyn & Bacon.

Armbruster, B. B., Lehr, F., & Osborn, J. (2001). *Put reading first: The research building blocks for teaching children to read.* Urbana, IL: Center for the Improvement of Early Reading Achievement.

Bear, D. R., Helman, L., Invernizzi, M., Templeton, S., & Johnston, F. (2007). *Words their way with English learners: Word study for phonics, vocabulary, and spelling instruction.* Upper Saddle River, NJ: Merrill/Prentice Hall.

Bear, D. R., Invernizzi, M., Templeton, S., & Johnston, F. (2008). *Words their way: Word study for phonics, vocabulary,*

and spelling instruction (4th ed.). Upper Saddle River, NJ: Merrill/ Prentice Hall.

Caldwell, J. S., & Leslie, L. (2005). *Intervention strategies to follow informal reading inventory assessment: So what do I do now?* Boston: Allyn & Bacon/Pearson.

Chamberlain, C. J. (2005). Literacy and technology: A world of ideas. In R. A. Karchmer, M. H. Mallette, J. Kara-Soteriou, & D. J. Leu, Jr. (Eds.), *Innovative approaches to literacy education: Using the Internet to support new literacies* (pp. 44–64). Newark, DE: International Reading Association.

Clay, M. M. (2005a). *Literacy lessons: Designed for individuals, part 2: Teaching procedures.* Portsmouth, NH: Heinemann.

Clay, M. M. (2005b). *Observation survey of early literacy achievement* (2nd ed.). Portsmouth, NH: Heinemann.

Clymer, T. (1963). The utility of phonic generalizations in the primary grades. *The Reading Teacher, 16*, 252–258.

Cooper, J. D., & Pikulski, J. J. (2003). *Houghton Mifflin reading* (California ed.). Boston: Houghton Mifflin.

Cramer, R. L. (1998). *The spelling connection: Integrating reading, writing, and spelling instruction.* New York: Guilford Press.

Cunningham, P. (1990). The Names Test: A quick assessment of decoding ability. *The Reading Teacher, 44*, 124–129.

Cunningham, P. M. (2007). Best practices in teaching phonological awareness and phonics. In L. B. Gambrell, L. M. Morrow, & M. Pressley (Eds.), *Best practices in literacy instruction* (pp. 159–177). New York: Guilford Press.

Cunningham, P. M. (2009). *Phonics they use: Words for reading and writing* (5th ed.). Boston: Allyn & Bacon/Pearson.

Cunningham, P. M., & Allington, R. L. (2007). *Classrooms that work: They can all read and write* (4th ed.). Boston: Allyn & Bacon.

Cunningham, P. M., & Cunningham, J. W. (1992). Making words: Enhancing the invented spelling-decoding connection. *The Reading Teacher, 46*, 106–115.

Cunningham, P. M., & Cunningham, J. W. (2002). What we know about how to teach phonics. In A. E. Farstrup & S. J. Samuels (Eds.), *What research has to say about reading instruction* (3rd ed., pp. 87–109). Newark, DE: International Reading Association.

Dahl, K. L., Scharer, P. L., Lawson, L. L., & Grogan, P. R. (2001). *Rethinking phonics: Making the best teaching decisions.* Portsmouth, NH: Heinemann.

Duffelmeyer, F. A., Kruse, A. E. Merkley, D. J., & Fyfe, S. A. (1994). Further validation and enhancement of the Names Test. *The Reading Teacher, 48*, 118–128.

Ganske, K. (2000). *Word journeys: Assessment-guided phonics, spelling, and vocabulary instruction.* New York: Guilford Press.

Gentry, J. R., & Gillet, J. W. (1993). *Teaching kids to spell.* Portsmouth, NH: Heinemann.

Gillon, G. T. (2004). *Phonological awareness: From research to practice.* New York: Guilford Press.

Griffith, F., & Olson, M. (1992). Phonemic awareness helps beginning readers break the code. *The Reading Teacher, 45*, 516–523.

Hanna, P. R., Hanna, J. S., Hodges, R. E., & Rudorf, E. H. (1966). *Phoneme-grapheme correspondences as cues to spelling improvement.* Washington, DC: U.S. Government Printing Office.

Invernizzi, M., Meier, J. D., & Juel, C. (2003). *Phonological Awareness Literacy Screening System.* Charlottesville: University of Virginia Press.

Ivey, G., & Baker, M. I. (2004). Phonics instruction for older students? Just say no. *Educational Leadership, 61*(6), 35–39.

Juel, C., Griffith, P. L., & Gough, P. B. (1986). Acquisition of literacy: A longitudinal study of children in first and second grade. *Journal of Educational Psychology, 78*, 243–255.

Kaminski, R. A., & Good, R. H., III. (1996). *Dynamic Indicators of Basic Early Literacy Skills.* Eugene: University of Oregon Center on Teaching and Learning.

Kinzer, C. K. (2005). The intersection of schools, communities, and technology: Recognizing children's use of new literacies. In R. A. Karchmer, M. H. Mallette, J. Kara-Soteriou, & D. J. Leu, Jr. (Eds.), *Innovative approaches to literacy education: Using the Internet to support new literacies* (pp. 65–82). Newark, DE: International Reading Association.

Klesius, J. P., Griffith, P. L., & Zielonka, P. (1991). A whole language and traditional instruction comparison: Overall effectiveness and development of the alphabetic principle. *Reading Research and Instruction, 30*, 47–61.

Lewkowicz, N. K. (1994). The bag game: An activity to heighten phonemic awareness. *The Reading Teacher, 47*, 508–509.

Mather, N., Sammons, J., & Schwartz, J. (2006). Adaptations of the Names Test: Easy to use phonics assessments. *The Reading Teacher, 60*, 114–122.

McCarrier, A., Pinnell, G. S., & Fountas, I. C. (2000). *Interactive writing: How language and literacy come together, K–2.* Portsmouth, NH: Heinemann.

McKenna, M. C. (2002). *Help for struggling readers: Strategies for grades 3–8.* New York: Guilford Press.

Mesmer, H. A. E., & Griffith, P. L. (2005). Everybody's selling it—But just what is explicit, systematic phonics instruction? *The Reading Teacher, 59*, 366–376.

National Reading Panel. (2000). *Teaching children to read: An evidence-based assessment of the scientific research literature on reading and its implications for reading instruction.* Washington, DC: National Institute of Child Health and Human Development.

Norman, K. A., & Calfee, R. C. (2004). Tile Test: A hands-on approach for assessing phonics in the early grades. *The Reading Teacher 58*, 42–52.

Peregoy, S. F., & Boyle, W. F. (2008). *Reading, writing, and learning in ESL: A resource book for teaching K–12 English learners* (5th ed.). Boston: Allyn & Bacon/Pearson.

Read, C. (1975). *Children's categorization of speech sounds in English* (NCTE Research Report No. 17). Urbana, IL: National Council of Teachers of English.

Riches, C., & Genesee, F. (2006). Literacy: Crosslinguistic and crossmodal issues. In F. Genesee, K. Lindholm-Leary, W. M. Saunders, & D. Christian (Eds.), *Educating English language learners: A synthesis of research evidence* (pp. 64–108). New York: Cambridge University Press.

Shefelbine, J. (1995). *Learning and using phonics in beginning reading* (Literacy research paper; volume 10). New York: Scholastic.

Snow, C., Burns, M. W., & Griffin, P. (1998). *Preventing reading difficulties in young children.* Washington, DC: National Academy Press.

Tompkins, G. E., & Collom, S. (2004). *Sharing the pen: Interactive writing with young children*. Upper Saddle River, NJ: Merrill/Prentice Hall.

Torgesen, J. K., & Bryant, B. R. (2004). *Test of Phonological Awareness* (2nd ed.). East Moline, IL: LinguiSystems.

Venezky, R. L. (1999). *The American way of spelling: The structure and origins of American English orthography*. New York: Guilford Press.

White, T. G. (2005). Effects of systematic and strategic analogy-based phonics on grade 2 students' word reading and reading comprehension. *Reading Research Quarterly, 40,* 234–255.

Wylie, R. E., & Durrell, D. D. (1970). Teaching vowels through phonograms. *Elementary English, 47,* 787–791.

Yopp, H. K. (1988). The validity and reliability of phonemic awareness tests. *Reading Research Quarterly, 23,* 159–177.

Yopp, H. K. (1992). Developing phonemic awareness in young children. *The Reading Teacher, 45,* 696–703.

Yopp, H. K. (1995). Read-aloud books for developing phonemic awareness: An annotated bibliography. *The Reading Teacher, 48,* 538–542.

Yopp, H. K., & Yopp, R. H. (2000). Supporting phonemic awareness development in the classroom. *The Reading Teacher, 54,* 130–143.

CHILDREN'S BOOK REFERENCES

Hutchins, P. (1989). *Don't forget the bacon!* New York: HarperCollins.

Most, B. (1996). *Cock-a-doodle-moo!* San Diego: Harcourt Brace.

Osborne, M. P. (2003). *High tide in Hawaii*. New York: Random House.

Park, B. (2003). *Junie B., first grader: Boss of lunch*. New York: Random House.

Root, P. (2004). *Rattletrap car*. Cambridge, MA: Candlewick Press.

Seuss, Dr. (1963). *Hop on pop*. New York: Random House.

Seuss, Dr. (1965). *Fox in socks*. New York: Random House.

Developing Fluent Readers and Writers

Ms. Williams's Students Learn High-Frequency Words

Ms. Williams's second graders are studying hermit crabs and their tide pool environments. A plastic habitat box with a hermit crab living inside sits in the center of each group of desks. As children care for their crustaceans, they observe the crabs. They've examined hermit crabs up close using magnifying glasses and identified the body parts. Ms. Williams helped them draw a diagram of a hermit crab on a large chart and label the body parts. They've compared hermit crabs to true crabs and examined their exoskeletons. They've also learned how to feed hermit crabs, how to get them to come out of their shells, and how they molt. And, they've conducted experiments to determine which environment hermit crabs prefer.

These second graders are using reading and writing as tools for learning. Eric Carle's *A House for Hermit Crab* (2005) is the featured book for this unit. Ms. Williams has read it aloud several times, and children are rereading it at the listening center. *Moving Day* (Kaplan, 1996), *Pagoo* (Holling, 1990), and other stories and informational books are available on a special shelf in the classroom library. Ms. Williams has read some aloud, and others children read independently or with buddies. Children make charts about hermit crabs that they post in the classroom and write about them in learning logs. One log entry is shown in the box below.

Ms. Williams and her second graders also write interesting and important vocabulary words related to hermit crabs on a word wall made on a sheet of butcher paper, divided into boxes for each letter. These words appear on their word wall:

coral	larvae	sea urchins
crustacean	molting	seaweed
eggs	pebbles	shells
enemies	pincers	shrimp
exoskeleton	regeneration	snails
lantern fish	scavenger	starfish
larva	sea anemone	tide pool

Then children refer to the words as they write about hermit crabs, and Ms. Williams uses them for various word study activities.

Ms. Williams integrates many components of reading instruction, including word recognition and fluency activities, into the unit on hermit crabs. To develop her second graders' ability to recognize many high-frequency words, she uses another word wall. This one differs from the hermit crab word wall, which contains only words related to these ocean animals. Her high-frequency word wall is a

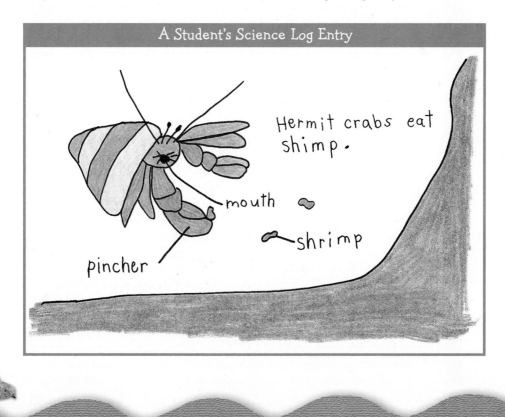

A Student's Science Log Entry

Hermit crabs eat shimp.

mouth

shrimp

pincher

brightly colored alphabet quilt with 26 blocks, one for each letter of the alphabet, displayed permanently on one wall of the classroom.

At the beginning of the school year, Ms. Williams and her students posted on the word wall the 70 high-frequency words that they were familiar with from first grade. Each word is written clearly on a small card, using print that's large enough so everyone can read it. Then each week, Ms. Williams adds three to five new words. At first, the words she chose were from her list of the 100 high-frequency words, and after finishing that list, she has begun choosing words from a list of the second 100 high-frequency words. She doesn't introduce the words in the order that they're presented in the list, but rather chooses words that she can connect to phonics lessons and literature focus units, and words that children misspell in their writing.

This week, Ms. Williams adds *soon, house, your,* and *you're* to the word wall. She chooses *soon* and *house* because these words are used in *A House for Hermit Crab* and because several children have recently asked her how to spell *house.* She chooses the homophones *your* and *you're* because children are confusing and misspelling these two words. She also has noticed that some children are confused about contractions, so she plans to review contractions, using *you're* as an example.

Ms. Williams has her students sit on the floor near the word wall to introduce and post the words on it. She uses a cookie sheet and large magnetic letters to introduce each new word. She explains that two of the new words—*house* and *soon*—are from *A House for Hermit Crab.* She scrambles the letters at the bottom of the cookie sheet and slowly builds the new word at the top of the sheet as children guess it. She begins with *h,* adds the *ou,* and several children call out "house." Ms. Williams continues adding letters, and when they are all in place, a chorus of voices says, "house." Then Kari places the new word card in the *H* square of the word wall, and children chant and clap as they say the word and spell it. Ms. Williams begins, "House, house, h-o-u-s-e," and children echo her chant. Then she calls on Enrique to begin the chant, and children echo him. Then Ms. Williams repeats the procedure with the three remaining words.

The next day, Ms. Williams and her students use interactive writing to compose sentences using each of the new words. They write these sentences:

> *The hermit crab has a good shell for a <u>house</u>. He likes it but <u>soon</u> he will move. "<u>You're</u> too small for me," he says. "I have to move, but I will always be <u>your</u> friend."*

Children take turns writing these sentences on a chart, and after rereading them, they underline the four new words. Each week, the children write sentences using the new word wall words. Ms. Williams and the children often reread the sentences they've written during previous weeks.

The next day, after children practice the new word wall words, Ms. Williams takes a few minutes to review contractions so that they understand that *you're* is a contraction of *you* and *are* and that the apostrophe indicates that a letter has been omitted. Then children volunteer other contractions. Michael identifies three: *I'm, can't,* and *don't.* The children use interactive writing to make a chart of contractions: They list the contractions and the two words that make up each one. Ms. Williams explains that she'll put the chart in the word work center and that they can use the information to make books about contractions.

After this practice with high-frequency words, children participate in activities at literacy centers while Ms. Williams meets with guided reading groups. Most of the center activities relate to the unit on hermit crabs and Eric Carle's book *A House for Hermit Crab,* but children also practice reading and writing high-frequency

Ms. Williams's Literacy Centers

Library Center
Children reread leveled books and other books about hermit crabs that were placed on a special shelf in the library. Ms. Williams includes *Moving Day* (Kaplan, 1996) (Level 7), *Hermit Crab* (Randell, 1994) (Level 8), and *Hermit's Shiny Shell* (Tuchman, 1997) (Level 10), three familiar books about hermit crabs, for children to reread.

Listening Center
Children use headphones to listen to an informational book about hermit crabs.

Retelling Center
Children sequence pictures of the events in the book and use them as a guide to retell the story.

Science Center
Children observe a hermit crab and make notes in their learning logs about its physical characteristics and eating habits.

Word Sort Center
Children sort words from *A House for Hermit Crab* into categories, including ocean animals and plants.

Word Wall Center
Children practice reading the word wall using pointers. Then they take a clipboard and a sheet of paper divided into 10 sections; the letters spelling h-e-r-m-i-t-c-r-a-b have been written in the sections. Children choose two words from the word wall beginning with each letter to write in each section on their papers.

Word Work Center
Children use magnetic letters to spell this week's high-frequency words—*house, soon, your*, and *you're*—and the words from the last 2 weeks. They also make a book of contractions with picture and sentence examples.

Writing Center
Children write "I Am a Hermit Crab" poems following the model posted at the center. They also write other books about hermit crabs.

words at two of the centers. The eight literacy centers in Ms. Williams's classroom are described above.

Each morning, a sixth-grade student aide comes to the classroom to monitor the children's work at the centers and provide assistance as needed. Ms. Williams worked with two sixth-grade teachers to train 10 students to serve as student aides, and they come to the classroom once every week or two on a rotating basis.

The second graders keep track of their work in centers using small booklets with eight sheets of paper that Ms. Williams calls their "center passports." The student aide marks their passports with stickers or stamps at each center after they finish the assignment, and children leave their written work in a basket at the center.

As a culminating activity, Ms. Williams and her students write a retelling of *A House for Hermit Crab*. The children compose the text, and Ms. Williams uses the Language Experience Approach to write their rough draft on chart paper so that everyone can see it. Children learn revision strategies as they fine-tune their retelling, and then Ms. Williams types the text on five sheets of paper, makes copies, and compiles booklets. Children each receive a copy of the booklet to read and illustrate. Later they'll take their booklets home to read to their families.

Ms. Williams reads their retelling aloud as children follow along and then join in the reading. They do choral reading as they read in small groups. The numbers on the left side indicate which group reads each sentence. As children read and reread the text aloud, they become increasingly fluent readers. Here's the last section of the class's retelling:

1 *Soon it was January.*

2 *Hermit Crab moved out of his house and the little crab moved in.*

3 *"Goodbye," said Hermit Crab.*
  "Be good to my friends."

4 *Soon Hermit Crab saw the perfect house.*

5 *It was a big, empty shell.*

1 *It looked a little plain but Hermit Crab didn't care.*

2 *He will decorate it*

3 *with sea urchins,*

4 *with sea anemones,*

5 *with coral,*

1 *with starfish,*

2 *with snails.*

ALL *So many possibilities!*

The underlined words are high-frequency words that are posted on the word wall in Ms. Williams's classroom; of the 68 words in this excerpt, 37 are high-frequency words! Also, two of the new words for this week, *soon* and *house*, are used twice.

As children learn to read, they move from word-by-word reading with little or no expression to fluent reading. Fluency is the ability to read quickly, accurately, and with expression, and to read fluently, they recognize most words automatically and identify unfamiliar words easily (Caldwell & Leslie, 2005). By third grade, most children have moved from word-by-word reading into fluent reading; however, 10–15% have difficulty learning to recognize words, and their learning to read is slowed (Allington, 2009). Fluency is an important component of reading instruction, especially in second and third grades, because researchers have found that fluent readers comprehend what they're reading better than less fluent readers do (National Reading Panel, 2000). Pikulski and Chard (2005) describe fluency as the bridge between decoding and comprehension.

Children become fluent readers through a combination of instruction and lots of reading experience. Through systematic phonics instruction, children learn how to identify unfamiliar words; as they read and reread hundreds of books during the primary grades, these words become familiar, and children learn to recognize them automatically. They also learn increasingly sophisticated strategies for identifying unfamiliar words, including syllabic and morphemic analysis, in which they break words into syllables and into root words and affixes.

At the same time children are becoming fluent readers, they're also becoming fluent writers. Through spelling instruction and lots of writing practice, children learn to spell many words automatically, apply capitalization and punctuation rules, and increase writing speed. They also learn strategies for spelling longer, multisyllabic words. Developing fluency is just as important for writers because both readers and writers must be able to focus their attention on meaning, not on decoding and spelling words.

LEARNING TO READ AND WRITE WORDS

Teachers have two goals as they teach children to read and write words. The first is to teach them to instantly recognize several hundred high-frequency words. Children need to be able to read and write these words automatically by the time they're third graders. The second is to equip them with strategies, or problem-solving techniques, that they can use to identify unfamiliar words—often longer, multisyllabic words— they come across during reading and need to spell during writing. Students learn and refine their use of these strategies between kindergarten and eighth grade.

Word Recognition

Students develop a large stock of words that they recognize automatically because it's impossible for them to analyze every word they encounter when reading or want to spell when writing; these recognizable words are called *sight words*. Through repeated reading and writing experiences, students develop automaticity, the ability to quickly recognize words they read and know how to spell words they're writing (LaBerge & Samuels, 1976; Samuels, 2004). The vital element in word recognition is learning each word's unique letter sequence.

High-Frequency Words. The most common words that readers and writers use again and again are called *high-frequency words*. There have been numerous attempts to identify specific lists of these words and to calculate their frequency in reading materials. Pinnell and Fountas (1998, p. 89) identified these 24 common words that kindergartners learn to read:

a	at	he	it	no	the
am	can	I	like	see	to
an	do	in	me	she	up
and	go	is	my	so	we

They also learn to write many of the words.

These words are part of the 100 high-frequency words, which account for more than half of the words people read and write. Children learn the rest of the 100 high-frequency words in first grade. Eldredge (2005) has identified the 300 highest-frequency words used in first-grade basal readers and trade books found in first-grade classrooms; these 300 words account for 72% of the words that beginning readers read. Figure 6–1 presents Eldredge's list of 300 high-frequency words; the 100 most common ones are marked with an asterisk. Children learn to read the last 200 words on the list during second and third grades.

It's essential that children learn to read and write high-frequency words, but many of these words are difficult to learn because they can't be easily decoded (Cunningham, 2009): Try sounding out *to*, *what*, and *could* and you'll see how difficult they are! Because these words can't be decoded easily, children learn to remember and recognize them automatically. A further complication is that many of these words are function words, so they don't carry much meaning. It's much easier to learn to recognize *whale* than *what*, because *whale* conjures up the image of the huge aquatic mammal, but *what* is abstract. *What*, however, is used much more frequently, and children must learn to recognize it.

Figure 6–1 ◆ The 300 High-Frequency Words

* a	children	great	looking	ran	through
* about	city	green	made	read	* time
* after	come	grow	make	red	* to
again	* could	* had	* man	ride	toad
* all	couldn't	hand	many	right	together
along	cried	happy	may	road	told
always	dad	has	maybe	room	* too
* am	dark	hat	* me	run	took
* an	* day	* have	mom	* said	top
* and	* did	* he	more	sat	tree
animals	* didn't	head	morning	* saw	truck
another	* do	hear	* mother	say	try
any	does	heard	mouse	* school	* two
* are	dog	help	Mr.	sea	under
* around	* don't	hen	Mrs.	* see	until
* as	door	* her	much	* she	* up
asked	* down	here	must	show	* us
* at	each	hill	* my	sister	* very
ate	eat	* him	name	sky	wait
away	end	* his	need	sleep	walk
baby	even	* home	never	small	walked
* back	ever	* house	new	* so	want
bad	every	* how	next	* some	wanted
ball	everyone	* I	nice	something	* was
* be	eyes	I'll	night	soon	water
bear	far	I'm	* no	started	way
* because	fast	* if	* not	stay	* we
bed	father	* in	nothing	still	* well
been	find	inside	* now	stop	* went
before	fine	* into	* of	stories	* were
began	first	* is	off	story	* what
behind	fish	* it	oh	sun	* when
best	fly	it's	old	take	where
better	* for	its	* on	tell	while
big	found	jump	once	than	* who
bird	fox	jumped	* one	* that	why
birds	friend	* just	only	that's	* will
blue	friends	keep	* or	* the	wind
book	frog	king	other	their	witch
books	* from	* know	* our	* them	* with
box	fun	last	* out	* then	wizard
boy	garden	left	* over	* there	woman
brown	gave	let	* people	these	words
* but	* get	let's	picture	* they	work
* by	girl	* like	pig	thing	* would
called	give	* little	place	* things	write
* came	go	live	play	* think	yes
* can	going	long	pulled	* this	* you
can't	good	look	* put	thought	your
cat	* got	looked	rabbit	three	* you're

From *Teach Decoding: How and Why* (2nd ed., pp. 119–120), by J. L. Eldredge, © 2005. Adapted by permission of Prentice Hall, Inc., Upper Saddle River, NJ.

*The first 100 most frequently used words, as shown in Figure 5–8 on p. 175.

Word Walls. Primary-grade teachers create word walls in their classrooms to display the high-frequency words the children are learning, as Ms. Williams did in the vignette at the beginning of the chapter. Some teachers use butcher paper or squares of construction paper for the word wall, and others use large pocket charts that they divide into sections for each letter of the alphabet. Word walls should be placed in a prominent, accessible location in the classroom so that everyone can see the words and new words can be added easily.

Teachers prepare word walls at the beginning of the school year and then add to them each week. Kindergarten teachers often begin by listing children's names on the word wall and then add the 24 highest-frequency words, one or two words per week, during the school year. First-grade teachers often begin with the 24 words introduced in kindergarten, and then add two to five words each week. Figure 6–2 presents a first-grade word wall with just over 100 words that were added during the school year. In second grade, teachers often begin the year with the easier half of the high-frequency words already on the word wall, and they add 100 more words during the school year. Third-grade teachers often test their students' knowledge of the 100 high-frequency words at the beginning of the year, add to the word wall any words that students can't read and write, and then continue with the next 200 high-frequency words so that everyone learns most of the 300 high-frequency words by the end of the school year.

Check the Compendium of Instructional Procedures, which follows Chapter 12, for more information on the highlighted terms.

Figure 6–2 ◆ A First-Grade Word Wall

A	B	C	D	E
a are	be	call	did	each
about as	been	called	didn't	eat
after at	boy	can	do	
all	but	can't	does	
am	by	come	don't	
and		could	down	

F	G	H	I	JK
find	get	had here	I into	just
first	go	has him	if is	know
for	good	have his	in it	
from		he how		
		her		

L	M	N	O	PQR
like	made must	no	of other	people
little	make my	not	on our	pretty
long	may	now	one out	
look	me		only over	
	more		or	

S	T	UV	W	XYZ
said	than there	up	was where	you
saw	that these	us	water which	your
see	the they	very	way who	
she	their this		we will	
so	them to		were with	
some	then two		what words	
should			when would	

Teachers can create word walls for older students, too. To assist struggling readers, teachers can post the 100 high-frequency words or some of the 300 high-frequency words on a classroom word wall, or they can make individual word lists for these students. Teachers can type up a list of words in alphabetical order and make copies to cut into bookmarks, to glue on a file folder, or to create personal dictionaries. Teachers who work with students who read and write on grade level can also make word walls to display more difficult common words. Figure 6–3 presents a list of 100 common words that fourth- through eighth-grade students need to learn. Some of the words, such as *himself*, *finally*, and *remember*, are more appropriate for fourth and fifth graders, and others, such as *necessary*, *foreign*, and *throughout*, are more appropriate for sixth through eighth graders. Some of these are commonly used words that students confuse with other words, including *desert* and *dessert* and *quiet* and *quite*.

Figure 6–3 ◆ 100 High-Frequency Words for Older Students

A	B	C	D	E
a lot	beautiful	caught	decided	either
again	because	certain	desert	embarrassed
all right	belief	clothes	different	enough
although	believe	committee	discussed	especially
another	beneath	complete	doesn't	etc.
anything	between			everything
around	board			everywhere
	breathe			excellent
	brought			experience

F G	H	I J	K	L
familiar	heard	immediately	knew	language
favorite	height	interesting	know	lying
field	herself	its	knowledge	
finally	himself	it's		
foreign	humorous			
friends	hungry			
frighten				

M	N	O	P	Q R
maybe	necessary	once	particular	quiet
	neighbor	ourselves	peace	really
			people	receive
			piece	recommend
			please	remember
			possible	restaurant
			probably	

S	T	U V	W	X Y Z
safety	their	until	weight	your
school	there	usually	where	you're
separate	themselves		whether	
serious	they're		whole	
since	though			
special	thought			
something	through			
success	throughout			
	together			

Word Wall

These first graders participate in daily word wall activities. In this teacher-directed activity, the children read the high-frequency words posted on the word wall and write them on dry-erase boards. They apply phonics skills as they make up riddles about words for their classmates to guess. For example: "What word begins with /g/ and rhymes with *pet*?" Children take turns creating and sharing riddles. One child solves the riddle, and everyone writes it on dry-erase boards. Then they hold their boards up so the teacher can check their work.

Teaching Word Recognition. Teachers carefully select the high-frequency words they introduce each week. They choose words that students are familiar with and use in conversation but can't read or write. The selected words may have been introduced in guided reading lessons, or they may be words that students misspelled recently in their writing. Even though the words are listed alphabetically in Figures 6–2 and 6–3, they aren't taught in that order; in the vignette, for example, Ms. Williams chose *soon* and *house* from *A House for Hermit Crab* and the homophones *your* and *you're*, which children were confusing in their writing.

Teaching high-frequency words isn't easy, because many of them have little or no meaning when they're used in isolation. Cunningham (2009) recommends this chant-and-clap procedure to practice the words being placed on the word wall:

1. **Introduce the words in context.** Teachers introduce the new words using a familiar book or with pictures or objects. For example, to introduce the words *for* and *from*, teachers might show a gift box, wrapped and tied with a bow, and with an attached gift tag labeled "for" and "from." Then teachers pass out extra gift tags they've made, and children read the words *for* and *from* and briefly talk about gifts they've given and received. Teachers also clarify that *for* isn't the number *four* and show children where the number *four* is written on the number chart posted in the classroom.

2. **Have children chant and clap the words.** Teachers introduce the new word cards that will be placed on the word wall and read the words. Then they begin a chant, "For, for, f-o-r," and clap their hands. Then children repeat the chant. After several repetitions, teachers begin a second chant, "From, from, f-r-o-m," and the children repeat the chant and clap their hands as they chant. Children practice chanting and clapping the words each day that week.

3. **Have children practice reading and writing the words.** Children create sentences using the high-frequency words on sentence strips and read them to classmates. Later, they cut them apart and practice rearranging the words. They also search for the words in big books and on charts posted around the classroom.

They use dry-erase boards and magnetic letters to practice spelling the words. To emphasize the sequence of letters in a word, they also sort word cards. For example, the words *for, from, four, fun, fish, fast, free, from, for, four, free,* and *fun* are written on cards, and children sort them into three piles: one pile for *for,* a second pile for *from,* and a third pile for all other words. Teachers direct children in some of these activities, and children participate in others at literacy centers.

4. **Have children read and write the words.** Authentic reading and writing activities are the best ways to practice high-frequency words because these common words are likely to be used often. During sharing sessions after independent reading and writing, teachers often ask children to point out where they read or wrote the high-frequency words they've been practicing. Teachers also point out high-frequency words during interactive read-alouds, shared reading, interactive writing activities, and other literacy activities.

Through this chant-and-clap procedure, teachers make the high-frequency words more concrete, and easily confused words are clarified and practiced.

A minilesson showing how a first-grade teacher focuses her students' attention on high-frequency words is presented on the next page. These first graders are learning high-frequency words from big books they're reading. Activities involving word walls are an important way to teach word recognition; reading and writing are two other ways. Children develop automatic word recognition by reading words. They read words in the context of stories and other books, and they read them on word lists and on word cards. Practice makes students more fluent readers and even has an impact on their comprehension.

Students also practice word recognition through writing because they write high-frequency words again and again. For example, when a first-grade class was studying animals, the children wrote riddle books. One first grader wrote this riddle book, entitled "What Is It?":

Page 1: *It is a bird.*
Page 2: *It can't fly but it can swim.*
Page 3: *It is black and white.*
Page 4: *It eats fish.*
Page 5: *What is it?*
Page 6: *A penguin.*

Of the words that the child wrote, more than half are among the 24 highest-frequency words! (These words are underlined.) Students refer to the word wall when they're writing so that they can spell words conventionally and write fluently.

Assessing Word Recognition. Because word recognition is so important in beginning reading, teachers assess children's developing word recognition regularly (Snow, Burns, & Griffin, 1998). Primary-grade teachers screen children at the beginning of the school year, monitor their progress several times during the year, and document their achievement at the end of the year. How often they monitor children's progress depends on their reading level and on the progress they're making.

Assessing children's word recognition is easy: Teachers have children individually read the words posted on the word wall or read high-frequency words on word cards or word lists. Kindergartners are usually tested on the 24 most common words, first graders on the 100 high-frequency words, second and third graders on the 300 high-frequency words. In addition, teachers can use commercial tests. Check the Assessment Tools feature on page 196 for more information on word-recognition assessment tools.

MiniLesson

TOPIC: Teaching High-Frequency Words
GRADE: First Grade
TIME: One 15-minute period

Miss Shapiro's goal is for her first graders to learn at least 75 of the 100 high-frequency words. She has a large word wall that's divided into sections for each letter. Each week, she introduces three new words and adds them to the word wall. She chooses words from the big book she's using for shared reading. On Monday, she introduces the new words and over the next four days, she focuses on them and reviews those she's introduced previously. To make the word study more authentic, the children often hunt for the word in reading materials available in the classroom; sometimes they look in familiar big books, in small books they're rereading, on charts of familiar poems and songs, or on Language Experience and interactive writing charts. On other days, the children create sentences using the words, which the teacher writes on sentence strips and displays in the classroom.

1 Introduce the Topic

"Let's read the D words on the word wall," Miss Shapiro says. As she points to the words, the class reads them aloud. "Which word is new this week?" she asks. The children respond, "do." Next, they read the H words and identify *here* as a new word, and then the M words and identify *my* as a new word. She asks individual children to reread the D, H, and M words on the word wall.

2 Share Examples

"Who can come up and point to our three new words for this week?" Miss Shapiro asks. Aaron eagerly comes to the word wall to point out *do, here*, and *my*. As he points to each word, Miss Shapiro writes it on the chalkboard, pronounces it, and spells it aloud. She and Aaron lead the class as they chant and clap the words: "Do, do, d-o, do!" "Here, here, h-e-r-e, here!" "My, my, m-y, my!"

3 Provide Information

"Let's look for *do, here*, and *my* in these books," Miss Shapiro suggests as she passes out a familiar big book to the children at each table. In each group, the children reread the book, pointing out *do, here*, and *my* each time they occur. The teacher circulates around the classroom, checking that the children notice the words.

4 Guide Practice

Miss Shapiro asks Aaron to choose three classmates to come to the chalkboard to spell the words with large magnetic letters; Daniel, Elizabeth, and Wills spell the words and read them aloud. Then Aaron passes out plastic bags with small magnetic letters and word cards to each pair of children. They read the word cards and spell the three words at their desks.

5 Assess Learning

On Friday, Miss Shapiro works with the first graders in small groups, asking them to locate the words in sentences they've written and to read the words individually on word cards.

Assessment Tools

Word Recognition

Teachers monitor children's growing ability to recognize high-frequency words as they listen to them read aloud and through these classroom tests:

◆ **High-Frequency Word Lists**

Teachers regularly have children read lists of high-frequency words and keep a record of which words children can identify. Children can read the high-frequency words posted on word walls or use grade-level lists of the high-frequency words; kindergartners are expected to read 24 words, first graders 100 words, second graders 200 words, and third graders 300 words. The high-frequency word lists presented in this chapter can be used; other options are the Dolch list of 220 sight words and Fry's list of 300 instant words, both of which are available in *Assessment for Reading Instruction* (McKenna & Stahl, 2003).

◆ **Observation Survey of Early Literacy Achievement (OS): Word Reading and Writing Vocabulary Subtests** (Clay, 2005)

Two subtests of the OS are used to assess children's knowledge of high-frequency words. In the Word Reading subtest, children read a list of 15 words that were selected from a list of the 45 highest-frequency words used in first-grade basal readers, and in the Writing Vocabulary subtest, they write a list of all the words they know (within a 10-minute time limit). The Word Reading subtest is administered individually, but small groups or the entire class can complete the Writing Vocabulary subtest together. The subtests and directions for administering and scoring them are included in Clay's *Observation Survey of Early Literacy Achievement* (2005), which is available from Heinemann.

◆ **Writing Samples**

Teachers examine samples of children's writing to examine whether writers are using high-frequency words and spelling them correctly. They can use the same word lists used to monitor children's progress in reading high-frequency words to assess their progress in writing these words.

Once children can read and write all of the high-frequency words on grade-level lists or they've become fluent readers and writers, it's not necessary to continue to monitor their progress.

Once children read fluently, word-recognition assessments aren't needed any longer; however, teachers in fourth through eighth grade do assess students who read below the third-grade level because when they can't recognize some of the 300 high-frequency words, they need instruction on the words they don't know.

Teachers also assess children's ability to write high-frequency words because these common words are as essential for writers as they are for readers. Beginning in kindergarten, children learn to spell many of the same words, such as *the*, *I*, and *you*, that they're learning to read; however, spelling development lags behind because it's more demanding to learn the letter sequences in a word and form the letters correctly in writing than it is to remember the word itself. Children usually can write more than half of the high-frequency words they can read. The number of words reflects the instruction children have received and how much writing they do.

Teachers use writing samples or spelling tests to screen children's development at the beginning of the school year. They informally monitor children's growth during the year, usually by examining their writing. At the middle of the school year and again at the end of the year, teachers administer another spelling test or collect additional writing samples to document children's learning. This assessment also ends after third grade unless students have difficulty spelling high-frequency words correctly.

Word Identification

Beginning readers encounter many unfamiliar words, and even fluent readers come upon words that they don't immediately recognize. Students use word-identification strategies to identify these unfamiliar words. Young children often depend on phonics to sound out unfamiliar words, but older students develop other strategies that use phonological information as well as semantic, syntactic, and pragmatic cues to identify words.

> **Be Strategic!**
>
> ## Word-Identification Strategies
>
> Students use these strategies to identify unfamiliar words when they're reading:
>
> ▶ Use phonic analysis
> ▶ Decode by analogy
> ▶ Divide into syllables
> ▶ Apply morphemic analysis
>
> Students' choice of strategy depends on their knowledge about words and the complexity of the unfamiliar word.

The four strategies that students learn to use to identify unfamiliar words are *phonic analysis*, *decoding by analogy*, *syllabic analysis*, and *morphemic analysis*. Writers use these same strategies to spell words. As with reading, young children depend on phonics to spell many, many words, but as they want to spell multisyllabic words, they apply other strategies to spelling. These four word-identification strategies are summarized in Figure 6–4.

Phonic Analysis. Students use what they have learned about phoneme-grapheme correspondences, phonics rules, and spelling patterns to decode words when they're reading and to spell words when they're writing. Even though English isn't a perfectly phonetic language, phonic analysis is a very useful strategy because almost every word has some phonetically regular parts. The words *have* and *come*, for example, are considered irregular words because the vowel sounds aren't predictable; however, the initial and final consonant sounds in both words are regular.

Figure 6–4 ◆ Word-Identification Strategies

Strategy	Description	Examples
Phonic Analysis	Students apply their knowledge of sound-symbol correspondences, phonics rules, and spelling patterns to read or write a word.	*peach* *spring* *blaze* *chin*
Decoding by Analogy	Students use their knowledge of phonograms to deduce the pronunciation or spelling of an unfamiliar word.	*flat* from *cat* *creep* from *sheep* *think* from *pink* *claw* from *saw*
Syllabic Analysis	Students break a multisyllabic word into syllables and then use their knowledge of phonics and phonograms to decode the word, syllable by syllable.	*cul-prit* *neg-a-tive* *sea-weed* *bi-o-de-grad-a-ble*
Morphemic Analysis	Students apply their knowledge of root words and affixes to read or write an unfamiliar word.	*trans-port* *astro-naut* *bi-cycle* *centi-pede*

Beginning readers often try to identify words based on a partial word analysis (Gough, Juel, & Griffith, 1992): They may guess at a word using the beginning sound or look at its overall shape as a clue to word identification; however, these aren't effective techniques. Through phonics instruction, students learn to focus on the letter sequences in words so that they examine the entire word as they identify it (Adams, 1990).

Researchers report that the big difference between students who identify words effectively and those who don't is whether they survey the letters in the words and analyze the interior components (Stanovich, 1992). Capable readers notice all or almost all letters in a word, whereas less capable readers don't completely analyze the letter sequences of words. Struggling readers with limited phonics skills often try to decode words by sounding out the beginning sound and then guessing at the word without using the other cueing systems to verify their guesses (Gaskins, Ehri, Cress, O'Hara, & Donnelly, 1996/1997). And, as you might imagine, their guesses are usually wrong. Sometimes they don't even make sense in the context of the sentence.

Decoding by Analogy. Students identify some words by associating them with words they already know; this strategy is known as *decoding by analogy* (Cunningham, 2004). When readers come to an unfamiliar word, such as *fright*, they might notice the phonogram *-ight* and figure out the word by analogy. Students use analogies to figure out the spelling of unfamiliar words as well; they might use the familar word *game* (*-ame* phonogram) to help them spell *frame*, for example. This strategy accounts for students' common misspelling of *they* as *thay*, because *they* rhymes with *day* and *say*.

This word-identification strategy is dependent on students' knowledge of phonograms. Students who can break words into onsets and rimes and substitute sounds in words are more successful than those who can't. Moreover, researchers have found that only students who know many sight words use this strategy because they must be able to identify patterns in familiar words to associate with those in unfamiliar words (Ehri & Robbins, 1992).

Teachers introduce decoding by analogy when they have students read and write "word families" using familiar phonograms. Using the *-ill* phonogram, for example, students can read or write *bill, chill, fill, hill, kill, mill, pill, quill, spill, still,* and *will*. They can add inflectional endings to create even more words, including *filling, hills,* and *spilled.* Two-syllable words can also be created using these words: *killer, refill, chilly,* and *hilltop.* Students read word cards, write the words using interactive writing, and use magnetic letters to spell the words to learn more about substituting beginning sounds, breaking words into parts, and spelling word parts. Teachers also share picture books that include several words representing a particular phonogram (Caldwell & Leslie, 2005). In Denise Fleming's *In the Tall, Tall Grass* (1995), for example, children can locate *-um* words (*strum, drum,* and *hum*), and in her *In the Small, Small Pond* (1998), they can read *-are* words (*care* and *share*) and *-ay* words (*way* and *spray*). Figure 6–5 lists books with words representing common phonograms. It's a big step, however, for students to move from these structured activities to using this strategy independently to identify unfamiliar words.

Syllabic Analysis. During the middle grades, students learn to divide words into syllables in order to read and write multisyllabic words such as *biodegradable, admonition,* and *unforgettable.* Once a word is divided into syllables, students use phonic analysis and decoding by analogy to pronounce or spell it. Identifying syllable boundaries is important, because these affect the pronunciation of the vowel sound. For example, compare the vowel sound in the first syllables of *cabin* and *cable.* For *cabin,* the syllable boundary is after *b,* whereas for *cable,* the division is before *b.* We can predict that the *a* in *cabin* will be short because the syllable follows the CVC pattern, and that the *a* in *cable* will be long because the syllable follows the CV pattern.

Figure 6–5 ◆ Books With Words Representing a Phonogram

Phonogram	Books
-ack	Shaw, N. E. (1996). *Sheep take a hike*. Boston: Houghton Mifflin.
-ail	Shaw, N. E. (1992). *Sheep on a ship*. Boston: Houghton Mifflin.
-are	Fleming, D. (1998). *In the small, small pond*. New York: Henry Holt.
-ash	Shaw, N. E. (2005). *Sheep eat out*. Boston: Houghton Mifflin.
-ay	Fleming, D. (1998). *In the small, small pond*. New York: Henry Holt.
-eep	Shaw, N. E. (1997). *Sheep in a jeep*. Boston: Houghton Mifflin.
-eet	Heiligman, D. (2005). *Fun dog, sun dog*. New York: Marshall Cavendish.
-ip	Fleming, D. (1995). *In the tall, tall grass*. New York: Henry Holt.
-og	Wood, A. (1992). *Silly Sally*. San Diego: Harcourt Brace.
-oose	Numeroff, L. J. (1991). *If you give a moose a muffin*. New York: HarperCollins.
-op	Shaw, N. E. (2005). *Sheep eat out*. Boston: Houghton Mifflin.
-ouse	Hoberman, M. A. (2007). *A house is a house for me*. New York: Puffin Books.
-own	Wood, A. (1992). *Silly Sally*. San Diego: Harcourt Brace.
-uck	Root, R. (2003). *One duck stuck*. Cambridge, MA: Candlewick Press.
-ug	Edwards, P. D. (1996). *Some smug slug*. New York: HarperCollins.
-um	Fleming, D. (1995). *In the tall, tall grass*. New York: Henry Holt.
-un	Heiligman, D. (2005). *Fun dog, sun dog*. New York: Marshall Cavendish.

The most basic rule about syllabication is that there's one vowel sound in each syllable. Consider the words *bit* and *bite*. *Bit* is a one-syllable word because there's one vowel letter representing one vowel sound. *Bite* is a one-syllable word, too, because even though there are two vowels, they represent one vowel sound. *Magic* and *curfew* are two-syllable words; there's one vowel letter and sound in each syllable in *magic*, but in the second syllable of *curfew*, the two vowels *ew* represent one vowel sound. Let's try a longer word: How many syllables are in *inconvenience*? There are six vowel letters representing four sounds in four syllables.

Syllabication rules are useful in teaching students how to divide words into syllables. Five of the most useful rules are listed in Figure 6–6. These 12 two-syllable words are from *A House for Hermit Crab* (Carle, 2005), the book Ms. Williams read in the vignette at the beginning of the chapter, and they illustrate all but one of the rules:

a-round	prom-ise	her-mit	with-out
pret-ty	ur-chin	nee-dles	cor-al
slow-ly	o-cean	ti-dy	com-plain

The first two rules focus on consonants, and the last three focus on vowels. The first rule, to divide between two consonants, is the most common rule; examples from the list include *her-mit* and *pret-ty*. The second rule deals with words where three consonants appear together in a word, such as *com-plain*: The word is divided

Figure 6–6 ◆ Syllabication Rules

Rules	Examples
• When two consonants come between two vowels in a word, divide syllables between the consonants.	cof-fee bor-der plas-tic jour-ney
• When there are more than two consonants together in a word, divide the syllables keeping the blends together.	em-ploy mon-ster en-trance bank-rupt
• When there is one consonant between two vowels in a word, divide the syllables after the first vowel.	ca-jole bo-nus plu-ral gla-cier
• If following the previous rule doesn't make a recognizable word, divide the syllables after the consonant that comes between the vowels.	doz-en ech-o meth-od cour-age
• When there are two vowels together that don't represent a long vowel sound or a diphthong, divide the syllables between the vowels.	cli-ent po-em cha-os li-on qui-et

between the *m* and the *p* in order to preserve the *pl* blend. The third and fourth rules involve the VCV pattern. Usually the syllable boundary comes after the first vowel, as in *ti-dy*, *o-cean*, and *a-round*; however, the division comes after the consonant in *cor-al* because dividing the word *co-ral* doesn't produce a recognizable word. The syllable boundary comes after the consonant in *without*, too, but this compound word has easily recognizable word parts. According to the fifth rule, words such as *qui-et* are divided between the two vowels because the vowels don't represent a vowel digraph or diphthong. This rule is the least common, and there were no examples of it in the story.

Teachers use minilessons to introduce syllabication and teach syllabication rules. During additional minilessons, students choose words from books they're reading and from thematic units for guided practice in breaking words into syllables. After identifying syllable boundaries, students pronounce and spell the words, syllable by syllable. Teachers also mark syllable boundaries on multisyllabic words on classroom word walls and create center activities in which students practice dividing words into syllables and building words using word parts. For example, after the word *compromise* came up in a social studies unit, a sixth-grade teacher developed a center activity in which students created two- and three-syllable words beginning with *com-* using syllable cards. Students created these words:

comic	*compliment*	*common*	*compromise*
companion	*complex*	*computer*	*comment*
complete	*commitment*	*complain*	*compartment*

After building these words, students brainstormed a list of additional words beginning with *com-*, including *complement*, *commuter*, *company*, *communicate*, *compass*, and *committee*.

Morphemic Analysis. Students examine the root word and affixes of longer unfamiliar words in order to identify them. A root word is a morpheme, the basic part of a word to which affixes are added. Many words are developed from a single root word; for example, the Latin words *portare* (to carry), *portus* (harbor), and *porta* (gate) are the sources of at least 12 English words: *deport*, *export*, *exporter*, *import*, *port*, *portable*, *porter*, *report*, *reporter*, *support*, *transport*, and *transportation*. Latin is the most common source of English root words; Greek and English are two other sources.

New Literacies
Visual Learning Software

Students use visual learning software to explore ideas and demonstrate their understanding through a combination of pictures and words. Inspiration® is a popular online graphics tool to help students visualize, think, organize, and learn (Silverman, 2005). It was developed for older students (grades 6–12), and a simpler version, Kidspiration®, was designed for children in kindergarten through fifth grade. Students use these software programs to practice strategies and skills they're learning in reading and across the curriculum. In word-identification activities, for example, they make maps and diagrams of words representing a phonogram, words with prefixes and suffixes, words sharing a root word, or etymological information about words (Gill, 2007). This software is especially useful for English learners: By visually representing information and adding links to show relationships, ELs convey their understanding more clearly than they could orally or in writing.

Kidspiration is an easy program for children to navigate. To begin, they choose the picture view on the starter screen and click on icons arranged on a tool bar to create graphic organizers, write words, search for appropriate images from the more than 3,000 pictures in the Symbol Library or create their own pictures, and add links to highlight relationships. There's a SuperGrouper tool that children use to categorize words, a word guide with a 13,000-word combined dictionary and thesaurus, and an audio feature that allows children to describe and document their work. In the writing view, their graphic organizers are transformed into skeleton compositions, and children expand the words into sentences and paragraphs. Afterward, they can export the texts into multimodal projects or print them.

Inspiration is similar to Kidspiration. Students create diagrams using the Inspiration software that can be transformed into outlines and used for writing and Web-based projects. They use tool bars to navigate the program, choose images from the Symbol Library that's loaded with more than one million pictures or design their own, consult a word guide with a combined dictionary and thesaurus, and monitor their spelling with a spell checker. Students integrate video and sound clips, record their own audio, use a hyperlink tool to connect to research documents and websites, and export Inspiration documents to word processing, PowerPoint, or other programs.

Both software programs include templates and a template wizard that teachers use to modify the diagrams and create their own. Teacher guidebooks and online resources are also available; these resources include diagram archives, curriculum packets, training videos, and case studies with real-life stories about how K–8 teachers and students have used these visual learning software programs.

It's important that students become comfortable using 21st-century technology. As they work with visual learning software, students learn to navigate the programs, transform information from visual to written modes, and craft multimodal projects. Kidspiration and Inspiration software programs are compatible with other emerging classroom technologies, including interactive whiteboards and handheld devices. Teachers are invited to download Kidspiration or Inspiration software with their complete symbol palettes at www.inspiration.com for a free 30-day trial, and afterward the software's available for purchase online.

Some root words are whole words, and others are word parts. Some root words have become free morphemes and can be used as separate words, but others can't. For instance, *cent* comes from the Latin root word *cent*, meaning "hundred." English treats the word as a root word that can be used independently and in combination with affixes, as in *century*, *bicentennial*, and *centipede*. The words *cosmopolitan*, *cosmic*, and *microcosm* come from the Greek root word *cosmo*, meaning "universe"; it isn't an independent root word in English. A list of Latin and Greek root words appears in Figure 6–7. English words such as *eye*, *tree*, and *water* are root words, too. New words are formed through compounding—for example, *eyelash*, *treetop*, and *waterfall*—and other English root words, such as *read*, combine with affixes, as in *reader* and *unreadable*.

Affixes are bound morphemes that are added to words: Prefixes are added at the beginning, as in *replay*, and suffixes are added to the end, as in *playing*, *playful*, and *player*. Like root words, some affixes are English and others come from Latin and Greek. Affixes often change a word's meaning, such as adding *un-* to *happy* to form *unhappy*. Sometimes they change the part of speech, too; for example, when *-tion* is added to *attract* to form *attraction*, the verb *attract* becomes a noun.

There are two types of suffixes: inflectional and derivational. Inflectional suffixes are endings that indicate verb tense and person, plurals, possession, and comparison; these suffixes are English. They influence the syntax of sentences. Here are some examples:

the *-ed* in *walked*	the *-es* in *beaches*
the *-ing* in *singing*	the *-'s* in *girl's*
the *-s* in *asks*	the *-er* in *faster*
the *-s* in *dogs*	the *-est* in *sunniest*

In contrast, derivational suffixes show the relationship of the word to its root word. Consider these words containing the root word *friend*: *friendly*, *friendship*, and *friendless*.

When a word's affix is "peeled off," the remaining word is usually a real word. For example, when the prefix *pre-* is removed from *preview* or the suffix *-er* is removed from *viewer*, the word *view* can stand alone. Some words include letter sequences that might be affixes, but because the remaining words can't stand alone, they aren't affixes. For example, the *in-* at the beginning of *include* is not a prefix because *clude* isn't a word. Similarly, the *-ic* at the end of *magic* is not a suffix because *mag* isn't a word. Sometimes, however, Latin and Greek root words cannot stand alone. One example is *legible*: The *-ible* is a suffix, and *leg* is the root word even though it can't stand alone. Of course, *leg*—meaning part of the body—is a word, but the root word *leg-* from *legible* isn't: It's a Latin root word, meaning "to read."

A list of derivational prefixes and suffixes is presented in Figure 6–8. White, Sowell, and Yanagihara (1989) researched affixes and identified the most common ones; these are marked with an asterisk in Figure 6–8. White and his colleagues recommend teaching the common derivational affixes to students in grades 4–8 because of their usefulness. Some of the most common prefixes are confusing, however, because they have more than one meaning; the prefix *un-*, for example, can mean *not* (e.g., *unclear*) or it can reverse the meaning of a word (e.g., *tie–untie*).

Teaching Word Identification. Word-level learning is an essential part of a balanced literacy program (Hiebert, 1991), and teaching minilessons about analogies and phonic, syllabic, and morphemic analysis is a useful way to help students focus on words. Teachers choose words for minilessons from books students are reading, as Ms. Williams did in the vignette, or from thematic units. The minilesson feature on page 205 shows how Mr. Morales teaches his sixth graders about morphemic analysis as part of a thematic unit on ancient civilizations.

Figure 6–7 ◆ Latin and Greek Root Words

Root	Language	Meaning	Sample Words
ann/enn	Latin	year	anniversary, annual, centennial, millennium, perennial, semiannual
arch	Greek	ruler	anarchy, archbishop, architecture, hierarchy, monarchy, patriarch
astro	Greek	star	aster, asterisk, astrology, astronaut, astronomy, disaster
auto	Greek	self	autobiography, automatic, automobile, autopsy, semiautomatic
bio	Greek	life	biography, biohazard, biology, biodegradable, bionic, biosphere
capit/capt	Latin	head	capital, capitalize, capitol, captain, caption, decapitate, per capita
cent	Latin	hundred	bicentennial, cent, centennial, centigrade, centipede, century, percent
circ	Latin	around	circle, circular, circus, circumspect, circuit, circumference, circumstance
cosmo	Greek	universe	cosmic, cosmopolitan, cosmos, microcosm
cred	Latin	believe	credit, creed, creditable, discredit, incredulity
cycl	Greek	wheel	bicycle, cycle, cyclist, cyclone, recycle, tricycle
dict	Latin	speak	contradict, dictate, dictator, prediction, verdict
gram	Greek	letter	cardiogram, diagram, grammar, monogram, telegram
graph	Greek	write	autobiography, biographer, cryptograph, epigraph, graphic, paragraph
jus/jud/jur	Latin	law	injury, injustice, judge, juror, jury, justice, justify, prejudice
lum/lus/luc	Latin	light	illuminate, lucid, luminous, luster, translucent
man	Latin	hand	manacle, maneuver, manicure, manipulate, manual, manufacture
mar/mer	Latin	sea	aquamarine, marine, maritime, marshy, mermaid, submarine
meter	Greek	measure	centimeter, diameter, seismometer, speedometer, thermometer
mini	Latin	small	miniature, minibus, minimize, minor, minimum, minuscule, minute
mort	Latin	death	immortal, mortality, mortuary, postmortem
ped	Latin	foot	biped, impede, pedal, pedestrian, pedicure
phono	Greek	sound	earphone, microphone, phonics, phonograph, saxophone, symphony
photo	Greek	light	photograph, photographer, photosensitive, photosynthesis
pod/pus	Greek	foot	gastropod, octopus, podiatry, podium, tripod
port	Latin	carry	exporter, import, port, portable, porter, reporter, support, transportation
quer/ques/quis	Latin	seek	query, quest, question, inquisitive, request
scope	Latin	see	horoscope, kaleidoscope, microscope, periscope, telescope
scrib/scrip	Latin	write	describe, inscription, postscript, prescribe, scribble, scribe, script
sphere	Greek	ball	atmosphere, atmospheric, hemisphere, sphere, stratosphere
struct	Latin	build	construct, construction, destruction, indestructible, instruct, reconstruct
tele	Greek	far	telecast, telegram, telegraph, telephone, telescope, telethon, television
terr	Latin	land	subterranean, terrace, terrain, terrarium, terrier, territory
vers/vert	Latin	turn	advertise, anniversary, controversial, divert, reversible, versus
vict/vinc	Latin	conquer	convince, convict, evict, invincible, victim, victor, victory
vis/vid	Latin	see	improvise, invisible, revise, supervisor, television, video, vision, visitor
viv/vit	Latin	live	revive, survive, vital, vitamin, vivacious, vivid, viviparous
volv	Latin	roll	convolutions, evolve, evolution, involve, revolutionary, revolver, volume

Figure 6–8 ◆ Derivational Affixes

Language	Prefixes	Suffixes
English	***over-** (too much): overflow **self-** (by oneself): self-employed ***un-** (not): unhappy ***un-** (reversal): untie **under-** (beneath): underground	**-ful** (full of): hopeful **-ish** (like): reddish **-less** (without): hopeless **-ling** (young): duckling ***-ly** (in the manner of): slowly ***-ness** (state or quality): kindness **-ship** (state of, art, or skill): friendship, seamanship **-ster** (one who): gangster **-ward** (direction): homeward ***-y** (full of): sleepy
Greek	**a-/an-** (not): atheist, anaerobic **amphi-** (both): amphibian **anti-** (against): antiseptic **di-** (two): dioxide **hemi-** (half): hemisphere **hyper-** (over): hyperactive **hypo-** (under): hypodermic **micro-** (small): microfilm **mono-** (one): monarch **omni-** (all): omnivorous **poly-** (many): polygon **sym-/syn-/sys-** (together): symbol, synonym, system	**-ism** (doctrine of): communism **-ist** (one who): artist **-logy** (the study of): zoology
Latin	**bi-** (two, twice): bifocal, biannual **contra-** (against): contradict **de-** (away): detract ***dis-** (not): disapprove ***dis-** (reversal): disinfect **ex-** (out): export ***il-/im-/in-/ir-** (not): illegible, impolite, inexpensive, irrational ***in-** (in, into): indoor **inter-** (between): intermission **mille-** (thousand): millennium ***mis-** (wrong): mistake **multi-** (many): multimillionaire **non-** (not): nonsense **post-** (after): postwar **pre-** (before): precede **quad-/quart-** (four): quadruple, quarter **re-** (again): repay ***re-/retro-** (back): replace, retroactive ***sub-** (under): submarine **super-** (above): supermarket **trans-** (across): transport **tri-** (three): triangle	**-able/-ible** (worthy of, can be): lovable, audible ***-al/-ial** (action, process): arrival, denial **-ance/-ence** (state or quality): annoyance, absence **-ant** (one who): servant **-ary/-ory** (person, place): secretary, laboratory **-cule** (very small): molecule **-ee** (one who is): trustee ***-er/-or/-ar** (one who): teacher, actor, liar **-ic** (characterized by): angelic **-ify** (to make): simplify **-ment** (state or quality): enjoyment **-ous** (full of): nervous ***-sion/-tion** (state or quality): tension, attraction **-ure** (state or quality): failure

From White, Sowell, & Yanagihara. Most commonly used affixes.

Minilesson

As part of a thematic unit on ancient civilizations, Mr. Morales introduces the concepts *democracy, monarchy, oligarchy,* and *theocracy* and adds the words to the word wall; however, he notices that many of his sixth graders have difficulty pronouncing the words and remembering what they mean even though they've read about them in the social studies textbook.

1 Introduce the Topic

Mr. Morales looks over the ancient civilizations word wall and reads aloud these words: *democracy, monarchy, oligarchy,* and *theocracy.* Marcos volunteers that he thinks that the words have something to do with kings or rulers, but he's not sure.

2 Share Examples

The teacher writes the words on the chalkboard, dividing them into syllables so that the sixth graders can pronounce them more easily. The students practice saying the words several times, but they're still puzzled about their meanings.

3 Provide Information

Mr. Morales explains that he can help them figure out the meaning of the words. "The words are Greek," he says, "and they have two word parts. If you know the meaning of the word parts, you'll be able to figure out the meaning of the words." He writes the four words and breaks them into word parts this way:

democracy = demo + cracy   monarchy = mono + archy
oligarchy = olig + archy   theocracy = theo + cracy

Then he explains that Marcos was right—the words have to do with kings and rulers: They describe different kinds of government. *Cracy* means *government* and *archy* means *leader.* The first word part tells more about the kind of government; one of them means *gods,* and the others mean *one, people,* and *few.* The students work in small groups to figure out that *democracy* means government by the people, *monarchy* means one leader, *oligarchy* means rule by a few leaders, and *theocracy* means government by the gods.

4 Guide Practice

The next day, Mr. Morales divides the class into four groups, and each group makes a poster to describe one of the four types of government. On each poster, students write the word, the two Greek word parts, and a definition. They also create an illustration based on what they've learned about this type of government. Afterward, students share their posters with the class and display them in the classroom.

5 Assess Learning

On the third day, Mr. Morales passes out a list of six sentences about the types of government taken from the social studies textbook and asks them to identify the type. He encourages the sixth graders to refer to the posters the class made as they complete the assignment. Afterward, he reviews their papers to determine which students can use the words correctly to identify the four types of government.

Guidelines

for Teaching Students to Identify Words

▶ Post high-frequency words on word walls.

▶ Teach students to read and spell high-frequency words in minilessons.

▶ Practice reading and writing high-frequency words through authentic literacy activities.

▶ Introduce key words before reading, and teach other words during and after reading.

▶ Model how to use word-identification strategies during interactive read-alouds and shared reading.

▶ Teach students to use phonic analysis, decoding by analogy, syllabic analysis, and morphemic analysis word-identification strategies.

▶ Use words from reading selections as examples in minilessons on word-identification strategies.

▶ Encourage students to apply word-identification strategies to both reading and spelling.

Fluent readers develop a large repertoire of sight words and use word-identification strategies to decode unfamiliar words. Less capable readers, in contrast, can't read as many words and don't use as many strategies for decoding words. Researchers have concluded again and again that students who don't become fluent readers depend on explicit instruction to learn how to identify words (R. W. Gaskins et al., 1991). The guidelines for teaching word identification are summarized above.

Assessing Students' Word Identification. Teachers use a combination of informal assessment tools and classroom tests to monitor students' ability to identify unfamiliar words and to determine which word-identification strategies they can use successfully. Teachers can often gauge students' progress as they listen to them read aloud and notice how they figure out the unfamiliar words they come across. Teachers also use the graded word lists and running records to analyze their progress according to grade-level standards. Check the Assessment Tools feature on the next page for more information about word-identification assessment tools.

How students spell words also provides information about their ability to identify words. When students use word-identification strategies to spell words correctly, it's likely that they're also using the strategies for reading; and when students depend on their phonics knowledge to spell words, they're probably depending on phonics to figure out unfamiliar words when they're reading.

WHAT IS FLUENCY?

Go to the Building Teaching Skills and Dispositions section of Chapter 6 on **MyEducationLab.com** to watch and listen as students and their teacher discuss fluency.

Fluency is the ability to read efficiently, and it's a bridge to comprehension (Allington, 2009). Fluent readers are better able to comprehend what they read because they automatically recognize most words and can apply word-identification strategies when they come across unfamiliar words (LaBerge & Samuels, 1976). Their reading is faster, and they read expressively (Kuhn & Rasinski, 2007). It's a milestone in students' reading achievement! In contrast, students who aren't fluent readers often read slowly and hesitantly. They devote most of their mental energy to identifying words, leaving few cognitive resources available for comprehension.

Assessment Tools

Word Identification

Teachers use a variety of classroom tests to determine whether students can identify unfamiliar words in grade-level texts and which word-identification strategies they use successfully.

◆ **Developmental Reading Assessment, Grades K–3 (DRA)** (Beaver, 2006) and **Developmental Reading Assessment, Grades 4–8** (Beaver & Carter, 2003)

Two versions of DRA are available, one for the primary grades and the other for middle and upper grades. Each one contains a collection of leveled books to use in assessing students' reading levels. Students read leveled books aloud while teachers take running records to analyze their reading. To examine students' ability to use word-identification strategies, teachers analyze the unfamiliar words that students identify correctly and those they can't to determine which strategies they're applying successfully.

◆ **The Names Test: A Quick Assessment of Decoding Ability** (Cunningham, 1990; Duffelmeyer et al., 1994; Mather, Sammons, & Schwartz, 2006)

The Names Test focuses on decoding, one of four ways to identify unfamiliar words. It measures third through eighth graders' ability to apply phoneme-grapheme correspondences, phonics rules, and spelling patterns to decode unfamiliar words. The test is a list of names that students read aloud. Teachers record students' errors and then analyze them to determine which phonics concepts students haven't acquired to plan for future instruction. This no-cost assessment is available online.

◆ **Phonological Awareness Literacy Screening (PALS) System: Word Recognition in Isolation Subtest** (Invernizzi, Meier, & Juel, 2003)

This PALS subtest consists of graded word lists that children read aloud; the highest level where children can read at least 15 words correctly is the instructional level. First- through third-grade teachers use the subtest to monitor children's accurate and automatic recognition of words, and kindergarten teachers administer the test when they believe a child is already reading. The PALS test is available free for Virginia teachers from the University of Virginia, and it can be purchased by teachers in other states.

◆ **Running Records**

Teachers take running records (Clay, 2005) as children read aloud to analyze their ability to identify unfamiliar words, and afterward they categorize children's errors to determine which word-identification strategies children use effectively and which ones they don't.

These assessments are used to evaluate children's progress toward becoming fluent readers, but once readers can read fluently, they aren't needed any longer.

Writing fluency is similar to reading fluency: Students need to be able to write quickly and easily so that their hands and arms don't hurt. Slow, laborious handwriting interferes with the expression of ideas. In addition, students must be able to spell high-frequency words automatically so that they can focus on the ideas they're writing about.

Components of Fluency

Fluency involves three components: accuracy, speed, and prosody (Rasinski, 2003). Too often, reading quickly is equated with fluency, and some assessment tools use speed as their only measure of fluency, but accurately identifying words and reading expressively are also critical components.

Accuracy. Accuracy is the ability to recognize familiar words automatically, without any conscious thought, and to identify unfamiliar words almost as quickly. It's crucial that students immediately recognize most of the words they're reading. When students have to stop to decode words in every sentence, their reading isn't fluent; it's an indication that the selection is too difficult. The conventional wisdom is that students can read a text successfully when they know at least 95% of the words, which is 19 of every 20 words or 95 of every 100 words. Allington (2009) challenges this notion, suggesting that students need to know 98 or 99% of the words in a text to read it fluently; otherwise, stopping again and again to use word-identification strategies to figure out the unfamiliar words places too much of a burden on readers.

Reading Speed. Reading speed refers to the rate at which students read; to read fluently, students need to orally read at least 100 words per minute. Most students reach this reading speed by third grade, and their reading rate continues to grow. By the time they're sixth graders, they'll read 150 words per minute, and adults typically read 250 words per minute or more. Of course, both children and adults vary their reading speed depending on the difficulty of what they're reading and their purpose, but excessively slow or fast reading is often a characteristic of dysfluent readers.

Prosody. The third component, prosody, is the ability to orally read sentences expressively, with appropriate phrasing and intonation. Dowhower (1991) describes prosody as "the ability to read in expressive rhythmic and melodic patterns" (p. 166). Students move from word-by-word reading with little or no expression to chunking words into phrases, attending to punctuation, and applying appropriate syntactic emphases. Fluent readers' oral reading approximates speech, and for their reading to be expressive, they have to recognize accurately and automatically most of the words they're reading and read quickly.

Dysfluent Readers

Young children read slowly, pointing at each word as they pronounce it, but as they learn to recognize more words and gain experience, their reading becomes faster and smoother. In second grade, most children develop a large bank of sight words that they recognize instantly so they're able to chunk the the words they're reading into longer phrases and add more expression to their oral reading. They apply what they've learned by listening to parents and teachers read aloud. In third grade, students' reading becomes fluent. They usually can read 100 words or more per minute and vary the emphasis they place on particular words and phrases to make their reading more meaningful. Some students, however, don't become fluent readers. They exemplify some of these characteristics:

◆ Students read slowly or too quickly.
◆ Students try to sound out phonetically irregular words.
◆ Students guess at words based on the beginning sound.
◆ Students don't remember a word the second or third time it is used in a passage.
◆ Students don't break multisyllabic words into syllables or root words to decode them.
◆ Students point at words as they read.
◆ Students repeat words and phrases.
◆ Students read without expression.
◆ Students read in a word-by-word manner.
◆ Students ignore punctuation marks.
◆ Students don't remember or understand what they read.

Allington (2009) offers three reasons why some students struggle to become fluent readers. First, these students regularly read books that are too difficult, instead of those at their instructional and independent levels. Second, they do very little actual reading. Struggling readers typically do much less reading than more capable readers, even though increasing reading volume is necessary to become better readers. Third, teachers frequently ask struggling readers to read aloud and then immediately interrupt them when they misread a word, rather than giving them time to notice and correct their error. In time, these students become more tentative, word-by-word readers who depend on teachers to monitor their reading instead of monitoring it themselves. Teachers can ensure that all students become fluent readers by providing them with books at their reading levels, scheduling more time for them to read interesting texts, and modifying their interactions with struggling readers so that they interrupt them less often and nurture their strategic behaviors.

Promoting Reading Fluency

Nonfluent readers can learn to read fluently (Allington, 2009). They may need to work on their accuracy, reading speed, or prosody, or on all three components of fluency. They may also need more reading practice—daily opportunities to read books at their reading levels to develop reading stamina. Rasinski (2003) identified four principles of fluency instruction:

- ◆ Teachers model fluent reading for students.
- ◆ Teachers provide oral support while students are reading.
- ◆ Teachers have students do repeated readings of brief texts.
- ◆ Teachers focus students' attention on chunking words into meaningful phrases.

The instructional recommendations that follow embody these principles.

Enhancing Accuracy. To become fluent readers, students learn to accurately and automatically recognize two kinds of words during the primary grades—high-frequency words that often can't be sounded out and phonetically regular words. Students who aren't fluent may need instruction on one or both types of words, depending on which words they can read. To teach high-frequency words, teachers present minilessons on the words and post them on a word wall in the classroom, and to teach phonetically regular words, teachers present minilessons on phonics skills. Then students need daily opportunities to practice the words they're learning in reading and writing activities.

Teaching Struggling Readers and Writers

Fluency
Struggling readers need to read fluently.

Many struggling readers don't read fluently, and their labored reading affects their comprehension. Allington (2006) examined the research about dysfluent readers and found that there's no single common problem; some have difficulty decoding words, whereas others read very slowly or in a monotone, ignoring phrasing and punctuation cues. Because struggling readers exhibit different fluency problems, it's essential to diagnose students and to plan instruction that's tailored to their instructional needs. To examine whether fluency is a problem, teachers listen to students read aloud in an appropriately leveled book and ask themselves these questions about their accuracy, reading speed, and prosody:

- *Does the student decode unfamiliar words quickly?*
- *Does the student know high-frequency words?*
- *Is the student's oral reading speed adequate for the text being read?*
- *Is the student's reading expressive?*

If struggling readers exhibit one or more problems, teachers provide instruction and involve them in activities, such as rereading familiar texts using repeated readings, using cross-age reading buddies for reading practice, and choral reading to develop reading speed and expression.

Teachers also ensure that struggling students have daily opportunities for independent reading in books that they can read comfortably. Too often, struggling readers try to read books like those that their classmates are reading, but they're usually too difficult. To increase reading volume, struggling readers need access to interesting books at their independent reading level and plenty of time to read, and to develop more interest in reading, students need to read fluently and comprehend what they're reading so they'll become confident that they're successful readers.

Most second graders move toward fluent reading, and Ms. Janusz spends a great deal of time talking about fluent reading, explaining its importance, teaching the components, and listening to her students read aloud to monitor their growth. Click on Rakie's December button to watch Ms. Janusz explain reading fluency during a guided reading lesson. Does she include the three components of fluency addressed in this chapter? Why do you think that she asks students to retell what they've just read? On this video clip, you can also listen to Rakie reading aloud. Next, click on Rakie's May button to listen to her reread *Click, Clack, Moo: Cows That Type*, by Doreen Cronin, and retell it to a classmate. It's one of her favorite books, and she's read it many times. Compare her accuracy, reading speed, and expression now with her fluency in December. Do you think that she's become a fluent reader?

myeducationlab

Improving Reading Speed. The best way to improve students' reading speed is repeated readings (Samuels, 1979), in which students practice reading aloud a book or an excerpt at their independent level three to five times, striving to improve their reading speed and decrease the number of errors with each reading. Teachers time students' reading and plot their speed on a graph so that improvements can be noted. Repeated readings also enhance students' ability to chunk words into meaningful phrases and read more expressively (Dowhower, 1989).

Teachers also have students reread passages as part of guided reading lessons when they want to improve students' reading speed. The teacher reads the passage aloud while students follow along or use echo reading, in which they repeat each phrase or sentence after the teacher reads it. After several repetitions, students read the passage one more time, this time independently. Teachers also set up rereading opportunities at a listening center; this activity is called Reading While Listening (Kuhn & Stahl, 2004). Students read along in a book as they listen to it read aloud.

Teaching Prosody. Schreider (1991) recommends teaching students how to phrase or chunk together parts of sentences in order to read with expression. Fluent readers seem to understand how to chunk parts of sentences into meaningful units, perhaps because they've been read to or have had many reading experiences themselves, but many struggling readers don't have this ability. Consider this sentence from *Sarah, Plain and Tall* (MacLachlan, 2004): "A few raindrops came, gentle at first, then stronger and louder, so that Caleb and I covered our ears and stared at each other without speaking" (p. 47). This sentence comes from the chapter describing a terrible storm that the pioneer family endured, huddled with their animals in their sturdy barn. Three commas help students read the first part of this sentence, but then they must decide how to chunk the second part.

Teachers work with nonfluent readers to break sentences into chunks and then read the sentences with expression. Teachers make copies of a page from a book students are reading so that they can mark pauses in longer sentences. Or, teachers can choose a sentence to write on the chalkboard, chunking it into phrases like this:

> A few raindrops came,
> gentle at first,
> then stronger and louder,
> so that Caleb and I
> covered our ears
> and stared at each other
> without speaking.

After chunking, students practice reading the sentence with classmates and individually. After working with one sentence, they work with a partner to choose another sentence to chunk and practice reading. Students who don't chunk words into phrases when they read aloud need many opportunities to practice chunking and rereading sentences.

Activities such as choral reading also help students improve their phrasing. In choral reading, students and the teacher take turns reading the text, as Ms. Williams and her students did in the vignette at the beginning of the chapter. Students provide support for each other because they're reading in small groups, and they learn to phrase sentences as they read together. Choral reading also improves students' reading speed because they read along with classmates.

One variation of choral reading is unison reading, in which the teacher and students read a text together (Reutzel & Cooter, 2008). The teacher is the leader and reads loudly enough to be heard above the group. Another variation is echo reading, in which the teacher reads a sentence with good phrasing and intonation, and then students read the same material again. If the students read confidently, the teacher moves to the next sentence. However, if students struggle to read the sentence, the teacher repeats the first sentence. These activities are especially useful for helping English learners to develop appropriate prosody.

Reading Practice. Students need many opportunities to practice reading and rereading books to develop fluency (Rasinski, 2003). The best books for reading practice are ones that students are interested in reading and that are written at their independent level; books for fluency practice should be neither too easy nor too difficult. Students should automatically recognize most words in the book, but if the book is extremely easy, it provides no challenge. And, when students read books that are too difficult, they read slowly because they stop again and again to identify unfamiliar words; this constant stopping reinforces nonfluent readers' already choppy reading style.

For reading practice, students often choose "pop" literature that's fun to read but rather ordinary. These books are often more effective than high-quality literature selections in helping children develop fluency because the vocabulary is more controlled, which allows students to be more successful. In addition, children like them because the stories are humorous or fantastic, or because they relate to their own lives. The popular Magic Tree House series, with coordinated stories and informational books, is written at the first- and second-grade reading levels, the time-travel stories in The Zack Files series at the second- and third-grade levels, and the hilarious Captain Underpants series at the third- and fourth-grade levels. A list of picture-book and chapter-book series written at the first- through fourth-grade levels is presented in Figure 6–9. More and more easy-to-read picture books and chapter books are becoming available each year, and many of them appeal to boys.

Teachers provide two types of daily opportunities for children to practice reading and rereading familiar stories and other books; some activities provide assisted practice, and others provide students with opportunities to read independently, without assistance. In assisted practice, students have a model to follow as they read or reread. Choral reading, readers theatre, and buddy reading are three examples. In choral reading, students experiment with different ways to read poems and other short texts (Rasinski, 2003). In readers theatre, students practice reading story scripts to develop fluency before reading the script to an audience of classmates. Researchers have found that practice reading using readers theatre scripts results in significant improvement in students' reading fluency (Griffith & Rasinski, 2004; Martinez, Roser, & Strecker, 1998/1999). In buddy reading, pairs of students who read at approximately the same level read or reread books together (Griffith & Rasinski, 2004). They choose a book that interests them and decide how they will read it. They may choose to read in unison or take turns reading aloud while the partner follows along. Sometimes when students are rereading familiar books, the student who isn't reading counts the errors that the reader makes and helps the reader with corrections afterward (Cunningham & Allington, 2007).

Figure 6–9 ◆ Popular Series of Picture Books and Chapter Books

Reading Level	Series	Description
1	Amelia Bedelia	Comical stories about a housekeeper who takes instructions literally.
	Fox and Friends	Stories about Fox, who likes to have everything his way.
	Pinky and Rex	Stories about two best friends, a boy named Pinky and a girl named Rex.
1–2	Arthur	Picture-book stories about an aardvark named Arthur.
	Henry and Mudge	Chapter-book stories about Henry and his 180-pound dog, Mudge.
	Junie B. Jones	Stories about a delightful girl who's always getting into trouble.
	The Magic Tree House	Stories about a magical tree house that transports children back in time and companion informational books.
	Third-Grade Detectives	Adventures featuring Todd and Noelle, two clever third graders.
2	Cam Jansen	Funny chapter books about a girl detective named Cam Jansen.
	Jigsaw Jones Mysteries	Stories featuring private eye Jigsaw Jones and his partner, Mila Yeh.
	Franklin	Picture-book stories featuring a gentle turtle-hero named Franklin.
	George and Martha	Stories about George and Martha, two hippo friends.
	Horrible Harry	Hilarious stories about Harry, who's a second-grade prankster.
	The Kids in Ms. Colman's Class	Chapter-book stories about a class of second graders.
2–3	Black Lagoon	Picture-book series deals with children's fears of the unknown.
	Marvin Redpost	Funny stories about third-grade Marvin Redpost.
	The Zack Files	Time-travel stories featuring a fifth grader named Zack.
	A to Z Mysteries	An alphabetical collection of mysteries.
3	Adventures of the Bailey School Kids	Chapter-book stories about the adventures of a diverse third-grade class.
	Hank the Cowdog	Fantastic chapter-book stories told by a cowdog named Hank.
	The Magic School Bus	Ms. Frizzle's adventures in her magic school bus.
	Secrets of the Droon	Fantasy adventures set in the magical world of Droon.
	Geronimo Stilton	Stories about Geronimo Stilton, a mouse who runs *The Rodent's Gazette*.
3–4	Amber Brown	Chapter-book stories about a spunky girl with a colorful name.
	Captain Underpants	Hilarious chapter-book stories about the superhero Captain Underpants.
	Time Warp Trio	Three friends travel back in time for adventure.

Developing Reading Stamina. Once students become fluent readers, the focus shifts to helping them develop reading stamina, or the strength to read silently for increasingly longer periods of time. Students develop this stamina through daily opportunities to read independently for extended periods. When students' reading is limited to reading basal reader selections, single chapters in novels, or magazine articles that can be completed in 15 or 20 minutes, they won't develop the endurance they need. Many teachers find that by sixth and seventh grades, their students can't read for more than 15 or 20 minutes at a time, or students complain about how tired they are or how hard reading is when they are asked to read for longer periods. It's crucial that students learn to read for longer periods of time so that they can handle novels and other chapter books and the lengthy texts they are asked to read on standardized tests.

Students develop this endurance through reading books at their independent level. Teachers typically include extended opportunities each day for independent reading of self-selected texts through Sustained Silent Reading at all grade levels. Kindergartners read for 5 to 10 minutes; in first grade, students begin by reading and rereading books for 10 to 15 minutes, and reach 20 minutes or more by the end of the school year. The time students spend reading gradually increases to at least 30 minutes a day in second and third grades, and students shift from oral to silent reading as they become fluent readers. In fourth and fifth grades, students' independent reading time increases to 40 or 45 minutes, and in sixth, seventh, and eighth grades, students spend 45 to 60 minutes a day reading. Students also benefit from doing additional independent reading at home.

Another way of looking at how students develop stamina is by the number of words they're expected to read. Many school districts now call for students to read 500,000 words in fourth grade and gradually increase the number of words until they read one million words in eighth grade. You may wonder how the number of words translates to books: Students in fourth, fifth, and sixth grades often read novels that are approximately 200 pages long, and these books typically have approximately 35,000 words; for example, *Esperanza Rising* (Ryan, 2000), *Loser* (Spinelli, 2002), and *Homeless Bird* (Whelan, 2000). Therefore, students need to read approximately 14 books to reach 500,000 words. Students who read two novels each month will reach the 500,000-word mark.

Students in seventh and eighth grades usually read longer books with 250 pages or more. Books with 250 pages, such as *Bud, Not Buddy* (Curtis, 1999), *Holes* (Sachar, 2003), and *Crispin: The Cross of Lead* (Avi, 2002), contain at least 50,000 words. Books containing more than 300 pages, such as *Harry Potter and the Chamber of Secrets* (Rowling, 1999), range from 75,000 to 100,000 words. Students need to read 10 to 20 books, depending on length, to reach one million words. So, students who read two books with 250 to 350 pages each month will reach the one million–word mark.

Why Is Round-Robin Reading No Longer Recommended? Round-robin reading is an outmoded oral reading activity in which the teacher calls on children to read aloud, one after the other (Johns & Berglund, 2006). Some teachers used round-robin reading in small groups and others used the procedure with the whole class, but neither version is advocated today. According to Opitz and Rasinski (1998), many problems are associated with round-robin reading. First of all, students may develop an inaccurate view of reading because they are expected to read aloud to the class without having opportunities to rehearse. Next, they may develop inefficient reading habits because they alter their silent reading speed to match the various speeds of classmates when they read aloud. Students signal their inattention and boredom by misbehaving as classmates read aloud. In addition to these problems for students who are listening, round-robin reading causes problems for some students when they are called upon to read: Struggling readers are often anxious or embarrassed when they read aloud.

Researchers agree that round-robin reading wastes valuable classroom time that could be spent on more meaningful oral and silent reading activities (Allington, 2009). Instead of round-robin reading, students should read books independently if they're at their reading level. If the books are too difficult, they can read with buddies, participate in shared reading, or listen to the teacher or another fluent reader read aloud. Also, they might listen to the teacher read the material aloud and then try reading it with a buddy or independently.

Nurturing English Learners

To become fluent readers, English learners need to read words accurately, quickly, and expressively, like native speakers do. It's very unlikely that they'll become fluent readers, however, before they learn to speak English fluently, because their lack of oral language proficiency limits their recognition of high-frequency words and use of word-learning strategies, and it interferes with their ability to understand word meanings, string words together into sentences, and read expressively (Peregoy & Boyle, 2008).

Many ELs speak and read English with a native-language accent, but their differences in pronunciation and intonation shouldn't hamper their reading fluency. Everyone has an accent, even native English speakers, so ELs should never be expected to eliminate their accents to be considered fluent readers.

The same types of instruction and practice activities that are recommended for native speakers are effective with English learners; however, ELs often need more time because they're learning to speak English at the same time they're learning to read. Teachers continue teaching high-frequency words and word-learning strategies until students learn them, and ELs need to spend more time every day reading texts at their independent reading level. It's often helpful to have students reread Language Experience Approach stories and other familiar texts, participate in choral reading activities, and engage in oral reading practice with buddies to get all the practice they need.

Developing Writing Fluency

To become fluent writers, students must be able to rapidly form letters and spell words automatically. Just as nonfluent readers read word by word and have to stop and decode many words, nonfluent writers write slowly, word by word, and have to stop and check the spelling of many words. In fact, some nonfluent writers write so slowly that they forget the sentence they're writing! Through varied, daily writing activities, students develop the muscular control to form letters quickly and legibly. They write high-frequency words again and again until they can spell them automatically. Being able to write fluently usually coincides with being able to read fluently because reading and writing practice are mutually beneficial (Shanahan, 1988; Tierney, 1983).

Students become fluent writers as they practice writing, and they need opportunities for both assisted and unassisted practice. Writing on dry-erase boards during interactive writing lessons is one example of assisted writing practice (Tompkins, 2008). The teacher and classmates provide support for students.

Quickwriting. Peter Elbow (1998) recommends using quickwriting to develop writing fluency. In quickwriting, students write rapidly and without stopping as they explore an idea. As part of the unit on hermit crabs, Ms. Williams asked the second-grade students to do a quickwrite listing what they had learned about hermit crabs. Here is Arlette's quickwrite:

 Hermit crabs live in tide pools. They have pincers and 10 legs in all. They can pinch you very hard. Ouch! They are crabs and they molt to grow and grow. They have to buro [borrow] shells to live in becus other anmels [animals] will eat them. They like to eat fish and shrimp. Sea enomes [anemones] like to live on ther shells.

Arlette listed a great deal of information that she'd learned about hermit crabs. She misspelled five words; some correct spellings are given in brackets. Arlette was able to write such a long quickwrite and to misspell so few words because she is already a fluent writer. While she was writing, she checked the hermit crab word wall and the high-frequency word wall in the classroom in order to spell *pincers*, *shrimp*, and *other*. She knew how to spell the other words and wrote them automatically.

In contrast, Jeremy is not yet a fluent writer. Here is his quickwrite:

The hermit crab liv in a hues [house]
he eat [eats] shimp [shrimp].

Jeremy writes slowly and laboriously. He stops to think of an idea before writing each sentence and starts each sentence on a new line. He rarely refers to the word walls in the classroom and spells most words phonetically. Even though Jeremy's writing is not as fluent as Arlette's, quickwriting is a useful activity for him because he'll become more fluent through practice.

Ms. Williams has her students quickwrite several times each week. They quickwrite to respond to a story she's read aloud or to write about what they're learning in science. She reads and responds to the quickwrites, and she writes the correct form of misspelled words at the bottom of the page so that students will notice the correct spelling. Once in a while, she has students revise and edit their quickwrites and make a final, published copy, but her goal is to develop writing fluency, not polished compositions.

Why Is Copying From the Chalkboard No Longer Recommended?
Some teachers write sentences and poems on the chalkboard for students to copy in the hope that this activity will develop writing fluency. Copying isn't very effective, though, because students are passively recording letters, not actively creating sentences, breaking the sentences into words, and spelling the words. In fact, sometimes students are copying sentences they can't even read, so the activity becomes little more than handwriting practice. It's much more worthwhile for students to write sentences to express their own ideas and to practice spelling the high-frequency words they're using.

Assessing Students' Reading and Writing Fluency

Primary-grade teachers monitor children's developing reading and writing fluency by observing them as they read and write. They assess children's reading fluency by listening to them read aloud and considering these questions:

Do students read most words automatically, or do they stop to decode many unfamiliar words?

Do students read quickly enough to understand what they're reading, or do they read too slowly or too fast?

Do students chunk words into phrases, or do they read word by word?

Do students read with expressively, or do they read in a monotone?

Teachers assess students' writing fluency in a similar manner. They observe students as they write and consider these questions:

Do students think of writing topics easily, or do they have trouble thinking of something to write?

Do students write quickly enough to complete the assignment, or do they write slowly or try to avoid writing?

Do students spell most words automatically, or do they stop to figure out the spelling of many words?

Do students write easily, or do they complain that their hands hurt?

Teachers use running records, informal reading inventories, and classroom tests to determine whether students are fluent readers, and document their progress. This Assessment Tools feature lists the tests and other assessment tools for evaluating students' development toward becoming fluent readers.

Assessment Tools

Reading Fluency

Teachers use one or more of these assessment tools as well as informal observation to determine students' reading speed and monitor their reading fluency:

◆ **Dynamic Indicators of Basic Early Literacy Skills (DIBELS): Oral Reading Fluency Subtest** (Kaminski & Good, 1996)

The Oral Reading Fluency subtest is a collection of graded passages used to measure first through third graders' reading speed, one component of fluency. In this individually administered test, children read aloud for one minute, and teachers mark errors; children's oral reading rate is the number of words they read correctly in a grade-level passage in one minute. The test is available on the DIBELS website.

◆ **Fluency Checks** (Johns & Berglund, 2006)

Teachers use these graded passages to monitor students' growth toward fluent reading. First- through eighth-grade passages are included in this assessment tool. The authors recommend that students be tested several times during the school year. Teachers listen to students read aloud as much of a narrative or expository passage as they can in one minute and mark errors on a scoring sheet. They also ask comprehension questions related to the portion of the passage that students read. Afterward, teachers calculate students' reading speed and score it against grade-level standards, and they rate their phrasing, expression, and attention to punctuation marks from strong to weak.

◆ **Informal Reading Inventories (IRIs)**

Teachers listen to students in grades 2–8 read aloud grade-level passages in an IRI and mark accuracy and prosody errors on scoring sheets. Accuracy errors include substituted words, mispronounced words, and skipped words; prosody errors include pauses, phrasing, and expressiveness. In addition, teachers use a stopwatch to record the time it takes students to read the passage and then calculate their reading rate (words read correctly per minute). They also examine students' accuracy errors to determine their knowledge of high-frequency words and their use of word-identification strategies.

◆ **Running Records**

Teachers, especially those who teach in the primary grades, take running records as students read leveled books. They time students' reading, mark errors on a copy of the text, and evaluate their phrasing and expressiveness. They compare students' fluency when reading familiar and unfamiliar books or books at their reading level with those at their grade level to determine whether students meet grade-level standards.

Until students become fluent readers, it's crucial that teachers monitor their developing accuracy, reading speed, and prosody. When students aren't making expected progress, teachers determine the source of the problem and provide instruction to address it. Once students are fluent, less frequent assessments are needed, but sometimes fluent readers will read less proficiently when the text is unfamiliar or too difficult.

Chapter 6
Review

How Effective Teachers Develop Fluent Readers and Writers

▶ Teachers teach students to read and spell the 300 high-frequency words.

▶ Teachers teach four word-identification strategies—phonic analysis, decoding by analogy, syllabic analysis, and morphemic analysis.

▶ Teachers use instructional procedures, including repeated reading, choral reading, and independent reading, to develop students' reading fluency.

▶ Teachers use instructional procedures, including quickwriting and independent writing, to develop students' writing fluency.

▶ Teachers ensure that students become fluent readers and writers by third grade.

PEARSON myeducationlab
Where the Classroom Comes to Life

Go to MyEducationLab at www.myeducationlab.com to deepen your understanding of the concepts presented in this chapter:

▶ Watch second graders learn about fluency and become more fluent readers by viewing video segments in the Literacy Portraits.
▶ Check your understanding of chapter concepts with the multiple-choice and essay quizzes in the Study Plan.
▶ Apply some of the main ideas discussed in the chapter in the Activities and Applications section of the website.
▶ Practice what you've learned in this chapter in Building Teaching Skills and Dispositions before applying the ideas in your own classroom.

PROFESSIONAL REFERENCES

Adams, M. J. (1990). *Beginning to read: Thinking and learning about print*. Cambridge, MA: MIT Press.

Allington, R. L. (2006). *What really matters for struggling readers: Designing research-based programs* (2nd ed.). Boston: Allyn & Bacon/Pearson.

Allington, R. L. (2009). *What really matters in fluency: Research-based best practices across the curriculum*. Boston: Allyn & Bacon/Pearson.

Beaver, J. (2006). *Developmental reading assessment, grades K–3* (2nd ed.). Upper Saddle River, NJ: Celebration Press/Pearson.

Beaver, J., & Carter, M. (2003). *Developmental reading assessment, grades 4–8*. Upper Saddle River, NJ: Celebration Press/Pearson.

Caldwell, J. S., & Leslie, L. (2005). *Intervention strategies to follow informal reading inventory assessment: So what do I do now?* Boston: Allyn & Bacon/Pearson.

Clay, M. M. (2005). *An observation survey of early literacy achievement* (2nd ed.). Portsmouth, NH: Heinemann.

Cunningham, P. (1990). The Names Test: A quick assessment of decoding ability. *The Reading Teacher, 44,* 124–129.

Cunningham, P. M. (2009). *Phonics they use: Words for reading and writing* (5th ed.). Boston: Allyn & Bacon.

Cunningham, P. M., & Allington, R. L. (2007). *Classrooms that work: They can all read and write*. Boston: Allyn & Bacon.

Dolch, E. W. (1936). A basic sight vocabulary. *Elementary School Journal, 36*, 456–460.

Dowhower, S. L. (1989). Repeated reading: Research into practice. *The Reading Teacher, 42*, 502–507.

Dowhower, S. L. (1991). Speaking of prosody: Fluency's unattended bedfellow. *Theory Into Practice, 30*, 165–173.

Duffelmeyer, F. A., Kruse, A. E., Merkley, D. J., & Fyfe, S. A. (1994). Further validation and enhancement of the Names Test. *The Reading Teacher, 48*, 118–128.

Ehri, L. C., & Robbins, C. (1992). Beginners need some decoding skill to read words by analogy. *Reading Research Quarterly, 27*, 13–26.

Elbow, P. (1998). *Writing without teachers* (2nd ed.). New York: Oxford University Press.

Eldredge, J. L. (2005). *Teach decoding: How and why* (2nd ed.). Upper Saddle River, NJ: Merrill/Prentice Hall.

Fry, E. (1980). The new instant word list. *The Reading Teacher, 34*, 284–289.

Gaskins, I. W., Ehri, L. C., Cress, C., O'Hara, C., & Donnelly, K. (1996/1997). Procedures for word learning: Making discoveries about words. *The Reading Teacher, 50*, 312–326.

Gaskins, R. W., Gaskins, J. W., & Gaskins, I. W. (1991). A decoding program for poor readers—and the rest of the class, too! *Language Arts, 68*, 213–225.

Gill, S. R. (2007). Learning about word parts with Kidspiration. *The Reading Teacher, 61*, 79–84.

Griffith, L. W., & Rasinski, T. V. (2004). A focus on fluency: How one teacher incorporated fluency with her reading curriculum. *The Reading Teacher, 58*, 126–137.

Gough, P. B., Juel, C., & Griffith, P. L. (1992). Reading, spelling, and the orthographic cipher. In P. B. Gough, L. C. Ehri, & R. Treiman (Eds.), *Reading acquisition* (pp. 35–48). Hillsdale, NJ: Erlbaum.

Hiebert, E. H. (1991). The development of word-level strategies in authentic literacy tasks. *Language Arts, 68*, 234–240.

Invernizzi, M., Meier, J. D., & Juel, C. (2003). *Phonological awareness literacy screening (PALS)*. Charlottesville: University of Virginia Press.

Johns, J. L., & Berglund, R. L. (2006). *Fluency: Strategies and assessments* (3rd ed.). Newark, DE: International Reading Association and Kendall/Hunt.

Kaminski, R. A., & Good, R. H., III. (1996). *Dynamic Indicators of Basic Early Literacy Skills (DIBELS)*. Eugene: University of Oregon Center on Teaching and Learning.

Koskinen, P. S., & Blum, I. H. (1986). Paired repeated reading: A classroom strategy for developing fluent reading. *The Reading Teacher, 40*, 70–75.

Kuhn, M. R., & Rasinski, T. (2007). Best practices in fluency instruction. In L. B. Gambrell, L. M. Morrow, &

M. Pressley (Eds.), *Best practices in literacy instruction* (3rd ed., pp. 204–219). New York: Guilford Press.

Kuhn, M. R., & Stahl, S. A. (2004). Fluency: A review of developmental and remedial practices. In R. B. Ruddell & N. J. Unrau (Eds.), *Theoretical models and processes of reading* (5th ed., pp. 412–453). Newark, DE: International Reading Association.

LaBerge, D., & Samuels, S. J. (1976). Toward a theory of automatic information processing in reading. In H. Singer & R. Ruddell (Eds.), *Theoretical models and processes of reading* (pp. 548–579). Newark, DE: International Reading Association.

Martinez, M., Roser, N. L., & Strecker, S. (1998/1999). "I never thought I could be a star": A readers theatre ticket to fluency. *The Reading Teacher, 52*, 326–334.

Mather, N., Sammons, J., & Schwartz, J. (2006). Adaptations of the Names Test: Easy to use phonics assessments. *The Reading Teacher, 60*, 114–122.

McKenna, M. C., & Stahl, S. A. (2003). *Assessment for reading instruction*. New York: Guilford Press.

National Reading Panel. (2000). *Teaching children to read: An evidence-based assessment of the scientific research literature on reading and its implications for reading instruction*. Washington, DC: National Institute of Child Health and Human Development.

Opitz, M. F., & Rasinski, T. V. (1998). *Good-bye round robin: Twenty-five effective oral reading strategies*. Portsmouth, NH: Heinemann.

Peregoy, S. F., & Boyle, O. F. (2008). *Reading, writing, and learning in ESL: A resource book for teaching K–12 English learners* (5th ed.). Boston: Allyn & Bacon/Pearson.

Pikulski, J. J., & Chard, D. J. (2005). Fluency: Bridge between decoding and reading comprehension. *The Reading Teacher, 58*, 510–519.

Pinnell, G. S., & Fountas, I. C. (1998). *Word matters: Teaching phonics and spelling in the reading/writing classroom*. Portsmouth, NH: Heinemann.

Rasinski, T. V. (2000). Speed does matter in reading. *The Reading Teacher, 54*, 146–151.

Rasinski, T. V. (2003). *The fluent reader*. New York: Scholastic.

Rasinski, T. V. (2004). Creating fluent readers. *Educational Leadership, 61*(6), 146–151.

Reutzel, D. R., & Cooter, R. B. (2008). *Teaching children to read* (5th ed.). Upper Saddle River, NJ: Merrill/Prentice Hall.

Samuels, S. J. (1979). The method of repeated readings. *The Reading Teacher, 32*, 403–408.

Samuels, S. J. (2004). Toward a theory of automatic information processing in reading, revisited. In R. B. Ruddell & N. J. Unrau (Eds.), *Theoretical models and processes of reading* (5th ed., pp. 1127–1148). Newark, DE: International Reading Association.

Schreider, P. A. (1991). Understanding prosody's role in reading acquisition. *Theory Into Practice, 30*, 158–164.

Shanahan, T. (1988). The reading-writing relationship: Seven instructional principles. *The Reading Teacher, 41*, 636–647.

Silverman, S. (2005). Getting connected: My experience as a collaborative Internet project coordinator. In R. A. Karchmer, M. H. Mallette, J. Kara-Soteriou, & D. J. Leu, Jr. (Eds.), *Innovative approaches to literacy education: Using the Internet to support new literacies* (pp. 103–120). Newark, DE: International Reading Association.

Snow, C. E., Burns, M. S., & Griffin, P. (Eds.). (1998). *Preventing reading difficulties in young children*. Washington, DC: National Academy Press.

Stanovich, K. E. (1992). Speculations on the causes and consequences of individual differences in early reading acquisition. In P. B. Gough, L. C. Ehri, & R. Treiman (Eds.), *Reading acquisition* (pp. 307–342). Hillsdale, NJ: Erlbaum.

Tierney, R. J. (1983). Writer-reader transactions: Defining the dimensions of negotiation. In P. L. Stock (Ed.), *Forum: Essays on theory and practice in the teaching of writing* (pp. 147–151). Upper Montclair, NJ: Boynton/Cook.

Tompkins, G. E. (2008). *Teaching writing: Balancing process and product* (5th ed.). Upper Saddle River, NJ: Merrill/Prentice Hall.

White, T. G., Sowell, J., & Yanagihara, A. (1989). Teaching elementary students to use word-part clues. *The Reading Teacher, 42*, 302–308.

CHILDREN'S BOOK REFERENCES

Avi. (2002). *Crispin: The cross of lead*. New York: Hyperion Books.

Carle, E. (2005). *A house for hermit crab*. New York: Aladdin Books.

Curtis, C. P. (1999). *Bud, not Buddy*. New York: Delacorte.

Fleming, D. (1995). *In the tall, tall grass*. New York: Henry Holt.

Fleming, D. (1998). *In the small, small pond*. New York: Henry Holt.

Holling, H. C. (1990). *Pagoo*. Boston: Houghton Mifflin.

Kaplan, R. (1996). *Moving day*. New York: Greenwillow.

MacLachlan, P. (2004). *Sarah, plain and tall*. New York: HarperTrophy.

Randell, B. (1994). *Hermit crab*. Crystal Lake, IL: Rigby Books.

Rowling, J. K. (1999). *Harry Potter and the chamber of secrets*. New York: Scholastic.

Ryan, P. M. (2000). *Esperanza rising*. New York: Scholastic.

Sachar, L. (2003). *Holes*. New York: Yearling.

Spinelli, J. (2002). *Loser*. New York: HarperCollins.

Tuchman, G. (1997). *Hermit's shiny shell*. New York: Macmillan/McGraw-Hill.

Whelan, G. (2000). *Homeless bird*. New York: HarperCollins.

CHAPTER 7

Expanding Students' Knowledge of Words

Mrs. Sanom's Word Wizards Club

Mrs. Sanom is the resource teacher at John Muir Elementary School, and she sponsors an after-school Word Wizards Club for fifth and sixth graders; the club meets for an hour on Wednesday afternoons. Nineteen students are club members this year; many of them are English learners. Mrs. Sanom teaches vocabulary lessons during the club meetings using costumes, books, and hands-on activities. She focuses on a different word-study topic each week; the topics include writing alliterations, choosing synonyms carefully, applying context clues to figure out unfamiliar words, using a dictionary and a thesaurus, understanding multiple meanings of words, choosing between homophones, adding prefixes and suffixes to words, and studying root words. She devised this club because many students have limited vocabularies, which affects their reading achievement. She displays two banners in her classroom: "Expanding Your Vocabulary Leads to School Success" and "Knowing Words Makes You Powerful." In the letters that club members write to Mrs. Sanom at the end of the school year, they report paying more attention to words an author uses, and they're better at using context clues to figure out the meaning of unfamiliar words. Most importantly, the students say that participation in the Word Wizards

Club gives them an appreciation for words that will last a lifetime. Rosie writes:

> *I love being a Word Wizard. I learned lots of new words and that makes me smart. I have a favorite word that is <u>hypothesis</u>. Did you know that I am always looking for more new words to learn? My Tio Mario gave me a dictionary because I wanted it real bad. I like looking for words in the dictionary and I like words with lots of syllables the best. I want to be in the club next year in 6th grade. Ok?*

At the first club meeting, Mrs. Sanom read aloud *Miss Alaineus: A Vocabulary Disaster* (Frasier, 2007), an outrageous yet touching story of a girl named Sage who loves words. In the story, Sage misunderstands the meaning of *miscellaneous*, but what begins as embarrassment turns into victory when she wins an award for her costume in the school's annual vocabulary parade. The students talked about the story in a grand conversation, and they decided that they want to dress in costumes and have a vocabulary parade themselves, just as Mrs. Sanom knew they would. They decided that they will have a vocabulary parade at the end of the year, and they'll invite their classmates to participate, too. "I like to dress in vocabulary costumes," Mrs. Sanom explained. "I plan to dress up in clothes or a hat that represents a vocabulary word at each club meeting." With that introduction, she reached into a shopping bag and pulled out an oversized, wrinkled shirt and put it on over her clothes. "Here is my costume," she announced. "Can you guess the word?" She modeled the shirt, trying to smooth the wrinkles, until a student guessed the word *wrinkled*.

The students talked about *wrinkle*, forms of the word (*wrinkled*, *unwrinkled*, and *wrinkling*), and the meanings. They checked the definitions of *wrinkle* in the dictionary. They understood the first meaning, "a crease or fold in clothes or skin," but the second meaning—"a clever idea or trick"—was more difficult. Mrs. Sanom called their idea to have a vocabulary parade "a new wrinkle" in her plans for the club, and then the students began to grasp the meaning.

The borders of each page in *Miss Alaineus* are decorated with words beginning with a specific letter; the first page has words beginning with A, the second page B, and so on. To immerse students in words, Mrs. Sanom asked them each to choose a letter from a box of plastic alphabet letters, turn to that page in the book, and then choose a word beginning with that letter from the border to use in an activity. The words they chose included *awesome*, *berserk*, *catastrophe*, and *dwindle*. Students wrote the word on the first page of their Word Wizard Notebooks (small, spiral-bound notebooks that Mrs. Sanom purchased for them), checked its meaning in a dictionary and wrote it beside the word, and then drew a picture to illustrate the meaning. While they worked, Mrs. Sanom wrote the words on the alphabetized word wall she posted in the classroom. Afterward, the students shared their words and illustrations in a tea party activity.

Mrs. Sanom has a collection of vocabulary books in her classroom library, and she gives brief book talks to introduce the books to the club members. She explains that the very best way to learn lots of words is to read every day, and she encourages students to choose a vocabulary book or another book from her library each week to read between club meetings. At the end of each meeting, she allows a few minutes for students to choose a book to take home to read.

At today's club meeting, Mrs. Sanom is wearing a broad-brimmed hat with two wrecked cars and a stop sign attached. The students check out Mrs. Sanom's costume because they know it represents a word—and that word is the topic of today's meeting. They quickly begin guessing words: "Is it *crash*?" Oscar asks. "I think the word is *accident*. My dad had a car accident last week," says Danielle. Ramon suggests, "Those cars are *wrecked*. Is that the word?" Mrs. Sanom commends the club members for their good guesses and says they're on the right track. To provide a little help, she draws a row of nine letter boxes on the chalkboard and fills in the first letter and the last four letters. Then Martha guesses it—*collision*. Mrs. Sanom begins a cluster on the chalkboard with the word *collision* written in the middle circle and related words on each ray. Students compare the noun *collision* and the verb *collide*. They also check the dictionary and a thesaurus for more information and write *crash, accident, wreck, hit, smashup*, and *collide* on the rays to complete the cluster. They talk about how and when to use *collide* and *collision*. Ramon offers, "I know a sentence: On 9-11, the terrorists' airplanes collided with the World Trade Center."

Mrs. Sanom explains that ships can be involved in collisions, too: A ship can hit another ship, or it can collide with something else in the water—an iceberg, for example. Several students know about the *Titanic*, and they share what they know about that ship's fateful ocean crossing. Mrs. Sanom selects *Story of the Titanic* (Kentley, 2001) from her text set of books about the *Titanic* and shows photos and drawings of the ship to provide more background information. They make a K-W-L chart, listing what they know in the K column and questions they want to find answers for in the W column. The students also make individual charts in their Word Wizard Notebooks.

Next, Mrs. Sanom presents a list of words using an overhead projector—some about the *Titanic* article they'll read and some not—for an exclusion brainstorming activity; the words include *unsinkable, crew, liner, passengers, voyage, airplane, catastrophe, ship, mountain, lifeboat*, and *general*. The students predict which words relate to the article and which don't. The word *general* stumps them because they think of it as an adjective meaning "having to do with the whole, not specific." A student checks the dictionary to learn about the second meaning—"a high-ranking military officer" (noun). The students are still confused, but after reading the article, they realize that the word *general* isn't related: The officer in charge of the *Titanic* (or any ship, for that matter) is called a *captain*.

Mrs. Sanom passes out copies of the one-page article and reads it aloud while students follow along. They discuss the article, talking and asking more questions about the needless tragedy. Then they complete the L section of the K-W-L chart and the exclusion brainstorming activity. Because the students are very interested in learning more about the disaster, Mrs. Sanom introduces her text set of narrative and informational books about the *Titanic*, including *Inside the Titanic* (Brewster, 1997), *Tonight on the Titanic* (Osborne & Osborne, 1995), *Titanic: A Nonfiction Companion to Tonight on the Titanic* (Osborne & Osborne, 2002), *On Board the Titanic: What It Was Like When the Great Liner Sank* (Tanaka, 1996), and *Voyage on the Great Titanic: The Diary of Margaret Ann Brady* (White, 1998). She invites the students to spend the last few minutes of the club meeting choosing a book from the text set to take home to read before the next meeting.

Mrs. Sanom wears a different costume or hat each week. Here are eight of her favorites:

bejeweled:	A silky shirt with "jewels" glued across the front
champion:	Racing shorts, tee shirt, and a medal on a ribbon worn around her neck
hocus-pocus:	A black top hat with a stuffed rabbit stuck inside, white gloves, and a magic wand

international: A dress decorated with the flags of many countries and a globe cut in half for a hat

mercury: A white sheet worn toga style and a baseball cap with wings on each side

slick: A black leather jacket, sunglasses, and hair slicked back with mousse

transparent: A clear plastic raincoat, clear plastic gloves, and a clear shower cap

vacant: A bird cage with a "for rent" sign worn as a hat with an artificial bird sitting on her shoulder

One week, however, Mrs. Sanom forgets to bring a costume, so after a bit of quick thinking, she decides to feature the word *ordinary*, and she wears her everyday clothes as her costume!

For their 17th weekly club meeting, Mrs. Sanom dressed as a queen with a flowing purple robe and a tiara on her head. The focus of the week was words beginning with Q, the 17th letter of the alphabet. They began by talking about queens—both historical queens such as Queen Isabella of Spain, who financed Christopher Columbus's voyage to the New World, and queens who are alive today. Next, Mrs. Sanom began a list of Q words with *queen*, and the students added words to it. They checked the Q page in alphabet books and examined dictionary entries for Q words. They chose interesting words, including *quadruped, quadruplet, qualify, quest,*

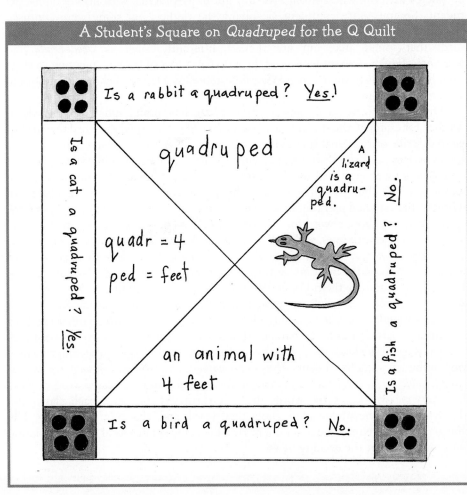

A Student's Square on *Quadruped* for the Q Quilt

quarantine, quintet, quiver, quench, and *quotation*. After they had more than 20 words on their list, Mrs. Sanom asked each student to choose a Q word, study it, and make a square poster to share what he or she learned. Afterward, Mrs. Sanom collected the posters, made a quilt from them, and hung the quilt on the wall outside the classroom. One student's square about *quadruped* is presented in the box on page 223, and it documents the student's understanding of root words.

Last week's topic was homographs, two or more words that are spelled alike but pronounced differently, such as *record, bow, read*, and *dove*. Mrs. Sanom was dressed with a big red ribbon bow tied around her waist and smaller red bows tied on pigtails. At the beginning of the club meeting, she retied the bow at her waist and then she bowed to the students. Ramon quickly guessed that the word was *bow*, but the concept of homographs was new to him and the other club members. Mrs. Sanom introduced the word *homograph*, explained the definition, and offered examples. Then she shared several homograph riddles from *The Dove Dove: Funny Homograph Riddles* (Terban, 1992), including "The nurse *wrapped* the bandage around the *injury*." The students solve the riddle by identifying the homograph that can replace the two highlighted words; for this riddle, the answer is *wound*.

Next, Mrs. Sanom divided the students into small groups, and she gave each group a different homograph riddle from Terban's book to solve. Then they shared the riddles with the whole group. As they got more practice with homographs, the students became more confident at solving the riddles, but some were confused about homophones and homographs. Mrs. Sanom explained that homophones are words that sound alike but are spelled differently, such as *wood–would* and *there–their–they're*. The students used the last 10 minutes of the club meeting to write about homographs in their Word Wizard Notebooks. They also chose new books to take home and read.

The Word Wizards make and wear word bracelets to highlight special words; in October, for example, the students made word bracelets that spell the word they'd chosen to describe or represent themselves, such as *genius, ornery*, or *sincere*. Mrs. Sanom's word was *sassy*, and she demonstrated how to make a bracelet using small alphabet beads strung on an elastic string. Then students followed her steps to make their own bracelets, which they proudly wear to school and show off to their classmates. In February, they studied patriotic words, such as *allegiance, citizen, equality, independence*, and *republic*, and chose a word for a second bracelet. They chose words after reading books with patriotic themes, such as Lynne Cheney's *America: A Patriotic Primer* (2002) and *A Is for America: An American Alphabet* (Scillian, 2001). For their third word bracelet, they chose the most interesting word from all the words they've collected on the word wall and in their Word Wizard Notebooks, including *valiant, awesome, phenomenon, plethora, incredulous, cryptic, guffaw, mischievous*, and *razzle-dazzle*.

The vocabulary parade is the highlight of the year. Every club member creates a costume and participates in the parade. Mrs. Sanom dresses as a wizard—a word wizard, that is—and she leads the parade from classroom to classroom in the intermediate wing of the school. The students dress as *camouflage, victory, shimmer, monarch, liberty, uncomfortable, fortune, emerald*, and *twilight*, for example, and they carry word cards so that everyone will know the words they represent. As they tour each classroom, Mrs. Sanom and the students talk about their words and what they're learning. The club members' parents come to school to view the parade, and a local television station films the parade for the evening news.

Check the Compendium of Instructional Procedures, which follows Chapter 12, for more information on the highlighted terms.

Students learn the meanings of words by being immersed in an environment that's rich with words, through lots of daily independent reading and interactive read-alouds, and through explicit instruction. As they read, students learn many, many words incidentally, and teachers reinforce students' learning in several important ways: They explicitly teach some words and word-learning strategies, and they foster students' interest in words (Graves, 2006). In the vignette, Mrs. Sanom engaged her fifth and sixth graders with words as they participated in lively Word Wizard Club activities.

Vocabulary learning can't be left to chance because students' word knowledge affects whether they comprehend what they're reading, write effectively, and learn content-area information (Stahl & Nagy, 2006). Children come to school with varying levels of word knowledge, both in the number of words they know and in the depth of their understanding. Students from low-income homes have less than half of the vocabulary that more affluent children possess, and some researchers estimate that they know one quarter to one fifth of the words that their classmates do. To make matters worse, this gap widens each year (Cunningham, 2009). Therefore, it's essential that teachers recognize the impact of socioeconomic level on students' vocabulary knowledge, support all students' vocabulary growth, and emphasize word learning for students who know fewer words.

HOW DO STUDENTS LEARN VOCABULARY WORDS?

Many students' vocabularies grow at an astonishing rate—about 3,000 words a year, or roughly 7 to 10 new words every day. By the time students graduate from high school, their vocabularies can reach 25,000 to 50,000 words or more. It seems obvious that to learn words at such a prolific rate, students learn words both in and outside of school, and they learn most words incidentally, not through explicit instruction. Reading has the greatest impact on students' vocabulary development, but other activities are important, too. For example, students learn words through family activities, hobbies, and vacations. Television also has a significant impact on vocabulary development, especially when students view educational programs and limit the amount of time they spend watching television each day.

Levels of Word Knowledge

Students develop knowledge about a word gradually, through repeated oral and written exposures to it. They move from not knowing a word at all to recognizing that they've seen the word before, and then to a level of partial knowledge where they have a general sense of the word or know one meaning. Finally, students know the word fully: They know multiple meanings of the word and can use it in a variety of ways (Nagy, 1988). Here are the four levels of word knowledge:

Unknown Word. Students don't recognize the word.

Initial Recognition. Students have seen or heard the word or can pronounce it, but they don't know the meaning.

Partial Word Knowledge. Students know one meaning of the word and can use it in a sentence.

Full Word Knowledge. Students know more than one meaning of the word and can use it in several ways. (Allen, 1999)

Once students reach the third level, they can usually understand the word in context and use it in writing. In fact, they don't reach the fourth level with every word they learn, but when they do develop full word knowledge, they're described as flexible word users because they understand the core meaning of a word and how it changes in different contexts (Stahl, 1999).

Incidental Word Learning

Students learn words incidentally, without explicit instruction, all the time, and because students learn so many words this way, teachers know that they don't have to teach the meaning of every unfamiliar word in a text. Students learn words from many sources, but researchers report that reading is the single largest source of vocabulary growth for students, especially after third grade (Swanborn & de Glopper, 1999). In addition, the amount of time students spend reading independently is the best predictor of vocabulary growth between second and fifth grades.

Independent Reading. Students need daily opportunities for independent reading in order to learn words, and they need to read books at their independent reading levels. If the books are too easy or too hard, students learn very few new words. The best way to provide opportunities for independent reading is reading workshop. Students choose books that they're interested in from age-appropriate and reading-level-suitable collections in their classroom libraries, and because they've chosen the books themselves, they're more likely to keep reading. Sustained Silent Reading (SSR) is another way to encourage wide reading. All students in a classroom or in the school spend 10 to 30 minutes or more silently reading appropriate books that they've chosen themselves. Even the teacher takes time to read, at the same time modeling how adults who enjoy reading make it part of their daily routine. Simply providing time for independent reading, however, doesn't guarantee that students will increase their vocabulary knowledge (Stahl & Nagy, 2006); students need to know how to use context clues and other word-learning strategies to figure out the meaning of unfamiliar words to increase their vocabulary. (Check pages 244–246 in this chapter to learn more about word-learning strategies.)

Reading Aloud to Students. Teachers also provide for incidental word learning when they read aloud stories, poems, and

---

Teaching Struggling Readers and Writers

Lots of Words

Struggling readers need to know more words.

One of the biggest challenges facing struggling readers is their limited word knowledge. Even though independent reading is an important way most students acquire a large vocabulary, it isn't enough for struggling students (Allington, 2006). Students who exhibit reading difficulties don't do as much reading as their classmates, and the books they read don't introduce them to grade-level vocabulary words. To expand students' vocabularies, it's essential that teachers provide both daily activities to draw students' attention to words and instruction on academic vocabulary and word-learning strategies. Cooper, Chard, and Kiger (2006) offer these instructional recommendations:

- *Nurture students' awareness of words using word walls, independent reading, and interactive read-alouds.*
- *Explicitly teach the meanings of 8–10 words each week by introducing key words before reading and providing worthwhile practice activities afterward.*
- *Develop students' ability to figure out the meaning of unfamiliar words.*

Teachers can accelerate students' vocabulary development by implementing a more-structured program with daily lessons based on these recommendations.

Sometimes teachers thwart students' vocabulary development. Allington (2006) identified three activities that waste instructional time: First, students shouldn't read books that are too difficult because they won't understand what they're reading. Next, teachers can't expect students to figure out the meaning of unfamiliar words when they're reading if they haven't been taught to use context clues or other word-learning strategies. Third, students shouldn't be given a list of words and asked to copy the definition for each word or write a sentence using it. These activities aren't recommended because they don't develop students' in-depth word knowledge.

Independent Reading
This third grader spends 30 minutes each day reading books she chooses herself from the classroom library. The books are interesting and appropriate for her reading level. So far this year, she's read 17 books! As she and her classmates read, they learn the meanings of hundreds of new words and additional meanings for familiar words incidentally. In addition, the third graders become more engaged in reading and feel their confidence soar. Students who participate in reading workshop, SSR, or another independent reading activity every day are more likely to become successful readers.

informational books. Daily read-aloud activities are important for students at all grade levels, kindergarten through eighth grade. Teachers use the interactive read-aloud procedure and focus on a few key words in the book, model how to use context clues to understand new words, and talk about the words after reading. Teachers use think-alouds when they model using context clues and other word-identification strategies. Two recent studies found that teachers enhance students' vocabulary knowledge and their comprehension when they add a focus on vocabulary to their read-alouds (Fisher, Frey, & Lapp, 2008; Santoro, Chard, Howard, & Baker, 2008).

Cunningham (2009) recommends that primary-grade teachers choose one picture book each week to read aloud and teach key vocabulary. Teachers read the book aloud one time and then present three new words from the book, each written on a word card. During the second reading, students listen for the words, and the teacher takes time to talk about each word's meaning using information available in the text and in the illustrations. Later, the teacher encourages students to practice using the new words when they talk and write about the book.

Although reading aloud is important for all students, it's especially important for struggling readers who typically read fewer books themselves, and because the books at their reading level have less sophisticated vocabulary words. In fact, researchers report that students learn as many words incidentally while listening to teachers read aloud as they do by reading themselves (Stahl, Richek, & Vandevier, 1991).

Why Is Vocabulary Knowledge Important?

Vocabulary knowledge and reading achievement are closely related: Students with larger vocabularies are more capable readers, and they know more strategies for figuring out the meanings of unfamiliar words than less capable readers do (Graves, 2006). Reading widely is the best way students learn new words, and that's one reason why capable readers have larger vocabularies: They simply do more reading, both in school and out of school.

The idea that capable readers learn more vocabulary because they read more is an example of the Matthew effect (Stanovich, 1986), which suggests that "the rich get richer and the poor get poorer" in vocabulary development and other components of reading. Capable readers become better readers because they read more, and the books they read are more challenging, with sophisticated vocabulary words. The gulf between more capable and less capable readers grows larger because less capable readers read less and the books they read aren't as challenging.

TEACHING STUDENTS TO UNLOCK WORD MEANINGS

Vocabulary instruction plays an important role in balanced literacy classrooms. Baumann, Kame'enui, and Ash (2003) and Graves (2006) identified these components of vocabulary instruction:

- Immerse students in words through listening, talking, reading, and writing
- Teach specific words through active involvement and multiple encounters with words
- Teach word-learning strategies so students can figure out the meanings of unfamiliar words
- Develop students' word consciousness, their awareness of and interest in words

Teachers address all of these components when they teach vocabulary. Too often, vocabulary instruction has emphasized only the second component, teaching specific words, without considering how to develop students' ability to learn words

Guidelines
for Teaching Vocabulary

▶ Choose key words for vocabulary instruction from books students are reading and from thematic units and highlight them on word walls.

▶ Engage students in word-study activities, such as word posters, word maps, and word sorts, so they can deepen their understanding of specific words.

▶ Teach minilessons about the meanings of individual words, vocabulary concepts, and word-learning strategies.

▶ Scaffold students as they develop full word knowledge by learning multiple meanings, how root words and affixes affect meaning, synonyms, antonyms, word histories, and figurative meanings.

▶ During interactive read-alouds, focus on specific high-utility words.

▶ Teach students to use word-learning strategies to unlock new words.

▶ Develop students' word consciousness by demonstrating curiosity about words, teaching students about words, and involving them in wordplay activities.

▶ Provide daily opportunities for students to read independently—at least 15–30 minutes in grades 1–3 and 30–60 minutes in grades 4–8.

independently and use them effectively. The feature on the preceding page lists guidelines for teaching vocabulary.

Word-Study Concepts

It's not enough to have students memorize one definition of a word; to develop full word knowledge, they need to learn more about a word (Stahl & Nagy, 2006). Consider the word *brave*: It can be used as an adjective, a noun, or a verb. It often means "showing no fear," but it can also mean an "American Indian warrior" or "to challenge or defy." These forms are related to the first meaning: *braver, bravest, bravely,* and *bravery.* Synonyms related to the first meaning include *courageous, bold, fearless, daring, intrepid, heroic,* and *valiant*; antonyms include *cowardly* and *frightened.* Our word *brave* comes from the Italian word *bravo.* Interestingly, the Italian word *bravo* and a related form—*bravissimo*—have entered English directly, and they're used to express great approval; these words mean "excellent," an obsolete meaning of *brave.* In addition, there's *bravado,* a Spanish word that means "a pretense of courage." As students learn some of this information about *brave,* they're better able to understand the word and use it orally and in writing.

As students learn about a word, they acquire a wide range of information. They learn one or more meanings for a word and synonyms and antonyms to compare and contrast meanings. Sometimes they confuse a word they're learning with a homonym that sounds or is spelled the same. Students also learn about idioms and figurative sayings that make our language more colorful. A seventh grader's investigation of the word *vaporize* is shown in Figure 7–1.

Multiple Meanings of Words. Many words have more than one meaning. For some words, multiple meanings develop for the noun and verb forms, but sometimes additional meanings develop in other ways. The word *bank,* for example, has these meanings:

> a piled-up mass of snow or clouds
> the slope of land beside a lake or river
> the slope of a road on a turn
> the lateral tilting of an airplane in a turn
> to cover a fire with ashes for slow burning
> a business establishment that receives and lends money
> a container in which money is saved
> a supply for use in emergencies (e.g., a blood bank)
> a place for storage (e.g., a computer's memory bank)
> to count on
> similar things arranged in a row (e.g., a bank of elevators)
> to arrange things in a row

You may be surprised that there are at least a dozen meanings for this common word. Some are nouns and others are verbs, but grammatical form alone doesn't account for so many meanings.

The meanings of *bank* come from three sources. The first five meanings come from a Viking word, and they're related because they all deal with something slanted or making a slanted motion. The next five come from the Italian word *banca,* a money changer's table. These meanings deal with financial banking except for the 10th

Figure 7–1 ◆ A Seventh Grader's Investigation of *Vaporize*

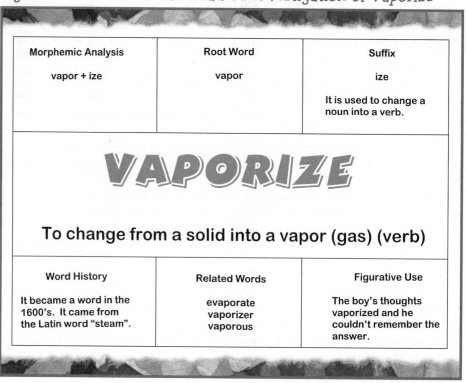

Morphemic Analysis	Root Word	Suffix
vapor + ize	vapor	ize It is used to change a noun into a verb.

VAPORIZE

To change from a solid into a vapor (gas) (verb)

Word History	Related Words	Figurative Use
It became a word in the 1600's. It came from the Latin word "steam".	evaporate vaporizer vaporous	The boy's thoughts vaporized and he couldn't remember the answer.

meaning, "to count on," which requires a bit more thought. We use the saying "to bank on" figuratively to mean "to depend on," but it began more literally from the actual counting of money on a table. The last two meanings come from the French word *banc*, meaning "bench." Words acquired multiple meanings as society became more complex and finer shades of meaning were necessary; for example, the meanings of *bank* as an emergency supply and a storage place are fairly new. As with many words with multiple meanings, it's just a linguistic accident that three original words from different languages with related meanings came to be spelled the same way (Tompkins & Yaden, 1986). A list of other common words with more than five meanings is shown in Figure 7–2.

Students gradually acquire additional meanings for words, and they usually learn these new meanings through reading. When a familiar word is used in a new way, students often notice the new application and may be curious enough to check the meaning in a dictionary.

Synonyms: Words With the Same Meaning. Words that have nearly the same meaning as other words are *synonyms*. English has so many synonyms because numerous words have been borrowed from other languages. Synonyms are useful because they're more precise. Think of all the synonyms for the word *cold: cool, chilly, frigid, icy, frosty,* and *freezing*. Each word has a different shade of meaning: *Cool* means moderately cold; *chilly* is uncomfortably cold; *frigid* is intensely cold; *icy* means very cold; *frosty* means covered with frost; and *freezing* is so cold that water changes into ice. English would be limited if we had only the word *cold*.

Teachers should carefully articulate the differences among synonyms. Nagy (1988) emphasizes that teachers should focus on teaching concepts and related words, not just provide single-word definitions using synonyms. For example, to tell a student that *frigid* means *cold* provides only limited information. And, when a student says, "I want my sweater because it's frigid in here," it shows that he or she doesn't understand the different degrees of cold; there's a big difference between *chilly* and *frigid*.

Antonyms: Words That Mean the Opposite. Words that express opposite meanings are *antonyms*. For the word *loud*, some antonyms are *soft, subdued, quiet, silent, inaudible, sedate, somber, dull,* and *colorless*. These antonyms express shades of meaning just as synonyms do, and some opposites are more appropriate for one meaning of *loud* than for another. When *loud* means *gaudy*, for instance, antonyms are *somber, dull,* and *colorless*; when *loud* means *noisy*, the opposites are *quiet, silent,* and *inaudible*.

Students learn to use a thesaurus to locate both synonyms and antonyms. *A First Thesaurus* (Wittels, 2001), *Scholastic Children's Thesaurus* (Bollard, 2006), and *The American Heritage Children's Thesaurus* (Hellweg, 2006) are three excellent reference books. Students need to learn how to use these handy references to locate more-effective words when they're revising their writing and during word-study activities.

Homonyms: Words That Confuse. Homonyms are confusing because even though these words have different meanings, they're either pronounced the same or spelled the same as other words. Homophones are words that sound alike but are spelled differently, such as *right–write, air–heir, to–too–two,* and *there–their–they're*. A list of homophones is presented in Figure 7–3. Sometimes students confuse the meanings of

Figure 7–2 ◆ Common Words With More Than Five Meanings

act	drive	lay	place	set	strike
air	dry	leave	plant	sharp	stroke
away	dull	line	plate	shine	strong
bad	eye	low	play	shoot	stuff
bar	face	make	point	short	sweep
base	fail	man	post	side	sweet
black	fair	mark	print	sight	swing
blow	fall	mind	quiet	sign	take
boat	fast	mine	rain	sing	thick
break	fire	natural	raise	sink	thing
carry	fly	new	range	slip	think
case	good	nose	rear	small	throw
catch	green	note	rest	sound	tie
change	hand	now	return	spin	tight
charge	have	off	rich	spread	time
check	head	open	ride	spring	touch
clear	heel	out	right	square	tough
color	high	paper	ring	stamp	train
count	hold	part	rise	star	trip
cover	hot	pass	roll	stay	turn
crack	house	pay	rule	step	under
cross	keep	pick	run	stick	up
crown	key	picture	scale	stiff	watch
cut	knock	piece	score	stock	way
draw	know	pitch	serve	stop	wear

these words, but more often they confuse their spellings. Most homophones are linguistic accidents, but *stationary* and *stationery* share an interesting history: *Stationery*, meaning paper and books, developed from *stationary*. In medieval England, merchants traveled from town to town selling their wares. The merchant who sold paper goods was the first to set up shop in one town. His shop was "stationary" because it didn't move, and he came to be the "stationer." The spelling difference between the two words signifies the semantic difference. In contrast, words with identical spellings but different meanings and pronunciations, such as the noun and verb forms of *wind* and the noun and adjective forms of *minute*, are homographs. Other examples include *live, read, bow, conduct, present,* and *record*.

There are many books of homonyms designed for children, including Gwynne's *The King Who Rained* (2006) and *A Chocolate Moose for Dinner* (2005), Barretta's *Dear Deer: A Book of Homophones* (2007), *The Dove Dove: Funny Homograph Riddles* (Terban, 1992), and *Eight Ate: A Feast of Homonym Riddles* (Terban, 2007a). Sharing these books with students helps to develop their understanding of homophones and homographs.

Figure 7–3 ◆ Homophones, Words That Sound Alike But Are Spelled Differently

air–heir	creak–creek	hour–our	peace–piece	shoot–chute
allowed–aloud	days–daze	knead–need	peak–peek–pique	side–sighed
ant–aunt	dear–deer	knew–new	peal–peel	slay–sleigh
ate–eight	dew–do–due	knight–night	pedal–peddle–petal	soar–sore
ball–bawl	die–dye	knot–not	plain–plane	soared–sword
bare–bear	doe–dough	know–no	pleas–please	sole–soul
be–bee	ewe–you	lead–led	pole–poll	some–sum
beat–beet	eye–I	leak–leek	poor–pore–pour	son–sun
berry–bury	fair–fare	lie–lye	praise–prays–preys	stairs–stares
billed–build	feat–feet	loan–lone	presence–presents	stake–steak
blew–blue	fined–find	made–maid	pride–pried	stationary–stationery
boar–bore	fir–fur	mail–male	prince–prints	steal–steel
board–bored	flair–flare	main–mane	principal–principle	straight–strait
bough–bow	flea–flee	manner–manor	profit–prophet	suite–sweet
brake–break	flew–flu	marshal–martial	quarts–quartz	tail–tale
brews–bruise	flour–flower	meat–meet–mete	rain–reign–rein	taught–taut
bridal–bridle	for–fore–four	medal–meddle–metal	raise–rays–raze	tear–tier
brows–browse	forth–fourth	might–mite	rap–wrap	their–there–they're
buy–by–bye	foul–fowl	mind–mined	red–read	threw–through
capital–capitol	gorilla–guerrilla	miner–minor	reed–read	throne–thrown
ceiling–sealing	grate–great	missed–mist	right–rite–write	tide–tied
cell–sell	grill–grille	moan–mown	ring–wring	to–too–tow
cellar–seller	groan–grown	morning–mourning	road–rode–rowed	toad–toed–towed
cent–scent–sent	guessed–guest	muscle–mussel	role–roll	toe–tow
chews–choose	hair–hare	naval–navel	root–route	troop–troupe
chic–sheik	hall–haul	none–nun	rose–rows	vain–vane–vein
chili–chilly	hay–hey	oar–or–ore	rung–wrung	wade–weighed
choral–coral	heal–heel	one–won	sail–sale	waist–waste
chord–cord–cored	hear–here	pail–pale	scene–seen	wait–weight
cite–sight–site	heard–herd	pain–pane	sea–see	wares–wears
close–clothes	hi–high	pair–pare–pear	seam–seem	way–weigh
coarse–course	hoarse–horse	passed–past	serf–surf	weak–week
colonel–kernel	hole–whole	patience–patients	sew–so–sow	wood–would

Figure 7–4 ◆ A Sixth Grader's Homophone Poster

Primary-grade teachers introduce homonyms and teach the easier pairs, including *see–sea, I–eye, right–write,* and *dear–deer.* In the upper grades, teachers focus on homographs and the homophones that students continue to confuse, such as *there–their–they're* and the more-sophisticated pairs, including *morning–mourning, flair–flare,* and *complement–compliment.* Teachers teach minilessons to explain the concept of homophones and homographs and have students make charts of the homophones and homographs; calling students' attention to the differences in spelling, meaning, and pronunciation helps to clarify the words. This explicit instruction is especially important for English learners (Jacobson, Lapp, & Flood, 2007). Students can also make homonym posters, as shown in Figure 7–4. On the posters, students draw pictures and write sentences to contrast homophones and homographs. Displaying these posters in the classroom reminds students of the differences between the words.

Etymologies: The History of the English Language. Glimpses into the history of the English language provide interesting information about word meanings and spellings (Tompkins & Yaden, 1986). The English language began in A.D. 447 when Angles, Saxons, and other Germanic tribes invaded England. This Anglo-Saxon English was first written down by Latin missionaries in approximately A.D. 750. The English of the period from 450 to 1100 is known as Old English. During this time, English was a very phonetic language and followed many German syntactic patterns. Many loan words, including *ugly, window, egg, they, sky,* and *husband,* were contributed by the marauding Vikings who plundered villages along the English coast.

Middle English (1100–1500) began with the Norman Conquest in 1066. William, Duke of Normandy, invaded England and became the English king. William, his lords, and the royals who accompanied him spoke French, so it became the official language of England for nearly 200 years. Many French loan words were added to the language, and French spellings were substituted for Old English spellings. For example, *night* was spelled *niht* and *queen* was spelled *cwen* in Old English to reflect how they were pronounced; their modern spellings reflect changes made by French scribes. Loan words from Dutch, Latin, and other languages were added to English during this period, too.

The invention of the printing press marks the transition from Middle English to Modern English (1500–present). William Caxton brought the first printing press to England in 1476, and soon books and pamphlets were being mass-produced. Spelling became standardized as Samuel Johnson and other lexicographers compiled dictionaries, even though English pronunciation of words continued to evolve. Loan words continued to flow into English from almost every language in the world. Exploration and colonization in North America and around the world accounted for many of the loan words. For example, *canoe* and *moccasin* are from Native American languages; *bonanza*, *chocolate*, and *ranch* are from Mexican Spanish; and *cafeteria*, *prairie*, and *teenager* are American English. Other loan words include *zero* (Arabic), *tattoo* (Polynesian), *robot* (Czech), *yogurt* (Turkish), *restaurant* (French), *dollar* (German), *jungle* (Hindi), and *umbrella* (Italian). Some words, such as *electric*, *democracy*, and *astronaut*, were created using Greek word parts. New words continue to be added to English every year, and these words reflect new inventions and cultural practices. Many new words today, such as *e-mail*, relate to the Internet. The word *Internet* is a recent word, too; it's less than 25 years old!

Students use etymological information in dictionaries to learn how particular words evolved and what the words mean. Etymological information is included in brackets at the beginning or end of dictionary entries. Here's the etymological information for three words:

> *democracy [1576, < MF < LL < Gr demokratia, demos (people) + kratia (cracy = strength, power)]*

The etymological information explains that the word *democracy* entered English in 1576 through French, and the French word came from Latin and before that Greek. In Greek, the word *demokratia* means "power to the people."

> *house [bef. 900, ME hous, OE hus]*

According to the etymological information, *house* is an Old English word that entered English before 900. It was spelled *hus* in Old English and *hous* in Middle English.

> *moose [1603, < Algonquin, "he who strips bark"]*

The etymological information explains that the word *moose* is Native American—from an Algonquin tribe in the northeastern United States—and entered English in 1603. It comes from the Algonquin word for "he who strips bark."

Even though words have entered English from around the world, the three main sources of words are English, Latin, and Greek. Upper-grade students can learn to identify the languages that these words came from; knowing the language backgrounds helps students to predict the spellings and meanings (Venezky, 1999). English words are usually one- or two-syllable common words that may or may not be phonetically regular, such as *fox*, *arm*, *Monday*, *house*, *match*, *eleven*, *of*, *come*, *week*, *horse*, *brother*, and *dumb*. Words with *ch* (pronounced as /ch/), *sh*, *th*, and *wh* digraphs are usually English, as in *church*, *shell*, *bath*, and *what*. Many English words are compound words or use comparative and superlative forms, such as *starfish*, *toothache*, *fireplace*, *happier*, *fastest*.

Many words from Latin are similar to comparable words in French, Spanish, or Italian, such as *ancient*, *judicial*, *impossible*, and *officer*. Latin words have related words or derivatives, such as *courage*, *courageous*, *encourage*, *discourage*, and *encouragement*. Also, many Latin words have *-tion/-sion* suffixes: *imitation*, *corruption*, *attention*, *extension*, and *possession*.

Greek words are the most unusual. Many are long words, and their spellings seem unfamiliar. The digraph *ph* is pronounced /f/, and the digraph *ch* is pronounced /k/ in Greek loan words, as in *autograph*, *chaos*, and *architect*. Longer words with *th*, such as *thermometer* and *arithmetic*, are Greek. The suffix *-ology* is Greek, as in the words *biology*, *psychology*, and *geology*. The letter *y* is used in place of *i* in the middle of some words, such as *bicycle* and *myth*. Many Greek words are composed of two parts: *bibliotherapy*, *microscope*, *biosphere*, *hypodermic*, and *telephone*. Figure 7–5 presents lists of words from English, Latin, and Greek that teachers can use for word sorts and other vocabulary activities.

Conceptually related words have developed from English, Latin, and Greek sources. Consider the words *tooth*, *dentist*, and *orthodontist*. *Tooth* is an English word, which explains its irregular plural form, *teeth*. *Dentist* is a Latin word; *dent* means "tooth" in Latin, and the suffix *-ist* means "one who does." The word *orthodontist* is Greek. *Ortho* means "straighten" and *dont* means "tooth"; therefore, *orthodontist*

Figure 7–5 ◆ Words From English, Latin, and Greek

English	Latin	Greek
apple	addiction	ache
between	administer	arithmetic
bumblebee	advantage	astronomy
child	beautiful	atomic
cry	capital	biology
cuff	confession	chaos
earth	continent	chemical
fireplace	delicate	democracy
fourteen	discourage	disaster
freedom	erupt	elephant
Friday	explosion	geography
get	fraction	gymnastics
have	fragile	helicopter
horse	frequently	hemisphere
knight	heir	hieroglyphics
know	honest	kaleidoscope
ladybug	identify	myth
lamb	January	octopus
lip	journal	phenomenal
lock	junior	photosynthesis
mouth	nation	pseudonym
out	occupy	rhinoceros
quickly	organize	rhythm
ride	principal	sympathy
silly	procession	telescope
this	salute	theater
twin	special	thermometer
weather	uniform	trophy
whisper	vacation	zodiac
wild	vegetable	zoo

means "one who straightens teeth." Other conceptually related triplets include the following:

book:	bookstore (E), bibliography (Gr), library (L)
eye:	eyelash (E), optical (Gr), binoculars (L)
foot:	foot-dragging (E), tripod (Gr), pedestrian (L)
great:	greatest (E), megaphone (Gr), magnificent (L)
see:	foresee (E), microscope (Gr), invisible (L)
star:	starry (E), astronaut (Gr), constellation (L)
time:	time-tested (E), chronological (Gr), contemporary (L)
water:	watermelon (E), hydrate (Gr), aquarium (L)

When students understand English, Latin, and Greek root words, they appreciate the relationships among words and their meanings.

Figurative Meanings of Words. Many words have both literal and figurative meanings: Literal meanings are the explicit, dictionary meanings, and figurative meanings are metaphorical or use figures of speech. For example, to describe *winter* as the coldest season of the year is literal, but to say that "winter has icy breath" is figurative. Two types of figurative language are idioms and comparisons.

Idioms are groups of words, such as "in hot water," that have a special meaning. Idioms can be confusing because they must be interpreted figuratively. "In hot water" is an old expression meaning "to be in trouble." In the Middle Ages, people had to protect themselves from robbers. When a robber tried to break into a house, the homeowner might pour boiling water from a second-floor window onto the head of the robber, who would then be "in hot water." There are hundreds of idioms in English, which we use every day to create word pictures that make language more colorful. Some examples are "out in left field," "a skeleton in the closet," "raining cats and dogs," and "a chip off the old block." A variety of books that explain idioms are available for students to examine, including the *Scholastic Dictionary of Idioms* (Terban, 2006), *Mad as a Wet Hen!: And Other Funny Idioms* (Terban, 2007c), *In a Pickle and Other Funny Idioms* (Terban, 2007b), *My Teacher Likes to Say* (Brennan–Nelson, 2004), and *There's a Frog in My Throat! 440 Animal Sayings a Little Bird Told Me* (Leedy, 2003).

Because idioms are figurative sayings, many students—and especially those who are English learners—have difficulty understanding them (Palmer, Shackelford, Miller, & Leclere, 2006/2007). It's crucial that teachers provide explicit instruction so that students move beyond the literal meanings of phrases. One way to help students learn about figurative language is to have them create idiom posters showing both literal and figurative meanings, as illustrated in Figure 7–6.

Metaphors and similes are comparisons that liken something to something else. A simile is a comparison signaled by the use of *like* or *as*: "The crowd was as rowdy as a bunch of marauding monkeys" and "My apartment was like an oven after the air-conditioning broke" are two examples. In contrast, a metaphor compares two things by implying that one is the other, without using *like* or *as*: "The children were frisky puppies playing in the yard" is an example. Metaphors are stronger comparisons, as these examples show:

She's as cool as a cucumber.
She's a cool cucumber.

In the moonlight, the dead tree looked like a skeleton.
In the moonlight, the dead tree was a skeleton.

Differentiating between the terms *simile* and *metaphor* is less important than understanding the meaning of comparisons in books students read and having students use comparisons to make their writing more vivid. For example, a sixth-grade student

Figure 7–6 ◆ A Sixth Grader's Idiom Poster for "In Hot Water"

compared anger to a thunderstorm using a simile. She wrote, "Anger is like a thunderstorm, screaming with thunder-feelings and lightning-words." Another student compared anger to a volcano. Using a metaphor, he wrote, "Anger is a volcano, erupting with poisonous words and hot-lava actions."

Students begin by learning traditional comparisons such as "happy as a clam" and "high as a kite," and then they learn to notice and invent fresh, unexpected comparisons. To introduce traditional comparisons to young children, teachers often use Audrey Wood's *Quick as a Cricket* (1982). Middle- and upper-grade students can invent new comparisons for stale expressions such as "butterflies in your stomach." In *Anastasia Krupnik* (1984), for example, Lois Lowry substituted "ginger ale in her knees" for the trite "butterflies in her stomach" to describe how nervous Anastasia felt when she stood in front of the class to read her poem.

Words to Study

Teachers highlight many words related to literature focus units and thematic units. They post these words on **word walls**, use many of them in word-study activities, and carefully choose some to teach directly. Teachers choose words that are essential to understanding the book or the unit, words that confuse students, and general-utility words students will use as they read other books or study other topics. Teachers should avoid words that aren't related to the book or unit and words that are too conceptually difficult for students understand.

Teachers are usually relieved to learn that students don't have to know all of the words in a book to read and comprehend it or listen to it read aloud. Of course, students vary in the number of unfamiliar words they can tolerate, depending on the topic of the book, their purpose for reading or listening, and the role of the unfamiliar words. It's unrealistic to assume that students will learn every word in a book or expect to teach every word.

Choosing Words to Study. It's impossible for teachers to teach all of the unfamiliar words that students come across in books they're reading or about topics they're studying during thematic units. Beck, McKeown, and Kucan (2002) have devised a tool to assist teachers in choosing which words to study. The researchers divide vocabulary words into three tiers or levels, and recommend that teachers focus on the words in the second tier:

Tier 1: Basic Words. These common words are used socially, in informal conversation at home and on the playground. Examples include *animal, clean,* and *laughing.* Native English-speaking students rarely require instruction about the meanings of these words.

Tier 2: Academic Words. These words are used more frequently in writing than in oral language, and students should learn their meanings because they have wide application across the curriculum. Students often understand the general concept represented by the word, but they don't recognize the specific word. Adding these words to their vocabulary allows them to express ideas more precisely. Examples include *community, evidence,* and *greedy.* Teaching these words has a powerful impact on students' vocabulary development.

Tier 3: Specialized Words. These technical words are content-specific and abstract. Examples include *minuend, osmosis,* and *suffrage.* They aren't used frequently enough to devote time to teaching them except as part of thematic units.

As teachers choose words for instruction and word-study activities, they focus on Tier 2 words even though words representing all three levels are written on word walls. During a fifth-grade unit on America in the 20th century, students learned to sing Woody Guthrie's folk ballad "This Land Is Your Land" (Guthrie, 1998) and then read Bonnie Christensen's biography, *Woody Guthrie: Poet of the People* (2001). The fifth graders created a word wall that included these words about Woody Guthrie:

ballads	*Great Depression*	*nightmare*	*spirit*
celebrate	*guitar*	*ordinary*	*stock market*
criss-cross	*hardship*	*original*	*tragedy*
depression	*harmonica*	*rallies*	*unfair*
desperate	*hitchhiked*	*restless*	*unions*
devastated	*lonesome*	*scorn*	*unsanitary*
drought	*migrant*	*severe*	*wandering*
Dust Bowl	*migration*	*sorrow*	*worries*

From this list, their teacher identified some words from the word wall as Tier 1, 2, and 3 words:

Tier 1 words: *guitar, harmonica, worries, nightmare, unfair, celebrates*

Tier 2 words: *ordinary, spirit, desperate, original, sorrow, tragedy*

Tier 3 words: *drought, Dust Bowl, stock market, Great Depression, unions, unsanitary*

There was only one Tier 1 word that needed to be taught: Not all the students knew what a harmonica was, so the teacher invited a friend who played the instrument to visit the classroom and play the harmonica. He focused on teaching Tier 2 words, and the students connected each word to Woody Guthrie and other American icons they'd studied. Because this was a social studies unit, the students read in their social studies textbooks about the Great Depression and learned some of the Tier 3 words.

Spotlighting Words on Word Walls. Teachers post word walls in the classroom; usually they're made from large sheets of butcher paper and divided into sections for each letter of the alphabet. Students and the teacher write interesting, confusing, and important words representing all three tiers on the word wall. Usually students choose the words to write on the word wall and may even do the writing themselves. Teachers add other important words that students haven't chosen. Words are added to the word wall as they come up in books students are reading or during a thematic unit, not in advance. Janet Allen (2007) says that word walls should be "a living part of the classroom with new words being added each day" (p. 120). Word walls are useful resources: Students locate words on the word wall that they want to use during a grand conversation or check the spelling of a word they're writing, and teachers use the words for word-study activities.

Some teachers use large pocket charts and word cards instead of butcher paper for their word walls. This way, the word cards can easily be used for word-study activities, and they can be sorted and rearranged on the pocket chart. After the book or unit is completed, teachers punch holes in one end of the cards and hang them on a ring. Then the collection of word cards can be placed in the writing center for students to use when they're writing.

Students also make individual word walls by dividing a sheet of paper into 20–24 boxes and labeling the boxes with the letters of the alphabet; they can put several letters together in one box. Then students write important words and phrases in the boxes as they read and discuss a book. Figure 7–7 shows a sixth grader's word wall for *Hatchet* (2007), a wilderness survival story by Gary Paulsen.

Figure 7–7 ◆ A Sixth Grader's Alphabetized Word Wall for *Hatchet*

A	B	C	D
alone	bush plane	Canadian wilderness	divorce
absolutely terrified	Brian Robeson	controls	desperation
arrows	bruised	cockpit	destroyed
aluminum cookset	bow & arrow	crash	disappointment
		careless	devastating
		campsite	
E	**F**	**G**	**H**
engine	fire	gut cherries	hatchet
emergency	fuselage	get food	heart attack
emptiness	fish		hunger
exhaustion	foolbirds		hope
	foodshelf		
	54 days		
I J	**K L**	**M N**	**O P Q**
instruments	lake	memory	pilot
insane		mosquitoes	panic
incredible wealth		mistakes	painful
		matches	porcupine quills
		mental journal	patience
		moose	
R	**S T**	**U V**	**W X Y Z**
rudder pedals	stranded	visitation rights	wilderness
rescue	secret	viciously thirsty	windbreaker
radio	survival pack	valuable asset	wreck
relative comfort	search	vicious whine	woodpile
raspberries	sleeping bag	unbelievable riches	wolf
roaring bonfire	shelter		
raft	starved		

Even though 25, 50, or more words may be added to the word wall, not all of them are explicitly taught. As they plan, teachers create lists of words that will probably be written on word walls during the unit. From this list, teachers choose the words—usually Tier 2 words that are critical to understanding the book or the unit—and these are the words they teach.

Nurturing English Learners

English learners often need more explicit instruction on words than native English speakers do. Sometimes English learners only need to have a word translated, but at other times, they're confused about a new meaning of a familiar word, or they're unfamiliar with both the underlying concept and words that describe it, and instruction is necessary.

Tier 1 Words. Tier 1 words are easier for English learners to learn because they often know these words in their native language; what they don't know are the equivalent English words. If teachers speak students' native language, they can translate the words and help students learn these English equivalents. English-speaking teachers often use pictures, pantomime, and demonstration to explain the words. It's often helpful for teachers to put together collections of small objects and pictures to share with students during literature focus units and thematic units.

Tier 2 Words. To build background knowledge, teachers preteach some unfamiliar words, including essential Tier 2 words, before students read a book or study a topic. Later, through explicit instruction and a variety of word-study activities, they teach other Tier 2 words. In addition, Calderon (2007) points out that ELs need to understand transition words and phrases, words with multiple meanings, and English words with cognates. Transition words, such as *consequently, yet, likewise, against, meanwhile, afterward,* and *finally,* are used to bridge ideas in sentences, paragraphs, and longer texts. Teachers can help ELs recognize these words and phrases, understand their meaning, and use them in their own writing.

Learning new meanings for familiar words is another Tier 2 activity. Some common words, such as *key, soft,* and *ready,* have less frequently used meanings that confuse English learners even though they're usually familiar with one or two of the meanings. Students also learn how to choose among related words. For example, *instrument* means a device for doing work; *tool* and *utensil* are also devices for doing work, but they don't mean exactly the same thing. *Instruments,* such as stethoscopes and scalpels, are used for doing complicated work; *tools,* such as hammers and screwdrivers, are used for skilled jobs, and *utensils* are simple devices, such as whisks and spoons, for working in the kitchen. Teachers also point out cognates, English words that are related to words in students' native language. Many Tier 2 words are Latin-based, so it's important to teach English learners who speak Spanish, Portuguese, Italian, and French to ask themselves whether an unfamiliar word is similar to a word in their native language.

Tier 3 Words. It's less important to teach these technical words because of their limited usefulness, and only a few words have cognates that students would know. Calderon (2007) recommends that teachers translate the words or briefly explain them. However, during thematic units, teachers do teach Tier 3 words that are important to understanding the big ideas being studied through a combination of instruction and word-study activities, including making word posters, doing word sorts, and completing semantic feature analyses.

Teaching Students About Words

Teachers explicitly teach students about specific words, usually Tier 2 words. McKeown and Beck (2004) emphasize that instruction should be rich, deep, and extended. That means that teachers provide multiple encounters with words; present a variety of information, including definitions, contexts, examples, and related words; and involve students in word-study activities so that they have multiple opportunities to interact with words. The procedure is time-consuming, but researchers report that students are more successful in learning and remembering word meanings this way (Beck, McKeown, & Kucan, 2002).

As teachers plan for instruction, they need to consider what students already know about a word. Sometimes the word is unfamiliar, or it represents a new concept. At other times, the word is familiar and students know one meaning, but they need to learn a new meaning. A word representing an unfamiliar concept usually takes the most time to teach, and a new meaning for a familiar word, the least.

Teachers use minilessons to teach students about specific words. They provide information about words, including both definitions and contextual information, and they engage students in activities to get them to think about and use words orally and in reading and writing. Sometimes teachers present minilessons before reading; at other times, they teach them after reading. The minilesson on page 242 shows how one teacher introduces vocabulary before reading a chapter in a content-area textbook.

Word-Study Activities

Students have opportunities to examine words and think more deeply about them as they participate in word-study activities (Allen, 2007). In some activities, they create visual representations of words, and in others, they categorize words or learn related words. Here's a list of word-study activities:

Word Posters. Students choose a word and write it on a small poster; then they draw and color a picture to illustrate it. They also use the word in a sentence on the poster. This is one way that students visualize the meaning of a word.

Word Maps. Students create a diagram to examine a word they're learning. They write the word, make a box around it, draw several lines from the box, and add information about the word in additional boxes they make at the end of each line. Three kinds of information typically included in a word map are a category for the word, examples, and characteristics or associations. Figure 7–8 shows a word map made by a fifth grader reading *Bunnicula: A Rabbit-Tale of Mystery* (Howe & Howe, 2006). Word maps are another way to visualize a word's meaning (Duffelmeyer & Banwart, 1992–1993).

Possible Sentences. To activate students' background knowledge about a topic and increase their curiosity before reading a book or a chapter in a content-area textbook, students write possible sentences using vocabulary words (Stahl & Kapinus, 1991). After reviewing the definitions of a set of 10 words, students work with classmates

Literacy Portraits: VIEWING GUIDE

The second graders in Ms. Janusz's class vary widely in their vocabulary knowledge. Some children have limited background knowledge and words to express ideas, but others are interested in many topics and know lots of words. Click on Jimmy's February button in the Literacy Profiles section of MyEducationLab at www.myeducationlab.com to watch a conference Ms. Janusz holds with him about a book he's reading during reading workshop. This informational book is about presidential elections. As they talk about the book, Jimmy uses sophisticated and technical vocabulary, including *democracy, electoral votes, snickering*, and *campaign slogan*, to discuss what he's learned. Most second graders aren't familiar with these concepts and don't use these words. How do you think Jimmy learned them? How does Ms. Janusz support his learning? Does his vocabulary knowledge correlate with his literacy level?

myeducationlab

MiniLesson

TOPIC: Introducing Content-Area Vocabulary Words
GRADE: Fifth Grade
TIME: Three 30-minute periods

Mrs. Cramer's fifth-grade class is involved in a social studies unit on immigration. The class has already created a K-W-L chart on immigration to activate students' background knowledge, and students have written about how and when their families came to the United States. They've also marked their countries of origin on a world map in the classroom. In this 3-day minilesson, Mrs. Cramer introduces six key vocabulary words before students read a chapter in their social studies textbook. Because many of her students are English learners, she takes more time to practice vocabulary before reading the chapter.

1 Introduce the Topic

Mrs. Cramer explains that after a week of studying immigration, the fifth graders are now getting ready to read the chapter about immigration in the social studies text. She places these five words written on word cards in a pocket chart and reads each one aloud: *culture, descendant, immigrant, prejudice*, and *pluralism*. She tells students that these words are used in the chapter and that it's important to be familiar with them before reading.

2 Share Examples

Mrs. Cramer distributes anticipation guides for students to rate their knowledge of the new words. The guide has four columns; the new words are listed in the left column, and the other three columns have these headings: I know the word well, I've heard of it, I don't know this word. For each word, the students put a checkmark in the appropriate column. At the end of the unit, they'll again rate their knowledge of the words and compare the two ratings to assess their learning.

3 Provide Information

Mrs. Cramer divides the students into small groups for a word sort. Each group receives a pack of 10 cards; the new vocabulary words are written on five of the cards and their definitions on the other cards. Students work together to match the words and definitions, and then Mrs. Cramer reviews the meaning of each word.

4 Guide Practice

The next day, the students repeat the word sort activity to review the meanings of the words. Next, they work with partners to complete a cloze activity: Mrs. Cramer has prepared a list of sentences taken from the chapter with the new words omitted, and students write the correct word in each blank. Then she reviews the sentences, explaining any sentences completed incorrectly.

5 Assess Learning

On the third day, Mrs. Cramer adds the new words to the word wall on immigration displayed in the classroom. Next, she models writing a quickwrite using the new words and other words from the word wall. Following the teacher's model, students write quickwrites using at least three of the new words and three other words from the word wall. Afterward, students use highlighters to mark the immigration-related words they've incorporated in their quickwrites. Later, Mrs. Cramer reads the quickwrites to assess the students' vocabulary knowledge.

to craft sentences using the words and afterward share them with the class. Then after reading, students review the sentences and revise those that aren't accurate.

Dramatizing Words. Students each choose a word and dramatize it for classmates, who then try to guess it. Sometimes an action is a more effective way to explain a word than a verbal definition. For example, a teacher teaching a literature focus unit on *Chrysanthemum* (Henkes, 1996), the story of a little girl who didn't like her name, dramatized the word *wilted* for her second graders when they didn't understand how a girl could wilt. Other words in *Chrysanthemum* that can easily be acted out include *humorous*, *sprouted*, *dainty*, and *wildly*. Dramatization is an especially effective activity for English learners.

Word Sorts. Students sort a collection of words taken from the word wall into two or more categories in a word sort (Bear, Invernizzi, Templeton, & Johnston, 2008). Usually students choose the categories they use for the sort, but sometimes the teacher chooses them. For example, words from a story might be sorted by character, or words from a thematic unit on machines might be sorted according to type of machine. The words can be written on cards, and then students sort a pack of word cards into piles. Or, students can cut apart a list of words, sort them into categories, and then paste the grouped words together on a sheet of paper.

Word Chains. Students choose a word and then identify three or four words to sequence before or after it to make a chain. For example, the word *tadpole* can be chained this way: *egg, tadpole, frog*; and the word *aggravate* can be chained like this: *irritate, bother, aggravate, annoy*. Students can draw and write their chains on a sheet of paper, or they can make a chain out of construction paper and write a word on each link.

Semantic Feature Analysis. Students learn the meanings of words that are conceptually related by examining their characteristics in a semantic feature analysis (Allen, 2007). Teachers select a group of related words, such as animals and plants in the rain forest or planets in the solar system, and then make a grid to classify them according to distinguishing characteristics (Pittelman, Heimlich, Berglund, & French, 1991; Rickelman & Taylor, 2006). Students analyze each

Figure 7-8 ◆ A Word Map for *Glistened*

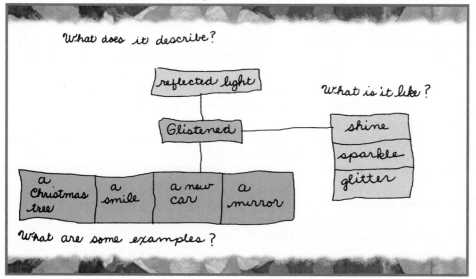

word, characteristic by characteristic, and they put checkmarks, circles, and question marks in each cell to indicate whether the word represents that characteristic. For example, on a semantic feature analysis about the rain forest, animals, plants, and people living in the rain forest are listed on one side of the grid and characteristics on the other. For the word *sloth*, students would add checkmarks in the grid to indicate that it is a mammal, lives in the canopy, goes to the forest floor, and has camouflage. They would add circles to indicate that a sloth is not colorful, not dangerous to people, not a plant, and not a bird or insect. If they aren't sure whether sloths are used to make medicine, they use a question mark.

These word-study activities provide opportunities for students to deepen their understanding of words listed on word walls, other words related to books they're reading, and words they're learning during thematic units. Students develop concepts, learn one or more meanings of words, and make associations among words through these activities. None of them require students to simply write words and their definitions or to use the words in sentences or a contrived story.

Word-Learning Strategies

When students come across an unfamiliar word while reading, there are a variety of things they can do: They can reread the sentence, analyze root words and affixes in the word, check a dictionary, sound out the word, look for context clues in the sentence, skip the word and keep reading, or ask the teacher or a classmate for help, for example (Allen, 1999). Some techniques, however, work better than others. After studying the research on ways to deal with unfamiliar words, Michael Graves (2006) has identified these three effective word-learning strategies:

- Using context clues
- Analyzing word parts
- Checking a dictionary

Be Strategic!

Word-Learning Strategies

When students are reading and come across an unfamiliar word, they use these strategies to figure out the word's meaning:

- Use context clues
- Analyze word parts
- Check a dictionary

These three strategies are effective when students know how to apply them and are interested in learning new words.

Capable readers know and use these strategies to figure out the meaning of unfamiliar words as they read. In contrast, less capable readers have fewer strategies available: They often depend on just one or two less effective strategies, such as sounding out the word or skipping it.

Graves (2006) recommends teaching students what to do when they encounter an unfamiliar word. They need to recognize when a word they're reading is unfamiliar and decide how important it is to know its meaning. If the word isn't important to the text, students skip it and continue reading, but if it is important, they need to take action. Here's the procedure he recommends that students use to figure out the meaning of an unfamiliar word:

1. Students reread the sentence containing the word.
2. Students use context clues to figure out the meaning of the word, and if that doesn't work, they continue to the next step.
3. Students examine the word parts, looking for familiar root words and affixes to aid in figuring out the meaning. If they're still not successful, they continue to the next step.
4. Students pronounce the word to see if they recognize it when they say it. If they still can't figure it out, they continue to the next step.
5. Students check the word in a dictionary or ask the teacher for help.

This procedure has the greatest chance of success because it incorporates all three word-learning strategies.

Using Context Clues. Students learn many words from context as they read. The surrounding words and sentences offer context clues; some clues provide information about the meaning of the word, and others provide information about the part of speech and how the word is used in a sentence. This contextual information helps students infer the meaning of the unfamiliar word. Illustrations also provide contextual information that helps readers identify words. The different types of context clues that readers use are presented in Figure 7–9. Interestingly, two or three types of contextual information are often found in the same sentence.

Nagy, Anderson, and Herman (1987) found that students who read books at their grade level have a 1 in 20 chance of learning the meaning of a word from context. Although that might seem insignificant, if students read 20,000 words a year and learn 1 of every 20 words from context, they will learn 1,000 words, or one third of their annual vocabulary growth. That's significant! How much time does it take to read 20,000 words? Nagy (1988) estimated that if teachers provide 30 minutes of daily reading time, students will learn an additional 1,000 words a year! It's interesting to note that both capable and less capable readers learn from context at about the same rate (Stahl, 1999).

The best way to teach students about context clues is by modeling. When teachers read aloud, they stop at a difficult word and do a think-aloud to show students how they use context clues to figure out its meaning. When the context provides enough information, teachers use the information and continue reading, but when the rest of the sentence or paragraph doesn't provide enough information, teachers use another strategy to figure out the meaning of the word.

Analyzing Word Parts. Students use their knowledge of prefixes, suffixes, and root words to unlock many multisyllabic words when they understand how word parts function. For example, *omnivorous*, *carnivorous*, and *herbivorous* relate to the foods that animals eat: *Omni* means "all," *carno* means "flesh," and *herb* means "vegetation." The common word part *vorous* comes from the Latin *vorare*, meaning "to swallow up." When students know *carnivorous* or *carnivore*, they use morphemic analysis to figure out the other words.

Go to the Building Teaching Skills and Dispositions section of Chapter 7 on **MyEducationLab.com** to hear second grader Michael discuss the strategies he uses to determine the meaning of unfamiliar words.

Figure 7–9 ◆ Six Types of Context Clues

Clue	Description	Sample Sentence
Definition	Readers use the definition in the sentence to understand the unknown word.	Some spiders spin silk with tiny organs called *spinnerets*.
Example-Illustration	Readers use an example or illustration to understand the unknown word.	Toads, frogs, and some birds are *predators* that hunt and eat spiders.
Contrast	Readers understand the unknown word because it's compared or contrasted with another word in the sentence.	Most spiders live for about one year, but *tarantulas* sometimes live for 20 years or more!
Logic	Readers think about the rest of the sentence to understand the unknown word.	An *exoskeleton* acts like a suit of armor to protect the spider.
Root Words and Affixes	Readers use their knowledge of root words and affixes to figure out the unknown word.	People who are terrified of spiders have *arachnophobia*.
Grammar	Readers use the word's function in the sentence or its part of speech to figure out the unknown word.	Most spiders *molt* five to ten times.

Teaching derivational prefixes and suffixes and non-English root words in fourth through eighth grades improves students' ability to unlock the meaning of unfamiliar words (Baumann, Edwards, Font, Tereshinski, Kame'enui, & Olejnik, 2002; Baumann, Font, Edwards, & Boland, 2005). For example, when students recognize that the Latin roots *-ann* and *-enn* mean "year," they can figure out the meanings of many of these words: *annual, biennial, perennial, centennial, bicentennial, millennium,* and *sesquicentennial*. Graves (2006) recommends that teachers teach morphemic analysis when non-English root words appear in books students are reading and during thematic units. Teachers break apart the words and discuss the word parts when they're posted on the word wall and through minilessons.

Checking the Dictionary. Looking up unfamiliar words in the dictionary is often frustrating because the definitions don't provide enough useful information or because words used in the definition are forms of the word being defined (Allen, 1999). Sometimes the definition that students choose—usually the first one—is the wrong one. Or, the definition doesn't make sense. For example, the word *pollution* is usually defined as "the act of polluting"—not a useful definition. Students could look for an entry for *polluting*, but they won't find it. They might notice an entry for *pollute*, where the first definition is "to make impure." The second definition is "to make unclean, especially with man-made waste," but even this definition may be difficult to understand.

Because dictionary definitions are most useful when a person is vaguely familiar with the word's meaning, teachers play an important role in dictionary work: They teach students how to read a dictionary entry and decide which definitions make sense, and they model the strategy when they're reading aloud and come across a word that's unfamiliar to most students. They also assist students by explaining the definitions that students locate, providing sample sentences, and comparing the word to related words and opposites.

Word Consciousness

Another component of vocabulary instruction is developing students' word consciousness, their interest in learning and using words (Graves & Watts-Taffe, 2002). According to Scott and Nagy (2004), word consciousness is "essential for vocabulary growth and comprehending the language of schooling" (p. 201). Students who have word consciousness exemplify these characteristics:

- Students use words skillfully, understanding the nuances of word meanings.
- Students gain a deep appreciation of words and value them.
- Students are aware of differences between social and academic language.
- Students understand the power of word choice.
- Students are motivated to learn the meaning of unfamiliar words.

Word consciousness is important because vocabulary knowledge is generative—that is, it transfers to and enhances students' learning of other words (Scott & Nagy, 2004).

The goal is for students to become more aware of words, manipulate them playfully, and appreciate their power. Teachers foster word consciousness in a variety of ways, as Mrs. Sanom did in the vignette at the beginning of the chapter. Most importantly, they model interest in words and precise use of vocabulary (Graves, 2006). To encourage students' interest in words, teachers share books about words, including *Max's Words* (Banks, 2006), *Word Wizard* (Falwell, 2006), and *The Boy Who Loved Words* (Schotter, 2006) with primary-grade students; and *Miss Alaineus: A Vocabulary Disaster* (Fraiser, 2007), *Baloney (Henry P.)* (Scieszka, 2005), and *Mom and Dad Are Palindromes* (Shulman, 2006) with older students. Next, they call students' attention to words by highlighting words of the day, posting words on word walls, and having students collect words from books they're reading. They promote wordplay by sharing riddles, jokes, puns, songs, and poems and encouraging students to experiment with words and use them in new ways. Figure 7–10 lists the types of wordplay. Through these activities, students become more powerful word users.

Assessing Students' Vocabulary Knowledge

It's difficult to assess students' vocabulary knowledge. There aren't any grade-level standards to indicate which words students should know or even how many words they need to learn. In addition, it's complicated because students learn words gradually,

Figure 7–10 ◆ Types of Wordplay

Type	Description	Examples
Alliteration	Repetition of a beginning consonant or vowel in neighboring words within a phrase or sentence. Sometimes sentences are called *tongue twisters*.	now or never do or die Peter Piper picked a peck of pickled peppers
Eponym	A person's name that has become a word.	teddy bear sandwich pasteurization
Hyperbole	An exaggerated statement.	I almost died laughing my feet are killing me I'm so hungry I could eat a horse
Onomatopoeia	A word that imitates a sound.	tick-tock kerplunk sizzling
Oxymoron	The combination of two normally contradictory words.	jumbo shrimp pretty ugly deafening silence
Palindrome	A word or phrase that reads the same forward or backward.	mom civic a man, a plan, a canal—Panama
Personification	A figure of speech that endows human traits or abilities to inanimate objects.	the old VW's engine coughed raindrops danced on my umbrella fear knocked on the door
Pig Latin	A language game where a speaker rearranges the sounds in words: The initial consonant sound of each word is moved to the end and *ay* is added after it; but when the word begins with a vowel, the initial sound isn't moved, but *ay* is added at the end.	cat = at-cay ice cream = ice-ay eam-cray pig Latin is fun = ig-pay atin-lay is-ay un-fay
Portmanteau	A word created by fusing two words to combine the meaning of both words. This wordplay was invented by Lewis Carroll in *Jabberwocky*.	spork (spoon + fork) brunch (breakfast + lunch) smog (smoke + fog)
Spoonerism	A tangle of words in which sounds are switched, often with a humorous effect. These "slips of the tongue," named for Reverend William Spooner (1844–1930), usually occur when a person is speaking quickly.	butterfly—flutterby go and take a shower—go and shake a tower save the whales—wave the sails

moving to deeper levels of "knowing" a word. Teachers typically monitor students' independent reading and use informal measures to evaluate their word knowledge, but several tests are available to measure students' vocabulary, and they're described in the Assessment Tools feature below.

Teachers often choose more-authentic measures of students' vocabulary knowledge because they're more useful than formal tests (Bean & Swan, 2006). These informal assessment tools show whether students have learned the words that were taught as well as the depth of their knowledge:

Observations. Teachers watch how students use new words during word-study activities, minilessons, and discussions. They also notice how students apply word-learning strategies during guided reading and when they're reading aloud.

Conferences. Teachers talk with students about the words they've used in word-study activities and in their writing. They also ask what students do when they come across an unfamiliar word and talk about word-learning strategies.

Assessment Tools

Vocabulary

Both informal assessments and standardized tests can be used to measure students' vocabulary knowledge, but tests often equate word knowledge with recognizing or being able to state a single definition of a word rather than assessing the depth of students' knowledge. Here are several norm-referenced vocabulary tests:

◆ **Peabody Picture Vocabulary Test-4 (PPVT-4)** (Dunn, Dunn, & Dunn, 2006)

The PPVT-4 is an individually administered assessment to screen students' vocabulary knowledge. The test can be used with K–8 students, but it's most commonly used with K–2 students showing limited verbal fluency. The PPVT-4 measures receptive vocabulary: The teacher says a word and asks the student to look at four pictures and identify the one that best illustrates the meaning of the word. Unfortunately, this test takes 10–15 minutes to administer, which makes it too time-consuming for regular classroom use. The PPVT-4 is available for purchase from the American Guidance Service.

◆ **Expressive Vocabulary Test-2 (EVT-2)** (Williams, 2006)

The EVT-2 is also an individual test that's used to screen K–8 students' knowledge of words. The EVT-2 is the expressive counterpart of the PPVT-4: The teacher points to a picture and asks the student to say a word that labels the picture or to provide a synonym for a word that's illustrated in the picture. This test is also very time-consuming for classroom teachers to use. It's available from the American Guidance Service.

◆ **Informal Reading Inventories (IRIs)**

Sometimes teachers in grades 2–8 use IRIs to assess students' vocabulary knowledge. One or two comprehension questions at each grade level focus on the meaning of words selected from the passage students have read. The usefulness of this assessment is limited, however, because so few questions deal with vocabulary and because students who read below grade level aren't tested on age-appropriate words.

Even though these tests aren't very useful in classroom settings, they are helpful in diagnosing struggling readers and English learners with limited word knowledge.

Rubrics. Teachers include items about vocabulary on rubrics to emphasize its importance. For oral-presentation rubrics, teachers emphasize the use of technical words related to the topic, and for writing, they emphasize precise vocabulary.

Tests. Teachers also create a variety of paper-and-pencil tests to monitor students' vocabulary knowledge. For example, they can have students complete a cloze passage using newly learned words, quickwrite about a word, create a word map or word chain about a word, or draw a picture to represent a word's meaning.

These informal assessments go beyond simply providing a definition or using a word in a sentence because students are actively involved in using the word in context.

Students also self-assess their word knowledge. Cunningham and Allington (2007) suggest having students self-assess their knowledge of specific words, using the levels of word knowledge. Teachers develop a list of five levels of word knowledge using language that's appropriate for their students and post it in the classroom. Here's a list developed by a sixth-grade teacher:

1 = I don't know this word at all.
2 = I've heard this word before, but I don't know the meaning.
3 = I think I know what this word means.
4 = I know one meaning for this word, and I can use it in a sentence.
5 = I know several meanings or other things about this word.

Teachers give students a list of words related to a book they're going to read or at the beginning of a thematic unit; students assess their word knowledge by writing a number to indicate their level of knowledge beside each word, and then they repeat the assessment at the end to see how their knowledge has grown. Or, before introducing a new word, teachers can informally ask students to raise their hands and show the number of fingers that corresponds with their level of knowledge about the word.

Chapter 7 Review

How Effective Teachers Expand Students' Knowledge of Words

▶ Teachers provide daily opportunities for students to read books independently and listen to them read aloud.

▶ Teachers categorize unfamiliar words into three tiers—basic words, academic words, and specialized words.

▶ Teachers teach Tier 2 words using explicit instruction and a variety of word-study activities.

▶ Teachers support students' development of word-learning strategies.

▶ Teachers nurture students' word consciousness.

PEARSON
myeducationlab
Where the Classroom Comes to Life

Go to MyEducationLab at www.myeducationlab.com to deepen your understanding of the concepts presented in this chapter:

▶ Investigate the second graders' growing knowledge of word-identification strategies by viewing video segments in the Literacy Portraits.

▶ Check your understanding of chapter concepts with the multiple-choice and essay quizzes in the Study Plan.

▶ Apply some of the main ideas discussed in the chapter in the Activities and Applications section of the website.

▶ Practice what you've learned in this chapter in Building Teaching Skills and Dispositions before applying the ideas in your own classroom.

PROFESSIONAL REFERENCES

Allen, J. (1999). *Words, words, words*. Portsmouth, NH: Heinemann.

Allen, J. (2007). *Inside words: Tools for teaching academic vocabulary, grades 4–12*. Portland, ME: Stenhouse.

Allington, R. L. (2006). *What really matters for struggling readers* (2nd ed.). Boston: Allyn & Bacon/Pearson.

Baumann, J. F., Edwards, E. C., Font, G., Tereshinski, C. A., Kame'enui, E. J., & Olejnik, S. (2002). Teaching morphemic and contextual analysis to fifth grade students. *Reading Research Quarterly, 37,* 150–176.

Baumann, J. F., Font, G., Edwards, E. C., & Boland, E. (2005). Strategies for teaching middle-grade students to use word-part and context clues to expand reading vocabulary. In E. Hiebert & M. L. Kamil (Eds.), *Teaching and learning vocabulary: Bringing research to practice* (pp. 179–205). Mahwah, NJ: Erlbaum.

Baumann, J. F., Kame'enui, E. J., & Ash, G. (2003). Research on vocabulary instruction: Voltaire redux. In J. Flood, D. Lapp, J. R. Squire, & J. M. Jensen (Eds.), *Handbook of research on teaching the English language arts* (2nd ed., pp. 752–785). Mahwah, NJ: Erlbaum.

Bean, R. M., & Swan, A. (2006). Vocabulary assessment: A key to planning vocabulary instruction. In C. C. Block & J. N. Mangieri (Eds.), *The vocabulary-enriched classroom: Practices for improving the reading performance of all students in grades 3 and up* (pp. 164–187). New York: Scholastic.

Bear, D. R., Invernizzi, M., Templeton, S., & Johnston, F. (2008). *Words their way: Word study for phonics, vocabulary, and spelling instruction* (4th ed.). Upper Saddle River, NJ: Merrill/Pearson.

Beck, I. L., McKeown, M. G., & Kucan, L. (2002). *Bringing words to life: Robust vocabulary instruction*. New York: Guilford Press.

Calderon, M. (2007). *Teaching reading to English language learners, grades 6–12*. Thousand Oaks, CA: Corwin Press.

Cooper, J. D., Chard, D. J., & Kiger, N. D. (2006). *The struggling reader: Interventions that work*. New York: Scholastic.

Cunningham, P. M. (2009). *What really matters in vocabulary: Research-based practices across the curriculum*. Boston: Allyn & Bacon/Pearson.

Cunningham, P. M., & Allington, R. L. (2007). *Classrooms at work: They can all read and write*. Boston: Allyn & Bacon.

Duffelmeyer, F. A., & Banwart, B. H. (1992–1993). Word maps for adjectives and verbs. *The Reading Teacher, 46,* 351–353.

Dunn, D. M., Dunn, L. W., & Dunn, L. M. (2006). *Peabody picture vocabulary test-4*. Bloomington, MN: American Guidance Service/Pearson.

Fisher, D., Frey, N., & Lapp, D. (2008). Shared readings: Modeling comprehension, vocabulary, text structures, and text features for older readers. *The Reading Teacher, 61,* 548–556.

Graves, M. F. (2006). *The vocabulary book: Learning and instruction*. New York: Teachers College Press.

Graves, M. F., & Watts-Taffe, S. M. (2002). The place of word consciousness in a research-based vocabulary program. In S. J. Samuels & A. E. Farstrup (Eds.), *What research has to say about reading instruction* (3rd ed., pp. 140–165). Newark, DE: International Reading Association.

Jacobson, J., Lapp, D., & Flood, J. (2007). A seven-step instructional plan for teaching English-language learners to comprehend and use homonyms, homophones, and homographs. *Journal of Adolescent and Adult Literacy, 51,* 98–111.

McKeown, M. G., & Beck, I. L. (2004). Direct and rich vocabulary instruction. In J. F. Baumann & E. B. Kame'enui (Eds.), *Vocabulary instruction: Research to practice* (pp. 13–27). New York: Guilford Press.

Nagy, W. E. (1988). *Teaching vocabulary to improve reading comprehension*. Urbana, IL: ERIC Clearinghouse on Reading and Communication Skills and the National Council of Teachers of English and the International Reading Association.

Nagy, W. E., Anderson, R. C., & Herman, P. A. (1987). Learning word meanings from context during normal reading. *American Educational Research Journal, 24,* 237–270.

Palmer, B. C., Shackelford, V. S., Miller, S. C., & Leclere, J. T. (2006/2007). Bridging two worlds: Reading comprehension, figurative language instruction, and the English-language learner. *Journal of Adolescent and Adult Literacy, 50,* 258–267.

Pittelman, S. D., Heimlich, J. E., Berglund, R. L., & French, M. P. (1991). *Semantic feature analysis: Classroom applications*. Newark, DE: International Reading Association.

Rickelman, R. J., & Taylor, D. B. (2006). Teaching vocabulary by learning content-area words. In C. C. Block & J. N. Mangieri (Eds.), *The vocabulary-enriched classroom: Practices for improving the reading performance of all students in grades 3 and up* (pp. 54–73). New York: Scholastic.

Santoro, L. E., Chard, D. J., Howard, L., & Baker, S. K. (2008). Making the *very* most of classroom read-alouds to promote comprehension and vocabulary. *The Reading Teacher, 61,* 396–408.

Scott, J. A., & Nagy, W. E. (2004). Developing word consciousness. In J. F. Baumann & E. J. Kame'enui (Eds.), *Vocabulary instruction: Theory to practice* (pp. 210–217). New York: Guilford Press.

Stahl, S. A. (1999). *Vocabulary development.* Cambridge, MA: Brookline Books.

Stahl, S. A., & Kapinus, B. (1991). Possible sentences: Predicting word meanings to teach content area vocabulary. *The Reading Teacher, 45,* 36–43.

Stahl, S. A., & Nagy, W. E. (2006). *Teaching word meanings.* Mahwah, NJ: Erlbaum.

Stahl, S. A., Richek, M. G., & Vandevier, R. (1991). Learning word meanings through listening: A sixth grade replication. In J. Zutell & S. McCormick (Eds.), *Learning factors/teacher factors: Issues in literacy research. Fortieth yearbook of the National Reading Conference* (pp. 185–192). Chicago: National Reading Conference.

Stanovich, K. E. (1986). Matthew effects in reading: Some consequences of individual differences in the acquisition of literacy. *Reading Research Quarterly, 21,* 360–406.

Swanborn, M. S. W., & de Glopper, K. (1999). Incidental word learning while reading: A meta-analysis. *Review of Educational Research, 69,* 261–285.

Tompkins, G. E., & Yaden, D. B., Jr. (1986). *Answering students' questions about words.* Urbana, IL: ERIC Clearinghouse on Reading and Communication Skills and the National Council of Teachers of English.

Venezky, R. L. (1999). *The American way of spelling: The structure and origins of American English orthography.* New York: Guilford Press.

Williams, K. T. (2006). *Expressive vocabulary test-2.* Bloomington, MN: American Guidance Service/Pearson.

CHILDREN'S BOOK REFERENCES

Banks, K. (2006). *Max's words.* New York: Farrar, Straus & Giroux.

Barretta, G. (2007). *Dear deer: A book of homophones.* New York: Holt.

Bollard, J. K. (2006). *Scholastic children's thesaurus.* New York: Scholastic.

Brennan-Nelson, D. (2004), *My teacher likes to say.* Chelsea, MI: Sleeping Bear Press.

Brewster, H. (1997). *Inside the Titanic.* Boston: Little, Brown.

Cheney, L. (2002). *America: A patriotic primer.* New York: Simon & Schuster.

Christensen, B. (2001). *Woody Guthrie: Poet of the people.* New York: Knopf.

Cole, J. (1997). *The magic school bus and the electric field trip.* New York: Scholastic.

Falwell, C. (2006). *Word wizard.* New York: Clarion Books.

Frasier, D. (2007). *Miss Alaineus: A vocabulary disaster.* New York: HarperCollins/Voyager Books.

Guthrie, W. (1998). *This land is your land.* New York: Little, Brown.

Gwynne, F. (2005). *A chocolate moose for dinner.* New York: Aladdin Books.

Gwynne, F. (2006). *The king who rained.* New York: Aladdin Books.

Hellweg, P. (2006). *The American Heritage children's thesaurus.* Boston: Houghton Mifflin.

Henkes, K. (1996). *Chrysanthemum.* New York: HarperTrophy.

Howe, D., & Howe, J. (2006). *Bunnicula: A rabbit-tale of mystery.* New York: Aladdin Books.

Kentley, E. (2001). *Story of the Titanic.* London: Dorling Kindersley.

Leedy, L. (2003). *There's a frog in my throat! 440 animal sayings a little bird told me.* New York: Holiday House.

Lowry, L. (1984). *Anastasia Krupnik.* New York: Yearling.

Osborne, W., & Osborne, M. P. (1995). *Tonight on the Titanic.* New York: Random House.

Osborne, W., & Osborne, M. P. (2002). *Titanic: A nonfiction companion to Tonight on the Titanic.* New York: Random House.

Paulsen, G. (2007). *Hatchet.* New York: Simon & Schuster.

Schotter, R. (2006). *The boy who loved words.* New York: Random House/Schwartz & Wade.

Scieszka, J. (2005). *Baloney (Henry P.).* New York: Puffin Books.

Scillian, D. (2001). *A is for America.* Chelsea, MI: Sleeping Bear Press.

Shulman, M. (2006). *Mom and dad are palindromes.* San Francisco: Chronicle Books.

Tanaka, S. (1996). *On board the Titanic: What it was like when the great liner sank.* New York: Hyperion Books.

Terban, M. (1992). *The dove dove: Funny homograph riddles.* New York: Clarion Books.

Terban, M. (2006). *Scholastic dictionary of idioms.* New York: Scholastic.

Terban, M. (2007a). *Eight ate: A feast of homonym riddles.* New York: Clarion Books.

Terban, M. (2007b). *In a pickle and other funny idioms.* New York: Clarion Books.

Terban, M. (2007c). *Mad as a wet hen!: And other funny idioms.* New York: Clarion Books.

White, E. E. (1998). *Voyage on the great Titanic: The diary of Margaret Ann Brady.* New York: Scholastic.

Wittels, H. (2001). *A first thesaurus.* New York: Golden Books.

Wood, A. (1982). *Quick as a cricket.* London: Child's Play.

Chapter 8

Facilitating Students' Comprehension: Reader Factors

Mrs. Donnelly Teaches Comprehension Strategies

Posters about comprehension strategies, including connecting, questioning, repairing, and summarizing, hang on the wall in Mrs. Donnelly's classroom. She introduced comprehension strategies by explaining that sixth graders think while they read, and they do different kinds of thinking. These kinds of thinking are called *strategies*. Her students made the posters as they studied each strategy. Tanner, Vincente, and Ashante's poster for monitoring is shown in the box on the next page.

One of the first strategies that Mrs. Donnelly taught was predicting, and even though her students were familiar with it, they didn't know why they were using it. She explained that predictions guide their thinking. Together they made a chart about the strategy and practiced making predictions as Mrs. Donnelly read *The Garden of Abdul Gasazi* (Van Allsburg, 1993), the story of an evil magician who hates dogs. The students made predictions about *The Garden of Abdul Gasazi* based on the title and the cover illustration, but making predictions got harder in the middle of the surrealistic story because they didn't know whether the dog would escape the magician's garden after he was turned into a duck. Mrs. Donnelly emphasized the importance of continuing to think about the story and to make predictions when it gets confusing. She stopped reading and talked first about why the dog was likely to be successful and then why he wouldn't be. Only about two thirds of the students predicted he would make it home safely, but he did.

The next day, they read *La Mariposa* (Jiménez, 1998), the autobiographical picture-book story about a migrant child with exceptional artistic ability. The title, which means "the butterfly," and the illustration on the cover of a boy flying toward the sun didn't provide enough information on which to base a prediction, so the students learned that sometimes they have to read a few pages before they can make useful predictions. After reading about Spanish-speaking Francisco's difficult first day of school in an English-only classroom, Norma figured out that the caterpillar the boy is watching in the classroom will become a butterfly, and that the boy on the front cover is flying like a butterfly, but she didn't know why that connection was important. Several students pointed out that the butterfly might symbolize freedom. Moises predicted that the boy will be rescued from the migrant tent city where he and his family live, and Lizette suggested that he will move to a bilingual classroom where his teacher will understand him and he will make friends. Even though those predictions were wrong, the students became more engaged in the story and were eager for their teacher to continue reading. Mrs. Donnelly wrote their predictions on small self-stick notes and attached them to the edge of the pages as she read. She modeled how to use these notes because she wanted to make their thinking more visible, and she explained that she wants them to use self-stick notes, too: "I want you to show me your thinking."

Sixth Graders' Strategy Poster	
Monitoring	
What is it?	It is checking that you are understanding what you are reading.
Why use it?	Monitoring helps you solve problems so you can be successful.
When?	You should use this strategy while you are reading.
What do you do?	1. Keep asking: Does this make sense? If you are understanding, keep reading, but if it doesn't make sense, take action to solve the problem. 2. Try these solutions: • Go back several pages or to the beginning of the chapter and reread. • Keep reading one or two more pages. • Reread the last prediction, connection, or summary you wrote. • Talk to a friend about the problem. • Write a quickwrite about the problem. • Talk to Mrs. Donnelly.

Next, she taught the connecting strategy using *So Far From the Sea* (Bunting, 1998), a story about life at a Japanese relocation camp during World War II. She explained that readers make three kinds of connections—text-to-self, text-to-world, and text-to-text. As she read each book aloud, she modeled making connections and encouraged the sixth graders to share their connections. Each time they made a connection, Mrs. Donnelly wrote it on a self-stick note; after she finished reading the book, she collected the notes, had the students sort them according to the kind of connection, and posted them in text-to-self, text-to-world, and text-to-text columns on a chart. The chart for *So Far From the Sea* is shown here.

Mrs. Donnelly reviewed each comprehension strategy because she wanted the sixth graders to be familiar with all of them. Next, she introduced *Joey Pigza Loses Control*, a Newbery Honor book by Jack Gantos (2005), so that students could practice integrating their use of the comprehension strategies in an authentic reading experience. Mrs. Donnelly explained that readers rarely use only one strategy; instead, they use many of them at the same time.

Mrs. Donnelly introduced the book: "This is a story about a boy named Joey who is about your age. His parents are divorced, and he's going to spend the summer with his dad. Joey is ADHD. His mother says he's 'wired,' and he uses medicine patches to

The Connections Chart About *So Far From the Sea*

Text-to-Self	Text-to-World	Text-to-Text
My grandmother takes flowers when she goes to the cemetery because one of her husbands died.	I know that in World War II, Americans were fighting the Japanese because of Pearl Harbor, and they were fighting Hitler and the Germans, too.	This story is like The Bracelet. That girl and her family were taken to a camp in the desert. It was miserable there and she didn't deserve to have to go.
My great-granddad had to go too, and it wasn't fair because he was a loyal American, but his parents were from Japan.	In the book it's World War II, but I'm thinking about our war in Iraq.	Another book I know is Journey to Topaz. Topaz was another war relocation center and it was a terrible prison, too.
I know how to make origami birds. My cousin and I learned last summer.		I've heard about a book called Anne Frank. She was Jewish and this sorta happened to her in Germany and she died, too.
We have an American flag on our car so everyone knows we love America.		

control his behavior. He doesn't know his dad very well, so he doesn't know what to expect. His mom tells him not to expect too much." She asks the sixth graders to think about what they know about divorced parents, summer vacations, and ADHD kids. They talk about what they know about each topic, and then they brainstorm these questions to stimulate their thinking about the story:

What is Joey's dad like?

Will they have fun together?

Will Joey be in the way?

Does he hope his parents will get back together?

Does Joey's dad love him?

Will Joey's dad disappoint him?

Will Joey disappoint his dad?

Will Joey's medicine work or will he be "wired"?

Will Joey's mom be lonely without him?

Will Joey stay with his dad all summer or come back home sooner?

Mrs. Donnelly passes out copies of the book and stacks of small self-stick notes for students to use to record their thinking as they read. They read the first chapter together, and then students continue to read on their own or with a partner. The book is contemporary realism, and it's easy reading for most students. Mrs. Donnelly chose it because it would be interesting but easy to read, so they'd have the cognitive resources available while reading to concentrate on their strategy use.

After reading the first chapter, the students come together to talk about it in a **grand conversation**. They begin by talking about what they remember from the chapter, and then Mrs. Donnelly reads the sentence from page 10 where Joey says this to his mom about the dad he doesn't know very well: "I just want him to love me as much as I already love him." She asks, "How do parents show that they love their children?" She hangs up a sheet of chart paper, divides it into two columns, and writes the question at the top of the first column. The students suggest a number of ways, including giving them presents, taking care of them, spending time with them, taking them to church, keeping them safe, and having dinner with them. Mrs. Donnelly writes their ideas under the question in the first column of the chart. Then she narrows the question and asks, "What do you think Joey is looking for from his dad?" Ashante says, "He wants his dad to pay attention to him." Leticia suggests, "He wants him to say 'I love you, son,' tell him he's missed him, and play basketball with him." Students continue to offer ideas, which Mrs. Donnelly adds to the chart. Then she asks, "How do kids show love to their parents?" and she writes the question at the top of the second column. The students suggest that children show their love by behaving, making their parents proud, being responsible, and doing their chores; she writes these answers under the question in the second column. Finally, Mrs. Donnelly asks, "What is Joey's dad expecting from his son?" It's much harder for the students to put themselves in this role. Henry offers, "I think he just wants to have him live with him every day." The sixth graders also reflect on their strategy use. Several students talk about predictions they made, and others share how they monitored their reading and made connections while they were reading.

After reading and discussing each chapter, the students collect the self-stick notes they've used to keep track of their thinking, and they write about the strategies they've used in a **double-entry journal**. Normally, double-entry journals have two columns, but Mrs. Donnelly asks the students to include three columns—she's calling it a triple-entry journal: They write what was happening in the text or copy a quote from the text in the first column, explain their thinking in the second column, and identify the strategy they used in the third column. Excerpts from Tanner's triple-entry thinking journal are shown below.

The students continue to read, discuss, and write about their strategy use as they read *Joey Pigza Loses Control*. After they've read half the book, Mrs. Donnelly brings the class together for a **minilesson**. She explains that she's reviewed their thinking journals and has noticed that students weren't summarizing very much. They talk about the summarizing strategy and how, when, and why they should use it. Mrs. Donnelly demonstrates how to summarize as she reads the beginning of the next chapter aloud, and then she encourages students to try to use the strategy as they read the next chapter.

Excerpts From Tanner's Triple-Entry Thinking Journal

Chapter	The Text	Your Thinking	The Strategy
1	Joey's mom warns him that his dad is wired like he is.	I'm thinking that this book is about a kid who doesn't know his dad and he's going to be disappointed by him. His Mom doesn't think it's going to be a good vacation.	Identifying big ideas
4	Joey's dad doesn't act like a dad and his Grandma doesn't act like a grandma.	My stomach feels queasy. Joey doesn't belong with these people. His dad doesn't stop talking to listen to him and his grandma doesn't even like him. I predict bad things are going to happen.	Predicting
7	After the game they go to the mall to see Leezy.	My mind is asking questions. Why would Carter let Joey drive the car to the mall? Why would his dad tell him it's OK to steal money out of the wishing pond? Is the author trying to show us what a terrible dad he is? We already know that.	Questioning
8	His dad thinks Joey doesn't need the patches and he won't let him have them.	What is wrong with his dad? The patch is medicine that he needs. I am so mad at his dad. That's all I can think. I'm glad my parents take good care of me.	Connecting
14	Joey calls his mom to come get him at the mall.	I think Joey is really a smart kid. He knows how to save himself. He calls his mom and she comes to get him. Joey is right to call his dad a J-E-R-K because that's what he is. The visit was a fiasco just like I predicted. This is a really great book and I want to read it all over again.	Evaluating

After they finish reading the book, the students have another grand conversation. They talk about how Joey's mom rescues him and how disillusioned Joey is about his dad. Next, they return to the list of questions they brainstormed before they began reading and talk about the questions and answers. Jake answers the question "Does Joey's dad love him?" this way: "I think his dad does love him but it's a strange kind of love because his dad is selfish. He loves him as much as he can, but it's not very good love." Lizette answers these two questions: "Will Joey's dad disappoint him?" and "Will Joey disappoint his dad?" She says, "I'm positive that Joey's dad disappointed him. His dad wasn't a good dad. The second question is harder to answer. I know Joey tried to be a good son, but it's impossible to satisfy his dad. His dad made him hyper and then got mad at him for being hyper."

Then they reread the chart they began after reading the first chapter about parents showing their love for their children and children showing their love for their parents. They talk about the things they learned that Joey wanted from his dad: for his dad to listen to him, to take care of him, to be responsible for him. They also talk about what Joey's dad wanted from him. Dillan explains, "I think Joey's dad wanted Joey to be his friend and to take care of him. I think Joey would be a better dad than his dad was." Then Mrs. Donnelly asks about Joey's mom: "Does Joey's mom love him?" Everyone agrees that she does, and they name many ways that she shows her love, including giving him money so he can call her, listening to him, worrying about him, hugging him, and telling him she loves him. They complete the chart by adding the new suggestions and then circling the behaviors that his dad exemplified in blue, his mom's in green, and Joey's in red. Later, students will use the information on this chart as they write an essay about how parents and children show their love for one another.

As they reflect on their strategy use, the students are amazed that they remember so much from the story and how well they understand it. Jake says, "I was thinking all the time in this story. I guess that's why I know so much about it. This thinking is a good idea." Richard agrees, saying, "I don't even have to remember to use strategies now. I just naturally think that way." Mrs. Donnelly smiles at Richard's comment. Her goal is for her students to use comprehension strategies independently. She'll continue to emphasize strategies and remind the sixth graders to use self-stick notes to track their thinking for several more months, but she'll gradually remove this scaffold once she sees that they've become strategic readers.

Comprehension is the goal of reading; it's the reason why people read. Students must understand what they're reading to learn from the experience; they must make sense of the words in the text to maintain interest; and they must enjoy reading to become lifelong readers. Mrs. Donnelly was teaching her students to use comprehension strategies in the vignette because strategic readers are more likely to comprehend what they're reading. Struggling readers, in contrast, are frustrated; they don't understand what they're reading, don't like to read, and aren't likely to read in the future.

Comprehension involves different levels of thinking, from literal to inferential, critical, and evaluative. The most basic level is literal comprehension: Readers pick out main ideas, sequence details, notice similarities and differences, and identify explicitly stated reasons. The higher levels differ from literal comprehension because readers use their own knowledge along with the information presented in the text. The second level is inferential comprehension. Readers use clues in the text, implied information, and their background knowledge to draw inferences. They make predictions, recognize cause and effect, and determine the author's purpose. Critical comprehension is next: Readers analyze symbolic meanings, distinguish fact from opinion, and draw conclusions. The most sophisticated level is evaluative comprehension: Readers judge the value of a text using generally accepted criteria and personal standards. They detect bias, identify faulty reasoning, determine the effectiveness of persuasive techniques, and assess the quality of a text. These levels point out the range of thinking readers do. Because it's important to involve students in higher-level thinking, teachers ask questions and involve students in activities that require them to use inferential, critical, and evaluative comprehension.

WHAT IS COMPREHENSION?

Comprehension is a creative, multifaceted thinking process in which students engage with the text (Tierney, 1990). You've read about the word *process* before—both reading and writing have been described as processes. A process is more complicated than a single action: It involves a series of behaviors that occur over time. The comprehension process begins during prereading as students activate their background knowledge and preview the text, and it continues to develop as students read, respond, explore, and apply their reading. Readers construct a mental "picture" or representation of the text and its interpretation through the comprehension process (Van Den Broek & Kremer, 2000).

Judith Irwin (1991) defines comprehension as a reader's process of using prior experiences and the author's text to construct meaning that's useful to that reader for a specific purpose. This definition emphasizes that comprehension depends on two factors: the reader and the text that's being read. Whether comprehension is successful, according to Sweet and Snow (2003), depends on the interaction of reader factors and text factors.

Reader and Text Factors

Readers are actively engaged with the text; they think about many things as they read to comprehend the text. For example, they do the following:

Activate prior knowledge
Examine the text to uncover its organization
Make predictions
Connect to their own experiences
Create mental images
Draw inferences
Notice symbols and other literary devices
Monitor their understanding

These activities can be categorized as reader and text factors (National Reading Panel, 2000). Reader factors include the background knowledge that readers bring to the reading process as well as the strategies they use while reading and their motivation and engagement during reading. Text factors include the author's ideas, the words the author uses to express those ideas, and how the ideas are organized and presented. Both reader factors and text factors affect comprehension. Figure 8–1 presents an

Figure 8–1 ◆ Overview of the Comprehension Factors

Type	Factor	Role in Comprehension
Reader	Background Knowledge	Students activate their world and literary knowledge to link what they know to what they're reading.
	Vocabulary	Students recognize the meaning of familiar words and apply word-learning strategies to understand what they're reading.
	Fluency	Students have adequate cognitive resources available to understand what they're reading when they read fluently.
	Comprehension Strategies	Students actively direct their reading, monitor their understanding, and troubleshoot problems when they occur.
	Comprehension Skills	Students automatically note details that support main ideas, sequence ideas, and use other skills.
	Motivation	Motivated students are more engaged in reading, more confident, and more likely to comprehend successfully.
Text	Genres	Genres have unique characteristics, and students' knowledge of them provides a scaffold for comprehension.
	Text Structures	Students recognize the important ideas more easily when they understand the patterns that authors use to organize text.
	Text Features	Students apply their knowledge of the conventions and literary devices used in texts to deepen their understanding.

overview of these two factors. This chapter focuses on reader factors, and Chapter 9 addresses text factors.

Prerequisites for Comprehension

In addition to reader and text factors, comprehension depends on three prerequisites: having adequate background knowledge about the topic and the genre, being familiar with most words in the text, and being able to read it fluently (Allington, 2006). When one of these requirements is lacking, students are unlikely to comprehend what they're reading (Cooper, Chard, & Kiger, 2006). Teachers can ameliorate students' difficulties through their instruction to increase the likelihood that students will be successful.

Background Knowledge. Having adequate background knowledge is a prerequisite because when students have both world knowledge and literary knowledge, it provides a bridge to a new text (Braunger & Lewis, 2006). When students don't have adequate background knowledge, the topic or genre of the text is unfamiliar and many words are new, they're likely to find the text very challenging, and it's unlikely that they'll be successful. Teachers use prereading activities to build students' background knowledge; first they determine whether students need world or literary knowledge and then provide experiences and information to develop their schema. They use a combination of experiences, visual representations, and talk to build knowledge. Involving students in authentic experiences such as taking field trips, participating in dramatizations, and examining artifacts is the best way to build background knowledge, but photos and pictures, picture books, websites, videos, and other visual representations can also be used. Talk is often the least effective way, especially for English learners, but sometimes explaining a concept or listing the characteristics of a genre does provide enough information.

Vocabulary. Students' knowledge of words plays a tremendous role in comprehension because it's difficult to comprehend a text that's loaded with unknown words. It's also possible that when students don't know many words related to a topic, they don't have adequate background knowledge either. Blachowicz and Fisher (2007) recommend creating a word-rich classroom environment to immerse students in words and teaching word-learning strategies so they can figure out the meaning of new words. In addition, teachers preteach key words when they're building background knowledge using K-W-L charts, graphic organizers, anticipation guides, and other prereading activities.

> Check the Compendium of Instructional Procedures, which follows Chapter 12, for more information on the highlighted terms.

Fluency. Fluent readers read quickly and efficiently. Because they recognize most words automatically, their cognitive resources aren't depleted by decoding unfamiliar words, and they can devote their attention to comprehension (Pressley, 2002a). In the primary grades, developing reading fluency is an important component of comprehension instruction because children need to learn to recognize words automatically so they can concentrate on comprehending what they're reading (Samuels, 2002). For many struggling readers, their lack of fluency severely affects their ability to understand what they read. Teachers help older struggling readers who aren't fluent readers by teaching or reteaching word-identification strategies, having students do repeated readings, and providing students with books at their reading levels so that they can be successful. When teachers use grade-level texts that are too difficult for struggling students, they read them aloud so that everyone can comprehend and participate in related activities.

Literacy Portraits:VIEWING GUIDE

Ms. Janusz regularly teaches her second graders about comprehension strategies, including predicting, connecting, visualizing, asking questions, and repairing. She introduces a strategy and demonstrates how to use it in a minilesson; next, she encourages students to practice using it as she reads books aloud. Then students start using the strategy themselves during guided reading lessons and reading workshop. Ms. Janusz monitors the students' strategy use as she observes and conferences with them. To see how Ms. Janusz works with Curt'Lynn as she's learning to make personal connections, go to the Literacy Profiles section of the MyEducationLab website and click on Curt'Lynn's November button. How does Ms. Janusz scaffold Curt'Lynn's learning? You might also check the student interviews to see Curt'Lynn and her classmates talk about comprehension strategies and their ability to use them.

myeducationlab

Comprehension Strategies

Comprehension strategies are thoughtful behaviors that students use to facilitate their understanding as they read (Afflerbach, Pearson, & Paris, 2008). Some strategies are *cognitive*—they involve thinking; others are *metacognitive*—students reflect on their thinking. For example, readers make predictions about a story when they begin reading: They wonder what will happen to the characters and whether they'll enjoy the story. Predicting is a cognitive strategy because it involves thinking. Readers also monitor their reading, and monitoring is a metacognitive strategy. They notice whether they're understanding; and if they're confused, they take action to solve the problem. For example, they may go back and reread or talk to a classmate to clarify their confusion. Students are being metacognitive when they are alert to the possibility that they might get confused, and they know several ways to solve the problem (Pressley, 2002b).

Students learn to use a variety of cognitive and metacognitive strategies to ensure that they comprehend what they're reading. Here's a list of the most important comprehension strategies:

- ◆ Activating background knowledge
- ◆ Connecting
- ◆ Determining importance
- ◆ Drawing inferences
- ◆ Evaluating
- ◆ Monitoring

- ◆ Predicting
- ◆ Questioning
- ◆ Repairing
- ◆ Setting a purpose
- ◆ Summarizing
- ◆ Visualizing

> **Be Strategic!**
>
> ## Comprehension Strategies
>
> Students use these strategies to understand texts they're reading:
>
> | | |
> |---|---|
> | ▶ Activate background knowledge | ▶ Monitor |
> | | ▶ Predict |
> | ▶ Connect | ▶ Question |
> | ▶ Determine importance | ▶ Repair |
> | | ▶ Set a purpose |
> | ▶ Draw inferences | ▶ Summarize |
> | ▶ Evaluate | ▶ Visualize |
>
> These 12 strategies emphasize how readers think during the reading process; they're reader factors.

Students use these comprehension strategies not only to understand what they're reading, but also for understanding while they're listening to books read aloud and when they're writing. For example, students use the determining importance strategy when they're listening or reading to identify the big ideas, and when they're writing, they organize their writing around the big ideas so that readers also will comprehend what they're reading. Figure 8–2 presents an overview of the comprehension strategies and explains how readers use them.

Activating Background Knowledge. Readers bring their background knowledge to every reading experience; in fact, they read a text differently depending on their prior experiences. Zimmermann and Hutchins (2003) explain that "the meaning you get from a piece is intertwined with the meaning you bring to it" (p. 45). Readers think about the topic before they begin reading and call up relevant information and related vocabulary to use while reading. The more background knowledge and prior experiences readers have about a topic, the more likely they are to successfully comprehend what they're reading (Harvey & Goudvis, 2007).

Teachers use a variety of prereading activities to scaffold students as they learn to activate their background knowledge, such as anticipation guides, exclusion brainstorming, graphic organizers, K-W-L charts, and prereading plans. Through these activities, students think about the topic they'll read about, use related vocabulary, and get interested in reading the text.

Connecting. Readers make three types of connections between the text and their background knowledge: text-to-self, text-to-world, and text-to-text connections (Harvey & Goudvis, 2007). In text-to-self connections, students link the ideas they're reading about to events in their own lives; these are personal connections. A story event or character may remind them of something or someone in their own lives, and information in a nonfiction book may remind them of a past experience. In text-to-world connections, students relate what they're reading to their "world" knowledge, learned both in and out of school. When students make text-to-text connections, they link the text or an element of it to another text they've read or to a familiar film or television program. Students often compare different versions of familiar folktales, novels and their sequels, and sets of books by the same author. Text-to-text connections require higher-level thinking, and they are often the most difficult, especially for students who have done less reading or who know less about literature.

Figure 8–2 ◆ Overview of the Comprehension Strategies

Strategy	What Readers Do	How It Aids Comprehension
Activating Background Knowledge	Readers make connections between what they already know and the information in the text.	Readers use their background knowledge to fill in gaps in the text and enhance their comprehension.
Connecting	Readers make text-to-self, text-to-world, and text-to-text links.	Readers personalize their reading by relating what they're reading to their background knowledge.
Determining Importance	Readers notice the big ideas in the text and the relationships among them.	Readers focus on the big ideas so they don't become overwhelmed with details.
Drawing Inferences	Readers use background knowledge and clues in the text to "read between the lines."	Readers move beyond literal thinking to grasp meaning that isn't explicitly stated in the text.
Evaluating	Readers evaluate both the text itself and their reading experience.	Readers assume responsibility for their own strategy use.
Monitoring	Readers supervise their reading experience, checking that they're understanding the text.	Readers expect the text to make sense, and they recognize when it doesn't so they can take action.
Predicting	Readers make thoughtful "guesses" about what will happen and then read to confirm their predictions.	Readers become more engaged in the reading experience and want to continue reading.
Questioning	Readers ask themselves literal and inferential questions about the text.	Readers use questions to direct their reading, clarify confusions, and make inferences.
Repairing	Readers identify a problem interfering with comprehension and then solve it.	Readers solve problems to regain comprehension and continue reading.
Setting a Purpose	Readers identify a broad focus to direct their reading through the text.	Readers focus their attention as they read according to the purpose they've set.
Summarizing	Readers paraphrase the big ideas to create a concise statement.	Readers have better recall of the big ideas when they summarize.
Visualizing	Readers create mental images of what they're reading.	Readers use the mental images to make the text more memorable.

One way that teachers teach this strategy is by making connection charts with three columns labeled *text-to-self*, *text-to-world*, and *text-to-text*. Then students write connections that they've made on small self-stick notes and post them in the correct column of the chart, as Mrs. Donnelly did in the vignette at the beginning of the chapter. Students can also make connection charts in their reading logs and write connections in each column. Later in the reading process, during the exploring and applying stages, students make connections as they assume the role of a character and are interviewed by classmates during hot seat, create open-mind portraits to share the character's thinking, or write simulated journals from the viewpoint of a character, for example.

Determining Importance. Readers sift through the text to identify the important ideas as they read because it isn't possible to remember everything (Harvey &

Goudvis, 2007; Keene & Zimmermann, 2007). Students learn to distinguish the big ideas and the details and to recognize what's important as they read and talk about the books they've read. This comprehension strategy is important because students need to be able to identify the big ideas in order to summarize.

Teachers often direct students toward the big ideas when they encourage them to make predictions. The way they introduce the text also influences students' thinking about what's important in the book they're about to read. Mrs. Donnelly's introduction of *Joey Pigza Loses Control* (Gantos, 2005), for instance, directed her sixth graders' thinking about the story and its theme. When students read stories, they make diagrams about the plot, characters, and setting, and these graphic organizers emphasize the big ideas. Similarly, students make diagrams that reflect the structure of the text when they read informational articles and books and chapters in content-area textbooks. Sometimes teachers provide the diagrams with the big ideas highlighted, but students often analyze the text to determine the big ideas and then create their own graphic organizers.

Drawing Inferences. Readers seem to "read between the lines" to draw inferences, but what they actually do is synthesize their background knowledge with the author's clues to ask questions that point toward inferences. Keene and Zimmermann (2007) explain that when readers draw inferences, they have "an opportunity to sense a meaning not explicit in the text, but which derives or flows from it" (p. 145). Readers make both unconscious and conscious inferences about characters in a story and its theme, the big ideas in a newspaper, magazine article, or informational book, and the author's purpose in a poem (Pressley, 2002a). In fact, readers may not even be aware that they're drawing inferences, but when they wonder why the author included this or omitted that information, they probably are.

Students often have to read a picture-book story or an excerpt from a chapter of a novel two or three times in order to draw inferences because at first they focused on literal comprehension, which has to precede higher-level thinking. Very capable students draw inferences on their own as they read, but other students don't notice opportunities to make them. Sometimes students do draw inferences when prompted by the teacher, but it's important to teach students how to draw inferences so that they can think more deeply when they read independently.

Teachers begin by explaining what inferences are, how inferential thinking differs from literal thinking, and why they're important. Then they teach these four steps in drawing inferences:

1. Activate background knowledge about topics related to the text.
2. Look for the author's clues as you read.
3. Ask questions, tying together background knowledge and the author's clues.
4. Draw inferences by answering the questions.

Teachers can create charts to make the steps more visible as students practice making inferences. Figure 8–3 shows an inference chart developed by a seventh-grade class as they read and analyzed *The Wretched Stone* (Van Allsburg, 1991). The story, told in diary format, is about a ship's crew that picks up a strange, glowing stone on a sea voyage. The stone captivates the sailors and has a terrible transforming effect on them. After reading the story and talking about what they understood and what confused them, students began making the chart. First, they completed the "background knowledge" column. The students thought about what they needed to know about to understand the story: the meaning of the word *wretched*, sailors, the author/illustrator Chris Van Allsburg, and the fantasy genre because fantasies are

Figure 8–3 ◆ The Seventh Graders' Inference Chart About *The Wretched Stone*

Background Knowledge	Clues in the Story	Questions	Inferences
• The word <u>wretched</u> means "causing misery." • The people who work on a ship are sailors or the crew. Usually they're hard workers but not readers and musicians. • Chris Van Allsburg writes and illustrates fantasy picture books. He has brown hair and a beard. He wears glasses. • In fantasies, magic and other impossible things happen.	• The captain's last name is Hope. • The crew can read, play music, and tell stories. • It's odd that the island isn't on any maps. • The odor on the island seems sweet at first, but then it stinks. • The crew stare at the glowing stone. They lose interest in reading and stop working. • The crew change into monkeys because they watch the stone. • Capt. Hope looks just like Chris Van Allsburg. • Sailors who could read recovered the quickest.	• Why did Chris Van Allsburg make himself the captain? • Was it a real island or was it magic? • What is the wretched stone? • Why did the sailors turn into monkeys? • Why did the sailors who could read get well faster?	• Chris Van Allsburg wrote this book with hope for kids. • The wretched stone is television. • This book is a warning that watching too much TV is bad for you. • He wants kids to spend more time reading books because reading is good for you. • He wants kids to watch less TV. • Watching television is like the odor on the island. It's sweet at first, but too much of it stinks and isn't good for you.

different from other types of stories. Then they reread the story, searching for clues that might affect the meaning. They noticed that the ship captain's name was Hope, the island was uncharted, and the sailors who could read recovered faster, and they wrote these clues in the second column. Next, they thought about questions they had about the story and wrote them in the third column of the chart. Finally, the teacher reread the book one more time; this time, students listened more confidently, recognizing clues and drawing the inferences they had missed earlier. Finally, they completed the last column of the chart with their inferences.

Evaluating. Readers reflect on their reading experience and evaluate the text and what they're learning (Owocki, 2003). As with the other comprehension strategies, students use the evaluating strategy throughout the reading process. They monitor their interest from the moment they pick up the book and judge their success in solving reading problems when they arise. They evaluate their reading experience, including these aspects:

Their ease in reading the text
The adequacy of their background knowledge
Their use of comprehension strategies
How they solved reading problems
Their interest and attention during reading

They also consider the text:

Whether they like the text
Their opinions about the author

The world knowledge they gain

How they'll use what they're learning

Students usually write about their reflections in reading log entries and talk about their evaluations in conferences with the teacher. Evaluating is important because it helps students assume more responsibility for their own learning.

New Literacies
Online Comprehension Strategies

Websites are dynamic learning contexts that create new challenges for readers because online texts differ from books, magazines, and other print texts in significant ways (Castek, Bevans-Mangelson, & Goldstone, 2006). Print texts are linear and unchanging; they contain a finite number of pages with information arranged in predictable narrative, informational, and poetic formats. Internet texts, in contrast, are multilayered, with unlimited multimodal information available through hypertext links.

Students use traditional comprehension strategies to read Web-based texts, but they use them in new ways (Coiro & Dobler, 2007; Leu, Kinzer, Coiro, & Cammack, 2004). Students use these five comprehension strategies to read online texts:

Activating Background Knowledge. Readers activate background knowledge about topics and text structures when they're reading both print and online texts. For Web-based texts, however, readers also need to know about informational websites and how to navigate search engines to locate useful ones.

Predicting. Students use predicting differently for online reading. When they're making choices about which hyperlinks to click on, readers predict which ones will be most useful. Making these predictions is important; otherwise, students get distracted or waste time finding their way back from unproductive links.

Evaluating. Students evaluate their reading experience and the text they're reading, no matter whether they're reading a print or a Web-based text, but when they're reading online, students use this strategy to determine the accuracy, objectivity, relevance, and quality of information at websites. It's crucial for Internet reading because anyone can post erroneous and biased information on the Web.

Monitoring. Students monitor their reading to determine whether what they're reading makes sense and so they can take action if they're confused. When they're reading online, students also monitor their navigational choices and decide whether the links they've clicked on are useful.

Repairing. Readers use the repairing strategy to fix comprehension problems when they're reading print and Web-based texts. For Internet reading, students also use this strategy to correct poor navigational choices and return to useful websites.

As researchers learn more about online reading, it's likely that they'll identify more ways students adapt traditional comprehension strategies.

Readers also learn new comprehension strategies that address the unique characteristics and complex applications of online texts (Coiro, 2003). In the New Literacies feature in Chapter 1, you read about coauthoring, a comprehension strategy that readers use to impose an organization on the information they read online (Leu, Kinzer, Coiro, & Cammack, 2004). More recently, Coiro and Dobler (2007) examined the strategies that sixth graders used for Internet reading and found that these students use a self-directed process of text construction. In this strategy routine, readers make a series of decisions as they move from one link to another, searching for information. They plan, predict, monitor, and evaluate each time they make a navigational choice. More than 25 years ago, Tierney and Pearson (1983) asserted that reading is a composing process, and these comprehension strategies emphasize the interrelatedness of reading and writing.

It's essential that teachers prepare students to use new 21st-century technology. Online reading isn't just a technology issue; websites have unique reader and text factors that affect comprehension (Henry, 2006). Students need to understand how print and Web-based texts differ so they can adjust how they apply traditional comprehension strategies and learn new ones to use for Internet texts.

Go to the Building
Teaching Skills and
Dispositions section of
Chapter 8 on
MyEducationLab.com
to hear second grader
Jimmy discuss the ways
in which he monitors his
comprehension.

Monitoring. Readers monitor their understanding as they read, although they may be aware that they're using this strategy only when their comprehension breaks down and they have to take action to solve their problem. Harvey and Goudvis (2007) describe monitoring as the inner conversation that students carry on in their heads with the text as they read—expressing wonder, making connections, asking questions, reacting to information, drawing conclusions, noticing confusions, for example.

Monitoring involves regulating reader and text factors at the same time. Readers often ask themselves these questions:

◆ What's my purpose for reading?
◆ Is this book too difficult for me to read on my own?
◆ Do I need to read the entire book or only parts of it?
◆ What's special about the genre of this book?
◆ How does the author use text structure?
◆ What is the author's viewpoint?
◆ Do I understand the meaning of the words I'm reading? (Pressley, 2002b)

Once students detect a problem, they shift into problem-solving mode to repair their comprehension.

Teachers use think-alouds to demonstrate the monitoring strategy during minilessons and when they're reading aloud to students. They show that capable readers ask themselves if they're understanding what they're reading or if they realize that they don't remember what they've just read and what they do when they run into difficulty. Students also write about their thinking on small self-stick notes and place them in their books, next to text that stimulated their thinking. Later, students share their notes during a discussion about how students monitor their reading.

Predicting. Readers make thoughtful "guesses" or predictions about what will happen or what they'll learn in the book they're reading. These guesses are based on what students already know about the topic and genre or on what they've read thus far. Students often make a prediction before beginning to read and several others at pivotal points in a text—no matter whether they're reading stories, informational books, or poems—and then as they read, they either confirm or revise their predictions. Predictions about nonfiction are different than for stories and poems; here students are generating questions about the topic that they would like to find answers to as they read.

When teachers share a big book with young children using shared reading, they prompt children to make predictions at the beginning of the book and again at key points during the reading. They model how to make reasonable predictions and use think-alouds to explain their thinking. When older students are reading novels, they often write their predictions on small self-stick notes while they're reading and stick them in their books to share with classmates in a discussion afterward.

Questioning. Readers ask themselves questions about the text as they read (Duke & Pearson, 2002). They ask self-questions out of curiosity, and as they use this strategy, they become more engaged with the text and want to keep reading to find answers (Harvey & Goudvis, 2007). These questions often lead to making predictions and drawing inferences. Students also ask themselves questions to clarify misunderstandings as they read. Students use this strategy throughout the reading process—to activate background knowledge and make predictions before reading, to engage with the text and clarify confusions during reading, and to evaluate and reflect on the text after reading.

Traditionally, teachers have been the question-askers and students have been the question-answerers, but when students learn to generate questions about the text, their comprehension improves. In fact, students comprehend better when they generate their own questions than when teachers ask questions (Duke & Pearson, 2002). Many students don't know how to ask questions to guide their reading, so it's important that teachers teach students how to do so. They model generating questions and then encourage students to do the same. Tovani (2000) suggests having students brainstorm a list of "I wonder" questions on a topic because they need to learn how to generate questions; in the vignette at the beginning of the chapter, for example, Mrs. Donnelly's sixth graders brainstormed questions before they began reading *Joey Pigza Loses Control* (Gantos, 2005).

The questions students ask shape their comprehension: If they ask literal questions, their comprehension will be literal, but if students generate inferential, critical, and evaluative questions, their comprehension will be higher-level. Question-Answer-Relationships (QARs) (Raphael, Highfield, & Au, 2006) is an effective way to teach students about the different types of questions they can ask about a text. QARs was developed for analyzing the end-of-chapter questions in content-area textbooks, but it's also useful for teaching students to categorize questions and ultimately to ask higher-level questions.

Repairing. Readers use repairing to fix comprehension problems that arise while reading (Zimmermann & Hutchins, 2003). When students notice that they're confused or bored, can't remember what they just read, or aren't asking questions, they need to use this strategy (Tovani, 2000). Repairing involves figuring out what the problem is and taking action to solve it: Sometimes students go back and reread or skip ahead and read, or they try questioning or another strategy that might help. At other times, they check the meaning of an unfamiliar word, examine the structure of a confusing sentence, learn more about an unfamiliar topic related to the text, or ask the teacher for assistance. These solutions are often referred to as *fix-up strategies.*

Setting a Purpose. Readers read for different reasons—for entertainment, to learn about a topic, for directions to accomplish a task, or to find the answer to a specific question, for instance—and the purposes they set direct their attention during reading (Tovani, 2000). Setting a purpose activates a mental blueprint, which aids in determining how readers focus their attention and how

Teaching Struggling Readers and Writers

Strategic Readers

Struggling students need to become strategic readers.

Struggling readers often complain that they don't understand what they're reading. Comprehension difficulties are due to a variety of problems, but one of the most common is that students don't read strategically (Cooper, Chard, & Kiger, 2006). They read passively, without using comprehension strategies to think about what they're reading. Without learning to thoughtfully engage in the reading process, it's unlikely that students who struggle with comprehension will improve very much.

The good news is that teachers can help struggling students become better readers by teaching them to use comprehension strategies to be more thoughtful readers (Allington, 2006). The most important comprehension strategies for struggling readers are activating background knowledge, determining importance, summarizing, questioning, visualizing, and monitoring.

As teachers teach comprehension strategies, they explain each strategy, including how, when, and why to use it, and they make the strategy visible by demonstrating how to use it during minilessons, interactive read-alouds, and guided reading lessons. They use think-alouds to show that capable readers are active thinkers while they're reading. Students participate in small-group and partner activities as they practice using the strategy and verbalize their thinking. At first, teachers provide lots of support, and they withdraw it slowly as students become responsible for using the strategy independently. Once students have learned to apply two or three strategies, they begin to use them together. Integrating strategy use is important because capable readers don't depend on a single comprehension strategy; instead, they have a repertoire of strategies available that they use as needed while they're reading (Allington, 2006).

they sort relevant from irrelevant information as they read (Blanton, Wood, & Moorman, 1990). Before they begin to read, students identify a single, fairly broad purpose that they sustain while reading the entire text; it must fit both students' reason for reading and the text. Students can ask themselves "Why am I going to read this text?" or "What do I need to learn from this book?" to help them set a purpose. It's important that students have a purpose when they read, because readers vary how they read and what they remember according to their purpose. When students don't have a purpose, they are likely to misdirect their attention and focus on unimportant ideas.

Summarizing. Readers pick out the most important ideas and the relationships among them and briefly restate them so they can be remembered (Harvey & Goudvis, 2007). It's crucial that students determine which ideas are the most important because if they focus on tangential ideas or details, their comprehension is compromised. To create effective summaries, students need to learn to paraphrase, or restate ideas in their own words.

Summarizing is a difficult task, but instruction and practice improve not only students' ability to summarize but their overall comprehension as well (Duke & Pearson, 2002). One way to teach students to summarize is to have them create graphic organizers after reading a chapter in a novel or a content-area textbook: They emphasize the big ideas and relationships among them in their diagram, and then they use the information to write a brief summary statement.

Visualizing. Readers create mental images of what they're reading (Harvey & Goudvis, 2007; Keene & Zimmermann, 2007). They often place themselves in the images they create, becoming a character in the story they're reading, traveling to that setting, or facing the conflict situations the characters face. Teachers sometimes ask students to close their eyes to help visualize the story or to draw pictures of the scenes and characters they visualize. How well students use visualization often becomes clear when they view film versions of books they've read: Students who are good visualizers are often disappointed with the film version and the actors who perform as the characters, but those who don't visualize are often amazed by the film and prefer it to the book.

Students use comprehension strategies at every stage in the reading process, but their activities vary from stage to stage, depending on the strategy being used. Figure 8–4 explains what readers do to comprehend at each stage and the strategies they use. Sometimes strategies are grouped into before reading, during reading, and after reading strategies, but that categorization doesn't work: Although setting a purpose is almost always a prereading strategy and monitoring and repairing are usually reading-stage strategies, students use connecting, drawing inferences, questioning, and other strategies in more than one stage.

Comprehension Skills

Even though there's controversy regarding the differences between comprehension strategies and skills, it's possible to identify some comprehension skills that students need to learn to become successful readers. These skills are related to strategies, but the big difference is that skills involve literal thinking. They're like questions to which there's one correct answer. One group of skills focus on main ideas and details. Students use the determining importance strategy to identify main ideas, and they use these related skills:

Figure 8–4 ◆ How the Comprehension Strategies Fit Into the Reading Process

Stage	What Readers Do	Strategies Readers Use
Prereading	Students prepare to read by setting purposes, thinking about the topic and genre of the text, and planning for the reading experience.	Activating background knowledge Predicting Questioning Setting a purpose
Reading	Students read the text silently or orally, thinking about it as they read, monitoring their understanding, and solving problems as they arise.	Monitoring Repairing All other strategies
Responding	Students share their reactions, making tentative and exploratory comments, asking questions, and clarifying confusions, by talking with classmates and the teacher and writing in reading logs.	Connecting Determining importance Drawing inferences Evaluating Questioning Visualizing
Exploring	Students reread parts of the text, examine it more analytically, and study the genre and author's craft.	Determining importance Drawing inferences Evaluating Summarizing
Applying	Students create projects to deepen their understanding of the text they've read and reflect on their reading experience.	Connecting Evaluating Questioning

Recognizing details
Noticing similarities and differences
Identifying topic sentences
Comparing and contrasting main ideas and details
Matching causes with effects
Sequencing details
Paraphrasing ideas
Choosing a good title for a text

In contrast, when main ideas and relationships among them aren't explicitly stated in the text, students use the drawing inferences strategy to comprehend them because higher-level thinking is required. Another group of comprehension skills are related to the evaluating strategy:

Recognizing the author's purpose
Detecting propaganda
Distinguishing between fact and opinion

Teachers teach these skills and students practice them until they become automatic procedures that don't require conscious thought or interpretation.

TEACHING STUDENTS ABOUT READER FACTORS

Comprehension instruction involves teaching students about comprehension and the strategies they use to understand what they're reading. The three components are explicit instruction, reading, and writing (Duke & Pearson, 2002). Researchers emphasize the need to establish the expectation that the books students read and the compositions they write will make sense (Duke & Pearson, 2002). Teachers create an expectation of comprehension in these ways:

- Involving students in authentic reading and writing activities every day
- Providing access to well-stocked classroom libraries
- Teaching students to use comprehension strategies
- Ensuring that students are fluent readers
- Providing opportunities for students to talk about the books they read
- Linking vocabulary instruction to underlying concepts

Teachers can't assume that students will learn to comprehend simply by doing lots of reading; instead, students develop an understanding of comprehension and what readers do to be successful through a combination of instruction and authentic reading activities (Block & Pressley, 2007). Guidelines for teaching comprehension are presented below.

Explicit Comprehension Instruction

The fact that comprehension is an invisible mental process makes it difficult to teach; however, through explicit instruction, teachers can make comprehension more visible. They explain what comprehension is and why it's important, and they model how they do it, by thinking aloud. Next, teachers encourage students to direct their thinking as they read, gradually releasing responsibility to students through guided and independent

Guidelines
for Teaching Comprehension

- Teach students about both reader and text factors.
- Teach comprehension strategies using a combination of explanations, demonstrations, think-alouds, and practice activities.
- Demonstrate how to use strategies through interactive read-alouds.
- Have students apply strategies in literacy activities as well as in thematic units.
- Teach groups of strategies in routines so that students learn to orchestrate their use of multiple strategies.
- Ask students to reflect on their use of individual strategies and strategy routines.
- Hang charts in the classroom of the strategies and strategy routines students are learning.
- Differentiate between strategies and skills so that students understand that strategies are problem-solving tactics and skills are automatic behaviors.

practice. Finally, they move students from focusing on a single comprehension strategy to integrating several strategies in routines. Mrs. Donnelly demonstrated the concept of gradual release in the vignette at the beginning of the chapter as she reviewed each comprehension strategy and had the students practice it as they read picture books; then she had them apply all the strategies as they read *Joey Pigza Loses Control* (Gantos, 2005).

Teaching Comprehension Strategies. Teachers teach individual comprehension strategies and then show students how to integrate several strategies simultaneously (Block & Pressley, 2007). They introduce each comprehension strategy in a series of minilessons. Teachers describe the strategy, model it for students as they read a text aloud, use it collaboratively with students, and provide opportunities for guided and then independent practice (Duke & Pearson, 2002); the independent practice is important because it's motivational. The minilesson feature on page 272 shows how Mrs. Macadangdang teaches her third graders to use the questioning strategy.

Teachers also support students' learning about comprehension strategies in other ways: Figure 8–5 suggests several activities for each strategy. Second graders practice questioning by asking questions instead of giving answers during a grand conversation, for example, and sixth graders practice connecting when they write favorite quotes in one column of a double-entry journal and then explain in the second column why each quote is meaningful. When teachers involve students in these activities, it's important to explain that students will be practicing a particular strategy as they complete an activity so that they think about what they're doing and how it's helping them to comprehend better.

Teaching Comprehension Routines. Once students know how to use individual strategies, they need to learn how to use routines or combinations of strategies because capable readers rarely use comprehension strategies one at a time (Duke & Pearson, 2002). In the vignette at the beginning of the chapter, for example, Mrs. Donnelly was teaching her sixth graders to use multiple strategies as they read *Joey Pigza Loses Control* (Gantos, 2005) and reflected on their strategy use in their thinking logs.

One of the most effective comprehension routines is *reciprocal teaching* (Palincsar & Brown, 1986). Students use predicting, questioning, clarifying, and summarizing strategies to figure out the meaning of a text, paragraph by paragraph. Teachers can use this instructional procedure with the whole class when students are reading chapters in content-area textbooks or in small groups, such as literature circles when students are reading novels (Oczkus, 2003).

Developing Comprehension Through Reading

Students need to spend lots of time reading authentic texts independently and talking about their reading with classmates and teachers. Having students read interesting books written at their reading level is the best way for them to apply comprehension strategies. As they read and discuss their reading, students are practicing what they're learning about comprehension. Reading a selection in a basal reader each week is not enough; instead, students need to read many, many books representing a range of genres during reading workshop or Sustained Silent Reading.

In addition to providing opportunities for students to read independently, teachers read books aloud to young children who are not yet fluent readers and to struggling readers who can't read age-appropriate books themselves. When teachers do the reading, students have more cognitive resources available to focus on comprehension.

MiniLesson

TOPIC: Teaching Students to Ask Self-Questions
GRADE: Third Grade
TIME: Three 30-minute periods

Mrs. Macadangdang (the students call her Mrs. Mac) introduced questioning by talking about why people ask questions and by asking questions about stories they were reading. She encouraged the third graders to ask questions, too. They made a list of questions for each chapter of *Chang's Paper Pony* (Coerr, 1993), a story set in the California gold rush era, as she read it aloud, and then they evaluated their questions, choosing the ones that focus on the big ideas and helped them understand the story better. Now all of her students can generate questions, so she's ready to introduce the questioning strategy.

1 Introduce the Topic

Mrs. Mac reads the list of comprehension strategies posted in the classroom that they've learned to use and explains, "Today, we're going to learn a new thinking strategy—questioning. Readers ask themselves questions while they're reading to help them think about the book." She adds "Questioning" to the list.

2 Share Examples

The teacher introduces *The Josefina Story Quilt* (Coerr, 1989), the story of a pioneer family going to California in a covered wagon. She reads aloud the first chapter, thinking aloud and generating questions about the story. Each time she says a question, she places in a pocket chart a sentence strip on which the question has already been written. Here are the questions: Why is Faith excited? Why are they going in a covered wagon? Who is Josefina? Can a chicken be a pet? Can Josefina do anything useful? Why is Faith crying?

3 Provide Information

Mrs. Mac explains, "Questions really turn your thinking on! I know it's important to think while I'm reading because it helps me understand. I like to ask questions about things I think are important and things that don't make sense to me." They reread the questions in the pocket chart and talk about the most helpful questions. Many students thought the question about the covered wagon was important, but as they continue reading, they'll learn that Josefina does indeed do something useful—she turns out to be a "humdinger of a watch dog" (p. 54)! Then Mrs. Mac reads aloud the second chapter, stopping often for students to generate questions. The students write their questions on sentence strips and add them to the pocket chart.

4 Guide Practice

The following day, Mrs. Mac reviews the questioning strategy, and students reread the questions for chapters 1 and 2. Then the students form pairs, get copies of the book, and read the next two chapters of *The Josefina Story Quilt* together, generating questions as they read. They write their questions on small self-stick notes and place them in the book. Mrs. Mac monitors students, noticing which ones need additional practice. Then the class comes together to share their questions and talk about the chapters they've read. On the third day, they read the last two chapters and generate more questions.

5 Assess Learning

As she monitored the students, Mrs. Mac made a list of students who needed more practice generating questions, and she'll work with them as they read another book together.

Figure 8–5 ◆ Ways to Teach the Comprehension Strategies

Strategy	Instructional Procedures
Activating Background Knowledge	• Students complete an anticipation guide. • Students do an exclusion brainstorming activity. • Students develop a K-W-L chart.
Connecting	• Students add text-to-self, text-to-world, and text-to-text connections to a class chart. • Students write a double-entry journal with quotes and reflections about each one. • Students become a character and participate in a hot seat activity.
Determining Importance	• Students create graphic organizers. • Students make posters highlighting the big ideas.
Drawing Inferences	• Students use small self-stick notes to mark clues in the text. • Students create charts with author's clues, questions, and inferences. • Students quickwrite about an inference they've made.
Evaluating	• Students write reflections and evaluations in reading logs. • Students conference with the teacher about a book they've read.
Monitoring	• Students think aloud to demonstrate how they monitor their reading. • Students write about their strategy use on small self-stick notes and in reading logs.
Predicting	• Students make and share predictions during read-alouds. • Students write a double-entry journal with predictions in one column and summaries in the other. • Students make predictions during guided reading lessons.
Questioning	• Students brainstorm a list of questions before reading. • Students ask questions during grand conversations and other discussions. • Students analyze the questions they pose using the QAR levels.
Repairing	• Students make personal charts of the ways they solve comprehension problems. • Students think aloud to demonstrate how they use the repairing strategy. • Students write about their repairs on small self-stick notes and place them in a book they're reading.
Setting a Purpose	• Students identify their purpose in a discussion before beginning to read. • Students write about their purpose in a reading log entry before beginning to read.
Summarizing	• Students write a summary using interactive writing. • Students create visual summaries on charts using words, diagrams, and pictures.
Visualizing	• Students create open-mind portraits of characters. • Students draw pictures of episodes from a book they're reading. • Students role-play episodes from a book they're reading.

Grand Conversations
These students have gathered together for a grand conversation to talk about chapters 6, 7, and 8 in a novel they're reading. The sixth graders share ideas, ask questions, and read and comment on excerpts from the book. Without raising their hands to be called on, the students take turns making comments. The teacher participates in the conversation to share her insights, ask questions, and clarify misconceptions. Later in the discussion, she'll focus on story elements and draw students' attention to the characters and talk about the similarities and differences among them.

Teachers often read books aloud when they introduce comprehension strategies so that they can model procedures and scaffold students' thinking.

Students also develop their comprehension abilities when they discuss the stories they're reading in grand conversations and informational books and chapters in content-area textbooks in other discussions. As students talk about their reading, draw inferences, ask questions to clarify confusions, and reflect on their use of the comprehension strategies, they elaborate and refine their comprehension.

Nurturing English Learners

Comprehension is often difficult for English learners, and there are a number of reasons why (Bouchard, 2005). Many ELs lack the background knowledge that's necessary for understanding the book they're attempting to read. Sometimes they lack culturally based knowledge, and at other times, they're unfamiliar with a genre or can't understand the meaning of figurative vocabulary. There can be a mismatch between the level of students' English proficiency and the reading level of the book too: Like all students, ELs won't understand what they're reading if the book is too difficult.

Teachers can address these issues by carefully choosing books that are appropriate for English learners, building their world and literary knowledge, and introducing key vocabulary words in advance. Peregoy and Boyle (2008) also point out that many ELs read texts passively, as if they were waiting for the information they're reading to organize itself and highlight the big ideas. To help these students become more active readers, teachers explicitly teach the comprehension strategies. During the lessons, teachers explain each strategy, including why it will help students become better readers and how and when to use it. They spend more time modeling how to apply each strategy and thinking aloud to share their thoughts. Next, teachers provide guided practice with the students working together in small groups and with partners, and they assist students as they use the strategy. Finally, students use the strategy independently and apply it in new ways.

Assessing Students' Comprehension

Teachers assess students' comprehension informally every day. They listen to the comments students make during grand conversations, conference with students about books they're reading, and examine their entries in reading logs, for example. They use informal assessment procedures such as the following to monitor students' use of comprehension strategies and their understanding of books they're reading:

Cloze Procedure. Teachers examine students' understanding of a text using the cloze procedure, in which students supply the deleted words in a passage taken from a text they've read. Although filling in the blanks may seem like a simple activity, it isn't because students need to consider the content of the passage, vocabulary words, and sentence structure to choose the exact word that was deleted.

Story Retellings. Teachers often have young children retell stories they've read or listened to read aloud to assess their literal comprehension (Morrow, 2002). Students' retellings should be coherent and well organized and should include the big ideas and important details. When teachers prompt students with questions and encourage them to "tell me more," they're known as *aided retellings*; otherwise they're *unaided retellings*. Teachers often use checklists and rubrics to score students' story retellings.

Running Records. Teachers use running records (Clay, 2007) to examine children's oral reading behaviors, analyze their comprehension, and determine their reading levels. Although they're most commonly used with young children, running records can also be used with older students. Children read a book, and afterward they orally retell it. Teachers encourage children to recall as much detail as possible, ask questions to prompt their recall, when necessary, and sometimes pose other comprehension questions to probe the depth of their understanding. Finally, they evaluate the completeness of the child's retelling.

Think-Alouds. Teachers assess students' ability to apply comprehension strategies by having them think aloud and share their thinking as they read a passage (Wilhelm, 2001). Students usually think aloud orally, but they can also write their thoughts on small self-stick notes that they place beside sections of text, write entries in reading logs, and do quickwrites.

Teachers also use other assessment tools, including tests, to evaluate students' comprehension; the Assessment Tools feature on page 276 presents more information about comprehension tests. No matter whether teachers are using informal assessments or tests to examine students' comprehension, they need to consider whether they're assessing literal, inferential, critical, or evaluative thinking. The emphasis in both assessment and instruction should be on higher-level comprehension.

Assessment Tools

Comprehension

Teachers use a combination of informal assessment procedures, including retelling and think-alouds, and commercially available tests to measure students' comprehension. Here are several tests that are commonly used in K–8 classrooms:

◆ **Comprehension Thinking Strategies Assessment** (Keene, 2006)

The Comprehension Thinking Strategies Assessment examines first through eighth graders' ability to use these strategies to think about fiction and nonfiction texts they're reading: activating background knowledge, determining importance, drawing inferences, noticing text structure, questioning, setting a purpose, and visualizing. As students read a passage, they pause and reflect on their strategy use. Teachers score students' responses using a rubric. This 30-minute test can be administered to individuals or to the class, depending on whether students' responses are oral or written. This flexible assessment tool can be used to evaluate students' learning after teaching a strategy, to survey progress at the beginning of the school year, or to document achievement at the end of the year. It's available from Shell Education.

◆ **Developmental Reading Assessment, Grades K–3 (DRA)** (Beaver, 2006)
Developmental Reading Assessment, Grades 4–8 (Beaver & Carter, 2003)

K–8 teachers use the DRA to determine students' reading levels, assess their strengths and weaknesses in word identification, fluency, and comprehension, and make instructional decisions. To measure comprehension, students read a leveled book and then retell what they've read. Their retellings are scored using a 4-point rubric. Both DRA levels are available from Celebration Press/Pearson.

◆ **Informal Reading Inventories (IRIs)**

Teachers use individually administered IRIs to assess students' comprehension of narrative and informational texts. Comprehension is measured by students' ability to retell what they've read and to answer questions about the passage. The questions examine how well students use literal and higher-level thinking and their knowledge about word meanings. A number of commercially published IRIs are available, including the following:

Analytical Reading Inventory (Woods & Moe, 2007)
Comprehensive Reading Inventory (Cooter, Flynt, & Cooter, 2007)
Critical Reading Inventory (Applegate, Quinn, & Applegate, 2008)
Qualitative Reading Inventory (Leslie & Caldwell, 2006)

These IRIs can be purchased from Pearson. Other IRIs accompany basal reading series. IRIs typically are designed for grades 1–8, but first- and second-grade teachers often find that running records provide more-useful information about beginning readers.

These tests provide valuable information about whether students meet grade-level comprehension standards.

MOTIVATION

Motivation is intrinsic, the innate curiosity that makes us want to figure things out. It involves feeling self-confident, believing you'll succeed, and viewing the activity as pleasurable (Guthrie & Wigfield, 2000). It's based on the engagement theory that you read about in the first chapter. Motivation is social, too: People want to socialize, share ideas, and participate in group activities. Motivation is more than one characteristic, however; it's a network of interacting factors (Alderman, 1999). Often students' motivation to become better readers and writers diminishes as they reach the middle grades, and struggling students demonstrate significantly less enthusiasm for reading and writing than other students do.

Many factors contribute to students' engagement or involvement in reading and writing. Some focus on teachers' role—what they believe and do—and others focus on students (Pressley, Dolezal, Raphael, Mohan, Roehrig, & Bogner, 2003; Unrau, 2004). Figure 8–6 summarizes the factors affecting students' engagement in literacy activities and what teachers can do to nurture students' interest.

Figure 8–6 ◆ Factors Affecting Students' Motivation

Roles	Factors	What Teachers Do
Teachers	Attitude	• Show students that you care about them. • Display excitement and enthusiasm about what you're teaching. • Stimulate students' curiosity and desire to learn.
	Community	• Create a nurturing and inclusive classroom community. • Insist that students treat classmates with respect.
	Instruction	• Focus on students' long-term learning. • Teach students to be strategic readers and writers. • Engage students in authentic activities. • Offer students choices of activities and reading materials.
	Rewards	• Employ specific praise and positive feedback. • Use external rewards only when students' interest is very low.
Students	Expectations	• Expect students to be successful. • Teach students to set realistic goals.
	Collaboration	• Encourage students to work collaboratively. • Minimize competition. • Allow students to participate in making plans and choices.
	Reading and Writing Competence	• Teach students to use reading and writing strategies. • Provide guided reading lessons for struggling readers. • Use interactive writing to teach writing skills to struggling writers. • Provide daily reading and writing opportunities.
	Choices	• Have students complete interest inventories. • Teach students to choose books at their reading levels. • Encourage students to write about topics that interest them.

Teachers' Role

Everything teachers do affects their students' interest and engagement with literacy, but four of the most important factors are teachers' attitude, the community teachers create, the instructional approaches they use, and their reward systems:

Attitude. It seems obvious that when teachers show that they care about their students and exhibit excitement and enthusiasm for learning, students are more likely to become engaged. Effective teachers also stimulate students' curiosity and encourage them to explore ideas. They emphasize intrinsic over extrinsic motivation because they understand that students' intrinsic desire to learn is more powerful than grades, rewards, and other extrinsic motivators.

Community. Students are more likely to engage in reading and writing when their classroom is a learning community that respects and nurtures everyone. Students and the teacher show respect for each other, and students learn how to work well with classmates in small groups. In a community of learners, students enjoy social interaction and feel connected to their classmates and their teacher.

Instruction. The types of literacy activities in which students are involved affect their interest and motivation. Turner and Paris (1995) compared authentic literacy activities such as reading and writing workshop with skills-based reading programs and concluded that students' motivation was determined by the daily classroom activities. They found that open-ended activities and projects in which students were in control of the processes they used and the products they created were the most successful.

Rewards. Many teachers consider using rewards to encourage students to do more reading and writing, but Alfie Kohn (2001) and others believe that extrinsic incentives are harmful because they undermine students' intrinsic motivation. Incentives such as pizzas, free time, or "money" to spend in a classroom "store" are most effective when students' interest is very low and they are reluctant to participate in literacy activities. Once students become more interested, teachers withdraw these incentives and use less tangible ones, including positive feedback and praise (Stipek, 2002).

Students' Role

Motivation isn't something that teachers or parents can force on students; rather, it's an innate, intrinsic desire that students must develop themselves. They're more likely to become engaged with reading and writing when they expect to be successful, when they work collaboratively with classmates, when they're competent readers and writers, and when they have opportunities to make choices and develop ownership of their work. Here are four factors that influence students' motivation:

Expectations. Students who feel they have little hope of success are unlikely to become engaged in literacy activities. Teachers play a big role in shaping students' expectations, and teacher expectations are often self-fulfilling (Brophy, 2004): If teachers believe that their students can be successful, it's more likely that they will be. Stipek (2002) found that in classrooms where teachers take a personal interest in their students and expect that all of them can learn, the students are more successful.

Collaboration. When students work with classmates in pairs and in small groups, they're often more interested and engaged in activities than when they read and write alone. Collaborative groups support students because they have opportunities to share ideas, learn from each other, and enjoy the collegiality of their classmates. Competition, in contrast, doesn't develop intrinsic motivation; instead, it decreases many students' interest in learning.

Reading and Writing Competence. Not surprisingly, students' competence in reading and writing affects their motivation: Students who read well are more likely to be motivated to read than those who read less well, and the same is true for writers. Teaching students how to read and write is an essential factor in developing their motivation. Teachers find that once struggling students improve their reading and writing performance, they become more interested.

Choices. Students want to have a say in which books they read and which topics they write about. By making choices, students develop more responsibility for their work and ownership of their accomplishments. Reading and writing workshop are instructional approaches that honor students' choices: In reading workshop, students choose books they're interested in reading and that are written at their reading level, and in writing workshop, students write about topics that interest them.

How to Engage Students in Reading and Writing

Oldfather (1995) conducted a 4-year study to examine the factors influencing students' motivation. She found that students were more highly motivated when they had opportunities for authentic self-expression as part of literacy activities. The students she interviewed reported that they were more highly motivated when they had ownership of the learning activities. Specific activities they mentioned included opportunities to do the following:

Express their own ideas and opinions
Choose topics for writing and books for reading
Talk about books they're reading
Share their writing with classmates
Pursue authentic activities—not worksheets—using reading, writing, listening, and talking

Ivey and Broaddus (2001) reported similar conclusions from their study of the factors that influence sixth graders' desire to read. Three of their conclusions are noteworthy. First, students are more interested in reading when their teachers make them feel confident and successful; a nurturing classroom community is an important factor. Second, students are more intrinsically motivated when they have ownership of their literacy learning. Students place great value on being allowed to choose interesting books and other reading materials. Third, students become more engaged with books when they have time for independent reading and opportunities to listen to the teacher read aloud. Students reported that they enjoy listening to teachers read aloud because teachers make books more comprehensible and more interesting through the background knowledge they provide.

Some students aren't strongly motivated to learn to read and write, and they adopt defensive tactics for avoiding failure rather than strategies for being successful (Paris, Wasik, & Turner, 1991). Unmotivated readers give up or remain passive, uninvolved in reading. Some students feign interest or pretend to be involved even though they aren't. Others don't think reading is important, and they choose to focus on other curricular areas—math or sports, for instance. Some students complain about feeling ill or that classmates are bothering them. They place the blame anywhere but on themselves.

Other students avoid reading and writing entirely; they just don't do it. Still others read books that are too easy for them or write short pieces so that they don't have to exert much effort. Even though these strategies are self-serving, students use them because they lead to short-term success. The long-term result, however, is devastating because these students fail to learn to read and write well. Because it takes quite a bit of effort to read and write strategically, it's especially important that students experience personal ownership of the literacy activities going on in their classrooms and know how to manage their own reading and writing behaviors.

Assessing Students' Motivation

Because students' motivation and engagement affect their success in reading as well as writing, it's important that teachers learn about their students and work to ensure that they're motivated and have positive attitudes about literacy. Teachers observe students and conference with them and their parents to understand students' reading and writing habits at home, their interests and hobbies, and their view of themselves as readers and writers. There are also surveys that teachers can administer to quickly estimate students' motivation toward reading and writing; these surveys are described in the Assessment Tools feature on the next page.

Comparing Capable and Less Capable Readers and Writers

Researchers have compared students who are capable readers and writers with other students who are less successful and have found some striking differences (Baker & Brown, 1984; Faigley, Cherry, Jolliffe, & Skinner, 1985; Paris, Wasik, & Turner, 1991). The researchers have found that more capable readers do the following:

- Read fluently
- View reading as a process of creating meaning
- Decode rapidly
- Have large vocabularies
- Understand the organization of stories, plays, informational books, poems, and other texts
- Use comprehension strategies
- Monitor their understanding as they read

Similarly, capable writers do the following:

- Vary how they write depending on the purpose for writing and the audience that will read the composition
- Use the writing process flexibly
- Focus on developing ideas and communicating effectively
- Turn to classmates for feedback on how they are communicating
- Monitor how well they are communicating in the piece of writing
- Use formats and structures for stories, poems, letters, and other texts
- Postpone attention to mechanical correctness until the end of the writing process

All of these characteristics of capable readers and writers relate to comprehension, and because these students know and use them, they are better readers and writers than students who don't use them.

A comparison of the characteristics of capable and less capable readers and writers is presented in Figure 8–7. Young children who are learning to read and write often exemplify many of the characteristics of less capable readers and writers, but older students who are less successful readers and writers also exemplify them.

Less successful readers exemplify few of the characteristics of capable readers or behave differently when they are reading and writing. Perhaps the most remarkable difference is that more capable readers view reading as a process of comprehending or creating meaning, whereas less capable readers focus on decoding. In writing, less capable writers make cosmetic changes when they revise, rather than changes to communicate

Assessment Tools

Motivation

Teachers assess students' motivation in several ways. They observe students as they read and write, read entries in their reading logs, and conference with them about their interests and attitudes. At the beginning of the school year, teachers often have students create interest inventories with lists of things they're interested in, types of books they like to read, and favorite authors. Teachers also administer attitude surveys. These surveys assess students' motivation:

◆ **Elementary Reading Attitude Survey** (McKenna & Kear, 1990)

The Elementary Reading Attitude Survey assesses first- through sixth-grade students' attitudes toward reading at home and in school. The 20 items begin with the stem "How do you feel . . ." and students mark one of four pictures of Garfield, the cartoon cat; each picture depicts a different emotional state, ranging from positive to negative. This survey enables teachers to quickly estimate their students' attitudes.

◆ **Motivation to Read Profile** (Gambrell, Palmer, Codling, & Mazzoni, 1996)

The Motivation to Read Profile consists of two parts, a group test and an individual interview. The test is a survey with 20 items about self-concept as a reader and the value of reading that students respond to using a 4-point Likert scale. The interview is a series of open-ended questions about the types of books students like best and where they get reading materials. Each part takes about 15 minutes to administer.

◆ **Reader Self-Perception Scale** (Henk & Melnick, 1995)

The Reader Self-Perception Scale measures how students feel about reading and about themselves as readers. It's designed for third to sixth graders. Students respond to "I think I am a good reader" and other statements using a 5-point Likert scale where responses range from "strongly agree" to "strongly disagree." Teachers score students' responses and interpret the results to determine both overall and specific attitude levels.

◆ **Writing Attitude Survey** (Kear, Coffman, McKenna, & Ambrosio, 2000)

The Writing Attitude Survey examines students' feelings about the writing process and types of writing. It has 28 items, including "How would you feel if your classmates talked to you about making your writing better?" It features Garfield, the cartoon cat, as in the Elementary Reading Attitude Survey. Students indicate their response by marking the picture of Garfield that best illustrates their feelings.

◆ **Writer Self-Perception Scale** (Bottomley, Henk, & Melnick, 1997/1998)

The Writer Self-Perception Scale assesses third through sixth graders' attitudes about writing and how they perceive themselves as writers. Students respond to statements such as "I write better than my classmates do," using the same 5-point Likert scale that the Reader Self-Perception Scale uses.

These attitude surveys were originally published in *The Reading Teacher* and are readily available at libraries, online, and in collections of assessment instruments, such as *Assessment for Reading Instruction* (McKenna & Stahl, 2003).

Figure 8–7 ◆ Capable and Less Capable Readers and Writers

Components	Reader Characteristics	Writer Characteristics
Belief Systems	Capable readers view reading as a comprehending process, but less capable readers view reading as a decoding process.	Capable writers view writing as communicating ideas, but less capable writers see writing as putting words on paper.
Purpose	Capable readers adjust their reading according to purpose, but less capable readers approach all reading tasks the same way.	Capable writers adapt their writing to meet demands of audience, purpose, and form, but less capable writers don't.
Fluency	Capable readers read fluently, whereas less capable readers read word by word, don't chunk words into phrases, and sometimes point at words as they read.	Capable writers sustain their writing for longer periods of time and pause as they draft to think and reread what they've written, whereas less capable writers write less and without pausing.
Background Knowledge	Capable readers relate what they're reading to their background knowledge, but less capable readers don't make this connection.	Capable writers gather and organize ideas before writing, but less capable writers don't plan before beginning to write.
Decoding/ Spelling	Capable readers identify unfamiliar words efficiently, but less capable readers make nonsensical guesses or skip over unfamiliar words and invent what they think is a reasonable text when they're reading.	Capable writers spell many words conventionally and use the dictionary to spell unfamiliar words, but less capable writers can't spell many high-frequency words, and they depend on phonics to spell unfamiliar words.
Vocabulary	Capable readers have larger vocabularies than less capable readers do.	Capable writers use more sophisticated words and figurative language than less capable writers do.
Strategies	Capable readers use a variety of strategies as they read, but less capable readers use fewer strategies or less effective ones.	Capable writers use many strategies effectively, but less capable writers use fewer strategies or less effective ones.
Monitoring	Capable readers monitor their comprehension, but less capable readers don't realize or take action when they don't understand.	Capable writers monitor that their writing makes sense, and they turn to classmates for revising suggestions, but less capable writers don't.

Adapted from Faigley, Cherry, Jolliffe, & Skinner, 1985; Paris, Wasik, & Turner, 1991.

meaning more effectively. These important differences indicate that capable students focus on comprehension and the strategies readers and writers use to understand what they read and to make sure that what they write will be comprehensible to others.

Another important difference between capable and less capable readers and writers is that those who are less successful aren't strategic. They are naive. They seem reluctant to use unfamiliar strategies or those that require much effort. They don't seem to be motivated or to expect that they'll be successful. Less capable readers and writers don't understand or use all stages of the reading and writing processes effectively. They don't monitor their reading and writing (Keene & Zimmermann, 2007). Or, if they do use strategies, they remain dependent on primitive ones. For example, as they read, less successful readers seldom look ahead or back into the text to clarify misunderstandings or make plans. Or, when they come to an unfamiliar word, they often stop reading, unsure of what to do. They may try to sound out an unfamiliar word, but if that's unsuccessful, they give up. In contrast, capable readers know a variety of strategies, and if one strategy isn't successful, they try another.

Less capable writers move through the writing process in a lockstep, linear approach. They use a limited number of strategies, most often a "knowledge-telling" strategy in which they write everything they know about a topic with little thought to choosing information to meet the needs of their readers or to organizing the information to put related ideas together (Faigley et al., 1985). In contrast, capable writers understand the recursive nature of the writing process and turn to classmates for feedback about how well they're communicating. They are more responsive to the needs of the audience that will read their writing, and they work to organize their writing in a cohesive manner.

This research on capable and less capable readers and writers has focused on comprehension differences and students' use of strategies. It's noteworthy that all research comparing readers and writers focuses on how students use strategies, not on their use of reading and writing skills.

Chapter 8
Review

How Effective Teachers Facilitate Students' Comprehension of Reader Factors

▶ Teachers understand that comprehension is a process involving both reader factors and text factors.

▶ Teachers ensure that students have adequate background knowledge, vocabulary, and fluency, the prerequisites for comprehension.

▶ Teachers understand how comprehension strategies support students' understanding of texts they're reading.

▶ Teachers teach students how to use comprehension strategies and skills.

▶ Teachers nurture students' motivation and engagement in literacy activities.

PEARSON
myeducationlab
Where the Classroom Comes to Life

Go to MyEducationLab at www.myeducationlab.com to deepen your understanding of the concepts presented in this chapter:

▶ Identify the comprehension strategies that Ms. Janusz's second graders have learned by viewing video segments in the Literacy Portraits.
▶ Check your understanding of chapter concepts with the multiple-choice and essay quizzes in the Study Plan.
▶ Apply some of the main ideas discussed in the chapter in the Activities and Applications section of the website.
▶ Practice what you've learned in this chapter in Building Teaching Skills and Dispositions before applying the ideas in your own classroom.

PROFESSIONAL REFERENCES

Afflerbach, P., Pearson, P. D., & Paris, S. G. (2008). Clarifying differences between reading skills and strategies. *The Reading Teacher, 61,* 364–373.

Alderman, M. K. (1999). *Motivation for achievement: Possibilities for teaching and learning.* Mahwah, NJ: Erlbaum.

Allington, R. L. (2006). *What really matters for struggling readers: Designing research-based programs* (2nd ed.). Boston: Allyn & Bacon/Pearson.

Applegate, M. D., Quinn, K. B., & Applegate, A. J. (2008). *The critical reading inventory: Assessing students' reading and thinking* (2nd ed.). Upper Saddle River. NJ: Merrill/Prentice Hall.

Baker, L., & Brown, A. (1984). Metacognitive skills of reading. In P. D. Pearson, M. Kamil, P. Mosenthal, & R. Barr (Eds.), *Handbook of reading research* (pp. 353–394). New York: Longman.

Beaver, J. (2006). *Developmental reading assessment, grades K–3* (2nd ed.). Upper Saddle River, NJ: Celebration Press/Pearson.

Beaver, J., & Carter, M. (2003). *Developmental reading assessment, grades 4–8.* Upper Saddle River, NJ: Celebration Press/Pearson.

Blachowicz, C. L. Z., & Fisher, P. J. (2007). Best practices in vocabulary instruction. In L. B. Gambrell, L. M. Morrow, & M. Pressley (Eds.), *Best practices in literacy instruction* (3rd ed., pp. 178–203). New York: Guilford Press.

Blanton, W. E., Wood, K. D., & Moorman, G. B. (1990). The role of purpose in reading instruction. *The Reading Teacher, 43,* 486–493.

Block, C. C., & Pressley, M. (2007). Best practices in teaching comprehension. In L. B. Gambrell, L. M. Morrow, & M. Pressley (Eds.), *Best practices in literacy instruction* (3rd ed., pp. 220–242). New York: Guilford Press.

Bottomley, D. M., Henk, W. A., & Melnick, S. A. (1997/1998). Assessing children's views about themselves as writers using the Writer Self-Perception Scale. *The Reading Teacher, 51,* 286–296.

Bouchard, M. (2005). *Comprehension strategies for English language learners.* New York: Scholastic.

Braunger, J., & Lewis, J. P. (2006). *Building a knowledge base in reading* (2nd ed.). Newark, DE: International Reading Association/National Council of Teachers of English.

Brophy, J. (2004). *Motivating students to learn* (2nd ed.). Mahwah, NJ: Erlbaum.

Castek, J., Bevans-Mangelson, J., & Goldstone, B. (2006). Reading adventures online: Five ways to introduce the new literacies of the Internet through children's literature. *The Reading Teacher, 59,* 714–728.

Clay, M. M. (2007). *An observation survey of early literacy achievement* (rev. ed.). Portsmouth. NH: Heinemann.

Coiro, J. (2003). Reading comprehension on the Internet: Expanding our understanding of reading comprehension to encompass new literacies. *The Reading Teacher, 56,* 458–464.

Coiro, J., & Dobler, E. (2007). Exploring the online reading comprehension strategies used by sixth-grade skilled readers to search for and locate information on the Internet. *Reading Research Quarterly, 42,* 214–257.

Cooper, J. D., Chard, D. J., & Kiger, N. D. (2006). *The struggling reader: Interventions that work.* New York: Scholastic.

Cooter, R. B., Jr., Flynt, E. S., & Cooter, K. S. (2007). *Comprehensive reading inventory.* Upper Saddle River. NJ: Merrill/Prentice Hall.

Cunningham, J. W. (1982). Generating interactions between schemata and text. In J. A. Niles & L. A. Harris (Eds.), *New inquiries in reading research and instruction* (pp. 42–47). Rochester, NY: National Reading Conference.

Duke, N. K., & Pearson, P. D. (2002). Effective practices for developing reading comprehension. In A. E. Farstrup & S. J. Samuels (Eds.), *What research has to say about reading instruction* (3rd ed., pp. 205–242). Newark, DE: International Reading Association.

Faigley, L., Cherry, R. D., Jolliffe, D. A., & Skinner, A. M. (1985). *Assessing writers' knowledge and processes of composing.* Norwood, NJ: Ablex.

Gambrell, L. B., Palmer, B. M., Codling, R. M., & Mazzoni, S. A. (1996). Assessing motivation to read. *The Reading Teacher, 49,* 518–533.

Guthrie, J. T., & Wigfield, A. (2000). Engagement and motivation in reading. In M. L. Kamil, P. B. Mosenthal, P. D. Pearson, & R. Barr (Eds.), *Handbook of reading research* (Vol. 3, pp. 403–422). New York: Erlbaum.

Harvey, S., & Goudvis, A. (2007). *Strategies that work: Teaching comprehension for understanding and engagement* (2nd ed.). Portland, ME: Stenhouse.

Henk, W. A., & Melnick, S. A. (1995). The Reader Self-Perception Scale (RSPS): A new tool for measuring how children feel about themselves as readers. *The Reading Teacher, 48,* 470–482.

Henry, L. A. (2006). SEARCHing for an answer: The critical role of new literacies while reading on the Internet. *The Reading Teacher, 59,* 614–627.

Irwin, J. W. (1991). *Teaching reading comprehension processes* (2nd ed). Boston: Allyn & Bacon.

Ivey, G., & Broaddus, K. (2001). "Just plain reading": A survey of what makes students want to read in middle school classrooms. *Reading Research Quarterly, 36,* 350–377.

Kear, D. J., Coffman, G. A., McKenna, M. C., & Ambrosio, A. L. (2000). Measuring attitude toward writing: A new tool for teachers. *The Reading Teacher, 54,* 10–23.

Keene, E. (2006). *Assessing comprehension thinking strategies.* Huntington Beach, CA: Shell Education.

Keene, E. O., & Zimmermann, S. (2007). *Mosaic of thought: The power of comprehension strategy instruction* (2nd ed.). Portsmouth, NH: Heinemann.

Kohn, A. (2001). *Punished by rewards: The trouble with gold stars, incentive plans, A's, praise, and other bribes*. Boston: Houghton Mifflin.

Leslie, L., & Caldwell, J. (2006). *Qualitative reading inventory* (4th ed.). Boston: Allyn & Bacon/Pearson.

Leu, D. J., Jr., Kinzer, C. K., Coiro, J., & Cammack, D. W. (2004). Toward a theory of new literacies emerging from the Internet and other communication technologies. In R. Ruddell & N. Unrau (Eds.), *Theoretical models and processes of reading* (5th ed., pp. 1570–1613). Newark, DE: International Reading Association.

McKenna, M. C., & Kear, D. J. (1990). Measuring attitudes toward reading: A new tool for teachers. *The Reading Teacher, 43*, 626–639.

McKenna, M. C., & Stahl, S. A. (2003). *Assessment for reading instruction*. New York: Guilford Press.

Morrow, L. M. (2002). *Organizing and managing the language arts block*. New York: Guilford Press.

National Reading Panel. (2000). *Teaching children to read: An evidence-based assessment of the scientific research literature on reading and its implications for reading instruction*. Washington, DC: National Institute of Child Health and Human Development.

Oczkus, L. D. (2003). *Reciprocal teaching at work: Strategies for improving reading comprehension*. Newark, DE: International Reading Association.

Oldfather, P. (1995). Commentary: What's needed to maintain and extend motivation for literacy in the middle grades. *Journal of Reading, 38*, 420–422.

Owocki, G. (2003). *Comprehension: Strategic instruction for K–3 students*. Portsmouth, NH: Heinemann.

Palinscar, A. S., & Brown, A. L. (1986). Interactive teaching to promote independent learning from text. *The Reading Teacher, 39*, 771–777.

Paris, S. G., Wasik, B. A., & Turner, J. C. (1991). The development of strategic readers. In R. Barr, M. L. Kamil, P. B. Mosenthal, & P. D. Pearson (Eds.), *Handbook of reading research* (Vol. 2, pp. 609–640). New York: Longman.

Peregoy, S. F., & Boyle, W. F. (2008). *Reading, writing, and learning in ESL: A resource book for teaching K–12 English learners* (5th ed.). Boston: Allyn & Bacon/Pearson.

Pressley, M. (2002a). Comprehension strategies instruction: A turn-of-the-century status report. In C. C. Block & M. Pressley (Eds.), *Comprehension instruction: Research-based best practices* (pp. 11–27). New York: Guilford Press.

Pressley, M. (2002b). Metacognition and self-regulated comprehension. In A. E. Farstrup & S. J. Samuels (Eds.), *What research has to say about reading instruction* (3rd ed., pp. 291–309). Newark, DE: International Reading Association.

Pressley, M., Dolezal, S. E., Raphael, L. M., Mohan, L., Roehrig, A. D., & Bogner, K. (2003). *Motivating primary-grade students*. New York: Guilford Press.

Raphael, T. E., Highfield, K., & Au, K. H. (2006). *QAR now: A powerful and practical framework that develops comprehension and higher-level thinking in all students*. New York: Scholastic.

Samuels, S. J. (2002). Reading fluency: Its development and assessment. In A. E. Farstrup & S. J. Samuels (Eds.), *What research has to say about reading instruction* (3rd ed., pp. 166–185). Newark, DE: International Reading Association.

Stipek, D. J. (2002). *Motivation to learn: Integrating theory and practice* (4th ed.). Boston: Allyn & Bacon.

Sweet, A. P., & Snow, C. E. (2003). Reading for comprehension. In A. P. Sweet & C. E. Snow (Eds.), *Rethinking reading comprehension* (pp. 1–11). New York: Guilford Press.

Tierney, R. J. (1990). Redefining reading comprehension. *Educational Leadership, 47*, 37–42.

Tierney, R., & Pearson, P. D. (1983). Toward a composing model of reading. *Language Arts, 60*, 568–580.

Tovani, C. (2000). *I read it, but I don't get it: Comprehension strategies for adolescent readers*. Portland, ME: Stenhouse.

Turner, J., & Paris, S. G. (1995). How literacy tasks influence children's motivation for literacy. *The Reading Teacher, 48*, 662–673.

Unrau, N. (2004). *Content area reading and writing: Fostering literacies in middle and high school cultures*. Upper Saddle River, NJ: Merrill/Prentice Hall.

Van Den Broek, P., & Kremer, K. E. (2000). The mind in action: What it means to comprehend during reading. In B. M. Taylor, M. F. Graves, & P. Van Den Broek (Eds.), *Reading for meaning: Fostering comprehension in the middle grades* (pp. 1–31). New York: Teachers College Press.

Wilhelm, J. D. (2001). *Improving comprehension with think-aloud strategies*. New York: Scholastic.

Woods, M. L., & Moe, A. J. (2007). *Analytical reading inventory* (8th ed.). Upper Saddle River. NJ: Merrill/Prentice Hall.

Zimmermann, S., & Hutchins, C. (2003). *Seven keys to comprehension: How to help your kids read it and get it!* New York: Three Rivers Press.

CHILDREN'S BOOK REFERENCES

Bunting, E. (1998). *So far from the sea*. Boston: Houghton Mifflin.

Coerr, E. (1989). *The Josefina story quilt*. New York: HarperCollins.

Coerr, E. (1993). *Chang's paper pony*. New York: HarperCollins.

Gantos, J. (2005). *Joey Pigza loses control*. New York: HarperCollins.

Jiménez, F. (1998). *La mariposa*. Boston: Houghton Mifflin.

Van Allsburg, C. (1991). *The wretched stone*. Boston: Houghton Mifflin.

Van Allsburg, C. (1993). *The garden of Abdul Gasazi*. Boston: Houghton Mifflin.

Facilitating Students' Comprehension: Text Factors

Mr. Abrams's Fourth Graders Learn About Frogs

The fourth graders in Mr. Abrams's class are studying frogs. They began by making a class **K-W-L chart** (Ogle, 1986), listing what they already know about frogs in the "K: What We Know" column and things they want to learn in the "W: What We Wonder" column. At the end of the unit, students will finish the chart by listing what they've learned in the "L: What We Have Learned" column. The fourth graders want to know how frogs and toads are different and if it is true that you get warts from frogs. Mr. Abrams assures them that they will learn the answers to many of their questions and makes a mental note to find the answer to their question about warts.

Aquariums with frogs and frog spawn are arranged in one area in the classroom. Mr. Abrams has brought in five aquariums and filled them with frogs he collected in his backyard and others he "rented" from a local pet store, and he has also brought in frog spawn from a nearby pond. The fourth graders are observing the frogs and the frog spawn daily and drawing diagrams and making notes in their learning logs.

Mr. Abrams sets out a text set with books about frogs representing the three genres—stories, informational books, and poetry books—on a special shelf in the classroom library. He reads many of the books aloud to the class. When he begins, he reads the title and shows students several pages and asks them whether the book is a story, an informational book, or a poem. After they determine the genre, they talk about their purpose for listening. For an informational book, the teacher writes a question or two on the chalkboard to guide their listening. After reading, the students answer the questions as part of their discussion. Students also read and reread many of these books during an independent reading time.

Mr. Abrams also has a class set of *Amazing Frogs and Toads* (Clarke, 1990), a nonfiction book with striking photograph illustrations and well-organized presentations of information. He reads it once with the whole class using shared reading, and they discuss the interesting information in the book. He divides the class into small groups, and each group chooses a question about frogs to research in the book. Students reread the book, hunting for the answer to their question. Mr. Abrams has already taught the students to use the table of contents and the index to locate facts in an informational book. After they locate and reread the information, they use the writing process to develop a poster to answer the question and share what they've learned. He meets with each group to help them organize their posters and revise and edit their writing.

From the vast amount of information in *Amazing Frogs and Toads*, Mr. Abrams chooses nine questions, which he designs to address some of the questions on the "W: What We Wonder" section of the K-W-L chart, to highlight important information in the text, and to focus on the five expository text structures, the organizational patterns used for nonfiction texts that students read and write. Mr. Abrams is teaching the fourth graders that informational books, like stories, have special organizational elements. Here are his questions organized according to the expository structures:

What are amphibians? (Description)

What do frogs look like? (Description)

What is the life cycle of a frog? (Sequence)

How do frogs eat? (Sequence)

How are frogs and toads alike and different? (Comparison)

Why do frogs hibernate? (Cause and Effect)

How do frogs croak? (Cause and Effect)

How do frogs use their eyes and eyelids? (Problem and Solution)

How do frogs escape from their enemies? (Problem and Solution)

After the students complete their posters, they share them with the class through brief presentations, and the posters are displayed in the classroom. Two of the students' posters are shown on page 288; the life cycle poster emphasizes the sequence structure, and the "Frogs Have Big Eyes" poster explains that the frog's eyes help it solve problems—finding food, hiding from enemies, and seeing underwater.

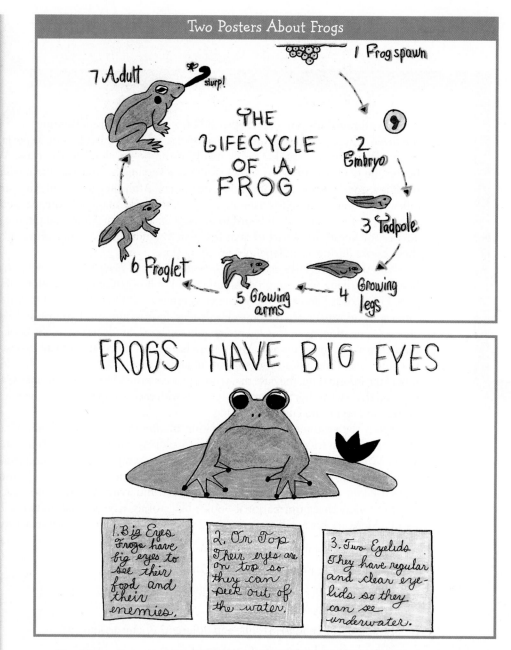

Two Posters About Frogs

Mr. Abrams's students use the information in the posters to write books about frogs. Students choose three posters and write one- to three-paragraph chapters to report the information from the poster. Students meet in **writing groups** to revise their rough drafts and then edit with a classmate and with Mr. Abrams. Finally, students word process their final copies and add illustrations, a title page, and a table of contents. Then they compile their books and "publish" them by sharing them with classmates from the author's chair.

Armin wrote this chapter on "Hibernation" in his book:

Hibernation means that an animal sleeps all winter long. Frogs hibernate because they are cold blooded and they might freeze to death if they didn't. They find a good place to sleep like a hole in the ground, or in a log, or under some leaves. They go to sleep and they do not eat, or drink, or go to the bathroom.

They sleep all winter and when they wake up it is spring. They are very, very hungry and they want to eat a lot of food. Their blood warms up when it is spring because the temperature warms up and when they are warm they want to be awake and eat. They are awake in the spring and in the summer, and then in the fall they start to think about hibernating again.

Jessica wrote this chapter on "The Differences Between Frogs and Toads" for her book:

You might think that frogs and toads are the same but you would be wrong. They are really different but they are both amphibians. I am going to tell you three ways they are different.

First of all, frogs really love water so they stay in the water or pretty close to it. Toads don't love water. They usually live where it is dry. This is a big difference between frogs and toads.

Second, you should look at frogs and toads. They look different. Frogs are slender and thin but toads are fat. Their skin is different, too. Frogs have smooth skin and toads have bumpy skin. I would say that toads are not pretty to look at.

Third, frogs have long legs but toads have short legs. That probably is the reason why frogs are wonderful jumpers and toads can't. They move slowly. They just hop. When you watch them move, you can tell that they are very different.

Frogs and toads are different kinds of amphibians. They live in different places, they look different, and they move in different ways. You can see these differences when you look at them and it is very interesting to study them.

Mr. Abrams helps his students develop a **rubric** to assess their books. The rubric addresses the following points about the chapters:

- The title describes the chapter.
- The information in each chapter is presented clearly.
- Vocabulary from the **word wall** is used in each chapter.
- The information in each chapter is written in one or more indented paragraphs.
- The information in each chapter has very few spelling, capitalization, and punctuation errors.
- There is a useful illustration in each chapter.

Other points on the rubric consider the book as a whole:

- The title page lists the title and the author's name.
- All pages in the book are numbered.
- The table of contents lists the chapters and the pages for each chapter.
- The title is written on the cover of the book.
- The illustrations on the cover of the book relate to frogs.

The students evaluate their books using a 4-point scale; Mr. Abrams also uses the rubric to assess their writing. He conferences with students and shares his scoring with them. Also, he helps the students set goals for their next writing project.

To end the unit, Mr. Abrams asks his students to finish the K-W-L chart. In the third column, "L: What We Have Learned," students list some of the information they have learned:

Tadpoles breathe through gills but frogs breathe through lungs.
Tadpoles are vegetarians but frogs eat worms and insects.
Snakes, rats, birds, and foxes are the frogs' enemies.

Some frogs in the rainforest are brightly colored and poisonous, too.
Some frogs are hard to see because they camouflage coloring.
Male frogs puff up their air sacs to croak and make sounds.
Frogs have teeth but they swallow their food whole.
Frogs have two sets of eyelids and one set is clear so frogs can see when they are underwater.
Frogs can jump ten times their body length but toads can't—they're hoppers.

Mr. Abrams stands back to reread the fourth graders' comments. "I can tell how much you've learned when I read the detailed information you've added in the L column," he remarks with a smile. He knows that one reason why his students are successful is because he taught them to use text structure as a tool for learning.

What readers know and do during reading has a tremendous impact on how well they comprehend, but comprehension involves more than just reader factors: It also involves text factors. Stories, informational books, and poems can be easier or more difficult to read depending on factors that are inherent in them (Harvey & Goudvis, 2007). Here are the three most important types of text factors:

Genres. The three broad categories of literature are stories, informational books or nonfiction, and poetry, and there are subgenres within each category. For example, science fiction, folktales, and historical fiction are subgenres of stories.

Text Structures. Authors use text structures to organize texts and emphasize the most important ideas. Sequence, comparison, and cause and effect, for example, are three internal patterns used to organize nonfiction texts.

Text Features. Authors use text features to achieve a particular effect in their writing. Literary devices and conventions include symbolism and tone in stories, headings and indexes in informational books, and page layout for poems.

When students understand how authors organize and present their ideas in texts, this knowledge about text factors serves as a scaffold, making comprehension easier (Meyer & Poon, 2004; Sweet & Snow, 2003). Text factors make a similar contribution to students' writing; students apply what they've learned about genres, text structures, and text features when they're writing (Mooney, 2001).

TEXT FACTORS OF STORIES

Stories are narratives about characters trying to overcome problems or deal with difficulties. They've been described as "waking dreams" that people use to find meaning in their lives. Children develop an understanding of what constitutes a story beginning in the preschool years when their parents read aloud to them, and they refine and expand their understanding of stories through literacy instruction at school (Applebee, 1978; Appleyard, 1994). Students learn about the subgenres of stories and read stories representing each one, examine the structural patterns that authors use to organize stories, and point out the narrative devices that authors use to breathe life into their stories.

Formats of Stories

Stories are available in picture-book and chapter-book formats. Picture books have brief texts, usually spread over 32 pages, in which text and illustrations combine to tell a story. The text is minimal, and the illustrations supplement the sparse text. The illustrations in many picture books are striking. Many picture books, such as *Rosie's Walk* (Hutchins, 2005), about a clever hen who outwits a fox, are for primary-grade students, but others, such as *Show Way* (Woodson, 2005), a multimedia story about the generations of women in the author's family, from slavery to the Civil Rights movement to the present, were written with middle-grade students in mind. Others are wordless picture books, such as *Flotsam* (Wiesner, 2006) and *The Red Book* (Lehman, 2004), in which the story is told entirely through the illustrations.

Novels are longer stories written in a chapter format. Most are written for older students, but Dan Greenburg's adventure series, The Zack Files, including *Just Add Water . . . and Scream!* (2003), is for students reading at the second- and third-grade levels. Chapter books for middle-grade students include *Shiloh* (Naylor, 2000) and *Esperanza Rising* (Ryan, 2002). Complex stories such as *Holes* (Sachar, 2003) are more suitable for upper-grade students. Chapter books have few illustrations, if any, because they don't usually play an integral role in the story.

Narrative Genres

Stories can be categorized in different ways, one of which is according to genres (Buss & Karnowski, 2000). Three general subcategories are folklore, fantasies, and realistic fiction. Figure 9–1 presents an overview of these narrative genres.

Folklore. Stories that began hundreds of years ago and were passed down from generation to generation by storytellers before being written down are *folk literature*. These stories, including fables, folktales, and myths, are an important part of our cultural heritage. Fables are brief narratives designed to teach a moral. The story format makes the lesson easier to understand, and the moral is usually stated at the end. Fables exemplify these characteristics:

- ◆ They are short, often less than a page long.
- ◆ The characters are usually animals.
- ◆ The characters are one-dimensional: strong or weak, wise or foolish.
- ◆ The setting is barely sketched; the stories could take place anywhere.
- ◆ The theme is usually stated as a moral at the end of the story.

The best-known fables, including "The Hare and the Tortoise" and "The Ant and the Grasshopper," are believed to have been written by a Greek slave named Aesop in the 6th century B.C. Individual fables hare been retold as picture-book stories, including *The Hare and the Tortoise* (Ward, 1999) and *The Lion and the Rat* (Wildsmith, 2007).

Folktales began as oral stories, told and retold by medieval storytellers as they traveled from town to town. The problem in a folktale usually revolves around one of four situations: a journey from home to perform a task, a journey to confront a monster, the miraculous change from a harsh home to a secure home, or a confrontation between a wise beast and a foolish beast. Here are other characteristics:

- ◆ The story often begins with the phrase "Once upon a time . . ."
- ◆ The setting is generalized and could be located anywhere.
- ◆ The plot structure is simple and straightforward.
- ◆ Characters are one-dimensional: good or bad, stupid or clever, industrious or lazy.
- ◆ The end is happy, and everyone lives "happily ever after."

Figure 9–1 ◆ Narrative Genres

Category	Genre	Description
Folklore	Fables	Brief tales told to point out a moral. For example: *Town Mouse, Country Mouse* (Brett, 2003) and *The Boy Who Cried Wolf* (Hennessy, 2006).
	Folktales	Stories in which heroes demonstrate virtues to triumph over adversity. For example: *Jouanah: A Hmong Cinderella* (Coburn, 1996) and *Rumpelstiltskin* (Zelinsky, 1996).
	Myths	Stories created by ancient peoples to explain natural phenomena. For example: *Why Mosquitoes Buzz in People's Ears* (Aardema, 2004) and *Raven* (McDermott, 2001).
	Legends	Stories, including hero tales and tall tales, that recount the courageous deeds of people who struggled against each other or against gods and monsters. For example: *John Henry* (Lester, 1999) and *The Adventures of Robin Hood* (Williams, 2007).
Fantasy	Modern Literary Tales	Stories written by modern authors that are similar to folktales. For example: *The Ugly Duckling* (Mitchell, 2007) and *Sylvester and the Magic Pebble* (Steig, 2006).
	Fantastic Stories	Imaginative stories that explore alternate realities and contain elements not found in the natural world. For example: *Jeremy Thatcher, Dragon Hatcher* (Coville, 2007b) and *Poppy* (Avi, 2005).
	Science Fiction	Stories that explore scientific possibilities. For example: *Aliens Ate My Homework* (Coville, 2007a) and *The Giver* (Lowry, 2006).
	High Fantasy	Stories that focus on the conflict between good and evil and often involve quests. For example: the Harry Potter series and *The Lion, the Witch and the Wardrobe* (Lewis, 2005).
Realistic Fiction	Contemporary Stories	Stories that portray today's society. For example: *Going Home* (Bunting, 1998) and *Seedfolks* (Fleischman, 2004b).
	Historical Stories	Realistic stories set in the past. For example: *Sarah, Plain and Tall* (MacLachlan, 2004) and *Roll of Thunder, Hear My Cry* (Taylor, 2001).

Some folktales are cumulative tales, such as *The Gingerbread Boy* (Galdone, 2008); these stories are built around the repetition of words and events. Others are talking animal stories; in these stories, such as *The Three Little Pigs* (Kellogg, 2002), animals act and talk like humans. The best-known folktales are fairy tales. They have motifs or small recurring elements, including magical powers, transformations, enchantments, magical objects, trickery, and wishes that are granted, and they feature witches, giants, fairy godmothers, and other fantastic characters. Well-known examples are *Cinderella* (Ehrlich, 2004) and *Jack and the Beanstalk* (Kellogg, 1997).

People around the world have created myths to explain natural phenomena. Some explain the seasons, the sun, the moon, and the constellations, and others tell how the mountains and other physical features of the earth were created. Ancient peoples used myths to explain many things that have since been explained by scientific investigations. Myths exemplify these characteristics:

◆ Myths explain creations.
◆ Characters are often heroes with supernatural powers.
◆ The setting is barely sketched.
◆ Magical powers are required.

For example, the Greek myth *King Midas: The Golden Touch* (Demi, 2002) tells about the king's greed, and the Native American myth *The Legend of the Bluebonnet* (dePaola, 1996) recounts how these flowers came to beautify the countryside. Other myths tell how animals came to be or why they look the way they do. Legends are myths about heroes who have done something important enough to be remembered in a story; they may have some basis in history but aren't verifiable. Stories about Robin Hood and King Arthur, for example, are legends. American legends about Johnny Appleseed, Paul Bunyan, and Pecos Bill are known as *tall tales*.

Fantasies. Fantasies are imaginative stories. Authors create new worlds for their characters, but these worlds must be based in reality so that readers will believe they exist. One of the most beloved fantasies is *Charlotte's Web* (White, 2004). Four types of fantasies are modern literary tales, fantastic stories, science fiction, and high fantasy.

Modern literary tales are related to folktales and fairy tales because they often incorporate many characteristics and conventions of traditional literature, but they've been written more recently and have identifiable authors. The best-known author of modern literary tales is Hans Christian Andersen, a Danish writer of the 1800s who wrote *The Snow Queen* (Ehrlich, 2006) and *The Ugly Duckling* (Mitchell, 2007). Other examples of modern literary tales include *Alexander and the Wind-Up Mouse* (Lionni, 2006) and *The Wolf's Chicken Stew* (Kasza, 1996).

Fantastic stories are realistic in most details, but some events require readers to suspend disbelief. Fantasies exemplify these characteristics:

◆ The events in the story are extraordinary; things that could not happen in today's world.
◆ The setting is realistic.
◆ Main characters are people or personified animals.
◆ Themes often deal with the conflict between good and evil.

Some are animal fantasies, such as *Babe: The Gallant Pig* (King-Smith, 2005). The main characters in these stories are animals endowed with human traits. Students often realize that the animals symbolize human beings and that these stories explore human relationships. Some are toy fantasies, such as *The Miraculous Journey of Edward Tulane* (DiCamillo, 2006). Toy fantasies are similar to animal fantasies except that the main characters are talking toys, usually stuffed animals or dolls. Other fantasies involve enchanted journeys during which wondrous things happen. The journey must have a purpose, but it is usually overshadowed by the thrill and delight of the fantastic world, as in Roald Dahl's *Charlie and the Chocolate Factory* (2007).

In science fiction stories, authors create a world in which science interacts with society. Many stories involve traveling through space to distant galaxies or meeting alien societies. Authors hypothesize scientific advancements and imagine technology of the future to create the plot. Science fiction exemplifies these characteristics:

- ◆ The story is set in the future.
- ◆ Conflict is usually between the characters and natural or mechanical forces, such as robots.
- ◆ The characters believe in the advanced technology.
- ◆ A detailed description of scientific facts is provided.

Time-warp stories in which the characters move forward and back in time are also classified as science fiction. Jon Scieszka's Time Warp Trio stories, including *Knights of the Kitchen Table* (2004), are popular with middle-grade students.

New Literacies
A New Generation of Books

Many of the best books for children and adolescents published since 2000 defy conventions, blur the lines between genres, and incorporate innovative forms. Because these texts require different reading strategies, they support students' learning about new literacies (Kiefer, Price-Dennis, & Ryan, 2006). *The Invention of Hugo Cabret* (Selznick, 2007), the first novel to win the Caldecott Medal, is a good example. Selznick combined storytelling, meticulous charcoal drawings, and cinematic techniques to create a touching story about Hugo, a 12-year-old orphan who lived in a Paris train station a century ago. Half of the 500-page novel is told through full-page illustrations, and to comprehend this story, readers must read the illustrations as carefully as they do the text.

Sometimes authors combine genres. *Love That Dog* (Creech, 2001), about a boy who learns the power of poetry, and *Becoming Joe Di Maggio* (Testa, 2005), about an Italian American kid who escapes his difficult life by listening to baseball games with his grandfather, are poetic narratives—stories told in verse. Students focus on the characters and the plot, but they're aware of the unique page layout and appreciate the figurative qualities of poetic language as they read.

Other authors invent multiple voices to develop their stories. *Day of Tears: A Novel in Dialogue* (Lester, 2005) tells about an 1859 slave auction in Georgia using different voices to emphasize the anguish of slave families and the greed of owners, and *Good Masters! Sweet Ladies! Voices From a Medieval Village* (Schlitz, 2007) is an award-winning collection of 23 monologues, each featuring a person living in and around an English manor in 1255. Students read flexibly, adjusting to a new viewpoint in each chapter. These stories can be read conventionally or presented as a reader's theatre or a play.

Book-length comics called *graphic novels* are a new genre, appealing to students of all ages and gaining respect from teachers and librarians. Babymouse is a sassy young mouse featured in *Babymouse: Queen of the World* (Holm, 2005) and numerous sequels. Fone Bone and his cousins engage in battles of good versus evil in *Bone: Out of Boneville* (Smith, 2005) and other books in this fantasy series. The wildly popular *Diary of a Wimpy Kid* (Kinney, 2007) and its sequels about Greg Heffley's trials and tribulations in middle school combine text and graphics. When students read graphic novels, they learn to examine all the details of every illustration and use their imagination to understand what's happening between frames.

Some wordless picture books incorporate the characteristics of graphic novels. *The Arrival* (Tan, 2007), for example, is a compelling story about an immigrant's journey to build a better future. Although the plot is straightforward, readers must study the illustrations to develop a sense of the immigrant's isolation, recognize the visual metaphors, and appreciate the themes.

Primary source materials are also being used to craft multi-genre stories. *Middle School Is Worse Than Meatloaf: A Year Told Through Stuff* (Holm, 2007) incorporates diary entries, refrigerator notes, IM screen messages, and cards from grandpa to recount a girl's day-to-day experiences; and *The Wall: Growing Up Behind the Iron Curtain* (Sís, 2007) combines drawings, diary entries, and photographs to create a powerful graphic memoir of the author's childhood in Soviet-ruled Prague, where children were encouraged to report on their parents and public displays of loyalty were required.

As 21st-century authors transform children's and adolescent literature, students are learning new strategies for exploring books that they can also use on the Internet. They learn to use a combination of visual and textual information to comprehend what they're reading and make connections across genres, text structures, and conventions.

Heroes confront evil for the good of humanity in high fantasy. The primary characteristic is the focus on the conflict between good and evil, as in C. S. Lewis's *The Lion, the Witch and the Wardrobe* (2005) and J. K. Rowling's Harry Potter stories. High fantasy is related to folk literature in that it's characterized by motifs and themes. Most stories include magical kingdoms, quests, tests of courage, magical powers, and super-human characters.

Realistic Fiction. These stories are lifelike and believable. The outcome is reasonable, and the story is a representation of action that seems truthful. Realistic fiction helps students discover that their problems aren't unique and that they aren't alone in experiencing certain feelings and situations. Realistic fiction also broadens students' horizons and allows them to experience new adventures. Two types are contemporary stories and historical stories.

Readers identify with characters who are their own age and have similar interests and problems in contemporary stories. In *The Higher Power of Lucky* (Patron, 2006), for example, students read about an eccentric 10-year-old girl named Lucky who finally comes to terms with her mother's death and finds stability in her life. Here are the characteristics of contemporary fiction:

◆ Characters act like real people or like real animals.
◆ The setting is in the world as we know it today.
◆ Stories deal with everyday occurrences or "relevant subjects."

Other contemporary stories include *Granny Torrelli Makes Soup* (Creech, 2005) and *I Am Not Joey Pigza* (Gantos, 2007).

In contrast, historical stories are set in the past. Details about food, clothing, and culture must be typical of the era in which the story is set because the setting influences the plot. These are the characteristics of this genre:

◆ The setting is historically accurate.
◆ Conflict is often between characters or between a character and society.
◆ The language is appropriate to the setting.
◆ Themes are universal, both for the historical period of the book and for today.

Examples of historical fiction include *Witness* (Hesse, 2001) and *Crispin: The Cross of Lead* (Avi, 2002). In these stories, students are immersed in historical events, they appreciate the contributions of people who have lived before them, and they learn about human relationships.

Elements of Story Structure

Stories have unique structural elements that distinguish them from other genres. The most important story elements are plot, characters, setting, point of view, and theme. They work together to structure a story, and authors manipulate them to develop their stories.

Plot. Plot is the sequence of events involving characters in conflict situations. It's based on the goals of one or more characters and the processes they go through to attain them (Lukens, 2006). The main characters want to achieve the goal, and other characters are introduced to prevent them from being successful. The story events are set in motion by characters as they attempt to overcome conflict and solve their problems. Figure 9–2 presents a list of stories with well-developed plots and other elements of story structure.

The most basic aspect of plot is the division of the main events into the beginning, middle, and end. In *The Tale of Peter Rabbit* (Potter, 2006), for instance, the three story parts are easy to pick out. As the story begins, Mrs. Rabbit sends her children out to play after warning them not to go into Mr. McGregor's garden. In the middle, Peter goes to Mr. McGregor's garden and is almost caught. Then Peter finds his way out of

Figure 9–2 ◆ Stories Illustrating the Elements of Story Structure

Plot

Brett, J. (2000). *Hedgie's surprise*. New York: Putnam. (P)

Fleming, D. (2003). *Buster*. New York: Henry Holt. (P)

Paulsen, G. (2007). *Hatchet*. New York: Simon & Schuster. (U)

Sachar, L. (2003). *Holes*. New York: Yearling. (U)

Steig, W. (2006). *Sylvester and the magic pebble*. New York: Aladdin Books. (P–M)

Characters

Cushman, K. (1994). *Catherine, called Birdy*. New York: HarperCollins. (U)

Dahl, R. (2007). *James and the giant peach*. New York: Puffin Books. (M–U)

Henkes, K. (1996). *Lilly's purple plastic purse*. New York: Greenwillow. (P)

Look, L. (2004). *Ruby Lu, brave and true*. New York: Atheneum. (P–M)

Lowry, L. (2006). *The giver*. New York: Delacorte. (U)

Setting

Bunting, E. (2006). *Pop's bridge*. San Diego: Harcourt. (P–M)

Curtis, C. P. (2000). *The Watsons go to Birmingham—1963*. New York: Laurel Leaf. (M–U)

Hale, S. (2005). *Princess Academy*. New York: Bloomsbury. (M–U)

Lowry, L. (1998). *Number the stars*. New York: Laurel Leaf. (M–U)

Patron, S. (2006). *The higher power of lucky*. New York: Atheneum. (U)

Point of View

Bunting, E. (2006). *One green apple*. New York: Clarion Books. (P–M)

Hesse, K. (2001). *Witness*. New York: Scholastic. (U)

Lewis, C. S. (2005). *The lion, the witch and the wardrobe*. New York: HarperCollins. (U)

MacLachlan, P. (2004). *Sarah, plain and tall*. New York: HarperTrophy. (M)

Pinkney, J. (2006). *The little red hen*. New York: Dial Books. (P)

Theme

Babbitt, N. (2007). *Tuck everlasting*. New York: Square Fish Books. (U)

Bunting, E. (1999). *Smoky night*. San Diego: Harcourt Brace. (M)

DiCamillo, K. (2006). *The miraculous journey of Edward Tulane*. Cambridge, MA: Candlewick Press. (M–U)

Naylor, P. R. (2000). *Shiloh*. New York: Aladdin Books. (M–U)

Woodson, J. (2001). *The other side*. New York: Putnam. (P–M)

P = primary grades (K–2); M = middle grades (3–5); U = upper grades (6–8)

the garden and gets home safely—the end of the story. Students can make a story map of the beginning-middle-end of a story using words and pictures, as the story map for *The Tale of Peter Rabbit* in Figure 9–3 shows.

Specific types of information are included in each part. In the beginning, the author introduces the characters, describes the setting, and presents a problem. Together, the characters, setting, and events develop the plot and sustain the theme through the story. In the middle, the plot unfolds, with each event preparing readers for what follows. Conflict heightens as the characters face roadblocks that keep them from solving their problems; how the characters tackle these problems adds suspense to keep readers interested. In the end, all is reconciled, and readers learn whether the characters' struggles are successful.

Conflict is the tension or opposition between forces in the plot, and it's what interests readers enough to continue reading the story (Lukens, 2006). Conflict occurs in these four ways:

Between a Character and Nature. Conflict between a character and nature occurs in stories in which severe weather plays an important role and in stories set in isolated geographic locations, such as *Holes* (Sachar, 2003), in which Stanley struggles to survive at Camp Green Lake, a boys' juvenile detention center.

Between a Character and Society. Sometimes the main character's activities and beliefs differ from those of others, and conflict arises between that character and society. In *The Witch of Blackbird Pond* (Speare, 2001), for example, Kit Tyler is accused of being a witch because she continues activities in a New England Puritan community that were acceptable in the Caribbean community where she grew up but aren't in her new home.

Between Characters. Conflict between characters is very common in children's literature. In *Tales of a Fourth Grade Nothing* (Blume, 2007), for instance, the never-ending conflict between Peter and his little brother, Fudge, is what makes the story entertaining.

Within a Character. The main character struggles to overcome challenges in his or her own life. In *Esperanza Rising* (Ryan, 2002), the title character must come to terms with her new life as a migrant worker after she leaves her family's ranch in Mexico.

Plot is developed through conflict that's introduced at the beginning, expanded in the middle, and finally resolved at the end. The development of the plot involves these components:

◆ A problem that introduces conflict is presented at the beginning of the story.
◆ Characters face roadblocks in attempting to solve the problem in the middle.
◆ The high point in the action occurs when the problem is about to be solved. This high point separates the middle and the end.
◆ The problem is solved and the roadblocks are overcome at the end of the story.

Figure 9–4 presents a plot diagram shaped like a mountain that incorporates these four components, which fifth graders completed after reading *Esperanza Rising* (Ryan, 2002). The problem in *Esperanza Rising* is that Esperanza and her mother must create a new life for themselves in California because they can't remain at their Mexican ranch home any longer. Certainly, there's conflict between characters here and conflict with society, too, but the most important conflict is within Esperanza as she leaves her comfortable life in Mexico to become a migrant laborer in California. Esperanza and her mother face many roadblocks. They become farm laborers, and the work is very difficult. Esperanza wants to bring her grandmother to join them, but they don't have enough money for her travel expenses. Then Esperanza's mother becomes ill, and Esperanza takes over her mother's work. Finally, Esperanza saves enough money to

Figure 9–3 ◆ A Beginning-Middle-End Story Map for *The Tale of Peter Rabbit*

Figure 9–4 ◆ A Plot Diagram for *Esperanza Rising*

Beginning	Middle	End
Esperanza has a wonderful childhood as a rich, pampered child in Mexico, but then her father dies and their ranch burns down. She and her mama leave Mexico to begin a new and different life in California.	Esperanza and her mama work as farm laborers but her mama gets very sick and is hospitalized for many months. Esperanza takes over her mama's work and she worries that her mother might die. She misses her Abuelita (grandmother) so she saves all the money she can so she can send for her. Then her money disappears.	Esperanza's mother gets well enough to leave the hospital and she learns that her friend Miguel used her money to bring her Abuelita to join them in California. Now Esperanza has adjusted to her new life.
Problem: Esperanza and her mother must flee Mexico and make a new life in California.	Roadblocks: 1. The work is very hard, there is very little money, and Esperanza is homesick. 2. Mama gets sick. 3. Some of the other workers want to strike. 4. Esperanza's money is missing.	High Point: Mama gets well enough to leave the hospital and Abuelita arrives.

bring her grandmother to California, but her money disappears. The high point of the action occurs when Esperanza's mother recovers enough to return to the farm labor camp, and it turns out that her money wasn't stolen after all: Esperanza's friend Miguel used it to bring her grandmother to California. As the story ends, the problem is solved: Esperanza adjusts to her new life in California with her mother and grandmother. *Esperanza* means "hope" in Spanish, and readers have reason to be optimistic that the girl and her family will create a good life for themselves.

Characters. Characters are the people or personified animals in the story. Characters are the most important structural element when stories are centered on a character or group of characters. Main characters have many character traits, both good and bad;

that is to say, they have all the characteristics of real people. Inferring a character's traits is an important part of comprehension: Through character traits, readers get to know a character well, and the character seems to come to life. A list of stories with fully developed main characters is included in Figure 9–2. Characters are developed in four ways:

Appearance. Readers learn about characters by the description of their facial features, body shapes, habits of dress, mannerisms, and gestures. On the first page of *Tacky the Penguin* (Lester, 1990), the illustration of Tacky wearing a bright floral shirt and a purple-and-white tie suggests to readers that Tacky is an "odd bird"! Lester confirms this impression as she describes how Tacky behaves.

Action. The best way to learn about characters is through their actions. In Van Allsburg's *The Stranger* (1986), readers deduce that the stranger is Jack Frost because of what he does: He watches geese flying south for the winter, blows a cold wind, labors long hours without becoming tired, has an unusual rapport with wild animals, and is unfamiliar with modern conveniences.

Dialogue. Authors use dialogue to breathe life into characters, develop their personalities, and spark reader interest. Also, dialogue is an effective way to move a story forward.

Monologue. Authors provide insight into characters by revealing their thoughts. In *Sylvester and the Magic Pebble* (Steig, 2006), thoughts and wishes are central to the story. Sylvester, a foolish donkey, wishes to become a rock, and he spends a miserable winter that way. Steig shares the donkey's thinking with readers: He thinks about his parents, who are frantic with worry, and readers learn how Sylvester feels in the spring when his parents picnic on the rock he has become.

Setting. The setting is generally thought of as the location where the story takes place, but it's only one aspect. There are the four aspects of setting:

Location. Many stories take place in predictable settings that don't contribute to a story's effectiveness, but sometimes the location is integral. For instance, the Boston Commons in *Make Way for Ducklings* (McCloskey, 2001) and the Alaskan North Slope in *Julie of the Wolves* (George, 2005) are artfully described and add uniqueness to the story.

Weather. Severe weather, such as a blizzard, a rainstorm, or a tornado, is crucial in some stories. A rainstorm is essential to the plot development in *Bridge to Terabithia* (Paterson, 2005), but in other books, the weather isn't mentioned because it doesn't affect the outcome of the story. Many stories take place on warm, sunny days.

Time Period. For stories set in the past or in the future, the time period is important. If *The Witch of Blackbird Pond* (Speare, 2001) and *Number the Stars* (Lowry, 1998) were set in different eras, for example, they would lose much of their impact. Today, few people would believe that Kit Tyler is a witch or that Jewish people are the focus of government persecution.

Time. This dimension involves both the time of day and the passage of time. Most stories take place during the day, except for scary stories that are set after dark. Many stories span a brief period of time. *Hatchet* (Paulsen, 2007) takes place in less than 2 months. Other stories, such as *The Ugly Duckling* (Mitchell, 2007), span a year—long enough for the main character to grow to maturity.

In some stories, the setting is barely sketched; these are called *backdrop settings*. The setting in many folktales, for instance, is relatively unimportant, and the convention "Once upon a time . . ." is enough to set the stage. In other stories, the setting is elaborated and essential to the story's effectiveness; these settings are called *integral settings* (Lukens, 2006). Stories with integral settings also are listed in Figure 9–2.

Point of View. Stories are written from a particular viewpoint, and this perspective determines to a great extent readers' understanding of the characters and events of the story (Lukens, 2006). Stories written from different viewpoints are presented in Figure 9–2. Here are the points of view:

First-Person Viewpoint. This point of view is used to tell a story through the eyes of one character using the first-person pronoun "I." The narrator, usually the main character, speaks as an eyewitness and a participant in the events. For example, in *The True Story of the 3 Little Pigs!* (Scieszka, 1996), the wolf tries to explain away his bad image in his version of the familiar folktale.

Omniscient Viewpoint. The author is godlike, seeing and knowing all. The author tells readers about the thought processes of each character without worrying about how the information is obtained. *Doctor De Soto* (Steig, 1990), a story about a mouse dentist who outwits a fox with a toothache, is told from the omniscient viewpoint. Steig lets readers know that the fox wants to eat the dentist as soon as his toothache is cured and that the mouse dentist is aware of the fox's thoughts and plans a clever trick.

Limited Omniscient Viewpoint. This viewpoint is used so that readers know the thoughts of one character. It's told in third person, and the author concentrates on the thoughts, feelings, and experiences of the main character or another important character. Gary Paulsen used this viewpoint for *Hatchet* (2007) to be able to explore both Brian's thoughts as he struggled to survive in the wilderness and his coming to terms with his parents' divorce.

Objective Viewpoint. Readers are eyewitnesses to the story and are confined to the immediate scene. They learn only what is visible and audible and are not aware of what any characters think. Most fairy tales, such as *Rumpelstiltskin* (Zelinski, 1996), are told from the objective viewpoint. The focus is on recounting events, not on developing the personalities of the characters.

Some stories are told from multiple viewpoints, such as *Seedfolks* (Fleischman, 2004b), the story of a community garden that brings hope to a blighted neighborhood, and *Witness* (Hesse, 2001), the story of what happened in 1924 when the Ku Klux Klan moved into a Vermont town. Each chapter is told from a first-person viewpoint by a different character.

Theme. Theme is the underlying meaning of a story; it embodies general truths about human nature (Lehr, 1991; Lukens, 2006). Themes usually deal with the characters' emotions and values, and can be stated either explicitly or implicitly: Explicit themes are stated clearly in the story, whereas implicit themes must be inferred. In a fable, the theme is often stated explicitly at the end, but in most stories, the theme emerges through the thoughts, speech, and actions of the characters as they try to overcome the obstacles that prevent them from reaching their goals. In *A Chair for My Mother* (Williams, 1993), for example, a young girl demonstrates the importance of sacrificing personal wants for her family's welfare as she and her mother collect money to buy a new chair after they lose all of their belongings in a fire.

Stories usually have more than one theme, and their themes generally can't be articulated with a single word. *Charlotte's Web* (White, 2004), for example, has several "friendship" themes, one explicitly stated and others that must be inferred. Friendship is a multidimensional theme—qualities of a good friend, unlikely friends, and sacrificing for a friend, for instance. Teachers probe students' thinking as they work to construct a theme and move beyond simplistic one-word labels. The minilesson featured on page 302 demonstrates how Mrs. Miller, a seventh-grade teacher, reviewed the concept of theme. Afterward, her students analyzed the theme of books they were reading in literature circles.

Check the Comp[...]
Instructional Procedures, which follows Chapter 12, for more information on the highlighted terms.

Narrative Devices

Authors use narrative devices to make their writing more vivid and memorable (Lukens, 2006). Figure 9–5 presents a list of literary devices used in stories. Imagery is probably the most commonly used convention; many authors use it as they paint rich word pictures that bring their characters and settings to life. Flashbacks are commonly used in stories, such as the Time Warp Trio series by Jon Scieszka and the Magic Tree House series by Mary Pope Osborne, where readers travel back in time for adventures. Authors also create symbols as they use one thing to represent something else. In Chris Van Allsburg's *The Wretched Stone* (1991), for example, the glowing stone that distracts the crew from reading, from spending time with their friends, and from doing their jobs symbolizes television or computers. To understand the theme of many stories, students must recognize symbols and what they represent. The author's style conveys the tone or overall feeling: Some stories are

Figure 9–5 ◆ Narrative Devices

Dialogue	Written conversation where characters speak to each other. Authors use dialogue to move the story forward while bringing the characters to life.
Flashback	An interruption, often taking readers back to the beginning of the story. Authors use flashbacks in time-warp stories where characters travel back in time to a particular historical period.
Foreshadowing	Hinting at events to come later in the story to build readers' expectations. Authors often use foreshadowing in the beginning of a story.
Imagery	Descriptive words and phrases used to create a picture in readers' minds. Authors also use metaphors and similes as they craft images.
Suspense	An excited uncertainty about the outcome of conflict in a story. Authors use suspense in the middle of the story as characters attempt to thwart one roadblock after another.
Symbolism	A person, place, or thing used to represent something else. For example, a lion often symbolizes courage and a dove symbolizes peace. Authors use symbols to enhance the theme of a story.
Tone	The overall feeling or mood in a story, ranging from humorous to serious and sad. Authors create the tone through their choice of words and use of other narrative devices.

MiniLesson

TOPIC: Analyzing the Theme
GRADE: Seventh Grade
TIME: 20 minutes

Mrs. Miller's seventh graders are studying the Middle Ages and are reading novels set in that period, such as *Catherine, Called Birdy* (Cushman, 1994), in literature circles. Mrs. Miller brings the class together to teach a minilesson on theme before asking the students in each literature circle to analyze the theme of the book they're reading.

1 Introduce the Topic

"It's time to talk about theme because most of you are reaching the end of the book you're reading," Mrs. Miller begins. "Before, I asked you to focus on the setting to learn more about medieval life as you were reading and discussing the book. Now, I want you to think about your book in a different way: I want you to think about the theme. Let's review: Theme is the universal message in the book. It might be about friendship, courage, acceptance, determination, or some other important quality."

2 Share Examples

Mrs. Miller uses *Hatchet* (Paulsen, 2007), a survival story that students read in September, as an example. "Did Brian save himself?" the teacher asks. Everyone agrees that he did. "So what is the theme of the story?" Mrs. Miller asks. Students identify survival as the theme, and Mrs. Miller asks them to explain it in a sentence. Jared suggests, "Sometimes you have to do a lot of disgusting things if you want to survive." Mrs. Miller agrees. Carole offers, "I think the theme is that you may not think that you have the guts and the brains to survive, but if you get trapped in the wilderness, you will find that you do." Again she agrees. Jo-Jo expresses the theme another way: "It's like in the movie *Castaway*. Brian has to get mad—really mad and a little crazy, too, but he gets mad enough to survive. You have to stand up and prove to yourself that you can survive." Again she agrees. Mrs. Miller draws a cluster on the chalkboard and writes *survival* in the center circle. Then she draws out rays and writes on them the sentences that the students offered.

3 Provide Information

"Theme isn't obvious the way plot, characters, and setting are," Mrs. Miller explains. She tells the class that in order to uncover the theme, they need to think about the conflicts facing the character and how the character goes about solving the problem. "Then you have to answer the question: 'What is the author trying to tell me about life?'"

4 Guide Practice

The minilesson ends as the students return to their literature circles to talk about the theme of their book. Mrs. Miller asks them to think of one or more one-word qualities and then to draw out at least three possible sentence-long themes. As they analyze the theme, they draw clusters on chart paper.

5 Assess Learning

Mrs. Miller moves from group to group, talking with students about theme. She checks their clusters and helps them draw out additional themes to add to the cluster.

humorous, some are uplifting celebrations of life, and others are sobering commentaries on society.

Looking at the Text Factors in a Story

Project Mulberry (Park, 2005) is a contemporary realistic novel about Julie Song, a seventh-grade Korean American girl, and her friend, Patrick, who team up to create a project to win a blue ribbon at the state fair. This multicultural novel is appropriate for fourth through eighth graders, and the reading level is fifth grade. Newbery Medal–winning author Linda Sue Park has written a lively, engaging first-person narrative. Julie is a compelling character, and her thoughts and actions drive the story forward. Her mother suggests that she and Patrick raise silkworms for their state fair project, but at first Julie isn't interested because she thinks it's too Korean; instead, she wants to do something "American."

Self-acceptance is the most important theme in this story. The conflict is within Julie as she struggles to fit in while honoring her Korean heritage. Another theme is prejudice: Julie fears that her mother may be racist because she doesn't want her to spend time with Mr. Dixon, the African American man who gives her mulberry leaves to feed to the silkworms. The story emphasizes the importance of doing small things to increase tolerance.

The most interesting feature in the book is a series of conversations between Julie and the book's author that are inserted between chapters. In these exchanges, Julie complains about her character and asks questions about how Ms. Park thinks of ideas and writes books. These witty conservations provide useful insights about the writing process. Most students will enjoy reading them, but those who don't can easily skip over them because they're set off from the rest of the story.

TEXT FACTORS OF INFORMATIONAL BOOKS

Stories have been the principal genre for reading and writing instruction in the primary grades because it's been assumed that constructing stories in the mind is a fundamental way of learning; however, many students prefer to read informational books, and they're able to understand them as well as they do stories (Stead & Duke, 2005). Certainly, students are interested in learning about their world—about the difference between dolphins and whales, how a road is built, threats to the environment of Antarctica, or Amelia Earhart's ill-fated flight around the world—and informational books provide this knowledge. Even young children read informational books to learn about the world around them.

Nonfiction Genres

Informational books provide facts about just about any topic you can think of. Consider, for example: *Flick a Switch: How Electricity Gets to Your Home* (Seuling, 2003), *Taj Mahal* (Arnold & Comora, 2007), *Saguaro Moon: A Desert Journal* (Pratt-Serafini, 2002), *The Brain* (Simon, 2006), *Groundhog Day!* (Gibbons, 2007), *Ancient Inca* (Gruber, 2006), and *Right Dog for the Job: Ira's Path From Service Dog to Guide Dog* (Patent, 2004). Some of these books are picture books that use a combination of text and illustrations to present information, and others are chapter books that depend primarily on the text to provide information.

Other books present information within a story context; the Magic School Bus series is perhaps the best known. In *The Magic School Bus and the Science Fair Expedition* (Cole, 2006), for example, Ms. Frizzle and her class travel through time to learn how scientific thinking developed. The page layout is innovative, with charts and reports containing factual information presented at the outside edges of most pages.

Alphabet Books. Many alphabet books are designed for young children who are learning to identify the letters of the alphabet. Some are predictable, featuring a letter and an illustration of a familiar object on each page, but others, such as *Alphabet Adventure* (Wood, 2001) and *The Alphabet Room* (Pinto, 2003), are more imaginative presentations. Other alphabet books are intended for older students. *The Alphabet From A to Y With Bonus Letter Z!* (Martin & Chast, 2007) is a clever wordplay book, and others, such as *SuperHero ABC* (McLeod, 2006) and *Q Is for Quark: A Science Alphabet Book* (Schwartz, 2001), provide a wealth of information about various topics. In these books, words representing each letter are explained in paragraph-long entries.

Biographies. Students read biographies to learn about a person's life. A wide range of biographies are available for children today, from those featuring well-known personalities, such as *Eleanor Roosevelt: A Life of Discovery* (Freedman, 1997), *Muhammad* (Demi, 2003), *Escape! The Story of the Great Houdini* (Fleischman, 2006), and *Isaac Newton* (Krull, 2006), to those about unsung heroes, such as *Delivering Justice: W. W. Law and the Fight for Civil Rights* (Haskins, 2006). These books are individual biographies because they focus on a single person; others are collective biographies with short vignettes about a group of people who are related in some way, such as *American Heroes* (Delano, 2005) and *Honky-Tonk Heroes and Hillbilly Angels: The Pioneers of Country and Western Music* (George-Warren, 2006). Only a few autobiographies are available for students, but the Meet the Author series of autobiographies for kindergarten through fifth-grade students and the Author at Work series for older students, from Richard C. Owen Publisher, are interesting to students who have read these authors' books. These autobiographies of contemporary authors, including Janet S. Wong's *Before It Wriggles Away* (2006) and Ralph Fletcher's *Reflections* (2007), include information about their lives and insights about their writing.

Expository Text Structures

Informational books are organized in particular ways called *expository text structures* (McGee & Richgels, 1985). Figure 9–6 describes these patterns, presents sample passages and cue words that signal use of each pattern, and suggests a graphic organizer for each structure. When readers are aware of these patterns, it's easier to understand what they're reading, and when writers use these structures to organize their writing, it's easier for readers to understand. Sometimes the pattern is signaled through the title, a topic sentence, or cue words, but sometimes it isn't. Here are the most common expository text structures:

Description. The author describes a topic by listing characteristics, features, and examples. Phrases such as *for example* and *characteristics are* cue this structure. When students delineate any topic, such as the Mississippi River, eagles, or Alaska, they use description.

Sequence. The author lists or explains items or events in numerical, chronological, or alphabetical order. Cue words for sequence include *first, second, third, next, then*, and *finally*. Students use this pattern to write directions for completing a math problem or the stages in an animal's life cycle. The events in a biography are often written in the sequence pattern, too.

Figure 9–6 ◆ The Five Expository Text Structures

Pattern	Graphic Organizer	Sample Passage
Description The author describes a topic by listing characteristics and examples. Cue words include *for example* and *characteristics are*.		The Olympic symbol consists of five interlocking rings. The rings represent the five continents from which athletes come to compete in the games. The rings are colored black, blue, green, red, and yellow. At least one of these colors is found in the flag of every country sending athletes to compete in the Olympic games.
Sequence The author lists items or events in numerical or chronological order. Cue words include *first, second, third, next, then*, and *finally*.	1. _____ 2. _____ 3. _____ 4. _____ 5. _____	The Olympic games began as athletic festivals to honor the Greek gods. The most important festival honored Zeus, the king of the gods, and this festival became the Olympic games in 776 B.C. They ended in A.D. 394, and no games were held for more than 1,500 years. Then the modern Olympics began in 1896. Almost 300 male athletes competed in the first modern Olympics. In the 1900 games, female athletes also competed. The games have continued every four years since 1896 except during World War II.
Comparison The author explains how two or more things are alike and/or how they're different. Cue words include *different, in contrast, alike, same as*, and *on the other hand*.	Alike Different	The modern Olympics is very different than the ancient games. While there were no swimming races, for example, there were chariot races. There were no female contestants, and all athletes competed in the nude. Of course, the ancient and modern Olympics are also alike in many ways. Some events, such as the javelin and discus throws, are the same. Some people say that cheating, professionalism, and nationalism in the modern games are a disgrace to the Olympic tradition, but according to ancient Greek writers, cheating, nationalism, and professionalism existed in their Olympics, too.
Cause and Effect The author lists one or more causes and the resulting effect or effects. Cue words include *reasons why, if . . . then, as a result, therefore*, and *because*.	Cause → Effect #1 Cause → Effect #2 Cause → Effect #3	There are several reasons why so many people attend the Olympic games or watch them on television. One reason is tradition. The name *Olympics* and the torch and flame remind people of the ancient games. People escape the ordinariness of daily life by attending or watching the Olympics. They like to identify with someone else's accomplishment. National pride is another reason, and an athlete's hard-earned victory becomes a nation's victory. There are national medal counts, and people keep track of how many medals their country's team has won.
Problem and Solution The author states a problem and lists one or more solutions. A variation is the question-and-answer format. Cue words include *problem is, dilemma is, puzzle is, solved*, and *question . . . answer*.	Problem → Solution	One problem with the modern Olympics games is that they're very expensive to operate. A stadium, pools, and playing fields must be built for the athletic events, and housing is needed for the athletes. And these facilities are used for only 2 weeks! In 1984, Los Angeles solved these problems by charging a fee for companies to be official sponsors. Many buildings that were already built in the Los Angeles area were also used. The Coliseum where the 1932 games were held was used again, and many local colleges became playing and living sites.

Figure 9–7 ◆ Informational Books Representing the Expository Text Structures

Description

Cooper, M. L. (2007). *Jamestown, 1607*. New York: Holiday House. (M–U)

Floca, B. (2007). *Lightship*. New York: Atheneum. (P–M)

Gibbons, G. (2007). *Groundhog day!* New York: Holiday House. (P)

Simon, S. (2007). *Snakes*. New York: HarperCollins. (M)

Sequence

Cole, J. (2006). *The magic school bus and the science fair expedition*. New York: Scholastic. (M)

Kelly, I. (2007). *It's a butterfly's life*. New York: Holiday House. (P)

Minor, W. (2006). *Yankee Doodle America: The spirit of 1776 from A to Z*. New York: Putnam. (M)

Royston, A. (2006). *The life and times of a drop of water: The water cycle*. Chicago: Raintree. (M)

Comparison

Bidner, J. (2007). *Is my cat a tiger? How your cat compares to its wild cousins*. New York: Lark Books. (M)

Jenkins, S. (2007). *Dogs and cats*. Boston: Houghton Mifflin. (M–U)

Munro, R. (2001). *The inside-outside book of Washington, DC*. San Francisco: Chronicle Books. (M–U)

Thomas, I. (2006). *Scorpion vs. tarantula*. Chicago: Raintree. (M)

Cause-Effect

Brown, C. L. (2006). *The day the dinosaurs died*. New York: HarperCollins. (P)

Burns, L. G. (2007). *Tracking trash: Flotsam, jetsam, and the science of ocean movement*. Boston: Houghton Mifflin. (M–U)

Collins, A. (2006). *Violent weather: Thunderstorms, tornadoes, and hurricanes*. Washington, DC: National Geographic. (M)

Rockwell, A. (2006). *Why are the ice caps melting? The dangers of global warming*. New York: HarperCollins. (P–M)

Problem-Solution

Bledsoe, L. J. (2006). *How to survive in Antarctica*. New York: Holiday House. (M–U)

Calmenson, S. (2007). *May I pet your dog? The how-to guide for kids meeting dogs (and dogs meeting kids)*. New York: Clarion Books. (P–M)

Morrison, M. (2006). *Mysteries of the sea: How divers explore the ocean depths*. Washington, DC: National Geographic. (M)

Thimmesh, C. (2006). *Team moon: How 400,000 people landed Apollo 11 on the moon*. Boston: Houghton Mifflin. (M–U)

Comparison. The author compares two or more things. *Different, in contrast, alike,* and *on the other hand* are cue words and phrases that signal this structure. When students compare and contrast book and movie versions of a story, reptiles and amphibians, or life in ancient Greece with life in ancient Egypt, they use this organizational pattern.

Cause and Effect. The author explains one or more causes and the resulting effect or effects. *Reasons why, if . . . then, as a result, therefore,* and *because* are words and phrases that cue this structure. Explanations of why dinosaurs became extinct, the effects of pollution, or the causes of the Civil War use this pattern.

Problem and Solution. The author states a problem and offers one or more solutions. A variation is the question-and-answer format, in which the writer poses a question and then answers it. Cue words and phrases include *the problem is, the puzzle is, solve,* and *question . . . answer.* Students use this structure when they write about why money was invented, why endangered animals should be saved, or why dams are needed to ensure a permanent water supply.

Figure 9–7 lists books exemplifying each of the expository text structures.

Nonfiction Features

Informational books have unique text features that stories and books of poetry normally don't have, such as margin notes and glossaries. The purpose of these features is to make text easier to read and to facilitate students' comprehension. Here's a list of nonfiction text features:

◆ Headings and subheadings to direct readers' attention to the big ideas
◆ Photographs and drawings to illustrate the big ideas
◆ Figures, maps, and tables to provide diagrams and detailed information visually
◆ Margin notes that provide supplemental information or direct readers to additional information on a topic
◆ Highlighted vocabulary words to identify key terms
◆ A glossary to assist readers in pronouncing and defining key terms
◆ Review sections or charts at the end of chapters or the entire book
◆ An index to assist readers in locating specific information

It's important that students understand these nonfiction text features so they can use them to make their reading more effective and improve their comprehension (Harvey & Goudvis, 2007).

Looking at the Text Factors in an Informational Book

The Down-to-Earth Guide to Global Warming (David & Gordon, 2007) is a 112-page paperback nonfiction book that explains global warming and its disastrous consequences using examples that students can relate to. It's organized into four sections: The first section explains global warming, the second examines weather changes, the next addresses extinction of plants and animals, and the fourth is a call to action. The authors present serious information in an entertaining way using concrete examples, and they provide practical suggestions to show students how they can help combat global warming in their homes and communities.

This informational book is reader-friendly; it incorporates most of the conventions of the nonfiction genre. Readers will find a table of contents and a "dear reader" letter at the beginning. Margin notes are used again and again to highlight important information and to add interesting facts. Key terms and important facts are printed in color and in a font that's larger than the surrounding text. Photos and cartoon illustrations add interest, and diagrams, pie charts, and maps make the information being presented easier to understand. In the back of the book are a glossary, an index, a bibliography, and suggestions for further reading, including websites for students to check out.

The authors use a problem-and-solution organizational structure: The problem is global warming, and the authors suggest ways that children can help to solve the problem, including recycling, conserving power, replacing conventional light bulbs with compact fluorescent light bulbs, using canvas bags instead of paper or plastic bags, and pursuing a career in the environmental field. Other text structures are also used within chapters. For example, the authors describe global warming, explain the water cycle, and identify effects of global warming that children can appreciate, such as worse allergies and less maple syrup for pancakes.

This brightly colored, inviting paperback book is appropriate for third through sixth graders, both for students who are interested in learning more about global warming and for those who are collecting information for a report or other project.

TEXT FACTORS OF POETRY

It's easy to recognize a poem because the text looks different than a page from a story or an informational book. Layout, or the arrangement of words on a page, is an important text factor. Poems are written in a variety of poetic forms, ranging from free verse to haiku, and poets use poetic devices to make their writing more effective. Janeczko (2003) explains that it's important to point out poetic forms and devices to establish a common vocabulary for talking about poems, and because poems are shorter than other types of text, it's often easier for students to examine the text, notice differences in poetic forms, and find examples of poetic devices that authors have used.

Formats of Poetry Books

Three types of poetry books are published for children. Picture-book versions of *The Midnight Ride of Paul Revere* (Longfellow, 2001) and other classic poems are the first type. In these books, each line or stanza is presented and illustrated on a page. Others are specialized collections of poems, either written by a single poet or related to a single theme, such as *Tour America: A Journey Through Poems and Art* (Siebert, 2006). Comprehensive anthologies are the third type, and these books feature 50 to 500 or more poems arranged by category. One of the best is Jack Prelutsky's *The Random House Book of Poetry for Children* (2000). A list of poetry books that includes examples of each format is presented in Figure 9–8.

Sometimes authors use narrative poems, usually free verse, to tell their stories. Karen Hesse's Newbery Medal–winning story, *Out of the Dust* (1999), focuses on the grim realities of living in the Oklahoma dust bowl, and *Witness* (2003) recounts the Ku Klux Klan infiltration into a sleepy Vermont town, told through 12 people's viewpoints. In *Locomotion* (2004), Jacqueline Woodson uses a collection of 60 poems to tell the sad but hopeful story of a New York City fifth grader who grieves and then slowly recovers after his parents are killed in a house fire. Sharon Creech's *Love That Dog* (2001) is a sweet novel written in the form of a boy's journal as he discovers the power and pleasures of poetry.

Figure 9–8　◆　Collections of Poetry

Picture-Book Versions of Single Poems

Carroll, L. (2007). *Jabberwocky* (C. Myers, illus.). New York: Jump at the Sun. (U)

Frost, R. (2001). *Stopping by woods on a snowy evening* (S. Jeffers, illus.). New York: Dutton. (M–U)

Thayer, E. L. (2006). *Casey at the bat.* Tonawanda, NY: Kids Can Press. (M–U)

Westcott, N. B. (2003). *The lady with the alligator purse.* New York: Little, Brown. (P)

Specialized Collections

Florian, D. (2007). *Comets, stars, the moon, and Mars: Space poems and paintings.* Orlando, FL: Harcourt. (M–U)

Havill, J. (2006). *I heard it from Alice Zucchini: Poems about the garden.* San Francisco: Chronicle Books. (P–M)

Issa, K. (2007). *Today and today.* New York: Scholastic. (M–U)

Kuskin, K. (2003). *Moon, have you met my mother? The collected poems of Karla Kuskin.* New York: HarperCollins. (P–M–U)

Larios, J. (2006). *Yellow elephant: A bright bestiary.* Orlando, FL: Harcourt. (P–M)

Prelutsky, J. (2006). *Behold the bold umbrellaphant and other poems.* New York: Greenwillow. (P–M)

Sidman, J. (2006). *Butterfly eyes and other secrets of the meadow.* Boston: Houghton Mifflin. (M–U)

Soto, G. (2006). *A fire in my hands.* Orlando, FL: Harcourt. (U)

Comprehensive Anthologies

Driscoll, M., & Hamilton, M. (Sels.). (2003). *A child's introduction to poetry.* New York: Black Dog & Leventhal. (P–M)

Paschem, E., & Raccah, D. (Sels.). (2005). *Poetry speaks to children.* Naperville, IL: Sourcebooks MediaFusion. (M)

Prelutsky, J. (Sel.). (2000). *The Random House book of poetry for children.* New York: Random House. (P–M–U)

Sword, E. H. (Sel.). (2007). *A child's anthology of poetry.* New York: HarperCollins/Ecco. (M–U)

Poetic Forms

Poets who write for K–8 students employ a variety of poetic forms; some are conventional, but others are innovative. Here are some of the more commonly used poetic forms:

Go to the Buildi
Teaching Skills a..u
Dispositions section of
Chapter 9 on
MyEducationLab.com to
watch second graders Rakie
and Michael write an
acrostic poem together.

Rhymed Verse. The most common type of poetry is rhymed verse, as in *My Parents Think I'm Sleeping* (Prelutsky, 2007) and *Today at the Bluebird Café: A Branchful of Birds* (Ruddell, 2007). Poets use various rhyme schemes, including limericks, and the effect of the rhyming words is a poem that's fun to read and listen to when it's read aloud.

Narrative Poems. Poems that tell a story are *narrative poems*. Perhaps our best-known narrative poem is Clement Moore's classic, "The Night Before Christmas." Other examples include Longfellow's *The Midnight Ride of Paul Revere* (2001), illustrated by Christopher Bing, and *Casey at the Bat* (Thayer, 2006).

Haiku. Haiku is a Japanese poetic form that contains just 17 syllables arranged in three lines of 5, 7, and 5 syllables. It's a concise form, much like a telegram, and the poems normally deal with nature, presenting a single clear image. Books of haiku to share with students include *Dogku* (Clements, 2007) and *Cool Melons—Turn to Frogs! The Life and Poems of Issa* (Gollub, 2004). The artwork in these picture books may give students ideas for illustrating their own haiku poems.

Free Verse. Unrhymed poetry is *free verse*. Word choice and visual images take on greater importance in free verse, and rhythm is less important than in other types of poetry. *The Friendly Four* (Greenfield, 2006) and *Canto Familiar* (Soto, 2007) are two collections of free verse. Poems for two voices are a unique form of free verse, written in two columns, side by side, and the columns are read simultaneously by two readers. The best-known collection is Paul Fleischman's Newbery Award–winning *Joyful Noise: Poems for Two Voices* (2004a).

Odes. These poems celebrate everyday objects, especially those things that aren't usually appreciated. The unrhymed poem, written directly to that object, tells what's good about the thing and why it's valued. The ode is a venerable poetic form, going back to ancient Greece. Traditionally, odes were sophisticated lyrical verses, such as Keats's "Ode to a Nightingale," but Chilean poet Pablo Neruda (2000) introduced this contemporary variation that's more informal. The best collection of odes for students is Gary Soto's *Neighborhood Odes* (2005), which celebrates everyday things, such as water sprinklers and tennis shoes, in the Mexican American community in Fresno, California, where he grew up.

Concrete Poems. The words and lines in concrete poems are arranged on the page to help convey the meaning. When the words and lines form a picture or outline the objects they describe, they're called *shape poems*. Sometimes the layout of words, lines, and stanzas is spread across a page or two to emphasize the meaning. *A Poke in the I: A Collection of Concrete Poems* (Janeczko, 2005) and *Doodle Dandies: Poems That Take Shape* (Lewis, 2002) are two collections of concrete poems.

To learn about other poetic forms, check *Handbook of Poetic Forms* (Padgett, 2007). Students use some of these forms when they write their own poems, including odes and concrete poems.

Poetry Unit
These fifth graders are studying Jack Prelutsky and reading his poems. They especially enjoy his CD of *The New Kid on the Block*. The students pick favorite poems and copy them on chart paper. Next, they choose a familiar tune, such as "Twinkle, Twinkle, Little Star" or "I've Been Working on the Railroad," that fits the cadence of the poem and sing the poem to that tune. Singing poems is a favorite daily activity. They're also writing their own verses collaboratively using Prelutsky's poetic forms, such as "My Fish Can Ride a Bicycle," that they will make into class books.

Poetic Devices

Poetic devices are especially important tools because poets express their ideas very concisely. Every word counts! Here are some of the poetic devices they use:

- Assonance: the type of alliteration where vowel sounds are repeated in nearby words.
- Consonance: the type of alliteration where consonant sounds are repeated in nearby words.
- Imagery: words and phrases that appeal to the senses and evoke mental pictures.
- Metaphor: a comparison between two unlikely things, without using *like* or *as*.
- Onomatopoeia: words that imitate sounds.
- Repetition: words, phrases, or lines that are repeated for special effect.
- Rhyme: words that end with similar sounds used at the end of the lines.
- Rhythm: the internal beat in a poem that's felt when poetry is read aloud.
- Simile: a comparison incorporating the word *like* or *as*.

Narrative and poetic devices are similar, and many of them, such as imagery and metaphor, are important in both genres.

Poets use other conventions, too. Capitalization and punctuation are used differently; poets choose where to use capital letters and whether or when to add punctuation marks. They think about the meaning they're conveying and the rhythm of their writing as they decide how to break poems into lines and whether to divide the lines into stanzas. Layout is another consideration: The arrangement of lines on the page is especially important in concrete poems, but it matters for all poems.

Looking at the Text Factors in a Book of Poetry

This Is Just to Say: Poems of Apology and Forgiveness (Sidman, 2007) is presented as a collection of poems written and compiled by Mrs. Merz's sixth graders at the Florence Scribner School as part of a poetry unit. In the introduction, student-editor Anthony K. explains that he and his classmates wrote the apology poems using William Carlos Williams's poem "This Is Just to Say" as a model, and then the recipients wrote poems of forgiveness back to the students.

The book is arranged in two parts. The first part, Apologies, contains the sixth graders' apology poems, with each student's poem featured on a separate page with a drawing of the student-author and other illustrations related to the content of the poem. Readers are told that the line drawings and mixed-media illustrations were created by Bao Vang, an artistic student in the class. The second part, Responses, contains the forgiveness poems that the sixth graders received. These poems are arranged in the same order as the apology poems, with each one on a separate page and accompanied by Bao's whimsical illustrations.

Short poems written on a wide variety of topics are included in this captivating anthology; some are humorous, and others heartfelt or sad. José, for example, wrote an apology to his dad for throwing a rock and breaking the garage window. Other topics include stealing brownies, the death of a pet, insensitive comments, and rough play during a dodge ball game. José's dad responds, telling him to forget about the broken window and expressing his pride in his son's accomplishments. Other recipients' poems convey feelings of love, grief, and acceptance.

Most of the poems follow the pattern of William Carlos Williams's model poem, but many of the students modified it to fit their ideas and words. A handful use different forms, including haiku, poems for two voices, odes, found poems, and free verse. The poems are typed in different fonts, and their arrangement on the page varies, too. The most striking feature of the poems is the range of voices: Some sound as if they were written by sixth-grade girls, some by boys, and others by siblings, parents, and grandparents.

In the author biography, Joyce Sidman confesses that she assumed the personas of the students and the recipients and wrote the poems in this book. Years before, she'd written an apology poem with a class of fourth graders and sent it to her mother who responded with a letter of forgiveness, and the idea for this book was born! This collection of poems is appropriate for third through sixth graders. Many of the poems can be used as models for students' writing, and teachers may want to have their students write their own collections of apology and forgiveness poems.

TEACHING STUDENTS ABOUT TEXT FACTORS

Researchers have documented that when teachers teach students about text factors, their comprehension increases (Fisher, Frey, & Lapp, 2008; Sweet & Snow, 2003). In addition, when students are familiar with the genres, organizational patterns, and literary devices in books they're reading, they're better able to create those text factors in their own writing (Buss & Karnowski, 2002). It's not enough to focus on stories, however; students need to learn about a variety of genres. In the vignette at the beginning of the chapter, Mr. Abrams used text factors to scaffold his students' learning about frogs. He taught them about the unique characteristics of informational books, emphasized text structures through the questions he asked, and used graphic organizers to help students visualize big ideas.

Minilessons

Teachers teach students about text factors directly—often through minilessons (Simon, 2005). They highlight a genre, explain its characteristics, and then read aloud books representing that genre, modeling their thinking about text factors. Later, students make charts of the information they're learning and hang them in the classroom. Similarly, teachers introduce structural patterns and have students examine how authors use them to organize a book or an excerpt from a book they're reading. Students often create graphic organizers to visualize the structure of informational books they're reading and appreciate how the organization emphasizes the big ideas (Opitz, Ford, & Zbaracki, 2006). Teachers also focus on the literary devices that authors use to make their writing more vivid and the conventions that make a text more reader-friendly. Students often collect sentences with narrative devices from stories they're reading and lines of poetry with poetic devices from poems to share with classmates, and they create charts with nonfiction features they've found in books to incorporate in reports they're writing.

Comprehension Strategies

It's not enough that students can name the characteristics of a myth, identify cue words that signal expository text structures, or define *metaphor* or *assonance*. The goal is for students to actually use what they've learned about text factors when they're reading and writing. The comprehension strategy they use when they're applying what they've learned is called *noticing text factors*; it involves considering genre, recognizing text structure, and attending to literary devices. Lattimer (2003) explains the strategy this way: Students need to think about "what to expect from a text, how to approach it, and what to take away from it" (p. 12). Teachers teach students about text factors through minilessons and other activities, but the last step is to help students internalize the information and apply it when they're reading and writing. One way teachers do this is by demonstrating how they use the strategy as they read books aloud using think-alouds (Harvey & Goudvis, 2007). Teachers also use think-alouds to demonstrate this strategy as they do modeled and shared writing.

Reading and Writing Activities

Students need opportunities to read books and listen to teachers read books aloud while they're learning about text factors. Lattimer (2003) recommends teaching genre studies where students learn about a genre while they're reading and exploring books representing that genre and then apply what they're learning through writing. For example, a small group of fifth graders wrote this poem for two voices as a project after reading *Number the Stars* (Lowry, 1998), the story of the friendship between two Danish girls, a Christian and a Jew, during World War II:

Literacy Portraits: VIEWING GUIDE

Ms. Janusz's classroom is filled with stories and informational books. She uses these books for instructional purposes, and plenty of books are available for students to read independently. These second graders know about genres. They can identify books representing each genre and talk about the differences between them. Ms. Janusz teaches minilessons on genres and points out the genre of books she's reading aloud. She doesn't call all books "stories." Go to the Literacy Profiles section of the MyEducationLab website and click on Rhiannon's Student Interview to watch her compare fiction and nonfiction. As you listen to Rhiannon, think about the information provided in this chapter. What conclusions can you draw about what Ms. Janusz has taught about text factors? Also, look at other video clips of Rhiannon to see how she applies her knowledge about genres in both reading and writing.

myeducationlab

I am Annemarie, a Christian.

I hate this war.

The Nazis want to kill my friend.
Why?
I want to help my friend.

My mother will take you to my uncle.
He's a fisherman.

He will hide you on his ship.

He will take you to Sweden.
To freedom.
I am Annemarie, a Christian.

I want to help my friend.

I hate this war.

I am Ellen, a Jew.
I hate this war.
The Nazis want to kill me.

Why?

Can you help me?

Your uncle is a fisherman?

He will hide me on his ship?

To freedom.

I am Ellen, a Jew.

I need the help of my friends
or I will die.
I hate this war.

The fifth graders' choice of this poetic form is especially appropriate because it highlights one of the story's themes: These characters are very much alike even though one is Christian and the other is Jewish. The students knew how to write poems for two voices because they participated in a genre study about poetry several months earlier.

Assessing Students' Knowledge of Text Factors

Although there aren't formal tests to assess students' knowledge of text factors, students demonstrate their knowledge in a variety of ways:

◆ Talk about the characteristics of the genre in book talks and grand conversations
◆ Use their understanding of story elements to explain themes in reading log entries
◆ Apply their knowledge of genre when writing in response to prompts for district and state writing assessments
◆ Document their understanding of text structures as they make graphic organizers
◆ Write poems that are patterned after poems they've read
◆ Choose sentences with literary devices when asked to share favorite sentences with the class from a book they're reading
◆ Incorporate literary devices in their own writing

It's up to teachers to notice how students are applying their knowledge about text factors, and to find new ways for students to share their understanding.

> **Be Strategic!**
>
> **Comprehension Strategies**
>
> Students apply what they've learned about text factors when they use these comprehension strategies:
>
> ▶ Consider genre
> ▶ Recognize text structure
> ▶ Attend to literary devices
>
> When students notice text factors, they're better able to understand what they're reading.

Chapter 9
Review

How Effective Teachers Facilitate Students' Comprehension of Text Factors

▶ Teachers teach students that stories have unique text factors: narrative genres, story elements, and narrative devices.

▶ Teachers teach students that informational books have unique text factors: nonfiction genres, expository text structures, and nonfiction features.

▶ Teachers teach students that poems have unique text factors: book formats, poetic forms, and poetic devices.

▶ Teachers encourage students to apply their knowledge of text factors when they're reading and writing.

PEARSON
myeducationlab
Where the Classroom Comes to Life

Go to MyEducationLab at www.myeducationlab.com to deepen your understanding of the concepts presented in this chapter:

▶ Evaluate the second graders' developing knowledge about fiction and nonfiction genres by viewing video segments in the Literacy Portraits.
▶ Check your understanding of chapter concepts with the multiple-choice and essay quizzes in the Study Plan.
▶ Apply some of the main ideas discussed in the chapter in the Activities and Applications section of the website.
▶ Practice what you've learned in this chapter in Building Teaching Skills and Dispositions before applying the ideas in your own classroom.

PROFESSIONAL REFERENCES

Applebee, A. N. (1978). *Child's concept of story: Ages 2–17*. Chicago: University of Chicago Press.

Appleyard, J. A. (1994) *Becoming a reader: The experience of fiction from childhood to adulthood*. New York: Cambridge University Press.

Buss, K., & Karnowski, L. (2000). *Reading and writing literary genres*. Newark, DE: International Reading Association.

Fisher, D., Frey, N., & Lapp, D. (2008). Shared readings: Modeling comprehension, vocabulary, text structures, and text features for older readers. *The Reading Teacher, 61*, 548–556.

Harvey, S., & Goudvis, A. (2007). *Strategies that work: Teaching comprehension for understanding and engagement* (2nd ed.). York, ME: Stenhouse.

Janeczko, P. B. (2003). *Opening a door: Reading poetry in the middle school classroom*. New York: Scholastic.

Kiefer, B. Z., Price-Dennis, D., & Ryan, C. L. (2006). Children's books in a multimodal age. *Language Arts, 84*, 92–98.

Lattimer, H. (2003). *Thinking through genre*. Portland, ME: Stenhouse.

Lehr, S. S. (1991). *The child's developing sense of theme: Responses to literature*. New York: Teachers College Press.

Lukens, R. J. (2006). *A critical handbook of children's literature* (8th ed.). Boston: Allyn & Bacon.

McGee, L. M., & Richgels, D. J. (1985). Teaching expository text structures to elementary students. *The Reading Teacher, 38*, 739–745.

Meyer, B. J. F., & Poon, L. W. (2004). Effects of structure strategy training and signaling on recall of text. In R. B. Ruddell & N. J. Unrau (Eds.), *Theoretical models and processes of reading* (5th ed., pp. 810–850). Newark, DE: International Reading Association.

of these stories in their basal readers and during literature circles, and Miss Paniccia has read others aloud. The stories they've been writing accompany the illustrations in *The Mysteries of Harris Burdick* (Van Allsburg, 1996).

The Chris Van Allsburg unit began in September when Miss Paniccia read aloud *Jumanji* (Van Allsburg, 1982), the story of two children who play a jungle adventure board game that comes to life. She also read aloud the sequel, *Zathura* (2002), about a space adventure board game, and students watched the movie version. They also made board games and wrote directions for playing them. She used the story to emphasize the importance of listening to directions in the classroom, following parents' directions at home, and reading directions on state achievement tests.

Miss Paniccia regularly teaches **minilessons** on writing strategies that students then apply in their own writing. She began with a series of lessons on revising and proofreading that students use in writing workshop. Next, she taught lessons about the elements of story structure. Posters about each story element hang in the classroom, testimony to the learning taking place there. Students apply what they've learned as they craft their own stories. They use the writing process, as shown in the box on page 322, to draft and refine their stories. Last year, these students took an afterschool touchtyping course, so they know the fundamentals of finger placement on the keyboard and are developing typing fluency as they use the AlphaSmart® word processing machines.

Month after month, the students have been writing stories. Seth's story for the illustration entitled "Mr. Linden's Library" is shown in the box on page 323. The illustration depicts a girl sleeping in bed with an open book beside her; vines are growing out of the book and spreading across her bed. As you read Seth's story, you'll see how his story developed from the illustration and how he applied what he's learned about story structure.

Today during writing workshop, Miss Paniccia is meeting with Alfonso, Martha, and Yimleej to proofread their stories and correct errors. Other students are word processing their last stories or printing out final copies and gluing them into their books. Miguel and Lindsey have finished their books, so they're helping classmates word process, transfer to the computer, and print out their stories. Miss Paniccia's optimistic that everyone will be finished by lunchtime tomorrow. She plans to start author's chair during writing workshop tomorrow: Students will take turns reading their favorite stories aloud to classmates. Author's chair is a popular classroom activity; most students are eager to share their stories, and their classmates enjoy listening to them because they've learned how to read with expression and hold their classmates' interest.

Last week, the students created this introductory page for their story collections:

> *Thirty years ago a man named Harris Burdick came by Peter Wenders's publishing office. Mr. Burdick claimed that he had written 15 stories and illustrated them. All he brought with him on that day were the illustrations with titles. The next day Harris Burdick was going to bring the stories to Mr. Wenders, but he never returned. In fact, Harris Burdick was never seen again.*
>
> *Chris Van Allsburg met with Mr. Wenders and that is where he came across the illustrations. Mr. Wenders handed Mr. Van Allsburg a dust-covered box full of*

Students' Writing Process Activities

Stage	Activity	Description
Prewriting	Story Cards	Students create story cards to develop their ideas, characters, setting, problem, climax, and solution.
	One-On-One	Students meet with a classmate to share their story cards and talk out their ideas.
Drafting	Rough Drafts	Students write their rough drafts in pencil, working from their story cards.
Revising	Writing Groups	Students meet with two classmates to share their rough drafts, getting feedback about their stories. Then they make revisions based on the feedback they received.
	Conference With Miss P.	They recopy their drafts in pen and have Miss Paniccia read and respond to their stories. Students make more revisions based on their teacher's feedback.
Editing	Proofreading	Students proofread their drafts and correct the errors they notice. Then they have two classmates proofread their drafts to identify and correct remaining spelling, capitalization, punctuation, and grammar errors.
	Word Processing	Students word process their stories using word processing machines. Then they transfer their stories to the classroom computer, put them into their own files, and print out a copy in a legible font.
	Conference With Miss P.	Students meet with Miss Paniccia to proofread and correct the remaining errors.
Publishing	Final Copy	Students print out a final copy, glue the pages into a book, and add illustrations.

drawings, and Chris Van Allsburg was inspired to reproduce them for children across the nation.

Right here in room 30, we have worked hard all year creating stories for the illustrations. Even though we have completed our stories, the mystery of Harris Burdick still remains.

It's a class collaboration: Miss Paniccia and the students developed the introduction together, and copies were made for each student. By collaborating, the teacher ensured that they had a useful introduction for their books.

After beginning the author study in September, Miss Paniccia continued to read stories each month. In October, she and her students read *The Stranger* (Van Allsburg, 1986), a story included in their basal readers. In the story, the Baileys take in an injured stranger, a man who doesn't speak or seem to know who he is, but he appears to be attuned with the seasons and has an amazing connection with wild animals. The stranger is Jack Frost, although it's never explicitly stated in the story. They take several days to read the story. On the first day, the teacher introduced the key vocabulary

Seth's Story About "Mr. Linden's Library"

"I would like to check out this book," Sally Olger said. The book that she wanted to check out was called <u>Adventures in the Wild</u>. She had skipped as she had gone up to the counter. Sally loved to go to this library. It was owned by Mr. Linden, so everybody just called it Mr. Linden's library.

The expression on the man at the counter's face changed when he saw the book that Sally was holding. The man warned Sally that if she left the book out on one page for over an hour, something dangerous would come out of the book.

Sally didn't really hear or care about what the man said. She checked out the book and started reading it in bed that night. The book was really interesting. It had tons of short stories in it. At 12:00 midnight, Sally turned the page to a story called "Lost in the Jungle," yawned, and fell asleep. At 1:00 A.M. vines started to grow out of the book. He had warned her about the book. Now it was too late. Soon Sally's whole room was covered in vines. By 2:00, they were making their way up the stairs.

BBBRRRRIIIIINNNNNNGGGGGG! went Sally's alarm clock.

"AAAAAAAHHHHHHHH!" screamed Sally. Now the whole house was covered in vines. Sally slowly made her way to her parents' bedroom through the vines and woke them up. They screamed too. As quickly as possible (which wasn't very fast) the Olgers got out of their house, got in their car and drove to the library. They told the man at the desk what had happened. He said that the only way to get rid of the vines was to cut their roots (they would be sticking right out of the book) and then haul all of the vines off to the dump. Luckily, the town dump wasn't very far away from the Olgers' house.

By the time Mr. Olger had found and cut the roots away from the book, Sally and Mrs. Olger had rounded up the whole neighborhood to help take the vines to the dump. By 5:00 P.M. in the afternoon they had cleared away all of the vines. Sally had learned her lesson to listen when someone warns you about something.

---

words, including *autumn*, *etched*, and *peculiar*, and the class previewed the story, examining the illustrations and making predictions. Miss Paniccia used a shared reading procedure: The students listened to the story read aloud on the professional CD that accompanies the textbook and followed along in their textbooks. Some inferred that the stranger is Jack Frost, but others didn't. That's when the teacher introduced the drawing inferences strategy, which she called "reading between the lines."

They read the story a second time, searching for clues that led their classmates to guess that the stranger is Jack Frost, and afterward made a cluster, a spider web–like diagram, with the clues. They wrote the words *The Stranger* in the center circle, drew out rays from this circle, and wrote these clues at the end of each one: he wears odd clothing, is confused by buttons, and works hard but doesn't get tired. Afterward, they completed page 156 in the Practice Book that accompanies the textbook as well as other pages that emphasize comprehension. Then Miss Paniccia asked students to closely examine the illustrations in the story. They noticed how the perspective in the illustrations varies to draw readers into the scenes and create the mood. The students read the story a third time with partners, talking about how Chris Van Allsburg used viewpoint in the illustrations.

In November, students read other books by Chris Van Allsburg in literature circles. Miss Paniccia presented book talks about these four books: *Two Bad Ants* (Van Allsburg, 1988), *Just a Dream* (Van Allsburg, 1990), *The Sweetest Fig* (Van Allsburg, 1993b), and *The Wreck of the Zephyr* (Van Allsburg, 1983). Then students formed small groups to read one of the books. They assumed roles and took on responsibilities in the small groups as they read and discussed the book. Then students read another of the books during a second literature circle in January.

Miss Paniccia read aloud the award-winning holiday story *The Polar Express* (Van Allsburg, 2005) in December. In the story, being able to hear Santa's bells jiggle represents belief in the magic of Christmas, so Miss Paniccia gave each student a small bell to jiggle each time it was mentioned in the story. The students discussed the story in a grand conversation; much of their discussion focused on the theme and how the author states it explicitly at the end of the story. "What an awesome story!" Hunter concluded, and his classmates agreed. They also talked about their own holiday traditions and wrote about them during writing workshop.

They continued to read other books by Chris Van Allsburg: In February, Miss Paniccia read *The Garden of Abdul Gasazi* (Van Allsburg, 1993a), and in March, she read *The Wretched Stone* (Van Allsburg, 1991). These books are difficult for students to comprehend because they have to make inferences: In *The Garden of Abdul Gasazi*, readers have to decide whether the magician really changes the dog into a duck, and in *The Wretched Stone*, they need to understand that the stone is a symbol, representing television, computers, or video games. Miss Paniccia taught a series of minilessons on drawing inferences, and she modeled the strategy as she reread the stories, showing the fourth graders how to use their background knowledge, the clues in the story, and self-questions to read between the lines. Then students reread the stories with partners, talked about clues in the stories, and made inferences as their teacher had.

In March, Miss Paniccia also taught a series of minilessons on the fantasy genre. Then students divided into small groups to reread the Chris Van Allsburg books and examine them for fantasy characteristics. They developed a chart with the titles of the books written across the top and the characteristics of fantasies written down the left side. Then they completed the chart by indicating how the characteristics are represented in each book.

This month, students are reading Chris Van Allsburg's books independently; some students are reading those they haven't yet read, and others are rereading favorite ones. As they read, they search for the white dog that Van Allsburg includes in each book. In some books, such as *The Garden of Abdul Gasazi*, the dog is alive, but in others, he's a puppet, a hood ornament, or a picture. In several books, only a small part of him shows; in *The Wretched Stone*, for example, you see only his tail on one page. In addition, they continue to notice the fantasy elements of the stories, they draw inferences when needed, and they reflect on Van Allsburg's use of perspective in his illustrations.

There's no one best way to teach reading and writing. Instead, teachers create a balanced literacy program using two or more approaches. Four of the most commonly used literacy programs for kindergarten through eighth grade are basal reading programs, literature focus units, literature circles, and reading and writing workshop. Miss Paniccia's author study in the vignette was successful because her literacy program was balanced with a combination of explicit instruction, small-group and whole-class literacy activities, and independent reading and writing opportunities.

By combining several instructional approaches, Miss Paniccia juggled the district's adopted basal reading program with other instructional approaches that enriched and extended her students' literacy learning.

TEACHING WITH BASAL READING PROGRAMS

Commercial reading programs, commonly called *basal readers*, have been a staple in reading instruction for 150 years. Before 1850, William Holmes McGuffey wrote the McGuffey Readers, the first textbooks published with increasingly challenging books designed for each grade level. The lessons featured literature selections that emphasized religious and patriotic values. Students used phonics to sound out words, studied vocabulary words in the context of stories, and practiced proper enunciation as they read aloud to classmates. These books were widely used until the beginning of the 20th century. The Scott Foresman basal reading program, introduced in 1930 and used through the 1960s, is probably the most famous; the first-grade textbooks featured stories about two children named Dick and Jane, their little sister Sally, their pets Puff and Spot, and their parents. The first-grade books relied on the repetition of words through contrived sentences such as "See Jane. See Sally. See Jane and Sally." to teach words. Students were expected to memorize words rather than use phonics to decode them. This whole-word method was known as "look and say." The Scott Foresman program has been criticized for its lack of phonics instruction as well as for centering stories on an "ideal" middle-class white family.

Today's basal readers include more authentic literature selections that celebrate diverse cultures, and they emphasize an organized presentation of strategies and skills, especially phonics in the primary grades. Kate Walsh (2003) reviewed five widely used series and found that they all provide visually stimulating artwork to engage students, similar methods of teaching decoding and comprehension, and teachers' guides with detailed lesson plans. She also uncovered a common problem: None of the programs provided for the sustained development of students' background knowledge, but when students don't develop a strong foundation of world and word knowledge, they have difficulty reading and understanding more conceptually demanding books, beginning at fourth-grade level. This drop in achievement is known as the "fourth-grade slump," and children from economically disadvantaged families are more likely to fall behind their classmates (Chall, Jacobs, & Baldwin, 1991).

Publishers of basal reading textbooks tout their programs as complete literacy programs containing all the materials needed for students to become successful readers. The accessibility of reading materials is one advantage: Teachers have copies of grade-level textbooks for every student. The instructional program is planned for them; teachers follow step-by-step directions to teach strategies and skills, and workbooks provide practice materials. An overview of basal reading programs is presented on page 326. It's unrealistic, however, to assume that any commercial reading program could be a complete literacy program. Teachers who have students reading above or below grade level need reading materials at their students' levels. In addition, students need many more opportunities to listen to books read aloud and to read and reread books than are provided in a basal reading program. In addition, a complete literacy program involves more than reading; students need opportunities to learn the writing process, draft and refine compositions, and learn writing strategies and skills.

OVERVIEW OF THE INSTRUCTIONAL APPROACH

Basal Reading Programs

TOPIC	DESCRIPTION
Purpose	To teach the strategies and skills that successful readers need using an organized program that includes grade-level reading selections, workbook practice assignments, and frequent testing.
Components	Basal reading programs involve five components: reading the selections in the grade-level textbook, instruction on strategies and skills, workbook assignments, independent reading opportunities, and a management plan that includes flexible grouping and regular assessment.
Theory Base	Basal reading programs are based on behaviorism because teachers provide explicit instruction and students are passive rather than active learners.
Applications	Basal reading programs organize instruction into units with weeklong lessons that include reading, strategy and skill instruction, and workbook activities. They should be used with other instructional approaches to ensure that students read books at their instructional levels and have opportunities to participate in writing projects.
Strengths	• Textbooks are aligned with grade-level standards. • Students read selections at their grade level. • Teachers teach strategies and skills in a sequential program, and students practice them through reading and workbook assignments. • The teacher's guide provides detailed instructions for teaching reading. • Assessment materials are included in the program.
Limitations	• Selections may be too difficult for some students and too easy for others. • Selections may lack the authenticity of good literature or not include a variety of genres. • Programs include many workbook assignments. • Most instruction is presented to the whole class.

Components of Basal Reading Programs

Even though there are a number of commercial programs available today, most include these components:

◆ Selections in grade-level textbooks
◆ Instruction about decoding and comprehension strategies and skills
◆ Workbook assignments
◆ Independent reading opportunities

Basal readers are recognized for their strong skills component: Teachers teach skills in a predetermined sequence, and students apply what they're learning in the textbook selections they read and the workbook assignments they complete.

Selections in Grade-Level Textbooks. Basal reading programs are organized into units on topics such as challenges, folktales, and friends. Each unit includes four to six weeklong lessons, each with a featured selection. The selections in the kindergarten and first-grade textbooks contain decodable text so that children can apply the phonics skills they're learning, but as students develop stronger word-identification skills and a bank of familiar high-frequency words, textbooks transition to literature selections that were originally published as trade books.

Everyone reads the same selections in the grade-level textbook each week, no matter their reading level. These commercial programs argue that it's important to expose all students to grade-level instruction because some students, especially minority students, have been denied equal access to instruction. The teacher's guide provides suggestions for supporting struggling readers and English learners. Many programs also provide video, audio, and Internet resources. Audiotapes of the selections, which teachers often play as students follow along in their copies of the textbook, are an especially useful resource. After this shared reading experience, some less successful readers can then read the selection, but many teachers complain that a few students can't read the selections no matter how much support they provide.

Instruction in Strategies and Skills. Teachers use basal reading programs to deliver explicit and systematic instruction that is aligned with state literacy outcomes and standards. Most textbooks include instruction in phonemic awareness, phonics, high-frequency words, word-identification skills, spelling, grammar, and writing mechanics (capitalization and punctuation). The programs also emphasize comprehension strategies, including evaluating, monitoring, predicting, questioning, summarizing, and visualizing.

The teacher's guide provides detailed lesson plans for teaching strategies and skills with each selection. Teachers explain the strategies and skills and model their use as they read with students, then students apply them as they read selections and complete workbook pages. Scope-and-sequence charts for each grade level that are included in the teacher's guide show the order for teaching strategies and skills and explain how they're introduced at one grade level and reinforced and expanded at the next level. These programs claim that it's their explicit, systematic instruction that ensures success.

Workbook Assignments. Students complete workbook pages before, during, and after reading each selection to reinforce instruction; 10 to 12 workbook pages that focus on phonics, vocabulary, comprehension, grammar, spelling, and writing accompany each selection. On these pages, students write words, letters, or sentences, match words and sentences, or complete graphic organizers.

Teachers vary how they use the workbook pages. Once students know how to complete a workbook page, such as the pages that focus on practicing spelling words, they work independently or with partners. However, for more-challenging assignments, such as those dealing with comprehension strategies or newly introduced skills, teachers have the whole class do the assignment together at their direction. Teachers also devise various approaches for monitoring students' completion of workbook assignments: They may have students check their own work, or they may grade the assignments themselves.

Independent Reading Opportunities. Most basal reading programs include a collection of easy, on-grade-level, and challenging paperback books for students to read independently. There are multiple copies of each book, and teachers set out some of these books for students to read after finishing each selection. Some of these books, especially in the primary grades, have been written to reinforce phonics skills and vocabulary words, but others are trade books. The goal is for the collection to meet the needs of all students, but sometimes teachers still need to supplement with much easier books for English learners or struggling readers.

Check the Compendium of Instructional Procedures, which follows Chapter 12, for more information on the highlighted terms.

When teachers implement basal reading programs, they use the reading process, even though many activities are different than in other approaches:

Prereading. Teachers follow directions in the teacher's guide to activate and build students' background knowledge, introduce vocabulary, teach word-identification and comprehension strategies, and preview the selection.

Reading. Students read the selection independently, but if it's too difficult, teachers read it aloud or play an audiotape before students read it themselves.

Responding. Teachers follow directions in the teacher's guide to enhance students' comprehension by asking questions about the author's purpose, modeling **think-alouds**, encouraging students to draw inferences, and summarizing the selection. Students also complete workbook assignments that focus on comprehension.

Exploring. Teachers teach phonics, word analysis, spelling, and grammar skills, and students practice the skills by completing workbook assignments. They also teach students about authors, genres, and text structures.

Applying. Students read related selections in the basal reader or in other books that accompany the program and participate in writing activities related to the selection or genre being studied.

One of the most striking differences is that students complete practice activities in workbooks during several of the stages rather than applying what they're learning in more authentic ways.

Materials Included in Basal Reading Programs

At the center of a basal reading program is the student textbook or anthology. In the primary grades, two or more books are provided at each grade level, and in fourth through sixth grades, there's usually one book. Most basal reading programs end in sixth grade. The books are colorful and inviting, often featuring pictures of children and animals on the covers of primary-level books and exciting adventures and fanciful locations on the covers of books for grades 4 through 6. The selections are grouped into units, and each unit includes stories, poems, and informational articles. Many multicultural selections have been added, and illustrations usually feature ethnically diverse people. Information about authors and illustrators is provided for many selections. Textbooks contain a table of contents and a glossary.

Commercial reading programs provide a wide variety of materials to support student learning. Consumable workbooks are probably the best-known support material; students write letters, words, and sentences in these books to practice phonics, comprehension, and vocabulary strategies and skills. Big books and kits with letter and word cards, wall charts, and manipulatives are available for kindergarten and first-grade programs. Black-line masters of parent letters are also available.

Some multimedia materials, including audiocassettes, CD-ROMs, and videos, are included, which teachers can use at listening centers and computer centers. Collections of trade books are available for each grade level to provide supplemental reading materials. In the primary grades, many books have decodable text to provide practice on phonics skills and high-frequency words; in the upper grades, the books are related to unit topics.

Basal reading programs also offer a variety of assessment tools. Teachers use placement evaluations or informal reading inventories to determine students' reading levels and for placement in reading groups. They use running records to informally monitor students' reading. There are also selection and unit tests to determine students' phonics, vocabulary, and comprehension achievement. Information is provided on how to administer the assessments and analyze the results.

A teacher's instructional guidebook is provided for each grade level. This oversize handbook gives comprehensive information about how to plan lessons, teach the selections, and assess students' progress. The selections are shown in reduced size in the guidebook, and each page includes background information about the selection, instructions for reading the selections, and ideas for coordinating skill and strategy instruction. In addition, information is presented about which supplemental books to use with each selection and how to assess students' learning. Figure 10–1 summarizes the materials provided in most basal reading programs.

Managing a Basal Reading Program

The teacher's guide provides a management plan for the basal reading program. Daily and weekly lesson plans are included with suggestions for pacing for each unit, ideas for flexible grouping, and regular assessment activities. There are letters to send home

Figure 10–1 ◆ Materials in Basal Reading Programs

Materials	Description
Textbook or Anthology	The student's book of reading selections. The selections are organized thematically and include literature from trade books. Often the textbook is available in a series of softcover books or a single hardcover book.
Big Books	Enlarged copies of books for shared reading. These books are used in kindergarten and first grade.
Supplemental Books	Collections of trade books for each grade level. Kindergarten-level books often feature familiar songs and wordless stories. First- and second-grade books often include decodable words for practicing phonics skills and high-frequency words. In grades 3 to 6, books are often related to unit themes.
Workbooks	Consumable books of phonics, comprehension, vocabulary, spelling, and grammar worksheets.
Transparencies	Color transparencies to use in teaching skills and strategies.
Black-Line Masters	Worksheets that teachers duplicate and use to teach skills and provide additional reading practice.
Kits	Alphabet cards, word cards, and other instructional materials. These kits are used in kindergarten through second grade.
Teacher's Guide	An oversize book that presents comprehensive information about how to teach reading using the basal reading program. The selections are shown in reduced size, and background information about the selection, instructions for teaching the selections, and instructions on coordinating skill and strategy instruction are given on each page. In addition, information is presented about which supplemental books to use with each selection and how to assess students' learning.
Parent Materials	Black-line masters that teachers duplicate and send home to parents. Information about the reading program and lists of ways parents can work with their children are included. These materials are available in English, Spanish, and several other languages.
Assessment Materials	A variety of assessments, including selection and unit tests, running records, and phonics inventories, are available along with teacher's guides.
Multimedia	Audiocassettes and CDs of some selections, related videos, and website connections are provided.

to parents at the beginning of each unit, usually available in several languages, as well as a variety of assessment materials, including phonics tests, end-of-lesson and end-of-unit tests, writing rubrics, and observation guidelines. Teachers are encouraged to assess students' learning regularly to monitor their progress and to evaluate the effectiveness of the instructional program.

TEACHING WITH LITERATURE FOCUS UNITS

Teachers plan literature focus units featuring popular and award-winning stories, informational books, or books of poetry. Some literature focus units feature a single book, either a picture book or a chapter book, whereas others feature several books for a genre unit or an author study. Teachers guide and direct students as they read and respond to a book, but the emphasis in this instructional approach is on teaching students about literature and developing lifelong readers. An overview of this instructional approach is shown on the next page.

Literature focus units include activities incorporating the five stages of the reading process:

Prereading. Teachers involve students in activities to build background knowledge and interest them in reading the book, including sharing book boxes, reading related books, showing DVDs, and talking about related topics.

Reading. Students read the featured selection independently, or the teacher reads it aloud or uses shared reading if it's too difficult for students to read themselves.

Responding. Students participate in grand conversations to talk about the book and write entries in reading logs to deepen their understanding.

Exploring. Students post vocabulary on word walls, participate in word-study activities, learn comprehension strategies, examine text factors, and research the book's author or related topics.

Applying. Students apply their learning as they create oral and written projects and share them with their classmates.

Through these activities, teachers guide students as they read and respond to high-quality literature.

Steps in Developing a Unit

Go to the Building Teaching Skills and Dispositions section of Chapter 10 on **MyEducationLab.com** to see an upper elementary class participating in a literature focus unit.

Teachers develop a literature focus unit through a series of steps, beginning with choosing the literature and setting goals, then identifying and scheduling activities, and finally deciding how to assess students' learning. Effective teachers don't simply follow directions in literature focus unit planning guides that are available for purchase in school supply stories; rather, they do the planning themselves because they're the ones who are most knowledgeable about their students, the time available for the unit, the strategies and skills they need to teach, and the activities they want to develop.

Usually literature focus units featuring a picture book are completed in 1 week, and units featuring a novel or other longer book are completed in 3 or 4 weeks. Genre and author units often last 3 or 4 weeks. Rarely, if ever, do literature focus units continue for more than a month. When teachers drag out a unit, they risk killing students' interest in that particular book or, worse yet, their interest in literature and reading.

OVERVIEW OF THE INSTRUCTIONAL APPROACH

Literature Focus Units

TOPIC	DESCRIPTION
Purpose	To teach reading through literature, using high-quality, grade-appropriate picture books and novels.
Components	Teachers involve students in three activities: Students read and respond to a trade book together as a class; the teacher teaches minilessons on phonics, vocabulary, and comprehension using the book they're reading; and students create projects to extend their understanding of the book.
Theory Base	Literature focus units represent a transition between teacher-centered and student-centered learning because the teacher guides students as they read a book. This approach reflects cognitive/information processing theory because teachers develop students' background knowledge, read aloud when students can't read fluently, and teach vocabulary words and comprehension strategies. It also reflects Rosenblatt's transactive theory because students participate in grand conversations and write in reading logs to deepen their comprehension, and critical literacy theory because issues of social justice often arise in the trade books.
Applications	Teachers teach units featuring a picture book or a novel, generally using books on a district-approved list, or units featuring a genre or author. Literature focus units are often alternated with another approach where students read books at their own reading levels.
Strengths	• Teachers select award-winning literature for these units. • Teachers scaffold students' comprehension as they read with the class or small groups. • Teachers teach minilessons on reading strategies and skills. • Students learn vocabulary through word walls and other activities. • Students learn about genres, story structure, and literary devices.
Limitations	• All students read the same book whether or not they like it and whether or not it's written at their reading level. • Many activities are teacher directed.

Step 1: Select the Literature. Teachers select the book for the literature focus unit—a picture-book story, a novel, an informational book, or a book of poetry. Teachers collect multiple copies so students will each have their own copy to read. Many school districts have class sets of selected books available; however, sometimes teachers have to ask administrators to purchase multiple copies or buy books themselves through book clubs.

Teachers collect related books for the text set, too, including other versions of the same story, sequels, other books written by the same author, or other books in the same genre. Teachers collect one or two copies of 10, 20, 30, or more books for the text set and add them to the classroom library for the unit. Books for the text set are placed on a special shelf or in a crate in the library center. At the beginning of the unit, teachers introduce the books and provide opportunities for students read them during independent reading time.

Teachers also identify and collect supplemental materials related to the featured selection, including puppets, stuffed animals, and toys; charts and diagrams; book boxes of materials to use in introducing the book; and information about the author and the illustrator. For many picture books, big-book versions are also available that can be used for shared reading. Teachers also locate multimedia resources, including videotapes of the featured selection, DVDs to provide background knowledge on the topic, and Internet sites about the author and the illustrator.

Step 2: Set Goals.   Teachers decide what they want their students to learn during the unit, and they connect the goals they set with state standards that their students are expected to learn.

Step 3: Develop a Unit Plan.   Teachers read or reread the selected book and then think about the focus they will use for the unit. Sometimes teachers focus on an element of story structure, the historical setting, wordplay, the author or genre, or a topic related to the book, such as weather or desert life. After determining the focus, they choose activities to use at each of the five stages of the reading process. Teachers often jot notes on a chart divided into sections for each stage; then they use the ideas they've brainstormed as they plan the unit. Generally, not all of the brainstormed activities will be used, but teachers select the most important ones according to their focus and the time available.

Step 4: Coordinate Grouping Patterns With Activities.   Teachers think about how to incorporate whole-class, small-group, partner, and individual activities into their unit plans. It's important that students have opportunities to read and write independently as well as to work with small groups and to come together as a class. If the book will be read together as a class, then students need opportunities to reread it with a buddy or to read related books independently. These grouping patterns should be alternated during various activities in the unit. Teachers often go back to their planning sheet and highlight activities with colored markers according to grouping patterns.

Step 5: Create a Time Schedule.   Teachers create a schedule that provides sufficient time for students to move through the five stages of the reading process and to complete the activities planned for the unit. They also plan minilessons to teach reading and writing strategies and skills identified in their goals and those needed for students to complete the unit activities. Teachers usually have a set time for minilessons in their weekly schedule, but sometimes they arrange their schedules to teach minilessons just before they introduce specific activities or assignments.

Step 6: Assessing Students.   Teachers often distribute unit folders in which students keep all their work. Keeping all the materials together makes the unit easier for both students and teachers to manage. Teachers also plan ways to document students' learning and assign grades. One type of record keeping is an assignment checklist, which is developed with students and distributed at the beginning of the literature focus unit. Students keep track of their work during the unit and sometimes negotiate to change the checklist as the unit evolves. Students keep the lists in their unit folders and mark off each item as it's completed. At the end of the unit, students turn in their assignment checklist and other completed work. Although this list doesn't include every activity students were involved in, it identifies those that will be graded.

Units Featuring a Picture Book

In literature focus units featuring picture books, younger children read predictable picture books or books with very little text, such as *Rosie's Walk* (Hutchins, 2005), a humorous story about a hen who walks leisurely around the barnyard, unwittingly leading the fox who is following her into one mishap after another; older students read more-sophisticated picture books with more-elaborate story lines, such as *Train to Somewhere* (Bunting, 2000), a story about an orphan train taking children to adoptive families in the West in the late 1800s. Teachers use the same six-step approach for developing units featuring a picture book for younger and older students.

Units Featuring a Novel

Teachers develop literature focus units using novels, such as *Bunnicula: A Rabbit-Tale of Mystery* (Howe & Howe, 2006), *Sarah, Plain and Tall* (MacLachlan, 2004), and *Number the Stars* (Lowry, 1998). The biggest difference between picture-book stories and novels is their length, and when teachers plan literature focus units featuring a novel, they need to decide how to schedule the reading of the book. Will students read one or two chapters each day? How often will they respond in reading logs or grand conversations? It's important that teachers reread the book to note the length of chapters and identify key points in the book where students will want time to explore and respond to the ideas presented there.

Figure 10–2 presents a 4-week lesson plan for Lois Lowry's *Number the Stars*, a story of friendship and courage set in Nazi-occupied Denmark during World War II. The daily routine during the first 2 weeks is as follows:

Reading. Students and the teacher read two chapters using shared reading.

Responding After Reading. Students participate in a grand conversation about the chapters they've read, write in reading logs, and add important words to the class word wall.

Minilesson. The teacher teaches a minilesson on a reading strategy or presents information about World War II or about the author.

More Reading. Students read related books from the text set independently.

The schedule for the last 2 weeks is different. During the third week, students choose a class project (interviewing people who were alive during World War II) and individual projects. They work in teams on activities related to the book and continue to read other books about the war. During the final week, students finish the class interview project and share their completed individual projects.

Units Featuring a Genre

During a genre unit, students learn about a particular genre, such as folktales, science fiction, or biographies. Students read several books illustrating the genre, participate in a variety of activities to deepen their knowledge about the genre's text factors, and sometimes apply what they've learned through a writing project. For example, after reading and comparing Cinderella tales from around the world, third graders often create picture books to retell their favorite version, and seventh graders who are studying the Middle Ages often write stories incorporating details that they've learned about the historical period. During a genre unit on biographies, fifth graders choose a person to research, read a biography, do more research on the Internet, and then write a biography to share what they learned; or during a genre unit on poetry, students write poems applying the forms of the poetry they've read.

Units Featuring an Author

During an author study, students learn about an author's life and read one or more books he or she has written. Most authors post websites where they share information about

Figure 10–2 ◆ A Lesson Plan for *Number the Stars*

	Monday	Tuesday	Wednesday	Thursday	Friday
Week 1	Build background on World War II The Resistance movement ML: Reading maps of Nazi-occupied Europe Read aloud The Lily Cupboard	Introduce NTS Begin word wall Read Ch. 1 & 2 Grand conversation Reading log Add to word wall Book talk on text set	Read Ch. 3 & 4 Grand conversation Reading log Word wall ML: Connecting with a character Read text set books	Read Ch. 5 Grand conversation Reading log Word wall ML: Visualizing Nazis in apartment (use drama)	Read Ch. 6 & 7 Grand conversation Reading log Word wall ML: Information about the author and why she wrote the book
Week 2	Read Ch. 8 & 9 Grand conversation Reading log Word wall ML: Compare home front and war front Read text set books	Read Ch. 10 & 11 Grand conversation Reading log Word wall ML: Visualizing the wake (use drama) ↑	Read Ch. 12 & 13 Grand conversation Reading log Word wall ML: Compare characters – make Venn diagram ↑	Read Ch. 14 & 15 Grand conversation Reading log Word wall ML: Make word maps of key words ↑	Finish book Grand conversation Reading log Word wall ML: Theme of book ↑
Week 3	Plan class interview project Choose individual projects Independent reading/projects ↑ ↑ ↑	Activities at Centers: 1. Story map 2. Word sort 3. Plot profile 4. Quilt ↑	↑	↑	↑
Week 4	Revise interviews Independent reading/ projects ↑	↑	Edit interviews Share projects	Make final copies	Compile interview book ↑

themselves, their books, and how they write, and each year more authors are writing autobiographies. As students learn about authors, they develop a concept of author; this awareness is important so that students will think of them as real people who eat breakfast, ride bikes, and take out the garbage, just as they do. When students think of authors as real people, they view reading in a more personal way. This awareness also carries over to their writing: Students gain a new perspective as they realize that they, too, can write books. They learn about the writing process that authors use, too.

In first grade, for example, many children read Eric Carle's books and experiment with his illustration techniques, and in the vignette at the beginning of the chapter, Miss Pannicia's students participated in a yearlong author study on Chris Van Allsburg. They read his fantasy picture books, hunted for the picture of the white dog that he includes in every book, and wrote their own fantasy stories based on *The Mysteries of Harris Burdick* (Van Allsburg, 1996). Figure 10–3 presents a list of recommended authors for author studies; the list is divided into primary-, middle-, and upper-grade levels, but many authors are appropriate for students at more than one level. Jerry Spinelli, for instance, writes books that appeal to both middle- and upper-grade students.

Managing Literature Focus Units

Literature focus units are somewhat teacher directed, and teachers play several important roles. They share their love of literature and direct students' attention to comprehension strategies and text factors. They model the strategies that capable readers use and guide students to read more strategically. They also scaffold students, providing

Figure 10–3 ◆ Recommended Authors for Author Studies

Primary Grades	Middle Grades	Upper Grades
Caroline Arnold	Eve Bunting	Avi
Jan Brett	Joanna Cole	Sharon Creech
Ashley Bryan	Gail Gibbons	Christopher Paul Curtis
Eric Carle	Nikki Giovanni	Paul Fleischman
Doreen Cronin	Eric Kimmel	Karen Hesse
Tomie dePaola	Patricia MacLachlan	Lois Lowry
Arthur Dorros	Phyllis Reynolds Naylor	Walter Dean Myers
Lois Ehlert	Patricia Polacco	Linda Sue Park
Denise Fleming	Pam Muñoz Ryan	Gary Paulsen
Kevin Henkes	Jon Scieszka	J. K. Rowling
Steven Kellogg	Jerry Spinelli	Louis Sachar
Patricia McKissack	Janet Stevens	Gary Soto
Rosemary Wells	Chris Van Allsburg	Suzanne Fisher Staples
Mo Willems	Carole Boston Weatherford	Jacqueline Woodson
Audrey Wood	David Wiesner	Laurence Yep

support and guidance so that students can be successful. Through this instruction and support, students learn about reading and literature, and they apply what they've learned as they participate in literature circles and reading workshop, two more student-centered approaches.

ORCHESTRATING LITERATURE CIRCLES

One of the best ways to nurture students' love of reading and ensure that they become lifelong readers is through literature circles—small, student-led book discussion groups that meet regularly in the classroom (Daniels, 2001). Sometimes literature circles are called *book clubs*. The reading materials are quality books of children's literature, including stories, poems, biographies, and other informational books, and what matters most is that students are reading something that interests them and is manageable. Students choose the books to read and form temporary groups. Next, they set a reading and discussion schedule. Then they read independently or with buddies and come together to talk about their reading in discussions that are like grand conversations. Sometimes the teacher meets with the group, and at other times, the group meets independently. A literature circle on one book may last from several days to a week or two, depending on the length of the book and the age of the students.

Key Features of Literature Circles

The three key features of literature circles are choice, literature, and response. As teachers organize for literature circles, they make decisions about these features: They structure the program so that students can make choices about what to read, and they develop a plan for response so that students can think deeply about books they're reading and respond to them.

Choice. Students make many choices in literature circles. They choose the books they'll read and the groups in which they participate. They share in setting the schedule for reading and discussing the book, and they choose the roles they assume in the discussions. They also choose how they will share the book with classmates. Teachers structure literature circles so that students have these opportunities, but even more important, they prepare students for making choices by creating a community of learners in their classrooms in which students assume responsibility for their learning and can work collaboratively with classmates.

Literature. The books chosen for literature circles should be interesting to students and at their reading level. The books must seem manageable to the students, especially during their first literature circles. Samway and Whang (1996) recommend choosing shorter books or picture books at first so that students don't become bogged down. It's also important that teachers have read and liked the books because otherwise they won't be able to do convincing book talks when they introduce them. In addition, they won't be able to contribute to the book discussions.

Students typically read stories during literature circles, but they can also read informational books or informational books paired with stories (Heller, 2006; Stien & Beed, 2004). Students read informational books related to thematic units or biographies during a genre unit. Second graders often choose books from the Magic Tree House series of easy-to-read chapter books that features pairs of fiction and nonfiction books, including *Hour of the Olympics* (Osborne, 1998) and *Olympics of Ancient Greece* (Osborne & Boyce, 2004), or the popular Magic School Bus picture-book series, including *The Magic School Bus Explores the Senses* (Cole, 1999).

Response. Students meet several times during a literature circle to discuss the book. Through these discussions, students summarize their reading, make connections, learn vocabulary, and explore the author's use of text factors. They learn that comprehension develops in layers. From an initial comprehension gained through reading, students deepen their understanding through the discussions. They learn to return to the text to reread sentences and paragraphs in order to clarify a point or state an opinion. Gilles (1998) examined children's talk during literature circle discussions and identified four types of talk, which are presented in Figure 10–4.

Karen Smith (1998) describes the discussions her students have as "intensive study," often involving several group meetings. At the first session, students share personal responses. They talk about the characters and events of the story, share favorite parts, and ask questions to clarify confusions. At the end of the first session, students and the teacher decide what they want to study at the next session, such as an element of story structure. Students prepare for the second discussion by rereading excerpts from the book related to the chosen focus. Then, during the second session, students talk about how the author used that element of story structure, and they often make charts and diagrams, such as an open-mind portrait, to organize their thoughts.

Students need many opportunities to respond to literature before they'll be successful in literature circles. One of the best ways to prepare students is by reading aloud to them and involving them in grand conversations (Peterson & Eeds, 2007). Teachers demonstrate ways to respond that are reflective and thoughtful, encourage students to respond to the books, and reinforce students' comments when they share their thoughts and feelings and talk about their use of comprehension strategies as they listened to the teacher reading aloud.

Some teachers have students assume roles and complete assignments in preparation for discussion group meetings (Daniels, 2001). One student is the discussion director, and he or she assumes the leadership role and directs the discussion. This student chooses topics and formulates questions to guide the discussion. Other students prepare by selecting a passage to read aloud, drawing a picture or making a graphic related to the book, or investigating a topic connected to the book. The roles are detailed in Figure 10–5. Although having students assume specific roles may seem artificial, it teaches them about the ways they can respond in literature circles.

Teachers often prepare assignment sheets for each of the roles their students assume during a literature circle and then pass out copies before students begin reading. Students complete one of the assignment sheets before each discussion. Figure 10–6 shows a "word wizard" assignment sheet that an eighth grader completed as he read *Holes* (Sachar, 2003), the story of a boy named Stanley Yelnats who is sent to a hellish

---

Figure 10–4 ◆ Types of Talk During Literature Circle Discussions

Talk About the Book

Students summarize their reading and talk about the book by applying what they've learned about text factors as they do the following:

- Retell events or big ideas
- Examine the theme or genre
- Explore the organizational elements or patterns the author used
- Find examples of literary devices

Talk About Connections

Students make connections between the book and their own lives, the world, and other literature they've read in these ways:

- Explain connections to their lives
- Compare this book to another book
- Make connections to a film or television show they've viewed

Talk About the Reading Process

Students think metacognitively and reflect on the strategies they used to read the book as they do the following:

- Reflect on how they used strategies
- Explain their reading problems and how they solved them
- Identify sections that they reread and why they reread them
- Talk about their thinking as they were reading
- Identify parts they understood or misunderstood

Talk About Group Process and Social Issues

Students use talk to organize the literature circle and maintain the discussion. They also examine social issues and current events related to the book, such as homelessness and divorce, as they do the following:

- Decide who will be group leader
- Determine the schedule, roles, and responsibilities
- Draw in nonparticipating students
- Bring the conversation back to the topic
- Extend the discussion to social issues and current events

Figure 10–5 ◆ Roles Students Play in Literature Circles

Role	Responsibilities
Discussion Director	The discussion director guides the group's discussion and keeps the group on task. To get the discussion started or to redirect it, the student may ask: • What did the reading make you think of? • What questions do you have about the reading? • What do you predict will happen next?
Passage Master	The passage master focuses on the literary merits of the book. This student chooses several memorable passages to share with the group and tells why each one wash chosen
Word Wizard	The word wizard is responsible for vocabulary. This student identifies four to six important, unfamiliar words from the reading and looks them up in the dictionary. He or she selects the most appropriate meaning and other interesting information about the word to share with the group.
Connector	The connector makes connections between the book and the students' lives. These connections might include happenings at school or in the community, current events or historical events from around the world, or something from the connector's own life. Or the connector can make comparisons with other books by the same author or on the same topic.
Summarizer	The summarizer prepares a brief summary of the reading to convey the big ideas to share with the group. This student often begins the discussion by reading the summary aloud to the group.
Illustrator	The illustrator draws a picture or diagram related to the reading. The illustration might relate to a character, an exciting event, or a prediction. The student shares the illustration with the group, and the group talks about it before the illustrator explains it.
Investigator	The investigator locates some information about the book, the author, or a related topic to share with the group. This student may search the Internet, check an encyclopedia or library book, or interview a person with special expertise on the topic.

Adapted from Daniels, 2001; Daniels & Bizar, 1998.

correctional camp where he finds a real friend, a treasure, and a new sense of himself. As word wizard, this student chose important words from the story to study. In the first column on the assignment sheet, he wrote the words and the pages on which they were found. Next, he checked the dictionary for each word's meaning, and in the second column listed several meanings when possible and placed checkmarks next to the appropriate meanings for how a word was used in the book. The student also checked the etymology of the word in the dictionary, and in the third column, he listed the language the word came from and when it entered English.

During the discussion about the second section of *Holes*, the word *callused* became important. The "word wizard" explained that *callused* means "toughened" and "hardened," and that in the story, Stanley and the other boys' hands became callused from

Figure 10–6 ◆ An Eighth Grader's Literature Circle Role Sheet

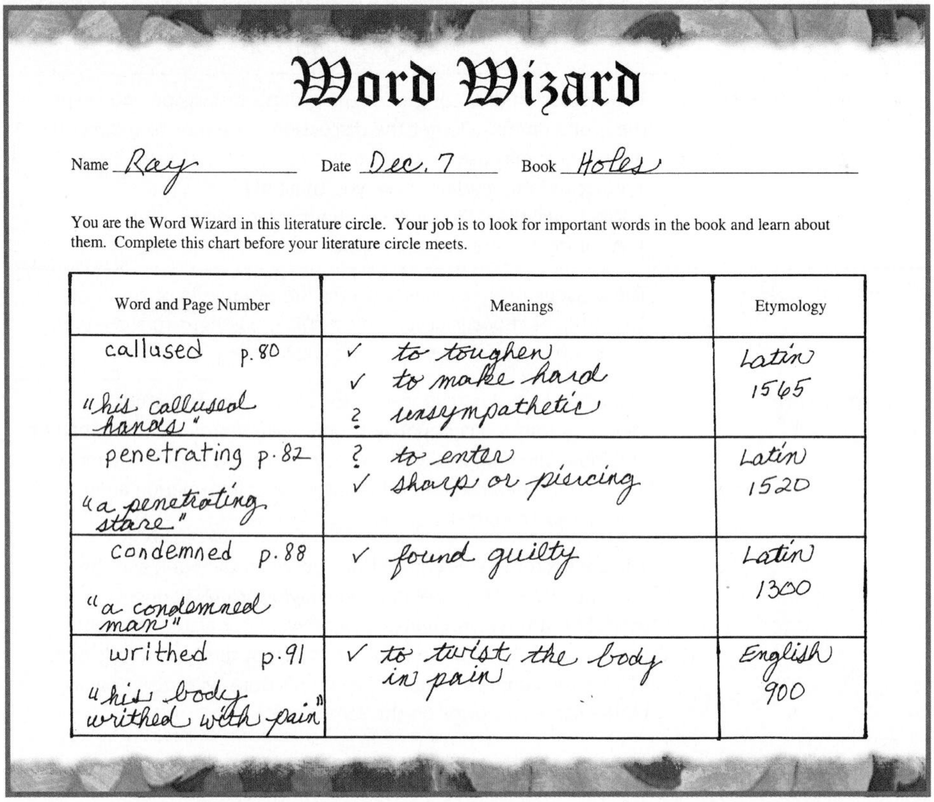

Word Wizard

Name **Ray**   Date **Dec. 7**   Book **Holes**

You are the Word Wizard in this literature circle. Your job is to look for important words in the book and learn about them. Complete this chart before your literature circle meets.

Word and Page Number	Meanings	Etymology
callused p. 80 "his callused hands"	✓ to toughen ✓ to make hard ? unsympathetic	Latin 1565
penetrating p. 82 "a penetrating stare"	? to enter ✓ sharp or piercing	Latin 1520
condemned p. 88 "a condemned man"	✓ found guilty	Latin 1300
writhed p. 91 "his body writhed with pain"	✓ to twist the body in pain	English 900

digging holes. He continued to say that the third meaning, "unsympathetic," didn't make sense. This comment provided an opportunity for the teacher to explain how *callused* could mean "unsympathetic," and students decided to make a chart to categorize characters in the story who had callused hands and those who were unsympathetic. The group concluded that the boys with callused hands were sympathetic to each other, but the adults at the correctional camp who didn't have callused hands were often unsympathetic and had callused hearts. Talking about the meaning of a single word—*callused*—led to a new and different way of looking at the characters in the story.

Literature circles are an effective instructional approach because of the three key features—choice, literature, and response. As students read and discuss books with classmates, they often become more engaged and motivated than in more teacher-directed approaches. The feature on page 341 presents an overview of literature circles.

Implementing Literature Circles

Teachers organize literature circles using a six-step series of activities.

Step 1: Select Books. Teachers prepare text sets with five to seven related titles and collect six or seven copies of each book. They give a brief book talk to introduce the books, and then students sign up for the one they want to read. Students need time to preview the books, and then they decide what to read after considering the topic and the difficulty level. Once in a while, students don't get to read their first choice, but they can always read it another time, perhaps during another literature circle or during reading workshop.

Step 2: Form Literature Circles. Students get together to read each book; usually no more than six students participate in a group. They begin by setting a schedule for reading and discussing the book within the time limits set by the teacher. Students also choose discussion roles so that they can prepare for the discussion after reading.

Step 3: Read the Book. Students read all or part of the book independently or with a partner, depending on the book's difficulty level. Afterward, students prepare for the discussion by doing the assignment for the role they assumed.

Step 4: Participate in a Discussion. Students meet to talk about the book; these grand conversations usually last about 30 minutes. The discussion director or another student who has been chosen as the leader begins the discussion, and then classmates continue as in any other grand conversation. They take turns sharing their responses according to the roles they assumed. The talk is meaningful because students talk about what interests them in the book.

Step 5: Teach Minilessons. Teachers teach minilessons before or after group meetings on a variety of topics, including asking insightful questions, completing role sheets, using comprehension strategies, and examining text factors (Daniels & Steineke, 2004). Teachers address the procedures that students use in small-group discussions as well as literary concepts and strategies and skills.

Step 6: Share With the Class. Students in each literature circle share the book they've read with their classmates through a book talk or another presentation.

OVERVIEW OF THE INSTRUCTIONAL APPROACH

Literature Circles

TOPIC	DESCRIPTION
Purpose	To provide students with opportunities for authentic reading and literary analysis.
Components	Students form literature circles to read and discuss books that they choose themselves. They often assume roles for the book discussion.
Theory Base	Literature circles reflect sociolinguistic, transactive, and critical literacy theories because students work in small, supportive groups to read and discuss books, and the books they read often involve cultural and social issues that require students to think critically.
Applications	Teachers often use literature circles in conjunction with a basal reading program or with literature focus units so students have opportunities to do independent reading and literary analysis.
Strengths	• Books are available at a variety of reading levels. • Students are more strongly motivated because they choose the books they read. • Students have opportunities to work with their classmates. • Students participate in authentic literacy experiences. • Students learn how to respond to literature. • Teachers may participate in discussions to help students clarify misunderstandings and think more critically about the book.
Limitations	• Teachers often feel a loss of control because students are reading different books. • Students must learn to be task oriented and to use time wisely to be successful. • Sometimes students choose books that are too difficult or too easy for them.

As students participate in literature circles, they're involved in activities representing all five stages of the reading process:

Prereading. Teachers give book talks, and then students choose books to read, form groups, and get ready to read by making schedules and choosing roles.

Reading. Students read the book independently or with a partner, and prepare for the group meeting.

Responding. Students talk about the book and take responsibility to come to the discussion prepared to participate actively.

Exploring. Teachers teach minilessons to rehearse literature circle procedures, learn comprehension strategies, and examine text factors.

Applying. Students give brief presentations to the class about the books they've read.

As students make choices and move through the reading process, they assume increasingly more responsibility for their own learning.

Using Literature Circles With Young Children

First and second graders can meet in small groups to read and discuss books, just as older, more experienced readers do (Frank, Dixon, & Brandts, 2001; Marriott, 2002; Martinez-Roldan & Lopez-Robertson, 1999/2000). These young children choose books at their reading levels, listen to the teacher read a book aloud, or participate in a shared reading activity. Children probably benefit from listening to a book read aloud two times or reading it several times before participating in the discussion. In preparation for the literature circle, children often draw and write reading log entries to share with the group. Or, they can write a letter to their group telling about the book. The literature circle often begins with one child sharing a reading log entry or letter with the small group.

Children meet with the teacher to talk about a book. The teacher guides the discussion at first and models how to share ideas and to participate in a discussion. The talk is meaningful because children share what interests them in the book, make text-to-self, text-to-world, and text-to-text connections, point out illustrations and other book features, ask questions, and discuss themes. Young children don't usually assume roles as older students do, but teachers often notice a few of the first and second graders beginning to take on leadership roles. During a literature circle, the other children in the classroom are usually reading books or writing in reading logs in preparation for their upcoming literature circle meeting with the teacher.

Managing Literature Circles

When teachers introduce literature circles, they teach students how to participate in small-group discussions and respond to literature. At first, many teachers participate in discussions, but they quickly step back as students become comfortable with the procedures and get engaged in the discussions.

Unfortunately, groups don't always work well. Sometimes conversations get off track because of disruptive behavior, or students monopolize the discussion, hurl insults at classmates, or exclude certain students. Clarke and Holwadel (2007) describe an inner-city sixth-grade classroom where literature circles deteriorated because of race, gender, and class tensions. They identified students' negative feelings toward classmates and their limited conversational skills as two problems they could address, and they improved the quality of literature circles in this classroom through these activities:

◆ **Minilessons.** The teachers taught minilessons to develop more-positive relationships among group members and build more-effective discussion skills, including learning how to listen to each other and take turns when talking (Daniels & Steineke, 2004).

◆ **Videotapes.** The teachers videotaped students participating in a literature circle and viewed it with group members to make them more aware of how their behavior affected their discussions. They talked about how the discussions went, identified problems, and brainstormed ways to solve them.

◆ **Books.** The teachers reconsidered the books they'd chosen and looked for books that might relate better to students' lives and inspire more-powerful discussions. These books were especially effective in this classroom: *Sang Spell* (Naylor, 1998), *Hush* (Woodson, 2002), *Slave Dancer* (Fox, 2001), and *Stargirl* (Spinelli, 2004).

◆ **Coaching.** The teachers became coaches to guide students in becoming more-effective participants. They modeled positive group behavior and appropriate discussion skills and demonstrated how to use their responses to deepen their understanding of a book. At times, they assumed the teacher role to ensure that everyone participated and to keep the discussion on track.

Even though some problems persisted, Clarke and Holwadel improved the quality of their students' literature circles. The classroom environment became more respectful, and students' improved conversation skills transferred to other discussions. And, once students became more successful, their interest in reading increased, too.

IMPLEMENTING READING AND WRITING WORKSHOP

Students are involved in authentic reading and writing projects during reading and writing workshop. This approach involves three key characteristics: time, choice, and response. First, students have large chunks of time and the opportunity to read and write. Instead of being add-ons for after students finish assignments, reading and writing become the core of the literacy curriculum.

Second, students assume ownership of their learning through self-selection of books they read and their topics for writing. Instead of reading books that the teacher has selected or reading the same book together as a group or class, students choose the books they want to read, books that are suitable to their interests and reading levels. Usually students choose whatever book they want to read—a story, a collection of poems, or an informational book—but sometimes teachers set parameters. For example, during a genre unit on science fiction, teachers ask students to select a science fiction story to read. During writing workshop, students plan their writing projects: They choose topics related to hobbies, content-area units, and other interests, and they also select the format for their writing. Often they choose to publish their writing as books.

The third characteristic is response. Students respond to books they're reading in reading logs that they share during conferences with the teacher. They also do book talks to share books they've finished reading with classmates. Similarly, in writing workshop, students share with classmates rough drafts of books and other compositions they're writing, and they share their completed and published compositions with genuine audiences.

Reading workshop and writing workshop are different types of workshops. Reading workshop fosters real reading of self-selected books. Students read hundreds of books during reading workshop. At the first-grade level, students might read or reread three or four books each day, totaling close to a thousand books during the school year, and older students read fewer, longer books. Even so, upper-grade teachers report that their students read between 25 and 100 books during the school year.

Similarly, writing workshop fosters real writing (and the use of the writing process) for genuine purposes and for authentic audiences. Each student writes and publishes as many as 50 to 100 short books in the primary grades and 20 to 25 longer books in the middle and upper grades. As they write, students come to see themselves as authors and become interested in learning about the authors of the books they read.

Teachers often use both workshops, or if their schedule doesn't allow, they may alternate the two. Schedules for reading and writing workshop at the first-, third-, sixth-, and eighth-grade levels are presented in Figure 10–7. Kindergarten teachers can implement reading and writing workshop in their classrooms, too (Cunningham & Shagoury, 2005); even though they do more of the reading and writing themselves, teachers involve 5-year-olds in authentic literacy experiences and teach them about comprehension strategies and text factors.

Reading and writing workshop can be used as the primary instructional approach in a classroom, or it can be used along with other instructional approaches to provide authentic opportunities for students to read and write. This approach is student centered because students make many choices and work independently as they read and write. Providing authentic activities and independent work opportunities reflects the constructivist theory, which emphasizes that learners create their own knowledge through exploration and experimentation.

Reading Workshop

Nancie Atwell introduced reading workshop in 1987 as an alternative to traditional reading instruction. In reading workshop, students read books that they choose themselves and respond to books through writing in reading logs and conferencing with teachers and classmates (Atwell, 1998). This approach represented a change in what teachers believe about how children learn and how literature should be used in the classroom. Whereas traditional reading programs emphasized dependence on a teacher's guide to determine how and when particular strategies and skills should be taught, reading workshop is an individualized reading program. Atwell developed reading workshop with her middle school students, but it's been adapted and used successfully at every grade level, first through eighth. There are several versions of reading workshop, but they usually contain five components: reading, responding, sharing, teaching minilessons, and reading aloud to students.

Reading. Students spend 30 to 60 minutes independently reading books. Students choose the books they read, often using recommendations from classmates. They also choose books on favorite topics—horses, science fiction, and dinosaurs, for example— or written by favorite authors, such as Audrey Wood, Chris Van Allsburg, and Louis Sachar. It's crucial that students be able to read the books they choose. Ohlhausen and Jepsen (1992) developed a strategy for choosing books called the *Goldilocks Strategy*. These teachers created three categories of books—"Too Easy" books, "Too Hard"

Figure 10–7 ◆ Schedules for Reading and Writing Workshop

First Grade

9:00–9:10	The teacher rereads several familiar big books. Then the teacher introduces a new big book and reads it aloud.
9:10–9:30	Children read matching small books independently and reread other familiar books.
9:30–9:40	Children choose one of the books they've read or reread during independent reading to draw and write a quickwrite.
9:40–9:50	Children share the favorite book and quickwrite.
9:50–10:05	The teacher teaches a reading/writing minilesson.
10:05–10:30	Children write independently on self-selected topics and conference with the teacher.
10:30–10:40	Children share their published books with classmates.
10:40–10:45	The class uses choral reading to enjoy poems and charts hanging in the classroom.

Third Grade

10:30–11:00	Students read self-selected books and respond to them in reading logs.
11:00–11:15	Students share with classmates books they have finished reading and do informal book talks about them. Students often pass the "good" books to classmates who want to read them next.
11:15–11:30	The teacher teaches a reading/writing minilesson.
11:30–11:55	The teacher reads aloud and afterward, students participate in a grand conversation.
	—Continued after lunch—
12:45–1:15	Students write books independently.
1:15–1:30	Students share their published books with classmates.

Sixth Grade

8:20–8:45	The teacher reads aloud a chapter book, and students talk about it in a grand conversation.
8:45–9:30	Students write independently and conference with the teacher.
9:30–9:40	The teacher teaches a reading/writing minilesson.
9:40–10:25	Students read self-selected books independently.
10:25–10:40	Students share published writings and give book talks about books they've read.

Eighth Grade

During alternating months, students participate in reading or writing workshop.

1:00–1:45	Students read or write independently.
1:45–2:05	The teacher presents a minilesson on a reading or writing procedure, concept, strategy, or skill.
2:05–2:15	Students share the books they've read or compositions they've published.

books, and "Just Right" books—using "The Three Bears" folktale as their model. The books in the "Too Easy" category were those students had read before or could read fluently; "Too Hard" books were unfamiliar and confusing; and books in the "Just Right" category were interesting, with just a few unfamiliar words. The books in each category vary according to the student's reading level. This approach works at any grade level. Figure 10–8 presents a chart about choosing books using the Goldilocks Strategy.

Classroom libraries need to contain literally hundreds of books, including books written at a range of reading levels, so that every student can find books to read. Primary teachers often worry about finding books that their students can handle independently. Predictable books, leveled books, easy-to-read books, and books that have been read aloud several times are often the most accessible for young children. Teachers need to introduce students—especially reluctant readers—to the books in the classroom library so that they can more effectively choose books to read. The best way to preview books is using a very brief book talk to interest students in the book. Teachers tell a little about the book, show the cover, and perhaps read the first paragraph or two.

Teachers often read their own books or a book of children's literature during reading workshop; through their example, they model the importance of reading. Teachers also conference with students about the books they're reading while the rest of the class reads. As they conference, they talk briefly and quietly with students about their reading. Students may also read aloud favorite quotes or an interesting passage to the teacher.

Responding. Students usually keep reading logs in which they write their initial responses to the books they're reading. Sometimes students dialogue with the teacher about the book they're reading; a journal allows for ongoing written conversation

Figure 10–8 ◆ The Goldilocks Strategy

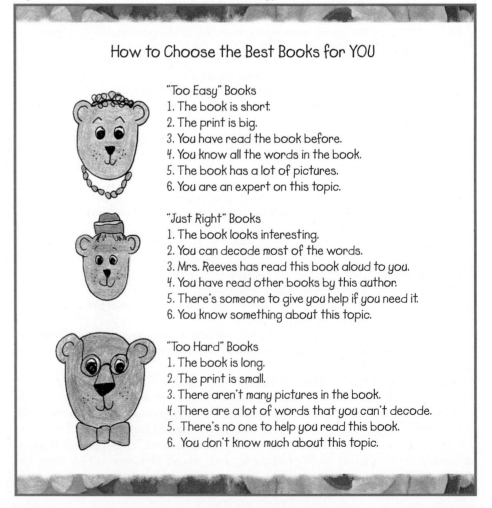

How to Choose the Best Books for YOU

"Too Easy" Books
1. The book is short.
2. The print is big.
3. You have read the book before.
4. You know all the words in the book.
5. The book has a lot of pictures.
6. You are an expert on this topic.

"Just Right" Books
1. The book looks interesting.
2. You can decode most of the words.
3. Mrs. Reeves has read this book aloud to you.
4. You have read other books by this author.
5. There's someone to give you help if you need it.
6. You know something about this topic.

"Too Hard" Books
1. The book is long.
2. The print is small.
3. There aren't many pictures in the book.
4. There are a lot of words that you can't decode.
5. There's no one to help you read this book.
6. You don't know much about this topic.

Figure 10-9 ◆ Response Patterns

Category	Pattern	Description
Immersion Responses	Understanding	Students write about their understanding of characters and plot. Their responses include personal interpretation as well as summarizing.
	Character Introspection	Students share their insights into the feelings and motives of a character. They often begin their comments with "I think . . ."
	Predicting	Students speculate about what will happen later in the story and confirm predictions they made previously.
	Questioning	Students ask "I wonder why" questions and write about confusions.
Involvement Responses	Character Identification	Students show personal identification with a character, sometimes writing "If I were _____, I would. . ." They express empathy, share related experiences from their own lives, and sometimes give advice to the character.
	Character Assessment	Students judge a character's actions and often use evaluative terms, such as *nice* or *dumb*.
	Story Involvement	Students reveal their involvement as they express satisfaction with how the story's developing. They may comment on their desire to continue reading or use terms such as *disgusting, weird*, or *awesome* to react to sensory aspects of the story.
Literary Connections	Connections	Students make text-to-self, text-to-world, text-to-text, and text-to-media (TV shows and movies) connections.
	Literary Evaluation	Students evaluate part or all of the book. They may offer "I liked/I didn't like" opinions and praise or condemn an author's style.

Adapted from Hancock, 2007.

between the teacher and individual students (Atwell, 1998). Responses often demonstrate students' reading strategies and offer insights into their thinking about literature. Seeing how students think about their reading helps teachers guide their learning.

Teachers play an important role in helping students expand and enrich their responses to literature. They collect students' reading logs periodically to monitor their responses. They write back and forth with students, with the idea that students write more if the teacher responds. However, because responding to students' journals is very time-consuming, teachers should keep their responses brief and not respond to every entry.

Hancock (2007) identified three types of response as students write about stories they're reading: immersion responses, involvement responses, and literary evaluation. The categories and the various patterns that exemplify each one are summarized in Figure 10–9. In most reading log entries, students write responses that address several patterns as they reflect on the story and explore their understanding.

In the first category, immersion responses, students indicate whether the book is making sense to them. They make inferences about characters, offer predictions, ask questions, or discuss confusions. Here are some responses excerpted from sixth graders' reading logs about *Bunnicula: A Rabbit-Tale of Mystery* (Howe & Howe, 2006):

I think the Monroes will find out what Chester and Harold are doing.

Can a bunny be a vampire? I don't think so. A bunny couldn't suck the blood out of a vegetable. They don't even have blood.

I guess Bunnicula really is a vampire.

I was right! I knew Harold and Chester would try to take care of Bunnicula. What I didn't know was that the Monroes would come home early.

I wonder why the vegetables are turning white. I know it's not Bunnicula but I don't know why.

In the second category, involvement responses, students show that they are personally involved with a character, often giving advice or judging a character's actions. They reveal their own involvement in the story as they express satisfaction with how the story is developing. Here are some examples:

I know how Chester and Harold feel. It's like when I got a new baby sister and everyone paid attention to her. I got ignored a lot.

If I were Bunnicula, I'd run away. He's just not safe in that house!

Gross!!! The vegetables are all white and there are two little fang holes in each one.

I just can't stop reading. This book is so cool. And it's funny, too.

In the third category, literary connections, students make connections and evaluate the book. They offer opinions, sometimes saying "I liked . . ." or "I didn't like . . ." and compare the book to others they've read. Here are some examples:

My dog is a lot like Harold. He gets on my bed with me and he loves snacks, but you should never feed a dog chocolate.

This is a great book! I know stuff like this couldn't happen but it would be awesome if it could. It's just fantasy but it's like I believe it.

This book is like <u>Charlotte's Web</u> because the animals can talk and have a whole life that the people in the story don't know about. But the books are different because <u>Bunnicula</u> is much funner than <u>Charlotte's Web</u>. It made me laugh and <u>Charlotte's Web</u> made me cry.

When students use only a few types of responses, teachers can teach minilessons to model the types of responses that students aren't using and ask questions to prompt students to think in new ways about the story they're reading.

Some students write minimal responses in journals. It's important that students choose books to read that they find personally interesting and that they feel free to share their thoughts, feelings, and questions with a trusted audience—usually the teacher. Sometimes writing entries on a computer and using e-mail to share them with students in another class or with other interested readers increase students' interest in writing more-elaborated responses.

During reading and responding, there's little or no talking because students are engrossed in reading and writing independently. Rarely do students interrupt classmates, go to the rest room, or get drinks of water, except in case of emergency, nor do they use reading workshop time to do homework or other schoolwork.

Sharing. For the last 15 minutes of reading workshop, the class gathers together to discuss books they've finished reading. Students talk about a book and why they liked it. Sometimes they read a brief excerpt aloud or formally pass the book to a classmate who wants to read it. Sharing is important because it helps students become a community to value and celebrate each other's accomplishments.

Minilessons. The teacher also spends 5 to 15 minutes teaching minilessons on reading workshop procedures, comprehension strategies, and text factors. Sometimes minilessons are taught to the whole class, and at other times, they're taught to small groups. At the beginning of the school year, teachers teach minilessons to the whole class on choosing books to read and other reading workshop procedures; later in the year, they teach minilessons on drawing inferences and other comprehension strategies and text factors. Teachers teach minilessons on particular authors when they introduce their books to the whole class and on literary genres when they set out collections of books representing a genre in the classroom library.

Reading Aloud to Students. Teachers use the interactive read-aloud procedure to read picture books and chapter books to the class as part of reading workshop. They choose high-quality literature that students might not be able to read themselves, award-winning books that they believe every student should be exposed to, or books that relate to a thematic unit. After reading, students talk about the book and share the reading experience. This activity is important because students listen to a book read aloud and respond to it together as a community of learners, not as individuals.

Even though reading workshop is different from other instructional approaches, students work through the same five stages of the reading process:

Prereading. Students choose books at their reading level to read and activate background knowledge as they look at the cover and think about the title.

Reading. Students read the books they've selected independently, at their own pace.

Responding. Students talk about the books they're reading when they conference with the teacher, and they often write responses in reading logs.

Exploring. Teachers teach students about text factors, authors, and comprehension strategies through minilessons.

Applying. Students often give book talks to their classmates about the books they've finished reading.

Is Sustained Silent Reading the Same as Reading Workshop? Sustained Silent Reading (SSR) is an independent reading time set aside during the school day for students in one class or the entire school to silently read self-selected books. It's used to increase the amount of reading students do and to encourage students to develop the habit of daily reading (Pilgreen, 2000). Reading workshop and SSR are similar. The goal of both programs is to provide opportunities for students to read self-selected books independently. Both programs work best in classrooms that are communities of learners. It seems obvious that students need to feel relaxed and comfortable in order to read for pleasure, and a community of learners is a place where students do feel comfortable because they are respected and valued by classmates and the teacher.

There are important differences, however. Reading workshop has five components—reading, responding, sharing, teaching minilessons, and reading aloud to students—whereas SSR has only one—reading. Reading workshop is recognized as an instructional approach because it includes both independent reading and instruction through minilessons. In contrast, SSR is a supplemental program without an instructional component.

Writing Workshop

Writing workshop is the best way to implement the writing process (Atwell, 1998; Fletcher & Portalupi, 2001). Students write on topics that they choose themselves and assume ownership of their writing and learning. At the same time, the teacher's role changes from being a provider of knowledge to serving as a facilitator and guide. The classroom becomes a community of writers who write and share their writing. There's a spirit of pride and acceptance in the classroom.

Students have writing folders in which they keep all papers related to the writing project they're working on. They also keep writing notebooks in which they jot down images, impressions, dialogue, and experiences that they can build upon for writing projects (Calkins, 1994). Students have access to different kinds of paper, some lined and some unlined, as well as writing instruments, including pencils and red and blue pens. They also have access to the classroom library because many times, students' writing grows out of books they've read. They may write a sequel to a book or retell a story from a different viewpoint. Primary-grade students often use patterns from books they've read to structure books they're writing.

As they write, students sit at desks or tables arranged in small groups. The teacher circulates around the classroom, conferencing briefly with students, and the classroom atmosphere is free enough that students converse quietly with classmates and move around to assist each other or share ideas. There's space for students to meet for writing groups, and often a sign-up sheet for writing groups is posted in the classroom. A table is available for the teacher to meet with individual students or small groups for conferences, writing groups, proofreading, and minilessons.

Writing workshop is a 60- to 90-minute period scheduled each day. During this time, students are involved in three components: writing, sharing, and minilessons. Sometimes a fourth activity, reading aloud to students, is added when it's not used in conjunction with reading workshop. The feature on page 351 presents an overview of the workshop approach.

Literacy Portraits: VIEWING GUIDE

The second graders in Ms. Janusz's classroom participate in writing workshop every morning. They use the writing process as they craft stories, poems, and informational books, usually on topics they've chosen themselves. Visit the Literacy Profiles section of the MyEducationLab website (www.myeducationlab.com), and click on Rakie's March button to watch her participate in writing workshop. Recently, Ms. Janusz taught a minilesson about how to write about a memory, and now Rakie's writing about a memory—a trip she took to Africa with her mom and sister. As you view the clip, try to identify some of the writing workshop activities that are described in this chapter. Since it's not possible to see every activity in one video clip, think about what might be going on during the other activities. Also, watch the video clip again to identify the stages of the writing process that Rakie's using.

myeducationlab

Writing.   Students spend 30 to 45 minutes or longer working independently on writing projects. Just as students in reading workshop choose books and read at their own pace, in writing workshop, they work at their own pace on writing projects they've chosen themselves. Most students move at their own pace through all five stages of the writing process, but young children often use an abbreviated process consisting of prewriting, drafting, and publishing.

Teachers conference with students as they write. Many teachers prefer moving around the classroom to meet with students rather than having students come to a table to meet with them: Too often, a line forms as students wait, and they lose precious writing time. Some teachers move around the classroom in a regular pattern, meeting with one fifth of the students each day. In this way, they are sure to conference with everyone during the week.

Other teachers spend the first 15 to 20 minutes of writing workshop stopping briefly to check on 10 or more students each day. Many use a zigzag pattern to get to all parts of the classroom each day. These teachers often kneel down beside each student, sit on the edge of the student's seat, or carry their own stool around to each student's desk. During the 1- or 2-minute conferences, teachers ask students what they're writing, listen to them read a paragraph or two, and then ask what they plan to do next. Then these teachers use the remaining time during writing workshop to conference more formally with students who are revising and editing their compositions. They identify strengths in students' writing, ask questions, and discover possibilities during revising conferences. Some teachers like to read the pieces themselves, and others like to listen to students read their papers aloud. As they interact with students, teachers model the kinds of responses that students are learning to give to each other.

As students meet to share their writing during revising and editing, they continue to develop as a community of writers. They share their rough drafts in writing groups composed of four or five students. Sometimes teachers join in, but students normally run the groups themselves. They take turns reading their rough drafts to each other

OVERVIEW OF THE INSTRUCTIONAL APPROACH ◆

Reading and Writing Workshop

TOPIC	DESCRIPTION
Purpose	To provide students with opportunities for authentic reading and writing activities.
Components	Reading workshop involves reading, responding, sharing, teaching minilessons, and reading aloud to students. Writing workshop consists of writing, sharing, and teaching minilessons.
Theory Base	The workshop approach reflects sociolinguistic and cognitive/information processing theories because students participate in authentic activities that encourage them to become lifelong readers and writers.
Applications	Teachers often use reading workshop in conjunction with a basal reading program or with literature focus units so students have opportunities to do independent reading. They often add writing workshop to any of the other instructional approaches so students have more sustained opportunities to use the writing process to develop and refine compositions.
Strengths	• Students read books that are appropriate for their reading levels. • Students are more motivated because they choose the books to read that interest them. • Students work through the stages of the writing process. • Activities are student directed, and students work at their own pace. • Teachers have opportunities to work individually with students during conferences.
Limitations	• Teachers often feel a loss of control because students are reading different books and working at different stages of the writing process. • Teachers have responsibility to teach minilessons on strategies and skills, in both whole-class groups and small groups. • Students must learn to be task oriented and to use time wisely to be successful.

and listen as their classmates offer compliments and suggestions for revision. Students also participate in revising and editing centers that are set up in the classroom. They know how to work at each center and the importance of working with classmates to make their writing better.

After proofreading their drafts with a classmate and then meeting with the teacher for final editing, students make the final copy of their writings. They often want to print out their writing on the computer so that it looks professional. Many times, students compile their final copies to make books, but sometimes they attach their writing to artwork, make posters, write letters that will be mailed, or perform scripts as skits or puppet shows. Not every piece is necessarily published; sometimes students decide not to continue with a piece of writing, and they file that piece in their writing folders and start something new.

Sharing. For the last 10 to 15 minutes of writing workshop, the class gathers together to share their new publications. Younger students often sit in a circle or gather together on a rug for sharing time. If an author's chair is available, each student sits in the special chair to read his or her composition aloud. After each sharing, classmates clap and offer compliments. They may also make other comments and suggestions, but the focus is on celebrating completed writing projects, not on revising the composition to make it better.

Minilessons. During this 5- to 30-minute period, teachers provide minilessons on writing workshop procedures, qualities of good writing, and writing strategies and skills, such as organizing ideas, proofreading, and using quotation marks to mark dialogue (Fletcher & Portalupi, 2007). In the middle and upper grades, teachers often display an anonymous piece of writing (perhaps from a student in another class or from a previous year). Students read the writing, and the teacher uses it to teach the lesson, which may focus on giving suggestions for revision, combining sentences, proofreading, or writing a stronger lead sentence. Teachers also select excerpts from books students are reading for minilessons to show how published authors use writing skills and strategies.

Writing workshop is the best way for students to apply the writing process: Teachers teach students how to complete the activities during each stage of the writing process, and then students practice what they have learned during writing workshop. Students move through the five stages of the writing process as they plan, draft, revise, edit, and, finally, publish their writing:

Prewriting. Students choose topics and set their own purposes for writing. Then they gather and organize ideas, often drawing pictures, making graphic organizers, or talking out their ideas with classmates.

Drafting. Students work independently to write their rough drafts.

Revising. Students participate in writing groups to share their rough drafts and get feedback to help them revise their writing.

Editing. Students work with classmates to proofread and correct mechanical errors in their writing, and they also meet with the teacher for a final editing.

Publishing. Students prepare a final "published" copy of their writing, and sit in the author's chair to read it to classmates.

As students participate in writing workshop, they gain valuable experience using the writing process.

Managing a Workshop Classroom

It takes time to establish a workshop approach because students need to develop new ways of working and learning, and they have to form a community of readers and writers in the classroom (Gillet & Beverly, 2001). For reading workshop, students need to know how to select books and other reading workshop procedures. For writing workshop, students need to know how to use the writing process to develop and refine a piece of writing, how to make books for their compositions, and other writing workshop procedures. Sometimes students complain that they don't know what to write about, but in time, they learn how to brainstorm possible topics and to keep a list of topics in their author's notebooks.

Teachers establish the workshop environment in their classroom, beginning on the first day of the school year. They provide time for students to read and write and teach them how to respond to books and to their classmates' writing. Through their interactions with students, the respect they show to students, and the way they model reading and writing, teachers establish the classroom as a community of learners.

Teachers develop a schedule for reading and writing workshop with time allocated for each component, as was shown in Figure 10–7. In their schedules, teachers allot as much time as possible for students to read and write. After developing the schedule, teachers post it in the classroom and talk with students about the activities and their expectations. Teachers teach the workshop procedures and continue to model them until students become comfortable with the routines. As students gain experience with the workshop approach, their enthusiasm grows and the workshop approach is successful.

Many teachers use a classroom chart, which Nancie Atwell (1998) calls "status of the class," to monitor students' work. At the beginning of reading workshop, students (or the teacher) record what book they are reading or if they're writing in a reading log, waiting to conference with the teacher, or browsing in the classroom library.

For writing workshop, students identify the stage of the writing process they're involved in. A sample writing workshop chart is shown in the Assessment Tools feature below. Teachers can also use the chart to award weekly "effort" grades, to have students indicate their need to conference with the teacher, or to have students announce that they are ready to share the book they've read or publish their writing. Teachers can review students' progress and note which students they need to meet with. When students fill in the chart themselves, they develop responsibility and a stronger desire to accomplish tasks they set for themselves.

Teachers take time during reading and writing workshop to observe students as they work together in small groups. Researchers who have observed in reading and writing workshop classrooms report that some students, even as young as first graders, are excluded from group activities because of gender, ethnicity, or socioeconomic status (Henkin, 1995); the socialization patterns in classrooms seem to reflect society's. Henkin recommends that teachers be alert to the possibility that boys might share books only with other boys or that some students won't find anyone willing to be their editing partner. If teachers see instances of discrimination, they should confront the situation directly and work to foster a classroom environment where students treat each other equitably.

Many teachers fear that when they implement the workshop approach in their classrooms, students' scores on standardized achievement tests will decline, even though teachers have reported either an increase in test scores or no change at all. Swift (1993) reported the results of a yearlong study comparing two groups of her students; one group read basal reader selections, and the other participated in reading workshop. The reading workshop group showed significantly greater improvement, and Swift also reported that students participating in reading workshop showed more-positive attitudes toward reading.

Assessment Tools

"Status of the Class" Chart

Writing Workshop Chart								
Names	Dates							
	3/15	3/16	3/17	3/18	3/19	3/22	3/23	3/24
Antonio	4	5	5	5	5	1	1	1 2
Bella	2	2	2 3	2	2	4	5	5
Charles	3	3 1	1	2	2 3	4	5	5
Dina	4 5	5	5	1	1	1	1	2 3
Dustin	3	3	4	4	4	5	5 1	1
Eddie	2 3	2	2 4	5	5	1	1 2	2 3
Elizabeth	2	3	3	4	4	4 5	5	1 2
Elsa	1 2	3 4	4 5	5	5	1	2	2

Code:
1 = Prewriting   2 = Drafting   3 = Revising   4 = Editing   5 = Publishing

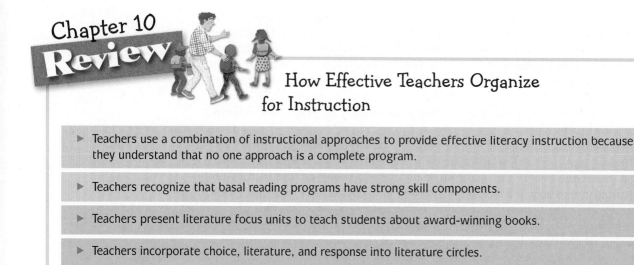

Chapter 10 Review

How Effective Teachers Organize for Instruction

▶ Teachers use a combination of instructional approaches to provide effective literacy instruction because they understand that no one approach is a complete program.

▶ Teachers recognize that basal reading programs have strong skill components.

▶ Teachers present literature focus units to teach students about award-winning books.

▶ Teachers incorporate choice, literature, and response into literature circles.

▶ Teachers provide opportunities for students to read self-selected books during reading workshop and write on self-selected topics during writing workshop.

PEARSON
myeducationlab
Where the Classroom Comes to Life

Go to MyEducationLab at www.myeducationlab.com to deepen your understanding of the concepts presented in this chapter:

▶ Analyze how Ms. Janusz organizes writing workshop by viewing video segments in the Literacy Portraits.
▶ Check your understanding of chapter concepts with the multiple-choice and essay quizzes in the Study Plan.
▶ Apply some of the main ideas discussed in the chapter in the Activities and Applications section of the website.
▶ Practice what you've learned in this chapter in Building Teaching Skills and Dispositions before applying the ideas in your own classroom.

PROFESSIONAL REFERENCES

Atwell, N. (1998). *In the middle: New understandings about reading and writing with adolescents* (2nd ed.). Upper Montclair, NJ: Boynton/Cook.

Calkins, L. M. (1994). *Teaching writing* (rev. ed.). Portsmouth, NH: Heinemann.

Chall, J. S., Jacobs, V. A., & Baldwin, L. E. (1991). *The reading crisis: Why poor children fall behind.* Cambridge, MA: Harvard University Press.

Clarke, L. W., & Holwadel, J. (2007). "Help! What is wrong with these literature circles and how can we fix them?" *The Reading Teacher, 61,* 20–29.

Cunningham, A., & Shagoury, R. (2005). *Starting with comprehension: Reading strategies for the youngest learners.* Portland, ME: Stenhouse.

Daniels, H. (2001). *Literature circles: Voice and choice in book clubs and reading groups.* York, ME: Stenhouse.

Daniels, H., & Bizar, M. (1998). *Methods that matter: Six structures for best practice classrooms.* York, ME: Stenhouse.

Daniels, H., & Steineke, N. (2004). *Mini-lessons for literature circles.* Portsmouth, NH: Heinemann.

Fletcher, R., & Portalupi, J. (2001). *Writing workshop: The essential guide.* Portsmouth, NH: Heinemann.

Fletcher, R., & Portalupi, J. (2007). *Craft lessons: Teaching writing K–8* (2nd ed.). York, ME: Stenhouse.

Frank, C. R., Dixon, C. N., & Brandts, L. R. (2001). Bears, trolls, and pagemasters: Learning about learners in book clubs. *The Reading Teacher, 54,* 448–462.

Gilles, C. (1998). Collaborative literacy strategies: "We don't need a circle to have a group." In K. G. Short & K. M. Pierce (Eds.), *Talking about books: Literature discussion groups in K–8 classrooms* (pp. 55–68). Portsmouth, NH: Heinemann.

Gillet, J. W., & Beverly, L. (2001). *Directing the writing workshop: An elementary teacher's handbook*. New York: Guilford Press.

Hancock, M. R. (2007). *Language arts: Extending the possibilities*. Upper Saddle River, NJ: Merrill/Prentice Hall.

Heller, M. F. (2006). Telling stories and talking facts: First graders' engagement in a nonfiction book club. *The Reading Teacher, 60*, 358–369.

Henkin, R. (1995). Insiders and outsiders in first-grade writing workshops: Gender and equity issues. *Language Arts, 72*, 429–434.

Marriott, D. (2002). *Comprehension right from the start: How to organize and manage book clubs for young readers*. Portsmouth, NH: Heinemann.

Martinez-Roldan, C. M., & Lopez-Robertson, J. M. (1999/2000). Initiating literature circles in a first grade bilingual classroom. *The Reading Teacher, 53*, 270–281.

Ohlhausen, M. M., & Jepsen, M. (1992). Lessons from Goldilocks: "Somebody's been choosing my books but I can make my own choices now!" *The New Advocate, 5*, 31–46.

Peterson, R., & Eeds, M. (2007). *Grand conversations: Literature groups in action*. New York: Scholastic.

Pilgreen, J. L. (2000). *The SSR handbook: How to organize and manage a sustained silent reading program*. Portsmouth, NH: Boynton/Cook/Heinemann.

Samway, K. D., & Whang, G. (1996). *Literature study circles in a multicultural classroom*. York, ME: Stenhouse.

Smith, K. (1998). Entertaining a text: A reciprocal process. In K. G. Short & K. M. Pierce (Eds.), *Talking about books: Literature discussion groups in K–8 classrooms* (pp. 17–31). Portsmouth, NH: Heinemann.

Stien, D., & Beed, P. L. (2004). Bridging the gap between fiction and nonfiction in the literature circle setting. *The Reading Teacher, 57*, 510–518.

Swift, K. (1993). Try reading workshop in your classroom. *The Reading Teacher, 46*, 366–371.

Walsh, K. (2003, Spring). Basal readers: The lost opportunity to build the knowledge that propels comprehension. *American Educator, 27*, 24–27.

CHILDREN'S BOOK REFERENCES

Bunting, E. (2000). *Train to somewhere*. New York: Clarion Books.

Cole, J. (1999). *The magic school bus explores the senses*. New York: Scholastic.

Fox, P. (2001). *Slave dancer*. New York: Atheneum.

Howe, D., & Howe, J. (2006). *Bunnicula: A rabbit-tale of mystery*. New York: Aladdin Books.

Hutchins, P. (2005). *Rosie's walk*. New York: Aladdin Books.

Lowry, L. (1998). *Number the stars*. New York: Laurel Leaf.

MacLachlan, P. (2004). *Sarah, plain and tall*. New York: HarperTrophy.

Naylor, P. R. (1998). *Sang spell*. New York: Atheneum.

Osborne, M. P. (1998). *Hour of the Olympics*. New York: Random House.

Osborne, M. P., & Boyce, N. P. (2004). *Olympics of Ancient Greece*. New York: Random House.

Sachar, L. (2003). *Holes*. New York: Yearling.

Spinelli, J. (2004). *Stargirl*. New York: Laurel Leaf.

Van Allsburg, C. (1982). *Jumanji*. Boston: Houghton Mifflin.

Van Allsburg, C. (1983). *Wreck of the Zephyr*. Boston: Houghton Mifflin.

Van Allsburg, C. (1986). *The stranger*. Boston: Houghton Mifflin.

Van Allsburg, C. (1988). *Two bad ants*. Boston: Houghton Mifflin.

Van Allsburg, C. (1990). *Just a dream*. Boston: Houghton Mifflin.

Van Allsburg, C. (1991). *The wretched stone*. Boston: Houghton Mifflin.

Van Allsburg, C. (1993a). *The garden of Abdul Gasazi*. Boston: Houghton Mifflin.

Van Allsburg, C. (1993b). *The sweetest fig*. Boston: Houghton Mifflin.

Van Allsburg, C. (1996). *The mysteries of Harris Burdick*. Boston: Houghton Mifflin.

Van Allsburg, C. (2002). *Zathura*. Boston: Houghton Mifflin.

Van Allsburg, C. (2005). *The polar express*. Boston: Houghton Mifflin.

Van Allsburg, C. (2006). *Probuditi*. Boston: Houghton Mifflin.

Woodson, J. (2002). *Hush*. New York: Scholastic.

ChapTer 11

Differentiating Reading and Writing Instruction

Mrs. Shasky Differentiates Instruction

The 31 students in Mrs. Shasky's sixth-grade class are reading *The Breadwinner* (Ellis, 2001), the story of a girl who seeks work disguised as a boy so that she can support her family during the Taliban era in Afghanistan. Before students began reading the novel, they participated in a webquest activity about Afghan culture at www.literacynet.org/cortez/ to learn basic information about Afghanistan and listen to an interview with the novel's author.

Today, some of the students are sitting on a sofa or lounging on floor pillows in the reading area in the back of the classroom; they're reading independently. Others are clustered around Mrs. Shasky, listening as she reads the same book aloud. She reads softly to avoid distracting the students reading in the back of the classroom. Some of the students close to Mrs. Shasky follow along in their copies, but others look at Mrs. Shasky, listening intently.

Mrs. Shasky provides two ways to read the novel because her students have a broad range of reading levels, from third through seventh grade. Her students who read at the fifth-, sixth-, and seventh-grade levels can read the book independently, but her 10 struggling readers who read at the third- and fourth-grade levels need extra support; that's why she reads the book aloud to them.

After she finishes reading the chapter, the class comes together for a **grand conversation**. Because the students have many questions about Afghanistan and life under Taliban rule, Mrs. Shasky often takes more of the discussion time than she would like to answer their questions, but gradually the students are developing the background knowledge they need to understand the story. This is the time when Mrs. Shasky teaches comprehension, so she asks inferential questions that require students to go beyond literal information. For example, she asks, "Why did the Taliban arrest Parvana's father?" Hector quickly answers with what he remembers reading in the novel: "Because he went to college in another country, and they don't want teachers to do that." Mrs. Shasky persists, "Why doesn't the Taliban want teachers or other people to study in another country?" No one has an idea, so Mrs. Shasky asks the question another way: "Lots of teachers in America go to other countries to study. You know that I went to visit schools in China last summer. Why is that a good idea?" The students offer several reasons—to learn about other people, to learn new things, and to learn new ways of teaching. "Wouldn't the Taliban want teachers to do these things, too?" Mrs. Shasky asks. Marisela replies, "No, the Taliban closed the schools because they want to control everyone. They don't like teachers who have new ideas because they could make trouble." "How could they make trouble?" Mrs. Shasky continues. Jared suggests, "Parvana's father and the other teachers could tell people that there is a better way to live, and then everyone could get together and fight the Taliban and kill them and have a free country like ours."

As they talk, several students add new words to the **word wall** posted on a nearby wall. The words they add include *burqa, hospitable, turban, chador, nan, exhaustion,* and *toshak.* Mrs. Shasky refers students to the word wall, and they use some of these words later in the morning during their word study period.

Literature study is only one part of Mrs. Shasky's literacy block; her schedule is shown on page 358. She differentiates instruction in several ways during the literacy block to ensure that her students are successful.

Mrs. Shasky begins the literacy block each morning with Accelerated Reader™. All students read independently in leveled books for 30 minutes, using books at their reading level, and complete online comprehension checks after each book. Mrs. Shasky supervises students as they read, moving from desk to desk and listening to individual students read. She also monitors their progress on the comprehension checks. A chart is posted in the classroom so students can track their reading growth.

Next, students participate in a literature study of a novel. Books are usually chosen from the district's recommended reading list for sixth grade, and Mrs. Shasky supplements with other books such as *The Breadwinner* that are timely or

	Ways Mrs. Shasky Differentiates Instruction	
Schedule	Grade-Level Students	Struggling Students
8:30–9:00 Accelerated Reader	Students read books at their reading level and check their comprehension online.	Students read books at their reading level and check their comprehension online.
9:00–10:00 Literature Study	Students read the featured novel independently and participate in grand conversations.	Students listen to the teacher read the featured novel aloud and participate in grand conversations.
10:00–10:15 Minilesson	Mrs. Shasky presents whole-class minilessons on grade-level literacy topics.	Mrs. Shasky presents whole-class minilessons on grade-level literacy topics and other minilessons for small groups according to need.
10:15–11:15 Activities/ Guided Reading	Students are involved in activities related to the featured novel.	Students participate in guided reading groups and work in small groups to do activities related to the featured novel.
11:15–11:45 Word Study	Students participate in whole-class and small-group word-study activities and lessons. They use an individualized approach to spelling.	Students participate in whole-class and small-group word-study activities and lessons. They use an individualized approach to spelling.

that she thinks would appeal to her students. The novel becomes a vehicle for teaching reading strategies and literary analysis.

The third activity is a minilesson. Mrs. Shasky teaches minilessons on comprehension strategies, literary analysis, and other grade-level standards; sometimes the whole class participates, and at other times, the lesson is designed for a specific group of students. She ties lessons to the novel they're reading, and her focus for this novel is on how authors use elements of story structure to develop theme. Right now, the students are overwhelmed by the devastating effects of war, but later during the unit, Mrs. Shasky redirects the focus to human rights. Today, she reviews character development with the whole class and explains that authors develop characters in four ways: through appearance, actions, talking, and thinking. She asks students to think about Parvana, the main character in *The Breadwinner*, and how the author, Deborah Ellis, developed her. As the students share ideas, Mrs. Shasky draws a weblike diagram on chart paper and writes Parvana's name in the center circle. She divides the diagram into four sections and writes *appearance*, *actions*, *talking*, and *thinking* in each section. Next, she writes a sentence or two that students have suggested in each section. Mrs. Shasky steps back and rereads the chart, and then she asks, "Which of the four ways of character development is most important in *The Breadwinner*? What is Deborah Ellis trying to tell us?" The students are torn between "appearance" and "actions." Nita says, "It's her clothes. She has to dress like a boy." Javier disagrees, "No, it's what she's doing. She is pretending to be a boy to help her family. That's what matters." With more discussion, most students agree with Javier. A student's copy of the character development diagram is shown on the next page.

Most of the students return to their desks to write in reading logs or work on activities, but Mrs. Shasky keeps a group of struggling readers who need more

---

A Character Diagram About Parvana

When she was a girl she kept her face covered and tried to be envisible.
She cut her hair and pretended to be a boy.

Appearance

She dressed as a boy to go to the markut and buy food.
She was a reader and writer.
She dug up graves.

Actions

(Parvana)

Talking

"I can do this".

"I am working to get my family back".

Thinking

She dident like the hard work but she did it to help her family.
She was very lonely.

---

practice writing summaries with her to write a summary statement about character development. She uses the Language Experience Approach to take the students' dictation quickly as they develop this summary statement, which they'll share with the whole class:

> *Deborah Ellis tells us about Parvana in four ways: appearance, actions, talking, and thinking. The most important way we learn about Parvana is by her actions. She pretends she is a boy to make money so her family doesn't starve.*

Next week, Mrs. Shasky will introduce human rights with his scenario: Imagine that when you wake up tomorrow morning, life as you know it is totally different—it's like Parvana's life. What will be different? How will you feel? What will you do? What won't you be able to do? Students will talk, draw, and write about the ways their lives would change. Mrs. Shasky will explain what human rights are, talk about the rights discussed in the Declaration of Independence and guaranteed in the Constitution's Bill of Rights, and have students play an interactive online game about human rights. Next, students will participate in differentiated activities to think more deeply about the human rights they enjoy and those denied to Parvana.

While students are working on activities, Mrs. Shasky meets with small groups of struggling readers for guided reading lessons. One group is reading at early third-grade level (Level M), the second group is reading at late third-grade/early fourth-grade level (Level P), and the third group is reading at fourth-grade level (Level R). She usually meets with two groups each day for 25 to 30 minutes each and they read short chapter books at their reading levels; they read and discuss one or two chapters each day, and then they are to reread the chapters independently or with a buddy before they meet again.

The group at the early third-grade level is reading Greenburg's wacky series, The Zack Files, about an amazing fifth grader named Zack. In the book they've just finished reading, *How I Went From Bad to Verse* (Greenburg, 2000), Zack is bitten by an insect and catches Rhyme Disease. He speaks only in rhyme, and worse yet, he floats above the ground and turns blue. Finally, his science teacher, Mrs. Coleman-Levin, cures him and his life returns to normal—at least until the next book. The students silently reread the last two chapters, and they talk again about Zack's weird symptoms and Mrs. Coleman-Levin's unusual cures.

Mrs. Shasky draws a chart about symptoms and cures on a dry-erase board beside her, and the students list the three symptoms that Zack exhibited (rhyming, floating, and blue skin) on the chart; then they explain how Mrs. Coleman-Levin cured each symptom. The students return to Chapter 8 to check that they remember the cures (wearing a reversible jacket, reciting a poem backward, and thinking happy thoughts) and then complete the chart.

These students also go through a ceremonial process of listing the book on a chart of the books they've read as a group. *How I Went From Bad to Verse* is number 28 on the list, and the students are amazed! "I've never read so many books before in my life," Ana comments, and the group agrees. "I told my Tio Roberto that I am a good reader now," Mark says. The students will take the book home tonight to read to their parents, a sibling, a grandparent, or a neighbor.

After conducting another guided reading group, Mrs. Shasky moves the class to the last segment of the literacy block: word study. Students do a combination of vocabulary and individualized spelling activities during word study. On Monday, Mrs. Shasky takes the entire 30 minutes for spelling. She administers the pretest, and students check it themselves. Then they choose the words they will study during the week and make two copies of their word list, one for themselves and one for Mrs. Shasky to keep. Because she's implemented an individualized spelling program, students study different words, depending on their developmental levels. The students practice their spelling words each day, and on Friday, they take the final test.

On Tuesday, Wednesday, and Thursday, students participate in vocabulary lessons to study the meanings of specific words, examine root words and affixes, and learn to use a dictionary and a thesaurus. They use words from the word wall for most activities. Over the past 5 weeks, Mrs. Shasky has taught lessons on these root words:

ann/enn (*year*): *annual, anniversary, millennium*
graph (*write*): *paragraph, autobiography, photograph*
mar/mer (*sea*): *mermaid, submarine, marsh*
tele (*far*): *telecast, telephone, telethon*
volv (*roll*): *revolution, evolution, revolver*

The students have made posters about these root words and brainstormed lists of words using them on chart paper, and they're displayed around the classroom. Today, students are examining words from the word wall to identify other root words.

Because Mrs. Shasky wants to do more to help her struggling readers, she developed a twice-a-week after-school intervention that she calls Shasky's Reading Club. She invited the 10 students reading at third- and fourth-grade levels to stay after school each Tuesday and Thursday to participate in the club. She began the club after parent conferences in early October; she explained the importance of providing these struggling readers with additional instruction and time for reading. All parents agreed to pick up their children after the reading club and to provide 30 minutes of independent reading time at home 4 days a week.

During the 45-minute reading club meeting, students read self-selected books independently and participate in guided reading groups. Mrs. Shasky is pleased to see these students' growth over the 4 months the club has been operating. She's noticed that her struggling students behave like her grade-level readers do during the school day: Instead of being reticent and unsure of themselves as they sometimes are during the school day, they participate willingly in discussions and confidently assume leadership roles.

As the club meeting begins, the 10 students have picked up books they're reading and settled on the sofa and on floor pillows in the back of the classroom. Mrs. Shasky checks that everyone has an appropriate book to read, and then she calls a group of 4 students reading at Level P (late third-/early fourth-grade level); they're reading Jon Scieszka's The Time Warp Trio series of easy-reading chapter books. In these stories, three modern-day friends warp back into history and find themselves in adventures. These students have already read *Your Mother Was a Neanderthal* (2004c) and *Tut Tut* (2004b).

Now they're reading *Knights of the Kitchen Table* (2004a), in which the boys travel back to the days of King Arthur. A giant and a dragon threaten Camelot, and the boys help King Arthur and his knights. The first few chapters were difficult because the students didn't know the King Arthur stories, but Mrs. Shasky told the stories to build their background knowledge. The vocabulary was unfamiliar, too—*vile knaves*, *methinks*, and *foul-mouthed enchanters*, for example—but now the group is into the story. They read about the boys reaching Camelot and meeting King Arthur, Queen Guenevere, and Merlin when they read Chapter 5 today in class. They begin by rereading the chapter and doing a read-around, where they take turns randomly reading aloud their favorite sentences from the chapter. Then Mrs. Shasky takes them on a text walk of Chapter 6, and they examine a full-page illustration of the giant. Hector predicts, "I think Sir Joe the Magnificent will kill the giant and the dragon." "You should say he will *slay* them. *Slay* means to kill," explains Jesus. Mrs. Shasky asks how the students might slay the giant and the dragon, and the boys quickly suggest using swords or guns, but the illustrations in Chapter 6 don't provide any clues.

Mrs. Shasky explains that this riddle is going to be important in the chapter: *Why did the giant wear red suspenders?* The students aren't familiar with suspenders, so Mrs. Shasky shows them a pair of her husband's. She models them and explains that sometimes her husband wears suspenders instead of a belt to hold his pants up.

Marisela, who has been listening quietly while the boys eagerly talked about slaying dragons and giants, asks, "Why did the giant wear suspenders?" The teacher explains that they'll learn the answer as they read the chapter, and then Marisela predicts, "You have to be smart to know the answer to a riddle, so I think those boys will use their brains to save Camelot." Mrs. Shasky smiles in agreement and says, "Let's read Chapter 6 to see if Marisela's prediction is right."

The students read the five-page chapter in less than 10 minutes, and while they're reading, Mrs. Shasky helps students decode several unfamiliar words and explains a confusing section when two boys ask about it. The group now knows the answer to the riddle: *Why did the giant wear red suspenders? To hold his pants up.* They like the riddle and show interest in reading more riddles. Mrs. Shasky says that she'll get some riddle books for them tomorrow. They continue to discuss the chapter, and Jesus sums up the group's feelings by saying, "Bleob [the giant] should be dead and gone by now. I just want to keep reading and find out what happens." Because the giant and the dragon do destroy themselves in the next chapter, Mrs. Shasky lets them take their books back to the reading corner and read the next chapter to find out what happens.

Then Mrs. Shasky calls a second group for a guided reading lesson while the other two groups continue reading on their own. The second group finishes reading with Mrs. Shasky when only several minutes remain before the reading club ends, so Mrs. Shasky joins the group in the back of the classroom and asks each student to briefly tell what he or she has been reading.

Teachers know that their students vary—in their interests and motivation, their background knowledge and prior experiences, and their culture and language proficiency as well as their reading and writing achievement—so it's important to take these individual differences into account as they plan for instruction. Differentiated instruction is based on this understanding that students differ in important ways. According to Tomlinson (2001), differentiated instruction "means 'shaking up' what goes on in the classroom so that students have multiple options for taking in information, making sense of ideas, and expressing what they learn" (p. 1). Differentiating instruction is especially important for struggling readers and writers who haven't been successful and who can't read grade-level textbooks and other reading materials.

In the vignette, for example, Mrs. Shasky modified her instruction to meet her students' needs and provided support for her struggling readers and writers so that they could be successful. First, she provided additional support for struggling students during regular classroom reading and writing activities: During the literature focus unit, Mrs. Shasky read aloud to students who couldn't read the featured novel independently. Second, she provided additional instruction for her struggling students: During the activities period, Mrs. Shasky taught **guided reading** lessons for those students. Third, she provided an after-school intervention program: Mrs. Shasky met with her struggling readers twice a week for Shasky's Reading Club and got these students' parents to commit to providing time for independent reading at home.

> Check the Compendium of Instructional Procedures, which follows Chapter 12, for more information on the highlighted terms.

WAYS TO DIFFERENTIATE INSTRUCTION

The expectation that all students are to meet the same literacy standards at each grade level implies that all students should receive the same instructional program, but teachers know that some of their students are working at grade level but others are struggling or advanced. Because students' achievement levels differ and their interests and preferred ways of learning vary, teachers modify their instructional programs so that all students can be successful. Tomlinson (2001) explains that in differentiated classrooms, "teachers provide specific ways for students to learn as deeply as possible and as quickly as possible without assuming one student's road map for learning is identical to anyone else's" (p. 2). Heacox (2002) characterizes differentiated instruction as rigorous, relevant, flexible, and complex:

Rigorous means that teachers provide challenging instruction that encourages students' active engagement in learning.

Relevant means that teachers address literacy standards to assure that students learn essential knowledge, strategies, and skills.

Flexible means that teachers use a variety of instructional procedures and grouping techniques to support students.

Complex means that teachers engage students in thinking deeply about books they're reading, compositions they're writing, and concepts they're learning.

It's crucial that teachers recognize the diversity of learners in 21st-century classrooms and understand that students don't need to participate in the same learning activities or read and write in whole-class groups all day long. A list of the characteristics of differentiated instruction is presented in Figure 11–1.

Figure 11-1 ◆ Characteristics of Differentiated Instruction

High Standards

Teachers maintain a commitment to meeting grade-level standards for all students.

Assessment-Instruction Link

Teachers use assessment procedures to diagnose students' needs and plan instruction to address those needs.

Flexible Grouping

Teachers have students work individually, in small groups and as a class, and they change grouping arrangements to reflect students' achievement levels and interests.

Reading Materials

Teachers teach with collections of books and other reading materials, written at varying difficulty levels.

Varied Instructional Activities

Teachers design activities with multiple options to meet students' instructional levels.

Instructional Modifications

Teachers modify instruction to respond to students' specific learning needs and continue to make adjustments during instruction to ensure that all students are successful.

Respect

Teachers respect students and value their work.

Academic Achievement

Teachers focus on individual students' academic achievement and success.

Adapted from Heacox, 2002; Robb, 2008; Tomlinson, 2001.

Teachers modify instruction in three ways: They modify the *content* that students need to learn, the instructional *process* used to teach students, and the *products* students create to demonstrate their learning (Heacox, 2002; Tomlinson, 2001):

Differentiating the Content. The content is the "what" of teaching, the literacy knowledge, strategies, and skills that students are expected to learn at each grade level. The content reflects state-mandated grade-level standards. Teachers concentrate on teaching the essential content, and to meet students' needs, they provide more instruction and practice for some students and less for others. For those who are already familiar with the content, they increase the complexity of instructional activities. Teachers decide how they will differentiate the content by assessing students' knowledge before they begin teaching, and then they match students with appropriate activities.

Differentiating the Process. The process is the "how" of teaching, the instruction that teachers provide, the instructional materials they use, and the activities in which students are involved to ensure that they're successful. Teachers group students for instruction and choose reading materials at appropriate levels of difficulty. They also make decisions about involving students in activities that allow them to process what they're learning through oral, written, or visual means.

Differentiating the Product. The product is the end result of learning; it demonstrates what students understand and how well they can apply what they've learned. Students usually create projects, such as posters, multimodal reports, board games, puppet shows, and new versions of stories. Teachers often vary the complexity of the projects they ask students to create by changing the level of thinking that's required to complete the project.

New Literacies
Computer-Based Reading Programs

Scholastic's Reading Counts! and Renaissance Learning's Accelerated Reader™ are two popular K–12 computer-based reading programs that manage students' daily reading practice. They are consistent with differentiated instruction because students choose books to read from a leveled collection and read at their own pace during an independent reading period. Afterward, students take computer-generated quizzes to check their comprehension, and the teacher retrieves computer-generated reports to track students' progress. More than half of the schools in the United States use one of these programs.

These programs provide students with daily opportunities for independent reading practice, and reading volume is related to achievement (Snow, Burns, & Griffin, 1998; Topping & Paul, 1999). Students who do more reading are better readers than those who do less reading. The programs are predicated on these principles:

- Students read authentic books at their reading levels.
- The quizzes provide frequent monitoring of students' comprehension.
- Teachers use the test results to quickly intervene with struggling students.
- Students' motivation grows as they read books and score well on the accompanying quizzes.

These principles reflect the balanced approach to reading instruction.

More than 100,000 books—stories, informational books, and magazine articles—are included in the Accelerated Reader collection, and approximately half that many are included in the Reading Counts! collection. Books in both programs have been leveled, and the reading level is clearly marked on each book. One potential problem is that a limited number of appropriate books are available for older struggling students because these students don't want to read childish books. Sometimes the book collections are housed in a special part of the school library, or teachers set out smaller collections of books at their students' reading levels in their classrooms.

Students take computer-generated quizzes after reading each book. Each quiz has 5 to 20 multiple-choice items, depending on the book's reading level; the questions focus on literal comprehension. The minimum passing score is 60%, and the optimal score is 85%. Students receive the results immediately after taking a quiz so they can learn from their errors and alert the teacher if they're having difficulty. The software provides information about students' comprehension, reading rates, and amount of reading they've done to assist teachers in monitoring their progress. The software also generates classroom, school, and district reports.

Researchers have found that students participating in these computer-based reading programs score higher on standardized tests than students in schools not using the programs; nonetheless, the programs are controversial for several reasons (Holmes & Brown, 2003; Schmidt, 2008). First, the quizzes focus on literal comprehension, not higher-level thinking. Proponents counter that the purpose is to determine whether students have read a book, not to assess higher-level comprehension. Next, detractors argue that students are limited in which books they can choose to read because they can read only those books in the collection that match their reading level, but proponents say that these programs involve only one independent reading time and that students can read any books they want at other times. Third, detractors contend that students often read the book with the goal of passing the quiz, rather than for enjoyment or to learn about an interesting topic, but proponents point out that students need to learn to read for a variety of purposes. Many teachers report liking the program because they can effectively manage students' independent reading and monitor their progress.

Teachers create a classroom culture that promotes acceptance of individual differences and is conducive to matching instruction to individual students. Having a classroom community where students respect their classmates and can work collaboratively is vital. They learn that students don't always do the same activity or read the same book, and they focus on their own work rather than on what their classmates are doing. Students become more responsible for their own learning and develop more confidence in their ability to learn.

Grouping for Instruction

Teachers use three grouping patterns: Sometimes students work together as a whole class, and at other times, they work in small groups or individually. Deciding which type of grouping to use depends on the teacher's purpose, the complexity of the activity, and students' specific learning needs. Small groups should be used flexibly to provide a better instructional match between students and their needs. In differentiated classrooms, students are grouped and regrouped often; they aren't always grouped according to achievement levels or with the same classmates.

Teachers use a combination of the three grouping patterns in each instructional program, but basal reading programs and literature focus units use primarily whole-class groups, literature circles are predominantly small-group programs, and reading and writing workshop feature mostly individual reading and writing activities. Nonetheless, each instructional program incorporates all three grouping patterns. The activities involved in each instructional program are categorized in Figure 11–2.

Teachers use the three types of groups for a variety of activities. Whole-class activities typically include interactive read-alouds and word walls. Guided reading and shared reading are small-group activities. Other activities, including the Language Experience Approach, open-mind portraits, and reading logs, are often done individually. Some activities, such as minilessons and interactive writing, are used with more than one type of group. In addition, when teachers introduce an activity, they have students work together as a class to learn the steps involved; then, once students understand the procedure, they work in small groups or individually.

Guided Reading. Teachers use guided reading to work with small groups of students who are reading books at their instructional level, with approximately 90–94% accuracy (Fountas & Pinnell, 1996, 2001). Students do the actual reading themselves,

Figure 11–2 ◆ The Grouping Patterns in Four Literacy Programs

Program	Whole Class	Small Groups	Individuals
Basal Readers	Introduce the book Teach vocabulary Teach strategies and skills Read the featured selection	Reread the selection Practice vocabulary and skills Work at centers	Complete workbook assignments Read related books
Literature Focus Units	Read a featured book Participate in grand conversations Teach minilessons Do word-study activities Learn about author and genre Create projects	Participate in grand conversations Teach minilessons Create projects	Respond in reading logs Read related books Create projects

Literature Circles	Introduce books	Read and discuss a book
		  together
			Choose a book to read
			Assume roles to contribute
			  to group discussions

Reading Workshop	Read aloud to students Teach minilessons Share books	Teach minilessons	Read self-selected books Conference with the teacher
Writing Workshop	Read aloud to students Teach minilessons Share writing from the author's chair	Teach minilessons Participate in writing groups Edit with a partner	Write on self-selected topics Conference with the teacher

although the teacher may read aloud with students to get them started on the first page or two. Beginning readers often mumble the words softly as they read, which helps the teacher keep track of students' reading and the decoding and comprehension strategies they're using and their level of fluency. Older students who are more fluent readers usually read silently during guided reading.

Teachers choose the books that students read during guided reading; the books are carefully chosen to reflect students' reading levels and their ability to use reading strategies. Teachers read the book in preparation for the lesson and plan how they'll teach it, considering how to develop students' background knowledge and which concepts and vocabulary to teach before students begin reading. They choose a strategy to teach, prepare for word-study activities, and plan other after-reading activities. Many teachers mark important teaching points in the book with little self-stick notes.

Guided reading lessons usually last approximately 20–30 minutes, and teachers meet with several groups each day. Primary-grade students read a book over a day or two, but older students often take a week or longer to complete a book.

Guided reading was developed to use with beginning readers, but teachers also use it with older students, especially English learners and struggling readers who need more teacher support to decode and comprehend books they're reading, learn reading strategies, and become independent readers. Sometimes guided reading is confused with round-robin reading and literature circles, but these three small-group instructional activities are different. In round-robin reading, an approach that's no longer recommended, students take turns reading aloud to the group rather than doing their own reading. In literature circles, students read books on their own with very limited teacher guidance.

Text Sets of Reading Materials

Teachers create text sets of books and other reading materials for students to read during literature focus units and thematic units. These collections include reading materials representing several genres, bookmarked Internet resources, and books that vary in difficulty level. If teachers can't locate a wide enough range of reading materials, they can create them with students to add to the text set. Figure 11–3 presents Mrs. Shasky's text set of books and Internet resources related to *The Breadwinner* (Ellis, 2001), Afghanistan, Muslim religious holidays, and Arab immigrants. The list includes all three books in Deborah Ellis's trilogy of stories about Parvana, and it features two books of poetry by Naomi Shihab Nye (2002a, 2002b), an esteemed Arab American poet and anthologist. Teachers use book talks to introduce books at the beginning of the unit and then display the books on a special shelf in the classroom library. They often read some of the books aloud to the class, have students read other books in literature circles, and encourage students to read additional books during reading workshop.

Text sets are only a small part of well-stocked classroom libraries. Teachers set out collections of stories, informational books, magazines, and books of poetry, written at a range of levels for students to read independently. They also make available lots of other books that are interesting, familiar, and easy enough for reluctant

Literacy Portraits: VIEWING GUIDE

Ms. Janusz uses flexible groups—whole class, small groups, buddies, and individuals—for instruction. Go to the Literacy Profiles section of MyEducationLab and watch these four video clips: Click on Michael's November button to see him reading a poem to the class; Rakie's December button to watch her participate in a guided reading group; Rhiannon's December button to view her reading individually with the teacher; and Curt'Lynn's March button to watch her read with a classmate. As you view these video segments, think about why Ms. Janusz grouped the students as she did. It's not enough to use varied grouping patterns; what matters most is that when students participate in a group, their learning is enhanced. When they set up groups, teachers consider their instructional goal, the activity, and group membership. How do you think Ms. Janusz's grouping patterns benefited these students' learning?

myeducationlab

Figure 11–3 ◆ A Text Set for *The Breadwinner*

Stories

Bunting, E. (2006). *One green apple*. New York: Clarion Books.

Ellis, D. (2001). *The breadwinner*. Toronto: Groundwood Books.

Ellis, D. (2003). *Parvana's journey*. Toronto: Groundwood Books.

Ellis, D. (2004). *Mud city*. Toronto: Groundwood Books.

Khan, R. (2004). *The roses in my carpets*. Markham, ON: Fitzhenry & Whiteside.

Oppenheim, S. L. (1997). *The hundredth name*. Honesdale, PA: Boyds Mills Press.

Informational Books

Banting, E. (2003). *Afghanistan: The culture*. Minneapolis, MN: Crabtree.

Banting, E. (2003). *Afghanistan: The land*. Minneapolis, MN: Crabtree.

Banting, E. (2003). *Afghanistan: The people*. Minneapolis, MN: Crabtree.

Haskins, J., & Benson, K. (2006). *Count your way through Afghanistan*. Minneapolis, MN: Millbrook Press.

Mobin-Uddin, A. (2007). *The best Eid ever*. Honesdale, PA: Boyds Mills Press.

Whitfield, S. (2008). *National Geographic countries of the world: Afghanistan*. Washington, DC: National Geographic Children's Books.

Wolf, B. (2003). *Coming to America: A Muslim family's story*. New York: Lee & Low.

Zucker, J. (2004). *Fasting and dates: A Ramadan and Eid-ul-Fitr story*. New York: Barron's.

Poetry

Nye, N. S. (Compiler). (2002). *The flag of childhood: Poems from the Middle East*. New York: Aladdin Books.

Nye, N. S. (2002). *19 varieties of gazelle: Poems of the Middle East*. New York: Greenwillow.

Websites and Webquests

Afghanistan for Kids
http://www.public.asu.edu/~apnilsen/afghanistan4kids/index2.html

The Breadwinner: A Prereading Webquest Activity for Grades 4–7
www.literacynet.org/cortez/

Kids in Afghanistan Scavenger Hunt
http://teacher.scholastic.com/scholasticnews/indepth/afghanistan/

No Music, no TV
http://www.timeforkids.com/TFK/kids/wr/article/0,28391,94545,00.html

Understanding Afghanistan: Land in Crisis
http://www.nationalgeographic.com/landincrisis/

and struggling students to read and reread on their own, including books they read the previous year.

Tiered Activities

To match students' needs, teachers create several tiered or related activities that focus on the same essential knowledge but vary in complexity (Robb, 2008). These activities are alternative ways of reaching the same goal because "one-size-fits-all" activities can't benefit on-grade-level students, support struggling readers, and challenge advanced students. Creating tiered lessons, according to Tomlinson (2001), increases the likelihood that all students will be successful. Even though the activities are different, they should be interesting and engaging and require the same amount of effort from students.

Teachers vary activities in several ways. First, they vary them by complexity of thinking. In recall-level activities, students identify, retell, or summarize; in analysis-level activities, they compare and categorize; and in synthesis-level activities, students evaluate, draw conclusions, and invent. Second, teachers vary activities according to the level of reading materials. They use books and other print and online materials written at students' reading level, or they vary the way the materials are shared with students. Third, teachers vary activities by the form of expression. Students are involved in visual, oral, and written expression as they complete an activity: Examples of visual expression

Tiered Activities
Teachers use tiered activities to maximize students' learning. These fourth graders are working on a tiered activity—a poster report about stagecoaches—based on Pam Muñoz Ryan's *Riding Freedom* (1998), the story of Charlotte Parkhurst, a legendary stagecoach driver during the California Gold Rush. The students have researched the vehicles and downloaded pictures from the Internet for their report. Today, they're revising their captions to include more facts. Later, they'll print out a "clean" copy, cut the captions apart, and attach them next to the pictures they've already glued on a poster.

are charts, posters, and dioramas; examples of oral expression are dramatizations, oral reports, and choral readings; and examples of written expression are stories, poems, and reports. Some activities require a combination of forms of expression; for example, students might write a poem from the viewpoint of a book character (written) and dress up as the character (visual) to read the poem aloud to the class (oral). Creating tiered activities doesn't mean that some students do more work and others do less; each activity must be equally interesting and challenging to the students.

Tomlinson (2001) suggests that teachers follow these steps to develop a tiered activity:

1. **Design an activity.** Teachers design an interesting activity that focuses on elemental knowledge and requires high-level thinking.
2. **Visualize a ladder.** Teachers visualize a ladder where the top rung represents advanced students, the middle rung on-grade-level students, and the bottom rung struggling students, and then they decide where the activity they've created fits on the ladder.
3. **Create other versions of the activity.** Teachers create one, two, or three versions of the activity at different levels of difficulty to meet the needs of their students. Versions can vary according to the difficulty level of reading materials they use, thinking levels, or forms of expression.
4. **Match activities to students.** Teachers decide which students will do each version of the activity.

It's important to make tiering invisible. Heacox (2002) recommends that teachers alternate the order in which activities are introduced to students, show similar enthusiasm for each one, and use neutral ways of identifying groups of students who will pursue each activity.

One of the literacy standards that Mrs. Shasky addressed as her sixth graders read and responded to *The Breadwinner* (Ellis, 2001) was to analyze the theme conveyed through the characters and the plot. She decided to explore the theme of human rights and, in particular, what happens when they're denied. She began by talking about human rights during a grand conversation as the class discussed the book, and students looked for examples of human rights that the Taliban denied to Parvana and her family. Later, students worked in small groups to create lists of human rights, including religious freedom, the right to safe food and drinking water, the right to speak your mind, the right to education, freedom to work and earn a living, civil rights, and equal rights for all people. They played the interactive game "Save the Bill of Rights" at the National Constitution Center's website (www.constitutioncenter.org/BillOf RightsGame) to learn more about the rights that Americans are guaranteed.

Once students understood what human rights were and could find examples of these rights and freedoms being denied in *The Breadwinner*, Mrs. Shasky designed this activity:

> *Information, please! Create a Venn diagram on chart paper to compare the human rights we have in America to those Parvana and her family had in Taliban-controlled Afghanistan. Then create a statement to summarize the information presented in the Venn diagram and write it underneath the diagram.*

Mrs. Shasky decided that this graphic activity was appropriate for her on-grade-level students. Here's the version she developed for her struggling students:

> *A celebration of human rights! Choose the human right that you value most and create a quilt square using color, images, and words to describe this right. Then we'll connect the squares and create a human rights quilt.*

Finally, Mrs. Shasky designed this activity for her advanced students:

> *Let's get involved! Students in our class are passionate about human rights and want to help people like Parvana and her family. Find a way for us to get involved, and create a brochure about your idea to share with everyone.*

The advanced students researched organizations that aid refugees and promote human rights, including UNICEF, Habitat for Humanity, Heifer International, and Doctors Without Borders, before they heard about Greg Mortenson's work building schools in Afghanistan that's described in *Three Cups of Tea: One Man's Mission to Promote Peace . . . One School at a Time* (Mortenson & Relin, 2007). The group proposed that that their class raise money to build a school through the Pennies for Peace program (www.penniesforpeace.org), and before long, the class had gotten the entire school and their local community involved!

Literacy Centers

Literacy centers contain meaningful, purposeful literacy activities that students can work at in small groups. Students practice phonics skills at the phonics center, sort word cards at the vocabulary center, or listen to books related to a book they're reading at the listening center. Figure 11–4 describes 20 literacy centers. Centers are usually organized in special places in the classroom or at groups of tables (Fountas & Pinnell, 1996).

Although literacy centers are generally associated with primary classrooms, they can be used effectively at all grade levels, even in seventh and eighth grades, to differentiate instruction. In most classrooms, the teacher works with a small group of students while the others work at centers, but sometimes all students work at centers at the same time.

The activities in these literacy centers relate to concepts, strategies, and skills that the teacher recently taught in minilessons, and they vary from simple to complex. Other center activities relate to books students are reading and to thematic units. Students manipulate objects, sort word cards, reread books, complete graphic organizers related to books, and practice skills in centers. Some literacy centers, such as reading and writing centers, are permanent, but others change according to the books students are reading and the activities planned. Teachers provide clear directions at the center so students know what to do and what they should do after they finish an activity.

Figure 11–4 ◆ Literacy Centers

Center	Description
Alphabet	Young children sing the ABC song, sort upper- and lowercase letters, read alphabet books, and practice other activities the teacher has introduced.
Author	Students examine information about authors they're studying, and interested students write letters to them.
Collaborative Books	Students write pages for a class book following the format indicated at the center, and the teacher compiles and binds the pages into a book afterward.
Computer	Students do word processing, read interactive books, complete webquests, search the Internet, and play online games.
Dramatic Play	Students work with puppets, small manipulative materials related to books they're reading, and book boxes as they retell stories and create sequels.
Grammar	Students examine grammar concepts, such as identifying parts of speech and marking capitalization and punctuation on sample compositions.
Informational Books	Students read nonfiction books on a special topic, complete graphic organizers emphasizing the big ideas, and examine genres and nonfiction features.
Library	Students look at books and magazines, choose appropriate books to read from text sets, read books classmates have written, and reread favorite books.
Listening	Students use a tape player and headphones to listen to stories and other books read aloud. Often copies of the books are available so students can read along.
Making Words	Students arrange letter cards to spell words using the procedure their teacher has taught them.
Message	Kindergartners write notes to classmates and post them on a message board. They also check for messages their classmates and the teacher have written to them.
Phonics	Children practice phonics concepts the teacher has introduced using a variety of small objects, picture cards, and games.
Pocket Charts	Children arrange sentence strips for a familiar poem or song in the pocket chart, and then they read or sing it. They also write new versions on sentence strips.
Poetry	Students read poems and locate examples of poetic devices. They also write poems, referring to charts describing various poetic formulas posted in the center.
Proofreading	Students proofread with partners and then use spellcheckers, high-frequency word lists, and dictionaries to correct mechanical errors in their rough drafts.
Sequencing	Students retell stories by sequencing story boards (made by cutting apart two copies of a picture book) or illustrations students have drawn.
Spelling	Students practice spelling words, do word sorts to review spelling concepts, and play spelling games at the center.
Stories	Students use copies of diagrams available at the center to examine story elements, narrative genres, and literary devices in stories they're reading.
Vocabulary	Students learn about idioms; match synonyms, homophones, or antonyms; make word posters or maps; and sort words according to meaning or structural form.
Writing	Students locate needed writing materials, work on writing projects, get feedback from classmates about their writing, and make books.

In some classrooms, students flow freely from one center to another according to their interests; in other classrooms, students are assigned to centers or are required to work at some "assigned" centers and choose among other "choice" centers. Students can sign attendance sheets when they work at each center or mark off their names on a class list posted there. Rarely do students move from center to center in a lockstep approach every 15 to 30 minutes; instead, they move from one center to the next when they finish what they're doing.

This Assessment Tools feature shows a checklist that eighth graders used as they worked at centers as part of a unit on the Constitution. Some centers are required;

Assessment Tools

An Eighth-Grade Centers Checklist

US Constitution Centers Checklist			
Center	**Activity**	**Student's Check**	**Teacher's Check**
Word Wall	Choose three words from the word wall and make word-study cards for each word.		
Puzzle Center	Complete the "Branches of Government" puzzle.		
Library Center	Use the informational books at the center to complete the Constitution time line.		
Internet Center	Research the Constitution on the Internet and complete the study guide.		
Writing Center	Study Howard Christy's painting "The Signing of the Constitution" and write a poem or descriptive essay about it.		
*Legislative Branch Center	Complete activities at this student-developed center.		
*Executive Branch Center	Complete activities at this student-developed center.		
*Judicial Branch Center	Complete activities at this student-developed center.		
*The Bill of Rights Center	Complete activities at this student-developed center.		
*Alphabet Book Center	Choose a letter and create a page for the Class Constitution Alphabet Book.		

they're marked with an asterisk. Students are expected to complete the "required" centers and two others of their choice. They put a checkmark in the "Student's Check" column when they finish work there. Students keep their checklists in their unit folders, and they add any worksheets or papers they do at the center. Having a checklist or another approach to monitor students' progress helps them develop responsibility for completing their assignments.

Differentiated Projects

Go to the Building Teaching Skills and Dispositions section of Chapter 11 on **MyEducationLab.com** to see the ways in which a teacher uses differentiated projects.

Students often create projects at the end of a unit to apply what they've learned and to bring closure to the unit. Possible projects include charts, murals, and other visual representations; poems, essays, and other compositions; PowerPoint reports, **readers theatre** productions, and other oral presentations; websites and other Internet products; and community-based projects that reflect students' synthesis of the big ideas and high-quality workmanship. Projects are an important part of differentiated instruction because students follow their interests, demonstrate what they've learned in authentic ways, and feel successful (Yatvin, 2004).

At the end of some units, students work together on a class project. When fifth graders are studying idioms, for example, they often create a collection of posters or write and compile a collaborative book about idioms, showing their literal and figurative meanings. Most of the time, however, students choose their own projects. Some students work independently or with a partner, and others work in small groups.

Projects are especially valuable for advanced students and struggling students (Yatvin, 2004). Advanced students have opportunities to pursue special interests and extend their learning beyond the classroom when they create projects. For example, they often choose to get involved in community and social issues that they're passionate about, such as homelessness, global warming, and disaster relief, through the projects they do. Similarly, struggling students are often more successful in demonstrating their learning when they work with classmates in small, collaborative groups and use their special talents and expertise, such as drawing, making oral presentations, and using computers, to create a high-quality project.

STRUGGLING READERS AND WRITERS

Why are some students more successful than others in learning to read and write? Researchers report that young children with strong oral language skills and in families where parents read aloud to them and provide other early literacy experiences are more likely to be successful in school. They've also found that children who aren't fluent English speakers, children whose parents had difficulty learning to read and write, and children from low-SES communities are more likely to have difficulty reaching grade-level proficiency in reading and writing (Strickland, 2002).

Struggling Readers

It's crucial to identify students at risk for reading problems early so these problems can be addressed quickly, before they're compounded. Fink (2006) identified these factors that predict early reading difficulty in kindergarten or first grade:

◆ Difficulty developing concepts about print, phonemic awareness, letter names, sound-symbol correspondences
◆ Slower response than classmates when asked to name letters and identify words
◆ Behavior that deviates from school norms

In addition, children with a family history of reading problems are more likely to experience difficulty in learning to read.

It's common for young children to make letter and word reversals (Fink, 2006); they often reverse the lowercase letters *b* and *d* and the words *was* and *saw*, for example. These reversals don't signify that students have a reading problem unless they persist beyond second grade.

Although many struggling readers are identified in the primary grades, other students who have been successful begin to exhibit reading problems in fourth or fifth grade. This phenomenon is known as the "fourth-grade slump" (Chall & Jacobs, 2003). Many teachers attribute this problem to the growing use of informational books and content-area textbooks that may be poorly written or that present unfamiliar topics using new vocabulary words.

Struggling readers exhibit a variety of difficulties. Some have ineffective decoding skills or don't read fluently, and others have insufficient vocabulary knowledge or difficulty understanding and remembering the author's message. Still others struggle because they're unfamiliar with English language structures. Figure 11–5 identifies some of the problems that struggling readers face and suggests ways to solve each one. When teachers suspect that a student is struggling, they take action and assess him or her to diagnose any problems, and they intervene if problems are present because expert instruction helps overcome reading difficulties (Snow, Burns, & Griffin, 1998).

Struggling Writers

Many students struggle with writing. It's easy to notice some of their problems when you examine the quality of their compositions: Some students have difficulty developing and organizing ideas, some struggle with word choice and writing complete sentences and effective transitions, and others have problems with spelling, capitalization, punctuation, and grammar skills. Other students struggle with the writing process and using writing strategies effectively. They may be unsure about what writers do as they develop and refine their compositions or the thinking that goes on during writing (Christenson, 2002). There are some students, too, who complain that their hands and arms hurt when they write, some who show little interest and do the bare minimum, and others who are so frustrated with writing that they refuse to write at all. Figure 11–6 lists some of the problems that struggling writers face and suggests ways to address each problem.

Struggling students need to learn more about writing and have more opportunities to practice writing in order to build their confidence and become more successful. Teachers address students' specific problem areas in their instruction, but high-quality instruction usually includes these five components:

Minilessons. Teachers teach students about the writing process, writing strategies and skills, qualities of good writing, and writing genres through minilessons. Students often examine anonymous student samples saved from previous years as part of their lessons, use rubrics to score these samples, and revise and edit weaker papers to apply what they're learning in the lesson. As part of minilessons, teachers also model how they write and think aloud about how to use writing strategies.

Interactive Writing. Teachers use interactive writing to craft a composition that's well developed and mechanically correct. As students take turns writing words and sentences on chart paper, the teacher reviews strategies and skills and monitors each student's knowledge. Students make their own copy as the composition is written on chart paper, which reinforces what they're learning.

Daily Opportunities to Write. Students need opportunities to apply what they're learning about writers and writing and to develop the stamina to see a

Figure 11–5 ◆ Ways to Address Struggling Readers' Problems

Component	Problem	Solutions
Concepts About Print	Student doesn't understand print concepts.	Use the Language Experience Approach to record the student's language and demonstrate concepts about print. Use shared reading and have the student point out examples of print concepts in big books. Have the student dictate and write messages.
Alphabet Knowledge	Student can't name letters or match upper- and lowercase letters.	Examine alphabet books with the student. Identify letters in the student's name and in environmental print. Teach the student to use the ABC song to identify specific letters. Teach the student to use an alphabet chart to identify matching letters. Play matching games with the student. Have the student sort upper- and lowercase letters. Compile an ABC book with the student.
Phonemic Awareness	Student can't manipulate speech sounds.	Sing songs, read poems, and have the student identify rhyming words. Have the student match rhyming picture cards. Pronounce individual sounds in a word and have the student orally blend them into words. Have the student orally segment words into individual sounds using Elkonin boxes. Have the student substitute beginning, medial, and ending sounds in words.
Decoding	Student can't identify high-frequency words.	Make a personal word wall with words the student recognizes. Use a routine to teach and practice high-frequency words. Have the student look for high-frequency words in familiar books. Have the student write words using magnetic letters or on a dry-erase board.
	Student can't identify consonant and vowel sounds.	Have the student sort objects or picture cards according to sounds. Have the student play phonics games, including those online. Have the student substitute initial consonants to create a list of words using a phonogram. Do interactive writing with the student.
	Student can't decode one-syllable words.	Involve the student in making words activities and word ladder games. Have the student spell words using magnetic letters or on a dry-erase board. Teach the student about vowel patterns. Have the student sort word cards according to vowel patterns. Teach the student to decode by analogy. Have the student read and write lists of words created from one phonogram. Do interactive writing with the student.
	Student can't identify multisyllabic words.	Teach a procedure for decoding multisyllabic words. Have the student remove prefixes and suffixes to identify the root word. Brainstorm lists of words from a single root word. Have the student write words with prefixes and suffixes on a dry-erase board. Do interactive writing with the student.
Fluency	Student omits, substitutes, or repeats words when reading.	Teach high-frequency words that the student doesn't know. Ensure that the level of reading materials is appropriate for the student. Have the student read the text quietly before reading it aloud. Have the student reread familiar texts, including big books and classroom charts. Use choral reading in small groups.

	Student reads word by word, without expression.	Have the student practice rereading easier texts to develop fluency. Have the student echo read, imitating the teacher's expression. Have the student do repeated readings. Break the text into phrases for the student to read aloud. Do choral reading in small groups.
Vocabulary	Student doesn't understand the meanings of words.	Create a K-W-L chart or do an anticipation guide before reading. Teach key vocabulary before reading. Have the student sort words from a book being read or a thematic unit. Have the student make diagrams and posters about key words. Read books aloud every day to build the student's vocabulary. Teach idioms, synonyms and antonyms, and word-learning strategies. Use tea party and semantic feature analysis to learn about words.
Comprehension	Student can't retell or answer questions after reading.	Build the student's background knowledge before reading. Ensure that the book is appropriate for the student. Read the book aloud instead of having the student read it. Teach the student how to retell a story. Have the student sequence story boards and use them to retell the story. Set a purpose for reading by having the student read a brief text to find the answer to one literal-level question.
	Student can't draw inferences or do higher-level thinking.	Read the book aloud instead of having the student read it. Do think-alouds to model drawing inferences and higher-level thinking. Teach comprehension strategies. Teach the student about text structure. Use the Questioning the Author procedure. Use QARs to teach the student about types of questions. Involve the student in small-group grand conversations and literature circles.
	Student is a passive reader.	Use the interactive read-aloud procedure. Teach the student to self-select books using the Goldilocks strategy. Teach the comprehension strategies. Have the student read a book with a partner or in a literature circle. To stimulate interest, have the student view the movie version before reading a novel. Involve the student in hot seat, grand conversations, and other participatory activities. Use the Questioning the Author procedure.
Study Skills	Student can't locate information in reference materials.	Teach the student to use an index to locate information. Have the student practice locating information in TV guides, dictionaries, almanacs, and other reference materials. Teach the student to skim and scan to find information in a text. Teach the student to navigate the Web to locate information online.
	Student can't take notes.	Demonstrate how to take notes using a graphic organizer or small self-stick notes. Make a copy of a text and have the student mark the big ideas with a highlighter pen. Have the student identify big ideas and create a graphic organizer to represent them. Have the student work with a partner to take notes on small self-stick notes.

Adapted from McKenna, 2002; Shanker & Cockrum, 2009.

Figure 11–6 ◆ Ways to Address Struggling Writers' Problems

Component	Problem	Solutions
Ideas	Student complains, "I don't know what to write."	Have the student • brainstorm a list of ideas and pick the most promising one. • talk with classmates to get ideas. • draw a picture to develop an idea. Suggest to the student several specific situations related to the assigned topic.
	Composition lacks focus.	After writing a draft, have the student highlight sentences that pertain to the focus, cut the other parts, and elaborate the highlighted ideas. Give the student a very focused assignment. In a minilesson, share samples of unfocused writing for the student to revise.
	Composition lacks interesting details.	Have the student • brainstorm words related to each of the five senses and then add some of the words to the composition. • draw a picture related to the topic of the composition and then add details reflected in the picture. In minilessons, • teach vivid verbs and adjectives. • teach the visualization strategy.
Organization	Composition lacks organization.	Help the student decide on paragraph organization before beginning to write. In minilessons, • teach the concept of "big idea" using many types of texts. • have the student examine the structure of sample compositions.
	Composition is divided into paragraphs, but some sentences in the paragraph don't belong.	Have the student • reread each paragraph, checking that each sentence belongs. • work with a partner to check sentences in each paragraph. In minilessons, • teach paragraph structure. • have the student examine paragraphs and locate sentences that don't belong.
	Composition lacks an exciting lead.	Have the student • try several leads with an experience, a question, a quotation, or a comparison. • get feedback about the effectiveness of the lead in a writing group. In a minilesson, have the student examine the leads in stories and informational books.
	Ideas in the composition aren't sequenced.	Write the sentences on sentence strips for the student to sequence. In a minilesson, teach sequence words, such as *first, next, last*, and *finally*.
	Composition follows a circular pattern.	Have the student create a graphic organizer before beginning to write. Assist the student in identifying the big idea for each paragraph before beginning to write. In a minilesson, teach sequence of ideas.
Word Choice	Composition lacks interesting vocabulary.	Have the student • refer to word walls posted in the classroom for vocabulary. • focus on adding more-interesting vocabulary words during revising. In a minilesson, have the student revise sample compositions to add interesting vocabulary.
Writing Process	Student doesn't reread or revise composition.	In minilessons, • model revision with sample compositions. • compare the quality of unrevised and revised compositions. Include revision as a requirement in the assessment rubric.

	Student doesn't make constructive revisions.	Use writing groups. Conference with the student to examine the revisions during the revising stage. Include substantive revision as a requirement on the assessment rubric. In minilessons, teach and model the types of revision.
	Student plagiarizes.	Use the writing process. Make the student accountable for clusters, graphic organizers, or note cards. Have the student do the research and writing in class, not at home. In a minilesson, teach the student how to take notes and develop a composition.
Mechanics	Composition is difficult to read because of misspelled words.	Have the student • refer to high-frequency and content-area word walls when writing. • edit with a partner. Conference with the student to correct remaining errors in the editing stage. Set high expectations. In minilessons, • teach the student to proofread. • have the student examine and correct errors in sample compositions. Encourage the student to do more reading.
	Composition is difficult to read because of capitalization and punctuation errors.	Have editing partners identify and correct capitalization and punctuation errors. Conference with the student to identify and correct remaining errors during editing. In minilessons, • teach capitalization and punctuation skills. • have the student examine sample compositions for errors and correct them.
	Composition is difficult to read because of grammar errors.	Have editing partners identify and correct grammar errors during the editing stage. Conference with the student to correct remaining errors during editing. In minilessons, • teach grammar concepts. • have the student examine and correct errors in sample compositions.
	Composition has weak sentence structure.	Have editing partners address sentence structure during the editing stage. In minilessons, • teach sentence structure. • teach sentence combining and then have the student practice it.
	Composition is difficult to read because of poor handwriting or messiness.	Have the student • use word processing. • use manuscript rather than cursive handwriting. • try various types of paper and writing instruments. Take the student's dictation, if necessary.
Motivation	Student does the bare minimum.	Conference with the student to determine why he/she is hesitant. Brainstorm ideas with the student during prewriting. In minilessons, • model how to expand a sentence into a paragraph. • have the student practice expanding a brief composition into a better-developed one.
	Student is too dependent on teacher approval.	Have the student • check with a classmate before coming to the teacher. • sign up for conferences with the teacher. Make sure the student understands expectations and procedures.
	Student refuses to write.	Conference with the student to determine and address the problem. Try Language Experience Approach and interactive writing. Have the student write a collaborative composition with a small group or a partner. Keep first writing assignments very short to ensure success.

composition from beginning to end. They also use writing as a tool for learning as they write in reading logs about books they're reading and in learning logs as part of thematic units.

Conferences. Teachers meet with individual students to talk about their writing, the writing process they use, and how they view themselves as writers. They ask questions such as these:

♦ What's one important thing you've learned about writing?
♦ What part of writing is easy for you? hard for you?
♦ How do you decide what changes to make in your writing?
♦ What would you like to learn next?
♦ Do you think of yourself as a good writer? Why? Why not?

Through these conversations, students learn to think metacognitively and reflect on the progress they've made.

Daily Opportunities to Read. Students need time to read books at their own reading level, and opportunities to listen to the teacher read aloud high-quality stories and informational books that they can't read independently to develop background knowledge, examine genres, become more strategic, and deepen their knowledge of vocabulary words.

Through a combination of instruction and practice, struggling students become more confident writers, develop stamina, and learn to craft well-organized and interesting compositions that are more mechanically correct.

Working With Struggling Students

Struggling students have significant difficulty learning to read and write. Some students are at risk for reading and writing problems in kindergarten and first grade, but others develop difficulties in fourth or fifth grade or even later. The best way to help these students is to prevent their difficulties in the first place by providing high-quality classroom instruction and adding an intervention, if it's needed (Cooper, Chard, & Kiger, 2006). Unfortunately, there's no quick fix for low-achieving students. Helping struggling students requires both high-quality classroom instruction and "a comprehensive and sustained intervention effort" (Allington, 2006, p. 141).

High-Quality Classroom Instruction. Teachers use a balanced approach to literacy that combines explicit instruction in decoding, fluency, vocabulary, comprehension, and writing along with daily opportunities for students to apply what they're learning in authentic literacy activities (Allington, 2006). It's standards driven and incorporates research-based procedures and activities. Teachers address these four components to enhance the literacy development of all students, including struggling readers and writers:

Differentiate instruction. Teachers adjust their instructional programs to match student needs using flexible grouping, tiered activities, and respectful tasks (Opitz & Ford, 2008). Results of ongoing assessment are used to vary instructional content, process, and assignments according to students' developmental levels, interests, and learning styles.

Use appropriate instructional materials. Most of the time, students read interesting books written at their reading levels in small groups or individually. Teachers usually have plenty of books available for on-grade-level readers, but finding appropriate books for struggling readers can be difficult. Figure 11–7 presents a list of easy-to-read paperback series for older struggling students. Teachers also choose award-winning books for literature focus units, but even though these "teaching-texts" are important, Allington (2006) recommends using a single text with the whole class only 25% of the time because students need more opportunities to read books at their reading levels.

Expand teachers' expertise. Teachers continue to grow professionally during their careers (Allington, 2006): They join professional organizations, participate in professional book clubs, attend workshops and conferences, and find answers to questions that puzzle them through teacher-inquiry projects. Figure 11–8 outlines some ways that teachers stretch their knowledge and teaching expertise.

Collaborate with literacy coaches. Literacy coaches are experienced teachers with special expertise in working with struggling readers and writers who support teachers (Casey, 2006). They work alongside teachers in their classrooms, demonstrating instructional procedures and evaluation techniques, and they collaborate with teachers to design instruction to address students' needs. Toll (2005) explains that "literacy coaching is not about telling others what to do, but rather bringing out the best in others" (p. 6). Through their efforts, teachers are becoming more expert, and schools are becoming better learning environments.

The quality of classroom instruction has a tremendous impact on how well students learn to read and write, and studies of exemplary teachers indicate that teaching expertise is the critical factor (Block, Oakar, & Hurt, 2002).

Interventions. Schools use intervention programs to address low-achieving students' reading and writing difficulties and accelerate their literacy learning (Cooper, Chard, & Kiger, 2006). They're used in addition to regular classroom instruction, not as a replacement for it. The classroom teacher or a specially trained reading teacher meets with struggling students on a daily basis. Using paraprofessionals is a widespread practice but not recommended because they aren't as effective as certified teachers (Allington, 2006). During interventions, teachers provide intensive, expert instruction to individuals or very small groups of no more than three students. Interventions take various forms: They can be provided by adding a second lesson during the regular school day, offering extra instruction in an after-school program, or holding extended-school-year programs during the summer. Figure 11–9 summarizes the recommendations for effective intervention programs.

Until recently, most interventions were designed for students in fourth through eighth grades who were already failing; now the focus has changed to early intervention to eliminate the pattern of school failure that begins early and persists throughout some students' lives (Strickland, 2002). Three types of interventions for preschoolers and students in the primary grades have been developed:

- Preventive programs to create more-effective early-childhood programs
- Family-focused programs to develop young children's awareness of literacy, parents' literacy, and parenting skills
- Early interventions to resolve reading and writing problems and accelerate literacy development for low-achieving K–3 students

Intervention programs still exist, of course, for older low-achieving students, but teachers are optimistic that earlier and more-intensive intervention will solve many of the difficulties that older students exhibit today.

Figure 11–7 ◆ Easy-to-Read Paperback Series

Reading Level	Series	Genre
2	A to Z Mysteries by Ron Roy (Random House)	Mystery
	Andrew Lost by J. C. Greenburg (Random House)	Informational
	Cam Jansen by David A. Adler (Puffin)	Adventure
	Jigsaw Jones Mysteries by James Preller (Scholastic)	Mystery
	Magic Tree House by Mary Pope Osborne (Random House)	Adventure
	Marvin Redpost by Louis Sachar (Random House)	Adventure
	Ricky Ricotta's Mighty Robots by Dav Pilkey (Scholastic)	Science Fiction
	Scooby-Do Mysteries by James Golsey (Scholastic)	Mystery
	The Zack Files (some are third-grade level) by Dan Greenburg (Grosset & Dunlap)	Fantasy
3	Abracadabra! by Peter Lerangis (Scholastic)	Mystery
	The Adventures of the Bailey School Kids by Debbie Dadey and Marcia Thornton Jones (Scholastic)	Adventure
	The Boxcar Children by Gertrude Chandler Warner (Albert Whitman)	Mystery
	Captain Underpants by Dav Pilkey (Scholastic)	Humor
	Hank the Cowdog by John R. Erickson (Puffin)	Fantasy
	The Magic School Bus Chapter Books by Joanna Cole (Scholastic)	Informational
	The Secrets of Droon by Tony Abbott (Scholastic)	Fantasy
	Sports by Matt Christopher (Little, Brown)	Sports
	The Unicorn's Secret by Kathleen Duey (Aladdin)	Fantasy
	The Zack Files (some are second-grade level) by Dan Greenburg (Grosset & Dunlap)	Fantasy
4	Animal Ark by Ben M. Baglio (Scholastic)	Animals
	The Babysitters Club by Ann M. Martin (Scholastic)	Adventure
	Deltora Quest by Emily Rodda (Scholastic)	Fantasy
	Dolphin Diaries by Ben M. Baglio (Scholastic)	Animals
	Encyclopedia Brown by Donald J. Sobol (Dutton)	Mystery
	Goosebumps by R. L. Stine (Scholastic)	Horror
	Guardians of Ga'hoole by Kathryn Lasky (Scholastic)	Fantasy
	Island/Everest/Dive Series by Gordon Korman (Scholastic)	Adventure
	Pyrates by Chris Archer (Scholastic)	Adventure
	The Time Warp Trio by Jon Scieszka (Puffin)	Fantasy
5	The Amazing Days of Abby Hayes by Anne Mazer (Scholastic)	Contemporary
	Animorphs by K. A. Applegate (Scholastic)	Science Fiction
	The Black Stallion by Walter Farley (Random House)	Animals
	Dinotopia by Peter David (Random House)	Science Fiction
	From the Files of Madison Finn by Laura Dower (Hyperion)	Contemporary
	Heartland by Lauren Brooke (Scholastic)	Animals
	The Saddle Club by Bonnie Bryant (Random House)	Animals
	Thoroughbred by Joanna Campbell (HarperCollins)	Animals

To prevent literacy problems and break the cycle of poverty in the United States, the federal government directs two early-intervention programs for economically disadvantaged children and their parents. The best-known program is Head Start, which began more than 40 years ago as part of President Lyndon Johnson's War on Poverty. It currently serves nearly one million children and their families each year. Young children grow rapidly in their knowledge of concepts about print and their understanding of literacy behaviors, but these remarkable gains aren't usually sustained after children start school. A newer program that began as part of the No Child Left Behind legislation is the Even Start Family Literacy Program, which integrates early-childhood education and literacy instruction for parents into one program.

Figure 11–8 ◆ Ways to Develop Professional Knowledge and Expertise

Professional Organizations
International Reading Association (IRA)
www.reading.org

National Council of Teachers of English (NCTE)
www.ncte.org

Teachers of English to Speakers of Other Languages (TESOL)
www.tesol.org

Journals
Journal of Adolescent and Adult Literacy (IRA)
Reading Online (www.readingonline.org) (IRA)
The Reading Teacher (IRA)

Language Arts (NCTE)
Voices From the Middle (NCTE)

Essential Teacher (TESOL)
The Internet TESOL Journal (iteslj.org) (TESOL)

Professional Books
Teachers read books about research-based instructional strategies, current issues, and innovative practices published by IRA, NCTE, TESOL, Heinemann, Scholastic, Stenhouse, and other publishers.

Literacy Workshops and Conferences
Teachers attend local, state, and national conferences sponsored by IRA, NCTE, and TESOL to learn more about teaching reading and writing, and they also attend workshops sponsored by local sites affiliated with the National Writing Project (NWP).

Collaboration
Teachers at one grade level or at one school can participate in teacher book clubs, view videos about classroom practices, and discuss ways to improve teaching and meet the needs of their students.

Teacher-Inquiry Projects
To learn how to conduct teacher research, consult one of these books: *The Art of Classroom Inquiry: A Handbook for Teacher-Researchers* (Hubbard & Power, 2003), *The Power of Questions: A Guide to Teacher and Student Research* (Falk & Blumenreich, 2005), and *What Works? A Practical Guide for Teacher Research* (Chiseri-Strater & Sunstein, 2006).

National Writing Project
Teachers attend programs at local National Writing Project sites and apply to participate at invitational summer institutes. To locate the nearest NWP site, check their website at www.nwp.org.

Figure 11-9 ◆ High-Quality Interventions

Scheduling
Interventions take place daily for 20–45 minutes, depending on students' age and instructional needs. Classroom teachers often provide the interventions as second reading lessons in the classroom or during after-school programs, but at other times, specially trained reading teachers provide the interventions.

Grouping
Teachers work with students individually or in small groups of no more than three students; larger groups of students, even when they exhibit the same reading or writing problems, aren't as effective.

Reading Materials
Teachers match students to books at their instructional level for lessons and at their independent level for voluntary reading. The reading materials should engage students and provide some challenge without frustrating them.

Instruction
Teachers provide lessons that generally include rereading familiar books, reading new books, word study (phonics, word identification, and vocabulary), and writing activities. The content of the lessons varies according to students' identified areas of difficulty.

Reading and Writing Practice
Teachers provide additional opportunities for students to spend time reading and writing to practice and apply what they're learning.

Assessment
Teachers monitor progress on an ongoing basis by observing students and collecting work samples. They also use diagnostic tests to document students' learning according to grade-level standards.

Professional Development
Teachers continue their professional development to improve their teaching expertise, and they ensure that the aides and volunteers who work in their classroom are well trained.

Home–School Partnerships
Teachers keep parents informed about students' progress and involve them in supporting independent reading and writing at home.

Two important school-based interventions are Reading Recovery® and Response to Intervention. These are early interventions that quickly identify students who are at risk of failing to avoid long-term reading and writing problems.

Reading Recovery is the most widely known intervention program for the lowest-achieving first graders (Clay, 1993, 2005a, 2005b). It involves 30-minute daily one-on-one tutoring by specifically trained and supervised teachers for 12 to 30 weeks. Reading Recovery lessons involve these components:

Rereading familiar books
Independently reading the book introduced in the previous lesson
Teaching decoding and comprehension strategies
Writing sentences
Reading a new book with teacher support

Once students reach grade-level standards and demonstrate that they can work independently in their classroom, they leave the program. The results of the intervention are impressive: 75% of students who complete the Reading Recovery program meet grade-level literacy standards and continue to be successful.

Response to Intervention (RTI) is a promising schoolwide initiative to identify struggling students quickly, promote effective classroom instruction, provide interventions, and increase the likelihood that students will be successful (Mellard & Johnson, 2008). It involves three tiers:

Tier 1: Screening and Prevention. Teachers provide high-quality instruction that's supported by scientifically based research, screen students to identify those at risk for academic failure, and monitor their progress. If students don't make adequate progress toward meeting grade-level standards, they move to Tier 2.

Tier 2: Early Intervention. Trained reading teachers provide enhanced, individualized instruction targeting students' specific areas of difficulty. If the intervention is successful and students' reading problems are resolved, they return to Tier 1; if they make some progress but need additional instruction, they remain in Tier 2; and if they don't show improvement, they move to Tier 3, where the intensity of intervention increases.

Tier 3: Intensive Intervention. Special education teachers provide more-intensive intervention to individual students and small groups and more-frequent progress monitoring. They focus on remedying students' problem areas and teaching compensatory strategies.

This schoolwide instruction and assessment program incorporates data-driven decision making, and special education teachers are optimistic that it will be a better way to diagnose learning-disabled students.

Improving classroom instruction, diagnosing students' specific reading and writing difficulties, and implementing intensive intervention programs to remedy students' literacy problems are three important ways that teachers work more effectively with struggling students. Research-based interventions, such as Reading Recovery and Response to Intervention, are changing the ways teachers work with students who struggle.

Chapter 11 Review

How Effective Teachers Differentiate Literacy Instruction

▸ Teachers differentiate instruction to meet the needs of all students, including those who struggle.

▸ Teachers understand that struggling readers have difficulties in decoding, fluency, vocabulary, and/or comprehension.

▸ Teachers understand that struggling writers lack knowledge about the qualities of good writing and the process that writers use.

▸ Teachers use a balanced approach to teach struggling students that incorporates explicit instruction, materials at students' reading levels, and more time for reading and writing.

▸ Teachers understand that interventions are additional instructional programs to remedy students' reading and writing difficulties.

Go to MyEducationLab at www.myeducationlab.com to deepen your understanding of the concepts presented in this chapter:

▶ Examine how Ms. Janusz uses grouping to enhance learning in her second-grade classroom by viewing video segments in the Literacy Portraits.

▶ Check your understanding of chapter concepts with the multiple-choice and essay quizzes in the Study Plan.

▶ Apply some of the main ideas discussed in the chapter in the Activities and Applications section of the website.

▶ Practice what you've learned in this chapter in Building Teaching Skills and Dispositions before applying the ideas in your own classroom.

PROFESSIONAL REFERENCES

Allington, R. L. (2006). *What really matter for struggling readers: Designing research-based programs* (2nd ed.). Boston: Allyn & Bacon.

Block, C., Oakar, M., & Hurt, N. (2002). The expertise of literacy teachers: A continuum from preschool–grade 5. *Reading Research Quarterly, 37,* 178–206.

Casey, K. (2006). *Literacy coaching: The essentials.* Portsmouth, NH: Heinemann.

Chall, J. S., & Jacobs, V. A. (2003). Poor children's fourth-grade slump. *American Educator, 27*(1), 14–15, 44.

Chiseri-Strater, E., & Sunstein, B. S. (2006). *What works? A practical guide for teacher research.* Portsmouth, NH: Heinemann.

Christenson, T. A. (2002). *Supporting struggling writers in the elementary classroom.* Newark, DE: International Reading Association.

Clay, M. M. (1993). *Reading Recovery: A guidebook for teachers in training.* Portsmouth, NH: Heinemann.

Clay, M. M. (2005a). *Literacy lessons: Designed for individuals (Part 1: Why? when? and how?).* Portsmouth, NH: Heinemann.

Clay, M. M. (2005b). *Literacy lessons: Designed for individuals (Part 2: Teaching procedures).* Portsmouth, NH: Heinemann.

Cooper, J. D., Chard, D. J., & Kiger, N. D. (2006). *The struggling reader: Interventions that work.* New York: Scholastic.

Falk, B., & Blumenreich, M. (2005). *The power of questions: A guide to teacher and student research.* Portsmouth, NH: Heinemann.

Fink, R. (2006). *Why Jane and John couldn't read—and how they learned: A new look at striving readers.* Newark, DE: International Reading Association.

Fountas, I. C., & Pinnell, G. S. (1996). *Guided reading: Good first teaching for all children.* Portsmouth, NH: Heinemann.

Fountas, I. C., & Pinnell, G. S. (2001). *Guiding readers and writers, grades 3–6.* Portsmouth, NH. Heinemann.

Heacox, D. (2002). *Differentiating instruction in the regular classroom: How to reach and teach all learners, grades 3–12.* Minneapolis, MN: Free Spirit Publishing.

Holmes, C. T., & Brown, C. L. (2003). *A controlled evaluation of a total school improvement process, School Renaissance* (Technical report). Athens: University of Georgia.

Hubbard, R. S., & Power, B. M. (2003). *The art of classroom inquiry: A handbook for teacher-researchers* (rev. ed.). Portsmouth, NH: Heinemann.

McKenna, M. C. (2002). *Help for struggling readers: Strategies for grades 3–8.* New York: Guilford Press.

Mellard, D. F., & Johnson, E. (2008). *RTI: A practitioner's guide to implementing Response to Intervention.* Thousand Oaks, CA: Corwin Press and the National Association of Elementary School Principals.

Mortenson, G., & Relin, D. O. (2007). *Three cups of tea: One man's mission to promote peace . . . one school at a time.* New York: Penguin.

Opitz, M. F., & Ford, M. P. (2008). *Do-able differentiation: Varying groups, texts, and supports to reach readers.* Portsmouth, NH: Heinemann.

Robb, L. (2008). *Differentiating reading instruction: How to teach reading to meet the needs of each student.* New York: Scholastic.

Schmidt, R. (2008). Really reading: What does Accelerated Reader teach adults and children? *Language Arts, 85,* 202–211.

Shanker, J. L., & Cockrum W. (2009). *Locating and correcting reading difficulties* (9th ed.). Boston: Allyn & Bacon/ Pearson.

Snow, C., Burns, S., & Griffin, P. (Eds.). (1998). *Preventing reading difficulties in young children.* Washington, DC: National Academy Press.

Strickland, D. S. (2002). The importance of effective early intervention. In A. E. Farstrup & S. J. Samuels (Eds.), *What research has to say about reading instruction* (3rd ed., pp. 261–290). Newark, DE: International Reading Association.

Toll, C. A. (2005). *The literacy coach's survival guide: Essential questions and practical answers*. Newark, DE: International Reading Association.

Tomlinson, C. A. (2001). *The differentiated classroom: Responding to the needs of all learners* (2nd ed.). Alexandria, VA: Association for Supervision and Curriculum Development.

Topping, K. J., & Paul, T. D. (1999). Computer-assisted assessment of practice at reading: A large scale survey using Accelerated Reader data. *Reading & Writing Quarterly, 15*, 213–231.

Yatvin, J. (2004). *A room with a differentiated view: How to serve ALL children as individual learners*. Portsmouth, NH: Heinemann.

CHILDREN'S BOOK REFERENCES

Ellis, D. (2001). *The breadwinner*. Toronto: Groundwood Books.

Greenburg, D. (2000). *How I went from bad to verse*. New York: Grosset & Dunlap.

Nye, N. S. (Compiler). (2002a). *The flag of childhood: Poems from the Middle East*. New York: Aladdin Books.

Nye, N. S. (2002b). *19 varieties of gazelle: Poems of the Middle East*. New York: Greenwillow.

Ryan, P. M. (1998). *Riding Freedom*. New York: Scholastic.

Scieszka, J. (2004a). *Knights of the kitchen table*. New York: Puffin Books.

Scieszka, J. (2004b). *Tut tut*. New York: Puffin Books.

Scieszka, J. (2004c). *Your mother was a neanderthal*. New York: Puffin Books.

CHAPTER 12

Reading and Writing in the Content Areas

Mrs. Zumwalt's Third Graders Create Multigenre Projects

Mrs. Zumwalt's third graders are studying ocean animals, and her focus is adaptation: How do animals adapt to survive in the ocean? As her students learn about ocean life, they take special notice of how individual animals adapt. For example, Alyssa learns that whelks have hard shells to protect them, Aidan knows that some small fish travel together in schools, Cody reports that clams burrow into the sand to be safe, and Christopher read that sea otters have thick fur to keep them warm in the cold ocean water. Students add what they're learning about adaptation to a chart hanging in the classroom.

A month ago, Mrs. Zumwalt began the thematic unit by passing out a collection of informational picture books from the text set on ocean animals for students to peruse. After they examined the books and read excerpts for 30 minutes or so, she brought them together to begin a K-W-L chart. This huge chart covers half of the back wall of the classroom; three sheets of poster paper hang vertically, side by side. The sheet on the left is labeled "K—What We Know About Ocean Animals." The middle sheet is labeled "W—What We Wonder About Ocean Animals," and the one on the right is labeled "L—What We Learned About

Ocean Animals." Mrs. Zumwalt asked what students already knew about ocean animals, and they offered many facts, including "sea stars can grow a lot of arms," "sharks have three rows of teeth," and "jellyfish and puffer fish are poisonous," which Mrs. Zumwalt recorded in the K column. They also asked questions, including "How can an animal live inside a jellyfish?" "Is it true that father seahorses give birth?" and "How do some fish light up?" which she wrote in the W column. Students continued to think of questions for several days, and Mrs. Zumwalt added them to the W column. At the end of the unit, students will add facts they've learned to the L column.

Mrs. Zumwalt talked about the six ocean habitats—seashore, open ocean, deep ocean, seabed, coral reefs, and polar seas—and the animals living in each one. She began with the seashore, and the students took a field trip to the Monterey Bay Aquarium to learn about the animals that live at the seashore. She focused on several animals in each habitat, reading aloud books and emphasizing how animals have adapted. For each habitat, they made a class chart about it, and students recorded information in their learning logs. They hung the charts in the classroom, and after all six habitats were introduced, Mrs. Zumwalt set out a pack of cards with names of animals and pictures of them for students to sort according to habitat. The box on page 388 shows the habitat sort.

Students have learning logs with 20 sheets of lined paper for writing, 10 sheets of unlined paper for drawing and charting, and 15 information sheets about ocean animals. There's also a page for a personal word wall that's divided into nine boxes and labeled with letters of the alphabet; students record words from the class word wall on their personal word walls. Mrs. Zumwalt introduces new words during her presentations and as she reads aloud books from the text set on ocean animals; then she adds them to the word wall.

Eight of her 20 third graders come from homes where Spanish is spoken, and these students struggle with oral and written English. Mrs. Zumwalt brings them together most days for an extra lesson while their classmates work on other activities. She either previews the next lesson she'll teach or the next book she'll read or reviews her last lesson or the last book she read. In this small-group setting, students talk about what they're learning, ask questions, examine artifacts and pictures, and practice vocabulary. They often create interactive writing charts to share what they've discussed with their classmates. Here is their chart about schools of fish:

There are two kinds of schools. Kids go to school to be smart and little fish travel in groups that are called "schools." Fish are safer when they stick together in schools.

Once the class became familiar with a variety of ocean animals, each student picked a favorite animal to study. They chose sting rays, dolphins, squids, sea anenomes, sand dollars, great white sharks, seals, penguins, sea turtles, jellyfish, octopuses, seahorses, pelicans, killer whales, barracudas, tunas, electric eels, lobsters, manatees, and squid. They researched their animals using the Internet and books in the text set; one of their best

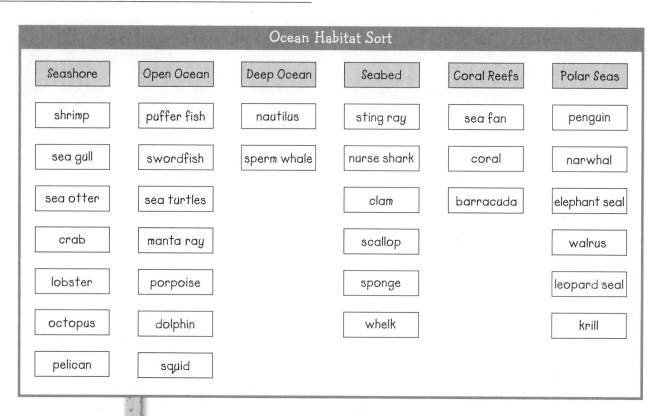

resources was the 11-volume encyclopedia *Aquatic Life of the World* (2001). Once they became experts, Mrs. Zumwalt introduced the idea of developing multigenre projects about the animals they'd studied. In multigenre projects, students create a variety of items representing different genres and package them in a box, on a display board, or in a notebook. Earlier in the year, the students worked collaboratively to develop a class multigenre project, so they were familiar with the procedure and format.

The students decided to create four items for their multigenre projects: an informational book with chapters about their animal's physical traits, diet, habitat, and enemies together with three other items. Other possible items included an adaptation poster, a life-cycle chart, a poem, an alliterative sentence, a diagram of the animal, and a pack of true/false cards about the animal. They plan to package their projects in cereal boxes brought from home and decorated with pictures, interesting information, and a big idea statement about how that animal has adapted to ocean life.

The third graders used the writing process to prepare their informational books. These students know how writers develop, draft, and refine their writing, and earlier in the year, they developed charts describing each stage of the writing process that now hang in the classroom. For prewriting, they used large, multicolored index cards to jot notes; the green one is for "Physical Traits," the yellow one is for "Diet," the blue one is for "Habitat," the purple one is for "Enemies," and the pink one is for other interesting information.

After students took notes using book resources from the text set and Internet resources, they shared the information they'd gathered one-on-one with classmates, who asked questions about things that confused them and encouraged the students to add more information about incomplete topics. Next, students wrote rough drafts and shared them with the partners they worked with earlier. Then they met in writing groups with Mrs. Zumwalt and several classmates and refined their drafts using the feedback they received from their group.

Now students are proofreading and correcting their revised drafts and creating published books. Once they correct the mechanical errors and meet with Mrs. Zumwalt for an editing conference, they recopy their drafts in their best handwriting, add illustrations, and compile the pages into a hardbound book. They're also preparing their boxes and the other items for their multigenre projects.

Christian researched pelicans; his informational book is shown here. For his other three items, he drew a life-cycle chart showing a pelican egg, a newly hatched bird in the nest, a young adult bird flapping its wings, and an older adult diving into the ocean for food; he made a Venn diagram comparing white and brown pelicans; and he wrote an alliterative sentence about pelicans using only words that begin with *p*. His multigenre project box is decorated with pictures of pelicans and interesting information he collected, including "their wings are nine feet long" and "pelicans can live to be 25 years old." The adaptation statement on his multigenre box reads, "Pelicans have web feet and they can dive underwater to catch their food to eat. That's how they can survive at the seashore."

Today, the students finish the K-W-L chart by adding comments about what they've learned about ocean animals. Cody offers that "octopuses can change shape

---

Christian's Informational Book About Pelicans

Chapter 1
Introduction
Pelicans are birds that live on the seashore. They have web feet for walking on sand and swimming. They can dive underwater to catch their food. That's how they live near the ocean.

Chapter 2
Physical Traits
Pelicans have some interesting physical traits. The pelican is easy to identify. They have big pouches and you can tell them by their big necks and plump bodies. The pelican has big legs and colors brown and white.

Chapter 3
Diet
Diet is what an animal eats. The pelican swallows a lot of fish. Pelicans gobble up meat. Pelicans attack sea stars and they chomp on seahorses.

Chapter 4
Habitat
A habitat is where an animal lives. The pelican lives in many countries. Pelicans are found where there's air and where it's warm. Some pelicans are now living in Monterey. Pelicans live by water, too.

Chapter 5
Enemies
Most animals are both prey and predator. That means animals are usually both the hunted and the hunter. The pelican eats seahorses and sea stars. Pelicans are hunted by sharks and people. Why do people hurt these birds? People dump waste into the water and it kills the fishes that the pelicans eat!

Chapter 6
Conclusion
I hope pelicans will always live in Monterey Bay but they could die if people dump pollution into the ocean and that would be very sad.

and color to camouflage themselves," Hernan reports that "dolphins' tails go up and down and fishes' tails go side to side," and Carlos adds that "jellyfish are related to sea anemones because neither one has teeth."

Next Monday afternoon, the third graders will share their completed multigenre boxes one-on-one with second graders, and that evening, they'll share them with their parents at back-to-school night. In preparation for this sharing, the students have been taking turns sharing their projects in the classroom. Each day, three students sit in the author's chair to show their projects and read their informational books aloud to the class.

Students read and write all through the school day as they learn science, social studies, and other content areas. Just as Mrs. Zumwalt's third graders learned about ocean animals through reading and writing, students at all grade levels— even kindergartners and first graders—use reading and writing as tools to learn about insects, the water cycle, pioneers, astronomy, and World War II. Teachers organize content-area study into thematic units and identify big ideas to investigate. Units are time-consuming because student-constructed learning takes time. Teachers can't try to cover every topic; if they do, their students will learn very little. Instead, teachers make careful choices as they plan units, because only a relatively few topics can be presented in depth during a school year. During thematic units, students need opportunities to question, discuss, explore, and apply what they're learning (Harvey, 1998).

Content-area textbooks are important resources that students use to learn about social studies, science, and other content areas, but they aren't a complete instructional program. Students need to know how to read content-area textbooks because these books differ from other reading materials: They have unique conventions and structures that students use as aids in reading and remembering the big ideas. Because many students find textbooks more challenging to read than other books, teachers need to know how to support their students' reading so that they will be successful.

CONNECTING READING AND WRITING

Reading and writing should be connected because reading has a powerful impact on writing, and vice versa (Tierney & Shanahan, 1996): When students read about a topic before writing, their writing is enhanced because of what they learn about the topic, and when they write about the ideas in a book they're reading, their comprehension is deepened because they're exploring big ideas and relationships among ideas. Making this connection is especially important when students are learning content-area information because of the added challenges that unfamiliar topics and technical vocabulary present.

There are other reasons for connecting reading and writing, too. Making meaning is the goal of both reading and writing: Students activate background knowledge, set purposes, and use many of the same strategies for reading and writing. In addition, the reading and writing processes are remarkably similar.

Reading Trade Books

A wide variety of high-quality picture books and chapter books are available today for teachers to use in teaching thematic units. Two outstanding science-related trade books, for example, are *Team Moon: How 400,000 People Landed Apollo 11 on the Moon* (Thimmesh, 2006), a stunning book that highlights the contributions of the people working behind the scenes on that space mission, and *Oh, Rats! The Story of Rats and People* (Marrin, 2006), a riveting book of facts about a champion of survival. Two notable trade books on social studies topics are *Freedom Riders: John Lewis and Jim Zwerg on the Front Lines of the Civil Rights Movement* (Bausum, 2006), a powerful book that contrasts black America and white America in the 1960s by tracing the journeys of two young men, and *One Thousand Tracings: Healing the Wounds of World War II* (Judge, 2007), a moving picture-book story of an American family who started a relief effort that reached 3,000 people in war-ravaged Europe. These books are entertaining and informative, and the authors' engaging writing styles and formats keep readers interested. They're relevant, too, because many students make connections to their own life experiences and background knowledge as they read these books, and teachers use them to build students' background knowledge at the beginning of a thematic unit.

Teachers share these trade books with students in many ways. They use interactive read-alouds to share some books that are too difficult for students to read on their own, and they feature others in literature focus units. They use related books at a range of reading levels for literature circles, and others for students to read independently during reading workshop. Because many books on social studies and science topics are available at a range of reading levels, teachers can find good books, many at their students' reading levels, to use in teaching in the content areas.

> Check the Compendium of Instructional Procedures, which follows this chapter, for more information on the highlighted terms.

Text Sets. Teachers collect text sets of books and other reading materials on topics to use in teaching thematic units, as Mrs. Zumwalt did in the vignette at the beginning of the chapter. Materials for text sets are carefully chosen to include different genres, a range of reading levels to meet the needs of all students in the class, and multimedia resources that present a variety of perspectives. It's especially important to include plenty of books and other materials that English learners and struggling readers can read (Robb, 2002).

Teachers collect as many different types of materials as possible, for example:

stories	newspaper articles
informational books	magazines
poems and songs	photographs
reference books	copies of primary source materials
encyclopedias	atlases and maps
websites and webquests	brochures and pamphlets
films and videos	models and diagrams

They collect single copies of some books and multiple copies of others to use for literature focus units and literature circles. Too often, teachers don't think about using magazines to teach social studies and science, but many excellent magazines are available, including *Click* and *National Geographic Explorer* for young children and *Cobblestone* and *Time for Kids* for older students. Some magazines are also available online, including *Time for Kids*. Figure 12–1 presents a list of print and online magazines for K–8 students.

Mentor Texts. Teachers use stories, informational books, and poems that students are familiar with to model quality writing (Dorfman & Cappelli, 2007). Picture books are especially useful mentor texts because they're short enough to be reread quickly. Teachers begin by rereading a mentor text and pointing out a specific feature such as adding punch with strong verbs, writing from a different perspective, or changing the tone by placing adjectives after nouns. Then students imitate the feature in brief collaborative compositions and in their own writing. Students have opportunities to experiment with literary devices, imitate sentence and book structures, try out new genres, or explore different page arrangements.

Informational books are often used as mentor texts to teach students about new genres, organizational structures, and page formats. For example, *Gone Wild: An Endangered Animal Alphabet* (McLimans, 2006) is a graphic masterpiece where letters

---

Figure 12–1 ◆ Magazines for Children and Adolescents

Format	Magazines
Print	*Appleseeds* (social studies) (M–U)
	Calliope (history) (M–U)
	Click (science) (P)
	Cobblestone (history) (M–U)
	Cricket (stories) (M–U)
	Dig (archeology) (M–U)
	Faces: People, Places, Cultures (multicultural) (M–U)
	Kids Discover (science and history themes) (M–U)
	Ladybug (stories, poems, and songs) (P)
	Muse (science and the arts) (M–U)
	National Geographic Explorer (geography and culture) (P)
	National Geographic for Kids (geography and culture) (M–U)
	Odyssey (science) (M–U)
	OWL (science) (U)
	Ranger Rick (nature) (M)
	Skipping Stones (multicultural) (M–U)
	Spider (stories and poems) (P–M)
	Sports Illustrated for Kids (sports) (M–U)
	Time for Kids (current events) (M–U)
	Your Big Backyard (nature) (P)
Online	*CobblestoneOnline.net* www.cobblestoneonline.net (history, social studies, science) (M–U)
	Dig www.digonsite.com (archeology) (M–U)
	Kids Newsroom www.kidsnewsroom.org (current events) (P–M)
	KidsPost www.washingtonpost.com/wp-srv/kidspost/orbit /kidspost.html (current events) (M–U)
	National Geographic for Kids www.kids.nationalgeographic.com (geography and culture) (M–U)
	Odyssey www.odysseymagazine.com (science) (M)
	OWL owlkids.com/ (science) (M–U)
	Ranger Rick www.nwf.org/rangerrick/ (nature) (M)
	Sports Illustrated for Kids www.sikids.com/ (sports) (M–U)
	Time for Kids www.timeforkids.com/ (current events) (M–U)
	Your Big Backyard www.nwf.org/kidzone/ (nature) (P)

P = primary grades (K–2); M = middle grades (3–5); U = upper grades (6–8)

Text Sets
These eighth graders are reading a novel as part of a text set about the Civil War. As they read, they enjoy the story and learn information at the same time. Other books in the text set include informational books and their social studies textbook. After finishing the novel, the students will preview the unit in their textbook, read other books in the text set, and then return to the textbook to read it thoroughly. The text set helps students expand their knowledge base about the Civil War, prepares them to read the textbook, and extends their learning.

of the alphabet are transformed into vulnerable animals and text boxes accompanying each letter provide information about the animal. Students can use the format of *Gone Wild* to write a class alphabet book during a science or social studies unit. Another excellent mentor text is *Good Masters! Sweet Ladies! Voices From a Medieval Village* (Schlitz, 2007), a collection of 23 first-person character sketches of young people living in an English village in 1255. Each character has a distinct personality and societal role, and historical notes are included in the margins. This book was designed as a play or a readers theatre presentation. During a unit on ancient Rome or World War II, for example, students can use this mentor text to write their own collection of character sketches and present them for students in other classrooms or their parents.

Teachers use mentor texts in minilessons to teach students how to make their writing more powerful, and students use these books as springboards for writing as part of thematic units. Dorfman and Cappelli (2007) explain that "mentor texts serve as snapshots into the future. They help students envision the kind of writers they can become" (p. 3).

Writing as a Learning Tool

Students use writing as a tool for learning during thematic units to take notes, categorize ideas, draw graphic organizers, and write summaries. The focus is on using writing to help students think and learn, not on spelling every word correctly. Nevertheless, students should use classroom resources, such as word walls, to spell most words correctly and write as neatly as possible so that they can reread their own writing. Armbruster, McCarthey, and Cummins (2005) also point out that writing to learn serves two other purposes as well: When students write about what they're learning, it helps them become better writers, and teachers can use students' writing to assess their learning.

Figure 12–2 ◆ A Page From a Second Grader's
Learning Log on Penguins

Learning Logs. Students use learning logs to record and react to what they are learning in social studies, science, or other content areas. Laura Robb (2003) explains that learning logs are "a place to think on paper" (p. 60). Students write in these journals to discover gaps in their knowledge and to explore relationships between what they're learning and their past experiences. Through these activities, students practice taking notes, writing descriptions and directions, and making graphic organizers. Figure 12–2 presents a page from a second grader's learning log about penguins. The chart shows that penguins have three enemies—leopard seals, skua gulls, and people.

Double-Entry Journals. Double-entry journals are just what the name suggests: Students divide their journal pages into two parts and write different types of information in each part (Daniels & Zemelman, 2004). They write important facts in one column and their reactions to the facts in the other column, or questions about the topic in the left column and answers in the right column. Figure 12–3 shows a sixth grader's double-entry journal written during a unit on drug prevention. In the left column, the student wrote information she was learning, and in the right column, she made personal connections to the information.

Simulated Journals. In some stories, such as *Catherine, Called Birdy* (Cushman, 1994), the author assumes the role of a character and writes a series of diary entries from the character's point of view. Here is an excerpt from one of Birdy's entries, which describes life in the Middle Ages:

12th Day of October

No more sewing and spinning and goose fat for me! Today my life is changed. How it came about is this:

We arrived at the abbey soon after dinner, stopping just outside the entry gate at the guest-house next to the mill. The jouncing cart did my stomach no kindness after jellied eel and potted lamb, so I was most relieved to alight. (Cushman, 1994, p. 25)

These books can be called *simulated journals*. They are rich with historical details and feature examples of both the vocabulary and the sentence structure of the period.

Figure 12–3 ◆ A Page From a Sixth Grader's Double-Entry Journal

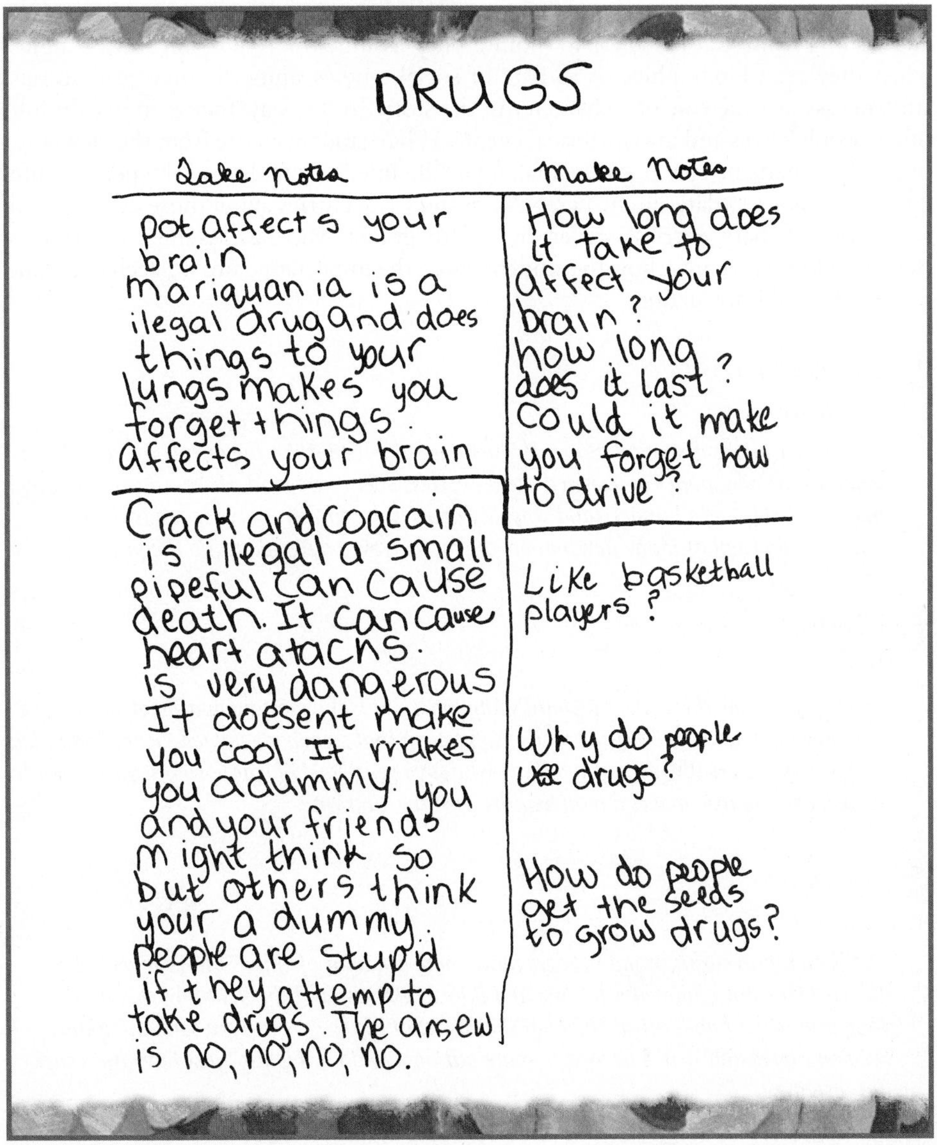

DRUGS

Take notes

pot affects your brain
mariguania is a ilegal drug and does things to your lungs makes you forget things.
affects your brain

Crack and coacain is illegal a small pipeful can cause death. It can cause heart atacks.
is very dangerous It doesent make you cool. It makes you a dummy. you and your friends might think so but others think your a dummy. people are stupid if they attempt to take drugs. The ansew is no, no, no, no.

Make Notes

How long does it take to affect your brain?
how long does it last? Could it make you forget how to drive?

Like basketball players?

Why do people use drugs?

How do people get the seeds to grow drugs?

At the end of the book, authors often include information about how they researched the period and explanations about the liberties they took with the characters or events that are recorded.

Scholastic has created two series of historical journals; one is for girls, and the other is for boys. *I Walk in Dread: The Diary of Deliverance Trembly, Witness to the Salem Witch Trials* (Fraustino, 2004), *A Picture of Freedom: The Diary of Clotee, a Slave Girl* (McKissack, 1997), and *Survival in the Storm: The Dust Bowl Diary of Grace Edwards* (Janke, 2002) are from the Dear America series; each book provides a glimpse into American history from a young girl's perspective. The My Name Is America series features books written from a boy's point of view. Three examples are *The Journal of Patrick Seamus Flaherty: United States Marine Corps* (White, 2002), *The Journal of Ben Uchida: Citizen 13559, Mirror Lake Internment Camp* (Denenberg, 1999), and *The Journal of Jesse Smoke: A Cherokee Boy, Trail of Tears, 1838* (Bruchac, 2001). These books are handsomely bound to look like old journals with heavy paper rough cut around the edges.

Students, too, can write simulated journals by assuming the role of another person and writing from that person's viewpoint. They assume the role of a historical figure when they read biographies or as part of social studies units. As they read stories, students assume the role of a character in the story. In this way, they gain insight into other people's lives and into historical events. When students write from the viewpoint of a famous person, they begin by making a "life line," a time line of the person's life. Then they pick key dates in the person's life and write entries about those dates. A look at a series of diary entries written by a fifth grader who has assumed the role of Benjamin Franklin shows how the student chose the important dates for each entry and wove in factual information:

 December 10, 1719

Dear Diary,

My brother James is so mad at me. He just figured out that I'm the one who wrote the articles for his newspaper and signed them Mistress Silence Dogood. He says I can't do any more of them. I don't understand why. My articles are funny. Everyone reads them. I bet he won't sell as many newspapers anymore. Now I have to just do the printing.

 February 15, 1735

Dear Diary,

I have printed my third "Poor Richard's Almanack." It is the most popular book in America and now I am famous. Everyone reads it. I pretend that somebody named Richard Saunders writes it, but it's really me. I also put my wise sayings in it. My favorite wise saying is "Early to bed, early to rise, makes a man healthy, wealthy, and wise."

 June 22, 1763

Dear Diary,

I've been an inventor for many years now. There are a lot of things I have invented like the Franklin stove (named after me) and bifocal glasses, and the lightning rod, and a long arm to get books off of the high shelves. That's how I work. I see something that we don't have and if it is needed, I figure out how to do it. I guess I just have the knack for inventing.

May 25, 1776

Dear Diary,

Tom Jefferson and I are working on the Declaration of Independence. The patriots at the Continental Congress chose us to do it but it is dangerous business. The Red Coats will call us traitors and kill us if they can. I like young Tom from Virginia. He'll make a good king of America some day.

April 16, 1790

Dear Diary,

I am dying. I only have a day or two to live. But it's OK because I am 84 years old. Not very many people live as long as I have or do so many things in a life. I was a printer by trade but I have also been a scientist, an inventor, a writer, and a statesman. I have lived to see the Philadelphia that I love so very much become part of a new country. Good-bye to my family and everyone who loves me.

Students can use simulated journals in two ways: as a journal or as a refined and polished composition—a demonstration-of-learning project. When students use simulated journals as a tool for learning, they write the entries as they are reading a book in order to get to know the character better, or during a thematic unit as they are learning about the historical period. In these entries, students are exploring concepts and making connections between what they are learning and what they already know. These journal entries are less polished than when students write a simulated journal as a culminating project for a unit. For a project, students plan out their journals carefully, choose important dates, and use the writing process to draft, revise, edit, and publish their journals. They often add covers typical of the historical period. For example, a simulated journal written as part of a unit on ancient Greece might be written on a long sheet of butcher paper and rolled like a scroll, or a pioneer journal might be backed with paper cut from a brown grocery bag to resemble an animal hide.

Quickwriting. Teachers use quickwriting during thematic units to activate background knowledge, monitor students' learning, and review big ideas (Readence, Moore, & Rickelman, 2000). Students write on a topic for 5 to 10 minutes, letting thoughts flow from their minds to their pens without focusing on mechanics or revisions. Young children often draw pictures or use a combination of drawing and writing to explore ideas.

Toward the end of a thematic unit on the solar system, for example, fourth graders each chose a word from the word wall for a quickwrite, and then they shared their writing with classmates. This is one student's quickwrite on Mars:

Mars is known as the red planet. Mars is Earth's neighbor. Mars is a lot like Earth. On Mars one day lasts 24 hours. It is the fourth planet in the solar system. Mars may have life forms. Two Viking ships landed on Mars. Mars has a dusty and rocky surface. The Viking ships found no life forms. Mars' surface shows signs of water long ago. Mars has no water now. Mars has no rings.

Quickwrites provide a good way of checking on what students are learning and an opportunity to clarify misconceptions. After students write, they usually share their quickwrites in small groups, and then one student in each group shares with the class. Sharing also takes about 10 minutes, so the entire activity can be completed in 20 minutes or less.

Figure 12–4 ◆ A Fifth Grader's Poster About Bees

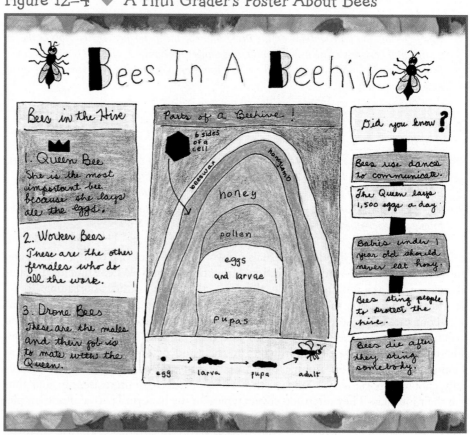

Writing to Demonstrate Learning

Students research topics and then use writing to demonstrate their learning. This writing is more formal, and students use the writing process to revise and edit their writing before making a final copy. Four types of writing to demonstrate learning are reports, essays, poems, and multigenre projects.

Reports. Reports are the best-known type of writing to demonstrate learning; students write many types of reports, ranging from posters to collaborative books and individual reports. Too often, students aren't exposed to report writing until they are faced with writing a term paper in high school, and then they're overwhelmed with learning how to take notes on note cards, organize information, write the paper, and compile a bibliography. There's absolutely no reason to postpone report writing; early, successful experiences with informative writing teach students about content-area topics as well as how to share information (Harvey, 1998; Tompkins, 2008). Here are five types of reports:

Posters. Students combine visual and verbal elements when they make posters (Moline, 1995). They draw pictures and diagrams and write labels and commentary. For example, students draw diagrams of the inner and outer planets in the solar system, identify the parts of a complex machine, label the clothing a Revolutionary War soldier wore and the supplies he carried, identify important events of a person's life on a life line, or chart the explorers' voyages to America and around the world on a map. Students plan the information they want to include in the poster and consider how to devise an attention-getting display using headings, illustrations, captions, boxes, and rules. They prepare a rough draft of their posters, section by section, and then revise and edit each section. Then they make a final copy of each section, glue the sections onto a sheet of posterboard, and share their posters with classmates as they would share finished pieces of writing. As part of a reading and writing workshop focusing on informational books, a fifth grader read *The Magic School Bus Inside a Beehive* (Cole, 1996) and created the poster shown in Figure 12–4 to share what he had learned.

"All About . . ." Books. The first reports that young children write are "All About . . ." books, in which they provide information about familiar topics, such as "Signs of Fall" and "Sea Creatures." Young children write an entire booklet on a single topic. Usually one piece of information and an illustration appear on each page. A page from a first grader's "All About Penguins" book is shown in Figure 12–5.

Alphabet Books. Students use the letters of the alphabet to organize the information they want to share in an alphabet book. These collaborative books

Figure 12–5 ◆ A Page From a First Grader's "All About Penguins" Book

Penguins lay eggs
and keep them
worm with ther
feets and ther
stomechs.

incorporate the sequence structure, because the pages are arranged in alphabetical order. Alphabet books such as *Z Is for Zamboni: A Hockey Alphabet* (Napier, 2002) and *The Queen's Progress: An Elizabethan Alphabet* (Mannis, 2003) can be used as models. Students begin by brainstorming information related to the topic being studied and identify a word or fact for each letter of the alphabet. Then they work individually, in pairs, or in small groups to compose pages for the book. The format for the pages is similar to the one used in alphabet books written by professional authors: Students write the letter in one corner of the page, draw an illustration, and write a sentence or paragraph to describe the word or fact. The text usually begins "_____ is for _____," and then a sentence or paragraph description follows. The "U" page from a fourth-grade class's alphabet book on the California missions is shown in Figure 12–6.

Class Collaborations. Students work together to write collaborative books. Sometimes students each write one page for the report, or they can work together in small groups to write chapters. Students create collaborative reports on almost any science or social studies topic. They write collaborative biographies; each student or small group writes about one event or accomplishment in the subject's life, and then the pages are assembled in chronological order. Or, students work in small groups to write chapters for a collaborative report on the planets in the solar system, ancient Egypt, or the Oregon Trail.

Individual Reports. Students also write individual reports during thematic units. They do "authentic" research, in which they explore topics that interest them or hunt for answers to questions that puzzle them (Harvey, 1998; Stead, 2002). Students read books and interview people with special knowledge to learn about their topics, and increasingly they're turning to the Internet for information. After learning about their topics, students write reports, using the writing process, to share their new knowledge.

Essays. Students write essays to explain, analyze, and persuade; sometimes their topics are personal, such as the death of a parent or adjusting to a new school, and at other times, they address national and international issues such as gun control, famine, and global warming. These compositions are short, usually no longer than two pages. They're classified as nonfiction but often include some story elements, especially in personal essays. Students write essays from their own viewpoints, and their voices should come clearly through the writing (Pryle, 2007). They learn to write personal essays, in which they recount an experience, shaping it to illustrate a theme or generalization; comparisons essays, in which they compare two or more things to emphasize important differences and sometimes offer an opinion; and persuasive essays, in which they try to persuade readers to accept an idea, agree with an opinion, or take a course of action.

Another type is the five-paragraph essay; it's tightly structured with the introduction, body, and conclusion divided into five paragraphs, as the name suggests. In the first paragraph, the writer introduces the topic, often using a thesis statement. In the next three paragraphs, the writer presents three ideas with supporting evidence and examples, one in each paragraph. In the last paragraph, the writer summarizes the ideas and restates the thesis. Use of the five-paragraph essay is very controversial: Proponents argue that it teaches students how to organize their thoughts, and opponents counter that its rigid structure limits thinking. In addition, essays can't always be organized into a predetermined number of paragraphs; instead, the topic and the

Figure 12–6 ◆ The "U" Page From a Fourth-Grade Class's Alphabet Book

Some of the Indians thought life was UNBEARABLE at the missions. They thought this because they couldn't hunt or do the things they were used to. Once they were at the missions they couldn't leave. They were sometimes beaten if they did.

writer's ideas drive the organization and determine the number of paragraphs (Robb, 2004). Because of its limitations, use of this type of essay isn't recommended.

Poetry. Students often write poems as projects after reading books and as part of thematic units. They write formula poems by beginning each line or stanza with a word or line, they create free-form poems, and they follow the structure of model poems as they create their own poems. Here are three poetry forms that students use to demonstrate content-area learning:

"I Am" Poems. Students assume the role of a person and write a poem from that person's viewpoint. They begin and end the poem (or each stanza) with "I am ____" and begin all the other lines with "I." For example, an eighth grader wrote an "I am" poem from the viewpoint of John F. Kennedy after reading a biography about the 35th president:

I am John Fitzgerald Kennedy.
I commanded a PT boat in World War II.
I saved my crew after a Japanese ship hit us.
I became a politician because that's
    what my dad wanted me to do.
I was elected the 35th president of the United States.
I said, "Ask not what your country can do for you—
    ask what you can do for your country."
I believed in equal rights for blacks and whites.
I began the Peace Corps to help the world live free.
I cried the tears of assassination because
Lee Harvey Oswald shot me dead.
I left my young family in America's love.
I am John Fitzgerald Kennedy.

Poems for Two Voices. Students take on two, often contrasting, roles to write poems for two voices. This unique form of free verse is arranged in two columns, side by side. The columns are read together by two readers or two groups of readers: One reader reads the left column, and the other reader reads the right column. When both readers have words—either the same words or different words—written on the same line, they read them simultaneously so that the poem sounds like a musical duet. The best-known book of poems for two voices is Paul Fleischman's Newbery Award–winning collection of insect poems, *Joyful Noise: Poems for Two Voices* (2004). Two eighth graders wrote the following poem during a unit on slavery, after learning about Harriet Tubman and her work with the Underground Railroad. The left column is written from the slave's perspective, and the right column from the conductor's.

FREEDOM!	*FREEDOM!*
	I hide slaves in my house;
	It is my moral duty.
I dodge the law wherever I go;	
I follow the north star.	
	I feed them until they get
	to the next stop.
I hide in closets and cellars	
and sleep whenever I can.	
	It is a big risk.
I am in grave danger.	
BUT IT'S WORTH IT!	*BUT IT'S WORTH IT!*
Harriet Tubman is the Moses	
of our people.	
	I am a conductor,
	helping her and her passengers
	along the way.
Once we reach Canada,	
we're free.	
Will freedom be sweet?	
	Oh, yes it will.
FREE AT LAST!	*FREE AT LAST!*

New Literacies
Webquests

Webquests are inquiry-oriented online projects that enhance students' learning by scaffolding their thinking and involving them in meaningful activities. In addition, these projects foster students' ability to use the Internet to search and retrieve information from websites and understand multimodal presentations of information (Ikpeze & Boyd, 2007). Too often, students waste time searching for Internet resources, but in webquests, the resources have been bookmarked so students can locate them easily. Webquests have these six components:

- **Introduction.** An engaging scenario is presented with background information and descriptions of the roles that students will assume, such as time traveler, botanist, superhero, or archeologist.
- **Task.** A description of the creative activity that students will accomplish during the webquest is provided, including open-ended questions to answer. Possible activities include making brochures, maps, graphs, or posters; writing poems, newspaper articles, letters, or songs; or creating board games or video-diaries.
- **Process.** The steps that students will follow to complete the task are presented.
- **Resources.** The bookmarked websites and any other resources that students will need are listed.
- **Evaluation.** A rubric is provided for students to use to self-assess their work. Teachers also use it to assess the quality of students' work.
- **Conclusion.** Opportunities are presented for students to share their experience, reflect on their learning, and pursue extensions.

These online learning projects were created by Bernie Dodge of San Diego State University in 1995. His website at http://webquest.org/ provides useful information about locating teacher-made webquests and creating your own online inquiry projects.

Webquests are quickly becoming popular. Teachers have created hundreds on a wide range of literature, social studies, science, and math topics that are available without charge on the Internet. A few websites are available for young children, but most are for older students. For example, in one webquest, students who have read *Hatchet* (Paulsen, 2006) embark on a wilderness journey and answer scavenger-hunt questions as they learn survival skills, and in another, students who are studying ancient Egypt travel back to 1250 B.C. to find King Tut's burial mask and decode the message hidden inside it. In these online inquiry projects, students assume roles, work in small groups to read Web-based information, and complete authentic tasks. Other webquest topics include roller coasters, chocolate, biomes, voting, polygons, World War II, and hurricanes, as well as picture books and novels that teachers often use in literature focus units, such as *The Outsiders* (Hinton, 2007) and *Whirligig* (Fleischman, 1999).

Most online resources for webquests are informational websites related to the topic, and most include multimodal features such as graphics, photos, maps, video clips, sound, and interactive activities. It's more difficult to locate good online resources for webquests featuring literature selections, but they generally include websites about the author and topics related to the story's characters, setting, or theme, such as gangs (*The Outsiders*) and drunk driving (*Whirligig*).

As with any instructional materials, teachers must carefully evaluate webquests before using them (Leu, Leu, & Coiro, 2004). Not surprisingly, some are much better than others. The webquests that teachers choose to use in their classrooms should include all six components described here, and resource links must still be active, or teachers need to replace them with new ones. In addition, teachers evaluate their quality: Will the webquest enhance students' understanding of the topic? promote higher-level thinking, including analysis and evaluation? develop new literacies?

Found Poems. Students create poems by culling words and phrases from a book they're reading and arranging the words and phrases into a free-form poem. Fourth graders created this poem about a Saguaro cactus after reading *Cactus Hotel* (Guiberson, 2007):

A young cactus sprouts up.

After 10 years only four inches high,

after 25 years two feet tall,

after 50 years 10 feet all.

A welcoming signal across the desert.

A Gila woodpecker,

a white-winged dove,

an elf owl

decide to stay.

After 60 years an arm grows,

the cactus hotel is 18 feet tall.

After 150 years 7 long branches

and holes of every size

in the cactus hotel.

Multigenre Projects. Students explore a science or social studies topic through several genres in a multigenre project (Allen, 2001). They combine content-area study with writing in significant and meaningful ways. Romano (2000) explains that the benefit of this approach is that each genre offers ways of learning and understanding that the others don't; students gain different understandings, for example, by writing a simulated journal entry, an alphabet book, and a time line. Teachers or students identify a *repetend*, a common thread or unifying feature for the project, which helps students move beyond the level of remembering facts to a higher, more analytical level of understanding. In the vignette at the beginning of the chapter, Mrs. Zumwalt's repetend was adaptation; in their multigenre projects, her students highlighted how the animal they studied adapted to life in the ocean.

Depending on the information they want to present and their repetend, students use a variety of genres such as these for their projects:

acrostics	found poems	websites
riddles	quotes	questions and answers
cartoons	songs	biographical sketches
reports	essays	simulated journals
letters	posters	videos
maps	word sorts	"I am" poems
photo galleries	Venn diagrams	alphabet books
time lines	book boxes	double-entry journals

Students generally use three or more genres in a multigenre project and include both textual and visual genres. What matters most is that the genres amplify and extend the repetend.

Not only can students create multigenre projects, but some authors use the technique in trade books; *The Magic School Bus and the Electric Field Trip* (Cole, 1999) and others in the Magic School Bus series are examples of multigenre books. Each book features a story about Ms. Frizzle and her students on a fantastic science adventure, and on the side panels of pages, a variety of explanations, charts, diagrams, and essays are presented. Together the story and informational side panels present a more complete, multigenre presentation or project. Other multigenre books for older students are *To Be a Slave* (Lester, 2005), *Nothing But the Truth* (Avi, 1993), *Lemony Snicket: The Unauthorized Autobiography* (Snicket, 2003), *Middle School Is Worse Than Meatloaf* (Holms, 2007), and *Ernest L. Thayer's Casey at the Bat: A Ballad of the Republic Sung in the Year 1888* (Bing, 2000).

CONTENT-AREA TEXTBOOKS

Textbooks have traditionally been the centerpiece of social studies and science classes, but these textbooks have shortcomings that limit their effectiveness. Too often, content-area textbooks are unappealing and too difficult for students to read and understand, and they cover too many topics superficially. It's up to teachers to plan instruction to make content-area textbooks more comprehensible and to supplement students' learning with other reading and writing activities during thematic units. A list of guidelines for using content-area textbooks is presented here.

Guidelines
for Using Content-Area Textbooks

▶ Teach students about the unique conventions of textbooks, and show how to use them as comprehension aids.

▶ Have students create questions before reading each section of a chapter and then read to find the answers.

▶ Introduce key terms before students read the textbook assignment.

▶ Have students focus on the big ideas instead of trying to remember lots of facts.

▶ Have students complete graphic organizers as they read because these visual representations emphasize the big ideas and the connections among them.

▶ Include small-group activities to make textbooks more comprehensible.

▶ Teach students to take notes about the big ideas as they read.

▶ Encourage students to be active readers, to ask themselves questions and to monitor their reading.

▶ Use the listen-read-discuss format when textbook assignments are too difficult for students to read on their own.

▶ Create text sets to supplement content-area textbooks.

Go to the Building Teaching Skills and Dispositions section of Chapter 12 on **MyEducationLab.com** to observe the ways in which students use the features of content-area textbooks to improve their comprehension.

Features of Content-Area Textbooks

Content-area textbooks look different than other types of books and have unique conventions, such as the following:

Headings and subheadings to direct readers' attention to the big ideas

Photographs and drawings to illustrate the big ideas

Charts and maps to provide detailed information visually

Margin notes to provide supplemental information or to direct readers to additional information on a topic

Highlighted words to identify key vocabulary

An index for locating specific information

A glossary to assist readers in pronouncing and defining technical words

Study questions at the end of the chapter to check readers' comprehension

These features make the textbook easier to read. It's essential that students learn to use them to make reading content-area textbooks more effective and improve their comprehension (Harvey & Goudvis, 2000). Teachers teach minilessons about these features and demonstrate how to use them to read more effectively.

Making Content-Area Textbooks More Comprehensible

Teachers use a variety of activities during each stage of the reading process to make content-area textbooks more "reader friendly" and to improve students' comprehension of what they've read. Figure 12–7 lists ways teachers can make content-area textbooks more comprehensible at each stage of the reading process. Teachers choose one or more activities at each stage to support their students' reading but never try to do all of the activities listed in the figure during a single reading assignment.

Stage 1: Prereading. Teachers prepare students to read the chapter and nurture their interest in the topic. There are four purposes:

◆ Activate and build students' background knowledge about the topic
◆ Introduce big ideas and technical words
◆ Set purposes for reading
◆ Preview the text

Teachers use a variety of activities to activate and build students' background knowledge about the topic, including developing K-W-L charts, reading aloud stories and informational books, reading information on websites, and viewing videos and DVDs. They also use the gamelike formats of anticipation guides and exclusion brainstorming to heighten students' interest. In anticipation guides, teachers introduce a set of statements on the topic of the chapter, students agree or disagree with each statement, and then they read the assignment to see if they were right. In exclusion brainstorming, students examine a list of words and decide which

ones they think are related to the textbook chapter and then read the chapter to check their predictions.

Teachers introduce the big ideas in a chapter when they create a **prereading plan** in which they present an idea discussed in the chapter and then have students brainstorm words and ideas related to it. They begin a **word wall** with some key words. Another activity is possible sentences, in which students compose sentences that might be in the textbook chapter using two or more vocabulary words from the chapter. Later, as they read the chapter, students check to see if their sentences are included or are accurate enough so that they could be used in the chapter.

Students are more successful when they have a purpose for reading. Teachers set the purpose through prereading activities, and they also can have students read the questions at the end of the chapter, assume responsibility for finding the answer to a specific question, and then read to find the answer. After reading, students share their answers with the class. To preview the chapter, teachers take students on a "text walk" page by page through the chapter, noting main headings, looking at illustrations, and reading diagrams and charts. Sometimes students turn the main headings into questions and prepare to read to find the answers to the questions or check the questions at the end of the chapter to determine the **question-answer-relationships**.

Teaching Struggling Readers and Writers

Content-Area Textbooks

Struggling readers need to know how to read content-area textbooks.

Struggling readers approach all reading assignments the same way—they open to the first page and read straight through—and afterward complain that they don't remember anything. This approach isn't successful because students aren't actively involved in the reading experience, and they're not taking advantage of the special features used in content-area textbooks, including headings, highlighted words, illustrations, end-of-chapter questions, and a glossary, that make the books easier to read.

Successful readers think about the text while they're reading, and the textbook features encourage students' active engagement. Before beginning to read, students activate their background knowledge by previewing the chapter. They read the introduction, the headings, the conclusion, and the end-of-chapter questions and examine photos and illustrations. They locate highlighted vocabulary words, use context clues to figure out the meaning of some words, and check the meaning of others in the glossary. Now they're thinking about the topic. As they read, students try to identify the big ideas and the relationships among them. They stop after reading each section to add information to a graphic organizer, take notes using small self-stick notes, or talk about the section with a classmate. After students finish reading the entire chapter, they make sure they can answer the end-of-chapter questions.

Teachers need to teach students how to read a content-area textbook, pointing out the special features and demonstrating how to use them. Next, students work in small groups or with partners as they practice using the features to engage their thinking and improve their comprehension. With guided practice and opportunities to work collaboratively with classmates, students can become more successful readers.

Stage 2: Reading. Students read the textbook chapter. There are three purposes:

- ◆ Ensure that students can read the assignment
- ◆ Assist students in identifying the big ideas
- ◆ Help students organize ideas and details

It's essential that students can read the chapter. Sometimes the prereading activities provide enough scaffolding so that students can read the assignment successfully, but sometimes they need more support. When students can't read the chapter, teachers have several options. They can read the chapter aloud before students read it independently, or students can read with a buddy. Teachers also can divide the chapter into sections and assign groups of students to read each section and report back to

Figure 12–7 ◆ Ways to Make Content-Area Textbooks More Comprehensible

Stage	Activities	
Prereading	K-W-L charts Text set of books Websites, videos, and DVDs Anticipation guides Exclusion brainstorming	Possible sentences Prereading plan Question-answer-relationships Text walk Word walls
Reading	Interactive read-aloud Buddy reading Small-group read and share	Reciprocal questioning Note taking Graphic organizers
Responding	Discussions Think-pair-square-share Graphic organizers	Learning logs Double-entry journals Quickwriting
Exploring	Word walls Word sorts Data charts	Semantic feature analysis Hot seat Tea party
Applying	Webquests PowerPoint presentations RAFT	Multigenre projects Oral reports Essays

the class; in this way, the reading assignment is shorter, and students can read along with their group members. Students learn the material from the entire chapter as they listen to classmates share their sections. After this sharing experience, students may then be able to go back and read the chapter.

Teachers help students identify and organize the big ideas in a variety of ways. Three of the best ways are reciprocal questioning, when students and the teacher ask questions and talk about each big idea as they read the chapter, taking notes about the big ideas, and completing graphic organizers that focus on the big ideas as they read.

Stage 3: Responding. Teachers help students develop and refine their comprehension in this stage as they think, talk, and write about the information they've read. There are three purposes:

◆ Clarify students' misunderstandings
◆ Help students summarize the big ideas
◆ Make connections to students' lives

Students talk about the big ideas, ask questions to clarify confusions, and make connections as they participate in class discussions. They also talk about the chapter in small groups. One popular technique is think-pair-square-share, in which students think about a topic individually for several minutes; then they pair up with classmates to share their thoughts and hear other points of view. Next, each pair of students gets together with another pair, forming a square, to share their thinking. Finally, students come back together as a class to discuss the topic.

Writing is another way for students respond: They do quickwrites, write in learning logs, or use double-entry journals to record quotes or important information from the chapter and make connections to their own lives. Students also write summaries in which they synthesize the big ideas and describe the relationships among them. Summary writing requires students to think strategically as they analyze what they've read to determine which ideas are important. The minilesson feature on page 410 shows how Mr. Surabian teaches his fourth graders to write summaries.

Stage 4: Exploring. Teachers ask students to dig into the text during the exploring stage to focus on vocabulary, examine the text, and analyze the big ideas. There are three purposes:

- ◆ Have students study vocabulary words
- ◆ Review the big ideas in the chapter
- ◆ Help students to connect the big ideas and details

As they study the technical words in the chapter, students post them on word walls, make posters to study their meaning, and do word sorts to emphasize the relationships among the big ideas. To focus on the big ideas, students make data charts to record information according to the big ideas or create a semantic feature analysis chart to classify important information Figure 12–8 shows an excerpt from a data chart that fourth graders made as they studied the regions of their state. Students often keep these charts and refer to them to write reports or create other projects. They also participate in hot seat and tea party to talk about what they're learning.

Stage 5: Applying. Teachers support students as they apply what they've learned by creating projects. There are three purposes:

- ◆ Expand students' knowledge about the topic
- ◆ Personalize students' learning
- ◆ Expect students to share their knowledge

Students participate in webquests, read additional books from the text set, conduct research online, and interview people to expand their knowledge, and then they share what they've learned by writing reports and essays, creating PowerPoint presentations and multigenre projects, presenting oral reports, and doing other projects.

Learning How to Study

Students are often asked to remember content-area material that they've read for a discussion, to take a test, or for an oral or written project. The traditional way to study is to memorize a list of facts, but it's more effective to use strategies that require students to think critically and to elaborate ideas. As they study, students need to do the following:

- ◆ Restate the big ideas in their own words
- ◆ Make connections among the big ideas
- ◆ Add details to each of the big ideas
- ◆ Ask questions about the importance of the ideas
- ◆ Monitor whether they understand the ideas

Minilesson

Mr. Surabian plans to teach his students how to write a summary; only a few of his students seem familiar with the term *summary writing*, and no one knows how to write one. Writing a summary is one of the state's fourth-grade standards, and the prompt for the writing assessment often requires summary writing. The teacher recognizes that his students need both instruction in how to write a summary and many opportunities to practice summary writing if they are to be successful on the state's achievement tests.

1 Introduce the Topic

Mr. Surabian explains that a summary is a brief statement of the main points of an article. He presents a poster with these characteristics of a summary:

▶ A summary tells the big ideas.

▶ A summary is organized to show connections between the big ideas.

▶ A summary has a generalization or a conclusion.

▶ A summary is written in a student's own words.

▶ A summary is brief.

2 Share Examples

Mr. Surabian shares a one-page article about Wilbur and Orville Wright and the summary he has written about it. The students check that the summary meets all of the characteristics on the poster. Then he shares a second article about mummification, and the students pick out the big ideas and highlight them. Next, Mr. Surabian draws a diagram to show the relationships among the ideas, and they develop a generalization or conclusion statement. Then he shares his summary, and the fourth graders check that he included the big ideas and that the summary meets all of the characteristics on the poster.

3 Provide Information

The next day, Mr. Surabian reviews the characteristics of a summary and shares an article about motorcycles. The students read it, identify and highlight the big ideas, draw a diagram to illustrate the relationships among the ideas, and create a generalization. After this preparation, they write a summary of the article. They check that their summary meets the characteristics listed on the classroom poster. On the third day, Mr. Surabian's students repeat the process with an article about rain forests.

4 Guide Practice

On the fourth day, Mr. Surabian shares an article about the Mississippi River. The students read and discuss it, identifying the big ideas, relationships among them, and possible conclusions. Then the teacher divides the students into small groups, and each group writes a summary. Afterward, they share their summaries and check them against the poster. The class repeats this activity the next day; this time, they read about porpoises. Mr. Surabian shortens the time spent discussing the article and identifying the big ideas and conclusions so that students must assume more responsibility for developing and writing the summary.

5 Assess Learning

Mr. Surabian assesses students' learning by monitoring them as they work in small groups. He identifies several students who need practice, and he plans additional minilessons with them.

Figure 12–8 ◆ An Excerpt From a Data Chart on California

REGION	VEGETATION	ANIMALS	PLACES	HISTORY	ECONOMY
North	Redwood tres	Grizzly Bears Salmon	Eureka Napa Valley	Sutter's Fort GOLD!	Logging Wine
North Coast	Redwood trees Giant Sequoia tres	Seals Sea Otters Monarch Butterflies	San Francisco	Chinatown Cable Cars Earthquake	Computers Ghirardelli chocolate Levis
South Coast	Palm tres Orange tres	Gray whales Condors	Los Angeles Hollywood	El Camino Real missions O.J. Simpson Earthquake	Disneyland TV + movies airplanes
Central Valley	Poppies	Quail	Fresno Sacramento	capital Pony Express Railroad	grapes Peaches Cotton Almond
Sierra Nevada	Giant Sequoia Lupine	Mule Deer Golden eagles Black Baers	Yosemite	John Muir	Skiing

Students use these five strategies as they study class notes, complete graphic organizers to highlight the big ideas, and orally rehearse by explaining the big ideas to themselves.

Taking Notes. When students take notes, they identify what is most important and then restate it in their own words. They select and organize the big ideas, identify organizational patterns, paraphrase and summarize information, and use abbreviations and symbols to take notes more quickly. Copying information verbatim is less effective than restating information because students are less actively involved in understanding what they're reading.

Students take notes in different ways: They can make outlines or bulleted lists; draw flow charts, webs, and other graphic organizers; or make double-entry journals with notes in one column and interpretations in the other column. Or, if students can mark on the text they're reading, they underline or highlight the big ideas and write notes in the margin.

Too often, teachers encourage students to take notes without teaching them how to do it. It's important that teachers share copies of notes they've taken so students see different styles of note taking, and that they demonstrate note taking—identifying the big ideas, organizing them, and restating information in their own words—as students read an article or an excerpt from a content-area textbook. Once students understand how to identify the big ideas and to state them in their own words, they need opportunities to practice note taking. First, they work in small groups to take notes collaboratively, and then they work with a partner.

Teachers often use study guides to direct students toward the big ideas when they read content-area textbooks. Teachers create the study guides using diagrams, charts, lists, and sentences, and students complete them as they read using information and vocabulary from the chapter. Afterward, they review their completed study guides with partners, small groups, or the whole class and check that their work is correct.

It's also important that teachers teach students how to review notes to study for quizzes and tests. Too often, students think they're done with notes once they've written them because they don't understand that the notes are a study tool.

Question-Answer-Relationships. Students use Taffy Raphael's question-answer-relationships (QARs) technique (1986) to understand how to answer questions written at the end of content-area textbook chapters. The technique teaches students to become aware of whether they are likely to find the answer to a question "right there" on the page, between the lines, or beyond the information provided in the text. By being aware of the requirements posed by a question, students are in a better position to answer it correctly and to use the activity as a study strategy.

The SQ3R Study Strategy. Students in the seventh and eighth grades also learn how to use the SQ3R study strategy, a five-step technique in which students survey, question, read, recite, and review as they study a content-area reading assignment. This study strategy, which incorporates before-, during-, and after-reading components, was devised in the 1930s and has been researched and thoroughly documented as a very effective technique (Topping & McManus, 2002).

Teachers introduce SQ3R and provide opportunities for students to practice each step. At first, students can work together as a class as they use the strategy with a text the teacher is reading to them. Then they can work with partners and in small groups before using the strategy individually. Teachers need to emphasize that if students simply begin reading the first page of the assignment without doing the first two steps, they won't be able to remember as much of what they read. When students are in a hurry and skip some of the steps, the strategy will not be as successful.

Why Aren't Content-Area Textbooks Enough?

Sometimes content-area textbooks are used as the entire instructional program in social studies or science, but that's not a good idea. Textbooks typically only survey topics; other instructional materials are needed to provide depth and understanding. Students need to read, write, and discuss topics. It is most effective to use the reading process and then extend students' learning with projects. Developing thematic units with content-area textbooks as one resource is a much better idea than using content-area textbooks as the only reading material.

THEMATIC UNITS

Thematic units are interdisciplinary units that integrate reading and writing with social studies, science, and other curricular areas. Students are often involved in planning the thematic units and identifying some of the questions they want to explore and the activities that interest them. Textbooks are used as a resource, but only one of many. Students explore topics that interest them and research answers to questions they have posed and are genuinely interested in answering. Students share their learning at the end of the unit, as Mrs. Zumwalt's students did in the vignette at the beginning of the chapter, and are assessed on what they have learned as well as on the processes they used in learning and working in the classroom.

How to Develop a Thematic Unit

To begin planning a thematic unit, teachers choose the general topic and determine the instructional focus using literacy and content-area standards. Next, teachers identify the resources they have available for the unit and develop their teaching plan, integrating content-area study with reading and writing activities. Here's an overview of the important considerations in developing a thematic unit:

1. **Determine the focus for the unit.** Teachers identify three or four big ideas to emphasize in the unit because the goal isn't to teach a collection of facts but to help students grapple with several big understandings. Teachers also choose which literacy and content-area standards to teach during the unit.

2. **Collect a text set of books.** Teachers collect stories, informational books, and poems on topics related to the unit for the text set and place them in a special area in the classroom library. Teachers will read aloud some books, and students will read others independently or in small groups. Other books are used for minilessons or as models or patterns for writing projects.

3. **Coordinate content-area textbook readings.** Teachers review the content-area textbook chapters related to the unit and decide how to use them most effectively. For example, they might use one as an introduction, have students read others during the unit, or read the chapters to review the big ideas. They also think about how to make the textbook more comprehensible, especially for English learners and struggling readers.

4. **Locate Internet and other multimedia materials.** Teachers locate websites, DVDs, maps, models, artifacts, and other materials for the unit. Some materials are used to build students' background knowledge and others to teach the big ideas. Also, students create multimedia materials to display in the classroom.

5. **Plan instructional activities.** Teachers think about ways to teach the unit using reading and writing as learning tools, brainstorm possible activities, and then develop a planning cluster with possible activities. They also make decisions about coordinating the thematic unit with a literature focus unit using one book related to the unit, literature circles featuring books from the text set, or reading and writing workshop.

6. **Identify topics for minilessons.** Teachers plan minilessons to teach strategies and skills related to reading and writing nonfiction as well as content-area topics related to the unit based on state standards as well as needs teachers have identified from students' work.

7. **Consider ways to differentiate instruction.** Teachers devise ways to use flexible grouping to adjust instruction to meet students' developmental levels and language proficiency levels, provide appropriate books and other instructional materials for all students, and scaffold struggling students and challenge high achievers with tiered activities and projects.

8. **Brainstorm possible projects.** Teachers think about projects students can develop to apply and personalize their learning at the end of the unit. This planning makes it possible for teachers to collect needed supplies and have suggestions ready for students who need assistance in choosing a project. Students usually work independently or in small groups, but sometimes the whole class works together on a project.

9. **Plan for assessment.** Teachers consider how they'll monitor students' learning and evaluate learning at the end of the unit. In this way, they can explain to students at the beginning of the unit how they will be evaluated and check to see that their assessment emphasizes students' learning of the big ideas.

After considering unit goals, standards to teach, the available resources, and possible activities, teachers are prepared to develop a time schedule, write lesson plans, and create rubrics and other assessment tools.

Nurturing English Learners

Teachers have two goals in mind as they consider how to accommodate English learners' instructional needs when they develop thematic units: They want to maximize students' opportunities to learn English and develop content-area knowledge, and they have to consider the instructional challenges facing their students and how to adjust instruction and assessment to meet their needs (Peregoy & Boyle, 2008).

Challenges in Learning Content-Area Information. English learners often have more difficulty learning during thematic units than during literacy instruction because of the additional language demands of unfamiliar topics, vocabulary words, and informational books (Rothenberg & Fisher, 2007). Here are the most important challenges facing many of these students:

English Language Proficiency. Students' ability to understand and communicate in English has an obvious effect on their learning. Teachers address this challenge by teaching English and content-area information together. They use realia and visual materials to support students' understanding of the topics they're teaching and simplify the language, when necessary, in their explanations of the big ideas. They consider the reading levels of the informational books and content-area textbooks they're using, and when students can't read these books themselves, they read them aloud. But if the books are still too difficult, they find others to use instead. Teachers also provide frequent opportunities for ELs to use the new vocabulary as they talk informally about the topics they're learning.

Background Knowledge. English learners often lack the necessary background knowledge about content-area topics, especially about American history, so teachers need to take time to expand students' knowledge base using artifacts, photos, models, picture books, videos, and field trips, and they need to make clear links between the topics and students' past experiences and previous thematic units; otherwise, the instruction won't be meaningful. Finding time to preteach this information isn't easy, but without it, English learners aren't likely to learn much during the unit. Teachers also involve all students, including ELs, in making **K-W-L charts**, doing **exclusion brainstorming**, and marking **anticipation guides** to activate their background knowledge.

Vocabulary. English learners are often unfamiliar with content-area vocabulary because these words aren't used in everyday conversation; they're technical terms, such as *prairie schooner, democracy, scavenger,* and *photosynthesis.* Because some words, such as *democracy,* are cognates, students who speak Spanish or another Latin-based language at home may be familiar with them, but other technical terms have entered English from other languages. Teachers address this challenge by preteaching key vocabulary words, posting words (with picture clues, if needed) on **word walls**, and using realia, photos, and picture books to introduce the words. They also involve students in a variety of vocabulary activities, including doing **word sorts**, making a **semantic feature analysis**, and drawing diagrams and posters about the words.

Reading. Informational books and content-area textbooks are different than stories: Authors organize information differently, incorporate special features, and use more-sophisticated sentence structures. In addition, nonfiction text is dense, packed with facts and technical vocabulary. Teachers address the challenge of an unfamiliar genre in three ways. First, they teach students about nonfiction books, including the expository text structures and the distinctive text features of this genre. Next, they teach the strategies that readers use to comprehend nonfiction books, including determining the big ideas and summarizing. Third, they teach ELs to make graphic organizers and take notes to highlight the big ideas and the relationships among them. Through this instruction, English learners are equipped with the necessary tools to read informational books and textbooks more effectively.

Writing. Writing is difficult for English learners because it reflects their English proficiency, but it also supports their learning of content knowledge and English. All students should use writing as a tool for learning during thematic units. As they **quickwrite**, draw graphic organizers, make charts and diagrams, take notes, and write in **learning logs**, they're grappling with the big ideas and the vocabulary they're learning. Students also use writing to demonstrate learning. This more-formal type of writing is much more difficult for English learners because of increased language demands. Teachers address this challenge by choosing a project that requires less writing or by having students work with partners or in small groups.

These challenges are primarily the result of the students' limited knowledge of English, and when teachers address them, ELs are more likely to be successful in learning content-area information and developing English language proficiency.

Adjusting Instruction. Teachers address the challenges facing English learners as they adjust instruction to maximize students' learning. They also find ways to maximize students' participation in instructional activities because many ELs avoid interacting with mainstream classmates or fear asking questions in class (Peregoy & Boyle, 2008; Rothenberg & Fisher, 2007). Here are some suggestions to guide teachers in adjusting their instruction:

◆ Use visuals and manipulatives, including artifacts, videos, photographs, and models
◆ Preteach big ideas and key vocabulary
◆ Teach students about expository text structures
◆ Practice taking notes with students
◆ Use graphic organizers and other diagrams to highlight relationships among big ideas
◆ Organize students to work in small collaborative groups and with partners
◆ Include frequent opportunities for students to talk informally about big ideas
◆ Provide opportunities for students to use oral language, reading, and writing
◆ Collect text sets, including picture books and online resources
◆ Use a textbook as only one resource
◆ Review big ideas and key vocabulary

These suggestions take into account students' level of English development, their limited background knowledge and vocabulary about many unit topics, and their reading and writing levels.

Choosing Alternative Assessments. Teachers monitor English learners' progress using a combination of observing them and asking questions. Too often, teachers ask ELs if they understand, but that usually isn't effective because they tend respond positively, even when they're confused. It's more productive to interact with students, talking with them about the activity they're involved in or asking questions about the book they're reading.

Teachers also devise alternative assessments to learn more about English learners' achievement when they have difficulty on regular evaluations (Rothenberg & Fisher, 2007). For example, instead of writing an essay, students can draw pictures or graphic organizers about the big ideas and add words from the word wall to label them to demonstrate their learning, or they can talk about what they've learned in a conference with the teacher. Instead of giving written tests, teachers can simplify the wording of the test questions and have ELs answer them orally. When it's important to have English learners create written projects, they'll be more successful if they work collaboratively in small groups. Portfolios are especially useful in documenting ELs' achievement. Students also place work samples in their portfolios to show what they've learned about content-area topics and how their English proficiency has developed.

A First-Grade Unit on Trees

During this 4-week unit, first graders learn about trees and their importance to people and animals. Students observe trees in their community and learn to identify the parts of a tree and types of trees. Teachers use the interactive read-aloud procedure to share books from the text set and list important words on the word wall. A collection of leaves, photos of trees, pictures of animals that live in trees, and products that come from trees is displayed in the classroom, and students learn about categorizing as they sort types of leaves, shapes of trees, foods that grow on trees and those that don't, and animals that live in trees and those that don't. Students learn how to use writing as a tool for learning as they make entries in learning logs, and teachers use interactive writing to make charts about the big ideas. They also view information on book-marked websites to learn more about trees. As a culminating activity, students plant a tree at their school or participate in a community tree-planting campaign. Figure 12–9 shows the planning cluster for this unit.

A Fourth-Grade Unit on Desert Ecosystems

During this 3-week unit, students investigate the plants, animals, and people that live in the desert and learn how they support each other. They keep learning logs in which they take notes and write reactions to books they're reading. Students divide into book clubs during the first week to read books about the desert. During the second week of the unit, students participate in an author study of Byrd Baylor, a woman who lives in the desert and writes about desert life, and they read many of her books. During the third week, students participate in reading workshop to read other desert books and reread favorites. To extend their learning, students create projects, including writing desert riddles, making a chart of a desert ecosystem, and drawing a desert mural. Together as a class, students write a desert alphabet book. A planning cluster for a unit on desert life is presented in Figure 12–10.

A Sixth-Grade Unit on Ancient Egypt

Students learn about this great ancient civilization during a monthlong unit. Key concepts include the influence of the Nile River on Egyptian life, the contributions of this civilization to contemporary America, a comparison of ancient to modern Egypt, and the techniques Egyptologists use to locate tombs of the ancient rulers and deci-pher Egyptian hieroglyphics. Students read books in literature circles and read other books from the text set independently. They also consult online resources and com-plete a webquest about ancient Egypt. Teachers teach minilessons on map-reading skills, taking notes from content-area textbooks, Egyptian gods, and writing poems. At the end of the unit, students create projects and share them on Egypt day, when they assume the roles of ancient Egyptians, dressing as ancient people did and eating foods of the period. Figure 12–11 presents a planning cluster for the unit.

Figure 12–9 ◆ A Planning Cluster for a First-Grade Unit on Trees

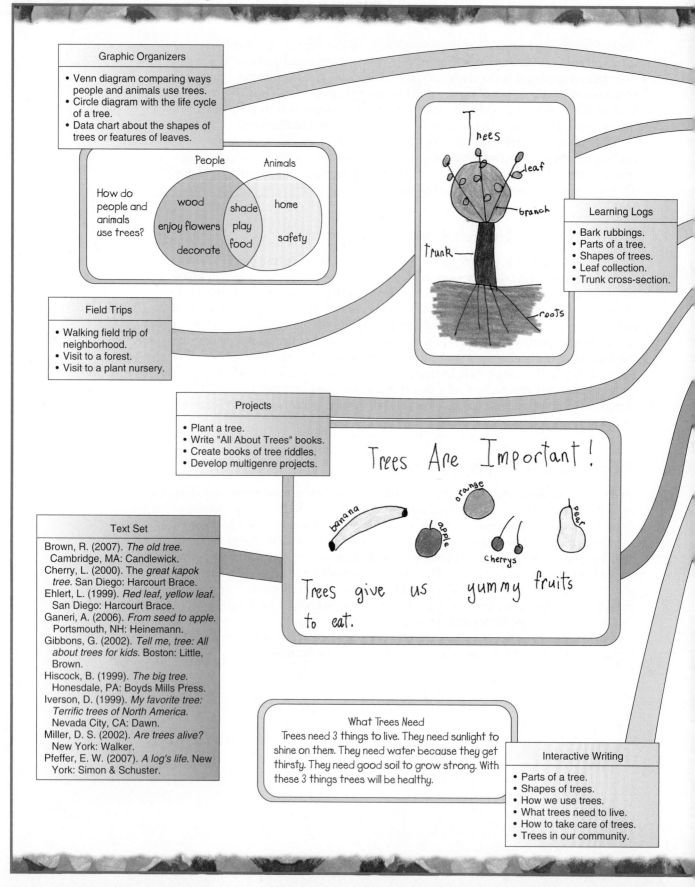

Graphic Organizers

- Venn diagram comparing ways people and animals use trees.
- Circle diagram with the life cycle of a tree.
- Data chart about the shapes of trees or features of leaves.

How do people and animals use trees?

People — Animals

wood
enjoy flowers
decorate
shade
play
food
home
safety

Trees
leaf
branch
trunk
roots

Learning Logs

- Bark rubbings.
- Parts of a tree.
- Shapes of trees.
- Leaf collection.
- Trunk cross-section.

Field Trips

- Walking field trip of neighborhood.
- Visit to a forest.
- Visit to a plant nursery.

Projects

- Plant a tree.
- Write "All About Trees" books.
- Create books of tree riddles.
- Develop multigenre projects.

Trees Are Important!

banana
orange
apple
cherrys
pear

Trees give us yummy fruits to eat.

Text Set

Brown, R. (2007). *The old tree.* Cambridge, MA: Candlewick.
Cherry, L. (2000). The *great kapok tree.* San Diego: Harcourt Brace.
Ehlert, L. (1999). *Red leaf, yellow leaf.* San Diego: Harcourt Brace.
Ganeri, A. (2006). *From seed to apple.* Portsmouth, NH: Heinemann.
Gibbons, G. (2002). *Tell me, tree: All about trees for kids.* Boston: Little, Brown.
Hiscock, B. (1999). *The big tree.* Honesdale, PA: Boyds Mills Press.
Iverson, D. (1999). *My favorite tree: Terrific trees of North America.* Nevada City, CA: Dawn.
Miller, D. S. (2002). *Are trees alive?* New York: Walker.
Pfeffer, E. W. (2007). *A log's life.* New York: Simon & Schuster.

What Trees Need

Trees need 3 things to live. They need sunlight to shine on them. They need water because they get thirsty. They need good soil to grow strong. With these 3 things trees will be healthy.

Interactive Writing

- Parts of a tree.
- Shapes of trees.
- How we use trees.
- What trees need to live.
- How to take care of trees.
- Trees in our community.

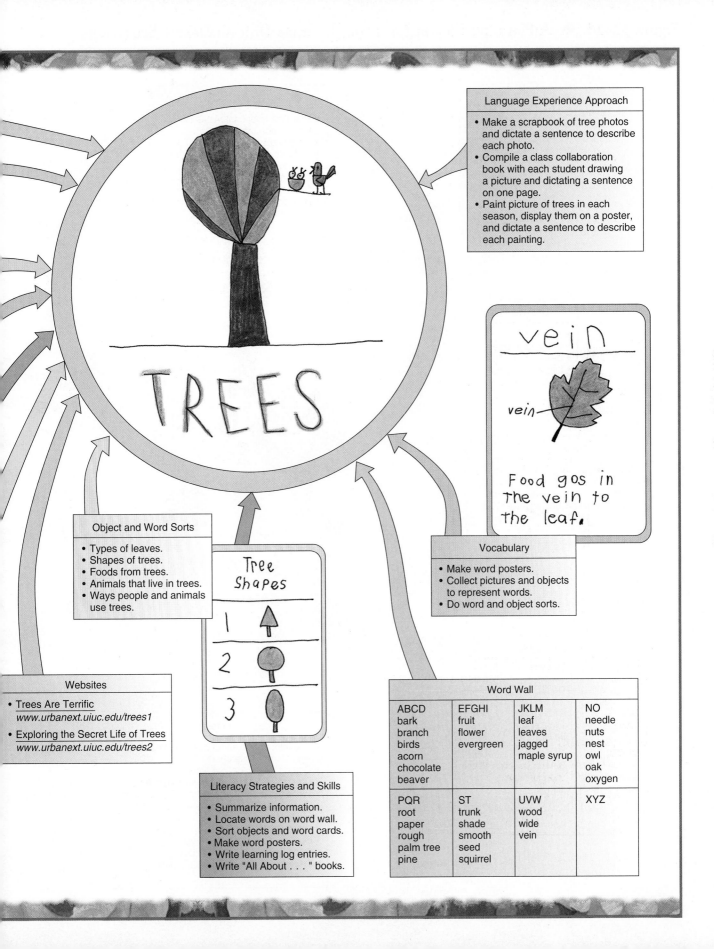

TREES

Language Experience Approach

- Make a scrapbook of tree photos and dictate a sentence to describe each photo.
- Compile a class collaboration book with each student drawing a picture and dictating a sentence on one page.
- Paint picture of trees in each season, display them on a poster, and dictate a sentence to describe each painting.

vein

vein

Food gos in the vein to the leaf.

Object and Word Sorts

- Types of leaves.
- Shapes of trees.
- Foods from trees.
- Animals that live in trees.
- Ways people and animals use trees.

Tree Shapes

1
2
3

Vocabulary

- Make word posters.
- Collect pictures and objects to represent words.
- Do word and object sorts.

Websites

- Trees Are Terrific
  www.urbanext.uiuc.edu/trees1
- Exploring the Secret Life of Trees
  www.urbanext.uiuc.edu/trees2

Literacy Strategies and Skills

- Summarize information.
- Locate words on word wall.
- Sort objects and word cards.
- Make word posters.
- Write learning log entries.
- Write "All About . . . " books.

Word Wall

ABCD	EFGHI	JKLM	NO
bark	fruit	leaf	needle
branch	flower	leaves	nuts
birds	evergreen	jagged	nest
acorn		maple syrup	owl
chocolate			oak
beaver			oxygen
PQR	ST	UVW	XYZ
root	trunk	wood	
paper	shade	wide	
rough	smooth	vein	
palm tree	seed		
pine	squirrel		

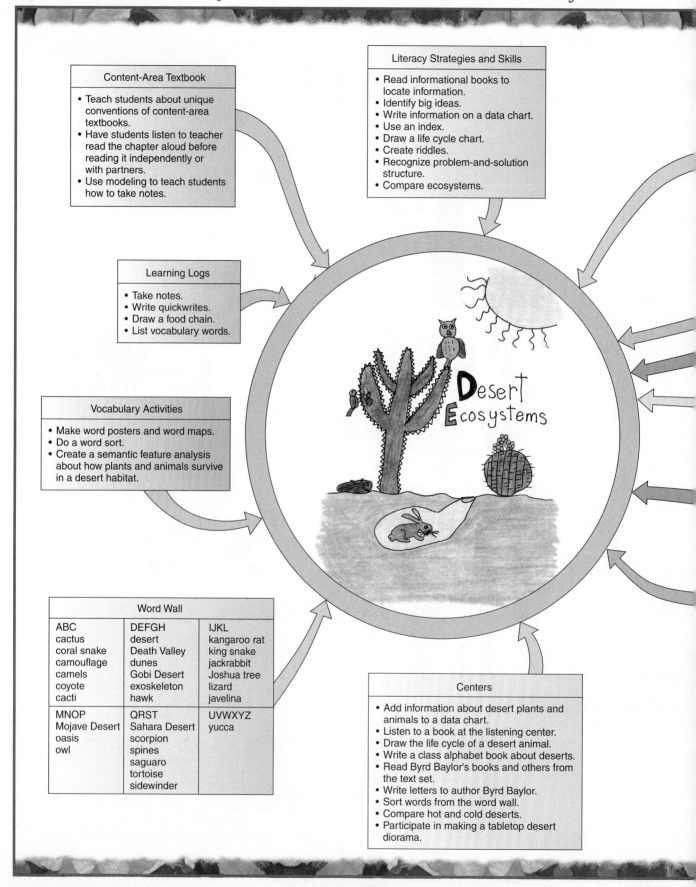

Content-Area Textbook

- Teach students about unique conventions of content-area textbooks.
- Have students listen to teacher read the chapter aloud before reading it independently or with partners.
- Use modeling to teach students how to take notes.

Literacy Strategies and Skills

- Read informational books to locate information.
- Identify big ideas.
- Write information on a data chart.
- Use an index.
- Draw a life cycle chart.
- Create riddles.
- Recognize problem-and-solution structure.
- Compare ecosystems.

Learning Logs

- Take notes.
- Write quickwrites.
- Draw a food chain.
- List vocabulary words.

Vocabulary Activities

- Make word posters and word maps.
- Do a word sort.
- Create a semantic feature analysis about how plants and animals survive in a desert habitat.

Word Wall

ABC	DEFGH	IJKL
cactus	desert	kangaroo rat
coral snake	Death Valley	king snake
camouflage	dunes	jackrabbit
camels	Gobi Desert	Joshua tree
coyote	exoskeleton	lizard
cacti	hawk	javelina
MNOP	QRST	UVWXYZ
Mojave Desert	Sahara Desert	yucca
oasis	scorpion	
owl	spines	
	saguaro	
	tortoise	
	sidewinder	

Centers

- Add information about desert plants and animals to a data chart.
- Listen to a book at the listening center.
- Draw the life cycle of a desert animal.
- Write a class alphabet book about deserts.
- Read Byrd Baylor's books and others from the text set.
- Write letters to author Byrd Baylor.
- Sort words from the word wall.
- Compare hot and cold deserts.
- Participate in making a tabletop desert diorama.

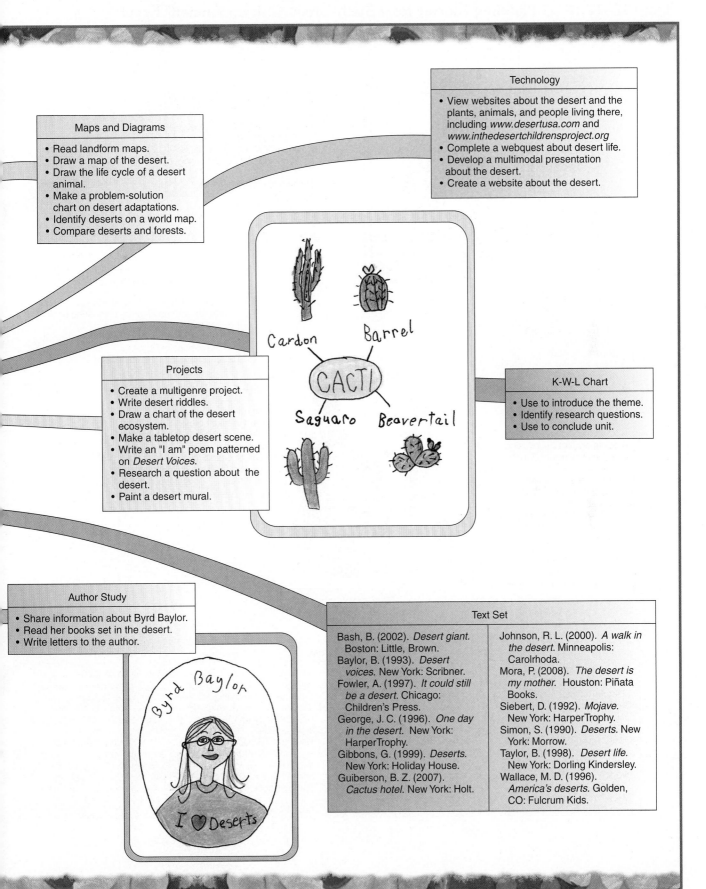

Maps and Diagrams

- Read landform maps.
- Draw a map of the desert.
- Draw the life cycle of a desert animal.
- Make a problem-solution chart on desert adaptations.
- Identify deserts on a world map.
- Compare deserts and forests.

Technology

- View websites about the desert and the plants, animals, and people living there, including *www.desertusa.com* and *www.inthedesertchildrensproject.org*
- Complete a webquest about desert life.
- Develop a multimodal presentation about the desert.
- Create a website about the desert.

Projects

- Create a multigenre project.
- Write desert riddles.
- Draw a chart of the desert ecosystem.
- Make a tabletop desert scene.
- Write an "I am" poem patterned on *Desert Voices*.
- Research a question about the desert.
- Paint a desert mural.

Cardon   Barrel

CACTI

Saguaro   Beavertail

K-W-L Chart

- Use to introduce the theme.
- Identify research questions.
- Use to conclude unit.

Author Study

- Share information about Byrd Baylor.
- Read her books set in the desert.
- Write letters to the author.

Byrd Baylor

I ♥ Deserts

Text Set

Bash, B. (2002). *Desert giant.* Boston: Little, Brown.

Baylor, B. (1993). *Desert voices.* New York: Scribner.

Fowler, A. (1997). *It could still be a desert.* Chicago: Children's Press.

George, J. C. (1996). *One day in the desert.* New York: HarperTrophy.

Gibbons, G. (1999). *Deserts.* New York: Holiday House.

Guiberson, B. Z. (2007). *Cactus hotel.* New York: Holt.

Johnson, R. L. (2000). *A walk in the desert.* Minneapolis: Carolrhoda.

Mora, P. (2008). *The desert is my mother.* Houston: Piñata Books.

Siebert, D. (1992). *Mojave.* New York: HarperTrophy.

Simon, S. (1990). *Deserts.* New York: Morrow.

Taylor, B. (1998). *Desert life.* New York: Dorling Kindersley.

Wallace, M. D. (1996). *America's deserts.* Golden, CO: Fulcrum Kids.

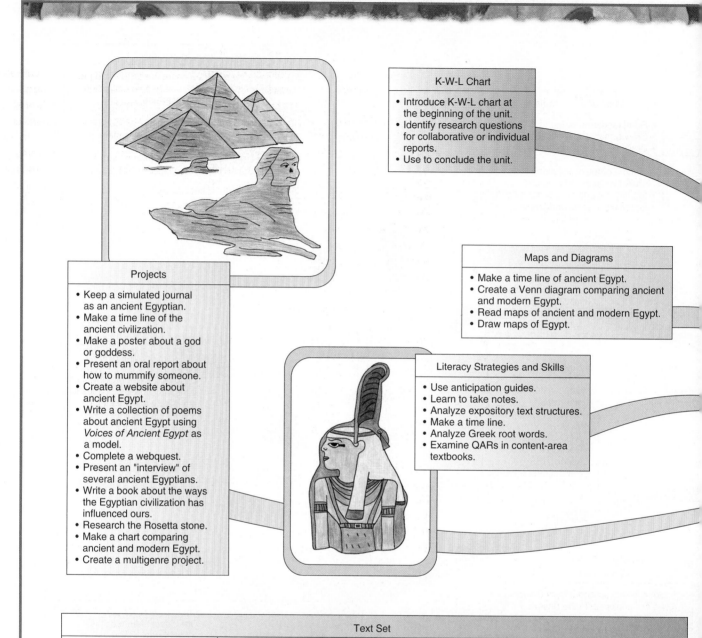

K-W-L Chart

- Introduce K-W-L chart at the beginning of the unit.
- Identify research questions for collaborative or individual reports.
- Use to conclude the unit.

Maps and Diagrams

- Make a time line of ancient Egypt.
- Create a Venn diagram comparing ancient and modern Egypt.
- Read maps of ancient and modern Egypt.
- Draw maps of Egypt.

Projects

- Keep a simulated journal as an ancient Egyptian.
- Make a time line of the ancient civilization.
- Make a poster about a god or goddess.
- Present an oral report about how to mummify someone.
- Create a website about ancient Egypt.
- Write a collection of poems about ancient Egypt using *Voices of Ancient Egypt* as a model.
- Complete a webquest.
- Present an "interview" of several ancient Egyptians.
- Write a book about the ways the Egyptian civilization has influenced ours.
- Research the Rosetta stone.
- Make a chart comparing ancient and modern Egypt.
- Create a multigenre project.

Literacy Strategies and Skills

- Use anticipation guides.
- Learn to take notes.
- Analyze expository text structures.
- Make a time line.
- Analyze Greek root words.
- Examine QARs in content-area textbooks.

Text Set

Aliki. (1985). *Mummies made in Egypt.* New York: HarperCollins.

Der Manueliàn, P. (1996). *Hieroglyphs from A to Z.* New York: Scholastic.

Giblin, J. C. (1993). *The riddle of the Rosetta stone.* New York: HarperCollins.

Gregory, K. (1999). *Cleopatra VII, daughter of the Nile.* New York: Scholastic.

Harris, G. (1993). *Gods and pharaohs from Egyptian mythology.* New York: Peter Bedrick.

Hart, G. (2004). *Ancient Egypt.* New York: DK Publishing.

Hinshaw, K. C. (2007). *Ancient Egypt.* San Francisco: Chronicle Books.

Honan, L. (1999). *Spend the day in ancient Egypt.* New York: Wiley.

Lattimore, D. N. (1995). *The winged cat: A tale of ancient Egypt.* New York: HarperCollins.

Macaulay, D. (1982). *Pyramid.* Boston: Houghton Mifflin.

Milton, J. (2000). *Hieroglyphs.* New York: Grosset & Dunlap.

Perl, L. (1990). *Mummies, tombs, and treasure: Secrets of ancient Egypt.* New York: Clarion Books.

Rubalcaba, J. (2007). *Ancient Egypt: Archaeology unlocks the secrets of Egypt's past.* Washington, DC: National Geographic Children's Books.

Stanley, D., & Vennema, P. (1997). *Cleopatra.* New York: HarperTrophy.

Winters, K. (2003). *Voices of ancient Egypt.* Washington, DC: National Geographic Children's Books.

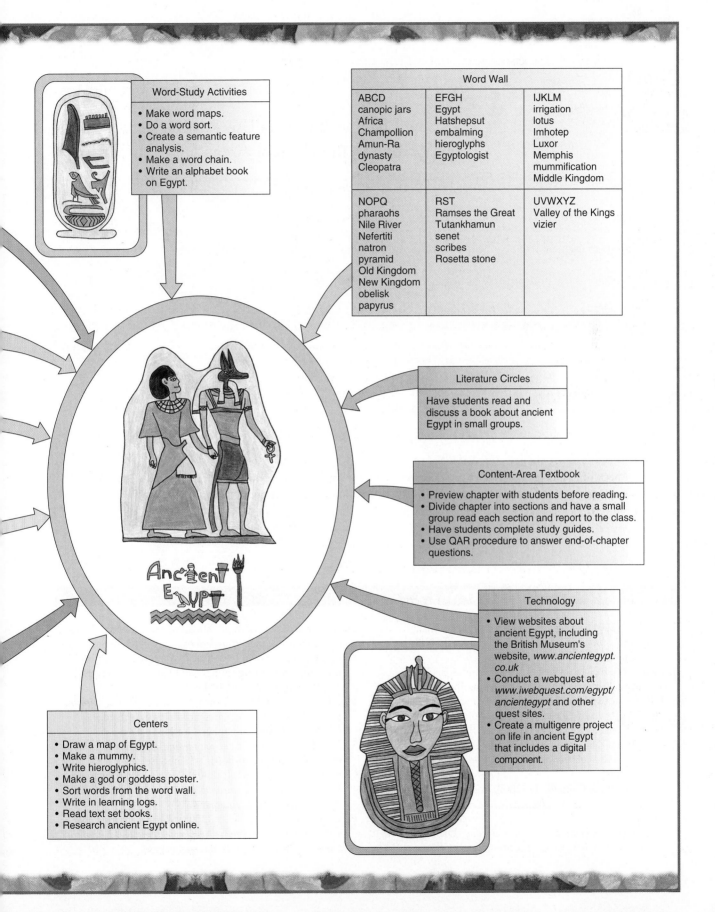

Word-Study Activities

- Make word maps.
- Do a word sort.
- Create a semantic feature analysis.
- Make a word chain.
- Write an alphabet book on Egypt.

Word Wall

ABCD	EFGH	IJKLM
canopic jars	Egypt	irrigation
Africa	Hatshepsut	lotus
Champollion	embalming	Imhotep
Amun-Ra	hieroglyphs	Luxor
dynasty	Egyptologist	Memphis
Cleopatra		mummification
		Middle Kingdom
NOPQ	**RST**	**UVWXYZ**
pharaohs	Ramses the Great	Valley of the Kings
Nile River	Tutankhamun	vizier
Nefertiti	senet	
natron	scribes	
pyramid	Rosetta stone	
Old Kingdom		
New Kingdom		
obelisk		
papyrus		

Literature Circles

Have students read and discuss a book about ancient Egypt in small groups.

Content-Area Textbook

- Preview chapter with students before reading.
- Divide chapter into sections and have a small group read each section and report to the class.
- Have students complete study guides.
- Use QAR procedure to answer end-of-chapter questions.

Technology

- View websites about ancient Egypt, including the British Museum's website, *www.ancientegypt. co.uk*
- Conduct a webquest at *www.iwebquest.com/egypt/ ancientegypt* and other quest sites.
- Create a multigenre project on life in ancient Egypt that includes a digital component.

Centers

- Draw a map of Egypt.
- Make a mummy.
- Write hieroglyphics.
- Make a god or goddess poster.
- Sort words from the word wall.
- Write in learning logs.
- Read text set books.
- Research ancient Egypt online.

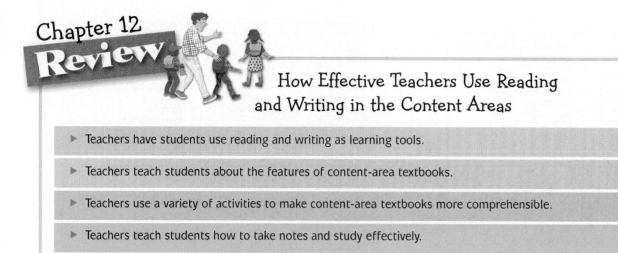

Chapter 12 Review

How Effective Teachers Use Reading and Writing in the Content Areas

▶ Teachers have students use reading and writing as learning tools.

▶ Teachers teach students about the features of content-area textbooks.

▶ Teachers use a variety of activities to make content-area textbooks more comprehensible.

▶ Teachers teach students how to take notes and study effectively.

▶ Teachers focus on big ideas in content-area units.

myeducationlab
PEARSON
Where the Classroom Comes to Life

Go to MyEducationLab at www.myeducationlab.com to deepen your understanding of the concepts presented in this chapter:

▶ Check your understanding of chapter concepts with the multiple-choice and essay quizzes in the Study Plan.
▶ Apply some of the main ideas discussed in the chapter in the Activities and Applications section of the website.
▶ Practice what you've learned in this chapter in Building Teaching Skills and Dispositions before applying the ideas in your own classroom.

PROFESSIONAL REFERENCES

Allen, C. A. (2001). *The multigenre research paper: Voice, passion, and discovery in grades 4–6.* Portsmouth, NH: Heinemann.

Armbruster, B. B., McCarthey, S. J., & Cummins, S. (2005). Writing to learn in elementary classrooms. In R. Indrisano & J. R. Paratore (Eds.), *Learning to write, writing to learn: Theory and research in practice* (pp. 71–96). Newark, DE: International Reading Association.

Daniels, H., & Zemelman, S. (2004). *Subjects matter: Every teacher's guide to content-area reading.* Portsmouth, NH: Heinemann.

Dorfman, L. R., & Cappelli, R. (2007). *Mentor texts: Teaching writing through children's literature, K–6.* Portland, ME: Stenhouse.

Harvey, S. (1998). *Nonfiction matters: Reading, writing, and research in grades 3–8.* York, ME: Stenhouse.

Harvey, S., & Goudvis, A. (2000). *Strategies that work: Teaching comprehension to enhance understanding.* York, ME: Stenhouse.

Ikpeze, C. H., & Boyd, F. B. (2007). Web-based inquiry learning: Facilitating thoughtful literacy with webquests. *The Reading Teacher, 60,* 644–654.

Leu, D. J., Leu, D. D., & Coiro, J. (2004). *Teaching with the Internet K–12: New literacies for new times* (4th ed.). Norwood, MA: Christopher-Gordon.

Moline, S. (1995). *I see what you mean: Children at work with visual information.* York, ME: Stenhouse.

Opitz, M. F., & Ford, M. P. (2008). *Do-able differentiation: Varying groups, texts, and supports to reach readers.* Portsmouth, NH: Heinemann.

Peregoy, S. F., & Boyle, O. F. (2008). *Reading, writing, and learning in ESL: A resource book for teaching K–12 English learners.* Boston: Allyn & Bacon/Pearson.

Pryle, M. (2007). *Teaching students to write effective essays*. New York: Scholastic.

Raphael, T. E. (1986). Teaching question-answer-relationships, revisited. *The Reading Teacher, 39*, 516–523.

Readence, J. E., Moore, D. W., & Rickelman, R. J. (2000). *Prereading activities for content area reading and learning* (3rd ed.). Newark, DE: International Reading Association.

Robb, L. (2002). Multiple texts: Multiple opportunities for teaching and learning. *Voices From the Middle, 9*(4), 28–32.

Robb, L. (2003). *Teaching reading in social studies, science, and math*. New York: Scholastic.

Robb, L. (2004). *Nonfiction writing: From the inside out*. New York: Scholastic.

Romano, T. (2000). *Blending genre, alternating style: Writing multiple genre papers*. Portsmouth, NH: Heinemann/Boynton/Cook.

Rothenberg, C., & Fisher, D. (2007). *Teaching English language learners: A differentiated approach*. Upper Saddle River, NJ: Merrill/Prentice Hall.

Stead, T. (2002). *Is that a fact? Teaching nonfiction writing K–3*. Portland, ME: Stenhouse.

Tierney, R. J., & Shanahan, T. (1996). Research on the reading-writing relationship: Interactions, transactions, and outcomes. In R. Barr, M. L. Kamil, P. Mosenthal, & P. D. Pearson (Eds.), *Handbook of reading research* (Vol. 2, pp. 246–280). Mahwah, NJ: Erlbaum.

Tompkins, G. E. (2008). *Teaching writing: Balancing process and product* (5th ed.). Upper Saddle River, NJ: Merrill/Prentice Hall.

Topping, D., & McManus, R. (2002). *Real reading, real writing: Content-area strategies*. Portsmouth, NH: Heinemann.

CHILDREN'S BOOK REFERENCES

Aquatic life of the world. (2001). New York: Marshall Cavendish.

Avi. (1993). *Nothing but the truth*. New York: Avon.

Bausum, A. (2006). *Freedom riders: John Lewis and Jim Zwerg on the front lines of the civil rights movement*. Washington, DC: National Geographic Children's Books.

Bing, C. (2000). *Ernest L. Thayer's Casey at the bat: A ballad of the republic sung in the year 1888*. Brooklyn, NY: Handprint Books.

Bruchac, J. (2001). *The journal of Jesse Smoke: A Cherokee boy, Trail of Tears, 1838*. New York: Scholastic.

Cole, J. (1996). *The magic school bus inside a beehive*. New York: Scholastic.

Cole, J. (1999). *The magic school bus and the electric field trip*. New York: Scholastic.

Cushman, K. (1994). *Catherine, called Birdy*. New York: HarperTrophy.

Denenberg, B. (1999). *The journal of Ben Uchida: Citizen 13559, Mirror Lake Internment Camp*. New York: Scholastic.

Fleischman, P. (1999). *Whirligig*. New York: Laurel Leaf.

Fleischman, P. (2004). *Joyful noise: Poems for two voices*. New York: HarperCollins.

Fraustino, L. R. (2004). *I walk in dread: The diary of Deliverance Trembly, witness to the Salem witch trials*. New York: Scholastic.

Guiberson, B. Z. (2007). *Cactus hotel*. New York: Henry Holt.

Hinton, S. E. (2007). *The outsiders*. New York: Viking.

Holms, J. L. (2007). *Middle school is worse than meatloaf*. New York: Atheneum.

Janke, K. (2002). *Survival in the storm: The dust bowl diary of Grace Edwards*. New York: Scholastic.

Judge, L. (2007). *One thousand tracings: Healing the wounds of World War II*. New York: Hyperion Books.

Lester, J. (2005). *To be a slave*. New York: Puffin Books.

Mannis, C. D. (2003). *The queen's progress: An Elizabethan alphabet*. New York: Viking.

Marrin, A. (2006). *Oh, rats! The story of rats and people*. New York: Dutton.

McKissack, P. C. (1997). *A picture of freedom: The diary of Clotee, a slave girl*. New York: Scholastic.

McLimans, D. (2006). *Gone wild: An endangered animal alphabet*. New York: Walker.

Napier, M. (2002). *Z is for Zamboni: A hockey alphabet*. Chelsea, MI: Sleeping Bear Press.

Paulsen, G. (2006). *Hatchet*. New York: Aladdin Books.

Schlitz, L. A. (2007). *Good masters! Sweet ladies! Voices from a medieval village*. Cambridge, MA: Candlewick Press.

Snicket, L. (2003). *Lemony Snicket: The unauthorized autobiography*. New York: HarperCollins.

Thimmesh, C. (2006). *Team moon: How 400,000 people landed Apollo 11 on the moon*. Boston: Houghton Mifflin.

White, E. E. (2002). *The journal of Patrick Seamus Flaherty: United States Marine Corps*. New York: Scholastic.

PART 4

Compendium of Instructional Procedures

Forty instructional procedures that effective teachers use to teach reading and writing are presented in this Compendium, with step-by-step directions. You've read about mini-lessons, hot seat, guided reading, K-W-L charts, interactive writing, word walls, and other procedures in this text; they were highlighted in orange to cue you to consult the Compendium for more detailed information. Teachers use these procedures in a variety of ways in their instructional programs. Here are three of the most important uses:

- ▶ Explicit instruction
- ▶ Authentic application activities
- ▶ Learning across the curriculum

To see some of these instructional procedures—making words and shared reading, for example—being used in real classrooms, go to the MyEducationLab website (www.myeducationlab.com).

Explicit Instruction

Teachers use some instructional procedures such as these to provide explicit instruction and guide practice activities:

- ▶ Guided reading
- ▶ Interactive writing
- ▶ Making words
- ▶ Minilessons
- ▶ Think-alouds
- ▶ Word ladders

Authentic Application Activities

Teachers use other instructional procedures for authentic application activities where students participate in real-life reading and writing projects. Here are some examples:

- ► Book talks
- ► Double-entry journals
- ► Grand conversations
- ► Hot seat
- ► Sustained Silent Reading
- ► Writing groups

Learning Across the Curriculum

Teachers use additional instructional procedures such as these to support students' learning across the curriculum and during thematic units:

- ► Anticipation guides
- ► K-W-L charts
- ► Learning logs
- ► Question-Answer-Relationships
- ► Tea party
- ► Word walls

Anticipation Guides

Teachers use anticipation guides (Head & Readence, 1986) to activate students' background knowledge before they read content-area textbooks and informational books. Teachers prepare a list of statements about the topic for students to discuss. Some of the statements are true, and others are incorrect or based on common misconceptions. Students discuss each statement and decide whether they agree with it. Then after reading the selection, students discuss the statements again and decide whether they agree with them. Usually students change some of their opinions, and they realize that they've refined their understanding of the subject through the activity.

An anticipation guide about immigration that eighth graders considered before reading a chapter in their social studies textbook included these statements:

There are more people immigrating to the United States today than ever before in history.

The government sets a quota for the number of people allowed to enter the United States each year.

Most people immigrate to the United States because they want to find better jobs and earn more money.

Aliens are people who are in the United States illegally.

Refugees are people who are forced to flee from their homeland because of war or other disasters.

Many immigrants have difficulty adjusting to the new ways of life in America.

You probably agree with some of these statements and disagree with others; perhaps you're unsure about a couple of them. Having these questions in mind when you begin reading gives you a purpose for reading and directs your attention to the big ideas. And, as you read, you might find that your initial assessment of one or two statements wasn't accurate, and when you repeat the assessment afterward, you'll make some changes.

Teachers follow these steps to develop and use anticipation guides:

1. *Identify several major concepts related to the reading assignment.* Teachers keep in mind students' knowledge about the topic and any misconceptions they might have about it.

2. *Develop a list of four to six statements.* Teachers compose statements that are general enough to stimulate discussion and are useful in clarifying misconceptions and make copies for students. The guide has space for students to mark whether they agree with each statement before and again after reading.

3. *Discuss the anticipation guide.* Teachers introduce the anticipation guide and have students respond to the statements. Working in small groups, in pairs, or individually, students decide whether they agree with each one. Then, as a class, students discuss their responses to each statement and defend their positions.

4. *Read the text.* Students read the text and compare their responses to what's stated in the reading material.

5. *Discuss each statement again.* Students talk about the statements again, citing information in the text that supports or refutes each one. Or, students can again respond to each of the statements and compare their answers before and after reading. When students use the anticipation guide, have them fold back their first set of responses on the left side of the paper and then respond to each item again on the right side of the paper.

Anticipation Guide on Gangs					
Before Reading		Gangs	After Reading		
Agree	Disagree		Agree	Disagree	
		1. Gangs are bad.			
		2. Gangs are exciting.			
		3. It is safe to be a gang member.			
		4. Gangs make a difference in a gang member's life.			
		5. Gangs fill a need.			
		6. Once you join a gang, it is very difficult to get out.			

Although anticipation guides are more commonly used before reading informational books and content-area textbooks, they can also be used to explore complex issues in novels, including homelessness, crime and punishment, and immigration. An eighth-grade class, for example, studied gangs in preparation for reading S. E. Hinton's *The Outsiders* (1997), and they completed the anticipation guide shown in the box above before and after reading the novel. The statements about gangs in the anticipation guide probe important points and lead to lively discussion and thoughtful responses.

Book Talks

Book talks are brief teasers that teachers give to introduce students to particular books and interest them in reading the books. Teachers show the book, summarize it without giving away the ending, and read a short excerpt aloud to hook students' interest. Then they pass the book off to an interested reader or place it in the classroom library for students to read.

Students use the same steps when they give book talks to share the books they've read during reading workshop. Here's a transcript of a third grader's book talk about Paula Danziger's *Amber Brown Is Not a Crayon* (2006):

This is my book: Amber Brown Is Not a Crayon. It's about these two kids—Amber Brown, who is a girl, and Justin Daniels, who is a boy. See? Here is their picture. They are in third grade, too, and their teacher—his name is Mr. Cohen—pretends to take them on airplane trips to the places they study. They move their chairs so that it is like they are on an airplane and Amber and Justin always put their chairs side by side. I'm going to read you the very beginning of the book. [She reads the first three pages aloud to the class.] This story is really funny and when you are reading you think the author is telling you the story instead of you reading it. And there are more stories about Amber Brown. This is the one I'm reading now — You Can't Eat Your Chicken Pox, Amber Brown [1995].

There are several reasons why this student and others in her class are so successful in giving book talks. The teacher has modeled how to give a book talk, and students are reading books that they've chosen—books they really like. In addition, these students are experienced in talking with their classmates about books.

Here are the steps in conducting a book talk:

1. *Select a book to share.* Teachers choose a new book to introduce to students or a book that students haven't shown much interest in. They familiarize themselves with the book by reading or rereading it.

2. *Plan a brief presentation.* Teachers plan how they will present the book to interest students in reading it. They usually begin with the title and author of the book, and they mention the genre or topic and briefly summarize the plot without giving away the ending. Teachers also decide why they liked the book and think about why students might be interested in it. Sometimes they choose a short excerpt to read and an illustration to show.

3. *Show the book and present the planned book talk.* Teachers present the book talk and show the book. Their comments are usually enough so that at least one student will ask to borrow the book to read.

Teachers use book talks to introduce students to books in the classroom library. At the beginning of the school year, teachers take time to introduce students to many of the books in the library, and during the year, they introduce new books that they add to the library. They also introduce the books for a literature circle, or a text set of books for a thematic unit (Gambrell & Almasi, 1996). During a seventh-grade unit on the Underground Railroad, for example, teachers might introduce five books about Harriet Tubman and the Underground Railroad and then have students form book groups to read one of them.

Choral Reading

Students use choral reading to orally share poems and other brief texts. This group reading activity provides students, especially struggling readers, with valuable oral reading practice. They learn to read more expressively and increase their reading fluency (Rasinski & Padak, 2004). In addition, it's a great activity for English learners because they practice reading aloud with classmates in a nonthreatening group setting (McCauley & McCauley, 1992). As they read with English-speaking classmates, they hear and practice English pronunciation of words, phrasing of words in a sentence, and intonation patterns.

Many arrangements for choral reading are possible: Students read the text together as a class or divide it and read sections in small groups. Or, individual students may read particular lines or stanzas while the class reads the rest of the text. Here are four arrangements:

- ◆ **Echo Reading.** A leader reads each line and the group repeats it.
- ◆ **Leader and Chorus Reading.** A leader reads the main part, and the group reads the refrain in unison.
- ◆ **Small-Group Reading.** The class divides into two or more groups, and each group reads part of the poem.
- ◆ **Cumulative Reading.** One student reads the first line or stanza, and another student joins in as each line or stanza is read to create a cumulative effect.

Students read the text aloud several times, experimenting with different arrangements until they decide which one conveys meaning most effectively.

Here are the steps in this instructional procedure:

1. *Select a poem to use for choral reading.* Teachers choose a poem or other text and copy it onto a chart or make multiple copies for students to read.

2. *Arrange the text for choral reading.* Teachers work with students to decide how to arrange the text. They add marks to the chart, or they have students mark individual copies so that they can follow the arrangement.

3. *Rehearse the poem.* Teachers read the poem with students several times at a natural speed, pronouncing words carefully.

4. *Have students read the poem aloud.* Teachers emphasize that students pronounce words clearly and read with expression. They can tape-record students' reading so that they can hear themselves, and sometimes students want to rearrange the choral reading after hearing an audiotape of their reading.

Choral reading makes students active participants in the poetry experience, and it helps them learn to appreciate the sounds, feelings, and magic of poetry. Many poems can be used for choral reading, and poems with repetitions, echoes, refrains, or questions and answers work well. Try these poems, for example:

"My Parents Think I'm Sleeping," by Jack Prelutsky (2007)

"I Woke Up This Morning," by Karla Kuskin (2003)

"Every Time I Climb a Tree," by David McCord (Paschen, 2005)

"Ode to La Tortilla," by Gary Soto (2005)

"The New Kid on the Block," by Jack Prelutsky (2008)

"Mother to Son," by Langston Hughes (2007)

"A Circle of Sun," by Rebecca Kai Dotlich (Yolen & Peters, 2007)

Poems written specifically for two readers are very effective, including Donald Hall's book-length poem *I Am the Dog/I Am the Cat* (1994), and Paul Fleischman's collection of insect poems, *Joyful Noise: Poems for Two Voices* (2004). Teachers can also use speeches, songs, and longer poems for choral reading. Try, for example, *Brother Eagle, Sister Sky: A Message From Chief Seattle* (Jeffers, 1993) and Woody Guthrie's *This Land Is Your Land* (2002).

Cloze Procedure

The cloze procedure is an informal diagnostic assessment that teachers use to gather information about readers' abilities to deal with the content and structure of texts they're reading (Taylor, 1953). Teachers construct a cloze passage by selecting an excerpt from a book—a story, an informational book, or a content-area textbook—that students have read and deleting every fifth word in the passage. The deleted words are replaced with blanks. Then students read the passage and add the missing words, using their knowledge of syntax (the order of words in English) and semantics (the meaning of words within sentences) to successfully predict the missing words in the text passage. Only the exact word is considered a correct answer.

Here's a cloze passage about wolves:

> *The leaders of a wolf pack are called the alpha wolves. There is an _____ male and an alpha _____ . They are usually the _____ and the strongest wolves _____ the pack. An alpha _____ fight any wolf that _____ to take over the _____. When the alpha looks _____ other wolf in the _____, the other wolf crouches _____ and tucks its tail _____ its hind legs. Sometimes _____ rolls over and licks _____ alpha wolf's face as _____ to say, "You are _____ boss."*

The missing words are *alpha, female, largest, in, will, tries, pack, the, eye, down, between, it, the, if,* and *the.*

The cloze procedure assesses sentence-level comprehension (Tierney & Readence, 2005). It's a useful classroom tool for determining which texts are at students' instructional levels and for monitoring students' understanding of novels they're reading. A caution, however: Cloze doesn't measure comprehension globally; it only assesses students' ability to use syntax and semantics within individual sentences and paragraphs.

Teachers follow these steps to use the cloze procedure:

1. ***Select a passage from a textbook or trade book.*** Teachers select a passage and retype it. The first sentence is typed exactly as it appears in the original text, but beginning with the second sentence, one of the first five words is deleted and replaced with a blank. Then every fifth word in the remainder of the passage is deleted and replaced with a blank.

2. ***Complete the cloze activity.*** Students read the passage all the way through once silently and then reread it and predict or "guess" the word that goes in each blank. They write the deleted words in the blanks.

3. ***Score students' work.*** Teachers award one point each time the missing word is identified. A percentage of correct answers is determined by dividing the number of points by the number of blanks. Compare the percentage of correct word placements with this scale:

61% or more correct replacements: independent reading level

41–60% correct replacements: instructional level

less than 40% correct replacements: frustration level

The cloze procedure can be used to judge students' reading level in unfamiliar books, or to assess students' comprehension after reading a book. When teachers use the cloze procedure to check students' comprehension, specific words, such as character names, facts related to the setting or key events, are deleted, rather than every fifth word. This assessment procedure can also be used to judge whether a particular book is appropriate for classroom instruction. Teachers prepare a cloze passage and have students follow the steps described here to predict the missing words (Jacobson, 1990). Then teachers score students' predictions and use a one-third to one-half formula to determine the text's appropriateness: If students correctly predict more than 50% of the deleted words, the passage is easy reading, but if they predict less than 30% of the missing words, the passage is too difficult for classroom instruction. The instructional range is 30–50% correct predictions (Reutzel & Cooter, 2008).

Students work together in small groups to make collaborative books. They each contribute one page or work with a classmate to write a page or a section of the book, using the writing process as they draft, revise, and edit their pages. Teachers often make class collaborations with students as a first bookmaking project and to introduce the stages of the writing process. Students write collaborative books to retell a favorite story, illustrate a poem with one line or a stanza on each page, or write an informational book or biography. The benefit of collaborative books is that students share the work so that the books are completed much more quickly and easily than individual books. Because students write only one page or section, it takes less time for teachers to conference with students and assist them with time-consuming revising and editing.

Teachers follow these steps in making a collaborative book:

1. *Choose a topic.* Teachers choose a topic related to a literature focus unit or thematic unit. Then students choose specific topics or pages to prepare.

2. *Introduce the page or section design for the book.* If students are each contributing one page for a class informational book on penguins, for example, they choose a fact or other piece of information about penguins to write. They might draw a picture related to the fact at the top of the page and write the fact underneath the picture. Teachers often model the procedure and write one page of the book together as a class before students begin working on their pages.

3. *Have students make rough drafts of their pages.* Students write rough drafts and share the pages in writing groups. They revise their pictures and text after getting feedback from classmates. Then they correct mechanical errors and make the final copy of their pages.

4. *Compile the pages to complete the book.* Students add a title page and covers. Older students might also prepare a table of contents, an introduction, and a conclusion, and add a bibliography at the end. To make the book sturdier, teachers often laminate the covers (or all pages in the book) and have the book bound.

5. *Make copies of the book for students.* Teachers often make copies of the book for each student. The specially bound copy is then placed in the class or school library.

As part of literature focus units, students often retell a story or create an innovation or new version of a story in a collaborative book. They can also retell a novel by having each student retell one chapter. Students also can illustrate a poem or song by writing one line or stanza on each page and then drawing or painting an illustration. *The Lady With the Alligator Purse* (Hoberman, 2003), *There Was an Old Lady Who Swallowed a Fly* (Taback, 1997), and *America the Beautiful* (Bates, 2003) are picture-book examples of song and poem retellings that students can examine before they write their own collaborative retellings.

Collaborative Books

A double-entry journal is a special type of reading log in which the pages are divided into two columns; students write different types of information in each column (Berthoff, 1981). In the left column, students write quotes from the story or informational book they're reading, and in the right column, they reflect on each quote. They may relate a quote to their own lives, react to it, write a question, or make some other connection. Excerpts from a fifth grader's double-entry journal about *The Lion, the Witch and the Wardrobe* (Lewis, 2005) are shown in the box on page 434. Teachers use double-entry journals to help students structure their thinking about a text (Tovani, 2000). The quotes that students select indicate what they think is important, and the responses they make in the right column reveal their understanding of what they've read.

Double-Entry Journals

Excerpts From a Fifth Grader's Double-Entry Journal About *The Lion, the Witch and the Wardrobe*

Quotes	Reflections
Chapter 1 I will tell you this is the sort of house where no one is going to mind what we do.	I remember the time that I went to Beaumont, Texas to stay with my aunt. My aunt's house was very large. She had a piano and she let us play it. She told us that we could do whatever we wanted to.
Chapter 5 "How do you know?" he asked, "that your sister's story is not true?"	It reminds me of when I was little and I had an imaginary place. I would go there in my mind. I made up all kinds of make-believe stories about myself in this imaginary place. One time I told my big brother about my imaginary place. He laughed at me and told me I was silly. But it didn't bother me because nobody can stop me from thinking what I want.
Chapter 15 Still they could see the shape of the great lion lying dead in his bonds. They're nibbling at the cords.	When Aslan died I thought about when my Uncle Carl died. This reminds me of the story where the lion lets the mouse go and the mouse helps the lion.

Students usually write double-entry journals independently after reading each chapter or two of a novel or informational book, and they follow these steps:

1. *Design journal pages.* Students divide the pages in their reading logs into two columns. They may label the left column "Quotes" and the right column "Comments" or "Reflections."

2. *Write quotes in journals.* As students read or immediately after reading, they copy one or more important or interesting quotes in the left column.

3. *Reflect on the quotes.* Students reread the quotes and make notes in the right column about their reasons for choosing each quote or what the quote means to them. Sometimes it's easier if students share the quotes with a reading buddy or in a grand conversation before they write comments or reflections in the right column.

Sometimes teachers change the headings for the two columns. Students can write "Reading Notes" in the left column and add "Reactions" in the right one. Young children can use the double-entry format in their journals (Macon, Bewell, & Vogt, 1991), labeling the left column "Predictions" and the right one "What Happened." In the left column, they write or draw what they think will happen before they begin to read, and afterward, they draw or write what actually happened in the right column.

Teachers use exclusion brainstorming to activate students' background knowledge and expand their understanding about a social studies or science topic before reading (Blachowicz, 1986). Teachers present a list of words, and students identify the ones that don't relate to the topic. Then after reading, students review the list of words and decide whether they chose correctly. Exclusion brainstorming is a useful prereading activity because as students talk about the words on the list to decide which ones aren't related, they refine their knowledge, think about some key vocabulary words, and develop a purpose for reading.

Exclusion Brainstorming

Here are the steps in exclusion brainstorming:

1. *Prepare a word list.* Teachers identify words related to an informational book or content-area textbook chapter that students will read and include a few words that don't fit with the topic. They write the list on the chalkboard or make copies for students.

2. *Read the list of words.* Teachers read the list, and then, in small groups or together as a class, students decide which words they think aren't related to the text and draw circles around those words.

3. *Learn about the topic.* Students read the text, noticing whether the words in the exclusion brainstorming exercise are mentioned in the text.

4. *Review the list.* Students check their exclusion brainstorming list and make corrections based on their reading. They put checkmarks by related words and cross out unrelated words, whether they circled them earlier or not.

Teachers use exclusion brainstorming as a prereading activity to familiarize students with key concepts and vocabulary before reading informational books and articles. An eighth-grade teacher prepared the list of words shown below before his students read an article on the Arctic Ocean; all of the words except *penguins, South Pole,* and *precipitation* are related to the Arctic Ocean. Students circled seven words as possibly unrelated, and after reading, they crossed out the three words that their teacher expected them to eliminate.

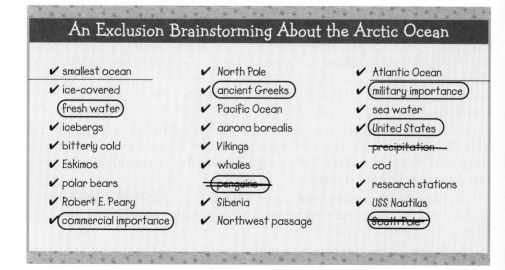

An Exclusion Brainstorming About the Arctic Ocean

✔ smallest ocean	✔ North Pole	✔ Atlantic Ocean
✔ ice-covered	✔ (ancient Greeks)	✔ (military importance)
(fresh water)	✔ Pacific Ocean	✔ sea water
✔ icebergs	✔ aurora borealis	✔ (United States)
✔ bitterly cold	✔ Vikings	~~precipitation~~
✔ Eskimos	✔ whales	✔ cod
✔ polar bears	~~(penguins)~~	✔ research stations
✔ Robert E. Peary	✔ Siberia	✔ USS Nautilus
✔ (commercial importance)	✔ Northwest passage	~~(South Pole)~~

Grand Conversations

Grand conversations are discussions about stories in which students explore the big ideas and reflect on their feelings (Peterson & Eeds, 2007). They're different than traditional discussions because they're student centered. Students do most of the talking as they voice their opinions and support their views with examples from the story. They talk about what puzzles them, what they find interesting, their personal connections to the story, connections to the world, and connections they see between this story and others they've read. Students usually don't raise their hands to be called on by the teacher; instead, they take turns and speak when no one else is speaking, much as adults do when they talk with friends. Students also encourage their classmates to contribute to the conversation. Even though teachers participate, the talk is primarily among the students.

Grand conversations have two parts. The first part is open ended: Students talk about their reactions to the book, and their comments determine the direction of the conversation; teachers share their responses, ask questions, and provide information. Later, teachers focus students' attention on one or two topics that they didn't talk about in the first part of the conversation. In order for English learners to participate successfully in grand conversations, they need to feel comfortable and safe in the group (Graves & Fitzgerald, 2003).

Teachers follow these steps in using this instructional procedure:

1. *Read the book.* Students read a story or part of story, or they listen to the teacher read it aloud.

2. *Prepare for the grand conversation.* Students think about the story by drawing pictures or writing in reading logs. This step is especially important when students don't talk much because with this preparation, they're more likely to have ideas to share with classmates.

3. *Have small-group conversations.* Students form small groups to talk about the story before getting together as a class. This step is optional and is generally used when students are uncomfortable about sharing with the whole class or when they need more time to talk about the story.

4. *Begin the grand conversation.* Students form a circle for the class conversation so that everyone can see each other. Teachers begin by asking, "Who would like to begin?" or "What are you thinking about?" One student makes a comment, and classmates take turns talking about the idea the first student introduced.

5. *Continue the conversation.* A student introduces a new idea, and classmates talk about it, sharing ideas, asking questions, and reading excerpts to make a point. Students limit their comments to the idea being discussed, and after students finish discussing this idea, a new one is introduced. To ensure that everyone participates, teachers often ask students to make no more than three comments until everyone has spoken at least once.

6. *Ask questions.* Teachers ask questions to direct students to aspects of the story that have been missed; for example, they might focus on an element of story structure or the author's craft. Or they may ask students to compare the book to the film version of the story or to other books by the same author.

7. *Conclude the conversation.* After all of the big ideas have been explored, teachers end the conversation by summarizing and drawing conclusions about the story or the chapter of the novel.

8. *Reflect on the conversation.* Students write (or write again) in reading logs to reflect on the ideas discussed in the grand conversation.

When students get together for a whole-class conversation during literature focus units, a feeling of community is established. Young children usually meet as a class; older students get together as a class when they're participating in a literature focus unit or listening to the teacher read a book aloud, but during literature circles, students meet in small groups because they're reading different books. When the entire class meets, students have only a few opportunities to talk, but when they meet in small groups, they have many more opportunities to share their ideas.

Guided Reading

Guided reading is a small-group instructional procedure that teachers use to read a book with a small group of students who read at approximately the same level. They select a book that students can read at their instructional level, that is, with approximately 90% accuracy, and they support students' reading and their use of reading strategies (Fountas & Pinnell, 1996). Students do the actual reading themselves, and they usually read silently at their own pace through the entire book. Emergent readers often mumble the words softly as they read, which helps the teacher keep track of students' reading and the strategies they're using.

Teachers use guided reading with young English learners just as they do with their native English-speaking classmates, and this instructional procedure can also be used with older ELs, especially if they aren't fluent readers and don't know how to use word-identification and comprehension strategies. It's important to choose the right books for older students—ones that are appropriate for their interests and their reading levels. Peregoy and Boyle (2008) point out that guided reading is effective because ELs experience success as they read interesting books in small, comfortable groups with teacher guidance.

Teachers adapt the procedure for guided reading to meet their students' needs, but they generally follow these steps:

1. *Choose an appropriate book.* Teachers choose a book that students in the small group can read with 90% accuracy. They collect copies of the book for each student.

2. *Introduce the book.* Teachers set the purpose for reading and show the book's cover, reading the title and the author's name. Next, they activate students' background knowledge on a topic related to the book, often introducing key vocabulary as they talk. Students "picture walk" through the book, looking at the illustrations, talking about them, and making predictions. And finally, teachers review one or more of the reading strategies they've already taught and remind these students to use them as they read.

3. *Have students read the book.* Teachers provide support to students with decoding and reading strategies as needed. Students either "mumble" read softly or read silently, depending on their reading level. Teachers observe students as they read and assess their use of word-identification and comprehension strategies. They help individual students decode unfamiliar words, deal with unfamiliar sentence structures, and comprehend ideas presented in the text whenever assistance is required. They offer prompts, such as "Look at how that word ends" or "Does that make sense?"

4. *Encourage students to respond.* Students talk about the book, ask questions, and relate it to others they've read, as in a grand conversation. Teachers also compliment students on the strategies they used while they were reading.

5. *Have students revisit the text.* Teachers use the text that students have just read to demonstrate a comprehension strategy, teach a phonics concept or word-identification skill, or review new vocabulary words.

6. *Provide opportunities for independent reading.* Teachers place the book in a book basket or in the classroom library so that students can reread it.

Teachers teach guided reading lessons to small groups of students using leveled books while their classmates are involved in other literacy activities; classmates are often reading independently, writing books, and doing phonics and spelling activities at centers. Teachers rotate the groups every 20–30 minutes so that students participate in a variety of teacher-directed and independent activities each day.

Hot Seat

Hot seat is a role-playing activity that builds students' comprehension. Students assume the persona of a character from a story, the featured person from a biography they're reading, or an author whose books they've read, and they sit in a chair designated as the "hot seat" to be interviewed by classmates. It's called *hot seat* because students have to think quickly and respond to their classmates' questions and comments. Wilhelm (2002) explains that through the hot seat activity, students explore the characters, analyze story events, draw inferences, and try out different interpretations. Students aren't intimidated by performing for classmates; in fact, in most classrooms, the activity is very popular. Students are usually eager for their turn to sit in the hot seat. They often wear a costume they've created when they assume the character's persona and share objects they've collected and artifacts they've made.

Here are the steps in the hot seat activity:

1. *Learn about the character.* Students prepare for the hot seat activity by reading a story or a biography to learn about the character they will impersonate.

2. *Create a costume.* Students design a costume appropriate for their character. In addition, they often collect objects or create artifacts to use in their presentations.

3. *Prepare opening remarks.* Students think about the most important things they'd like to share about the character and plan what they'll say at the beginning of the activity.

4. *Introduce the character.* One student sits in front of classmates in a chair designated as the "hot seat," tells a little about the character he or she is role-playing using a first-person viewpoint (e.g., "I was the first person to step onto the moon's surface"), and shares artifacts.

5. *Ask questions and make comments.* Classmates ask thoughtful questions to learn more about the character and offer advice, and the student remains in the role to respond to them.

6. *Summarize the ideas.* The student doing the role-play selects a classmate to summarize the important ideas that were presented about the character. The student in the hot seat clarifies any misunderstandings and adds any big ideas that classmates don't mention.

During literature focus units, students take turns role-playing characters and being interviewed. Students representing different characters can also come together for a conversation—a group hot seat activity. For example, during a literature focus unit on *The View From Saturday* (Kongisburg, 1998), the story of a championship sixth-grade Academic Bowl team that's told from the perspectives of the team members, students representing Noah, Nadia, Ethan, Julian, and their teacher, Mrs. Olinski, take turns sitting on the hot seat, or they come together to talk about the story. Similarly, when students are participating in literature circles, they can take turns role-playing characters from the story they're reading, or each student in the group can assume the persona of a different character at the same time for a group hot seat activity.

Teachers use interactive read-alouds to share books with students. The focus is on enhancing students' comprehension by engaging them in the reading process before, during, and after reading. Teachers introduce the book and activate students' background knowledge before beginning to read. Next, they engage students during reading through conversation and other activities. Afterward, they involve students in responding to the book. What's most important is how teachers engage students while they're reading aloud (Fisher, Flood, Lapp, & Frey, 2004).

Teachers often engage students by pausing periodically to talk about what's just been read. The timing is crucial: When reading stories, it's more effective to stop where students can make predictions and connections, after episodes that students might find confusing, and just before the ending becomes clear. When reading nonfiction, teachers stop to talk about big ideas as they're presented, briefly explain technical terms, and emphasize connections among the ideas. Teachers often read a poem from beginning to end once, and then stop as they're rereading it for students to play with words, notice poetic devices, and repeat favorite words and lines. The box below lists interactive techniques that teachers use. Deciding how often to pause for an activity and knowing when to continue reading develop through practice and vary from one group of students to another.

Teachers follow these steps to conduct interactive read-alouds:

1. *Pick a book.* Teachers choose award-winning and other high-quality books that are appropriate for students and that fit into their instructional programs.

2. *Prepare to share the book.* Teachers practice reading the book to ensure that they can read it fluently and to decide where to pause and engage students with the text; they write prompts on self-stick notes to mark these pages. Teachers also think about how they'll introduce the book and highlight difficult vocabulary words.

3. *Introduce the book.* Teachers activate students' background knowledge, set a clear purpose for listening, and preview the text.

4. *Read the book interactively.* Teachers read the book aloud, modeling fluent reading. They stop periodically to ask questions to focus students on specific points in the text and involve them in other activities.

5. *Involve students in after-reading activities.* Students participate in discussions and other response activities.

Interactive Read-Alouds

Interactive Techniques	
Stories	• Make and revise predictions at pivotal points. • Share personal, world, and literary connections. • Draw a picture of a character or an event. • Assume the persona of a character and share the character's thoughts. • Reenact a scene from the story.
Nonfiction	• Ask questions or share information. • Raise hands when specific information is read. • Restate the headings as questions. • Take notes. • Complete graphic organizers.
Poetry	• Add sound effects. • Mumble read along with the teacher. • Repeat lines after the teacher. • Clap when rhyming words, alliteration, or other poetic devices are heard.

Teachers use this instructional procedure whenever they're reading aloud, no matter whether it's an after-lunch read-aloud period or during a literature focus unit, reading workshop, or a thematic unit. Reading aloud has always been an important activity in kindergarten and first-grade classrooms. Sometimes teachers think they should read to children only until they learn to read, but reading aloud to share the excitement of books, especially those that students can't read themselves, should remain an important part of the literacy program at all grade levels. Older students report that when they listen to the teacher read aloud, they get more interested in the book and understand it better, and the experience often makes them want to read it themselves (Ivey, 2003).

Interactive Writing

Teachers use interactive writing to create a message with students and write it on chart paper (Button, Johnson, & Furgerson, 1996). The text is composed by the group, and the teacher guides students as they write it word by word. Students take turns writing known letters and familiar words, adding punctuation marks, and marking spaces between words. As students participate in creating and writing the text on chart paper, they also write it on small dry-erase boards. Afterward, students read and reread the text using shared reading at first, and then read it independently.

Interactive writing is used to demonstrate how writing works and show students how to construct words using their knowledge of sound-symbol correspondences and spelling patterns, and it's a powerful instructional procedure to use with English learners, no matter whether they're first graders or eighth graders (Tompkins & Collom, 2004). It was developed by the well-known English educator Moira McKenzie, who based it on Don Holdaway's work in shared reading (Fountas & Pinnell, 1996).

Teachers follow these steps to do interactive writing with small groups of students or the entire class:

1. *Collect materials for interactive writing.* Teachers collect chart paper, colored marking pens, white correction tape, an alphabet chart, magnetic letters or letter cards, and a pointer. They also collect these materials for individual students' writing: small dry-erase boards, pens, and erasers.

2. *Set a purpose.* Teachers present a stimulus activity or set a purpose for interactive writing. Often they read or reread a trade book as a stimulus, but students also share daily news summarize or information they're learning in social studies or science.

3. *Choose a sentence to write.* Teachers negotiate the text—often a sentence or two—with students. Students repeat the sentence several times and segment it into words. The teacher also helps the students remember the sentence as it is written.

4. *Pass out writing supplies.* Teachers distribute individual dry-erase boards, pens, and erasers for students to use to write the text individually as it is written together as a class on chart paper. They periodically ask students to hold their boards up so they can see what the students are writing.

5. *Write the first sentence.* The teacher and students slowly pronounce the first word, "stretching" it out, and students identify the sounds and the letters that represent them and write the letters on chart paper. The teacher chooses students to write letters and words, depending on their knowledge of phonics and spelling. They use one color pen, and the teacher uses another color to write words students can't spell to keep track of how much writing students are able to do. Teachers have an alphabet poster with upper- and lowercase letters available for students to refer to

when they're unsure how to form a letter, and white correction tape (sometimes called "boo-boo" tape) to correct poorly formed letters and misspellings. After writing each word, one student serves as the "spacer" and uses his or her hand to mark the space between words. This procedure is repeated to write each word in the sentence, and students reread the sentence from the beginning after each new word is completed. When appropriate, teachers point out capital letters, punctuation marks, and other conventions of print.

6. Write additional sentences. Teachers follow the procedure described in the fifth step to write the remaining sentences to finish the text.

7. Display the completed text. After completing the message, teachers post the chart in the classroom and have students reread it using shared reading or independent reading. Students often reread interactive charts when they "read the room," and teachers use the charts in teaching high-frequency words and phonics concepts.

Interactive writing can be used as part of literature focus units, in social studies and science thematic units, and for many other purposes, too. Here are some uses:

Write predictions before reading	Write responses after reading
Write letters and other messages	Write information or facts
Make K-W-L charts	Create new versions of a familiar text
Write class poems	Make posters

When students begin interactive writing in kindergarten, they use letters to represent the beginning sounds in words and write familiar words such as *the*, *a*, and *is*. As they learn more about sound-symbol correspondences and spelling patterns, they do more of the writing. Once they're writing words fluently, students do interactive writing in small groups. Each group member uses a different color pen and takes turns writing words. They also sign their names in color on the page so that the teacher can track which words each student wrote.

K-W-L Charts

Teachers use K-W-L charts during thematic units to activate students' background knowledge about a topic and to scaffold them as they ask questions and organize the information they're learning (Ogle, 1986). Teachers create a K-W-L chart by hanging up three sheets of butcher paper on a classroom wall and labeling them *K*, *W*, and *L*; the letters stand for "What We **K**now," "What We **W**onder," and "What We **L**earned." A K-W-L chart developed by a kindergarten class as they were hatching chicks is shown on page 442. The teacher did the actual writing on the K-W-L chart, but the children generated the ideas and questions. It often takes several weeks to complete this activity because teachers introduce the K-W-L chart at the beginning of a unit and use it to identify what students already know and what they wonder about the topic. Toward the end of the unit, students complete the last section of the chart, listing what they've learned.

This procedure helps students activate background knowledge, combine new information with prior knowledge, and learn technical vocabulary related to a thematic unit. Students become curious and more engaged in the learning process, and teachers can introduce complex ideas and technical vocabulary in a nonthreatening way. Teachers direct, scribe, and monitor the development of the K-W-L chart, but it's the students' talk that makes this such a powerful instructional procedure. Students use talk to explore ideas as they create the K and W columns and to share new knowledge as they complete the L column.

Teachers follow these steps:

1. Post a K-W-L chart. Teachers post a large chart on the classroom wall, divide it into three columns, and label them *K* (What We **K**now), *W* (What We **W**onder), and *L* (What We **L**earned).

2. Complete the K column. At the beginning of a thematic unit, teachers ask students to brainstorm what they know about the topic and write this information in the K column. Sometimes students suggest information that isn't correct; these statements should be turned into questions and added to the W column.

3. Complete the W column. Teachers write the questions that students suggest in the W column. They continue to add questions to the W column during the unit.

4. Complete the L column. At the end of the unit, students reflect on what they've learned, and teachers record this information in the L column of the chart.

Sometimes teachers organize the information on the K-W-L chart into categories to highlight the big ideas and to help students remember more of what they're learning; this procedure is called K-W-L Plus (Carr & Ogle, 1987). Teachers either provide three to six big-idea categories when they introduce the chart, or they ask students to decide on categories after they brainstorm information about the topic for the K column. Students then focus on these categories as they complete the L column, classify-

A Kindergarten Class's K-W-L Chart on Baby Chicks

K	W	L
What We <u>K</u>now	What We <u>W</u>ant to Learn	What We <u>L</u>earned
They hatch from eggs.	Are their feet called wabbly?	Chickens' bodies are covered with feathers.
They sleep.	Do they live in the woods?	Chickens have 4 claws.
They can be yellow or other colors.	What are their bodies covered with?	Yes, they do have stomachs.
They have 2 legs.		
They have 2 wings.	How many toes do they have?	Chickens like to play in the sun.
They eat food.		
They have a tail.	Do they have a stomach?	They like to stay warm.
They live on a farm.		
They are little.	What noises do they make?	They live on farms.
They have beaks.		
They are covered with fluff.	Do they like the sun?	

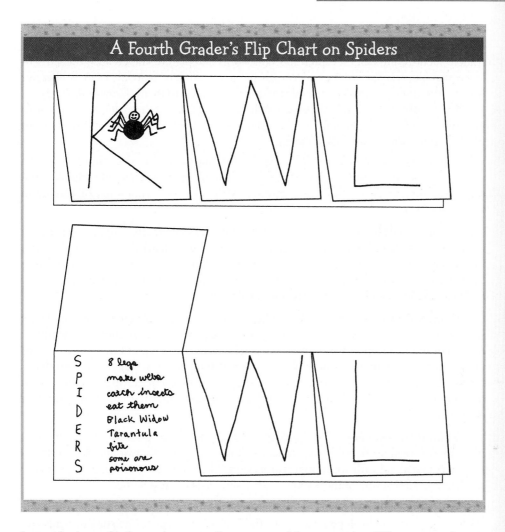

A Fourth Grader's Flip Chart on Spiders

S 8 legs
P make webs
I catch insects
D eat them
E Black Widow
R Tarantula
S bite
  some are
  poisonous

ing each piece of information according to one of the categories. When categories are used, it's easier to make sure students learn about each of the big ideas being presented.

Students also make individual K-W-L charts. As with class K-W-L charts, they brainstorm what they know about a topic, identify questions, and list what they've learned. They can make their charts in learning logs or construct flip books with K, W, and L columns. Students make individual flip charts by folding a legal-size sheet of paper in half, lengthwise, cutting the top flap into thirds, and labeling the flaps K, W, and L. Then students lift the flaps to write in each column, as shown here. Checking how students complete their L columns is a good way to monitor their learning.

Language Experience Approach

The Language Experience Approach (LEA) is a reading and writing procedure that's based on students' language and experiences (Ashton-Warner, 1965). A student dictates words and sentences about an experience, and the teacher writes the dictation. As the words and sentences are written, the teacher models how written language works. The text becomes the student's reading material. Because the language comes from the student and because the content is based on his or her experiences, the student is usually able to read the text. It's an effective way to help children begin reading; even those who haven't been successful with other types of reading activities can read what they've dictated.

Teachers use LEA to create reading materials that English learners can read. The EL cuts pictures out of magazines and glues them in a book. Then the teacher and the student identify and label several important words in a picture and create a related sentence that the teacher writes underneath it for the student to read. LEA is effective because the texts students create and read are meaningful to them (Crawford, 2003).

This flexible procedure can be used with the entire class, with small groups, and with individual students, depending on the teacher's purpose. Teachers follow these steps when working with individual students:

1. *Provide an experience.* The experience that serves as the stimulus for the writing can be an experience shared in school, a book read aloud, a field trip, or some other experience that the student is familiar with, such as having a pet or playing in the snow.

2. *Talk about the experience.* The teacher and the student talk about the experience to generate words and review the experience so that the student's dictation will be more interesting and complete. Teachers often begin with an open-ended question, such as "What are we going to write about?" The student talks about the experience to clarify and organize ideas and use more-specific vocabulary.

3. *Record the student's dictation.* The teacher takes the student's dictation. If the student hesitates, the teacher rereads what has been written and encourages him or her to continue. Teachers print neatly and spell words correctly, but they preserve students' language as much as possible. It's a great temptation to change the student's language to their own, in either word choice or grammar, but editing should be kept to a minimum so that students don't get the impression that their language is inferior or inadequate.

4. *Read the text aloud.* The teacher reads the text aloud, pointing at each word as it's read; this reading reminds the student of the content of the text and demonstrates how to read it aloud with appropriate intonation. Then the student reads along with the teacher, and after several joint readings, he or she reads the text alone.

5. *Make sentence strips.* The teacher rewrites the text on sentence strips that the student keeps in an envelope attached to the back of the paper. The student reads and sequences the sentence strips, and once he or she can read them smoothly, the student cuts the strips into individual words. He or she arranges the words into the familiar sentence and then creates new sentences with the word cards.

6. *Add word cards to word bank.* The student adds the word cards to his or her word bank (a small box that holds the word cards) after working with this text. They use these word cards for a variety of activities, including word sorts.

LEA is often used to create texts students can read and use as a resource for writing. For example, during a thematic unit on insects, first graders learned about ladybugs and created a big book with this dictated text:

Part 1: What Ladybugs Do

Ladybugs are helper insects. They help people because they eat aphids. They make the earth pretty. They are red and they have 7 black spots. Ladybugs keep their wings under the red wing cases. Their wings are transparent and they fly with these wings. Ladybugs love to eat aphids. They love them so much that they can eat 50 aphids in one day!

Part 2: How Ladybugs Grow

Ladybugs live on leaves in bushes and in tree trunks. They lay eggs that are sticky and yellow on a leaf. The eggs hatch and out come tiny and black larvae. They like to eat aphids, too. Next the larva becomes a pupa and then it changes into a ladybug. When the ladybugs first come out of the pupa, they are yellow but they change into red and their spots appear. Then they can fly.

Part 3: Ladybugs Are Smart

Ladybugs have a good trick so that the birds won't eat them. If a bird starts to attack, the ladybug turns over on her back and squeezes a stinky liquid from her legs. It smells terrible and makes the bird fly away.

Each part was written on a large sheet of paper, and the pages were bound into a book. After reading and rereading the book, the children each chose a sentence to be written on a sentence strip. Some children wrote their own sentences, and the teacher wrote them for others. They practiced reading their sentences, next they cut the sentences apart and rearranged them, and finally they used the sentences in writing their own "All About Ladybugs" books.

Learning Logs

Students write in learning logs as part of thematic units. Learning logs, like other journals, are booklets of paper in which students record information they're learning, write questions, summarize big ideas, draw diagrams, and reflect on their learning. Their writing is impromptu, and the emphasis is on using writing as a learning tool rather than creating polished products. Even so, students should be encouraged to work carefully and to spell content-related words posted on the word wall correctly. Teachers monitor students' logs, and they can quickly see how well students understand the big ideas they're learning.

Students each construct learning logs at the beginning of a thematic unit and then make entries in them during the unit. Here are the steps in this instructional procedure:

1. *Prepare learning logs.* At the beginning of a thematic unit, students construct learning logs using a combination of lined and unlined paper that's stapled into booklets with tagboard or laminated construction-paper covers.

2. *Have students use their learning logs.* Students take notes, draw diagrams, list vocabulary words, do quickwrites, and write summaries.

3. *Monitor students' entries.* Teachers read students' learning logs and answer their questions and clarify confusions.

4. *Have students write reflections.* Teachers often have students review their entries at the end of the thematic unit and write a reflection about what they've learned during the unit.

Students use learning logs during social studies units to make notes and respond to information they're learning as they read informational books and content-area textbooks. During a thematic unit on pioneers, for example, students do these activities in learning logs:

◆ Write questions to investigate during the unit
◆ Draw and label pictures of covered wagons
◆ List items the pioneers carried west

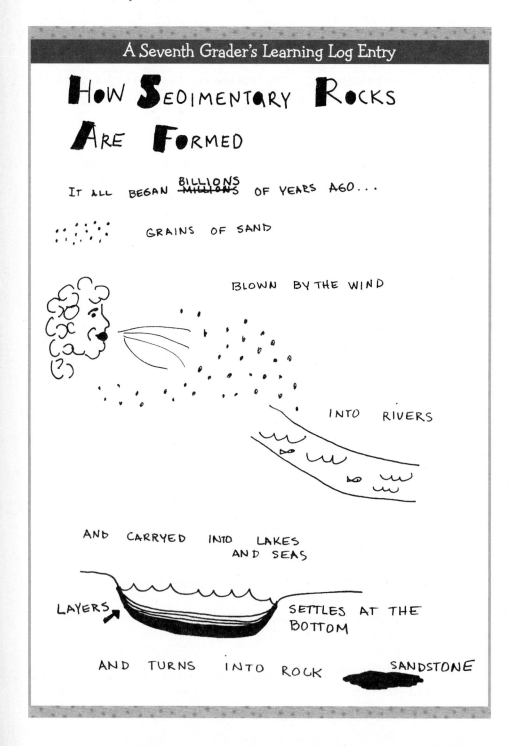

A Seventh Grader's Learning Log Entry

HOW SEDIMENTARY ROCKS ARE FORMED

IT ALL BEGAN BILLIONS ~~MILLIONS~~ OF YEARS AGO...

GRAINS OF SAND

BLOWN BY THE WIND

INTO RIVERS

AND CARRYED INTO LAKES AND SEAS

LAYERS

SETTLES AT THE BOTTOM

AND TURNS INTO ROCK   SANDSTONE

◆ Mark the Oregon Trail on a map of the United States
◆ Write responses to videos about pioneers
◆ Write a rough draft of a poem about life on the Oregon Trail
◆ Write a letter to the teacher at the end of the unit listing five things they learned

Learning logs are used for similar purposes in science units. During a unit on rocks and minerals, for example, seventh graders drew graphic organizers that they completed as they read a chapter in the science textbook, compiled lab reports as they did experiments, did quickwrites after watching videos, and drew diagrams and charts about scientific information. One student drew a series of illustrations to explain how sedimentary rocks form in the entry shown on the preceding page.

Making words is a teacher-directed spelling activity in which students arrange letter cards to spell words (Cunningham & Cunningham, 1992). Teachers choose key words from books students are reading that exemplify particular phonics or spelling patterns for students to practice. Then they prepare a set of letter cards that small groups of students or individual students can use to spell words. The teacher leads students as they create a variety of words using the letters. For example, after reading *Diary of a Spider* (Cronin, 2005), a group of first graders built these short-*i* and long-*i* words using the letters in the word *spider*: *is, sip, rip, dip, drip, side, ride,* and *ripe*. After spelling these words, students used all of the letters to spell the key word—*spider*. As students make words, they're practicing what they know about sound-symbol correspondences and spelling patterns, and teachers get feedback on what students understand, correct confusions, and review phonics and spelling concepts when necessary.

Making Words

Teachers often use this activity with small groups of English learners to practice spelling strategies and skills. It's effective because ELs collaborate with classmates, and the activity is both nonthreatening and hands-on. Sometimes teachers bring together a group of ELs to do a making words activity as a preview before doing it with the whole class (or afterward as a review), and sometimes a different word is used to reinforce a spelling pattern that they're learning.

Here are the steps in making words:

1. Make letter cards. Teachers prepare a set of small letter cards with multiple copies of each letter, especially common letters such as *a, e, i, r, s,* and *t*, printing the lowercase letterform on one side and the uppercase form on the reverse. They package the cards letter by letter in small plastic bags or partitioned plastic boxes.

2. Choose a word. Teachers choose a word to use in the word-making activity, and without disclosing it, have a student distribute the needed letter cards to classmates.

3. Name the letter cards. Teachers ask students to name the letter cards and arrange them on their desks with consonants in one group and vowels in another.

4. Make words. Students use the letter cards to spell words containing two, three, four, five, six, or more letters, and they list the words they can spell on a chart. Teachers monitor students' work and encourage them to fix any misspelled words.

5. Share words. Teachers have students identify two-letter words they made with the letter cards and continue to report longer and longer words until they identify the chosen word made using every letter card. After students share all of the words, teachers suggest any words they missed and point out recently taught spelling patterns.

A Sixth-Grade Making Words Activity Using the Word *Hieroglyphics*

h i e r o g l y p h i c s

2	3	4	5	6	7
go	her	hope	cries	prices	crisply
he	she	high	horse	highly	spicier
or	yes	hero	chose	chores	hospice
so	ice	rose	girls	psycho	
is	pig	rice	chili	higher	
hi	hop	chip	Chile	crispy	
	cry	iris	crisp		
	shy	pigs	shore		
	lie	girl	spice		
	pie	core	spire		
	ore	rosy	choir		
		goes	price		
		pier			

Teachers choose words for word-making lessons from books they are reading with students. For example, for Eric Carle's *A House for Hermit Crab* (2005), *hermit crabs* offers many word-making possibilities; and for *Number the Stars* (Lowry, 1998), *resistance fighters* can be used. Teachers also choose words for making words activities from thematic units. While a sixth-grade class was studying ancient Egypt, they completed the making words activity shown here using the word *hieroglyphics*. Teachers can get additional ideas for word-making activities using books that Patricia Cunningham and Dorothy Hall have compiled (1994a, 1994b).

Minilessons

Teachers teach short, focused lessons called *minilessons* on literacy strategies and skills (Atwell, 1998; Hoyt, 2000). Topics include how to write an entry in a reading log, use commas in a series, draw inferences, and use sentence combining. In these lessons, teachers introduce a topic and connect it to the reading or writing students are involved in, provide information, and supervise as students practice the topic. Minilessons usually last 15 to 30 minutes, and sometimes teachers extend the lesson over several days as students apply the topic in reading and writing activities. The best time to teach a minilesson is when students will have immediate opportunities to apply what they're learning.

It's not enough to simply explain strategies and skills or remind students to use them. Minilessons are an effective way to teach strategies and skills so that students actually do learn to use them. Teachers must actively engage students, encourage and scaffold them while they're learning, and then gradually withdraw their support (Dorn & Soffos, 2001).

Teachers follow these steps to present minilessons to small groups and to the whole class:

1. *Introduce the topic.* Teachers introduce the strategy or skill by naming it and making a connection between the topic and activities going on in the classroom.

2. *Share examples.* Teachers show how to use the topic with examples from students' own writing or from books students are reading.

3. *Provide information.* Teachers provide information, explaining and demonstrating the strategy or skill.

4. *Supervise practice.* Students practice using the strategy or skill with teacher supervision.

5. *Assess learning.* Teachers monitor students' progress and evaluate their use of newly learned strategies or skills.

Teachers teach minilessons on literacy strategies and skills as a part of literature focus units, reading and writing workshop, and other instructional approaches. Other minilessons focus on instructional procedures, such as how to use a dictionary or share writing from the author's chair, and concepts, such as homophones or adjectives.

Open-Mind Portraits

Students draw open-mind portraits to help them think more deeply about a character, reflect on story events from the character's viewpoint, and analyze the theme (McLaughlin & Allen, 2001). The portraits have two parts: the character's face on the top, "portrait" page, and several "thinking" pages revealing the character's thoughts at pivotal points in the story. The two pages of a fourth grader's open-mind portrait on Sarah, the mail-order bride in *Sarah, Plain and Tall* (MacLachlan, 2004), is shown on page 450. The words and pictures on the "thinking" page represent her thoughts at the end of the story.

Students follow these steps to make open-mind portraits while they're reading a story or immediately afterward:

1. *Make a portrait of a character.* Students draw and color a large portrait of the head and neck of a character in a story they're reading.

2. *Cut out the "portrait" and "thinking" pages.* Students cut out the portrait and attach it with a brad or staple on top of several more sheets of drawing paper. It's important that students place the brad or staple at the top of the portrait so that there's space available to draw and write on the "thinking" pages.

3. *Design the "thinking" pages.* Students lift the portrait page and draw and write about the character's thoughts at key points in the story.

4. *Share the completed open-mind portraits.* Students share their portraits with classmates and talk about the words and pictures they chose to include on the "thinking" pages.

Students create open-mind portraits to think more deeply about a character in a story they're reading in literature focus units and literature circles. They often reread parts of the story to recall specific details about the character's appearance before they draw the portrait, and they write several entries in a simulated journal to start thinking from that character's viewpoint before making the "thinking" pages. In addition to making open-mind portraits of characters in stories they're reading, students can make open-mind portraits of historical figures as part of social studies units, and of well-known personalities after reading biographies.

An Open-Mind Portrait of Sarah From *Sarah, Plain and Tall*

Prereading Plan

Teachers use the prereading plan (PReP) to diagnose and build necessary background knowledge before students read informational books and content-area textbooks (Langer, 1981; Vacca & Vacca, 2008). Teachers introduce a key concept discussed in the reading assignment and ask students to brainstorm related words and ideas. Teachers and students talk about the concept, and afterward students quickwrite to reflect on it. This activity is especially important for English learners who have limited background knowledge about a topic and technical vocabulary so that they'll be prepared to read informational books or content-area textbooks. An added benefit is that students' interest in the topic often increases as they participate in this activity.

Teachers follow these steps when they use this instructional procedure:

1. *Discuss a key concept.* Teachers introduce a key concept using a word, phrase, object, or picture to initiate a discussion.

2. *Brainstorm.* Teachers ask students to brainstorm words about the topic and record their ideas on a chart. They also help students make connections among the brainstormed ideas.

3. *Introduce vocabulary.* Teachers present additional vocabulary words that students need to read the assignment and clarify any misconceptions.

4. *Quickwrite about the topic.* Teachers have students quickwrite about the topic using words from the brainstormed list.

5. *Share the quickwrites.* Students share their quickwrites with the class, and teachers ask questions to help classmates clarify and elaborate their thinking.

6. *Read the assignment.* Students read the assignment and relate what they're reading to what they learned before reading.

Teachers use this instructional procedure during thematic units. Before reading a social studies textbook chapter about the Bill of Rights, for example, an eighth-grade teacher used PReP to introduce the concept that citizens have freedoms and responsibilities. Students brainstormed this list during a discussion about the Bill of Rights:

guaranteed in the Constitution	*James Madison*
1791	*10 amendments*
citizens	*freedom of speech*
freedom of religion	*owning guns and pistols*
homes can't be searched without a search warrant	*act responsibly*
limits on these freedoms for everyone's good	*serve on juries*
"life, liberty, and the pursuit of happiness"	*right to a jury trial*
no cruel or unusual punishments	*vote intelligently*

Then before reading the chapter, students wrote quickwrites to make personal connections to the ideas they'd brainstormed. Here is one student's quickwrite:

> *I always knew America was a free country but I thought it was because of the Declaration of Independence. Now I know that the Bill of Rights is a list of our freedoms. There are 10 freedoms in the Bill of Rights. I have the freedom to go to any church I want, to own guns, to speak my mind, and to read newspapers. I never thought of serving on a jury as a freedom and my Mom didn't either. She was on a jury about a year ago and she didn't want to do it. It took a whole week. Her boss didn't like her missing work. The trial was about someone who robbed a store and shot a man but he didn't die. I'm going to tell her that it is important to do jury duty. When I am an adult, I hope I get to be on a jury of a murder trial. I want to protect my freedoms and I know it is a citizen's responsibility, too.*

When the teacher read this student's quickwrite, she noticed that the student confused the number of amendments with the number of freedoms listed in the amendments, so she clarified the misunderstandings individually with her.

Question-Answer-Relationships

Taffy Raphael's Question-Answer-Relationships (QARs) procedure teaches students to be consciously aware of whether they are likely to find the answer to a comprehension question "right there" on the page, between the lines, or beyond the information provided in the text so that they're better able to answer it (Raphael, Highfield, & Au, 2006). Students use the QAR procedure when they're reading both narrative and expository texts and answering comprehension questions independently.

This procedure differentiates among the types of questions and the kinds of thinking required to answer them: Some questions require only literal thinking whereas others demand higher levels of thinking. Here are Raphael's four types of questions:

◆ **Right There Questions.** Readers find the answer "right there" in the text, usually in the same sentence as words from the question. These are literal-level questions.

◆ **Think and Search Questions.** The answer is in the text, but readers must search for it in different parts of the text and put the ideas together. These are inferential-level questions.

◆ **Author and Me Questions.** Readers use a combination of the author's ideas and their own to answer the question. These questions combine inferential and application levels.

◆ **On My Own Questions.** Readers use their own ideas to answer the question; sometimes they don't need to read the text to answer it. These are application- and evaluation-level questions.

The first two types of questions are known as "in the book" questions because the answers can be found in the book, and the last two types are "in the head" questions because they require information and ideas not presented in the book. An eighth grader's chart describing these types of questions is shown below.

Here are the steps in the QAR procedure:

1. *Read the questions first.* Students read the questions as a preview before reading the text to give them an idea of what to think about as they read.

2. *Predict how to answer the questions.* Students consider which of the four types each question represents and the level of thinking required to answer it.

3. *Read the text.* Students read the text while thinking about the questions they will answer afterward.

4. *Answer the questions.* Students reread the questions, determine where to find the answers, locate the answers, and write them.

5. *Share answers.* Students read their answers aloud and explain how they answered the questions. Students should again refer to the type of question and whether the answer was "in the book" or "in the head."

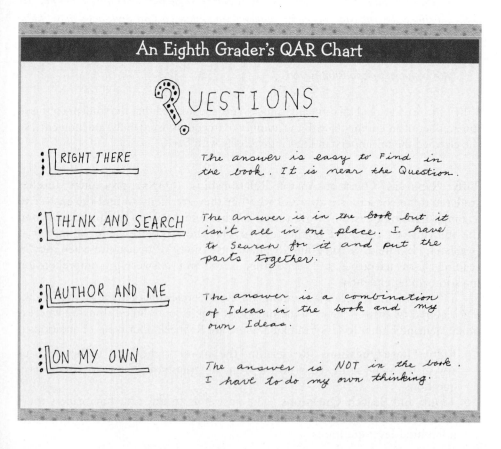

An Eighth Grader's QAR Chart

QUESTIONS

RIGHT THERE — The answer is easy to find in the book. It is near the Question.

THINK AND SEARCH — The answer is in the book but it isn't all in one place. I have to search for it and put the parts together.

AUTHOR AND ME — The answer is a combination of Ideas in the book and my own Ideas.

ON MY OWN — The answer is NOT in the book. I have to do my own thinking.

Students use the QAR procedure whenever they're expected to answer questions after reading a story, informational book, or content-area textbook. They can also write their own "in the book" and "in the head" questions. An eighth-grade teacher, for instance, asked his students to write questions representing the four levels in their reading logs as they were reading *The Giver* (Lowry, 2006). Here are some of their questions:

Right There Questions

What was the first color Jonas could see?
What does a Receiver do?

Think and Search Questions

How is Jonas different than the other people?
Why did Rosemary ask to be released?

Author and Me Questions

What happened to Jonas and Gabe at the end of the book?
Was the Giver an honorable person?

On My Own Questions

What would you have done if you were Jonas?
Could this happen in the United States?

Students also write questions when reading informational books and content-area textbooks.

Questioning the Author

Questioning the Author (QtA) teaches students how to construct meaning from a text. Isabel Beck and Margaret McKeown (2006) developed this instructional procedure to encourage students to question texts, particularly content-area textbooks, that they read. Students learn to view texts as fallible products written by authors who make errors and sometimes don't write as clearly as they should. Once students understand this tenet of fallibility, they read differently than they have before. Too often, students assume that if they don't understand something, it's because they aren't smart or don't read well enough.

Teachers teach students to ask questions, called *queries*, and talk about the text with classmates while they're reading to make sense of it. Queries support students as they develop comprehension. Sometimes the focus is on a single sentence, and at other times, it's on a paragraph or longer chunk of text in these whole-class discussions. Teachers and students ask queries such as these:

What is the author trying to tell us here?
What is the author talking about here?
How does this fit with what the author told us before?
Why is the author telling us this?

As students respond to questions like these, they share ideas and work together to construct meaning.

Teachers use six discussion moves as they orchestrate the discussion:

◆ **Marking.** Teachers draw attention to particular ideas students have expressed.
◆ **Turning-Back.** Teachers return responsibility for exploring the text to students and turn students' attention back to the text.
◆ **Revoicing.** Teachers interpret and rephrase students' ideas that they're struggling to express.
◆ **Recapping.** Teachers summarize the big ideas.

◆ **Modeling.** Teachers make their thinking public as they talk about a point students may have missed.

◆ **Annotating.** Teachers provide information during a discussion. (Beck & McKeown, 2006)

Although teachers prompt students to think more deeply, they should do less talking than the students do.

They follow these steps as they teach QtA to the whole class:

1. *Analyze the text.* Teachers identify the big ideas that they want students to focus on and decide how to segment the text to facilitate students' comprehension.

2. *Develop queries.* Teachers brainstorm a list of queries to ask about the big ideas in each segment. For example: "What's the author trying to tell us?" and "Why did the author say _____?" These queries are used to encourage students to probe the ideas, facilitate their discussion, and extend their understanding. Teachers often jot them on self-stick notes that they place in their copy of the book students are reading.

3. *Have students read.* Students read the first segment of text, stopping at a predetermined point to talk about what they've read.

4. *Ask queries.* Teachers present a query to begin the discussion. Students respond by sharing their interpretations, reading excerpts from the text, questioning ideas, clarifying confusions, and talking together to deepen their understanding. Teachers orchestrate the discussion using marking, revoicing, modeling, and the other discussion moves, and they ask additional questions based on the students' comments, including "Do you agree with what _____ said?" and "How does this information connect with what you already know?"

5. *Repeat reading and asking queries.* Teachers repeat steps 3 and 4 as students read and discuss each segment of text.

6. *Discuss the text.* Teachers lead a discussion based on students' responses to the queries to bring closure to the reading experience. They raise issues of accuracy and viewpoint; invite students to make personal, world, and textual connections; and compare this text to other books on the same topic or to other books by the same author.

Teachers explain the central tenet of QtA, that authors and their texts are fallible, at the beginning of the school year to give students more confidence in their abilities to read and understand books. They also teach students how to ask questions and talk about a text so that they're ready to use QtA whenever they're reading difficult texts. Teachers can use this procedure during literature focus units or literature circles whenever students have difficulty understanding a particular passage, and they use it during thematic units when they're reading chapters in content-area textbooks and other informational books.

Quickwriting

Quickwriting is an impromptu writing activity in which students explore a topic or respond to a question (Brozo & Simpson, 2007). They write for five to 10 minutes, letting their thoughts flow without stopping to make revisions or correct misspelled words; the focus is on generating ideas and developing writing fluency. Students think about ideas, reflect on what they know about a topic, ramble on paper, and make connections among ideas. Here's a series of quickwrites that a fifth grader wrote as she listened to her teacher read aloud *The Higher Power of Lucky* (Patron, 2006), an award-winning story of a plucky 10-year-old girl named Lucky who tries to surmount her problems and bring stability to her life:

Prompt: Why do you think the main character is named Lucky?

I don't know. At this point I don't think Lucky is lucky at all. Her mom died and her dad doesn't want her. She seems pretty unlucky. All that I can think is that Lucky is going to get more lucky at the end of the book. I hope something really good happens to her because she deserves it.

Prompt: Do you think Brigitte will abandon Lucky?

Lucky is really afraid that Brigitte will go back home to Paris. I don't think Brigitte is going to leave. It would be a really mean thing to do and Brigitte is sort of a mom and moms don't do that. I also think it's bad for a girl to have to worry about being abandoned. That's really sad. I predict that Lucky will have a real family at the end of the book.

Prompt: What happened when Lucky hit bottom?

It happened when she ran away from home. There was a bad dust storm and Miles was lost and it was her fault that Miles was lost. She was wearing Brigitte's beautiful red dress and she probably ruined it. I thought she'd get in big trouble and maybe she'd even die and so would Miles and her dog but it didn't happen that way. Everybody in town drove their cars out to the caves to find her and they were so happy to see her and Miles that they didn't even get mad. Lots of good things happened. Best of all, she found out that Brigitte was going to adopt her and would always be her mom. I love this book.

Students wrote their quickwrites after the teacher finished reading each chapter or two, and the quickwrites helped them reflect on what was happening in the story and prepare for the grand conversations.

Here are the steps in this instructional procedure:

1. *Choose a topic.* Students choose a topic or question (or the teacher assigns one) for the quickwrite, and they write it at the top of their papers.

2. *Write about the topic.* Students write sentences and paragraphs to explore the topic for 5 to 10 minutes. They focus on interesting ideas, make connections between the topic and their own lives, and reflect on their reading or learning. They rarely, if ever, stop writing to reread or correct errors in what they've written.

3. *Read quickwrites.* Students meet in small groups to read their quickwrites, and then one student in each group is chosen to share with the class. That student rereads his or her quickwrite in preparation for sharing with the whole class and adds any missing words and completes any unfinished thoughts.

4. *Share chosen quickwrites.* Students in each group who have been chosen to share their quickwrites with the whole class take turns reading them aloud.

5. *Write a second time.* Sometimes students write a second time on the same topic or on a new topic that emerged through writing and sharing; this second quickwrite is usually more focused than the first. Or students can expand their first quickwrite after listening to classmates share theirs or after learning more about the topic.

Teachers use quickwriting to promote thinking during literature focus units and thematic units. They're used as a warm-up at the beginning of a lesson or to promote reflection at the end of a lesson. Sometimes students identify the topics or questions for the quickwrite, and at other times, the teacher provides them. Quickwrites are also an effective prewriting procedure (Routman, 2004). Students often do several quick-writes to explore what they know about a topic before beginning to write; they brain-storm ideas and vocabulary, play with language, and identify ideas they need to learn more about before moving on to the drafting stage.

RAFT

Teachers use RAFT to create projects and other assignments to enhance students' comprehension of novels they're reading and information they're learning in thematic units (Holston & Santa, 1985). RAFT is an acronym for *role, audience, format,* and *topic,* and teachers consider these four dimensions as they design projects:

◆ **Role.** The role is the person or people the student becomes for this project. Sometimes students take on the role of a book character, historical figure, or con-temporary personality, such as Oprah, and at other times, they are themselves.

◆ **Audience.** The audience is the person or people who will read or view this proj-ect. They may include students, teachers, parents, or community members, as well as simulated audiences, such as book characters and historical personalities.

◆ **Format.** The format is the genre or activity that students create. It might be a letter, brochure, cartoon, journal, poster, essay, newspaper article, speech, or digital scrapbook.

◆ **Topic.** The topic is the subject of the project. It may be an issue related to the text, an essential question, or something of personal interest.

When students develop projects, they process ideas and information in different ways as they assume varied viewpoints and complete projects directed to specific audiences. Their thinking is imaginative and interpretive; in contrast, students' comprehension tends to be more literal when they do more-traditional assignments, such as writing answers to questions.

RAFT is an effective way to differentiate instruction by providing tiered activi-ties: Projects on the same text or topic can be adjusted according to students' achievement levels, English proficiency, and interests. For example, a seventh-grade teacher developed the chart of RAFT ideas on the next page for the Newbery Honor Book *The Wednesday Wars* (Schmidt, 2007); this coming-of-age novel chronicles the everyday trials of Holling Hoodhood, who is at odds with his seventh-grade English teacher, Mrs. Baker.

Teachers follow these steps to use RAFT after reading a book or studying a topic during a thematic unit:

1. *Establish the purpose.* Teachers reflect on what they want students to learn through this activity and consider how it can enhance students' comprehension of a book they're reading or a social studies or science topic they're learning.

2. *Prepare a RAFT chart.* Teachers prepare a RAFT chart of possible projects by brainstorming roles, choosing audiences, identifying genres and other formats for projects, and listing topics.

3. *Read the book or study the topic.* Students read and discuss a book or learn about a topic before they create RAFT projects.

RAFT Ideas for *The Wednesday Wars*

Role	Audience	Format	Topic
Holling and William Shakespeare	Our class	Interview	Explain "To thine own self be true" and other life lessons.
Mrs. Baker	Her son, a U.S. soldier in Vietnam	Letter	Tell why you took such an interest in Holling.
You	Our class	Poster	Describe the cultural and political uproar of the 1960s.
You	Newbery Award committee	Persuasive essay	Present reasons why this book should win the Newbery Award.
Bullies	Students at Camillo Jr. High	Speech	Research bullying, and explain how to deal with bullies.
Mai Thi (Holling's classmate)	Our class	Digital scrapbook	Share information about Vietnam and the war's effect on you and your home country.
Holling	Mrs. Baker	Letter, written when Holling is 30 years old	Explain how you've followed Mrs. Baker's advice: "Learn everything you can—everything. And then use all that you have learned to be a wise and good man."

4. *Choose projects.* Sometimes teachers assign the same project for all students, but at other times, they vary the assignment for small groups or let students choose a project from the RAFT chart.

5. *Create projects.* Students create their projects using the writing process and get feedback from the teacher as they work.

6. *Shared completed projects.* Students share their projects with small groups or the whole class and other appropriate audiences.

RAFT is usually an applying-stage activity because students develop these projects after reading and discussing a novel or after studying a social studies or science topic, but it can also be used in preparation for grand conversations or literature circle discussions. In addition, many teachers use RAFT as a prewriting activity to help students understand the relationships among topics, formats or genres, authors, and readers.

Readers Theatre

Readers theatre is a dramatic performance of a script by a group of readers (Black & Stave, 2007). Students each assume a part, rehearse by reading and rereading their characters' lines in the script, and then do a performance for their classmates. Students can read scripts in trade books and textbooks, or they can create their own scripts. The box on page 458 lists 10 books of narrative and informational scripts. What's valuable about readers theatre is that students interpret the story with their voices, without using much action. They may stand or sit, but they must carry the whole communication of the plot, characterization, mood, and theme by using their voices, gestures, and facial expressions. In addition, readers theatre avoids many of the problems inherent in theatrical productions: Students don't memorize their parts; elaborate props, costumes, and backdrops aren't needed; and long, tedious hours aren't spent rehearsing.

There are many reasons to recommend readers theatre. Students have opportunities to read good literature, and through this procedure they engage with text, interpret characters, and bring the text to life (Keehn, Martinez, & Roser, 2005; Worthy & Prater, 2002). Moreover, English learners and other students who are not yet fluent readers gain valuable oral reading practice in a relaxed small-group setting. They practice reading high-frequency words, increase their reading speed, learn how to phrase and chunk words in sentences, and read with more expression.

Teachers follow these steps as they work with a small group or the whole class:

1. *Select a script.* Students select a script and then read and discuss it as they would any story. Afterward, they volunteer to read each part.

2. *Rehearse the reading.* Students decide how to use their voice, gestures, and facial expressions to interpret the characters they're reading. They read the script several times, striving for accurate pronunciation, voice projection, and appropriate inflections. Less rehearsal is needed for an informal, in-class presentation than for a more formal production; nevertheless, interpretations should always be developed as fully as possible.

3. *Stage the reading.* Readers theatre can be presented on a stage or in a corner of the classroom. Students stand or sit in a row and read their lines. They stay in position through the production or enter and leave according to the characters' appearances "onstage." If readers are sitting, they stand to read their lines; if they're standing, they step forward to read. The emphasis isn't on production quality; rather, it's on the interpretive quality of readers' voices and expressions. Costumes and props aren't necessary; however, adding a few small props enhances interest as long as they don't interfere with the interpretive quality of the reading.

Students create their own readers theatre scripts from stories they've read and about topics related to thematic units (Flynn, 2007). When students are creating a script, it's important to choose a story with lots of conversation; any parts that don't

Readers Theatre Scripts

Barchers, S. I. (1997). *50 fabulous fables: Beginning readers theatre*. Portsmouth, NH: Teacher Ideas Press.

Barchers, S. I., & Pfeffinger, C. R. (2006). *More readers theatre for beginning readers*. Portsmouth, NH: Teacher Ideas Press.

Fredericks, A. D. (2007). *Nonfiction readers theatre for beginning readers*. Portsmouth, NH: Teacher Ideas Press.

Laughlin, M. K., Black, P. T., & Loberg, M. K. (1991). *Social studies readers theatre for children: Scripts and script development*. Portsmouth, NH: Teacher Ideas Press.

Martin, J. M. (2002). *12 fabulously funny fairy tale plays*. New York: Scholastic.

Pugliano-Martin, C. (1999). *25 just-right plays for emergent readers*. New York: Scholastic.

Shepard, A. (2005). *Stories on stage: Children's plays for reader's theater with 15 play scripts from 15 authors*. Olympia, WA: Shepard.

Wolf, J. M. (2002). *Cinderella outgrows the glass slipper and other zany fractured fairy tale plays*. New York: Scholastic.

Wolfman, J. (2004). *How and why stories for readers theatre*. Portsmouth, NH: Teacher Ideas Press.

Worthy, J. (2005). *Readers theatre for building fluency: Strategies and scripts for making the most of this highly effective, motivating, and research-based approach to oral reading*. New York: Scholastic.

include dialogue can become narrator parts. Depending on the number of narrator parts, one to four students can share the narrator duties. Teachers often make photocopies of the story for students to mark up or highlight as they develop the script. Sometimes students simply use their marked-up copies as the finished script, and at other times, they retype the finished script, omitting the unnecessary parts.

Reading Logs

Reading logs are journals in which students write their reactions and opinions about books they're reading or listening to the teacher read aloud. Through their reading log entries, students clarify misunderstandings, explore ideas, and deepen their comprehension (Barone, 1990; Hancock, 2008). They also add lists of words from the word wall, diagrams about story elements, and information about authors and genres (Tompkins, 2008). For a chapter book, students write after reading every chapter or two, and they often write single entries after reading picture books or short stories. Often students write a series of entries about a collection of books written by the same author, such as books by Eric Carle or Chris Van Allsburg, or about versions of the same folktale or fairy tale.

Sometimes students choose what they'll write about in reading log entries, and at other times, they respond to questions or prompts that teachers have prepared. Both student-choice and teacher-directed entries are useful: When students choose their own topics, they delve into their own ideas and questions, sharing what's important to them, and when teachers prepare prompts, they direct students' thinking to topics and questions that students might otherwise miss. When teachers know their students well and are familiar with the books students are reading, they choose the best mix of student-choice and teacher-directed entries.

Students follow these steps as they write independently in reading logs:

1. Prepare reading logs. Students make reading logs by stapling paper into booklets, and they write the title of the book on the cover.

2. Write entries. Students write their reactions and reflections about the book or chapter. Sometimes they choose their own topics, and at other times, teachers pose topics and questions. Students often summarize events and make connections to the book. They also list interesting or unfamiliar words, jot down memorable quotes, and take notes about characters, plot, or other story elements.

3. Share entries. Students share their reading logs with teachers so they can monitor students' work. Teacher also write comments back to students about their interpretations and reflections.

Students at all grade levels can write and draw reading log entries to help them understand stories they're reading and listening to read aloud during literature focus units and literature circles (Daniels, 2001). As a sixth-grade class read *The Giver* (Lowry, 2006), a Newbery Award–winning story of a not-so-perfect society, students discussed each chapter and brainstormed several possible titles for the chapter. Then they wrote entries in their reading logs and labeled each chapter with the number and the title they felt was most appropriate. The following three reading log entries show how a sixth grader grappled with the idea of "release":

Chapter 18: "Release"

I think release is very rude. People have a right to live where they want to. Just because they're different they have to go somewhere else. I think release is when you have to go and live elsewhere. If you're released you can't come back to the community.

Chapter 19: "Release—The Truth"

It is so mean to kill people that didn't do anything bad. They kill perfectly innocent peo-ple. Everyone has a right to live. The shot is even worse to give them. They should be able to die on their own. If I were Jonas I would probably go insane. The people who kill the people that are to be released don't know what they're doing.

Chapter 20: "Mortified"

I don't think that Jonas is going to be able to go home and face his father. What can he do? Now that he knows what release is he will probably stay with The Giver for the rest of his life until he is released.

After reading and discussing Chapter 18, this student doesn't understand that "release" means "killing," but he grasps the awful meaning of the word as he reads Chapter 19.

Reciprocal Questioning

Teachers use reciprocal questioning to involve students more actively in reading and understanding informational texts (Ciardello, 1998). In this instructional procedure, teachers segment content-area textbook chapters and informational books and articles into sentences or paragraphs, and teachers and students read a segment and ask each other questions about the text they've read. Students and teachers ask these types of questions during reciprocal questioning:

◆ Questions about the meaning of particular words
◆ Questions that are answered directly in the text
◆ Questions that can be answered using common knowledge about the world
◆ Questions that relate the text to students' own lives
◆ "I wonder why" questions that go beyond the information provided in the text
◆ Questions that require students to locate information not contained in the text

This procedure is effective because students read more purposefully when they read to create questions and to prepare to answer questions than when they're reading inde-pendently to finish an assignment.

    Teachers follow these steps as they implement reciprocal questioning:

    1. *Prepare for the reciprocal questioning activity.* Teachers read the text and chunk it into segments. They choose the length of a segment—from a sentence to a paragraph or two—depending on the complexity of the material being presented and students' reading levels.

    2. *Introduce the assignment.* Teachers introduce the reading assignment and have students silently read a small segment of the text.

    3. *Ask questions.* Students ask several questions about the text they've just read; the teacher closes the book and answers the questions as fully as possible.

    4. *Reverse roles.* This time, the teacher questions the students after they've read a segment of text and closed their books. Teachers model asking a range of questions, from factual to interpretive questions. Or students and the teacher can alternate asking and answering questions after reading each segment of text.

    5. *Repeat steps 2, 3, and 4 to read and discuss more of the text.* At an appropri-ate point, the teacher asks students to predict what information they expect to read and learn in the rest of the text, and then students continue reading the rest of the assign-ment independently.

Questions About *The Real McCoy: The Life of an African-American Inventor*

Page 1	What does "the real McCoy" mean?	S
	Who was Elijah McCoy?	S
	What did he invent?	S
Page 2	Was Elijah McCoy born in the United States?	T
	Do you think Elijah's parents ever knew Harriet Tubman?	T
	Was Elijah McCoy free or a slave?	T
Page 3	Did Elijah McCoy learn to read and write?	S
	What did Elijah McCoy like to do?	S
	Do you think he was a smart boy?	T
Page 4	Why did Elijah McCoy go to Scotland?	T
	What did he study in college?	T
Page 5	When did Elijah come to the United States?	S
	Why was it hard for him to get a job?	S
	What was the only job he could find?	S
Page 6	What does a fireman do on a train?	T
	Was it a good job?	S
Page 7	What was Elijah's other job?	S
	What does an oilman do?	S
Page 8	What was Elijah's invention?	T
	What does <u>lubrication</u> mean?	T
Page 9	What does <u>skeptical</u> mean?	S
	What does the saying "the real McCoy" mean?	T

Teachers use reciprocal questioning to support students' reading of difficult nonfiction texts. For example, a fifth-grade teacher used reciprocal questioning to read *The Real McCoy: The Life of an African-American Inventor* (Towle, 1993), an informational book about Elijah McCoy, whose name became an eponym. Because there is only a paragraph or two of text on each page of this picture book, it works well for reciprocal questioning. The teacher began by talking about words and phrases that came from people's names, such as *Levi's*. A list of the questions that students and the teacher asked is presented above; questions that students asked are marked with *S*, and questions asked by the teacher are marked with *T*. After the class read the first nine pages together, the teacher asked students to predict what the rest of the book was about, and the students read the rest of the book independently. After reading, students made a lifeline of the events in this African American inventor's life.

Rubrics

Rubrics are scoring guides that teachers use to assess students' writing (Spandel, 2005). These guides usually have 4, 5, or 6 levels, ranging from high to low, and assessment criteria are described at each level. Students receive a copy of the rubric as they begin writing so that they understand what's expected and how they'll be assessed. Depending on the rubric's intricacy, teachers mark the assessment criteria either while they're reading students' writing or immediately afterward and then determine the overall score for the piece of writing.

The assessment criteria on some rubrics describe general qualities of effective writing, such as ideas, organization, word choice, and mechanics, but in others, they focus on genre characteristics. Teachers often use genre-specific rubrics to assess stories, reports, letters, and autobiographies. No matter which assessment criteria are used, the same criteria are addressed at each level. If a criterion addresses sentence fluency, for example, descriptors about sentence fluency are included at each level; the statement "contains short, choppy sentences" might be used at the lowest level and "uses sentences that vary in length and style" at the highest level. Each level represents a one-step improvement in students' application of that criterion.

Rubrics can be constructed with any number of levels, but it's easier to show growth in students' writing when the rubric has more levels. Much more improvement is needed for students to move from one level to another if the rubric has 4 levels than if it has 6 levels. A rubric with 10 levels would be even more sensitive to student growth, but rubrics with many levels are harder to construct and more time-consuming to use. Researchers usually recommend that teachers use rubrics with either 4 or 6 levels so that there is no middle score—each level is either above or below the middle—because teachers are inclined to score students at the middle level, when there is one.

Rubrics are often used for determining proficiency levels and assigning grades. The level that is above the midpoint is usually designated as "proficient," "competent," or "passing"—that's a 3 on a 4-point rubric and a 4 on a 5- or 6-point rubric. The levels on a 6-point rubric can be described this way:

1 = minimal level	4 = proficient level
2 = beginning or limited level	5 = excellent level
3 = developing level	6 = superior level

Teachers also equate levels to letter grades.

These scoring guides help students become better writers because they lay out the qualities that constitute excellence and clarify teachers' expectations so students understand how the assignment will be assessed. Students, too, can use rubrics to improve their writing: Based on the rubric's criteria, they can examine their rough drafts and decide how to revise their writing to make it more effective. In addition, Vicki Spandel (2005) claims that rubrics are time savers: She says that rubrics drastically reduce the time it takes to read and respond to students' writing because the criteria on the rubric guide the assessment and reduce the need to write lengthy comments back to students.

Teachers follow these steps:

1. Choose a rubric. Teachers choose a rubric that's appropriate to the writing project or create one that reflects the assignment.

2. Introduce the rubric. Teachers distribute copies of the rubric to students and talk about the criteria used at each level, focusing on the requirements at the proficient level.

3. Have students self-assess their writing. Students use the rubric to self-assess their writing as part of the revising stage. They highlight phrases in the rubric or check off items that best describe their writing. Then they determine which level has the most highlighted words or checkmarks; that level is the overall score, and students circle it.

4. Assess students' writing. Teachers assess students' writing by highlighting phrases in the rubric or checking off items that best describe the composition. Then they assign the overall score by determining which level has the most highlighted words or checkmarks and circle it.

5. *Conference with students.* Teachers talk with students about the assessment, identifying strengths and weaknesses. Then students set goals for the next writing assignment.

Students use rubrics during writing workshop or whenever they're using the writing process to draft and refine a piece of writing. Many commercially prepared rubrics are currently available: State departments of education post rubrics for mandated writing tests on their websites, and school districts hire teams of teachers or consultants to develop writing rubrics for each grade level. Spandel (2005) provides rubrics that assess the six traits of writing. Other rubrics are provided with basal reading programs, in professional books for teachers, and on the Internet.

Even though commercially prepared rubrics are convenient, they may not be appropriate for some groups of students or for specific writing assignments. The rubrics may have only 4 levels when 6 would be better, or they may have been designed for a different grade level. They also may not address a specific genre, or they may have been written for teachers, not in kid-friendly language. Because of these limitations, teachers often decide to develop their own rubrics or adapt commercial rubrics to meet their own needs.

In this reading-stage activity, teachers observe individual students as they read aloud and record information to analyze their reading fluency (Clay, 2000). They calculate the percentage of words the student reads correctly and then analyze the miscues or errors. Teachers make a checkmark on a copy of the text as the student reads each word correctly and use other marks to indicate words that the student doesn't know or mispronounces.

Teachers conduct running records with individual students using these steps:

1. *Choose a book.* Teachers have the student choose an excerpt at least 100 words in length from a book he or she is reading for the assessment. For beginning readers, the text can be shorter.

2. *Take the running record.* As the student reads the excerpt aloud, the teacher records information about the words read correctly as well as those misread. The teacher makes checkmarks on a copy of the text for each word read correctly and uses other marks for miscues. The box on page 464 shows how to mark miscues.

3. *Calculate the percentage of miscues.* Teachers calculate the percentage of miscues by dividing the number of miscues by the total number of words read. When the student makes 5% or fewer errors, the book is considered to be at the student's independent level. When there are 6–10% errors, the book is at the student's instructional level, and when there are more than 10% errors, the book is too difficult—the student's frustration level.

4. *Analyze the miscues.* Teachers look for patterns in the miscues in order to determine how the student is growing as a reader and what strategies and skills should be taught next.

Many teachers conduct running records on all their students at the beginning of the school year and at the end of grading periods. In addition, teachers do running records more often during guided reading groups and with students who aren't making expected progress in reading to diagnose their reading problems and make instructional decisions.

Running Records

How to Mark Miscues

Miscue	Explanation	Marking
Incorrect word	If the student reads a word incorrectly, the teacher writes the incorrect word and the correct word under it.	take / taken
Self-correction	If the student self-corrects an error, the teacher writes SC (for "self-correction") following the incorrect word.	for SC / from
Unsuccessful attempt	If the student attempts to pronounce a word, the teacher records each attempt and adds the correct text underneath.	be-běf-before / before
Skipped word	If the student skips a word, the teacher marks the error with a dash.	— / the
Inserted word	If the student says words that are not in the text, the teacher writes an insertion symbol (caret) and records the inserted words.	not / ^
Supplied word	If the student can't identify a word, the teacher supplies it and writes T above the word.	T / which
Repetition	If the student repeats a word or phrase, it isn't scored as a miscue, but the teacher notes it by making a checkmark for each repetition.	✓✓✓ / so

Semantic Feature Analysis

Teachers create a semantic feature analysis to help students examine the characteristics of vocabulary words or content-area concepts (Pittelman, Heimlich, Berglund, & French, 1991). They draw a grid for the analysis with words or concepts listed on one axis and the characteristics or components listed on the other. Students reading a novel, for example, can do a semantic feature analysis with vocabulary words listed on one axis and the characters' names on the other; they decide which words relate to which characters and use pluses and minuses to mark the relationships on the grid. Teachers often do a semantic feature analysis with the whole class, but students can work in small groups or individually to complete the grid. The examination should be done as a whole-class activity, however, so that students can share their insights.

Here are the steps in doing a semantic feature analysis:

1. *Create a grid.* Teachers create a grid with vocabulary or concepts listed on the vertical axis and characteristics or categories on the horizontal axis.

2. *Complete the grid.* Students complete the grid, cell by cell, by considering the relationship between each item on the vertical axis and the items on the horizontal axis. Then they mark the cell with a plus to indicate a relationship, a minus to indicate no relationship, and a question mark when they're unsure.

3. *Examine the grid.* Students and the teacher examine the grid for patterns and then draw conclusions based on the patterns.

Teachers have students do a semantic feature analysis as part of a literature focus unit or a thematic unit. In a thematic unit on immigration, for example, fifth-grade class did a semantic feature analysis, shown on the next page, to review what they were learning about America as a culturally pluralistic society. They listed the groups of peo-

Fifth Graders' Semantic Feature Analysis on Immigration

	Arrived in the 1600s	Arrived in the 1700s	Arrived in the 1800s	Arrived in the 1900s	Came to to Ellis Island	Came for religious freedom	Came for safety	Came for opportunity	Were refugees	Experienced prejudice
English	+	+	–	–	–	+	–	+	–	–
Africans	+	+	+	–	–	–	–	–	–	+
Irish	–	–	+	–	–	–	+	+	+	+
Other Europeans	–	+	+	+	+	–	+	+	+	+
Jews	–	–	+	+	+	+	+	–	+	+
Chinese	–	–	+	–	–	–	–	–	–	+
Latinos	–	–	–	+	–	–	–	+	–	+
Southeast Asians	–	–	–	+	–	–	+	+	+	+

Code: + = yes
     – = no
     ? = don't know

ple who immigrated to the United States on one axis and historical features on the other. Next, they completed the grid by marking each cell. Afterward, the students examined it for patterns and identified these big ideas:

Different peoples immigrated to America at different times.

The Africans who came as slaves were the only people who were brought to America against their will.

The English were the only immigrants who didn't suffer prejudice.

Shared Reading

Teachers use shared reading to read authentic literature—stories, informational books, and poems—with students who couldn't read those books independently (Holdaway, 1979). Teachers read the book aloud, modeling fluent reading, and then they read the book again and again for several days. The focus for the first reading is students' enjoyment. Teachers draw students' attention to concepts about print, comprehension, and interesting words and sentences during the next couple of readings. Finally, students focus on decoding particular words during the last reading or two.

Students are actively involved in shared reading. Teachers encourage them to make predictions and to chime in on reading repeated words and phrases. Individual students or small groups take turns reading brief parts once they begin to recognize words and phrases. Students examine interesting features that they notice in the book—punctuation marks, illustrations, tables of contents, for example—and teachers point out others. They also talk about the book, both while they're reading and afterward. Shared reading builds on students' experience listening to their parents read bedtime stories (Fisher & Medvic, 2000).

Teachers follow these steps to use shared reading with the whole class or small groups of students:

1. *Introduce the text.* Teachers talk about the book or other text by activating or building background knowledge on topics related to the book and by reading the title and the author's name aloud.

2. *Read the text aloud.* Teachers read the story aloud to students, using a pointer (a dowel rod with a pencil eraser on the end) to track as they read. They invite students to be actively involved by making predictions and by joining in the reading, if the story is repetitive.

3. *Have a* grand conversation. Students talk about the story, ask questions, and share their responses.

4. *Reread the story.* Students take turns using the pointer to track the reading and turning pages. Teachers invite students to join in reading familiar and predictable words. Also, they take opportunities to teach and use graphophonic cues and reading strategies while reading. Teachers vary the support that they provide, depending on students' reading expertise.

5. *Continue the process.* Teachers continue to reread the story with students over a period of several days, again having students turn pages and take turns using the pointer to track the text while reading. They encourage students who can read the text to read along with them.

6. *Have students read independently.* After students become familiar with the text, teachers distribute individual copies of the book or other text for students to read independently and use for a variety of activities.

Teachers use shared reading during literature focus units, literature circles, and thematic units. When doing shared reading with young children, teachers use enlarged texts, including big books, poems written on charts, Language Experience stories, and interactive writing charts, so that students can see the text and read along. Teachers also use shared reading techniques to read books that older students can't read themselves (Allen, 2002). Students each have a copy of the novel, content-area textbook, or other book, and the teacher and students read together. The teacher or another fluent reader reads aloud while students follow along in the text, reading to themselves.

Sketch-to-Stretch

Sketch-to-stretch is a tool for helping students deepen their comprehension of stories they've read (Short & Harste, 1996). Students work in small groups to draw pictures or diagrams that represent what the story means to them, not pictures of their favorite character or episode. In particular, they focus on theme and on symbols to represent the theme as they make sketch-to-stretch drawings (Dooley & Maloch, 2005). An added benefit is that students learn that stories rarely have only one interpretation and that by reflecting on the characters and events, they usually discover one or more themes.

Students need many opportunities to experiment with this activity before they move beyond drawing pictures of the story events or characters to be able to think symbolically. It's helpful to introduce this instructional procedure through a minilesson and to draw several sketches together as a class before students do their own. With practice, students learn that there isn't a single correct interpretation, and teachers help students focus on the interpretation rather than on their artistic talents. The box below shows a fourth grader's sketch-to-stretch made after reading *The Ballad of Lucy Whipple* (Cushman, 1996), a story set during the California gold rush. The sketch-to-stretch emphasizes two themes of the book—you make your own happiness, and home is where you are.

Teachers follow these steps as they implement this instructional procedure:

1. *Read and respond to a story.* Students read a story or several chapters of a longer book, and they respond to the story in a grand conversation or in reading logs.

2. *Discuss the themes.* Students and the teacher talk about the themes in the story and ways to symbolize meanings. Teachers remind students that there are many ways to represent the meaning of an experience, and they explain that students can use lines, colors, shapes, symbols, and words to visually represent what a story means to them. They talk about possible meanings and ways they might visually represent these meanings.

3. *Draw the sketches.* Students work in small groups to draw sketches that reflect what the story means to them. Teachers emphasize that students should focus on their thinking about the meaning of the story, not on their favorite part, and that there's no single correct interpretation of the story. They also remind students that the artistic quality of their drawings is less important than their interpretation.

A Fourth Grader's Sketch-to-Stretch About *The Ballad of Lucy Whipple*

4. *Share the sketches.* Students meet in small groups to share their sketches and talk about the symbols they used. Teachers encourage classmates to study each student's sketch and tell what they think the student is trying to convey.

5. *Share some sketches with the class.* Each group chooses one sketch from their group to share with the class.

6. *Revise sketches and make final copies.* Students add to their sketches based on feedback they received and ideas from classmates, and then they make a final copy of their sketches.

Students can use sketch-to-stretch whenever they're reading stories. In literature circles, for example, students create sketch-to-stretch drawings about themes and symbols that they share during group meetings (Whitin, 2002). Through this sharing, students gain insights about their classmates' thinking and clarify their own understanding. The same is true when students create and share sketch-to-stretch drawings during literature focus units.

Story Boards

Story boards are cards on which the illustrations and text from a picture book have been attached. Teachers make story boards by cutting apart two copies of a picture book and gluing the pages on pieces of tagboard. The most important use of story boards is to sequence the events of a story by lining the cards up on a chalkboard tray or hanging them on a clothesline. Once the pages of the picture book have been laid out, students visualize the story and its structure in new ways and examine the illustrations more closely. For example, students arrange story boards from *How I Became a Pirate* (Long, 2003) to retell the story and pick out the beginning, middle, and end. They use story boards to identify the dream sequences in the middle of *Abuela* (Dorros, 1997) and compare versions of folktales, such as *The Mitten* (Brett, 1989; Tresselt, 1989) and *The Woodcutter's Mitten* (Koopmans, 1995).

Teachers use this instructional procedure because it allows students to manipulate and sequence stories and examine illustrations more carefully. Story boards are especially useful tools for English learners who use them to preview a story before reading or to review the events in a story after reading. ELs also draw story boards because they can often share their understanding better through art than through language. In addition, story boards present many opportunities for teaching comprehension when only one copy of a picture book is available.

Teachers generally use story boards with a small group of students or with the whole class, but individual students can reexamine them as part of center activities. Here are the steps:

1. *Collect two copies of a book.* Teachers use two copies of a picture book for the story boards. Paperback copies are preferable because they're less expensive. In a few picture books, all the illustrations are on right-hand or left-hand pages, so only one copy is needed.

2. *Cut the books apart.* Teachers remove the covers and separate the pages, evening out the cut edges.

3. *Attach the pages to pieces of cardboard.* Teachers glue each page or double-page spread to a piece of cardboard, making sure that pages from each book are alternated so that each illustration is included.

4. *Laminate the cards.* Teachers laminate the cards so that they can withstand use by students.

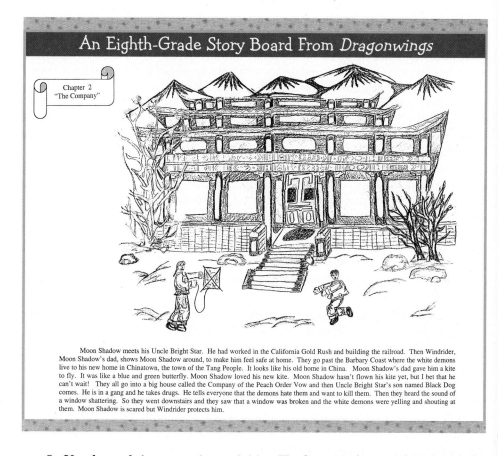

An Eighth-Grade Story Board From *Dragonwings*

Chapter 2
"The Company"

Moon Shadow meets his Uncle Bright Star. He had worked in the California Gold Rush and building the railroad. Then Windrider, Moon Shadow's dad, shows Moon Shadow around, to make him feel safe at home. They go past the Barbary Coast where the white demons live to his new home in Chinatown, the town of the Tang People. It looks like his old home in China. Moon Shadow's dad gave him a kite to fly. It was like a blue and green butterfly. Moon Shadow loved his new kite. Moon Shadow hasn't flown his kite yet, but I bet that he can't wait! They all go into a big house called the Company of the Peach Order Vow and then Uncle Bright Star's son named Black Dog comes. He is in a gang and he takes drugs. He tells everyone that the demons hate them and want to kill them. Then they heard the sound of a window shattering. So they went downstairs and they saw that a window was broken and the white demons were yelling and shouting at them. Moon Shadow is scared but Windrider protects him.

5. *Use the cards in sequencing activities.* Teachers use the story board cards for a number of activities, including sequencing, story structure, rereading, and word-study activities.

Students use story boards for a variety of activities during literature focus units. For a sequencing activity, teachers pass out the cards in a random order, and students line up around the classroom to sequence the story events. Story boards can also be used when only a few copies of a picture book are available so that students can identify words for the word wall, notice literary language, examine an element of story structure, or study the illustrations. When students read novels, they create their own story boards. Partners work together to create a story board for one chapter: They make a poster with a detailed drawing illustrating events in the chapter and write a paragraph-length summary of it. Two eighth graders' story board summarizing Chapter 2 of *Dragonwings* (Yep, 1975) is shown here.

Teachers use story retelling to monitor students' comprehension (Morrow, 1985). Teachers sit one-on-one with individual students in a quiet area of the classroom and ask them to retell a story they've just read or listened to read aloud. While the student is retelling, teachers use a teacher-made scoring sheet to mark the information that the student includes. If the student hesitates or doesn't finish retelling the story, teachers ask questions, such as "What happened next?" When they retell a story, students organize the information they remember to provide a personalized summary that reveals their level of comprehension (Hoyt, 1999).

Story Retelling

Teachers can't assume that students already know how to retell stories, even though many do. Through explanations and demonstrations of the retelling procedure, students learn what's expected of them. Students also need to practice retelling stories before they'll be good at it. They can retell stories with a classmate and to their parents at home.

Once teachers begin listening to students retell stories, they notice that students who understand a story retell it differently than those who don't. Good comprehenders' retellings make sense: They reflect the organization of the story and include all of the important story events. In contrast, weak comprehenders often recall events haphazardly or omit important events, especially those in the middle of the story.

Retelling is an instructional tool as well as an assessment tool. McKenna and Stahl (2003) explain that through story retelling, students expand their oral language, enhance their use of comprehension strategies, and deepen their knowledge of story structure. When students participate regularly in retelling activities, their comprehension improves as they learn to focus on the big ideas in the story, and their oral language abilities are enhanced as they incorporate sentence patterns, vocabulary, and phrases from stories into their own talk.

Teachers usually share a story with the class and then follow these steps as individual students retell it:

1. *Introduce the story.* Teachers introduce the story by reading the title, examining the cover of the book, or talking about a topic related to the story. They also explain that students will be asked to retell the story afterward.

2. *Read and discuss the story.* Students read the story or listen to it read aloud. When students are reading the story themselves, it's essential that the story is at their reading level. Afterward, they talk about the story, sharing ideas and clarifying confusions.

3. *Create a graphic organizer.* Students create a graphic organizer or a series of drawings to guide their retelling. (This step is optional, but it's especially helpful for students who have difficulty retelling stories.)

4. *Have a student retell the story.* Teachers ask students to individually retell the story in their own words, asking questions, if necessary, to elicit more information:

Who was the story about?

What happened next?

Where did the story take place?

What did the character do next?

How did the story end?

5. *Mark the scoring guide.* Teachers assess the retelling using a scoring guide that they mark as the student retells the story. The scoring guide lists important information about characters and events in the story, usually organized into beginning, middle, and end sections. As they listen to the student's retelling, teachers place checkmarks by each piece of information that the student recalls. If a student omits important information, teachers ask questions to prompt the student's recall, and they write P beside information that was recalled with prompting.

Teachers often use this instructional procedure during literature focus units and guided reading to monitor students' comprehension of stories they've read and listened to read aloud. Students can also retell informational books; in these retellings, the focus is on summarizing the big ideas and their relationships rather than on story events (Flynt & Cooter, 2005). Their retellings should address these questions:

What are the big ideas?

How are the big ideas structured?

What is the author's purpose?

What did students learn that they didn't already know?

For students to remember the big ideas they're learning, it's essential that they make personal, world, and textual connections to them. They need adequate background knowledge about a topic to make connections—and if they can't make any connections, it's unlikely they'll understand or remember the big ideas.

Sustained Silent Reading

Sustained Silent Reading (SSR) is an independent reading time set aside during the school day for students in one class or the entire school to silently read self-selected books (Gardiner, 2005). In some schools, everyone—students, teachers, principals, secretaries, and custodians—stops to read, usually for a 15- to 30-minute period. SSR is a popular reading activity that's known by a variety of names, including "drop everything and read" (DEAR), "sustained quiet reading time" (SQUIRT), and "our time to enjoy reading" (OTTER).

Teachers use SSR to increase the amount of reading students do every day and to develop their ability to read silently and without interruption (Hunt, 1967). SSR follows these guidelines:

◆ Students choose the books they read.
◆ Students read silently.
◆ The teacher serves as a model by reading.
◆ Students choose one book or other reading material for the entire reading time.
◆ The teacher sets a timer for a predetermined, uninterrupted time period, usually 15–30 minutes.
◆ Everyone participates.
◆ The teacher doesn't keep records or evaluate students on their performance. (Pilgreen, 2000)

Even though SSR was specifically developed without follow-up activities, many teachers use a few carefully selected and brief follow-up activities to sustain students' interest in reading books. For example, students often discuss their reading with a partner, or volunteers give **book talks** to tell the whole class about their books. As students listen to one another, they get ideas about books that they might like to read. In some classrooms, students develop a ritual of passing on the books they've finished reading to interested classmates.

Through numerous studies, SSR has been found to be beneficial in developing students' reading ability—fluency, vocabulary, and comprehension (Krashen, 1993; Marshall, 2002; Pilgreen, 2000). In addition, it promotes a positive attitude toward reading and encourages students to develop the habit of daily reading. Because students choose the books they'll read, they have the opportunity to develop their own tastes and preferences as readers.

Teachers follow these steps in implementing this instructional procedure:

1. Set aside a time for SSR. Teachers allow time every day for uninterrupted, independent reading; it may last for only 10 minutes in first-grade classrooms or 20 to 30 minutes or more in the upper grades. Teachers often begin with a 10-minute period and then extend the time as students build endurance and want to continue reading.

2. Ensure that students have books to read. Students read independently in books they keep at their desks. Beginning readers often reread three or four leveled readers that they've already read during SSR.

3. *Set a timer for a predetermined time.* Teachers set the timer for the SSR reading period. To ensure that students aren't disturbed during SSR, some teachers place a "do not disturb" sign on the door.

4. *Read along with students.* Teachers read a book, magazine, or newspaper for pleasure while students read to model what capable readers do and to show that reading is a pleasurable activity.

When all teachers in a school are working together to set up SSR, they meet to set a daily time for this special reading activity and lay the ground rules for the program. Many schools have SSR first thing in the morning or at some other convenient time during the day. What's most important is that SSR is held every day at the same time, and that all students and adults in the school stop what they're doing to read. If teachers use the time to grade papers or work with individual students, the program won't be effective. The principal and other staff members should also make a habit of visiting a different classroom each day to join in the reading activity.

Tea Party

Students participate in a tea party to read or reread excerpts from a story, informational book, or content-area textbook. It's an active, participatory activity with students moving around the classroom and socializing with classmates as they read short excerpts aloud to each other and talk about them (Beers, 2003). Teachers choose and make copies of excerpts, back them with tagboard, and laminate them. Then they distribute the excerpts to students, provide some rehearsal time, and have students participate in the tea party activity.

Teachers often use tea party as a prereading activity to introduce a new chapter in a content-area textbook. They usually select the excerpts in order to introduce big ideas and related vocabulary, familiarize students with a new text, and build background knowledge. At other times, teachers invite students to reread favorite excerpts to celebrate a book they've finished reading. When tea party is used as a postreading activity, students review big ideas, summarize the events in a story, or focus on an element of story structure. Students can also create vocabulary cards, each featuring a word from the word wall, its definition, and an illustration. After making the cards, students participate in a tea party, sharing their word cards and explaining the words to their classmates.

This instructional procedure is especially valuable for English learners because students have opportunities to build background knowledge before reading and review texts after reading in a supportive, social classroom environment (Rea & Mercuri, 2006). It's important that teachers choose excerpts that are written at English learners' reading levels or adapt them so that these students will be able to read them fluently.

Teachers follow these steps as they implement tea party:

1. *Make the cards.* Teachers make cards with excerpts from a story, informational book, or content-area textbook that students are reading. They laminate the cards, or they use sentence strips with younger students.

2. *Practice reading.* Students practice reading the excerpts to themselves several times until they can read them fluently.

3. *Share excerpts.* Students move around the classroom, stopping to read their excerpts to classmates. When students pair up, they take turns reading their excerpts. After the first student reads, both students discuss the text; then the other student reads and both students comment on the second student's text. Then students move apart and find other classmates to read their cards to.

Tea Party Cards With Information About Ecology

Recycling means using materials over and over or making them into new things instead of throwing them away.	Acid rain happens when poisonous gases from factories and cars get into rain clouds. Then the gases mix with rain and fall back to earth. It is harmful to our environment and to the people and animals on earth.
Plastic bottles, plastic forks, and plastic bags last forever! A big problem with plastic is that it doesn't biodegrade. Instead of filling landfills with plastic, it should be recycled.	Many cities have air filled with pollution called smog. This pollution is so bad that the sky looks brown, not blue.
The ozone layer around the earth protects us from the harmful rays of the sun. This layer is being damaged by gases called chloro-fluorocarbons or CFCs. These gases are used in air conditioners, fire extinguishers, and styrofoam.	Americans cut down 850 million trees last year to make paper products. Sound like a lot of trees? Consider this: One tree can be made into approximately 700 grocery bags, and a large grocery store uses about that many bags in an hour!

4. *Share excerpts with the class.* Students return to their desks after 10 to 15 minutes, and teachers invite several students to read their excerpts to the class or talk about what they learned through the tea party activity.

Tea party is a good way to celebrate the conclusion of a literature focus unit or a thematic unit, and the activity reinforces the main ideas taught during the unit. Teachers also use tea party to introduce a thematic unit by choosing excerpts from informational books or content-area textbooks that present the main ideas and key vocabulary to be taught during the unit. The box above shows six tea party cards from a class set that a seventh-grade teacher used to introduce a unit on ecology. The teacher collected some of the sentences and paragraphs from informational books and a textbook chapter that students would read, and she wrote other selections herself. Students read and discussed the excerpts and began a word wall with the key words. These two activities activated students' background knowledge about ecology and began to build new concepts.

Think-Alouds

Teachers use the think-aloud procedure to teach students how to direct and monitor their thinking during reading (Wilhelm, 2001). By making their thinking explicit, they're demonstrating what capable readers do implicitly (Keene & Zimmerman, 2007). After they watch teachers think aloud, students practice the procedure by thinking aloud about the literacy strategies they're learning. As they think aloud, students respond to the text, identify big ideas, ask self-questions, make connections, figure out how to solve problems that arise, and reflect on their use of strategies. This procedure is valuable because students learn to be more active readers. They learn how to think metacognitively and to regulate their own cognitive processes (Baker, 2002).

Teachers use these steps to teach students to think aloud:

1. *Choose a book.* Teachers who work with younger children usually choose a big book, and those who teach older students often make copies of an excerpt from a book they're reading aloud to the class to demonstrate how to think aloud.

2. *Plan the think-aloud.* Teachers decide which strategies they want to demonstrate, where they'll pause, and the kinds of thinking they want to share.

3. *Demonstrate a think-aloud.* Teachers read the text, pausing to think aloud, explaining what they're thinking and how they're using a strategy or solving a reading problem. They often use these "I" sentence starters to talk about their thinking:

I wondered if . . .

This makes me think of . . .

I was confused by . . .

I didn't understand why . . .

I think the big idea is . . .

I reread this part because . . .

4. *Annotate the text.* Teachers write a small self-stick note about their thinking and attach it next to the text that prompted the think-aloud. They often use a word or phrase, such as *picture in my mind*, *context clues*, or *reread*, to quickly document their thinking.

5. *Continue thinking aloud.* Teachers continue reading the book, pausing to think aloud again and annotate the text with additional notes about their thinking.

6. *Reflect on the procedure.* Teachers review their annotations, talk about their strategy use, and reflect on the usefulness of think-alouds as a tool for comprehending what they're reading.

7. *Repeat the procedure.* Teachers read another book and have students take turns thinking aloud and annotating the text. Once students are familiar with the procedure, they practice doing think-alouds in small groups and with partners.

Once students know how to think aloud, teachers can use this procedure as an assessment tool. During student–teacher conferences, students reflect on their reading and evaluate how well they use particular strategies, and they think about what they could do differently to comprehend more effectively. Students can also refer to their annotations and write reflections about their use of particular strategies.

Word Ladders

Word ladders are games where students change one word into another through a series of steps, altering a single letter at each step. The goal is to use as few steps as possible to change the first word into the last word. This type of puzzle was invented by Lewis Carroll, author of *Alice in Wonderland*, in 1878. Typically, the first and last words are related in some way, such as *fall–down*, *slow–fast*, and *trick–treat*, and all the middle words must be real words. A well-known word ladder is *cat–dog*, which can be solved in three steps: *cat–cot–dot–dog*.

A *Cat–Dog* Word Ladder	
The teacher says:	Students write:
Begin with the word *cat*.	cat
Change the vowel to form another word for *bed*, sometimes the kind of bed you use when you're camping.	cot
Change one letter to form a word that means "a tiny, round mark."	dot
Finally, change the final consonant to make a word that goes with the first word, *cat*.	dog

Teachers can create a variation of word ladders to practice phonics, spelling, and vocabulary skills with their students (Rasinski, 2006). They guide students to build a series of words as they provide graphophonemic and semantic clues about the words. Like traditional word ladder puzzles, each word comes from the previous word, but students may be asked to add, delete, or change one or more letters from the previous word to make a new word. Students write the words vertically in list form so they can see the words they've written. A *cat–dog* word ladder is shown above. Teachers make their own word ladders to reinforce the phonics concepts and spelling patterns their students are learning; in this case, it's not necessary to ensure that the first and last words are related as in traditional word ladders. A word ladder to practice words with the short and long sounds of /oo/ is shown on page 476.

Here's the procedure for using word ladders:

1. Create the word ladder. Teachers create a word ladder with 5 to 15 words, choosing words from spelling lists or phonics lessons, and they write clues for each word, trying to incorporate a combination of graphophonemic and semantic clues.

2. Pass out supplies. Teachers often have students use dry-erase boards and marking pens for this activity, but they can also use blank paper or paper with word ladders already drawn on them.

3. Do the word ladder. Teachers read the clues they've prepared and have students write the words. Students take turns identifying the words and spelling them correctly. When necessary, teachers provide additional clues and explain any unfamiliar words, phonics rules, or spelling patterns.

4. Review the word ladder. Once students complete the word ladder, they reread the words and talk about any words they had difficulty writing. They also volunteer other words they can write using these letters.

Word ladders are a fun way for students to practice the phonics skills they're learning and, at the same time, think about the meanings of words. The activity's gamelike format makes it engaging for students and teachers. To see more word ladders, check Rasinski's (2005a, 2005b) books of easy-to-use word ladder games for second through sixth graders; word ladder games are also available on the Internet.

An /oo/ Word Ladder

The teacher says:	Students write:
Write the word *good*. We're practicing words with *oo* today.	good
Change the beginning sound to write the past tense of *stand*. The word is *stood*.	stood
Change the ending sound to write a word that means "a seat without arms or a back."	stool
Change the beginning sound to write a word that means the opposite of *warm*.	cool
Add two letters—one before and one after the *c*—to spell where we are right now.	school
Change the beginning sound to spell *tool*.	tool
Drop a letter to make a word that means *also*.	too
Change the first letter to write a word that means "a place where people can go to see wild animals."	zoo
Add a letter to *zoo* to spell the sound a car makes.	zoom
Change the beginning sound—use two letters for this blend—to spell something we use for sweeping.	broom
Change one letter to spell a word that means *creek*.	brook
Change the beginning sound to make a word that means "a dishonest person."	crook

Word Sorts

Students use word sorts to examine and categorize words according to their meanings, sound-symbol correspondences, or spelling patterns (Bear, Invernizzi, Templeton, & Johnston, 2008). The purpose of word sorts is to help students focus on conceptual and phonological features of words and identify recurring patterns. For example, as students sort cards with words such as *stopping, eating, hugging, running,* and *raining,* they discover the rule for doubling the final consonant in short-vowel words before adding an inflectional ending.

Teachers choose categories for word sorts, depending on instructional goals or students' developmental levels:

◆ Rhyming words, such as words that rhyme with *ball, fat, car,* and *rake*
◆ Consonant sounds, such as pictures of words beginning with *r* or *l*
◆ Sound-symbol relationships, such as words in which the final *y* sounds like long *i* (*cry*) and others in which the final *y* sounds like long *e* (*baby*)
◆ Spelling patterns, such as long-*e* words with various spelling patterns (*sea, greet, be, Pete*)
◆ Number of syllables, such as *pig, happy, afternoon,* and *television*
◆ Root words and affixes
◆ Conceptual relationships, such as words related to different characters in a story or to big ideas in a thematic unit

Many of the words chosen for word sorts come from books students are reading or thematic units. The boxes on the next page show two word sorts using words from *Holes* (Sachar, 2003); the first is a conceptual sort and the second is a grammar sort.

A Concept Sort Using Words From *Holes*

Stanley	Zero	Camp Green Lake	Mr. Sir	The Warden	The Escape
unlucky	nobody	wasteland	grotesque	Ms. Walker	miracle
sneakers	Hector Zeroni	guards	cowboy hat	holes	sploosh
Caveman	confession	investigation	swollen	venom	thumbs-up sign
overweight	homeless	yellow-spotted lizard	tattoo	miserable	impossible
callused	Clyde Livingston's shoes	scorpions	sunflower seeds	fingernail polish	ledges
million dollars	digger	girl scout camp	guard	make-up kit	Big Thumb
suitcase	frail	temperature	tougher	freckles	happiness

A Grammar Sort Using Words From *Holes*

Adjectives	Nouns	Verbs	Adverbs
half-opened	wasteland	chewing	surely
scratchy	curiosity	waits	previously
tougher	fossil	howled	quickly
desolate	allergies	startled	well
throbbing	pitchfork	watches	intently
metallic	warden	gazes	supposedly
shriveled	sneakers	wiggled	always
callused	Caveman	scooped	angrily

Word sorts are effective for English learners because students build skills to understand how English differs from their native language, and they develop knowledge to help them predict meaning through spelling (Bear, Helman, Invernizzi, & Templeton, 2007). Because word sorts can be done in small groups, teachers can choose words for the sorts that are appropriate for students' developmental levels.

Here are the steps for conducting a word sort:

1. *Choose a topic.* Teachers choose a language skill or content-area topic for the word sort and decide whether it will be an open or closed sort. In an open sort, students determine the categories themselves based on the words they're sorting. In a closed sort, teachers present the categories as they introduce the sorting activity.

2. *Compile a list of words.* Teachers compile a list of 6 to 20 words, depending on grade level, that exemplify particular categories, and they write the words on small cards. Or, small picture cards can be used.

3. *Introduce the sorting activity.* If it's a closed sort, teachers present the categories and have students sort word cards into these categories. If it's an open sort, students identify the words and look for possible categories. Students arrange and rearrange the cards until they are satisfied with the sorting. Then they add category labels.

4. *Make a permanent record.* Students make a permanent record of their sort by gluing the word cards onto a large sheet of construction paper or poster board or by writing the words on a sheet of paper.

5. *Share word sorts.* Students share their word sorts with classmates, explaining the categories they used (for open sorts).

Teachers use word sorts to teach phonics, spelling, and vocabulary. During literature focus units, students sort vocabulary words according to the beginning, middle, or end of the story or according to character. During thematic units, students sort vocabulary words according to big ideas.

Word Walls

Word walls are collections of words posted in the classroom that students use for word-study activities and refer to when they're writing (Wagstaff, 1999). Teachers make word walls using construction-paper squares or sheets of butcher paper that have been divided into alphabetized sections. Students and the teacher write on the word wall interesting, confusing, or other important words from books they're reading and about big ideas they're learning during thematic units. Usually students choose the words to write on the word wall, and they may even do the writing themselves, but teachers add any important Tier 2 words that students haven't chosen.

A second type of word wall for high-frequency words is used in primary-grade classrooms: Teachers hang large sheets of construction paper, one for each letter of the alphabet, on a wall of the classroom, and then post high-frequency words such as *the, is, are, you, what,* and *to* as they're introduced (Cunningham, 2005; Lynch, 2005). This word wall remains on display, and additional words are added throughout the year. In kindergarten classrooms, teachers begin the school year by placing word cards with students' names on the wall chart and add common environmental print, such as *K-Mart* and *McDonald's.* Later in the year, they add words such as *I, love, the, you, Mom, Dad, good,* and other words that students want to be able to read and write.

Teachers usually create word walls with the whole class, and they follow these steps:

1. *Prepare the word wall.* Teachers prepare a blank word wall in the classroom from sheets of construction paper or butcher paper, dividing it into 12 to 24 boxes and labeling the boxes with letters of the alphabet.

2. *Introduce the word wall.* Teachers introduce the word wall and write several key words on it before beginning to read.

3. *Add words to the word wall.* Students suggest "important" words for the word wall as they are reading a book or participating in thematic-unit activities. Students and the teacher write the words in the alphabetized blocks, making sure to write large enough so that most students can see the words. If a word is misspelled, it's corrected because students will be using the words in various activities. Sometimes the teacher adds a small picture or writes a synonym for a difficult word, puts a box around the root word, or writes the plural form or other related words nearby.

4. *Use the word wall.* Teachers use the word wall for a variety of vocabulary activities, and students refer to the word wall when they're writing.

Teachers use word walls during literature focus units and thematic units, and primary-grade teachers also teach high-frequency words using word walls. They involve students in a variety of word-study activities. For example, students do quickwrites using words from the word wall and refer to the word wall when they're writing journal entries and books. Teachers also use words from the word wall for word sorts and tea party activities. In addition, primary-grade teachers use words from high-frequency word walls for phonics and other word-study activities. One example is a popular word hunt game: Teachers distribute small dry-erase boards and have students identify and write words from the word wall on their boards according to the clues they provide. For example, teachers say "Find the word that begins like _____," "Look for the word that rhymes with _____," "Find the word that alphabetically follows _____," or "Think of the word that means the opposite of _____," depending on what students are learning. Students read and reread the words, apply phonics and word-study concepts, and practice spelling high-frequency words as they play this game.

Writing Groups

During the revising stage of the writing process, students meet in writing groups to share their rough drafts and get feedback on how well they're communicating (Tompkins, 2008). Writing group members offer compliments about things writers have done well and make suggestions for improvement. Their comments reflect these topics and other aspects of the writer's craft:

leads	word choice	voice
dialogue	sentences	rhyme
endings	character development	sequence
description	point of view	flashbacks
ideas	organization	alliterations

These topics are used for both compliments and suggestions. When students are offering a compliment, they might say, "I liked your lead. It grabbed me and made me keep listening," and when they're making a suggestion, they say, "I wonder if you could start with a question to make your lead more interesting. Maybe you could say, 'Have you ever ridden in a police car? Well, that's what happened to me!'"

Teaching students how to share their rough drafts in a writing group and offer constructive feedback isn't easy. When teachers introduce revision, they model appropriate responses because students may not know how to offer specific and meaningful comments tactfully. Teachers and students can brainstorm a list of appropriate compliments and suggestions and post it in the classroom to refer to. Comments should usually begin with "I," not "you." Notice the difference in tone in these two sentence stems: "I wonder if . . ." versus "You need to . . ." Here are some ways to begin compliments:

I like the part where . . .

I learned how . . .

I like the way you described . . .

I like how you organized the information because . . .

Students also offer suggestions about how classmates can revise their writing. It's important that students phrase what they say in helpful ways. Here are some ways to begin suggestions:

I got confused in the part about . . .

I wonder if you need a closing . . .

I'd like you to add more about . . .

I wonder if these paragraphs are in the right order . . .

I think you might want to combine these sentences . . .

Student-writers also ask classmates for help with specific problems they've identified. Looking to classmates for feedback is a big step in learning to revise. Here are some questions writers can ask:

What do you want to know more about?

Is there a part that I should throw away?

What details can I add?

What do you think is the best part of my writing?

Are there some words I need to change?

Writing groups work effectively once students understand how to support and help their classmates by offering compliments, making suggestions, and asking questions.

Revising is the most difficult part of the writing process because it's hard for students to stand back and evaluate their writing objectively in order to make changes to communicate more effectively. As students participate in writing groups, they learn how to accept compliments and suggestions and to provide useful feedback to classmates.

Teachers teach students how to use this instructional procedure so that they can then work in small groups to get ideas for revising their writing. Here are the steps:

1. *Read drafts aloud.* Students take turns reading their rough drafts aloud to the group. Everyone listens politely, thinking about compliments and suggestions they will make after the writer finishes reading. Only the writer looks at the composition because when classmates look at it, they quickly notice and comment on mechanical errors, even though the emphasis during revising is on content. Listening to the writing read aloud keeps the focus on content.

2. *Offer compliments.* After listening to the rough draft read aloud, classmates in the writing group tell the writer what they liked about the composition. These positive comments should be specific, focusing on strengths, rather than the often-heard "I liked it" or "It was good"; even though these are positive comments, they don't provide effective feedback.

3. *Ask clarifying questions.* Writers ask for assistance with trouble spots they identified earlier when rereading their writing, or they may ask questions that reflect more general concerns about how well they're communicating.

4. *Offer other revision suggestions.* Members of the writing group ask questions about things that were unclear to them and make suggestions about how to revise the rough draft.

5. *Repeat the process.* Members of the writing group repeat the process so that all students can share their rough drafts. The first four steps are repeated for each student's composition.

6. *Make plans for revision.* Students each make a commitment to revise their writing based on the comments and suggestions of the group members. The final decision on what to revise always rests with the writers themselves, but with the understanding that their rough drafts aren't perfect comes the realization that some revision will be necessary. When students verbalize their planned revisions, they're more likely to complete the revision stage.

Students meet in writing groups whenever they're using the writing process. Once they've written a rough draft, students are ready to share their writing and get some feedback from classmates. They often meet with the same writing group throughout the school year, or students can form groups when they're ready to get feedback about their rough drafts. Many teachers have students sign up on the chalkboard; this way, whenever four students are ready, they form a group. Both established and spontaneously formed groups can be effective. What matters most is that students get feedback about their writing when they need it.

PROFESSIONAL REFERENCES

Allen, J. (2002). *On the same page: Shared reading beyond the primary grades.* York, ME: Stenhouse.

Ashton-Warner, S. (1965). *Teacher.* New York: Simon & Schuster.

Atwell, N. (1998). *In the middle: New understandings about writing, reading, and learning.* Portsmouth, NH: Heinemann/ Boynton/Cook.

Baker, L. (2002). Metacognition in comprehension instruction. In C. C. Block & M. Pressley (Eds.), *Comprehension instruction: Research-based best practices* (pp. 77–95). New York: Guilford Press.

Barone, D. (1990). The written responses of young children: Beyond comprehension to story understanding. *The New Advocate, 3,* 49–56.

Bear, D. R., Helman, L., Invernizzi, M., & Templeton, S. R. (2007). *Words their way with English learners: Word study for spelling, phonics, and vocabulary instruction.* Upper Saddle River, NJ: Merrill/Prentice Hall.

Bear, D. R., Invernizzi, M., Templeton, S., & Johnston, F. (2008). *Words their way: Word study for phonics, vocabulary, and spelling instruction* (4th ed.). Upper Saddle River, NJ: Merrill/Prentice Hall.

Beck, I. L., & McKeown, M. G. (2006). *Improving comprehension with questioning the author: A fresh and expanded view of a powerful approach.* New York: Scholastic.

Beers, K. (2003). *When kids can't read, what teachers can do.* Portsmouth, NH: Heinemann.

Berthoff, A. E. (1981). *The making of meaning.* Montclair, NJ: Boynton/Cook.

Blachowicz, C. L. Z. (1986). Making connections: Alternatives to the vocabulary notebook. *Journal of Reading, 29,* 643–649.

Black, A., & Stave, A. M. (2007). *A comprehensive guide to readers theatre: Enhancing fluency and comprehension in middle school and beyond.* Newark, DE: International Reading Association.

Brozo, W. G., & Simpson, M. L. (2007). *Content literacy for today's adolescents: Honoring diversity and building competence* (5th ed.). Upper Saddle River, NJ: Prentice Hall.

Button, K., Johnson, M. J., & Furgerson, P. (1996). Interactive writing in a primary classroom. *The Reading Teacher, 49,* 446–454.

Carr, E., & Ogle, D. (1987). K-W-L Plus: A strategy for comprehension and summarization. *Journal of Reading, 31,* 626–631.

Ciardello, A. V. (1998). Did you ask a good question today? *Journal of Adolescent and Adult Literacy, 42,* 210–220.

Clay, M. M. (2000). *Running records for classroom teachers.* Portsmouth, NH: Heinemann.

Crawford, A. N. (2003). Communicative approaches to second-language acquisition: The bridge to second-language literacy. In G. G. Garcia (Ed.), *English learners: Reaching the highest level of English literacy* (pp. 152–181). Newark, DE: International Reading Association.

Cunningham, P. M. (2005). *Phonics they use: Words for reading and writing* (4th ed.). New York: HarperCollins.

Cunningham, P. M., & Cunningham, J. W. (1992). Making words: Enhancing the invented spelling-decoding connection. *The Reading Teacher, 46,* 106–115.

Cunningham, P. M., & Hall, D. P. (1994a). *Making big words.* Parsippany, NJ: Good Apple.

Cunningham, P. M., & Hall, D. P. (1994b). *Making words.* Parsippany, NJ: Good Apple.

Daniels, H. (2001). *Literature circles: Voice and choice in book clubs and reading groups.* York, ME: Stenhouse.

Dooley. C. M., & Maloch, B. (2005). Exploring characters through visual representations. In N. L. Roser & M. G. Martinez (Eds.), *What a character! Character study as a guide to literary meaning making in grades K–8* (pp. 111–123). Newark, DE: International Reading Association.

Dorn, L. J., & Soffos, C. (2001). *Shaping literate minds: Developing self-regulated learners.* York, ME: Stenhouse.

Farr, R., & Tone, B. (1994). *Portfolio and performance assessment: Helping students evaluate their progress as readers and writers.* Fort Worth, TX: Harcourt Brace.

Fisher, B., & Medvic, E. F. (2000). *Perspectives on shared reading: Planning and practice.* Portsmouth, NH: Heinemann.

Fisher, D., Flood, K., Lapp, D., & Frey, N. (2004). Interactive read-alouds: Is there a common set of implementation practices? *The Reading Teacher, 58,* 8–17.

Flynn, R. M. (2007). *Dramatizing the content with curriculum-based readers theatre, grades 6–12.* Newark, DE: International Reading Association.

Flynt, E. S., & Cooter, R. B., Jr. (2005). Improving middle-grades reading in urban schools: The Memphis Comprehension Framework. *The Reading Teacher, 58,* 774–780.

Fountas, I. C., & Pinnell, G. S. (1996). *Guided reading: Good first teaching for all children.* Portsmouth, NH: Heinemann.

Gambrell, L. B., & Almasi, J. F. (Eds.). (1996). *Lively discussions! Fostering engaged reading.* Newark, DE: International Reading Association.

Gardiner, S. (2005). *Building students' literacy through SSR.* Alexandria, VA: Association for Supervision and Curriculum Development.

Graves, M. F., & Fitzgerald, J. (2003). Scaffolding reading experiences for multilingual classrooms. In G. G. Garcia (Ed.), *English learners: Reaching the highest level of English literacy* (pp. 96–124). Newark, DE: International Reading Association.

Hancock, M. R. (2008). *A celebration of literature and response: Children, books, and teachers in K–8 classrooms* (3rd ed.). Upper Saddle River, NJ: Merrill/Prentice Hall.

Head, M. H., & Readence, J. E. (1986). Anticipation guides: Meaning through prediction. In E. K. Dishner, T. W. Bean, J. E. Readence, & D. W. Moore (Eds.), *Reading in the content areas* (2nd ed., pp. 229–234). Dubuque, IA: Kendall/Hunt.

Holdaway, D. (1979). *Foundations of literacy.* Auckland, NZ: Ashton Scholastic.

Holston, V., & Santa, C. (1985). RAFT: A method of writing across the curriculum that works. *Journal of Reading, 28,* 456–457.

Hoyt, L. (1999). *Revisit, reflect, retell: Strategies for improving reading comprehension.* Portsmouth, NH: Heinemann.

Hoyt, L. (2000). *Snapshots.* Portsmouth, NH: Heinemann.

Hunt, L. (1967). Evaluation through teacher-pupil conferences. In T. C. Barrett (Ed.), *The evaluation of children's reading achievement* (pp. 111–126). Newark, DE: International Reading Association.

Ivey, G. (2003). "The teacher makes it more explainable" and other reasons to read aloud in the intermediate grades. *The Reading Teacher, 56,* 812–814.

Jacobson, J. M. (1990). Group vs. individual completion of a cloze passage. *Journal of Reading, 33,* 244–250.

Keehn, S., Martinez, M. G., & Roser, N. L. (2005). Exploring character through readers theatre. In N. L. Roser & M. G. Martinez (Eds.), *What a character! Character study as a guide to literary meaning making in grades K–8* (pp. 96–110). Newark, DE: International Reading Association.

Keene, E. O., & Zimmerman, S. (2007). *Mosaic of thought: The power of comprehension strategy instruction* (2nd ed.). Portsmouth, NH: Heinemann.

Krashen, S. (1993). *The power of reading.* Englewood, CO: Libraries Unlimited.

Langer, J. A. (1981). From theory to practice: A prereading plan. *Journal of Reading, 25,* 152–157.

Lynch, J. (2005). *High frequency word walls.* New York: Scholastic.

Macon, J. M., Bewell, D., & Vogt, M. E. (1991). *Responses to literature: Grades K–8*. Newark, DE: International Reading Association.

Marshall, J. C. (2002). *Are they really reading? Expanding SSR in the middle grades*. Portland, ME: Stenhouse.

McCauley, J. K., & McCauley, D. S. (1992). Using choral reading to promote language learning for ESL students. *The Reading Teacher, 45,* 526–533.

McKenna, M. C., & Stahl, S. A. (2003). *Assessment for reading instruction*. New York: Guilford Press.

McLaughlin, M., & Allen, M. B. (2001). *Guided comprehension: A teaching model for grades 3–8*. Newark, DE: International Reading Association.

Morrow, L. M. (1985). Retelling stories: A strategy for improving children's comprehension, concept of story structure, and oral language complexity. *Elementary School Journal, 85,* 647–661.

Ogle, D. M. (1986). K-W-L: A teaching model that develops active reading of expository text. *The Reading Teacher, 39,* 564–570.

Peregoy, S. F., & Boyle, O. F. (2008). *Reading, writing, and learning in ESL: A resource book for K–12 teachers* (5th ed.). Boston: Allyn & Bacon/Pearson.

Peterson, R., & Eeds, M. (2007). *Grand conversations: Literature groups in action* (updated ed.). New York: Scholastic.

Pilgreen, J. L. (2000). *The SSR handbook: How to organize and manage a sustained silent reading program*. Portsmouth, NH: Boynton/Cook/Heinemann.

Pittelman, S. D., Heimlich, J. E., Berglund, R. L., & French, M. P. (1991). *Semantic feature analysis: Classroom applications*. Newark, DE: International Reading Association.

Raphael, T. E., Highfield, K., & Au, K. H. (2006). *QAR now: A powerful and practical framework that develops comprehension and higher-level thinking in all students*. New York: Scholastic.

Rasinski, T. (2005a). *Daily word ladders: Grades 2–3*. New York: Scholastic.

Rasinski, T. (2005b). *Daily word ladders: Grades 4–6*. New York: Scholastic.

Rasinski, T. (2006). Developing vocabulary through word building. In C. C. Block & J. N. Mangieri (Eds.), *The vocabulary-enriched classroom: Practices for improving the reading performance of all students in grades 3 and up* (pp. 36–53). New York: Scholastic.

Rasinski, T., & Padak, N. (2004). *Effective reading strategies: Teaching children who find reading difficult*. Upper Saddle River, NJ: Merrill/Prentice Hall.

Rea, D. M., & Mercuri, S. P. (2006). *Research-based strategies for English language learners: How to teach goals and meet standards, K–8*. Portsmouth, NH: Heinemann.

Reutzel, D. R., & Cooter, R. B., Jr. (2008). *Teaching children to read: From basals to books* (5th ed.). Upper Saddle River, NJ: Merrill/Prentice Hall.

Routman, R. (2004). *Writing essentials: Raising expectations and results while simplifying teaching*. Portsmouth, NH: Heinemann.

Short, K. G., & Harste, J. (1996). *Creating classrooms for authors and inquirers*. Portsmouth, NH: Heinemann.

Spandel, V. (2005). *Creating writers: Through 6-trait writing assessment and instruction* (4th ed.). Boston: Allyn & Bacon.

Taylor, W. L. (1953). "Cloze procedure": A new tool for measuring readability. *Journalism Quarterly, 30,* 415–433.

Tierney, R. J., & Readence, J. E. (2005). *Reading strategies and practices: A compendium* (6th ed.). Boston: Allyn & Bacon.

Tompkins, G. E. (2008). *Teaching writing: Balancing process and product* (5th ed.). Upper Saddle River, NJ: Merrill/Prentice Hall.

Tompkins, G. E., & Collom, S. (Eds.). (2004). *Sharing the pen: Interactive writing with young children*. Upper Saddle River, NJ: Merrill/Prentice Hall.

Tovani, C. (2000). *I read it, but I don't get it: Comprehension strategies for adolescent readers*. York, ME: Stenhouse.

Vacca, R. T., & Vacca, J. L. (2008). *Content area reading: Literacy and learning across the curriculum* (9th ed.). Boston: Allyn & Bacon/Pearson.

Wagstaff, J. (1999). *Teaching reading and writing with word walls*. New York: Scholastic.

Whitin, P. E. (2002). Leading into literature circles through the sketch-to-stetch strategy. *The Reading Teacher, 55,* 444–450.

Wilhelm, J. D. (2001). *Improving comprehension with think-aloud strategies*. New York: Scholastic.

Wilhelm, J. D. (2002). *Action strategies for deepening comprehension*. New York: Scholastic.

Worthy, J., & Prater, K. (2002). "I thought about it all night": Readers theatre for reading fluency and motivation. *The Reading Teacher, 56,* 294–297.

CHILDREN'S BOOK REFERENCES

Bates, K. L. (2003). *America the beautiful*. New York: Putnam.

Brett, J. (1989). *The mitten*. New York: Putnam.

Carle, E. (2005). *A house for hermit crab*. New York: Aladdin Books.

Cronin, D. (2005). *Diary of a spider*. New York: HarperCollins.

Cushman, K. (1996). *The ballad of Lucy Whipple*. New York: Clarion Books.

Danziger, P. (1995). *You can't eat your chicken pox, Amber Brown*. New York: Putnam.

Danziger, P. (2006). *Amber Brown is not a crayon*. New York: Scholastic.

Dorros, A. (1997). *Abuela*. New York: Puffin Books.

Fleischman, P. (2004). *Joyful noise: Poems for two voices*. New York: HarperTrophy.

Guthrie, W. (2002). *This land is your land*. Boston: Little, Brown.

Hall, D. (1994). *I am the dog/I am the cat*. New York: Dial Books.

Hinton, S. E. (1997). *The outsiders*. New York: Puffin Books.

Hoberman, M. A. (2003). *The lady with the alligator purse*. Boston: Little, Brown.

Hughes, L. (2007). *The dream keeper and other poems*. New York: Knopf.

Jeffers, S. (1993). *Brother eagle, sister sky: A message from Chief Seattle*. New York: Puffin Books.

Konigsburg, E. L. (1998). *The view from Saturday*. New York: Aladdin Books.

Koopmans, L. (1995). *The woodcutter's mitten*. New York: Crocodile Books.

Kuskin, K. (2003). *Moon, have you met my mother? The collected poems of Karla Kuskin*. New York: HarperCollins.

Lewis, C. S. (2005). *The lion, the witch and the wardrobe*. New York: HarperCollins.

Long, M. (2003). *How I became a pirate*. San Diego: Harcourt.

Lowry, L. (1998). *Number the stars*. New York: Laurel Leaf.

Lowry, L. (2006). *The giver*. New York: Delacorte.

MacLachlan, P. (2004). *Sarah, plain and tall*. New York: HarperTrophy.

Paschen, E. (Ed.). (2005). *Poetry speaks to children*. Naperville, IL: Sourcebooks/MediaFusion.

Patron, S. (2006). *The higher power of Lucky*. New York: Atheneum.

Prelutsky, J. (2007). *My parents think I'm sleeping*. New York: Greenwillow.

Prelutsky, J. (2008). *The Random House book of poetry*. New York: Greenwillow.

Sachar, L. (2003). *Holes*. New York: Yearling.

Schmidt, G. D. (2007). *The Wednesday wars*. New York: Clarion Books.

Soto, G. (2005). *Neighborhood odes*. San Diego: Harcourt.

Taback, S. (1997). *There was an old lady who swallowed a fly*. New York: Viking.

Towle, W. (1993). *The real McCoy: The life of an African-American inventor*. New York: Scholastic.

Tresselt, A. (1989). *The mitten*. New York: HarperTrophy.

Yolen, J., & Peters, A. F. (Eds.). (2007). *Here's a little poem*. Cambridge, MA: Candlewick Press.

GLOSSARY

Aesthetic reading Reading for pleasure.

Affix A syllable added to the beginning (prefix) or end (suffix) of a word to change the word's meaning (e.g., *il-* in *illiterate* and *-al* in *national*).

Alphabetic principle The assumption underlying alphabetical language systems that each sound has a corresponding graphic representation (or letter).

Antonyms Words with opposite meanings (e.g., *good–bad*).

Applying The fifth stage of the reading process, in which readers go beyond the text to use what they have learned in another literacy experience, often by making a project or reading another book.

Authentic Activities and materials related to real-world reading and writing.

Automaticity Identifying words accurately and quickly.

Background knowledge A student's knowledge or previous experiences about a topic.

Basal readers Reading textbooks that are leveled according to grade.

Basal reading program A collection of student textbooks, workbooks, teacher's manuals, and other materials and resources for reading instruction used in kindergarten through sixth grade.

Big books Enlarged versions of picture books that teachers read with children, usually in the primary grades.

Blend To combine the sounds represented by letters to pronounce a word.

Bound morpheme A morpheme that is not a word and cannot stand alone (e.g., *-s, tri-*).

Closed syllable A syllable ending in a consonant sound (e.g., *make, duck*).

Cloze An activity in which students replace words that have been deleted from a text.

Cluster A spiderlike diagram used to collect and organize ideas after reading or before writing; also called a *map* or a *web*.

Comprehension The process of constructing meaning using both the author's text and the reader's background knowledge for a specific purpose.

Concepts about print Basic understandings about the way print works, including the direction of print, spacing, punctuation, letters, and words.

Consonant A speech sound characterized by friction or stoppage of the airflow as it passes through the vocal tract; usually any letter except *a, e, i, o,* and *u.*

Consonant digraph Two adjacent consonants that represent a sound not represented by either consonant alone (e.g., *th–this, ch–chin, sh–wash, ph–telephone*).

Content-area reading Reading in social studies, science, and other areas of the curriculum.

Context clue Information from the words or sentences surrounding a word that helps to clarify the word's meaning.

Cueing systems The phonological, semantic, syntactic, and pragmatic information that students rely on as they read.

Decoding Using word-identification strategies to pronounce and attach meaning to an unfamiliar word.

Diagnosis Determining specific problems readers are having, generally using a test.

Differentiated instruction Procedures for assisting students in learning, providing options, challenging students, and matching books to students to maximize their learning.

Diphthong A sound produced when the tongue glides from one sound to another; it is represented by two vowels (e.g., *oy–boy, ou–house, ow–how*).

Drafting The second stage of the writing process, in which writers pour out ideas in a rough draft.

Echo reading The teacher or other reader reads a sentence and a group of students reread or "echo" what was read.

Editing The fourth stage of the writing process, in which writers proofread to identify and correct spelling, capitalization, punctuation, and grammar errors.

Efferent reading Reading for information.

Elkonin boxes A strategy for segmenting sounds in a word that involves drawing a box to represent each sound.

Emergent literacy Children's early reading and writing development before conventional reading and writing.

Environmental print Signs, labels, and other print found in the community.

Etymology The origin and history of words; the etymological information is enclosed in brackets in dictionary entries.

Explicit instruction Systematic instruction of concepts, strategies, and skills that builds from simple to complex.

Exploring The fourth stage of the reading process, in which readers reread the text, study vocabulary words, and learn strategies and skills.

Expository text Nonfiction.

Family literacy Home–school partnerships to enhance students' literacy development.

Fluency Reading smoothly, quickly, and with expression.

Free morpheme   A morpheme that can stand alone as a word (e.g., *book*, *cycle*).

Frustration level   The level of reading material that is too difficult for a student to read successfully.

Genre   A category of literature such as folklore, science fiction, biography, or historical fiction, or a writing form.

Goldilocks principle   A strategy for choosing "just right" books.

Grand conversation   A small-group or whole-class discussion about literature.

Grapheme   A written representation of a sound using one or more letters.

Graphic organizers   Diagrams that provide organized visual representations of information from texts.

Graphophonemic   Referring to sound-symbol relationships.

Guided reading   Students work in small groups to read as independently as possible a text selected and introduced by the teacher.

High-frequency word   A common English word, usually a word among the 100 or 300 most common words.

Homographic homophones   Words that sound alike and are spelled alike but have different meanings (e.g., baseball *bat* and the animal *bat*).

Homographs   Words that are spelled alike but are pronounced differently (e.g., a *present* and to *present*).

Homonyms   Words that sound alike but are spelled differently (e.g., *sea–see*, *there–their–they're*); also called *homophones*.

Hyperbole   A stylistic device involving obvious exaggerations.

Imagery   The use of words and figurative language to create an impression.

Independent reading level   The level of reading material that a student can read independently with high comprehension and an accuracy level of 95–100%.

Inflectional endings   Suffixes that express plurality or possession when added to a noun (e.g., *girls*, *girl's*), tense when added to a verb (e.g., *walked*, *walking*), or comparison when added to an adjective (e.g., *happier*, *happiest*).

Informal reading inventory (IRI)   An individually administered reading test composed of word lists and graded passages that are used to determine students' independent, instructional, and frustration levels and listening capacity levels.

Instructional reading level   The level of reading material that a student can read with teacher support and instruction with 90–94% accuracy.

Interactive writing   A writing activity in which students and the teacher write a text together, with the students taking turns to do most of the writing themselves.

Intervention   Intense, individualized instruction for struggling readers to solve reading problems and accelerate their growth.

Invented spelling   Students' attempts to spell words that reflect their developing knowledge about the spelling system.

K-W-L   An activity to activate background knowledge and set purposes for reading an informational text and to bring closure after reading. The letters stand for What I (We) K̲now, What I (We) W̲onder, and What I (We) L̲earned.

Language Experience Approach (LEA)   A student's dictated composition is written by the teacher and used as a text for reading instruction; it is generally used with beginning readers.

Leveling books   A method of estimating the difficulty level of a text.

Lexile scores   A method of estimating the difficulty level of a text.

Listening capacity level   The highest level of graded passage that can be comprehended well when read aloud to the student.

Literacy   The ability to read and write.

Literal comprehension   The understanding of what is explicitly stated in a text.

Literature circle   An instructional approach in which students meet in small groups to read and respond to a book.

Literature focus unit   An approach to reading instruction in which the whole class reads and responds to a piece of literature.

Long vowels   The vowel sounds that are also names of the alphabet letters: /ā/ as in *make*, /ē/ as in *feet*, /ī/ as in *ice*, /ō/ as in *coat*, and /ū/ as in *rule*.

Lowercase letters   The letters that are smaller and usually different from uppercase letters.

Metacognition   Students' awareness of their own thought and learning processes.

Metaphor   A comparison expressed directly, without using *like* or *as*.

Minilesson   Explicit instruction about literacy procedures, concepts, strategies, and skills that are taught to individual students, small groups, or the whole class, depending on students' needs.

Miscue analysis   A strategy for categorizing and analyzing a student's oral reading errors.

Mood   The tone of a story or poem.

Morpheme   The smallest meaningful part of a word; sometimes it is a word (e.g., *cup*, *hope*), and sometimes it is not a whole word (e.g., *-ly*, *bi-*).

Narrative   A story.

New literacies   The ability to use digital and multimodal technologies to communicate and learn effectively.

Onset   The part of a syllable (or one-syllable word) that comes before the vowel (e.g., *str* in *string*).

Open syllable   A syllable ending in a vowel sound (e.g., *sea*).

Orthography   The spelling system.

Personification   Figurative language in which objects and animals are represented as having human qualities.

Phoneme   A sound; it is represented in print with slashes (e.g., /s/ and /th/).

Phoneme-grapheme correspondence   The relationship between a sound and the letter that represents it.

Phonemic awareness   The ability to manipulate the sounds in words orally.

Phonics   Predictable relationships between phonemes and graphemes.

Phonics instruction   Teaching the relationships between letters and sounds and how to use them to read and spell words.

Phonological awareness   The ability to identify and manipulate phonemes, onsets and rimes, and syllables; it includes phonemic awareness.

Phonology   The sound system of language.

Polysyllabic   Containing more than one syllable.

Pragmatics   The social use system of language.

Prediction   A strategy in which students predict what will happen in a story and then read to verify their guesses.

Prefix   A syllable added to the beginning of a word to change the word's meaning (e.g., *re-* in *reread*).

Prereading   The first stage of the reading process, in which readers activate background knowledge, set purposes, and make plans for reading.

Prevention   Identifying potentially struggling readers and providing appropriate instruction so that failure is avoided.

Prewriting   The first stage of the writing process, in which writers gather and organize ideas for writing.

Proofreading   Reading a composition to identify and correct spelling and other mechanical errors.

Prosody   The ability to orally read sentences expressively, with appropriate phrasing and intonation.

Publishing   The fifth stage of the writing process, in which writers make the final copy of their writing and share it with an audience.

Quickwrite   An activity in which students explore a topic through writing.

Readability formula   A method of estimating the difficulty level of a text.

Reading   The second stage of the reading process, in which readers read the text for the first time using independent reading, shared reading, or guided reading, or by listening to it read aloud.

Reading rate   Reading speed, usually reported as the average number of words read correctly in 1 minute.

Reading workshop   An approach in which students read self-selected texts independently.

Reciprocal teaching   An activity in which the teacher and students take turns modeling the use of strategies.

Responding   The third stage of the reading process, in which readers respond to the text, often through grand conversations and by writing in reading logs.

Revising   The third stage of the writing process, in which writers clarify meaning in the writing.

Rhyming   Words with the same rime sound (e.g., *white*, *bright*).

Rime   The part of a syllable (or one-syllable word) that begins with the vowel (e.g., *ing* in *string*).

Scaffolding   The support a teacher provides to students as they read and write.

Segment   To pronounce a word slowly, saying each sound distinctly.

Semantics   The meaning system of language.

Shared reading   The teacher reads a book aloud with a group of children as they follow along in the text, often using a big book.

Short vowels   The vowel sounds represented by /ă/ as in *cat*, /ĕ/ as in *bed*, /ĭ/ as in *big*, /ŏ/ as in *hop*, and /ŭ/ as in *cut*.

Simile   A comparison expressed using *like* or *as*.

Skill   An automatic processing behavior that students use in reading and writing, such as sounding out words, recognizing antonyms, and capitalizing proper nouns.

Strategy   A problem-solving behavior that students use in reading and writing, such as predicting, monitoring, visualizing, and summarizing.

Struggling reader or writer   A student who isn't meeting grade-level expectations in reading or writing.

Suffix   A syllable added to the end of a word to change the word's meaning (e.g., *-y* in *hairy*, *-ful* in *careful*).

Sustained Silent Reading (SSR)   Independent reading practice in which all adults and students in the class or in the school stop what they are doing and spend time (20–30 minutes) reading a self-selected book.

Syllable   An uninterrupted segment of speech that includes a vowel sound (e.g., *get*, *a-bout*, *but-ter-fly*, *con-sti-tu-tion*).

Symbol   The author's use of an object to represent something else.

Synonyms   Words that mean nearly the same thing (e.g., *road–street*).

Syntax   The structural system of language or grammar.

Text   Words appearing in print.

Trade book   A published book that is not a textbook; the type of books in bookstores and libraries.

Uppercase letters   The letters that are larger and are used as first letters in a name or at the beginning of a sentence; also called "capital letters."

Vowel A voiced speech sound made without friction or stoppage of the airflow as it passes through the vocal tract; the letters *a, e, i, o, u*, and sometimes *w* and *y*.

Vowel digraph Two or more adjacent vowels in a syllable that represent a single sound (e.g., *bread, eight, pain, saw*).

Word families Groups of words that rhyme (e.g., *ball, call, fall, hall, mall, tall*, and *wall*).

Word identification Strategies that students use to decode words, such as phonic analysis, analogies, syllabic analysis, and morphemic analysis.

Word sort A word-study activity in which students group words into categories.

Word wall An alphabetized chart posted in the classroom listing words students are learning.

Writing genres Forms of writing, such as stories, friendly letters, essays, and poems.

Writing process The process in which students use prewriting, drafting, revising, editing, and publishing to develop and refine a composition.

Writing workshop An approach in which students use the writing process to write books and other compositions on self-selected topics.

Zone of proximal development The distance between a child's actual developmental level and his or her potential developmental level that can be reached with scaffolding by the teacher or classmates.

Author and Title INDEX

Subject INDEX

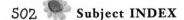

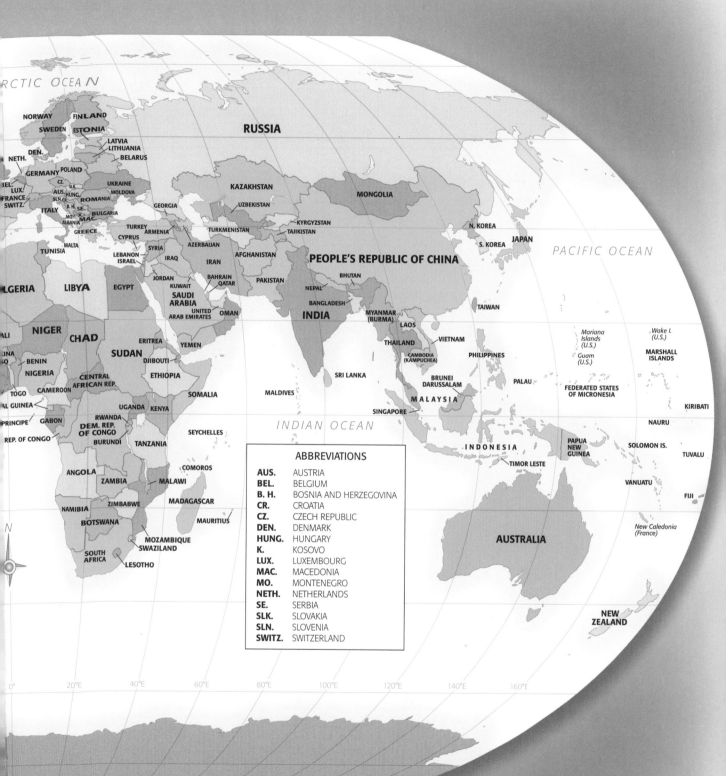

ARCTIC OCEAN

NORWAY
FINLAND
SWEDEN
ESTONIA
LATVIA
LITHUANIA
DEN.
BELARUS
NETH.
GERMANY POLAND
BEL.
LUX.
CZ.
SLK.
AUS. HUNG.
FRANCE
SLN. CR.
ROMANIA
SWITZ.
B. H. SE.
ITALY
MO. K.
MAC.
ALBANIA
BULGARIA
GREECE
MALTA
TUNISIA

RUSSIA

KAZAKHSTAN
MONGOLIA

UKRAINE
MOLDOVA
GEORGIA
UZBEKISTAN
KYRGYZSTAN
TURKMENISTAN
TAJIKISTAN
N. KOREA
TURKEY
ARMENIA
S. KOREA
JAPAN
CYPRUS
AZERBAIJAN
AFGHANISTAN
SYRIA
LEBANON
IRAQ
IRAN
PEOPLE'S REPUBLIC OF CHINA
ISRAEL
JORDAN
BAHRAIN
KUWAIT
QATAR
PAKISTAN
NEPAL
BHUTAN
ALGERIA
LIBYA
EGYPT
SAUDI
ARABIA
UNITED
ARAB EMIRATES
OMAN
INDIA
BANGLADESH
MYANMAR
(BURMA)
TAIWAN

PACIFIC OCEAN

LAOS
MALI
NIGER
CHAD
ERITREA
YEMEN
SUDAN
DJIBOUTI
THAILAND
VIETNAM
BURKINA
ETHIOPIA
CAMBODIA
(KAMPUCHEA)
PHILIPPINES
TOGO
CAMEROON
CENTRAL
AFRICAN REP.
SOMALIA
SRI LANKA
BENIN
NIGERIA
BRUNEI
DARUSSALAM
EQUATORIAL GUINEA
UGANDA
KENYA
MALDIVES
PALAU
PRINCIPE
GABON
RWANDA
DEM. REP.
OF CONGO
SEYCHELLES
MALAYSIA
REP. OF CONGO
BURUNDI
TANZANIA
SINGAPORE
KIRIBATI

Mariana
Islands
(U.S.)
Wake I.
(U.S.)
Guam
(U.S.)
MARSHALL
ISLANDS

FEDERATED STATES
OF MICRONESIA

NAURU

INDIAN OCEAN

COMOROS
ANGOLA
ZAMBIA
MALAWI
NAMIBIA
ZIMBABWE
MADAGASCAR
BOTSWANA
MAURITIUS
MOZAMBIQUE
SWAZILAND
SOUTH
AFRICA
LESOTHO

INDONESIA
TIMOR LESTE

PAPUA
NEW
GUINEA

SOLOMON IS.

TUVALU

VANUATU

FIJI

New Caledonia
(France)

AUSTRALIA

NEW
ZEALAND

ABBREVIATIONS

AUS.	AUSTRIA
BEL.	BELGIUM
B. H.	BOSNIA AND HERZEGOVINA
CR.	CROATIA
CZ.	CZECH REPUBLIC
DEN.	DENMARK
HUNG.	HUNGARY
K.	KOSOVO
LUX.	LUXEMBOURG
MAC.	MACEDONIA
MO.	MONTENEGRO
NETH.	NETHERLANDS
SE.	SERBIA
SLK.	SLOVAKIA
SLN.	SLOVENIA
SWITZ.	SWITZERLAND

0° 20°E 40°E 60°E 80°E 100°E 120°E 140°E 160°E

THE ESSENTIAL WORLD HISTORY

VOLUME II: SINCE 1500

SEVENTH EDITION

WILLIAM J. DUIKER
The Pennsylvania State University

JACKSON J. SPIELVOGEL
The Pennsylvania State University

WADSWORTH
CENGAGE Learning·

Australia • Brazil • Japan • Korea • Mexico • Singapore • Spain • United Kingdom • United States

WADSWORTH
CENGAGE Learning®

The Essential World History, Volume II: Since 1500,
Seventh Edition
William J. Duiker, Jackson J. Spielvogel

Senior Publisher: Suzanne Jeans

Acquiring Sponsoring Editor: Brooke Barbier

Senior Development Editor: Margaret McAndrew Beasley

Assistant Editor: Jamie Bushell

Editorial Assistant: Katie Coaster

Senior Media Editor: Lisa Ciccolo

Market Development Manager: Melissa Larmon

Senior Content Project Manager: Jane Lee

Senior Art Director: Cate Rickard Barr

Production Technology Analyst: Jeff Joubert

Manufacturing Planner: Sandra Milewski

Rights Acquisition Specialist, Image: Jennifer Meyer Dare

Rights Acquisition Specialist, Text: Jennifer Meyer Dare

Production Service: Orr Book Services

Text Designer: Shawn Girsberger

Cover Designer: Emily Chionchio, Roycroft Design

Cover Image: *Carnival*, 1951 (oil on masonite), Bazile, Castera (1923–1965)/Private Collection/ Galerie Bonheur, St. Louis, Missouri, USA/ The Bridgeman Art Library.

Compositor: Cenveo

For product information and technology assistance, contact us at
Cengage Learning Customer & Sales Support, 1-800-354-9706

For permission to use material from this text or product,
submit all requests online at **www.cengage.com/permissions**.
Further permissions questions can be emailed to
permissionrequest@cengage.com.

Library of Congress Control Number: 2012921058

ISBN-13: 978-1-133-93477-6
ISBN-10: 1-133-93477-3

Wadsworth
20 Channel Center Street
Boston, MA 02210
USA

Cengage Learning is a leading provider of customized learning solutions with office locations around the globe, including Singapore, the United Kingdom, Australia, Mexico, Brazil and Japan. Locate your local office at **international.cengage.com/region**.

Cengage Learning products are represented in Canada by Nelson Education, Ltd.

For your course and learning solutions, visit **www.cengage.com**. Purchase any of our products at your local college store or at our preferred online store **www.cengagebrain.com**.
Instructors: Please visit **login.cengage.com** and log in to access instructor-specific resources.

Printed in Canada
2 3 4 5 16 15 14 13

ABOUT THE AUTHORS

WILLIAM J. DUIKER is liberal arts professor emeritus of East Asian studies at The Pennsylvania State University. A former U.S. diplomat with service in Taiwan, South Vietnam, and Washington, D.C., he received his doctorate in Far Eastern history from Georgetown University in 1968, where his dissertation dealt with the Chinese educator and reformer Cai Yuanpei. At Penn State, he has written widely on the history of Vietnam and modern China, including the widely acclaimed *The Communist Road to Power in Vietnam* (revised edition, Westview Press, 1996), which was selected for a Choice Outstanding Academic Book Award in 1982–1983 and 1996–1997. Other recent books are *China and Vietnam: The Roots of Conflict* (Berkeley, 1987); *Sacred War: Nationalism and Revolution in a Divided Vietnam* (McGraw-Hill, 1995); and *Ho Chi Minh: A Life* (Hyperion, 2000), which was nominated for a Pulitzer Prize in 2001. While his research specialization is in the field of nationalism and Asian revolutions, his intellectual interests are considerably more diverse. He has traveled widely and has taught courses on the history of communism and non-Western civilizations at Penn State, where he was awarded a Faculty Scholar Medal for Outstanding Achievement in the spring of 1996.

TO YVONNE,
FOR ADDING SPARKLE TO THIS BOOK, AND TO MY LIFE
W.J.D.

JACKSON J. SPIELVOGEL is associate professor emeritus of history at The Pennsylvania State University. He received his Ph.D. from The Ohio State University, where he specialized in Reformation history under Harold J. Grimm. His articles and reviews have appeared in such journals as *Moreana, Journal of General Education, Catholic Historical Review, Archiv für Reformationsgeschichte,* and *American Historical Review.* He has also contributed chapters or articles to *The Social History of the Reformation, The Holy Roman Empire: A Dictionary Handbook, Simon Wiesenthal Center Annual of Holocaust Studies,* and *Utopian Studies.* His work has been supported by fellowships from the Fulbright Foundation and the Foundation for Reformation Research. At Penn State, he helped inaugurate the Western civilization courses as well as a popular course on Nazi Germany. His book *Hitler and Nazi Germany* was published in 1987 (sixth edition, 2010). He is the author of *Western Civilization* published in 1991 (eighth edition, 2012). Professor Spielvogel has won five major university-wide teaching awards. During the year 1988–1989, he held the Penn State Teaching Fellowship, the university's most prestigious teaching award. In 1996, he won the Dean Arthur Ray Warnock Award for Outstanding Faculty Member and in 2000 received the Schreyer Honors College Excellence in Teaching Award.

TO DIANE,
WHOSE LOVE AND SUPPORT MADE IT ALL POSSIBLE
J.J.S.

BRIEF CONTENTS

DETAILED CONTENTS

DOCUMENTS

MAPS

FEATURES

PREFACE

FOR SEVERAL MILLION YEARS after primates first appeared on the surface of the earth, human beings lived in small communities, seeking to survive by hunting, fishing, and foraging in a frequently hostile environment. Then suddenly, in the space of a few thousand years, there was an abrupt change of direction as human beings in a few widely scattered areas of the globe began to master the art of cultivating food crops. As food production increased, the population in those areas rose correspondingly, and people began to congregate in larger communities. Governments were formed to provide protection and other needed services to the local population. Cities appeared and became the focal point of cultural and religious development. Historians refer to this process as the beginnings of civilization.

For generations, historians in Europe and the United States pointed to the rise of such civilizations as marking the origins of the modern world. Courses on Western civilization conventionally began with a chapter or two on the emergence of advanced societies in Egypt and Mesopotamia and then proceeded to ancient Greece and the Roman Empire. From Greece and Rome, the road led directly to the rise of modern civilization in the West.

There is nothing inherently wrong with this approach. Important aspects of our world today can indeed be traced back to these early civilizations, and all human beings the world over owe a considerable debt to their achievements. But all too often this interpretation has been used to imply that the course of civilization has been linear in nature, leading directly from the emergence of agricultural societies in ancient Mesopotamia to the rise of advanced industrial societies in Europe and North America. Until recently, most courses on world history taught in the United States routinely focused almost exclusively on the rise of the West, with only a passing glance at other parts of the world, such as Africa, India, and East Asia. The contributions made by those societies to the culture and technology of our own time were often passed over in silence.

Two major reasons have been advanced to justify this approach. Some have argued that it is more important that young minds understand the roots of their own heritage than that of peoples elsewhere in the world. In many cases, however, the motivation for this Eurocentric approach has been the belief that since the time of Socrates and Aristotle Western civilization has been the sole driving force in the evolution of human society.

Such an interpretation, however, represents a serious distortion of the process. During most of the course of human history, the most advanced civilizations have been not in the West, but in East Asia or the Middle East. A relatively brief period of European dominance culminated with the era of imperialism in the late nineteenth century, when the political, military, and economic power of the advanced nations of the West spanned the globe. During recent generations, however, that dominance has gradually eroded, partly as a result of changes taking place within Western societies and partly because new centers of development are emerging elsewhere on the globe—notably in Asia, with the growing economic strength of China and India and many of their neighbors.

World history, then, has been a complex process in which many branches of the human community have taken an active part, and the dominance of any one area of the world has been a temporary rather than a permanent phenomenon. It will be our purpose in this book to present a balanced picture of this story, with all respect for the richness and diversity of the tapestry of the human experience. Due attention must be paid to the rise of the West, of course, since that has been the most dominant aspect of world history in recent centuries. But the contributions made by other peoples must be given adequate consideration as well, not only in the period prior to 1500 when the major centers of civilization were located in Asia, but also in our own day, when a multipolar picture of development is clearly beginning to emerge.

Anyone who wishes to teach or write about world history must decide whether to present the topic as an integrated whole or as a collection of different cultures. The world that we live in today, of course, is in many respects an interdependent one in terms of economics as well as culture and communications, a reality that is often expressed by the phrase "global village." The convergence of peoples across the surface of the earth into an integrated world system began in early times and intensified after the rise of capitalism in the early modern era. In growing recognition of this trend, historians trained in global history, as well as instructors in the growing number of world history courses, have now begun to speak and write of a "global approach" that turns attention away from the study of individual civilizations and focuses instead on the "big picture" or, as the world historian Fernand Braudel termed it, interpreting world history as a river with no banks.

On the whole, this development is to be welcomed as a means of bringing the common elements of the evolution of human society to our attention. But this approach also involves two problems. For the vast majority of their time on earth, human beings have lived in partial or virtually total isolation from each other. Differences in climate, location, and geographic features have created human societies very different from each other in culture and historical experience. Only in relatively recent times (the commonly accepted date has long been the beginning of the age of European exploration at the end of the fifteenth century, but some would now push it back to the era of the Mongol Empire or even further) have cultural interchanges begun to create a common "world system," in which events taking place in one part of the world are rapidly transmitted throughout the globe, often with momentous consequences. In recent generations, of course, the process of global interdependence has been proceeding even more rapidly. Nevertheless, even now the process is by no means complete, as ethnic and regional differences continue to exist and to shape the course of world history. The tenacity of these differences and sensitivities is reflected not only in the rise of internecine conflicts in such divergent areas as Africa, India, and Eastern Europe, but also in the emergence in recent years of such regional organizations as the African Union, the Association for the Southeast Asian Nations, and the European Union.

The second problem is a practical one. College students today are all too often not well informed about the distinctive character of civilizations such as China and India and, without sufficient exposure to the historical evolution of such societies, will assume all too readily that the peoples in these countries have had historical experiences similar to ours and will respond to various stimuli in a similar fashion to those living in western Europe or the United States. If it is a mistake to ignore those forces that link us together, it is equally a mistake to underestimate those factors that continue to divide us and to differentiate us into a world of diverse peoples.

Our response to this challenge has been to adopt a global approach to world history while at the same time attempting to do justice to the distinctive character and development of individual civilizations and regions of the world. The presentation of individual cultures is especially important in Parts I and II, which cover a time when it is generally agreed that the process of global integration was not yet far advanced. Later chapters begin to adopt a more comparative and thematic approach, in deference to the greater number of connections that have been established among the world's peoples since the fifteenth and sixteenth centuries. Part V consists of a series of chapters that center on individual regions of the world

while at the same time focusing on common problems related to the Cold War and the rise of global problems such as overproduction and environmental pollution.

We have sought balance in another way as well. Many textbooks tend to simplify the content of history courses by emphasizing an intellectual or political perspective or, most recently, a social perspective, often at the expense of sufficient details in a chronological framework. This approach is confusing to students whose high school social studies programs have often neglected a systematic study of world history. We have attempted to write a well-balanced work in which political, economic, social, religious, intellectual, cultural, and military history have been integrated into a chronologically ordered synthesis.

Features of the Text

To enliven the past and let readers see for themselves the materials that historians use to create their pictures of the past, we have included several **primary sources** (boxed documents) in each chapter that are keyed to the discussion in the text. The documents include examples of the religious, artistic, intellectual, social, economic, and political aspects of life in different societies and reveal in a vivid fashion what civilization meant to the individual men and women who shaped it by their actions. Questions at the end of each source aid students in analyzing the documents.

Each chapter has a **lengthy introduction** to help maintain the continuity of the narrative and to provide a synthesis of important themes. Anecdotes in the chapter introductions dramatically convey the major theme or themes of each chapter. A **timeline** at the end of each chapter enables students to see the major developments of an era at a glance and within cross-cultural categories, while the more **detailed chronologies** reinforce the events discussed in the text. An **annotated bibliography** at the end of each chapter reviews the most recent literature on each period and also gives references to some of the older, "classic" works in each field.

Maps and extensive illustrations serve to deepen the reader's understanding of the text. **Map captions** are designed to enrich students' awareness of the importance of geography to history, and numerous **spot maps** enable students to see at a glance the region or subject being discussed in the text. Map captions also include a question to guide students' reading of the map. To facilitate understanding of cultural movements, illustrations of artistic works discussed in the text are placed near the discussions. **Chapter outlines and focus questions, including critical thinking questions**, at the beginning of each chapter give students a useful overview and guide them to the main subjects of each chapter. The focus questions are then repeated at the beginning of each major section in the chapter to reinforce the main themes. A **glossary of important terms** (boldfaced in the text when they are introduced and defined) is provided at the back of the book to maximize reader comprehension. A **guide to pronunciation** is now provided in parentheses in the text, following the first mention of a complex name or term.

Comparative essays, keyed to the seven major themes of world history (see p. xxxx), enable us to more concretely draw comparisons and contrasts across geographic, cultural, and chronological lines. Some new essays have been added to the seventh edition. **Comparative illustrations**, also keyed to the seven major themes of world history, continue to be a feature in each chapter. Both the comparative essays and the comparative illustrations conclude with focus questions to help students develop their analytical skills. We hope that the comparative essays and the comparative illustrations will assist instructors who wish to encourage their students to adopt a comparative approach to their understanding of the human experience.

The **Film & History** feature, now appearing in many chapters, presents a brief analysis of the plot as well as the historical significance, value, and accuracy of popular films. New features have been added on films such as *Gladiator*, *Marie Antoinette*, and *Letters from Iwo Jima*.

The **Opposing Viewpoints** feature presents a comparison of two or three primary sources to facilitate student analysis of historical documents. This feature has been expanded and now appears in almost every chapter. Focus questions are included to help students evaluate the documents.

New to This Edition

After reexamining the entire book and analyzing the comments and reviews of many colleagues who have found the book to be a useful instrument for introducing their students to world history, we have also made a number of other changes for the seventh edition.

We have continued to strengthen the global framework of the book, but not at the expense of reducing the attention assigned to individual regions of the world. New material, including new comparative sections, has been added to most chapters to help students be aware of similar developments globally.

The enthusiastic response to the primary sources (boxed documents) led us to evaluate the content of each document carefully and add new documents throughout the text, including new comparative documents in the Opposing Viewpoints features.

The **Suggested Reading** sections at the end of each chapter have been thoroughly updated and are organized under subheadings to make them more useful. New illustrations were added to every chapter. **Chapter Notes** appear at the end of the book.

A new format has been added to the end of each chapter. The **Chapter Summary** is illustrated with thumbnail images of chapter illustrations and combined with a **Chapter Timeline**. A **Chapter Review** has been added to assist students in studying the chapter. This review includes **Upon Reflection** essay questions and a list of **Key Terms** from the chapter.

Also new to the seventh edition are **historiographical subsections**, which examine how and why historians differ in their interpretation of specific topics. To keep up with the ever-growing body of historical scholarship, new or revised material has been added throughout the book on many topics (see the specific notes below).

Chapter-by-Chapter Content Revisions

Chapter 1 New and revised material on early humans; new historiographical subsection: "The Spread of Humans: Out of Africa or Multiregional?"; new material on gender roles in the Neolithic Age; new material on the role of Kushite monarchs in Egypt; new material on the early history of Israel; new historiographical subsection: "Was There a United Kingdom of Israel?"; new material on Zoroastrianism.

Chapter 2 New Opposing Viewpoints feature: "The Search for Truth"; new historiographical subsection: "Who Were the Aryans?"; revised sections on Vedic religion and class and caste in India.

Chapter 3 Revised opening vignette and Map 3.1; new Opposing Viewpoints feature: "A Debate over Good and Evil"; new material on the following: Shang religion, Qin politics, and cities in ancient China; new historiographical subsections: "The Shang Dynasty: China's Mother Culture?" and "Are All Hydraulic Societies Despotic?"

Chapter 4 New material on Greek religion, with special emphasis on the Olympic games; new Opposing Viewpoints feature: "Women in Athens and Sparta"; new material on the Greek impact on Roman civilization; new historiographical subsection: "The Legacy: Was Alexander Great?"

Chapter 5 New Film & History feature on *Gladiator*; new historiographical subsection: "What Caused the Fall of the Western Roman Empire?"; new material on Han political, economic, and social policies; new section on "A Comparison of Rome and China."

Chapter 6 New material on the following: the Olmecs, including their use of chocolate, and Wari culture in South America; revised chapter summary to include more comparisons with other ancient cultures; new historiographical subsections: "The Olmecs: Mother Culture or First Among Equals?" and "The Mystery of Mayan Decline."

Chapter 7 New document: "Winning Hearts and Minds in Murcia"; new paragraph on the meaning of *jihad*; expanded discussion of Arab scholarship; revised opening vignette; new historiographical subsection: "Moorish Spain: An Era of 'Cultural Tolerance'?"; new comparative illustration on medieval mapmaking.

Chapter 8 New document: "The Nyanga Meet the Pygmies of Gabon"; new historiographical subsection: "Africa: A Continent Without History?"; new "Critical Thinking" question; revised content on Axum, Kush, Bantu migrations, and Swahili culture; new information on the origins of agriculture in Africa.

Chapter 9 Revised chapter title and Map 9.1; new historiographical subsection: "When Did the Indians Become Hindus?"; new material on early migrations to Southeast Asia and rice culture.

Chapter 10 Shortened opening section; new material on the following: civil service examinations, Tang land reforms, and the decline of noble families; expanded discussions of women's roles and the role of the emperor and popular religion; new Opposing Viewpoints feature: "A Meeting of Two Worlds" (exchange of letters between Pope Innocent IV and the Mongols); two new historiographical subsections: "The Mongols: A Reputation Undeserved?" and "Why Were Zhenghe's Voyages Abandoned?"; new document: "Beautiful Women: The Scapegoats of Legend"; new comparative illustration on "The Two Worlds of Tang China."

Chapter 11 New historiographical subsection: "Was Japan a Feudal Society?"; new document: "How the Earth Was Formed."

Chapter 12 New Opposing Viewpoints feature: "Lords and Vassals in Europe and Japan"; new material on England and France; new section on the Iberian kingdoms; new historiographical subsection: "What Were the Effects of the Crusades?"

Chapter 13 Clarified use of terms Later Roman Empire, Eastern Roman Empire, and Byzantine Empire; new material on the Byzantine capital of Constantinople as a "God-guarded city"; new Opposing Viewpoints feature: "Causes of the Black Death: Contemporary Views"; new document: "Christian Crusaders Capture Constantinople"; new historiographical subsection: "Was There a Renaissance for Women?"

Chapter 14 Added material on Latin America from Chapter 18; new historiographical subsection: "Christopher Columbus: Hero or Villain?"; revised comparative essay on "The Columbian Exchange"; new material on Africa.

Chapter 15 New material on religious piety on the eve of the Reformation; new material on the impact of the Reformation on common people as seen in the Peasants' War; new material on the Catholic Reformation; new historiographical subsection: "Catholic Reformation or Counter-Reformation?"; new material in comparative illustration of Louis XIV and Kangzi.

Chapter 16 Reorganized section on the Mughals; new document: "Designing the Perfect Society" (on *Jalali's Ethics*); new historiographical subsection: "The Mughal Dynasty: A 'Gunpowder Empire'?"

Chapter 17 New material on seizure of Taiwan; new document: "Be My Brother, or I'll Bash Your Head In!" (on Japanese-Korean war); new historiographical subsection: "The Qing Economy: Ready for Takeoff?"; revised section on Korea.

Chapter 18 Moved discussion of Latin American society to Chapter 14; new material on French colonization; new document: "British Victory in India"; new Film & History feature on *Marie Antoinette*; new material on the French monarchy on the eve of the Revolution.

Chapter 19 New material on the Industrial Revolution in Great Britain and the United States; new material on working laws; new material on the emergence of a world economy; new historiographical subsection: "Did Industrialization Bring an Improved Standard of Living?"

Chapter 20 New material on Zapata; new material on positive aspects of American society; new material on education and the Catholic Church.

Chapter 21 New comparative essay on "Imperialisms Old and New"; new historiographical subsection: "Imperialism: The Balance Sheet"; revised material on Africa and traditional resistance.

Chapter 22 Revised sections on the Chinese economy, Japan's "closed country" policy, and Meiji reforms; revised comparative essay on "Imperialism and the Global Environment"; new Opposing Viewpoints feature: "The Wonders of Western Civilization: Two Views"; new historiographical subsection: "What Explains Japanese Uniqueness?"

Chapter 23 New historiographical subsection: "The Assassination of Francis Ferdinand: A Blank Check?"; new material on the global nature of World War I; new material on the impact of Woodrow Wilson's rhetoric on self-determination for the colonial world; new Opposing Viewpoints feature: "Three Voices of Peacemaking."

Chapter 24 Expanded section on Palestine between the wars; new section on the rise of nationalism in Egypt; new Opposing Viewpoints feature: "Islam in the Modern World: Two Views" (Atatürk and Iqbal); added comparison of Latin America and Asian countries; new historiographical subsection: "Taisho Democracy: An Aberration?"

Chapter 25 New material on the war in Asia; new material and new illustration on the Battle of Stalingrad; new material on the Holocaust; new section entitled "World War II and the European Colonies: Decolonization"; new Film & History feature, *Letters from Iwo Jima*.

Chapter 26 Reorganized material on Dien Bien Phu and Taiwan; revised and reduced material on denazification.

Chapter 27 New historiographical subsection: "Why Did the Soviet Union Collapse?"; new document: "The Rights and Duties of Soviet Citizens"; new Opposing Viewpoints feature: "Students Appeal for Democracy" (on Tiananmen Square demonstrations); revised and updated section on China.

Chapter 28 New material on France, Germany, Great Britain, Eastern Europe, Russia, and the United States; new material on the European Union and the euro; new material on the West and Islam; new discussion of green urban planning, including new comparative illustration on "Green Urbanism"; new material on popular culture; new Opposing Viewpoints feature: "Islam and the West: Secularism in France."

Chapter 29 New comparative illustration on "Wealth and Poverty in the Middle East"; new Film & History feature on *Persepolis*; new historiographical subsection: "The Destiny of Africa: Unity or Diversity?"; updated material on the Middle East.

Chapter 30 Expanded section on Pakistan; new material on the following: Hindu-Muslim relations, caste and sexual relations, and Indian literature; new historiographical subsection: "What Is the Future of India?"; updated material on Indonesia; revised sections on Japanese politics and society.

Epilogue New material on global communications and global financial markets.

Because courses in world history at American and Canadian colleges and universities follow different chronological divisions, a one-volume comprehensive edition, a two-volume edition of this text, and a volume covering events to 1500 are being made available to fit the needs of instructors. Teaching and learning ancillaries include the following.

Instructor Resources

PowerLecture DVD with ExamView® and JoinIn®
ISBN-10: 113394406X | ISBN-13: 9781133944065
This dual platform, all-in-one multimedia resource includes the Instructor's Resource Manual; Test Bank including essay questions, key term identifications, multiple choice, and true/false questions; Microsoft® PowerPoint® slides of both lecture outlines and images and maps from the text that can be used as offered, or customized by importing personal lecture slides or other material; and JoinIn® PowerPoint® slides with clicker content. Also included is ExamView, an easy-to-use assessment and tutorial system that allows instructors to create, deliver, and customize tests in minutes. Instructors can build tests with as many as 250 questions using up to twelve question types, and using ExamView's complete word-processing capabilities, they can enter an unlimited number of new questions or edit existing ones.

eInstructor's Resource Manual Prepared by Dave Pretty of Winthrop University. This manual has many features, including instructional objectives, chapter outlines, thought/discussion questions for the primary sources, possible class lecture topics, student research and project topics, relevant worldwide websites/resources, and relevant video collections. Available on the instructor's companion website.

WebTutor™ on Blackboard
ISBN-10: 1285083245 | ISBN-13: 9781285083247 PAC
ISBN-10: 1285083199 | ISBN-13: 9781285083193 IAC
With WebTutor's text-specific, preformatted content and total flexibility, instructors can easily create and manage their own custom course website. WebTutor's course management tool gives instructors the ability to provide virtual office hours, post syllabi, set up threaded discussions, track student progress with the quizzing material, and much more. For students, WebTutor offers real-time access to a full array of study tools, including animations and videos that bring the book's topics to life, plus chapter outlines, summaries, learning objectives, glossary flashcards (with audio), practice quizzes, and weblinks.

WebTutor™ on WebCT®
ISBN-10: 1285083237 | ISBN-13: 9781285083230 PAC
ISBN-10: 1285083202 | ISBN-13: 9781285083209 IAC
With WebTutor's text-specific, preformatted content and total flexibility, instructors can easily create and manage their own custom course website. WebTutor's course management tool gives instructors the ability to provide virtual office hours, post syllabi, set up threaded discussions, track student progress with the quizzing material, and much more. For students, WebTutor offers real-time access to a full array of study tools, including animations and videos that bring the book's topics to life, plus chapter outlines, summaries, learning objectives, glossary flashcards (with audio), practice quizzes, and web links.

CourseMate

ISBN-10: 1285083482 | ISBN-13: 9781285083483 PAC
ISBN-10: 128508344X | ISBN-13: 9781285083445 IAC
ISBN-10:1285083318 | ISBN-13: 9781285083315 SSO

Cengage Learning's History CourseMate brings course concepts to life with interactive learning, study, and exam preparation tools that support the printed textbook. History CourseMate includes an integrated eBook; interactive teaching and learning tools including quizzes, flashcards, videos, and more; and EngagementTracker, a first-of-its-kind tool that monitors student engagement in the course. Learn more at www.cengagebrain.com.

Aplia

ISBN-10: 1285083032 | ISBN-13: 9781285083032 1-term PAC
ISBN-10: 1285083075 | ISBN-13: 9781285083070 1-term IAC
ISBN-10: 1285083024 | ISBN-13: 9781285083025 2-term PAC
ISBN-10: 1285083067 | ISBN-13: 9781285083063 2-term IAC

Aplia™ is an online interactive learning solution that improves comprehension and outcomes by increasing student effort and engagement. Founded by a professor to enhance his own courses, Aplia provides automatically graded assignments with detailed, immediate explanations on every question. The interactive assignments have been developed to address the major concepts covered in *The Essential World History*, seventh edition, and are designed to promote critical thinking and engage students more fully in their learning. Question types include questions built around animated maps, primary sources such as newspaper extracts, and imagined scenarios, such as engaging in a conversation with Benjamin Franklin or finding a diary and having to fill in some blank words; more in-depth primary source question sets that address a major topic with a number of related primary sources; and questions that promote deeper analysis of historical evidence. Images, video clips, and audio clips are incorporated into many of the questions. Students get immediate feedback on their work (not only what they got right or wrong, but why), and they can choose to see another set of related questions if they want to practice further. A searchable eBook is available inside the course as well so that students can easily reference it as they are working. Map-reading and writing tutorials are available as well to get students off to a good start.

Aplia's simple-to-use course management interface allows instructors to post announcements, upload course materials, host student discussions, e-mail students, and manage the gradebook; personalized support from a knowledgeable and friendly support team also offers assistance in customizing assignments to the instructor's course schedule. To learn more and view a demo for this book, visit www.aplia.com.

CourseReader

CourseReader is an online collection of primary and secondary sources that lets you create a customized electronic reader in minutes. With an easy-to-use interface and assessment tool, you can choose exactly what your students will be assigned—simply search or browse Cengage Learning's extensive document database to preview and select your customized collection of readings. In addition to print sources of all types (letters, diary entries, speeches, newspaper accounts, and more), the collection includes a growing number of images and video and audio clips.

Each primary source document includes a descriptive headnote that puts the reading into context and is further supported by both critical thinking and multiple-choice questions designed to reinforce key points. For more information, visit www.cengage.com/coursereader.

Cengagebrain.com

Save your students time and money. Direct them to www.cengagebrain.com for a choice of formats and savings and a better chance to succeed in your class. *Cengagebrain.com*, Cengage Learning's online store, is a single destination for more than 10,000 new textbooks, eTextbooks, eChapters, study tools, and audio supplements. Students have the freedom to purchase à la carte exactly what they need when they need it. Students can save 50 percent on the electronic textbook and can pay as little as $1.99 for an individual eChapter.

Student Resources

Book Companion Site
ISBN-10: 1133939007 | ISBN-13: 9781133939009

A website for students features a wide assortment of resources to help students master the subject matter. The website, prepared by Alan Hester of Greenville Technical College, includes a glossary, flashcards, focus questions, sample quizzes, suggested readings, and primary source links.

CL eBook

This interactive multimedia eBook links out to rich media assets such as video and MP3 chapter summaries. Through this eBook, students can also access primary sources, audio chapter summaries, zoomable and animated maps, web field trips, and more than 25 videos. Available at www.cengagebrain.com.

Doing History: Research and Writing in the Digital Age, 2e
ISBN-10: 1133587887 | ISBN-13: 9781133587880

Prepared by Michael J. Galgano, J. Chris Arndt, and Raymond M. Hyser of James Madison University.

Whether you're starting down the path as a history major or simply looking for a straightforward and systematic guide to writing a successful paper, you'll find this text to be an indispensable handbook to historical research. This text's "soup to nuts" approach to researching and writing about history addresses every step of the process, from locating your sources and gathering information, to writing clearly and making proper use of various citation styles to avoid plagiarism. You'll also learn how to make the most of every tool available to you—especially the technology that helps you conduct the process efficiently and effectively. The second edition includes a special appendix linked to CourseReader (see above), where you can examine and interpret primary sources online.

The History Handbook, 2e
ISBN-10: 049590676X | ISBN-13: 9780495906766
Prepared by Carol Berkin of Baruch College, City University of New York, and Betty Anderson of Boston University. This book teaches students both basic and history-specific study skills such as how to take notes, get the most out of lectures and readings, read primary sources, research historical topics, and correctly cite sources. Substantially less expensive than comparable skill-building texts, *The History Handbook* also offers tips for conducting Internet research and evaluating online sources. Additionally, students can purchase and download the eAudio version of *The History Handbook* or any of its eighteen individual units at www.cengagebrain.com to listen to on the go.

Writing for College History, 1e
ISBN-10: 061830603X | ISBN-13: 9780618306039
Prepared by Robert M. Frakes of Clarion University. This brief handbook for survey courses in American history, Western civilization/European history, and world civilization guides students through the various types of writing assignments they encounter in a history class. Providing examples of student writing and candid assessments of student work, this text focuses on the rules and conventions of writing for the college history course.

The Modern Researcher, 6e
ISBN-10: 0495318701 | ISBN-13: 9780495318705
Prepared by Jacques Barzun and Henry F. Graff of Columbia University. This classic introduction to the techniques of research and the art of expression is widely used in history courses, but is also appropriate for writing and research methods courses in other departments. Barzun and Graff thoroughly cover every aspect of research, from the selection of a topic through the gathering of material, analysis, writing, revision, and publication of

findings. They present the process not as a set of rules but through actual cases that put the subtleties of research in a useful context. Part One covers the principles and methods of research; Part Two covers writing, speaking, and getting one's work published.

Reader Program
Cengage Learning publishes a number of readers; some contain exclusively primary sources, others are devoted to essays and secondary sources, and still others provide a combination of primary and secondary sources. All of these readers are designed to guide students through the process of historical inquiry. Visit Cengage.com/history for a complete list of readers.

Rand McNally Historical Atlas of the World
ISBN-10: 0618841911 | ISBN-13: 9780618841912
This valuable resource features more than seventy maps that portray the rich panoply of the world's history from preliterate times to the present. They show how cultures and civilizations were linked and how they interacted. The maps make it clear that history is not static. Rather, it is about change and movement across time. The maps show change by presenting the dynamics of expansion, cooperation, and conflict. This atlas includes maps that display the world from the beginnings of civilization; the political development of all major areas of the world; expanded coverage of Africa, Latin America, and the Middle East; the current Islamic world; and world population change in 1900 and 2000.

Document Exercise Workbook
Volume 1: ISBN-10: 0534560830 | ISBN-13: 9780534560836
Volume 2: ISBN-10: 0534560849 | ISBN-13: 9780534560843
Prepared by Donna Van Raaphorst of Cuyahoga Community College. This collection of exercises is based around primary sources. Available in two volumes.

Custom Options

Nobody knows your students like you, so why not give them a text that is tailored to their needs? Cengage Learning offers custom solutions for your course—whether that involves making a small modification to *The Essential World History* to match your syllabus or combining multiple sources to create something truly unique. You can pick and choose chapters, include your own material, and add additional map exercises along with the *Rand McNally Atlas* to create a text that fits the way you teach. Ensure that your students get the most out of their textbook dollar by giving them exactly what they need. Contact your Cengage Learning representative to explore custom solutions for your course.

ACKNOWLEDGMENTS

BOTH AUTHORS GRATEFULLY acknowledge that without the generosity of many others, this project could not have been completed.

William Duiker would like to thank Kumkum Chatterjee and On-cho Ng for their helpful comments about issues related to the history of India and premodern China. His longtime colleague Cyril Griffith, now deceased, was a cherished friend and a constant source of information about modern Africa. Art Goldschmidt has been of invaluable assistance in reading several chapters of the manuscript, as well as in unraveling many of the mysteries of Middle Eastern civilization. Finally, he remains profoundly grateful to his wife, Yvonne V. Duiker, Ph.D. She has not only given her usual measure of love and support when this appeared to be an insuperable task, but she has also contributed her own time and expertise to enrich the sections on art and literature, thereby adding life and sparkle to this, as well as the earlier editions of the book. To her, and to his daughters Laura and Claire, he will be forever thankful for bringing joy to his life.

Jackson Spielvogel would like to thank Art Goldschmidt, David Redles, and Christine Colin for their time and ideas. Daniel Haxall of Kutztown University provided valuable assistance with materials on postwar art, popular culture, Postmodern art and thought, and the digital age. He is especially grateful to Kathryn Spielvogel for her work as research associate. Above all, he thanks his family for their support. The gifts of love, laughter, and patience from his daughters, Jennifer and Kathryn, his sons, Eric and Christian, and his daughters-in-law, Liz and Laurie, and his sons-in-law, Daniel and Eddie, were especially valuable. He also wishes to acknowledge his grandchildren, Devyn, Bryn, Drew, Elena, Sean, Emma, and Jackson, who bring great joy to his life. Diane, his wife and best friend, provided him with editorial assistance, wise counsel, and the loving support that made a project of this magnitude possible.

Thanks to Wadsworth's comprehensive review process, many historians were asked to evaluate our manuscript. We are grateful to the following for the innumerable suggestions that have greatly improved our work:

Henry Abramson
Florida Atlantic University

Eric H. Ash
Wayne State University

William Bakken
Rochester Community College

Suzanne Balch-Lindsay
Eastern New Mexico University

Michael E. Birdwell
Tennessee Technological University

Eric Bobo
Hinds Community College

Michael Bonislawski
Cambridge College

Connie Brand
Meridien Community College

Eileen Brown
Norwalk Community College

Paul Buckingham
Morrisville State College

Thomas Cardoza
University of California, San Diego

Alistair Chapman
Westmont College

Nupur Chaudhuri
Texas Southern University

Richard Crane
Greensboro College

Wade Dudley
East Carolina University

E. J. Fabyan
Vincennes University

Kenneth Faunce
Washington State University

Jamie Garcia
Hawaii Pacific University

Steven Gosch
University of Wisconsin—Eau Claire

Donald Harreld
Brigham Young University

Janine C. Hartman
University of Connecticut

Greg Havrilcsak
University of Michigan—Flint

Thomas Hegerty
University of Tampa

Sanders Huguenin
University of Science and Arts of Oklahoma

Ahmed Ibrahim
Southwest Missouri State University

C. Barden Keeler
Gulf Coast High School

Marilynn Fox Kokoszka
Orchard Ridge Campus, Oakland Community College

James Krippner-Martinez
Haverford College

Oscar Lansen
University of North Carolina—Charlotte

David Leinweber
Oxford College, Emory University

Susie Ling
Pasadena City College

Moira Maguire
University of Arkansas at Little Rock

Andrew McGreevy
Ohio University

Daniel Miller
Calvin College

Michael Murdock
Brigham Young University

Mark Norris
Grace College

Elsa A. Nystrom
Kennesaw State University

S. Mike Pavelec
Hawaii Pacific University

Matthew Phillips
Kent State University

Randall L. Pouwels
University of Central Arkansas

Margaret Power
Illinois Institute of Technology

Pamela Sayre
Henry Ford Community College

Philip Curtis Skaggs
Grand Valley State University

Laura Smoller
University of Arkansas at Little Rock

Beatrice Spade
University of Southern Colorado

Jeremy Stahl
Middle Tennessee State University

Clif Stratton
Washington State University

Kate Transchel
California State University, Chico

Justin Vance
Hawaii Pacific University

Lorna VanMeter
Ball State University

Michelle White
University of Tennessee at Chattanooga

Edna Yahil
Washington State University—Swiss Center

The authors are truly grateful to the people who have helped us to produce this book. We especially want to thank Clark Baxter, whose faith in our ability to do this project was inspiring. Margaret McAndrew Beasley thoughtfully, wisely, efficiently, and pleasantly guided the overall development of this edition. We also thank Brooke Barbier for her valuable editorial insights. We want to express our gratitude to John Orr, whose good humor, well-advised suggestions, and generous verbal support made the production process easier. Pat Lewis was, as usual, a truly outstanding copyeditor. Abigail Baxter provided valuable assistance in obtaining illustrations and permissions for the illustrations.

THEMES FOR UNDERSTANDING WORLD HISTORY

AS THEY PURSUE their craft, historians often organize their material on the basis of themes that enable them to ask and try to answer basic questions about the past. Such is our intention here. In preparing the seventh edition of this book, we have selected several major themes that we believe are especially important in understanding the course of world history. Thinking about these themes will help students to perceive the similarities and differences among cultures since the beginning of the human experience.

In the chapters that follow, we will refer to these themes frequently as we advance from the prehistoric era to the present. Where appropriate, we shall make comparisons across cultural boundaries or across different time periods. To facilitate this process, we have included a comparative essay in each chapter that focuses on a particular theme within the specific time period covered by that chapter. For example, the comparative essay in Chapter 6 deals with the human impact on the natural environment during the premodern era, while the essay in Chapter 30 discusses the same issue in the contemporary world. Each comparative essay is identified with a particular theme, although many essays touch on multiple themes.

We have sought to illustrate these themes through the use of comparative illustrations in each chapter. These illustrations are comparative in nature and seek to encourage the reader to think about thematic issues in cross-cultural terms, while not losing sight of the unique characteristics of individual societies. Our seven themes, each divided into two subtopics, are listed below.

1. Politics and Government The study of politics seeks to answer certain basic questions that historians have about the structure of a society: How were people governed? What was the relationship between the ruler and the ruled? What people or groups of people (the political elites) held political power? What actions did people take to guarantee their security or change their form of government?

2. Art and Ideas We cannot understand a society without looking at its culture, or the common ideas, beliefs, and patterns of behavior that are passed on from one generation to the next. Culture includes both high culture and popular culture. High culture consists of the writings of a society's thinkers and the works of its artists. A society's popular culture encompasses the ideas and experiences of ordinary people. Today, the media have embraced the

term *popular culture* to describe the current trends and fashionable styles.

3. Religion and Philosophy Throughout history, people have sought to find a deeper meaning to human life. How have the world's great religions, such as Hinduism, Buddhism, Judaism, Christianity, and Islam, influenced people's lives? How have they spread to create new patterns of culture in other parts of the world?

4. Family and Society The most basic social unit in human society has always been the family. From a study of family and social patterns, we learn about the different social classes that make up a society and their relationships with one another. We also learn about the role of gender in individual societies. What different roles did men and women play in their societies? How and why were those roles different?

5. Science and Technology For thousands of years, people around the world have made scientific discoveries and technological innovations that have changed our world. From the creation of stone tools that made farming easier to advanced computers that guide our airplanes, science and technology have altered how humans have related to their world.

6. Earth and the Environment Throughout history, peoples and societies have been affected by the physical world in which they live. Climatic changes alone have been an important factor in human history. Through their economic activities, peoples and societies, in turn, have also made an impact on their world. Human activities have affected the physical environment and even endangered the very existence of entire societies and species.

7. Interaction and Exchange Many world historians believe that the exchange of ideas and innovations is the driving force behind the evolution of human societies. Knowledge of agriculture, writing and printing, metalworking, and navigational techniques, for example, spread gradually from one part of the world to other regions and eventually changed the face of the entire globe. The process of cultural and technological exchange took place in various ways, including trade, conquest, and the migration of peoples.

A NOTE TO STUDENTS ABOUT LANGUAGES AND THE DATING OF TIME

ONE OF THE MOST difficult challenges in studying world history is coming to grips with the multitude of names, words, and phrases in unfamiliar languages. Unfortunately, this problem has no easy solution. We have tried to alleviate the difficulty, where possible, by providing an English-language translation of foreign words or phrases, a glossary, and a pronunciation guide in parentheses in the text. The issue is especially complicated in the case of Chinese because two separate systems are commonly used to transliterate the spoken Chinese language into the Roman alphabet. The Wade-Giles system, invented in the nineteenth century, was the most frequently used until recent years, when the pinyin system was adopted by the People's Republic of China as its own official form of transliteration. We have opted to use the latter, as it appears to be gaining acceptance in the United States, but the initial use of a Chinese word is accompanied by its Wade-Giles equivalent in parentheses for the benefit of those who may encounter the term in their outside reading.

In our examination of world history, we also need to be aware of the dating of time. In recording the past, historians try to determine the exact time when events occurred. World War II in Europe, for example, began on September 1, 1939, when Adolf Hitler sent German troops into Poland, and ended on May 7, 1945, when Germany surrendered. By using dates, historians can place events in order and try to determine the development of patterns over periods of time.

If someone asked you when you were born, you would reply with a number, such as 1994. In the United States, we would all accept that number without question, because it is part of the dating system followed in the Western world (Europe and the Western Hemisphere). In this system, events are dated by counting backward or forward from the birth of Christ (assumed to be the year 1). An event that took place 400 years before the birth of Christ would commonly be dated 400 B.C. (before Christ). Dates after the birth of Christ are labeled as A.D. These letters stand for the Latin words *anno domini*, which mean "in the year of the Lord" (or the year of the birth of Christ). Thus, an event that took place 250 years after the birth of Christ is written A.D. 250, or in the year of the Lord 250. It can also be written as 250, just as you would not give your birth year as A.D. 1994, but simply as 1994.

Some historians now prefer to use the abbreviations B.C.E. ("before the common era") and C.E. ("common era") instead of B.C. and A.D. This is especially true of world historians who prefer to use symbols that are not so Western or Christian oriented. The dates, of course, remain the same. Thus, 1950 B.C.E. and 1950 B.C. are the same year, as are A.D. 40 and 40 C.E. In keeping with the current usage by many world historians, this book will use the terms B.C.E. and C.E.

Historians also make use of other terms to refer to time. A decade is 10 years; a century is 100 years; and a millennium is 1,000 years. The phrase "fourth century B.C.E." refers to the fourth period of 100 years counting backward from 1, the assumed date of the birth of Christ. Since the first century B.C.E. would be the years 100 B.C.E. to 1 B.C.E., the fourth century B.C.E. would be the years 400 B.C.E. to 301 B.C.E. We could say, then, that an event in 350 B.C.E. took place in the fourth century B.C.E.

The phrase "fourth century C.E." refers to the fourth period of 100 years after the birth of Christ. Since the first period of 100 years would be the years 1 to 100, the fourth period or fourth century would be the years 301 to 400. We could say, then, for example, that an event in 350 took place in the fourth century. Likewise, the first millennium B.C.E. refers to the years 1000 B.C.E. to 1 B.C.E.; the second millennium C.E. refers to the years 1001 to 2000.

The dating of events can also vary from people to people. Most people in the Western world use the Western calendar, also known as the Gregorian calendar after Pope Gregory XIII who refined it in 1582. The Hebrew calendar, on the other hand, uses a different system in which the year 1 is the equivalent of the Western year 3760 B.C.E., considered by Jews to be the date of the creation of the world. Thus, the Western year 2013 is the year 5773 on the Jewish calendar. The Islamic calendar begins year 1 on the day Muhammad fled from Mecca, which is the year 622 on the Western calendar.

THE PEOPLES OF MESOPOTAMIA AND EGYPT, like the peoples of India and China, built the first civilizations. Blessed with an abundant environment in their fertile river valleys, beginning around 3000 B.C.E. they built technologically advanced societies, developed cities, and struggled with the problems of organized states. They developed  writing to keep records and created literature. They constructed monumental architecture to please their gods, symbolize their power, and preserve their culture for all time. They developed new political, military, social, and religious structures to deal with the basic problems of human existence and organization. These first literate civilizations left detailed records that allow us to view how they grappled with three of the fundamental problems that humans have pondered: the nature of human relationships, the nature of the universe, and the role of divine forces in that cosmos. Although other peoples would provide different answers from those of the Mesopotamians and Egyptians, they posed the questions, gave answers, and wrote them down. Human memory begins with the creation of civilizations.

By the middle of the second millennium B.C.E., much of the creative impulse of the Mesopotamian and Egyptian civilizations was beginning to wane. Around 1200 B.C.E., the decline of the Hittites and Egyptians had created a power vacuum that allowed a number of small states to emerge and flourish temporarily. All of them were eventually overshadowed by the rise of the great empires of the Assyrians and Persians. The Assyrian Empire had been the first to unite almost all of the ancient Middle East. Even larger, however, was the empire of the Great Kings of Persia. The many years of peace that the Persian Empire brought to the Middle East facilitated trade and the general wellbeing of its peoples. It is no wonder that many peoples expressed their gratitude for being subjects of the Great Kings of Persia. Among these peoples were the Israelites, who created no empire but nevertheless left an important spiritual legacy. The evolution of monotheism created in Judaism one of the world's greatest religions; Judaism in turn influenced the development of both Christianity and Islam.

While the peoples of North Africa and the Middle East were actively building the first civilizations, a similar process was getting under way in India. The first civilization in India arose in the Indus River valley during the fourth millennium B.C.E. This Harappan civilization made significant political and social achievements for some two thousand years until the coming of the Aryans finally brought its end around 1500 B.C.E. The Aryans established political control throughout all of India and created a new Indian civilization. Two of the world's great religions, Hinduism and Buddhism, began in India. With its belief in reincarnation, Hinduism provided justification for the rigid class system of India. Buddhism was the product of one man, Siddhartha Gautama, whose simple message in the sixth century B.C.E. of achieving wisdom created a new spiritual philosophy that came to rival Hinduism.

With the rise of the Mauryan dynasty in the fourth century B.C.E., the distinctive features of a great civilization began to be clearly visible. It was extensive in its scope, embracing the entire Indian subcontinent and eventually, in the form of Buddhism  and Hinduism, spreading to China and Southeast Asia. But the underlying ethnic, linguistic, and cultural diversity of the Indian people posed a constant challenge to the unity of the state. After the collapse of the Mauryas, the subcontinent would not come under a single authority again for several hundred years.

In the meantime, another great experiment was taking place far to the northeast, across the Himalaya Mountains. Like many other civilizations of antiquity, the first Chinese state was concentrated on a major river system. Beginning around 1600 B.C.E., the Shang dynasty created the first flourishing Chinese civilization. Under the Shang, China developed organized government, a system of writing, and advanced skills in the making of bronze vessels. During the Zhou dynasty, China began to adopt many of the features that characterized Chinese civilization for centuries. Especially important politically was the "mandate from Heaven," which, it was believed, gave kings a divine right to rule. The family, with its ideal of filial piety, also emerged as a powerful economic and social unit.

Once embarked on its own path toward the creation of a complex society, China achieved results that were in all respects the equal of its counterparts elsewhere. A new dynasty—the Han—then established a vast empire that lasted over four hundred years. During the glory years of the Han dynasty (202 B.C.E.–221 C.E.), China extended the boundaries of its empire far into the sands of central Asia

and southward along the coast of the South China Sea into what is modern-day Vietnam. Chinese culture appeared to be unrivaled, and its scientific and technological achievements were unsurpassed.

Unlike the great centralized empires of the Persians and the Chinese, ancient Greece consisted of a larger number of small, independent city-states, most of which had populations of only a few thousand. Despite the small size of their city-states, these ancient Greeks created a civilization that was the fountainhead of Western culture. In Classical Greece (c. 500–338 B.C.E.), Socrates, Plato, and Aristotle established the foundations of Western philosophy. Western literary forms are largely derived from Greek poetry and drama. Greek notions of harmony, proportion, and beauty have remained the touchstones for all subsequent Western art. A rational method of inquiry, so important to modern science, was conceived in ancient Greece. Many political terms are

Greek in origin, and so too are concepts of the rights and duties of citizenship, especially as they were conceived in Athens, the first great democracy. The Greeks raised and debated the fundamental questions about the purpose of human existence, the structure of human society, and the nature of the universe that have concerned thinkers ever since.

For all of their brilliant accomplishments, however, the Greeks were unable to rise above the divisions and rivalries that caused them to fight each other and undermine their own civilization. Of course, their cultural contributions have outlived their political struggles. And the Hellenistic era, which emerged after the Greek city-states had lost their independence in 338 B.C.E. and Alexander the Great had defeated the Persian Empire and carved out a new kingdom in the Middle East, made possible the spread of Greek ideas to larger areas. New philosophical concepts captured the minds of many. Significant achievements were made in art, literature, and science. Greek culture spread throughout the Middle East and

made an impact wherever it was carried. Although the Hellenistic world achieved a degree of political stability, by the late third century B.C.E. signs of decline were beginning to multiply, and the growing power of Rome would eventually endanger the Hellenistic world.

In the eighth and seventh centuries B.C.E., the Latin-speaking community of Rome emerged as an actual city. Between 509 and 264 B.C.E., the expansion of this city brought about the union of almost all of Italy under Rome's control. Even more dramatically, between 264 and 133 B.C.E., Rome expanded to the west and east and became master of the Mediterranean Sea and its surrounding territories, creating one of the largest empires in antiquity. Rome's republican institutions proved inadequate for the task of ruling an empire, however, and after a series of bloody civil wars, Octavian created a new order that would rule the empire in an orderly fashion. His successors established a Roman imperial state.

The Roman Empire experienced a lengthy period of peace and prosperity between 14 and 180 C.E. During this era, trade flourished and the provinces were governed efficiently. In the course of the third century, however, the Roman Empire came near to collapse due to invasions, civil wars, and economic decline. Although the emperors Diocletian and Constantine brought new life to the so called Late Empire, their efforts shored up the empire only temporarily. In its last two hundred years, as Christianity, with its new ideals of spiritual equality and respect for human life, grew, a slow transformation of the Roman world took place. The Germanic invasions greatly accelerated this process. Beginning in 395, the empire divided into western and eastern parts, and in 476, the Roman Empire in the west came to an end.

Although the western Roman Empire lived on only as an idea, Roman achievements were bequeathed to the future. The Romance languages of today (French, Italian, Spanish, Portuguese, and Romanian) are based on Latin. Western practices of impartial justice and trial by jury owe much to Roman law. As great builders, the Romans left monuments to their skills throughout Europe, some of which, such as aqueducts and roads, are still in use today.

The fall of ancient empires did not mark the end of civilization. After 500 C.E., new societies eventually rose on the ashes of the ancient empires, while new civilizations were on the verge of creation across the oceans in the continents of North and South America. The Maya and Aztecs were especially successful in developing advanced and prosperous civilizations in Central America. Both cultures built elaborate cities with pyramids, temples, and palaces. Both were polytheistic and practiced human sacrifice as a major part of their religions. Mayan civilization collapsed in the ninth century, whereas the Aztecs fell to Spanish invaders in the sixteenth century. In the fifteenth century,

another remarkable civilization—that of the Inka—flourished in South America. The Inkan Empire was carefully planned and regulated, which is especially evident in the extensive network of roads that connected all parts of the empire. However, the Inka, possessing none of the new weapons of the Spaniards, eventually fell to the foreign conquerors.

All of these societies in the Americas developed in apparently total isolation from their counterparts elsewhere in the world. This lack of contact with other human beings deprived them of access to developments taking place in Africa, Asia, and Europe. They did not know of the wheel, for example, and their written languages were not as sophisticated as those in other parts of the world. In other respects, however, their cultural achievements were the equal of those realized elsewhere. One development that the peoples of the Americas lacked was the knowledge of firearms. In a few short years, tiny bands of Spanish explorers were able to conquer the magnificent civilizations of the Americas and turn them into ruins.

After the collapse of Roman power in the west, the eastern Roman Empire, centered in Constantinople, continued in the eastern Mediterranean and eventually emerged as the unique Christian civilization known as the Byzantine Empire, which flourished for hundreds of years. One of the greatest challenges to the Byzantine Empire, however, came from a new force—Islam, a new religion that arose in the Arabian peninsula at the beginning of the seventh century C.E. and spread rapidly throughout the Middle East. It was the work of a man named Muhammad. After Muhammad's death, his successors organized the Arabs and set in motion a great expansion. Arab armies moved westward across North Africa and into Spain, as well as eastward into the Persian Empire, conquering Syria and Mesopotamia. Internal struggles, however, soon weakened the empire, although the Abbasid dynasty established an Arab empire in 750 that flourished for almost five hundred years.

Like other empires in the region, however, the Arab Empire did not last. Nevertheless, Islam brought a code of law and a written language to societies that had previously not had them. By creating a flourishing trade network stretching from West Africa to East Asia, Islam also brought untold wealth to thousands and a better life to millions. By the end of the thirteenth century, the Arab Empire was no more than a memory. But it left a powerful legacy in Islam, which remains one of the great religions of the world. In succeeding centuries, Islam began to penetrate into Africa and across the Indian Ocean into the islands of Southeast Asia.

The mastery of agriculture gave rise to three early civilizations in northern Africa: Egypt, Kush, and Axum. Later, new states emerged in different parts of Africa, some of them strongly influenced by the spread of Islam. Ghana, Mali, and Songhai were three prosperous trading states that flourished in West Africa between the twelfth and fifteenth centuries. Zimbabwe, which emerged around 1300, played an important role in the southern half of Africa. Africa was also an active participant in emerging regional and global trade with the Mediterranean world and across the Indian Ocean. Although the state-building process in sub-Saharan Africa was still in its early stages compared with the ancient civilizations of India, China, and Mesopotamia, in many respects the new African states were as impressive and sophisticated as their counterparts elsewhere in the world.

In the fifteenth century, a new factor came to affect Africa. Fleets from Portugal began to probe southward along the coast of West Africa. At first, their sponsors were in search of gold and slaves, but when Portuguese ships rounded the southern coast of Africa by 1500, they began to seek to dominate the trade of the Indian Ocean as well. The new situation posed a challenge to the peoples of Africa, whose states would be severely tested by the demands of the Europeans.

The peoples of Africa were not the only ones to confront a new threat from Europe at the beginning of the sixteenth century. When the Portuguese sailed across the Indian Ocean, they sought to reach India, where a new empire capable of rivaling the great kingdom of the Mauryas was in the throes of creation. Between 500 and 1500, Indian civilization had faced a number of severe challenges. One was an ongoing threat from beyond the mountains in the northwest. This challenge, which began in the eleventh century, led to the takeover of all of northern India in the eleventh century by Turkish warriors, who were Muslims. A second challenge came from the tradition of internal rivalry that had marked Indian civilization for hundreds of years and that continued almost without interruption down to the sixteenth century. The third challenge was the religious divisions between Hindus and Buddhists, and later between Hindus and Muslims, that existed throughout much of this period.

During the same period that Indian civilization faced these challenges at home, it was having a profound impact on the emerging states of Southeast Asia. Situated at the crossroads between two oceans and two great civilizations, Southeast Asia has long served as a bridge linking peoples and cultures. When complex societies

began to appear in the region, they were strongly influenced by the older civilizations of neighboring China and India. All the young states throughout the region—Vietnam, Angkor, Thailand, the Burmese kingdom of Pagan, and several states on the Malayan peninsula and Indonesian archipelago—were affected by foreign ideas and adopted them as a part of their own cultures. At the same time, the Southeast Asian peoples, like the Japanese, put their own unique stamp on the ideas that they adopted. The result was a region marked by cultural richness and diversity yet rooted in the local culture.

One of the civilizations that spread its shadow over the emerging societies of Southeast Asia was China. Between the sixth and fifteenth centuries, China was ruled by a series of strong dynasties and had advanced in many ways. The industrial and commercial sectors had grown considerably in size, complexity, and technological capacity. In the countryside, a flourishing agriculture bolstered China's economic prosperity. The civil service provided for a stable government bureaucracy and an avenue of upward mobility that was virtually unknown elsewhere in the world. China's achievements were unsurpassed throughout the world and made it a civilization that was the envy of its neighbors.

And yet some things had not changed. By 1500, China was still a predominantly agricultural society, with wealth based primarily on the ownership of land. Commercial activities flourished but remained under a high level of government regulation. China also remained a relatively centralized empire based on an official ideology that stressed the virtue of hard work, social conformity, and hierarchy. In foreign affairs, the long frontier struggle with the nomadic peoples along the northern and western frontiers continued unabated.

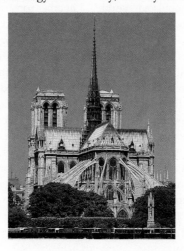

Along the fringes of Chinese civilization were a number of other agricultural societies that were beginning to follow a pattern of development similar to that of China, although somewhat later in time. All of these early agricultural societies were eventually influenced to some degree by their great neighbor. Vietnam remained under Chinese rule for a thousand years. Korea retained its separate existence but was long a tributary state of China and in many ways followed China's cultural example. Cut off from the mainland by 120 miles of ocean, the Japanese had little contact with the outside world during most of their early development. However, once the Japanese became acquainted with Chinese culture, they were quick to take advantage of the opportunity. In the space of a few decades, the young state adopted many features of Chinese society and culture and thereby introduced major changes into the Japanese way of life. Nevertheless, Japan was a society that was able to make use of ideas imported from beyond its borders without endangering its customs, beliefs, and institutions. Japan retained both its political independence and its cultural uniqueness.

After the collapse of the Roman Empire in the fifth century, a new European civilization slowly began to emerge in western Europe. The coronation of Charlemagne, the descendant of a Germanic tribe converted to Christianity, as Roman emperor in 800 symbolized the fusion of the three chief components of the new European civilization: the German tribes, the Roman legacy, and the Christian church. Charlemagne's Carolingian Empire fostered the idea of a distinct European identity. With the disintegration of that empire, power fell into the hands of many different lords, who came to constitute a powerful group of nobles that dominated the political, economic, and social life of Europe. But quietly and surely, within this world of castles and private power, kings gradually began to extend their public power and laid the foundations for the European kingdoms that in one form or another have dominated European politics ever since.

European civilization began to flourish in the High Middle Ages (1000–1300). The revival of trade, the expansion of towns and cities, and the development of a money economy did not mean the end of a predominantly rural European society, but they did offer new opportunities for people to expand and enrich their lives. At the same time, the High Middle Ages also gave birth to an intellectual and spiritual revival that transformed European society. However, fourteenth-century Europe was challenged by an overwhelming number of disintegrative forces but proved remarkably resilient. Elements of recovery in the age of the Renaissance made the fifteenth century a period of significant artistic, intellectual, and political change in Europe. By the second half of the fifteenth century, the growth of strong, centralized monarchical states made possible the dramatic expansion of Europe into other parts of the world.

The Emergence of New World Patterns (1500–1800)

HISTORIANS OFTEN REFER to the period from the sixteenth through eighteenth centuries as the early modern era. During these years, several factors were at work that created the conditions of our own time.

From a global perspective, perhaps the most noteworthy event of the period was the extension of the maritime trade network throughout the entire populated world. The Chinese had inaugurated the process with their groundbreaking voyages to East Africa in the early fifteenth century. The primary instrument of that expansion, however, was a resurgent Europe, which exploded onto the world scene with the initial explorations of the Portuguese and the Spanish at the end of the fifteenth century and then gradually came to dominate shipping on international trade routes during the next three centuries.

Some contemporary historians argue that it was this sudden burst of energy from Europe that created the first truly global economic network. According to Immanuel Wallerstein, one of the leading proponents of this theory, the Age of Exploration led to the creation of a new "world system" characterized by the emergence of global trade networks dominated by the rising force of European capitalism, which now began to scour the periphery of the system for access to markets and cheap raw materials.

Many historians, however, qualify Wallerstein's view and point to the Mongol expansion beginning in the thirteenth century or even to the rise of the Arab Empire in the Middle East a few centuries earlier as signs of the creation of a global communications network enabling goods and ideas to travel from one end of the Eurasian supercontinent to the other.

Whatever the truth of this debate, there are still many reasons for considering the end of the fifteenth century to be a crucial date in world history. In the first place, it marked the end of the long isolation of the Western Hemisphere from the rest of the inhabited world. This in turn led to the creation of the first truly global network of ideas and commodities, which would introduce plants, ideas, and (unfortunately) many new diseases to all humanity (see the comparative essay in Chapter 14). Second, the period gave birth to a stunning increase in trade and manufacturing that stimulated major economic changes not only in Europe but in other parts of the world as well.

The period from 1500 to 1800, then, was an incubation period for the modern world and the launching pad for an era of European domination that would reach fruition in the nineteenth century. To understand why the West emerged as the leading force in the world at that time, it is necessary to grasp the factors that were at work in Europe and why they were absent in other major civilizations around the globe.

Historians have identified improvements in navigation, shipbuilding, and weaponry that took place in Europe in the early modern era as essential elements in the Age of Exploration. As we have seen, many of these technological advances were based on earlier discoveries that had taken place elsewhere—in China, India, and the Middle East—and

Batavia, Java, 1780//© The Art Archive at Art Resource, NY

had then been brought to Europe on Muslim ships or along the trade routes through Central Asia. But it was the capacity and the desire of the Europeans to enhance their wealth and power by making practical use of the discoveries of others that was the significant factor in the equation and enabled them to dominate international sea lanes and create vast colonial empires in the Western Hemisphere.

European expansion was not fueled solely by economic considerations, however. As in the rise of Islam, religion played a major role in motivating the European Age of Exploration in the early modern era. Although Christianity was by no means a new faith in the sixteenth century (as Islam had been at the moment of Arab expansion), the world of Christendom was in the midst of a major period of conflict with the forces of Islam, a rivalry that had been exacerbated by the conquest of the Byzantine Empire by the Ottoman Turks in 1453.

Although the claims of Portuguese and Spanish adventurers that their activities were motivated primarily by a desire to bring the word of God to non-Christian peoples certainly included a considerable measure of self-delusion and hypocrisy, there seems no reason to doubt that religious motives played a meaningful role in the European Age of Exploration. Religious motives were perhaps less evident in the activities of the non-Catholic powers that entered the competition beginning in the seventeenth century. English and Dutch merchants and officials were more inclined to be motivated purely by the pursuit of economic profit.

Conditions in many areas of Asia were less conducive to these economic and political developments. In China, a centralized monarchy continued to rely on a prosperous agricultural sector as the economic foundation of the empire. In Japan, power was centralized under the powerful Tokugawa shogunate, and the era of peace and stability that ensued saw an increase in manufacturing and commercial activity. But Japanese elites, after initially expressing interest in the outside world, abruptly shut the door on European trade and ideas in an effort to protect Japan from external contamination.

In the societies of India and the Middle East, commerce and manufacturing had played a vital role in the life of societies since the emergence of the Indian Ocean trade network in the first centuries C.E. But beginning in the eleventh century, the area had suffered through an extended period of political instability, marked by invasions by nomadic peoples from Central Asia. The violence of the period and the local rulers' lack of experience in promoting maritime commerce had a severe depressing effect on urban manufacturing and commerce.

In the early modern era, then, Europe was best placed to take advantage of the technological innovations that had become increasingly available. With its political stability, sources of capital, and a "modernizing elite," it was well equipped to wrest the greatest benefit from the new conditions. Whereas other regions were beset by internal obstacles or had deliberately turned inward to seek their destiny, Europe now turned outward to seek a new and dominant position in the world. Nevertheless, significant changes were taking place in other parts of the world as well, and many of these changes had relatively little to do with the situation in the West. As we shall see, the impact of European expansion on the rest of the world was still limited at the end of the eighteenth century. Though European political authority was firmly established in a few key areas, such as the Spice Islands and Latin America, traditional societies remained relatively intact in most regions of Africa and Asia. And processes at work in these societies were often operating independently of events in Europe and would later give birth to forces that acted to restrict or shape the Western impact. One of these forces was the progressive emergence of centralized states, some of them built on the concept of ethnic unity. ◆

New Encounters: The Creation of a World Market

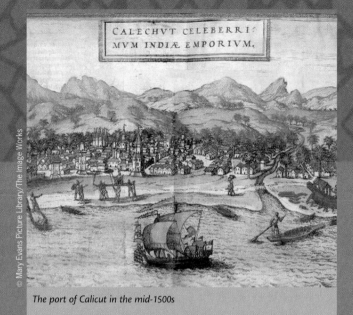

The port of Calicut in the mid-1500s

CHAPTER OUTLINE AND FOCUS QUESTIONS

An Age of Exploration and Expansion

Q How did Muslim merchants expand the world trade network at the end of the fifteenth century?

The Portuguese Maritime Empire

Q Why were the Portuguese so successful in taking over the spice trade?

The Conquest of the ''New World''

Q How did Portugal and Spain acquire their empires in the Americas, and how did their methods of governing their colonies differ?

Africa in Transition

Q What were the main features of the African slave trade, and what effects did European participation have on traditional African practices?

Southeast Asia in the Era of the Spice Trade

Q What were the main characteristics of Southeast Asian societies, and how were they affected by the coming of Islam and the Europeans?

CRITICAL THINKING

Q How was European expansion into the rest of the world both a positive and a negative experience for Europeans and non-Europeans?

WHEN THE PORTUGUESE FLEET arrived at the town of Calicut (KAL-ih-kuht) (now known as Kozhikode) on the western coast of India, in the spring of 1498, fleet commander Vasco da Gama (VAHSH-koh dah GAHM-uh) ordered a landing party to go ashore to contact the local authorities. The first to greet them, a Muslim merchant from Tunisia, said, "May the Devil take thee! What brought thee hither?" "Christians and spices," replied the visitors. "A lucky venture, a lucky venture," replied the Muslim. "Plenty of rubies, plenty of emeralds! You owe great thanks to God, for having brought you to a country holding such riches!"[1]

Such words undoubtedly delighted the Portuguese, who concluded that the local population appeared to be Christians. Although it later turned out that they were mistaken—the local faith was a form of Hinduism—their spirits were probably not seriously dampened, for God was undoubtedly of less immediate importance than gold and glory to sailors who had become the first Europeans since the ancient Greeks to sail across the Indian Ocean. They left two months later with a cargo of spices and the determination to return soon with a larger fleet.

Vasco da Gama's voyage to India inaugurated a period of European expansion into Asia that lasted several hundred years and had effects that are still felt today. Eventually, it resulted in a Western takeover of existing trade routes in the Indian Ocean and the establishment of colonies throughout Asia, Africa, and Latin America. In later years, Western historians would describe the era as an "Age of Discovery" that significantly broadened the maritime trade network and set the stage for the emergence of the modern world.

In fact, however, the voyages of Vasco da Gama and his European successors were only the latest stage in a process that had begun generations earlier, at a time when European explorations were still restricted to the North Atlantic. As we saw in Chapter 10, Chinese fleets under Admiral Zhenghe had roamed the Indian Ocean for several years during the early fifteenth century, linking the Middle Kingdom with societies as distant as the Middle East and the coast of East Africa. Although the Chinese voyages were short in duration and had few lasting effects, the world of Islam was also expanding its reach, as Muslim traders blazed new trails into Southeast Asia and across the Sahara to the civilizations along the banks of the Niger River. It was, after all, a Muslim from North Africa who greeted the Portuguese when they first appeared off the coast of India. In this chapter, we turn our attention to the stunning expansion in the scope and volume of commercial and cultural contacts that took place in the generations preceding and following da Gama's historic voyage to India, as well as to the factors that brought about this expansion. 🖎

An Age of Exploration and Expansion

Q FOCUS QUESTION: How did Muslim merchants expand the world trade network at the end of the fifteenth century?

The voyage of Vasco da Gama has customarily been seen as a crucial step in the opening of trade routes to the East. In the sense that the voyage was a harbinger of future European participation in the spice trade, this view has merit. In fact, however, as has been pointed out in earlier chapters, the Indian Ocean had been a busy thoroughfare for centuries. The spice trade had been carried on by sea in the region since the days of the legendary Queen of Sheba, and Chinese junks had sailed to the area in search of cloves and nutmeg since the Tang dynasty (see Chapter 10).

Islam and the Spice Trade

By the fourteenth century, Muslim ships were transporting a growing percentage of the spice trade. Muslims, either Arabs or Indian converts, had taken part in the Indian Ocean trade for centuries, and by the thirteenth century Islam had established a presence in seaports on the islands of Sumatra and Java. In 1292, the Venetian traveler Marco Polo observed that Muslims were engaging in missionary activity in Sumatra: "This kingdom is so much frequented by the Saracen merchants that they have converted the natives to the Law of Mahomet—I mean the townspeople only, for the hill people live for all the world like beasts, and eat human flesh, as well as other kinds of flesh, clean or unclean."[2]

But the major impetus for the spread of Islam in Southeast Asia came in the early fifteenth century, with the foundation of a new sultanate at Malacca (muh-LAK-uh). The founder was Paramesvara (pahr-uh-muss-VAHR-uh), a vassal of the Hindu state of Majapahit (mah-jah-PAH-hit) on Java, who had been based first on Sumatra and then at Tumasik (tuh-MAH-sik) (modern Singapore), at the tip of the Malay peninsula. In the early fifteenth century, Paramesvara moved to Malacca

The Strait of Malacca

to take advantage of its strategic location. As a sixteenth-century visitor from Portugal would observe, Malacca "is a city that was made for commerce; . . . the trade and commerce between the different nations for a thousand leagues on every hand must come to Malacca."[3]

Shortly after its founding, Malacca was visited by a Chinese fleet under the command of Admiral Zhenghe (see Chapter 10). To protect his patrimony from local rivals, Paramesvara accepted Chinese vassalage and cemented the new relationship by making an official visit to the Ming emperor in Beijing (see the box on p. 356). More importantly, perhaps, he also converted to Islam, a move that would have enhanced Malacca's ability to participate in the trade that passed through the strait, much of which was dominated by Muslim merchants. Within a few years, Malacca had become the leading economic power in the region and helped to promote the spread of Islam to trading ports throughout the islands of Southeast Asia, including Java, Borneo, Sulawesi (soo-lah-WAY-see), and the Philippines.

A Chinese Description of Malacca

INTERACTION & EXCHANGE

Malacca, located on the west coast of the Malay peninsula, first emerged as a major trading port in the early fifteenth century, when its sultan, Paramesvara, avoided Thai rule with the aid of the emperor of China. This description of the area was written by a naval officer who served in one of the famous Chinese fleets that visited the city in the early fifteenth century.

Ma Huan, *Description of a Starry Raft*

This place did not formerly rank as a kingdom. It can be reached from Palembang on the monsoon in eight days. The coast is rocky and desolate, the population sparse. The country [used to] pay an annual tax of 40 taels of gold to Siam. The soil is infertile and yields low. In the interior there is a mountain from [the slopes of] which a river takes its rise. The [local] folk pan the sands [of this river] to obtain tin, which they melt into ingots called *tou*. These weigh 1 kati 4 taels standard weight. [The inhabitants] also weave banana fiber into mats. Apart from tin, no other product enters into [foreign] trade. The climate is hot during the day but cool at night. [Both] sexes coil their hair into a knot. Their skin resembles black lacquer, but there are [some] white-complexioned folk among them who are of Chinese descent. The people esteem sincerity and honesty. They make a living by panning tin and catching fish. Their houses are raised above the ground. [When constructing them] they refrain from joining planks and restrict the building to the length of a [single] piece of timber. When they wish to retire, they spread their bedding side by side. They squat on their haunches when taking their meals. The kitchen and all its appurtenances is [also] raised [on the stilts]. The goods [used in trading at Malacca] are blue and white porcelain, colored beads, colored taffetas, gold and silver. In the seventh year of Yung-lo [1409], the imperial envoy, the eunuch Cheng-Ho [Zhenghe], and his lieutenants conferred [on the ruler], by Imperial command, a pair of silver seals, and a headdress, girdle and robe. They also set up a tablet [stating that] Malacca had been raised to the rank of a kingdom, but at first Siam refused to recognize it. In the thirteenth year [of Yung-lo] [1415], the ruler [of Malacca, desirous of] showing his gratitude for the Imperial bounty, crossed the ocean and, accompanied by his consort and son, came to court with tribute. The Emperor rewarded him [appropriately], whereupon [the ruler of Malacca] returned to his [own] country.

Q *Why was Malacca such an important center of world trade?*

Source: From Harry J. Banda and John A. Larkin, eds. *The World of Southeast Asia: Selected Historical Readings,* Harper & Row, 1967.

The Spread of Islam in West Africa

In the meantime, Muslim trade and religious influence continued to expand south of the Sahara into the Niger River valley in West Africa. Muslim traders—first Arabs and later African converts—crossed the desert carrying Islamic values, political culture, and legal traditions along with their goods. The early stage of state formation had culminated with the kingdom of Mali under the renowned Mansa Musa (see Chapter 8).

THE EMPIRE OF SONGHAI With the decline of Mali in the late fifteenth century, a new power eventually appeared: the empire of Songhai (song-GY). Its founder was Sonni Ali, a local chieftain who seized Timbuktu from its Berber overlords in 1468 and then sought to restore the formidable empire of his predecessors. Sonni Ali was criticized by Muslim scholars for supporting traditional religious practices, but under his rule, Songhai emerged as a major trading state (see Map 14.1). Shortly after his death in 1492, one of his military commanders seized power as king under the name Askia Mohammed (r. 1493–1528).

The new ruler, a fervent Muslim, increasingly relied on Islamic institutions and ideology to strengthen national unity and centralize authority. After his return from a pilgrimage to Mecca, Askia Mohammed tried to revive Timbuktu as a major center of Islamic learning, although many of his subjects—especially in rural

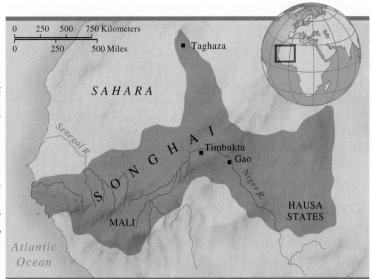

© Cengage Learning. Adapted from Geoffrey Barraclough, ed. *Times Atlas of World History* (Maplewood, N.J.: Hammond Inc., 1978), p. 160.

MAP 14.1 The Songhai Empire. Songhai was the last of the great states to dominate the region of the Niger River valley prior to the European takeover in the nineteenth century.

Q *What were the predecessors of the Songhai Empire in the region? What explains the importance of the area in African history?*

areas—continued to resist conversion to Islam. He did preside over a significant increase in trans-Saharan trade (notably in salt and gold), which provided a steady source of income to Songhai (see the box on p. 358). After his death, however, centrifugal forces within Songhai eventually led to its breakup. In 1591, Moroccan forces armed with firearms conquered the city to gain control over the gold trade in the region.

A New Player: Europe

For almost a millennium, Catholic Europe had largely been confined to one area. Its one major attempt to expand beyond those frontiers, the Crusades, ultimately had failed. Of course, Europe had never completely lost contact with the outside world: in particular, with the revival of trade in the High Middle Ages, European merchants began to travel more frequently to Asia and Africa. Nevertheless, Europe's contacts with non-European civilizations remained limited until the fifteenth century, when Europeans began to embark on a remarkable series of overseas journeys. What caused European seafarers to undertake such dangerous voyages to the ends of the earth?

Europeans had long been attracted to the East. Myths and legends of an exotic land of great riches were widespread in the Middle Ages, but the most informative description of the East was provided by Marco Polo of Venice, who wrote an account of his experiences at the court of the great Mongol ruler Khubilai Khan in the thirteenth

century (see Chapter 10). In the fourteenth century, however, the conquests of the Ottoman Turks and then the breakup of the Mongol Empire reduced Western traffic to the East. With the closing of the overland routes, a number of people in Europe became interested in the possibility of reaching Asia by sea.

THE MOTIVES An economic motive thus looms large in Renaissance European expansion (see Chapter 13). Merchants, adventurers, and government officials had high hopes of finding precious metals and a direct source for the spices of the East, which continued to be transported to Europe via Arab intermediaries but were outrageously expensive. Europeans did not hesitate to express their desire to share in the wealth. As one Spanish conquistador (kahn-KEES-tuh-dor) explained, he and his kind went to the Americas to "serve God and His Majesty, to give light to those who were in darkness, and to grow rich, as all men desire to do."[4]

This statement expresses another major reason for the overseas voyages—religious zeal. A crusading mentality was particularly strong in Portugal and Spain, where the Muslims had largely been driven out in the Middle Ages. Prince Henry the Navigator of Portugal, an outspoken advocate of European expansion, was said to be motivated by "his great desire to make increase in the faith of our Lord Jesus Christ and to bring him all the souls that should be saved." Although most scholars believe that the religious motive was secondary to economic considerations, it would be foolish to overlook the genuine desire to convert the heathen to Christianity. Hernán Cortés (hayr-NAHN kor-TAYSS *or* kor-TEZ), the conqueror of Mexico, asked his Spanish rulers if it was not their duty to ensure that the native Mexicans were "introduced into and instructed in the holy Catholic faith."[5]

THE MEANS If "God, glory, and gold" were the primary motives, what made the voyages possible? First of all, the expansion of Europe was a state enterprise, tied to the growth of centralized monarchies during the Renaissance. By the second half of the fifteenth century, European monarchies had increased both their authority and their resources and were in a position to turn their energies beyond their borders. That meant the invasion of Italy for France, but for Portugal, a state not strong enough to pursue power in Europe, it meant going abroad. The Spanish scene was more complex, since the Spanish monarchy was strong enough by the sixteenth century to pursue power both on the Continent and beyond.

The Great City of Timbuktu

INTERACTION & EXCHANGE

After its founding in the twelfth century, Timbuktu became a great center of Islamic learning and a fabled city of mystery and riches to Europeans. In the sixteenth century, Timbuktu was still a major commercial center on the trade route through the Sahara. This description of the city was written in 1526 by Leo Africanus, a Muslim from the Islamic state of Granada and one of the great travelers of his time.

Leo Africanus, *History and Description of Africa*

Here are many shops of artificers and merchants, and especially of such as weave linen and cotton cloth. And hither do the Barbary merchants bring cloth of Europe. All the women of this region, except the maid-servants, go with their faces covered, and sell all necessary victuals. The inhabitants, and especially strangers there residing, are exceeding rich, insomuch that the king that now is, married both his daughters to rich merchants. Here are many wells containing sweet water; and so often as the river Niger overfloweth, they convey the water thereof by certain sluices into the town. Corn, cattle, milk, and butter this region yieldeth in great abundance: but salt is very scarce here; for it is brought hither by land from Taghaza which is 500 miles distant. When I myself was here, I saw one camel's load of salt sold for 80 ducats. The rich king of Timbuktu hath many plates and scepters of gold, some whereof weigh

1,300 pounds: and he keeps a magnificent and well-furnished court. When he travelleth any whither he rideth upon a camel which is led by some of his noblemen; and so he doth likewise when he goeth forth to warfare, and all his soldiers ride upon horses. Whoever will speak unto this king must first fall down before his feet, and then taking up earth must first sprinkle it upon his own head and shoulders: which custom is ordinarily observed by . . . ambassadors from other princes. He hath always 3,000 horsemen, and a number of footmen that shoot poisoned arrows, attending upon him. They have often skirmishes with those that refuse to pay tribute, and so many as they take, they sell unto the merchants of Timbuktu. . . . Here are great store of doctors, judges, priests, and other learned men, that are bountifully maintained at the king's cost and charges, and hither are brought divers manuscripts or written books out of Barbary, which are sold for more money than any other merchandise. The coin of Timbuktu is of gold without any stamp or superscription but in matters of small value they use certain shells brought hither out of the kingdom of Persia. . . . The inhabitants are people of gentle and cheerful disposition, and spend a great part of the night singing and dancing through all the streets of the city.

 What role did the city of Timbuktu play in regional commerce, according to this author? What were the chief means of payment?

Source: From *The History and Description of Africa*, by Leo Africanus (New York: Burt Franklin).

At the same time, by the end of the fifteenth century European states had a level of knowledge and technology that enabled them to regularly engage in voyages beyond Europe. In the thirteenth and fourteenth centuries, navigators and mathematicians began to produce *portolani* (pohr-tuh-LAH-nee), detailed charts that provided information on coastal contours, distances between ports, and compass readings. The *portolani* were valuable for voyages in European waters, but because they were drawn on a flat surface and did not account for the curvature of the earth, they were of little use for longer overseas voyages. Only when seafarers began to venture beyond the coasts of Europe did they begin to accumulate information about the actual shape of the earth and

how to measure it. By the end of the fifteenth century, cartography had developed to the point that Europeans possessed fairly accurate maps of the known world.

In addition, Europeans had developed remarkably seaworthy ships as well as new navigational techniques. European shipbuilders had mastered the use of the sternpost rudder (an import from China) and learned how to combine the use of lateen sails with a square rig. With these innovations, they could construct ships mobile enough to sail against the wind and engage in naval warfare and also large enough to be armed with heavy cannons and carry a substantial amount of goods. In addition, new navigational aids such as the compass (a Chinese invention) and the astrolabe (an instrument, reportedly

Museo de la Torre del Oro, Seville//© Gianni Dagli Orti/
The Art Archive at Art Resource, NY

Marine Museum, Lisbon/© Gianni Dagli Orti/
The Art Archive at Art Resource, NY

European Warships During the Age of Exploration. Prior to the fifteenth century, most European ships were either small craft with triangular, lateen sails used in the Mediterranean or slow, unwieldy square-rigged vessels operating in the North Atlantic. By the sixteenth century, European naval architects began to build **caravels** (KER-uh-velz) (left), which combined the maneuverability and speed offered by lateen sails (widely used by sailors in the Indian Ocean) with the carrying capacity and seaworthiness of the square-riggers. For a century, caravels were the feared "raiders of the oceans." Eventually, as naval technology progressed, European warships developed in size and firepower, as the illustration of Portuguese carracks on the right shows.

devised by Arab sailors, that was used to measure the altitude of the sun and the stars above the horizon) enabled sailors to explore the high seas with confidence.

The Portuguese Maritime Empire

Q **FOCUS QUESTION:** Why were the Portuguese so successful in taking over the spice trade?

Portugal took the lead in exploration when it began exploring the coast of Africa under the sponsorship of Prince Henry the Navigator (1394–1460), who hoped both to find a Christian kingdom to be an ally against the Muslims and to acquire new trade opportunities for Portugal. In 1419, he founded a school for navigators, and shortly thereafter, Portuguese fleets began probing southward along the western coast of Africa in search of gold. In 1441, Portuguese ships reached the Senegal River, just north of Cape Verde. They found no gold, but brought home a cargo of black Africans, most of whom were sold as slaves to wealthy buyers elsewhere in Europe. Within a few years, an estimated thousand slaves were shipped annually from the area back to Lisbon.

Continuing southward, in 1471 the Portuguese discovered a new source of gold along the southern coast of the hump of West Africa (an area henceforth known to

Europeans as the Gold Coast). A few years later, they established contact with the state of Kongo, near the mouth of the Congo River in Central Africa, and with the inland state of Benin, north of the Gold Coast.

The Portuguese in India

Hearing reports of a route to India around the southern tip of Africa, Portuguese sea captains continued their probing (see Map 14.2). In 1487, Bartolomeu Dias (bar-toh-loh-MAY-oo DEE-uhs) rounded the Cape of Good Hope, but fearing a mutiny from his crew, he returned home without continuing onward. Ten years later, a fleet under the command of Vasco da Gama rounded the cape and stopped at several ports controlled by Muslim merchants along the coast of East Africa, including Sofala, Kilwa, and Mombasa. Then da Gama's fleet crossed the Arabian Sea and arrived at Calicut on the Indian coast on May 18, 1498. The Portuguese crown had sponsored the voyage with the clear objective of destroying the Muslim monopoly over the spice trade, which had intensified since the Ottoman conquest of Constantinople in 1453 (see Chapter 13). Calicut was a major entrepôt (ON-truh-poh) on the route from the Spice Islands to the Mediterranean, but the ill-informed Europeans believed it was the source of the spices themselves. Da Gama returned to Europe with a cargo of ginger and cinnamon that earned the investors a profit of several thousand percent.

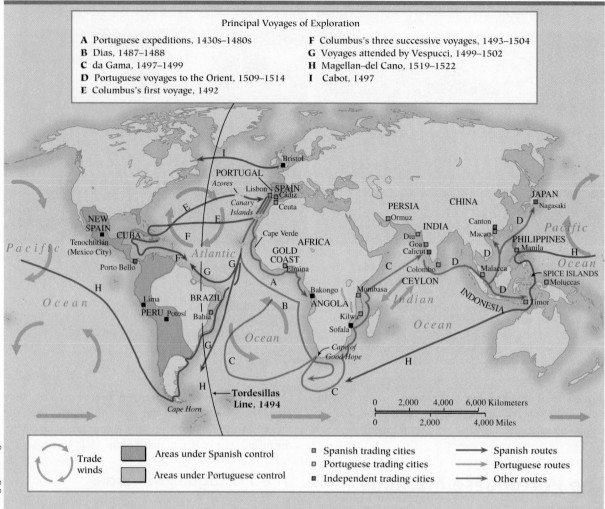

Principal Voyages of Exploration

A Portuguese expeditions, 1430s–1480s
B Dias, 1487–1488
C da Gama, 1497–1499
D Portuguese voyages to the Orient, 1509–1514
E Columbus's first voyage, 1492

F Columbus's three successive voyages, 1493–1504
G Voyages attended by Vespucci, 1499–1502
H Magellan–del Cano, 1519–1522
I Cabot, 1497

MAP 14.2 European Voyages and Possessions in the Sixteenth and Seventeenth Centuries.
This map indicates the most important voyages launched by Europeans during their momentous
Age of Exploration in the sixteenth and seventeenth centuries.

Q *Why did Vasco da Gama sail so far into the South Atlantic on his voyage to Asia?*

The Search for Spices

During the next years, the Portuguese set out to gain control of the spice trade. In 1510, Admiral Afonso de Albuquerque (ah-FAHN-soh day AL-buh-kur-kee) established his headquarters at Goa (GOH-uh), on the western coast of India. From there, the Portuguese raided Arab shippers, provoking the following comment from an Arab source: "[The Portuguese] took about seven vessels, killing those on board and making some prisoner. This was their first action, may God curse them."[6] In 1511, Albuquerque seized Malacca and put the local Muslim population to the sword. Control of Malacca not only provided the Portuguese with a way

station en route to the Spice Islands, known today as the Moluccas (muh-LUHK-uhz), but also gave them a means to destroy the Arab spice trade network by blocking passage through the Strait of Malacca.

From Malacca, the Portuguese sent **The Spice Islands**

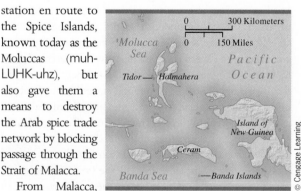

expeditions farther east, to China in 1514 and to the Spice Islands. There they signed a treaty with a local sultan for the purchase of cloves for the European market. Within a few years, they had managed to seize control of the spice trade from Muslim traders and had garnered substantial profits for the Portuguese monarchy.

Why were the Portuguese so successful? Basically, their success was a matter of guns and seamanship. The Portuguese by no means possessed a monopoly on the use of firearms and explosives, but they used the maneuverability of their light ships to maintain their distance while bombarding the enemy with their powerful cannons. Such tactics gave them a military superiority over lightly armed rivals that they were able to exploit until the arrival of other European forces several decades later.

New Rivals Enter the Scene

Portugal's efforts to dominate the trade of the Indian Ocean were never totally successful, however. The Portuguese lacked both the numbers and the wealth to overcome local resistance and colonize the Asian regions. Moreover, their massive investments in ships and laborers for their empire (hundreds of ships and hundreds of thousands of workers in shipyards and overseas bases) proved very costly. The empire was simply too large and Portugal too small to maintain it, and by the end of the sixteenth century, the Portuguese were being severely challenged by rivals.

THE SPANISH   First came the Spanish, whose desire to find a westward route to the East Indies had already led Queen Isabella to sponsor the voyage of Christopher Columbus across the Atlantic in 1492. Two years later, in an effort to head off conflict between the two countries, the Treaty of Tordesillas (tor-day-SEE-yass) divided the newly discovered world into Portuguese and Spanish spheres of influence. Thereafter, the route east around the Cape of Good Hope was reserved for the Portuguese, while the route across the Atlantic (except for the eastern hump of South America) was assigned to Spain (see Map 14.2 on p. 360).

Eventually convinced that the lands Columbus had reached were not the Indies, the Spanish continued to seek a route to the Spice Islands. In 1519, a Spanish fleet under the command of the Portuguese sea caption Ferdinand Magellan sailed around the southern tip of South America, proceeded across the Pacific Ocean, and landed in the Philippine Islands. Although Magellan and some forty of his crew were killed in a skirmish with the local population, one of the two remaining ships sailed on to the Moluccas and thence around the world via the Cape of Good Hope. In the words of a contemporary historian,

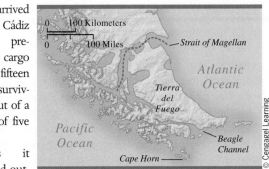

Cape Horn and the Strait of Magellan

they arrived in Cádiz "with precious cargo and fifteen men surviving out of a fleet of five sail."[7]

As it turned out, the Spanish could not follow up on Magellan's accomplishment, and in 1529, they sold their rights in the Moluccas to the Portuguese. But Magellan's voyage was not a total loss. The Spanish managed to consolidate their control over the Philippines, which eventually became a major Spanish base in the carrying trade across the Pacific. Spanish galleons carried silk and other luxury goods to Acapulco in exchange for silver from the mines of Mexico.

THE ENGLISH AND THE DUTCH   The primary threat to the Portuguese toehold in Southeast Asia, however, came from the English and the Dutch. In 1591, the first English expedition to the Indies through the Indian Ocean returned to London with a cargo of pepper. Nine years later, a private joint-stock company, the East India Company, was founded to provide a stable source of capital for future voyages. In 1608, an English fleet landed at Surat (SOOR-et), on the northwestern coast of India. Trade with Southeast Asia soon followed.

The Dutch were quick to follow suit, and the first Dutch fleet arrived in India in 1595. In 1602, the Dutch East India Company was established under government sponsorship and was soon actively competing with the English and the Portuguese. In 1641, the Dutch seized Malacca, one of the linchpins of Portugal's trading empire in Asia.

The Conquest of the "New World"

Q   FOCUS QUESTION: How did Portugal and Spain acquire their empires in the Americas, and how did their methods of governing their colonies differ?

While the Portuguese were seeking access to the spice trade by sailing eastward through the Indian Ocean, the Spanish attempted to reach the same destination by sailing westward across the Atlantic. Although the Spanish came to overseas discovery and exploration later than the Portuguese, their greater resources enabled them to establish a far grander overseas empire.

The Voyages

In the late fifteenth century, knowledgeable Europeans were aware that the earth was round but had little understanding of its size or the extent of the continent of Asia. Convinced that the earth's circumference was smaller than contemporaries believed and that Asia was larger, Christopher Columbus (1451–1506), an Italian from Genoa, maintained that Asia could be reached by sailing due west instead of eastward around Africa. He persuaded Queen Isabella of Spain to finance an expedition, which reached the Americas in October 1492 and explored the coastline of Cuba and the neighboring island of Hispaniola (his-puhn-YOH-luh or ees-pahn-YAH-luh). Columbus believed that he had reached Asia and in three subsequent voyages (1493, 1498, and 1502) sought in vain to find a route through the outer islands to the Asian mainland.

Other navigators, however, realized that Columbus had discovered a new frontier altogether. State-sponsored explorers joined the race to what Europeans called the "New World." A Venetian, John Cabot, explored the New England coastline under a license from King Henry VII of England. The continent of South America was discovered accidentally by the Portuguese captain Pedro Cabral (PAY-droh kuh-BRAHL) in 1500. Amerigo Vespucci (ahm-ay-REE-goh vess-POO-chee), a Florentine, accompanied several voyages and wrote a series of letters describing the lands he observed. The publication of these letters led to the name "America" (after Amerigo) for the new lands.

The Conquests

The territories that Europeans referred to as the New World actually contained flourishing civilizations populated by millions of people. But the Americas were new to the Europeans, who quickly saw opportunities for conquest and exploitation. With Portugal clearly in the lead in the race to exploit the riches of the Indies, the importance of these lands was magnified in the minds of the Spanish.

The Spanish **conquistadors** were a hardy lot of mostly upper-class individuals motivated by a typical sixteenth-century blend of glory, greed, and religious zeal. Although sanctioned by the Castilian crown, these groups were financed and outfitted privately, not by the government.

Their superior weapons, organizational skills, and determination brought the conquistadors incredible success. In 1519, a Spanish expedition led by Hernán Cortés landed at Veracruz, on the Gulf of Mexico. Marching to Tenochtitlán (teh-nahch-teet-LAHN) with a small contingent of troops, Cortés received a friendly welcome from the Aztec monarch Moctezuma Xocoyotzin

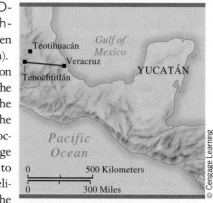

The Arrival of Hernán Cortés in Mexico

(mahk-tuh-ZOO-muh shoh-koh-YAHT-seen) (often called Montezuma).

But tensions soon erupted between the Spaniards and the Aztecs. When the Spanish took Moctezuma hostage and began to destroy Aztec religious shrines, the local population revolted and drove the invaders from the city. Meanwhile, the Aztecs were beginning to suffer the first effects of the diseases brought by the Europeans, which would eventually wipe out the majority of the local population. With assistance from the state of Tlaxcallan (tuh-lah-SKAH-lahn), Cortés finally succeeded in vanquishing the Aztecs (see the comparative illustration on p. 363). Within months, their magnificent city and its temples, believed by the conquerors to be the work of Satan, had been destroyed.

A similar fate awaited the powerful Inka Empire in South America. Between 1531 and 1536, an expedition led by Francisco Pizarro (frahn-CHESS-koh puh-ZAHR-oh) (1470–1541) destroyed Inka power high in the Peruvian Andes. Here, too, the Spanish conquests were undoubtedly facilitated by the previous arrival of European diseases, which had decimated the local population.

THE PORTUGUESE IN BRAZIL Meanwhile, the Portuguese crown had established the colony of Brazil, basing its claim on the Treaty of Tordesillas, which had allocated the eastern coast of South America to the Portuguese sphere of influence. Like their Spanish rivals, the Portuguese initally saw their new colony as a source of gold and silver, but they soon discovered that profits could be made in other ways as well. A formal administrative system was instituted in Brazil in 1549, and Portuguese migrants arrived to establish plantations to produce sugar, coffee, and other tropical products for export to Europe.

Governing the Empires

While Portugal came to dominate Brazil, Spain established a colonial empire that included Central America, most of South America, and parts of North America. Within the lands of Central and South America, a new civilization arose that we have come to call Latin America (see Map 14.3).

Latin America rapidly became a multiracial society. Already by 1501, Spanish rulers allowed intermarriage between Europeans and the inhabitants of the Americas,

COMPARATIVE ILLUSTRATION

POLITICS & GOVERNMENT

The Spaniards Conquer a New World.
The Spanish perception of their arrival in the Americas was quite different from that of the indigenous peoples. In the European painting shown above, the encounter was a peaceful one, and the upturned eyes of Columbus and his fellow voyagers imply that their motives were spiritual rather than material. The image below, drawn by an Aztec artist, expresses a dramatically different point of view, as the Spanish invaders, assisted by their Indian allies, use superior weapons against the bows and arrows of their adversaries to bring about the conquest of Mexico.

Q *What does the Aztec painting show the viewer about the nature of the conflict between the two contending armies?*

---

whom the Europeans called Indians. Their offspring were known as **mestizos** (mess-TEE-zohz). In addition, over three centuries, as many as 8 million African slaves were brought to Spanish and Portuguese America to work the plantations (see "The Slave Trade" later in this chapter). **Mulattoes** (muh-LAH-tohz)—the offspring of Africans and whites—joined mestizos and descendants of whites, Africans, and local Indians to produce a unique multiracial society.

THE STATE AND THE CHURCH IN COLONIAL LATIN AMERICA In administering their colonial empires in the Americas, both Portugal and Spain tried to keep the most important posts of colonial government in the hands of Europeans. Nevertheless, the distance from the home countries meant that colonial officials would have considerable autonomy in implementing their monarchs' policies.

At the head of the administrative system that the Portuguese established for Brazil was the position of governor-general. The governor-general developed a bureaucracy but had at best only loose control over the captains-general, who were responsible for governing the districts into which Brazil was divided.

To rule his American empire, the king of Spain appointed **viceroys**. The first viceroyalties were established for New Spain (Mexico) in 1535 and for Peru in 1543. Viceroyalties were in turn subdivided into smaller units. All of the major government positions were held by Spaniards. For **creoles**—American-born descendants of Europeans—the chief opportunity to hold a government post was in city councils.

From the beginning, the Spanish and Portuguese rulers were determined to convert the indigenous peoples of the Americas to Christianity. Consequently, the Catholic

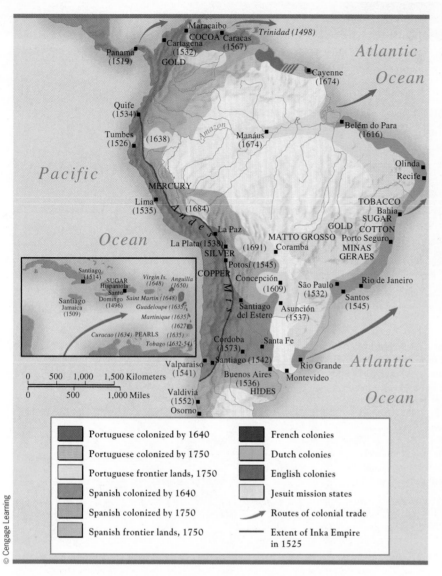

Maracaibo
COCOA Caracas
Cartagena (1567)
(1532)
Panama GOLD
(1519)
Trinidad (1498)

Atlantic
Ocean

Cayenne
(1674)

Quife
(1534)

Belém do Para
(1616)

Tumbes
(1526) (1638)

Manáus
(1674)

Amazon

Pacific

Olinda
Recife

MERCURY

Lima (1684)
(1535)

Andes

La Paz
La Plata(1538)
SILVER
Potosí (1545)
COPPER
Concepción
(1609)

TOBACCO
Bahia
SUGAR
GOLD COTTON
MATTO GROSSO Porto Seguro,
(1691) Coramba MINAS
GERAES

São Paulo
(1532)

Rio de Janeiro

Ocean

Santiago
(1514)
SUGAR
Hispaniola
Santo
Santiago Domingo
Jamaica (1496)
(1509)
Virgin Is.
(1648) Anguilla
(1650)
Saint Martin (1648)
Guadeloupe (1635)
Martinique (1635)
(1627)
Curacao (1634) PEARLS (1635)
Tobago (1632-54)

Santiago
del Estero

Asunción
(1537)

Santos
(1545)

Córdoba
(1573)

Santa Fe

0 500 1,000 1,500 Kilometers

0 500 1,000 Miles

Valparaiso
(1541)
Santiago (1542)
Buenos Aires
(1536)
Valdivia HIDES
(1552)
Osorno

Rio Grande
Montevideo

Atlantic

Ocean

Portuguese colonized by 1640   French colonies

Portuguese colonized by 1750   Dutch colonies

Portuguese frontier lands, 1750   English colonies

Spanish colonized by 1640   Jesuit mission states

Spanish colonized by 1750   Routes of colonial trade

Spanish frontier lands, 1750   Extent of Inka Empire
in 1525

MAP 14.3 Latin America from c. 1500 to 1750. From the sixteenth century, Latin America was largely the colonial preserve of the Spanish, although Portugal dominated Brazil. The Latin American colonies supplied the Spanish and Portuguese with gold, silver, sugar, tobacco, cotton, and animal hides.

Q *How do you explain the ability of Europeans to dominate such large areas of Latin America?*

orders, many of them of aristocratic background, often operated outside their establishments by running schools and hospitals. The nun Sor Juana Inés de la Cruz (SAWR HWAH-nuh ee-NAYSS day lah KROOZ) (1651–1695) became one of seventeenth-century Latin America's best-known literary figures. She wrote poetry and prose and urged that women be educated.

EXPLOITING THE RICHES OF THE AMERICAS Both the Portuguese and the Spanish sought to profit economically from their colonies. One source of wealth came from the gold and silver that the Europeans sought so avidly. One Aztec observer commented that the Spanish conquerors "longed and lusted for gold. Their bodies swelled with greed, and their hunger was ravenous; they hungered like pigs for that gold."[8] Rich silver deposits were exploited in Mexico and southern Peru (modern Bolivia). When the mines at Potosí (poh-toh-SEE) in Peru were opened in 1545, the value of precious metals imported into Europe quadrupled. Between 1503 and 1650, an estimated 16 million kilograms (17,500 tons) of silver and 185,000 kilograms (200 tons) of gold entered the port of Seville in Spain.

In the long run, however, agriculture proved to be more rewarding. The American colonies became sources of raw materials for Spain and Portugal as sugar, tobacco, chocolate, precious woods, animal hides, and other natural products made their way to Europe. In turn, the mother countries supplied their colonists with manufactured goods (see Map 14.4).

To produce these goods, colonial authorities initially tried to rely on local sources of human labor. Spanish policy toward the Indians was a combination of confusion, misguided paternalism, and cruel exploitation. Queen Isabella declared the Indians to be subjects of Castile and instituted the *encomienda* **system**, under which European

Church played an important role in the colonies—a role that added considerably to church power. As Catholic missionaries fanned out across the Spanish Empire, the church built hospitals, orphanages, and schools to instruct the Indians in the rudiments of reading, writing, and arithmetic. To facilitate their efforts, missionaries often brought Indians to live in mission villages where they could be converted, taught trades, and encouraged to grow crops, all under the control of the church.

For women in the colonies, Catholic nunneries provided outlets other than marriage. Women in religious settlers received grants of land and could collect tribute from the indigenous peoples and use them as laborers. In return, the holders of an *encomienda* (en-koh-MYEN-duh) were supposed to protect the Indians and supervise their spiritual and material needs. In practice, this meant that the settlers were free to implement the system as they pleased. Spanish settlers largely ignored their distant government and brutally used the Indians to pursue their own economic interests. Indians were put to work on sugar plantations and in the gold and silver mines.

Forced labor, starvation, and especially disease took a fearful toll on Indian lives. With little or no natural resistance to European diseases, the Indians were ravaged by smallpox, measles, and typhus brought by the Europeans. Although estimates vary, in some areas at least half of the local population probably died of European diseases. On Hispaniola alone, out of an initial population of 100,000 when Columbus arrived in 1493, only 300 Indians survived by 1570. In 1542, largely in response to the publications of

CHRONOLOGY	Spanish and Portuguese Activities in the Americas
Christopher Columbus's first voyage to the Americas	1492
Portuguese fleet arrives in Brazil	1500
Columbus's last voyages	1502–1504
Spanish conquest of Mexico	1519–1522
Francisco Pizarro's conquest of the Inkas	1531–1536
Viceroyalty of New Spain established	1535
Formal colonial administrative system established in Brazil	1549

Bartolomé de Las Casas (bahr-toh-loh-MAY day lahs KAH-sahs), the government abolished the *encomienda* system and provided more protection for the Indians (see the box on p. 366). By then, however, the indigenous population had been decimated by disease, causing the Spanish

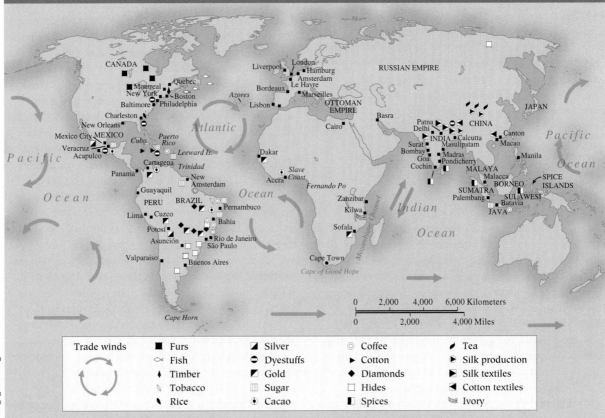

MAP 14.4 Patterns of World Trade Between 1500 and 1800. This map shows the major products that were traded by European merchants throughout the world during the era of European exploration.

 What were the primary sources of gold and silver, so sought after by Columbus and his successors?

OPPOSING ✕ VIEWPOINTS

The March of Civilization

INTERACTION & EXCHANGE

As Europeans began to explore new parts of the world in the fifteenth century, they were convinced that it was their duty to introduce civilized ways to the heathen peoples they encountered. This attitude is reflected in the first selection, which describes the Spanish captain Vasco Núñez de Balboa (BAHS-koh NOON-yez day bal-BOH-uh) in 1513, when from a hill on the Isthmus of Panama he first laid eyes on the Pacific Ocean.

Bartolomé de Las Casas (1474–1566) was a Dominican monk who participated in the conquest of Cuba and received land and Indians in return for his efforts. But in 1514, he underwent a radical transformation that led him to believe that the Indians had been cruelly mistreated by his fellow Spaniards. He spent the remaining years of his life (he lived to the age of ninety-two) fighting for the Indians. The second selection is taken from his most influential work, *Brevísima Relación de la Destrucción de las Indias,* known to English readers as *The Tears of the Indians.* This work was largely responsible for the reputation of the Spanish as inherently "cruel and murderous fanatics." Many scholars today feel that Las Casas may have exaggerated his account to shock his contemporaries into action.

Gonzalo Fernández de Ovieda, *Historia General y Natural de las Indias*

On Tuesday, the twenty-fifth of September of the year 1513, at ten o'clock in the morning, Captain Vasco Núñez, having gone ahead of his company, climbed a hill with a bare summit, and from the top of this hill saw the South Sea. Of all the Christians in his company, he was the first to see it. He turned back toward his people, full of joy, lifting his hands and his eyes to Heaven, praising Jesus Christ and his glorious Mother the Virgin, Our Lady. Then he fell upon his knees on the ground and gave great thanks to God for the mercy He had shown him, in allowing him to discover that sea, and thereby to render so great a service to God and to the most serene Catholic Kings of Castile, our sovereigns. . . .

And he told all the people with him to kneel also, to give the same thanks to God, and to beg Him fervently to allow them to see and discover the secrets and great riches of that sea and coast, for the greater glory and increase of the Christian faith, for the conversion of the Indians, natives of those southern regions, and for the fame and prosperity of the royal throne of Castile and of its sovereigns present and to come. All the people cheerfully and willingly did as they were bidden; and the Captain made them fell a big tree and make from it a tall cross, which they erected in that same place, at the top of the hill from which the South Sea had first been seen.

Bartolomé de Las Casas, *The Tears of the Indians*

There is nothing more detestable or more cruel than the tyranny which the Spaniards use toward the Indians for the getting of pearl. Surely the infernal torments cannot much exceed the anguish that they endure, by reason of that way of cruelty; for they put them under water some four or five ells deep, where they are forced without any liberty of respiration, to gather up the shells wherein the Pearls are; sometimes they come up again with nets full of shells to take breath, but if they stay any while to rest themselves, immediately comes a hangman row'd in a little boat, who as soon as he hath well beaten them, drags them again to their labor. Their food is nothing but filth, and the very same that contains the Pearl, with small portion of that bread which that Country affords; in the first whereof there is little nourishment; and as for the latter, it is made with great difficulty, besides that they have not enough of that neither for sustenance; they lie upon the ground in fetters, lest they should run away; and many times they are drown'd in this labor, and are never seen again till they swim upon the top of the waves; oftentimes they also are devoured by certain sea monsters, that are frequent in those seas. Consider whether this hard usage of the poor creatures be consistent with the precepts which God commands concerning charity to our neighbor, by those that cast them so undeservedly into the dangers of a cruel death, causing them to perish without any remorse or pity, or allowing them the benefit of the Sacraments, or the knowledge of Religion; it being impossible for them to live any time under the water; and this death is so much the more painful, by reason that by the coarctation of the breast, while the lungs strive to do their office, the vital parts are so afflicted that they die vomiting the blood out of their mouths.

(Continued)

Their hair also, which is by nature black, is hereby changed and made of the same color with that of the sea Wolves; their bodies are also so besprinkled with the froth of the sea, that they appear rather like monsters than men.

 Can the sentiments expressed by Vasco Núñez be reconciled with the treatment accorded to the Indians as described by Las Casas? Which selection do you think better describes the behavior of the Spaniards in the Americas? Compare the treatment of the Indians described here with the treatment of African slaves described in the selection on p. 373.

Sources: Gonzalo Fernández de Ovieda, *Historia General y Natural de las Indias.* From *The Age of Reconnaissance* by J.H. Parry (International Thomson Publishing, 1969), p. 233–234. Bartolomé de Las Casas, *The Tears of the Indians.* From *The Tears of the Indians,* Bartolome de Las Casas. Copyright © 1970 by The John Lilburne Company Publishers.

and eventually the Portuguese to import African slaves to replace the Indians in the sugar fields.

The Competition Intensifies

The success of the Spanish and the Portuguese in exploiting the riches of the Americas soon attracted competition from other European states. The Dutch formed the Dutch West India Company in 1621, but although it made some inroads in Brazil and the Caribbean (see Map 14.3), the company's profits were never large enough to cover its expenditures. Dutch settlements were also established in North America. The colony of New Netherland stretched from the mouth of the Hudson River as far north as present-day Albany, New York.

By the second half of the seventeenth century, however, the Dutch commercial empire in the Americas had begun to decline as years of rivalry and warfare with the English and French took their toll. In 1664, the English seized New Netherland and renamed it New York, and the Dutch West India Company soon went bankrupt. In 1663, Canada became the property of the French crown and was administered as a French province. But the French never provided adequate men or money for their North American possessions and, by the early eighteenth century, had begun to cede some of them to the English.

The English, meanwhile, had proceeded to create a colonial empire along the Atlantic seaboard of North America. Although their early efforts did not lead to quick profits, the desire to escape from religious oppression combined with economic interests could result in successful colonization, as the Massachusetts Bay Company demonstrated. The Massachusetts colony had only 4,000 settlers in its early years, but by 1660, their numbers had swelled to 40,000.

Christopher Columbus: Hero or Villain?

For centuries, Christopher Columbus has generally been viewed in a positive light. By discovering the Western Hemisphere, he opened up the world and laid the foundations for the modern global economy. Recently, however, some historians have begun to challenge the image of Columbus as a heroic figure and view him instead as a symbol of European colonial repression and a prime mover in the virtual extinction of the peoples and cultures of the Americas (see the comparative essay "The Columbian Exchange" on p. 368).

Certainly, they have a point. As we have seen, the immediate consequences of Columbus's voyages were tragic for countless peoples. Columbus himself viewed the indigenous peoples that he encountered with condescension, describing them as naïve innocents who could be exploited to increase the wealth and power of Spain. As a consequence, his men frequently treated the local population brutally.

But is it fair to blame Columbus for possessing many of the character traits and prejudices common to his era? To do so is to demand that an individual transcend the limitations of his time and adopt the values of a future generation. Perhaps it is better to note simply that Columbus and his contemporaries showed relatively little understanding and sympathy for the cultural values of peoples who lived beyond the borders of their own civilization, a limitation that would probably apply to one degree or another to all generations, including our own. Whether Columbus was a hero or a villain will remain a matter of debate. That he and his contemporaries played a key role in the emergence of the modern world is a matter on which there can be no doubt.

The Columbian Exchange

In the Western world, the discovery of the Americas has traditionally been viewed in a largely positive sense, as the first step in a process that expanded the global trade network and eventually led to increased economic well-being and the spread of civilization throughout the world. In recent years, however, that view has come under sharp attack from some observers, who point out that for the peoples of the Americas, the primary legacy of the European conquest was not improved living standards but harsh colonial exploitation and the spread of pestilential diseases that devastated local populations.

Certainly, the record of the European conquistadors leaves much to be desired, and the voyages of Columbus were not of universal benefit to his contemporaries or to later generations. They not only resulted in the destruction of vibrant civilizations in the Americas but also led ultimately to the enslavement of millions of Africans.

But to focus solely on the evils committed in the name of exploration and civilization misses a larger point and obscures the long-term ramifications of the Age of Exploration. The age of European expansion that began with Prince Henry the Navigator and Christopher Columbus was only the latest in a series of population movements that included the spread of nomadic peoples across Central Asia and the expansion of Islam out of the Middle East. In fact, the migration of peoples in search of a better livelihood has been a central theme since the dawn of prehistory. Virtually all of the migrations involved acts of unimaginable cruelty and the forcible displacement of peoples and societies.

In retrospect, it seems clear that the consequences of such broad population movements are too complex to be summed up in moral or ideological simplifications. The Mongol invasions and the expansion of Islam are two examples of movements that brought benefits as well as costs for the affected peoples. By the same token, the European conquest of the Americas not only brought the destruction of cultures and dangerous new diseases but also initiated an exchange of plant and animal species that has been beneficial for peoples throughout the globe. The introduction of the horse, the cow, and various grain crops vastly increased food production in the Americas. The cultivation of corn, manioc, and the potato, all of them products of the Western Hemisphere, has had the same effect in Asia, Africa, and Europe. The **Columbian**

Collections of the Library of Congress, Washington, DC

Massacre of the Indians. This sixteenth-century engraving is an imaginative treatment of what was probably an all-too-common occurrence as the Spanish attempted to enslave the American peoples and convert them to Christianity.

Exchange, as it is sometimes called, has had far-reaching consequences that transcend facile moral judgments.

The opening of the Americas had other long-term ramifications as well. The importation of vast amounts of gold and silver fueled a price revolution that for years distorted the Spanish economy. At the same time, the increase in liquid capital was a crucial factor in the growth of commercial capitalism that set the stage for the global economy of the modern era. Some have even suggested that the precious metals that flowed into European treasuries may have helped finance the Industrial Revolution (see Chapter 19).

Viewed in that context, the Columbian Exchange, whatever its moral failings, ultimately brought benefits to peoples throughout the world. For some, the costs were high, and it can be argued that the indigenous peoples of the Americas might have better managed the transformation on their own. But the "iron law" of history operates at its own speed and does not wait for laggards. For good or ill, the Columbian Exchange marks a major stage in the transition between the traditional and the modern world.

Q *How can the costs and benefits of the Columbian Exchange be measured? What standards would you apply in attempting to measure them?*

Africa in Transition

 FOCUS QUESTION: What were the main features of the African slave trade, and what effects did European participation have on traditional African practices?

Although the primary objective of the Portuguese in rounding the Cape of Good Hope was to find a sea route to the Spice Islands, they soon discovered that profits were to be made en route, along the eastern coast of Africa.

Europeans in Africa

In the early sixteenth century, a Portuguese fleet seized a number of East African port cities, including Kilwa, Sofala, and Mombasa, and built forts along the coast in an effort to control the trade in the area (see Map 14.2 on p. 360). Above all, the Portuguese wanted to monopolize the trade in gold, which was mined by Bantu workers in the hills and then shipped to Sofala on the coast (see Chapter 8). For centuries, the gold trade had been monopolized by local Bantu-speaking Shona peoples at Zimbabwe. In the fifteenth century, it had come under the control of a Shona dynasty known as the Mwene Mutapa (MWAY-nay moo-TAH-puh). At first, the Mwene Mutapa found the Europeans useful as an ally against local rivals, but by the end of the sixteenth century, the Portuguese had forced the local ruler to grant them large tracts of land. The Portuguese lacked the personnel, the capital, and the expertise to dominate the local trade, however, and in the late seventeenth century, a vassal of the Mwene Mutapa succeeded in driving them from the plateau.

The first Europeans to settle in southern Africa were the Dutch. In 1652, the Dutch set up a way station at the Cape of Good Hope to serve as a base for their fleets en route to the East Indies. Eventually, the settlement developed into a permanent colony as Dutch farmers, known as **Boers** (BOORS or BORS) and speaking a Dutch dialect that evolved into Afrikaans, began to settle outside the city of Cape Town. With its temperate climate and absence of tropical diseases, the territory was practically the only land south of the Sahara that the Europeans had found suitable for habitation.

The Slave Trade

The European exploration of the African coastline had little apparent significance for most peoples living in the interior of the continent, except for a few who engaged in direct or indirect trade with the foreigners. But for peoples living on or near the coast, the impact was often great indeed. As the trade in slaves increased during the sixteenth through the eighteenth centuries, thousands, and then millions, were removed from their homes and forcibly exported to plantations in the Western Hemisphere.

THE ARRIVAL OF THE EUROPEANS As we saw in Chapter 8, there were different forms of slavery in Africa before the arrival of the Europeans. For centuries, slaves—often captives seized in battle—had been used in many African societies as agricultural laborers or as household servants. After the expansion of Islam south of the Sahara in the eighth century, a vigorous traffic in slaves developed, as Arab merchants traded for slaves to be transported to the Middle East. Slavery also existed in many European countries, where a few slaves from Africa or Slavic-speaking peoples captured in war in the regions near the Black Sea (the English word *slave* derives from "Slav") were used for domestic purposes or as agricultural workers.

With the arrival of the Europeans in the fifteenth century, the African slave trade changed dramatically, although the shift did not occur immediately. At first, the Portuguese simply replaced European slaves with African ones. But the discovery of the Americas in the 1490s and the planting of sugarcane in South America and the islands of the Caribbean changed the situation. Cane sugar was native to Indonesia and had first been introduced to Europeans from the Middle East during the Crusades. But when the Ottoman Empire seized much of the eastern Mediterranean (see Chapter 16), the Europeans needed to seek out new areas suitable for cultivation.

The primary impetus to the sugar industry came from the colonization of the Americas. During the sixteenth century, plantations were established along the eastern coast of Brazil and on several Caribbean islands. Because the cultivation of cane sugar is an arduous process demanding large quantities of labor, the new plantations required more workers than could be provided by the local Indian population, many of whom had died of diseases as described earlier. Since the climate and soil of much of West Africa were not especially conducive to the cultivation of sugar, African slaves began to be shipped to Brazil and the Caribbean to work on the plantations. The first were sent from Portugal, but in 1518, a Spanish ship carried the first boatload of African slaves directly from Africa to the Americas.

GROWTH OF THE SLAVE TRADE During the next two centuries, the trade in slaves increased by massive proportions. An estimated 275,000 enslaved Africans were exported to other countries during the sixteenth century, with 2,000 going annually to the Americas alone. The total climbed to over a million during the next century and jumped to 6 million in the eighteenth century, when the trade spread from West and Central Africa to East Africa. It has been estimated that altogether as many as

A Sugar Plantation. To meet the growing European demand for sugar in the sixteenth century, sugar plantations were established in suitable areas throughout South America and the Caribbean islands. Shown here is a plantation established by the French on the island of Hispaniola. The backbreaking nature of the work is evident, as slaves imported from Africa cut the sugarcane and bring it to the mill for crushing and transformation into raw sugar. The inset shows a contemporary sugar plantation on the island of St. Kitts.

10 million African slaves were transported to the Americas between the early sixteenth and the late nineteenth centuries (see Map 14.5). As many as 2 million were exported to other areas during the same period.

THE MIDDLE PASSAGE   One reason for these astonishing numbers was the tragically high death rate. In what is often called the **Middle Passage**, the arduous voyage from Africa to the Americas, losses were frequently appalling. Although figures on the number of slaves who died on the journey are almost entirely speculative, during the first shipments, up to one-third may have died of disease or malnourishment. Even among crew members, mortality rates were sometimes as high as one in four. Later merchants became more efficient and reduced losses to about 10 percent. Still, the future slaves were treated inhumanely, chained together in the holds of ships reeking with the stench of human waste and diseases carried by vermin.

Ironically, African slaves who survived the brutal voyage fared somewhat better than whites after their arrival. Mortality rates for Europeans in the West Indies were ten to twenty times higher than in Europe, and death rates for new arrivals in the islands averaged more than 125 per 1,000 annually. But the figure for Africans, many of whom had developed at least a partial immunity to yellow fever, was only about 30 per 1,000.

The reason for these staggering death rates was clearly more than maltreatment, although that was certainly a factor. As we have seen, the transmission of diseases from one continent to another brought high death rates among those lacking immunity. African slaves were somewhat less susceptible to European diseases than the American Indian populations. Indeed, they seem to have possessed a degree of immunity, perhaps because their ancestors had developed antibodies to diseases common to the Old World from centuries of contact via the trans-Saharan trade. The Africans would not have had immunity to native American diseases, however.

SOURCES OF SLAVES   Slaves were obtained by traditional means. When Europeans first began to take part in the slave trade, they would normally purchase slaves from local African merchants at the infamous slave markets in exchange for gold, guns, or other European manufactured goods such as textiles or copper or iron utensils. At first, local slave traders obtained their supply from immediately surrounding regions, but as demand increased, they had to move farther inland to locate their victims. A few local rulers became concerned about the

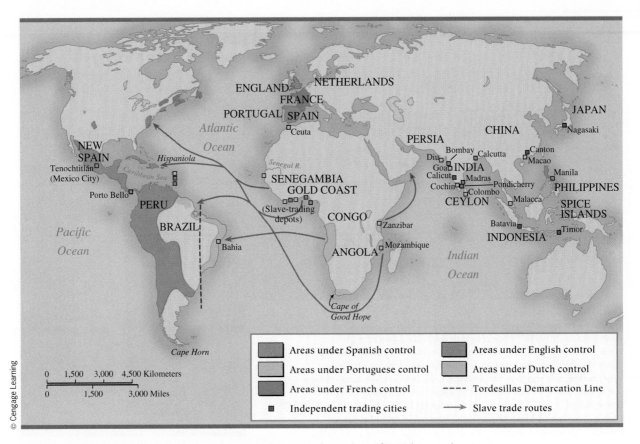

MAP 14.5 **The Slave Trade.** Beginning in the sixteenth century, the trade in African slaves to the Americas became a major source of profit for European merchants. This map traces the routes taken by slave-trading ships, as well as the territories and ports of call of European powers in the seventeenth century.

Q *What were the major destinations for the slave trade?*

impact of the slave trade on their societies. In a letter to the king of Portugal in 1526, King Afonso of Kongo complained that "so great, Sire, is the corruption and licentiousness that our country is being completely depopulated."[9] More frequently, however, local monarchs viewed the slave trade as a source of income, and many launched forays against defenseless villages in search of victims (see the box on p. 373).

THE EFFECTS OF THE SLAVE TRADE The effects of the slave trade varied from area to area. It might be assumed that the practice would have led to the depopulation of vast areas of the continent. This did occur in some areas, notably in modern Angola, south of the mouth of the Congo River, and in thinly populated areas in East Africa, but it was less true in West Africa. There high birthrates were often able to counterbalance the loss of able-bodied adults, and the introduction of new crops from

the Western Hemisphere, such as maize, peanuts, and manioc, led to an increase in food production that made it possible to support a larger population. One of the many cruel ironies of history is that while the institution of slavery was a tragedy for many, it benefited others.

Still, there is no denying that from a moral point of view, the slave trade represented a tragic loss for millions of Africans, for families as well as individuals. As many as 20 percent of those sold to European slavers were children, a statistic that may be partly explained by the fact that many European countries had enacted regulations that permitted more children than adults to be transported aboard the ships.

How did Europeans justify cruelty of such epidemic proportions? Some rationalized that slave traders were only carrying on a tradition that had existed for centuries throughout the Mediterranean and African world. In fact, African intermediaries were active in the process and were often able to dictate the price, volume, and availability of

Gateway to Slavery. Of the 12 million slaves shipped from Africa to other parts of the world, some passed through this doorway (right) on Gorée (GOR-ay) (left), a small island off the coast of Senegal, near Cape Verde. Beginning in the sixteenth century, European traders shipped Africans from this region to the Americas to be used as slave labor on sugar plantations. Some victims were kept in a prison on the island, which was first occupied by the Portuguese and later by the Dutch, the British, and the French. The sign by the doorway reads, "From this door, they would embark on a voyage with no return, eyes fixed on an infinity of suffering."

slaves to European purchasers. Other Europeans eased their consciences by noting that slaves would now be exposed to the Christian faith.

Political and Social Structures in a Changing Continent

Of course, the Western economic penetration of Africa had other dislocating effects. The importation of manufactured goods from Europe undermined the foundations of local cottage industry and impoverished countless families. The introduction of firearms intensified political instability and civil strife. As the European demand for slaves increased, African slave traders began to use their newly purchased guns to raid neighboring villages in search of captives, initiating a chain of violence that created a climate of fear and insecurity. Old polities were undermined, and new regimes ruled by rapacious "merchant princes" began to proliferate on the coast.

At the same time, the impact of the Europeans should not be exaggerated. Only in a few isolated areas, such as South Africa and Mozambique, were permanent European settlements established. Elsewhere, at the insistence of African rulers and merchants, European influence generally did not penetrate beyond the coastal regions. Nevertheless, inland areas were often affected by events taking place elsewhere. In the western Sahara, for example, the diversion of trade routes toward the coast led to the weakening of the old Songhai trading empire and its eventual conquest by a vigorous new Moroccan dynasty in the late sixteenth century.

European influence had a more direct impact along the coast of West Africa, but no European colonies were established there before 1800. Most of the numerous African states in the area from Cape Verde to the delta of the Niger River were sufficiently strong to resist Western encroachments. Some, like the powerful Ashanti kingdom, established in 1680 on the Gold Coast, profited substantially from the rise in seaborne commerce. Some states, particularly along the so-called Slave Coast, in what is now Benin and Togo, or in the densely populated Niger River delta, took an active part in the slave trade. The demands of slavery and the temptations to profit, however, also contributed to the increase in conflict among the states in the area.

A Slave Market in Africa

FAMILY & SOCIETY

Traffic in slaves had been carried on in Africa since the kingdom of the pharaohs in ancient Egypt. But the slave trade increased dramatically after the arrival of the Europeans. The following passage by a Dutch observer describes a slave market in Africa and the conditions on the ships that carried the slaves to the Americas.

Slavery in Africa: A Firsthand Report

Not a few in our country fondly imagine that parents here sell their children, men their wives, and one brother the other. But those who think so deceive themselves, for this never happens on any other account but that of necessity, or some great crime; most of the slaves that are offered to us are prisoners of war, who are sold by the victors as their booty.

When these slaves come to Fida, they are put in prison all together; and when we treat concerning buying them, they are brought out into a large plain. There, by our surgeons, whose province it is, they are thoroughly examined, even to the smallest member, and that naked too, both men and women, without the least distinction or modesty. Those that are approved as good are set on one side; and the lame or faulty are set by as invalids. . . .

The invalids and the maimed being thrown out, . . . the remainder are numbered, and it is entered who delivered them. In the meanwhile, a burning iron, with the arms or name of the companies, lies in the fire, with which ours are marked on the breast. This is done that we may distinguish them from the slaves of the English, French, or others (which are also marked with their mark), and to prevent the Negroes exchanging them for worse, at which they have a good hand.

I doubt not but this trade seems very barbarous to you, but since it is followed by mere necessity, it must go on; but we take all possible care that they are not burned too hard, especially the women, who are more tender than the men.

When we have agreed with the owners of the slaves, they are returned to their prison. There from that time forward they are kept at our charge, costing us two pence a day a slave; which serves to subsist them, like our criminals, on bread and water. To save charges, we send them on board our ships at the very first opportunity, before which their masters strip them of all they have on their backs so that they come aboard stark naked, women as well as men. In this condition they are obliged to continue, if the master of the ship is not so charitable (which he commonly is) as to bestow something on them to cover their nakedness.

You would really wonder to see how these slaves live on board, for though their number sometimes amounts to six or seven hundred, yet by the careful management of our masters of ships, they are so regulated that it seems incredible. And in this particular our nation exceeds all other Europeans, for the French, Portuguese and English slave ships are always foul and stinking; on the contrary, ours are for the most part clean and neat.

The slaves are fed three times a day with indifferent good victuals, and much better than they eat in their own country. Their lodging place is divided into two parts, one of which is appointed for the men, the other for the women, each sex being kept apart. Here they lie as close together as it is possible for them to be crowded.

We are sometimes sufficiently plagued with a parcel of slaves which come from a far inland country who very innocently persuade one another that we buy them only to fatten and afterward eat them as a delicacy. When we are so unhappy as to be pestered with many of this sort, they resolve and agree together (and bring over the rest to their party) to run away from the ship, kill the Europeans, and set the vessel ashore, by which means they design to free themselves from being our food.

I have twice met with this misfortune; and the first time proved very unlucky to me, I not in the least suspecting it, but the uproar was quashed by the master of the ship and myself by causing the abettor to be shot through the head, after which all was quiet.

Q *What is the author's overall point of view with respect to the institution of slavery? Does he justify the practice? How does he think Dutch behavior compares with that of other European countries?*

Source: From *The Great Travelers*, vol. I, Milton Rugoff, ed. Copyright © 1960 by Simon & Schuster. Used with permission of Milton Rugoff.

Manioc, Food for the Millions. One of the plants native to the Americas that European adventurers took back to the Old World was manioc (also known as cassava or yuca). A tuber like the potato, manioc is a prolific crop that grows well in poor, dry soils, but it lacks the high nutrient value of grain crops such as wheat and rice and for that reason never became popular in Europe (except as a source of tapioca). It was introduced to Africa in the seventeenth century. Because it flourishes in dry climates and can be preserved easily for consumption at a later date, it eventually became a staple food for up to one-third of the population of that continent. Shown at the left is a manioc plant growing in East Africa. On the right, a Brazilian farmer on the Amazon River sifts peeled lengths of manioc into fine grains that will be dried into flour.

This was especially true in the region of the Congo River, where Portuguese activities eventually led to the splintering of the Kongo Empire and two centuries of strife among its successor states. Similarly, in East Africa, Portuguese activities led to the decline and eventual collapse of the Mwene Mutapa. Northward along the coast, in present-day Kenya and Tanzania, African rulers, assisted by Arab forces from the Arabian peninsula, expelled the Portuguese from Mombasa in 1728. Swahili culture now regained some of its earlier dynamism, but with much shipping now diverted to the route around the Cape of Good Hope, the area never completely recovered and was increasingly dependent on the export of slaves and ivory obtained through contacts with African states in the interior.

CHRONOLOGY	The Penetration of Africa
Life of Prince Henry the Navigator	1394–1460
Portuguese ships reach the Senegal River	1441
Bartolomeu Dias sails around the tip of Africa	1487
First boatload of slaves to the Americas	1518
Dutch way station established at Cape of Good Hope	1652
Ashanti kingdom established in West Africa	1680
Portuguese expelled from Mombasa	1728

Southeast Asia in the Era of the Spice Trade

Q FOCUS QUESTION: What were the main characteristics of Southeast Asian societies, and how were they affected by the coming of Islam and the Europeans?

As noted earlier, Southeast Asia would be affected in various ways by the expansion of the global trade network that began to accelerate in the fifteenth century. Not only did the Muslim faith begin to make inroads in the region, but the seizure of Malacca by the Portuguese in 1511 inaugurated a period of conflict among various European competitors for control of the spice trade. At first, the rulers of most of the local states were able to fend off these challenges and maintain their independence. As we shall see in a later chapter, however, the reprieve was only temporary.

The Arrival of the West

As we have seen, the Spanish soon followed the Portuguese into Southeast Asia. By the seventeenth century, the Dutch, English, and French had begun to join the scramble for rights to the lucrative spice trade.

Within a short time, the Dutch, through the well-financed Dutch East India Company (Vereenigde Oost-Indische Compagnie, or VOC), succeeded in elbowing

© William J. Duiker

© William J. Duiker

COMPARATIVE ILLUSTRATION

Bringing Lumber to Java. Long before the Europeans arrived, a brisk trade was taking place throughout the Indonesian islands and the South China Sea. Many of the goods were carried on sturdy boats—called pinisi—that were manned by the Bugi (BOO-gih), a trading people who lived mainly in the eastern islands. The trade continues today, as these cargo ships in the harbor of Jakarta attest. The Bugi were also feared as pirates, giving rise to the once-familiar parental admonition to children, "Don't let the bogyman get you!" The bas-relief in the inset from the temple of Borobudur, is a rare example of a sailing vessel in the ninth century C.E.

Q *What role did Southeast Asia play in the global trade network?*

their rivals out of the spice trade and began to consolidate their control over the area. On the island of Java, where they established a fort at Batavia (buh-TAY-vee-uh) (today's Jakarta) in 1619 (see the illustration on p. 353), the Dutch found it necessary to bring the inland regions under their control to protect their position. Rather than establishing a formal colony, however, they tried to rule through the local aristocracy. On Java and Sumatra, the VOC established pepper plantations, which became the source of massive profits for Dutch merchants in Amsterdam. Elsewhere they attempted to monopolize the clove trade by limiting cultivation of the crop to one island. By the end of the eighteenth century, the Dutch had succeeded in bringing almost the entire Indonesian archipelago under their control.

Competition among the European naval powers for territory and influence continued to intensify throughout the region, however, and prospects for the future were ominous. In island groups scattered throughout the Pacific Ocean, local rulers were already finding it difficult to resist the growing European presence. The results were sometimes tragic, as indigenous cultures were overwhelmed under the impact of Western material civilization, which often left a sense of rootlessness and psychic stress in its wake.

The arrival of the Europeans had somewhat less impact in the Indian subcontinent and in mainland Southeast Asia, where cohesive monarchies in Burma, Thailand, and Vietnam resisted foreign encroachment. In addition, the coveted spices did not thrive on the mainland, so the Europeans' efforts were far less determined

An Exchange of Royal Correspondence

INTERACTION & EXCHANGE

In 1681, King Louis XIV of France wrote a letter to the "king of Tonkin" (the Trinh family head, then acting as viceroy to the Vietnamese ruler) requesting permission for Christian missionaries to proselytize in Vietnam. The latter politely declined the request on the grounds that such activity was prohibited by ancient custom. In fact, Christian missionaries had been active in Vietnam for years, and their intervention in local politics had aroused the anger of the court in Hanoi.

A Letter to the King of Tonkin from Louis XIV

Most high, most excellent, most mighty, and most magnanimous Prince, our very dear and good friend, may it please God to increase your greatness with a happy end!

We hear from our subjects who were in your Realm what protection you accorded them. We appreciate this all the more since we have for you all the esteem that one can have for a prince as illustrious through his military valor as he is commendable for the justice which he exercises in his Realm. We have even been informed that you have not been satisfied to extend this general protection to our subjects but, in particular, that you gave effective proofs of it to Messrs. Deydier and de Bourges. We would have wished that they might have been able to recognize all the favors they received from you by having presents worthy of you offered you; but since the war which we have had for several years, in which all of Europe had banded together against us, prevented our vessels from going to the Indies, at the present time, when we are at peace after having gained many victories and expanded our Realm through the conquest of several important places, we have immediately given orders to the Royal Company to establish itself in your kingdom as soon as possible, and have commanded Messrs. Deydier and de Bourges to remain with you in order to maintain a good relationship between our subjects and yours, also to warn us on occasions that might present themselves when we might be able to give you proofs of our esteem and of our wish to concur with your satisfaction as well as with your best interests.

By way of initial proof, we have given orders to have brought to you some presents which we believe might be agreeable to you. But the one thing in the world which we desire most, both for you and for your Realm, would be to obtain for your subjects who have already embraced the law of the only true God of heaven and earth, the freedom to profess it, since this law is the highest, the noblest, the most sacred, and especially the most suitable to have kings reign absolutely over the people.

We are even quite convinced that, if you knew the truths and the maxims which it teaches, you would give first of all to your subjects the glorious example of embracing it. We wish you this incomparable blessing together with a long and happy reign, and we pray God that it may please Him to augment your greatness with the happiest of endings.

Written at Saint-Germain-en-Laye, the 10th day of January, 1681,

Your very dear and good friend,
Louis

Answer from the King of Tonkin to Louis XIV

The King of Tonkin sends to the King of France a letter to express to him his best sentiments, saying that he was happy to learn that fidelity is a durable good of man and that justice is the most important of things. Consequently practicing of fidelity and justice cannot but yield good results. Indeed, though France and our Kingdom differ as to mountains, rivers, and boundaries, if fidelity and justice reign among our villages, our conduct will express all of our good feelings and contain precious gifts. Your communication, which comes from a country which is a thousand leagues away, and which proceeds from the heart as a testimony of your sincerity, merits repeated consideration and infinite praise. Politeness toward strangers is nothing unusual in our country. There is not a stranger who is not well received by us. How then could we refuse a man from France, which is the most celebrated among the kingdoms of the world and which for love of us wishes to frequent us and bring us merchandise? These feelings of fidelity and justice are truly worthy to be applauded. As regards your wish that

(Continued)

we should cooperate in propagating your religion, we do not dare to permit it, for there is an ancient custom, introduced by edicts, which formally forbids it. Now, edicts are promulgated only to be carried out faithfully; without fidelity nothing is stable. How could we disdain a well-established custom to satisfy a private friendship? . . .

We beg you to understand well that this is our communication concerning our mutual acquaintance. This then is my letter. We send you herewith a modest gift, which we offer you with a glad heart.

This letter was written at the beginning of winter and on a beautiful day.

Q *Compare the king of Tonkin's response to Louis XIV with the answer that the Mongol emperor Kuyuk Khan gave to the pope in 1244 (see p. 263). Which do you think was more conciliatory?*

Source: From *The World of Southeast Asia: Selected Historical Readings* by Harry J. Benda and John A. Larkin, eds. Copyright © 1967 by Harper & Row, Publishers.

---

there. The Portuguese did establish limited trade relations with several mainland states, including the Thai kingdom at Ayuthaya (ah-yoo-TY-yuh), Burma, Vietnam, and the remnants of the old Angkor kingdom in Cambodia. By the early seventeenth century, other nations had followed and had begun to compete actively for trade and missionary privileges.

In Vietnam, the arrival of Western merchants and missionaries in the mid-seventeenth century coincided with a period of internal conflict among ruling groups in the country. The European powers characteristically began to intervene in local politics, with the Portuguese and the Dutch supporting rival factions. By the end of the century, when it became clear that economic opportunities were limited, most European states abandoned their factories (trading stations) in the area. French missionaries attempted to remain, but were hampered by the local authorities, who viewed the Catholic insistence that converts give their primary loyalty to the pope as a threat to the legal status and prestige of the Vietnamese emperor (see the box on p. 376).

State and Society in Precolonial Southeast Asia

Between 1400 and 1800, Southeast Asia experienced the last flowering of traditional culture before the advent of European rule in the nineteenth century. Although the coming of the Europeans had an immediate and direct impact in some areas, notably the Philippines and parts of the Malay world, in most areas Western influence was still relatively limited.

Nevertheless, Southeast Asian societies were changing in subtle ways—in trade patterns, means of livelihood,

and religious beliefs. In some ways, these changes accentuated the differences between individual states in the region. Yet beneath these differences was an underlying commonality of life for most people. Despite the diversity of cultures and religious beliefs, Southeast Asians were in most respects closer to each other than to peoples outside the region. For the most part, the states and peoples of Southeast Asia were still in control of their own destiny.

RELIGION AND KINGSHIP During the early modern era, both Buddhism and Islam became well established in Southeast Asia, and Christianity began to attract some converts, especially in the Philippines (see the comparative illustration on p. 378). Buddhism was dominant in lowland areas on the mainland, from Burma to Vietnam. At first, Muslim influence was felt mainly on the Malay peninsula and along the northern coast of Java and Sumatra, where local traders regularly encountered Muslim merchants from foreign lands.

CHRONOLOGY	The Spice Trade	
Vasco da Gama lands at Calicut in southwestern India	1498
Albuquerque establishes base at Goa	1510
Portuguese seize Malacca	1511
Portuguese ships land in southern China	1514
Magellan's voyage around the world	1519–1522
English East India Company established	1600
Dutch East India Company established	1602
English arrive at Surat in northwestern India	1608
Dutch fort established at Batavia	1619

COMPARATIVE ILLUSTRATION

RELIGION & PHILOSOPHY

The Face of Christianity in America and Asia. As Europeans began to spread through the Americas and Asia in the sixteenth and seventeenth centuries, the churches that they built reflected the styles that had become popular in their own countries. The photograph on the left shows a Baroque cathedral in Mexico City, the headquarters of Spanish rule in Central America. It was erected on the site of the Aztec temple to the sun god at Tenochtitlán, using materials from the dismantled Aztec pyramids. The Dutch preferred a less ornate approach, as seen in the rose-colored church in Malacca shown at the right, erected after their takeover of that trading port in 1641.

Q *How did the spread of Christianity in America and Asia in the sixteenth and seventeenth centuries compare with the expansion of Islam in earlier times?*

Buddhism and Islam also helped shape Southeast Asian political institutions. As the political systems began to mature, they evolved into four main types: Buddhist kings, Javanese kings, Islamic sultans, and Vietnamese emperors (for Vietnam, which was strongly influenced by China, see Chapter 11). In each case, institutions and concepts imported from abroad were adapted to local circumstances.

The Buddhist style of kingship took shape between the eleventh and the fifteenth centuries. It became the predominant political system in the mainland Buddhist states—Burma, Ayuthaya, Laos, and Cambodia. Its dominant feature was the godlike character of the monarch, who was considered by virtue of his *karma* to be innately superior to other human beings and served as a link between humans and the cosmos.

The Javanese model was a blend of Buddhist and Islamic political traditions. Like their Buddhist counterparts, Javanese monarchs possessed a sacred quality and maintained the balance between the sacred and the material world.

The Islamic model was found mainly on the Malay peninsula and along the coast of the Indonesian archipelago. In this pattern, the head of state was a sultan, who was viewed as a mortal, although he still possessed some magical qualities.

THE ECONOMY During the early period of European penetration, the economy of most Southeast Asian societies was still based on agriculture, although by the sixteenth century, commerce was growing, especially in the cities that were beginning to proliferate along the coasts or on navigable rivers. In part, this was because agriculture itself was becoming more commercialized as cash crops like sugar and spices replaced subsistence farming in rice or other cereals in some areas.

Regional and interregional trade were already expanding before the coming of the Europeans. Southeast Asia's location enabled it to become a focal point in a widespread trading network. Spices, of course, were the mainstay of the interregional trade, but other products were exchanged as well. Tin (mined in Malaya since the tenth century), copper, gold, tropical fruits and other agricultural products, cloth, gems, and luxury goods were exported in exchange for manufactured goods, ceramics, and high-quality textiles such as silk from China.

Society

In general, Southeast Asians probably enjoyed a higher living standard than most of their contemporaries elsewhere in Asia. Although most of the population was poor by modern Western standards, hunger was not widespread. Several factors help explain this relative prosperity. First, most of Southeast Asia has been blessed by a salubrious climate. The uniformly high temperatures and the abundant rainfall enable as many as two or even three crops to be grown each year. Second, although the soil in some areas is poor, the alluvial deltas on the mainland are fertile, and the volcanoes of Indonesia periodically spew forth rich volcanic ash that renews the soil of Sumatra and Java. Finally, with some exceptions, most of Southeast Asia was relatively thinly populated.

Social institutions tended to be fairly homogeneous throughout Southeast Asia. Compared with China and India, there was little social stratification, and the nuclear family predominated. In general, women fared better in the region than elsewhere in Asia. Daughters often had the same inheritance rights as sons, and family property was held jointly between husband and wife. Wives were often permitted to divorce their husbands, and monogamy was the rule rather than the exception. Although women were usually restricted to specialized work, such as making ceramics, weaving, or transplanting the rice seedlings into the main paddy fields, and rarely possessed legal rights equal to those of men, they enjoyed a comparatively high degree of freedom and status in most societies in the region and were sometimes involved in commerce.

CHAPTER SUMMARY

During the fifteenth century, the pace of international commerce increased dramatically. Chinese fleets visited the Indian Ocean while Muslim traders extended their activities into the Spice Islands and sub-Saharan West Africa. Then the Europeans burst onto the world scene. Beginning with the seemingly modest ventures of the Portuguese ships that sailed southward along the West African coast, the process accelerated with the epoch-making voyages of Christopher Columbus to the Americas and Vasco da Gama to the Indian Ocean in the 1490s. Soon a number of other European states had entered the fray, and by the end of the eighteenth century, they had created a global trade network dominated by Western ships and Western power that distributed foodstuffs, textile goods, spices, and precious minerals from one end of the globe to the other.

In less than three hundred years, the European Age of Exploration changed the face of the world. In some areas, such as the Americas and the Spice Islands, it led to the destruction of indigenous civilizations and the establishment of European colonies. In others, as in Africa, South Asia, and mainland Southeast Asia, it left local regimes intact but had a strong impact on local societies and regional trade patterns. In some areas, it led to an irreversible decline in traditional institutions and values, setting in motion a corrosive process that has not been reversed to this day.

At the time, many European observers viewed the process in a favorable light. Not only did it expand world trade and foster the exchange of new crops and discoveries between the Old and New Worlds, but it also introduced Christianity to "heathen peoples" around the globe. Many modern historians have been much more critical, concluding that European activities during the sixteenth and seventeenth centuries created a "tributary mode of production" based on European profits from unequal terms of trade that foreshadowed the exploitative relationship characteristic of the later colonial period. Other scholars have questioned

that contention, however, and argue that although Western commercial operations had a significant impact on global trade patterns, they did not—at least not before the nineteenth century—usher in an era of dominance over the rest of the world. Muslim merchants were long able to evade European efforts to eliminate them from the spice trade, and the trans-Saharan caravan trade was relatively unaffected by European merchant shipping along the West African coast. In the meantime, powerful empires continued to hold sway over the lands washed by the Muslim faith. Beyond the Himalayas, Chinese emperors in their new northern capital of Beijing retained proud dominion over all the vast territory of continental East Asia. We shall deal with these regions, and how they confronted the challenges of a changing world, in Chapters 16 and 17.

CHAPTER TIMELINE

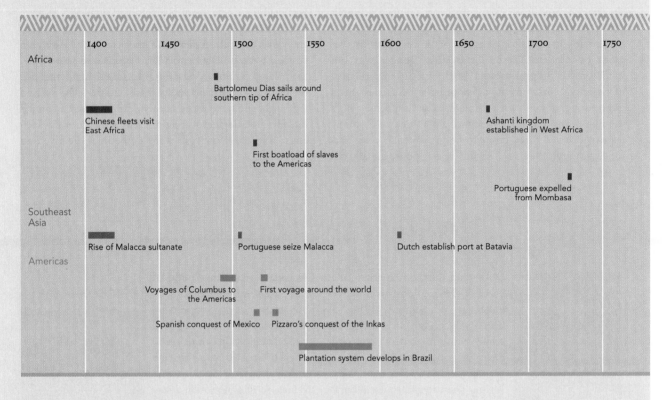

CHAPTER REVIEW

Upon Reflection

Q What were some of the key features of the Columbian Exchange, and what effects did they have on the world trade network?

Q How did the expansion of European power during the Age of Exploration compare with the expansion of the Islamic empires in the Middle East a few centuries earlier?

Q Why were the Spanish conquistadors able to complete their conquest of Latin America so quickly when their contemporaries failed to do so in Africa and Southeast Asia?

Key Terms

portolani (p. 358)
caravels (p. 359)
conquistadors (p. 362)
mestizos (p. 363)
mulattoes (p. 363)
viceroys (p. 363)
creoles (p. 363)
encomienda **system** (p. 364)
encomienda (p. 365)
Columbian Exchange (p. 368)
Boers (p. 369)
Middle Passage (p. 370)

Suggested Reading

EUROPEAN EXPANSION On the technological aspects of European expansion, see **F. Fernandez-Armesto, ed.,** *The Times Atlas of World Exploration* (New York, 1991), and **R. C. Smith,** *Vanguard of Empire: Ships of Exploration in the Age of Columbus* (Oxford, 1993). Also see **A. Pagden,** *Lords of All the World: Ideologies of Empire in Spain, Britain, and France, c. 1500–c. 1800* (New Haven, Conn., 1995). For an overview of the advances in map making that accompanied the Age of Exploration, see **T. Lester,** *The Fourth Part of the World: The Race to the Ends of the Earth, and the Epic Story of the Map That Gave America Its Name* (New York, 2009). Also see **A. Gurney,** *Compass: A Story of Exploration and Innovation* (New York, 2004), and **W. Bernstein's** impressive *A Splendid Exchange: How Trade Shaped the World* (New York, 2008).

COUNTRY-SPECIFIC STUDIES A gripping work on the conquistadors is **H. Thomas,** *Conquest: Montezuma, Cortés, and the Fall of Old Mexico* (New York, 1993). On the Dutch, see **J. I. Israel,** *Dutch Primacy in World Trade, 1585–1740* (Oxford, 1989). British activities are chronicled in **S. Sen,** *Empire of Free Trade: The East India Company and the Making of the Colonial Marketplace* (Philadelphia, 1998), and **Anthony Wild's** elegant work *The East India Company: Trade and Conquest from 1600* (New York, 2000).

THE SPICE TRADE The effects of European trade in Southeast Asia are discussed in **A. Reid,** *Southeast Asia in the Age of Commerce, 1450–1680* (New Haven, Conn., 1989). On the spice trade, see **A. Dalby,** *Dangerous Tastes: The Story of Spices* (Berkeley, Calif., 2000), and **J. Turner,** *Spice: The History of a Temptation* (New York, 2004).

THE SLAVE TRADE On the African slave trade, see **P. E. Lovejoy,** *Transformations in Slavery: A History of Slavery in Africa* (Cambridge, 1983), and **P. Manning,** *Slavery and African Life* (Cambridge, 1990). **H. Thomas,** *The Slave Trade* (New York, 1997), provides a useful overview.

WOMEN For a brief introduction to women's experiences during the Age of Exploration and global trade, see **S. Hughes** and **B. Hughes,** *Women in World History,* vol. 2 (Armonk, N.Y., 1997). The native American female experience with the European encounter is presented in **R. Gutierrez,** *When Jesus Came the Corn Mothers Went Away: Marriage, Sexuality, and Power in New Mexico, 1500–1846* (Stanford, Calif., 1991).

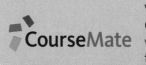

Visit the CourseMate website at www.cengagebrain.com for additional study tools and review materials for this chapter.

Europe Transformed:
Reform and State Building

A nineteenth-century engraving showing Martin Luther before the Diet of Worms

© bpk, Berlin/Art Resource, NY

CHAPTER OUTLINE
AND FOCUS QUESTIONS

The Reformation of the Sixteenth Century

Q What were the main tenets of Lutheranism and Calvinism, and how did they differ from each other and from Catholicism?

Europe in Crisis, 1560–1650

Q Why is the period between 1560 and 1650 in Europe considered an age of crisis?

Response to Crisis: The Practice of Absolutism

Q What was absolutism, and what were the main characteristics of the absolute monarchies that emerged in France, Prussia, Austria, and Russia?

England and Limited Monarchy

Q How and why did England avoid the path of absolutism?

The Flourishing of European Culture

Q How did the artistic and literary achievements of this era reflect the political and economic developments of the period?

CRITICAL THINKING

Q What was the relationship between European overseas expansion (as traced in Chapter 14) and political, economic, and social developments in Europe?

ON APRIL 18, 1521, A LOWLY MONK stood before the emperor and princes of Germany in the city of Worms (VAWRMZ). He had been called before this august gathering to answer charges of heresy, charges that could threaten his very life. The monk was confronted with a pile of his books and asked if he wished to defend them all or reject a part. Courageously, Martin Luther defended them all and asked to be shown where any part was in error on the basis of "Scripture and plain reason." The emperor was outraged by Luther's response and made his own position clear the next day: "Not only I, but you of this noble German nation, would be forever disgraced if by our negligence not only heresy but the very suspicion of heresy were to survive. After having heard yesterday the obstinate defense of Luther, I regret that I have so long delayed in proceeding against him and his false teaching. I will have no more to do with him." Luther's appearance at Worms set the stage for a serious challenge to the authority of the Catholic Church. This was by no means the first crisis in the church's 1,500-year history, but its consequences were more far-reaching than anyone at Worms in 1521 could have imagined.

After the disintegrative patterns of the fourteenth century, Europe began a remarkable recovery that encompassed a revival of arts and letters in the fifteenth century, known as the Renaissance, and a religious renaissance in the sixteenth century, known as the Reformation. The resulting religious division of Europe (Catholics versus Protestants) was instrumental in beginning a series of wars that dominated much of European history from 1560 to 1650 and exacerbated the economic and social crises that were besetting the region.

One of the responses to the crises of the seventeenth century was a search for order. The most general trend was an extension of monarchical power as a stablizing force. This development, which historians have called **absolutism** or *absolute monarchy*, was most evident in France during the flamboyant reign of Louis XIV, regarded by some as the perfect embodiment of an absolute monarch.

But absolutism was not the only response to the search for order in the seventeenth century. Other states, such as England, reacted very differently to domestic crises, and another system emerged in which monarchs were limited by the power of their representative assemblies. Absolute and limited monarchy were the two poles of seventeenth-century state building.

The Reformation of the Sixteenth Century

 FOCUS QUESTION: What were the main tenets of Lutheranism and Calvinism, and how did they differ from each other and from Catholicism?

The **Protestant Reformation** is the name given to the religious reform movement that divided the western Christian church into Catholic and Protestant groups. Although the Reformation began with Martin Luther in the early sixteenth century, several earlier developments had set the stage for religious change.

Background to the Reformation

Changes in the fifteenth century—the age of the Renaissance—helped prepare the way for the dramatic upheavals in sixteenth-century Europe.

THE GROWTH OF STATE POWER In the first half of the fifteenth century, European states had continued the disintegrative patterns of the previous century. In the second half of the fifteenth century, however, recovery had set in, and attempts had been made to reestablish the centralized power of monarchical governments. To characterize

the results, some historians have used the label "Renaissance states"; others have spoken of the "**new monarchies**," especially those of France, England, and Spain at the end of the fifteenth century (see Chapter 13).

What was new about these Renaissance monarchs was their concentration of royal authority, their attempts to suppress the nobility, their efforts to control the church in their lands, and their desire to obtain new sources of revenue in order to increase royal power and enhance the military forces at their disposal. Like the rulers of fifteenth-century Italian states, the Renaissance monarchs were often crafty men obsessed with the acquisition and expansion of political power. Of course, none of these characteristics was entirely new; a number of medieval monarchs, especially in the thirteenth century, had also exhibited them. Nevertheless, the Renaissance period marks a significant expansion of centralized royal authority.

No one gave better expression to the Renaissance preoccupation with political power than Niccolò Machiavelli (nee-koh-LOH mahk-ee-uh-VEL-ee) (1469–1527), an Italian who wrote *The Prince* (1513), one of the most influential works on political power in the Western world. Machiavelli's major concerns in *The Prince* were the acquisition, maintenance, and expansion of political power as the means to restore and maintain order. In the Middle Ages, many political theorists stressed the ethical side of a prince's activity—how a ruler ought to behave based on Christian moral principles. Machiavelli bluntly contradicted this approach: "For the gap between how people actually behave and how they ought to behave is so great that anyone who ignores everyday reality in order to live up to an ideal will soon discover he had been taught how to destroy himself, not how to preserve himself."[1] Machiavelli was among the first Western thinkers to abandon morality as the basis for the analysis of political activity. The same emphasis on the ends justifying the means, or on achieving results regardless of the methods employed, had in fact been expressed a thousand years earlier by a court official in India named Kautilya (kow-TIL-yuh) in his treatise on politics, the *Arthasastra* (ar-thuh-SAS-truh) (see Chapter 2).

SOCIAL CHANGES IN THE RENAISSANCE Social changes in the fifteenth century also helped to create an environment in which the Reformation of the sixteenth century could occur. After the severe economic reversals and social upheavals of the fourteenth century, the European economy gradually recovered as manufacturing and trade increased in volume.

As noted in Chapter 12, society in the Middle Ages was divided into three estates: the clergy, or First Estate, whose preeminence was grounded in the belief that people should be guided to spiritual ends; the nobility, or Second Estate, whose privileges rested on the principle that nobles provided security and justice for society; and the peasants and inhabitants of the towns and cities, the Third Estate. Although this social order continued into the Renaissance, some changes also became evident.

Throughout much of Europe, the landholding nobles faced declining real incomes during most of the fourteenth and fifteenth centuries. Many members of the old nobility survived, however, and new blood also infused their ranks. By 1500, the nobles, old and new, who constituted between 2 and 3 percent of the population in most countries, still dominated society, as they had done in the Middle Ages, holding important political posts and serving as advisers to the king.

Except in the heavily urban areas of northern Italy and Flanders, peasants made up the overwhelming mass of the Third Estate—they constituted 85 to 90 percent of the total European population. Serfdom had decreased as the manorial system continued to decline. Increasingly, the labor dues owed by peasants to their lord were converted into rents paid in money. By 1500, especially in western Europe, more and more peasants were becoming legally free. At the same time, peasants in many areas resented their social superiors and sought a greater share of the benefits coming from their labor. In the sixteenth century, the grievances of the peasants, especially in Germany, led many of them to support religious reform movements.

Inhabitants of towns and cities, originally merchants and artisans, constituted the remainder of the Third Estate. But by the fifteenth century, the Renaissance town or city had become more complex. At the top of urban society were the patricians, whose wealth from capitalistic enterprises in trade, industry, and banking enabled them to dominate their urban communities economically, socially, and politically. Below them were the petty burghers—the shopkeepers, artisans, guildmasters, and guildsmen—who were largely concerned with providing goods and services for local consumption. Below these two groups were the propertyless workers earning pitiful wages and the unemployed, living squalid and miserable lives. These poor city-dwellers made up 30 to 40 percent of the urban population. The pitiful conditions of the lower groups in urban society often led them to support calls for radical religious reform in the sixteenth century.

THE IMPACT OF PRINTING The Renaissance witnessed the development of printing, which made an immediate impact on European intellectual life and thought. Printing from hand-carved wooden blocks had been done in the West since the twelfth century and in China even before that. What was new in the fifteenth century in Europe was multiple printing with movable metal type. The development of printing from movable type was a gradual process that culminated sometime between 1445 and 1450; Johannes Gutenberg (yoh-HAH-nuss GOO-ten-bayrk)

of Mainz (MYNTS) played an important role in bringing the process to completion. Gutenberg's Bible, completed in 1455 or 1456, was the first true book produced from movable type.

By 1500, there were more than a thousand printers in Europe, who collectively had published almost 40,000 titles (between 8 and 10 million copies). Probably half of these books were religious—Bibles and biblical commentaries, books of devotion, and sermons.

The printing of books encouraged scholarly research and the desire to attain knowledge. Printing also stimulated the development of an ever-expanding lay reading public, a development that had an enormous impact on European society. Indeed, without the printing press, the new religious ideas of the Reformation would never have spread as rapidly as they did in the sixteenth century. Moreover, printing allowed European civilization to compete for the first time with the civilization of China.

PRELUDE TO REFORMATION During the second half of the fifteenth century, the new Classical learning of the Italian Renaissance spread to the European countries north of the Alps and spawned a movement called **Christian humanism** or **northern Renaissance humanism**, whose major goal was the reform of Christendom. The Christian humanists believed in the ability of human beings to reason and improve themselves and thought that through education in the sources of Classical, and especially Christian, antiquity, they could instill an inner piety or an inward religious feeling that would bring about a reform of the church and society. To change society, then, they believed they must first change the human beings who composed it.

The most influential of all the Christian humanists was Desiderius Erasmus (dez-i-DEER-ee-us i-RAZZ-mus) (1466–1536), who formulated and popularized the reform program of Christian humanism. He called his conception of religion "the philosophy of Christ," by which he meant that Christianity should be a guiding philosophy for the direction of daily life rather than the system of dogmatic beliefs and practices that the medieval church seemed to stress. No doubt his work helped prepare the way for the Reformation; as contemporaries proclaimed, "Erasmus laid the egg that Luther hatched."

CHURCH AND RELIGION ON THE EVE OF THE REFORMATION Corruption in the Catholic Church was another factor that encouraged people to want reform. Between 1450 and 1520, a series of popes—called the Renaissance popes—failed to meet the church's spiritual needs. The popes were supposed to be the spiritual leaders of the Catholic Church, but as rulers of the Papal States, they were all too often involved in worldly concerns. Julius II (1503–1513), the fiery "warrior-pope," personally led armies against his enemies, much to the disgust of pious Christians, who viewed the pope as a spiritual leader. As one intellectual wrote, "How, O bishop standing in the room of the Apostles, dare you teach the people the things that pertain to war?" Many high church officials regarded their church offices mainly as opportunities to advance their careers and their wealth, and many ordinary parish priests seemed ignorant of their spiritual duties.

While the leaders of the church were failing to meet their responsibilities, ordinary people were clamoring for meaningful religious expression and certainty of salvation. As a result, for some the process of salvation became almost mechanical. As more and more people sought certainty of salvation through veneration of **relics** (bones or other objects intimately association with the saints), collections of relics grew. Frederick the Wise, elector of Saxony and Martin Luther's prince, had amassed nearly 19,000 relics to which were attached **indulgences** that could reduce one's time in purgatory by 1,443 years. (An indulgence is a remission, after death, of all or part of the punishment due to sin.) Other people sought certainty of salvation in more spiritual terms by participating in the popular mystical movement known as the Modern Devotion, which downplayed religious dogma and stressed the need to follow the teachings of Jesus.

Martin Luther and the Reformation in Germany

Martin Luther (1483–1546) was a monk and a professor at the University of Wittenberg (VIT-ten-bayrk), where he lectured on the Bible. Probably sometime between 1513 and 1516, through his study of the Bible, he arrived at an answer to a problem—the assurance of salvation—that had disturbed him since his entry into the monastery.

Catholic doctrine had emphasized that both faith and good works were required for a Christian to achieve personal salvation. In Luther's eyes, human beings, weak and powerless in the sight of an almighty God, could never do enough good works to merit salvation. Through his study of the Bible, Luther came to believe that humans are saved not through their good works but through faith in the promises of God, made possible by the sacrifice of Jesus on the cross. This doctrine of salvation, or justification by grace through faith alone, became the primary doctrine of the Protestant Reformation (**justification by faith** is the act by which a person is made deserving of salvation). Because Luther had arrived at this doctrine from his study of the Bible, the Bible became for Luther, as for all other Protestants, the chief guide to religious truth.

Luther did not see himself as a rebel, but he was greatly upset by the widespread selling of indulgences. Especially offensive in his eyes was the monk Johann Tetzel, who hawked indulgences with the slogan: "As soon as the coin in the coffer [money box] rings, the soul from purgatory springs." Greatly angered, in 1517 Luther issued a stunning indictment of the abuses in the sale of indulgences, known as the Ninety-Five Theses. Thousands of copies were printed and quickly spread to all parts of Germany.

Unable to accept Luther's ideas, the church excommunicated him in January 1521. He was also summoned to appear before the imperial diet or Reichstag (RYKHSS-tahk) of the Holy Roman Empire, convened by the newly elected Emperor Charles V (1519–1556). Ordered to recant the heresies he had espoused, Luther refused and made the famous reply that became the battle cry of the Reformation:

> Unless I am convicted by Scripture and plain reason—I do not accept the authority of popes and councils, for they have contradicted each other—my conscience is captive to the Word of God. I cannot and I will not recant anything, for to go against conscience is neither right nor safe. Here I stand, I cannot do otherwise. God help me. Amen.[2]

Members of the Reichstag were outraged and demanded that Luther be arrested and delivered to the emperor. But Luther's ruler, Elector Frederick of Saxony, stepped in and protected him.

During the next few years, Luther's movement began to grow and spread. As it made an impact on the common people, it also created new challenges. This was especially true when the Peasants' War erupted in 1524. Social discontent created by their pitiful conditions became entangled with religious revolt as the German peasants looked to Martin Luther for support. But when the peasants took up arms and revolted against their landlords, Luther turned against them and called on the German princes, who in Luther's eyes were ordained by God to maintain peace and order, to crush the rebels. By May 1525, the German princes had ruthlessly suppressed the peasant hordes. By this time, Luther found himself dependent on the state authorities for the growth of his reformed church.

Luther now succeeded in gaining the support of many of the rulers of the three hundred or so German states that made up the Holy Roman Empire. These rulers quickly took control of the churches in their territories. The Lutheran churches in Germany (and later in Scandinavia) became territorial or state churches in which the state supervised the affairs of the church. As part of the development of these state-dominated churches, Luther also instituted new religious services to replace the Catholic Mass. These focused on Bible reading, preaching the word of God, and singing hymns.

POLITICS AND RELIGION IN THE GERMAN REFORMATION From its very beginning, the fate of Luther's movement was closely tied to political affairs. In 1519, Charles I, king of Spain and the grandson of Emperor Maximilian, was elected Holy Roman Emperor as Charles V. Charles V ruled over an immense empire, consisting of Spain and its

A Reformation Woodcut. In the 1520s, after Luther's return to Wittenberg, his teachings began to spread rapidly, ending ultimately in a reform movement supported by state authorities. Pamphlets containing picturesque woodcuts were important in the spread of Luther's ideas. In the woodcut shown here, the crucified Jesus attends Luther's service on the left, while on the right the pope is at a table selling indulgences.

overseas possessions, the traditional Austrian Habsburg lands, Bohemia, Hungary, the Low Countries, and the kingdom of Naples in southern Italy. Politically, Charles wanted to maintain his enormous empire; religiously, he hoped to preserve the unity of his empire in the Catholic faith.

The internal political situation in the Holy Roman Empire was not in Charles's favor, however. Although all the German states owed loyalty to the emperor, in the Middle Ages these states had become quite independent of imperial authority. By the time Charles V was able to bring military forces to Germany in 1546, Lutheranism had become well established, and the Lutheran princes were well organized. Unable to defeat them, Charles was forced to negotiate a truce. Religious warfare in Germany came to an end in 1555 with the Peace of Augsburg (OUKS-boork). The division of Christianity was formally acknowledged; Lutheran states were to have the same legal rights as Catholic states. Although the German states were now free to choose between Catholicism and Lutheranism, the peace settlement did not recognize the principle of religious toleration for individuals. The right of each German ruler to determine the religion of his subjects was accepted, but not the right of the subjects to choose their own religion. With the Peace of Augsburg, what had at first been merely feared was now certain: the ideal of Christian unity was forever lost. The rapid spread of new Protestant groups made this a certainty.

The Spread of the Protestant Reformation

Switzerland was home to two major Reformation movements: Zwinglianism and Calvinism. Ulrich Zwingli (OOL-rikh TSFING-lee) (1484–1531) was ordained a priest in 1506 and accepted an appointment as a cathedral priest in the Great Minster of Zürich (ZOOR-ik *or* TSIH-rikh) in 1518. Zwingli's preaching of the Gospel caused such unrest that in 1523 the city council decided to institute evangelical reforms. Relics and images were abolished; all paintings and decorations were removed from the churches and replaced by whitewashed walls. The Mass was replaced by a new liturgy consisting of Scripture reading, prayer, and sermons. Monasticism, pilgrimages, the veneration of saints, clerical celibacy, and the pope's authority were all abolished as remnants of papal Christianity.

As his movement began to spread to other cities in Switzerland, Zwingli sought an alliance with Martin Luther and the German reformers. Although both the German and the Swiss reformers realized the need for unity to defend against the opposition of the Catholic authorities, they were unable to agree on the interpretation of the Lord's Supper, the sacrament of Communion (see the box on p. 387). Zwingli believed that the scriptural words "This is my body, this is my blood" should be taken figuratively, not literally, and refused to accept

A Reformation Debate: Conflict at Marburg

RELIGION & PHILOSOPHY

Debates played a crucial role in the Reformation period. They were a primary instrument for introducing the Reformation in innumerable cities as well as a means of resolving differences among like-minded Protestant groups. This selection contains an excerpt from the vivacious and often brutal debate between Luther and Zwingli over the sacrament of the Lord's Supper at Marburg in 1529. The two protagonists failed to reach agreement.

The Marburg Colloquy, 1529

THE HESSIAN CHANCELLOR FEIGE: My gracious prince and lord [Landgrave Philip of Hesse] has summoned you for the express and urgent purpose of settling the dispute over the sacrament of the Lord's Supper. . . . Let everyone on both sides present his arguments in a spirit of moderation, as becomes such matters. . . . Now then, Doctor Luther, you may proceed.

LUTHER: Noble prince, gracious lord! Undoubtedly the colloquy is well intentioned. . . . Although I have no intention of changing my mind, which is firmly made up, I will nevertheless present the grounds of my belief and show where the others are in error. . . . Your basic contentions are these: In the last analysis you wish to prove that a body cannot be in two places at once, and you produce arguments about the unlimited body which are based on natural reason. I do not question how Christ can be God and man and how the two natures can be joined. For God is more powerful than all our ideas, and we must submit to his word. Prove that Christ's body is not there where the Scripture says, "This is my body!" Rational proofs I will not listen to. . . . God is beyond all mathematics and the words of God are to be revered and carried out in awe. It is God who commands, "Take, eat, this is my body."
I request, therefore, valid scriptural proof to the contrary.

Luther writes on the table in chalk, "This is my body," and covers the words with a velvet cloth.

OECOLAMPADIUS [leader of the reform movement in Basel and a Zwinglian partisan]: The sixth chapter of John clarifies the other scriptural passages. Christ is not speaking there about a local presence. "The flesh is of no avail," he says. It is not my intention to employ rational, or geometrical, arguments—neither am I denying the power of God—but as long as I have the complete faith I will speak from that. For Christ is risen; he sits at the right hand of God; and so he cannot be present in the bread. Our view is neither new nor sacrilegious, but is based on faith and Scripture. . . .

ZWINGLI: I insist that the words of the Lord's Supper must be figurative. This is ever apparent, and even required by the article of faith: "taken up into heaven, seated at the right hand of the Father." Otherwise, it would be absurd to look for him in the Lord's Supper at the same time that Christ is telling us that he is in heaven. One and the same body cannot possibly be in different places. . . .

LUTHER: I call upon you as before: your basic contentions are shaky. Give way, and give glory to God!

ZWINGLI: And we call upon you to give glory to God and to quit begging the question! The issue at stake is this: Where is the proof of your position? I am willing to consider your words carefully—no harm meant! You're trying to outwit me. I stand by this passage in the sixth chapter of John, verse 63, and shall not be shaken from it. You'll have to sing another tune.

LUTHER: You're being obnoxious.

ZWINGLI: (*excitedly*) Don't you believe that Christ was attempting in John 6 to help those who did not understand?

LUTHER: You're trying to dominate things! You insist on passing judgment! Leave that to someone else! . . . It is your point that must be proved, not mine. But let us stop this sort of thing. It serves no purpose.

ZWINGLI: It certainly does! It is for you to prove that the passage in John 6 speaks of a physical repast.

LUTHER: You express yourself poorly and make about as much progress as a cane standing in a corner. You're going nowhere.

ZWINGLI: No, no, no! This is the passage that will break your neck!

(Continued)

LUTHER: Don't be so sure of yourself. Necks don't break this way. You're in Hesse, not Switzerland.

Q How did the positions of Zwingli and Luther on the sacrament of the Lord's Supper differ? What was the purpose of this debate? Based on this example, why did many Reformation debates lead to further hostility rather than compromise and unity between religious and sectarian opponents? What implication did this have for the future of the Protestant Reformation?

Source: "The Marburg Colloquy," edited by Donald Ziegler, from GREAT DEBATES OF THE REFORMATION, edited by Donald Ziegler, copyright © 1969 by Donald Ziegler.

Luther's insistence on the real presence of the body and blood of Christ "in, with, and under the bread and wine." In October 1531, war erupted between the Swiss Protestant and Catholic states. Zürich's army was routed, and Zwingli was found wounded on the battlefield. His enemies killed him, cut up his body, burned the pieces, and scattered the ashes. The leadership of Swiss Protestantism now passed to John Calvin, the systematic theologian and organizer of the Protestant movement.

CALVIN AND CALVINISM John Calvin (1509–1564) was educated in his native France, but after converting to Protestantism, he was forced to flee to the safety of Switzerland. In 1536, he published the first edition of the *Institutes of the Christian Religion*, a masterful synthesis of Protestant thought that immediately secured his reputation as one of the new leaders of Protestantism.

On most important doctrines, Calvin stood very close to Luther. He adhered to the doctrine of justification by faith alone to explain how humans achieved salvation. But Calvin also placed much emphasis on the absolute sovereignty of God or the all-powerful nature of God— what Calvin called the "power, grace, and glory of God." One of the ideas derived from his emphasis on the absolute sovereignty of God—**predestination**—gave a unique cast to Calvin's teachings. This "eternal decree," as Calvin called it, meant that God had predestined some people to be saved (the elect) and others to be damned (the reprobate). According to Calvin, "He has once for all determined, both whom He would admit to salvation, and whom He would condemn to destruction."[3] Although Calvin stressed that there could be no absolute certainty of salvation, his followers did not always make this distinction. The practical psychological effect of predestination was to give later Calvinists an unshakable conviction that they were doing God's work on earth, making Calvinism a dynamic and activist faith.

In 1536, Calvin began working to reform the city of Geneva. He was able to fashion a tightly organized church order that employed both clergy and laymen in the service of the church. The Consistory, a special body for enforcing moral discipline, functioned as a court to oversee the moral life, daily behavior, and doctrinal orthodoxy of Genevans and to admonish and correct deviants. Citizens of Geneva were punished for such varied "crimes" as dancing, singing obscene songs, drunkenness, swearing, and playing cards.

Calvin's success in Geneva enabled the city to become a vibrant center of Protestantism. Following Calvin's lead, missionaries trained in Geneva were sent to all parts of Europe. Calvinism became established in France, the Netherlands, Scotland, and central and eastern Europe, and by the mid-sixteenth century, Calvin's Geneva stood as the fortress of the Reformation.

THE ENGLISH REFORMATION The English Reformation was rooted in politics, not religion. King Henry VIII (1509–1547) had a strong desire to divorce his first wife, Catherine of Aragon, with whom he had a daughter, Mary, but no male heir. The king wanted to marry Anne Boleyn (BUH-lin *or* buh-LIN), with whom he had fallen in love. Impatient with the pope's unwillingness to grant him an annulment of his marriage, Henry turned to England's own church courts. As archbishop of Canterbury and head of the highest church court in England, Thomas Cranmer ruled in May 1533 that the king's marriage to Catherine was "absolutely void." At the beginning of June, Anne was crowned queen, and three months later, a child was born; much to the king's disappointment, the baby was a a girl (the future Queen Elizabeth I).

In 1534, at Henry's request, Parliament moved to finalize the break of the Church of England with Rome. The Act of Supremacy of 1534 declared that the king was "the only supreme head on earth of the Church of England," a position that gave him control of doctrine, clerical appointments, and discipline. Although Henry VIII had broken with the papacy, little change occurred in matters of doctrine, theology, and ceremony. Some of his supporters, including Archbishop Cranmer, sought a religious reformation as well as an administrative one, but Henry was unyielding. But he died in 1547 and was succeeded by his son, the underage and sickly Edward VI (1547–1553), and during Edward's reign, Cranmer and others inclined toward Protestant doctrines were able to move the Church of England (or Anglican Church) in a more Protestant direction. New acts of Parliament gave the clergy the right to marry and created a new Protestant church service.

Edward VI was succeeded by Mary (1553–1558), a Catholic who attempted to return England to Catholicism. Her actions aroused much anger, however, especially when "bloody Mary" burned more than three hundred Protestant heretics. By the end of Mary's reign, England was more Protestant than it had been at the beginning.

The Social Impact of the Protestant Reformation

The Protestants were especially important in developing a new view of the family. Because Protestantism had eliminated any idea of special holiness for celibacy and had abolished both monasticism and a celibate clergy, the family could be placed at the center of human life, and a new stress on "mutual love between man and wife" could be extolled (see the comparative essay "Marriage in the Early Modern World" on p. 390).

But were doctrine and reality the same? Most often, reality reflected the traditional roles of husband as the ruler and wife as the obedient servant whose chief duty was to please her husband. Luther stated it clearly:

> The rule remains with the husband, and the wife is compelled to obey him by God's command. He rules the home and the state, wages war, defends his possessions, tills the soil, builds, plants, etc. The woman on the other hand is like a nail driven into the wall . . . so the wife should stay at home and look after the affairs of the household, as one who has been deprived of the ability of administering those affairs that are outside and that concern the state. She does not go beyond her most personal duties.[4]

Obedience to her husband was not a wife's only role; her other important duty was to bear children. To Calvin and Luther, this function of women was part of the divine plan, and for most Protestant women, family life was their only destiny. Overall, the Protestant Reformation did not noticeably alter women's subordinate place in society.

The Catholic Reformation

By the mid-sixteenth century, Lutheranism had become established in Germany and Scandinavia and Calvinism in Scotland, Switzerland, France, the Netherlands, and eastern Europe. In England, the split from Rome had resulted in the creation of a national church. The situation in Europe did not look particularly favorable for the Roman Catholic Church. Nevertheless, the Catholic Church underwent a revitalization in the sixteenth century that gave it new strength.

CATHOLIC REFORMATION OR COUNTER-REFORMATION? But was this revitalization a **Catholic Reformation** or a Counter-Reformation? Some historians prefer the term *Counter-Reformation* to focus on the aspects that were a direct reaction against the Protestant movement. Historians who prefer the term *Catholic Reformation* point out that elements of reform were already present in the Catholic Church at the end of the fifteenth century and the beginning of the sixteenth century. Especially noticeable were the calls for reform from the religious orders of the Franciscans, Dominicans, and Augustinians. Members of these groups put particular emphasis on preaching to laypeople. Another example was the Oratory of Divine Love. First organized in Italy in 1497, the Oratory was an informal group of clergy and laymen who worked to foster reform by emphasizing personal spiritual development and outward acts of charity. Its members included a Spanish archbishop, Cardinal Ximenes (khee-MAY-ness), who was especially active in using Christian humanism to reform the church in Spain.

No doubt, both positions on the nature of the reformation of the Catholic Church contain elements of truth. The Catholic Reformation revived the best features of medieval Catholicism and then adjusted them to meet new conditions, as is most apparent in the emergence of a new mysticism, closely tied to the traditions of Catholic piety, and the revival of monasticism by the regeneration of older religious orders and the founding of new orders.

THE SOCIETY OF JESUS Of all the new religious orders, the most important was the Society of Jesus, known as the Jesuits; it was founded by a Spanish nobleman, Ignatius of Loyola (ig-NAY-shuss of loi-OH-luh) (1491–1556). Loyola brought together a small group of individuals who were recognized as a religious order by the pope in 1540. The new order was grounded on the principles of absolute obedience to the papacy, a strict hierarchical order for the society, the use of education to achieve its goals, and a dedication to engage in "conflict for God." A special vow of absolute obedience to the pope made the Jesuits an important instrument for papal policy. Jesuit missionaries proved singularly successful in restoring Catholicism to parts of Germany and eastern Europe.

Another prominent Jesuit activity was the propagation of the Catholic faith among non-Christians. Francis Xavier (ZAY-vee-ur) (1506–1552), one of the original members of the Society of Jesus, carried the message of

Marriage in the Early Modern World

FAMILY & SOCIETY

Marriage is an ancient institution. In China, myths about the beginnings of Chinese civilization maintained that the rites of marriage began with the primordial couple Fuxi and Nugun and that these rites actually preceded such discoveries as fire, farming, and medicine. In the early modern world, family and marriage were inseparable and at the center of all civilizations.

In the early modern period, the family was still at the heart of Europe's social organization. For the most part, people viewed the family in traditional terms, as a patriarchal institution in which the husband dominated his wife and children. The upper classes in particular thought of the family as a "house," an association whose collective interests were more important than those of its individual members. Parents (especially fathers) generally selected marriage partners for their children, based on the interests of the family. When the son of a French noble asked about his upcoming marriage, the father responded, "Mind your own business." Details were worked out well in advance, sometimes when children were only two or three years old, and were set out in a legally binding contract. An important negotiating point was the size of the dowry, money presented by the wife's family to the groom upon marriage. The dowry could be a large sum, and all families were expected to provide dowries for their daughters.

Arranged marriages were not unique to Europe but were common throughout the world. In China, marriages were normally arranged for the benefit of the family, often by a go-between, and the groom and bride were usually not consulted. Frequently, they did not meet until the marriage ceremony. Love was obviously not a reason for marriage and in fact was often viewed as a detriment because it could distract the married couple from their responsibility to the larger family unit. In Japan too, marriages were arranged, often by the heads of dominant families in rural areas, and the new wife moved in with the family of her husband. In India, not only were marriages arranged, but it was not uncommon

Marriage Ceremonies. At the left is a detail of a marriage ceremony in Italy from a fresco painted by Domenico di Bartolo in 1443. At the right is a seventeenth-century Mughal painting from India showing Shah Jahan, the Mughal emperor (with halo). He is riding to the wedding celebration of his son, who rides before him.

Santa Maria della Scala Hospital, Siena//© Alfredo Dagli Orti/The Art Archive at Art Resource, NY

© The Granger Collection, New York

(Continued)

for women to be married before the age of ten. In colonial Latin America, parents selected marriage partners for their children and often chose a dwelling for the couple as well. In many areas, before members of the lower classes could marry, they had to offer gifts to the powerful noble landlords in the region and obtain their permission. These nobles often refused to allow women to marry in order to keep them as servants.

Arranged marriages were the logical result of a social system in which men dominated and women's primary role was to bear children, manage the household, and work in the fields. Not until the nineteenth century did a feminist movement emerge in Europe to improve the rights of women. By the beginning of the twentieth century, that movement had spread to other parts of the world. The New Culture Movement in China, for example, advocated the free choice of spouses. Although the trend throughout the world is toward allowing people to choose their mates, in some places, especially in rural communities, families continue to play an active role in selecting marriage partners.

Q *In what ways were marriage practices similar in the West and East during the early modern period? Were there any significant differences?*

Catholic Christianity to the East. After attracting tens of thousands of converts in India, he traveled to Malacca and the Moluccas before finally reaching Japan in 1549. He spoke highly of the Japanese: "They are a people of excellent morals—good in general and not malicious."[5] Thousands of Japanese, especially in the southernmost islands, became Christians. In 1552, Xavier set out for China but died of fever before he reached the mainland.

Although conversion efforts in Japan proved short-lived, Jesuit activity in China, especially that of the Italian Matteo Ricci (ma-TAY-oh REE-chee), was more long-lasting. Recognizing the Chinese pride in their own culture, the Jesuits attempted to draw parallels between Christian and Confucian concepts and to show the similarities between Christian morality and Confucian ethics. For their part, the missionaries were much impressed with many aspects of Chinese civilization, and reports of their experiences heightened European curiosity about this great society on the other side of the world.

A REFORMED PAPACY A reformed papacy was another important factor in the development of the Catholic Reformation. The involvement of Renaissance popes in dubious finances and Italian political and military affairs had created numerous sources of corruption. It took the jolt of the Protestant Reformation to bring about serious reform. Pope Paul III (1534–1549) perceived the need for change and took the audacious step of appointing a reform commission to ascertain the church's ills. The commission's report in 1537 blamed the church's problems on the corrupt policies of popes and cardinals. Paul III also formally recognized the Jesuits and summoned the Council of Trent.

THE COUNCIL OF TRENT In March 1545, a group of high church officials met in the city of Trent on the border between Germany and Italy and initiated the Council of Trent, which met intermittently from 1545 to 1563 in three major sessions. The final decrees of the Council of Trent reaffirmed traditional Catholic teachings in opposition to Protestant beliefs. Scripture and tradition were affirmed as equal authorities in religious matters; only the church could interpret Scripture. Both faith and good works were declared necessary for salvation. Belief in purgatory and in the use of indulgences was strengthened, although the selling of indulgences was prohibited.

After the Council of Trent, the Roman Catholic Church possessed a clear body of doctrine and a unified structure under the acknowledged supremacy of the popes. Although the Roman Catholic Church had become one Christian denomination among many, the church entered a new phase of its history with a spirit of confidence.

Europe in Crisis, 1560–1650

Q FOCUS QUESTION: Why is the period between 1560 and 1650 in Europe considered an age of crisis?

Between 1560 and 1650, Europe experienced religious wars, revolutions and constitutional crises, economic and social disintegration, and a witchcraft craze. It was truly an age of crisis.

Politics and the Wars of Religion in the Sixteenth Century

By 1560, Calvinism and Catholicism had become activist religions dedicated to spreading the word of God as they interpreted it. Although their struggle for the minds and hearts of Europeans was at the center of the religious wars of the sixteenth century, economic, social, and political forces also played important roles in these conflicts.

THE FRENCH WARS OF RELIGION (1562–1598) Religion was central to the French civil wars of the sixteenth century. The growth of Calvinism had led to persecution by the French kings, but the latter did little to stop the spread of Calvinism. Huguenots (HYOO-guh-nots) (as the French Calvinists were called) constituted only about 7 percent of the population, but 40 to 50 percent of the French nobility became Huguenots, including the house of Bourbon (boor-BOHN), which stood next to the Valois (val-WAH) in the royal line of succession. The conversion of so many nobles made the Huguenots a potentially dangerous political threat to monarchical power. Still, the Calvinist minority was greatly outnumbered by the Catholic majority, and the Valois monarchy was staunchly Catholic.

For thirty years, battles raged in France between Catholic and Calvinist parties. Finally, in 1589, Henry of Navarre, the political leader of the Huguenots and a member of the Bourbon dynasty, succeeded to the throne as Henry IV (1589–1610). Realizing, however, that he would never be accepted by Catholic France, Henry converted to Catholicism. With his coronation in 1594, the Wars of Religion had finally come to an end. The Edict of Nantes (NAHNT) in 1598 solved the religious problem by acknowledging Catholicism as the official religion of France while guaranteeing the Huguenots the right to worship and to enjoy all political privileges, including the holding of public offices.

PHILIP II AND MILITANT CATHOLICISM The greatest advocate of militant Catholicism in the second half of the sixteenth century was King Philip II of Spain (1556–1598), the son and heir of Charles V. Philip's reign ushered in an age of Spanish greatness, both politically and culturally. Philip II had inherited from his father Spain, the Netherlands, and possessions in Italy and the Americas. To strengthen his control, Philip insisted on strict conformity to Catholicism and strong monarchical authority. Achieving the latter was not an easy task, because each of the lands of his empire had its own structure of government.

Philip's attempt to strengthen his control over the Spanish Netherlands, which consisted of seventeen provinces (the modern Netherlands and Belgium), soon led to a revolt. The nobles, who stood to lose the most politically, strongly opposed Philip's efforts. Religion also became a major catalyst for rebellion when Philip attempted to crush Calvinism. Violence erupted in 1566, and the revolt became organized, especially in the northern provinces, where the Dutch, under the leadership of William of Nassau, the prince of Orange, offered growing resistance. The struggle dragged on for decades until 1609, when the war ended with a twelve-year truce that virtually recognized the independence of the northern provinces. These seven northern provinces, which called themselves the United Provinces of the Netherlands, became the core of the modern Dutch state.

To most Europeans at the beginning of the seventeenth century, Spain still seemed the greatest power of the age, but the reality was quite different. The Spanish treasury was empty, the armed forces were obsolescent, and the government was inefficient. Spain continued to play the role of a great power, but real power had shifted to England.

THE ENGLAND OF ELIZABETH When Elizabeth Tudor, the daughter of Henry VIII and Anne Boleyn, ascended the throne in 1558, England was home to fewer than 4 million people. Yet during her reign (1558–1603), the small island kingdom became the leader of the Protestant nations of Europe and laid the foundations for a world empire.

Intelligent, cautious, and self-confident, Elizabeth moved quickly to solve the difficult religious problem she inherited from her half-sister, Queen Mary. Elizabeth's religious policy was based on moderation and compromise. She repealed the Catholic laws of Mary's reign, and a new Act of Supremacy designated Elizabeth as "the only supreme governor" of both church and state. The Church of England under Elizabeth was basically Protestant, but it was of a moderate bent that kept most people satisfied.

Caution and moderation also dictated Elizabeth's foreign policy. Nevertheless, Elizabeth was gradually drawn into conflict with Spain. Having resisted for years the idea of invading England as too impractical, Philip II of Spain was finally persuaded to do so by advisers who assured him that the people of England would rise against their queen when the Spaniards arrived. A successful invasion of England would mean the overthrow of heresy and the return of England to Catholicism. Philip ordered preparations for a fleet of warships, the *armada*, to spearhead the invasion of England.

The armada was a disaster. The Spanish fleet that finally set sail had neither the ships nor the manpower that Philip had planned to send. Battered by a number of encounters with the English, the Spanish fleet sailed back to Spain by a northward route around Scotland and Ireland, where it was further pounded by storms.

Economic and Social Crises

The period of European history from 1560 to 1650 witnessed severe economic and social crises as well as political upheaval. Economic contraction began to be evident

Procession of Queen Elizabeth I. Intelligent and learned, Elizabeth Tudor was familiar with Latin and Greek and spoke several European languages. Served by able administrators, Elizabeth ruled for nearly forty-five years and generally avoided open military action against any major power. This picture, painted near the end of her reign, shows the queen in a ceremonial procession.

in some parts of Europe by the 1620s. In the 1630s and 1640s, as imports of silver from the Americas declined, economic recession intensified, especially in the Mediterranean area.

POPULATION DECLINE Population trends of the sixteenth and seventeenth centuries also reveal Europe's worsening conditions. The population of Europe increased from 60 million in 1500 to 85 million by 1600, the first major recovery of the European population since the devastation of the Black Death in the mid-fourteenth century. By 1650, however, records indicate a decline in the population, especially in central and southern Europe. Europe's longtime adversaries—war, famine, and plague—continued to affect population levels. These problems created social tensions, some of which were manifested in an obsession with witches.

WITCHCRAFT MANIA Hysteria over witchcraft affected the lives of many Europeans in the sixteenth and seventeenth centuries. Perhaps more than 100,000 people were prosecuted throughout Europe on charges of witchcraft. As more and more people were brought to trial, the fear of

witches, as well as the fear of being accused of witchcraft, escalated to frightening levels (see the box on p. 394).

Common people—usually those who were poor and without property—were more likely to be accused of witchcraft. Indeed, where lists are given, those mentioned most often are milkmaids, peasant women, and servant girls. In the witchcraft trials of the sixteenth and seventeenth centuries, more than 75 percent of the accused were women, most of them single or widowed and many over fifty years old.

That women should be the chief victims of witchcraft trials was hardly accidental. Nicholas Rémy (nee-koh-LAH ray-MEE), a witchcraft judge in France in the 1590s, found it "not unreasonable that this scum of humanity, i.e., witches, should be drawn chiefly from the feminine sex." To another judge, it came as no surprise that witches would confess to sexual experiences with Satan: "The Devil uses them so, because he knows that women love carnal pleasures, and he means to bind them to his allegiance by such agreeable provocations."[6]

By the mid-seventeenth century the witchcraft hysteria had begun to subside. As governments grew stronger, fewer magistrates were willing to accept the unsettling

A Witchcraft Trial in France

FAMILY & SOCIETY

Persecutions for witchcraft reached their high point in the sixteenth and seventeenth centuries, when tens of thousands of people were brought to trial. In this excerpt from the minutes of a trial in France in 1652, we can see why the accused witch stood little chance of exonerating herself.

The Trial of Suzanne Gaudry

28 May, 1652. . . . Interrogation of Suzanne Gaudry, prisoner at the court of Rieux. . . . During interrogations on May 28 and May 29, the prisoner confessed to a number of activities involving the devil.

Deliberation of the Court—June 3, 1652

The undersigned advocates of the Court have seen these interrogations and answers. They say that the aforementioned Suzanne Gaudry confesses that she is a witch, that she had given herself to the devil, that she had renounced God, Lent, and baptism, that she has been marked on the shoulder, that she has cohabited with the devil and that she has been to the dances, confessing only to have cast a spell upon and caused to die a beast of Philippe Cornié. . . .

Third Interrogation, June 27

This prisoner being led into the chamber, she was examined to know if things were not as she had said and confessed at the beginning of her imprisonment.

—Answers no, and that what she has said was done so by force.

Pressed to say the truth, that otherwise she would be subjected to torture, having pointed out to her that her aunt was burned for this same subject.

—Answers that she is not a witch. . . .

She was placed in the hands of the officer in charge of torture, throwing herself on her knees, struggling to cry, uttering several exclamations, without being able, nevertheless, to shed a tear. Saying at every moment that she is not a witch.

The Torture

On this same day, being at the place of torture.

This prisoner, before being strapped down, was admonished to maintain herself in her first confessions and to renounce her lover.

—Says that she denies everything she has said, and that she has no lover. Feeling herself being strapped down, says that she is not a witch, while struggling to cry . . . and upon being asked why she confessed to being one, said that she was forced to say it.

Told that she was not forced, that on the contrary she declared herself to be a witch without any threat.

—Says that she confessed it and that she is not a witch, and being a little stretched [on the rack] screams ceaselessly that she is not a witch.

Asked if she did not confess that she had been a witch for twenty-six years.

—Says that she said it, that she retracts it, crying that she is not a witch.

Asked if she did not make Philippe Cornié's horse die, as she confessed.

—Answers no, crying Jesus-Maria, that she is not a witch.

The mark having been probed by the officer, in the presence of Doctor Bouchain, it was adjudged by the aforesaid doctor and officer truly to be the mark of the devil.

Being more tightly stretched upon the torture rack, urged to maintain her confessions.

—Said that it was true that she is a witch and that she would maintain what she had said.

Asked how long she has been in subjugation to the devil.

—Answers that it was twenty years ago that the devil appeared to her, being in her lodgings in the form of a man dressed in a little cowhide and black breeches. . . .

Verdict

July 9, 1652. In the light of the interrogations, answers, and investigations made into the charge against Suzanne Gaudry, . . . seeing by her own confessions that she is said to have made a pact with the devil, received the mark from him, . . . and that following this, she had renounced God, Lent, and baptism and had let herself be known carnally by him, in which she received satisfaction. Also, seeing that she is said to have been a part of nocturnal carols and dances.

For expiation of which the advice of the undersigned is that the office of Rieux can legitimately condemn the aforesaid Suzanne Gaudry to death, tying her to a gallows, and strangling her to death, then burning her body and burying it here in the environs of the woods.

Why were women, particularly older women, especially vulnerable to accusations of witchcraft? What "proofs" are offered here that Suzanne Gaudry had consorted with the devil? What does this account tell us about the spread of witchcraft persecutions in the seventeenth century?

Source: From *Witchcraft in Europe, 1100–1700: A Documentary History* by Alan Kors and Edward Peters (Philadelphia: University of Pennsylvania Press, 1972), pp. 266–275. Used with permission of the publisher.

and divisive conditions generated by the trials of witches. Moreover, by the beginning of the eighteenth century, more and more people were questioning altogether their old attitudes toward religion and found it especially contrary to reason to believe in the old view of a world haunted by evil spirits.

ECONOMIC TRENDS IN THE SEVENTEENTH CENTURY

In the course of the seventeenth century, new economic trends also emerged. Historians refer to the economic practices of the seventeenth century as **mercantilism**. According to the mercantilists, the prosperity of a nation depended on a plentiful supply of bullion (gold and silver). For this reason, it was desirable to achieve a favorable balance of trade in which goods exported were of greater value than those imported, promoting an influx of gold and silver payments that would increase the quantity of bullion. Furthermore, to encourage exports, governments should stimulate and protect export industries and trade by granting trade monopolies, encouraging investment in new industries through subsidies, importing foreign artisans, and improving transportation systems by building roads, bridges, and canals. By placing high tariffs on foreign goods, a government could reduce imports and prevent them from competing with domestic industries. Colonies were also deemed valuable as sources of raw materials and markets for finished goods.

Mercantilist theory on the role of colonies was matched in practice by Europe's overseas expansion. With the development of colonies and trading posts in the Americas and the East, Europeans embarked on an adventure in international commerce in the seventeenth century. Although some historians speak of a nascent world economy, we should remember that local, regional, and intra-European trade still predominated. At the end of the seventeenth century, for example, English imports totaled 360,000 tons, but only 5,000 tons came from the East Indies. What made the transoceanic trade rewarding, however, was not the volume but the value of its goods. Dutch, English, and French merchants were bringing back products that were still consumed largely by the wealthy but were beginning to make their way into the lives of artisans and merchants. Pepper and spices from the Indies, West Indian and Brazilian sugar, and Asian coffee and tea were becoming more readily available to European consumers.

The commercial expansion of the sixteenth and seventeenth centuries was made easier by new forms of commercial organization, especially the **joint-stock company**. Individuals bought shares in a company and received dividends on their investment while a board of directors ran the company and made the important business decisions. The return on investments could be spectacular. The joint-stock company made it easier to raise large amounts of capital for world trading ventures.

Despite the growth of commercial capitalism, most of the European economy still depended on an agricultural system that had experienced few changes since the thirteenth century. At least 80 percent of Europeans still worked on the land. Almost all of the peasants of western Europe were free of serfdom, although many still owed a variety of feudal dues to the nobility. Despite the expanding markets and rising prices, European peasants saw little or no improvement in their lot as they faced increased rents and fees and higher taxes imposed by the state.

Seventeenth-Century Crises: Revolution and War

During the first half of the seventeenth century, a series of rebellions and civil wars rocked the domestic stability of many European governments. A devastating war that affected much of Europe also added to the sense of crisis.

THE THIRTY YEARS' WAR (1618–1648) The Thirty Years' War began in 1618 in the Germanic lands of the Holy Roman Empire as a struggle between Catholic forces, led by the Habsburg Holy Roman Emperors, and Protestant—primarily Calvinist—nobles in Bohemia who rebelled against Habsburg authority (see Map 15.1). What began as a struggle over religious issues soon became a wider conflict perpetuated by political motivations as both minor and major European powers—Denmark, Sweden, France, and Spain—entered the war. The competition for European leadership between the Bourbon dynasty of France and the Habsburg dynasties of Spain and the Holy Roman Empire was an especially important factor. Nevertheless, most of the battles were fought on German soil (see the box on p. 397).

The war in Germany was officially ended in 1648 by the Peace of Westphalia, which proclaimed that all German states, including the Calvinist ones, were free to determine their own religion. The major contenders gained new territories, and France emerged as the dominant nation in Europe. The more than three hundred entities that made up the Holy Roman Empire were recognized as independent states, and each was given the power to conduct its own foreign policy; this brought an end to the Holy Roman Empire and ensured German disunity for another two hundred years. The Peace of Westphalia made it clear that political motives, not religious convictions, had become the guiding force in public affairs.

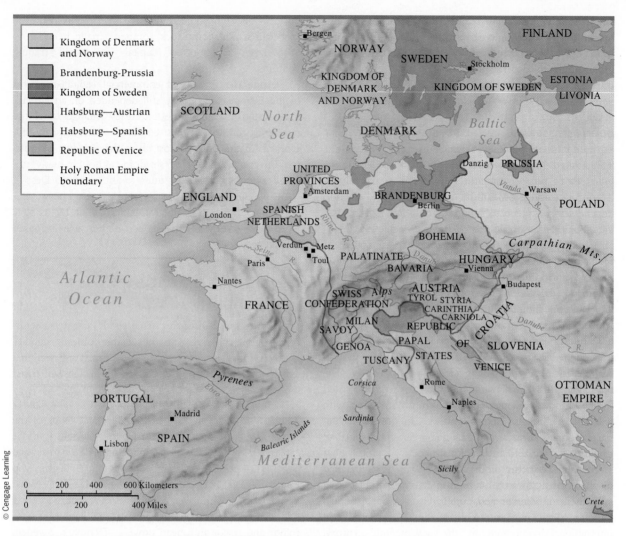

MAP 15.1 **Europe in the Seventeenth Century.** This map shows Europe at the time of the Thirty Years' War (1618–1648). Although the struggle began in Bohemia and much of the fighting took place in the Germanic lands of the Holy Roman Empire, the conflict became a Europe-wide struggle.

Q *Which countries engaged in the war were predominantly Protestant, which were Catholic, and which were mixed?*

A MILITARY REVOLUTION? By the seventeenth century, war was playing an increasingly important role in European affairs. Military power was considered essential to a ruler's reputation and power; thus, the pressure to build an effective military machine was intense. Some historians believe that the changes that occurred in the science of warfare between 1560 and 1650 constituted a military revolution.

These changes included increased use of firearms and cannons, greater flexibility and mobility in tactics, and better-disciplined and better-trained armies. These innovations necessitated standing armies, based partly on conscription, which grew ever larger and more expensive as the seventeenth century progressed. Such armies could be maintained only by levying heavier taxes, making war an economic burden and an ever more important part of the early modern European state. The creation of large bureaucracies to supervise the military resources of the state contributed to the growth in the power of governments.

The Face of War in the Seventeenth Century

FAMILY & SOCIETY

We have a firsthand account of the face of war in Germany from a picaresque novel called *Simplicius Simplicissimus,* written by Jakob von Grimmelshausen (YAH-kop fun GRIM-ulz-how-zun). The author's experiences as a soldier in the Thirty Years' War give his descriptions of the effect of the war on ordinary people a certain vividness and reality. This selection describes the fate of a peasant farm, an experience all too familiar to thousands of German peasants between 1618 and 1648.

Jakob von Grimmelshausen, *Simplicius Simplicissimus*

The first thing these horsemen did in the nice back rooms of the house was to put in their horses. Then everyone took up a special job, one having to do with death and destruction. Although some began butchering, heating water, and rendering lard, as if to prepare for a banquet, others raced through the house, ransacking upstairs and down; not even the privy chamber was safe, as if the golden fleece of Jason might be hidden there. Still others bundled up big packs of cloth, household goods, and clothes, as if they wanted to hold a rummage sale somewhere. What they did not intend to take along they broke and spoiled. Some ran their swords into the hay and straw, as if there hadn't been hogs enough to stick. Some shook the feathers out of beds and put bacon slabs, hams, and other stuff in the ticking, as if they might sleep better on these. Others knocked down the hearth and broke the windows, as if announcing an everlasting summer. They flattened out copper and pewter dishes and baled the ruined goods. They burned up bedsteads, tables, chairs, and benches, though there were yards and yards of dry firewood outside the kitchen. Jars and crocks, pots and casseroles all were broken, either because they preferred their meat broiled or because they thought they'd eat only one meal with us. In the barn, the hired girl was handled so roughly that she was unable to walk away, I am ashamed to report. They stretched the hired man out flat on the ground, stuck a wooden wedge in his mouth to keep it open, and emptied a milk bucket full of stinking manure drippings down his throat; they called it a Swedish cocktail. He didn't relish it and made a very wry face. By this means they forced him to take a raiding party to some other place where they carried off men and cattle and brought them to our farm. Among those were my father, mother, and [sister] Ursula.

Then they used thumbscrews, which they cleverly made out of their pistols, to torture the peasants, as if they wanted to burn witches. Though he had confessed to nothing as yet, they put one of the captured hayseeds in the bake-oven and lighted a fire in it. They put a rope around someone else's head and tightened it like a tourniquet until blood came out of his mouth, nose, and ears. In short, every soldier had his favorite method of making life miserable for peasants, and every peasant had his own misery. My father was, as I thought, particularly lucky because he confessed with a laugh what others were forced to say in pain and martyrdom. No doubt because he was the head of the household, he was shown special consideration; they put him close to a fire, tied him by his hands and legs, and rubbed damp salt on the bottoms of his feet. Our old nanny goat had to lick it off and this so tickled my father that he could have burst laughing. This seemed so clever and entertaining to me—I had never seen or heard my father laugh so long—that I joined him in laughter, to keep him company or perhaps to cover up my ignorance. In the midst of such glee he told them the whereabouts of hidden treasure much richer in gold, pearls, and jewelry than might have been expected on a farm.

I can't say much about the captured wives, hired girls, and daughters because the soldiers didn't let me watch their doings. But I do remember hearing pitiful screams from various dark corners and I guess that my mother and our Ursula had it no better than the rest.

 What does this document reveal about the effect of war on ordinary Europeans?

Source: Excerpt from *The Adventure of Simplicius Simplicissimus* by Hans Jacob Chistoffel von Grimmelshausen, translated by George Schulz-Behren, © 1993 Camden House/Boydell & Brewer, Rochester, New York.

Response to Crisis: The Practice of Absolutism

 FOCUS QUESTION: What was absolutism, and what were the main characteristics of the absolute monarchies that emerged in France, Prussia, Austria, and Russia?

Many people responded to the crises of the seventeenth century by searching for order. An increase in monarchical power became an obvious means for achieving stability. The result was what historians have called absolutism or absolute monarchy, in which the sovereign power or ultimate authority in the state rested in the hands of a king who claimed to rule by divine right—the idea that kings received their power from God and were responsible to no one but God. Late-sixteenth-century political theorists believed that sovereign power consisted of the authority to make laws, levy taxes, administer justice, control the state's administrative system, and determine foreign policy.

France Under Louis XIV

France during the reign of Louis XIV (1643–1715) has traditionally been regarded as the best example of the practice of absolute or **divine-right monarchy** in the seventeenth century. French culture, language, and manners reached into all levels of European society. French diplomacy and wars overwhelmed the political affairs of western and central Europe. The court of Louis XIV seemed to be imitated everywhere in Europe (see the comparative illustration on p. 399).

POLITICAL INSTITUTIONS One of the keys to Louis's power was his ability to control the central policy-making machinery of government because it was part of his own court and household. The royal court, located in the magnificent palace at Versailles (vayr-SY) served three purposes simultaneously: it was the personal household of the king, the location of central governmental machinery, and the place where powerful subjects came to find favors and offices for themselves and their clients. The greatest danger to Louis's personal rule came from the very high nobles and princes of the blood (the royal princes), who considered it their natural role to assert the policy-making role of royal ministers. Louis eliminated this threat by removing them from the royal council, the chief administrative body of the king, and enticing them to his court at Versailles, where he could keep them preoccupied with court life and out of politics. Instead of the high nobility and royal princes, Louis relied for his ministers on nobles who came from relatively new aristocratic families. His

ministers were expected to be subservient: "I had no intention of sharing my authority with them," Louis said.

Louis's domination of his ministers and secretaries gave him control of the central policy-making machinery of government and thus authority over the traditional areas of monarchical power: the formulation of foreign policy, the making of war and peace, the assertion of the secular power of the crown against any religious authority, and the ability to levy taxes to fulfill these functions. Louis had considerably less success with the internal administration of the kingdom, however.

THE ECONOMY AND THE MILITARY The cost of building palaces, maintaining his court, and pursuing his wars made finances a crucial issue for Louis XIV. He was most fortunate in having the services of Jean-Baptiste Colbert (ZHAHN-bap-TEEST kohl-BAYR) (1619–1683) as controller general of finances. Colbert sought to increase the wealth and power of France by general adherence to mercantilism, which advocated government intervention in economic activities for the benefit of the state. To decrease imports and increase exports, Colbert granted subsidies to individuals who established new industries. To improve communications and the transportation of goods internally, he built roads and canals. To decrease imports directly, Colbert raised tariffs on foreign goods.

The increase in royal power that Louis pursued led the king to develop a professional army numbering 100,000 men in peacetime and 400,000 in time of war. To achieve the prestige and military glory befitting an absolute monarch as well as to ensure the domination of his Bourbon dynasty over European affairs, Louis waged four wars between 1667 and 1713. His ambitions roused much of Europe to form coalitions that were determined to prevent the certain destruction of the European balance of power by Bourbon hegemony. Although Louis added some territory to France's northeastern frontier and established a member of his own Bourbon dynasty on the throne of Spain, he also left France impoverished and surrounded by enemies.

Absolutism in Central and Eastern Europe

During the seventeenth century, a development of great importance for the modern Western world took place with the appearance in central and eastern Europe of three new powers: Prussia, Austria, and Russia.

PRUSSIA Frederick William the Great Elector (1640–1688) laid the foundation for the Prussian state. Realizing that the land he had inherited, known as Brandenburg-Prussia, was a small, open territory with no natural frontiers for defense, Frederick William built an army of

COMPARATIVE ILLUSTRATION

POLITICS & GOVERNMENT

Sun Kings, West and East. At the end of the seventeenth century, two powerful rulers held sway in kingdoms that dominated the affairs of the regions around them. Both rulers saw themselves as favored by divine authority—Louis XIV of France as a divine-right monarch and Kangxi (KANG-shee) of China as possessing the mandate of Heaven. Thus, both rulers saw themselves not as divine beings but as divinely ordained beings whose job was to govern organized societies. On the left, Louis XIV, who ruled France from 1643 to 1715, is seen in a portrait by Hyacinthe Rigaud (ee-ah-SANT ree-GOH) that captures the king's sense of royal dignity and grandeur. One person at court said of Louis XIV: "Louis XIV's vanity was without limit or restraint." On the right, Kangxi, who ruled China from 1661 to 1722, is seen in a nineteenth-century portrait that shows him seated in majesty on his imperial throne. A dedicated ruler, Kangxi once wrote, "One act of negligence may cause sorrow all through the country, and one moment of negligence may result in trouble for hundreds and thousands of generations."

Q *Although these rulers practiced very different religions, why did they justify their powers in such a similar fashion?*

40,000 men, the fourth largest in Europe. To sustain this force, he established the General War Commissariat to levy taxes for the army and oversee its growth. The Commissariat soon evolved into an agency for civil government as well. The new bureaucratic machine became the elector's chief instrument for governing the state. Many of its officials were members of the Prussian landed aristocracy, the Junkers (YOONG-kers), who also served as officers in the all-important army.

In 1701, Frederick William's son Frederick (1688–1713) officially gained the title of king. Elector Frederick III became King Frederick I, and Brandenburg-Prussia simply Prussia. In the eighteenth century, Prussia emerged as a great power in Europe.

AUSTRIA The Austrian Habsburgs had long played a significant role in European politics as Holy Roman Emperors, but by the end of the Thirty Years' War, their hopes of creating an empire in Germany had been dashed. In the seventeenth century, the house of Austria created a new empire in eastern and southeastern Europe.

The nucleus of the new Austrian Empire remained the traditional Austrian hereditary possessions: Lower and Upper Austria, Carinthia, Carniola, Styria, and Tyrol. To these had been added the kingdom of Bohemia and parts of northwestern Hungary. After the defeat of the Turks in 1687 (see Chapter 16), Austria took control of all of Hungary, Transylvania, Croatia, and Slovenia, thus establishing the Austrian Empire in southeastern Europe.

Interior of Versailles: The Hall of Mirrors. Pictured here is the exquisite Hall of Mirrors in King Louis XIV's palace at Versailles. Located on the second floor, the hall overlooks the park below. Three hundred and fifty-seven mirrors were placed on the wall opposite the windows to create an illusion of even greater width. Careful planning went into every detail of the interior decoration. Even the doorknobs were specially designed to reflect the magnificence of Versailles. This photo shows the Hall of Mirrors after the restoration work that was completed in June 2007, a project that took three years, cost 12 million euros (more than $16 million), and included the restoration of the Bohemian crystal chandeliers.

By the beginning of the eighteenth century, the house of Austria had assembled an empire of considerable size.

The Austrian monarchy, however, never became a highly centralized, absolutist state, primarily because it contained so many different national groups. The Austrian Empire remained a collection of territories held together by the Habsburg emperor, who was archduke of Austria, king of Bohemia, and king of Hungary. Each of these regions had its own laws and political life.

FROM MUSCOVY TO RUSSIA   A new Russian state had emerged in the fifteenth century under the leadership of the principality of Muscovy and its grand dukes. In the sixteenth century, Ivan IV (1533–1584) became the first ruler to take the title of *tsar* (the Russian word for *Caesar*). Ivan expanded the territories of Russia eastward and crushed the power of the Russian nobility. He was known as Ivan the Terrible because of his ruthless deeds, among them stabbing his son to death in a heated argument. When Ivan's dynasty came to an end in 1598, it was followed by a period of anarchy that did not end until the Zemsky Sobor (ZEM-skee suh-BOR), or national assembly, chose Michael Romanov (ROH-muh-nahf) as the new tsar, establishing a dynasty that lasted more than three hundred years. One of its most prominent members was Peter the Great.

Peter the Great (1689–1725) was an unusual character. A towering, strong man at 6 feet 9 inches tall, Peter enjoyed a low kind of humor—belching contests and crude jokes—and vicious punishments, including floggings, impalings, and roastings. Peter got a firsthand view of the West when he made a trip there in 1697–1698 and returned to Russia with a firm determination to westernize or Europeanize Russia. He was especially eager to borrow European technology in order to create the army and navy he needed to make Russia a great power.

As could be expected, one of his first priorities was the reorganization of the army and the creation of a navy. Employing both Russians and Europeans as officers, he conscripted peasants for twenty-five-year stints of service to build a standing army of 210,000 men and at the same time formed the first navy Russia had ever had.

To impose the rule of the central government more effectively throughout the land, Peter divided Russia into provinces. Although he hoped to create a "police state," by which he meant a well-ordered community governed in accordance with law, few of his bureaucrats shared his concept of loyalty to the state. Peter hoped to evoke a sense of civic duty among his people, but his own forceful personality created an atmosphere of fear that prevented any such sentiment.

The object of Peter's domestic reforms was to make Russia into a great state and military power. His primary goal was to "open a window to the west," meaning an ice-free port easily accessible to Europe. This could only be achieved on the Baltic, but at that time, the Baltic coast was controlled by Sweden, the most important power in northern Europe. A long and hard-fought war with Sweden won Peter the lands he sought. In 1703, Peter began the construction of a new city, Saint Petersburg, his window to the west and a symbol that Russia was looking westward to Europe. Under Peter, Russia became a great military power and, by his death in 1725, an important European state.

England and Limited Monarchy

Q FOCUS QUESTION: How and why did England avoid the path of absolutism?

Not all states were absolutist in the seventeenth century. One of the most prominent examples of resistance to absolute monarchy came in England, where king and Parliament struggled to determine the roles each should play in governing England.

Conflict Between King and Parliament

With the death of Queen Elizabeth I in 1603, the Tudor dynasty became extinct, and the Stuart line of rulers was inaugurated with the accession to the throne of Elizabeth's cousin, King James VI of Scotland, who became James I (1603–1625) of England. James espoused the divine right of kings, a viewpoint that alienated Parliament, which had grown accustomed under the Tudors to act on the premise that monarch and Parliament together ruled England as a "balanced polity." Then, too, the Puritans—Protestants within the Anglican Church who, inspired by Calvinist theology, wished to eliminate every trace of Roman Catholicism from the Church of England—were alienated by the king's strong defense of the Anglican Church. Many of England's gentry, mostly well-to-do landowners, had become Puritans, and they formed an important and substantial part of the House of Commons, the lower house of Parliament. It was not wise to alienate these men.

The conflict that had begun during the reign of James came to a head during the reign of his son Charles I (1625–1649). Like his father, Charles believed in divine-right monarchy, and religious differences also added to the hostility between Charles I and Parliament. The king's attempt to impose more ritual on the Anglican Church struck the Puritans as a return to Catholic practices. When Charles tried to force the Puritans to accept his religious policies, thousands of them went off to the "howling wildernesses" of America.

Civil War and Commonwealth

Grievances mounted until England finally slipped into a civil war (1642–1648) won by the parliamentary forces, due largely to the New Model Army of Oliver Cromwell, the only real military genius of the war. The New Model Army was composed primarily of more extreme Puritans known as the Independents, who, in typical Calvinist fashion, believed they were doing battle for God. As Cromwell wrote in one of his military reports, "Sir, this is none other but the hand of God; and to Him alone belongs the glory." We might give some credit to Cromwell; his soldiers were well trained in the new military tactics of the seventeenth century.

After the execution of Charles I on January 30, 1649, Parliament abolished the monarchy and the House of Lords and proclaimed England a republic or commonwealth. But Cromwell and his army, unable to work effectively with Parliament, dispersed it by force and established a military dictatorship. After Cromwell's death in 1658, the army decided that military rule was no longer feasible and restored the monarchy in the person of Charles II (1660–1685), the son of Charles I.

Restoration and a Glorious Revolution

Charles II was sympathetic to Catholicism, and Parliament's suspicions were aroused in 1672 when he took the audacious step of issuing the Declaration of Indulgence, which suspended the laws that Parliament had passed against Catholics and Puritans after the restoration of the monarchy. Parliament forced the king to suspend the declaration.

The accession of James II (1685–1688) to the crown virtually guaranteed a new constitutional crisis for England. An open and devout Catholic, his attempt to further Catholic interests made religion once more a primary cause of conflict between king and Parliament. James named Catholics to high positions in the government, army, navy, and universities. Parliamentary outcries against James's policies stopped short of rebellion because the members knew that he was an old man and that his successors were his Protestant daughters Mary and

CHRONOLOGY	Absolute and Limited Monarchy
France	
Louis XIV	1643–1715
Brandenburg-Prussia	
Frederick William the Great Elector	1640–1688
Elector Frederick III (King Frederick I)	1688–1713
Russia	
Ivan IV the Terrible	1533–1584
Peter the Great	1689–1725
First trip to the West	1697–1698
Construction of Saint Petersburg begins	1703
England	
Civil wars	1642–1648
Commonwealth	1649–1653
Charles II	1660–1685
Declaration of Indulgence	1672
James II	1685–1688
Glorious Revolution	1688
Bill of Rights	1689

The Bill of Rights

POLITICS & GOVERNMENT

In 1688, the English experienced a bloodless revolution in which the Stuart king James II was replaced by Mary, James's daughter, and her husband, William of Orange. After William and Mary had assumed power, Parliament passed a Bill of Rights that specified the rights of Parliament and laid the foundation for a constitutional monarchy.

The Bill of Rights

Whereas the said late King James II having abdicated the government, and the throne being thereby vacant, his Highness the prince of Orange (whom it hath pleased Almighty God to make the glorious instrument of delivering this kingdom from popery and arbitrary power) did (by the device of the lords spiritual and temporal, and diverse principal persons of the Commons) cause letters to be written to the lords spiritual and temporal, being Protestants, and other letters to the several counties, cities, universities, boroughs, and Cinque Ports, for the choosing of such persons to represent them, as were of right to be sent to parliament, to meet and sit at Westminster upon the two and twentieth day of January, in this year 1689, in order to such an establishment as that their religion, laws, and liberties might not again be in danger of being subverted; upon which letters elections have been accordingly made.

And thereupon the said lords spiritual and temporal and Commons, pursuant to their respective letters and elections, being now assembled in a full and free representation of this nation, taking into their most serious consideration the best means for attaining the ends aforesaid, do in the first place (as their ancestors in like case have usually done), for the vindication and assertion of their ancient rights and liberties, declare:

1. That the pretended power of suspending laws, or the execution of laws, by regal authority, without consent of parliament is illegal.

2. That the pretended power of dispensing with the laws, or the execution of law by regal authority, as it hath been assumed and exercised of late, is illegal.

3. That the commission for erecting the late court of commissioners for ecclesiastical causes, and all other commissions and courts of like nature, are illegal and pernicious.

4. That levying money for or to the use of the crown by pretense of prerogative, without grant of parliament, for longer time or in other manner than the same is or shall be granted, is illegal.

5. That it is the right of the subjects to petition the king, and all commitments and prosecutions for such petitioning are illegal.

6. That the raising or keeping a standing army within the kingdom in time of peace, unless it be with consent of parliament, is against law.

7. That the subjects which are Protestants may have arms for their defense suitable to their conditions, and as allowed by law.

8. That election of members of parliament ought to be free.

9. That the freedom of speech, and debates or proceedings in parliament, ought not to be impeached or questioned in any court or place out of parliament.

10. That excessive bail ought not to be required, nor excessive fines imposed, nor cruel and unusual punishments inflicted.

11. That jurors ought to be duly impaneled and returned, and jurors which pass upon men in trials for high treason ought to be freeholders.

12. That all grants and promises of fines and forfeitures of particular persons before conviction are illegal and void.

13. And that for redress of all grievances, and for the amending, strengthening, and preserving of the laws, parliament ought to be held frequently.

How did the Bill of Rights lay the foundation for a constitutional monarchy in England?

Source: From *The Statutes: Revised Edition* (London: Eyre & Spottiswoode, 1871), Vol. 2, pp. 10–12.

Anne, born to his first wife. But on June 10, 1688, a son was born to James II's second wife, also a Catholic. Suddenly, the specter of a Catholic hereditary monarchy loomed large. A group of prominent English noblemen invited the Dutch chief executive, William of Orange, husband of James's daughter Mary, to invade England. William and Mary raised an army and invaded England while James, his wife, and their infant son fled to France. With little bloodshed, England had undergone its "Glorious Revolution."

In January 1689, Parliament offered the throne to William and Mary, who accepted it along with the provisions of the Bill of Rights (see the box above). The Bill of Rights affirmed Parliament's right to make laws and levy taxes. The rights of citizens to keep arms and have a jury trial were also confirmed. By deposing one king and establishing another, Parliament had destroyed the divine-right theory of kingship (William was, after all, king by grace of Parliament, not God) and asserted its right to participate in the government. Parliament did not have complete control of the government, but it now had the right to participate in affairs of state. Over the next century, it would gradually prove to be the real authority in the English system of **limited (constitutional) monarchy**.

The Flourishing of European Culture

Q **FOCUS QUESTION:** How did the artistic and literary achievements of this era reflect the political and economic developments of the period?

Despite religious wars and the growth of absolutism, European culture continued to flourish. The era was blessed with a number of prominent artists and writers.

Art: The Baroque

The artistic movement known as the **Baroque** (buh-ROHK) dominated the Western artistic world for a century and a half. The Baroque began in Italy in the last quarter of the sixteenth century and spread to the rest of Europe and Latin America. Baroque artists sought to harmonize the Classical ideals of Renaissance art with the spiritual feelings of the sixteenth-century religious revival. In large part, Baroque art and architecture reflected the search for power that was characteristic of much of the seventeenth century. Baroque churches and palaces featured richly ornamented facades, sweeping staircases, and an overall splendor meant to impress people. Kings and princes wanted not only their subjects, but also other kings and princes to be in awe of their power.

Baroque painting was known for its use of dramatic effects to arouse the emotions, especially evident in the works of Peter Paul Rubens (1577–1640), a prolific artist and an important figure in the spread of the Baroque from Italy to other parts of Europe. In his artistic masterpieces, bodies in violent motion, heavily fleshed nudes, a dramatic use of light and shadow, and rich sensuous pigments converge to express intense emotions.

Art: Dutch Realism

The supremacy of Dutch commerce in the seventeenth century was paralleled by a brilliant flowering of Dutch

Louvre, Paris//© RMN-Grand Palais/Art Resource, NY

Peter Paul Rubens, *The Landing of Marie de' Medici at Marseilles.* The Flemish painter Peter Paul Rubens played a key role in spreading the Baroque style from Italy to other parts of Europe. In *The Landing of Marie de' Medici at Marseilles*, Rubens made dramatic use of light and color, bodies in motion, and luxurious nudes to heighten the emotional intensity of the scene. This was one of a cycle of twenty-one paintings dedicated to the queen mother of France.

painting. Wealthy patricians and burghers of Dutch urban society commissioned works of art for their guildhalls, town halls, and private dwellings. The interests of this burgher society were reflected in the subject matter of many Dutch paintings: portraits of themselves, group portraits of their military companies and guilds, landscapes, seascapes, genre scenes, still lifes, and the interiors of their residences. Neither Classical nor Baroque, Dutch painters were primarily interested in the realistic portrayal of secular everyday life.

A Golden Age of Literature in England

In England, writing for the stage reached new heights between 1580 and 1640. The golden age of English literature is often called the Elizabethan Era because much of the English cultural flowering occurred during Elizabeth's reign. Elizabethan literature exhibits the exuberance and pride associated with English exploits at the time. Of all the forms of Elizabethan literature, none expressed the energy and intellectual versatility of the era better than drama. And no dramatist is more famous or more accomplished than William Shakespeare (1564–1614).

Shakespeare was a "complete man of the theater." Although best known for writing plays, he was also an actor and a shareholder in the chief acting company of the time, the Lord Chamberlain's Company, which played in various London theaters. Shakespeare is to this day hailed as a genius. A master of the English language, he imbued its words with power and majesty. And his technical proficiency was matched by incredible insight into human psychology. Whether writing tragedies or comedies, Shakespeare exhibited a remarkable understanding of the human condition.

CHAPTER SUMMARY

In the last chapter, we observed how the movement of Europeans beyond Europe began to change the shape of world history. But what had made this development possible? After all, the Reformation of the sixteenth century, initially begun by Martin Luther, had brought about the religious division of Europe into Protestant and Catholic camps. By the middle of the sixteenth century, it was apparent that the religious passions of the Reformation era had brought an end to the religious unity of medieval Europe. The religious division (Catholics versus Protestants) was instrumental in beginning a series of religious wars that were complicated by economic, social, and political forces that also played a role.

The crises of the sixteenth and seventeenth centuries soon led to a search for a stable, secular order of politics and made possible the emergence of a system of nation-

states in which power politics took on an increasing significance. Within those states, there slowly emerged some of the machinery that made possible a growing centralization of power. In those states called absolutist, strong monarchs with the assistance of their aristocracies took the lead in providing the leadership for greater centralization. In this so-called age of absolutism, Louis XIV, the Sun King of France, was the model for other rulers. Strong monarchy also prevailed in central and eastern Europe, where three new powers made their appearance: Prussia, Austria, and Russia.

But not all European states followed the pattern of absolute monarchy. Especially important were developments in England, where a series of struggles between king and Parliament took place in the seventeenth century. In the long run, the landed aristocracy gained power at the expense of the monarchs, thus laying the foundations for a constitutional government in which Parliament provided the focus for the institutions of centralized power.

In all the major European states, a growing concern for power and dynamic expansion led to larger armies and greater conflict, stronger economies, and more powerful governments. From a global point of view, Europeans—with their strong governments, prosperous economies, and strengthened military forces—were beginning to dominate other parts of the world, leading to a growing belief in the superiority of their civilization.

Yet despite Europeans' increasing domination of global trade markets, they had not achieved their goal of diminishing the power of Islam, first pursued during the Crusades. In fact, as we shall see in the next chapter, in the midst of European expansion and exploration, three new and powerful Muslim empires were taking shape in the Middle East and South Asia.

CHAPTER TIMELINE

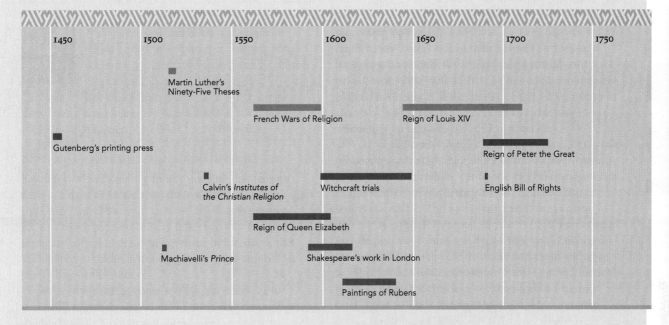

1450   1500   1550   1600   1650   1700   1750

Martin Luther's
Ninety-Five Theses

French Wars of Religion   Reign of Louis XIV

Gutenberg's printing press

Reign of Peter the Great

Calvin's *Institutes of*   Witchcraft trials   English Bill of Rights
the Christian Religion

Reign of Queen Elizabeth

Machiavelli's *Prince*   Shakespeare's work in London

Paintings of Rubens

CHAPTER REVIEW

Upon Reflection

Q What role did politics play in the success of the Protestant Reformation?

Q What did Louis XIV hope to accomplish in his domestic and foreign policies? To what extent did he succeed?

Q What role did the gentry play in seventeenth-century England?

Key Terms

absolutism (p. 383)
Protestant Reformation (p. 383)
new monarchies (p. 383)
Christian humanism (northern Renaissance humanism) (p. 384)
relics (p. 385)
indulgences (p. 385)
justification by faith (p. 385)
predestination (p. 388)
Catholic Reformation (p. 389)
mercantilism (p. 395)
joint-stock company (p. 395)
divine-right monarchy (p. 398)
limited (constitutional) monarchy (p. 403)
Baroque (p. 403)

Suggested Reading

THE REFORMATION: GENERAL WORKS Basic surveys of the Reformation period include **J. D. Tracy,** *Europe's Reformations, 1450–1650* (Oxford, 1999), and **D. MacCulloch,** *The Reformation* (New York, 2003). Also see the brief work by **U. Rublack,** *Reformation Europe* (Cambridge, 2005).

THE PROTESTANT AND CATHOLIC REFORMATIONS On Martin Luther's life, see **H. A. Oberman,** *Luther: Man Between God and the Devil* (New York, 1992), and the brief biography by **M. Marty,** *Martin Luther* (New York, 2004). A good survey of the English Reformation is **A. G. Dickens,** *The English Reformation,* 2nd ed. (New York, 1989). On John Calvin, see **W. G. Naphy,** *Calvin and the Consolidation of the Genevan Reformation* (Philadelphia, 2003). A good introduction to the Catholic Reformation can be found in **R. P. Hsia,** *The World of Catholic Renewal, 1540–1770* (Cambridge, 1998).

EUROPE IN CRISIS, 1560–1650 On the French Wars of Religion, see **R. J. Knecht,** *The French Wars of Religion, 1559–1598,* 2nd ed. (New York, 1996). The fundamental study of the Thirty Years' War is **P. H. Wilson,** *The Thirty Years War, Europe's Tragedy* (Cambridge, Mass., 2009). Witchcraft hysteria can be examined in **R. Briggs,** *Witches and Neighbours: The Social and Cultural Context of European Witchcraft,* 2nd ed. (Oxford, 2002).

ABSOLUTE AND LIMITED MONARCHY A solid and very readable biography of Louis XIV is **J. Levi,** *Louis XIV* (New York, 2004). See **P. H. Wilson,** *Absolutism in Central Europe* (New York, 2000), on both Prussia and Austria. On Peter the Great, see **P. Bushkovitz,** *Peter the Great* (Oxford, 2001). On the English Civil War, see **D. Purkiss,** *The English Civil War* (New York, 2006).

EUROPEAN CULTURE For a general survey of Baroque culture, see **F. C. Marchetti et al.,** *Baroque, 1600–1770* (New York, 2005). The literature on Shakespeare is enormous. For a biography, see **A. L. Rowse,** *The Life of Shakespeare* (New York, 1963).

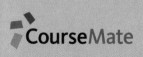

Visit the CourseMate website at **www.cengagebrain.com** for additional study tools and review materials for this chapter.

The Muslim Empires

Turks fight Christians at the Battle of Mohács.

Topkapi Museum Istanbul/© Gianni Dagli Orti/The Art Archive at Art Resource, NY

CHAPTER OUTLINE
AND FOCUS QUESTIONS

The Ottoman Empire

Q What was the ethnic composition of the Ottoman Empire, and how did the government of the sultan administer such a diverse population? How did Ottoman policy in this regard compare with the policies applied in Europe and Asia?

The Safavids

Q How did the Safavid Empire come into existence, and what led to its collapse?

The Grandeur of the Mughals

Q What role did Islam play in the Mughal Empire, and how did the Mughals' approach to religion compare with that of the Ottomans and the Safavids? What might explain the differences?

┌─ CRITICAL THINKING ─────────────────
Q What were the main characteristics of each of the Muslim empires, and in what ways did they resemble each other? How were they distinct from their European counterparts?
└──────────────────────────────────────

THE OTTOMAN ARMY, led by Sultan Suleyman the Magnificent, arrived at Mohács, on the plains of Hungary, on an August morning in 1526. The Turkish force numbered about 100,000 men, and its weapons included three hundred new long-range cannons. Facing them was a somewhat larger European force, clothed in heavy armor but armed with only one hundred older cannons.

The battle began at noon and was over in two hours. The flower of the Hungarian cavalry had been destroyed, and 20,000 foot soldiers had drowned in a nearby swamp. The Ottomans had lost fewer than two hundred men. Two weeks later, they seized the Hungarian capital at Buda and prepared to lay siege to the nearby Austrian city of Vienna. Europe was in a panic, but Mohács was to be the high point of Turkish expansion in Europe.

In launching their Age of Exploration, European rulers had hoped that by controlling global markets, they could cripple the power of Islam and reduce its threat to the security of Europe. But the Christian nations' dream of expanding their influence around the globe at the expense of their great Muslim rival had not entirely been achieved. On the contrary, the Muslim world, which appeared to have entered a period of decline with the collapse of the Abbasid caliphate during the era of the Mongols, managed to revive in the shadow of Europe's Age of Exploration, a period that also saw the rise of three great Muslim empires. These powerful Muslim states—those of the Ottomans, the Safavids, and the Mughals—dominated the Middle East and the South Asian subcontinent and brought a measure of stability to a region that had been in turmoil for centuries.

The Ottoman Empire

 FOCUS QUESTIONS: What was the ethnic composition of the Ottoman Empire, and how did the government of the sultan administer such a diverse population? How did Ottoman policy in this regard compare with the policies applied in Europe and Asia?

The Ottoman Turks were among the various Turkic-speaking nomadic peoples who had spread westward from Central Asia in the ninth, tenth, and eleventh centuries. The first to appear were the Seljuk Turks, who initially attempted to revive the declining Abbasid caliphate in Baghdad. Later they established themselves in the Anatolian peninsula at the expense of the Byzantine Empire. Turks served as warriors or administrators, while the peasants who tilled the farmland were mainly Greek.

The Rise of the Ottoman Turks

In the late thirteenth century, a new group of Turks under the tribal leader Osman (os-MAHN) (1280–1326) began to consolidate their power in the northwestern corner of the Anatolian peninsula. At first, the Osman Turks were relatively peaceful and engaged in pastoral pursuits, but as the Seljuk Empire began to disintegrate in the early fourteenth century, they began to expand and founded the Osmanli (os-MAHN-lee) dynasty, with its capital at Bursa (BURR-suh). The Osmanlis later came to be known as the Ottomans.

The Ottomans gained a key advantage by seizing the Bosporus and the Dardanelles, between the Mediterranean and the Black Seas. The Byzantine Empire, of course, had controlled the area for centuries, serving as a buffer between the Muslim Middle East and the Latin West. The Byzantines, however, had been severely weakened by the sack of Constantinople in the Fourth Crusade in 1204 and the Western occupation of much of the empire for the next half century. In 1345, Ottoman forces under their leader Orkhan (or-KHAHN) I (1326–1360) crossed the Bosporus for the first time to support a usurper against the Byzantine emperor in Constantinople. Setting up their first European base at Gallipoli (gah-LIP-poh-lee) at the Mediterranean entrance to the Dardanelles, Turkish forces expanded gradually into the Balkans and allied with fractious Serbian and Bulgar

forces against the Byzantines. In these unstable conditions, the Ottomans gradually established permanent settlements throughout the area, where Turkish provincial governors, called **beys** (BAYS) (from the Turkish *beg*, "knight"), drove out the previous landlords and collected taxes from the local Slavic peasants. The Ottoman leader now began to claim the title of **sultan** (SUL-tun) or sovereign of his domain.

In 1360, Orkhan was succeeded by his son Murad I (moo-RAHD) (1360–1389), who consolidated Ottoman power in the Balkans and gradually reduced the Byzantine emperor to a vassal. Murad now began to build up a strong military administration based on the recruitment of Christians into an elite guard. Called **Janissaries** (JAN-nih-say-reez) (from the Turkish *yeni chert*, "new troops"), they were recruited from the local Christian population in the Balkans and then converted to Islam and trained as foot soldiers or administrators. One of the major advantages of the Janissaries was that they were directly subordinated to the sultanate and therefore owed their loyalty to the person of the sultan. Other military forces were organized by the beys and were thus loyal to their local tribal leaders.

The Janissary corps also represented a response to changes in warfare. As the knowledge of firearms spread in the late fourteenth century, the Turks began to master the new technology, including siege cannons and muskets (see the comparative essay "The Changing Face of War" on p. 409). The traditional nomadic cavalry charge was now outmoded and was superseded by infantry forces armed with muskets. Thus, the Janissaries provided a well-armed infantry who served both as an elite guard to protect the palace and as a means of extending Turkish control in the Balkans. With his new forces, Murad defeated the Serbs at the famous Battle of Kosovo (KAWSS-suh-voh) in 1389 and ended Serbian hegemony in the area.

Expansion of the Empire

Under Murad's successor, Bayazid (by-uh-ZEED) I (1389–1402), the Ottomans advanced northward, annexed Bulgaria, and slaughtered the French cavalry at a major battle on the Danube. When Mehmet (meh-MET) II (1451–1481) succeeded to the throne, he was determined to capture Constantinople. Already in control of the Dardanelles, he ordered the construction of a major fortress on the Bosporus just north of the city, which put the Turks in a position to strangle the Byzantines.

THE FALL OF CONSTANTINOPLE The last Byzantine emperor issued a desperate call for help from the Europeans, but only the Genoese came to his defense. With 80,000 troops ranged against only 7,000 defenders,

COMPARATIVE ESSAY

The Changing Face of War

SCIENCE & TECHNOLOGY

"War," as the renowned French historian Fernand Braudel once observed, "has always been a matter of arms and techniques. Improved techniques can radically alter the course of events." Braudel's remark was directed to the situation in the Mediterranean region during the sixteenth century, when the adoption of artillery changed the face of warfare and gave enormous advantages to the countries that stood at the head of the new technological revolution. But it could as easily have been applied to the present day, when potential adversaries possess weapons capable of reaching across oceans and continents.

One crucial aspect of military superiority, of course, lies in the nature of weaponry. From the invention of the bow and arrow to the advent of the atomic era, the possession of superior instruments of war has provided a distinct advantage against a poorly armed enemy. It was at least partly the possession of bronze weapons, for example, that enabled the invading Hyksos to conquer Egypt during the second millennium B.C.E.

Mobility is another factor of vital importance. During the second millennium B.C.E., horse-drawn chariots revolutionized the art of war from the Mediterranean Sea to the Yellow River valley in northern China. Later, the invention of the stirrup enabled mounted warriors to shoot bows and arrows from horseback, a technique applied with great effect by the Mongols as they devastated civilizations across the Eurasian supercontinent.

To protect themselves from marauding warriors, settled societies began to erect massive walls around their cities and fortresses. That in turn led to the invention of siege weapons like the catapult and the battering ram. The Mongols allegedly even came up with an early form of chemical warfare, hurling human bodies infected with the plague into the bastions of their enemies.

The invention of explosives launched the next great revolution in warfare. First used as a weapon of war by the Tang dynasty in China, explosives were brought to

© William J. Duiker

Roman troops defeat Celtic warriors in this detail from the Great Altar of Pergamum.

the West by the Turks, who used them with great effectiveness in the fifteenth century against the Byzantine Empire. But the Europeans quickly mastered the new technology and took it to new heights, inventing handheld firearms and mounting iron cannons on their warships. The latter represented a significant advantage to European fleets as they began to compete with rivals for control of the Indian and Pacific Oceans.

The twentieth century saw revolutionary new developments in the art of warfare, from armored vehicles to airplanes to nuclear arms. But as weapons grow ever more fearsome, they are more risky to use, resulting in the paradox of the Vietnam War, when lightly armed Viet Cong guerrilla units were able to fight the world's mightiest army to a virtual standstill. As the Chinese military strategist Sun Tzu had long ago observed, victory in war often goes to the smartest, not the strongest.

 Why were the Europeans, rather than other peoples, able to make effective use of firearms to expand their influence throughout the rest of the world?

Mehmet laid siege to Constantinople in 1453. In their attack on the city, the Turks made use of massive cannons with 26-foot barrels that could launch stone balls weighing up to 1,200 pounds each. The Byzantines stretched heavy chains across the Golden Horn, the inlet that forms the city's harbor, to prevent a naval attack

The Turkish Conquest of Constantinople. Mehmet II put a stranglehold on the Byzantine capital of Constantinople with a surprise attack by Turkish ships, which were dragged overland and placed in the water behind the Byzantines' defense lines. In addition, the Turks made use of massive cannons that could launch stone balls weighing up to 1,200 pounds each. The heavy bombardment of the city walls presaged a new kind of warfare in Europe. Notice the fanciful Gothic interpretation of the city in this contemporary French miniature of the siege.

from the north and prepared to make their final stand behind the 13-mile-long wall along the western edge of the city. But Mehmet's forces seized the tip of the peninsula north of the Golden Horn and then dragged their ships overland across the peninsula from the Bosporus and put them into the water behind the chains. Finally, the walls were breached; the Byzantine emperor died in the final battle.

THE ADVANCE INTO WESTERN ASIA AND AFRICA With their new capital at Constantinople, renamed Istanbul, the Ottoman Turks had become a dominant force in the Balkans and the Anatolian peninsula. They now began to advance to the east against the Shi'ite kingdom of the Safavids (sah-FAH-weeds) in Persia (see "The Safavids"

later in this chapter), which had been promoting rebellion among the Anatolian tribal population and disrupting Turkish trade through the Middle East. After defeating the Safavids at a major battle in 1514, Emperor Selim (seh-LEEM) I (1512–1520) consolidated Turkish control over the territory that had been ancient Mesopotamia and then turned his attention to the Mamluks (MAM-looks) in Egypt, who had failed to support the Ottomans in their struggle against the Safavids. The Mamluks were defeated in Syria in 1516; Cairo fell a year later. Now controlling several of the holy cities of Islam, including Jerusalem, Mecca, and Medina, Selim declared himself to be the new caliph, or successor to Muhammad. During the next few years, Turkish armies and fleets advanced westward along the African coast, occupying Tripoli, Tunis, and Algeria and eventually penetrating almost to the Strait of Gibraltar (see Map 16.1).

The impact of Turkish rule on the peoples of North Africa was relatively light. Like their predecessors, the Turks were Muslims, and they preferred where possible to administer their conquered regions through local rulers. The central government appointed **pashas** (PAH-shuz) who collected taxes (and then paid a fixed percentage as tribute to the central government), maintained law and order, and were directly responsible to Istanbul. The Turks ruled from coastal cities like Algiers, Tunis, and Tripoli and made no attempt to control the interior beyond maintaining the trade routes through the Sahara to the trading centers along the Niger River. Meanwhile, local pirates along the Barbary Coast—the northern coast of Africa from Egypt to the Atlantic Ocean—competed with their Christian rivals in raiding shipping in the Mediterranean.

By the seventeenth century, the links between the imperial court in Istanbul and its appointed representatives in North Africa had begun to decline. Some pashas were dethroned by local elites, while others, such as the bey of Tunis, became hereditary rulers. Even Egypt, whose agricultural wealth and control over the route to the Red Sea made it the most important country in the area to the Turks, gradually became autonomous under a new official class of Janissaries.

TURKISH EXPANSION IN EUROPE After their conquest of Constantinople in 1453, the Turks tried to extend their territory in Europe. Under the leadership of Suleyman (SOO-lay-mahn) I the Magnificent (1520–1566), Turkish forces advanced up the Danube, seizing Belgrade in 1521 and winning a major victory over the Hungarians at the Battle of Mohács (MOH-hach) on the Danube in 1526. Subsequently, the Turks overran most of Hungary, moved into Austria, and advanced as far as Vienna, where they were finally repulsed in 1529. At the

Bibliothèque Nationale, Paris/The Bridgeman Art Library

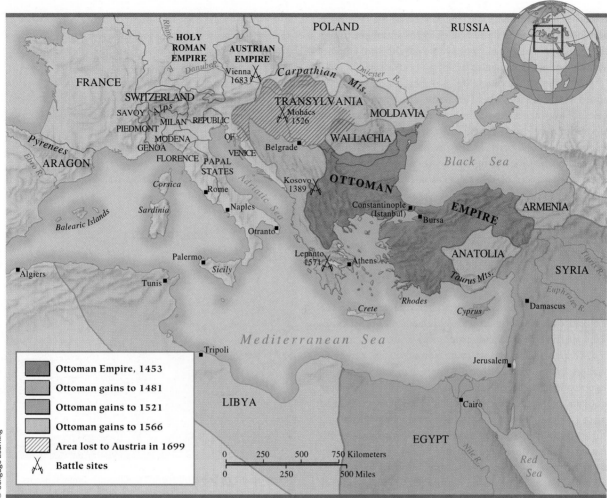

MAP 16.1 **The Ottoman Empire.** This map shows the territorial growth of the Ottoman Empire from the eve of the conquest of Constantinople in 1453 to the end of the seventeenth century, when a defeat at the hands of Austria led to the loss of a substantial portion of central Europe.

Q *Where did the Ottomans come from?*

same time, they extended their power into the western Mediterranean and threatened to turn it into a Turkish lake until a large Turkish fleet was destroyed by the Spanish at Lepanto (LEH-pahn-toh *or* LIH-pan-toh) in 1571.

In the second half of the seventeenth century, the Ottoman Empire again took the offensive. By mid-1683, the Ottomans had marched through the Hungarian plain and laid siege to Vienna. Repulsed by a mixed army of Austrians, Poles, Bavarians, and Saxons, the Turks retreated and were pushed out of Hungary by a new European coalition. Although they retained the core of their empire, the Ottoman Turks would never again be a threat to Europe. The Turkish empire held together for the rest of the seventeenth and the eighteenth centuries, but it faced new challenges from the ever-growing

Austrian Empire in southeastern Europe and the new Russian giant to the north.

The Nature of Turkish Rule

Like other Muslim empires in Persia and India, the Ottoman political system was the result of the evolution of tribal institutions into a sedentary empire. At the apex of the Ottoman system was the sultan, who was the supreme authority in both a political and a military sense. The origins of this system can be traced back to the bey, who as tribal leader was a first among equals, who could claim loyalty from his chiefs only as long as he could provide them with booty and grazing lands. Disputes were settled by tribal law, while Muslim laws were secondary. Tribal leaders collected taxes—or booty—from areas under their control and sent one-fifth on to the bey. Both administrative and military power were centralized under the bey, and the capital was wherever the bey and his administration happened to be.

But with the rise of empire came the adoption of Byzantine traditions of rule. The status and prestige of the sultan now increased relative to the subordinate tribal leaders. Court rituals inherited from the Byzantines and Persians were adopted, as was a centralized administrative system that increasingly isolated the sultan in his palace. The position of the sultan was hereditary, with a son, although not necessarily the eldest, always succeeding the father. This practice led to chronic succession struggles upon the death of individual sultans, and the losers were often executed (strangled with a silk bowstring) or imprisoned. Heirs to the throne were assigned as provincial governors to provide them with experience.

THE HAREM   The heart of the sultan's power was in the Topkapi (tahp-KAH-pee) Palace in the center of Istanbul. Topkapi (meaning "cannon gate") was constructed in 1459 by Mehmet II and served as an administrative center as well as the private residence of the sultan and his family. Eventually, it had a staff of 20,000 employees. The private domain of the sultan was called the **harem** ("sacred place"). Here he resided with his concubines. Normally, a sultan did not marry but chose several concubines as his favorites; they were accorded this status after they gave birth to sons. When a son became a sultan, his mother became known as the queen mother and served as adviser to the throne. This tradition, initiated by the influential wife of Suleyman the Magnificent, often resulted in considerable authority for the queen mother in affairs of state.

Members of the harem, like the Janissaries, were often of slave origin and formed an elite element in Ottoman society. Since the enslavement of Muslims was forbidden, slaves were taken among non-Islamic peoples. Some concubines were prisoners selected for the position, while others were purchased or offered to the sultan as a gift. They were then trained and educated like the Janissaries in a system called *devshirme* (dev-SHEER-may) ("collection"). *Devshirme* had originated in the practice of requiring local clan leaders to provide prisoners to the sultan as part of their tax obligation. Talented males were given special training for eventual placement in military or administrative positions, while their female counterparts were trained for service in the harem, with instruction in reading, the Qur'an, sewing and embroidery, and musical performance. They were ranked according to their status, and some were permitted to leave the harem to marry officials.

Unique to the Ottoman Empire from the fifteenth century onward was the exclusive use of slaves to produce its royal heirs. Contrary to myth, few of the women of the

Recruitment of the Children. The Ottoman Empire, like its Chinese counterpart, sought to recruit its officials on the basis of merit. Through the *devshirme* system, youthful candidates were selected from the non-Muslim population in villages throughout the empire. In this painting, an imperial officer is counting coins to pay for the children's travel expenses to Istanbul, where they will undergo extensive academic and military training. Note the concern of two of the mothers and a priest as they question the official, who undoubtedly underwent the process himself as a child. As they leave their family and friends, the children carry their worldly possessions in bags slung over their shoulders.

imperial harem were used for sexual purposes, as the majority were members of the sultan's extended family— sisters, daughters, widowed mothers, and in-laws, with their own personal slaves and entourage. Contemporary European observers compared the atmosphere in the Topkapi harem to a Christian nunnery, with its hierarchical organization, enforced chastity, and rule of silence.

Because of their proximity to the sultan, the women of the harem often wielded so much political power that the era has been called "the sultanate of women." Queen mothers administered the imperial household and engaged in diplomatic relations with other countries while controlling the marital alliances of their daughters with senior officials or members of other royal families in the region. One princess was married seven separate times from the age of two after her previous husbands died either in battle or by execution.

ADMINISTRATION OF THE GOVERNMENT The sultan ruled through an imperial council that met four days a week and was chaired by the chief minister known as the **grand vizier** (veh-ZEER) (Turkish *vezir*). The sultan often attended behind a screen, whence he could privately indicate his desires to the grand vizier. The latter presided over the imperial bureaucracy. Like the palace guard, the bureaucrats were not an exclusive group but were chosen at least partly by merit from a palace school for training officials. Most officials were Muslims by birth, but some talented Janissaries became senior members of the bureaucracy, and almost all the later grand viziers came from the *devshirme* system.

Local administration during the imperial period was a product of Turkish tribal tradition and was similar in some respects to fief-holding in Europe. The empire was divided into provinces and districts governed by officials who, like their tribal predecessors, combined civil and military functions. Senior officials were assigned land in fief by the sultan and were then responsible for collecting taxes and supplying armies to the empire. These lands were then farmed out to the local cavalry elite called the *sipahis* (suh-pah-heez), who obtained their salaries by exacting taxes from all peasants in their fiefdoms.

Religion and Society in the Ottoman World

Like most Turkic-speaking peoples throughout the Middle East, the Ottoman ruling elites were Sunni Muslims. Ottoman sultans had claimed the title of caliph ("defender of the faith") since the early sixteenth century and thus were theoretically responsible for guiding the flock and maintaining Islamic law, the *Shari'a*. In practice, the sultan assigned these duties to a supreme religious authority, who administered the law and maintained schools for educating Muslims. Islamic law and customs were applied to all Muslims in the empire. Like their rulers, most Turkic-speaking people were Sunni Muslims, but some communities were attracted to Sufism (see Chapter 7) or other heterodox doctrines. The government tolerated such activities as long as their practitioners remained loyal, but in the early sixteenth century, unrest among these groups—some of whom converted to the Shi'ite version of Islam—outraged the conservative *ulama* and eventually led to war against the Safavids (see "The Safavids" later in this chapter).

THE TREATMENT OF MINORITIES Non-Muslims— mostly Orthodox Christians (Greeks and Slavs), Jews, and

CHRONOLOGY	The Ottoman Empire	
Reign of Osman I		1280–1326
Ottoman Turks cross the Bosporus		1345
Murad I consolidates Turkish power in the Balkans		1360
Ottomans defeat the Serbian army at Kosovo		1389
Reign of Mehmet II the Conqueror		1451–1481
Turkish conquest of Constantinople		1453
Turks defeat the Mamluks in Syria and seize Cairo		1516–1517
Reign of Suleyman I the Magnificent		1520–1566
Turks defeat the Hungarians at Battle of Mohács		1526
Defeat of the Turks at Vienna		1529
Battle of Lepanto		1571
Second siege of Vienna		1683

Armenian Christians—formed a significant minority within the empire, which treated them with relative tolerance. Non-Muslims were compelled to pay a head tax (because of their exemption from military service), and they were permitted to practice their religion or convert to Islam, although Muslims were prohibited from adopting another faith. Most of the population in European areas of the empire remained Christian, but in some places, such as the territory now called Bosnia, substantial numbers converted to Islam.

Technically, women in the Ottoman Empire were subject to the same restrictions that afflicted their counterparts in other Muslim societies, but their position was ameliorated to some degree by various factors. In the first place, non-Muslims were subject to the laws and customs of their own religions; thus, Orthodox Christian, Jewish, and Armenian Christian women were spared some of the restrictions applied to their Muslim sisters. In the second place, Islamic laws as applied in the Ottoman Empire defined the legal position of women comparatively tolerantly. Women were permitted to own and inherit property, including their dowries. They could not be forced into marriage and in certain cases were permitted to seek a divorce. As we have seen, women often exercised considerable influence in the palace and in a few instances even served as senior officials, such as governors of provinces. The relatively tolerant attitude toward women in Ottoman-held territories has been ascribed by some to Turkish tribal traditions, which took a more egalitarian view of gender roles than the sedentary societies of the region did.

The Ottomans in Decline

By the seventeenth century, signs of internal rot had begun to appear in the empire, although the first loss of

A Turkish Discourse on Coffee

INTERACTION & EXCHANGE

Coffee was first introduced to Turkey from the Arabian peninsula in the mid-sixteenth century and supposedly came to Europe during the Turkish siege of Vienna in 1529. The following account was written by Katib Chelebi (kah-TEEB CHEL-uh-bee), a seventeenth-century Turkish author who, among other things, compiled an extensive encyclopedia and bibliography. Here, in *The Balance of Truth*, he describes how coffee entered the empire and the problems it caused for public morality. (In the Muslim world, as in Europe and later in colonial America, the drinking of coffee was associated with coffeehouses, where rebellious elements often gathered to promote antigovernment activities.) Chelebi died in Istanbul in 1657, reportedly while drinking a cup of coffee.

Katib Chelebi, *The Balance of Truth*

[Coffee] originated in Yemen and has spread, like tobacco, over the world. Certain sheikhs, who lived with their dervishes in the mountains of Yemen, used to crush and eat the berries . . . of a certain tree. Some would roast them and drink their water. Coffee is a cold dry food, suited to the ascetic life and sedative of lust. . . .

It came to Asia Minor by sea, about 1543, and met with a hostile reception, *fetwas* [decrees] being delivered against it. For they said, Apart from its being roasted, the fact that it is drunk in gatherings, passed from hand to

hand, is suggestive of loose living. It is related of Abul-Suud Efendi that he had holes bored in the ships that brought it, plunging their cargoes of coffee into the sea. But these strictures and prohibitions availed nothing. . . . One coffeehouse was opened after another, and men would gather together, with great eagerness and enthusiasm, to drink. Drug addicts in particular, finding it a life-giving thing, which increased their pleasure, were willing to die for a cup.

Storytellers and musicians diverted the people from their employments, and working for one's living fell into disfavor. Moreover the people, from prince to beggar, amused themselves with knifing one another. Toward the end of 1633, the late Ghazi Gultan Murad, becoming aware of the situation, promulgated an edict, out of regard and compassion for the people, to this effect: Coffeehouses throughout the Guarded Domains shall be dismantled and not opened hereafter. Since then, the coffeehouses of the capital have been as desolate as the heart of the ignorant. . . . But in cities and towns outside Istanbul, they are opened just as before. As has been said above, such things do not admit of a perpetual ban.

Q *Why did coffee come to be regarded as a dangerous substance in the Ottoman Empire? Were the authorities successful in suppressing its consumption?*

Source: From *The Balance of Truth* by Katib Chelebi, translated by G.L. Lewis, copyright 1927.

imperial territory did not occur until 1699, when Transylvania and much of Hungary were ceded to Austria in the Treaty of Karlowitz (KARL-oh-vits). Apparently, a number of factors were involved. In the first place, the administrative system inherited from the tribal period began to break down. Although the *devshirme* system of training officials continued, *devshirme* graduates were now permitted to marry and inherit property and to enroll their sons in the palace corps. Thus, they were gradually transformed from a meritocratic administrative elite into a privileged and often degenerate hereditary caste. Local administrators were corrupted and taxes rose as the central bureaucracy lost its links with rural areas. Constant wars depleted the treasury, and transport and communications were neglected. Interest in science and technology, once a hallmark of the Arab Empire, was in decline.

In addition, the empire was beset by economic difficulties caused by the diversion of trade routes away from the eastern Mediterranean and the price inflation brought about by the influx of cheap American silver.

Other signs of change were the increasing material affluence and the impact of Western ideas and customs. Sophisticated officials and merchants began to mimic the habits and lifestyles of their European counterparts, dressing in the European fashion, purchasing Western furniture and art objects, and ignoring Muslim strictures against the consumption of alcohol and sexual activities outside marriage. During the sixteenth and early seventeenth centuries, coffee and tobacco were introduced into polite Ottoman society, and cafés for their consumption began to appear in the major cities (see the box above). One sultan in the early seventeenth century issued a decree prohibiting the

Photo credits: © Fergus O'Brien//Getty Images; © William J. Duiker

The Suleymaniye Mosque, Istanbul. The magnificent mosques built under the patronage of Suleyman the Magnificent are a great legacy of the Ottoman Empire and a fitting supplement to Hagia Sophia, the cathedral built by the Byzantine emperor Justinian in the sixth century C.E. Towering under a central dome, these mosques seem to defy gravity and, like European Gothic cathedrals, convey a sense of weightlessness. The Suleymaniye (soo-lay-MAHN-ee-eh) Mosque is one of the most impressive and most graceful in Istanbul. A far cry from the seventh-century desert mosques constructed of palm trunks, the Ottoman mosques stand among the architectural wonders of the world. Under the massive dome, the interior of the Suleymaniye Mosque offers a quiet refuge for prayer and reflection, bathed in muted sunlight and the warmth of plush carpets, as shown in the inset photo.

consumption of both coffee and tobacco, arguing (correctly, no doubt) that many cafés were nests of antigovernment intrigue. He even began to wander incognito through the streets of Istanbul at night. Any of his subjects detected in immoral or illegal acts were summarily executed and their bodies left on the streets as an example to others.

There were also signs of a decline in competence within the ruling family. Whereas the first sultans reigned twenty-seven years on average, later ones averaged only thirteen years, suggesting an increase in turmoil within the ruling cliques. The throne now went to the oldest surviving male, while his rivals were kept secluded in a latticed cage and thus had no governmental experience if they succeeded to rule. Later sultans also became less involved in government, and more power flowed to the office of the grand vizier, called the **Sublime Porte** (PORT), or to eunuchs and members of the harem. Palace intrigue increased as a result.

Ottoman Art

The Ottoman sultans were enthusiastic patrons of the arts and maintained large ateliers of artisans and artists, primarily at the Topkapi Palace in Istanbul but also in other important cities of the vast empire. The period from Mehmet II in the fifteenth century to the early eighteenth century witnessed the flourishing of pottery, rugs, silk and other textiles, jewelry, arms and armor, and calligraphy. All adorned the palaces of the rulers, testifying to their opulence and exquisite taste. The artists came from all parts of the realm and beyond.

ARCHITECTURE By far the greatest contribution of the Ottoman Empire to world art was its architecture, especially the magnificent mosques of the second half of the sixteenth century. Traditionally, prayer halls in mosques were divided by numerous pillars that supported small individual domes, creating a private, forestlike atmosphere. The Turks, however, modeled their new mosques on the open floor plan of the Byzantine church of Hagia Sophia (completed in 537), which had been turned into a mosque by Mehmet II, and began to push the pillars toward the outer wall to create a prayer hall with an uninterrupted central area under one large dome. With this plan, large numbers of believers could worship in unison in accordance with Muslim preference. By the mid-sixteenth century, the greatest of all Ottoman architects, Sinan (si-NAHN), began erecting the first of his eighty-one mosques with an uncluttered prayer area. Each was topped by an imposing dome, and often, as at Edirne, the entire building was framed with four towering narrow minarets. By emphasizing its vertical lines, the minarets camouflaged the massive stone bulk of the structure and gave it a feeling of incredible lightness. These four graceful minarets would find new expression sixty years later in India's white marble Taj Mahal (see "Mughal Culture" later in this chapter).

Earlier, in the thirteenth-century the Seljuk Turks of Anatolia had created beautiful tile decorations with two-color mosaics. Now Ottoman artists invented a new glazed tile art with painted flowers and geometrical designs in brilliant blue, green, yellow, and their own secret "tomato red." Entire walls, both interior and exterior, were covered with the painted tiles, which adorned palaces as well as mosques.

TEXTILES   The sixteenth century also witnessed the flourishing of textiles and rugs. The Byzantine emperor Justinian had introduced the cultivation of silkworms to the West in the sixth century, and the silk industry resurfaced under the Ottomans. Perhaps even more famous than Turkish silks are the rugs. But whereas silks were produced under the patronage of the sultans, rugs were a peasant industry. Each village boasted its own distinctive design and color scheme for the rugs it produced.

The Safavids

Q   FOCUS QUESTION: How did the Safavid Empire come into existence, and what led to its collapse?

After the collapse of the empire of Tamerlane in the early fifteenth century, the area extending from Persia into Central Asia lapsed into anarchy. The Uzbeks (ooz-BEKS), Turkic-speaking peoples from Central Asia, were the chief political and military force in the area. From their capital at Bukhara (boh-KAHR-uh *or* boo-KAH-ruh), east of the Caspian Sea, they maintained a semblance of control over the highly fluid tribal alignments until the emergence of the Safavid dynasty in Persia at the beginning of the sixteenth century.

The Safavid dynasty was founded by Shah Ismail (IS-mah-eel) (1487–1524), the descendant of Sheikh Safi al-Din (SAH-fee ul-DIN) (hence the name *Safavid*), who traced his origins to Ali, the fourth *imam* of the Muslim faith. In the early fourteenth century, Safi had been the leader of a community of Turkic-speaking tribespeople in Azerbaijan, near the Caspian Sea. Safi's community was only one of many Sufi mystical religious groups throughout the area. In time, the doctrine spread among

nomadic groups throughout the Middle East and was transformed into the more activist Shi'ite version of Islam. Its adherents were known as "red heads" because they wore a distinctive red cap with twelve folds, meant to symbolize allegiance to the twelve *imams* of the Shi'ite faith.

In 1501, after Ismail's forces seized much of Iran and Iraq, he proclaimed himself the shah of a new Persian state. Baghdad was subdued in 1508 and the Uzbeks and their capital at Bokhara shortly thereafter. Ismail now sent Shi'ite preachers into Anatolia to proselytize and promote rebellion among Turkish tribal peoples in the Ottoman Empire. In retaliation, the Ottoman sultan, Selim I, advanced against the Safavids in Iran and won a major battle near Tabriz (tah-BREEZ) in 1514. But Selim could not maintain control of the area, and Ismail regained Tabriz a few years later.

The Ottomans returned to the attack in the 1580s and forced the new Safavid shah, Abbas (uh-BAHS) I the Great (1587–1629), to sign a punitive peace acceding to the loss of much territory. The capital was subsequently moved from Tabriz in the northwest to Isfahan (is-fah-HAHN) in the south. Still, it was under Shah Abbas that the Safavids reached the zenith of their glory. He established a system similar to the Janissaries in Turkey to train administrators to replace the traditional warrior elite. He also used the period of peace to strengthen his army, now armed with modern weapons, and in the early seventeenth century, he attempted to regain the lost territories. Although he had some initial success, war resumed in the 1620s, and a lasting peace was not achieved until 1638 (see Map 16.2).

Abbas the Great had managed to strengthen the dynasty significantly, and for a time after his death in 1629, it remained stable and vigorous. But succession conflicts plagued the dynasty. Partly as a result, the power of the more militant Shi'ites began to increase at court and in Safavid society at large. The intellectual freedom that had characterized the empire at its height was curtailed under the pressure of religious orthodoxy, and Iranian women, who had enjoyed considerable freedom and influence during the early empire, were forced to withdraw into seclusion and behind the veil. Meanwhile, attempts to suppress the religious beliefs of minorities led to increased popular unrest. In the early eighteenth century, Afghan warriors took advantage of local revolts to seize the capital of Isfahan, forcing the remnants of the Safavid ruling family to retreat to Azerbaijan, their original homeland. As the Ottomans seized territories along the western border, the empire finally collapsed in 1723. Eventually, order was restored by the military adventurer Nadir Shah Afshar (NAH-der shah ahf-SHAR), who launched an extended series of campaigns that restored the country's borders and even occupied the Mughal capital of Delhi (see "The Shadows Lengthen" later in this

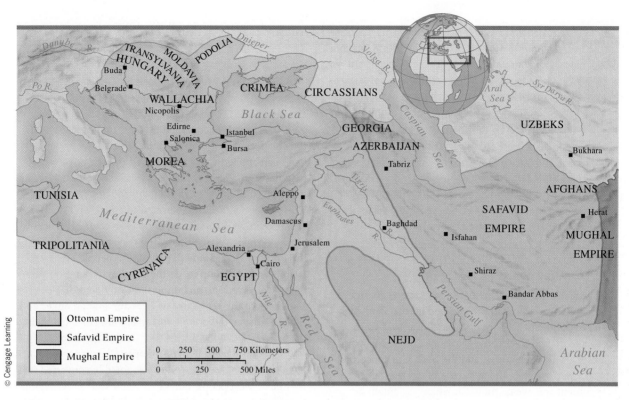

MAP 16.2 The Ottoman and Safavid Empires, c. 1683. During the seventeenth century, the Ottoman and Safavid Empires contested vigorously for hegemony in the eastern Mediterranean and the Middle East. This map shows the territories controlled by each state in the late seventeenth century.

Q *Which states shared control over the ancient lands in the Tigris and Euphrates valleys? In which modern-day countries are those lands?*

chapter). After his death, the Zand dynasty ruled until the end of the eighteenth century.

Safavid Politics and Society

Like the Ottoman Empire, Persia under the Safavids was a mixed society The Safavids had come to power with the support of nomadic Turkic-speaking tribal groups, and leading elements from those groups retained considerable influence. But the majority of the population were Iranian; most were farmers or townspeople, with attitudes inherited from the relatively sophisticated and urbanized culture of pre-Safavid Iran. Faced with the problem of integrating unruly Turkic-speaking tribal peoples with the sedentary Persian-speaking population of the urban areas, the Safavids used the Shi'ite faith as a unifying force (see the box on p. 418). The shah himself acquired an almost divine quality and claimed to be the spiritual leader of all Islam. Shi'ism was declared the state religion.

Although there was a landed aristocracy, aristocratic power and influence were firmly controlled by strong-minded shahs, who confiscated aristocratic estates when possible and brought them under the control of the crown. Appointment to senior positions in the bureaucracy was by merit rather than birth.

The Safavid shahs took a direct interest in the economy and actively engaged in commercial and manufacturing activities, although there was also a large and affluent urban bourgeoisie. Like the Ottoman sultan, one shah regularly traveled the city streets incognito to check on the honesty of his subjects. When he discovered that a baker and butcher were overcharging for their products, he had the baker cooked in his own oven and the butcher roasted on a spit.

At its height, Safavid Iran was a worthy successor to the great Persian empires of the past, although it was

CHRONOLOGY	The Safavids	
Ismail seizes Iran and Iraq and becomes shah of Persia		1501
Ismail conquers Baghdad and defeats Uzbeks		1508
Reign of Shah Abbas I		1587–1629
Truce achieved between Ottomans and Safavids		1638
Collapse of the Safavid Empire		1723

The Religious Zeal of Shah Abbas the Great

RELIGION & PHILOSOPHY

Shah Abbas I, probably the greatest of the Safavid rulers, expanded the borders of his empire into areas of the southern Caucasus inhabited by Christians and other non-Muslim peoples. After Persian control was assured, he instructed that the local populations be urged to convert to Islam for their own protection and the glory of God. In this passage, his biographer, the Persian historian Eskander Beg Monshi (es-KAHN-der bayg MAHN-shee), recounts the story of that effort.

Eskander Beg Monshi, "The Conversion of a Number of Christians to Islam"

This year the Shah decreed that those Armenians and other Christians who had been settled in [the southern Caucasus] and had been given agricultural land there should be invited to become Muslims. Life in this world is fraught with vicissitudes, and the Shah was concerned lest, in a period when the authority of the central government was weak, these Christians . . . might be subjected to attack by the neighboring Lor tribes (who are naturally given to causing injury and mischief), and their women and children carried off into captivity. In the areas in which these Christian groups resided, it was the Shah's purpose that the places of worship which they had built should become mosques, and the muezzin's call should be heard in them, so that these Christians might assume the guise of Muslims, and their future status accordingly be assured. . . .

Some of the Christians, guided by God's grace, embraced Islam voluntarily; others found it difficult to abandon their Christian faith and felt revulsion at the idea. They were encouraged by their monks and priests to remain steadfast in their faith. After a little pressure had been applied to the monks and priests, however, they desisted, and these Christians saw no alternative but to embrace Islam, though they did so with reluctance. The women and children embraced Islam with great enthusiasm, vying with one another in their eagerness to abandon their Christian faith and declare their belief in the unity of God. Some five thousand people embraced Islam. As each group made the Muslim declaration of faith, it received instruction in the Koran and the principles of the religious law of Islam, and all bibles and other Christian devotional material were collected and taken away from the priests.

In the same way, all the Armenian Christians who had been moved to [the area] were also forcibly converted to Islam. . . . Most people embraced Islam with sincerity, but some felt an aversion to making the Muslim profession of faith. True knowledge lies with God! May God reward the Shah for his action with long life and prosperity!

Q How do Shah Abbas's efforts to convert nonbelievers to Islam compare with similar programs by Muslim rulers in India, as described in Chapter 9? What did the author of this selection think about the conversions?

Source: From Eskander Beg Monshi in *History of Shah Abbas The Great*, Vol. II by Roger M. Savory by Westview Press, 1978.

---

probably not as wealthy as its Mughal and Ottoman neighbors to the east and west. Hemmed in by the sea power of the Europeans to the south and by the land power of the Ottomans to the west, the early Safavids had no navy and were forced to divert overland trade with Europe through southern Russia to avoid an Ottoman blockade. In the early seventeenth century, the situation improved when Iranian forces, in cooperation with the English, seized the island of Hormuz (hawr-MOOZ) from Portugal and established a new seaport on the southern coast at Bandar Abbas (BUHN-der uh-BAHS). As a consequence, commercial ties with Europe began to increase.

Safavid Art and Literature

Persia witnessed an extraordinary flowering of the arts during the reign of Shah Abbas I. His new capital of Isfahan was a grandiose planned city with wide visual perspectives and a sense of order almost unique in the region. Shah Abbas ordered his architects to position his palaces, mosques, and bazaars around a massive rectangular polo ground. Much of the original city is still in good condition and remains the gem of modern Iran. The immense mosques are richly decorated with elaborate blue tiles. The palaces are delicate structures with unusual

The Royal Academy of Isfahan. Along with institutions such as libraries and hospitals, theological schools were often included in the mosque compound. One of the most sumptuous was the Royal Academy of Isfahan, built by the shah of Persia in the early eighteenth century. This view shows the large courtyard surrounded by arcades of student rooms, reminiscent of the arrangement of monks' cells in European cloisters.

slender wooden columns. These architectural wonders of Isfahan epitomize the grandeur, delicacy, and color that defined the Safavid golden age. To adorn the splendid buildings, Safavid artisans created imaginative metalwork, tile decorations, and original and delicate glass vessels.

Textiles, however, were the area of greatest productivity. Silk weaving based on new techniques became a national industry. The silks depicted birds, animals, and flowers in a brilliant mass of color with silver and gold threads. Above all, carpet weaving flourished, stimulated by the great demand for Persian carpets in the West.

The long tradition of Persian painting continued into the Safavid era, but changed dramatically in two ways during the second half of the sixteenth century. First, taking advantage of the growing official toleration of portraiture, painters began to highlight the inner character of their subjects. Secondly, since royal patronage was not always forthcoming, artists sought to attract a larger audience by producing individual paintings that promoted their own distinctive styles and proudly bore their own signature.

The Grandeur of the Mughals

Q FOCUS QUESTIONS: What role did Islam play in the Mughal Empire, and how did the Mughals' approach to religion compare with that of the Ottomans and the Safavids? What might explain the differences?

In retrospect, the period from the sixteenth to the eighteenth centuries can be viewed as a high point of traditional culture in India. The era began with the creation of one of the subcontinent's greatest empires—that of the Mughals (MOO-guls). For the first time since the

Mauryan dynasty, the entire subcontinent was united under a single government, with a common culture that inspired admiration and envy throughout the entire region.

The Mughal Empire reached its peak in the sixteenth century under the famed Emperor Akbar (AK-bar) and maintained its vitality under a series of strong rulers for another century (see Map 16.3). Then the dynasty began to weaken, a process that was hastened by the challenge of the foreigners arriving by sea. The Portuguese, who first arrived in 1498, were little more than an irritant. Two centuries later, however, Europeans began to seize control of regional trade routes and to meddle in the internal politics of the subcontinent. By the end of the eighteenth century, nothing remained of the empire but a shell. But some historians see the seeds of decay less in the challenge from abroad than in internal weakness—in the very nature of the empire itself, which was always more a heterogeneous collection of semiautonomous political forces than a centralized empire in the style of neighboring China.

The Founding of the Empire

When the Portuguese fleet led by Vasco da Gama arrived at the port of Calicut in 1498, the Indian subcontinent was still divided into a number of Hindu and Muslim kingdoms. But it was on the verge of a new era of unity that would be brought about by a foreign dynasty—the Mughals. Like so many recent rulers of northern India, the founders of the Mughal Empire were not natives of India but came from the mountainous region north of the Ganges River. The founder of the dynasty, known to history as Babur (BAH-burr) (1483–1530), had an illustrious pedigree. His father was descended from the great Asian conqueror Tamerlane, his mother from the Mongol conqueror Genghis Khan.

Babur had inherited a fragment of Tamerlane's empire in a valley of the Syr Darya (SEER DAHR-yuh) River

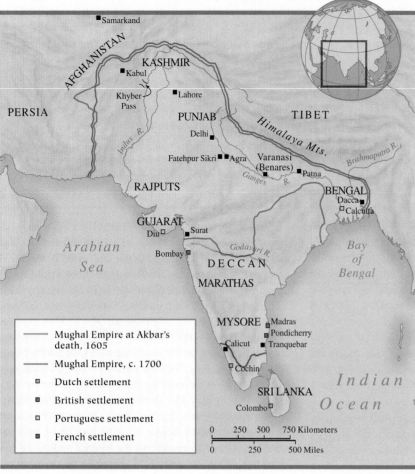

Map source: © Cengage Learning. Adapted from Geoffrey Barraclough, ed., *Times Atlas of World History* (Maplewood, N.J.: Hammond, Inc., 1978), p. 173.

Map labels: Samarkand, AFGHANISTAN, KASHMIR, Kabul, Khyber Pass, Lahore, PERSIA, PUNJAB, Delhi, TIBET, *Himalaya Mts.*, Fatehpur Sikri, Agra, Varanasi (Benares), *Brahmaputra R.*, *Ganges R.*, Patna, RAJPUTS, BENGAL, Dacca, Calcutta, *Indus R.*, GUJARAT, Diu, Surat, *Arabian Sea*, Bombay, *Godavari R.*, DECCAN, *Bay of Bengal*, MARATHAS, MYSORE, Madras, Pondicherry, Calicut, Tranquebar, *Indian Ocean*, Cochin, SRI LANKA, Colombo

Legend:
— Mughal Empire at Akbar's death, 1605
— Mughal Empire, c. 1700
▫ Dutch settlement
▪ British settlement
▫ Portuguese settlement
▪ French settlement

0   250   500   750 Kilometers
0   250   500 Miles

MAP 16.3 The Mughal Empire. This map shows the expansion of the Mughal Empire from the death of Akbar in 1605 to the rule of Aurangzeb at the end of the seventeenth century.

Q *In which cities on the map were European settlements located? When did each group of Europeans arrive, and how did the settlements spread?*

Babur's success was due in part to his vigor and his charismatic personality, which earned him the undying loyalty of his followers. His son and successor Humayun (hoo-MY-yoon) (1530–1556) was, in the words of one British historian, "intelligent but lazy." In 1540, he was forced to flee to Persia, where he lived in exile for sixteen years. Finally, with the aid of the Safavid shah of Persia, he returned to India and reconquered Delhi in 1555 but died the following year, reportedly from injuries suffered in a fall after smoking opium.

Humayun was succeeded by his son Akbar (1556–1605). Born while his father was in exile, Akbar was only fourteen when he mounted the throne. Illiterate but highly intelligent and industrious, Akbar set out to extend his domain, then limited to the Punjab (puhn-JAHB) and the upper Ganges River valley. "A monarch," he remarked, "should be ever intent on conquest, otherwise his neighbors rise in arms against him. The army should be exercised in warfare, lest from want of training they become self-indulgent."[1] By the end of his life, he had brought Mughal rule to most of the subcontinent, from the Himalaya Mountains to the Godavari (goh-DAH-vuh-ree) River in central India and from Kashmir to the mouths of the Brahmaputra (brah-muh-POO-truh) and the Ganges. In so doing, Akbar had created the greatest Indian empire since the Mauryan dynasty nearly two thousand years earlier. Though it appeared highly centralized from the outside, the empire was actually a collection of semiautonomous principalities ruled by provincial elites and linked together by the overarching majesty of the Mughal emperor.

Akbar and Indo-Muslim Civilization

Although Akbar was probably the greatest of the conquering Mughal monarchs, like his famous predecessor

(see Map 16.2 on p. 417). Driven south by the rising power of the Uzbeks and then the Safavid dynasty in Persia, Babur and his warriors seized Kabul in 1504 and, thirteen years later, crossed the Khyber Pass to India.

Following a pattern that we have seen before, Babur began his rise to power by offering to help an ailing dynasty against its opponents. Although his own forces were far smaller than those of his adversaries, he possessed advanced weapons, including artillery, and used them to great effect. His use of mobile cavalry was particularly successful against the massed forces, supplemented by mounted elephants, of his enemy. In 1526, with only 12,000 troops against an enemy force nearly ten times that size, Babur captured Delhi (DEL-ee). Over the next years, he continued his conquests in northern India, until his early death in 1530 at the age of forty-seven.

Asoka, he is best known for the humane character of his rule. Above all, he accepted the diversity of Indian society and took steps to reconcile his Muslim and Hindu subjects.

RELIGION AND THE STATE   Though raised an orthodox Muslim, Akbar had been exposed to other beliefs during his childhood and had little patience with the pedantic views of Muslim scholars at court. As emperor, he displayed a keen interest in other religions, not only tolerating Hindu practices and taking a Hindu princess as one of his wives but also welcoming the expression of Christian views by his Jesuit advisers (the Jesuits first sent a mission to Agra in 1580). He patronized classical Indian arts and architecture and abolished many of the restrictions faced by Hindus in a Muslim-dominated society.

During his later years, Akbar became steadily more hostile to Islam. To the dismay of many Muslims at court, he sponsored a new form of worship called the Divine Faith (*Din-i-Ilahi*), which combined characteristics of several religions with a central belief in the infallibility of all decisions reached by the emperor. The new faith aroused deep hostility in Muslim circles and rapidly vanished after his death.

ADMINISTRATIVE REFORMS   Akbar also extended his innovations to the imperial administration. The empire was divided into provinces, and the administration of each province was modeled after the central government, with departments for military, financial, commercial, and legal affairs. Senior officials in each department reported directly to their counterparts in the capital city.

Although the upper ranks of the government continued to be dominated by nonnative Muslims, a substantial proportion of lower-ranking officials were Hindus, and a few Hindus were appointed to positions of importance. At first, most officials were paid salaries, but later they were ordinarily assigned sections of land for their temporary use; they kept a portion of the taxes paid by the local peasants in lieu of a salary. These local officials, known as *zamindars* (zuh-meen-DAHRZ), were expected to forward the rest of the taxes from the lands under their control to the central government. *Zamindars* often recruited a number of military and civilian retainers and accumulated considerable power in their localities.

The same tolerance that marked Akbar's attitude toward religion and administration extended to the legal system. While Muslims were subject to the Islamic codes (the *Shari'a*), Hindu law applied in areas settled by Hindus, who after 1579 were no longer required to pay the unpopular *jizya* (JIZ-yuh), or poll tax on non-Muslims. Punishments for crime were mild by the standards of the day, and justice was administered in a relatively impartial and efficient manner.

A HARMONIOUS SOCIETY   A key element in Akbar's vision of the ideal social order was the concept of harmony, meaning that each individual and group within the empire would play their assigned role and contribute to the welfare of society as a whole. This concept of social harmony was based in part on his vision of a world shaped by the laws of Islam as transmitted by Muhammad (*Shari'a*), but it also corresponded to the deep-seated indigenous belief in the importance of class hierarchy, as expressed in the Indian class and caste system (see the box on p. 422). In its overall conception, it bears a clear resemblance to the social structure adopted by the Mughals' contemporaries to the west, the Ottoman Empire.

Overall, Akbar's reign was a time of peace and prosperity. Although all Indian peasants were required to pay about one-third of their annual harvest to the state through the *zamindars*, in general the system was applied fairly, and when drought struck in the 1590s, the taxes were reduced or even suspended altogether. Thanks to a long period of relative peace and political stability, commerce and manufacturing flourished. Foreign trade, in particular, thrived as Indian goods, notably textiles, tropical food products, spices, and precious stones, were exported in exchange for gold and silver. Tariffs on imports were low. Much of the foreign commerce was handled by Arab traders, since the Indians, like their Mughal rulers, did not care for travel by sea. Internal trade, however, was dominated by large merchant castes, who also were active in banking and handicrafts.

Akbar's Successors

Akbar died in 1605 and was succeeded by his son Jahangir (juh-HAHN-geer) (1605–1628). During the early years of his reign, Jahangir continued to strengthen central control over the vast empire. Eventually, however, his grip began to weaken (according to his memoirs, he "only wanted a bottle of wine and a piece of meat to make merry"), and the court fell under the influence of one of his wives, the Persian-born Nur Jahan (NOOR juh-HAHN) (see the box on p. 423). The empress took advantage of her position to enrich her own family and arranged for her niece Mumtaz Mahal (MOOM-tahz muh-HAHL) to marry her husband's third son and ultimate successor, Shah Jahan (1628–1657). When Shah Jahan succeeded to the throne, he quickly demonstrated the single-minded quality of his grandfather (albeit in a much more brutal manner), ordering the assassination of all of his rivals in order to secure his position.

THE REIGN OF SHAH JAHAN   During a reign of three decades, Shah Jahan maintained the system established by his predecessors while expanding the boundaries of the empire by successful campaigns in the Deccan

Designing the Perfect Society

POLITICS & GOVERNMENT

In the late fifteenth century, the Persian author Muhammad ibn Asad Jalal ud-din al-Dawwani (al-da-WAH-nee) (1427–1501) wrote an essay on the ideal society entitled *Jalali's Ethics*. The work later attracted favorable notice at the Mughal court in India and eventually was paraphrased by Emperor Akbar's famous adviser Abu'l Fazl Allami (uh-BUL FAYZ-ul ahl-LAHM-mee). It thus provides insight into the political and social views of key officials in Mughal India during the reign of its most famous ruler.

Jalali's Ethics

In order to preserve this political equipoise, there is a correspondence to be maintained between the various classes. Like as the equipoise of bodily temperament is affected by intermixture and correspondence of four elements, the equipoise of the political temperament is to be sought for in the correspondence of four classes.

1. *Men of the pen*, such as lawyers, divines, judges, bookmen, statisticians, geometricians, astronomers, physicians, poets. In these and their exertions in the use of their delightful pens, the subsistence of the faith and of the world itself is vested and bound up. They occupy the place in politics that water does among the elements. Indeed, to persons of ready understanding, the similarity of knowledge and water is as clear as water itself, and as evident as the sun that makes it so.

2. *Men of the sword*, such as soldiers, fighting zealots, guards of forts and passes, etc.; without whose exercise of the impetuous and vindictive sword, no arrangement of the age's interests could be effected; without the havoc of whose tempest-like energies, the materials of corruption, in the shape of rebellious and disaffected persons, could never be dissolved and dissipated. These then occupy the place of fire, their resemblance to it is too plain to require demonstration; no rational person need call in the aid of fire to discover it.

3. *Men of business*, such as merchants, capitalists, artisans, and craftsmen by whom the means of emolument and all other interests are adjusted; and through whom the remotest extremes enjoy the advantage and safeguard of each other's most peculiar commodities. The resemblance of these to air—the auxiliary of growth and increase in vegetables—the reviver of spirit in animal life—the medium of the undulation and movement of which all sorts of rare and precious things traverse the hearing to arrive at the headquarters of human nature—is exceedingly manifest.

4. *Husbandmen*, such as seedsmen, bailiffs, and agriculturists—the superintendents of vegetation and preparers of provender; without whose exertions the continuance of the human kind must be cut short. These are, in fact, the only producers of what had no previous existence; the other classes adding nothing whatever to subsisting products, but only transferring what subsists already from person to person, from place to place, and from form to form. How close these come to the soil and surface of the earth—the point to which all the heavenly circles refer—the scope to which all the luminaries of the purer world direct their rays—the stage on which wonders are displayed—the limit to which mysteries are confined—must be universally apparent.

In like manner then as in the composite organizations the passing of any element beyond its proper measure occasions the loss of equipoise, and is followed by dissolution and ruin, in political coalition, no less, the prevalence of any one class over the other three overturns the adjustment and dissolves the junction. Next attention is to be directed to the condition of the individuals composing them, and the place of every one determined according to his right.

How does the social class system described here compare with the traditional division of classes in premodern India?

Source: A. T. Embree (ed.), *Sources of Indian Tradition: From the Beginning to 1800*, Vol. I, 2nd ed. (New York, 1988), pp. 431–432.

The Power Behind the Throne

POLITICS & GOVERNMENT

During his reign, the Mughal emperor Jahangir became addicted to alcohol and opium. Because of his weakened condition, his Persian wife, Nur Jahan, began to rule on his behalf. She served as the de facto ruler of India, exerting influence in both internal and foreign affairs. Although the extent of Nur Jahan's influence was often criticized at court, her performance impressed many European observers, as these remarks by an English visitor attest.

Nur Jahan, Empress of Mughal India

If anyone with a request to make at Court obtains an audience or is allowed to speak, the King hears him indeed, but will give no definite answer of Yes or No, referring him promptly to Asaf Khan, who in the same way will dispose of no important matter without communicating with his sister, the Queen, and who regulates his attitude in such a way that the authority of neither of them may be diminished. Anyone then who obtains a favour must thank them for it, and not the King. . . .

Her abilities were uncommon; for she rendered herself absolute, in a government in which women are thought incapable of bearing any part. Their power, it is true, is sometimes exerted in the harem; but, like the virtues of the magnet, it is silent and unperceived. Nur Jahan stood forth in public; she broke through all restraint and custom, and acquired power by her own address, more than by the weakness of Jahangir. . . .

Her former and present supporters have been well rewarded, so that now most of the men who are near the King owe their promotion to her, and are consequently under . . . obligations to her. . . . Many misunderstandings result, for the King's orders or grants of appointments, etc., are not certainties, being of no value until they have been approved by the Queen.

 Based on this description, how does the position that Nur Jahan occupied in Mughul government compare with the roles played by other female political figures in China, Africa, and Europe? What do all of these women have in common?

Source: From *Nur Jahan: Empress of Mughal India* by Ellison Banks Findly. Oxford University Print on Demand, 1993.

Plateau and against Samarkand, north of the Hindu Kush. But Shah Jahan's rule was marred by his failure to deal with the growing domestic problems. He had inherited a nearly empty treasury because of Empress Nur Jahan's penchant for luxury and ambitious charity projects. Though the majority of his subjects lived in grinding poverty, Shah Jahan's frequent military campaigns and expensive building projects put a heavy strain on the imperial finances and compelled him to raise taxes. At the same time, the government did little to improve rural conditions. In a country where transport was primitive (it often took three months to travel the 600 miles between Patna, in the middle of the Ganges River valley, and Delhi) and drought conditions frequent, the dynasty made few efforts to increase agricultural efficiency or to improve the roads, although a grand trunk road was eventually constructed between the capital Agra (AH-gruh) and Lahore (luh-HOHR), a growing city several hundred miles to the northwest. A Dutch merchant in

Gujarat (goo-juh-RAHT) described conditions during a famine in the mid-seventeenth century:

> As the famine increased, men abandoned towns and villages and wandered helplessly. It was easy to recognize their condition: eyes sunk deep in head, lips pale and covered with slime, the skin hard, with the bones showing through, the belly nothing but a pouch hanging down empty, knuckles and kneecaps showing prominently. One would cry and howl for hunger, while another lay stretched on the ground dying in misery; wherever you went, you saw nothing but corpses.[2]

In 1648, Shah Jahan moved his capital from Agra to Delhi and built the famous Red Fort in his new capital city. But he is best known for the Taj Mahal (tahj muh-HAHL) in Agra, widely considered to be the most beautiful building in India, if not in the entire world (see the comparative illustration on p. 430). The story is a romantic one—that the Taj was built by the emperor in memory of his wife Mumtaz Mahal, who had died giving birth to her thirteenth child at the age of thirty-nine. But the reality has a less attractive side: the expense of the building, which employed 20,000 masons over twenty years, forced the government to raise agricultural taxes, further impoverishing many Indian peasants.

RULE OF AURANGZEB Succession struggles returned to haunt the dynasty in the mid-1650s when Shah Jahan's illness led to a struggle for power between his sons Dara Shikoh (DA-ruh SHIH-koh) and Aurangzeb (ow-rang-ZEB). Dara Shikoh was described by his contemporaries as progressive and humane, but he apparently lacked political acumen and was outmaneuvered by Aurangzeb (1658–1707), who had Dara Shikoh put to death and then imprisoned his father in the fort at Agra.

Aurangzeb is one of the most controversial individuals in the history of India. A man of high principle, he attempted to eliminate many of what he considered to be India's social evils, prohibiting the immolation of widows on their husband's funeral pyre (*sati*), the castration of eunuchs, and the exaction of illegal taxes. With less success, he tried to forbid gambling, drinking, and prostitution. But Aurangzeb, a devout and somewhat doctrinaire Muslim, also adopted a number of measures that reversed the policies of religious tolerance established by his predecessors. The building of new Hindu temples was prohibited, and the Hindu poll tax was restored. Forced conversions to Islam were resumed, and non-Muslims were driven from the court. Aurangzeb's heavy-handed religious policies led to a revival of Hindu fervor. The last years of his reign saw considerable domestic unrest and a number of revolts against imperial authority.

THE SHADOWS LENGTHEN During the eighteenth century, Mughal power was threatened from both within and without. Fueled by the growing power and autonomy of the local gentry and merchants, rebellious groups throughout the empire, from the Deccan to the Punjab, began to reassert local authority and reduce the power of the Mughal emperor to that of a "tinsel sovereign." Increasingly divided, India was vulnerable to attack from abroad. In 1739, Delhi was sacked by the Persians, who left it in ashes.

A number of obvious reasons for the virtual collapse of the Mughal Empire can be identified, including the draining of the imperial treasury and the decline in competence of the Mughal rulers. But it should also be noted that even at its height under Akbar, the empire was a loosely knit collection of heterogeneous principalities held together by the authority of the throne, which tried to combine Persian concepts of kingship with the Indian tradition of decentralized power. Decline set in when centrifugal forces gradually began to predominate over centripetal ones.

The Impact of European Power in India

As we have seen, the first Europeans to arrive were the Portuguese. Although they established a virtual monopoly over regional trade in the Indian Ocean, they did not seek to penetrate the interior of the subcontinent but focused on establishing way stations en route to China and the Spice Islands. The situation changed at the end of the sixteenth century, when the English and the Dutch appeared on the scene. Soon both powers were in active competition with Portugal, and with each other, for trading privileges in the region (see the box on p. 425).

Penetration of the new market was not easy. When the first English fleet arrived at Surat (SOOR-et), a thriving port on the northwestern coast of India, in 1608, their request for trading privileges was rejected by Emperor Jahangir. Needing lightweight Indian cloth to trade for spices in the East Indies, the English persisted, and in 1616, they were finally permitted to install their own ambassador at the imperial court in Agra. Three years later, the first English factory (trading station) was established at Surat.

During the next several decades, the English presence in India steadily increased while Mughal power gradually waned. By midcentury, additional English factories had been established at Fort William (now the great city of Kolkata, formerly Calcutta) on the Hoogly River near the Bay of Bengal and in 1639 at Madras (muh-DRAS *or* muh-DRAHS) (Chennai) on the southeastern coast. From there, English ships carried Indian-made cotton goods to the East Indies, where they were bartered for spices, which were shipped back to England.

English success in India attracted rivals, including the Dutch and the French. The Dutch abandoned their interests to concentrate on the spice trade in the mid-seventeenth century, but the French were more persistent and established factories of their own. For a brief period, under the ambitious empire builder Joseph François Dupleix (zho-ZEF frahn-SWAH doo-PLAY), the French competed successfully with the British, even capturing Madras from a British garrison in 1746. But the military genius of Sir Robert Clive (CLYV), an aggressive British administrator and empire builder who eventually became the chief representative of the East India Company in the subcontinent, and the refusal of the French government to provide financial support for Dupleix's efforts eventually left the French with only their fort at Pondicherry (pon-duh-CHEH-ree) and a handful of small territories on the southeastern coast.

OPPOSING ✕ VIEWPOINTS

The Capture of Port Hoogly

INTERACTION & EXCHANGE

In 1632, the Mughal ruler, Shah Jahan, ordered an attack on the city of Hoogly (HOOG-lee), a fortified Portuguese trading post on the northeastern coast of India. For the Portuguese, who had profited from half a century of triangular trade involving India, China, and various countries in the Middle East and Southeast Asia, the loss of Hoogly hastened the decline of their influence in the region. Presented here are two contemporary versions of the battle. The first, from the *Padshahnama* (pad-shah-NAHM-uh) (*Book of Kings*), relates the course of events from the Mughal point of view. The second account is by John Cabral, a Jesuit missionary who was resident in Hoogly at the time.

The *Padshahnama*

During the reign of the Bengalis, a group of Frankish [European] merchants . . . settled in a place one *kos* from Satgaon . . . and, on the pretext that they needed a place for trading, they received permission from the Bengalis to construct a few edifices. Over time, due to the indifference of the governors of Bengal, many Franks gathered there and built dwellings of the utmost splendor and strength, fortified with cannons, guns, and other instruments of war. It was not long before it became a large settlement and was named Hoogly. . . . The Franks' ships trafficked at this port, and commerce was established, causing the market at the port of Satgaon to slump. . . . Of the peasants of those places, they converted some to Christianity by force and others through greed and sent them off to Europe in their ships. . . .

Since the improper actions of the Christians of Hoogly Port toward the Muslims were accurately reflected in the mirror of the mind of the Emperor before his accession to the throne, when the imperial

banners cast their shadows over Bengal, and inasmuch as he was always inclined to propagate the true religion and eliminate infidelity, it was decided that when he gained control over this region he would eradicate the corruption of these abominators from the realm.

John Cabral, *Travels of Sebastian Manrique, 1629–1649*

Hugli continued at peace all the time of the great King Jahangir. For, as this Prince, by what he showed, was more attached to Christ than to Mohammad and was a Moor in name and dress only. . . . Sultan Khurram [Shah Jahan] was in everything unlike his father, especially as regards the latter's leaning towards Christianity. . . . He declared himself the mortal enemy of the Christian name and the restorer of the law of Mohammad. . . . He sent a *firman* [order] to the Viceroy of Bengal, commanding him without reply or delay, to march upon the Bandel of Hugli and put it to fire and the sword. He added that, in doing so, he would render a signal service to God, to Mohammad, and to him. . . .

Consequently, on a Friday, September 24, 1632, . . . all the people [the Portuguese] embarked with the utmost secrecy. . . . Learning what was going on, and wishing to be able to boast that they had taken Hugli by storm, they [the imperialists] made a general attack on the Bandel by Saturday noon. They began by setting fire to a mine, but lost in it more men than we. Finally, however, they were masters of the Bandel.

> **Q** How do these two accounts of the Battle of Hoogly differ? Is there any way to reconcile the two accounts into a single narrative?

Source: From *King of the World: a Mughal manuscript from the Royal Library*, Windsor Castle, trans. by Wheeler Thackston, text by Milo Cleveland Beach and Ebba Koch (London: Thames and Hudson, 1997), p. 59.

In the meantime, Clive began to consolidate British control in Bengal (ben-GAHL), where the local ruler had attacked Fort William and imprisoned the local British population in the infamous Black Hole of Calcutta (an underground prison for holding the prisoners, many of whom died in captivity). In 1757, a small British force numbering about three thousand defeated a Mughal-led army over ten times that size in the Battle of Plassey (PLASS-ee). As part of the spoils of victory, the British East India Company exacted from the now-decrepit Mughal court the authority to collect taxes from extensive lands in the area surrounding Calcutta. Less than ten

The Grandeur of the Mughals ❧ **425**

A Pepper Plantation. During the Age of Exploration, pepper was one of the spices most sought by European adventurers. Unlike cloves and nutmeg, it was found in other areas in Asia besides the Indonesian archipelago. Shown here is a French pepper plantation in southern India. Eventually, the French were driven out of the Indian subcontinent by the British and retained only a few tiny enclaves along the coast.

years later, British forces seized the reigning Mughal emperor in a skirmish at Buxar (buk-SAHR), and the British began to consolidate their economic and administrative control over Indian territory through the surrogate power of the now powerless Mughal court (see Map 16.4).

To officials of the East India Company, the expansion of their authority into the interior of the subcontinent probably seemed like a simple commercial decision, a way to obtain guaranteed revenues to pay for the increasingly expensive military operations in India. To historians, it marks a major step in the gradual transfer of all of the Indian subcontinent to the British East India Company and later, in 1858, to the British crown. The process was more haphazard than deliberate.

ECONOMIC DIFFICULTIES The company's takeover of vast landholdings, notably in the eastern Indian states of Orissa (uh-RIH-suh) and Bengal, may have been a windfall for enterprising British officials, but it was a disaster for the Indian economy. In the first place, it resulted in the transfer of capital from the local Indian aristocracy to company officials, most of whom sent their profits back to Britain. Second, it hastened the destruction of once healthy local industries because British goods such as machine-made textiles were imported duty-free into India to compete against local products. Finally, British expansion hurt the peasants. As the British took over the administration of the land tax, they also applied British law, which allowed

the lands of those unable to pay the tax to be confiscated. In the 1770s, a series of massive famines led to the death of an estimated one-third of the population in the areas under company administration. The British government attempted to resolve the problem by assigning tax lands to the local revenue collectors (*zamindars*) in the hope of transforming them into English-style rural gentry, but many collectors themselves fell into bankruptcy and sold their lands to absentee bankers while the now landless peasants remained in abject poverty. It was hardly an auspicious beginning to "civilized" British rule.

RESISTANCE TO THE BRITISH As a result of such problems, Britain's rise to power in India did not go unchallenged. Astute Indian commanders avoided pitched battles with the well-armed British troops but harassed and ambushed them in the manner of guerrillas in our time. Haidar Ali (HY-dur AH-lee), one of Britain's primary rivals for control in southern India, said:

> You will in time understand my mode of warfare. Shall I risk my cavalry which cost a thousand rupees each horse, against your cannon ball which cost two pice? No! I will march your troops until their legs swell to the size of their bodies. You shall not have a blade of grass, nor a drop of water. I will hear of you every time your drum beats, but you shall not know where I am once a month. I will give your army battle, but it must be when I please, and not when you choose.[3]

Bibliothèque Nationale, Paris//© The Art Archive at Art Resource, NY

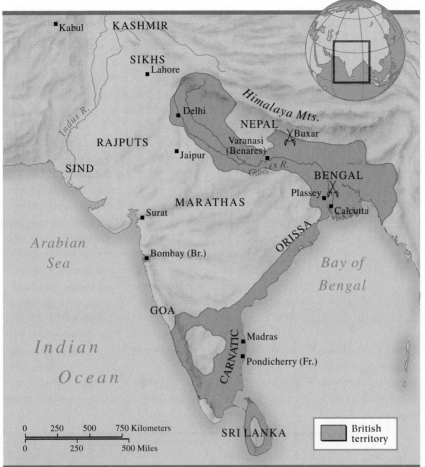

MAP 16.4 **India in 1805.** By the early nineteenth century, much of the Indian subcontinent had fallen under British domination.

Q *Where was the capital of the Mughal Empire located?*

Unfortunately for India, not all of its commanders were as astute as Haidar Ali. In the last years of the eighteenth century, the stage was set for the final consolidation of British rule over the subcontinent.

The Mughal Dynasty: A "Gunpowder Empire"?

To some recent historians, the success of the Mughals, like that of the Ottomans and the Safavids, was due to their mastery of the techniques of modern warfare, especially the use of firearms. In this view, firearms played a central role in the rise of all three empires to regional hegemony. Accordingly, some scholars have labeled them "gunpowder empires." Although technical prowess in the art of warfare was undoubtedly a key element in their success, we should not forget that other factors, such as dynamic leadership, political acumen, and ardent followers

motivated by religious zeal, were at least equally important.

In the case of the Mughals, the "gunpowder empire" thesis has been challenged by historian Douglas Streusand, who argues that the Mughals used "the carrot and the stick" to extend their authority, relying not just on heavy artillery but also on other forms of siege warfare and the offer of negotiations. Once in power, the Mughals created an empire in which the semiautonomous provinces were held together as much by the majesty of the Mughal emperor as by the barrel of a gun. Even today, many Indians regard Akbar as the country's greatest ruler, a tribute not only to his military success but also to the humane policies adopted during his reign.

Society Under the Mughals: A Synthesis of Cultures

The Mughals were the last of the great traditional Indian dynasties. Like so many of their predecessors since the fall of the Guptas nearly a thousand years before, the Mughals were Muslims. But like the Ottoman Turks, the best Mughal rulers did not simply impose Islamic institutions and beliefs on the predominantly Hindu population; they combined Muslim with Hindu and even Persian concepts and cultural values in a unique social and cultural synthesis. The new faith of Sikhism, founded in the early sixteenth century in an effort to blend both faiths (see Chapter 9), undoubtedly benefited from the mood of syncretism promoted by the Mughal court.

To be sure, Hindus sometimes attempted to defend themselves and their religious practices against the efforts of some Mughal monarchs to impose the Islamic religion and Islamic mores on the indigenous population. In some cases, despite official prohibitions, Hindu men forcibly married Muslim women and then converted them to the native faith, while converts to Islam normally lost all of their inheritance rights within the Indian family. Government orders to destroy Hindu temples were often the Indian Ocean from the Red Sea and the Persian Gulf to the Strait of Malacca and the Indonesian archipelago. High-quality cloth from India was especially prized, and the country's textile industry made it, in the words of one historian, "the industrial workshop of the world."

Long-term stability led to increasing commercialization and the spread of wealth to new groups within Indian society. The Mughal era saw the emergence of an affluent landed gentry and a prosperous merchant class. Members of prestigious castes from the pre-Mughal period reaped many of the benefits of the increasing wealth, but some of these changes transcended caste boundaries and led to the emergence of new groups who achieved status and wealth on the basis of economic achievement rather than traditional kinship ties. During the late eighteenth century, this economic prosperity was shaken by the decline of the Mughal Empire and the increasing European presence. But many prominent Indians reacted by establishing commercial relationships with the foreigners. For a time, such relationships often worked to the Indians' benefit. Later, as we shall see, they would have cause to regret the arrangement.

THE POSITION OF WOMEN Whether Mughal rule had much effect on the lives of ordinary Indians seems

ignored by local officials, sometimes as the result of bribery or intimidation. Although the founding emperor Babur expressed little admiration for the country he had subjected to his rule, ultimately Indian practices had an influence on the Mughal elites, as many Mughal chieftains married Indian women and adopted Indian forms of dress.

In some areas, Emperor Akbar's tireless effort to bring about a blend of Middle Eastern and South Asian religious and cultural values paid rich dividends, as substantial numbers of Indians decided to convert to the Muslim faith during the centuries of Mughal rule. Some were undoubtedly attracted to the egalitarian characteristics of Islam, but others found that the mystical and devotional qualities promoted by Sufi missionaries corresponded to local traditions. This was especially true in Bengal, on the eastern edge of the Indian subcontinent, where Hindu practices were not as well established and where forms of religious devotionalism had long been popular.

THE ECONOMY Although much of the local population in the subcontinent lived in grinding poverty, punctuated by occasional periods of widespread famine, the first centuries of Mughal rule were in some respects a period of relative prosperity for the region. India was a leading participant in the growing foreign trade that crisscrossed

The Palace of the Winds at Jaipur. Built by the maharaja of Jaipur (JY-poor) in 1799, this imposing building, part of a palace complex, is today actually only a facade. Behind the intricate pink sandstone window screens, the women of the palace were able to observe city life while at the same time remaining invisible to prying eyes. The palace, like most of the buildings in the city of Jaipur, was constructed of sandstone, a product of the nearby desert of Rajasthan (RAH-juh-stahn).

somewhat problematic. The treatment of women is a good example. Women had traditionally played an active role in Mongol tribal society—many actually fought on the battlefield alongside the men—and Babur and his successors often relied on the women in their families for political advice. Women from aristocratic families were often awarded honorific titles, received salaries, and were permitted to own land and engage in business. Women at court sometimes received an education, and aristocratic women often expressed their creative talents by writing poetry, painting, or playing music. Women of all classes were adept at spinning thread, either for their own use or to sell to weavers to augment the family income. They sold simple cloth to local villages and fine cottons, silks, and wool to the Mughal court.

To a certain degree, these Mughal attitudes toward women may have had an impact on Indian society. Women were allowed to inherit land, and some even possessed *zamindar* rights. Women from mercantile castes sometimes took an active role in business activities. At the same time, however, as Muslims, the Mughals subjected women to certain restrictions under Islamic law. On the whole, these Mughal practices coincided with and even accentuated existing tendencies in Indian society. The Muslim practice of isolating women and preventing them from associating with men outside the home (**purdah**) was adopted by many upper-class Hindus as a means of enhancing their status or protecting their women from unwelcome advances by Muslims in positions of authority. In other ways, Hindu practices were unaffected. The custom of *sati* continued to be practiced despite efforts by the Mughals to abolish it, and child marriage (most women were betrothed before the age of ten) remained common. Women were still instructed to obey their husbands without question and to remain chaste.

Mughal Culture

The era of the Mughals was one of synthesis in culture as well as in politics and religion. The Mughals combined Islamic themes with Persian and indigenous motifs to produce a unique style that enriched and embellished Indian art and culture. The Mughal emperors were zealous patrons of the arts and enticed painters, poets, and artisans from as far away as the Mediterranean. Apparently, the generosity of the Mughals made it difficult to refuse a trip to India. It was said that they would reward a poet with his weight in gold.

ARCHITECTURE   Undoubtedly, the Mughals' most visible achievement was in architecture. Here they integrated Persian and Indian styles in a new and sometimes breathtakingly beautiful form best symbolized by the Taj Mahal, built by the emperor Shah Jahan in the mid-seventeenth century (see the comparative illustration on p. 430). Although the human and economic cost of the Taj tarnishes the romantic legend of its construction, there is no denying the beauty of the building. It had evolved from a style that originated several decades earlier with the tomb of Humayun.

Humayun's mausoleum had combined Persian and Islamic motifs ina square building finished in red sandstone and topped with a dome. The Taj brought the style to perfection. Working with a model created by his Persian architect, Shah Jahan raised the dome and replaced the red sandstone with brilliant white marble. The entire surface of the exterior and interior is decorated with cut-stone geometrical patterns, delicate black stone tracery, or intricate inlay of colored precious stones in floral and Qur'anic arabesques. The technique of creating dazzling floral mosaics of lapis lazuli, malachite, carnelian, turquoise, and mother of pearl may have been introduced by Italian artists at the Mughal court. Shah Jahan spent his last years imprisoned in a room in the Red Fort at Agra; from his windows, he could see the beautiful memorial to his beloved wife.

The Taj was by no means the only magnificent building erected during the Mughal era. Akbar, who, in the words of a contemporary, "[dressed] the work of his mind and heart in the garment of stone and clay," was the first of the great Mughal builders. His first palace at Agra, the Red Fort, was begun in 1565. A few years later, he ordered the construction of a new palace at Fatehpur Sikri (fah-tay-POOR SIK-ree), 26 miles west of Agra. The new palace was built in honor of a Sufi mystic who had correctly forecast the birth of a son to the emperor. In gratitude, Akbar decided to build a new capital city and palace on the site of the mystic's home in the village of Sikri. Over a period of fifteen years, from 1571 to 1586, a magnificent new city in red sandstone was constructed. Although the city was abandoned before completion and now stands almost untouched, it is a popular destination for tourists and pilgrims.

PAINTING   The other major artistic achievement of the Mughal period was painting. Like so many other aspects of Mughal India, painting blended two cultures. While living in exile, Emperor Humayun had learned to admire Persian miniatures. On his return to India in 1555, he invited two Persian masters to live in his palace and introduce the technique to his adopted land. His successor, Akbar, appreciated the new style and popularized it with his patronage. He established a state workshop at Fatehpur Sikri for two hundred artists, mostly Hindus, who worked under the guidance of the Persian masters to create the Mughal school of painting.

The "Akbar style" combined Persian with Indian motifs, such as the use of extended space and the

COMPARATIVE ILLUSTRATION

ART & IDEAS

The Taj Mahal: Symbol of the Exotic East. The Taj Mahal, completed in 1653, was built by the Mughal emperor Shah Jahan as a tomb to glorify the memory of his beloved wife. Raised on a marble platform above the Jumna River, the Taj is dramatically framed by contrasting twin red sandstone mosques, magnificent gardens, and a long reflecting pool that mirrors and magnifies its beauty. The effect is one of monumental size, near blinding brilliance, and delicate lightness, a startling contrast to the heavier and more masculine Baroque style then popular in Europe. The inset at the upper right shows an example of the exquisite inlay of precious stones that adorns the façade. The Taj Mahal inspired many imitations, including the Royal Pavilion at Brighton, England (inset at lower right), constructed in 1815 to commemorate the British victory over Napoleon at Waterloo. The Pavilion is a good example of the way Europeans portrayed the "exotic" East.

Q *How does Mughal architecture, as exemplified by the Taj Majal, compare with the mosques erected by builders such as Sinan in the Ottoman Empire?*

portrayal of physical human action, characteristics not usually seen in Persian art. Akbar also apparently encouraged the imitation of European art forms, including the portrayal of Christian subjects, the use of perspective, lifelike portraits, and the shading of colors in the Renaissance style. The depiction of the human figure in Mughal painting outraged orthodox Muslims at court, but Akbar argued that the painter, "in sketching anything that has life . . . must come to feel that he cannot bestow individuality upon his work, and is thus forced to think of God, the Giver of Life, and will thus increase in knowledge."[4]

LITERATURE The development of Indian literature was held back by the absence of printing, which was not introduced until the end of the Mughal era. Literary works were inscribed by calligraphers, and one historian has estimated that the library of Agra contained more than 24,000 volumes. Poetry, in particular, flourished

under the Mughals, who established poet laureates at court. Poems were written in the Persian style and in the Persian language. In fact, Persian became the official language of the court until the sack of Delhi in 1739.

Another aspect of the long Mughal reign was a revival of Hindu devotional literature, much of it dedicated to Krishna and Rama. The retelling of the Ramayana in the vernacular culminated in the sixteenth-century Hindi version by the great poet Tulsidas (tool-see-DAHSS) (1532–1623). His *Ramcaritmanas* (RAM-kah-rit-MAH-nuz) presents the devotional story with a deified Rama and Sita. Tulsidas's genius was in combining the conflicting cults of Vishnu and Shiva into a unified and overwhelming love for the divine, which he expressed in some of the most moving of all Indian poetry. The *Ramcaritmanas* has eclipsed its two-thousand-year-old Sanskrit ancestor in popularity and even became the basis of an Indian television series in the late 1980s.

CHAPTER SUMMARY

The three empires discussed in this chapter exhibited a number of striking similarities. First of all, they were Muslim in their religious affiliation, although the Safavids were Shi'ite rather than Sunni, a distinction that often led to mutual tensions and conflict. More important, perhaps, they were all of nomadic origin, and the political and social institutions that they adopted carried the imprint of their preimperial past. Once they achieved imperial power, however, all three ruling dynasties displayed an impressive capacity to administer a large empire and brought a degree of stability to peoples who had all too often lived in conditions of internal division and war.

The rise of these powerful Muslim states coincided with the opening period of European expansion at the end of the fifteenth century and the beginning of the sixteenth. The military and political talents of these empires helped protect much of the Muslim world from the resurgent forces of Christianity. In fact, the Ottoman Turks carried their empire into the heart of Christian Europe and briefly reached the gates of the great city of Vienna. By the end of the eighteenth century, however, the Safavid dynasty had imploded, and the powerful Mughal Empire was in a state of virtual collapse. Only the Ottoman Empire was still functioning. Yet it too had lost much of its early expansionistic vigor and was showing signs of internal decay.

The reasons for the decline of these empires have inspired considerable debate among historians. One factor was undoubtedly the expansion of European power into the Indian Ocean and the Middle East. But internal causes were probably more important in the long run. All three empires experienced growing factionalism within the ruling elite, incompetent leadership, and the emergence of divisive forces in the empire at large—factors that have marked the passing of traditional empires since early times. Climate change (the region was reportedly hotter and drier after the beginning of the seventeenth century) may have been a contributing factor. Paradoxically, one of the greatest strengths of these empires—their mastery of gunpowder—may have simultaneously been a serious weakness in that it allowed them to develop a complacent sense of security. With little incentive to turn their attention to new developments in science and technology, they were increasingly vulnerable to attack by the advanced nations of the West.

The Muslim empires, however, were not the only states in the Old World that were able to resist the first outward thrust of European expansion. Farther to the east, the mature civilizations in China and Japan faced down a similar challenge from Western merchants and missionaries. Unlike their counterparts in South Asia and the Middle East, as the nineteenth century dawned, they continued to thrive.

CHAPTER TIMELINE

1450	1500	1550	1600	1650	1700	1750

Turks defeat Mamluks in Syria and seize Cairo

Battle of Lepanto

Ottomans evicted from central Europe

Ottoman Turks capture Constantinople

Reign of Suleyman I (the Magnificent)

Ismail becomes shah of Persia

Ismail conquers Baghdad from Uzbeks

Reign of Shah Abbas I

Collapse of Safavid Empire

Babur seizes Delhi

Reign of Shah Jahan

Death of Aurangzeb

Reign of Akbar

Building of Taj Mahal

Upon Reflection

Q How did the social policies adopted by the Ottomans compare with those of the Mughals? What similarities and differences do you detect, and what might account for them?

Q What is meant by the phrase "gunpowder empires," and to what degree did the Muslim states discussed here conform to this description?

Q What role did women play in the Ottoman, Safavid, and Mughal Empires? What might explain the similarities and differences? How did the treatment of women in these states compare with their treatment in other parts of the world?

Key Terms

bey (p. 408)
sultan (p. 408)
Janissaries (p. 408)
pashas (p. 410)
harem (p. 412)
devshirme (p. 412)
grand vizier (p. 413)
sipahis (p. 413)
Sublime Porte (p. 415)
zamindars (p. 421)
purdah (p. 429)

Suggested Reading

CONSTANTINOPLE A dramatic recent account of the Muslim takeover of Constantinople is provided by **R. Crowley** in *1453: The Holy War for Constantinople and the Clash of Islam and the West* (New York, 2005). Crowley acknowledges his debt to the classic by **S. Runciman,** *The Fall of Constantinople, 1453* (Cambridge, 1965).

OTTOMAN EMPIRE Two useful general surveys of Ottoman history are **C. Finkel,** *Osman's Dream: The History of the Ottoman Empire* (Jackson, Tenn., 2006),

and **J. Goodwin,** *Lords of the Horizons: A History of the Ottoman Empire* (London, 2002).

For the argument that the decline of the Ottoman Empire was not inevitable, see **E. Karsh et al.,** *Empires of the Sand: The Struggle for Mastery in the Middle East, 1789–1923* (Cambridge, Mass., 2001).

THE SAFAVIDS On the Safavids, see **R. M. Savory,** *Iran Under the Safavids* (Cambridge, 1980). For a thoughtful if scholarly account of the reasons for the rise of the Safavid Empire, see **R. J. Abisaab,** *Converting Persia: Shia Islam and the Safavid Empire, 1501–1736* (London, 2004).

THE MUGHALS For an elegant overview of the Mughal Empire and its cultural achievements, see **A. Schimmel,** *The Empire of the Great Mughals: History, Art and Culture,* trans. **C. Attwood** (London, 2004). The Mughal Empire is analyzed in a broad Central Asian context in **R. C. Foltz,** *Mughal India and Central Asia* (Karachi, 1998).

There are a number of specialized works on various aspects of the period. The concept of "gunpowder empires" is persuasively analyzed in **D. E. Streusand,** *The Formation of the Mughal Empire* (Delhi, 1989). Economic issues predominate in much recent scholarship. For example, see **O. Prakash,** *European Commercial Enterprise in Pre-Colonial India* (Cambridge, 1998). Finally, **K. N. Chaudhuri,** *Trade and Civilization in the Indian Ocean: An Economic History from the Rise of Islam to 1750* (Cambridge, 1985), views Indian commerce in the perspective of the regional trade network throughout the Indian Ocean.

For treatments of all three Muslim empires in a comparative context, see **J. J. Kissling et al.,** *The Last Great Muslim Empires* (Princeton, N.J., 1996). On the impact of Islam in the subcontinent, see **R. Eaton, ed.,** *Essays on Islam and Indian History* (New Delhi, 2000).

WOMEN OF THE OTTOMAN AND MUGHAL EMPIRES For a detailed presentation of women in the imperial harem, consult **L. P. Peirce,** *The Imperial Harem: Women and Sovereignty in the Ottoman Empire* (Oxford, 1993). The fascinating story of the royal woman who played an important role behind the scenes is found in **E. B. Findly,** *Nur Jahan: Empress of Mughal India* (Oxford, 1993).

ART AND ARCHITECTURE On the art of this era, see **R. C. Craven,** *Indian Art: A Concise History,* rev. ed. (New York, 1997); **J. Bloom** and **S. Blair,** *Islamic Arts* (London, 1997); **M. C. Beach** and **E. Koch,** *King of the World: The Padshahnama* (London, 1997); and **M. Hattstein** and **P. Delius,** *Islam: Art and Architecture* (Königswinter, Germany, 2004).

CourseMate Visit the CourseMate website at www.cengagebrain.com for additional study tools and review materials for this chapter.

Emperor Kangxi

The East Asian World

CHAPTER OUTLINE
AND FOCUS QUESTIONS

China at Its Apex

Q Why were the Manchus so successful at establishing a foreign dynasty in China, and what were the main characteristics of Manchu rule?

Changing China

Q How did the economy and society of China change during the Ming and Qing eras, and to what degree did these changes seem to be leading toward an industrial revolution on the European model?

Tokugawa Japan

Q How did the society and economy of Japan change during the Tokugawa era, and how did Japanese culture reflect those changes?

Korea and Vietnam

Q To what degree did developments in Korea during this period reflect conditions in China and Japan? What were the unique aspects of Vietnamese civilization?

CRITICAL THINKING

Q How did China and Japan respond to the coming of the Europeans, and what explains the differences in their approach? What impact did European contacts have on these two East Asian civilizations through the end of the eighteenth century?

IN DECEMBER 1717, Emperor Kangxi (KANG-shee) returned from a hunting trip north of the Great Wall and began to suffer from dizzy spells. Conscious of his approaching date with mortality—he was now nearly seventy years of age—the emperor called together his sons and leading government officials in the imperial palace and issued an edict summing up his ideas on the art of statecraft. Rulers, he declared, should sincerely revere Heaven's laws as their fundamental strategy for governing the country. Among other things, those laws required that the ruler show concern for the welfare of the people, practice diligence, protect the state from its enemies, choose able advisers, and strike a careful balance between leniency and strictness, principle and expedience. That, he concluded, was all there was to it.[1]

Any potential successor to the throne would have been well advised to attend to the emperor's advice. Kangxi was not only one of the longest reigning of all Chinese rulers but also one of the wisest. His era was one of peace and prosperity, and after a half century of his rule, the empire was now at the zenith of its power and influence. As his life approached its end, Heaven must indeed have been pleased at the quality of his stewardship.

As for the emperor's edict, it clearly reflected the genius of Confucian teachings at their best and, with its emphasis on prudence, compassion, and tolerance, has a timeless quality that applies to our age as well as to the golden age of the Qing (CHING) dynasty.

Kangxi reigned during one of the most glorious eras in the long history of China. Under the Ming (MING) and the early Qing dynasties, the empire expanded its borders to a degree not seen since the Han and the Tang. Chinese culture was the envy of its neighbors and earned the admiration of many European visitors, including Jesuit priests and Enlightenment philosophers.

On the surface, China appeared to be an unchanging society patterned after the Confucian vision of a "golden age" in the remote past. This indeed was the image presented by China's rulers, who referred constantly to tradition as a model for imperial institutions and cultural values. Although few observers could have been aware of it at the time, however, China was changing—and rather rapidly.

A similar process was under way in neighboring Japan. A vigorous new shogunate (SHOH-gun-ut *or* SHOH-gun-ayt) called the Tokugawa (toh-goo-GAH-wah) rose to power in the early seventeenth century and managed to revitalize the traditional system in a somewhat more centralized form that enabled it to survive for another 250 years. But major structural changes were taking place in Japanese society, and by the nineteenth century, tensions were growing as the gap between theory and reality widened.

One of the many factors contributing to the quickening pace of change in both countries was contact with the West, which began with the arrival of Portuguese ships in Chinese and Japanese ports in the first half of the sixteenth century. The Ming and the Tokugawa initially opened their doors to European trade and missionary activity. Later, however, Chinese and Japanese rulers became concerned about the corrosive effects of Western ideas and practices and attempted to protect their traditional societies from external intrusion. But neither could forever resist the importunities of Western trading nations; nor were they able to inhibit the societal shifts that were taking place within their borders. When the doors to the West were finally reopened in the mid-nineteenth century, both societies were ripe for radical change. 🖉

China at Its Apex

Q FOCUS QUESTION: Why were the Manchus so successful at establishing a foreign dynasty in China, and what were the main characteristics of Manchu rule?

In 1514, a Portuguese fleet dropped anchor off the coast of China, just south of the Pearl River estuary and present-day Hong Kong. It was the first direct contact between the Chinese Empire and the West since the arrival of the Venetian adventurer Marco Polo two centuries earlier, and it opened an era that would eventually change the face of China and, indeed, all the world.

From the Ming to the Qing

Marco Polo had reported on the magnificence of China after visiting Beijing (bay-ZHING) during the reign of Khubilai Khan, the great Mongol ruler. By the time the Portuguese fleet arrived off the coast of China, of course, the Mongol Empire had long since disappeared. It had gradually weakened after the death of Khubilai Khan and was finally overthrown in 1368 by a massive peasant rebellion under the leadership of Zhu Yuanzhang (JOO yoo-wen-JAHNG), who had declared himself the founding emperor of a new Ming (Bright) dynasty (1369–1644).

As we have seen, the Ming inaugurated a period of territorial expansion westward into Central Asia and southward into Vietnam while consolidating control over China's vast heartland. At the same time, between 1405 and 1433 the dynasty sponsored a series of voyages under Admiral Zhenghe (JEHNG-huh) that spread Chinese influence far into the Indian Ocean. Then suddenly the voyages were discontinued, and the dynasty turned its attention to domestic concerns (see Chapter 10).

FIRST CONTACTS WITH THE WEST Despite the Ming's retreat from active participation in maritime trade, when the Portuguese arrived in 1514, China was in command of a vast empire that stretched from the steppes of Central Asia to the China Sea, from the Gobi Desert to the tropical rain forests of Southeast Asia. From the lofty perspective of the imperial throne in Beijing, the Europeans could only have seemed like an unusually exotic form of barbarian to be placed within the familiar framework of the tributary system, the hierarchical arrangement in which rulers of all other countries were regarded as "younger brothers" of the Son of Heaven. Indeed, the bellicose and uncultured behavior of the Portuguese so outraged Chinese officials that they expelled the Europeans, but after further negotiations, the Portuguese were permitted to occupy the tiny territory of Macao (muh-KOW), a foothold they would retain until the end of the twentieth century.

Initially, the arrival of the Europeans did not have much impact on Chinese society. Direct trade between Europe and China was limited, and Portuguese ships became involved in the regional trade network, carrying silk from China to Japan in return for Japanese silver. Eventually, the Spanish also began to participate, using the Philippines as an anchor in the galleon trade between China and the great silver mines in the Americas.

More influential than trade, perhaps, were the ideas introduced by Christian missionaries, who first received permission to reside in China in the last quarter of the sixteenth century. Among the most active and the most effective were highly educated Jesuits, who were familiar with European philosophical and scientific developments. Court officials were particularly impressed by the visitors' ability to predict the exact time of a solar eclipse, an event that the Chinese viewed with extreme reverence.

Recognizing the Chinese pride in their own culture, the Jesuits attempted to draw parallels between Christian and Confucian concepts (for example, they identified the Western concept of God with the Chinese character for Heaven) and to show the similarities between Christian morality and Confucian ethics. European inventions such as the clock, the prism, and various astronomical and musical instruments impressed Chinese officials, hitherto deeply imbued with a sense of the superiority of Chinese civilization, and helped Western ideas win acceptance at court. An elderly Chinese scholar expressed his wonder at the miracle of eyeglasses:

> White glass from across the Western Seas
> Is imported through Macao:
> Fashioned into lenses big as coins,
> They encompass the eyes in a double frame.
> I put them on—it suddenly becomes clear;
> I can see the very tips of things!
> And read fine print by the dim-lit window
> Just like in my youth.[2]

For their part, the missionaries were much impressed with many aspects of Chinese civilization, and reports of their experiences heightened European curiosity about this great society on the other side of the world (see the box on p. 436). By the late seventeenth century, European philosophers and political thinkers had begun to praise Chinese civilization and to hold up Confucian institutions and values as a mirror to criticize their counterparts in the West.

THE MING BROUGHT TO EARTH During the late sixteenth century, the Ming began to decline as a series of weak rulers led to an era of corruption, concentration of landownership, and ultimately peasant rebellions and tribal unrest along the northern frontier. The inflow of vast amounts of foreign silver to pay for Chinese goods resulted in an alarming increase in inflation. Then the arrival of the English and the Dutch, whose ships preyed on the Spanish galleon trade between Asia and the Americas, disrupted the silver trade; silver imports plummeted, severely straining the Chinese economy by raising the value of the metal relative to that of copper. Crop yields declined due to harsh weather, and the resulting scarcity made it difficult for the government to provide food in times of imminent starvation. High taxes, necessitated in part because corrupt officials siphoned off revenues, led to rural unrest and violent protests among urban workers.

As always, internal problems were accompanied by unrest along the northern frontier. Following long precedent, the Ming had attempted to pacify the frontier tribes by forging alliances with them and granting trade privileges. One of the alliances was with the Manchus (man-CHOOZ)—also known as the Jurchen (roor-ZHEN)—the descendants of peoples who had briefly established a kingdom in northern China during the early thirteenth century. The Manchus, a mixed agricultural and hunting people, lived northeast of the Great Wall in the area known today as Manchuria (man-CHUR-ee-uh).

At first, the Manchus were satisfied with consolidating their territory and made little effort to extend their rule south of the Great Wall. But during the first decades of the seventeenth century, a major epidemic devastated the population in many areas of the country. The suffering brought on by the epidemic helped spark a vast peasant revolt led by Li Zicheng (lee zuh-CHENG) (Li Tzu-ch'eng) (1604–1651), a postal worker in central China who had been dismissed from his job as part of a cost-saving measure by the imperial court. In the 1630s, Li managed to extend the revolt throughout the country, and his forces finally occupied the capital of Beijing in 1644. The last Ming emperor committed suicide by hanging himself from a tree in the palace gardens.

But Li was unable to hold his conquest. The overthrow of the Ming dynasty presented a great temptation to the Manchus. With the assistance of many military commanders who had deserted from the Ming, they conquered Beijing on their own (see Map 17.1). Li Zicheng's army disintegrated, and the Manchus declared the creation of a new dynasty: the Qing (Ch'ing, or Pure), which lasted from 1644 until 1911. Once again, China was under foreign rule.

The Greatness of the Qing

The accession of the Manchus to power in Beijing was not universally applauded. Some Ming loyalists fled to

The Art of Printing

ART & IDEAS

Europeans obtained much of their early information about China from the Jesuits who served at the Ming court in the sixteenth and seventeenth centuries. Clerics such as the Italian Matteo Ricci (ma-TAY-oh REE-chee) (1552–1610), who arrived in China in 1601, found much to admire in Chinese civilization. Here Ricci expresses a keen interest in Chinese printing methods, which at that time were well in advance of the techniques used in the West. Later Christian missionaries expressed strong interest in Confucian philosophy and Chinese ideas of statecraft.

Matteo Ricci, *The Diary of Matthew Ricci*

The art of printing was practiced in China at a date somewhat earlier than that assigned to the beginning of printing in Europe, which was about 1405. It is quite certain that the Chinese knew the art of printing at least five centuries ago, and some of them assert that printing was known to their people before the beginning of the Christian era, about 50 B.C.E. Their method of printing differs widely from that employed in Europe, and our method would be quite impracticable for them because of the exceedingly large number of Chinese characters and symbols. . . .

Their method of making printed books is quite ingenious. The text is written in ink, with a brush made of very fine hair, on a sheet of paper which is inverted and pasted on a wooden tablet. When the paper has become thoroughly dry, its surface is scraped off quickly and with great skill, until nothing but a fine tissue bearing the characters remains on the wooden tablet. Then, with a steel graver, the workman cuts away the surface following the outlines of the characters until these alone stand out in low relief. From such a block a skilled printer can make copies with incredible speed, turning out as many as fifteen hundred copies in a single day. . . . This scheme of engraving wooden blocks is well adapted for the large and complex nature of the Chinese characters, but I do not think it would lend itself very aptly to our European type, which could hardly be engraved upon wood because of its small dimensions.

Their method of printing has one decided advantage, namely, that once these tablets are made, they can be preserved and used for making changes in the text as often as one wishes. Additions and subtractions can also be made as the tablets can be readily patched. . . . We have derived great benefit from this method of Chinese printing, as we employ the domestic help in our homes to strike off copies of the books on religious and scientific subjects which we translate into Chinese from the languages in which they were written originally. In truth, the whole method is so simple that one is tempted to try it for himself after once having watched the process. The simplicity of Chinese printing is what accounts for the exceedingly large numbers of books in circulation here and the ridiculously low prices at which they are sold.

 How did the Chinese method of printing differ from that used in Europe at that time? What were its advantages?

Source: From *China in the Sixteenth Century*, by Matthew Ricci, translated by Louis J. Gallagher. Copyright © 1942 and renewed 1970 by Louis J. Gallagher, S.J.

Southeast Asia, but others continued their resistance to the new rulers from inside the country. To make it easier to identify the rebels, the government ordered all Chinese to adopt Manchu dress and hairstyles. All Chinese males were to shave their foreheads and braid their hair into a queue (KYOO); those who refused were to be executed. As a popular saying put it, "Lose your hair or lose your head."[3]

But the Manchus eventually proved to be more adept at adapting to Chinese conditions than their predecessors, the Mongols. Unlike the latter, who had tried to impose their own methods of ruling, the Manchus adopted the Chinese political system (although, as we shall see, they retained their distinct position within it) and were gradually accepted by most Chinese as the legitimate rulers of the country.

Like all of China's great dynasties, the Qing was blessed with a series of strong early rulers who pacified the country, rectified many of the most obvious social and economic inequities, and restored peace and prosperity. For the Ming dynasty, these strong emperors had been Zhu Yuanzhang and Yongle (YOONG-luh); under

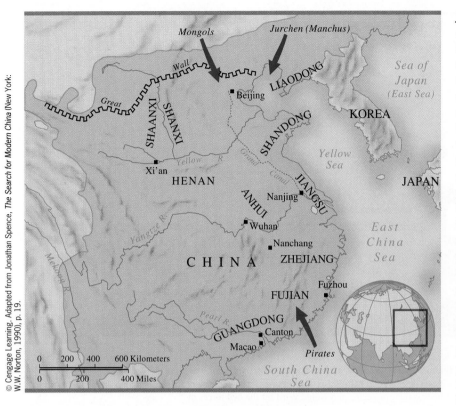

MAP 17.1 China and Its Enemies During the Late Ming Era. During the seventeenth century, the Ming dynasty faced challenges on two fronts: from China's traditional adversaries, nomadic groups north of the Great Wall, and from new arrivals, European merchants who had begun to press for trading privileges along the southern coast.

Q *How did these threats differ from those faced by previous dynasties in China?*

Jesuits, reached their height. The emperor was quite tolerant of the Christians, and several Jesuit missionaries became influential at court. Several hundred court officials converted to Christianity, as did an estimated 300,000 ordinary Chinese. But the Christian effort was ultimately undermined by squabbling among the Western religious orders over the Jesuit policy of accommodating local beliefs and practices in order to facilitate conversion. Jealous Dominicans and Franciscans complained to the pope, who issued an edict ordering all missionaries and converts to conform to the official orthodoxy set forth in Europe. At first, Kangxi attempted to resolve the problem by appealing directly to the Vatican, but the pope was uncompromising. After Kangxi's death, his successor began to suppress Christian activities throughout China.

THE REIGN OF QIANLONG Kangxi's achievements were carried on by his successors, Yongzheng (YOONG-jehng) (Yung Cheng, 1722–1736) and Qianlong (1736–1795). Like Kangxi, Qianlong was known for his diligence, tolerance, and intellectual curiosity, and he too combined vigorous military action against the unruly tribes along the frontier with active efforts to promote economic prosperity, administrative efficiency, and scholarship and artistic excellence. The result was continued growth for the Manchu Empire throughout much of the eighteenth century.

But it was also under Qianlong that the first signs of the internal decay of the Manchu dynasty began to appear. The clues were familiar ones. Qing military campaigns along the frontier were expensive and placed heavy demands on the imperial treasury. As the emperor aged, he became less astute in selecting his subordinates and fell under the influence of corrupt elements at court.

Corruption at the center led inevitably to unrest in rural areas, where higher taxes, bureaucratic venality, and rising pressure on the land because of the growing population had produced economic hardship. The heart of the unrest was in central China, where discontented peasants who had recently been settled on infertile land launched

the Qing, they would be Kangxi (K'ang Hsi) and Qianlong (CHAN-loong) (Chien Lung). The two Qing monarchs ruled China for well over a century, from the middle of the seventeenth century to the end of the eighteenth, and were responsible for much of the greatness of Manchu China.

THE REIGN OF KANGXI Kangxi (1661–1722) was arguably the greatest ruler in Chinese history. Ascending to the throne at the age of seven, he was blessed with diligence, political astuteness, and a strong character and began to take charge of Qing administration while still an adolescent. During the six decades of his reign, Kangxi not only stabilized imperial rule by pacifying the restive peoples along the northern and western frontiers but also managed to make the dynasty acceptable to the general population. As an active patron of arts and letters, he cultivated the support of scholars through a number of major projects.

During Kangxi's reign, the activities of the Western missionaries, Dominicans and Franciscans as well as

© Cengage Learning. Adapted from Jonathan Spence, *The Search for Modern China* (New York: W.W. Norton, 1990), p. 19.

The Temple of Heaven. This temple, located in the capital city of Beijing, is one of the most significant historical structures in China. Built in 1420 at the order of the Ming emperor Yongle, it was the site of the emperor's annual appeal to Heaven for a good harvest. In this important ceremony, the emperor demonstrated to his subjects that he was their protector and would ward off the evil forces in nature. Yongle's temple burned to the ground in 1889 but was immediately rebuilt following the original design.

a revolt known as the White Lotus Rebellion (1796–1804). The revolt was eventually suppressed but at great expense.

QING POLITICS One reason for the success of the Manchus was their ability to adapt to their new environment. They retained the Ming political system with relatively few changes. They also tried to establish their legitimacy as China's rightful rulers by stressing their

devotion to the principles of Confucianism. Emperor Kangxi ostentatiously studied the sacred Confucian classics and issued a "sacred edict" that proclaimed to the entire empire the importance of the moral values established by the master (see the box on p. 452).

Still, the Manchus, like the Mongols, were ethnically, linguistically, and culturally different from their subject population. The Qing attempted to cope with this reality by adopting a two-pronged strategy. As one part of this strategy, the Manchus, representing less than 2 percent of the entire population, were legally defined as distinct from everyone else in China. The Manchu nobles retained their aristocratic privileges, while their economic base was protected by extensive landholdings and revenues provided from the state treasury. Other Manchus were assigned farmland and organized into military units, called **banners**, which were stationed as separate units in various strategic positions throughout China. These "bannermen" were the primary fighting force of the empire. Ethnic Chinese were prohibited from settling in Manchuria and were still compelled to wear their hair in a queue as a sign of submission to the ruling dynasty.

But while the Qing attempted to protect their distinct identity within an alien society, they also recognized the need to bring ethnic Chinese into the top ranks of imperial

CHRONOLOGY	China During the Early Modern Era
Rise of Ming dynasty	1369
Voyages of Zhenghe	1405–1433
Portuguese arrive in southern China	1514
Matteo Ricci arrives in China	1601
Li Zicheng occupies Beijing	1644
Manchus seize China	1644
Reign of Kangxi	1661–1722
Treaty of Nerchinsk	1689
First English trading post at Canton	1699
Reign of Qianlong	1736–1795
Lord Macartney's mission to China	1793
White Lotus Rebellion	1796–1804

administration. Their solution was to create a **dyarchy**, a system in which all important administrative positions were shared equally by Chinese and Manchus. Meanwhile, the Manchus themselves, despite official efforts to preserve their separate language and culture, were increasingly assimilated into Chinese civilization.

CHINA ON THE EVE OF THE WESTERN ONSLAUGHT Unfortunately for China, the decline of the Qing dynasty occurred just as China's modest relationship with the West was about to give way to a new era of military confrontation and increased pressure for trade. The first problems came in the north, where Russian traders seeking skins and furs began to penetrate the region between Siberian Russia and Manchuria. Earlier the Ming dynasty had attempted to deal with the Russians by the traditional method of placing them in a tributary relationship.

But the tsar refused to play by Chinese rules. His envoys to Beijing ignored the tribute system and refused to perform the **kowtow** (the ritual of prostration and touching the forehead to the ground before the emperor), the classic symbol of fealty demanded of all foreign ambassadors to the Chinese court. Formal diplomatic relations were finally established in 1689, when the Treaty of Nerchinsk (ner-CHINSK) settled the boundary dispute and provided for regular trade between the two countries. Through such arrangements, the Manchus were able not only to pacify the northern frontier but also to extend their rule over Xinjiang (SHIN-jyahng) and Tibet to the west and southwest (see Map 17.2).

Dealing with the foreigners who arrived by sea was more difficult. By the end of the seventeenth century, the English had replaced the Portuguese as the dominant force in European trade. Operating through the East India

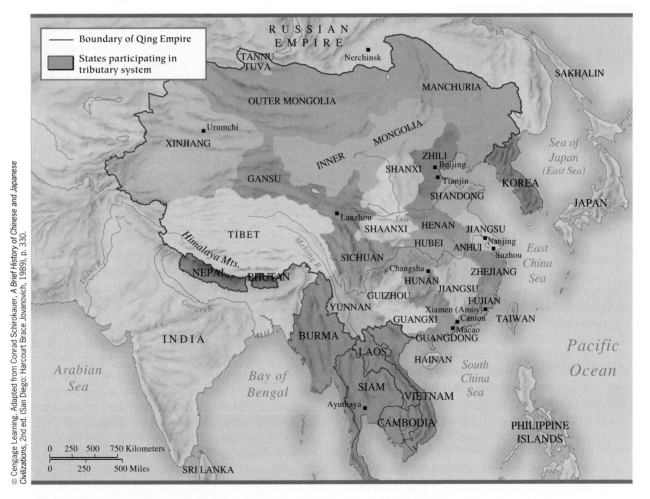

© Cengage Learning. Adapted from Conrad Schirokauer, *A Brief History of Chinese and Japanese Civilizations*, 2nd ed. (San Diego: Harcourt Brace Jovanovich, 1989), p. 330.

MAP 17.2 The Qing Empire in the Eighteenth Century. The boundaries of the Chinese Empire at the height of the Qing dynasty in the eighteenth century are shown on this map.

 What areas were linked in tributary status to the Chinese Empire, and how did they benefit the empire?

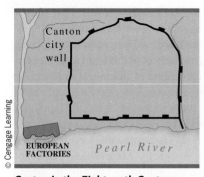

Canton in the Eighteenth Century

Company, which served as both a trading unit and the administrator of English territories in Asia, the English established their first trading post at Canton (KAN-tun) in 1699. Over the next decades, trade with China, notably the export of tea and silk to England, increased rapidly. To limit contact between Chinese and Europeans, the Qing licensed Chinese trading firms at Canton to be the exclusive conduit for trade with the West. Eventually, the Qing confined the Europeans to a small island just outside the city wall and permitted them to reside there only from October through March.

For a while, the British tolerated this system, but by the end of the eighteenth century, the British government became restive at the uneven balance of trade between the two countries, which forced the British to ship vast amounts of silver bullion to China in exchange for its silks, porcelains, and teas. In 1793, a mission under Lord Macartney visited Beijing to press for liberalization of trade restrictions. A compromise was reached on the kowtow (Macartney was permitted to bend on one knee as was the British custom), but Qianlong expressed no interest in British manufactured products (see the box on p. 441). An exasperated Macartney compared the Chinese Empire to "an old, crazy, first-rate man-of-war" that had once awed its neighbors "merely by her bulk and appearance" but was now destined under incompetent leadership to be "dashed to pieces on the shore."[4] With his contemptuous dismissal of the British request, the emperor had inadvertently sowed the seeds for a century of humiliation.

Changing China

Q FOCUS QUESTION: How did the economy and society of China change during the Ming and Qing eras, and to what degree did these changes seem to be leading toward an industrial revolution on the European model?

During the Ming and Qing dynasties, China remained a predominantly agricultural society; nearly 85 percent of its people were farmers. But although most Chinese still lived in rural villages, the economy was undergoing a number of changes.

The Population Explosion

In the first place, the center of gravity was continuing to shift steadily from the north to the south. In the early centuries of Chinese civilization, the administrative and economic center of gravity was clearly in the north. By the early Qing, the economic breadbasket of China was located along the Yangtze River and regions to the south. One concrete indication of this shift occurred during the Ming dynasty, when Emperor Yongle ordered the renovation of the Grand Canal to facilitate the shipment of rice from the Yangtze delta to the food-starved north.

Moreover, the population was beginning to increase rapidly (see the comparative essay "The Population Explosion" on p. 442). For centuries, China's population had remained within a range of 50 to 100 million, rising in times of peace and prosperity and falling in periods of foreign invasion and internal anarchy. During the Ming and the early Qing, however, the population increased from an estimated 70 to 80 million in 1390 to more than 300 million at the end of the eighteenth century. There were probably several reasons for this population increase: the relatively long period of peace and stability under the early Qing; the introduction of new crops from the Americas, including peanuts, sweet potatoes, and maize; and the planting of a new species of faster-growing rice from Southeast Asia.

Of course, this population increase meant much greater population pressure on the land, smaller farms, and a razor-thin margin of safety in case of climatic disaster. The imperial court attempted to deal with the problem through various means, most notably by preventing the concentration of land in the hands of wealthy landowners. Nevertheless, by the eighteenth century, almost all the land that could be irrigated was already under cultivation, and the problems of rural hunger and landlessness became increasingly serious.

Seeds of Industrialization

Another change during the early modern period in China was the steady growth of manufacturing and commerce. Taking advantage of the long era of peace and prosperity, merchants and manufacturers began to expand their operations beyond their immediate provinces. Commercial networks began to operate on a regional and sometimes even a national basis, as trade in silk, metal and wood products, porcelain, cotton goods, and cash crops like cotton and tobacco developed rapidly. Foreign trade also expanded as Chinese merchants set up extensive contacts with countries in Southeast Asia. As Chinese tea, silk, and porcelain became ever more popular in other parts of the world, the trade surplus grew as the country's exports greatly outnumbered its imports.

The Tribute System in Action

INTERACTION & EXCHANGE

In 1793, the British emissary Lord Macartney visited the Qing Empire to request the opening of formal diplomatic and trading relations between his country and China. Emperor Qianlong's reply, addressed to King George III of Britain, illustrates how the imperial court in Beijing viewed the world. King George could not have been pleased. The document provides a good example of the complacency with which the Celestial Empire viewed the world beyond its borders.

A Decree of Emperor Qianlong

An Imperial Edict to the King of England: You, O King, are so inclined toward our civilization that you have sent a special envoy across the seas to bring to our Court your memorial of congratulations on the occasion of my birthday and to present your native products as an expression of your thoughtfulness. On perusing your memorial, so simply worded and sincerely conceived, I am impressed by your genuine respectfulness and friendliness and greatly pleased.

As to the request made in your memorial, O King, to send one of your nationals to stay at the Celestial Court to take care of your country's trade with China, this is not in harmony with the state system of our dynasty and will definitely not be permitted. Traditionally people of the European nations who wished to render some service under the Celestial Court have been permitted to come to the capital. But after their arrival they are obliged to wear Chinese court costumes, are placed in a certain residence, and are never allowed to return to their own countries. This is the established rule of the Celestial Dynasty with which presumably you, O King, are familiar. Now you, O King, wish to send one of your nationals to live in the capital, but he is not like the Europeans who come to Peking [Beijing] as Chinese employees, live there, and never return home again, nor can he be allowed to go and come and maintain any correspondence. This is indeed a useless undertaking.

Moreover the territory under the control of the Celestial Court is very large and wide. There are well-established regulations governing tributary envoys from the outer states to Peking, giving them provisions (of food and traveling expenses) by our post-houses and limiting their going and coming. There has never been a precedent for letting them do whatever they like. Now if you, O King, wish to have a representative in Peking, his language will be unintelligible and his dress different from the regulations; there is no place to accommodate him. . . .

The Celestial Court has pacified and possessed the territory within the four seas. Its sole aim is to do its utmost to achieve good government and to manage political affairs, attaching no value to strange jewels and precious objects. The various articles presented by you, O King, this time are accepted by my special order to the office in charge of such functions in consideration of the offerings having come from a long distance with sincere good wishes. As a matter of fact, the virtue and prestige of the Celestial Dynasty having spread far and wide, the kings of the myriad nations come by land and sea with all sorts of precious things. Consequently there is nothing we lack, as your principal envoy and others have themselves observed. We have never set much store on strange or ingenious objects, nor do we need any more of your country's manufactures.

Q *What reasons did the emperor give for refusing Macartney's request to have a permanent British ambassador in Beijing? How did the tribute system differ from the principles of international relations as practiced in the West?*

Source: Reprinted by permission of the publisher from *China's Response to the West: A Documentary Survey, 1839–1923,* by Ssu-yu Teng and John King Fairbank, pp. 24–27, Cambridge, Mass.: Harvard University Press, copyright © 1954, 1979 by the President and Fellows of Harvard College, copyright renewed 1982 by Ssu-yu Teng and John King Fairbank.

THE QING ECONOMY: READY FOR TAKEOFF? In recent years, a number of historians have suggested that because of these impressive advances, by the end of the eighteenth century China was poised to make the transition from an agricultural to a predominantly manufacturing and commercial economy—a transition that began to take place in western Europe with the onset of the Industrial Revolution in the late eighteenth century (see Chapter 19).

Certainly, in most respects the Chinese economy in the mid-Qing era was as advanced as any of its counterparts around the world. China's achievements in technology

COMPARATIVE ESSAY

The Population Explosion

EARTH & ENVIRONMENT

Between 1700 and 1800, Europe, China, and, to a lesser degree, India and the Ottoman Empire experienced a dramatic growth in population. In Europe, the population grew from 120 million people to almost 200 million by 1800; China, from less than 200 million to 300 million during the same period.

Four factors were important in causing this population explosion. First, better growing conditions, made possible by an improvement in climate, affected wide areas of the world and enabled people to produce more food. Summers in both China and Europe became warmer beginning in the early eighteenth century. Second, by the eighteenth century, people had begun to develop immunities to the epidemic diseases that had caused such widespread loss of life between 1500 and 1700. The movements of people by ship after 1500 had led to devastating epidemics. For example, the arrival of Europeans in Mexico introduced smallpox, measles, and chicken pox to a native population that had no immunities to European diseases. In 1500, between 11 and 20 million people lived in the area of Mexico; by 1650, only 1.5 million remained. Gradually, however, people developed immunities to these diseases.

A third factor in the population increase was the availability of new foods. As a result of the Columbian Exchange (see the box on p. 368 in Chapter 14), American food crops—such as corn, potatoes, and sweet potatoes—were carried to other parts of the world, where they became important food sources. China had imported a new species of rice from Southeast Asia that had a shorter harvest cycle than that of existing varieties. These new foods provided additional sources of nutrition that enabled more people to live for a longer time. At the same time, land development and canal building in the eighteenth century also enabled government authorities to move food supplies to areas threatened with crop failure and famine.

Finally, the use of new weapons based on gunpowder allowed states to control larger territories and maintain a new degree of order. The early rulers of the Qing dynasty, for example, pacified the Chinese Empire and ensured a long period of peace and stability. Absolute monarchs achieved similar goals in a number of European states. Thus, in the eighteenth century, deaths from violence and from diseases were declining at the same time that food supplies were increasing, thereby making possible the beginning of the world population explosion that persists to this day.

Festival of the Yam. With the spread of a few major food crops, new sources of nutrition became available to feed more people. The importance of the yam to the Ashanti people of West Africa is evident in this celebration of a yam festival at harvest time in 1817.

© Lambeth Palace Library, London/The Bridgeman Art Library

 What were the main reasons for the dramatic expansion in the world's population during the early modern era?

over the past centuries were unsurpassed, and a perceptive observer at the time might well have concluded that the Manchu Empire would be highly competitive with the most advanced nations around the world for the indefinite future.

Nevertheless, a number of factors made it unlikely that China would advance rapidly into the industrial age. In the first place, the mercantile class was not as independent in China as in some European societies. Trade and manufacturing in China remained under the firm control of the state. In addition, political and social prejudices against commercial activity remained strong. Reflecting an ancient preference for agriculture over manufacturing and trade, the state levied heavy taxes on manufacturing and commerce while attempting to keep agricultural taxes low.

Haggling Over the Price of Tea. An important item in the China trade of the eighteenth and early nineteenth centuries was tea, which had become extremely popular in Great Britain. This painting depicts the various stages of growing, processing, and marketing tea leaves. In the background, workers are removing tender young leaves from the bushes. In the foreground, British and Chinese merchants bargain over the price. After being dried, the leaves are packed into chests and loaded on vessels for shipment abroad.

To a considerable degree, these views were shared by the population at large, as the scholar-gentry continued to dominate intellectual fashions in China throughout the early Qing period. Chinese elites in general had little interest in the natural sciences or economic activities and often viewed them as a threat to their own dominant status within Chinese society as a whole. The commercial middle class, lacking social status and an independent position in society, had little say in intellectual matters.

At the root of such attitudes was the lingering influence of Neo-Confucianism, which remained the official state doctrine in China down to the end of the Qing dynasty. Although the founding fathers of Neo-Confucianism had originally focused on the "investigation of things," as time passed its practitioners tended to emphasize the elucidation of moral principles rather than the expansion of scientific knowledge. Though the Chinese economy was gradually being transformed from an agricultural to a commercial and industrial giant, scholars tended to look back to antiquity, rather than to empirical science, as the prime source for knowledge of the natural world and human events. The result was an intellectual environment that valued continuity over change and tradition over innovation.

The Chinese reaction to European clock-making techniques provides an example. In the early seventeenth century, the Jesuit priest Matteo Ricci introduced advanced European clocks driven by weights or springs. The emperor was fascinated and found the clocks more reliable than Chinese timekeepers. Over the next decades, European timepieces became a popular novelty at court, but the Chinese expressed little curiosity about the technology involved, provoking one European observer to remark that playthings like cuckoo clocks "will be received here with much greater interest than scientific instruments or *objets d'art*."[5]

Daily Life in Qing China

Daily life under the Ming and early Qing dynasties continued to follow traditional patterns. As in earlier periods, Chinese society was organized around the family. The ideal family unit in Qing China was the joint family, in which as many as three or even four generations lived under the same roof. When sons married, they brought their wives to live with them in the family homestead. Unmarried daughters would also remain in the house. Aging parents and grandparents remained under the same roof and were cared for by younger members of the household until they died. This ideal did not always correspond to reality, however, since many families did not possess sufficient land to support a large household.

THE FAMILY The family continued to be important in early Qing times for much the same reasons as in earlier times. As a labor-intensive society based primarily on the cultivation of rice, China needed large families to help with the harvest and to provide security for parents too old to work in the fields. Sons were particularly prized, not only because they had strong backs but also because they would raise their own families under the parental roof. With few opportunities for employment outside the family, sons had little choice but to remain with their parents and help on the land. Within the family, the oldest male was king, and his wishes theoretically had to be obeyed by all family members. Arranged marriages were the norm, and the primary consideration in selecting a spouse was whether the union would benefit the family as a whole. The couple themselves usually had no say in the matter and might not even meet until the marriage ceremony. Not only was love considered unimportant in marriage, but it was often viewed as undesirable because it would draw the attention of the husband and wife away from their primary responsibility to the larger family unit.

Although this emphasis on filial piety might seem to represent a blatant disregard for individual rights, the obligations were not all on the side of the children. The father was expected to provide support for his wife and children and, like the ruler, was supposed to treat those in his care with respect and compassion. All too often, however, the male head of the family was able to exact his privileges without performing his responsibilities in return.

Beyond the joint family was the clan. Sometimes called a lineage, a clan was an extended kinship unit consisting of dozens or even hundreds of joint and nuclear families linked together by a clan council of elders and a variety of other common social and religious functions. The clan served a number of useful purposes. Some clans possessed lands that could be rented out to poorer families, or richer families within the clan might provide land for the poor. Since there was no general state-supported educational system, sons of poor families might be invited to study in a school established in the home of a more prosperous relative. If the young man succeeded in becoming an official, he would be expected to provide favors and prestige for the clan as a whole.

THE ROLE OF WOMEN In traditional China, the role of women had always been inferior to that of men. A sixteenth-century Spanish visitor to South China observed that Chinese women were "very secluded and virtuous, and it was a very rare thing for us to see a woman in the cities and large towns, unless it was an old crone."[6] Women were more visible, he said, in rural areas, where they frequently could be seen working in the fields.

The concept of female inferiority had deep roots in Chinese history. This view was embodied in the belief that only a male would carry on sacred family rituals and that men alone had the talent to govern others. Only males could aspire to a career in government or scholarship. Within the family system, the wife was clearly subordinated to the husband. Legally, she could not divorce her husband or inherit property. The husband, however, could divorce his wife if she did not produce male heirs, or he could take a second wife as well as a concubine for his pleasure. A widow suffered especially because she had to either raise her children on a single income or fight off her former husband's greedy relatives, who would coerce her to remarry since, by law, they would

then inherit all of her previous property and her original dowry.

Female children were less desirable because of their limited physical strength and because a girl's parents would have to pay a dowry to the parents of her future husband. Female children normally did not receive an education, and in times of scarcity when food was in short supply, daughters might even be put to death.

Though women were clearly inferior to men in theory, this was not always the case in practice. Capable women often compensated for their legal inferiority by playing a strong role within the family. Women were often in charge of educating the children and handled the family budget. Some privileged women also received training in the Confucian classics, although their schooling was generally for a shorter time and less rigorous than that of their male counterparts. A few produced significant works of art and poetry.

Cultural Developments

During the late Ming and the early Qing dynasties, traditional culture in China reached new heights of achievement. With the rise of a wealthy urban class, the demand for art, porcelain, textiles, and literature grew significantly.

THE RISE OF THE CHINESE NOVEL During the Ming dynasty, a new form of literature appeared that eventually evolved into the modern Chinese novel. Although considered less respectable than poetry and nonfiction prose, these groundbreaking works (often written anonymously or under pseudonyms) were enormously popular, especially among well-to-do urban dwellers.

Written in a colloquial style, the new fiction was characterized by a realism that resulted in vivid portraits of Chinese society. Many of the stories sympathized with society's downtrodden—often helpless maidens—and dealt with such crucial issues as love, money, marriage, and power. Adding to the realism were sexually explicit passages that depicted the private side of Chinese life. Readers delighted in sensuous tales that, no matter how pornographic, always professed a moral lesson; the villains were punished and the virtuous rewarded.

The Dream of the Red Chamber is generally considered China's most distinguished popular novel. Published in 1791, it tells of the tragic love between two young people caught in the financial and moral disintegration of a powerful Chinese clan. The hero and the heroine, both sensitive and spoiled, represent the inevitable decline of the Chia family and come to an equally inevitable tragic end, she in death and he in an unhappy marriage to another.

THE ART OF THE MING AND THE QING During the Ming and the early Qing, China produced its last outpouring of traditional artistic brilliance. Although most of the creative work was modeled on past examples, the art of this period is impressive for its technical perfection and breathtaking quantity.

In architecture, the most outstanding example is the Imperial City in Beijing. Building on the remnants of the palace of the Yuan dynasty, the Ming emperor Yongle ordered renovations when he returned the capital to Beijing in 1421. Succeeding emperors continued to add to the palace, but the basic design has not changed since the Ming era. Surrounded by high walls, the immense compound is divided into a maze of private apartments and offices and an imposing ceremonial quadrangle with a series of stately halls for imperial audiences and banquets. The grandiose scale, richly carved marble, spacious gardens, and graceful upturned roofs all contribute to the splendor of the "Forbidden City."

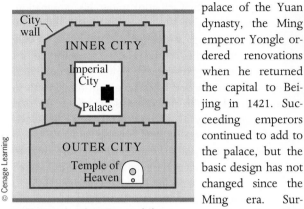

Beijing Under the Ming and the Manchus, 1400–1911

The decorative arts flourished in this period, especially the intricately carved lacquerware and the boldly shaped and colored cloisonné (kloi-zuh-NAY or KLWAH-zuh-nay), a type of enamelwork in which thin metal bands separate the areas of colored enamel. Silk production reached its zenith, and the best-quality silks were highly prized in Europe, where chinoiserie (sheen-wah-zuh-REE or shee-nwahz-REE), as Chinese art of all kinds was called, was in vogue. Perhaps the most famous of all the achievements of the Ming era was its blue-and-white porcelain, still prized by collectors throughout the world.

During the Qing dynasty, artists produced great quantities of paintings, mostly for home consumption. Inside the Forbidden City in Beijing, court painters worked alongside Jesuit artists and experimented with Western techniques. Most scholarly painters and the literati, however, totally rejected foreign techniques and became obsessed with traditional Chinese styles. As a result, Qing painting became progressively more repetitive and stale.

The Imperial City in Beijing. During the fifteenth century, the Ming dynasty erected an immense imperial city on the remnants of the palace of Khubilai Khan in Beijing. Surrounded by 6½ miles of walls, the enclosed compound is divided into a maze of private apartments and offices; it also includes an imposing ceremonial quadrangle with stately halls for imperial audiences and banquets. Because it was off-limits to commoners, the compound was known as the Forbidden City. The fearsome lion shown in the inset, representing the omnipotence of the Chinese Empire, guards the entrance to the private apartments of the palace.

World-Class China Ware. Ming porcelain was desired throughout the world for its delicate blue-and-white floral decorations. The blue coloring was produced with cobalt that had originally been brought from the Middle East along the Silk Road and was known in China as "Mohammedan blue." In the early seventeenth century, the first Ming porcelain arrived in the Netherlands, where it was called *kraak* because it had been loaded on two Portuguese ships known as carracks seized by the Dutch fleet. It took Dutch artisans more than a century to learn how to produce a porcelain as fine as the examples brought from China.

Tokugawa Japan

Q FOCUS QUESTION: How did the society and economy of Japan change during the Tokugawa era, and how did Japanese culture reflect those changes?

At the end of the fifteenth century, the traditional Japanese system was at a point of near anarchy. With the decline in the authority of the Ashikaga (ah-shee-KAH-guh) shogunate at Kyoto (KYOH-toh), clan rivalries had exploded into an era of warring states. Even at the local level, power was frequently diffuse. The typical daimyo (DYM-yoh) (great lord) domain had often become little more than a coalition of fief-holders held together by a loose allegiance to the manor lord. Nevertheless, Japan was on the verge of an extended era of national unification and peace under the rule of its greatest shogunate—the Tokugawa.

The Three Great Unifiers

The process began in the mid-sixteenth century with the emergence of three very powerful political figures, Oda Nobunaga (1568–1582), Toyotomi Hideyoshi (1582–1598), and Tokugawa Ieyasu (1598–1616). In 1568, Oda Nobunaga (OH-dah noh-buh-NAH-guh), the son of a samurai (SAM-uh-ry) and a military commander under the Ashikaga shogunate, seized the imperial capital of Kyoto and placed the reigning shogun (SHOH-gun) under his domination. During the next few years, the brutal and ambitious Nobunaga attempted to consolidate his rule throughout the central plains by defeating his rivals and suppressing the power of the Buddhist estates, but he was killed by one of his generals in 1582 before the process was complete. He was succeeded by Toyotomi Hideyoshi (toh-yoh-TOH-mee hee-day-YOH-shee), a farmer's son who had worked his way up through the ranks to become a military commander. Hideyoshi located his capital at Osaka (oh-SAH-kuh), where he built a castle to accommodate his headquarters, and gradually extended his power outward to the southern islands of Shikoku (shee-KOH-koo) and Kyushu (KYOO-shoo) (see Map 17.3). By 1590, he had persuaded most of the daimyo on the Japanese islands to accept his authority and created a national currency. Then he invaded Korea in an abortive effort to export his rule to the Asian mainland (see "Korea: In a Dangerous Neighborhood" later in this chapter).

Despite their efforts, however, neither Nobunaga nor Hideyoshi was able to eliminate the power of the local daimyo. Both were compelled to form alliances with some daimyo in order to destroy other more powerful rivals. At the conclusion of his conquests in 1590, Toyotomi Hideyoshi could claim to be the supreme proprietor of all registered lands in areas under his authority. But he then reassigned those lands as fiefs to the local daimyo, who declared their allegiance to him. The daimyo in turn began to pacify the countryside, carrying out extensive "sword hunts" to disarm the population and attracting samurai to their service. The Japanese tradition of decentralized rule had not yet been overcome.

After Hideyoshi's death in 1598, Tokugawa Ieyasu (toh-koo-GAH-wah ee-yeh-YAH-soo), the powerful daimyo of Edo (EH-doh) (modern Tokyo), moved to fill the vacuum. Neither Hideyoshi nor Oda Nobunaga had claimed the title of shogun, but Ieyasu named himself shogun in 1603, initiating the most powerful and long-lasting of all Japanese shogunates. The Tokugawa rulers completed the restoration of central authority begun by Nobunaga and Hideyoshi and remained in power until 1868, when a war dismantled the entire system. As a contemporary phrased it, "Oda pounds the national rice

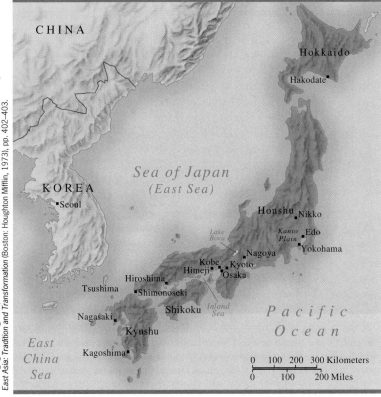

© Cengage Learning. Adapted from John K. Fairbank, Edwin O. Reischauer, and Albert M. Craig, *East Asia: Tradition and Transformation* (Boston: Houghton Mifflin, 1973), pp. 402–403.

MAP 17.3 Tokugawa Japan. This map shows the Japanese islands during the long era of the Tokugawa shogunate. Key cities, including the shogun's capital of Edo (Tokyo), are shown.

Q *Where was the imperial court located?*

cake, Hideyoshi kneads it, and in the end Ieyasu sits down and eats it."[7]

Opening to the West

The unification of Japan took place almost simultaneously with the coming of the Europeans. Portuguese traders sailing in a Chinese junk that may have been blown off course by a typhoon had landed on the islands in 1543. Within a few years, Portuguese ships were stopping at Japanese ports on a regular basis to take part in the regional trade between Japan, China, and Southeast Asia. The first Jesuit missionary, Francis Xavier (ZAY-vee-ur), arrived in 1549.

Initially, the visitors were welcomed. The curious Japanese were fascinated by tobacco, clocks, spectacles, and other European goods, and local daimyo were interested in purchasing all types of European weapons and armaments (see the box on p. 448). Oda Nobunaga and Toyotomi Hideyoshi found the new firearms helpful in defeating their enemies and unifying the islands. The effect on Japanese military architecture was particularly striking as local lords began to erect castles on the European model, many of which still exist today.

Musée des Arts Asiatiques-Guimet, Paris,// © RMN-Grand Palais/ Art Resource, NY

Arrival of the Portuguese at Nagasaki. Portuguese traders, dressed in billowing pantaloons and broad-brimmed hats, landed in Japan by accident in 1543. In a few years, they were arriving regularly, taking part in a regional trade network involving Japan, China, and Southeast Asia. In these panels done in black lacquer and gold leaf, we see a late-sixteenth-century Japanese interpretation of Portuguese merchants at Nagasaki. Normally, Japanese screens are read from right to left, but this one is read left to right. Having arrived by ship, the Portuguese proceed in splendor to the Jesuit priests waiting in a church on the right.

A Present For Lord Tokitaka

SCIENCE & TECHNOLOGY

The Portuguese introduced firearms to Japan in the sixteenth century, and Japanese warriors were quick to explore the possibilities of these new weapons. In this passage, the daimyo of a small island off the southern tip of Japan receives an explanation of how to use the new weapons and is fascinated by the results. Note how Lord Tokitaka (toh-kuh-TAH-kuh) attempts to understand the procedures in terms of traditional Daoist beliefs.

The Japanese Discover Firearms

"There are two leaders among the traders, the one called Murashusa, and the other Christian Mota. In their hands they carried something two or three feet long, straight on the outside with a passage inside, and made of a heavy substance. The inner passage runs through it although it is closed at the end. At its side there is an aperture which is the passageway for fire. Its shape defies comparison with anything I know. To use it, fill it with powder and small lead pellets. Set up a small . . . target on a bank. Grip the object in your hand, compose your body, and closing one eye, apply fire to the aperture. Then the pellet hits the target squarely. The explosion is like lightning and the report like thunder. Bystanders must cover their ears. . . . This thing with one blow can smash a mountain of silver and a wall of iron. If one sought to do mischief in another man's domain and he was touched by it, he would lose his life instantly. Needless to say this is also true for the deer and stag that ravage the plants in the fields."

Lord Tokitaka saw it and thought it was the wonder of wonders. He did not know its name at first nor the details of its use. Then someone called it "iron-arms," although it was not known whether the Chinese called it so, or whether it was so called only on our island. Thus, one day, Tokitaka spoke to the two alien leaders through an interpreter: "Incapable though I am, I should like to learn about it." Whereupon, the chiefs answered, also through an interpreter: "If you wish to learn about it,

we shall teach you its mysteries." Tokitaka then asked, "What is its secret?" The chief replied: "The secret is to put your mind aright and close one eye." Tokitaka said: "The ancient sages have often taught how to set one's mind aright, and I have learned something of it. If the mind is not set aright, there will be no logic for what we say or do. Thus, I understand what you say about setting our minds aright. However, will it not impair our vision for objects at a distance if we close an eye? Why should we close an eye?" To which the chiefs replied: "That is because concentration is important in everything. When one concentrates, a broad vision is not necessary. To close an eye is not to dim one's eyesight but rather to project one's concentration farther. You should know this." Delighted, Tokitaka said: "That corresponds to what Lao Tzu has said, 'Good sight means seeing what is very small.'"

That year the festival day of the Ninth Month fell on the day of the Metal and the Boar. Thus, one fine morning the weapon was filled with powder and lead pellets, a target was set up more than a hundred paces away, and fire was applied to the weapon. At first the people were astonished; then they became frightened. But in the end they all said in unison: "We should like to learn!" Disregarding the high price of the arms, Tokitaka purchased from the aliens two pieces of the firearms for his family treasure. As for the art of grinding, sifting, and mixing of the powder, Tokitaka let his retainer, Shinokawa Shoshiro, learn it. Tokitaka occupied himself, morning and night, and without rest in handling the arms. As a result, he was able to convert the misses of his early experiments into hits—a hundred hits in a hundred attempts.

Q *How did Lord Tokitaka use Daoist concepts to explain something unfamiliar to him? What impact did the introduction of firearms have on Japanese society at the time?*

Source: From *Sources of Japanese Tradition* by William Theodore de Bary, Carol Gluck, and Arthur E. Tiedemann. Copyright © 2005 by Columbia University Press. Reprinted with permission of the publisher.

The missionaries also had some success in converting a number of local daimyo, some of whom may have been motivated in part by the desire for commercial profits. By the end of the sixteenth century, thousands of Japanese in the southernmost islands of Kyushu and Shikoku had become Christians. But papal claims to the loyalty of all Japanese Christians and the European habit of intervening in local politics soon began to arouse suspicion in official circles. Missionaries added to the problem by deliberately destroying local idols and shrines and turning some temples into Christian schools or churches.

THE CHRISTIANS ARE EXPELLED Inevitably, the local authorities reacted. In 1587, Toyotomi Hideyoshi issued an edict prohibiting further Christian activities within his domains. Japan, he declared, was "the land of the Gods," and the destruction of shrines by the foreigners was "something unheard of in previous ages."[8] The Jesuits were ordered to leave the country within twenty days. Hideyoshi was careful to distinguish missionary from trading activities, however, and merchants were permitted to continue their operations.

The Jesuits protested the expulsion, and eventually Hideyoshi relented, permitting them to continue proselytizing as long as they were discreet. But he refused to repeal the edicts, and when the aggressive activities of newly arrived Spanish Franciscans aroused his ire, he ordered the execution of nine missionaries and a number of their Japanese converts. When the missionaries continued to interfere in local politics, Tokugawa Ieyasu ordered the eviction of all missionaries in 1612.

At first, Japanese authorities hoped to maintain commercial relations with European countries even while suppressing the Western religion, but eventually they decided to regulate foreign trade more closely and closed the two major foreign factories on the island of Hirado (heh-RAH-doh) and at Nagasaki (nah-gah-SAH-kee). The sole remaining opening to the West was at the island of Deshima (deh-SHEE-muh *or* deh-JEE-muh) in Nagasaki harbor, where in 1609 a small Dutch community was given permission to engage in limited trade with Japan (the Dutch, unlike the Portuguese and the Spanish, had not allowed missionary activities to interfere with their commercial interests). Dutch ships were permitted to dock at Nagasaki harbor only once a year and, after close inspection, were allowed to remain for two or three months. Conditions on the island of Deshima itself were quite confining: the Dutch physician Engelbert Kaempfer complained that the Dutch lived in "almost perpetual imprisonment."[9] Nor were the Japanese free to engage in foreign trade. A small amount of commerce took place with China and other parts of Asia, but Japanese subjects of the shogunate were forbidden to leave the country on penalty of death.

The Tokugawa "Great Peace"

Once in power, the Tokugawa attempted to strengthen the system that had governed Japan for more than three hundred years. They followed precedent in ruling through the *bakufu* (buh-KOO-foo *or* bah-KOO-fuh),

composed now of a coalition of daimyo, and a council of elders. But the system was more centralized than it had been previously. Now the shogunate government played a dual role. It set national policy on behalf of the emperor in Kyoto while simultaneously governing the shogun's own domain, which included about one-quarter of the national territory as well as the three great cities of Edo, Kyoto, and Osaka. As before, the state was divided into separate territories, called domains (**han**), which were ruled by a total of about 250 individual daimyo.

In theory, the daimyo were essentially autonomous in that they were able to support themselves from taxes on their lands (the shogunate received its own revenues from its extensive landholdings). In actuality, the shogunate was able to guarantee their loyalty by compelling the daimyo to maintain two residences, one in their own domains and the other at Edo, and to leave their families in Edo as hostages for the daimyo's good behavior. Keeping up two residences also put the Japanese nobility in a difficult economic position. Some were able to defray the high costs by concentrating on cash crops such as sugar, fish, and forestry products; but most were rice producers, and their revenues remained roughly the same throughout the period. The daimyo were also able to protect their economic interests by depriving their samurai retainers of their proprietary rights over the land and transforming them into salaried officials. The fief thus became a stipend, and the personal relationship between the daimyo and his retainers gradually gave way to a bureaucratic authority.

CHRONOLOGY	Japan and Korea During the Early Modern Era
First phonetic alphabet in Korea	Fifteenth century
Portuguese merchants arrive in Japan	1543
Francis Xavier arrives in Japan	1549
Rule of Oda Nobunaga	1568–1582
Seizure of Kyoto	1568
Rule of Toyotomi Hideyoshi	1582–1598
Edict prohibiting Christianity in Japan	1587
Japan invades Korea	1592
Death of Hideyoshi and withdrawal of the Japanese army from Korea	1598
Rule of Tokugawa Ieyasu	1598–1616
Creation of Tokugawa shogunate	1603
Dutch granted permission to trade at Nagasaki	1609
Order evicting Christian missionaries	1612
Yi dynasty of Korea declares fealty to China	1630s

A Japanese Castle. In imitation of European castle architecture, the Japanese perfected a new type of fortress-palace in the early seventeenth century. Strategically placed high on a hilltop, constructed of heavy stone with tiny windows, and fortified by numerous watchtowers and massive walls, these strongholds were impregnable to arrows and catapults. They served as a residence for the local daimyo, while the castle compound also housed his army and contained the seat of local government. Himeji (HEE-meh-jee) Castle, shown here, is one of the most beautiful in Japan.

Most of this commercial expansion took place in the major cities and the castle towns, where the merchants and artisans lived along with the samurai, who were clustered in neighborhoods surrounding the daimyo's castle. Banking flourished, and paper money became the normal medium of exchange in commercial transactions. Merchants formed guilds not only to control market conditions but also to facilitate government control and the collection of taxes. Under the benign if somewhat contemptuous supervision of Japan's noble rulers, a Japanese merchant class gradually began to emerge from the shadows to play a significant role in the life of the Japanese nation. Some historians view the Tokugawa era as the first stage in the rise of an indigenous form of capitalism.

Eventually, the increased pace of industrial activity spread beyond the cities into rural areas. As in Great Britain, cotton was a major factor. Cotton had been introduced to China during the Song dynasty and had spread to Korea and Japan shortly thereafter. Traditionally, cotton cloth had been too expensive for the common people, who instead wore clothing made of hemp. Imports increased during the sixteenth century, however, when cotton cloth began to be used for uniforms, matchlock fuses, and sails. Eventually, technological advances reduced the cost, and specialized communities for producing cotton cloth began to appear in the countryside and were gradually transformed into towns. By the eighteenth century, cotton had firmly replaced hemp as the cloth of choice for most Japanese.

The Tokugawa also tinkered with the social system by limiting the size of the samurai class and reclassifying samurai who supported themselves by tilling the land as commoners. In fact, with the long period of peace brought about by Tokugawa rule, the samurai gradually ceased to be a warrior class and were required to live in the castle towns. As a gesture to their glorious past, samurai were still permitted to wear their two swords, and a rigid separation was maintained between persons of samurai status and the nonaristocratic segment of the population.

SEEDS OF CAPITALISM The long period of peace under the Tokugawa shogunate made possible a dramatic rise in commerce and manufacturing, especially in the growing cities of Edo, Kyoto, and Osaka. By the mid-eighteenth century, Edo, with a population of more than one million, was one of the largest cities in the world. The growth of trade and industry was stimulated by a rising standard of living—driven in part by technological advances in agriculture and an expansion of arable land—and the voracious appetites of the aristocrats for new products.

Not everyone benefited from the economic changes of the seventeenth and eighteenth centuries, however, notably the samurai, who were barred by tradition and prejudice from commercial activities. Most samurai still relied on their revenues from rice lands, which were often insufficient to cover their rising expenses; consequently, they fell heavily into debt. Others were released from servitude to their lord and became "masterless samurai." Occasionally, these unemployed warriors—known as **ronin** (ROH-nihn), or "wave men"—revolted or plotted against the local authorities.

LAND PROBLEMS The effects of economic developments on the rural population during the Tokugawa era are harder to estimate. Some farm families benefited by exploiting the growing demand for cash crops. But not all prospered. Most peasants continued to rely on rice cultivation and were whipsawed between declining profits and rising costs and taxes (as daimyo expenses increased, land taxes often took up to 50 percent of the annual harvest). Many were forced to become tenants or to work as wage laborers on the farms of wealthy neighbors or in village industries. When rural conditions in some areas became desperate, peasant revolts erupted. According to one estimate, nearly seven thousand disturbances took place during the Tokugawa era.

Some Japanese historians, influenced by a Marxist view of history, have interpreted such evidence as an indication that the Tokugawa economic system was highly exploitative, with feudal aristocrats oppressing powerless peasants. Recent scholars, however, have tended to adopt a more balanced view, maintaining that in addition to agriculture, manufacturing and commerce experienced extensive growth. Some point out that although the population doubled in the seventeenth century, a relatively low rate for the time period, so did the amount of cultivable land, while agricultural technology made significant advances.

The relatively low rate of population growth probably meant that Japanese peasants were spared the kind of land hunger that many of their counterparts in China faced. Recent evidence indicates that the primary reasons for the relatively low rate of population growth were late marriage, abortion, and infanticide.

Life in the Village

The changes that took place during the Tokugawa era had a major impact on the lives of ordinary Japanese. In some respects, the result was an increase in the power of the central government at the village level. The shogunate increasingly relied on Confucian maxims advocating obedience and hierarchy to enhance its authority with the general population. Decrees from the *bakufu* instructed the peasants on all aspects of their lives, including their eating habits and their behavior (see the box on p. 452). At the same time, the increased power of the government led to more autonomy from the local daimyo for the peasants. Villages now had more control over their local affairs.

At the same time, the Tokugawa era saw the emergence of the nuclear family (*ie*) as the basic unit in Japanese society. In previous times, Japanese peasants had few legal rights. Most were too poor to keep their conjugal family unit intact or to pass property on to their children. Many lived at the manorial residence or worked as servants in the households of more affluent villagers. Now, with farm income on the rise, the nuclear family took on the same form as in China, although without the joint family concept. The Japanese system of inheritance was based on primogeniture (pry-moh-JEN-ih-chur). Family property was passed on to the eldest son, although younger sons often received land from their parents to set up their own families after marriage.

THE ROLE OF WOMEN Another result of the changes under the Tokugawa was that women were somewhat more restricted than they had been previously. The rights of females were especially restricted in the samurai class, where Confucian values were highly influential. Male heads of households had broad authority over property, marriage, and divorce; wives were expected to obey their husbands on pain of death. Males often took concubines or homosexual partners, while females were expected to remain chaste. The male offspring of samurai parents studied the Confucian classics in schools established by the daimyo, while females were reared at home, where only the fortunate might receive a rudimentary training in reading and writing Chinese characters. Nevertheless, some women were able to become accomplished poets and painters since, in aristocratic circles, female literacy was prized for enhancing the refinement, social graces, and moral virtue of the home.

Women were similarly at a disadvantage among the common people. Marriages were arranged, and as in China, the new wife moved in with the family of her husband. A wife who did not meet the expectations of her spouse or his family was likely to be divorced. Still, gender relations were more egalitarian than among the nobility. Women were generally valued as childbearers and homemakers, and both men and women worked in the fields. Coeducational schools were established in villages and market towns, and about one-quarter of the students were female. Poor families, however, often put infant daughters to death or sold them into prostitution.

Such attitudes toward women operated within the context of the increasingly rigid stratification of Japanese society. Deeply conservative in their social policies, the Tokugawa rulers established strict legal distinctions between the four main classes in Japan (warriors, artisans, peasants, and merchants). Intermarriage between classes was forbidden in theory, although sometimes the prohibitions were ignored in practice. Below these classes were Japan's outcasts, the *eta* (AY-tuh). Formerly, they were permitted to escape their status, at least in theory. The Tokugawa made their status hereditary and enacted severe discriminatory laws against them, regulating their place of residence, their dress, and even their hairstyles.

OPPOSING ✕ VIEWPOINTS

Some Confucian Commandments

FAMILY & SOCIETY

Although the Qing dynasty was of foreign origin, its rulers found Confucian maxims convenient for maintaining the social order. In 1670, the great emperor Kangxi issued the Sacred Edict to popularize Confucian values among the common people. The edict was read publicly at periodic intervals in every village in China and set the standard for behavior throughout the empire. Like the Qing dynasty in China, the Tokugawa shoguns attempted to keep their subjects in line with decrees that carefully prescribed all kinds of behavior. Yet a subtle difference in tone can be detected in these two documents. Whereas Kangxi's edict tended to encourage positive behavior, the decree of the Tokugawa shogunate focused more on actions that were prohibited or discouraged.

Kangxi's Sacred Edict

1. Esteem most highly filial piety and brotherly submission, in order to give due importance to the social relations.
2. Behave with generosity toward your kindred, in order to illustrate harmony and benignity.
3. Cultivate peace and concord in your neighborhoods, in order to prevent quarrels and litigations.
4. Recognize the importance of husbandry and the culture of the mulberry tree, in order to ensure a sufficiency of clothing and food.
5. Show that you prize moderation and economy, in order to prevent the lavish waste of your means.
6. Give weight to colleges and schools, in order to make correct the practice of the scholar.
7. Extirpate strange principles, in order to exalt the correct doctrine.
8. Lecture on the laws, in order to warn the ignorant and obstinate.
9. Elucidate propriety and yielding courtesy, in order to make manners and customs good.
10. Labor diligently at your proper callings, in order to stabilize the will of the people.
11. Instruct sons and younger brothers, in order to prevent them from doing what is wrong.
12. Put a stop to false accusations, in order to preserve the honest and good.

13. Warn against sheltering deserters, in order to avoid being involved in their punishment.
14. Fully remit your taxes, in order to avoid being pressed for payment.
15. Unite in hundreds and tithing, in order to put an end to thefts and robbery.
16. Remove enmity and anger, in order to show the importance due to the person and life.

Maxims for Peasant Behavior in Tokugawa Japan

1. Young people are forbidden to congregate in great numbers.
2. Entertainments unsuited to peasants, such as playing the samisen or reciting ballad dramas, are forbidden.
3. Staging sumo matches is forbidden for the next five years.
4. The edict on frugality issued by the *han* at the end of last year must be observed.
5. Social relations in the village must be conducted harmoniously.
6. If a person has to leave the village for business or pleasure, that person must return by ten at night.
7. Father and son are forbidden to stay overnight at another person's house. An exception is to be made if it is to nurse a sick person.
8. Corvée [obligatory labor] assigned by the *han* must be performed faithfully.
9. Children who practice filial piety must be rewarded.
10. One must never get drunk and cause trouble for others.
11. Peasants who farm especially diligently must be rewarded.
12. Peasants who neglect farm work and cultivate their paddies and upland fields in a slovenly and careless fashion must be punished.
13. The boundary lines of paddy and upland fields must not be changed arbitrarily.
14. Recognition must be accorded to peasants who contribute greatly to village political affairs.
15. Fights and quarrels are forbidden in the village.
16. The deteriorating customs and morals of the village must be rectified.

(Continued)

17. Peasants who are suffering from poverty must be identified and helped.

18. This village has a proud history compared to other villages, but in recent years bad times have come upon us. Everyone must rise at six in the morning, cut grass, and work hard to revitalize the village.

19. The punishments to be meted out to violators of the village code and gifts to be awarded the deserving are to be decided during the last assembly meeting of the year.

Q *In what ways did Kangxi's set of commandments conform to the principles of State Confucianism? How do these standards compare with those applied in Japan?*

Sources: Kangxi's Sacred Edict. From *Popular Culture in Late Imperial China* by David Johnson et al. Copyright © 1985 The Regents of the University of California. Maxims for Peasant Behavior in Tokugawa Japan. From Chi Nakane and Oishi Shinsabura, *Tokugawa Japan: The Social and Economic Antecedents of Modern Japan* (Japan, University of Tokyo, 1990), pp. 51–52. Translated by Conrad Totman. Copyright 1992 by Columbia University Press.

Tokugawa Culture

Under the Tokugawa, a vital new set of cultural values began to appear, especially in the cities. This innovative era witnessed the rise of popular literature written by and for the townspeople. With the development of woodblock printing in the early seventeenth century, literature became available to the common people, literacy levels rose, and lending libraries increased the accessibility of the printed word.

THE LITERATURE OF THE NEW MIDDLE CLASS The best examples of this new urban fiction are the works of Saikaku (SY-kah-koo) (1642–1693), considered one of Japan's finest novelists. Saikaku's greatest novel, *Five Women Who Loved Love*, relates the amorous exploits of five women of the merchant class. Based partly on real-life experiences, it broke from the Confucian ethic of wifely fidelity to her husband and portrayed women who were willing to die for love—and all but one eventually did. Despite the tragic circumstances, the tone of the novel is upbeat and sometimes comic, and the author's wry comments prevent the reader from becoming emotionally involved with the heroines' misfortunes.

In the theater, the rise of Kabuki (kuh-BOO-kee) threatened the long dominance of the *No* (NOH) play, replacing the somewhat restrained and elegant thematic and stylistic approach of the classical drama with a new emphasis on violence, music, and dramatic gestures. Significantly, the new drama emerged not from the rarefied world of the court but from the new world of entertainment and amusement (see the comparative illustration on p. 454). Its very commercial success, however, led to difficulties with the government, which periodically attempted to restrict or even suppress it. Early Kabuki was often performed by prostitutes, and shogunate officials, fearing that such activities could have a corrupting effect on the nation's morals, prohibited women from appearing on the stage; at the same time, they attempted to create a new professional class of male actors to impersonate female characters on stage.

In contrast to the popular literature of the Tokugawa period, poetry persevered in its more serious tradition. The most exquisite poetry was produced in the seventeenth century by the greatest of all Japanese poets, Basho (BAH-shoh) (1644–1694). He was concerned with the search for the meaning of existence and the poetic expression of his experience. With his love of Daoism and Zen Buddhism, Basho found answers to his quest for the meaning of life in nature, and his poems are grounded in seasonal imagery. The following are among his most famous poems:

> The ancient pond
> A frog leaps in
> The sound of the water.
>
> On the withered branch
> A crow has alighted—
> The end of autumn.

His last poem, dictated to a disciple only three days before his death, succinctly expressed his frustration with the unfinished business of life:

> On a journey, ailing—
> my dreams roam about
> on a withered moor.

Like all great artists, Basho made his poems seem effortless and simple. He speaks directly to everyone, everywhere.

TOKUGAWA ART Art also reflected the dynamism and changes in Japanese culture under the Tokugawa regime. The shogun's order that all daimyo and their families live every other year in Edo set off a burst of building as provincial rulers competed to erect the most magnificent mansion. Furthermore, the shoguns themselves constructed splendid castles adorned with sumptuous, almost ostentatious decor and furnishings. And the prosperity of

COMPARATIVE ILLUSTRATION

FAMILY & SOCIETY

Popular Culture: East and West. By the seventeenth century, a popular culture distinct from the elite culture of the nobility was beginning to emerge in the urban worlds of both the East and the West. At the top is a festival scene from the pleasure district of Kyoto known as the Gion. Spectators on a balcony are enjoying a colorful parade of floats and costumed performers. The festival originated as a celebration of the passing of a deadly epidemic in medieval Japan. On the right below is a scene from the celebration of Carnival on the Piazza Sante Croce in Florence, Italy. Carnival was a period of festivities before Lent, celebrated primarily in Roman Catholic countries. It became an occasion for indulgence in food, drink, games, and practical jokes as a prelude to the austerity of the forty-day Lenten season from Ash Wednesday to Easter.

Q *Do festivals such as these still exist in our own day? What purpose might they serve?*

the newly rising merchant class added fuel to the fire. Japanese paintings, architecture, textiles, and ceramics all flourished during this affluent era.

Although Japan was isolated from the Western world during much of the Tokugawa era, Japanese art was enriched by ideas from other cultures. Japanese pottery makers borrowed both techniques and designs from Korea to produce handsome ceramics. The passion for "Dutch learning" inspired Japanese to study Western medicine, astronomy, and languages and also led to experimentation with oil painting and Western ideas of perspective and the interplay of light and dark. Europeans desired Japanese lacquerware and metalwork, inlaid with ivory and mother-of-

pearl, and especially the ceramics, which were now as highly prized as those of the Chinese.

Perhaps the most famous of all Japanese art of the Tokugawa era is the woodblock print. Genre painting, or representations of daily life, began in the sixteenth century and found its new mass-produced form in the eighteenth-century woodblock print. The now literate mercantile class was eager for illustrated texts of the amusing and bawdy tales that had circulated in oral tradition. Some prints depict entire city blocks filled with people, trades, and festivals, while others show the interiors of houses; thus, they provide us with excellent visual documentation of the times. Others portray the "floating

© The Art Institute of Chicago/The Bridgeman Art Library

Evening Bell at the Clock. As woodblock prints became a popular form of pictorial expression in Tokugawa Japan, the painter Suzuki Haranobu (SOO-ZOO-kee hah-ROO-noh-boo) (c. 1725–1770) used the technique to portray scenes of daily life in the homes of ordinary Japanese. In the print shown here, a Japanese woman dries herself with a towel, while her companion looks up at a chiming clock on the dresser.

world" of the entertainment quarter, with scenes of carefree revelers enjoying the pleasures of life.

One of the most renowned of the numerous blockprint artists was Utamaro (OO-tah-mah-roh) (1754–1806), who painted erotic and sardonic women in everyday poses, such as walking down the street, cooking, or drying their bodies after a bath. Hokusai (HOH-kuh-sy) (1760–1849) was famous for *Thirty-Six Views of Mount Fuji*, a new and bold interpretation of the Japanese landscape.

Korea and Vietnam

Q FOCUS QUESTIONS: To what degree did developments in Korea during this period reflect conditions in China and Japan? What were the unique aspects of Vietnamese civilization?

On the fringes of the East Asian mainland, two of China's close neighbors sought to preserve their fragile independence from the expansionistic tendencies of the powerful Ming and Qing dynasties.

Korea: In a Dangerous Neighborhood

While Japan under the Tokugawa shogunate moved steadily out from the shadows of the Chinese Empire by creating a unique society with its own special characteristics, the Yi (YEE) dynasty in Korea continued to pattern itself, at least on the surface, after the Chinese model. The dynasty had been founded by the military commander Yi Song Gye (YEE song yee) in the late fourteenth century and immediately set out to establish close political and cultural relations with the Ming dynasty. From their new capital at Seoul (SOHL), located on the Han (HAHN) River in the center of the peninsula, the Yi rulers accepted a tributary relationship with their powerful neighbor and engaged in the wholesale adoption of Chinese institutions and values. As in China, the civil service examinations tested candidates on their knowledge of the Confucian classics, and success was viewed as an essential step toward upward mobility.

There were differences, however. As in Japan, the dynasty continued to restrict entry into the bureaucracy to members of the aristocratic class, known in Korea as the *yangban* (YAHNG-ban) (or "two groups," civilian and military). At the same time, the peasantry remained in serflike conditions, working on government estates or on the manor holdings of the landed elite. A class of slaves, called *chonmin* (CHAWN-min), labored on government plantations or served in certain occupations, such as butchers and entertainers, considered beneath the dignity of other groups in the population.

Eventually, Korean society began to show signs of independence from Chinese orthodoxy. In the fifteenth century, a phonetic alphabet for writing the Korean spoken language (*hangul*) was devised. Although it was initially held in contempt by the elites and used primarily as a teaching device, eventually it became the medium for private correspondence and the publishing of fiction for a popular audience. At the same time, changes were taking place in the economy, where rising agricultural production contributed to a population increase and the appearance of a small urban industrial and commercial sector, and in society, where the long domination of the *yangban* class began to weaken. As their numbers increased and their power and influence declined, some *yangban* became merchants or even moved into the ranks of the peasantry, further blurring the distinction between the aristocratic class and the common people.

Meanwhile, the Yi dynasty faced continual challenges to its independence from its neighbors. Throughout much of the sixteenth century, the main threat came from the north, where Manchu forces harassed Korean lands just south of the Yalu (YAH-loo) River (see Map 17.3 on p. 447). By the 1580s, however, the larger threat

Be My Brother, or I'll Bash Your Head In!

INTERACTION & EXCHANGE

In 1590, Toyotomi Hideyoshi defeated the last of his enemies and brought the islands of Japan under his rule. Shortly thereafter, an emissary from the Yi dynasty in Korea presented him with a letter congratulating him on his success. In his reply, presented here, Hideyoshi disclosed his plan to conquer the Chinese mainland and bring all of East Asia under his control. In a thinly veiled warning, which disclosed his megalomaniacal ambition, he demanded that the Yi ruler support his forthcoming attack on China. If not, he declared, Japan would exact terrible revenge. But the Korean king was more fearful of his powerful neighbor to the west and rejected Hideyoshi's demand for an alliance with Japan. Thereupon Hideyoshi attacked Korea in the so-called Imjin (IM-jin) War (1592–1598), which caused tremendous hardship throughout the peninsula.

Hideyoshi, Imperial Regent of Japan, to His Excellency the King of Korea

I read your epistle from afar with pleasure, opening and closing the scroll again and again to savor the aroma of your distinguished presence.

Now, then: This empire is composed of more than sixty provinces, but for years the country was divided, the polity disturbed, civility abandoned, and the realm unresponsive to imperial rule. Unable to stifle my indignation at this, I subjugated the rebels and struck down the bandits within the span of three or four years. As far away as foreign regions and distant islands, all is now in my grasp.

As I privately consider the facts of my background, I recognize it to be that of a rustic and unrefined minor retainer. Nevertheless: As I was about to be conceived, my dear mother dreamt that the wheel of the sun had entered her womb. The diviner declared, "As far as the sun shines, so will the brilliance of his rule extend. When he reaches his prime, the Eight Directions will be enlightened through his benevolence and the Four Seas replete with the glory of his name. How could anyone doubt this?" As a result of this miracle, anyone who turned against me was automatically crushed. Whomever I fought, I never failed to conquer. Now that the realm has been thoroughly pacified, I caress and nourish the people, solacing the orphaned and the desolate. Hence my subjects live in plenty and the revenue produced by the land has increased ten-thousand-fold over the past. Since this empire originated, never has the imperial court seen such prosperity or the capital city such grandeur as now.

Man born on this earth, though he live to a ripe old age, will as a rule not reach a hundred years. Why should I rest, then, grumbling in frustration, where I am? Disregarding the distance of the sea and mountain reaches that lie in between, I shall in one fell swoop invade Great Ming. I have in mind to introduce Japanese customs and values to the four hundred and more provinces of that country and bestow upon it the benefits of imperial rule and culture for the coming hundred million years.

Your esteemed country has done well to make haste in attending on our court. Where there is farsightedness, grief does not come near. Those who lag behind [in offering homage], however, will not be granted pardon, even if this is a distant land of little islands lying in the sea. When the day comes for my invasion of Great Ming and I lead my troops to the staging area, that will be the time to make our neighborly relations flourish all the more. I have no other desire but to spread my fame throughout the Three Countries, this and no more.

I have received your regional products as itemized. Stay healthy and take care.

Hideyoshi
Imperial Regent of Japan

Q *How did Hideyoshi justify his ambitious plan to bring all of eastern Asia under his control?*

Source: From W. T. de Bary, et al., *Sources of Japanese Tradition* 2nd ed., Vol. I (New York, 2001), pp. 466–467, citing Zoku Zenrin Kokuho Ki xxx, in Zoku gunsho ruiju, demivol. I, fasc. 881, 404, JSAE.

came from the east in the form of a newly united Japan. During much of the sixteenth century, leading Japanese daimyo had been involved in a protracted civil war, as Oda Nobunaga, Toyotomi Hideyoshi, and Tokugawa Ieyasu strove to solidify their control over the islands. Of the three, only Hideyoshi lusted for an empire beyond the seas. Although born to a commoner family, he harbored visions of grandeur and in the late 1580s announced plans to attack the Ming Empire (see the box above). When the Korean king Sonjo (SOHN-joe) (1567–1608) refused

Hideyoshi's offer of an alliance, in 1592 the latter launched an invasion of the Korean peninsula.

At first the campaign went well, and Japanese forces, wreaking death and devastation throughout the countryside, advanced as far as the Korean capital at Seoul. But eventually the Koreans, under the inspired leadership of the military commander Yi Sunshin (YEE-soon-SHIN) (1545–1598), who designed fast but heavily armed ships that could destroy the more cumbersome landing craft of the invading forces, managed to repel the attack and safeguard their independence. The respite was brief, however. By the 1630s, a new threat from the Manchus had emerged from across the northern border. A Manchu force invaded northern Korea in the 1630s and eventually compelled the Yi dynasty to promise allegiance to the new imperial government in Beijing. Korea was relatively untouched by the arrival of European merchants and missionaries, although information about Christianity was brought to the peninsula by Koreans returning from tribute missions to China, and a small Catholic community was established there in the late eighteenth century.

Vietnam: The Perils of Empire

Vietnam—or Dai Viet (dy VEE-et), as it was known at the time—had managed to avoid the fate of many of its neighbors during the seventeenth and eighteenth centuries. Isolated from the major maritime routes that passed through the region, the country was only peripherally involved in the spice trade with the West and had not suffered the humiliation of losing territory to European colonial powers. In fact, Dai Viet followed an imperialist path of its own, defeating the trading state of Champa to the south and imposing its suzerainty over the rump of the old Angkor empire—today known as Cambodia. The state of Dai Viet now extended from the Chinese border to the shores of the Gulf of Siam.

But expansion undermined the cultural integrity of traditional Vietnamese society, as those migrants who settled in the marshy Mekong River delta developed a "frontier spirit" far removed from the communal values long practiced in the old national heartland of the Red River valley. By the seventeenth century, a civil war had split Dai Viet into two squabbling territories in the north and south, providing European powers with the opportunity to meddle in the country's internal affairs to their own benefit. In 1802, with the assistance of a French adventurer long active in the region, a member of the southern royal family managed to reunite the country under the new Nguyen (NGWEN) dynasty, which lasted until 1945.

To placate China, the country was renamed Vietnam (South Viet), and the new imperial capital was established in the city of Hué (HWAY), a small river port roughly equidistant from the two rich river valleys that provided the country with its chief sustenance, wet rice. The founder of the new dynasty, who took the reign title of Gia Long, fended off French efforts to promote Christianity among his subjects and sought to promote traditional Confucian values among an increasingly diverse population.

CHAPTER SUMMARY

When Christopher Columbus sailed from southern Spain in his three ships in August 1492, he was seeking a route to China and Japan. He did not find it, but others eventually did. In 1514, Portuguese ships arrived on the coast of southern China. Thirty years later, a small contingent of Portuguese merchants became the first Europeans to set foot on the islands of Japan.

At first, the new arrivals were welcomed, if only as curiosities. Eventually, several European nations established trade relations with China and Japan, and Christian missionaries of various religious orders were active in both countries and in Korea as well. But their success was short-lived. Europeans eventually began to be perceived as detrimental to law and order, and during the seventeenth century, the majority of the foreign merchants and missionaries were evicted from all three countries. From that time until the middle of the nineteenth century, China, Japan, and Korea were relatively little affected by events taking place beyond their borders.

That fact led many observers to assume that the societies of East Asia were essentially stagnant, characterized by agrarian institutions and values reminiscent of those of the feudal era in Europe. As we have seen, however, that picture is misleading, for all three countries were evolving and by the early nineteenth century were quite different from what they had been three centuries earlier.

Ironically, these changes were especially marked in Tokugawa Japan, a seemingly "closed" country, but one where traditional classes and institutions were under increasing strain, not only from the emergence of a new merchant class but also from the centralizing tendencies of the powerful Tokugawa shogunate. On the mainland as well, the popular image in the West of a "changeless China" was increasingly divorced from reality, as social and economic conditions were marked by a growing complexity, giving birth to tensions that by the middle of the nineteenth century would strain the Qing dynasty to its very core.

By the beginning of the nineteenth century, then, powerful tensions, reflecting a growing gap between ideal and reality, were at work in both Chinese and Japanese society. Under these conditions, both countries were soon forced to face a new challenge from the aggressive power of an industrializing Europe.

CHAPTER TIMELINE

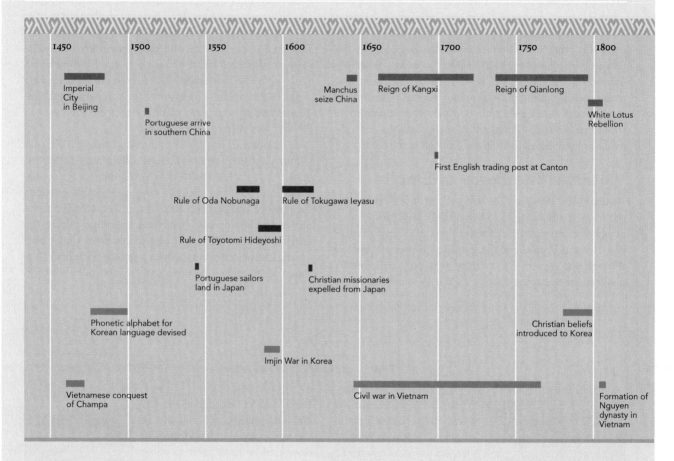

CHAPTER REVIEW

Upon Reflection

Q What factors at the end of the eighteenth century might have served to promote or to impede China's transition to an advanced industrial and market economy? Which factors do you think were the most important? Why?

Q Some historians have declared that during the Tokugawa era the Japanese government essentially sought to close the country to all forms of outside influence. Is that claim justified? Why or why not?

Q What was the nature of Sino-Korean relations during the early modern era? How did they compare with Chinese policies toward Vietnam?

Key Terms

banners (p. 438)
dyarchy (p. 439)
kowtow (p. 439)
han (p. 449)
ronin (p. 450)
eta (p. 451)
yangban (p. 455)
chonmin (p. 455)

Suggested Reading

CHINA UNDER THE MING AND QING DYNASTIES
Reliable surveys with a readable text are **T. Brook,** *The Troubled Empire: China in the Yuan and Ming Dynasties* (Cambridge, Mass., 2010), and **W. Rowe,** *China's Last Empire: Great Qing* (Cambridge, Mass., 2009). For fascinating vignettes of Chinese social conditions, see **J. Spence,** *Return to Dragon Mountain: Memories of a Late Ming Man* (New York, 2007) and *Treason by the Book* (New York, 2001).

 L. Brockey, *Journey to the East: The Jesuit Mission to China, 1579–1724* (Cambridge, Mass., 2007), is an account of China's first encounter with Europe. For a defense of Chinese science, see **B. Elman,** *On Their Own Terms: Science in China, 1550–1900* (Cambridge, Mass., 2005). **J. E. Wills Jr.,** *Mountains of Fame: Portraits in Chinese History* (Princeton, N.J., 1994), is an interesting collection of biographies from across the gamut of Chinese history.

CHINESE LITERATURE AND ART The best surveys of Chinese literature are **S. Owen,** *An Anthology of Chinese Literature: Beginnings to 1911* (New York, 1996), and **V. Mair,** *The Columbia Anthology of Traditional Chinese Literature* (New York, 1994). For a comprehensive introduction to the Chinese art of this period, see **M. Sullivan,** *The Arts of China,* 4th ed. (Berkeley, Calif., 1999), and **C. Clunas,** *Art in China* (Oxford, 1997). For the best introduction to the painting of this era, see **J. Cahill,** *Chinese Painting* (New York, 1977).

JAPAN AND KOREA C. Totman, *A History of Japan,* 2nd ed. (Cambridge, Mass., 2005), is a reliable survey of Japanese history. For a more detailed analysis, see **J. W. Hall, ed.,** *The Cambridge History of Japan,* vol. 4 (Cambridge, 1991). Social issues are explored in **W. Farris,** *Japan's Medieval Population* (Honolulu, 2006). **B. Bodart-Baily,** *Kaempfer's Japan: Tokugawa Culture Observed* (Honolulu, 1999), is a first-hand account by a Western visitor to Tokugawa Japan. On Korea, see **M. Seth,** *A Concise History of Korea: From the Neolithic Period Through the Nineteenth Century* (Lanham, Md., 2006).

WOMEN IN CHINA AND JAPAN For a brief introduction to women in the Ming and Qing dynasties as well as the Tokugawa era, see **S. Hughes** and **B. Hughes,** *Women in World History,* vol. 2 (Armonk, N.Y., 1997), and **S. Mann** and **Y. Cheng, eds.,** *Under Confucian Eyes: Writings on Gender in Chinese History* (Berkeley, Calif., 2001). Also see **D. Ko, J. K. Haboush,** and **J. R. Piggott, eds.,** *Women and Confucian Culture in Premodern China, Korea, and Japan* (Berkeley, Calif., 2003). On women's literacy in seventeenth-century China, see **D. Ko,** *Teachers of the Inner Chambers: Women and Culture in Seventeenth-Century China* (Stanford, Calif., 1994). Most valuable is the collection of articles edited by **G. L. Bernstein,** *Re-Creating Japanese Women, 1600–1945* (Berkeley, Calif., 1991).

JAPANESE LITERATURE AND ART Of specific interest on Japanese literature of the Tokugawa era is **D. Keene,** *World Within Walls: Japanese Literature of the Pre-Modern Era, 1600–1867* (New York, 1976). For the most comprehensive and accessible overview of Japanese art, see **P. Mason,** *Japanese Art* (New York, 1993).

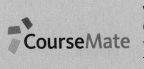

Visit the CourseMate website at www.cengagebrain.com for additional study tools and review materials for this chapter.

The West on the Eve of a New World Order

The storming of the Bastille

CHAPTER OUTLINE AND FOCUS QUESTIONS

Toward a New Heaven and a New Earth: An Intellectual Revolution in the West

Q Who were the leading figures of the Scientific Revolution and the Enlightenment, and what were their main contributions?

Economic Changes and the Social Order

Q What changes occurred in the European economy in the eighteenth century, and to what degree were these changes reflected in social patterns?

Colonial Empires and Revolution in the Americas

Q What colonies did the British and French establish in the Americas, and how did their methods of administering their colonies differ?

Toward a New Political Order and Global Conflict

Q What do historians mean by the term *enlightened absolutism*, and to what degree did eighteenth-century Prussia, Austria, and Russia exhibit its characteristics?

The French Revolution

Q What were the causes, the main events, and the results of the French Revolution?

The Age of Napoleon

Q Which aspects of the French Revolution did Napoleon preserve, and which did he destroy?

CRITICAL THINKING

Q In what ways were the American Revolution, the French Revolution, and the seventeenth-century English revolutions alike? In what ways were they different?

IN PARIS ON THE MORNING of July 14, 1789, a mob of eight thousand men and women in search of weapons streamed toward the Bastille (bass-STEEL), a royal armory filled with arms and ammunition. The Bastille was also a state prison, and although it held only seven prisoners at the time, in the eyes of these angry Parisians, it was a glaring symbol of the government's despotic policies. It was defended by the marquis de Launay (mar-KEE duh loh-NAY) and a small garrison of 114 men. The attack on the Bastille began in earnest in the early afternoon, and after three hours of fighting, de Launay and the garrison surrendered. Angered by the loss of ninety-eight protesters, the victors beat de Launay to death, cut off his head, and carried it aloft in triumph through the streets of Paris. When King Louis XVI was told the news of the fall of the Bastille by the duc de La Rochefoucauld-Liancourt (dook duh lah-RUSH-foo-koh-lee-ahn-KOOR), he exclaimed, "Why, this is a revolt." "No, Sire," replied the duc. "It is a revolution."

The French Revolution was a key factor in the emergence of a new world order. Historians have often portrayed the eighteenth century as the final phase of an old Europe that would be forever changed by the violent upheaval and reordering of society associated with the French Revolution. Before the Revolution, the old order—still largely agrarian, dominated by kings and landed aristocrats, and grounded in privileges for nobles, clergy, towns, and provinces—seemed to continue a basic pattern that had prevailed in Europe since medieval times. As the century drew to a close, however, a new intellectual order based on rationalism and secularism emerged, and demographic, economic, social, and political patterns were beginning to change in ways that proclaimed the arrival of a new and more modern order.

The French Revolution demolished the institutions of the old regime and established a new order based on individual rights, representative institutions, and a concept of loyalty to the nation rather than to the monarch. The revolutionary upheavals of the era, especially in France, created new liberal and national political ideals, summarized in the French revolutionary slogan, "Liberty, Equality, Fraternity," that transformed France and then spread to other European countries and the rest of the world.

Toward a New Heaven and a New Earth: An Intellectual Revolution in the West

Q FOCUS QUESTION: Who were the leading figures of the Scientific Revolution and the Enlightenment, and what were their main contributions?

In the seventeenth century, a group of scientists set the Western world on a new path known as the **Scientific Revolution**, which gave Europeans a new way of viewing the universe and their place in it. The Scientific Revolution affected only a small number of Europe's educated elite. But in the eighteenth century, this changed dramatically as a group of intellectuals popularized the ideas of the Scientific Revolution and used them to undertake a dramatic reexamination of all aspects of life. The widespread impact of these ideas on their society has caused historians ever since to call the eighteenth century in Europe the Age of Enlightenment.

The Scientific Revolution

The Scientific Revolution ultimately challenged conceptions and beliefs about the nature of the external world that had become dominant by the Late Middle Ages.

TOWARD A NEW HEAVEN: A REVOLUTION IN ASTRONOMY Medieval philosophers had used the ideas of Aristotle, Ptolemy (the greatest astronomer of antiquity, who lived in the second century C.E.), and Christianity to form the Ptolemaic (tahl-uh-MAY-ik) or **geocentric theory** of the universe. In this conception, the universe was seen as a series of concentric spheres with a fixed or motionless earth at its center. Composed of material substance, the earth was imperfect and constantly changing. The spheres surrounding the earth were made of a crystalline, transparent substance and moved in circular orbits around the earth. The heavenly bodies, believed to number ten in 1500, were pure orbs of light, embedded in the moving, concentric spheres. Working outward from the earth, the first eight spheres contained the moon, Mercury, Venus, the sun, Mars, Jupiter, Saturn, and the fixed stars. The ninth sphere imparted to the eighth sphere of the fixed stars its daily motion, while the tenth sphere was frequently described as the prime mover that moved itself and imparted motion to the other spheres. Beyond the tenth sphere was the Empyrean Heaven—the location of God and all the saved souls. Thus, God and the saved souls were at one end of the universe and humans were at the center.

Nicolaus Copernicus (NEE-koh-lowss kuh-PURR-nuh-kuss) (1473–1543), a Polish mathematician, felt that Ptolemy's geocentric system failed to accord with the observed motions of the heavenly bodies and offered his **heliocentric** (sun-centered) **theory** as a more accurate explanation. Copernicus argued that the sun was motionless at the center of the universe. The planets revolved around the sun in the order of Mercury, Venus, the earth, Mars, Jupiter, and Saturn. The moon, however, revolved around the earth. Moreover, what appeared to be the movement of the sun around the earth was really explained by the earth's daily rotation on its axis and its journey around the sun each year. But Copernicus did not reject the idea that the heavenly spheres moved in circular orbits.

The next step in destroying the geocentric conception and supporting the Copernican system was taken by Johannes Kepler (yoh-HAHN-us KEP-lur) (1571–1630). A brilliant German mathematician and astronomer, Kepler arrived at laws of planetary motion that confirmed Copernicus's heliocentric theory. In his first law, however, he revised Copernicus by showing that the orbits of the planets around the sun were not circular but elliptical, with the sun at one focus of the ellipse rather than at the center.

Kepler's work destroyed the basic structure of the Ptolemaic system. People could now think in new terms of the actual paths of planets revolving around the sun in elliptical orbits. But important questions remained. For example, what were the planets made of? An Italian

Medieval Conception of the Universe. As this sixteenth-century illustration shows, the medieval cosmological view placed the earth at the center of the universe, surrounded by a series of concentric spheres. The earth was imperfect and constantly changing, while the heavenly bodies that surrounded it were perfect and incorruptible. Beyond the tenth and final sphere was heaven, where God and all the saved souls were located. (The circles read, from the center outward: 1. Moon, 2. Mercury, 3. Venus, 4. Sun, 5. Mars, 6. Jupiter, 7. Saturn, 8. Firmament of the Stars, 9. Crystalline Sphere, 10. Prime Mover, and at the end, Empyrean Heaven—Home of God and All the Elect, that is, saved souls.)

The Copernican System. The Copernican system was presented in *On the Revolutions of the Heavenly Spheres*, published shortly before Copernicus's death. As shown in this illustration from the first edition, Copernicus maintained that the sun was the center of the universe while the planets, including the earth, revolved around it. Moreover, the earth rotated daily on its axis. (The circles read, from the center outward: Sun; VII. Mercury, orbit of 80 days; VI. Venus; V. Earth, with the moon, orbit of one year; IIII. Mars, orbit of 2 years; III. Jupiter, orbit of 12 years; II. Saturn, orbit of 30 years; I. Immobile Sphere of the Fixed Stars.)

scientist achieved the next important breakthrough to a new cosmology by answering that question.

Galileo Galilei (gal-li-LAY-oh GAL-li-lay) (1564–1642) taught mathematics and was the first European to make systematic observations of the heavens by means of a telescope, inaugurating a new age in astronomy. Galileo turned his telescope to the skies and made a remarkable series of discoveries: mountains on the moon, four moons revolving around Jupiter, and sunspots. Galileo's observations seemed to destroy yet another aspect of the traditional cosmology in that the universe seemed to be composed of material similar to that of earth rather than a perfect, unchanging substance.

Galileo's revelations, published in *The Starry Messenger* in 1610, made Europeans aware of a new picture of the universe. But the Catholic Church condemned Copernicanism and ordered Galileo to abandon the Copernican thesis. The church attacked the Copernican system because it threatened not only Scripture but also an entire conception of the universe. The heavens were no longer a spiritual world but a world of matter.

By the 1630s and 1640s, most astronomers had come to accept the new conception of the universe. Nevertheless, the problem of explaining motion in the universe and tying together the ideas of Copernicus, Galileo, and Kepler had not yet been done. This would be the work of an Englishman who has long been considered the greatest genius of the Scientific Revolution.

Isaac Newton (1642–1727) taught at Cambridge University, where he wrote his major work, *Mathematical Principles of Natural Philosophy*, known simply as the *Principia* (prin-SIP-ee-uh) by the first word of its Latin title. In the *Principia*, Newton defined the three laws of motion that govern the planetary bodies, as well as objects on earth. Crucial to his argument was the universal law of gravitation, which explained why the planetary bodies did not go off in straight lines but continued in elliptical orbits about the sun. In mathematical terms, Newton explained that every object in the universe is attracted to every other object by a force called gravity.

Newton had demonstrated that one mathematically proven universal law could explain all motion in the

COMPARATIVE ESSAY

The Scientific Revolution

SCIENCE & TECHNOLOGY

When Catholic missionaries began to arrive in China during the sixteenth century, they marveled at the many accomplishments of Chinese civilization, including woodblock printing and the civil service examination system. In turn, their hosts were impressed with European inventions such as the spring-driven clock and eyeglasses.

It is not surprising that the Western visitors were impressed with what they saw in China, for that country had long been at the forefront of human achievement. After the sixteenth century, however, Europe would take the lead in science and technology, a phenomenon that would ultimately bring about the Industrial Revolution and begin a transformation of human society that would lay the foundations of the modern world.

Why did Europe suddenly become the engine for rapid change in the seventeenth and eighteenth centuries? One factor was the shift in the European worldview from a metaphysical to a materialist perspective and the growing inclination among European intellectuals to question first principles. In contrast to China, where, for example, Song dynasty thinkers had used the "investigation of things" to analyze and confirm principles first established by Confucius and his contemporaries, empirical scientists in early modern Europe rejected received religious ideas, developed a

The telescope—a European invention.

new conception of the universe, and sought ways to improve material conditions around them.

Why were European thinkers more interested in practical applications of their discoveries than their counterparts elsewhere? No doubt the literate mercantile and propertied elites of Europe were attracted to the new science because it offered new ways to exploit resources for profit. Some early scientists made it easier for these groups to accept the new ideas by showing how they could be applied to specific industrial and technological needs. Galileo, for example, consciously appealed to the material interests of the educated elite when he explained that the science of mechanics would be quite useful "when it becomes necessary to build bridges or other structures over water, something occurring mainly in affairs of great importance."

Finally, the political changes taking place in Europe may also have contributed. Many European states enlarged their bureaucratic machinery and consolidated their governments in order to collect the revenues and amass the armies needed to compete militarily with rivals. Political leaders desperately sought ways to enhance their wealth and power and grasped eagerly at new tools that might guarantee their survival and prosperity.

Q Why did the Scientific Revolution emerge in Europe and not in China?

universe. At the same time, the Newtonian synthesis created a new cosmology in which the universe was seen as one huge, regulated machine that operated according to natural laws in absolute time, space, and motion. Newton's **world-machine** concept dominated the modern worldview until the twentieth century, when Albert Einstein's concept of relativity created a new picture of the universe.

EUROPE, CHINA, AND SCIENTIFIC REVOLUTIONS A question that arises is why the Scientific Revolution

occurred in Europe and not in China. In the Middle Ages, China had been the most technologically advanced civilization in the world. After 1500, that distinction passed to the West (see the comparative essay "The Scientific Revolution" above). Historians are not sure why. Some have contrasted the sense of order in Chinese society with the competitive spirit existing in Europe. Others have emphasized China's ideological viewpoint that favored living in harmony with nature rather than trying to dominate it.

One historian has even suggested that China's civil service system drew the "best and the brightest" into government service, to the detriment of other occupations.

Background to the Enlightenment

The impetus for political and social change in the eighteenth century stemmed in part from the **Enlightenment**. The Enlightenment was a movement of intellectuals who were greatly impressed with the accomplishments of the Scientific Revolution. When they used the word *reason*— one of their favorite words—they were advocating the application of the **scientific method** to the understanding of all life. All institutions and all systems of thought were subject to the rational, scientific way of thinking if people would only free themselves from the shackles of outmoded traditions, especially religious ones. If Isaac Newton could discover the natural laws regulating the world of nature, they too, by using reason, could find the laws that governed human society. This belief in turn led them to hope that they could create a better society than the one they had inherited. *Reason, natural law, hope, progress*—these were the buzzwords in the heady atmosphere of eighteenth-century Europe.

Major sources of inspiration for the Enlightenment were Isaac Newton and his fellow Englishman John Locke (1632–1704). Newton had contended that the world and everything in it worked like a giant machine. Enchanted by the grand design of this world-machine, the intellectuals of the Enlightenment were convinced that by following Newton's rules of reasoning, they could discover the natural laws that governed politics, economics, justice, and religion.

John Locke's theory of knowledge also made a great impact. In his *Essay Concerning Human Understanding* (1690), Locke denied the existence of innate ideas and argued that every person was born with a *tabula rasa* (TAB-yuh-luh RAH-suh), a blank mind:

> Let us then suppose the mind to be, as we say, white paper, void of all characters, without any ideas. How comes it to be furnished? Whence comes it by that vast store which the busy and boundless fancy of man has painted on it with an almost endless variety? Whence has it all the materials of reason and knowledge? To this I answer, in one word, from experience. . . . Our observation, employed either about external sensible objects or about the internal operations of our minds perceived and reflected on by ourselves, is that which supplies our understanding with all the materials of thinking.[1]

By denying innate ideas, Locke implied that people were molded by their environment, by whatever they perceived through their senses from their surrounding world. By changing the environment and subjecting people to proper influences, they could be changed and a new society created. And how should the environment be changed? Newton had paved the way: reason enabled enlightened people to discover the natural laws to which all institutions should conform.

The Philosophes and Their Ideas

The intellectuals of the Enlightenment were known by the French term *philosophes* (fee-loh-ZAHFS), although they were not all French and few were philosophers in the strict sense of the term. The **philosophes** were literary people, professors, journalists, economists, political scientists, and, above all, social reformers. Although it was a truly international and cosmopolitan movement, the Enlightenment also enhanced the dominant role being played by French culture; Paris was its recognized capital. Most of the leaders of the Enlightenment were French. The French philosophes, in turn, affected intellectuals elsewhere and created a movement that touched the entire Western world, including the British and Spanish colonies in the Americas. (The terms *British* and *British* began to be used after 1707 when the Act of Union united England and Scotland.)

To the philosophes, the role of philosophy was not just to discuss the world but to change it. A spirit of rational criticism was to be applied to everything, including religion and politics. Spanning almost a century, the Enlightenment evolved with each succeeding generation, becoming more radical as new thinkers built on the contributions of their predecessors. A few individuals, however, dominated the landscape so completely that we can gain insight into the core ideas of the philosophes by focusing on the three French giants—Montesquieu, Voltaire, and Diderot.

MONTESQUIEU   Charles de Secondat (SHARL duh suh-KAHN-da), the baron de Montesquieu (MOHN-tess-kyoo) (1689–1755), came from the French nobility. In his most famous work, *The Spirit of the Laws* (1748), Montesquieu attempted to apply the scientific method to the comparative study of governments to ascertain the "natural laws" governing the social and political relationships of human beings. Montesquieu distinguished three basic kinds of governments: republic, monarchy, and despotism.

Montesquieu used England as an example of monarchy, and his analysis of England's constitution led to his most lasting contribution to political thought—the importance of checks and balances achieved by means of a **separation of powers**. He believed that England's system, with its separate executive, legislative, and judicial powers that served to limit and control each other, provided the greatest freedom and security for a state. His work was eventually read by American political leaders, who incorporated its principles into the U.S. Constitution.

VOLTAIRE   The greatest figure of the Enlightenment was François-Marie Arouet (frahn-SWAH-ma-REE ahr-WEH), known simply as Voltaire (vohl-TAYR) (1694–1778). Son of a prosperous middle-class family from Paris, he studied law, but achieved his first success as a playwright. Voltaire was a prolific author and wrote an almost endless stream of pamphlets, novels, plays, letters, philosophical essays, and histories.

Voltaire was especially well known for his criticism of traditional religion and his strong attachment to the ideal of religious toleration. As he grew older, Voltaire became ever more strident in his denunciations. "Crush the infamous thing," he thundered—the infamous thing being religious fanaticism, intolerance, and superstition.

Throughout his life, Voltaire championed not only religious tolerance but also **deism**, a religious outlook shared by most other philosophes. Deism was built on the Newtonian world-machine, which implied the existence of a mechanic (God) who had created the universe. To Voltaire, the universe was like a clock, and God was the clockmaker who had created it, set it in motion, and allowed it to run according to its own natural laws.

DIDEROT   Denis Diderot (duh-NEE dee-DROH) (1713–1784), the son of a skilled craftsman, became a writer so that he could be free to study many subjects and languages. One of Diderot's favorite topics was Christianity, which he condemned as fanatical and unreasonable.

Diderot's most famous contribution was the *Encyclopedia*, or *Classified Dictionary of the Sciences, Arts, and Trades*, a twenty-eight-volume compendium of knowledge that he edited and referred to as the "great work of his life." Its purpose, according to Diderot, was to "change the general way of thinking." It did precisely that, becoming a major weapon of the philosophes' crusade against the old French society. The contributors included many philosophes who attacked religious intolerance and advocated social, legal, and political improvements that would lead to a society that was more cosmopolitan, more tolerant, more humane, and more reasonable. The *Encyclopedia* was sold to doctors, clergymen, teachers, lawyers, and even military officers, thus spreading the ideas of the Enlightenment.

TOWARD A NEW "SCIENCE OF MAN"   The Enlightenment belief that Newton's scientific methods could be used to discover the natural laws underlying all areas of human life led to the emergence of what the philosophes called a "science of man," or what we would call the social sciences. In a number of areas, such as economics, politics, and education, the philosophes arrived at natural laws that they believed governed human actions.

Adam Smith (1723–1790), often viewed as one of the founders of the discipline of economics, believed that individuals should be free to pursue their own economic self-interest. Through their actions, all society would ultimately benefit. Consequently, the state should in no way interrupt the free play of natural economic forces by imposing government regulations on the economy but should leave it alone, a doctrine that subsequently became known as **laissez-faire** (less-ay-FAYR) (French for "leave it alone"). In Smith's view, government had only three basic functions: it should protect society from invasion (army), defend its citizens from injustice (police), and keep up certain public works, such as roads and canals, that private individuals could not afford.

THE LATER ENLIGHTENMENT   By the late 1760s, a new generation of philosophes began to move beyond their predecessors' beliefs. Most famous was Jean-Jacques Rousseau (ZHAHNH-ZHAHK roo-SOH) (1712–1778), whose political beliefs were presented in two major works. In his *Discourse on the Origins of the Inequality of Mankind*, Rousseau argued that people had adopted laws and governors in order to preserve their private property. In the process, they had become enslaved by government. What, then, should people do to regain their freedom? In his celebrated treatise *The Social Contract* (1762), Rousseau found an answer in the concept of the social contract whereby an entire society agreed to be governed by its general will. Each individual might have a particular will contrary to the general will, but if the individual put his particular will (self-interest) above the general will, he should be forced to abide by the general will. "This means nothing less than that he will be forced to be free," said Rousseau, because the general will, being ethical and not just political, represented what the entire community ought to do.

Another influential treatise by Rousseau was his novel *Émile*, one of the Enlightenment's most important works on education. Rousseau's fundamental concern was that education should foster, rather than restrict, children's natural instincts. Rousseau's own experiences had shown him the importance of the emotions. He sought a balance between heart and mind, between emotion and reason.

But Rousseau did not necessarily practice what he preached. His own children were sent to orphanages, where many children died at a young age. Rousseau also viewed women as "naturally" different from men. In *Émile*, Sophie, Émile's intended wife, was educated for her role as wife and mother by learning obedience and nurturing skills that would enable her to provide loving care for her husband and children. Not everyone in the eighteenth century, however, agreed with Rousseau.

THE "WOMAN QUESTION" IN THE ENLIGHTENMENT   For centuries, many male intellectuals had argued that the nature of women made them inferior to men and made

The Rights of Women

Mary Wollstonecraft responded to an unhappy childhood in a large family by seeking to lead an independent life. Few occupations were available for middle-class women in her day, but she survived by working as a governess to aristocratic children. All the while, she wrote and developed her ideas on the rights of women. This excerpt is taken from her *Vindication of the Rights of Woman*, written in 1792. This work established her reputation as the foremost British feminist thinker of the eighteenth century.

Mary Wollstonecraft, *Vindication of the Rights of Woman*

It is a melancholy truth—yet such is the blessed effect of civilization—the most respectable women are the most oppressed; and, unless they have understandings far superior to the common run of understandings, taking in both sexes, they must, from being treated like contemptible beings, become contemptible. How many women thus waste life away the prey of discontent, who might have practiced as physicians, regulated a farm, managed a shop, and stood erect, supported by their own industry, instead of hanging their heads surcharged with the dew of sensibility, that consumes the beauty to which it at first gave luster. . . .

Proud of their weakness, however, [women] must always be protected, guarded from care, and all the rough toils that dignify the mind. If this be the fiat of fate, if they will make themselves insignificant and contemptible, sweetly to waste "life away," let them not expect to be valued when their beauty fades, for it is the fate of the fairest flowers to be admired and pulled to pieces by the careless hand that plucked them. In how many ways do I wish, from the purest benevolence, to impress this truth on my sex; yet I fear that they will not listen to a truth that dear-bought experience has brought home to many an agitated bosom, nor willingly resign the privileges of rank and sex for the privileges of humanity, to which those have no claim who do not discharge its duties. . . .

Would men but generously snap our chains, and be content with rational fellowship instead of slavish obedience, they would find us more observant daughters, more affectionate sisters, more faithful wives, and more reasonable mothers—in a word, better citizens. We should then love them with true affection, because we should learn to respect ourselves; and the peace of mind of a worthy man would not be interrupted by the idle vanity of his wife.

What picture did Wollstonecraft paint of the women of her day? Why were they in such a deplorable state? Why did Wollstonecraft suggest that both women and men were at fault for the "slavish" situation of females?

Source: From *First Feminists: British Women, 1578–1799* by Moira Ferguson. Copyright © 1985. Reprinted with permission of Indiana University Press.

---

male domination of women necessary and right. In the Scientific Revolution, however, some women had made notable contributions. Maria Winkelmann (VINK-ul-mahn) in Germany, for example, was an outstanding practicing astronomer. Nevertheless, when she applied for a position as assistant astronomer at the Berlin Academy, for which she was highly qualified, she was denied the post by the academy's members, who feared that hiring her would establish a precedent ("mouths would gape").

Female thinkers in the eighteenth century disagreed with this attitude and offered suggestions for improving conditions for women. The strongest statement of the rights of women was advanced by the English writer Mary Wollstonecraft (WULL-stun-kraft) (1759–1797),

viewed by many as the founder of modern European **feminism**.

In her *Vindication of the Rights of Woman* (1792), Wollstonecraft pointed out two contradictions in the views of women held by such Enlightenment thinkers as Rousseau. To argue that women must obey men, she said, was contrary to the beliefs of those same individuals that a system based on the arbitrary power of monarchs over their subjects or slave owners over their slaves was wrong. The subjection of women to men was equally wrong. Furthermore, the Enlightenment was based on an ideal of reason innate in all human beings. If women have reason, then they should have the same rights as men to obtain an education and engage in economic and political life (see the box above).

Antoine Watteau, *The Pilgrimage to Cythera*. Antoine Watteau was one of the most gifted painters in eighteenth-century France. His portrayal of aristocratic life reveals a world of elegance, wealth, and pleasure. In this painting, Watteau depicts a group of aristocratic lovers about to depart from the island of Cythera, where they have paid homage to Venus, the goddess of love.

Culture in an Enlightened Age

Although the Baroque style that had dominated the seventeenth century continued to be popular, by the 1730s, a new style of decoration and architecture known as **Rococo** (ruh-KOH-koh) had spread throughout Europe. Unlike the Baroque, which stressed power, grandeur, and movement, Rococo emphasized grace, charm, and gentle action. Rococo rejected strict geometrical patterns and had a fondness for curves; it liked to follow the wandering lines of natural objects, such as seashells and flowers. Highly secular, its lightness and charm spoke of the pursuit of pleasure, happiness, and love.

Some of Rococo's appeal is evident in the work of Antoine Watteau (AHN-twahn wah-TOH) (1684–1721), whose lyrical views of aristocratic life, refined, sensual, and civilized, with gentlemen and ladies in elegant dress, revealed a world of upper-class pleasure and joy. Underneath that exterior, however, was an element of sadness as the artist revealed the transitory nature of pleasure, love, and life.

HIGH CULTURE Historians have grown accustomed to distinguishing between a civilization's high culture and its popular culture. **High culture** is the literary and artistic culture of the educated and wealthy ruling classes; **popular culture** is the written and unwritten culture of the masses, most of which has traditionally been passed down

orally. By the eighteenth century, the two forms were beginning to blend, owing to the expansion of both the reading public and publishing. Whereas French publishers issued 300 titles in 1750, about 1,600 were being published yearly in the 1780s. Although many of these books were still aimed at small groups of the educated elite, many were also directed to the new reading public of the middle classes, which included women and even urban artisans.

POPULAR CULTURE The distinguishing characteristic of popular culture is its collective nature. Group activity was especially common in the *festival*, a broad name used to cover a variety of celebrations: community festivals; annual festivals, such as Christmas and Easter; and the ultimate festival, Carnival, which was celebrated in the Mediterranean world of Spain, Italy, and France as well as in Germany and Austria.

Carnival began after Christmas and lasted until the start of Lent, the forty-day period of fasting and purification leading up to Easter. Because people were expected to abstain from meat, sex, and most recreations during Lent, Carnival was a time of great indulgence when heavy consumption of food and drink was the norm. It was a time of intense sexual activity as well. Songs with double meanings that would ordinarily be considered offensive could be sung publicly at this time of year. A float of Florentine "keymakers," for example, sang this ditty to the ladies: "Our tools are fine, new and useful. We always carry them with us. They are good for anything. If you want to touch them, you can."[2]

Economic Changes and the Social Order

 FOCUS QUESTION: What changes occurred in the European economy in the eighteenth century, and to what degree were these changes reflected in social patterns?

The eighteenth century in Europe witnessed the beginning of economic changes that ultimately had a strong impact on the rest of the world.

New Economic Patterns

Europe's population began to grow around 1750 and continued to increase steadily. The total European population was probably around 120 million in 1700, 140 million in 1750, and 190 million in 1790. A falling death rate was perhaps the most important reason for this population growth. Of great significance in lowering death rates was the disappearance of bubonic plague, but so was diet. More plentiful food and better transportation of food supplies led to improved nutrition and relief from devastating famines.

More plentiful food was in part a result of improvements in agricultural practices and methods in the eighteenth century, especially in Britain, parts of France, and the Low Countries. Food production increased as more land was farmed, yields per acre increased, and climate improved. Also important to the increased yields was the cultivation of new vegetables, including two important American crops, the potato and maize (Indian corn). Both had been brought to Europe from the Americas in the sixteenth century.

In European industry in the eighteenth century, textiles were the most important product and were still mostly produced by master artisans in guild workshops. But in many areas textile production was shifting to the countryside through the "putting-out" or "domestic" system. A merchant-capitalist entrepreneur bought the raw materials, mostly wool and flax, and "put them out" to rural workers who spun them into yarn and then wove the yarn into cloth on simple looms. The entrepreneurs sold the finished product, made a profit, and used it to purchase more raw materials. This system also became known as the **cottage industry** because the spinners and weavers did their work in their own cottages.

Overseas trade boomed in the eighteenth century. Some historians speak of the emergence of a true global economy, with patterns of trade that interlocked Europe, Africa, the East, and the Americas (see Map 18.1). One important pattern involved the influx of gold and silver into Spain from its colonial American empire. Much of this gold and silver made its way to Britain, France, and the Netherlands in return for manufactured goods. British, Dutch, and French merchants in turn used their profits to buy tea, spices, silk, and cotton goods from China and India to sell in Europe.

Commercial capitalism created enormous prosperity for some European countries. By 1700, Spain, Portugal, and the Dutch Republic, which had earlier monopolized overseas trade, found themselves increasingly overshadowed by France and England, which built enormously profitable colonial empires in the course of the eighteenth century. After the French lost the Seven Years' War in 1763, Britain emerged as the world's strongest overseas trading nation, and London became the world's greatest port.

European Society in the Eighteenth Century

The pattern of Europe's social organization, first established in the Middle Ages, continued well into the eighteenth century. Society was still divided into the traditional "orders" or "estates" determined by heredity.

Because society was still mostly rural in the eighteenth century, the peasantry constituted the largest social group, about 85 percent of Europe's population. There were rather wide differences within this group, however, especially between free peasants and serfs. In eastern Germany, eastern Europe, and Russia, serfs remained tied to the lands of their noble landlords. In contrast, peasants in Britain, northern Italy, the Low Countries, Spain, most of France, and some areas of western Germany were largely free.

The nobles, who constituted only 2 to 3 percent of the European population, played a dominating role in society. Being born a noble automatically guaranteed a place at the top of the social order, with all its attendant privileges and rights. Nobles, for example, were exempt from many forms of taxation. Since medieval times, landed aristocrats had functioned as military officers, and eighteenth-century nobles held most of the important offices in the administrative machinery of state and controlled much of the life of their local districts.

Townspeople were still a distinct minority of the total population except in the Dutch Republic, Britain, and parts of Italy. At the end of the eighteenth century, about one-sixth of the French population lived in towns of two thousand people or more. The biggest city in Europe was London, with a million inhabitants; Paris was a little more than half that size.

Many cities in western and even central Europe had a long tradition of **patrician** oligarchies that dominated town and city councils. Just below the patricians stood

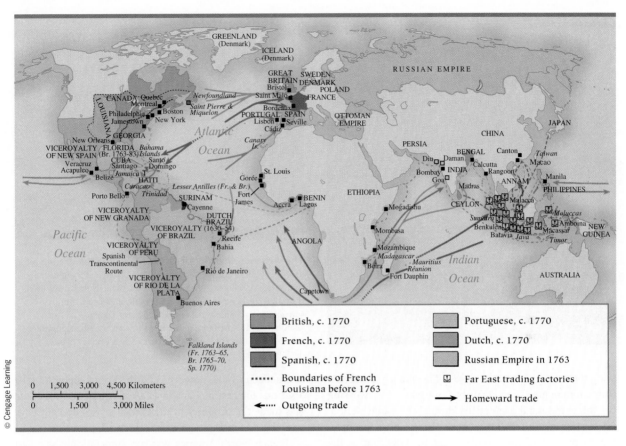

MAP 18.1 **Global Trade Patterns of the European States in the Eighteenth Century.** New patterns of trade interlocked Europe, Africa, the East, and the Americas. Dutch, English, French, Spanish, and Portuguese colonies had been established in North and South America, and the ships of these nations followed the trade routes across the Atlantic, Pacific, and Indian Oceans.

Q *With what regions did Britain conduct most of its trade?*

the upper crust of the middle classes: nonnoble office-holders, financiers and bankers, merchants, wealthy *rentiers* (rahn-TYAYS) who lived off their investments, and important professionals, including lawyers. Another large urban group consisted of the lower middle class, made up of master artisans, shopkeepers, and small traders. Below them were the laborers or working classes and a large group of unskilled workers who served as servants, maids, and cooks at pitifully low wages.

Colonial Empires and Revolution in the Americas

Q FOCUS QUESTION: What colonies did the British and French establish in the Americas, and how did their methods of administering their colonies differ?

The first colonial empires in the Americas had been established in the sixteenth century by Spain and Portugal

(see Chapter 14). By the early seventeenth century, however, both Portugal and Spain were facing challenges from the Dutch, English, and French, who sought to create their own colonial empires in the Western Hemisphere, both in the West Indies and on the North American continent.

The West Indies

Both the French and British colonial empires in the Americas ultimately included large parts of the West Indies. The British held Barbados, Jamaica, and Bermuda, and the French possessed Saint-Dominique, Martinique, and Guadeloupe. On these tropical islands, both the British and the French developed plantations, worked by African slaves, to produce tobacco, cotton, coffee, and sugar, all products increasingly in demand in Europe.

The "sugar factories," as the sugar plantations in the Caribbean were called, played an especially prominent role. By the 1780s, Jamaica, one of Britain's most important colonies, was producing 50,000 tons of sugar annually

The Aristocratic Way of Life. The desire of British aristocrats for both elegance and greater privacy was fulfilled by the eighteenth-century country house. The painting on the right, by Richard Wilson, shows a typical English country house of the eighteenth century, surrounded by a simple and serene landscape. Thomas Gainsborough's *Coversation in the Park*, shown at the left, captures the relaxed life of two aristocrats in the park of their country estate.

with the labor of 200,000 slaves. The French colony of Saint-Dominique (later Haiti) had 500,000 slaves working on three thousand plantations during the same period. This colony produced 100,000 tons of sugar a year, supplying 40 percent of the world's sugar by 1789, but at the expense of a high death rate from the brutal treatment of the slaves. It is not surprising that Saint-Dominique saw the first successful slave uprising in 1793.

British North America

Although Spain had claimed all of North America as part of its empire, other nations largely ignored its claims. The first permanent English settlement in North America was established in 1607 at Jamestown, in what is now Virginia. The settlers barely survived, making it clear that colonizing American lands was not necessarily conducive to quick profits. The Massachusetts colony fared much better; its initial 4,000 settlers had increased to 40,000 by 1660. By the eighteenth century, British North America consisted of thirteen colonies. They were thickly populated, containing about 1.5 million people by 1750, and were also prosperous.

French North America

The French also established a colonial empire in North America. In 1534, the French explorer Jacques Cartier (ZHAHK kar-TYAY) had discovered the Saint Lawrence River and laid claim to Canada as a French possession. Not until Samuel de Champlain (sa-my-ELL duh shahm-PLAN *or* SHAM-playn) established a settlement

at Quebec in 1608, however, did the French begin to take a serious interest in Canada as a colony. In 1663, Canada was made the property of the French crown and administered by a French governor like a French province.

French North America was run autocratically as a vast trading area, where valuable furs, leather, fish, and timber were acquired. The inability of the French state to persuade its people to emigrate to its Canadian possessions, however, left the territory thinly populated. Already in 1713, the French began to cede some of their American possessions to their British rival. As a result of the Seven Years' War, they surrendered the rest of their Canadian lands to Britain in 1763 (see "Changing Patterns of War: Global Confrontation" later in this chapter).

The American Revolution

By the mid-eighteenth century, increasing trade and industry had led to a growing middle class in Britain that favored expansion of trade and world empire. These people found a spokesman in William Pitt the Elder (1708–1778), who became prime minister in 1757 and began to expand the British Empire. In North America, after the end of the Seven Years' War, Great Britain controlled Canada and the lands east of the Mississippi.

The Americans and the British had different conceptions of how the empire should be governed, however. In eighteenth-century Britain, the king or queen and Parliament shared power, with Parliament gradually gaining the upper hand. The monarch chose ministers who were responsible to the crown and who set policy and guided Parliament. Parliament had the power to make laws, levy taxes, pass budgets, and indirectly influence the ministers. The British envisioned Parliament as the supreme authority throughout the empire, but the Americans had their own representative assemblies. They believed that neither king nor Parliament should interfere in their internal affairs and that no tax could be levied without the consent of their own assemblies. After the Seven Years' War, when the British tried to obtain new revenues from the colonies to pay for the cost of defending them, the colonists resisted. An attempt to levy new taxes by the Stamp Act of 1765 led to riots and the law's quick repeal.

Crisis followed crisis until 1776, when the colonists declared their independence from Great Britain. On July 4, 1776, the Second Continental Congress approved a declaration of independence drafted by Thomas Jefferson. A stirring political document, the Declaration of Independence affirmed the Enlightenment's natural rights of "life, liberty, and the pursuit of happiness" and declared the colonies to be "free and independent states absolved from all allegiance to the British crown." The war for American independence had formally begun.

Of great importance to the colonies' cause was support from foreign countries eager to gain revenge for earlier defeats at the hands of the British. French officers and soldiers served in the American Continental Army under George Washington as commander in chief. When the British army of General Cornwallis was forced to surrender to a combined American and French army and French fleet under Washington at Yorktown in 1781, the British decided to call it quits. The Treaty of Paris, signed in 1783, recognized the independence of the American colonies and granted the Americans control of the territory from the Appalachians to the Mississippi River.

BIRTH OF A NEW NATION The thirteen American colonies had gained their independence, but fear of concentrated power caused them to have little enthusiasm for establishing a strong central government, and so the Articles of Confederation, ratified in 1781, did not create one. A movement for a different form of national government soon arose. In the summer of 1787, fifty-five delegates—wealthy, politically experienced, and well educated—convened in Philadelphia to revise the Articles of Confederation, but decided instead to devise a new constitution.

The proposed U.S. Constitution established a central government distinct from and superior to governments of the individual states. The central or federal government was divided into three branches, each with some power to check the others. A president would serve as the chief executive with the power to execute laws, veto the legislature's acts, supervise foreign affairs, and direct military forces. Legislative power was vested in the second branch of government, a bicameral legislature composed of the Senate, elected by the state legislatures, and the House of Representatives, elected directly by the people. A supreme court and other courts "as deemed necessary" by Congress provided the third branch of government. They would enforce the Constitution as the "supreme law of the land."

The Constitution was approved by the states—by a slim margin. Important to its success was a promise to add a bill of rights as the new government's first piece of business. Accordingly, in March 1789, the new Congress enacted the first ten amendments to the Constitution, known as the Bill of Rights. These guaranteed freedom of religion, speech, press, petition, and assembly, as well as the right to bear arms, protection against unreasonable searches and arrests, trial by jury, due process of law, and protection of property rights. Many of these rights were derived from the **natural rights** philosophy of the eighteenth-century philosophes. Is it any wonder that many European intellectuals saw the American Revolution as the embodiment of the Enlightenment's political dreams?

Toward a New Political Order and Global Conflict

Q FOCUS QUESTION: What do historians mean by the term *enlightened absolutism*, and to what degree did eighteenth-century Prussia, Austria, and Russia exhibit its characteristics?

There is no doubt that Enlightenment thought had some impact on the political development of European states in the eighteenth century. The philosophes believed there were certain natural rights, which should not be withheld from any person. These rights included equality before the law, freedom of religious worship, freedom of speech and press, and the rights to assemble, hold property, and pursue happiness. But how were these natural rights to be established and preserved? Most philosophes believed that people needed to be ruled by an enlightened ruler, by which they meant a ruler who would allow religious toleration, freedom of speech and press, and the rights of private property; foster the arts, sciences, and education; and, above all, obey the laws and enforce them fairly. Only strong monarchs seemed capable of overcoming vested interests and effecting the needed reforms. Therefore, reforms should come from above (from absolute rulers) rather than from below (from the people).

Many historians once assumed that a new type of monarchy emerged in the later eighteenth century, which they called *enlightened despotism* or **enlightened absolutism**. Monarchs such as Frederick II of Prussia, Catherine the Great of Russia, and Joseph II of Austria supposedly followed the philosophes' advice and ruled by enlightened principles. Recently, however, scholars have questioned the usefulness of the concept of enlightened absolutism. We can determine the extent to which it can be applied by examining the major "enlightened absolutists" of the late eighteenth century.

Prussia

Frederick II, known as Frederick the Great (1740–1786), was one of the best-educated and most cultured monarchs of the eighteenth century. He was well versed in Enlightenment thought and even invited Voltaire to live at his court for several years. A believer in the king as the "first servant of the state," Frederick was a conscientious ruler who enlarged the Prussian army (to 200,000 men) and kept a strict watch over the bureaucracy.

For a time, Frederick seemed quite willing to make enlightened reforms. He abolished the use of torture except in treason and murder cases and also granted limited freedom of speech and press, as well as complete religious toleration. His efforts were limited, however, as he kept Prussia's rigid social structure and serfdom intact and avoided any additional reforms.

The Austrian Empire of the Habsburgs

The Austrian Empire had become one of the great European states by the beginning of the eighteenth century. Yet it was difficult to rule because it was a sprawling conglomerate of nationalities, languages, religions, and cultures (see Map 18.2).

MAP 18.2 **Europe in 1763.** By the mid-eighteenth century, five major powers dominated Europe—Prussia, Austria, Russia, Britain, and France. Each sought to enhance its power both domestically, through a bureaucracy that collected taxes and ran the military, and internationally, by capturing territory or preventing other powers from doing so.

Q *Given the distribution of Prussian and Habsburg holdings, in what areas of Europe were they most likely to compete for land and power?*

Joseph II (1780–1790) believed in the need to sweep away anything standing in the path of reason. As he said, "I have made Philosophy the lawmaker of my empire; her logical applications are going to transform Austria." Joseph's reform program was far-reaching. He abolished serfdom, abrogated the death penalty, and established the principle of equality of all before the law. Joseph instituted drastic religious reforms as well, including complete religious toleration.

Joseph's program proved overwhelming for Austria, however. He alienated the nobility by freeing the serfs and alienated the church by his attacks on the monastic establishment. Joseph realized his failure when he wrote the epitaph for his own gravestone: "Here lies Joseph II, who was unfortunate in everything that he undertook." His successors undid many of his reforms.

Russia Under Catherine the Great

Catherine II the Great (1762–1796) was an intelligent woman who was familiar with the works of the philosophes and seemed to favor enlightened reforms. But she was skeptical about impractical theories. She did consider the idea of a new law code that would recognize the principle of the equality of all people in the eyes of the law. But in the end she did nothing, knowing that her success depended on the support of the Russian nobility. In 1785, she gave the nobles a charter that exempted them from taxes. Catherine's policy of favoring the landed nobility led to even worse conditions for the Russian peasants and sparked a rebellion, but it soon faltered and collapsed. Catherine responded with even harsher measures against the peasantry.

Above all, Catherine proved a worthy successor to Peter the Great in her policies of territorial expansion westward into Poland and southward to the Black Sea. Russia spread southward by defeating the Turks. Russian expansion westward occurred at the expense of neighboring Poland. In three partitions of Poland, Russia gained about 50 percent of Polish territory.

Enlightened Absolutism Reconsidered

Of the rulers we have discussed, only Joseph II sought truly radical changes based on Enlightenment ideas. Both Frederick II and Catherine II liked to talk about enlightened reforms, and they even attempted some. But neither ruler's policies seemed seriously affected by Enlightenment thought. Necessities of state and maintenance of the existing system took precedence over reform. Indeed, many historians maintain that Joseph, Frederick, and Catherine were all primarily concerned for the power and well-being of their states. In the final analysis, heightened state power was used to create armies and wage wars to gain more power.

At the same time, the ability of enlightened rulers to make reforms was limited by political and social realities. Everywhere in Europe, the hereditary aristocracy was still the most powerful class. As the chief beneficiaries of a system based on traditional rights and privileges, the nobles were not willing to support a political ideology that trumpeted the principle of equal rights for all. The first serious challenge to their supremacy would come with the French Revolution, an event that blew open the door to the world of modern politics.

Changing Patterns of War: Global Confrontation

The philosophes condemned war as a foolish waste of life and resources. Despite their words, the rivalries and costly struggles among the European states continued unabated in the eighteenth century. Europe consisted of a number of self-governing, individual states that were chiefly guided by the self-interest of the ruler. And as Frederick the Great of Prussia said, "The fundamental rule of governments is the principle of extending their territories."

By far the most dramatic confrontation was the Seven Years' War. Although it began in Europe, it soon turned into a global conflict fought in Europe, India, and North America. In Europe, the British and Prussians fought the Austrians, Russians, and French. With his superb army and military skill, Frederick the Great of Prussia was able for some time to defeat the Austrian, French, and Russian armies. Eventually, however, his forces were gradually worn down and faced utter defeat until a new Russian tsar withdrew Russia's troops from the conflict. A stalemate ensued, ending the European conflict in 1763.

The struggle between Britain and France in the rest of the world had more decisive results. In India, local rulers allied with British and French troops fought a number of battles. Ultimately, the British under Robert Clive won out, not because they had better forces but because they were more persistent (see the box on p. 474). By the Treaty of Paris in 1763, the French withdrew and left India to the British.

The greatest conflicts of the Seven Years' War took place in North America, where it was known as the French and Indian War. Despite initial French successes, the British went on to seize Montreal, the Great Lakes area, and the Ohio valley. The French were forced to make peace. By the Treaty of Paris, they ceded Canada and the lands east of the Mississippi to Britain. Their ally Spain transferred Spanish Florida to British control; in return, the French gave their Louisiana territory to the Spanish. By 1763, Great Britain had become the world's greatest colonial power. For France, the loss of its empire was soon followed by an even greater internal upheaval.

British Victory in India

POLITICS & GOVERNMENT

The success of the British against the French in India was due to Robert Clive, who, in this excerpt from one of his letters, describes his famous victory at Plassey, north of Calcutta, on June 23, 1757. This battle demonstrated the inability of native Indian soldiers to compete with Europeans and signified the beginning of British control in Bengal. Clive claimed to have a thousand Europeans, two thousand sepoys (local soldiers), and eight cannons available for this battle.

Robert Clive's Account of His Victory at Plassey

At daybreak we discovered the [governor's army] moving toward us, consisting, as we since found, of about fifteen thousand horse and thirty-five thousand foot, with upwards of forty pieces of cannon. They approached apace, and by six began to attack with a number of heavy cannon, supported by the whole army, and continued to play on us very briskly for several hours, during which our situation was of the utmost service to us, being lodged in a large grove with good mud banks. To succeed in an attempt on their cannon was next to impossible, as they were planted in a manner round us and at considerable distances from each other. We therefore remained quiet in our post, in expectation of a successful attack upon their camp at night. About noon the enemy drew off their artillery and retired to their camp. . . .

On finding them make no great effort to dislodge us, we proceeded to take possession of one or two more eminences lying very near an angle of their camp, from whence, and an adjacent eminence in their possession, they kept a smart fire of musketry upon us. They made several attempts to bring out their cannon, but our advanced fieldpieces played so warmly and so well upon them that they were always driven back. Their horse exposing themselves a good deal on this occasion, many of them were killed, and among the rest four or five officers of the first distinction; by which the whole army being visibly dispirited and thrown into some confusion, we were encouraged to storm both the eminence and the angle of their camp, which were carried at the same instant, with little or no loss; though the latter was defended (exclusively of blacks) by forty French and two pieces of cannon; and the former by a large body of blacks, both horse and foot. On this a general rout ensued, and we pursued the enemy six miles, passing upwards of forty pieces of cannon they had abandoned, with an infinite number of carts and carriages filled with baggage of all kinds. . . . It is computed there are killed of the enemy about five hundred.

Our loss amounted to only twenty-two killed and fifty wounded, and those chiefly blacks.

In what ways, if any, would Clive's account likely have been different if the Battle of Plassey had occurred in Europe? According to the letter, what role did native Indians seemingly play in the battle? Why does Clive give them such little mention?

Source: From *Readings in European History*, vol. 2, by James Harvey Robinson (Lexington, Mass.: Ginn and Co., 1906).

The French Revolution

Q FOCUS QUESTION: What were the causes, the main events, and the results of the French Revolution?

The year 1789 witnessed two far-reaching events, the beginning of a new United States of America under its revamped constitution and the eruption of the French Revolution. Compared with the American Revolution a decade earlier, the French Revolution was more complex, more violent, and far more radical in its attempt to construct both a new political and a new social order.

Background to the French Revolution

The root causes of the French Revolution must be sought in the condition of French society. Before the Revolution, France was a society grounded in privilege and inequality. Its population of 27 million was divided, as it had been since the Middle Ages, into three orders or estates.

SOCIAL STRUCTURE OF THE OLD REGIME   The first estate consisted of the clergy and numbered about 130,000 people who owned approximately 10 percent of the land. Clergy were exempt from the *taille* (TY), France's chief tax. Clergy were also radically divided: the higher clergy, stemming from aristocratic families, shared the interests of the nobility, while the parish priests were often poor commoners.

The second estate consisted of the nobility, composed of about 350,000 people who owned about 25 to 30 percent of the land. The nobility continued to play an important role in French society, holding many of the leading positions in the government, the military, the law courts, and the higher church offices. The nobles sought to expand their power at the expense of the monarchy and to maintain their positions in the military, church, and government. Common to all nobles were tax exemptions, especially from the *taille*.

The third estate, or the commoners, constituted the overwhelming majority of the French population. They were divided by vast differences in occupation, level of education, and wealth. The peasants, who constituted 75 to 80 percent of the total population, were by far the largest segment of the third estate. They owned about 35 to 40 percent of the land, although more than half had little or no land on which to survive. Serfdom no longer existed on any large scale in France, but French peasants still had obligations to their local landlords that they deeply resented. These "relics of feudalism," or aristocratic privileges, had survived from an earlier age and included the payment of fees for the use of village facilities, such as the flour mill, community oven, and winepress.

Another part of the third estate consisted of skilled craftspeople, shopkeepers, and other urban wage earners. In the eighteenth century, these groups suffered a decline in purchasing power as consumer prices rose faster than wages. Their daily struggle for survival led many of these people to play an important role in the Revolution, especially in Paris.

About 8 percent of the population, or 2.3 million people, constituted the bourgeoisie or middle class, who owned about 20 to 25 percent of the land. This group included merchants, industrialists, and bankers who had benefited from the economic prosperity after 1730. The bourgeoisie also included professional people—lawyers, holders of public offices, doctors, and writers. Many members of the bourgeoisie had their own grievances because they were often excluded from the social and political privileges monopolized by nobles.

Moreover, the new political ideas of the Enlightenment proved attractive to both the aristocracy and the bourgeoisie. Both elites, long accustomed to a new socioeconomic reality based on wealth and economic achievement, were increasingly frustrated by a monarchical system resting on privileges and on an old and rigid social order based on the concept of estates. The opposition of these elites to the **old order** led them ultimately to drastic action against the monarchical **old regime**. In a real sense, the Revolution had its origins in political grievances.

OTHER PROBLEMS FACING THE FRENCH MONARCHY   Although France had enjoyed fifty years of economic expansion, bad harvests in 1787 and 1788 and the beginnings of a manufacturing depression had resulted in food shortages, rising prices for food and other goods, and unemployment in the cities. The number of poor, estimated at almost one-third of the population, reached crisis proportions on the eve of the Revolution.

The French monarchy seemed incapable of dealing with the new social realities. Louis XVI (1774–1792) had become king in 1774 at the age of twenty; he knew little about the operations of the French government and lacked the energy to deal decisively with state affairs. His wife, Marie Antoinette (ma-REE ahn-twahn-NET), was a spoiled Austrian princess who devoted much of her time to court intrigues (see the Film & History feature on p. 476). As France's crises worsened, neither Louis nor his queen seemed able to fathom the depths of despair and discontent that soon led to violent revolution.

The immediate cause of the French Revolution was the near collapse of government finances. Costly wars and royal extravagance drove French governmental expenditures ever higher. On the verge of a complete financial collapse, the government of Louis XVI was finally forced to call a meeting of the Estates-General, the French parliamentary body that had not met since 1614. The Estates-General consisted of representatives from the three orders of French society. In the elections for the Estates-General, the government had ruled that the third estate should get double representation (it did, after all, constitute 97 percent of the population). Consequently, while both the first estate (the clergy) and the second estate (the nobility) had about three hundred delegates each, the third estate had almost six hundred representatives, most of whom were lawyers from French towns.

From Estates-General to National Assembly

The Estates-General opened at Versailles on May 5, 1789. The first issue was whether voting should be by order or by head (each delegate having one vote). Traditionally, each order would vote as a group and have one vote. That meant that the first and second estates could outvote the third estate two to one. The third estate demanded that each deputy have one vote. With the assistance of liberal nobles and clerics, that would give the

Marie Antoinette (2006)

The film *Marie Antoinette* (2006), directed by Sofia Coppola, is based on Antonia Fraser's book, *Marie Antoinette: A Journey* (2001). The film begins in 1770 with the marriage of Marie Antoinette (Kirsten Dunst), the daughter of Empress Maria Theresa of Austria (Marianne Faithful), to Louis (Jason Schwartzman), the heir to the French throne. Four years later, Marie Antoinette became queen of France, and in 1793, she would go to the guillotine. Although the Revolution is briefly mentioned near the end, the majority of the film focuses on the early experiences of a young woman thrust into the court of Versailles.

Perhaps the best part of the film is the portrayal of life at Versailles. Under intense scrutiny due to her Austrian heritage and unfamiliar with court protocol, Marie Antoinette makes several early missteps. She refuses to speak to Louis XV's mistress, the comtesse du Barry (Asia Argento), because the comtesse threatens Marie Antoinette's position as the highest-ranking woman at court. By ignoring the king's mistress, however, she appears to insult the king.

An even greater challenge for Marie Antoinette is her need to produce an heir to the French throne. Her young husband, whose interests include hunting and lock making, fails to consummate their marriage for seven years. During this time, Marie Antoinette faces increasing pressure from her mother, who has produced sixteen children while ruling the Austrian Empire. Bored but aware that she must remain chaste, Marie Antoinette turns to frivolous pursuits—outings in Paris, gambling, and, above all, buying clothes. In 1782 alone, she commissions ninety-three gowns made of silk and other expensive fabrics.

After the birth of her first child in 1777, Marie Antoinette begins to withdraw from the court. After

Columbia/American Zoetrope/Sony/The Kobal Collection at Art Resource, NY

Marie Antoinette (Kirsten Dunst) at Versailles.

1783, she spends most of time in the Petit Trianon, a small palace on the grounds of Versailles. Although she is spending more time with her children and less on frivolity, her estrangement from the court only worsens her reputation with the French public.

Filmed at Versailles, the film captures the grandeur and splendor of eighteenth-century royal life. But the movie received unfavorable reviews when it opened in France, in part because it uses contemporary music by artists such as The Cure and The Strokes and includes modern products such as Converse sneakers. Although the flurry of costumes and music can be distracting, they also convey the rebelliousness of a young woman, frustrated and bored, isolated yet always on display.

third estate a majority. When the first estate declared in favor of voting by order, the third estate responded dramatically. On June 17, 1789, the third estate declared itself the "National Assembly" and prepared to draw up a constitution. This was the first step in the French Revolution because the third estate had no legal right to act as the National Assembly. Louis XVI sided with the first estate and prepared to use force to dissolve the Estates-General.

The common people, however, saved the third estate from the king's forces. On July 14, a mob of Parisians stormed the Bastille, a royal armory, and proceeded to dismantle it, brick by brick. Louis XVI was soon informed that the royal troops were unreliable. Louis's acceptance of that reality signaled the collapse of royal authority; the king could no longer enforce his will.

At the same time, popular revolts broke out throughout France, both in the cities and in the countryside

COMPARATIVE ILLUSTRATION

POLITICS & GOVERNMENT

Revolution and Revolt in France and China. Both France and China experienced revolutionary upheaval in the late eighteenth and nineteenth centuries. In both countries, common people often played an important role. At the right is a scene from the storming of the Bastille in 1789. This early action by the people of Paris ultimately led to the overthrow of the French monarchy. At the top is an episode during the Taiping Rebellion, a major peasant revolt in the mid-nineteenth century in China. An imperial Chinese army is shown recapturing the city of Nanjing from Taiping rebels in 1864.

Q *What role did common people play in revolutionary upheavals in France and China in the eighteenth and nineteenth centuries?*

(see the comparative illustration above). Behind the popular uprising was a growing resentment of the entire landholding system, with its fees and obligations. The fall of the Bastille and the king's apparent capitulation to the demands of the third estate now led peasants to take matters into their own hands. The peasant rebellions that occurred throughout France had a great impact on the National Assembly meeting at Versailles.

Destruction of the Old Regime

One of the first acts of the National Assembly was to abolish the rights of landlords and the fiscal exemptions of nobles, clergy, towns, and provinces. Three weeks later, the National Assembly adopted the Declaration of the Rights of Man and the Citizen. This charter of basic liberties proclaimed freedom and equal rights for all men and access to public office based on talent. All citizens were to have the right to take part in the legislative process. Freedom of speech and the press was coupled with the outlawing of arbitrary arrests.

But did the declaration's ideal of equal rights for "all men" also include women? Many deputies insisted that it did, provided that, as one said, "women do not hope to exercise political rights and functions." Olympe de Gouges (oh-LAMP duh GOOZH), a playwright, refused to accept this exclusion of women from political rights. Echoing the words of the official declaration, she penned the Declaration of the Rights of Woman and the Female Citizen, in which she insisted that women should have all the same rights as men (see the box on p. 478). The National Assembly ignored her demands.

OPPOSING ✕ VIEWPOINTS

The Natural Rights of the French People: Two Views

POLITICS & GOVERNMENT

One of the important documents of the French Revolution, the Declaration of the Rights of Man and the Citizen was adopted on August 26, 1789, by the National Assembly. The declaration affirmed that "men are born and remain free and equal in rights," that governments must protect these natural rights, and that political power is derived from the people.

Olympe de Gouges (the pen name used by Marie Gouze) was a butcher's daughter who wrote plays and pamphlets. She argued that the Declaration of the Rights of Man and the Citizen did not apply to women and composed her own Declaration of the Rights of Woman and the Female Citizen in 1791.

Declaration of the Rights of Man and the Citizen

1. Men are born and remain free and equal in rights. Social distinctions can only be founded upon the general good.
2. The aim of all political association is the preservation of the natural and imprescriptible rights of man. These rights are liberty, property, security, and resistance to oppression.
3. The principle of all sovereignty resides essentially in the nation. No body or individual may exercise any authority which does not proceed directly from the nation.
4. Liberty consists in being able to do everything which injures no one else. . . .
6. Law is the expression of the general will. Every citizen has a right to participate personally or through his representative in its formation. It must be the same for all, whether it protects or punishes. All citizens being equal in the eyes of the law are equally eligible to all dignities and to all public positions and occupations according to their abilities and without distinction except that of their virtues and talents.
7. No person shall be accused, arrested, or imprisoned except in the cases and according to the forms prescribed by law. . . .
10. No one shall be disturbed on account of his opinions, including his religious views, provided their

manifestation does not disturb the public order established by law.

11. The free communication of ideas and opinions is one of the most precious of the rights of man. Every citizen may, accordingly, speak, write and print with freedom, being responsible, however, for such abuses of this freedom as shall be defined by law.
12. The security of the rights of man and of the citizen requires public military force. These forces are, therefore, established for the good of all and not for the personal advantage of those to whom they shall be entrusted.
14. All the citizens have a right to decide either personally or by their representatives as to the necessity of the public contribution, to grant this freely, to know to what uses it is put, and to fix the proportion, the mode of assessment, and of collection, and the duration of the taxes.
15. Society has the right to require of every public agent an account of his administration.
16. A society in which the observance of the law is not assured nor the separation of powers defined has no constitution at all.
17. Property being an inviolable and sacred right, no one shall be deprived thereof except where public necessity, legally determined, shall clearly demand it, and then only on condition that the owner shall have been previously and equitably indemnified.

Declaration of the Rights of Woman and the Female Citizen

Mothers, daughters, sisters and representatives of the nation demand to be constituted into a national assembly. Believing that ignorance, omission, or scorn for the rights of woman are the only causes of public misfortunes and of the corruption of governments, the women have resolved to set forth in a solemn declaration the natural, inalienable, and sacred rights of woman in order that this declaration, constantly exposed before all the members of the society, will ceaselessly remind them of their rights and duties. . . .

Consequently, the sex that is as superior in beauty as it is in courage during the sufferings of maternity recognizes and declares in the presence and under the

(Continued)

auspices of the Supreme Being, the following Rights of Woman and of Female Citizens.

1. Woman is born free and lives equal to man in her rights. Social distinctions can be based only on the common utility.

2. The purpose of any political association is the conservation of the natural and imprescriptible rights of woman and man; these rights are liberty, property, security, and especially resistance to oppression.

3. The principle of all sovereignty rests essentially with the nation, which is nothing but the union of woman and man; no body and no individual can exercise any authority which does not come expressly from [the nation].

4. Liberty and justice consist of restoring all that belongs to others; thus, the only limits on the exercise of the natural rights of woman are perpetual male tyranny; these limits are to be reformed by the laws of nature and reason. . . .

6. The law must be the expression of the general will; all female and male citizens must contribute either personally or through representatives to its formation; it must be the same for all: male and female citizens, being equal in the eyes of the law, must be equally admitted to all honors, positions, and public employment according to their capacity and without other distinctions besides those of their virtues and talents.

7. No woman is an exception; she is accused, arrested, and detained in cases determined by law. Women, like men, obey this rigorous law. . . .

10. No one is to be disquieted for his very basic opinions; woman has the right to mount the scaffold; she must equally have the right to mount the rostrum, provided that her demonstrations do not disturb the legally established public order.

11. The free communication of thought and opinions is one of the most precious rights of woman, since

that liberty assured the recognition of children by their fathers. . . .

12. The guarantee of the rights of woman and the female citizen implies a major benefit; this guarantee must be instituted for the advantage of all, and not for the particular benefit of those to whom it is entrusted. . . .

14. Female and male citizens have the right to verify, either by themselves or through their representatives, the necessity of the public contribution. This can only apply to women if they are granted an equal share, not only of wealth, but also of public administration, and in the determination of the proportion, the base, the collection, and the duration of the tax.

15. The collectivity of women, joined for tax purposes to the aggregate of men, has the right to demand an accounting of his administration from any public agent.

16. No society has a constitution without the guarantee of rights and the separation of powers; the constitution is null if the majority of individuals comprising the nation have not cooperated in drafting it.

17. Property belongs to both sexes whether united or separate; for each it is an inviolable and sacred right; no one can be deprived of it, since it is the true patrimony of nature, unless the legally determined public need obviously dictates it, and then only with a just and prior indemnity.

Q *What "natural rights" does the first document proclaim? To what extent was this document influenced by the writings of the philosophes? What rights for women does the second document enunciate? Given the nature and scope of the arguments in favor of natural rights and women's rights in these two documents, what key effects on European society would you attribute to the French Revolution?*

Sources: Declaration of the Rights of Man and the Citizen. Excerpt from THOMAS CARLYLE, THE FRENCH REVOLUTION: A HISTORY, VOL. I, (GEORGE BELL AND SONS, LONDON, 1902), PP. 346–348. Declaration of the Rights of Woman and the Female Citizen. From *Women in Revolutionary Paris, 1789–1795: Selected Documents Translated with Notes and Commentary.* Translated with notes and commentary by Darline Gay Levy, Harriet Branson Applewhite, and Mary Durham Johnson. Copyright © 1979 by the Board of Trustees of the University of Illinois. Used with permission of the editors and the University of Illinois Press.

Because the Catholic Church was seen as an important pillar of the old order, it too was reformed. Most of the lands of the church were seized. Under the Civil Constitution of the Clergy, which was adopted on July 12, 1790, bishops and priests were to be elected by the people and paid by the state. The Catholic Church, still an important institution in the life of the French people, now became an enemy of the Revolution.

By 1791, the National Assembly had completed a new constitution that established a limited constitutional monarchy. There was still a monarch (now called "king of the French"), but sovereign power was vested in the new Legislative Assembly, which would make the laws. The Legislative Assembly was to sit for two years and consist of 745 representatives elected by an indirect system that preserved power in the hands of the more affluent members of society. A small group of 50,000 electors chose the deputies.

Thus, the old order had been destroyed, but the new order had many opponents—Catholic priests, nobles, lower classes hurt by the rising cost of living, peasants opposed to dues that had still not been eliminated, and political clubs like the Jacobins (JAK-uh-binz) that offered more radical solutions. The king also made things difficult for the new government when he sought to flee France in June 1791 and almost succeeded before being recognized, captured, and brought back to Paris. In this unsettled situation, under a discredited and seemingly disloyal monarch, the new Legislative Assembly held its first session in October 1791. France's relations with the rest of Europe soon led to Louis's downfall.

On August 27, 1791, the monarchs of Austria and Prussia, fearing that revolution would spread to their countries, invited other European monarchs to use force to reestablish monarchical authority in France. The French fared badly in the fighting in the spring of 1792, and a frantic search for scapegoats began. As one observer noted, "Everywhere you hear the cry that the king is betraying us, the generals are betraying us, that nobody is to be trusted; . . . that Paris will be taken in six weeks by the Austrians. . . . We are on a volcano ready to spout flames."[3] Defeats in war coupled with economic shortages led to renewed political demonstrations, especially against the king. In August 1792, radical political groups in Paris took the king captive and forced the Legislative Assembly to suspend the monarchy and call for a national convention, chosen on the basis of universal male suffrage, to decide on the future form of government. The French Revolution was about to enter a more radical stage.

The Radical Revolution

In September 1792, the newly elected National Convention began its sessions. Dominated by lawyers and other professionals, two-thirds of its deputies were under forty-five, and almost all had gained political experience as a result of the Revolution. Almost all distrusted the king. As a result, the convention's first step on September 21 was to abolish the monarchy and establish a republic. On January 21, 1793, the king was executed, and the destruction of the old regime was complete. But the execution of the king created new enemies for the Revolution both at home and abroad.

In Paris, the local government, known as the Commune, whose leaders came from the working classes, favored radical change and put constant pressure on the convention, pushing it to ever more radical positions. Meanwhile, peasants in the west and inhabitants of the major provincial cities refused to accept the authority of the convention.

A foreign crisis also loomed. By the beginning of 1793, after the king had been executed, most of Europe—an informal coalition of Austria, Prussia, Spain, Portugal, Britain, the Dutch Republic, and even Russia—aligned militarily against France. Grossly overextended, the French armies began to experience reverses, and by late spring, France was threatened with invasion.

A NATION IN ARMS To meet these crises, the convention gave broad powers to an executive committee of twelve known as the Committee of Public Safety, which came to be dominated by Maximilien Robespierre (mak-see-meel-YENH ROHBZ-pyayr). For a twelve-month period, from 1793 to 1794, the Committee of Public Safety took control of France. To save the Republic from its foreign foes, on August 23, 1793, the committee decreed a levy-in-mass, or universal mobilization of the nation:

> Young men will fight, young men are called to conquer. Married men will forge arms, transport military baggage and guns and will prepare food supplies. Women, who at long last are to take their rightful place in the revolution and follow their true destiny, will forget their futile tasks: their delicate hands will work at making clothes for soldiers; they will make tents and they will extend their tender care to shelters where the defenders of the *Patrie* [nation] will receive the help that their wounds require. Children will make lint of old cloth. It is for them that we are fighting: children, those beings destined to gather all the fruits of the revolution, will raise their pure hands toward the skies. And old men, performing their missions again, as of yore, will be guided to the public squares of the cities where they will kindle the courage of young warriors and preach the doctrines of hate for kings and the unity of the Republic.[4]

In less than a year, the French revolutionary government had raised an army of 650,000, and by 1795 it had pushed the allies back across the Rhine and even conquered the Austrian Netherlands.

The French revolutionary army was an important step in the creation of modern **nationalism**. Previously, wars had been fought between governments or ruling dynasties by relatively small armies of professional soldiers.

The new French army was the creation of a "people's" government; its wars were now "people's" wars, involving the entire nation. But when dynastic wars became people's wars, warfare increased in ferocity and lack of restraint. The wars of the French revolutionary era opened the door to the total war of the modern world.

REIGN OF TERROR To meet the domestic crisis, the National Convention and the Committee of Public Safety launched the Reign of Terror. Revolutionary courts were instituted to protect the Republic from its internal enemies. In the course of nine months, 16,000 people were officially killed under the blade of the guillotine—a revolutionary device designed for the quick and efficient separation of heads from bodies.

Revolutionary armies were set up to bring recalcitrant cities and districts back under the control of the National Convention. The Committee of Public Safety decided to make an example of Lyons (LYOHNH), which had defied the authority of the National Convention. By April 1794, some 1,880 citizens of Lyons had been executed. When the guillotine proved too slow, cannon fire was used to blow condemned men into open graves. A German observed:

> Whole ranges of houses, always the most handsome, burnt. The churches, convents, and all the dwellings of the former patricians were in ruins. When I came to the guillotine, the blood of those who had been executed a few hours beforehand was still running in the street. . . . I said to a group of [radicals] that it would be decent to clear away all this human blood. Why should it be cleared? one of them said to me. It's the blood of aristocrats and rebels. The dogs should lick it up.[5]

EQUALITY AND SLAVERY: REVOLUTION IN HAITI Early in the French Revolution, the desire for equality led to a discussion of what to do about slavery. A club called Friends of the Blacks advocated the abolition of slavery, which was achieved in France in September 1791. But French planters in the West Indies, who profited greatly from the use of slaves on their sugar plantations, opposed the abolition of slavery in the French colonies. On February 4, 1794, however, the National Convention, guided by ideals of equality, abolished slavery in the colonies.

In one French colony, slaves had already rebelled. In 1791, black slaves in the French colony of Saint-Domingue (the western third of the island of Hispaniola), inspired by the revolution in France, revolted against French plantation owners. Led by Toussaint L'Ouverture (too-SANH loo-vayr-TOOR) (1746–1803), a son of African slaves, more than 100,000 black slaves rose in revolt and seized control of Hispaniola. Later, an army sent by Napoleon captured L'Ouverture, who died in captivity in France. But the French soldiers, weakened by disease, soon succumbed to the slave forces. On January 1, 1804, the western part of Hispaniola, now called Haiti, became the first independent state in Latin America. One of the French revolutionary ideals had triumphed abroad.

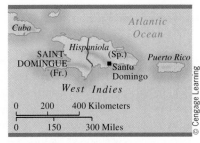

Revolt in Saint-Dominique

Reaction and the Directory

By the summer of 1794, the French had been successful on the battlefield against their foreign foes, making the Terror less necessary. But the Terror continued because Robespierre, who had come to dominate the Committee of Public Safety, became obsessed with purifying the body politic of all the corrupt. Many deputies in the National Convention began to fear that they were not safe while Robespierre was free to act and gathered enough votes to condemn him. Robespierre was guillotined on July 28, 1794.

After the death of Robespierre, a reaction set in as more moderate middle-class leaders took control. The Reign of Terror came to a halt, and the National Convention reduced the power of the Committee of Public Safety. In August, a new constitution was drafted that reflected the desire for a stability that did not sacrifice the ideals of 1789. Five directors—the Directory—acted as the executive authority.

The period of the Revolution under the Directory (1795–1799) was an era of stagnation and corruption. At the same time, the Directory faced political enemies from both the left and the right of the political spectrum. On

CHRONOLOGY	The French Revolution
Meeting of Estates-General	May 5, 1789
Formation of National Assembly	June 17, 1789
Fall of the Bastille	July 14, 1789
Declaration of the Rights of Man and the Citizen	August 26, 1789
Civil Constitution of the Clergy	July 12, 1790
Flight of the king	June 20–21, 1791
Attack on the royal palace	August 10, 1792
Abolition of the monarchy	September 21, 1792
Execution of the king	January 21, 1793
Levy-in-mass	August 23, 1793
Execution of Robespierre	July 28, 1794
Adoption of Constitution of 1795 and the Directory	August 22, 1795

Napoleon and Psychological Warfare

POLITICS & GOVERNMENT

In 1796, at the age of twenty-seven, Napoleon Bonaparte was given command of the French army in Italy, where he won a series of stunning victories. His use of speed, deception, and surprise to overwhelm his opponents is well known. In this selection from a proclamation to his troops in Italy, Napoleon also appears as a master of psychological warfare.

Napoleon Bonaparte, Proclamation to French Troops in Italy (April 26, 1796)

Soldiers:

In a fortnight you have won six victories, taken twenty-one standards [flags of military units], fifty-five pieces of artillery, several strong positions, and conquered the richest part of Piedmont [in northern Italy]; you have captured 15,000 prisoners and killed or wounded more than 10,000 men You have won battles without cannon, crossed rivers without bridges, made forced marches without shoes, camped without brandy and often without bread. Soldiers of liberty, only republican troops could have endured what you have endured. Soldiers, you have our thanks! The grateful *Patrie* [nation] will owe its prosperity to you.

The two armies which but recently attacked you with audacity are fleeing before you in terror; the wicked men who laughed at your misery and rejoiced at the thought of the triumphs of your enemies are confounded and trembling.

But, soldiers, as yet you have done nothing compared with what remains to be done. . . . Undoubtedly the greatest obstacles have been overcome; but you still have battles to fight, cities to capture, rivers to cross. Is there one among you whose courage is abating? No. . . . All of you are consumed with a desire to extend the glory of the French people; all of you long to humiliate those arrogant kings who dare to contemplate placing us in fetters; all of you desire to dictate a glorious peace, one which will indemnify the *Patrie* for the immense sacrifices it has made; all of you wish to be able to say with pride as you return to your villages, "I was with the victorious army of Italy!"

Q *What themes did Napoleon use to play on the emotions of his troops and inspire them to greater efforts? Do you think Napoleon believed these words? Why or why not?*

Source: From *A Documentary Survey of the French Revolution* by John Hall Stewart, ed. Copyright © 1951 by Macmillan College Publishing Company, renewed 1979 by John Hall Stewart.

the right, royalists continued their efforts to restore the monarchy. On the left, radical hopes of power were revived by continuing economic problems. Battered from both sides, unable to solve the country's economic problems, and still carrying on the wars inherited from the Committee of Public Safety, the Directory increasingly relied on the military to maintain its power. This led to a coup d'état in 1799 in which the popular military general Napoleon Bonaparte seized power.

The Age of Napoleon

Q FOCUS QUESTION: Which aspects of the French Revolution did Napoleon preserve, and which did he destroy?

Napoleon dominated both French and European history from 1799 to 1815. He had been born in Corsica in 1769

shortly after France had annexed the island. The young Napoleone Buonaparte (his birth name) was sent to France to study in one of the new military schools and was a lieutenant when the Revolution broke out in 1789. The Revolution and the European war that followed gave him new opportunities, and Napoleon rose quickly through the ranks. In 1794, at the age of only twenty-five, he was made a brigadier general. Two years later, he commanded the French armies in Italy, where he won a series of victories and returned to France as a conquering hero (see the box above). After a disastrous expedition to Egypt, Napoleon returned to Paris, where he participated in the coup that gave him control of France. He was only thirty years old.

After the coup of 1799, a new form of the Republic—called the Consulate—was proclaimed in which Napoleon, as first consul, controlled the entire executive authority of government. He had overwhelming influence over the

The Coronation of Napoleon. In 1804, Napoleon restored monarchy to France when he became Emperor Napoleon I. In the coronation scene painted by Jacques-Louis David, Napoleon is shown crowning his wife, the empress Josephine, while the pope looks on. The painting shows Napoleon's mother seated in the box in the background, even though she was not at the ceremony.

legislature, appointed members of the administrative bureaucracy, commanded the army, and conducted foreign affairs. In 1802, Napoleon was made consul for life, and in 1804, he returned France to monarchy when he became Emperor Napoleon I.

Domestic Policies

One of Napoleon's first domestic policies was to establish peace with the oldest and most implacable enemy of the Revolution, the Catholic Church. In 1801, Napoleon arranged a concordat with the pope that recognized Catholicism as the religion of a majority of the French people. In return, the pope agreed not to challenge the confiscation of church lands during the Revolution.

Napoleon's most enduring domestic achievement was his codification of the laws. Before the Revolution, France had some three hundred local legal systems. During the Revolution, efforts were made to prepare a single code of laws for the nation, but it remained for Napoleon to bring the work to completion in the famous Civil Code. It preserved most of the revolutionary gains by recognizing the equality of all citizens before the law, the abolition of serfdom and feudalism, and religious toleration. Property rights were also protected.

Napoleon also developed a powerful, centralized administration and worked hard to develop a bureaucracy of capable officials. Early on, the regime showed that it cared little whether officials had acquired their expertise in royal or revolutionary bureaucracies. Promotion, whether in civil or military offices, was based not on rank or birth but on ability only. This principle of a government career open to talent was, of course, what many bourgeois had wanted before the Revolution.

In his domestic policies, then, Napoleon both destroyed and preserved aspects of the Revolution. Although equality was preserved in the law code and the opening of careers to talent, the creation of a new aristocracy, the strong protection accorded to property rights, and the use of conscription for the military made it clear that much equality had been lost. Liberty was replaced by an initially benevolent despotism that grew increasingly arbitrary. Napoleon shut down sixty of France's seventy-three newspapers.

Napoleon's Empire

When Napoleon became consul in 1799, France was at war with a second European coalition of Russia, Great Britain, and Austria. Napoleon realized the need for a pause and made a peace treaty in 1802. But in 1803 war was renewed with Britain, which was soon joined by Austria, Russia, and Prussia in the Third Coalition. In a series of battles from 1805 to 1807, Napoleon's Grand Army defeated the Austrian, Prussian, and Russian armies, giving Napoleon the opportunity to create a new European order.

THE GRAND EMPIRE From 1807 to 1812, Napoleon was the master of Europe. His Grand Empire was composed of three major parts: the French Empire, dependent states, and allied states (see Map 18.3). Dependent states were under the rule of Napoleon's relatives; these came to include Spain, the Netherlands, the kingdom of Italy, the Swiss Republic, the Grand Duchy of Warsaw, and the Confederation of the Rhine (a union of all German states except Austria and Prussia). Allied states were those defeated by Napoleon and forced to join his struggle against Britain; these included Prussia, Austria, Russia, and Sweden.

Within his empire, Napoleon sought acceptance of certain revolutionary principles, including legal equality, religious toleration, and economic freedom. In the inner core and dependent states of his Grand Empire, Napoleon tried to destroy the old order. Nobility and clergy

MAP 18.3 Napoleon's Grand Empire. Napoleon's Grand Army won a series of victories against Austria, Prussia, and Russia that gave the French emperor full or partial control over much of Europe by 1807.

Q *On the Continent, what was the overall relationship between distance from France and degree of French control, and how can you account for this?*

everywhere in these states lost their special privileges. He decreed equality of opportunity with offices open to talent, equality before the law, and religious toleration.

Napoleon hoped that his Grand Empire would last for centuries, but it collapsed almost as rapidly as it had been formed. As long as Britain ruled the waves, it was not subject to military attack. Napoleon hoped to invade Britain, but he could not overcome the British navy's decisive defeat of a combined French-Spanish fleet at Trafalgar in 1805. To defeat Britain, Napoleon turned to his **Continental system**. An alliance put into effect between 1806 and 1808, it attempted to prevent British goods from reaching the European continent in order to weaken Britain economically and destroy its capacity to wage war. But the Continental system failed. Allied states resented it; some began to cheat and others to resist.

Napoleon also encountered new sources of opposition. His conquests made the French hated oppressors and aroused the patriotism of the conquered people. A Spanish uprising, aided by the British, kept a French force of 200,000 pinned down for years.

THE FALL OF NAPOLEON The beginning of Napoleon's downfall came in 1812 with his invasion of Russia. The refusal of the Russians to remain in the Continental system left Napoleon with little choice. Although aware of the risks in invading such a huge country, he knew that if the Russians were allowed to challenge the Continental system unopposed, others would follow suit. In June 1812, he led his Grand Army of more than 600,000 men into Russia. His hopes for victory depended on quickly defeating the Russian armies, but the Russian forces retreated and refused to give battle, torching their own villages to keep Napoleon's army from finding food. When the Russians did stop to fight at Borodino, Napoleon won an indecisive and costly victory. When the remaining troops of the Grand Army arrived in Moscow, they found the city ablaze. Lacking food and supplies, Napoleon abandoned Moscow late in October and made a retreat across Russia in terrible winter conditions. Only 40,000 of the original 600,000 men arrived back in Poland in January 1813.

This military disaster led other European states to rise up and attack the crippled French army. Paris was captured in March 1814, and Napoleon was sent into exile on the island of Elba, off the coast of Italy. Meanwhile, the Bourbon monarchy was restored in the person of Louis XVIII, brother of the executed king. (Louis XVII, son of Louis XVI, had died in prison at age ten.) Napoleon, bored on Elba, slipped back into France. When troops were sent to capture him, Napoleon opened his coat and addressed them: "Soldiers of the 5th regiment, I am your Emperor. . . . If there is a man among you would kill his Emperor, here I am!" No one fired a shot. Shouting "Vive l'Empereur! Vive l'Empereur," the troops went over to his side, and Napoleon entered Paris in triumph on March 20, 1815. The powers that had defeated him pledged once more to fight him. Napoleon raised another army and moved to attack the allied forces stationed in what is now Belgium. At Waterloo on June 18, Napoleon met a combined British and Prussian army under the duke of Wellington and suffered a bloody defeat. This time, the victorious allies exiled him to Saint Helena, a small, forsaken island in the South Atlantic, off the coast of Africa. Only Napoleon's memory continued to haunt French political life.

CHAPTER SUMMARY

In the Scientific Revolution, the Western world overthrew the medieval, Ptolemaic worldview and arrived at a new conception of the universe: the sun at the center, the planets as material bodies revolving around the sun in elliptical orbits, and an infinite rather than finite world. With the changes in the conception of "heaven" came changes in the conception of "earth." Highly influenced by the new worldview created by the Scientific Revolution, the philosophes of the eighteenth century hoped to create a new society by using reason to discover the natural laws that governed it. They attacked traditional religion as the enemy and developed the new "sciences of man" in economics, politics, and education. Together, the Scientific Revolution of the seventeenth century and the Enlightenment of the eighteenth century constituted an intellectual revolution that laid the foundations for a modern worldview based on rationalism and secularism.

Everywhere in Europe at the beginning of the eighteenth century, the old order remained strong. Nobles, clerics, towns, and provinces all had privileges. Everywhere in the eighteenth century, monarchs sought to enlarge their bureaucracies to raise taxes to support large standing armies. The existence of these armies led to wars on a worldwide scale. Although the wars resulted in few changes in Europe, British victories enabled Great Britain to emerge as the world's greatest naval and colonial power. Meanwhile, in Europe increased demands for taxes to support these wars led to attacks on the old order and a desire for change not met by the ruling monarchs. At the same time, a growing population as well as changes in finance, trade, and industry created tensions that undermined the foundations of the old order. Its inability to deal with these changes led to a revolutionary outburst at the end of the eighteenth century that marked the beginning of the end for the old order.

The revolutionary era of the late eighteenth century was a time of dramatic political transformations. Revolutionary upheavals, beginning in North America and continuing in France, spurred movements for political liberty

and equality. The documents promulgated by these revolutions, the Declaration of Independence and the Declaration of the Rights of Man and the Citizen, embodied the fundamental ideas of the Enlightenment and created a liberal political agenda based on a belief in popular sovereignty—the people as the source of political power—and the principles of liberty and equality. Liberty meant, in theory, freedom from arbitrary power as well as the freedom to think, write, and worship as one chose. Equality meant equality in rights, although it did not include equality between men and women.

CHAPTER TIMELINE

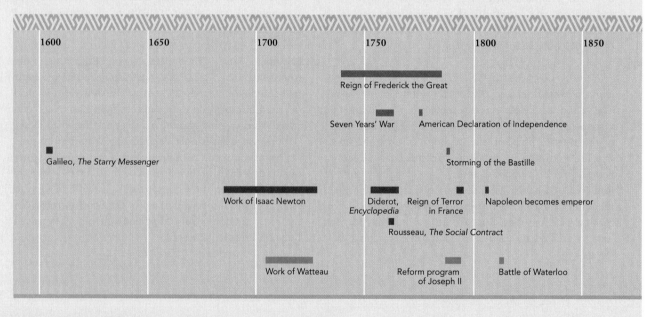

CHAPTER REVIEW

Upon Reflection

Q What was the impact of the intellectual revolution of the seventeenth and eighteenth centuries on European society?

Q How was France changed by the revolutionary events between 1789 and 1799, and who benefited the most from these changes?

Q In what ways did Napoleon's policies reject the accomplishments of the French Revolution? In what ways did his policies strengthen those accomplishments?

Key Terms

Scientific Revolution (p. 461)
geocentric theory (p. 461)
heliocentric theory (p. 461)
world-machine (p. 463)
Enlightenment (p. 464)
scientific method (p. 464)
philosophes (p. 464)
separation of powers (p. 464)
deism (p. 465)
laissez-faire (p. 465)
feminism (p. 466)

Industrialization and the rise of national consciousness also transformed the nature of war itself. New weapons of mass destruction created the potential for a new kind of warfare that reached beyond the battlefield into the very heartland of the enemy's territory, while the concept of nationalism transformed war from the sport of kings to a matter of national honor and commitment. Since the French Revolution, governments had relied on mass conscription to defend the nation, while their engines of destruction reached far into enemy territory to destroy the industrial base and undermine the will to fight. This trend was amply demonstrated in the two world wars of the twentieth century.

In the end, then, industrial power and nationalism, the very factors that had created the conditions for European global dominance, contained the seeds for the decline of that dominance. These seeds germinated during the 1930s, when the Great Depression sharpened international competition and mutual antagonism, and then sprouted in the ensuing conflict, which spanned the entire globe. By the time World War II came to an end, the once powerful countries of Europe were exhausted, leaving the door ajar for the emergence of two new global superpowers, the United States and the Soviet Union, and for the collapse of the Europeans' colonial empires.

Europeans had begun to explore the world in the fifteenth century, but even as late as 1870, they had not yet completely penetrated North America, South America, Australia, or most of Africa. In Asia and Africa, with few exceptions, the Western presence was limited to trading posts. Between 1870 and 1914, Western civilization expanded into the rest of the Americas and Australia, while the bulk of Africa and Asia was divided into European colonies or spheres of influence. Two major events explain this remarkable expansion: the migration of many Europeans to other parts of the world due to population growth and the revival of imperialism, which was made possible by the West's technological advances. Beginning in the 1880s, European states began an intense scramble for overseas territory. This revival of imperialism—the "new imperialism," some have called it—led Europeans to carve up Asia and Africa.

What was the overall economic effect of imperialism on the subject peoples? For most of the population in colonial areas, Western domination was rarely beneficial and often destructive. Although some merchants, large landowners, and traditional hereditary elites undoubtedly prospered under the expanding imperialistic economic order, the majority of colonial peoples, urban and rural alike, probably suffered considerable hardship as a result of the policies adopted by their foreign rulers.

Some historians point out, however, that for all its inequities, there was a positive side to the colonial system as well. The expansion of markets and the beginnings of a modern transportation and communications network, while bringing few immediate benefits to the colonial peoples, offered considerable promise for future economic growth. At the same time, colonial peoples soon learned the power of nationalism, and in the twentieth century, nationalism would become a powerful force in the rest of the world as nationalist revolutions moved through Asia, Africa, and the Middle East. Moreover, the exhaustive struggles of two world wars sapped the power of the European states, and the colonial powers no longer had the energy or the wealth to maintain their colonial empires after World War II. ◈

The Beginnings of Modernization: Industrialization and Nationalism in the Nineteenth Century

A meeting of the Congress of Vienna

CHAPTER OUTLINE
AND FOCUS QUESTIONS

The Industrial Revolution and Its Impact

Q What were the basic features of the new industrial system created by the Industrial Revolution, and what effects did the new system have on urban life, social classes, family life, and standards of living?

The Growth of Industrial Prosperity

Q What was the Second Industrial Revolution, and what effects did it have on economic and social life? What were the main ideas of Karl Marx, and what role did they play in politics and the union movement in the late nineteenth and early twentieth centuries?

Reaction and Revolution: The Growth of Nationalism

Q What were the major ideas associated with conservatism, liberalism, and nationalism, and what role did each ideology play in Europe between 1800 and 1850? What were the causes of the revolutions of 1848, and why did these revolutions fail?

National Unification and the National State, 1848–1871

Q What actions did Cavour and Bismarck take to bring about unification in Italy and Germany,

respectively, and what role did war play in their efforts?

The European State, 1871–1914

Q What general political trends were evident in the nations of western Europe in the late nineteenth and early twentieth centuries, and to what degree were those trends also apparent in the nations of central and eastern Europe? How did the growth of nationalism affect international affairs during the same period?

---CRITICAL THINKING---
Q In what ways was the development of industrialization related to the growth of nationalism?

IN SEPTEMBER 1814, hundreds of foreigners began to converge on Vienna, the capital of the Austrian Empire. Many were members of European royalty—kings, archdukes, princes, and their wives—accompanied by their diplomatic advisers and scores of servants. Their congenial host was the Austrian emperor, Francis I, who never tired of regaling his guests with concerts, glittering balls, and sumptuous feasts. One participant remembered, "Eating, fireworks, public illuminations. For eight or ten days, I haven't been able to work at all. What a life!" Of course, not every waking hour was spent in pleasure during this gathering of notables, known to history as the Congress of Vienna. The guests were also representatives of all the states that had fought Napoleon, and their real business was to arrange a peace settlement after almost a decade of war. On June 8, 1815, they finally completed their task.

The forces of upheaval unleashed during the French revolutionary and Napoleonic wars were temporarily quieted in 1815 as rulers sought to restore stability by reestablishing much of the old order to a Europe ravaged by war. But the Western world had been changed, and it would not readily go back to the old system. New ideologies, especially liberalism and nationalism, products of the upheaval initiated in France, had become too powerful to be contained. The forces of change called forth revolts that periodically shook the West and culminated in a spate of revolutions in 1848. Some of the revolutions were successful; most were not. And yet by 1870, many of the goals sought by the liberals and nationalists during the first half of the nineteenth century seemed to have been achieved. National unity became a reality in Italy and Germany, and many Western states developed parliamentary features. Between 1870 and 1914, these newly constituted states experienced a time of great tension. Europeans engaged in a race for colonies that intensified existing antagonisms among the European states, while the creation of huge conscript armies and enormous military establishments heightened tensions among the major powers.

During the late eighteenth and early nineteenth centuries, another revolution—an industrial one—transformed the economic and social structure of Europe and spawned the industrial era that has characterized modern world history. ✍

The Industrial Revolution and Its Impact

Q FOCUS QUESTION: What were the basic features of the new industrial system created by the Industrial Revolution, and what effects did the new system have on urban life, social classes, family life, and standards of living?

During the Industrial Revolution, Europe shifted from an economy based on agriculture and handicrafts to an economy based on manufacturing by machines and automated factories. The Industrial Revolution triggered an enormous leap in industrial production that relied largely on coal and steam, which replaced wind and water as new sources of energy to drive laborsaving machines. In turn, these machines called for new ways of organizing human labor to maximize the benefits and profits from the new machines. As factories replaced shop and home workrooms, large numbers of people moved from the countryside to the cities to work in the new factories. The creation of a wealthy industrial middle class and a huge industrial working class (or proletariat) substantially transformed traditional social relationships. Finally, the Industrial Revolution altered how people related to nature, ultimately creating an environmental crisis that in the twentieth century came to be recognized as a danger to human existence itself.

The Industrial Revolution in Great Britain

The Industrial Revolution began in Britain in the 1780s. Improvements in agricultural practices in the eighteenth century led to a significant increase in food production. British agriculture could now feed more people at lower prices with less labor; even ordinary families did not have to use most of their income to buy food, giving them the wherewithal to purchase manufactured goods. At the same time, rapid population growth in the second half of the eighteenth century provided a pool of surplus labor for the new factories of the emerging British industry.

In the course of its eighteenth-century wars, Great Britain had assembled a vast colonial empire at the expense of its leading rivals, the Dutch Republic and France. That empire's many markets gave British industrialists a ready outlet for their manufactured goods. British exports quadrupled from 1660 to 1760. Crucial to Britain's successful industrialization was the ability to produce cheaply the articles in greatest demand. The traditional methods of cottage industry could not keep up with the growing demand for cotton clothes throughout Britain and its vast colonial empire. Faced with this problem, British cloth manufacturers readily adopted the new methods of manufacturing that a series of inventions provided. In so doing, these individuals ignited the Industrial Revolution.

CHANGES IN TEXTILE PRODUCTION The invention of the flying shuttle enabled weavers to weave faster on a loom, thereby doubling their output. This created shortages of yarn until James Hargreaves's spinning jenny, perfected by 1768, allowed spinners to produce more yarn. Edmund Cartwright's loom, powered by water and invented in 1787, allowed the weaving of cloth to catch up with the spinning of yarn. It was now more efficient to bring workers to the machines and organize their labor collectively in factories located next to rivers, the source of power for these early machines.

The invention of the steam engine pushed the cotton industry to even greater heights of productivity. In the 1760s, a Scottish engineer, James Watt (1736–1819), built an engine powered by steam that could pump water from mines three times as quickly as previous engines. In 1782, Watt developed a rotary engine that could turn a shaft and thus drive machinery. Steam power could now be applied to spinning and weaving cotton, and before long, cotton mills using steam engines were multiplying across Britain. Fired by coal, these steam engines could be located anywhere.

The boost given to cotton textile production by these technological changes was readily apparent. In 1760, Britain had imported 2.5 million pounds of raw cotton, which was farmed out to cottage industries. In 1787, the British imported 22 million pounds of cotton; most of it was spun on machines, some powered by water in large mills. By 1840, some 366 million pounds of cotton—now Britain's most important product in value—were being imported. By this time, British cotton goods were sold everywhere in the world.

OTHER TECHNOLOGICAL CHANGES The British iron industry was also radically transformed. Britain had always had large reserves of iron ore, but at the beginning of the eighteenth century, iron production had changed little since the Middle Ages and still depended heavily on charcoal. In the 1780s, Henry Cort developed a system called puddling, in which coke, derived from coal, was used to burn away impurities in pig iron (crude iron) and produce an iron of high quality. A boom then ensued in the British iron industry. By 1852, Britain was producing almost 3 million tons of iron annually, more than the rest of the world combined.

The new high-quality wrought iron was in turn used to build new machines and ultimately new industries. In 1804, Richard Trevithick (TREV-uh-thik) pioneered the first steam-powered locomotive on an industrial rail line in southern Wales. It pulled 10 tons of ore and seventy people at 5 miles per hour. Better locomotives soon followed. Engines built by George Stephenson and his son proved superior, and it was Stephenson's *Rocket* that was used on the first public railway line, which opened in 1830, extending 32 miles from Liverpool to Manchester. *Rocket* sped along at 16 miles per hour. Within twenty years, locomotives were traveling at 50 miles per hour. By 1840, Britain had almost 6,000 miles of railroads.

The railroad was important to the success and maturing of the Industrial Revolution. The availability of a cheaper and faster means of transportation had a ripple effect on the growth of the industrial economy. As the prices of goods fell, markets grew larger; increased sales meant more factories and more machinery, thereby reinforcing the self-sustaining aspect of the Industrial Revolution—a development that marked a fundamental break with the traditional European economy. Continuous, self-sustaining economic growth came to be a fundamental characteristic of the new economy.

THE INDUSTRIAL FACTORY Another visible symbol of the Industrial Revolution was the factory (see the comparative illustration on p. 493). From its beginning, the factory created a new labor system. Factory owners wanted to use their new machines constantly. Workers were therefore obliged to work regular hours and in shifts to keep the machines producing at a steady rate. Early factory workers, however, came from rural areas, where they were used to a different pace of life. Peasant farmers worked hard, especially at harvest time, but they were also used to periods of inactivity.

Early factory owners therefore had to institute a system of work discipline that would accustom employees to working regular hours and doing the same work over and over. Of course, such work was boring, and factory owners resorted to detailed regulations and tough methods to accomplish their goals. Adult workers were fined for a wide variety of minor infractions, such as being a few minutes late for work, and dismissed for more serious misdoings, especially drunkenness, which courted disaster in the midst of dangerous machinery. Employers found that dismissals and fines worked well for adult employees; in a time when great population growth had produced large masses of unskilled labor, dismissal meant disaster. Children were less likely to understand the implications of dismissal, so they were disciplined more directly—often by beating. As the nineteenth century progressed, the second and third generations of workers came to view a regular workweek as a natural way of life.

By the mid-nineteenth century, Great Britain had become the world's first and richest industrial nation. Britain was the "workshop, banker, and trader of the world." It produced half of the world's coal and manufactured goods; in 1850, its cotton industry alone was equal in size to the industries of all other European countries combined.

The Spread of Industrialization

From Britain, industrialization spread to the continental countries of Europe and the United States, though at different times and speeds. First to be industrialized on the Continent were Belgium, France, and the German states. Their governments actively encouraged industrialization by, among other things, setting up technical schools to train engineers and mechanics and providing funds to build roads, canals, and railroads. By 1850, a network of iron rails had spread across Europe.

Textile Factories, West and East. The development of the factory changed the relationship between workers and employers as workers had to adjust to a new system of discipline that required them to work regular hours under close supervision. At the top is an 1851 illustration that shows women working in a British cotton factory. The factory system came later to the rest of the world than it did to Britain. Shown at the bottom is one of the earliest industrial factories in Japan, the Tomioka silk factory, built in the 1870s. Note that although women are doing the work in both factories, the managers are men.

Q *What do you think were the major differences and similarities between British and Japanese factories (see also the box on p. 496)?*

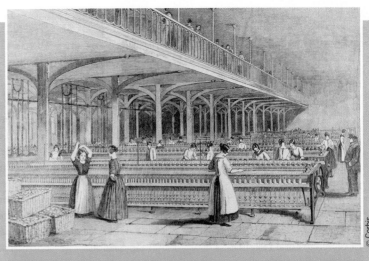

© Corbis

© The Granger Collection, New York

The Industrial Revolution also transformed the new nation in North America, the United States. In 1800, six out of every seven American workers were farmers, and there were no cities with more than 100,000 people. By 1860, the population had sextupled to 30 million people (larger than Great Britain), nine U.S. cities had populations over 100,000, and only 50 percent of American workers were farmers.

In sharp contrast to Britain, the United States was a large country. Thousands of miles of roads and canals were built linking east and west. The steamboat facilitated transportation on the Great Lakes, Atlantic coastal waters, and rivers. Most important in the development of an American transportation system was the railroad, which was needed to transport the abundant raw materials found throughout the country. Beginning with 100 miles in 1830, by 1865 the United States was crisscrossed by more than 35,000 miles of railroad track. This transportation revolution turned the United States into a single massive market for the manufactured goods of the Northeast, the early center of American industrialization. By the end of the nineteenth century, with its growing manufacturing sector, abundant raw materials, and elaborate transportation system, the United States had become the world's second-largest industrial nation.

Limiting the Spread of Industrialization to the Rest of the World

Before 1870, the industrialization that was transforming western and central Europe and the United States did not extend in any significant way to the rest of the world (see the comparative essay "The Industrial Revolution" on p. 494). Even in eastern Europe, industrialization

COMPARATIVE ESSAY

The Industrial Revolution

SCIENCE & TECHNOLOGY

Why some societies were able to embark on the road to industrialization during the nineteenth century and others were not has long been debated. Some historians have pointed to the cultural characteristics of individual societies, such as the Protestant work ethic in parts of Europe or the tradition of social discipline and class hierarchy in Japan. Others have placed more emphasis on practical reasons. To the historian Peter Stearns, for example, the availability of capital, natural resources, a network of trade relations, and navigable rivers all helped stimulate industrial growth in nineteenth-century Britain. By contrast, the lack of urban markets for agricultural goods (which reduced landowners' incentives to introduce mechanized farming) is sometimes cited as a reason for China's failure to set out on its own path toward industrialization.

To some observers, the ability of western European countries to exploit the resources of their colonies in Asia, Africa, and Latin America was crucial to their industrial success. In this view, the Age of Exploration led to the creation of a new "world system" characterized by the emergence of global trade networks, propelled by the rising force of European capitalism in pursuit of precious metals, markets, and cheap raw materials.

These views are not mutually exclusive. In his recent book *The Great Divergence: China, Europe, and the Making of the Modern World Economy,* Kenneth Pomeranz argued that coal resources and access to the cheap raw materials of the Americas were both assets for Great Britain as it became the first to industrialize.

The Steam Engine. Pictured here is an early steam engine developed by James Watt. The steam engine revolutionized the production of cotton goods and helped usher in the factory system.

Clearly, this controversy has no single answer. In any event, the coming of the industrial age had a number of lasting consequences for the world at large. On the one hand, the material wealth of the nations that successfully passed through the process increased significantly. In many cases, the creation of advanced industrial societies strengthened democratic institutions and led to a higher standard of living for the majority of the population. It also helped reduce class barriers and bring about the emancipation of women from many of the legal and social restrictions that had characterized the previous era.

On the other hand, not all the consequences of the Industrial Revolution were beneficial. In the industrializing societies themselves, rapid economic change often led to widening disparities in wealth and a sense of rootlessness and alienation among much of the population. Although some societies were able to manage these problems with a degree of success, others experienced a breakdown of social values and widespread political instability. In the meantime, the transformation of Europe into a giant factory sucking up raw materials and spewing manufactured goods out to the entire world had a wrenching impact on traditional societies whose own economic, social, and cultural foundations were forever changed by absorption into the new world order.

 What were the positive and negative consequences of the Industrial Revolution?

lagged far behind. Russia, for example, was still largely rural and agricultural, ruled by an autocratic regime that preferred to keep the peasants in serfdom.

In other parts of the world where they had established control (see Chapter 21), newly industrialized European states pursued a deliberate policy of preventing the growth of mechanized industry. India provides an excellent example. In the eighteenth century, India had been one of the world's greatest exporters of cotton cloth produced by hand labor. In the first half of the nineteenth century, much of India fell under the control of the British East India Company. With British control came inexpensive textiles produced in British factories. As the indigenous Indian textile industry declined, thousands of Indian spinners and handloom weavers lost their jobs, forcing many to turn to growing raw materials, such as cotton, wheat, and tea, for export to Britain, while buying British-made finished goods. In a similar fashion elsewhere, the rapidly industrializing nations of Europe worked to thwart the spread of the Industrial Revolution to their colonial dominions.

Social Impact of the Industrial Revolution

Eventually, the Industrial Revolution revolutionized the social life of Europe and the world. This change was already evident in the first half of the nineteenth century in the growth of cities and the emergence of new social classes.

POPULATION GROWTH AND URBANIZATION The European population had already begun to increase in the eighteenth century, but the pace accelerated in the nineteenth century. Between 1750 and 1850, the total European population almost doubled, rising from 140 million to 266 million. The key to this population growth was a decline in death rates as wars and major epidemic diseases, such as plague and smallpox, became less frequent. Thanks to the increase in the food supply, more people were also better fed and more resistant to disease.

Throughout Europe, cities and towns grew dramatically in the first half of the nineteenth century, a phenomenon related to industrialization. By 1850, especially in Great Britain and Belgium, cities were rapidly becoming home to many industries. With the steam engine, factories could be located in urban centers where they had ready access to transportation facilities and large numbers of new arrivals from the country looking for work.

In 1800, Great Britain had one major city, London, with a population of one million, and six cities with populations between 50,000 and 100,000. Fifty years later, London's population had swelled to 2,363,000, and there were nine cities with populations over 100,000 and eighteen cities with populations between 50,000 and 100,000. More than 50 percent of the British population lived in towns and cities by 1850. Urban populations also grew on the Continent, but less dramatically.

The dramatic growth of cities in the first half of the nineteenth century resulted in miserable living conditions for many of the inhabitants. Located in the center of most industrial towns were the row houses of the industrial workers. Rooms were small and frequently overcrowded, as a government report of 1838 in Britain revealed: "There were 63 families where there were at least five persons to one bed; and there were some in which even six were packed in one bed, lying at the top and bottom—children and adults."[1]

Sanitary conditions were appalling; sewers and open drains were common on city streets: "In the centre of this street is a gutter, into which the refuse of animal and vegetable matters of all kinds, the dirty water from the washing of clothes and of the houses, are all poured, and there they stagnate and putrefy."[2] Unable to deal with human excrement, early industrial cities smelled horrible and were extraordinarily unhealthy. Towns and cities were death traps: deaths outnumbered births in most large cities in the first half of the nineteenth century; only a constant influx of people from the country kept them alive and growing.

NEW SOCIAL CLASSES: THE INDUSTRIAL MIDDLE CLASS The rise of industrial capitalism produced a new middle-class group. The bourgeoisie was not new; it had existed since the emergence of cities in the Middle Ages. Originally, the bourgeois or burgher was a town dweller, active as a merchant, official, artisan, lawyer, or man of letters. As wealthy townspeople bought land, the original meaning of the word *bourgeois* became lost, and the term came to include people involved in commerce, industry, and banking as well as professionals such as teachers, physicians, and government officials.

The new industrial middle class was made up of the people who constructed the factories, purchased the machines, and figured out where the markets were (see the box on p. 496). Their qualities included resourcefulness, single-mindedness, resolution, initiative, vision, ambition, and often, of course, greed. As Jedediah Strutt, a cotton manufacturer said, "Getting of money . . . is the main business of the life of men."

Members of the industrial middle class sought both to reduce the barriers between themselves and the landed elite and at the same time to separate themselves from the laboring classes below. In the first half of the nineteenth century, the working class was actually a mixture of different groups, but in the course of the century, factory workers came to form an industrial **proletariat** that constituted a majority of the working class.

NEW SOCIAL CLASSES: THE INDUSTRIAL WORKING CLASS Early industrial workers faced wretched working conditions. Work shifts ranged from twelve to sixteen hours a day, six days a week, with a half hour for lunch and dinner. Workers had no security of employment and no minimum wage. The worst conditions were in the cotton mills, where temperatures were especially debilitating.

Attitudes of the Industrial Middle Class in Britain and Japan

SCIENCE & TECHNOLOGY

In the nineteenth century, a new industrial middle class in Great Britain took the lead in creating the Industrial Revolution. Japan did not begin to industrialize until after 1870 (see Chapter 22). There, too, an industrial middle class emerged, although there were also important differences in the attitudes of business leaders in Britain and Japan. Some of these differences can be seen in these documents. The first is an excerpt from the book *Self-Help* (1859) by Samuel Smiles, who believed that people succeed through "individual industry, energy, and uprightness." The other two selections are by Shibuzawa Eiichi (shih-boo-ZAH-wah EH-ee-chee), a Japanese industrialist who supervised textile factories. Although his business career began in 1873, he did not write his autobiography, the source of his first excerpt, until 1927.

Samuel Smiles, *Self-Help*

"Heaven helps those who help themselves" is a well-worn maxim, embodying in a small compass the results of vast human experience. The spirit of self-help is the root of all genuine growth in the individual; and, exhibited in the lives of many, it constitutes the true source of national vigor and strength. Help from without is often enfeebling in its effects, but help from within invariably invigorates. Whatever is done for men or classes, to a certain extent takes away the stimulus and necessity of doing for themselves; and where men are subjected to overguidance and overgovernment, the inevitable tendency is to render them comparatively helpless. . . .

National progress is the sum of individual industry, energy, and uprightness, as national decay is of individual idleness, selfishness, and vice. . . . If this view be correct, then it follows that the highest patriotism and philanthropy consist, not so much in altering laws and modifying institutions as in helping and stimulating men to elevate and improve themselves by their own free and independent action as individuals. . . .

Many popular books have been written for the purpose of communicating to the public the grand secret of making money. But there is no secret whatever about it, as the proverbs of every nation abundantly testify. . . . "A penny saved is a penny gained."— "Diligence is the mother of good-luck."—"No pains no gains."—"No sweat no sweet."—"Sloth, the key of poverty"—"Work, and thou shalt have."—"He who will not work, neither shall he eat."—"The world is his, who has patience and industry."

Shibuzawa Eiichi, *Autobiography*

I . . . felt that it was necessary to raise the social standing of those who engaged in commerce and industry. By way of setting an example, I began studying and practicing the teachings of the *Analects of Confucius*. It contains teachings first enunciated more than twenty-four hundred years ago. Yet it supplies the ultimate in practical ethics for all of us to follow in our daily living. It has many golden rules for businessmen. For example, there is a saying: "Wealth and respect are what men desire, but unless a right way is followed, they cannot be obtained; poverty and lowly position are what men despise, but unless a right way is found, one cannot leave that status once reaching it." It shows very clearly how a businessman must act in this world.

Shibuzawa Eiichi on Progress

One must beware of the tendency of some to argue that it is through individualism or egoism that the State and society can progress most rapidly. They claim that under individualism, each individual competes with the others, and progress results from this competition. But this is to see merely the advantages and ignore the disadvantages, and I cannot support such a theory. Society exists, and a State has been founded. Although people desire to rise to positions of wealth and honor, the social order and the tranquillity of the State will be disrupted if this is done egoistically. Men should not do battle in competition with their fellow men. Therefore, I believe that in order to get along together in society and serve the State, we must by all means abandon this idea of independence and self-reliance and reject egoism completely.

 What are the major similarities and differences between the business attitudes of Samuel Smiles and Shibuzawa Eiichi? How do you explain the differences?

Sources: Samuel Smiles, *Self-Help.* From Samuel Smiles, *Self-Help*, London, 1859. Shibuzawa Eiichi, *Autobiography* and Shibuzawa Eiichi on Progress. Shibuzawa Eiichi, *The Autobiography of Shibuzawa Eiichi: From Peasant to Entrepreneur*, 1927 (Tokyo: University of Tokyo Press, 1994).

One report noted that "in the cotton-spinning work, these creatures are kept, fourteen hours in each day, locked up, summer and winter, in a heat of from eighty to eighty-four degrees." Mills were also dirty, dusty, and unhealthy.

Conditions in the coal mines were also harsh. Although steam-powered engines were used to lift coal to the top of the mines, inside the mines, men still had to dig the coal out while horses, mules, women, and children pulled coal carts on rails to the lift. Cave-ins, explosions, and gas fumes were a way of life. The cramped conditions—tunnels were often only 3 or 4 feet high—and constant dampness led to deformed bodies and ruined lungs.

Both children and women worked in large numbers in early factories and mines. Children had been an important part of the family economy in preindustrial times, working in the fields or carding and spinning wool at home. In the Industrial Revolution, however, child labor was exploited more than ever. The owners of cotton factories found child labor very helpful. Children had a particular delicate touch as spinners of cotton, and their small size enabled them to crawl under machines to gather loose cotton. Moreover, children were more easily trained to do factory work. Above all, children were a cheap supply of labor. In 1821, about half of the British population was under twenty years of age. Hence, children made up an abundant supply of labor, and they were paid only about one-sixth to one-third of what a man was paid. Children as young as seven worked twelve to fifteen hours per day, six days a week, in the cotton mills.

By 1830, women and children made up two-thirds of the cotton industry's labor. Under the Factory Act of 1833, however, which prohibited employment of children under the age of nine and restricted the working hours of those under eighteen, child labor declined but did not disappear. In 1838, children under eighteen still made up 29 percent of the total workforce in the cotton mills. As the number of children employed declined, women came to dominate the labor forces of the early factories, making up 50 percent of the labor force in textile (cotton and woolen) factories before 1870. They were mostly unskilled laborers and were paid half or less of what men received.

DID INDUSTRIALIZATION BRING AN IMPROVED STANDARD OF LIVING? During the first half of the nineteenth century, industrialization altered the lives of Europeans, especially the British, as they left their farms and moved to cities to work in factories. But did they experience a higher standard of living during this time? Some historians argue that industrialization increased employment and lowered the price of consumer goods, thus improving the way people lived. They also maintain that household income rose because several family members could now hold wage-paying jobs. Other historians argue

that wage labor initially made life worse for many families. They maintain that employment in the early factories was highly volatile as employers quickly dismissed workers whenever demand declined. Wages were not uniform, and families lived in cramped and unsanitary conditions in the early industrial cities. Families continued to spend most of their income on food and clothing. Most historians agree that members of the middle class were the real gainers in the early Industrial Revolution and that industrial workers had to wait until the second half of the nineteenth century to begin to reap the benefits of industrialization.

The Growth of Industrial Prosperity

Q **FOCUS QUESTIONS:** What was the Second Industrial Revolution, and what effects did it have on economic and social life? What were the main ideas of Karl Marx, and what role did they play in politics and the union movement in the late nineteenth and early twentieth centuries?

After 1870, the Western world experienced a dynamic age of material prosperity. The new industries, new sources of energy, and new goods of the Second Industrial Revolution led people to believe that their material progress reflected human progress.

New Products

The first major change in industrial development between 1870 and 1914 was the substitution of steel for iron. New methods of shaping steel made it useful for constructing lighter, smaller, and faster machines and engines, as well as railways, ships, and armaments. In 1860, Great Britain, France, Germany, and Belgium produced 125,000 tons of steel; by 1913, the total was 32 million tons.

Electricity was a major new form of energy that could be easily converted into other forms of energy—such as heat, light, and motion—and moved relatively effortlessly through space over transmitting wires. In the 1870s, the first commercially practical generators of electrical current were developed, and by 1910, hydroelectric power stations and coal-fired steam-generating plants enabled homes and factories in whole neighborhoods to be tied into a single, common source of power.

Electricity spawned a number of inventions. The light-bulb, developed independently by the American Thomas Edison and the Briton Joseph Swan, permitted homes and cities to be illuminated by electric lights. By the 1880s, streetcars and subways powered by electricity had appeared in major European cities. Electricity also

Model T. By 1916, Ford's factories were producing 735,000 cars a year. In 1903, at Kitty Hawk, North Carolina, brothers Orville and Wilbur Wright made the first flight in a fixed-wing airplane. The first regular passenger air service was established in 1919.

New Patterns

Industrial production grew rapidly at this time because of the greatly increased sales of manufactured goods. An increase in real wages for workers after 1870, combined with lower prices for manufactured goods because of reduced transportation costs, made it easier for Europeans to buy consumer products. In the cities, the first department stores began to sell a host of new consumer goods made possible by the development of the steel and electrical industries. The desire to own sewing machines, clocks, bicycles, electric lights, and typewriters was rapidly generating a new consumer ethic that has been a crucial part of the modern economy.

Not all nations benefited from the Second Industrial Revolution. Between 1870 and 1914, Germany replaced Great Britain as the industrial leader of Europe. Moreover, by 1900, Europe was divided into two economic zones. Great Britain, Belgium, France, the Netherlands, Germany, the western part of the Austro-Hungarian Empire, and northern Italy constituted an advanced industrialized core that had a high standard of living, decent systems of transportation, and relatively healthy and educated peoples (see Map 19.1). Another part of Europe, the backward and little industrialized area to the south and east, consisting of southern Italy, most of Austria-Hungary, Spain, Portugal, the Balkan kingdoms, and Russia, was still largely agricultural and relegated by the industrial countries to providing food and raw materials.

Emergence of a World Economy

The economic developments of the late nineteenth century, combined with the transportation revolution that saw the growth of marine transport and railroads, fostered a true world economy. By 1900, Europeans were receiving beef and wool from Argentina and Australia, coffee from Brazil, iron ore from Algeria, and sugar from Java. Until the Industrial Revolution, European countries had imported more from Asia than they had exported, but now foreign countries provided markets for the surplus manufactured goods of Europe. European capital was also invested abroad to develop railways, mines, electrical power plants, and banks. With its capital, industries, and military might, Europe dominated the world economy by the beginning of the twentieth century.

An Age of Progress. Between 1871 and 1914, the Second Industrial Revolution led many Europeans to believe that they were living in an age of progress when science would solve most human problems. This illustration is taken from a special issue of *The Illustrated London News* celebrating the Diamond Jubilee of Queen Victoria in 1897. On the left are scenes from 1837, when Victoria came to the British throne; on the right are scenes from 1897. The vivid contrast underscored the magazine's conclusion: "The most striking . . . evidence of progress during the reign is the ever increasing speed which the discoveries of physical science have forced into everyday life. Steam and electricity have conquered time and space to a greater extent during the last sixty years than all the preceding six hundred years witnessed."

transformed the factory. Conveyor belts, cranes, machines, and machine tools could all be powered by electricity and located anywhere. Similarly, a revolution in communications began when Alexander Graham Bell invented the telephone in 1876 and Guglielmo Marconi (gool-YEL-moh mahr-KOH-nee) sent the first radio waves across the Atlantic in 1901.

The development of the internal combustion engine, fired by oil and gasoline, provided a new source of power and gave rise to ocean liners as well as to the airplane and the automobile. In 1900, world production stood at 9,000 cars, but an American, Henry Ford, revolutionized the automotive industry with the mass production of the

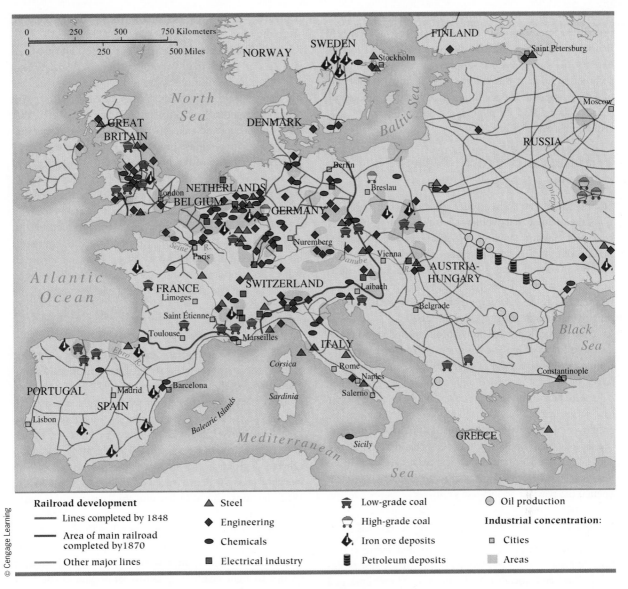

MAP 19.1 **The Industrial Regions of Europe at the End of the Nineteenth Century.** By the end of the nineteenth century, the Second Industrial Revolution—in steelmaking, electricity, petroleum, and chemicals—had spurred substantial economic growth and prosperity in western and central Europe; it also sparked economic and political competition between Great Britain and Germany.

Q *What correlation, if any, was there between industrial growth and political developments in the nineteenth century?*

Map legend:

Railroad development
— Lines completed by 1848
— Area of main railroad completed by 1870
— Other major lines

▲ Steel
◆ Engineering
⬬ Chemicals
◼ Electrical industry

⛏ Low-grade coal
⛏ High-grade coal
⚒ Iron ore deposits
⬓ Petroleum deposits

○ Oil production

Industrial concentration:
◻ Cities
▨ Areas

© Cengage Learning

The Spread of Industrialization

After 1870, industrialization began to spread beyond western and central Europe and North America. Especially noticeable was its rapid development, fostered by governments, in Russia and Japan. A surge of industrialization began in Russia in the 1890s under the guiding hand of Sergei Witte (syir-GYAY VIT-uh), the minister of finance. Witte pushed the government to support massive railroad construction. By 1900, 35,000 miles of track had been laid. Witte's program also made possible the rapid growth of a modern steel and coal industry, making Russia by 1900 the fourth-largest producer of steel, behind the United States, Germany, and Great Britain. At the same time, Russia was also turning out half of the world's oil production.

In Japan, the imperial government took the lead in promoting industry (see Chapter 22). The government financed industries, built railroads, brought foreign experts to train Japanese employees in new industrial techniques, and instituted a universal educational system based on applied science. By the end of the nineteenth century, Japan had developed key industries in tea, silk, armaments, and shipbuilding.

Women and Work: New Job Opportunities

During the nineteenth century, working-class organizations maintained that women should remain at home to bear and nurture children. Working-class men argued that keeping women out of industrial work would ensure the moral and physical well-being of families. In reality, however, when their husbands were unemployed, women had to do low-wage work at home or labor part-time in sweatshops to support their families.

The Second Industrial Revolution opened the door to new jobs for women. The development of larger industrial plants and the expansion of government services created a large number of service and white-collar jobs. The increased demand for white-collar workers at relatively low wages coupled with a shortage of male workers led employers to hire women. Women found new opportunities as telephone operators, typists, secretaries, file clerks, and salesclerks. Compulsory education necessitated more teachers, and the development of modern hospital services opened the way for an increase in nurses.

Organizing the Working Classes

The desire to improve their working and living conditions led many industrial workers to form socialist political parties and socialist trade unions. These emerged after 1870, but the theory that made them possible had been developed more than two decades earlier in the work of Karl Marx. **Marxism** made its first appearance on the eve of the revolutions of 1848 with the publication of a short treatise titled *The Communist Manifesto*, written by two Germans, Karl Marx (1818–1883) and Friedrich Engels (FREE-drikh ENG-ulz) (1820–1895).

MARXIST THEORY Marx and Engels began their treatise with the statement that "the history of all hitherto existing society is the history of class struggles." Throughout history, oppressor and oppressed have "stood in constant opposition to one another."[3] One group of people—the oppressors—owned the means of production and thus had the power to control government and society. Indeed, government itself was but an instrument of the ruling class. The other group, which

depended on the owners of the means of production, were the oppressed.

The **class struggle** continued in the industrialized societies of Marx's day. According to Marx, "Society as a whole is more and more splitting up into two great hostile camps, into two great classes directly facing each other: Bourgeoisie and Proletariat." Marx predicted that the struggle between the bourgeoisie and the proletariat would ultimately break into open revolution, "where the violent overthrow of the bourgeoisie lays the foundation for the sway of the proletariat." The fall of the bourgeoisie "and the victory of the proletariat are equally inevitable."[4] For a while, the proletariat would form a dictatorship to reorganize the means of production, but then the state—itself an instrument of the bourgeois interests—would wither away. Since classes had arisen from the economic differences that would have been abolished, the end result would be a classless society (see the box on p. 501).

SOCIALIST PARTIES In time, Marx's ideas were picked up by working-class leaders who formed socialist parties. Most important was the German Social Democratic Party (SPD), which emerged in 1875 and espoused revolutionary Marxist rhetoric while organizing itself as a mass political party competing in elections for the Reichstag (RYKHSS-tahk), the lower house of parliament. Once in the Reichstag, SPD delegates worked to achieve legislation to improve the condition of the working class. When it received 4 million votes in the 1912 elections, the SPD became the largest single party in Germany.

Socialist parties also emerged in other European states. In 1889, leaders of the various socialist parties formed the Second International, an association of national socialist groups to fight against capitalism worldwide. (The First International had failed in 1872.) The Second International took some coordinated actions—May Day (May 1), for example, was made an international labor holiday—but differences often wreaked havoc at the organization's congresses.

Marxist parties divided over the issue of **revisionism**. Pure Marxists believed in violent revolution that would bring the collapse of capitalism and socialist ownership of the means of production. But others, called revisionists, rejected **revolutionary socialism** and argued that workers must organize mass political parties and work with other progressive elements to gain reforms. Evolution by democratic means, not revolution, would achieve the desired goal of socialism.

Another force working for evolutionary rather than revolutionary socialism was the development of trade unions. In Great Britain, unions won the right to strike in

The Classless Society

FAMILY & SOCIETY

In *The Communist Manifesto*, Karl Marx and Friedrich Engels projected that the struggle between the bourgeoisie and the proletariat would end with the creation of a classless society. In this selection, they discuss the steps by which that classless society would be reached.

Karl Marx and Friedrich Engels, *The Communist Manifesto*

We have seen . . . that the first step in the revolution by the working class is to raise the proletariat to the position of ruling class. . . . The proletariat will use its political supremacy to wrest, by degrees, all capital from the bourgeoisie, to centralize all instruments of production in the hands of the State, i.e., of the proletariat organized as the ruling class; and to increase the total of productive forces as rapidly as possible.

Of course, in the beginning, this cannot be effected except by means of despotic inroads on the rights of property, and on the conditions of bourgeois production; by means of measures, therefore, which appear economically insufficient and untenable, but which, in the course of the movement, outstrip themselves, necessitate further inroads upon the old social order, and are unavoidable as a means of entirely revolutionizing the mode of production.

These measures will of course be different in different countries.

Nevertheless, in the most advanced countries, the following will be pretty generally applicable:

1. Abolition of property in land and application of all rents of land to public purposes.
2. A heavy progressive or graduated income tax.
3. Abolition of all right of inheritance. . . .
5. Centralization of credit in the hands of the State, by means of a national bank with State capital and an exclusive monopoly.

6. Centralization of the means of communication and transport in the hands of the State.
7. Extension of factories and instruments of production owned by the State. . . .
8. Equal liability of all to labor. Establishment of industrial armies, especially for agriculture.
9. Combination of agriculture with manufacturing industries; gradual abolition of the distinction between town and country, by a more equable distribution of the population over the country.
10. Free education for all children in public schools. Abolition of children's factory labor in its present form. . . .

When, in the course of development, class distinctions have disappeared, and all production has been concentrated in the whole nation, the public power will lose its political character. Political power, properly so called, is merely the organized power of one class for oppressing another. If the proletariat during its contest with the bourgeoisie is compelled, by the force of circumstances, to organize itself as a class, if, by means of a revolution, it makes itself the ruling class, and, as such, sweeps away by force the old conditions of production, then it will, along with these conditions, have swept away the conditions for the existence of class antagonisms and of classes generally, and will thereby have abolished its own supremacy as a class.

In place of the old bourgeois society, with its classes and class antagonisms, we shall have an association, in which the free development of each is the condition for the free development of all.

Q *How did Marx and Engels define the proletariat? The bourgeoisie? Why did Marxists come to believe that this distinction was paramount for understanding history? For shaping the future?*

Source: From *The Communist Manifesto* by Karl Marx and Friedrich Engels.

---

the 1870s. Soon after, factory workers began to organize into trade unions so that they could use the strike to improve their conditions. By 1900, British trade unions had 2 million members; by 1914, the number had risen to almost 4 million. Trade unions in the rest of Europe had varying degrees of success, but by the outbreak of World War I, they had made considerable progress in bettering the living and working conditions of the laboring classes.

Reaction and Revolution: The Growth of Nationalism

 FOCUS QUESTIONS: What were the major ideas associated with conservatism, liberalism, and nationalism, and what role did each ideology play in Europe between 1800 and 1850? What were the causes of the revolutions of 1848, and why did these revolutions fail?

Industrialization was a major force for change as it led the West into the machine-dependent modern world. Another major force for change was nationalism, which transformed the political map of Europe in the nineteenth century.

The Conservative Order

After the defeat of Napoleon, European rulers moved to restore much of the old order. This was the goal of the great powers—Great Britain, Austria, Prussia, and Russia—when they met at the Congress of Vienna in 1814 to arrange a final peace settlement after the Napoleonic wars. The leader of the congress was the Austrian foreign minister, Prince Klemens von Metternich (KLAY-menss fun MET-ayr-nikh) (1773–1859), who claimed that he was guided at Vienna by the principle of **legitimacy**. To reestablish peace and stability in Europe, he considered it necessary to restore the legitimate monarchs who would preserve traditional institutions. This had already been done in France with the restoration of the Bourbon monarchy and in a number of other states, but it did not stop the great powers from grabbing territory, often from the smaller, weaker states (see Map 19.2).

The peace arrangements of 1815 were only the beginning of a conservative reaction determined to contain the liberal and nationalist forces unleashed by the French Revolution. Metternich and his kind were representatives of the ideology known as **conservatism**. Most conservatives favored obedience to political authority, believed that organized religion was crucial to social order, hated revolutionary upheavals, and were unwilling to accept either the liberal demands for civil liberties and representative governments or the nationalistic aspirations generated

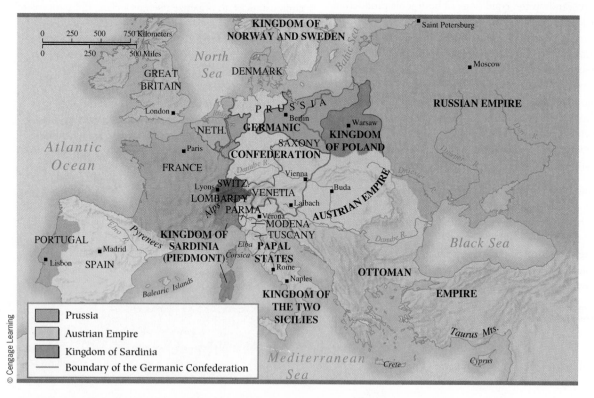

MAP 19.2 Europe After the Congress of Vienna, 1815. The Congress of Vienna imposed order on Europe based on the principles of monarchical government and a balance of power. Monarchs were restored in France, Spain, and other states recently under Napoleon's control, and much territory changed hands, often at the expense of the small, weak states.

 How did Europe's major powers manipulate territory to decrease the probability that France could again threaten the Continent's stability?

by the French revolutionary era. After 1815, the political philosophy of conservatism was supported by hereditary monarchs, government bureaucracies, landowning aristocracies, and revived churches, both Protestant and Catholic. The conservative forces were dominant after 1815.

One method used by the great powers to maintain the new status quo they had constructed was the Concert of Europe, according to which Great Britain, Russia, Prussia, and Austria (and later France) agreed to convene periodically to take steps that would maintain the peace in Europe. Eventually, the great powers adopted a principle of **intervention**, asserting that they had the right to send armies into countries where there were revolutions to restore legitimate monarchs to their thrones.

Forces for Change

Although conservative governments throughout Europe strived to restore the old order after 1815, powerful forces for change—liberalism and nationalism—were also at work. **Liberalism** owed much to the eighteenth-century Enlightenment and the American and French Revolutions; it was based on the idea that people should be as free from restraint as possible.

Politically, liberals came to hold a common set of beliefs. Chief among them was the protection of civil liberties, or the basic rights of all people, which included equality before the law; freedom of assembly, speech, and the press; and freedom from arbitrary arrest. All of these freedoms should be guaranteed by a written document, such as the American Bill of Rights. In addition to religious toleration for all, most liberals advocated separation of church and state. Liberals also demanded the right of peaceful opposition to the government in and out of parliament and the making of laws by a representative assembly (legislature) elected by qualified voters. Thus, many liberals believed in a constitutional monarchy or constitutional state with limits on the powers of government to prevent despotism and in written constitutions that would guarantee these rights. Liberals were not democrats, however. They thought that the right to vote and hold office should be open only to men of property. Liberals also believed in *laissez-faire* economic principles that rejected state interference in the regulation of wages and work hours. As a political philosophy, liberalism was adopted by middle-class men, especially industrial middle-class men, who favored voting rights for themselves so that they could share power with the landowning classes.

Nationalism was an even more powerful ideology for change. Nationalism arose out of an awareness of being part of a community that has common institutions, traditions, language, and customs. This community constitutes a "nation," and it would be the focus of the individual's primary loyalty. Nationalism did not become a popular force for change until the French Revolution. From then on, nationalists came to believe that each nationality should have its own government. Thus, the Germans, who were not united, wanted national unity in a German nation-state with one central government. Subject peoples, such as the Hungarians, wanted to establish their own autonomy rather than be subject to a German minority in the multinational Austrian Empire.

Nationalism thus posed a threat to the existing political order. A united Germany, for example, would upset the balance of power established at Vienna in 1815, and an independent Hungarian state would mean the breakup of the Austrian Empire. Because many European states were multinational, conservatives tried hard to repress the radical threat of nationalism. The conservative order dominated much of Europe after 1815, but the forces of liberalism and nationalism, first generated by the French Revolution, continued to grow as that second great revolution, the Industrial Revolution, expanded and brought in new groups of people who wanted change. In 1848, these forces for change erupted.

The Revolutions of 1848

Revolution in France was the spark for revolts in other countries. While the lower middle class, workers, and peasants were suffering from a severe industrial and agricultural depression, the government's persistent refusal to lower the property qualification for voting angered the disenfranchised members of the middle class. When the government of King Louis-Philippe (1830–1848) refused to make changes, opposition grew and finally overthrew the monarchy on February 24, 1848. A group of moderate and radical republicans established a provisional government and called for the election by universal male suffrage of a "constituent assembly" to draw up a new constitution.

The new constitution, ratified on November 4, 1848, established the Second Republic, with a single legislature elected to three-year terms by universal male suffrage and a president, also elected by universal male suffrage to a four-year term. In the elections for the presidency held in December 1848, Charles Louis Napoleon Bonaparte (1808–1873), the nephew of the famous French ruler, won a resounding victory. Within four years, President Louis Napoleon would become Emperor Napoleon III and establish an authoritarian regime.

News of the 1848 revolution in France led to upheaval in central Europe as well (see the box on p. 504). The Vienna settlement in 1815 had recognized the existence of thirty-eight sovereign states (called the Germanic Confederation) in what had once been the Holy Roman

Response to Revolution: Two Perspectives

POLITICS & GOVERNMENT

Based on their political beliefs, Europeans responded differently to the specter of revolution that haunted Europe in the first half of the nineteenth century. The first excerpt is taken from a speech by Thomas Babington Macaulay (muh-KAHL-lee) (1800–1859), a historian and a member of the British Parliament. Macaulay spoke in Parliament on behalf of the Reform Act of 1832, which extended the right to vote to the industrial middle classes of Britain. A revolution in France in 1830 that had resulted in some gains for the upper bourgeoisie had influenced his belief that it was better to reform than to have a political revolution.

The second excerpt is taken from the *Reminiscences* of Carl Schurz (SHOORTS) (1829–1906). Like many liberals and nationalists in Germany, Schurz received the news of the 1848 revolution in France with great expectations for change in the German states. After the failure of the German revolution, Schurz emigrated to the United States and eventually became a U.S. senator.

Thomas Babington Macaulay, Speech of March 2, 1831

My hon[orable] friend the member of the University of Oxford tells us that, if we pass this law, England will soon be a Republic. The reformed House of Commons will, according to him, before it has sat ten years, depose the King, and expel the Lords from their House. . . . His proposition is, in fact, this—that our monarchical and aristocratical institutions have no hold on the public mind of England; that these institutions are regarded with aversion by a decided majority of the middle class. . . . Now, sir, if I were convinced that the great body of the middle class in England look with aversion on monarchy and aristocracy, I should be forced, much against my will, to come to this conclusion, that monarchical and aristocratical institutions are unsuited to this country. Monarchy and aristocracy, valuable and useful as I think them, are still valuable and useful as means, and not as ends. The end of government is the happiness of the people; and I do not conceive that, in a country like this, the happiness of the people can be promoted by a form of government in which the middle classes place no confidence. . . . But, sir, I am fully

convinced that the middle classes sincerely wish to uphold the royal prerogatives, and the constitutional rights of the Peers. . . .

But let us know our interest and our duty better. Turn where we may—within, around—the voice of great events is proclaiming to us, "Reform, that you may preserve." Now, therefore, while everything at home and abroad forebodes ruin to those who persist in a hopeless struggle against the spirit of the age; now, . . . take counsel, not of prejudice, not of party spirit . . . but of history, of reason. . . . Save property divided against itself. Save the multitude, endangered by their own ungovernable passions. Save the aristocracy, endangered by its own unpopular power. Save the greatest, and fairest, and most highly civilized community that ever existed, from calamities which may in a few days sweep away all the rich heritage of so many ages of wisdom and glory. The danger is terrible. The time is short. If this Bill should be rejected, I pray to God that none of those who concur in rejecting it may ever remember their votes with unavailing regret, amidst the wreck of laws, the confusion of ranks, the spoliation of property, and the dissolution of social order.

Carl Schurz, *Reminiscences*

One morning, toward the end of February, 1848, I sat quietly in my attic-chamber, . . . when suddenly a friend rushed breathlessly into the room, exclaiming: "What, you sitting here! Do you not know what has happened?"

"No; what?"

"The French have driven away Louis Philippe and proclaimed the republic."

. . . We tore down the stairs, into the street, to the market-square. . . . Although it was still forenoon, the market was already crowded with young men talking excitedly. . . What did we want there? This probably no one knew. But since the French had driven away Louis Philippe and proclaimed the republic, something of course must happen here, too. . . .

The next morning . . . [we were] impelled by a feeling that now we had something more important [than our classes] to do—to devote ourselves to the affairs of the fatherland. And this we did by seeking as quickly as

(Continued)

possible again the company of our friends, in order to discuss what had happened and what was to come.

In these conversations, excited as they were, certain ideas and catchwords worked themselves to the surface, which expressed more or less the feelings of the people. Now had arrived in Germany the day for the establishment of "German Unity," and the founding of a great, powerful national German Empire. In the first line the convocation of a national parliament. Then the demands for civil rights and liberties, free speech, free press, the right of free assembly, equality before the law, a freely elected representation of the people with legislative power, responsibility of ministers, self-government of the communes, the right of the people to carry arms, the formation of a civic guard with elective officers, and so on—in short, that which was called a "constitutional form of government on a broad democratic basis." Republican ideas were at first only sparingly expressed. But the word *democracy* was soon on all tongues, and many, too, thought it a matter of course that if the princes should try to withhold from the people the rights and liberties demanded, force would take the

place of mere petition. Of course the regeneration of the fatherland must, if possible, be accomplished by peaceable means. . . . I was dominated by the feeling that at last the great opportunity had arrived for giving to the German people the liberty which was their birthright and to the German fatherland its unity and greatness, and that it was now the first duty of every German to do and to sacrifice everything for this sacred object.

Q *What arguments did Macaulay use to support the Reform Act of 1832? Was he correct? Why or why not? Why was Carl Schurz so excited when he heard the news about the revolution in France? Do you think being a university student helps explain his reaction? Why or why not? What differences do you see in the approaches of these two writers? What do these selections tell you about the development of politics in the German states and Britain in the nineteenth century?*

Sources: Thomas Babington Macaulay, Speech of March 2, 1831. From *Speeches, Parliamentary and Miscellaneous* by Thomas B. Macaulay (New York: Hurst Co., 1853), vol. 1, pp. 20–21, 25–26. Carl Schurz, *Reminiscences*. From *The Reminiscences of Carl Schurz* by Carl Schurz (New York: The McClure Co., 1907), vol. 1, pp. 112–113.

Empire. Austria and Prussia were the two great powers; the other states varied considerably in size. In 1848, cries for change caused many German rulers to promise constitutions, a free press, jury trials, and other liberal reforms. In Prussia, King Frederick William IV (1840–1861) agreed to establish a new constitution and work for a united Germany.

The promise of unity reverberated throughout the German states as governments allowed elections by universal male suffrage for deputies to an all-German parliament called the Frankfurt Assembly. Its purpose was to fulfill a liberal and nationalist dream—the preparation of a constitution for a new united Germany. But the assembly failed to achieve its goal. The members had no real means of compelling the German rulers to accept the constitution they had drawn up. German unification was not achieved; the revolution had failed.

The Austrian Empire needed only the news of the revolution in Paris to erupt in flames in March 1848. The Austrian Empire was a multinational state, containing at least eleven ethnically distinct peoples, including Germans, Czechs, Magyars (Hungarians), Slovaks, Romanians, Serbians, and Italians. The Germans, though only

a quarter of the population, were economically dominant and played a leading role in government. The Hungarians, however, wanted their own legislature. In March, demonstrations in Buda, Prague, and Vienna led to the dismissal of Metternich, the Austrian foreign minister and archsymbol of the conservative order, who fled abroad. In Vienna, revolutionary forces took control of the capital and demanded a liberal constitution. Hungary was given its own legislature and a separate national army.

Austrian officials had made concessions to appease the revolutionaries, but they were determined to reestablish firm control. As in the German states, they were increasingly encouraged by the divisions between radical and moderate revolutionaries. By the end of October 1848, Austrian military forces had crushed the rebels in Vienna, but it was only with the assistance of a Russian army of 140,000 men that the Hungarian revolution was finally put down in 1849. The revolutions in the Austrian Empire had failed.

Revolutions in Italy also failed. The Congress of Vienna had established nine states in Italy, including the kingdom of Sardinia in the north, ruled by the house of Savoy; the kingdom of the Two Sicilies (Naples and

Austrian Students in the Revolutionary Civil Guard. In 1848, revolutionary fervor swept the European continent and toppled governments in France, central Europe, and Italy. In the Austrian Empire, students joined the revolutionary civil guard in taking control of Vienna and forcing the Austrian emperor to call a constituent assembly to draft a liberal constitution.

Sicily); the Papal States; a handful of small duchies; and the important northern provinces of Lombardy and Venetia (vuh-NEE-shuh), which were part of the Austrian Empire. Italy was largely under Austrian domination, but a new movement for Italian unity known as Young Italy led to initially successful revolts in 1848. By 1849, however, the Austrians had reestablished complete control over Lombardy and Venetia, and the old order also prevailed in the rest of Italy.

Throughout Europe in 1848–1849, moderate, middle-class liberals and radical workers soon divided over their aims, and the failure of the revolutionaries to stay united soon led to the reestablishment of authoritarian regimes. In other parts of the Western world, revolutions took somewhat different directions (see Chapter 20).

Nationalism in the Balkans: The Ottoman Empire and the Eastern Question

The Ottoman Empire had long been in control of much of the Balkans in southeastern Europe. By the beginning of the nineteenth century, however, the Ottoman Empire was in decline, and authority over its outlying territories in the Balkans waned. As a result, European governments, especially those of Russia and Austria, began to take an active interest in the disintegration of the empire. The "Eastern Question," as it came to be called, troubled European diplomats throughout the century.

When the Russians invaded the Ottoman provinces of Moldavia (mohl-DAY-vee-uh) and Wallachia (wah-LAY-kee-uh), the Ottoman Turks declared war on Russia

on October 4, 1853. In the following year, on March 28, Great Britain and France, fearful of Russian gains, declared war on Russia. The Crimean War, as the conflict came to be called, was poorly planned and poorly fought. Heavy losses caused the Russians to sue for peace. By the Treaty of Paris in 1856, Russia agreed to allow Moldavia and Wallachia to be placed under the protection of all the great powers.

The Crimean War destroyed the Concert of Europe. Austria and Russia, the chief powers maintaining the status quo in the first half of the nineteenth century, were now enemies because Austria had failed to support Russia in the war. Russia, defeated and humiliated by the obvious failure of its armies, withdrew from European affairs for the next two decades. Great Britain, disillusioned by its role in the war, also pulled back from continental affairs. Austria, paying the price for its neutrality, was now without friends among the great powers. This new international situation opened the door for the unification of Italy and Germany.

National Unification and the National State, 1848–1871

Q FOCUS QUESTION: What actions did Cavour and Bismarck take to bring about unification in Italy and Germany, respectively, and what role did war play in their efforts?

The revolutions of 1848 had failed, but within twenty-five years, many of the goals sought by liberals and nationalists during the first half of the nineteenth century were achieved. Italy and Germany became nations, and many European states were led by constitutional monarchs.

The Unification of Italy

The Italians were the first to benefit from the breakdown of the Concert of Europe. In 1850, Austria was still the dominant power on the Italian peninsula. After the failure of the revolution of 1848–1849, more and more Italians looked to the northern Italian state of Piedmont, ruled by the house of Savoy, as their best hope to achieve the unification of Italy. It was, however, doubtful that the little state could provide the necessary leadership until King Victor Emmanuel II (1849–1878; 1861–1878 as king of Italy) named Count Camillo di Cavour (kuh-MEEL-oh dee kuh-VOOR) (1810–1861) prime minister in 1852.

Cavour pursued a policy of economic expansion that increased government revenues and enabled Piedmont to equip a large army. Then, allied with the French emperor, Napoleon III, Cavour defeated the Austrians and gained control of Lombardy. Cavour's success caused nationalists in some northern Italian states (Parma, Modena, and Tuscany) to overthrow their governments and join Piedmont.

Meanwhile, in southern Italy, Giuseppe Garibaldi (joo-ZEP-pay gar-uh-BAHL-dee) (1807–1882), a dedicated Italian patriot, raised an army of a thousand volunteers called Red Shirts because of the color of their uniforms. Garibaldi's forces swept through Sicily and then crossed over to the mainland and began a victorious march up the Italian peninsula. Naples, and with it the kingdom of the Two Sicilies, fell in September 1860. Ever the patriot, Garibaldi chose to turn over his conquests to Cavour's Piedmontese forces. On March 17, 1861, the new kingdom of Italy was proclaimed under a centralized government subordinated to the control of Piedmont and King Victor Emmanuel II. The task of unification was not yet complete, however. Venetia in the north was taken from Austria in 1866. The Italian army annexed the city of Rome on September 20, 1870, and it became the new capital of the united Italian state.

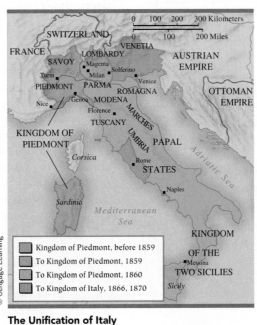

The Unification of Italy

CHRONOLOGY	The Unification of Italy
Victor Emmanuel II	1849–1878
Count Cavour becomes prime minister of Piedmont	1852
Garibaldi's invasion of the Two Sicilies	1860
Kingdom of Italy is proclaimed	March 17, 1861
Italy's annexation of Venetia	1866
Italy's annexation of Rome	1870

The Unification of Germany

After the failure of the Frankfurt Assembly to achieve German unification in 1848–1849, Germans increasingly looked to Prussia for leadership in the cause of German unification. Prussia had become a strong, prosperous, and authoritarian state, with the Prussian king in firm control of both the government and the army. In 1862, King William I (1861–1888) appointed a new prime minister, Count Otto von Bismarck (OT-toh fun BIZ-mark) (1815–1898). Bismarck has often been portrayed as the ultimate realist, the foremost nineteenth-century practitioner of *Realpolitik* (ray-AHL-poh-lee-teek)—the "politics of reality." He said, "Not by speeches and majorities will the great questions of the day be decided—that was the mistake of 1848–1849—but by iron and blood."[5] Opposition to his domestic policy determined Bismarck on an active foreign policy, which led to war and German unification.

After defeating Denmark with Austrian help in 1864 and gaining control over the duchies of Schleswig (SHLESS-vik) and Holstein (HOHL-shtyn), Bismarck goaded the Austrians into a war on June 14, 1866. The Austrians were barely defeated at Königgrätz (kur-nig-GRETS) on July 3, but Prussia now organized the northern German states into the North German Confederation. The southern German states, largely Catholic, remained independent but signed military alliances with Prussia due to their fear of France, their western neighbor.

Prussia now dominated all of northern Germany, but Bismarck realized that France would never be content with a strong German state to its east because of the potential threat to French security. Bismarck goaded the French into declaring war on Prussia on July 15, 1870. The Prussian armies advanced into France, and at Sedan (suh-DAHN) on September 2, 1870, they captured an entire French army and the French emperor Napoleon III himself. Paris capitulated on January 28, 1871. France had to give up the provinces of Alsace (al-SASS) and Lorraine (luh-RAYN) to the new German state, a loss that left the French burning for revenge.

Even before the war had ended, the southern German states had agreed to enter the North German Confederation. On January 18, 1871, in the Hall of Mirrors in Louis XIV's palace at Versailles, William I was proclaimed kaiser (KY-zur) (emperor) of the Second German Empire

The Unification of Germany

(the first was the medieval Holy Roman Empire). German unity had been achieved by the Prussian monarchy and the Prussian army. The Prussian leadership of German unification meant the triumph of authoritarian, militaristic values over liberal, constitutional sentiments in the development of the new German state. With its industrial resources and military might, the new state had become the strongest power on the Continent. A new European balance of power was at hand.

CHRONOLOGY	The Unification of Germany
King William I of Prussia	1861–1888
Danish War	1864
Austro-Prussian War	1866
Franco-Prussian War	1870–1871
German Empire is proclaimed	January 18, 1871

The Unification of Germany. Under Prussian leadership, a new German empire was proclaimed on January 18, 1871, in the Hall of Mirrors in the palace of Versailles. King William of Prussia became Emperor William I of the Second German Empire. Otto von Bismarck, who had been so instrumental in creating the new German state, is shown here, resplendently attired in his white uniform, standing at the foot of the throne.

Nationalism and Reform: The European National State at Mid-Century

Unlike nations on the Continent, Great Britain managed to avoid the revolutionary upheavals of the first half of the nineteenth century. In the early part of the century, Great Britain was governed by the aristocratic landowning classes that dominated both houses of Parliament. But in 1832, to avoid turmoil like that on the Continent, Parliament passed a reform bill that increased the number of male voters, chiefly by adding members of the industrial middle class (see the box on p. 504). By allowing the industrial middle class to join the landed interests in ruling Britain, Britain avoided revolution in 1848.

In the 1850s and 1860s, the British liberal parliamentary system made both social and political reforms that enabled the country to remain stable. Another reason for Britain's stability was its continuing economic growth. After 1850, middle-class prosperity was at last coupled with improvements for the working classes as real wages for laborers increased more than 25 percent between

The Young Victoria (2009)

Directed by Jean-Marc Vallée, *The Young Victoria* is an imaginative and yet relatively realistic portrayal of the early years of the young woman who became Britain's longest-reigning monarch. The film begins in 1836 when the seventeen-year-old Victoria (Emily Blunt) is the heir to the throne. Her controlling mother, the duchess of Kent (Miranda Richardson), schemes to prevent her daughter from ascending the throne by trying to create a regency for herself and her paramour, Sir John Conroy (Mark Strong). The mother and Conroy fail, and Victoria succeeds to the throne after the death of her uncle, King William IV (Jim Broadbent), in 1837. The movie also shows the impact that Lord Melbourne (Paul Bettany), the prime minister, had on the young queen. Indeed, Victoria's attachment to Melborne led to considerable discontent among her subjects. Central to the film, however, is the romantic portrayal of the wooing of Victoria by her young German cousin, Prince Albert of Sax-Coburg-Gotha (Rupert Friend). The film accurately conveys the deep and abiding love that developed between Victoria and Albert.

With its castle and cathedral settings, the film is a visual treat but also contains some inaccuracies. Victoria is shown painting with her right hand, although she was actually left-handed. The facts are also embellished at times for dramatic effect. Although there was an assassination attempt on the queen, Prince Albert was not shot while trying to protect her. Both shots fired by

GK Films/The Kobal Collection at Art Resource, NY

The coronation of Victoria (Emily Blunt) as queen of England

the would-be assassin went wide of the mark. The banquet scene in which King William IV insults the duchess of Kent is accurate and uses many of the king's actual words, but its consequences are not. The duchess did not leave the room, and Victoria did not remain calm, but broke into tears. Finally, except for a passing reference to Victoria's concern for workers' housing conditions, this romantic movie makes no attempt to portray the political and social issues of Victoria's time.

1850 and 1870. The British sense of national pride was well reflected in Queen Victoria (1837–1901), whose sense of duty and moral respectability reflected the attitudes of her age, which has ever since been known as the Victorian Age (see the Film & History feature above)

After the revolution of 1848, France moved toward the restoration of monarchy. Four years after his election as president, Louis Napoleon restored an authoritarian empire. On December 2, 1852, he assumed the title of Napoleon III (the first Napoleon had abdicated in favor of his son, Napoleon II, in 1814). The Second Empire had begun.

The first five years of Napoleon III's reign were a spectacular success. He took many steps to expand industrial growth. Government subsidies fostered the rapid construction of railroads as well as harbors, roads, and canals. The major French railway lines were completed during Napoleon III's reign, and iron production tripled. Napoleon III also undertook a vast reconstruction of the city of Paris.

The medieval Paris of narrow streets and old city walls was destroyed and replaced by a modern Paris of broad boulevards, spacious buildings, an underground sewage system, a new public water supply, and gas streetlights.

In the 1860s, as opposition to his rule began to mount, Napoleon III began to liberalize his regime. He gave the Legislative Corps more say in affairs of state, including debate over the budget. Liberalization policies worked initially; in a plebiscite in May 1870 on whether to accept a new constitution that might have inaugurated a parliamentary regime, the French people gave Napoleon III a resounding victory. This triumph was short-lived, however. War with Prussia in 1870 brought Napoleon III's ouster, and a republic was proclaimed.

Although nationalism was a major force in nineteenth-century Europe, one of the most powerful states, the Austrian Empire, managed to frustrate the desire of its numerous ethnic groups for self-determination. After the

Emancipation: Serfs and Slaves

FAMILY & SOCIETY

Although overall their histories have been quite different, Russia and the United States shared a common feature in the 1860s. They were the only states in the Western world that still had large enslaved populations (the Russian serfs were virtually slaves). The leaders of both countries issued emancipation proclamations within two years of each other. The first excerpt is taken from the imperial decree of March 3, 1861, which freed the Russian serfs. The second excerpt is from Abraham Lincoln's Emancipation Proclamation, issued on January 1, 1863.

Alexander II's Imperial Decree, March 3, 1861

By the grace of God, we, Alexander II, Emperor and Autocrat of all the Russias, King of Poland, Grand Duke of Finland, etc., to all our faithful subjects, make known:

Called by Divine Providence and by the sacred right of inheritance to the throne of our ancestors, we took a vow in our innermost heart to respond to the mission which is intrusted to us as to surround with our affection and our Imperial solicitude all our faithful subjects of every rank and of every condition, from the warrior, who nobly bears arms for the defense of the country, to the humble artisan devoted to the works of industry; from the official in the career of the high offices of the State to the laborer whose plough furrows the soil. . . .

We thus came to the conviction that the work of a serious improvement of the condition of the peasants was a sacred inheritance bequeathed to us by our ancestors, a mission which, in the course of events, Divine Providence called upon us to fulfill. . . .

In virtue of the new dispositions above mentioned, the peasants attached to the soil will be invested within a term fixed by the law with all the rights of free cultivators. . . .

At the same time, they are granted the right of purchasing their close, and, with the consent of the proprietors, they may acquire in full property the arable lands and other appurtenances which are allotted to them as a permanent holding. By the acquisition in full property of the quantity of land fixed, the peasants are free from their obligations toward the proprietors for land thus purchased, and they enter definitely into the condition of free peasant-landholders.

Lincoln's Emancipation Proclamation, January 1, 1863

Now therefore, I, Abraham Lincoln, President of the United States, by virtue of the power in me vested as Commander-in-Chief of the Army and Navy of the United States in time of actual armed rebellion against the authority and government of the United States, and as a fit and necessary war measure for suppressing such rebellion, do, on this 1st day of January, A.D. 1863, and in accordance with my purpose to do so, . . . order and designate as the States and parts of States wherein the people thereof, respectively, are this day in rebellion against the United States the following, to wit:

Arkansas, Texas, Louisiana, . . . Mississippi, Alabama, Florida, Georgia, South Carolina, North Carolina, and Virginia. . . .

And by virtue of the power for the purpose aforesaid, I do order and declare that all persons held as slaves within said designated States and parts of States are, and henceforward shall be free; and that the Executive Government of the United States, including the military and naval authorities thereof, will recognize and maintain the freedom of said persons.

Q *What changes did Tsar Alexander II's emancipation of the serfs initiate in Russia? What effect did Lincoln's Emancipation Proclamation have on the southern "armed rebellion"? What reasons did each leader give for his action?*

Sources: Alexander II's Imperial Decree, March 3, 1861. From Annual Register (New York: Longmans, Green, 1861), p. 207. Lincoln's Emancipation Proclamation, January 1, 1863. From *U.S. Statutes at Large* (Washington, D.C., Government Printing Office, 1875), vol. 12, pp. 1268–1269.

Habsburgs had crushed the revolutions of 1848–1849, they restored centralized, autocratic government. But Austria's defeat at the hands of the Prussians in 1866 forced the Austrians to deal with the fiercely nationalistic Hungarians.

The result was the negotiated *Ausgleich* (OWSS-glykh), or Compromise, of 1867, which created the dual monarchy of Austria-Hungary. Each part of the empire now had its own constitution, its own legislature, its own governmental bureaucracy, and its own capital (Vienna for Austria and Budapest for Hungary). Holding the two states together were a single monarch—Francis Joseph (1848–1916) was emperor of Austria and king of Hungary—and a common army, foreign policy, and system of finances. The *Ausgleich* did not, however, satisfy the other nationalities that make up the Austro-Hungarian Empire.

At the beginning of the nineteenth century, Russia was overwhelmingly rural, agricultural, and autocratic. The Russian imperial autocracy, based on soldiers, secret police, and repression, withstood the revolutionary fervor of the first half of the nineteenth century. But defeat in the Crimean War in 1856 led even staunch conservatives to realize that Russia was falling hopelessly behind the western European powers. Tsar Alexander II (1855–1881) decided to make serious reforms.

Serfdom was Russia's most burdensome problem. On March 3, 1861, Alexander issued his emancipation edict (see the box on p. 510). Peasants were now free to own property and marry as they chose. But the redistribution of land instituted after emancipation was not favorable to them. The government provided land for the peasants by purchasing it from the landlords, but the landowners often kept the best lands. The peasants soon found that they had inadequate amounts of arable land to support themselves.

Nor were the peasants completely free. The state compensated the landowners for the land given to the peasants, but the peasants were to repay the state in long-term installments. To ensure that the payments were made, peasants were subjected to the authority of their *mir* (MEER), or village commune, which was collectively responsible for the payments to the government. Since the communes were responsible for the payments, they were reluctant to allow peasants to leave. Emancipation, then, led not to free, landowning peasants on the Western model but to unhappy, land-starved peasants who largely followed the old ways of agricultural production.

The European State, 1871–1914

Q FOCUS QUESTIONS: What general political trends were evident in the nations of western Europe in the late nineteenth and early twentieth centuries, and to what degree were those trends also apparent in the nations of central and eastern Europe? How did the growth of nationalism affect international affairs during the same period?

Throughout much of Europe by 1870, the national state had become the focus of people's loyalties. Only in Russia, eastern Europe, Austria-Hungary, and Ireland did national groups still struggle for independence.

Within the major European states, considerable progress was made in achieving such liberal practices as constitutions and parliaments, but it was largely in the western European states that **mass politics** became a reality. Reforms encouraged the expansion of political democracy through voting rights for men and the creation of mass political parties. At the same time, however, similar reforms were strongly resisted in parts of Europe where the old political forces remained strong.

Western Europe: The Growth of Political Democracy

By 1871, Great Britain had a functioning two-party parliamentary system. For the next fifty years, Liberals and Conservatives alternated in power. Both parties were dominated by aristocratic landowners and upper-middle-class businesspeople. The parties competed in passing laws that expanded the right to vote. By 1918, all males over twenty-one and women over thirty could vote. Political democracy was soon accompanied by social welfare measures for the working class.

The growth of trade unions, which advocated more radical economic change, and the emergence in 1900 of the Labour Party, which dedicated itself to workers' interests, caused the Liberals, who held the government from 1906 to 1914, to realize that they would have to create a program of social welfare or lose the workers' support. Therefore, they voted for a series of social reforms. The National Insurance Act of 1911 provided benefits for workers in case of sickness and unemployment. Additional legislation provided a small pension for those over seventy. Although both the benefits and the tax increase were modest, they were the first hesitant steps toward the future British welfare state.

In France, the confusion that ensued after the collapse of the Second Empire finally ended in 1875 when an improvised constitution established the Third Republic, which lasted sixty-five years. France's parliamentary system was weak, however, because the existence of a dozen political parties forced the premier (or prime minister) to depend on a coalition of parties to stay in power. The Third Republic was notorious for its changes of government. Nevertheless, by 1914, the Third Republic commanded the loyalty of most French people.

Central and Eastern Europe: Persistence of the Old Order

The constitution of the new imperial Germany begun by Chancellor Otto von Bismarck in 1871 provided for a bicameral legislature. The lower house of the German parliament, the Reichstag, was elected by universal male suffrage, but it did not have ministerial responsibility. Government ministers were responsible to the emperor, not the parliament. The emperor also commanded the armed forces and controlled foreign policy and the bureaucracy.

During the reign of Emperor William II (1888–1918), Germany continued to be an "authoritarian, conservative, military-bureaucratic power state." By the end of William's reign, Germany had become the strongest military and industrial power on the Continent, but the rapid change had also helped produce a society torn between modernization and traditionalism. With the expansion of industry and cities came demands for true democracy. Conservative forces, especially the landowning nobility and industrialists, tried to block the movement for democracy by supporting William II's activist foreign policy. Expansion abroad, they believed, would divert people's attention from the yearning for democracy at home.

After the creation of the dual monarchy of Austria-Hungary in 1867, the Austrian part received a constitution that theoretically established a parliamentary system. In practice, however, Emperor Francis Joseph largely ignored parliament, ruling by decree when parliament was not in session. The problem of the various nationalities also remained unsolved. The German minority that governed Austria felt increasingly threatened by the Czechs, Poles, and other Slavic groups within the empire. Their agitation in the parliament for autonomy led prime ministers after 1900 to ignore the parliament and rely increasingly on imperial decrees to govern.

In Russia, the assassination of Alexander II in 1881 convinced his son and successor, Alexander III (1881–1894), that reform had been a mistake, and he lost no

time in persecuting both reformers and revolutionaries. When Alexander III died, his weak son and successor, Nicholas II (1894–1917), began his rule with his father's conviction that the absolute power of the tsars should be preserved: "I shall maintain the principle of autocracy just as firmly and unflinchingly as did my unforgettable father."[6] But conditions were changing.

Industrialization progressed rapidly in Russia after 1890, and with industrialization came factories, an industrial working class, and the development of socialist parties, including the Marxist Social Democratic Party and the Social Revolutionaries. Although repression forced both parties to go underground, the growing opposition to the regime finally exploded into revolution in 1905.

The defeat of the Russians by the Japanese in 1904–1905 encouraged antigovernment groups to rebel against the tsarist regime. Nicholas II granted civil liberties and created a legislative assembly, the Duma (DOO-muh), elected directly by a broad franchise. But real constitutional monarchy proved short-lived. By 1907, the tsar had curtailed the power of the Duma and relied again on the army and bureaucracy to rule Russia.

International Rivalries and the Winds of War

Between 1871 and 1914, Europe was mostly at peace. Wars did occur (including wars of conquest in the non-Western world), but none involved the great powers. Bismarck had realized in 1871 that the emergence of a unified Germany as the most powerful state on the Continent (see Map 19.3) had upset the balance of power established at Vienna in 1815. Fearful of a possible anti-German alliance between France and Russia, and possibly even Austria, Bismarck made a defensive alliance with Austria in 1879. Three years later, this alliance was enlarged with the addition of Italy, angry with the French over conflicting colonial ambitions in North Africa. The Triple Alliance of 1882—Germany, Austria-Hungary, and Italy—committed the three powers to a defensive alliance against France. At the same time, Bismarck maintained a separate treaty with Russia.

When Emperor William II cashiered Bismarck in 1890 and took over direction of Germany's foreign policy, he embarked on an activist foreign policy dedicated to enhancing German power by finding, as he put it, Germany's rightful "place in the sun." One of his changes in Bismarck's foreign policy was to drop the treaty with Russia, which he viewed as being at odds with Germany's alliance with Austria. The ending of the alliance brought France and Russia together, and in 1894, the two powers concluded a military alliance. During the next ten years, German policies caused the British to draw closer

CHRONOLOGY	The National State, 1870–1914
Great Britain	
Formation of Labour Party	1900
National Insurance Act	1911
France	
Republican constitution (Third Republic)	1875
Germany	
Bismarck as chancellor	1871–1890
Emperor William II	1888–1918
Austria-Hungary	
Emperor Francis Joseph	1848–1916
Russia	
Tsar Alexander III	1881–1894
Tsar Nicholas II	1894–1917
Russo-Japanese War	1904–1905
Revolution	1905

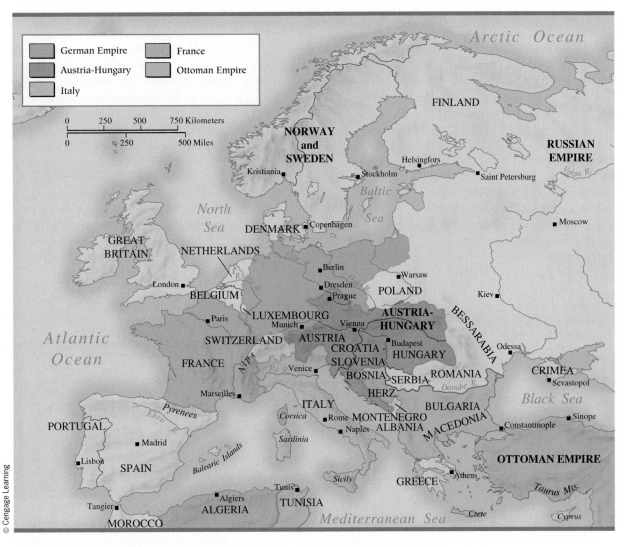

MAP 19.3 **Europe in 1871.** German unification in 1871 upset the balance of power established at Vienna in 1815 and eventually led to a realignment of European alliances. By 1907, Europe was divided into two opposing camps: the Triple Entente of Great Britain, Russia, and France and the Triple Alliance of Germany, Austria-Hungary, and Italy.

Q *How was Germany affected by the formation of the Triple Entente?*

to France. By 1907, an alliance of Great Britain, France, and Russia—known as the Triple Entente (ahn-TAHNT)—stood opposed to the Triple Alliance of Germany, Austria-Hungary, and Italy. Europe became divided into two opposing camps that became more and more inflexible and unwilling to compromise. A series of crises in the Balkans between 1908 and 1913 set the stage for World War I.

CRISIS IN THE BALKANS During the nineteenth century, the Balkan provinces of the Ottoman Empire had gradually gained their freedom, although the rivalry

between Austria and Russia complicated the process. By 1878, Greece, Serbia, Romania, and Montenegro (mahn-tuh-NEE-groh) had become independent. Bulgaria, though not totally independent, was allowed to operate autonomously under Russian protection. Bosnia and Herzegovina (HAYRT-suh-guh-VEE-nuh) were placed under Austrian protection; Austria could occupy but not annex them.

Nevertheless, in 1908, Austria did annex the two Slavic-speaking territories. Serbia was outraged because the annexation dashed the Serbs' hopes of creating a large Serbian kingdom that would unite most of the southern

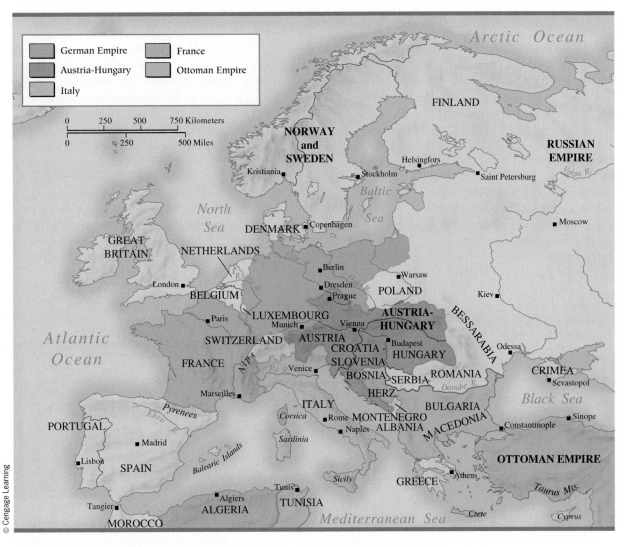

Slavs. The Russians, as protectors of their fellow Slavs, supported the Serbs and opposed the Austrian action. Backed by the Russians, the Serbs prepared for war against Austria. At this point, William II intervened and demanded that the Russians accept Austria's annexation of Bosnia and Herzegovina or face war with Germany. Weakened from their defeat in the Russo-Japanese War in 1904–1905, the Russians backed down but vowed revenge. Two wars between the Balkan states in 1912–1913 further embittered the inhabitants of the region and generated more tensions among the great powers.

The Balkans in 1913

© Cengage Learning

Serbia's desire to create a large Serbian kingdom remained unfulfilled. In their frustration, Serbian nationalists blamed the Austrians. Austria-Hungary was convinced that Serbia was a mortal threat to its empire and must at some point be crushed. As Serbia's chief supporters, the Russians were determined not to back down again in the event of a confrontation with Austria or Germany in the Balkans. The allies of Austria-Hungary and Russia were also determined to be more supportive of their respective allies in another crisis. By the beginning of 1914, two armed camps viewed each other with suspicion.

CHAPTER SUMMARY

In 1815, a conservative order had been reestablished throughout Europe, but the forces of liberalism and nationalism, unleashed by the French Revolution and now reinforced by the spread of industrialization, were pushing Europe into a new era of political and social change. Industrialization spread rapidly from Great Britain to the Continent and United States. As cities grew, the plight of Europe's new working class became the focus of new political philosophies, notably the work of Karl Marx who sought to liberate the oppressed proletariat. At the same time, middle-class industrialists adopted the political philosophy of liberalism, espousing freedom in politics and in economic activity. By the mid-nineteenth century, nationalism threatened the status quo in divided Germany and Italy and the multiethnic Austrian Empire.

In 1848, revolutions erupted across the Continent. A republic with universal manhood suffrage was established in France, but within four years, it had given way to the Second Empire. The Frankfurt Assembly worked to create a unified Germany, but it also failed. In the Austrian Empire, the liberal demands of the Hungarians and other nationalities were eventually put down, In Italy, too, uprisings against Austrian rule failed when conservatives regained control.

By 1871, nationalist forces had prevailed in Germany and Italy. The combined activities of Count Cavour and

Giuseppe Garibaldi finally led to the unification of Italy in 1870. Under the guidance of Otto von Bismarck, Prussia engaged in wars with Denmark, Austria, and France before it finally achieved the goal of Germany national unification in 1871. Reform characterized developments in other Western states. Austria created the

dual monarchy of Austria-Hungary. Russia's defeat in the Crimean War led to reforms under Alexander II, which included the freeing of the Russian serfs.

Between 1871 and 1914, the functions of the national state began to expand as social insurance measures such as protection against illnesses and old age were adopted to appease the working masses. Liberal and democratic reforms, especially in western Europe, brought the possibility for greater participation in the political process. Nevertheless, large minorities, especially in the multiethnic empires controlled by the Austrians, Ottomans, and Russians, had not achieved the goal of their own national states. Meanwhile, the collapse of the Ottoman Empire caused Russia and Austria to set their sights on territories in the Balkans. As Germany's power increased, the European nations formed new alliances that helped maintain a balance of power but also led to the creation of large armies. The alliances also generated tensions that were unleashed when Europeans were unable to resolve a series of crises in the Balkans and rushed into the catastrophic carnage of World War I.

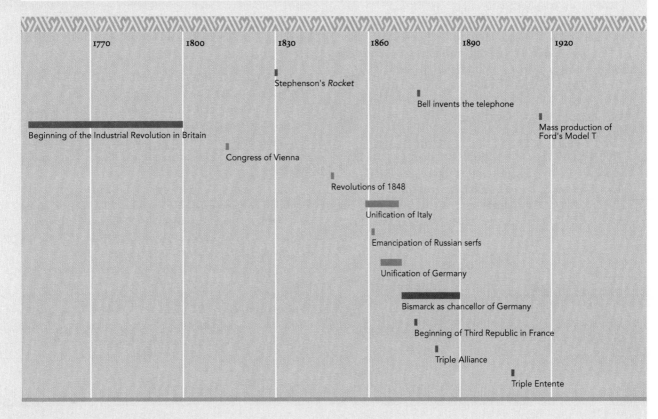

1770   1800   1830   1860   1890   1920

Stephenson's *Rocket*

Bell invents the telephone

Mass production of Ford's Model T

Beginning of the Industrial Revolution in Britain

Congress of Vienna

Revolutions of 1848

Unification of Italy

Emancipation of Russian serfs

Unification of Germany

Bismarck as chancellor of Germany

Beginning of Third Republic in France

Triple Alliance

Triple Entente

CHAPTER REVIEW

Upon Reflection

Q What are the major similarities and differences between the First and Second Industrial Revolutions?

Q What were the chief ideas associated with liberalism and nationalism, and how were these ideas put into practice in the first half of the nineteenth century?

Q To what extent were the major goals of establishing liberal practices and achieving the growth of political democracy realized in Great Britain, France, Germany, Austria-Hungary, and Russia between 1871 and 1914?

Key Terms

proletariat (p. 495)
Marxism (p. 500)
class struggle (p. 500)
revisionism (p. 500)
revolutionary socialism (p. 500)
legitimacy (p. 502)
conservatism (p. 502)

intervention (p. 503)
liberalism (p. 503)
nationalism (p. 503)
Realpolitik (p. 507)
Ausgleich (p. 510)
mass politics (p. 511)

Suggested Reading

THE INDUSTRIAL REVOLUTION AND ITS IMPACT A good introduction to the Industrial Revolution is **J. Horn,** *The Industrial Revolution* (Westport, Conn., 2007). On the role of the British, see **K. Morgan,** *The Birth of Industrial Britain: Social Change, 1750–1850* (New York, 2004). A work on female labor patterns is **J. Rendall,** *Women in an Industrializing Society: England, 1750–1880* (Oxford, 2002).

For a global approach to the modern economy, see **K. Pomeranz,** *The Great Deliverance: China, Europe, and the Making of the Modern World Economy* (Princeton, N.J., 2002).

THE GROWTH OF INDUSTRIAL PROSPERITY The Second Industrial Revolution is well covered in **A. S. Milward** and **S. B. Saul**, *The Development of the Economies of Continental Europe, 1850–1914* (Cambridge, Mass., 1977). The impact of the new technology on European thought is imaginatively discussed in **S. Kern**, *The Culture of Time and Space, 1880–1914*, rev. ed. (Cambridge, Mass., 2003). On Marx, the standard work is **D. McLellan**, *Karl Marx: His Life and Thought*, 4th ed. (New York, 2006).

THE GROWTH OF NATIONALISM, 1814–1848 For a good survey of the nineteenth century, see **R. Gildea**, *Barricades and Borders: Europe, 1800–1914*, 3rd ed. (Oxford, 2003). Also valuable is **T. C. W. Blanning, ed.**, *Nineteenth Century: Europe, 1789–1914* (Oxford, 2000).

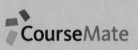

Visit the CourseMate website at www.cengagebrain.com for additional study tools and review materials for this chapter.

For a survey of the period 1814–1848, see **M. Lyons**, *Postrevolutionary Europe, 1815–1856* (New York, 2006). The best introduction to the revolutions of 1848 is **J. Sperber**, *The European Revolutions, 1848–1851*, 2nd ed. (New York, 2005).

NATIONAL UNIFICATION AND THE NATIONAL STATE, 1848–1871 The unification of Italy can be examined in **B. Derek** and **E. F. Biagini**, *The Risorgimento and the Unification of Italy*, 2nd ed. (London, 2002). The unification of Germany can be pursued first in a biography of Bismarck, **E. Feuchtwanger**, *Bismarck* (London, 2002).

Louis Napoleon's role can be examined in **J. F. McMillan**, *Napoleon III* (New York, 1991). On the Austrian Empire, see **R. Okey**, *The Habsburg Monarchy* (New York, 2001). Imperial Russia is covered in **T. Chapman**, *Imperial Russia, 1801–1905* (London, 2001). On Victorian Britain, see **W. L. Arnstein**, *Queen Victoria* (New York, 2005).

THE EUROPEAN STATE, 1871–1914 The domestic politics of the period can be examined in the general works listed above. See also **J. Sperber**, *Europe 1850–1914* (New York, 2009).

The Americas and Society and Culture in the West

A portrait of Toussaint L'Ouverture, leader of the Haitian independence movement

CHAPTER OUTLINE AND FOCUS QUESTIONS

┌─ CRITICAL THINKING ─────────────────

Q In what ways were the intellectual and cultural developments in the Western world between 1800 and 1914 related to the economic, social, and political developments?

NATIONALISM—one of the major forces for change in Europe in the nineteenth century—also affected Latin America as the colonial peoples there overthrew their Spanish and Portuguese masters and began the process of creating new national states. An unusual revolution in Haiti preceded the main independence movements. François-Dominique Toussaint L'Ouverture (frahn-SWAH-doh-muh-NEEK too-SANH loo-vayr-TOOR), the grandson of an African king, was born a slave in Saint-Domingue (san doh-MAYNG)—the western third of the island of Hispaniola, a French sugar colony—in 1746. Educated by his godfather, Toussaint was able to amass a small private fortune through his own talents and the generosity of his French master. When black slaves in Saint-Domingue, inspired by news of the French Revolution, revolted in 1791, Toussaint became their leader. For years, Toussaint and his ragtag army struck at the French. By 1801, after his army had come to control Saint-Domingue, Toussaint assumed the role of ruler and issued a constitution that freed all slaves.

But Napoleon Bonaparte refused to accept Toussaint's control of France's richest colony and sent a French army of 23,000 men under General Leclerc (luh-KLAHR), his brother-in-law, to crush the rebellion. Although yellow fever took its toll on the French, their superior numbers and weapons enabled them to gain the upper hand. Toussaint was tricked into surrendering in 1802 by Leclerc's promise: "You will not find a more sincere friend than myself." Instead, Toussaint was arrested, put in chains, and shipped to France, where he died a year later in a dungeon. The western part of Hispaniola, now called Haiti, however, became the first independent state in Latin America when Toussaint's lieutenants drove out the French forces in 1804. Haiti was only one of a number of places in the Americas where new nations were formed during the nineteenth century. Indeed, nation building was prominent in North America as the United States and Canada expanded.

As national states in both the Western Hemisphere and Europe were evolving in the nineteenth century, significant changes were occurring in society and culture. The rapid economic changes of the nineteenth century led to the emergence of mass society in the Western world, which meant improvements for the lower classes, who benefited from the extension of voting rights, a better standard of living, and universal education. The coming of mass society also created new roles for the governments of nation-states, which now fostered national loyalty, created mass armies by conscription, and took more responsibility for public health and housing in their cities. Cultural and intellectual changes paralleled these social developments, and after 1870, Western philosophers, writers, and artists began exploring modern cultural expressions that questioned traditional ideas and increasingly provoked a crisis of confidence.

Latin America in the Nineteenth and Early Twentieth Centuries

Q **FOCUS QUESTIONS:** What role did liberalism and nationalism play in Latin America between 1800 and 1870? What were the major economic, social, and political trends in Latin America in the late nineteenth and early twentieth centuries?

The Spanish and Portuguese colonial empires in Latin America had been integrated into the traditional monarchical structure of Europe for centuries. When that structure was challenged, first by the ideas of the Enlightenment and then by the upheavals of the Napoleonic era, Latin America encountered the possibility of change. How it responded to that possibility, however, was determined in part by conditions unique to the region.

The Wars for Independence

By the end of the eighteenth century, the ideas of the Enlightenment and the new political ideals stemming from the successful revolution in North America were beginning to influence the creole elites (descendants of Europeans who became permanent inhabitants of Latin America). The principles of the equality of all people in the eyes of the law, free trade, and a free press proved very attractive. Sons of creoles, such as Simón Bolívar (see-MOHN boh-LEE-var) (1783–1830) and José de San Martín (hoh-SAY day san mar-TEEN) (1778–1850) who became leaders of the independence movement, even went to European universities, where they imbibed the ideas of the Enlightenment. These Latin American elites, joined by a growing class of merchants, especially resented the domination of their trade by Spain and Portugal.

NATIONALISTIC REVOLTS IN LATIN AMERICA The creole elites soon began to use their new ideas to denounce the rule of the Iberian monarchs and the peninsulars (Spanish and Portuguese officials who resided in Latin America for political and economic gain). As Bolívar said in 1815, "It would be easier to have the two continents meet than to reconcile the spirits of Spain and America."[1] When Napoleon Bonaparte toppled the monarchies of Spain and Portugal, the authority of the Spaniards and Portuguese in their colonial empires was weakened, and between 1807 and 1825, a series of revolts enabled most of Latin America to become independent.

As described in the chapter-opening vignette, the first revolt was actually a successful slave rebellion. Led by Toussaint L'Ouverture (1746–1803), the revolt resulted in the formation of Haiti as the first independent postcolonial state in Latin America in 1804.

Beginning in 1810, Mexico, too, experienced a revolt, fueled initially by the desire of the creole elites to overthrow the rule of the peninsulars. The first real hero of Mexican independence was Miguel Hidalgo y Costilla (mee-GEL ee-THAHL-goh ee kahs-TEE-yuh), a parish priest in a small village about 100 miles from Mexico City. Hidalgo, who had studied the French Revolution, roused the local Indians and mestizos, many of whom were suffering from a major famine, to free themselves from the Spanish. On September 16, 1810, a crowd of Indians and mestizos, armed with clubs, machetes, and a few guns, quickly formed a mob army and attacked the Spaniards, shouting, "Long live independence and death to the Spaniards." But Hidalgo was not a good organizer, and his forces were soon crushed. A military court sentenced Hidalgo to death, but his memory lived on. In fact, September 16, the first day of the uprising, is celebrated as Mexico's Independence Day.

The participation of Indians and mestizos in Mexico's revolt against Spanish control frightened both creoles and peninsulars. Fearful of the masses, they cooperated in defeating the popular revolutionary forces. The elites—both creoles and peninsulars—then decided to overthrow Spanish rule as a way of preserving their own power. They selected a creole military leader, Augustín de Iturbide (ah-goo-STEEN day ee-tur-BEE-day), as their leader and the first emperor of Mexico in 1821. The new government fostered neither political nor economic changes, and it soon became apparent that Mexican independence had benefited primarily the creole elites.

Independence movements elsewhere in Latin America were likewise the work of elites—primarily creoles—who overthrew Spanish rule and set up new governments that they could dominate. José de San Martín of Argentina and Simón Bolívar of Venezuela, leaders of the independence movement, were both members of the creole elite, and both were hailed as the liberators of South America.

THE EFFORTS OF BOLÍVAR AND SAN MARTÍN Simón Bolívar has long been regarded as the George Washington of Latin America. Born into a wealthy Venezuelan family, he was introduced as a young man to the ideas of the Enlightenment. While in Rome in 1805 to witness the coronation of Napoleon as king of Italy, he committed himself to free his people from Spanish control. He vowed, "I swear before the God of my fathers, by my fathers themselves, by my honor and by my country, that my arm shall not rest nor my mind be at peace until I have broken the chains that bind me by the will and power of Spain."[2] When he returned to South America, Bolívar began to lead the bitter struggle for independence in Venezuela as well as other parts of northern South America. Although he was acclaimed as the "liberator" of Venezuela in 1813 by the people, it was not until 1821 that he definitively defeated Spanish forces there. He went on to liberate Colombia, Ecuador, and Peru. Already in 1819, he had become president of Venezuela, at the time part of a federation that included Colombia and Ecuador. Bolívar was well aware of the difficulties in establishing stable republican governments in Latin America (see the box on p. 520).

While Bolívar was busy liberating northern South America from the Spanish, José de San Martín was concentrating his efforts on the southern part of the continent. Son of a Spanish army officer in Argentina, San Martín himself went to Spain and pursued a military career in the Spanish army. In 1811, after serving twenty-two years, he learned of the liberation movement in his native Argentina, abandoned his military career in Spain, and returned to his homeland in March 1812. Argentina had already been freed from Spanish control, but San Martín believed that the Spaniards must be removed from all of South America if any nation was to remain free. In January 1817, he led his forces over the high Andes Mountains, an amazing feat in itself. Two-thirds of their pack mules and horses died during the difficult journey. Many of the soldiers suffered from lack of oxygen and severe cold while crossing mountain passes more than 2 miles above sea level. The arrival of San Martín's troops in Chile completely surprised the Spaniards, whose forces were routed at the Battle of Chacabuco (chahk-ah-BOO-koh) on February 12, 1817.

In 1821, San Martín moved on to Lima, Peru, the center of Spanish authority. Convinced that he would be unable to complete the liberation of all of Peru, San Martín welcomed the arrival of Bolívar and his forces. As he wrote to Bolívar, "For me it would have been the height of happiness to end the war of independence under the orders of a general to whom [South] America owes its freedom. Destiny orders it otherwise, and one must resign oneself to it."[3] Highly disappointed, San Martín left South America for Europe, where he remained until his death in 1850. Meanwhile, Bolívar took on the task of crushing the last significant Spanish army at Ayacucho (ah-ya-KOO-choh) on December 9, 1824. By then, Peru, Uruguay, Paraguay, Colombia, Venezuela, Argentina, Bolivia, and Chile had all become free states. In 1823, the Central American states became independent

Simón Bolívar on Government in Latin America

POLITICS & GOVERNMENT

Simón Bolívar is acclaimed as the man who liberated Latin America from Spanish control. His interest in history and the ideas of the Enlightenment also led him to speculate on how Latin American nations would be governed after their freedom was obtained. This selection is taken from a letter that he wrote to the British governor of Jamaica.

Simón Bolívar, *The Jamaica Letter*

It is . . . difficult to foresee the future fate of the New World, to set down its political principles, or to prophesy what manner of government it will adopt. . . . We inhabit a world apart, separated by broad seas. We are young in the ways of almost all the arts and sciences, although in a certain manner, we are old in the ways of civilized society. . . . But we scarcely retain a vestige of what once was; we are, moreover, neither Indian nor European, but a species midway between the legitimate proprietors of this country and the Spanish usurpers. In short, though Americans by birth we derive our rights from Europe, and we have to assert these rights against the rights of the natives, and at the same time we must defend ourselves against the invaders. This places us in a most extraordinary and involved situation. . . .

The role of the inhabitants of the American hemisphere has for centuries been purely passive. Politically they were nonexistent. We are still in a position lower than slavery, and therefore it is more difficult for us to rise to the enjoyment of freedom. . . . States are slaves because of either the nature or the misuse of their constitutions; a people is therefore enslaved when the government, by its nature or its vices, infringes on and usurps the rights of the citizen or subject. Applying these principles, we find that America was denied not only its freedom but even an active and effective tyranny. . . .

It is harder, Montesquieu has written, to release a nation from servitude than to enslave a free nation. This truth is proven by the annals of all times, which reveal that most free nations have been put under the yoke, but very few enslaved nations have recovered their liberty. Despite the convictions of history, South Americans have made efforts to obtain liberal, even perfect, institutions, doubtless out of that instinct to aspire to the greatest possible happiness, which, common to all men, is bound to follow in civil societies founded on the principles of justice, liberty, and equality. But are we capable of maintaining in proper balance the difficult charge of a republic? Is it conceivable that a newly emancipated people can soar to the heights of liberty . . . ? Such a marvel is inconceivable and without precedent. There is no reasonable probability to bolster our hopes.

More than anyone, I desire to see America fashioned into the greatest nation in the world, greatest not so much by virtue of her area and wealth as by her freedom and glory. Although I seek perfection for the government of my country, I cannot persuade myself that the New World can, at the moment, be organized as a great republic. Since it is impossible, I dare not desire it; yet much less do I desire to have all America a monarchy because this plan is not only impracticable but also impossible. Wrongs now existing could not be righted, and our emancipation would be fruitless. The American states need the care of paternal governments to heal the sores and wounds of despotism and war.

Q *What problems did Bolívar foresee for Spanish America's political future? Do you think he believed in democracy? Why or why not?*

Source: Simón Bolívar, *Selected Writings*, ed. H. A. Bierck, trans. L Berrand (New York, 1951), pp. 106, 108, 112–114.

and in 1838–1839 divided into five republics (Guatemala, El Salvador, Honduras, Costa Rica, and Nicaragua). Earlier, in 1822, the prince regent of Brazil had declared Brazil's independence from Portugal.

INDEPENDENCE AND THE MONROE DOCTRINE In the early 1820s, only one major threat remained to the newly won independence of the Latin American states. Reveling in their success in crushing rebellions in Spain and Italy, the victorious continental European powers favored the use of troops to restore Spanish control in Latin America. This time, Britain's opposition to intervention prevailed. Eager to gain access to an entire continent for investment and trade, the British proposed joint

The Liberators of South America. José de San Martín and Simón Bolívar are hailed as the leaders of the South American independence movement. In the painting on the left, by Théodore Géricault (zhay-rih-KOH), a French Romantic painter, San Martín is shown leading his troops at the Battle of Chacabuco in Chile in 1817. The painting on the right shows Bolívar leading his troops across the Andes in 1823 to fight in Peru. This depiction of impeccably uniformed troops moving in perfect formation through the snow of the Andes, by the Chilean artist Franco Gomez, is, of course, highly unrealistic.

action with the United States against European interference in Latin America. Distrustful of British motives, President James Monroe acted alone in 1823, guaranteeing the independence of the new Latin American nations and warning against any further European intervention in the Americas under what is known as the Monroe Doctrine. Even more important to Latin American independence than American words was Britain's navy. All of the continental European powers were reluctant to challenge British naval power, which stood between Latin America and any European invasion force.

The Difficulties of Nation Building

As Simón Bolívar had foreseen, the new Latin American nations (see Map 20.1), most of which began as republics, faced a number of serious problems between 1830 and 1870. The wars for independence themselves had resulted in a staggering loss of population, property, and livestock. At the same time, disputes arose between nations over their precise boundaries.

POLITICAL DIFFICULTIES The new nations of Latin America established republican governments, but they had had no experience in ruling themselves. Due to the insecurities prevalent after independence, strong leaders known as **caudillos** (kah-DEEL-yohz *or* kow-THEEL-yohz) came to power. Caudillos at the national level were generally one of two types. One group, who supported the elites, consisted of autocrats who controlled (and often abused) state revenues, centralized power, and kept the new national states together. Sometimes they were also modernizers who built roads and canals, ports, and schools. These caudillos were usually supported by the Catholic Church, the rural aristocracy, and the army, which emerged from the wars of independence as a powerful political force that often made and deposed governments. Many caudillos, in fact, were former army leaders.

In contrast, other caudillos were supported by the masses, became extremely popular, and served as instruments for radical change. Juan Manuel de Rosas (WAHN mahn-WEL day ROH-sas), for example, who led

MAP 20.1 Latin America in the First Half of the Nineteenth Century. Latin American colonies took advantage of Spain's weakness during the Napoleonic wars to fight for independence, beginning with Argentina in 1810 and spreading throughout the region over the next decade with the help of leaders like Simón Bolívar and José de San Martín.

Q *How many South American countries are sources of rivers that feed the Amazon, and roughly what percentage of the continent is contained within the Amazon's watershed?*

Argentina from 1829 to 1852, became very popular by favoring Argentine interests against foreigners.

ECONOMIC PATTERNS Although political independence brought economic independence, old patterns were quickly reestablished. Instead of Spain and Portugal, Great Britain now dominated the Latin American economy. British merchants arrived in large numbers, and British investors poured in funds, especially into the mining industry. Old trade patterns soon reemerged. Since Latin America served as a source of raw materials and foodstuffs for the industrializing nations of Europe and the United States, exports—especially wheat, tobacco, wool, sugar, coffee, and hides—to the North Atlantic countries increased noticeably. At the same time, finished consumer goods, especially textiles, were imported in increasing quantities, causing a decline in industrial production in Latin America. The emphasis on exporting raw materials and importing finished products ensured the ongoing domination of the Latin American economy by foreigners.

SOCIAL CONDITIONS A fundamental underlying problem for all of the new Latin American nations was the persistent domination of society by the landed elites. Large estates remained an important aspect of Latin America's economic and social life. After independence, the size of these estates expanded even more. By 1848, the Sánchez Navarro (SAHN-ches nuh-VAH-roh) family in Mexico owned seventeen haciendas (hah-see-EN-duhz), or plantations, covering 16 million acres. Estates were often so large that they could not be farmed efficiently. As one Latin American newspaper put it, "The huge fortunes have the unfortunate tendency to grow even larger, and their owners possess vast tracts of land, which lie fallow and abandoned. Their greed for land does not equal their ability to use it intelligently and actively."[4]

Land remained the basis of wealth, social prestige, and political power throughout the nineteenth century. The Latin American elites tended to identify with European standards of progress, which worked to their benefit, while the masses gained little. Landed elites ran governments, controlled courts, and maintained the system of debt peonage that provided large landowners with a supply of cheap labor. These landowners made enormous profits by concentrating on specialized crops for export, such as coffee, while the masses, left without land to grow basic food crops, lived in dire poverty.

Tradition and Change in the Latin American Economy and Society

After 1870, Latin America began to experience an era of rapid economic growth based to a large extent on the export of a few basic commodities, such as wheat and beef from Argentina, coffee from Brazil, nitrates from Chile, coffee and bananas from Central America, and sugar and silver from Peru. These foodstuffs and raw materials were exchanged for finished goods—textiles, machines, and luxury goods—from Europe and the United States. Despite their economic growth, Latin American nations remained economic colonies of Western nations.

Old patterns also still largely prevailed in society. Rural elites dominated their estates and their workers. Although slavery was abolished by 1888, former slaves and their descendants were at the bottom of their society. The Indians remained poverty-stricken.

One result of the new prosperity that came from increased exports was growth in the middle sectors of Latin American society—lawyers, merchants, shopkeepers, businesspeople, schoolteachers, professors, bureaucrats, and military officers. These middle sectors, which made up only 5 to 10 percent of the population, depending on the country, were hardly large enough in numbers to constitute a true middle class. Nevertheless, after 1900, the middle sectors continued to expand. They lived in the cities, sought education and decent incomes, and increasingly saw the United States as the model to emulate, especially in regard to industrialization and education.

As Latin American exports increased, so did the working class, and that in turn led to the growth of labor unions, especially after 1914. Radical unions often advocated the use of the general strike as an instrument for change. By and large, however, the governing elites succeeded in stifling the political influence of the working class by restricting workers' right to vote.

The need for industrial labor also led Latin American countries to encourage immigration from Europe. Between 1880 and 1914, 3 million Europeans, primarily Italians and Spaniards, settled in Argentina. More than 100,000 Europeans, mostly Italian, Portuguese, and Spanish, arrived in Brazil each year between 1891 and 1900.

As in Europe and the United States, industrialization led to urbanization, evident in both the emergence of new cities and the rapid growth of old ones. Buenos Aires (the "Paris" of South America) had 750,000 inhabitants by 1900 and 2 million by 1914—a fourth of Argentina's population.

Political Change in Latin America

Latin America also experienced a political transformation after 1870. Large landowners began to take a more direct interest in national politics and even in governing. In Argentina and Chile, for example, landholding elites controlled the governments, and although they produced constitutions similar to those of the United States and European nations, they ensured that they would maintain power by restricting voting rights.

In some countries, large landowners supported dictators who would protect their interests. José de la Cruz Porfirio Díaz (hoh-SAY day lah KROOZ por-FEER-yoh DEE-ahs) (1830–1915), who ruled Mexico from 1876 to 1910, created a conservative, centralized government with the support of the army, foreign capitalists, large landowners, and the Catholic Church. Nevertheless, there were forces for change in Mexico that led to revolution in 1910.

During Díaz's dictatorial regime, the real wages of the working class declined. Moreover, 95 percent of the rural population owned no land, while about a thousand families owned almost all of Mexico. When a liberal landowner, Francisco Madero (frahn-SEES-koh muh-DERR-oh) (1873–1913), forced Díaz from power, he opened the door to a wider revolution. Madero's ineffectiveness triggered a demand for agrarian reform led by

CHRONOLOGY	Latin America	
Revolt in Mexico		1810
Bolívar and San Martín free most of South America		1810–1824
Augustín de Iturbide becomes emperor of Mexico		1821
Brazil gains independence from Portugal		1822
Monroe Doctrine		1823
Rule of Porfirio Díaz in Mexico		1876–1910
Mexican Revolution begins		1910

Emiliano Zapata (eh-mee-LYAH-noh zup-PAH-tuh) (1873–1919), who aroused the masses of landless peasants and began to seize the estates of the wealthy landholders. The ensuing revolution caused untold destruction to the Mexican economy. Finally, a new constitution in 1917 established a strong presidency, initiated land reform policies, established limits on foreign investors, and set an agenda for social welfare for workers.

By this time, a new power had begun to wield its influence over Latin America. By 1900, the United States, which had begun to emerge as a great world power, began to interfere in the affairs of its southern neighbors. As a result of the Spanish-American War (1898), Cuba became a U.S. protectorate, and Puerto Rico was annexed outright by the United States. American investments in Latin America soon followed; so did American resolve to protect these investments. Between 1898 and 1934, American military forces were sent to Cuba, Mexico, Guatemala, Honduras, Nicaragua, Panama, Colombia, Haiti, and the Dominican Republic to protect American interests. At the same time, the United States became the chief foreign investor in Latin America.

Emiliano Zapata. The inability of Francisco Madero to carry out far-reaching reforms led to a more radical upheaval in the Mexican countryside. Emiliano Zapata led a band of Indians in a revolt against the large landowners of southern Mexico and issued his own demands for land reform.

The North American Neighbors: The United States and Canada

Q **FOCUS QUESTIONS:** What role did nationalism and liberalism play in the United States and Canada between 1800 and 1870? What economic, social, and political trends were evident in the United States and Canada between 1870 and 1914?

Whereas Latin America had been colonized by Spain and Portugal, the colonies established in North America were part of the British Empire and thus differed in various ways from their southern neighbors. Although they gained their freedom from the British at different times, both the United States and Canada emerged as independent and prosperous nations whose political systems owed much to British political thought. In the nineteenth century, both the United States and Canada faced difficult obstacles in achieving national unity.

The Growth of the United States

The U.S. Constitution, ratified in 1789, committed the United States to two of the major influences of the first half of the nineteenth century, liberalism and nationalism. Initially, this constitutional commitment to national unity was challenged by divisions over the power of the federal government versus the individual states. A strong force for national unity came from the Supreme Court while John Marshall (1755–1835) was chief justice from 1801 to 1835. Marshall made the Supreme Court into an important national institution by asserting the right of the Court to overrule an act of Congress if the Court found it to be in violation of the Constitution. Under Marshall, the Supreme Court contributed further to establishing the supremacy of the national government by curbing the actions of state courts and legislatures.

The election of Andrew Jackson (1767–1845) as president in 1828 opened a new era in American politics, the era of mass democracy. The electorate was expanded by dropping property qualifications; by the 1830s, suffrage had been extended to almost all adult white males. During the period from 1815 to 1850, the traditional liberal belief in the improvement of human beings was also given concrete expression through the establishment of detention schools for juvenile delinquents and new penal institutions, both motivated by the liberal belief that the right kind of environment would rehabilitate wayward individuals.

SLAVERY AND THE COMING OF WAR By the mid-nineteenth century, however, American national unity was increasingly threatened by the issue of slavery. Both North and South had grown dramatically in population during the first half of the nineteenth century, but in different ways. The cotton economy and social structure of the South were based on the exploitation of enslaved black Africans and their descendants. Although the importation of new slaves had been barred in 1808, there were 4 million slaves in the South by 1860—four times the number sixty years earlier. The cotton economy depended on plantation-based slavery, and the South was determined to maintain its slaves. In the North, many people feared the spread of slavery into western territories. The issue first arose in the 1810s as new states were being created by the rush of settlers beyond the Mississippi. The free states of the North feared the prospect of a slave-state majority in the national government.

As polarization over the issue of slavery intensified, compromise became less feasible. When Abraham Lincoln, the man who had said in a speech in Illinois in 1858 that "this government cannot endure permanently half slave and half free," was elected president in November 1860, the die was cast. Lincoln, the Republicans' second presidential candidate, carried only 2 of the 1,109 counties in the South; the Republican Party was not even on the ballot in ten southern states. On December 20, 1860, a South Carolina convention voted to repeal the state's ratification of the U.S. Constitution. In February 1861, six more southern states did the same, and a rival nation, the Confederate States of America, was formed. In April, fighting erupted between North and South.

THE CIVIL WAR The American Civil War (1861–1865) was an extraordinarily bloody struggle, a foretaste of the total war to come in the twentieth century. More than 600,000 soldiers died, either in battle or from deadly infectious diseases spawned by filthy camp conditions. The northern, or Union, forces enjoyed a formidable advantage in numbers of troops and material resources, but to southerners, those assets were not decisive. As they saw it, the Confederacy only had to defend the South from invasion, whereas the Union had to conquer the South. Southerners also believed that the dependence of manufacturers in the North and the European countries on southern raw cotton would lead to antiwar sentiment in the North and support abroad for the South.

All these southern calculations meant little in the long run. Over a period of four years, the Union states of the North mobilized their superior assets and gradually wore down the Confederate forces of the South. As the war dragged on, it had the effect of radicalizing public opinion in the North. What began as a war to save the Union became a war against slavery. On January 1, 1863, Lincoln issued his Emancipation Proclamation, declaring most of the nation's slaves "forever free" (see the box on p. 510 in Chapter 19). An increasingly effective Union blockade of the ports of the South, combined with a shortage of fighting men, made the Confederate cause desperate by the end of 1864. The final push of Union troops under General Ulysses S. Grant forced General Robert E. Lee's Confederate Army to surrender on April 9, 1865. Although problems lay ahead, the Union victory reunited the country and confirmed that the United States would thereafter again be "one nation, indivisible."

The Rise of the United States

Four years of bloody civil war had restored American national unity. The old South had been destroyed; one-fifth of its adult white male population had been killed, and 4 million black slaves had been freed. For a while at least, a program of radical change in the South was attempted. Slavery was formally abolished by the Thirteenth Amendment to the Constitution in 1865, and the Fourteenth and Fifteenth Amendments extended citizenship to blacks and gave black men the right to vote. Radical Reconstruction in the early 1870s tried to create a new South based on the principle of the equality of black and white people, but the changes were soon mostly undone. Militia organizations, such as the Ku Klux Klan, used violence to discourage blacks from voting. A new system of sharecropping made blacks once again economically dependent on white landowners. New state laws made it nearly impossible for blacks to exercise their right to vote. By the end of the 1870s, supporters of white supremacy were back in power everywhere in the South.

The Dead at Antietam. National unity in the United States dissolved over the issue of slavery and led to a bloody civil war that cost 600,000 American lives. This photograph shows the southern dead after the Battle of Antietam on September 17, 1862. The invention of photography in the 1830s made it possible to document the horrors of war in the most graphic manner.

PROSPERITY AND PROGRESSIVISM Between 1860 and 1914, the United States made the shift from an agrarian to a mighty industrial nation. American heavy industry stood unchallenged in 1900. In that year, the Carnegie Steel Company alone produced more steel than Great Britain's entire steel industry. Industrialization also led to urbanization. Whereas 20 percent of Americans lived in cities in 1860, more than 40 percent did in 1900. Four-fifths of the population growth came from migration. Eight to 10 million Americans moved from rural areas into the cities, and 14 million foreigners came from abroad.

The United States had become the world's richest nation and greatest industrial power. Yet serious questions remained about the quality of American life. In 1890, the richest 9 percent of Americans owned an incredible 71 percent of all the wealth. Labor unrest over unsafe working conditions, strict work discipline, and periodic cycles of devastating unemployment led workers to organize. By the turn of the century, one national organization, the American Federation of Labor, had emerged as labor's dominant voice. Its lack of real power, however, was reflected in its membership figures. In 1900, it included only 8.4 percent of the American industrial labor force.

During the so-called Progressive Era after 1900, reform swept the United States. Efforts to improve living conditions in the cities included attempts to eliminate corrupt machine politics. At the state level, reforming governors sought to achieve clean government by introducing elements of direct democracy, such as direct primaries for selecting nominees for public office. State governments also enacted economic and social legislation, such as laws that governed hours, wages, and working conditions, especially for women and children.

State laws were ineffective in dealing with nationwide problems, however, and a Progressive movement soon developed at the national level. The Meat Inspection Act and Pure Food and Drug Act of 1906 provided for a limited degree of federal regulation of industrial practices. The presidency of Woodrow Wilson (1913–1921) witnessed the enactment of a graduated federal income tax and the establishment of the Federal Reserve System, which permitted the national government to play a role in important economic decisions formerly made by bankers. Like European nations, the United States was slowly adopting policies that broadened the functions of the state.

THE UNITED STATES AS A WORLD POWER At the end of the nineteenth century, the United States began to expand abroad. The Samoan Islands in the Pacific became the first important American colony; the Hawaiian Islands were next. By 1887, American settlers had gained control of the sugar industry on the Hawaiian Islands. As more Americans settled in Hawaii, they sought political power. When Queen Liliuokalani (LIL-ee-uh-woh-kuh-LAH-nee) (1838–1917) tried to strengthen the monarchy in order to keep the islands for the Hawaiian people, the U.S. government sent Marines to "protect" American lives. The queen was deposed, and Hawaii was annexed by the United States in 1898.

The defeat of Spain in the Spanish-American War in 1898 expanded the American empire to include Cuba, Puerto Rico, Guam, and the Philippines. Although the Filipinos appealed for independence, the Americans refused to grant it. As President William McKinley said, the United States had a duty "to educate the Filipinos and uplift and Christianize them," a remarkable statement in view of the fact that most of them had been Roman Catholics for centuries. It took three years and 60,000 troops to pacify the Philippines and establish U.S. control. By the beginning of the twentieth century, the United States had become another Western imperialist power.

The Making of Canada

North of the United States, the process of nation building was also making progress. Under the Treaty of Paris in 1763, Canada—or New France, as it was called—passed into the hands of the British. By 1800, most Canadians favored more autonomy, although the colonists disagreed on the form this autonomy should take. Upper Canada (now Ontario) was predominantly English speaking, whereas Lower Canada (now Quebec) was dominated by French Canadians. A dramatic increase in immigration to Canada from Great Britain (almost one million immigrants between 1815 and 1850) also fueled the desire for self-government.

In 1837, a number of Canadian groups rose in rebellion against British authority. Although the rebellions were crushed by the following year, the British government now began to seek ways to satisfy some of the Canadian demands. The U.S. Civil War proved to be a turning point. Fearful of American designs on Canada during the war, the British government finally capitulated to Canadian demands. In 1867, Parliament established the Dominion of Canada, with its own constitution. Canada now possessed a parliamentary system and ruled itself, although foreign affairs still remained under the control of the British government.

Canada faced problems of national unity between 1870 and 1914. At the beginning of 1870, the Dominion of Canada had only four provinces: Quebec, Ontario, Nova Scotia, and New Brunswick. With the addition of two more provinces in 1871—Manitoba and British Columbia—the Dominion now extended from the Atlantic Ocean to the Pacific. As the

Canada, 1914

CHRONOLOGY   The United States and Canada

United States
Election of Andrew Jackson	1828
Election of Abraham Lincoln and secession of South Carolina	1860
Civil War	1861–1865
Lincoln's Emancipation Proclamation	1863
Surrender of Robert E. Lee's Confederate Army	April 9, 1865
Spanish-American War	1898
Presidency of Woodrow Wilson	1913–1921

Canada
Rebellions	1837–1838
Formation of the Dominion of Canada	1867
Transcontinental railroad	1885
Wilfred Laurier as prime minister	1896

first prime minister, John Macdonald (1815–1891) moved to strengthen Canadian unity. He pushed for the construction of a transcontinental railroad, which was completed in 1885 and opened the western lands to industrial and commercial development. This also led to the incorporation of two more provinces—Alberta and Saskatchewan—into the Dominion of Canada in 1905.

Real unity was difficult to achieve, however, because of the distrust between the English-speaking majority and the French-speaking Canadians living primarily in Quebec. Wilfred Laurier (LOR-ee-ay), who became the first French Canadian prime minister in 1896, was able to reconcile Canada's two major groups and resolve the issue of separate schools for French Canadians. During Laurier's administration, industrialization boomed, especially the production of textiles, furniture, and railway equipment. Hundreds of thousands of immigrants, primarily from central and eastern Europe, also flowed into Canada. Many settled on lands in the west, thus helping populate Canada's vast territories.

The Emergence of Mass Society

Q FOCUS QUESTION: What is meant by the term *mass society*, and what were its main characteristics?

While new states were developing in the Western Hemisphere in the nineteenth century, a new kind of society—a **mass society**—was emerging in Europe, especially in the second half of the nineteenth century, as a result of rapid economic and social changes. For the lower classes, mass society brought voting rights, an improved standard of living, and access to education. At the same time, however, mass society also made possible the development of organizations that manipulated the populations of the **nation-states**. To understand this mass society, we need to examine some aspects of its structure.

The New Urban Environment

One of the most important consequences of industrialization and the population explosion of the nineteenth century was urbanization. In the course of the nineteenth century, more and more people came to live in cities. In 1800, city dwellers constituted 40 percent of the population in Britain, 25 percent in France and Germany, and only 10 percent in eastern Europe. By 1914, urban residents had increased to 80 percent of the population in Britain, 45 percent in France, 60 percent in Germany, and 30 percent in eastern Europe. The size of cities also expanded dramatically, especially in industrialized countries. Between 1800 and 1900, London's population grew from 960,000 to 6.5 million and Berlin's from 172,000 to 2.7 million.

Urban populations grew faster than the general population primarily because of the vast migration from rural areas to cities. But cities also grew faster in the second half of the nineteenth century because health and living conditions were improving as urban reformers and city officials used new technology to improve urban life. Following the reformers' advice, city governments set up boards of health to improve the quality of housing and instituted regulations requiring all new buildings to have running water and internal drainage systems.

Middle-class reformers also focused on the housing needs of the working class. Overcrowded, disease-ridden slums were seen as dangerous not only to physical health but also to the political and moral health of the entire nation. V. A. Huber, a German housing reformer, wrote in 1861: "Certainly it would not be too much to say that the home is the communal embodiment of family life. Thus, the purity of the dwelling is almost as important for the family as is the cleanliness of the body for the individual."[5] To Huber, good housing was a prerequisite for stable family life, and without stable family life, society would fall apart.

Early efforts to attack the housing problem emphasized the middle-class, liberal belief in the power of private enterprise. By the 1880s, as the number and size of cities continued to mushroom, governments concluded that private enterprise could not solve the housing crisis. In 1890, a British law empowered local town councils to construct cheap housing for the working classes. More

and more, governments were stepping into areas of activity that they would not have touched earlier.

The Social Structure of Mass Society

At the top of European society stood a wealthy elite, constituting but 5 percent of the population while controlling between 30 and 40 percent of its wealth. In the course of the nineteenth century, landed aristocrats had joined with the most successful industrialists, bankers, and merchants (the wealthy upper middle class) to form a new elite. Marriage also united the two groups. Daughters of business tycoons gained titles, while aristocratic heirs gained new sources of cash. Members of this elite, whether aristocratic or middle class in background, assumed leadership roles in government bureaucracies and military hierarchies.

The middle classes included a variety of groups. Below the upper middle class was a group that included lawyers, doctors, and members of the civil service, as well as business managers, engineers, architects, accountants, and chemists benefiting from industrial expansion. Beneath this solid and comfortable middle group was a lower middle class of small shopkeepers, traders, manufacturers, and prosperous peasants.

Standing between the lower middle class and the lower classes were new groups of white-collar workers who were the product of the Second Industrial Revolution. They were the salespeople, bookkeepers, bank tellers, telephone operators, and secretaries. Though often paid little more than skilled laborers, these white-collar workers were committed to middle-class ideals of hard work, Christian morality, and propriety.

Below the middle classes on the social scale were the working classes, who constituted almost 80 percent of the European population. Many of them were landholding peasants, agricultural laborers, and sharecroppers, especially in eastern Europe. The urban working class included skilled artisans in such traditional trades as cabinetmaking, printing, and jewelry making, along with semiskilled laborers, such as carpenters, bricklayers, and many factory workers. At the bottom of the urban working class stood the largest group of workers, the unskilled laborers. They included day laborers, who worked irregularly for very low wages, and large numbers of domestic servants, most of whom were women.

The Experiences of Women

In the nineteenth century, women remained legally inferior, economically dependent, and largely defined by family and household roles. Women struggled to change their status throughout the century.

MARRIAGE AND THE FAMILY Many women in the nineteenth century aspired to the ideal of femininity popularized by writers and poets. Alfred Lord Tennyson's poem *The Princess* expressed it well:

> Man for the field and woman for the hearth:
> Man for the sword and for the needle she:
> Man with the head and woman with the heart:
> Man to command and woman to obey;
> All else confusion.

This traditional characterization of the sexes, based on socially defined gender roles, was elevated to the status of universal male and female attributes in the nineteenth century. As the chief family wage earners, men worked outside the home for pay, while women were left with the care of the family, for which they were paid nothing. For most of the century, marriage was viewed as the only honorable career available to most women.

The most significant development in the modern family was the decline in the number of offspring born to the average woman. While some historians attribute the decline to more widespread use of coitus interruptus, or male withdrawal before ejaculation, others have emphasized female control of family size through abortion and even infanticide or abandonment. That a change in attitude occurred was apparent in the development of a movement to increase awareness of birth control

methods. Europe's first birth control clinic opened in Amsterdam in 1882.

The family was the central institution of middle-class life. Men provided the family income while women focused on household and child care. The use of domestic servants in many middle-class homes, made possible by an abundant supply of cheap labor, reduced the amount of time middle-class women had to spend on household chores. At the same time, by reducing the number of children in the family, mothers could devote more time to child care and domestic leisure.

The middle-class family fostered an ideal of togetherness. The Victorians created the family Christmas with its Yule log, Christmas tree, songs, and exchange of gifts. In the United States, Fourth of July celebrations changed from drunken revels to family picnics by the 1850s.

Women in working-class families were more accustomed to hard work. Daughters in working-class families were expected to work until they married; even after marriage, they often did piecework at home to help support the family. For the children of the working classes, childhood was over by the age of nine or ten, when they became apprentices or were employed at odd jobs.

Between 1890 and 1914, however, family patterns among the working class began to change. High-paying jobs in heavy industry and improvements in the standard of living made it possible for working-class families to depend on the income of husbands and the wages of grown children. By the early twentieth century, some working-class mothers could afford to stay at home, following the pattern of middle-class women.

THE MOVEMENT FOR WOMEN'S RIGHTS Modern European feminism, or the movement for women's rights, had its beginnings during the French Revolution, when some women advocated equality for women based on the doctrine of natural rights. In the 1830s, a number of women in the United States and Europe, who worked together in several reform movements, argued for the right of women to divorce and own property. These early efforts were not overly successful; women did not gain the right to their own property until 1870 in Britain, 1900 in Germany and 1907 in France.

Divorce and property rights were only a beginning for the women's movement, however. Some middle- and upper-middle-class women gained access to higher education, and others sought entry into

A Middle-Class Family. Nineteenth-century middle-class moralists considered the family the fundamental pillar of a healthy society. The family was a crucial institution in middle-class life, and togetherness constituted one of the important ideals of the middle-class family. This painting by William P. Frith, titled *Many Happy Returns of the Day*, shows a family birthday celebration for a little girl in which grandparents, parents, and children are taking part. The servant at the left holds the presents for the little girl.

occupations dominated by men. The first to fall was teaching. As medical training was largely closed to women, they sought alternatives in the development of nursing. Nursing pioneers included the British nurse Florence Nightingale, whose efforts during the Crimean War (1854–1856), along with those of Clara Barton in the American Civil War (1861–1865), transformed nursing into a profession of trained, middle-class "women in white."

By the 1840s and 1850s, the movement for women's rights had entered the political arena with the call for equal political rights. Many feminists believed that the right to vote was the key to all other reforms to improve the position of women. **Suffragists** had one basic aim: the right of women to full citizenship in the nation-state.

The British women's movement was the most vocal and active in Europe. In 1903, Emmeline Pankhurst (PANK-hurst) (1858–1928) and her daughters, Christabel and Sylvia, founded the Women's Social and Political Union, which enrolled mostly middle- and upper-class women. The members of Pankhurst's organization realized the value of the media and staged unusual publicity stunts to call attention to their demands. Derisively labeled "suffragettes" by male politicians, they pelted government officials with eggs, chained themselves to lampposts, smashed the windows of department stores on fashionable shopping streets, burned railroad cars, and went on hunger strikes in jail.

Before World War I, the demands for women's rights were being heard throughout Europe and the United States, although only in Norway and some American states did women receive the right to vote before 1914. It would take the dramatic upheaval of World War I before male-dominated governments capitulated on this basic issue. At the same time, at the turn of the twentieth century, a number of "new women" became prominent. These women rejected traditional feminine roles (see the box on p. 531) and sought new freedom outside the household and new roles other than those of wives and mothers.

Education in an Age of Mass Society

Education in the early nineteenth century was primarily for the elite or the wealthier middle class, but between 1870 and 1914, most Western governments began to offer at least primary education to both boys and girls between the ages of six and twelve. States also assumed responsibility for better training of teachers by establishing teacher-training schools. By the beginning of the twentieth century, many European states, especially in northern and western Europe, were providing state-financed primary schools, salaried and trained teachers, and free, compulsory elementary education.

Why did Western nations make this commitment to **mass education**? One reason was industrialization. The new firms of the Second Industrial Revolution demanded skilled labor. Both boys and girls with an elementary education had new possibilities of jobs beyond their villages or small towns, including white-collar jobs in railways and subways, post offices, banking and shipping firms, teaching, and nursing. Mass education furnished the trained workers industrialists needed. For most students, elementary education led to apprenticeship and a job.

The chief motive for mass education, however, was political. The expansion of suffrage created the need for a more educated electorate. In parts of Europe where the Catholic Church remained in control of education, implementing a mass education system reduced the influence of the church over the electorate. Even more important, however, mass compulsory education instilled patriotism and nationalized the masses, providing an opportunity for even greater national integration. As people lost their ties to local regions and even to religion, nationalism supplied a new faith (see the comparative essay "The Rise of Nationalism" on p. 533).

Compulsory elementary education created a demand for teachers, and most of them were women. Many men viewed the teaching of children as an extension of women's "natural role" as nurturers of children. Moreover, females were paid lower salaries, in itself a considerable incentive for governments to encourage the establishment of teacher-training institutes for women. The first female colleges were really teacher-training schools. It was not until the beginning of the twentieth century that women were permitted to enter the male-dominated universities.

Leisure in an Age of Mass Society

With the Industrial Revolution came new forms of leisure. Work and leisure became opposites as leisure came to be viewed as what people do for fun after work. The new leisure hours created by the industrial system— evening hours after work, weekends, and eventually a week or two in the summer—largely determined the contours of the new **mass leisure**.

New technology created novel experiences for leisure, such as the Ferris wheel at amusement parks, while the subways and streetcars of the 1880s meant that even the working classes were no longer dependent on neighborhood facilities but could make their way to athletic games, amusement parks, and dance halls. Railroads could take people to the beaches on weekends.

By the late nineteenth century, team sports had also developed into another important form of mass leisure. Unlike the old rural games, which were spontaneous and

OPPOSING ⚔ VIEWPOINTS

Advice to Women: Two Views

FAMILY & SOCIETY

Industrialization had a strong impact on middle-class women as strict gender-based social roles became the norm. Men worked outside the home to support the family, while women provided for the needs of their children and husband at home. In the first selection, *Woman in Her Social and Domestic Character* (1842), Elizabeth Poole Sanford gives advice to middle-class women on their proper role and behavior.

Although a majority of women probably followed the nineteenth-century middle-class ideal, an increasing number of women fought for women's rights. The second selection is taken from the third act of Henrik Ibsen's 1879 play *A Doll's House*, in which the character Nora Helmer declares her independence from her husband's control.

Elizabeth Poole Sanford, *Woman in Her Social and Domestic Character*

The changes wrought by Time are many. . . .

It is thus that the sentiment for woman has undergone a change. The romantic passion which once almost deified her is on the decline; and it is by intrinsic qualities that she must now inspire respect. She is no longer the queen of song and the star of chivalry. But if there is less of enthusiasm entertained for her, the sentiment is more rational, and, perhaps, equally sincere; for it is in relation to happiness that she is chiefly appreciated.

And in this respect it is, we must confess, that she is most useful and most important. Domestic life is the chief source of her influence; and the greatest debt society can owe to her is domestic comfort. . . . A woman may make a man's home delightful, and may thus increase his motives for virtuous exertion. She may refine and tranquilize his mind—may turn away his anger or allay his grief. Her smile may be the happy influence to gladden his heart, and to disperse the cloud that gathers on his brow. And in proportion to her endeavors to make those around her happy, she will be esteemed and loved. She will secure by her excellence that interest and that regard which she might formerly claim as the privilege of her sex, and will really merit the deference which was then conceded to her as a matter of course. . . .

Nothing is so likely to conciliate the affections of the other sex as a feeling that woman looks to them for support and guidance. In proportion as men are themselves superior, they are accessible to this appeal. On the contrary, they never feel interested in one who seems disposed rather to offer than to ask assistance. There is, indeed, something unfeminine in independence. It is contrary to nature, and therefore it offends. We do not like to see a woman affecting tremors, but still less do we like to see her acting the amazon. A really sensible woman feels her dependence. She does what she can; but she is conscious of inferiority, and therefore grateful for support. She knows that she is the weaker vessel, and that as such she should receive honor. In this view, her weakness is an attraction, not a blemish.

Henrik Ibsen, *A Doll's House*

NORA: Yes, it's true, Torvald. When I was living at home with Father, he told me his opinions and mine were the same. If I had different opinions, I said nothing about them, because he would not have liked it. He used to call me his doll-child and played with me as I played with my dolls. Then I came to live in your house.

HELMER: What a way to speak of our marriage!

NORA *(Undisturbed):* I mean that I passed from Father's hands into yours. You arranged everything to your taste and I got the same tastes as you; or pretended to—I don't know which—both, perhaps; sometimes one, sometimes the other. When I look back on it now, I seem to have been living here like a beggar, on handouts. I lived by performing tricks for you, Torvald. . . . I must stand quite alone if I am ever to know myself and my surroundings; so I cannot stay with you.

HELMER: You are mad! I shall not allow it! I forbid it!

NORA: It's no use your forbidding me anything now. I shall take with me only what belongs to me; from you I will accept nothing, either now or later. . . .

HELMER: Forsake your home, your husband, your children! And you don't consider what the world will say.

NORA: I can't pay attention to that. I only know that I must do it.

(Continued)

HELMER: This is monstrous! Can you forsake your holiest duties?

NORA: What do you consider my holiest duties?

HELMER: Need I tell you that? Your duties to your husband and children.

NORA: I have other duties equally sacred.

HELMER: Impossible! What do you mean?

NORA: My duties toward myself.

HELMER: Before all else you are a wife and a mother.

NORA: That I no longer believe. Before all else I believe I am a human being just as much as you are—or at least that I should try to become one. I know that most people agree with you, Torvald, and that they say so in books. But I can no longer be satisfied with what most people say and what is in books. I must think things out for myself and try to get clear about them.

Q *According to Elizabeth Sanford, what is the proper role of women? What forces in nineteenth-century European society merged to shape Sanford's understanding of "proper" gender roles? In Ibsen's play, what challenges does Nora Helmer make to Sanford's view of the proper role and behavior of wives? Why is her husband so shocked? Why did Ibsen title this play* A Doll's House?

Sources: Elizabeth Poole Sanford, *Woman in Her Social and Domestic Character*. From Elizabeth Poole Sanford, *Woman in Her Social and Domestic Character* (Boston: Otis, Broaders & Co., 1842), pp. 5–7, 15–16. Henrik Ibsen, *A Doll's House*. From *Henrik Ibsen, A Doll's House*, Act III, 1879, as printed in *Roots of Western Civilization* by Wesley D. Camp, John Wiley & Sons, 1983.

often chaotic activities, the new sports were strictly organized with sets of rules and officials to enforce them. These rules were the products of organized athletic groups, such as the English Football Association (1863) and the American Bowling Congress (1895). The development of urban transportation systems made possible the construction of stadiums where thousands could attend, making mass spectator sports into a big business.

Cultural Life: Romanticism and Realism in the Western World

Q FOCUS QUESTION: What were the main characteristics of Romanticism and Realism?

At the end of the eighteenth century, a new intellectual movement known as **Romanticism** emerged to challenge the ideas of the Enlightenment. The Enlightenment stressed reason as the chief means for discovering truth. Although the Romantics by no means disparaged reason, they tried to balance its use by stressing the importance of feeling, emotion, and imagination as sources of knowing.

The Characteristics of Romanticism

Many Romantics had a passionate interest in the past. They revived medieval Gothic architecture and left European countrysides adorned with pseudo-medieval castles and cities bedecked with grandiose neo-Gothic cathedrals, city halls, and parliamentary buildings. Literature, too, reflected this historical consciousness. The novels of Walter Scott (1771–1832) became European best-sellers in the first half of the nineteenth century. *Ivanhoe*, in which Scott sought to evoke the clash between Saxon and Norman knights in medieval England, became one of his most popular works.

Many Romantics also had a deep attraction to the exotic and unfamiliar. In an exaggerated form, this preoccupation gave rise to so-called **Gothic literature**, chillingly evident in Mary Shelley's *Frankenstein* and Edgar Allan Poe's short stories of horror (see the box on p. 534). Some Romantics even tried to bring the unusual into their own lives by experimenting with cocaine, opium, and hashish to achieve drug-induced altered states of consciousness.

To the Romantics, poetry was the direct expression of the soul and therefore ranked above all other literary forms. Romantic poetry gave full expression to one of the most important characteristics of Romanticism: love of nature, especially evident in the poetry of William Wordsworth (1770–1850). His experience of nature was almost mystical as he claimed to receive "authentic tidings of invisible things":

> One impulse from a vernal wood
> May teach you more of man,
> Of Moral Evil and of good,
> Than all the sages can.[6]

Romantics believed that nature served as a mirror into which humans could look to learn about themselves.

COMPARATIVE ESSAY

The Rise of Nationalism

POLITICS & GOVERNMENT

Like the Industrial Revolution, the concept of nationalism originated in eighteenth-century Europe, where it was the product of a variety of factors, including the spread of printing and the replacement of Latin with vernacular languages, the secularization of the age, and the experience of the French revolutionary and Napoleonic eras. The French were the first to show what a nation in arms could accomplish, but peoples conquered by Napoleon soon created their own national armies. At the beginning of the nineteenth century, peoples who had previously focused their identity on a locality or a region, on loyalty to a monarch or to a particular religious faith, now shifted their political allegiance to the idea of a nation, based on ethnic, linguistic, or cultural factors. The idea of the nation had explosive consequences: by 1920, the world's three largest multiethnic states—imperial Russia, Austria-Hungary, and the Ottoman Empire—had all given way to a number of individual nation-states.

The idea of establishing political boundaries on the basis of ethnicity, language, or culture had a broad appeal throughout Western civilization, but it also had unintended consequences. Although the concept provided the basis for a new sense of community that was tied to liberal thought in the first half of the nineteenth century, it also gave birth to ethnic tensions and hatred in the second half of the century that resulted in bitter disputes and contributed to the competition between nation-states that eventually erupted into world war. Governments, following the lead of the radical government in Paris during the French Revolution, took full advantage of the rise of a strong

Museo Civico, Modigliana/© Alfredo Dagli Orti/The Art Archive at Art Resource, NY

Garibaldi. Giuseppe Garibaldi was a dedicated patriot and an outstanding example of the Italian nationalism that led to the unification of Italy by 1870.

national consciousness and transformed war into a demonstration of national honor and commitment. Universal schooling enabled states to arouse patriotic enthusiasm and create national unity. Most soldiers who joyfully went to war in 1914 were convinced that their nation's cause was just.

Although the concept of nationalism was initially the product of conditions in modern Europe, it soon spread to other parts of the world. A few societies, such as Vietnam, had already developed a strong sense of national identity, but most of the peoples in Asia and Africa lived in multiethnic and multireligious communities and were not yet ripe for the spirit of nationalism. As we shall see, the first attempts to resist European colonial rule were often based on religious or ethnic identity, rather than on the concept of denied nationhood. But the imperialist powers, which at first benefited from the lack of political cohesion among their colonial subjects, eventually reaped what they had sowed. As the colonial peoples became familiar with Western concepts of democracy and self-determination, they too began to manifest a sense of common purpose that helped knit together the different elements in their societies to oppose colonial regimes and create the conditions for the emergence of future nations. For good or ill, the concept of nationalism had now achieved global proportions. We shall explore such issues, and their consequences, in greater detail in the chapters that follow.

> **Q** *What is nationalism? How did it arise, and what impact did it have on the history of the nineteenth and twentieth centuries?*

Gothic Literature: Edgar Allan Poe

ART & IDEAS

American writers and poets made significant contributions to the movement of Romanticism. Although Edgar Allan Poe (1809–1849) was influenced by the German Romantic school of mystery and horror, many literary historians give him the credit for pioneering the modern short story. This selection from the conclusion of "The Fall of the House of Usher" gives a feeling for the nature of so-called Gothic literature.

Edgar Allan Poe, "The Fall of the House of Usher"

No sooner had these syllables passed my lips, than—as if a shield of brass had indeed, at the moment, fallen heavily upon a floor of silver—I became aware of a distinct, hollow, metallic, and clangorous, yet apparently muffled, reverberation. Completely unnerved, I leaped to my feet; but the measured rocking movement of Usher was undisturbed. I rushed to the chair in which he sat. His eyes were bent fixedly before him, and throughout his whole countenance there reigned a stony rigidity. But, as I placed my hand upon his shoulder, there came a strong shudder over his whole person; a sickly smile quivered about his lips; and I saw that he spoke in a low, hurried, and gibbering murmur, as if unconscious of my presence. Bending closely over him, I at length drank in the hideous import of his words.

"Not hear it?—yes, I hear it, and have heard it. Long-long-long-many minutes, many hours, many days, have I heard it—yet I dared not—oh, pity me, miserable wretch that I am!—I dared not—I *dared* not speak! *We have put her living in the tomb!* Said I not that my senses were acute? I now tell you that I heard her first feeble movements in the hollow coffin. I heard them—many, many days ago—yet I dared not—*I dared not speak!* And now—to-night— . . . the rending of her coffin, and the grating of the iron hinges of her prison, and her struggles within the coppered archway of the vault! Oh whither shall I fly? Will she not be here anon? Is she not hurrying to upbraid me for my haste? Have I not heard her footstep on the stair? Do I not distinguish that heavy and horrible beating of her heart? MADMAN!"—here he sprang furiously to his feet, and shrieked out his syllables, as if in the effort he were giving up his soul— "MADMAN! I TELL YOU THAT SHE NOW STANDS WITHOUT THE DOOR!" As if in the superhuman energy of his utterance there had been found the potency of a spell, the huge antique panels to which the speaker pointed threw slowly back, upon the instant, their ponderous and ebony jaws. It was the work of the rushing gust—but then without those doors there DID stand the lofty and enshrouded figure of the lady Madeline of Usher. There was blood upon her white robes, and the evidence of some bitter struggle upon every portion of her emaciated frame. For a moment she remained trembling and reeling to and fro upon the threshold, then, with a low moaning cry, fell heavily inward upon the person of her brother, and in her violent and now final death-agonies, bore him to the floor a corpse, and a victim to the terrors he had anticipated.

Q *What were the aesthetic aims of Gothic literature? How did it come to be called "Gothic"? How did its values relate to those of the Romantic movement as a whole?*

Source: From *Selected Prose and Poetry*, Edgar Allan Poe, copyright © 1950 by Holt, Rinehart, and Winston, Inc.

Like the literary arts, the visual arts were also deeply affected by Romanticism. To Romantic artists, all artistic expression was a reflection of the artist's inner feelings; a painting should mirror the artist's vision of the world and be the instrument of his own imagination.

Eugène Delacroix (oo-ZHEN duh-lah-KRWAH) (1798–1863) was one of the most famous French exponents of the Romantic school of painting. Delacroix visited North Africa in 1832 and was strongly impressed by its vibrant colors and the brilliant dress of the people. His paintings came to exhibit two primary characteristics—a fascination with the exotic and a passion for color. Both are apparent in his *Women of Algiers*. In Delacroix, theatricality and movement combined with a daring use of color. Many of his works reflect his own belief that "a painting should be a feast to the eye."

Eugène Delacroix, *Women of Algiers.* A characteristic of Romanticism was its love of the exotic and unfamiliar. In his *Women of Algiers*, Delacroix reflected this fascination with the exotic. In this portrayal of harem concubines from North Africa, the clothes and jewelry of the women combine with their calm facial expressions to create an atmosphere of peaceful sensuality. At the same time, Delacroix's painting reflects his preoccupation with light and color.

A New Age of Science

With the Industrial Revolution came a renewed interest in basic scientific research. By the 1830s, new scientific discoveries led to many practical benefits that caused science to have an ever-greater impact on European life.

In biology, the Frenchman Louis Pasteur (LWEE pass-TOOR) (1822–1895) discovered the germ theory of disease, which had enormous practical applications in the development of modern scientific medical practices. In chemistry, the Russian Dmitri Mendeleev (di-MEE-tree men-duh-LAY-ef) (1834–1907) in the 1860s classified all the material elements then known on the basis of their atomic weights and provided the systematic foundation for the periodic law.

The popularity of scientific and technological achievement produced a widespread acceptance of the **scientific method** as the only path to objective truth and objective reality. This in turn undermined the faith of many people in religious revelation. It is no accident that the nineteenth century was an age of increasing **secularization**, evident in the belief that truth was to be found in the concrete material existence of human beings. No one did more to create a picture of humans as material beings that were simply part of the natural world than Charles Darwin.

In 1859, Charles Darwin (1809–1882) published *On the Origin of Species by Means of Natural Selection*. The basic idea of this book was that all plants and animals had evolved over a long period of time from earlier and simpler forms of life, a principle known as **organic evolution**. In every species, he argued, "many more individuals of

each species are born than can possibly survive." This results in a "struggle for existence." Darwin believed that some organisms were more adaptable to the environment than others, a process that he called **natural selection**. Those that were naturally selected for survival ("survival of the fit") reproduced and thrived. The unfit did not and became extinct. The fit who survived passed on small variations that enhanced their survival until, from Darwin's point of view, a new and separate species emerged. In *The Descent of Man*, published in 1871, he argued for the animal origins of human beings. Humans were not an exception to the rule governing other species.

Realism in Literature and Art

The name **Realism** was first applied in 1850 to describe a new style of painting and soon spread to literature. The literary Realists of the mid-nineteenth century rejected Romanticism. They wanted to deal with ordinary characters from actual life rather than Romantic heroes in exotic settings. They also sought to avoid emotional language by using close observation and precise description, an approach that led them to write novels rather than poems.

The leading novelist of the 1850s and 1860s, the Frenchman Gustave Flaubert (goo-STAHV floh-BAYR) (1821–1880), perfected the Realist novel. His *Madame Bovary* (1857) was a straightforward description of barren and sordid provincial life in France. Emma Bovary is trapped in a marriage to a drab provincial doctor. Impelled by the images of romantic love she has read

Gustave Courbet, *The Stonebreakers.* Realism, largely developed by French painters, aimed at a lifelike portrayal of the daily activities of ordinary people. Gustave Courbet was the most famous of the Realist artists. As is evident in *The Stonebreakers*, he sought to portray things as they really appear. He shows an old road builder and his young assistant in their tattered clothes, engrossed in their dreary work of breaking stones to construct a road.

about in novels, she seeks the same thing for herself in adulterous love affairs but is ultimately driven to suicide.

By the second half of the nineteenth century, Realism had also made inroads into the Latin American literary scene. There, Realist novelists focused on the injustices of their society, evident in the work of Clorinda Matto de Turner (kloh-RIN-duh MAH-toh day TUR-nerr) (1852–1909). Her *Aves sin Nido* (*Birds Without a Nest*) was a brutal revelation of the pitiful living conditions of the Indians in Peru. She blamed the Catholic Church in particular for much of their misery.

In art, too, Realism became dominant after 1850. Gustave Courbet (goo-STAHV koor-BAY) (1819–1877), the most famous artist of the Realist school, reveled in realistic portrayals of everyday life. His subjects were factory workers, peasants, and the wives of saloonkeepers. "I have never seen either angels or goddesses, so I am not interested in painting them," he exclaimed. One of his famous works, *The Stonebreakers*, painted in 1849, shows two road workers engaged in the deadening work of breaking stones to build a road.

Toward the Modern Consciousness: Intellectual and Cultural Developments

Q FOCUS QUESTION: What intellectual and cultural developments in the late nineteenth and early twentieth centuries "opened the way to a modern consciousness," and how did this consciousness differ from earlier worldviews?

Before 1914, many people in the Western world continued to believe in the values and ideals that had been generated by the Scientific Revolution and the Enlightenment. The idea that human beings could improve themselves and achieve a better society seemed to be proved by a rising standard of living, urban comforts, and mass education. It was easy to think that the human mind could make sense of the universe. Between 1870 and 1914, though, radically new ideas challenged these optimistic views and opened the way to a modern consciousness.

A New Physics

Science was one of the chief pillars underlying the optimistic and rationalistic view of the world that many Westerners shared in the nineteenth century. Supposedly based on hard facts and cold reason, science offered a certainty of belief in the orderliness of nature. The new physics dramatically altered that perspective.

Throughout much of the nineteenth century, Westerners adhered to the mechanical conception of the universe postulated by the classic physics of Isaac Newton. In this perspective, the universe was viewed as a giant machine in which time, space, and matter were objective realities that existed independently of the observers. Matter was thought to be composed of indivisible and solid material bodies called atoms.

Albert Einstein (YN-styn) (1879–1955), a German-born patent officer working in Switzerland, questioned this view of the universe. In 1905, Einstein published his special theory of relativity, which stated that space and time are not absolute but relative to the observer. Neither space nor time had an existence independent of human experience. As Einstein later explained simply to a journalist: "It was formerly believed that if all material things disappeared out of the universe, time and space would be left. According to the **relativity theory**, however, time and space disappear together with the things."[7] Einstein concluded that matter was nothing but another form of energy. His epochal formula $E = mc^2$—stating that each particle of matter is equivalent to its mass times the square of the velocity of light—was the key theory explaining the vast energies contained within the atom. It led to the atomic age.

Sigmund Freud and the Emergence of Psychoanalysis

At the turn of the twentieth century, the Viennese physician Sigmund Freud (SIG-mund *or* ZIG-munt FROID) (1856–1939) advanced a series of theories that undermined optimism about the rational nature of the human mind. Freud's thought, like the new physics, added to the uncertainties of the age. His major ideas were published in 1900 in *The Interpretation of Dreams*.

According to Freud, human behavior was strongly determined by the unconscious, by past experiences and internal forces of which people were largely oblivious. For Freud, human behavior was no longer truly rational but rather instinctive or irrational. He argued that painful and unsettling experiences were blotted from conscious awareness but still continued to influence behavior since they had become part of the unconscious (see the box on p. 538). Repression of these thoughts began in childhood. Freud devised a method, known as **psychoanalysis**, by which a psychotherapist and patient could probe deeply into the memory and retrace the chain of repression all the way back to its childhood origins. By making the conscious mind aware of the unconscious and its repressed contents, the patient's psychic conflict was resolved.

The Impact of Darwin: Social Darwinism and Racism

In the second half of the nineteenth century, scientific theories were sometimes wrongly applied to achieve other ends. For example, Charles Darwin's principle of organic evolution was applied to the social order as **social Darwinism**, the belief that societies were organisms that evolved through time from a struggle with their environment. Such ideas were used in a radical way by rabid nationalists and racists. In their pursuit of national greatness, extreme nationalists insisted that nations, too, were engaged in a "struggle for existence" in which only the fittest survived.

ANTI-SEMITISM   Anti-Semitism had a long history in European civilization, but in the nineteenth century, as a result of the ideals of the Enlightenment and the French Revolution, Jews were increasingly granted legal equality in many European countries. Many Jews now left the ghetto and became assimilated into the cultures around them. Many became successful as bankers, lawyers, scientists, scholars, journalists, and stage performers.

These achievements represent only one side of the picture, however. In Germany and Austria during the 1880s and 1890s, conservatives founded right-wing anti-Jewish parties that used anti-Semitism to win the votes of traditional lower-middle-class groups who felt threatened by the new economic forces of the times. The worst treatment of Jews at the turn of the century, however, occurred in eastern Europe, where 72 percent of the entire world Jewish population lived. Russian Jews were forced to live in certain regions of the country, and persecutions and pogroms were widespread. Hundreds of thousands of Jews decided to emigrate to escape the persecution.

Many Jews went to the United States, although some moved to Palestine, which soon became the focus of a Jewish nationalist movement called **Zionism**. For many Jews, Palestine, the land of ancient Israel, had long been the land of their dreams. Settlement in Palestine was difficult, however, because it was then part of the Ottoman

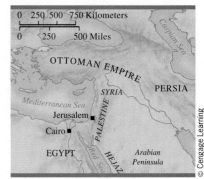

Palestine in 1900

Empire, which was opposed to Jewish immigration. Despite the problems, the First Zionist Congress, which met in Switzerland in 1897, proclaimed as its aim the creation of a "home in Palestine secured by public law" for the Jewish people. In 1900, around a thousand Jews migrated to Palestine, and the trickle rose to about three thousand a year between 1904 and 1914, keeping the Zionist dream alive.

The Culture of Modernity

The revolution in physics and psychology was paralleled by a revolution in literature and the arts. Before 1914, writers and artists were rebelling against the traditional literary and artistic styles that had dominated European cultural life since the Renaissance. The changes that they produced have since been called **Modernism**.

At the beginning of the twentieth century, a group of writers known as the Symbolists caused a literary revolution. Primarily interested in writing poetry and strongly influenced by the ideas of Freud, the Symbolists believed

Freud and the Concept of Repression

ART & IDEAS

Freud's psychoanalytical theories resulted from his attempt to understand the world of the unconscious. This excerpt is taken from a lecture given in 1909 in which Freud described how he arrived at his theory of the role of repression.

Sigmund Freud, *Five Lectures on Psychoanalysis*

I did not abandon [the technique of encouraging patients to reveal forgotten experiences], however, before the observations I made during my use of it afforded me decisive evidence. I found confirmation of the fact that the forgotten memories were not lost. They were in the patient's possession and were ready to emerge in association to what was still known by him; but there was some force that prevented them from becoming conscious and compelled them to remain unconscious. The existence of this force could be assumed with certainty, since one became aware of an effort corresponding to it if, in opposition to it, one tried to introduce the unconscious memories into the patient's consciousness. The force which was maintaining the pathological condition became apparent in the form of resistance on the part of the patient.

It was on this idea of resistance, then, that I based my view of the course of psychical events in hysteria. In order to effect a recovery, it had proved necessary to remove these resistances. Starting out from the mechanism of cure, it now became possible to construct quite definite ideas of the origin of the illness. The same forces which, in the form of resistance, were now offering opposition to the forgotten material's being made conscious, must formerly have brought about the forgetting and must have pushed the pathogenic experiences in question out of consciousness. I gave the name of "repression" to this hypothetical process, and I considered that it was proved by the undeniable existence of resistance.

The further question could then be raised as to what these forces were and what the determinants were of the repression in which we now recognized the pathogenic mechanism of hysteria. A comparative study of the pathogenic situations which we had come to know through the cathartic procedure made it possible to answer this question. All these experiences had involved the emergence of a wishful impulse which was in sharp contrast to the subject's other wishes and which proved incompatible with the ethical and aesthetic standards of his personality. There had been a short conflict, and the end of this internal struggle was that the idea which had appeared before consciousness as the vehicle of this irreconcilable wish fell a victim to repression, was pushed out of consciousness with all its attached memories, and was forgotten. Thus, the incompatibility of the wish in question with the patient's ego was the motive for the repression; the subject's ethical and other standards were the repressing forces. An acceptance of the incompatible wishful impulse or a prolongation of the conflict would have produced a high degree of unpleasure; this unpleasure was avoided by means of repression, which was thus revealed as one of the devices serving to protect the mental personality.

Q *According to Freud, how did he discover the existence of repression? What function does repression perform?*

Source: Reprinted from *Five Lectures on Psychoanalysis* by Sigmund Freud. Translated and edited by James Strachey, W. W. Norton & Company, Inc. Copyright 1909, 1910 by Sigmund Freud. Copyright © 1961 by James Strachey. Copyright renewed 1989.

that an objective knowledge of the world was impossible. The external world was not real but only a collection of symbols that reflected the true reality of the individual human mind.

The period from 1870 to 1914 was one of the most fertile in the history of art. By the late nineteenth century, artists were seeking new forms of expression. The preamble to modern painting can be found in **Impressionism**, a movement that originated in France in the 1870s when a group of artists rejected the studios and museums and went out into the countryside to paint nature directly.

An important Impressionist painter was Berthe Morisot (BAYRT mor-ee-ZOH) (1841–1895), who believed

Musée Fabre, Montpellier//© Erich Lessing/Art Resource, NY

© Christie's Images Ltd./SuperStock

COMPARATIVE ILLUSTRATION

ART & IDEAS

Painting—West and East. Berthe Morisot, the first female painter to join the Impressionists, developed her own unique style. Her gentle colors and strong use of pastels are especially evident in *Young Girl by the Window*, seen at the left. The French Impressionist style also spread abroad. One of the most outstanding Japanese artists of the time was Kuroda Seiki (koor-OH-duh SAY-kee) (1866–1924), who returned from nine years in Paris to open a Western-style school of painting in Tokyo. Shown at the right is his *Under the Trees*, an excellent example of the fusion of contemporary French Impressionist painting with the Japanese tradition of courtesan prints.

Q What differences and similarities do you notice in these two paintings?

that women had a special vision that she described as "more delicate than that of men." She made use of lighter colors and flowing brushstrokes (see the comparative illustration above). Near the end of her life, she lamented the refusal of men to take her work seriously: "I don't think there has ever been a man who treated a woman as an equal, and that's all I would have asked, for I know I'm worth as much as they."[8]

In the 1880s, a new movement known as **Post-Impressionism** arose in France and soon spread to other European countries. A famous Post-Impressionist was the tortured and tragic figure Vincent van Gogh (van GOH *or* vahn GOK) (1853–1890). For van Gogh, art was a spiritual experience. He was especially interested in color and believed that it could act as its own form of language.

By the beginning of the twentieth century, the belief that the task of art was to represent "reality" had lost much of its meaning. The growth of photography gave artists one reason to reject Realism. Invented in the 1830s, photography became popular and widespread after 1888

when George Eastman created the first Kodak camera for the mass market. What was the point of an artist's doing what the camera did better? Unlike the camera, which could only mirror reality, artists could create reality.

By 1905, one of the most important figures in modern art was just beginning his career. Pablo Picasso (PAHB-loh pi-KAH-soh) (1881–1973) was from Spain but settled in Paris in 1904. Picasso was extremely flexible and painted in a remarkable variety of styles. He was instrumental in the development of a new style called **Cubism** that used geometrical designs as visual stimuli to re-create reality in the viewer's mind.

The modern artist's flight from "visual reality" reached a high point in 1910 with the beginning of **abstract painting**. A Russian who worked in Germany, Vasily Kandinsky (vus-YEEL-yee kan-DIN-skee) (1866–1944) was one of its founders. Kandinsky sought to avoid representation altogether. He believed that art should speak directly to the soul. To do so, it must avoid any reference to visual reality and concentrate on line and color.

Pablo Picasso, *Les Demoiselles d'Avignon*.

Pablo Picasso, a major pioneer and activist of modern art, experimented with a remarkable variety of modern styles. *Les Demoiselles d'Avignon* (lay dem-wah-ZEL dah-vee-NYONH) was the first great example of Cubism, which one art historian called "the first style of this [twentieth] century to break radically with the past." Geometrical shapes replace traditional forms, forcing the viewer to re-create reality in his or her own mind. The head at the upper right of the painting reflects Picasso's attraction to aspects of African art, as is evident from the mask included at the left.

© Dr. Werner Muensterberger Collection, London/The Bridgeman Art Library

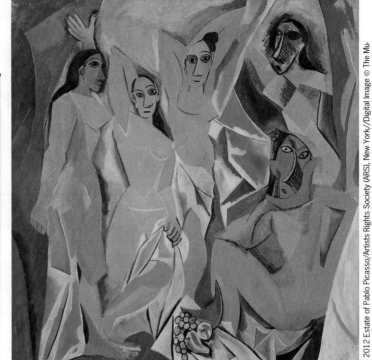

© 2012 Estate of Pablo Picasso/Artists Rights Society (ARS), New York//Digital Image © The Museum of Modern Art/Licensed by Scala/Art Resource, NY

CHAPTER SUMMARY

Since the sixteenth century, much of the Western Hemisphere had been under the control of Great Britain, Spain, and Portugal. But between 1776 and 1826, an age of revolution in the Atlantic world led to the creation of the United States and nine new nations in Latin America. Canada and other nations in Latin America followed in the course of the nineteenth century. This age of revolution was an expression of the force of nationalism, which had first emerged as a political ideology at the end of the eighteenth century. Influential, too, were the ideas of the Enlightenment that had made an impact on intellectuals and political leaders in both North and South America.

The new nations that emerged in the Western Hemisphere did not, however, develop without challenges to their national unity. Latin American nations often found it difficult to establish stable republics and resorted to strong leaders who used military force to govern.

And although Latin American nations had achieved political independence, they found themselves economically dependent on Great Britain as well as their northern neighbor. The United States dissolved into four years of bloody civil war before reconciling, and Canada achieved only questionable unity owing to distrust between the English-speaking majority and the French-speaking minority.

By the second half of the nineteenth century, much of the Western world was experiencing a new mass society in which the lower classes in particular benefited from the right to vote, a higher standard of living, and new schools that provided them with some education. New forms of mass transportation, combined with new work patterns, enabled large numbers of people to enjoy weekend trips to amusement parks and seaside resorts, as well as to participate in new mass leisure activities.

The cultural revolutions before 1914 produced anxiety and a crises of confidence in Western civilization. Albert Einstein showed that time and space were relative to the observer, that matter was simply another form of energy, and that the old Newtonian view of the universe was no longer valid. Sigmund Freud added to the uncertainties of the age with his argument that human behavior was governed not by reason but by the unconscious. Some intellectuals used the ideas of Charles Darwin to argue that in the struggle of race and nations, only the fittest survive. Collectively, these new ideas helped create a modern consciousness that questioned most Europeans' optimistic faith in reason, the rational structure of nature, and the certainty of progress. As we shall see in Chapter 23, the devastating experiences of World War I would turn this culture of uncertainty into a way of life after 1918.

CHAPTER TIMELINE

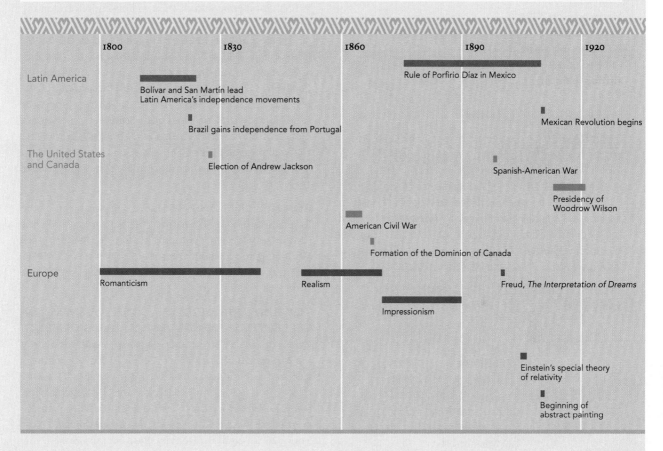

	1800	1830	1860	1890	1920

Latin America
Rule of Porfirio Díaz in Mexico
Bolívar and San Martín lead Latin America's independence movements
Brazil gains independence from Portugal
Mexican Revolution begins

The United States and Canada
Election of Andrew Jackson
Spanish-American War
Presidency of Woodrow Wilson
American Civil War
Formation of the Dominion of Canada

Europe
Romanticism
Realism
Freud, *The Interpretation of Dreams*
Impressionism
Einstein's special theory of relativity
Beginning of abstract painting

CHAPTER REVIEW

Upon Reflection

Q What were the similarities and dissimilarities in the development of Latin American nations, the United States, and Canada in the nineteenth century?

Q How were the promises and problems of the new mass society reflected in education, leisure, and the experiences of women?

Q How is Modernism evident in literature and the arts between 1870 and 1914? How do these literary and artistic products reflect the political and social developments of the age?

Key Terms

caudillos (p. 521)
mass society (p. 527)
nation-states (p. 528)
suffragists (p. 530)
mass education (p. 530)
mass leisure (p. 530)

Romanticism (p. 532)
Gothic literature (p. 532)
scientific method (p. 535)
secularization (p. 535)
organic evolution (p. 535)
natural selection (p. 535)
Realism (p. 535)
relativity theory (p. 537)
psychoanalysis (p. 537)
social Darwinism (p. 537)
Zionism (p. 537)
Modernism (p. 537)
Impressionism (p. 538)
Post-Impressionism (p. 539)
Cubism (p. 539)
abstract painting (p. 539)

Suggested Reading

LATIN AMERICA For general surveys of Latin American history, see **M. C. Eakin,** *The History of Latin America: Collision of Cultures* (New York, 2007), and **P. Bakewell,** *A History of Latin America* (Oxford, 1997). On the wars for independence, see **J. C. Chasteen,** *Americanos: Latin America's Struggle for Independence* (Oxford, 2008). On the economic history of Latin America, see **V. Bulmer-Thomas,** *The Economic History of Latin America Since Independence,* 2nd ed. (New York, 2003).

THE UNITED STATES AND CANADA On the United States in the first half of the nineteenth century, see

D. W. Howe, *What God Hath Wrought: The Transformation of America, 1815–1848* (Oxford, 2007). The definitive one-volume history of the American Civil War is **J. M. McPherson,** *Battle Cry of Freedom: The Civil War Era* in the Oxford History of the United States series (New York, 2003). On the second half of the nineteenth century, see **L. Gould,** *America in the Progressive Era, 1890–1914* (New York, 2001). For a general history of Canada, see **S. W. See,** *History of Canada* (Westport, N.Y., 2001).

THE EMERGENCE OF MASS SOCIETY IN THE WEST For a good introduction to housing reform on the Continent, see **N. Bullock** and **J. Read,** *The Movement for Housing Reform in Germany and France, 1840–1914* (Cambridge, 1985). There are good overviews of women's experiences in the nineteenth century in **B. Smith,** *Changing Lives: Women in European History Since 1700,* rev. ed. (Lexington, Mass., 2005). On various aspects of education, see **M. J. Maynes,** *Schooling in Western Europe: A Social History* (Albany, N.Y., 1985). A concise and well-presented survey of leisure patterns is **G. Cross,** *A Social History of Leisure Since 1600* (State College, Pa., 1989).

ROMANTICISM AND REALISM On the ideas of the Romantics, see **M. Cranston,** *The Romantic Movement* (Oxford, 1994). For an introduction to the arts, see **W. Vaughan,** *Romanticism and Art* (New York, 1994). On Realism, **J. Malpas,** *Realism* (Cambridge, 1997), is a good introduction.

TOWARD THE MODERN CONSCIOUSNESS: INTELLECTUAL AND CULTURAL DEVELOPMENTS On Freud, see **P. D. Kramer,** *Sigmund Freud: Inventor of the Modern Mind* (New York, 2006). European racism is analyzed in **N. MacMaster,** *Racism in Europe, 1870–2000* (New York, 2001). On Modernism, see **P. Gay,** *Modernism: The Lure of Heresy* (New York, 2007). Very valuable on modern art are **G. Crepaldi,** *The Impressionists* (New York, 2002), and **B. Denvir,** *Post-Impressionism* (New York, 1992).

Visit the CourseMate website at www.cengagebrain.com for additional study tools and review materials for this chapter.

The High Tide of Imperialism

Revere the conquering heroes: Establishing British rule in Africa

CHAPTER OUTLINE AND FOCUS QUESTIONS

The Spread of Colonial Rule

Q What were the causes of the new imperialism of the nineteenth century, and how did it differ from European expansion in earlier periods?

The Colonial System

Q What types of administrative systems did the various colonial powers establish in their colonies, and how did these systems reflect the general philosophy of colonialism?

India Under the British Raj

Q What were some of the major consequences of British rule in India, and how did they affect the Indian people?

Colonial Regimes in Southeast Asia

Q Which Western countries were most active in seeking colonial possessions in Southeast Asia, and what were their motives in doing so?

Empire Building in Africa

Q What factors were behind the "scramble for Africa," and what impact did it have on the continent?

The Emergence of Anticolonialism

Q How did the subject peoples respond to colonialism, and what role did nationalism play in their response?

CRITICAL THINKING

Q What were the consequences of the new imperialism of the nineteenth century for the colonies of the European powers? How should the motives and stated objectives of the imperialist countries be evaluated?

IN 1877, THE BRITISH empire builder Cecil Rhodes drew up his last will and testament. He bequeathed his fortune, achieved as a diamond magnate in South Africa, to two of his close friends. He instructed them to use the inheritance to form a secret society aimed at bringing about "the extension of British rule throughout the world, the perfecting of a system of emigration from the United Kingdom . . . especially the occupation by British settlers of the entire continent of Africa, the Holy Land, the valley of the Euphrates, the Islands of Cyprus and Candia [Crete], the whole of South America. . . . The ultimate recovery of the United States of America as an integral part of the British Empire . . . then finally the foundation of so great a power as to hereafter render wars impossible and promote the best interests of humanity."[1]

Preposterous as such ideas sound today, they serve as a graphic reminder of the hubris that characterized the worldview of Rhodes and many of his contemporaries during the age of imperialism, as well as the complex union of moral concern and vaulting ambition that motivated their actions on the world stage.

Through their efforts, Western colonialism spread throughout much of the non-Western world during the nineteenth and early twentieth centuries. Spurred by the demands of the Industrial Revolution, a few powerful Western states—notably, Great Britain, France, Germany, Russia, and the United States—competed avariciously for consumer markets and raw materials for their expanding economies. By the end of the nineteenth century, virtually all of the traditional societies in Asia and Africa were under direct or indirect colonial rule. As the new century began, the Western imprint on Asian and African societies, for better or for worse, appeared to be a permanent feature of the political and cultural landscape.

The Spread of Colonial Rule

Q FOCUS QUESTION: What were the causes of the new imperialism of the nineteenth century, and how did it differ from European expansion in earlier periods?

In the nineteenth century, a new phase of Western expansion into Asia and Africa began. Whereas before 1800 European aims in the East could be summed up as "Christians and spices" and Western gold and silver were exchanged for cloves, silk, and porcelain, now European nations began to view Asian and African societies as markets for the prodigious output of European factories and as sources of the raw materials needed to fuel the Western industrial machine. This relationship between the West and African and Asian societies has been called the **new imperialism** (see the comparative essay on p. 545).

The Motives

The reason for this change, of course, was the Industrial Revolution. Now industrializing countries in the West needed vital raw materials that were not available at home, as well as reliable markets for the goods produced in their factories. The latter factor became increasingly crucial as producers discovered that their home markets could not absorb their entire output and that they had to export to make a profit. When consumer demand lagged, economic depression threatened.

The relationship between colonialism and national survival was expressed directly by the French politician Jules Ferry (ZHOOL feh-REE) in 1885. A policy of "containment or abstinence," he warned, would set France on "the broad road to decadence" and initiate its decline into a "third- or fourth-rate power." British imperialists, convinced by the theory of social Darwinism that in the struggle between nations, only the fit are victorious and survive, agreed. As the British professor of mathematics Karl Pearson argued in 1900, "The path of progress is strewn with the wrecks of nations; traces are everywhere to be seen of the [slaughtered remains] of inferior races. . . . Yet these dead people are, in very truth, the stepping stones on which mankind has arisen to the higher intellectual and deeper emotional life of today."[2]

For some, colonialism had a moral purpose, whether to promote Christianity or to build a better world. The British colonial official Henry Curzon (CURR-zun) declared that the British Empire "was under Providence, the greatest instrument for good that the world has seen." To Cecil Rhodes, the most famous empire builder of his day, the extraction of material wealth from the colonies was only a secondary matter. "My ruling purpose," he remarked, "is the extension of the British Empire."[3] That British Empire, on which, as the saying went, "the sun never set," was the envy of its rivals and was viewed as the primary source of British global dominance during the second half of the nineteenth century.

The Tactics

With the change in European motives for colonization came a shift in tactics. Earlier, European states had generally been satisfied to deal with existing independent states rather than attempting to establish direct control over vast territories. There had been exceptions where state power was at the point of collapse (as in India), where European economic interests were especially intense (as in Latin America and the East Indies), or where there was no centralized authority (as in North America and the Philippines). But for the most part, the Western presence had been limited to controlling regional trade networks and establishing a few footholds where the foreigners could carry on trade and missionary activity.

After 1800, the demands of industrialization in Europe created a new set of dynamics. Maintaining access to raw materials such as tin and rubber and setting up markets for European products required more extensive control over colonial territories. As competition for colonies increased, the colonial powers sought to solidify their hold over their territories to protect them from attack by their rivals. After 1880, the quest for colonies became a scramble as all the major European states, now joined by the United States and Japan, engaged in a global land grab. In many cases, economic interests were secondary to security concerns or the demands of national prestige. In Africa, for example, the British engaged in a struggle with their rivals to protect their interests in the Suez Canal and the Red Sea.

Imperialisms Old and New

INTERACTION & EXCHANGE

Originally, the word *imperialism* (derived from the Latin meaning "to command") was used to describe certain types of political entities. An empire was larger than a kingdom and comprised more than one nation or people, all ruled by an emperor who represented one dominant ethnic or religious group within the territory. Good examples include the Roman Empire, the Chinese Empire, the Mongol Empire in Central Asia, the empires of Ghana and Mali in West Africa, and perhaps the Inkan Empire in South America.

In the nineteenth century, as Western expansion into Asia and Africa gathered strength, it became fashionable to call that process "imperialism" as well. In this instance, the expansion was motivated by the efforts of capitalist states in the West to seize markets, cheap raw materials, and lucrative avenues for investment in the countries beyond Western civilization. Eventually, it resulted in the creation of colonies ruled by the imperialist powers. In this interpretation, the primary motives behind imperial expansion were economic. In his influential book *Imperialism: A Study*, published in 1902, the British political economist John A. Hobson promoted this view, maintaining that modern imperialism was a direct consequence of the modern industrial economy.

As historians began to analyze the phenomenon, however, many became convinced that the motivations of the imperial powers were not simply economic. As Hobson himself conceded, economic concerns were inevitably tinged with political overtones and questions of national grandeur and moral purpose. To nineteenth-century Europeans, economic wealth, national status, and political power went hand in hand with the possession of a colonial empire. To global strategists, colonies brought tangible benefits in balance-of-power politics as well as economic profits, and many nations pursued colonies as much to gain

Gateway to India. Built in the Roman imperial style by the British to commemorate the visit to India of King George V and Queen Mary in 1911, the Gateway to India was erected at the water's edge in the harbor of Bombay (now Mumbai), India's greatest port city. For thousands of British citizens arriving in India, the Gateway to India was the first view of their new home and a symbol of the power and majesty of the British raj.

advantage over their rivals as to acquire territory for its own sake.

After World War II, when colonies throughout Asia and Africa were replaced by independent nations, a new term *neocolonialism* appeared to describe the situation in which imperialist nations cede formal political independence to their former colonies, but continue to exercise control by various political and economic means. Hence, many critics argue, Western imperialism has not disappeared in the former colonial territories but has simply found other ways to maintain its influence. We will discuss this issue further in Part V.

 What were the principal motives of the major trading nations for seizing colonies in Asia and Africa in the late nineteenth century?

By 1900, almost all the societies of Africa and Asia were either under full colonial rule or, as in China and the Ottoman Empire, at a point of virtual collapse. Only a handful of states, including Thailand, Afghanistan, Iran, Ethiopia, and Japan, managed to escape internal disintegration or subjection to colonial rule. For the most part, the exceptions were the result of good fortune rather

than design. Thailand escaped subjugation primarily because officials in London and Paris found it more convenient to transform the country into a buffer state than to fight over it. Ethiopia and Afghanistan survived not only because of their long tradition of fierce resistance to outside threats, but also because of their remote location and mountainous terrain. Only Japan managed to avoid the common fate through a concerted strategy of political and economic reform.

The Colonial System

Q FOCUS QUESTION: What types of administrative systems did the various colonial powers establish in their colonies, and how did these systems reflect the general philosophy of colonialism?

Now that they had control of most of the world, what did the colonial powers do with it? As we have seen, their primary objective was to exploit the natural resources of the subject areas and to open up markets for manufactured goods and capital investment from the mother country. In some cases, that goal could be realized in cooperation with local political elites, whose loyalty could be earned, or purchased, by economic rewards or by confirming them in their positions of authority and status in a new colonial setting. Sometimes, however, this policy of **indirect rule** was not feasible because local leaders refused to cooperate with their colonial masters or even actively resisted. In such cases, the imperialists resorted to **direct rule**, removing the local elites from power and replacing them with officials from the mother country.

In general, the societies most likely to actively resist colonial conquest were those with a long tradition of national cohesion and independence, such as Burma and Vietnam in Asia and the African Muslim states in northern Nigeria and Morocco. In those areas, the colonial powers encountered more resistance and consequently tended to dispense with local collaborators and govern directly. In some parts of Africa, the Indian subcontinent, and the Malay peninsula, where the local authorities, for whatever reason, were willing to collaborate with the imperialist powers, indirect rule was more common.

Overall, colonialism in India, Southeast Asia, and Africa exhibited many similarities but also some differences. Some of these variations can be traced to differences among the colonial powers themselves. The French, for example, often tried to impose a centralized administrative system on their colonies that mirrored the system in use in France, while the British sometimes attempted to transform local aristocrats into the equivalent of the landed gentry at home in Britain. Other differences stemmed from conditions in the colonies themselves.

The Philosophy of Colonialism

To justify their rule, the colonial powers appealed in part to the time-honored maxim of "might makes right." That attitude received pseudoscientific validity from the concept of social Darwinism, which maintained that only societies that aggressively adapted to changing circumstances would survive and prosper in a world governed by the Darwinian law of "survival of the fittest."

Some people, however, were uncomfortable with such a brutal view and sought a moral justification that appeared to benefit the victim. Here again, social Darwinism pointed the way. By bringing the benefits of Western democracy, capitalism, and Christianity to tradition-ridden societies, the colonial powers were enabling primitive peoples to adapt to the challenges of the modern world. Buttressed by such comforting theories, sensitive Westerners could ignore the brutal aspects of colonialism and persuade themselves that in the long run, the results would be beneficial for both sides (see the box on p. 547). Few were

The Company Resident and His Puppet. The British East India Company gradually replaced the sovereigns of the once independent Indian states with puppet rulers who carried out the company's policies. Here we see the company's resident dominating a procession in Tanjore in 1825, while the Indian ruler, Sarabhoji, follows like an obedient shadow. As a boy, Sarabhoji had been educated by European tutors and had filled his life and home with English books and furnishings.

© Art Media, Victoria and Albert Museum, London/HIP/The Image Works

White Man's Burden, Black Man's Sorrow

One of the justifications for imperialism was that the "more advanced" white peoples had a moral responsibility to raise "ignorant" indigenous peoples to a higher level of civilization. Few captured this notion better than the British poet Rudyard Kipling (1865–1936) in his poem *The White Man's Burden*. Directed to the United States, it became famous throughout the English-speaking world.

That moral responsibility, however, was often misplaced or, even worse, laced with hypocrisy. Few observers described the destructive effects of Western imperialism on the African people as well as Edmund Morel, a British journalist whose book *The Black Man's Burden* pointed out some of the more harmful aspects of colonialism in the Belgian Congo.

Rudyard Kipling, *The White Man's Burden*

Take up the White Man's burden—
Send forth the best ye breed—
Go bind your sons to exile
To serve your captives' need;
To wait in heavy harness,
On fluttered folk and wild—
Your new-caught sullen peoples,
Half-devil and half-child.

Take up the White Man's burden—
In patience to abide,
To veil the threat of terror
And check the show of pride;
By open speech and simple,
An hundred times made plain
To seek another's profit,
And work another's gain.

Take up the White Man's burden—
The savage wars of peace—
Fill full the mouth of Famine
And bid the sickness cease;
And when your goal is nearest

The end for others sought,
Watch Sloth and heathen Folly
Bring all your hopes to nought.

Edmund Morel, *The Black Man's Burden*

It is [the Africans] who carry the "Black man's burden." They have not withered away before the white man's occupation. Indeed . . . Africa has ultimately absorbed within itself every Caucasian and, for that matter, every Semitic invader, too. In hewing out for himself a fixed abode in Africa, the white man has massacred the African in heaps. The African has survived, and it is well for the white settlers that he has. . . .

What the partial occupation of his soil by the white man has failed to do; what the mapping out of European political "spheres of influence" has failed to do; what the Maxim and the rifle, the slave gang, labour in the bowels of the earth and the lash, have failed to do; what imported measles, smallpox and syphilis have failed to do; whatever the overseas slave trade failed to do; the power of modern capitalistic exploitation, assisted by modern engines of destruction, may yet succeed in accomplishing.

For from the evils of the latter, scientifically applied and enforced, there is no escape for the African. Its destructive effects are not spasmodic; they are permanent. In its permanence resides its fatal consequences. It kills not the body merely, but the soul. It breaks the spirit. It attacks the African at every turn, from every point of vantage. It wrecks his polity, uproots him from the land, invades his family life, destroys his natural pursuits and occupations, claims his whole time, enslaves him in his own home.

 According to Kipling, why should Western nations take up the "white man's burden"? What was the "black man's burden," in the eyes of Edmund Morel?

Sources: Rudyard Kipling, *The White Man's Burden*. From Rudyard Kipling, "The White Man's Burden," *McClure's Magazine* 12 (Feb. 1899). Edmund Morel, *The Black Man's Burden*. Edmund Morel, *Black Man's Burden*, Metro Books, 1972.

as adept at describing this "civilizing mission" as the French governor-general of French Indochina Albert Sarraut (ahl-BAYR sah-ROH). While admitting that colonialism was originally an "act of force" undertaken for profit, he insisted that by redistributing the wealth of the earth, the colonial process would result in a better life for all: "Is it just, is it legitimate that such [an uneven distribution of resources] should be indefinitely prolonged? . . . No! . . . Humanity is distributed throughout the globe. No race, no people has the right or power to isolate itself egotistically from the movements and necessities of universal life."[4]

But what if historically and culturally the societies of Asia and Africa were fundamentally different from those of the West and could not, or would not, be persuaded to transform themselves along Western lines? In that case, a policy of cultural transformation could not be expected to succeed and could even lead to disaster.

ASSIMILATION OR ASSOCIATION? In fact, colonial theorists never decided the issue. The French, who were most inclined to philosophize about the problem, adopted the terms **assimilation** (which implied an effort to transform colonial societies in the Western image) and **association** (implying collaboration with local elites while leaving local traditions alone) to describe the two alternatives and then proceeded to vacillate between them. French policy in Indochina, for example, began as one of association but switched to assimilation under pressure from those who felt that colonial powers owed a debt to their subject peoples. But assimilation (which in any case was never accepted as feasible or desirable by many colonial officials) aroused resentment among the local population, many of whom opposed the destruction of their native traditions. In the end, the French abandoned the attempt to justify their presence and resorted to ruling by force of arms.

Other colonial powers had little interest in the issue. The British, whether out of a sense of pragmatism or of racial superiority, refused to entertain the possibility of assimilation and treated their subject peoples as culturally and racially distinct.

India Under the British Raj

Q FOCUS QUESTION: What were some of the major consequences of British rule in India, and how did they affect the Indian people?

By 1800, the once glorious empire of the Mughals (MOO-guls) had been reduced by British military power to a shadow of its former greatness. During the next decades, the British consolidated their control over the Indian subcontinent. Some territories were taken over directly, first by the East India Company and later by the British crown; others were ruled indirectly through their local maharajas (mah-huh-RAH-juhs) and rajas (RAH-juhs).

Colonial Reforms

Not all of the effects of British rule were bad. British governance over the subcontinent brought order and stability to a society that had been rent by civil war. By the early nineteenth century, British control had led to a relatively honest and efficient government that in many respects operated to the benefit of the average Indian. One benefit was the heightened attention given to education. Through the efforts of the British administrator Thomas Babington Macaulay (muh-KAHL-lee) (1800–1859), a new school system was established to train the children of Indian elites, and the British civil service examination was introduced (see the box on p. 549). The instruction of young girls also expanded, primarily in order to make them better wives and mothers for the educated male population. In 1875, a Madras (muh-DRAS or muh-DRAHS) medical college accepted its first female student.

British rule also brought an end to some of the more inhumane aspects of Indian tradition. The practice of *sati* (suh-TEE) was outlawed, and widows were legally permitted to remarry. The British also attempted to put an end to the endemic brigandage (known as *thuggee*, which gave rise to the English word *thug*) that had plagued travelers in India since time immemorial. Railroads, the telegraph, and the postal service were introduced to India shortly after they appeared in Great Britain. Work began on the main highway from Calcutta to Delhi (DEL-ee) in 1839 (see Map 21.1), and the first rail network in northern India was opened in 1853.

The Costs of Colonialism

But the Indian people paid a high price for the peace and stability brought by the British **raj** (RAHJ) (from the Indian *raja*, or prince). Perhaps the most flagrant cost was economic. While British entrepreneurs and a small percentage of the local population reaped financial benefits from British rule, it brought hardship to millions in both the cities and the rural areas. The introduction of British textiles put thousands of Bengali women out of work and severely damaged the local textile industry.

In rural areas, the British introduced the *zamindar* (zuh-meen-DAHR) system (see Chapter 16) in the misguided expectation that it would facilitate the collection of taxes and create a new landed gentry, who could, as in Britain, become the conservative foundation of imperial rule. But the local gentry took advantage of this new authority to increase taxes and force the less fortunate peasants to become tenants or lose their land entirely. British officials

Indian in Blood, English in Taste and Intellect

FAMILY & SOCIETY

As a member of the Supreme Council of India in the early 1830s, Thomas Babington Macaulay drew up an educational policy for Britain's Indian subjects. In his *Minute on Education*, he considered the claims of English and various local languages to become the vehicle for educational training and decided in favor of the former. If Indian elites were taught about Western civilization, he argued, they would "form a class who may be interpreters between us and the millions whom we govern; a class of persons, Indian in blood and color, but English in taste, in opinions, in morals, and in intellect." Later Macaulay became a prominent historian. The debate over the relative benefits of English and the various Indian languages continues today.

Thomas Babington Macaulay, *Minute on Education*

We have a fund to be employed as government shall direct for the intellectual improvement of the people of this country. The simple question is, what is the most useful way of employing it?

All parties seem to be agreed on one point, that the dialects commonly spoken among the natives of this part of India contain neither literary or scientific information, and are, moreover so poor and rude that, until they are enriched from some other quarter, it will not be easy to translate any valuable work into them. . . .

What, then, shall the language [of education] be? One half of the Committee maintain that it should be the English. The other half strongly recommend the Arabic and Sanskrit. The whole question seems to me to be, which language is the best worth knowing?

I have no knowledge of either Sanskrit or Arabic—but I have done what I could to form a correct estimate of their value. I have read translations of the most celebrated Arabic and Sanskrit works. I have conversed both here and at home with men distinguished by their proficiency in the Eastern tongues. I am quite ready to take the Oriental learning at the valuation of the Orientalists themselves. I have never found one among them who could deny that a single shelf of a good European library was worth the whole native literature of India and Arabia. . . .

It is, I believe, no exaggeration to say, that all the historical information which has been collected from all the books written in the Sanskrit language is less valuable than what may be found in the most paltry abridgments used at preparatory schools in England. In every branch of physical or moral philosophy the relative position of the two nations is nearly the same.

Q *How did Macaulay justify the teaching of the English language in India? How might a critic have responded?*

Source: From Speeches by *Lord Macaulay, With His Minute on Indian Education* by Thomas B. MacAuley. AMS Press, 1935.

---

also made few efforts during the nineteenth century to introduce democratic institutions or values. As one senior political figure remarked in Parliament in 1898, democratic institutions "can no more be carried to India by Englishmen . . . than they can carry ice in their luggage."[5]

The British also did little to bring modern science and technology to India. Some limited industrialization took place, notably in the manufacturing of textiles and jute (used in making rope). The first textile mill opened in 1856. Seventy years later, there were eighty mills in the city of Bombay (now Mumbai) alone. Nevertheless, the lack of local capital and the advantages given to British imports prevented the emergence of other vital new commercial and manufacturing operations.

Foreign rule also had a psychological effect on the Indian people. Although many British colonial officials sincerely tried to improve the lot of the people under their charge, British arrogance and contempt for native tradition cut deeply into the pride of many Indians, especially those of high caste, who were accustomed to a position of superior status in India. Educated Indians trained in the Anglo-Indian school system for a career in the civil service, as well as Eurasians born to mixed marriages, often imitated the behavior and dress of their rulers, speaking English, eating Western food, and taking up European leisure activities, but many rightfully wondered where their true cultural loyalties lay (see the comparative illustration on p. 551).

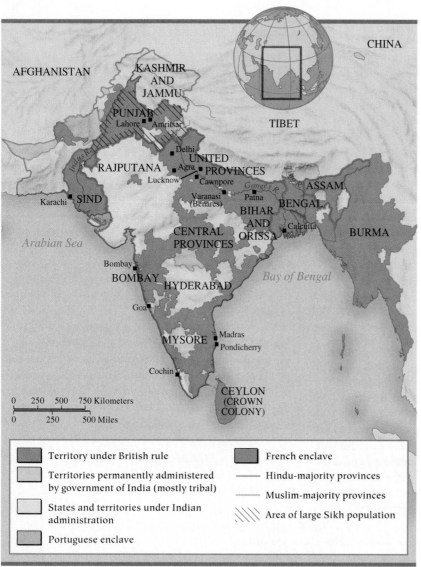

MAP 21.1 India Under British Rule, 1805–1931. This map shows the different forms of rule that the British applied in India under their control.

Q *Where were the major cities of the subcontinent located, and under whose rule did they fall?*

Colonial Regimes in Southeast Asia

Q FOCUS QUESTION: Which Western countries were most active in seeking colonial possessions in Southeast Asia, and what were their motives in doing so?

In 1800, only two societies in Southeast Asia were under effective colonial rule: the Spanish Philippines and the Dutch East Indies. During the nineteenth century,

however, European interest in Southeast Asia increased rapidly, and by 1900, virtually the entire area was under colonial rule (see Map 21.2).

"Opportunity in the Orient": The Colonial Takeover in Southeast Asia

The process began after the Napoleonic wars, when the British, by agreement with the Dutch, abandoned their claims to territorial possessions in the East Indies in return for a free hand in the Malay peninsula. In 1819, the colonial administrator Stamford Raffles founded a new British colony on the island of Singapore at the tip of the peninsula. Singapore became a major stopping point for traffic en route to and from China and other commercial centers in the region.

During the next decades, the pace of European penetration into Southeast Asia accelerated. The British attacked Burma in 1826 and eventually established control there, arousing fears in France that the British might acquire a monopoly of trade in South China. In 1858, the French launched an attack against Vietnam. Though it was not a total success, the Nguyen (NGWEN) dynasty in Vietnam was ultimately forced to cede some territories. A generation later, French rule was extended over the remainder of the country. By 1900, French seizure of neighboring Cambodia and Laos had led to the creation of the French-ruled Indochinese Union.

After the French conquest of Indochina, Thailand was the only remaining independent state on the Southeast Asian mainland. Under the astute leadership of two remarkable rulers, King Mongkut (MAHNG-koot) (1851–1868) and his son, King Chulalongkorn (CHOO-luh-lahng-kom) (1868–1910), the Thai attempted to introduce Western learning and maintain relations with the

COMPARATIVE ILLUSTRATION

INTERACTION & EXCHANGE

Cultural Influences—East and West. When Europeans moved into Asia in the nineteenth century, some Asians began to imitate European customs for prestige or social advancement. Seen at the left, for example, is a young Vietnamese during the 1920s dressed in Western sports clothes, learning to play tennis. Sometimes, however, the cultural influence went the other way. At the right, an English nabob, as European residents in India were often called, apes the manner of an Indian aristocrat, complete with harem and hookah, the Indian water pipe. The paintings on the wall, however, are in the European style.

Q *Compare and contrast the artistic styles of these two paintings. What message do they send to the viewer?*

major European powers without undermining internal stability or inviting an imperialist attack. In 1896, the British and the French agreed to preserve Thailand as an independent buffer zone between their possessions in Southeast Asia.

The final piece in the colonial edifice in Southeast Asia was put in place during the Spanish-American War in 1898 (see Chapter 20), when U.S. naval forces under Commodore George Dewey defeated the Spanish fleet in Manila Bay. President William McKinley agonized over the fate of the Philippines but ultimately decided that the moral thing to do was to turn the islands into an American colony to prevent them from falling into the hands of the Japanese. In fact, the Americans (like the Spanish before them) found the islands a convenient jumping-off point for the China trade (see Chapter 22). The mixture of moral idealism and desire for profit was reflected in a speech given in the U.S. Senate in January 1900 by Senator Albert Beveridge of Indiana:

> Mr. President, the times call for candor. The Philippines are ours forever, "territory belonging to the United States," as the Constitution calls them. And just beyond the Philippines are China's illimitable markets. We will not retreat from

either. . . . We will not renounce our part in the mission of our race, trustee, under God, of the civilization of the world. And we will move forward to our work, not howling out regrets like slaves whipped to their burdens, but with gratitude for a task worthy of our strength, and thanksgiving to Almighty God that He has marked us as His chosen people, henceforth to lead in the regeneration of the world.[6]

Not all Filipinos agreed with Beveridge's portrayal of the situation. Under the leadership of Emilio Aguinaldo (ay-MEEL-yoh ah-gwee-NAHL-doh), guerrilla forces fought bitterly against U.S. troops to establish their independence from both Spain and the United States. But America's first war against guerrilla forces in Asia was a success, and the bulk of the resistance collapsed in 1901. President McKinley had his stepping-stone to the rich markets of China.

The Nature of Colonial Rule

In Southeast Asia, the colonial powers were primarily concerned with economic profit and tried wherever possible to work with local elites to facilitate the exploitation

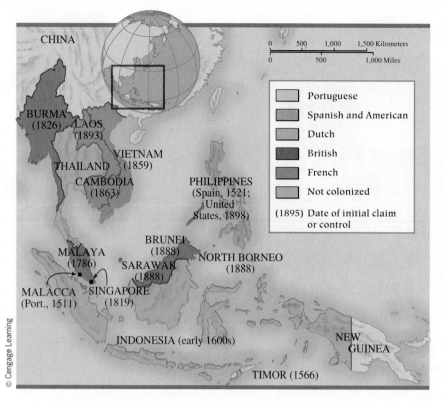

MAP 21.2 **Colonial Southeast Asia.** This map shows the spread of European colonial rule into Southeast Asia from the sixteenth century to the end of the nineteenth. Malacca, initially seized by the Portuguese in 1511, was taken by the Dutch in the seventeenth century and then by the British one hundred years later.

Q *What was the significance of Malacca?*

Map legend:
- Portuguese
- Spanish and American
- Dutch
- British
- French
- Not colonized

(1895) Date of initial claim or control

Map labels: CHINA; BURMA (1826); LAOS (1893); VIETNAM (1859); THAILAND; CAMBODIA (1863); PHILIPPINES (Spain, 1521; United States, 1898); BRUNEI (1888); SARAWAK (1888); NORTH BORNEO (1888); MALAYA (1786); MALACCA (Port., 1511); SINGAPORE (1819); INDONESIA (early 1600s); NEW GUINEA; TIMOR (1566)

Scale: 0 500 1,000 1,500 Kilometers / 0 500 1,000 Miles

© Cengage Learning

the southern provinces in the Mekong delta but governed the north as a protectorate, with the emperor retaining titular authority from his palace in Hué (HWAY). The French adopted a similar policy in Cambodia and Laos, where local rulers were left in charge with French advisers to counsel them.

Whatever method was used, the colonial regimes were slow to create democratic institutions. The first legislative councils and assemblies were composed almost exclusively of European residents in the colonies. The first representatives from the indigenous population were wealthy and politically conservative. When Southeast Asians complained, the French official Albert Sarraut advised patience: "I will treat you like my younger brothers, but do not forget that I am the older brother. I will slowly give you the dignity of humanity."[7] Only gradually and reluctantly did colonial officials begin to broaden the franchise.

Colonial officials were also slow to adopt educational reforms. Although the introduction of Western education was one of the justifications of colonialism, officials soon discovered that educating local elites could backfire. Colonial societies often had few jobs for lawyers, engineers, and architects, leading to a mass of unemployed intellectuals ready to take out their frustrations on the colonial regime. As one French official noted in voicing his opposition to increasing the number of schools in Vietnam, educating the locals meant not "one coolie less, but one rebel more."

of natural resources. Indirect rule was less costly than training European administrators and had a less corrosive impact on the local culture. In the Dutch East Indies, for example, officials of the Dutch East India Company (or VOC, the initials of its Dutch name) entrusted local administration to the indigenous aristocracy, who maintained law and order and collected taxes in return for a payment from the VOC. The British followed a similar practice in Malaya. While establishing direct rule over the crucial commercial centers of Singapore and Malacca, the British allowed local Muslim rulers to maintain power in the interior of the peninsula.

ADMINISTRATION AND EDUCATION Indirect rule, though convenient and inexpensive, was not always feasible. In some instances, local resistance to the colonial conquest made such a policy impossible. In Burma, the staunch opposition of the monarchy and other traditionalist forces caused the British to abolish the monarchy and administer the country directly through their colonial government in India. In Indochina, the French used both direct and indirect means. They imposed direct rule on

ECONOMIC DEVELOPMENT Colonial powers were equally reluctant to take up the "white man's burden" in the area of economic development. As we have seen, their primary goals were to secure cheap raw materials and to maintain markets for manufactured goods. Colonial policy therefore concentrated on exporting raw materials—teakwood from Burma; rubber and tin from Malaya; spices, tea and coffee, and palm oil from the East Indies; and sugar and copra (the meat of a coconut) from the Philippines.

In some Southeast Asian colonial societies, a measure of industrial development did take place to meet the

Government Hill in Singapore. After occupying Singapore early in the nineteenth century, the British turned what was once a pirate lair into an important commercial seaport. Like other colonial port cities, Singapore became home to a rich mixture of peoples, who came to work as merchants, urban laborers, and craftsmen in the new imperial marketplace. The multiracial character of the colony is evident in this mid-nineteenth-century painting by a British artist. People of various ethnic backgrounds stroll on Government Hill, with the busy harbor in the background.

A Rubber Plantation. Natural rubber was one of the most important cash crops in European colonies in Asia. Rubber trees, native to the Amazon River basin in Brazil, were transplanted to Southeast Asia, where they became a major source of profit. Workers on the plantations received few benefits, however. Once the sap of the tree (known as latex and shown on the left) was extracted, it was hardened and pressed into sheets (shown on the right) and then sent to Europe for refining.

needs of the European population and local elites. Major manufacturing cities like Rangoon in lower Burma, Batavia (buh-TAY-vee-uh) on the island of Java, and Saigon (sy-GAHN) in French Indochina grew rapidly. Most large industrial and commercial establishments were owned and managed by Europeans, however, or, in some cases, by Indian or Chinese merchants.

COLONIALISM AND THE COUNTRYSIDE Despite the growth of an urban economy, the vast majority of people continued to farm the land. Many continued to live by subsistence agriculture, but the colonial policy of emphasizing cash crops for export also led to the creation of a plantation agriculture in which peasants worked for poverty-level wages on rubber and tea plantations owned by Europeans. Many laborers were "shanghaied" (the English term originated from the practice of recruiting workers, often from the docks and streets of Shanghai, by the use of force, alcohol, or drugs) to work on the plantations, where conditions were often so inhumane that thousands died. High taxes, imposed by colonial governments to pay for administrative costs or improvements in the local infrastructure, were a heavy burden for poor peasants.

The situation was made even more difficult by the dramatic growth of the population as improved sanitation and medical treatment resulted in lower rates of infant mortality. The population of the island of Java, for example, increased from about a million in the precolonial era to about 40 million at the end of the nineteenth century. Under these conditions, the rural areas could no longer support the growing populations, and many young people fled to the cities to seek jobs in factories or shops.

As in India, colonial rule brought some benefits to Southeast Asia. It led to the beginnings of a modern economic infrastructure and to what is sometimes called a "modernizing elite" dedicated to the creation of an advanced industrialized society. The development of an export market helped create an entrepreneurial class in rural areas. This happened, for example, on the outer islands of the Dutch East Indies (such as Borneo and Sumatra), where small growers of rubber trees, palm trees for oil, coffee, tea, and spices began to share in the profits of the colonial enterprise.

Empire Building in Africa

Q FOCUS QUESTION: What factors were behind the "scramble for Africa," and what impact did it have on the continent?

Before 1800, European economic interests in Africa had been relatively limited, providing little incentive for the penetration of the interior or the political takeover of the coastal areas. The slave trade, the main source of European profit during the eighteenth century, could be carried on by using African rulers and merchants as intermediaries. Disease, political instability, the lack of transportation, and the generally unhealthy climate all deterred Europeans from more extensive efforts in Africa. The situation began to change in the nineteenth century, as the growing need for industrial materials created a reason for the imperialist countries to increase their economic presence in the continent.

The Growing European Presence in West Africa

As the new century dawned, the slave trade was in decline, in part because of the efforts of humanitarians in several European countries. Dutch merchants effectively ceased trafficking in slaves in 1795, and the Danes stopped in 1803. In 1808, the slave trade was declared illegal in both Great Britain and the United States. The British began to apply pressure on other nations to follow suit, and most did so after the end of the Napoleonic wars in 1815, leaving only Portugal and Spain as practitioners of the trade south of the equator. In the meantime, the demand for slaves began to decline in the Western Hemisphere. When slavery was abolished in the United States in 1863 and in Cuba and Brazil seventeen years later, the slave trade across the Atlantic was effectively brought to an end. It continued to exist, although at a reduced rate, along the Swahili coast in East Africa.

As the Atlantic slave trade declined, Europeans became more interested in so-called legitimate trade. Exports of peanuts, timber, hides, and palm oil from West Africa increased substantially during the first decades of the nineteenth century, while imports of textile goods and other manufactured products rose.

CHRONOLOGY	Imperialism in Asia	
Stamford Raffles arrives in Singapore	1819
British attack lower Burma	1826
British rail network opens in northern India	1853
Sepoy Rebellion	1857
French attack Vietnam	1858
British and French agree to neutralize Thailand	1896
Commodore Dewey defeats Spanish fleet in Manila Bay	1898
French create Indochinese Union	1900

European governments also began to push for a more permanent presence along the coast. During the early nineteenth century, the British established settlements along the Gold Coast and in Sierra Leone, where they set up agricultural plantations for freed slaves who had returned from the Western Hemisphere or had been liberated by British ships while en route to the Americas. A similar haven for ex-slaves was developed with the assistance of the United States in Liberia. The French occupied the area around the Senegal River near Cape Verde, where they attempted to develop peanut plantations.

The European presence in West Africa led to the emergence of a new class of Africans educated in Western culture and often employed by Europeans. Many became Christians, and some studied in European or American universities. At the same time, tensions were increasing between Europeans and African governments. Most African states were able to maintain their independence from this creeping European encroachment, called "**informal empire**" by some historians, but the prospects for the future were ominous. When local groups attempted to organize to protect their interests, the British stepped in and annexed the coastal states as the British colony of Gold Coast in 1874. At about the same time, the British extended an informal protectorate over warring ethnic groups in the Niger delta (see Map 21.3).

Imperialist Shadow over the Nile

A similar process was under way in the Nile valley. There had long been interest in shortening the trade route to the East by digging a canal across the isthmus separating the Mediterranean from the Red Sea. In 1798, Napoleon had unsuccessfully invaded Egypt in an effort to cement French power in the eastern Mediterranean and open a faster route to India. French troops landed in Egypt and destroyed the ramshackle Mamluk (MAM-look) regime, but the British counterattacked and destroyed the French fleet. The British restored the Mamluks to power, but in 1805 Muhammad Ali (1769–1849), an Ottoman army officer, seized control.

During the next three decades, Muhammad Ali introduced a series of reforms to bring Egypt into the modern world. He modernized the army, set up a public education system (supplementing the traditional religious education provided in Muslim schools), and sponsored the creation of a small industrial sector producing refined sugar, textiles, munitions, and even ships. Muhammad Ali also extended

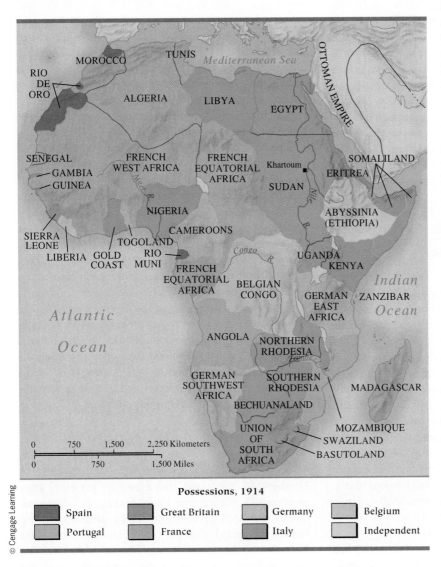

Possessions, 1914

- Spain
- Portugal
- Great Britain
- France
- Germany
- Italy
- Belgium
- Independent

MAP 21.3 Africa in 1914. By the start of the twentieth century, virtually all of Africa was under some form of European rule. The territorial divisions established by colonial powers on the continent of Africa on the eve of World War I are shown here.

Q *Which European countries possessed the most colonies in Africa? Why did Ethiopia remain independent?*

Egyptian authority southward into the Sudan and eastward into Arabia, Syria, and northern Iraq and even threatened to seize Istanbul itself. To prevent the possible collapse of the Ottoman Empire, the British and the French recognized Muhammad Ali as the hereditary **pasha** (PAH-shuh) of Egypt under the loose authority of the Ottoman government.

The growing economic importance of the Nile valley, along with the development of steam navigation, made the heretofore visionary plans for a Suez canal more urgent. In 1869, construction of the canal was completed under the direction of Ferdinand de Lesseps (fer-DEE-nahn duh le-SEPS), a French entrepreneur. The project brought little immediate benefit to Egypt, however. The construction cost thousands of lives and left the Egyptian government deep in debt, forcing it to depend increasingly on foreign financial support. When an army revolt against growing foreign influence broke out in 1881, the British stepped in to protect their investment (they had bought Egypt's canal company shares in 1875) and established an informal protectorate that would last until World War I.

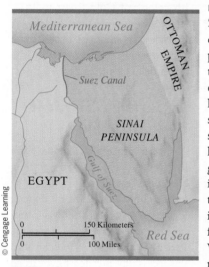

The Suez Canal

Rising discontent in the Sudan added to Egypt's growing internal problems. In 1881, the Muslim cleric Muhammad Ahmad (AH-mahd) (1844–1885), known as the Mahdi (MAH-dee) (in Arabic, the "rightly guided one"), led a religious revolt that brought much of the upper Nile under his control. The famous British general Charles Gordon led a military force to Khartoum (kahr-TOOM) to restore Egyptian authority, but his besieged army was captured in 1885 by the Mahdi's troops, thirty-six hours before a British rescue mission reached Khartoum. Gordon himself died in the battle (see the Film & History feature on p. 557).

The weakening of Turkish rule in the Nile valley had a parallel to the west, where local viceroys in Tripoli, Tunis, and Algiers had begun to establish their autonomy. In 1830, the French, on the pretext of protecting shipping from pirates, seized the area surrounding Algiers and integrated it into the French Empire. In 1881, the French imposed a protectorate on neighboring Tunisia; only Tripoli and Cyrenaica (seer-uh-NAY-uh-kuh), the territories comprising modern Libya, remained under Turkish rule.

Arab Merchants and European Missionaries in East Africa

As always, events in East Africa followed their own distinctive pattern. Whereas the Atlantic slave trade was in decline, demand for slaves was increasing on the other side of the continent due to the growth of plantation agriculture in the region. The French introduced sugar to the island of Réunion (ray-yoo-NYAHN) early in the century, and plantations of cloves (introduced from the Moluccas) were established under Omani Arab ownership on the island of Zanzibar (ZAN-zi-bar). Zanzibar itself became the major shipping port along the east coast during the early nineteenth century, and the sultan of Oman, who had reasserted Arab suzerainty over the region after the collapse of Portuguese authority, established his capital there in 1840.

The tenacity of the slave trade in East Africa—Zanzibar was now the largest slave market in Africa—drew Christian missionaries to the region during the middle of the century. The most renowned was the Scottish doctor David Livingstone (LIV-ing-stuhn) (1813–1873), who arrived in Africa in 1841. Because Livingstone spent much of his time exploring the interior of the continent, discovering Victoria Falls in the process, he was occasionally criticized for being more explorer than missionary. But Livingstone was convinced that it was his divinely appointed task to bring Christianity to the continent, and his passionate opposition to slavery did much to win public support for the abolitionist cause. Public outcries caused the British to redouble their efforts to bring the slave trade to an end, and in 1873 shortly after Livingstone's death, the slave market at Zanzibar was finally closed as the result of pressure from London.

Bantus, Boers, and British in the South

Nowhere in Africa did the European presence grow more rapidly than in the south. During the eighteenth century, the Boers (BOORS *or* BORS), Afrikaans-speaking farmers descended from the original Dutch settlers of the Cape Colony, began to migrate eastward. After the British seized the cape during the Napoleonic wars, the Boers' eastward migration intensified, culminating in the Great Trek of the mid-1830s. In part, the Boers' departure was provoked by the British attitude toward the local population. Slavery was abolished in the British Empire in 1834, and the British government was

Khartoum (1966)

The mission of General Charles Gordon to Khartoum in 1884 was one of the most dramatic news stories of the late nineteenth century. Gordon was already renowned for his successful efforts to bring an end to the practice of slavery in North Africa and his role in helping suppress the Taiping Rebellion in China in the 1860s (see Chapter 22). But the Khartoum affair not only marked the culmination of his storied career but also symbolized the struggle in Britain between advocates and opponents of imperial expansion. The battle for Khartoum became an object lesson in modern British history.

Proponents of British imperial expansion argued that the country must project its power in the Nile valley to protect the Suez Canal, its main trade route to the East. Critics argued that imperial overreach would inevitably entangle the country in unwinnable wars in far-off places. The movie *Khartoum*, filmed in Egypt and London, captures the ferocity of the battle for the Nile as well as its significance for the future of the British Empire. General Gordon, stoically played by the American actor Charlton Heston, is a devout Christian who has devoted his life to carrying out the moral imperative of imperialism. When peace in the Sudan (then a British protectorate) is threatened by the forces of the Muslim mystic Muhammad Ahmad—known as the Mahdi—Gordon leads a mission to Khartoum under orders to prevent catastrophe there. But Prime Minister William Ewart Gladstone, admirably portrayed by the British actor Ralph Richardson, fears that Gordon's messianic desire to save the Sudan will entrap the government in an unwinnable war; he thus orders

Cinerama/United Artists/The Kobal Collection at Art Resource, NY

General Charles Gordon (Charlton Heston) astride his camel in Khartoum, Sudan.

Gordon to evacuate the city. The most fascinating character in the film is the Mahdi (played brilliantly by Sir Laurence Olivier), who believes that he has a sacred mandate to carry the Prophet's words to the global Muslim community.

The film reaches a climax with the clash of wills in the battle for control of Khartoum. Although the film's portrayal of a face-to-face meeting between Gordon and the Mahdi is not based on fact, the narrative serves as an object lesson on the dangers of imperial overreach and as an eerie foretaste of the clash between Islam and Christendom in our own day.

---

generally more sympathetic to the rights of the local African population than were the Afrikaners (ah-fri-KAH-nurz), many of whom believed that white superiority was ordained by God. Eventually, the Boers formed their own independent republics—the Orange Free State and the South African Republic, usually called the Transvaal (trans-VAHL) (see Map 21.4).

Although the Boer occupation of the eastern territory was initially facilitated by internecine warfare among the local inhabitants, the new settlers met some resistance. In the early nineteenth century, the Zulus (ZOO-looz), a Bantu people led by a talented ruler named Shaka (SHAH-kuh), engaged in a series of wars with the Europeans that ended only when Shaka was overthrown.

The Scramble for Africa

At the beginning of the 1880s, most of Africa was still independent. European rule was limited to the fringes of the continent, such as Algeria, the Gold Coast, and South Africa. Other areas like Egypt, lower Nigeria, Senegal (sen-ni-GAHL), and Mozambique (moh-zam-BEEK) were under loose protectorates. But the pace of European penetration was accelerating.

The scramble began in the mid-1880s when several European states, including Belgium, France, Germany, and Great Britain, engaged in a feeding frenzy to seize a piece of the African cake before the plate had been picked clean. By 1900, virtually all of the continent had

The Sunday Battle. When Boer "trekkers" arrived in the Transvaal in the 1830s and 1840s, they were bitterly opposed by the Zulus, a Bantu-speaking people who resisted European encroachments on their territory for decades. This 1847 lithograph depicted thousands of Zulu warriors engaged in battle with their European rivals. Zulu resistance was not finally quelled until the end of the nineteenth century.

been placed under some form of European rule. The British consolidated their authority over the Nile valley and seized additional territories in East Africa (see Map 21.3 on p. 555). The French advanced eastward from Senegal into the central Sahara. They also occupied Madagascar and other territories in West and Central Africa. The Germans claimed the hinterland opposite Zanzibar, as well as coastal strips in West and Southwest Africa, and King Leopold (LAY-oh-polt) II (1835–1909) of Belgium claimed the Congo for his own personal use. Italy entered the contest in 1911–1912 and seized the territories that comprise modern Libya.

What had sparked the imperialist hysteria that brought an end to African independence? Although trade between Europe and Africa had increased, it was probably not sufficient, by itself, to justify the risks and expense of conquest. More important than economic interests were the rivalries among the European states that led them to engage in imperialist takeovers out of fear that if they did not, another state would. As one British diplomat remarked, a protectorate at the mouth of the Niger River would be an "unwelcome burden," but a French protectorate there would be "fatal." Hence, as in Southeast Asia, statesmen felt compelled to obtain colonies as a hedge against future actions by rivals. Notably,

the British solidified their control over the entire Nile valley to protect the Suez Canal from the French.

Another consideration might be called the "missionary factor," as European missionaries lobbied for colonial takeovers to facilitate their efforts to convert the African population. The concept of social Darwinism and the "white man's burden" persuaded many that they had a duty to introduce the African people to the benefits of Western civilization. Even David Livingstone believed that missionary work and economic development had to go hand in hand, pleading with his fellow Europeans to introduce the "three Cs" (Christianity, commerce, and civilization) to the continent. How much easier that task would be if African peoples were under benevolent European rule!

There were more prosaic reasons as well. Advances in Western technology and European superiority in firearms made it easier than ever for a small European force to defeat superior numbers (see the box on p. 560). Furthermore, life expectancy for Europeans living in Africa had improved. With the discovery that quinine (from the bark of the cinchona tree) could provide partial immunity from malaria, the mortality rate for Europeans living in Africa dropped dramatically. By the end of the century, European residents in tropical Africa faced only slightly higher risks of death by disease than individuals living in Europe.

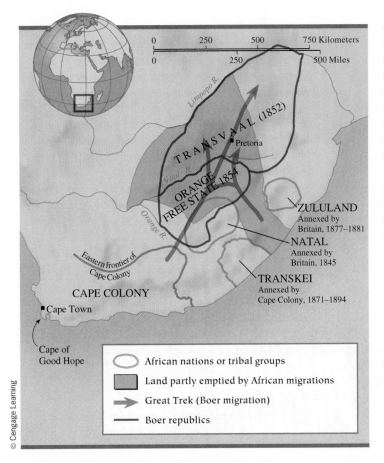

MAP 21.4 The Struggle for Southern Africa. European settlers from the Cape Colony expanded into adjacent areas of southern Africa during the nineteenth century. The arrows indicate the routes taken by the Afrikaans-speaking Boers.

Q *Who were the Boers, and why did they migrate eastward?*

Under these circumstances, King Leopold of Belgium used missionary activities as an excuse to claim vast territories in the Congo River basin—Belgium, he said, as "a small country, with a small people," needed a colony to enhance its image.[8] The royal land grab set off a race among European nations to stake claims throughout sub-Saharan Africa. Leopold ended up with the territories south of the Congo River, while France occupied areas to the north. Rapacious European adventurers established plantations in the new Belgian Congo to grow rubber, palm oil, and other valuable export products. Conditions for African workers were so abysmal that an international outcry led in 1903 to the formation of a commission under British consul Roger Casement to investigate. The commission's report, issued in 1904, helped to bring about reforms.

Meanwhile, in East Africa, Germany annexed the colony of Tanganyika (tan-gan-YEE-kuh). To avert violent clashes among the great powers, the German chancellor, Otto von Bismarck, convened a conference in Berlin in 1884 to set ground rules for future annexations of African territory. Like the famous Open Door Notes fifteen years later (see Chapter 22), the conference combined high-minded resolutions with a hardheaded recognition of practical interests. The delegates called for free commerce in the Congo and along the Niger River as well as for further efforts to end the slave trade. At the same time, the participants recognized the inevitability of the imperialist dynamic, agreeing only that future annexations of African territory should not be recognized until effective occupation had been demonstrated. No African delegates were present at the conference.

During the next few years, African territories were annexed without provoking a major confrontation between the Western powers, but in 1898, Britain and France reached the brink of conflict at Fashoda (fuh-SHOH-duh), a small town in the Sudan. The French had been advancing eastward across the Sahara with the objective of controlling the regions around the upper Nile. British and Egyptian troops then marched southward to head off the French. After a tense face-off, the French government backed down, and British authority over the area was secured.

Colonialism in Africa

Having seized Africa in what could almost be described as a fit of hysteria, the European powers had to decide what to do with it. With economic concerns relatively limited except for isolated areas like the gold mines in the Transvaal and copper deposits in the Belgian Congo, interest in Africa declined, and most European governments settled down to govern their new territories with the least effort and expense possible. In many cases, this meant a form of indirect rule similar to what the British used in the princely states in India.

INDIRECT RULE IN WEST AFRICA For British administrators, the stated goal of indirect rule was to preserve African political traditions. The desire to limit cost was one reason for this approach, but it may also have been due to the conviction that Africans were inherently inferior and thus incapable of adopting European customs and institutions. In any event, indirect rule entailed relying on existing political elites and institutions. In some areas, the British simply asked a local ruler to formally accept British authority. Sometimes the Africans did the

The Ndebele Rebellion

SCIENCE & TECHNOLOGY

As British forces advanced northward from the Cape Colony toward the Zambezi River in the 1890s, they overran the Ndebele (uhn-duh-BEE-lee) people, who occupied rich lands near the site of the ruins of Great Zimbabwe (zim-BAHB-way). Angered by British brutality, Ndebele warriors revolted in 1896 to throw off their oppressors. Despite the Ndebele's great superiority in numbers, British units possessed the feared Maxim gun, which mowed down African attackers by the hundreds. Faced with defeat, the Ndebele king, Lobengula (loh-beng-GOO-luh), fled into the hills and committed suicide. In the following account, a survivor describes the conflict.

Ndansi Kumalo, *A Personal Account*

We surrendered to the white people and were told to go back to our homes and live our usual lives and attend to our crops. But the white men sent native police who did abominable things; they were cruel and assaulted a lot of our people and helped themselves to our cattle and goats. . . . They interfered with our wives and molested them. . . . We thought it best to fight and die rather than bear it. . . .

We knew that we had very little chance because their weapons were so much superior to ours. But we meant to fight to the last, feeling that even if we could not beat them we might at least kill a few of them and so have some sort of revenge. . . .

I remember a fight . . . when we charged the white men. There were some hundreds of us; the white men also were many. We charged them at close quarters: we thought we had a good chance to kill them but the Maxims were too much for us. . . . Many of our people were killed in this fight. . . .

We were still fighting when we heard that [Cecil] Rhodes was coming and wanted to make peace with us. It was best to come to terms he said, and not go shedding blood like this on both sides. . . . So peace was made. Many of our people had been killed, and now we began to die of starvation; and then came the rinderpest [an infectious disease] and the cattle that were still left to us perished. We could not help thinking that all these dreadful things were brought by the white people.

Q *How would you characterize the relationship between the Ndebele people and the British? How can the behavior of the British as described in this account be reconciled with the concept of the "white man's burden"?*

Source: From Margery Perham, *Ten Africans* (London: Faber & Faber, 1963), pp. 72–75.

---

asking, as in the case of the African leaders in Cameroons who wrote to Queen Victoria:

We *wish* to have your laws in our towns. We want to have every *fashion* altered; also we will do according to your Consul's *word*. Plenty wars here in our country. Plenty murder and plenty idol worshippers. Perhaps these *lines* of our writing will look to you as an *idle* tale.

We have *spoken* to the English consul plenty times about having an English *government* here. We never have answer from you, so we wish to write you *ourselves*.[9]

Nigeria offers a typical example of British indirect rule. British officials maintained the central administration, but local authority was assigned to local chiefs, with British district officers serving as intermediaries. The local authorities were expected to maintain law and order

and to collect taxes. Local customs were generally left undisturbed, although slavery was abolished. A dual legal system was instituted that applied African laws to Africans and European laws to foreigners.

Although such a system did not severely disrupt local institutions, it had some undesirable consequences. It was essentially a fraud since British administrators made all major decisions and the local authorities merely enforced them. Moreover, indirect rule served to perpetuate the autocratic system often in use prior to colonial takeover.

THE BRITISH IN EAST AFRICA The situation was somewhat different in East Africa, especially in Kenya, which had a relatively large European population. The local government had encouraged white settlers to

© Universal Images Group/Getty Images

Legacy of Shame. By the mid-nineteenth century, most European nations had prohibited the trade in African slaves, but slavery continued to exist in Africa well into the next century. The most flagrant example was in the Belgian Congo, where the mistreatment of conscript laborers led to a popular outcry and the formation of a commission to investigate and recommend reforms. Shown here are two members of a chain gang in the Belgian Congo. The photograph was taken in 1904.

CHRONOLOGY	Imperialism in Africa	
Dutch abolish slave trade in Africa		1795
Napoleon invades Egypt		1798
Slave trade declared illegal in Great Britain		1808
French seize Algeria		1830
Boers' Great Trek in southern Africa		1830s
Sultan of Oman establishes capital at Zanzibar		1840
David Livingstone arrives in Africa		1841
Slavery abolished in the United States		1863
Suez Canal completed		1869
Zanzibar slave market closed		1873
British establish Gold Coast colony		1874
British establish informal protectorate over Egypt		1881
Berlin Conference on Africa		1884
Charles Gordon killed at Khartoum		1885
Confrontation at Fashoda		1898
Boer War		1899–1902
Casement Commission report on the Belgian Congo		1904
Union of South Africa established		1910

migrate to the area as a means of promoting economic development. Fertile farmlands in the central highlands were reserved for Europeans, while specified reserve lands were set aside for Africans. The presence of a substantial European minority (although, in fact, they represented only about 1 percent of the entire population) affected Kenya's political development. The white settlers sought self-government and dominion status similar to that granted to Canada and Australia. The British government, however, was not willing to risk provoking racial tensions with the African majority and agreed only to establish separate government organs for the European and African populations.

BRITISH RULE IN SOUTH AFRICA The British used a different system in southern Africa, which had a high percentage of European settlers. The situation was complicated by the division between the English-speaking and Afrikaner elements, which intensified after gold and diamonds were discovered in the Boer republic of the Transvaal. After Cecil Rhodes, prime minister of the Cape Colony, attempted to bring the Transvaal under British rule, the so-called Boer War broke out between Britain and the Boer republics in 1899. Guerrilla resistance by the Boers was fierce, but the vastly superior forces of the British were able to prevail by 1902. To compensate the Afrikaners for the loss of independence, the British government agreed that only whites would vote in the now essentially self-governing colony. Nevertheless, the brutalities committed during the war (the British introduced an institution later known as the concentration camp) had left bitterness on both sides.

In 1910, the British agreed to the creation of the independent Union of South Africa, which combined the old Cape Colony and Natal (nuh-TAHL) with the Boer republics. The new union adopted a representative government, but only for the European population, while the African reserves of Basutoland (buh-SOO-toh-land), now Lesotho (luh-SOH-toh); Bechuanaland (bech-WAH-nuh-land), now Botswana (baht-SWAH-nuh); and Swaziland (SWAH-zee-land) were subordinated directly to the crown. The union was free to manage its domestic affairs and possessed considerable autonomy in foreign relations. Formal British rule was also extended to the lands south of the Zambezi River, which were eventually divided into the territories of Northern and Southern Rhodesia. Southern Rhodesia attracted many British immigrants, and in 1922, after a popular referendum, it became a crown colony.

DIRECT RULE   Most other European nations governed their African possessions through a form of direct rule. The prototype was the French system, which reflected the centralized administrative system used in France. At the top was a French governor-general, who was appointed from Paris. At the provincial level, French commissioners were assigned to deal with local administrators, who were required to be conversant in French.

The French ideal was to assimilate their African subjects into French culture rather than preserving their local traditions. Africans were eligible to run for office and to serve in the French National Assembly, and a few were appointed to high positions in the colonial administration. Such policies reflected the relative absence of racist attitudes in French society, as well as the conviction among the French of the superiority of Gallic culture.

After World War I, European colonial policy in Africa entered a more formal phase that specialists in African studies call "**high colonialism**." The administrative network was extended into outlying areas, where it was represented by a district official and defended by a small African army under European command. The colonial system was viewed more formally as a moral and social responsibility, a "sacred trust" to be maintained by the civilized countries until the Africans became capable of self-government. Greater attention was given to improving social services, including education, medicine and sanitation, and communications. More emphasis was placed on economic development to enable the colonies to become self-sufficient. More Africans served in colonial administrations, although rarely in positions of responsibility. At the same time, race consciousness probably increased. Segregated clubs, schools, and churches were established as more European officials brought their wives and began to raise families in the colonies. European feelings of superiority to their African subjects led to countless examples of cruelty. Although the institution of slavery was discouraged, African workers were often subjected to harsh conditions as they were put to use in promoting the cause of imperialism.

WOMEN IN COLONIAL AFRICA   The colonial era had a mixed impact on the rights and status of women in Africa. Sexual relationships changed profoundly, sometimes in ways that could justly be described as beneficial.

Colonial governments attempted to bring an end to forced marriage, bodily mutilation such as clitoridectomy (clit-er-ih-DEK-toh-mee), and polygamy. Missionaries introduced women to Western education and encouraged them to organize to defend their interests.

But the colonial system had some unfavorable consequences as well. Previously, African women had benefited from the matrilineal system and their traditional role as the primary agricultural producers. Under colonialism, European settlers not only took the best land for themselves but also tended to deal exclusively with males, encouraging them to develop lucrative cash crops using new techniques, while women were restricted to traditional farming methods. African men applied chemical fertilizer to the fields, but women continued to use manure. Men began to use bicycles and eventually trucks for transport, but women still carried goods on their heads. In British colonies, Victorian attitudes of female subordination led to restrictions on women's freedom, and positions in government that they had formerly held were now closed to them.

The Emergence of Anticolonialism

Q **FOCUS QUESTION:** How did the subject peoples respond to colonialism, and what role did nationalism play in their response?

Thus far we have looked at the colonial experience primarily from the point of view of the colonial powers. Equally important is the way the subject peoples reacted to the experience. In this chapter, we will deal with the initial response, which can be described in most cases as "traditional resistance." Later, however, many people in the colonized societies began to turn to nationalism as a means of preserving their ethnic, cultural, or religious identity. We will deal with that stage in more detail in Chapter 24.

Stirrings of Nationhood

As noted earlier, nationalism involves an awareness of being part of a community that possesses common institutions, traditions, language, and customs (see the comparative essay "The Rise of Nationalism" in Chapter 20). In the nineteenth century, few societies met such criteria. Even today, most modern states contain a variety of ethnic, religious, and linguistic communities, each with its own sense of cultural and national identity. Another question is how nationalism differs from other forms of tribal, religious, or linguistic affiliation. Should every group that resists assimilation into a larger political entity be called nationalist?

Such questions complicate the study of nationalism and make agreement on a definition elusive. The dilemmas are especially complex when discussing Asia and Africa, where most societies are deeply divided by ethnic, linguistic, and religious differences and the very term *nationalism* is a foreign concept imported from the West. Before the colonial era, most traditional societies in Africa and Asia were formed on the basis of religious beliefs, ethnic loyalties, or devotion to hereditary monarchies. Although some individuals may have identified themselves as members of a particular national group, others viewed themselves as subjects of a king, members of a lineage group, or adherents to a particular religion.

The advent of European colonialism brought the consciousness of modern nationhood to many of these societies. The creation of colonies with defined borders and a powerful central government led to the weakening of local ethnic and religious loyalties. The introduction of Western ideas of citizenship and representative government—even though they usually were not replicated in the colonies themselves—produced a desire for participation in the affairs of government. At the same time, the appearance of a new elite class based on alleged racial or cultural superiority aroused a shared sense of resentment among the subject peoples. By the first quarter of the twentieth century, political movements dedicated to the overthrow of colonial rule and the creation of modern nations had arisen throughout much of the non-Western world.

Modern nationalism, then, was both a product of colonialism and a reaction to it. But a sense of nationhood does not emerge full-blown in a society. The rise of modern nationalism is a process that begins among a few members of the educated elite (most commonly among articulate professionals such as lawyers, teachers, journalists, and doctors) and then spreads gradually to the mass of the population. Even after national independence has been realized, it is often questionable whether a mature sense of nationhood has been created, since local ethnic, linguistic, or religious ties often continue to predominate over loyalty to the larger community (see Chapter 29).

Traditional Resistance: A Precursor to Nationalism

The beginnings of modern nationalism can be found in the initial resistance by the indigenous peoples to the colonial conquest. Although such resistance was essentially motivated by the desire to defend traditional institutions and thus was not strictly "nationalist," it did reflect a primitive concept of nationhood in that it aimed at protecting the homeland from the invader. After independence was achieved, governments of new nations often hailed early resistance movements as the precursors of twentieth-century nationalist movements. Thus, traditional resistance to colonial conquest may be viewed as the first stage in the development of modern nationalism.

Such resistance took various forms. For the most part, it was led by the existing ruling class, although in some instances traditionalists continued their opposition even after resistance by the rulers had ceased. In India, Tipu Sultan (tih-POO SUL-tun) fought the British in the Deccan after the collapse of the Mughal dynasty. Similarly, after the decrepit monarchy in Vietnam had bowed to French pressure, civilian and military officials set up an organization called Can Vuong (kahn VWAHNG) (literally, "save the king") and continued their own resistance campaign without imperial sanction.

Sometimes traditional resistance to Western penetration took the form of peasant revolts. In traditional Asian societies, peasant discontent with high taxes, official corruption, rising debt, and famine had often led to uprisings. Under colonialism, rural conditions frequently deteriorated as population density increased and peasants were driven off the land to make way for plantation agriculture. Angry peasants then vented their frustration at the foreign invaders. For example, in Burma, the Buddhist monk Saya San (SAH-yuh SAHN) led a peasant uprising against the British. Similar unrest occurred in India, where *zamindars* and rural villagers alike resisted government attempts to increase tax revenues. A peasant uprising took place in Algeria in 1840.

OPPOSITION TO COLONIAL RULE IN AFRICA Because of Africa's size and its ethnic, religious, and linguistic diversity, resistance to the European invaders was often sporadic and uncoordinated, but fierce nonetheless. The uprising led by the Mahdi in the Sudan was only the most dramatic example. In South Africa, the Zulus engaged in a bitter war of resistance to Boer colonists arriving from the Cape Colony. Later they fought against the British occupation of their territory and were not finally subdued until the end of the century. In West Africa, the Ashanti ruling class led a bitter struggle against the British with broad-based popular support. The lack of modern weapons was decisive, however, and African resistance forces eventually suffered defeat throughout the continent (see the box on p. 560). The one exception was Ethiopia where, at the Battle of Adowa (AH-doo-wah) in 1896, the modernized army created by Emperor Menelik (MEN-il-ik), who had prudently purchased modern European weapons, was able to fend off an Italian invasion force and preserve the country's national independence well into the next century.

THE SEPOY REBELLION Perhaps the most famous uprising against European authority in the mid-nineteenth century was the revolt of the **sepoys** (SEE-poiz) in India. The sepoys (from the Turkish *sipahis*, cavalrymen or soldiers) were Indian troops hired by the East India Company to protect British interests. Unrest within Indian units of the colonial army had been common since early in the century, when it had been sparked by economic issues, religious sensitivities, or nascent anticolonial sentiment. In 1857, tension erupted when the British adopted the new Enfield rifle for use by sepoy infantrymen. The rifle was a muzzleloader that used paper cartridges covered with animal fat and lard; because the cartridge had to be bitten off, it broke strictures against high-class Hindus' eating animal products and Muslim prohibitions against eating pork. Protests among sepoy units in northern India turned into a full-scale mutiny, supported by uprisings in rural districts in various parts of the country. But the revolt lacked clear goals, and discord between Hindus and Muslims prevented them from coordinating operations. Although the Indian troops fought bravely and outnumbered the British six to one, they were poorly organized, and the British forces (often supplemented by sepoy troops) suppressed the rebellion.

Still, the revolt frightened the British and led to a number of reforms. The proportion of Indian troops in the army was reduced, and precedence was given to ethnic groups likely to be loyal to the British, such as the Sikhs (SEEKS *or* see-ikhz) of Punjab (pun-JAHB) and the Gurkhas (GUR-kuhz), an upland people from Nepal (nuh-PAHL). The British also decided to suppress the final remnants of the hapless Mughal dynasty, which had supported the mutiny, and turned responsibility for the administration of the subcontinent over to the crown.

Like the Sepoy Rebellion, traditional resistance movements usually met with little success. Peasants armed with pikes and spears were no match for Western armies possessing the most terrifying weapons then known to human society. In a few cases, such as the revolt of the Mahdi at Khartoum, the local peoples were able to defeat the invaders temporarily. But such successes were rare, and the late nineteenth century witnessed the seemingly inexorable march of the Western powers, armed with the Gatling gun (the first rapid-fire weapon and the precursor of the modern machine gun), to mastery of the globe.

THE PATH OF COLLABORATION Not all Asians and Africans reacted to a colonial takeover by choosing the path of violent resistance. Some found elements to admire in Western civilization and compared it favorably with their own traditional practices and institutions (see the box on p. 565). Even in sub-Saharan Africa, where the colonial record was often at its most brutal, some elites supported the imposition of colonial authority.

The decision to collaborate with the colonial administration was undoubtedly often motivated by self-interest. In those cases, the collaborators might be treated with scorn or even hostility by their contemporaries, especially those who had chosen resistance. On occasion, however, the decision was reached only after painful consideration of the alternatives. Whatever the circumstances, the decision often divided friends and families, as occurred with two onetime childhood friends in central Vietnam, when one chose resistance and the other collaboration (see the box on p. 566).

Not all colonial subjects, of course, felt required to choose between resistance and collaboration. Most simply lived out their lives without engaging in the political arena. Even so, in some cases their actions had an impact on their country's future. A prime example was Ram Mohan Roy (RAHM moh-HUHN ROI). A *brahmin* from Bengal (ben-GAHL), Roy founded the Brahmo Samaj (BRAH-moh suh-MAHJ) (Society of Brahma) in 1828 to help his fellow Hindus defend their faith against verbal attacks from British acquaintances. Roy was by no means a hidebound traditionalist. He opposed such practices as *sati* and recognized the benefit of introducing the best aspects of European culture into Indian society. He probably had no intention of promoting Indian independence by his action, but by encouraging his countrymen to defend their traditional values against the onslaught of Western civilization, he helped to promote the first stirrings of nationalist sentiment in nineteenth-century India.

Imperialism: The Balance Sheet

Few periods of history are as controversial as the era of imperialism. To defenders of the colonial enterprise like the poet Rudyard Kipling, imperialism was the "white man's burden," a disagreeable but necessary phase in the evolution of human society (see the box on p. 547).

Critics disagree, portraying imperialism as a tragedy of major proportions. The insatiable drive of the advanced economic powers for access to raw materials and markets created an exploitative environment that transformed the vast majority of colonial peoples into a permanent underclass while restricting the benefits of modern technology to a privileged few. In this view, Kipling's "white man's burden" was a hypocritical gesture to hoodwink the naive and salve the guilty feelings of those who recognized imperialism for what it was—a savage act of rape. In the blunt words of two Western critics of imperialism: "Why is Africa (or for that matter Latin America and much of Asia) so poor? . . . The answer is very brief: we have made it poor."[10]

The Civilizing Mission in Egypt

FAMILY & SOCIETY

In many cases, European occupation served to sharpen class divisions in traditional societies. This occurred in Egypt, where many elites benefited after the British protectorate was established in the early 1880s. Ordinary Egyptians, less inclined to adopt foreign ways, seldom profited from the European presence. In response, British administrators showed little patience for those who failed to recognize the superiority of Western civilization. The governor-general, Lord Cromer (KROHmer), remarked in exasperation, "The mind of the Oriental, . . . like his picturesque streets, is eminently wanting in symmetry. His reasoning is of the most slipshod description." Cromer was especially irritated at the treatment of women, arguing that the seclusion of women and the wearing of the veil were the chief causes of Islamic backwardness.

Such views were echoed by some Egyptian elites, who embraced the colonialists' condemnation of traditional ways. The French-educated lawyer Qassim Amin was an example. His book *The Liberation of Women*, published in 1899 and excerpted here, precipitated a heated debate between those who considered Western nations the liberators of Islam and those who reviled them as oppressors.

Qassim Amin, *The Liberation of Women*

European civilization advances with the speed of steam and electricity, and has even overspilled to every part of the globe so that there is not an inch that he [European man] has not trodden underfoot. Any place he goes he takes control of its resources . . . and turns them into profit . . . and if he does harm to the original inhabitants, it is only that he pursues happiness in this world and seeks it wherever he may find it. . . . For the most part he uses his intellect, but when circumstances require it, he deploys force. He does not seek glory from his possessions and colonies, for he has enough of this through his intellectual achievements and scientific inventions. What drives the Englishman to dwell in India and the French in Algeria . . . is profit and the desire to acquire resources in countries where the inhabitants do not know their value or how to profit from them.

When they encounter savages they eliminate them or drive them from the land, as happened in America . . . and is happening now in Africa. . . . When they encounter a nation like ours, with a degree of civilization, with a past, and a religion . . . and customs and . . . institutions . . . they deal with its inhabitants kindly. But they do soon acquire its most valuable resources, because they have greater wealth and intellect and knowledge and force. . . . [The veil constituted] a huge barrier between woman and her elevation, and consequently a barrier between the nation and its advance.

Why did Qassim Amin believe that Western culture would be beneficial to Egyptian society? How might a critic of colonialism have responded?

Source: From Leila Ahmen, *Women and Gender in Islam* (New Haven, CT: Yale University Press, 1992), pp. 152–160.

Defenders of the colonial enterprise sometimes concede that there were gross inequities in the system but point out that there was a positive side as well. The expansion of markets and the beginnings of a modern transportation and communications network, while bringing few immediate benefits to the colonial peoples, laid the groundwork for future economic growth. The introduction of new ways of looking at human freedom, the relationship between the individual and society, and democratic principles set the stage for the adoption of such ideas after the restoration of independence following World War II. Finally, the colonial experience offered a new approach to the traditional relationship between men and women. Although colonial rule was by no means uniformly beneficial to women in African and Asian societies, their growing awareness of the struggle for equality by women in the West gave them a weapon to use against long-standing barriers of custom and legal discrimination.

Between these two irreconcilable views, where does the truth lie? This chapter has contended that neither extreme position is justified. The consequences of

OPPOSING ✕ VIEWPOINTS

To Resist or Not to Resist

INTERACTION & EXCHANGE

How to respond to colonial rule could be an excruciating problem for political elites in many Asian countries. Not only did resistance often seem futile but it could even add to the suffering of the indigenous population. Hoang Cao Khai (HWANG cow KY) and Phan Dinh Phung (FAN din FUNG) were members of the Confucian scholar-gentry from the same village in Vietnam. Yet they reacted in dramatically different ways to the French conquest of their country. Their exchange of letters, reproduced here, illustrates the dilemmas they faced.

Hoang Cao Khai's Letter to Phan Dinh Phung

Soon, it will be seventeen years since we ventured upon different paths of life. How sweet was our friendship when we both lived in our village. . . . At the time when the capital was lost and after the royal carriage had departed, you courageously answered the appeals of the King by raising the banner of righteousness. It was certainly the only thing to do in those circumstances. No one will question that.

But now the situation has changed and even those without intelligence or education have concluded that nothing remains to be saved. How is it that you, a man of vast understanding, do not realize this? . . . You are determined to do whatever you deem righteous. . . . But though you have no thoughts for your own person or for your own fate, you should at least attend to the sufferings of the population of a whole region. . . .

Until now your actions have undoubtedly accorded with your loyalty. May I ask however what sin our people have committed to deserve so much hardship? I would understand your resistance, did you involve but your family for the benefit of a large number. As of now, hundreds of families are subject to grief; how do you have the heart to fight on? I venture to predict that, should you pursue your struggle, not only will the population of our village be destroyed but our entire country will be transformed into a sea of blood and a mountain of bones. It is my hope that men of your superior morality and honesty will pause a while to appraise the situation.

Reply of Phan Dinh Phung to Hoang Cao Khai

In your letter, you revealed to me the causes of calamities and of happiness. You showed me clearly where advantages and disadvantages lie. All of which sufficed to indicate that your anxious concern was not only for my own security but also for the peace and order of our entire region. I understood plainly your sincere arguments.

I have concluded that if our country has survived these past thousand years when its territory was not large, its army not strong, its wealth not great, it was because the relationships between king and subjects, fathers and children, have always been regulated by the five moral obligations. In the past, the Han, the Sung, the Yuan, the Ming time and again dreamt of annexing our country and of dividing it up into prefectures and districts within the Chinese administrative system. But never were they able to realize their dream. Ah! if even China, which shares a common border with our territory, and is a thousand times more powerful than Vietnam, could not rely upon her strength to swallow us, it was surely because the destiny of our country had been willed by Heaven itself.

The French, separated from our country until the present day by I do not know how many thousand miles, have crossed the oceans to come to our country. Wherever they came, they acted like a storm, so much so that the Emperor had to flee. The whole country was cast into disorder. Our rivers and our mountains have been annexed by them at a stroke and turned into a foreign territory.

Moreover, if our region has suffered to such an extent, it was not only from the misfortunes of war. You must realize that wherever the French go, there flock around them groups of petty men who offer plans and tricks to gain the enemy's confidence. . . . They use every expedient to squeeze the people out of their possessions. That is how hundreds of misdeeds, thousands of offenses have been perpetrated. How can the French not be aware of all the suffering that the rural population has had to endure? Under these

(Continued)

(Opposing Viewpoints Continued)

circumstances, is it surprising that families should be disrupted and the people scattered?

My friend, if you are troubled about our people, then I advise you to place yourself in my position and to think about the circumstances in which I live. You will understand naturally and see clearly that I do not need to add anything else.

 Explain briefly the reasons advanced by each writer to justify his actions. Which argument do you think would have earned more support from contemporaries? Why?

Source: From Truong Buu Lam, *Patterns of Vietnamese Response to Foreign Intervention*, Monograph Series No. 11. Southeast Asian Studies, Yale University, 1967. Dist. By Celler Book Shop, Detroit, MI.

---

colonialism have been more complex than either its defenders or its critics would have us believe. While the colonial peoples received little immediate benefit, overall the imperialist era brought about a vast expansion of the international trade network and created at least the potential for societies throughout Africa and Asia to play an active and rewarding role in the new global economic arena. If, as the historian William McNeill believes, the introduction of new technology through cross-cultural encounters is the driving force of change in world history, then Western imperialism, whatever its faults, helped to open the door to such change, much as the rise of the Arab empire and the Mongol invasions hastened the process of global economic development in an earlier time.

Still, the critics have a point. Although colonialism introduced the peoples of Asia and Africa to new technology and the expanding global marketplace, it was unnecessarily brutal and all too often failed to realize the exalted claims of its promoters. Existing economic networks—often potentially valuable as a foundation for later economic development—were ruthlessly swept aside to provide markets for Western manufactured goods. Potential sources of local industrialization were nipped in the bud to avoid competition for factories in Amsterdam, London, Pittsburgh, or Manchester. Training in Western democratic ideals and practices was ignored out of fear that the recipients might use them as weapons against the ruling authorities.

The fundamental weakness of colonialism, then, was that it was ultimately based on the self-interests of the colonial powers. When those interests collided with the needs of the colonial peoples, those of the former always triumphed. However sincerely the David Livingstones, Albert Sarrauts, and William McKinleys of the world were convinced of the rightness of their civilizing mission, the ultimate result was to deprive the colonial peoples of the right to make their own choices about their own destiny. Sophisticated, age-old societies that could have been left to respond to the technological revolution in their own way were squeezed dry of precious national resources under the false guise of a "civilizing mission." As the sociologist Clifford Geertz remarked in his book *Agricultural Involution: The Processes of Ecological Change in Indonesia*, the tragedy is not that the colonial peoples suffered through the colonial era but that they suffered for nothing.

CHAPTER SUMMARY

By the first quarter of the twentieth century, virtually all of Africa and a good part of South and Southeast Asia  were under some form of colonial rule. With the advent of the age of imperialism, a global economy was finally established, and the domination of Western civilization over the civilizations of Africa and Asia appeared to be complete.

The imperialist rush for colonies did not take place without opposition. In most areas of the world, local governments and peoples resisted the onslaught, sometimes to the bitter end. But with few exceptions, they were unable to overcome the fearsome new warships and firearms that the Industrial Revolution in Europe had brought into being.

Chapter Summary ❦ **567**

Although the material benefits and democratic values of the occupying powers aroused admiration from observers in much of the colonial world, in the end it was weapons, more than ideas, that ushered in the age of imperialism.

Africa and southern Asia were not the only areas of the world that were buffeted by the winds of Western expansionism in the late nineteenth century. The nations of eastern Asia, and those of Latin America and the Middle East as well, were also affected in significant ways.

The consequences of Western political, economic, and military penetration varied substantially from one region to another, however, and therefore require separate treatment. The experience of East Asia will be dealt with in the next chapter. That of Latin America and the Middle East will be discussed in Chapter 24. In these areas, new rivals—notably the United States, Russia, and Japan—entered the scene and played an active role in the process. By the end of the nineteenth century, the rush to secure colonies had circled the world.

CHAPTER TIMELINE

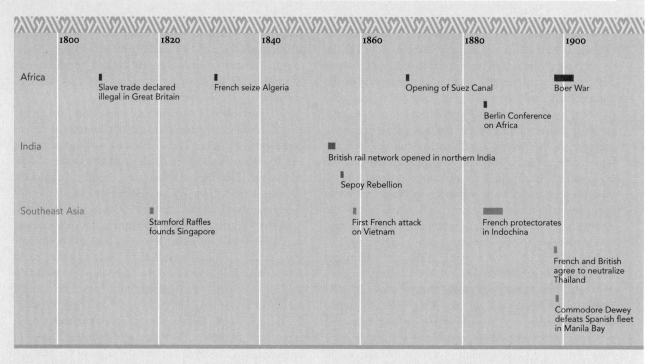

	1800	1820	1840	1860	1880	1900

Africa
- Slave trade declared illegal in Great Britain
- French seize Algeria
- Opening of Suez Canal
- Boer War
- Berlin Conference on Africa

India
- British rail network opened in northern India
- Sepoy Rebellion

Southeast Asia
- Stamford Raffles founds Singapore
- First French attack on Vietnam
- French protectorates in Indochina
- French and British agree to neutralize Thailand
- Commodore Dewey defeats Spanish fleet in Manila Bay

CHAPTER REVIEW

Upon Reflection

Q What arguments have been advanced to justify the European takeover of societies in Asia and Africa during the latter part of the nineteenth century? To what degree are such arguments justified?

Q The colonial powers adopted two basic philosophies in seeking to govern their conquered territories in Asia and Africa—assimilation and association. What were the principles behind these philosophies, and how did they work in practice? Which do you believe was more successful?

Q What was the purpose of the Berlin Conference of 1884, and how successful was it at achieving that purpose? What was the impact of the conference for the European powers and for Africa?

Key Terms

imperialism (p. 544)
indirect rule (p. 546)
direct rule (p. 546)
assimilation (p. 548)
association (p. 548)
raj (p. 548)
informal empire (p. 555)
pasha (p. 556)
high colonialism (p. 562)
sepoys (p. 564)

Suggested Reading

IMPERIALISM AND COLONIALISM There are a number of good works on the subject of imperialism and colonialism. For a study that directly focuses on the question of whether colonialism was beneficial to subject peoples, see **D. K. Fieldhouse,** *The West and the Third World: Trade, Colonialism, Dependence, and Development* (Oxford, 1999). Also see **D. B. Abernathy,** *Global Dominance: European Overseas Empires, 1415–1980* (New Haven, Conn., 2000). For a defense of the British imperial mission, see **N. Ferguson,** *Empire: The Rise and Demise of the British World Order* (New York, 2003).

IMPERIALIST AGE IN AFRICA On the imperialist age in Africa, above all see **B. Vandervoort,** *Wars of Imperial Conquest in Africa, 1830–1914* (Bloomington, Ind., 1998), and **T. Pakenham,** *The Scramble for Africa* (New York, 1991). The three-sided conflict in South Africa is ably analyzed in **M. Meredith,** *Diamonds, Gold, and War: The British, the Boers, and the Making of South Africa* (New York, 2007). The scandal in the Belgian Congo is chronicled in **A. Hothschild,** *King Leopold's Ghost: A Story of Greed, Terror, and Heroism in Central Africa* (New York, 1999). Also informative is **R. O. Collins, ed.,** *Historical Problems of Imperial Africa* (Princeton, N.J., 1994).

INDIA For an overview of the British takeover and administration of India, see **S. Wolpert,** *A New History of India,* 8th ed. (New York, 2008). **C. A. Bayly,** *Indian Society and the Making of the British Empire* (Cambridge, 1988), is a scholarly analysis of the impact of British conquest on the Indian economy. Also see **A. Wild's** elegant *East India Company: Trade and Conquest from 1600* (New York, 2000). In a provocative work, *Ornamentalism: How the British Saw Their Empire* (Oxford, 2000), **D. Cannadine** argues that it was class and not race that motivated British policy in the subcontinent. In *The Last Mughal: The Fall of a Dynasty: Delhi 1857* (New York, 2007), **W. Dalrymple** argues that religion was the key issue in provoking the Sepoy Rebellion. Also see **N. Dirks,** *The Scandal of Empire: India and the Creation of Imperial Britain* (Cambridge, Mass., 2007).

COLONIAL AGE IN SOUTHEAST ASIA General studies of the colonial period in Southeast Asia are rare because most authors focus on specific areas. For an overview by several authors, see **N. Tarling, ed.,** *The Cambridge History of Southeast Asia,* vol. 3 (Cambridge, 1992).

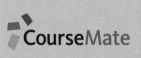

Visit the CourseMate website at www.cengagebrain.com for additional study tools and review materials for this chapter.

Shadows over the Pacific: East Asia Under Challenge

The Macartney mission to China, 1793

CHAPTER OUTLINE AND FOCUS QUESTIONS

The Decline of the Manchus

Q Why did the Qing dynasty decline and ultimately collapse, and what role did the Western powers play in this process?

Chinese Society in Transition

Q What political, economic, and social reforms were instituted by the Qing dynasty during its final decades, and why were they not more successful in reversing the decline of Manchu rule?

A Rich Country and a Strong State: The Rise of Modern Japan

Q To what degree was the Meiji Restoration a "revolution," and to what extent did it succeed in transforming Japan?

CRITICAL THINKING

Q How did China and Japan each respond to Western pressures in the nineteenth century, and what were the implications of their different responses for each nation's history?

THE BRITISH EMISSARY Lord Macartney had arrived in Beijing in 1793 with a caravan loaded with gifts for the emperor. Flags provided by the Chinese proclaimed in Chinese characters that the visitor was an "ambassador bearing tribute from the country of England." But the tribute was in vain, for Macartney's request for an increase in trade between the two countries was flatly rejected, and he left Beijing with nothing to show for his efforts. Not until half a century later would the Qing dynasty—at the point of a gun—agree to the British demand for an expansion of commercial ties.

In fact, the Chinese emperor Qianlong had responded to his visitor's requests with polite but poorly disguised condescension. To Macartney's proposal that a British ambassador be stationed in Beijing, the emperor replied that such a request was "not in harmony with the state system of our dynasty and will definitely not be permitted." He also rejected the British envoy's suggestion that regular trade relations be established between the two countries. We receive all sorts of precious things as gifts from the myriad nations, replied the Celestial Emperor. "Consequently," he added, "there is nothing we lack, as your principal envoy and others have themselves observed. We have never set much store on strange or ingenious objects, nor do we need more of your country's manufactures."

Historians have often viewed the failure of Macartney's mission as a reflection of the disdain of Chinese rulers toward their counterparts in other countries and their serene confidence in the superiority of Chinese civilization in a world inhabited by barbarians. If that was the case, Qianlong's confidence was misplaced, for as the eighteenth century came to an end, China faced a growing challenge not only from the escalating power and ambitions of the West, but also from its own internal weakness. When British demands for the right to carry out trade and missionary activities in China were rejected, Britain resorted to force and in the Opium War, which broke out in 1839, gave Manchu troops a sound thrashing. A humiliated China was finally forced to open its doors. 🖎

The Decline of the Manchus

FOCUS QUESTION: Why did the Qing dynasty decline and ultimately collapse, and what role did the Western powers play in this process?

In 1800, the Qing (CHING) (Ch'ing) or Manchu dynasty was at the height of its power. China had experienced a long period of peace and prosperity under the rule of two great emperors, Kangxi (kang-SHEE) and Qianlong (CHAN-loong). Its borders were secure, and its culture and intellectual achievements were the envy of the world. Its rulers, hidden behind the walls of the Forbidden City in Beijing (bay-ZHING), had every reason to describe their patrimony as the "Central Kingdom." But a little over a century later, humiliated and harassed by the black ships and big guns of the Western powers, the Qing dynasty, the last in a series that had endured for more than two thousand years, collapsed in the dust (see Map 22.1).

Historians once assumed that the primary reason for the rapid decline and fall of the Manchu dynasty was the intense pressure applied by the Western powers. Now, however, most historians believe that internal changes played a major role in the dynasty's collapse and that at least some of its problems during the nineteenth century were self-inflicted.

Both explanations have some validity. Like so many of its predecessors, after an extended period of growth, the Qing dynasty began to suffer from the familiar dynastic ills of official corruption, peasant unrest, and incompetence at court. Such weaknesses were probably exacerbated by the rapid growth in population. The long era of peace, the introduction of new crops from the Americas, and the cultivation of new, fast-ripening strains of rice enabled the Chinese population to double between 1550 and 1800 and to reach the unprecedented level of 400 million by the end of the nineteenth century. Even without the Western powers, the Manchus were probably destined to repeat the fate of their imperial predecessors. The ships, guns, and ideas of the foreigners simply highlighted the growing weakness of the dynasty and likely hastened its demise. In doing so, Western imperialism exerted an indelible impact on the history of modern China—but as a contributing, not a causal, factor.

Opium and Rebellion

By 1800, Westerners had been in contact with China for more than two hundred years, but Western traders were limited to a small commercial outlet at Canton. This arrangement was not acceptable to the British, however. Not only did they chafe at being restricted to a tiny enclave, but the growing British appetite for Chinese tea created a severe balance-of-payments problem. After the failure of Macartney's mission in 1793, Lord Amherst led another mission to China in 1816, but it managed only to worsen the already strained relations between the two countries. The British solution was opium, which was grown in northeastern India and then shipped to China. Opium had been grown in southwestern China for several hundred years but had been used primarily for medicinal purposes. Now, as imports increased, popular demand for the addictive product in southern China became insatiable despite an official prohibition on its use. Soon bullion was flowing out of the Chinese imperial treasury into the pockets of British merchants.

The Chinese became concerned and tried to negotiate. In 1839, Lin Zexu (LIN dzeh-SHOO) (Lin Tse-hsu; 1785–1850), a Chinese official appointed to curtail the opium trade, appealed to Queen Victoria on both moral and practical grounds and threatened to prohibit the sale of rhubarb (widely used as a laxative in nineteenth-century Europe) to Great Britain if she did not respond (see the box on p. 573). But moral principles paled before the lure of commercial profits, and the British continued to promote the opium trade, arguing that if the Chinese did not want the opium, they did not have to buy it. Lin Zexu attacked on three fronts, imposing penalties on smokers, arresting dealers, and seizing supplies from importers as they attempted to smuggle the drug into China. The last tactic caused his downfall. When he blockaded the foreign factory area in Canton to force traders to hand over their opium, the British government, claiming that it could not permit British subjects "to be exposed to insult and injustice," launched a naval expedition to punish the Manchus and force them to open China to foreign trade.[1]

THE OPIUM WAR The Opium War (1839–1842) lasted three years and demonstrated the superiority of British firepower and military tactics. British warships destroyed Chinese coastal and river forts and seized the offshore

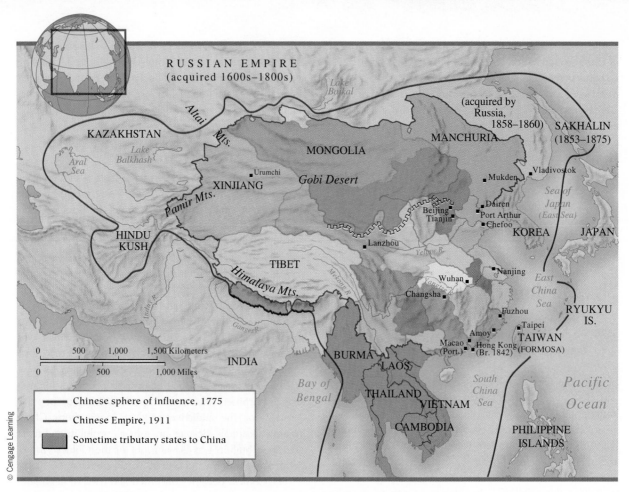

MAP 22.1 **The Qing Empire.** Shown here is the Qing Empire at the height of its power in the late eighteenth century, together with its shrunken boundaries at the moment of dissolution in 1911.

Q How do China's tributary states on this map differ from those in Map 17.2? Which of them fell under the influence of foreign powers during the nineteenth century?

island of Zhoushan (JOE-shahn), near the mouth of the Yangtze River. When a British fleet sailed virtually unopposed up the Yangtze to Nanjing (nan-JING) and cut off the supply of "tribute grain" from southern to northern China, the Qing finally agreed to British terms. In the Treaty of Nanjing in 1842, the Chinese agreed to open five coastal ports to British trade, limit tariffs on imported British goods, grant extraterritorial rights to British citizens in China, and pay a substantial indemnity to cover the costs of the war. China also agreed to cede the island of Hong Kong (dismissed by a senior British official as a "barren rock") to Great Britain. Nothing was said in the treaty about the opium trade, which continued unabated until it was brought under control through Chinese government efforts in the early twentieth century.

Although the Opium War has traditionally been considered the beginning of modern Chinese history,

probably few Chinese at the time viewed it that way. This was not the first time that a ruling dynasty had been forced to make concessions to foreigners, and the opening of five coastal ports to the British hardly constituted a serious threat to the empire. Although a few concerned Chinese argued that the court should learn more about European civilization, others contended that China had nothing to learn from the barbarians and that borrowing foreign ways would undercut the purity of Confucian civilization.

For the time being, the Manchus attempted to deal with the foreigners in the traditional way of playing them off against each other. Concessions granted to the British were offered to other Western nations, including the United States, and soon foreign concession areas were operating in treaty ports along the Chinese coast from Canton to Shanghai (SHANG-hy).

A Letter of Advice to the Queen

INTERACTION & EXCHANGE

Lin Zexu was the Chinese imperial commissioner in Canton at the time of the Opium War. Prior to the conflict, he attempted to use reason and the threat of retaliation to persuade the British to stop smuggling opium into China. The following selection is from a letter that he wrote to Queen Victoria. In it, he appeals to her conscience while showing the condescension that the Chinese traditionally displayed to the rulers of other countries.

Lin Zexu, Letter to Queen Victoria

The kings of your honorable country by a tradition handed down from generation to generation have always been noted for their politeness and submissiveness. . . . Privately we are delighted with the way in which the honorable rulers of your country deeply understand the grand principles and are grateful for the Celestial grace. . . . The profit from trade has been enjoyed by them continuously for two hundred years. This is the source from which your country has become known for its wealth.

But after a long period of commercial intercourse, there appear among the crowd of barbarians both good persons and bad, unevenly. Consequently there are those who smuggle opium to seduce the Chinese people and so cause the spread of the poison to all provinces. . . .

The wealth of China is used to profit the barbarians. That is to say, the great profit made by barbarians is all taken from the rightful share of China. By what right do they then in return use the poisonous drug to injure the Chinese people? . . . Let us ask, where is your conscience? I have heard that the smoking of opium is very strictly forbidden by your country; that is because the harm caused by opium is clearly understood. Since it is not permitted to do harm to your own country, then even less should you let it be passed on to the harm of other countries—how much less to China! Of all that China exports to foreign countries, there is not a single thing which is not beneficial to people. . . . Take tea and rhubarb, for example; the foreign countries cannot get along for a single day without them. . . . On the other hand, articles coming from the outside to China can only be used as toys. We can take them or get along without them. Nevertheless our Celestial Court lets tea, silk, and other goods be shipped without limit and circulated everywhere without begrudging it in the slightest. This is for no other reason but to share the benefit with the people of the whole world. . . .

May you, O King, check your wicked and sift your vicious people before they come to China, in order to guarantee the peace of your nation, to show further the sincerity of your politeness and submissiveness, and to let the two countries enjoy together the blessings of peace. . . . After receiving this dispatch will you immediately give us a prompt reply regarding the details and circumstances of your cutting off the opium traffic. Be sure not to put this off.

Q *How did Lin Zexu seek to persuade Queen Victoria to prohibit the sale of opium in China? To what degree are his arguments persuasive?*

Source: Reprinted by permission of the publisher from *China's Response to the West: A Documentary Survey, 1839–1923*, by Ssu-yu Teng and John K. Fairbank, pp. 19, 24–27, Cambridge, Mass.: Harvard University Press. Copyright © 1954, 1979 by the President and Fellows of Harvard College, copyright © renewed 1982 by Ssu-yu Teng and John King Fairbank.

THE TAIPING REBELLION In the meantime, the Qing's failure to deal with internal economic problems led to a major peasant revolt that shook the foundations of the empire. On the surface, the Taiping (TY-ping) (T'ai p'ing) Rebellion owed something to the Western incursion; the leader of the uprising, Hong Xiuquan (HOONG shee-oo-CHWAHN) (Hung Hsiu-ch'uan), a failed examination candidate, was a Christian convert who viewed himself as a younger brother of Jesus and hoped to establish what he referred to as a "Heavenly Kingdom of Supreme Peace." But there were many local causes as well. The rapid increase in population forced millions of peasants to eke out a living as sharecroppers or landless laborers. Official corruption and incompetence led to the whipsaw of increased taxes and a decline in government services; even the Grand Canal was allowed to silt up, hindering the shipment of grain. In 1853, the rebels seized

The Opium War. The Opium War, waged between China and Great Britain between 1839 and 1842, was China's first conflict with a European power. Lacking modern military technology, the Chinese suffered a humiliating defeat. In this painting, heavily armed British steamships destroy unwieldy Chinese junks. China's humiliation at sea was a legacy of its rulers' lack of interest in maritime matters since the mid-fifteenth century, when Chinese junks were among the most advanced ships in the world.

Nanjing, but that proved to be their high-water mark. Plagued by factionalism, the rebellion gradually lost momentum and was finally suppressed in 1864, but by then more than 25 million people had been killed, the vast majority of them civilians.

One reason for the dynasty's failure to deal effectively with the internal unrest was its continuing difficulties with the Western imperialists. In 1856, the British and the French, still smarting from the restrictions on trade and on their missionary activities, launched a new series of attacks and seized Beijing in 1860. As punishment, British troops destroyed the imperial summer palace outside the city. In the ensuing Treaty of Tianjin (TYAHN-jin) (Tientsin), the Qing agreed to humiliating new concessions: the legalization of the opium trade, the opening of additional ports to foreign trade, and the cession of the peninsula of Kowloon (KOW-loon) (opposite the island of Hong Kong) to the

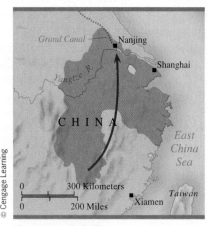

The Taiping Rebellion

British (see Map 22.2). Additional territories in the north were ceded to Russia.

Efforts at Reform

By the late 1870s, the old dynasty was well on the road to internal disintegration. To fend off the Taiping Rebellion, the Manchus had had to rely on armed forces under regional command, but now many of these regional commanders refused to disband their units and continued to collect local taxes for their own use. The dreaded pattern of imperial breakdown, so familiar in Chinese history, was beginning to appear again.

Finally, the court began to listen to reform-minded officials, who advocated a new policy called **self-strengthening**, in which Western technology would be adopted while Confucian principles and institutions were maintained intact. This policy, popularly known by its slogan "East for Essence, West for Practical Use," remained China's guiding standard for nearly a quarter of a century. Some even called for reforms in education and

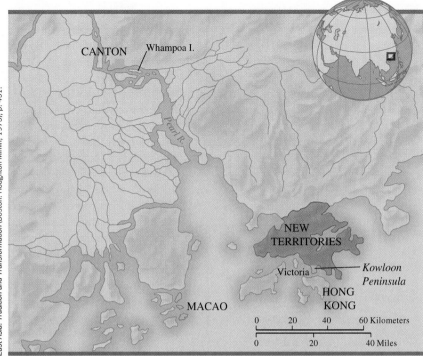

MAP 22.2 Canton and Hong Kong. This map shows the estuary of the Pearl River in southern China, an important area of early contact between China and Europe.

Q *What was the importance of Canton? What were the New Territories, and when were they annexed by the British?*

Manchus attempted to modernize the military and build an industrial base without disturbing the essential elements of traditional Chinese civilization. Railroads, weapons arsenals, and shipyards were built, but the value system remained unchanged.

In the end, the results spoke for themselves. During the last decades of the century, the European penetration of China intensified. Rapacious imperialists began to bite off the outer edges of the empire. The Gobi Desert north of the Great Wall, Central Asia, and Tibet, all inhabited by non-Chinese peoples and never fully assimilated into the Chinese Empire, were gradually lost. In the north and northwest, the main beneficiary was Russia, which forced the court to cede territories north of the Amur (ah-MOOR) River in Siberia. Competition between Russia and Great Britain prevented either power from seizing Tibet outright but enabled Tibetan authorities to revive their local autonomy. In the south, British and French advances in mainland Southeast Asia removed Burma and Vietnam from their traditional status as vassals to the Manchu court. Even more ominous were the foreign spheres of influence in the Chinese heartland, where local commanders were willing to sell exclusive commercial, railroad-building, or mining privileges.

The disintegration of the Manchu dynasty accelerated as the century came to an end. In 1894, the Qing went to war with Japan over Japanese incursions into the Korean peninsula, which threatened China's long-held suzerainty over the area (see "Joining the Imperialist Club" later in this chapter). The Chinese were roundly defeated, confirming to some critics the failure of the policy of self-strengthening by halfway measures. In 1897, Germany, a new entry in the race for spoils in East Asia, used the murder of two German missionaries by Chinese rioters as a pretext to demand territories in the Shandong (SHAHN-doong) (Shantung) peninsula. The imperial court granted the demand, setting off a scramble for territory (see Map 22.3). Russia demanded the Liaodong (LYOW-doong) peninsula with its ice-free port at Port Arthur, and Great Britain obtained a hundred-year lease on the New Territories, adjacent to Hong Kong, as well as a coaling station in northern China.

in China's hallowed political institutions. Pointing to British power and prosperity, the journalist Wang Tao (wahng TOW ["ow" as in "how"]) (Wang T'ao, 1828–1897) remarked, "The real strength of England . . . lies in the fact that there is a sympathetic understanding between the governing and the governed, a close relationship between the ruler and the people. . . . My observation is that the daily domestic political life of England actually embodies the traditional ideals of our ancient Golden Age."[2] Such democratic ideas were too radical for most moderate reformers, however. Zhang Zhidong (JANG jee-DOONG) (Chang Chih-tung), a leading court official, countered:

> The doctrine of people's rights will bring us not a single benefit but a hundred evils. Are we going to establish a parliament? . . . Even supposing the confused and clamorous people are assembled in one house, for every one of them who is clear-sighted, there will be a hundred others whose vision is beclouded; they will converse at random and talk as if in a dream—what use will it be?[3]

The Climax of Imperialism

For the time being, Zhang Zhidong's arguments won the day. During the last quarter of the nineteenth century, the

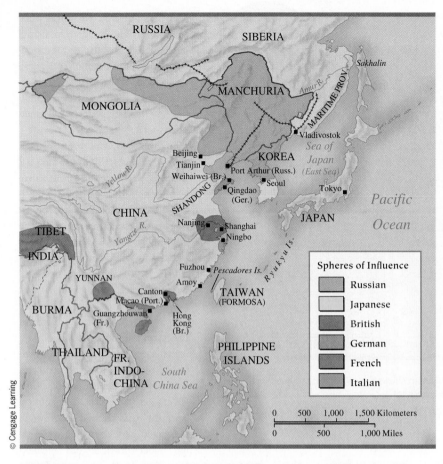

MAP 22.3 **Foreign Possessions and Spheres of Influence About 1900.** At the end of the nineteenth century, China was being carved up like a melon by foreign imperialist powers.

Q *Which of the areas marked on the map were removed from Chinese control during the nineteenth century?*

emperor incarcerated in the palace. With Cixi's palace coup, the so-called One Hundred Days of reform came to an end.

OPENING THE DOOR During the next two years, foreign pressure on the dynasty intensified. With encouragement from the British, who hoped to avert a total collapse of the Manchu Empire, in 1899 U.S. Secretary of State John Hay proposed that the imperialist powers join together to ensure equal access to the China market for all states and to guarantee the territorial and administrative integrity of the Chinese Empire. Though probably motivated more by the United States' preference for open markets than by a benevolent wish to protect China, the so-called **Open Door Notes** did have the practical effect of reducing the imperialist hysteria over access to China. The "gentlemen's agreement" about the Open Door (it was not a treaty, but merely a nonbinding expression of intent) quelled fears in Britain, France, Germany, and Russia that other powers would take advantage of the dynasty's weakness to dominate the China market.

Although the Open Door brought a measure of sanity to imperialist meddling in East Asia, it unfortunately came too late to stop the explosion known as the Boxer Rebellion. The Boxers, so-called because of the physical exercises they performed (similar to the more martial forms of tai chi), were a secret society operating primarily in rural areas in northern China. Provoked by a damaging drought and high unemployment caused in part by

The government responded with yet another effort at reform. In 1898, the progressive Confucian scholar Kang Youwei (KAHNG yow-WAY) (K'ang Yu-wei) won the support of the young Guangxu (gwahng-SHOO) (Kuang Hsu) emperor for a comprehensive reform program patterned after recent measures in Japan. During the next several weeks, the emperor issued edicts calling for political, administrative, and educational reforms. Not surprisingly, Kang's proposals were opposed by conservatives, who saw little advantage and much risk in copying the West. More important, the new program was opposed by the emperor's aunt, the Empress Dowager Cixi (TSE-shee) (Tz'u Hsi; 1835–1908), the real power at court. Cixi had begun her career as a concubine to an earlier emperor. After his death, she became a dominant force at court and in 1878 placed her infant nephew, the future Guangxu emperor, on the throne. For two decades, she ruled in his name as regent. With the aid of conservatives in the army, she arrested and executed several of the reformers and had the

The International Expeditionary Force Advances to Beijing to Suppress the Boxers

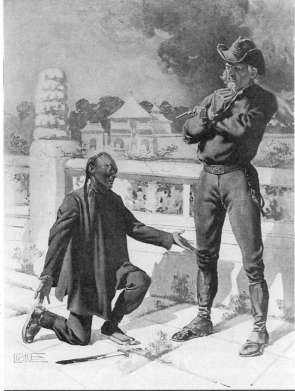

Leslie's Illustrated Newspaper, October 14, 1900

Justice or Mercy? Uncle Sam Decides. In the summer of 1900, Chinese rebels known as Boxers besieged Western embassies in the imperial capital of Beijing. Western nations, including the United States, dispatched troops to North China to rescue their compatriots. In this cartoon, which appeared in a contemporary American newsmagazine, China figuratively seeks pardon from a stern Uncle Sam.

foreign activity (the introduction of railroads and steamships, for example, undercut the livelihood of barge workers on the rivers and canals), the Boxers attacked foreign residents and besieged the foreign legation quarter in Beijing until an international expeditionary force arrived in the late summer of 1900. As punishment, the foreign troops destroyed temples in the capital suburbs, and the Chinese government was compelled to pay a heavy indemnity to the foreign governments involved in suppressing the uprising.

The Collapse of the Old Order

During the next few years, the old dynasty tried desperately to reform itself. The empress dowager, who had long resisted change, now embraced a number of reforms. The venerable civil service examination system was replaced by a new educational system based on the Western model. In 1905, a commission was formed to study constitutional changes; over the next years, legislative assemblies were established at the provincial level, and elections for a national assembly were held in 1910.

Such moves helped shore up the dynasty temporarily, but history shows that the most dangerous period for an authoritarian system is when it begins to reform itself, because change breeds instability and performance rarely matches rising expectations. Such was the case in China. The new provincial elite, composed of merchants, professionals, and reform-minded gentry, became impatient with the slow pace of change and were disillusioned to find that the new assemblies were to be primarily advisory. The reforms also had little meaning for peasants, artisans, miners, and transportation workers, whose standard of living was being eroded by rising taxes and official venality. Rising rural unrest was an ominous sign of deep-seated resentment.

THE RISE OF SUN YAT-SEN The first physical manifestations of future revolution appeared during the last decade of the nineteenth century with the formation of the Revive China Society by the young radical Sun Yat-sen (SOON yaht-SEN) (1866–1925). Born in a village south of Canton, Sun was educated in Hawaii and returned to China to practice medicine. Soon he turned his full attention to the ills of Chinese society.

At first, Sun's efforts yielded few positive results, but in 1905, he managed to unite radical groups from across China in the so-called Revolutionary Alliance, or Tongmenghui (toong-meng-HWAY) (T'ung Meng Hui). Its program was based on Sun's **"three people's principles"** of nationalism (meaning primarily the elimination of Manchu rule over China), democracy, and people's livelihood. It called for a three-stage process beginning with a military takeover and ending with a constitutional democracy (see the box on p. 578). Although the organization was small and relatively inexperienced, it benefited from rising popular discontent.

Program for a New China

POLITICS & GOVERNMENT

In 1905, Sun Yat-sen united a number of anti-Manchu groups into a single organization called the Revolutionary Alliance (Tongmenghui). The new organization eventually formed the core of his Guomindang (gwoh-min-DAHNG), or Nationalist Party. This excerpt is from the organization's manifesto, published in 1905 in Tokyo. Note that Sun believed that the Chinese people were not ready for democracy and required a period of tutelage to prepare them for constitutional government. This formula would be adopted by many other political leaders in Asia and Africa after World War II.

Sun Yat-sen, *Manifesto for the Tongmenghui*

By order of the Military Government, . . . the Commander-in-Chief of the Chinese National Army proclaims the purposes and platform of the Military Government to the people of the nation:

Therefore we proclaim to the world in utmost sincerity the outline of the present revolution and the fundamental plan for the future administration of the nation.

1. *Drive out the Tartars:* The Manchus of today were originally the eastern barbarians beyond the Great Wall. . . . when China was in a disturbed state they came inside Shanhaikuan, conquered China, and enslaved our Chinese people. The extreme cruelties and tyrannies of the Manchu government have now reached their limit. With the righteous army poised against them, we will overthrow that government, and restore our sovereign rights.

2. *Restore China:* China is the China of the Chinese. The government of China should be in the hands of the Chinese. After driving out the Tartars we must restore our national state. . . .

3. *Establish the Republic:* Now our revolution is based on equality, in order to establish a republican government. All our people are equal and all enjoy political rights. . . .

4. *Equalize land ownership:* The good fortune of civilization is to be shared equally by all the people of the nation. We should improve our social and economic organization, and assess the value of all the land in the country. Its present price shall be received by the owner, but all increases in value resulting from reform and social improvements after the revolution shall belong to the state, to be shared by all the people, in order to create a socialist state, where each family within the empire can be well supported, each person satisfied, and no one fail to secure employment. . . .

The above four points will be carried out in three steps in due order. The first period is government by military law. When the righteous army has arisen, various places will join the cause. . . . Evils like the oppression of the government, the greed and graft of officials, . . . the cruelty of tortures and penalties, the tyranny of tax collections, the humiliation of the queue [the requirement that all Chinese males braid their hair]—shall all be exterminated together with the Manchu rule. Evils in social customs, such as the keeping of slaves, the cruelty of foot binding, the spread of the poison of opium, should also all be prohibited. . . .

The second period is that of government by a provisional constitution. When military law is lifted in each *hsien* [district], the Military Government shall return the right of self-government to the local people. . . .

The third period will be government under the constitution. Six years after the provisional constitution has been enforced a constitution shall be made. The military and administrative powers of the Military Government shall be annulled; the people shall elect the president, and elect the members of parliament to organize the parliament.

Q *What were Sun Yat-sen's key proposals to transform China into a modern society? How does his program compare with the so-called Meiji reforms in Japan, discussed later in this chapter?*

Source: Excerpt from *Sources of Chinese Tradition* by William Theodore De Bary. Copyright © 1960 by Columbia University Press, New York. Reprinted with permission of the publisher.

FILM & HISTORY

The Last Emperor (1987)

On November 14, 1908, the Chinese emperor Guangxu died in Beijing. One day later, Empress Dowager Cixi passed away as well. A three-year-old boy, to be known in history as Henry Puyi, ascended the throne. Three years later, the Qing dynasty collapsed, and the deposed monarch lived out the remainder of his life in a China lashed by political turmoil and violence.

The Last Emperor (1987), directed by the Italian filmmaker Bernardo Bertolucci, is a brilliant portrayal of the experience of one hapless individual in a nation caught up in a seemingly endless revolution. The film evokes the fading majesty of the last days of imperial China, the chaos of the warlord era, and the terrors of the Maoist period, when the last shreds of Puyi's personality are shattered under the pressure of Communist brainwashing. The main character, who never appears to grasp what is happening to his country, lives and dies a nonentity.

The film, based on Puyi's autobiography, benefits from having been filmed partly onsite in the Imperial

Yanco/Tao/Recorded Picture Co/The Kobal Collection at Art Resource, NY

Three-year-old Puyi (Richard Vuu), the last emperor of China, watches an emissary approach at the Imperial Palace.

City. The only major Western actor in the movie is the veteran film star Peter O'Toole, who plays Puyi's tutor.

THE REVOLUTION OF 1911 In October 1911, Sun's followers launched an uprising in the industrial center of Wuhan (WOO-HAHN), in central China. With Sun traveling in the United States, the insurrection lacked leadership, but the decrepit government's inability to react quickly encouraged political forces at the provincial level to take measures into their own hands. The dynasty was now in a state of virtual collapse: the empress dowager had died in 1908, one day after her nephew; the throne was occupied by China's "last emperor," the infant Puyi (POO-YEE) (P'u Yi). Sun's party lacked the military strength and political base needed to seize the initiative, however, and was forced to turn to a representative of the old order, General Yuan Shikai (yoo-AHN shee-KY) (Yuan Shih-k'ai). Yuan had been put in charge of the imperial forces sent to suppress the rebellion, but now he abandoned the Manchus and acted on his own behalf. In negotiations with Sun Yat-sen's party (Sun himself had arrived in China in January 1912), he agreed to serve as president of a new Chinese republic. The old dynasty and the age-old system that it had attempted to preserve were no more (see the Film & History feature above).

Although the dynasty was gone, Sun and his followers were unable to consolidate their gains. Their program was based on Western liberal democratic principles aimed at the urban middle class, but the middle class in China was too small to form the basis for a new political order. The vast majority of the Chinese people still lived on the land. Sun had hoped to win their support with a land reform program, but few peasants had participated in the revolution. In failing to create new institutions and values to provide a framework for change, the events of 1911 were less a revolution than a collapse of the old order. Under the weight of imperialism and its own internal weaknesses, the old dynasty had crumbled before new political and social forces were ready to fill the vacuum.

What China had experienced was part of a historical process that was bringing down traditional empires across the globe, both in regions threatened by Western imperialism and in Europe itself, where tsarist Russia, the Austro-Hungarian Empire, and the Ottoman Empire all came to an end not long after the collapse of the Qing. The circumstances of their demise differed. The

Austro-Hungarian Empire was dismembered by the victorious allies after World War I, and the fate of tsarist Russia was directly linked to that conflict. Still, all four regimes bore some responsibility for their fate in that they had failed to meet the challenges posed by the times. All had responded to the forces of industrialization and popular participation in the political process with hesitation and reluctance, and their attempts at reform were too little and too late. All paid the supreme price for their folly.

Chinese Society in Transition

Q FOCUS QUESTION: What political, economic, and social reforms were instituted by the Qing dynasty during its final decades, and why were they not more successful in reversing the decline of Manchu rule?

The growing Western presence in China during the late nineteenth and early twentieth centuries obviously had a major impact on Chinese society. Hence, until recently historians commonly asserted that the arrival of the Europeans shook China out of centuries of slumber and launched it on the road to revolutionary change. As we now know, however, Chinese society was already in a state of transition when the European penetration began to accelerate in the mid-nineteenth century. The growth of industry and trade was particularly noticeable in the cities, where a national market for such commodities as oil, copper, salt, tea, and porcelain had developed. The foundation of an infrastructure more conducive to the rise of a money economy appeared to be in place. In the countryside, new crops introduced from abroad significantly increased food production and aided population growth. The Chinese economy had never been more productive or more complex.

The Economy: The Drag of Tradition

Whether these changes by themselves in the absence of outside intervention would have led to an industrial revolution and a capitalist economy on the Western model is impossible to know. Certainly, a number of obstacles would have made it difficult for China to embark on the Western path if it had wished to do so.

Although industrial production was on the rise, it was still based almost entirely on traditional methods. There was no uniform system of weights and measures, and the banking system was still primitive by European standards. The use of paper money, invented by the Chinese centuries earlier, was still relatively limited. The transportation system, which had been neglected since the end of the Yuan dynasty, was increasingly chaotic. There were few paved roads, and the Grand Canal, long the most efficient means of carrying goods from north to south, was silting up.

The Chinese also borrowed less Western technology than they might have. Foreign manufacturing enterprises could not legally operate in China until the last decade of the nineteenth century, and their methods had little influence beyond the concession areas in the coastal cities. Chinese efforts to imitate Western methods, notably in shipbuilding and weapons manufacture, were dominated by the government and often suffered from mismanagement.

Equally serious problems persisted in the countryside. The rapid increase in population had led to smaller plots and burgeoning numbers of tenant farmers. Rice as a staple of the diet was increasingly being replaced by less nutritious foods, many of which depleted the soil, already under pressure from the dramatic increase in population. Some farmers benefited from switching to commercial agriculture to supply the markets of the growing coastal cities, but the shift entailed a sizable investment. Many farmers went so deeply into debt that they eventually lost their land. In the meantime, the traditional patron-client relationship was frayed as landlords moved to the cities to take advantage of the glittering urban lifestyle introduced by the West.

Some of these problems can undoubtedly be ascribed to the growing Western presence. But the court's hesitant efforts to cope with these challenges suggest that the most important obstacle was at the top: Qing officials often seemed overwhelmed by the combination of external pressure and internal strife. At a time when other traditional societies, such as Russia, the Ottoman Empire, and Japan, were making vigorous attempts to modernize their economies, the Manchu court, along with much of the elite class, still exhibited an alarming degree of complacency.

THE IMPACT OF IMPERIALISM In any event, with the advent of the imperialist era the question of whether China left to itself would have experienced an industrial revolution became academic. Imperialism created serious distortions in the local economy that resulted in massive changes in Chinese society during the twentieth century. Whether the Western intrusion was beneficial or harmful is debated to this day. The Western presence undoubtedly accelerated the development of the Chinese economy in some ways: the introduction of modern means of production, transport, and communications; the creation of an export market; and the steady integration of the Chinese market into the global economy. To many Westerners at the time, it was self-evident that such changes would ultimately benefit the Chinese people (see the comparative essay "Imperialism and the Global Environment" on p. 581). In their view, by supplying (in the

Imperialism and the Global Environment

EARTH & ENVIRONMENT

Beginning in the 1870s, European states engaged in an intense scramble for territory in Asia and Africa. Within the empires created by this "new imperialism," the Western powers redrew political boundaries to meet their needs and paid no attention to existing political, linguistic, or religious divisions. In Africa, for example, the Europeans often drew boundaries that divided distinctive communities between colonies or included two hostile communities within the same colony; those boundaries often became the boundaries of the countries of modern Africa.

Similarly, Europeans paid little heed to the requirements of their colonial subjects but instead organized the economies of their empires to meet their own needs in the world market. In the process, Europeans often dramatically altered the global environment. Westerners built railways and ports, drilled for oil, and dug mines for gold, tin, iron ore, and copper. Although the extraction of such resources often resulted in enormous profits, the colonial powers, not the indigenous population, were the prime beneficiaries. At the same time, these projects transformed and often scarred the natural landscape.

Landscapes were even more dramatically altered by Europe's demand for cash crops. Throughout vast regions of Africa and Asia, woodlands were cleared to make way for plantations. In Ceylon (modern Sri Lanka) and India, the British cut down vast tropical forests to plant row upon row of tea bushes. The Dutch razed forests in the East Indies to plant cinchona trees imported from Peru. (Quinine, used to treat malaria, was derived from the trees' bark.) In Indochina, the French replaced extensive forests with rubber, sugar, and coffee plantations. Local workers provided the labor for these vast plantations, usually at pitiful wages.

In many areas, precious farmland was turned over to the cultivation of cash crops. In the Dutch East Indies, farmers were forced to plow up rice fields to make way for the cultivation of sugar. In West Africa, overplanting of cash crops damaged fragile grasslands and turned parts of the Sahel (suh-HAYL or suh-HEEL) into a wasteland.

European states greatly profited from this transformed environment, however. To the British botanist John Christopher Willis, their actions were entirely justified. In *Agriculture in the Tropics: An Elementary Treatise*, written in 1909, he commented:

> Whether planting in the tropics will always continue to be under European management is another question, but the northern powers will not permit that the rich and as yet comparatively undeveloped countries of the tropics should be entirely wasted by being devoted merely to the supply of the food and clothing wants of their own people, when they can also supply the wants of the colder zones in so many indispensable products.

Q *How did the effects of imperialism on the environment in colonial countries compare with the impact of the Industrial Revolution in Europe and North America?*

© Transcendental Graphics/Getty Images

Picking Tea Leaves in Ceylon. In this 1900 photograph, women on a plantation in Ceylon (Sri Lanka) pick tea leaves for shipment abroad. The British cut down vast stands of tropical forests in Ceylon and India to grow tea to satisfy demand back home.

catch phrase of the day) "oil for the lamps of China," the West was providing a backward society with an opportunity to move up a notch or two on the ladder of human evolution.

Not everyone agreed. The Russian Marxist Vladimir Lenin contended that Western imperialists hindered the process of structural change in preindustrial societies by thwarting the rise of a local industrial and commercial sector in order to maintain colonies as markets for Western manufactured goods and sources of cheap labor and materials. Fellow Marxists in China such as Mao Zedong (see Chapter 24) later asserted that if the West had not intervened, China would have found its own road to capitalism and thence to socialism and communism.

Many historians today would say that such explanations are too simplistic. By shaking China out of its traditional mind-set, imperialism accelerated the change that had begun in the late Ming and early Qing periods and forced the Chinese to adopt new ways of thinking and acting. At the same time, China paid a heavy price in the destruction of its local industry while many of the profits flowed abroad. Although industrial revolution is inevitably a painful process, the Chinese found the experience doubly painful because it was foisted on them from the outside.

Daily Life in Qing China

In 1800, daily life for most Chinese was not substantially different from what it had been centuries earlier. Most were farmers, whose lives were governed by the harvest cycle, village custom, and family ritual. Their roles in society were fixed by the time-honored principles of Confucian social ethics. Male children, at least the more fortunate ones, were educated in the Confucian classics, while females remained in the home or in the fields. All children were expected to obey their parents, and all wives to submit to their husbands.

A visitor to China a hundred years later would have seen a very different society, although one still recognizably Chinese. Change was most striking in the coastal cities, where the educated and affluent had been affected by the Western presence. Confucian social institutions and behavioral norms were declining rapidly in influence, while those of Europe and North America were on the ascendant. Change was much less noticeable in the countryside, but even there, the customary bonds had been frayed.

Some of the change can be traced to the educational system. During the nineteenth century, the importance of a Confucian education steadily declined as up to half of the degree holders had purchased their degrees. After 1906, when the government abolished the civil service examinations, a Confucian education ceased to be the key to a successful career, and Western-style education became more desirable. The old dynasty attempted to establish an educational system on the Western model with universal education at the elementary level. The effect was greatest in the cities, where public schools, missionary schools, and other private institutions educated a new generation of Chinese with little knowledge of or respect for the past.

CHANGING ROLES FOR WOMEN The status of women was also in transition. During the mid-Qing era, women were still expected to remain in the home. Their status as useless sex objects was painfully symbolized by

Women with Bound Feet. To provide the best possible marriage for their daughters, upper-class families began to perform foot binding during the Song dynasty. Eventually, the practice spread to all social classes. Although small feet were supposed to denote a woman of leisure, most Chinese women with bound feet worked, mainly in textiles and handicrafts, to supplement the family income.

the practice of foot binding, which had probably originated among court entertainers in the Tang dynasty. By the mid-nineteenth century, more than half of all adult women probably had bound feet.

During the second half of the century, signs of change began to appear. Women began to seek employment in factories—notably in cotton mills and in the silk industry. Some women participated in the Taiping Rebellion and the Boxer movement, and a few fought beside men in the 1911 revolution. Qiu Jin (chee-oo JIN), a well-known female revolutionary, wrote a manifesto calling for women's liberation and then organized a revolt against the Manchu government, only to be captured and executed at the age of thirty-two in 1907.

By the end of the century, educational opportunities for women began to appear for the first time. Christian missionaries opened some girls' schools, mainly in the foreign concession areas. Although only a small number of women were educated in these schools, they had a significant impact as progressive intellectuals began to argue that ignorant women produced ignorant children. In 1905, the court announced plans to open public schools for girls, but few such schools ever materialized. The government also began to take steps to discourage foot binding, initially with only minimal success.

© Royal Geographical Society/Alamy

Emperor Meiji and the Charter Oath. In 1868, reformist elements overthrew the Tokugawa shogunate and initiated an era of rapid modernization. Their intentions were announced in a charter oath of five articles promulgated in April 1868. In this contemporary print, the young Emperor Meiji listens to the reading of the Charter Oath in his palace in Kyoto.

traditional in that power remained in the hands of a ruling oligarchy. The system permitted the traditional ruling class to retain its influence and economic power while acquiescing in the emergence of new institutions and values.

MEIJI ECONOMICS With the end of the daimyo domains, the government needed a new system of landownership that would transform the rural population from indentured serfs into citizens. To do so, it enacted a land reform program that redefined the domain lands as the private property of the tillers while compensating the previous owners with government bonds. A new land tax, set at an annual rate of 3 percent of the land's estimated value, was then imposed to raise revenue for the government. The tax proved to be a lucrative source of income for the government, but it was onerous for the farmers, who had previously paid a fixed percentage of their harvest to the landowner. In bad years, many peasants were unable to pay their taxes and were forced to sell their lands to wealthy neighbors. Eventually, the government reduced the tax to 2.5 percent of the land value. Still, by the end of the century, about 40 percent of all farmers were tenants.

With its budget needs secured, the government turned to the promotion of industry with the objective of guaranteeing Japan's survival against the challenge of Western imperialism. Building on the small but growing industrial economy that existed under the Tokugawa, the Meiji reformers provided massive stiumulus in the form of financial subsidies, training, foreign advisers, improved transport and communications, and a universal educational system emphasizing applied science. Unlike China, Japan relied very little on foreign capital.

During the late Meiji era, Japan's industrial sector began to grow. Besides tea and silk, key industries included weaponry, shipbuilding, and sake (SAH-kee) (fermented rice wine). From the start, the distinctive feature of the Meiji model was the intimate relationship between government and private business. Once an individual enterprise or industry was on its feet, it was turned over entirely to private ownership, although the

political ideas. The Liberal Party favored a model that would vest supreme authority in the parliament as the representative of the people. The Progressive Party called for the distribution of power between the legislative and executive branches, with a slight nod to the latter.

THE CONSTITUTION OF 1890 During the 1870s and 1880s, these factions competed for preeminence. In the end, the Progressives emerged victorious. The Meiji Constitution, which was adopted in 1890, was based on the Bismarckian model with authority vested in the executive branch; the imperialist faction was pacified by the statement that the constitution was the gift of the emperor. The Meiji oligarchs would handpick the cabinet. The upper house of parliament would be appointed and have equal legislative powers with the lower house, called the Diet, whose members would be elected. The core ideology of the state, called the *kokutai* (koh-kuh-TY), or national polity, embodied the concept of the uniqueness of the Japanese system based on the supreme authority of the emperor. The ancient practice of Shinto was transformed into a virtual national religion, and its traditional ceremonies were performed at all important events in the imperial court.

The result was a system that was democratic in form but despotic in practice, modern in appearance but still government often continued to play some role. One historian has explained the process:

> [The Meiji government] pioneered many industrial fields and sponsored the development of others, attempting to cajole businessmen into new and risky kinds of endeavor, helping assemble the necessary capital, forcing weak companies to merge into stronger units, and providing private entrepreneurs with aid and privileges of a sort that would be corrupt favoritism today. All this was in keeping with Tokugawa traditions that business operated under the tolerance and patronage of government. Some of the political leaders even played a dual role in politics and business.[4]

From the workers' perspective, the Meiji reforms had a less attractive side. Industrial growth was subsized by funds provided by the new land tax, but the tax imposed severe hardships on the peasants, many of whom fled to the cities, where they provided an abundant source of cheap labor. As in Europe during the early Industrial Revolution, workers toiled for long hours in the coal mines and textile mills, often under horrendous conditions. Reportedly, coal miners on a small island in Nagasaki harbor worked naked in temperatures up to 130 degrees Fahrenheit. If they tried to escape, they were shot.

BUILDING A MODERN SOCIAL STRUCTURE By the late Tokugawa era, the rigidly hierarchical social order was beginning to disintegrate. Rich merchants were buying their way into the ranks of the samurai, and Japanese of all classes were abandoning their rice fields and moving into the cities. Nevertheless, community and hierarchy still formed the basis of society. The lives of all Japanese were determined by their membership in various social organizations—their family, village, and social class. Membership in a particular social class determined a person's occupation and social relationships with others. Women in particular were constrained by the "**three obediences**": child to father, wife to husband, and widow to son. Husbands could easily obtain a divorce, but wives could not (allegedly, a husband could divorce his wife if she drank too much tea or talked too much). Marriages were arranged, and the average age at marriage for females was sixteen years. Females did not share inheritance rights with males, and few received any education outside the family.

The Meiji reformers destroyed much of the traditional social system. With the abolition of hereditary rights in 1871, the legal restrictions of the past were brought to an end with a single stroke. Special privileges for the aristocracy were abolished, as were the legal restrictions on the *eta* (AY-tuh), the traditional slave class (numbering about 400,000 in the 1870s). Another key focus of the reformers was the army. The Sat-Cho reformers had been struck by

the weakness of the Japanese forces in clashes with Western powers and set out to create a military that could compete in the modern world. The old feudal army based on the traditional warrior class was abolished, and an imperial army based on universal conscription was formed in 1871.

Education also underwent major changes. Recognizing the need for universal education including technical subjects, the Meiji leaders adopted the American model of a three-tiered system culminating in a series of universities and specialized institutes. They also sent bright students to study abroad and brought foreign scholars to Japan to teach in the new schools, where much of the content was inspired by Western models. In another break with tradition, women for the first time were given an opportunity to get an education.

These changes were included in the Imperial Rescript on Education that was issued in 1890, but the rescript also emphasized the traditional Confucian virtues of filial piety and loyalty to the state. One reason for issuing the Imperial Rescript was concern that Western individualistic ideas might dilute the traditional Japanese emphasis on responsibility to the community.

Indeed, Western ideas and fashions had become the rage in elite circles, and the ministers of the first Meiji government were known as the "dancing cabinet" because of their addiction to Western-style ballroom dancing. Young people began to imitate the clothing styles, eating habits, and social practices of their European and American counterparts (see the box on p. 587).

TRADITIONAL VALUES AND WOMEN'S RIGHTS Nevertheless, the self-proclaimed transformation of Japan into a "modern society" by no means detached the country entirely from its traditional moorings. Although an educational order in 1872 increased the percentage of Japanese women exposed to public education, conservatives soon began to impose restrictions and bring about a return to more traditional social relationships. As we have seen, the Imperial Rescript on Education in 1890 stressed the Confucian virtues of filial piety, patriotism, and loyalty to the family and community. Traditional values were given a firm legal basis in the Constitution of 1890, which restricted the franchise to males and defined individual liberties as "subject to the limitations imposed by law," and by the Civil Code of 1898, which de-emphasized individual rights and treated women within the context of their role in the family.

By the end of the century, however, changes were under way as women began to play a crucial role in the nation's effort to modernize. Urged by their parents to augment the family income, as well as by the government to fulfill their patriotic duty, young girls went en

The Wonders of Western Civilization: Two Views

INTERACTION & EXCHANGE

As information about the West began to penetrate East Asian societies during the nineteenth century, it aroused considerable interest and discussion. Some found much to admire in Western science and democracy, as the first selection demonstrates. Published in 1891 by the Chinese intellectual Wang Xiji (wahng SHEE-jee) (Wang Hsi-ch'i), it is a generally laudatory description of European society written by a hypothetical Chinese visitor.

Other Asian observers, however, found the lavish praise and imitation of Western ways somewhat ridiculous. In the second selection, published in 1871, the Japanese writer Kanagaki Rebun (REE-bun) mocks his compatriots who imitate Western practices. He begins by heaping scorn on those Japanese who now eat beef simply because it is popular in the West.

Wang Xiji, *A Chinese Description of Europe*

Europe (*Ou-lo-pa*) is one of the five great continents. . . . Though it is smaller than the other four continents, its soil is fertile, its products are plentiful, it has many talented people and many famous places. For this reason, Europe's power in the present world is pre-eminent, and it has become a leading force in the five continents. Yet in ancient times its people hunted for a living, ate meat, and wore skins. Their customs were barbaric, and their spirit was wild and free. But during our own Shang period (2000 B.C.E.) Greece and other countries gradually came under the influence of the Orient. For the first time they began to till fields and manufacture products, build cities, and dig lakes. . . . Before long, writing and civilization began to flourish. Thus, they became beautiful like the countries of the East. . . .

Now for their machines. When they first invented them, they just relied on common sense. They tried this and rejected that, without ever finding out from anyone else how it ought to be done. However, they did some research and found people who investigated the fine points and propagated their usage. In this way they gradually developed all their machines such as steamships, steam trains, spinning machines, mining and canal-digging machines, and all machines for making weapons and gunpowder. Things improved day to day and helped enrich the nation and benefit the people. Day by day they became more prosperous and will keep on becoming so.

Kanagaki Rebun, *The Beefeater*

Excuse me, but the beef is certainly a most delicious thing, isn't it? Once you get accustomed to its taste, you can never go back to deer or wild boar again. I wonder why we in Japan haven't eaten such a clean thing before? For over 1,620—or is it 1,630—years people in the West have been eating huge quantities of beef. . . . We really should be grateful that even people like ourselves can now eat beef, thanks to the fact that Japan is steadily becoming a truly civilized country.

In the West they're free of superstitions. There it's the custom to do everything scientifically, and that's why they've invented amazing things like the steamship and the steam engine. Did you know that . . . they bring down wind from the sky with balloons? . . . Of course, there are good reasons behind these inventions. If you look at a map of the world you'll see some countries marked "tropical," which means that's where the sun shines closest. The people in those countries are all burnt black by the sun. The king of that part of the world tried all kinds of schemes before he hit on what is called a balloon. That's a big round bag they fill with air high up in the sky. They bring the bag down and open it, causing the cooling air inside the bag to spread out all over the country. That's a great invention. On the other hand, in Russia, which is a cold country where the snow falls even in summer and the ice is so thick that people can't move, they invented the steam engine. You've got to admire them for it. I understand that they modeled the steam engine after the flaming chariot of hell, but anyway, what they do is to load a crowd of people on a wagon and light a fire in a pipe underneath. They keep feeding the fire inside the pipe with a coal, so that the people riding on top can travel a great distance completely oblivious to the cold. Those people in the West can think up inventions like that, one after the other.

Q *Which of these two views of European society in the late nineteenth century appears to be more accurate? Why?*

Sources: Wang Xiji, *A Chinese Description of Europe.* A Chinese Description of Europe. Kanagaki Rebun, *The Beefeater.* Excerpt from *Modern Japanese Literature,* Donald Keene, ed. (New York: Grove Press, 1960), pp. 32–33.

"In the Beginning, We Were the Sun"

FAMILY & SOCIETY

One aspect of Western thought that the Meiji reformers did not seek to imitate was the idea of gender equality. Although Japanese women sometimes tried to be "modern" like their male counterparts, Japanese society as a whole continued to treat women differently. In 1911, a young woman named Hiratsuka Raicho (hee-RAHT-soo-kuh RAY-choh) founded a journal named *Seito* (SAY-toh) (Blue Stockings) to promote the liberation of women in Japan. Her goal was to encourage women to develop their own latent talents, rather than to demand legal changes. The following document is the proclamation that was issued at the creation of the Seito Society. Compare it with Mary Wollstonecraft's discussion of the rights of women in Chapter 18.

Hiratsuka Raicho, Proclamation at the Founding of the Seito Society

Freedom and Liberation! Oftentimes we have heard the term "liberation of women." But what is it then? . . . Assuming that women are freed from external oppression, liberated from constraint, given the so-called higher education, employed in various occupations, given [the] franchise, and provided an opportunity to be independent from the protection of their parents and husbands, and to be freed from the little confinement of their homes, can all of these be called liberation of women? They may provide proper surroundings and opportunities to let us fulfill the true goal of liberation. Yet they remain merely the means, and do not represent our goal or ideals.

However, I am unlike many intellectuals in Japan who suggest that higher education is not necessary for women. Men and women are endowed by nature to have equal faculties. Therefore, it is odd to assume that one of the sexes requires education while the other does not. This may be tolerated in a given country and in a given age, but it is fundamentally a very unsound proposition.

I bemoan the facts that there is only one private college for women in Japan, and that there is no tolerance on man's part to permit entrance of women into many universities maintained for men. However, what benefit is there when the intellectual level of women becomes similar to that of men? Men seek knowledge in order to escape from their lack of wisdom and lack of enlightenment. They want to free themselves. . . . Yet multifarious thought can darken true wisdom, and lead men away from nature. . . .

Now, what is the true liberation which I am seeking? It is none other than to provide an opportunity for women to develop fully their hidden talents and hidden abilities. We must remove all the hindrances that stand in the way of women's development, whether they be external oppression or lack of knowledge. And above and beyond these factors, we must realize that we are the masters in possession of great talents, for we are the bodies which enshrine the great talents.

Q *What did Hiratsuka Raicho think was necessary to bring about the liberation of women in Meiji Japan? Were her proposals similar to those set forth by her counterparts in the West?*

Source: From John David Lu, *Sources of Japanese Tradition* (New York: McGraw-Hill, 1974), vol II, pp. 118–119, from CHUO KOREN, November 1965, pp. 354–357.

---

masse to work in textile mills. From 1894 to 1912, women represented 60 percent of the Japanese labor force. Thanks to them, by 1914, Japan was the world's leading exporter of silk and dominated cotton manufacturing. Without the revenues earned from textile exports, Japan might have required an infusion of foreign capital to develop its heavy industry and military.

Japanese women received few rewards for their contribution, however. In 1900, new regulations prohibited women from joining political organizations or attending public meetings. Beginning in 1905, a group of independent-minded women petitioned the Japanese parliament to rescind this restriction. Although the regulation was not repealed until 1922, calls for women's rights increasingly were heard (see the box above).

Joining the Imperialist Club

Traditionally, Japan had not been an expansionist country, but now the Japanese began to emulate the Western approach to foreign affairs as well as Western domestic policies. This is perhaps not surprising. The Japanese felt particularly vulnerable in the world economic arena. Their territory was small, lacking in resources, and densely populated, and they had no natural outlet for expansion. To observant Japanese, the lessons of history were clear. Western nations had amassed wealth and power not only because of their democratic systems and high level of education but also because of their colonies. The Japanese began their program of territorial expansion close to home (see Map 22.4). In 1874, after a brief conflict with China, Japan was able to claim suzerainty over the Ryukyu (RYOO-kyoo) Islands, long tributary to the Chinese Empire. Two years later, Japanese naval pressure forced Korea to open three ports to Japanese commerce.

During the early nineteenth century, Korea had followed Japan's example and attempted to isolate itself from outside contact except for periodic tribute missions to China. Christian missionaries, mostly Chinese or French, were vigorously persecuted. But Korea's problems were basically internal. In the early 1860s, a peasant revolt, inspired in part by the Taiping Rebellion in China, caused considerable devastation before being crushed in 1864. In succeeding years, the Yi (YEE) dynasty sought to strengthen the country by returning to traditional values and fending off outside intrusion, but rural poverty and official corruption remained rampant. A U.S. fleet sought to open the country in 1871 but was driven off with considerable loss of life.

Korea's most persistent suitor, however, was Japan, which was determined to bring an end to Korea's dependency status with China and modernize it along Japanese lines. In 1876, Korea agreed to open three ports to Japanese commerce in return for Japanese recognition of Korean independence. During the 1880s, Sino-Japanese rivalry over Korea intensified. When a new peasant rebellion broke out in Korea in 1894, China and Japan intervened on opposite sides (see the box on p. 590). During the war, the Japanese navy destroyed the Chinese fleet and seized the Manchurian city of Port Arthur. In the Treaty of Shimonoseki, the Chinese were forced to recognize the independence of Korea and cede Taiwan (TY-WAHN) and the Liaodong peninsula with its strategic naval base at Port Arthur to Japan.

Shortly thereafter, under pressure from the European powers, the Japanese returned the Liaodong peninsula to China, but in the early twentieth century, they went back on the offensive. Rivalry with Russia over influence in Korea led to increasingly strained relations between the two countries. In 1904, Japan launched a surprise attack on the Russian naval base at Port Arthur, which Russia had taken from China in 1898. The Japanese armed forces were weaker, but Russia faced difficult logistical problems along its new Trans-Siberian Railway and severe political instability at home. In 1905, after Japanese warships sank almost the entire Russian fleet off the coast of Korea, the Russians agreed to a humiliating peace, ceding the Liaodong peninsula back to Japan, as well as southern Sakhalin (SAK-uh-leen) and the Kurile (KOOR-il or koo-REEL) Islands. Russia also agreed to abandon its political and economic influence in Korea and southern Manchuria, which now came increasingly under Japanese control. The Japanese victory stunned the world, including the colonial peoples of Southeast Asia, who now began to realize that the white race was not necessarily invincible.

During the next few years, the Japanese consolidated their position in northeastern Asia, annexing Korea in 1908 as an integral part of Japan. When the Koreans protested, Japanese reprisals resulted in thousands of deaths. The United States was the first to recognize the annexation in return for Tokyo's declaration of respect for U.S. authority in the Philippines. In 1908, the United States recognized Japanese interests in the region in return for Japanese acceptance of the principles of the Open Door. But mutual suspicion between the two countries was growing, sparked in part by U.S. efforts to restrict immigration from all Asian countries.

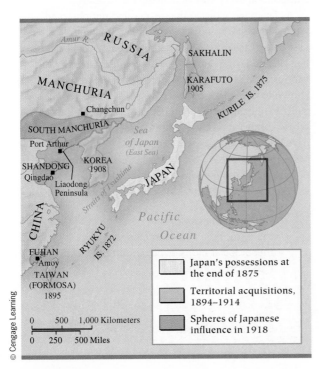

© Cengage Learning

MAP 22.4 Japanese Overseas Expansion During the Meiji Era. Beginning in the late nineteenth century, Japan ventured beyond its home islands and became an imperialist power. The extent of Japanese colonial expansion through World War I is shown here.

 Which parts of imperial China came under Japanese influence?

OPPOSING ✕ VIEWPOINTS

Two Views of the World

INTERACTION & EXCHANGE

During the nineteenth century, China's hierarchical way of looking at the outside world came under severe challenge, not only from Western countries but also from the rising power of Japan, which accepted the Western view that a colonial empire was the key to national greatness. Japan's first objective was Korea, long a dependency of China, and in 1894, the competition between China and Japan in the Korean peninsula led to war. The following declarations of war by the rulers of the two countries are revealing. Note the Chinese use of the derogatory term *Wojen* ("dwarf people") in referring to the Japanese.

Declaration of War Against China

Korea is an independent state. She was first introduced into the family of nations by the advice and guidance of Japan. It has, however, been China's habit to designate Korea as her dependency, and both openly and secretly to interfere with her domestic affairs. At the time of the recent insurrection in Korea, China despatched troops thither, alleging that her purpose was to afford a succor to her dependent state. We, in virtue of the treaty concluded with Korea in 1882, and looking to possible emergencies, caused a military force to be sent to that country.

Wishing to procure for Korea freedom from the calamity of perpetual disturbance, and thereby to maintain the peace of the East in general, Japan invited China's cooperation for the accomplishment of the object. But China, advancing various pretexts, declined Japan's proposal. . . . Such conduct on the part of China is not only a direct injury to the rights and interests of this Empire, but also a menace to the permanent peace and tranquility of the Orient. . . . In this situation, . . . we find it impossible to avoid a formal declaration of war against China.

Declaration of War Against Japan

Korea has been our tributary for the past two hundred odd years. She has given us tribute all this time, which is a matter known to the world. For the past dozen years or so Korea has been troubled by repeated insurrections and we, in sympathy with our small tributary, have as repeatedly sent succor to her aid. . . . This year another rebellion was begun in Korea, and the King repeatedly asked again for aid from us to put down the rebellion. We then ordered Li Hung-chang to send troops to Korea; and they having barely reached Yashan the rebels immediately scattered. But the *Wojen*, without any cause whatever, suddenly sent their troops to Korea, and entered Seoul, the capital of Korea, reinforcing them constantly until they have exceeded ten thousand men. In the meantime the Japanese forced the Korean king to change his system of government, showing a disposition every way of bullying the Koreans. . . .

As Japan has violated the treaties and not observed international laws, and is now running rampant with her false and treacherous actions commencing hostilities herself, and laying herself open to condemnation by the various powers at large, we therefore desire to make it known to the world that we have always followed the paths of philanthropy and perfect justice throughout the whole complications, while the *Wojen*, on the other hand, have broken all the laws of nations and treaties which it passes our patience to bear with. Hence we commanded Li Hung-chang to give strict orders to our various armies to hasten with all speed to root the *Wojen* out of their lairs.

Compare the worldviews of China and Japan at the end of the nineteenth century as reflected in these declarations. Which point of view do you find more persuasive?

Source: From MacNair, *Modern Chinese History*, pp. 530–534, quoted in Franz Schurmann and Orville Schell, eds., *The China Reader: Imperial China* (New York: Vintage, 1967), pp. 251–259.

Japanese Culture in Transition

The wave of Western technology and ideas that entered Japan in the second half of the nineteenth century greatly altered traditional Japanese culture. Literature in particular was affected as European models eclipsed the repetitive and frivolous tales of the Tokugawa era. Dazzled by this "new" literature, Japanese authors began translating and imitating the imported models. Experimenting with Western verse, Japanese poets were influenced by such styles as Symbolism, and in later decades by Dadaism

(DAH-duh-iz-um) and Surrealism, although some traditional poetry was still composed.

As the Japanese invited technicians, engineers, architects, and artists from Europe and the United States to teach their "modern" skills to a generation of eager students, Western artistic techniques and styles were adopted on a massive scale. Japanese architects and artists created huge buildings of steel and reinforced concrete adorned with Greek columns and cupolas, oil paintings reflecting the European concern with depth perception and shading, and bronze sculptures of secular subjects.

Cultural exchange also went the other way as Japanese arts and crafts, porcelains, textiles, fans, folding screens, and woodblock prints became the vogue in Europe and North America. Japanese art influenced Western painters such as Vincent van Gogh, Edgar Degas (duh-GAH), and James Whistler, who experimented with flatter compositional perspectives and unusual poses. Japanese gardens, with their exquisite attention to the positioning of rocks and falling water, became especially popular.

After the initial period of mass absorption of Western art, a reaction occurred at the end of the nineteenth century as many artists returned to pre-Meiji techniques. In 1889, the Tokyo School of Fine Arts (today the Tokyo National University of Fine Arts and Music) was founded to promote traditional Japanese art. Over the next decades, Japanese art underwent a dynamic resurgence, reflecting the nation's emergence as a prosperous and powerful state. While some Japanese artists attempted to

CHRONOLOGY	Japan and Korea in the Era of Imperialism
Commodore Perry arrives in Tokyo Bay	1853
Townsend Harris Treaty	1858
Fall of Tokugawa shogunate	1868
U.S. fleet fails to open Korea	1871
Feudal titles abolished in Japan	1871
Japanese imperial army formed	1871
Meiji Constitution adopted	1890
Imperial Rescript on Education	1890
Treaty of Shimonoseki awards Taiwan to Japan	1895
Russo-Japanese War	1904–1905
Korea annexed by Japan	1908

synthesize native and foreign techniques, others found inspiration in past artistic traditions.

The Meiji Restoration: A Revolution from Above

Japan's transformation from a feudal, agrarian society to an industrializing, technologically advanced society in little more than half a century has frequently been described by outside observers (if not by the Japanese themselves) in almost miraculous terms. Some historians have questioned this characterization, pointing out that

Collection Ministry of Foreign Affairs, Tokyo//© Art Resource, NY

The Ginza in Downtown Tokyo. This 1877 woodblock print shows the Ginza, a major commercial thoroughfare in downtown Tokyo, with modern brick buildings and a horse-drawn streetcar. The focus of public attention is a new electric streetlight. In combining traditional form with modern content, this print symbolizes the unique ability of the Japanese to borrow ideas from abroad while preserving much of the essence of their traditional culture.

the achievements of the Meiji leaders were spotty. In *Japan's Emergence as a Modern State*, the Canadian historian E. H. Norman lamented that the **Meiji Restoration** was an "incomplete revolution" because it did not end the economic and social inequities of feudal society or enable the common people to participate fully in the governing process. Although the *genro* were enlightened in many respects, they were also despotic and elitist, and the distribution of wealth remained as unequal as it had been under the old system.[5]

Moreover, Japan's transformation into a major industrial nation was by no means complete by the beginning of the new century. Until at least the outbreak of World War I in 1914, the majority of manufactured goods were produced by traditional cottage industries, rather than by modern factories. The integration of the Japanese economy into the global marketplace was also limited, and foreign investment played a much smaller role than in most comparable economies in the West.

These criticisms are persuasive, although most of them could also be applied to most other societies going through the early stages of industrialization. In any event, from an economic perspective, the Meiji Restoration was certainly one of the great success stories of modern times. Not only did the Meiji leaders put Japan firmly on the path to economic and political development, but they also managed to remove the unequal treaty provisions that had been imposed at mid-century. Japanese achievements are especially impressive when compared with the difficulties experienced by China, which was not only unable to bring about significant changes in its traditional society but had not even reached a consensus on the need for doing so. Japan's achievements more closely resemble those of Europe, but whereas the West needed a century and a half to achieve significant industrial development, the Japanese realized it in forty years.

One of the distinctive features of Japan's transition from a traditional to a modern society was that it took place for the most part without violence or the kind of social or political revolution that occurred in so many other countries. The Meiji Restoration, which began the process, has been called a "revolution from above," a comprehensive restructuring of Japanese society by its own ruling group.

WHAT EXPLAINS JAPANESE UNIQUENESS? The differences between the Japanese response to the West and the responses of China and many other nations in the region have sparked considerable debate among students of comparative history. In this and previous chapters, we have already discussed some of the reasons why China—along with most other countries in Asia and Africa—had not begun to enter an industrial revolution of its own by the end of the nineteenth century. The puzzle then becomes, why was Japan apparently uniquely positioned to make the transition to an advanced industrial economy?

A number of explanations have been offered. Some have argued that Japan's success was partly due to good fortune. Lacking abundant natural resources, it was exposed to less pressure from the West than many of its neighbors. That argument is problematic, however, and would probably not have been accepted by Japanese observers at the time. Nor does it explain why nations under considerably less pressure, such as Laos and Nepal, did not advance even more quickly. All in all, the luck hypothesis is not very persuasive.

Some explanations have already been suggested in this book. Japan's unique geographic position was certainly a factor. China, a continental nation with a heterogeneous ethnic composition, was distinguished from its neighbors by its Confucian culture. By contrast, Japan was an island nation, ethnically and linguistically homogeneous, and had never been conquered. Unlike the Chinese or many other peoples in the region, the Japanese had little to fear from cultural change in terms of its effect on their national identity. The fact that the emperor, the living symbol of the nation, had adopted change ensured that his subjects could follow in his footsteps without fear.

In addition, a number of other factors may have played a role. Japanese values, with their emphasis on practicality and military achievement, may have contributed. Finally, the Meiji also benefited from the fact that the pace of urbanization and commercial and industrial development had already begun to quicken under the Tokugawa. Having already lost their traditional feudal role and much of the revenue from their estates, the Japanese aristocracy—daimyo and samurai alike—could discard sword and kimono and don modern military uniforms or Western business suits and still feel comfortable in both worlds.

Whatever the case, as the historian W. G. Beasley has noted, the Meiji Restoration was possible because aristocratic and capitalist elements managed to work together to bring about drastic change. Japan, it was said, was ripe for change, and nothing could have been more suitable as an antidote for the collapsing old system than the Western emphasis on wealth and power. It was a classic example of challenge and response.

THE FUSION OF EAST AND WEST The final product was an amalgam of old and new, Japanese and foreign, forming a new civilization that was still uniquely Japanese. There were some undesirable consequences, however. Because Meiji politics was essentially despotic,

Japanese leaders were able to fuse key traditional elements such as the warrior ethic and the concept of feudal loyalty with the dynamics of modern industrial capitalism to create a state totally dedicated to the possession of material wealth and national power. This combination of *kokutai* and capitalism, which one scholar has described as a form of "Asian fascism," was highly effective but explosive in its international manifestation. Like modern Germany, which also entered the industrial age directly from feudalism, Japan eventually engaged in a policy of repression at home and expansion abroad to achieve its national objectives. In Japan, as in Germany, it took defeat in war to disconnect the drive for national development from the feudal ethic and bring about the transformation to a pluralistic society dedicated to living in peace and cooperation with its neighbors.

CHAPTER SUMMARY

Few areas of the world resisted the Western incursion as stubbornly and effectively as East Asia. Although military, political, and economic pressure by the European powers was relatively intense during this era, two of the main states in the area were able to retain their independence while the third—Korea—was temporarily absorbed by one of its larger neighbors. Why the Chinese and the Japanese were able to prevent a total political and military takeover by foreign powers is an interesting question. One key reason was that both had a long history as well-defined states with a strong sense of national community and territorial cohesion. Although China had frequently been conquered, it had retained its sense of unique culture and identity. Geography, too, was in its favor. As a continental nation, China was able to survive partly because of its sheer size. Japan possessed the advantage of an island location.

Even more striking, however, are the different ways in which the two states attempted to deal with the challenge. While the Japanese chose to face the problem in a pragmatic manner, borrowing foreign ideas and institutions that appeared to be of value and at the same time were not in conflict with traditional attitudes and customs, China agonized over the issue for half a century while conservative elements fought a desperate battle to retain a maximum of the traditional heritage intact.

This chapter has discussed some of the possible reasons for those differences. In retrospect, it is difficult to avoid the conclusion that the Japanese approach was more effective. Whereas the Meiji leaders were able to set in motion an orderly transition from a traditional to an advanced society, in China the old system collapsed in disorder, leaving chaotic conditions that were still not rectified a generation later. China would pay a heavy price for its failure to respond coherently to the challenge.

But the Japanese "revolution from above" was by no means an unalloyed success. Ambitious efforts by Japanese leaders to carve out a share in the spoils of empire led to escalating conflict with China as well as with rival Western powers and in the early 1940s to global war. We will deal with that issue in Chapter 25. Meanwhile, in Europe, a combination of old rivalries and the effects of the Industrial Revolution were leading to a bitter regional conflict that eventually engulfed the entire world.

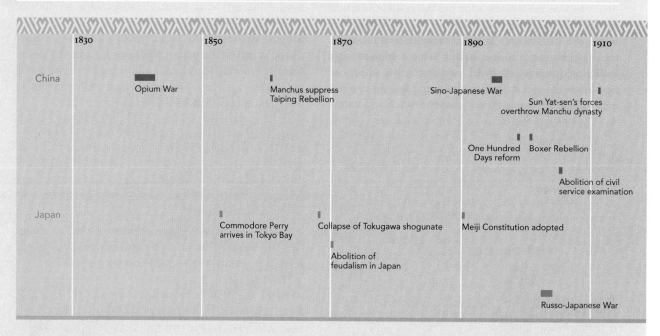

Timeline:

China
- Opium War (c. 1840)
- Manchus suppress Taiping Rebellion (c. 1864)
- Sino-Japanese War (1894)
- One Hundred Days reform (1898)
- Boxer Rebellion (1900)
- Abolition of civil service examination (1905)
- Sun Yat-sen's forces overthrow Manchu dynasty (1911)

Japan
- Commodore Perry arrives in Tokyo Bay (1853)
- Collapse of Tokugawa shogunate (1868)
- Abolition of feudalism in Japan
- Meiji Constitution adopted (1889)
- Russo-Japanese War (1905)

CHAPTER REVIEW

Upon Reflection

Q What were some of the key reasons why the Meiji reformers were so successful in launching Japan on the road to industrialization? Which of those reasons also applied to China under the Manchus?

Q What impact did colonial rule have on the environment in the European colonies in Asia and Africa during the nineteenth century? Did some of these same factors apply in China and Japan?

Q How did Western values and institutions influence Chinese and Japanese social mores and traditions during the imperialist era?

Key Terms

self-strengthening (p. 574)
Open Door Notes (p. 576)
three people's principles (p. 577)
sakoku (p. 583)
genro (p. 584)
kokutai (p. 585)
three obediences (p. 586)
eta (p. 586)
Meiji Restoration (p. 592)

Suggested Reading

CHINA For a general overview of modern Chinese history, see **I. C. Y. Hsu, *The Rise of Modern China,*** 6th ed. (Oxford, 2000). Also see **J. Spence's** stimulating ***The Search for Modern China*** (New York, 1990).

On the Taiping Rebellion, **J. Spence, *God's Chinese Son: The Taiping Heavenly Kingdom of Hong Xiuquan*** (New York, 1996), has become a classic. Social issues are dealt with in **E. S. Rawski, *The Last Emperors: A Social History of Qing Imperial Institutions*** (Berkeley, Calif., 1998). On the Manchus' attitude toward modernization, see **D. Pong, *Shen Pao-chen and China's Modernization in the Nineteenth Century*** (New York, 1994). For a series of stimulating essays on various aspects of China's transition to modernity, see **Wenhsin Yeh, ed., *Becoming Chinese: Passages to Modernity and Beyond*** (Berkeley, Calif., 2000).

Sun Yat-sen's career is explored in **M. C. Bergère, Sun Yat-sen,** trans. **J. Lloyd** (Stanford, Calif., 2000). **S. Seagraves's *Dragon Lady: The Life and Legend of the Last Empress of China*** (New York, 1992), is a revisionist treatment of Empress Dowager Cixi. On the Boxer Rebellion, see **D. Preston, *The Boxer Rebellion: The Dramatic Story of China's War on Foreigners That Shook the World in the Summer of 1900*** (Berkeley, Calif., 2001).

JAPAN The Meiji period of modern Japan is covered in **M. B. Jansen, ed.,** *The Emergence of Meiji Japan* (Cambridge, 1995). Also see **D. Keene,** *Emperor of Japan: Meiji and His World, 1852–1912* (New York, 2000). See also **C. Gluck,** *Japan's Modern Myths: Ideology in the Late Meiji Period* (Princeton, N.J., 1985). To understand the role of the samurai in the Meiji Revolution, see **E. Ikegami,** *The Taming of the Samurai: Honorific Individualism and the Making of Modern Japan* (Cambridge, 1995).

On the international scene, **W. Lafeber,** *The Clash: U.S.-Japanese Relations Throughout History* (New York, 1997), is slow reading but a good source of information. The U.S. role in opening Japan to the West is analyzed in **G. Feifer,** *Breaking Open Japan: Commodore Perry, Lord Abe, and American Imperialism in 1853* (Washington, D.C., 2007). On the Russo-Japanese War, **R. Connaughton,** *Rising Sun and Tumbling Bear: Russia's War with Japan* (London, 2003), is one of several good offerings. The best introduction to Japanese art is **P. Mason,** *History of Japanese Art* (New York, 1993).

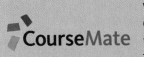

Visit the CourseMate website at **www.cengagebrain.com** for additional study tools and review materials for this chapter.

The Beginning of the Twentieth-Century Crisis: War and Revolution

Canadian soldiers prepare for an attack at the Battle of the Somme.

CHAPTER OUTLINE AND FOCUS QUESTIONS

The Road to World War I

Q What were the long-range and immediate causes of World War I?

The Great War

Q Why did the course of World War I turn out to be so different from what the belligerents had expected? How did World War I affect the belligerents' governmental and political institutions, economic affairs, and social life?

Crisis in Russia and the End of the War

Q What were the causes of the Russian Revolution of 1917, and why did the Bolsheviks prevail in the civil war and gain control of Russia?

An Uncertain Peace

Q What problems did Europe and the United States face in the 1920s?

In Pursuit of a New Reality: Cultural and Intellectual Trends

Q How did the cultural and intellectual trends of the post–World War I years reflect the crises of the time as well as the lingering effects of the war?

CRITICAL THINKING

Q What was the relationship between World War I and the Russian Revolution?

ON JULY 1, 1916, BRITISH and French infantry forces attacked German defensive lines along a 25-mile front near the Somme (SUHM) River in France. Each soldier carried almost 70 pounds of equipment, making it "impossible to move much quicker than a slow walk." German machine guns soon opened fire: "We were able to see our comrades move forward in an attempt to cross No-Man's Land, only to be mown down like meadow grass," recalled one British soldier. "I felt sick at the sight of this carnage and remember weeping." In one day, more than 21,000 British soldiers died. After six months of fighting, the British had advanced 5 miles; one million British, French, and German soldiers had been killed or wounded.

Philip Gibbs, an English war correspondent, described what he saw in the German trenches that the British forces overran: "Victory! . . . Some of the German dead were young boys, too young to be killed for old men's crimes, and others might have been old or young. One could not tell because they had no faces, and were just masses of raw flesh in rags of uniforms. Legs and arms lay separate without any bodies thereabout."

World War I (1914–1918) was the defining event of the twentieth-century Western world. Overwhelmed by the size of its battles, the extent of its casualties, and its impact on all facets of life, contemporaries referred to it simply as the "Great War." The Great War was all the more disturbing to Europeans because it came after a period that many believed to have been an age of progress. Material prosperity and a fervid belief in scientific and technological advances had convinced many people that the world stood on the verge of creating the utopia that humans had dreamed of for centuries. The historian Arnold Toynbee expressed what the era before the war had meant to his generation:

> [We had expected] that life throughout the world would become more rational, more humane, and more democratic and that, slowly, but surely, political democracy would produce greater social justice. We had also expected that the progress of science and technology would make mankind richer, and that this increasing wealth would gradually spread from a minority to a majority. We had expected that all this would happen peacefully. In fact we thought that mankind's course was set for an earthly paradise.[1]

After 1918, it was no longer possible to maintain naive illusions about the progress of Western civilization. As World War I was followed by revolutionary upheavals, the mass murder machines of totalitarian regimes, and the destructiveness of World War II, it became all too apparent that instead of a utopia, Western civilization had become a nightmare. World War I and the revolutions it spawned can properly be seen as the first stage in the crisis of the twentieth century. 🖎

The Road to World War I

Q FOCUS QUESTION: What were the long-range and immediate causes of World War I?

On June 28, 1914, the heir to the Austrian throne, Archduke Francis Ferdinand, was assassinated in the Bosnian city of Sarajevo (sar-uh-YAY-voh). Although this event precipitated the confrontation between Austria and Serbia that led to World War I, underlying forces had been propelling Europeans toward armed conflict for a long time.

Nationalism and Internal Dissent

The system of nation-states that had emerged in Europe in the second half of the nineteenth century (see Map 23.1) had led to intense competition. Rivalries over colonies and trade intensified during an era of frenzied imperialist expansion, while the division of Europe's great powers into two loose alliances (Germany, Austria, and Italy on one side and France, Great Britain, and Russia on the other) only added to the tensions. The series of crises that tested these alliances in the 1900s and early 1910s had left European states embittered, eager for revenge, and willing to go to war to preserve the power of their national states.

The growth of nationalism in the nineteenth century had yet another serious consequence. Not all ethnic groups had achieved the goal of nationhood. Slavic minorities in the Balkans and the multiethnic Habsburg Empire, for example, still dreamed of creating their own national states. So did the Irish in the British Empire and the Poles in the Russian Empire.

National aspirations, however, were not the only source of internal strife at the beginning of the twentieth century. Socialist labor movements had grown more powerful and were increasingly inclined to use strikes, even violent ones, to achieve their goals. Some conservative leaders, alarmed at the increase in labor strife and class division, even feared that European nations were on the verge of revolution. Did these statesmen opt for war in 1914 because they believed that "prosecuting an active foreign policy," as some Austrian leaders expressed it, would smother "internal troubles"? Some historians have argued that the desire to suppress internal disorder may have encouraged some leaders to take the plunge into war in 1914.

Militarism

The growth of large mass armies after 1900 not only heightened the existing tensions in Europe but also made it inevitable that if war did come, it would be extremely destructive. **Conscription**—obligatory military service—had been established as a regular practice in most Western countries before 1914 (the United States and Britain were major exceptions). European military machines had doubled in size between 1890 and 1914. The Russian army was the largest, with 1.3 million men, but the French and Germans were not far behind, with 900,000 each. The British, Italian, and Austrian armies numbered between 250,000 and 500,000 soldiers.

Militarism, however, involved more than just large armies. As armies grew, so did the influence of military leaders, who drew up vast and complex plans for quickly mobilizing millions of men and enormous quantities of supplies in the event of war. Fearful that changing these plans would cause chaos in the armed forces, military leaders insisted that the plans could not be altered. In the crises during the summer of 1914, the generals' lack of flexibility forced European political leaders to make decisions for military instead of political reasons.

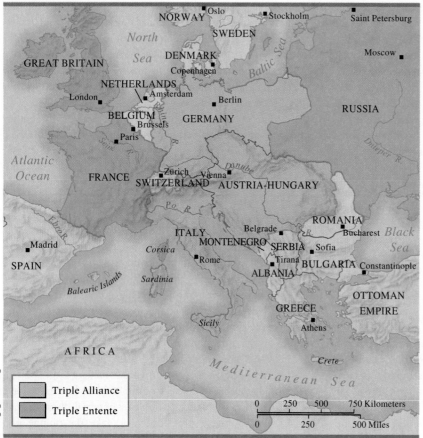

MAP 23.1 **Europe in 1914.** By 1914, two alliances dominated Europe: the Triple Entente of Britain, France, and Russia and the Triple Alliance of Germany, Austria-Hungary, and Italy. Russia sought to bolster fellow Slavs in Serbia, whereas Austria-Hungary was intent on increasing its power in the Balkans and thwarting Serbia's ambitions. Thus, the Balkans became the flash point for World War I.

Q *Which nonaligned nations were positioned between the two alliances?*

Slavic minorities to contend with, was equally set on preventing that possibility. Many Europeans perceived the inherent dangers in this explosive situation. The British ambassador to Vienna wrote in 1913:

> Serbia will some day set Europe by the ears, and bring about a universal war on the Continent. . . . I cannot tell you how exasperated people are getting here at the continual worry which that little country causes to Austria under encouragement from Russia. . . . It will be lucky if Europe succeeds in avoiding war as a result of the present crisis. The next time a Serbian crisis arises . . . , I feel sure that Austria-Hungary will refuse to admit of any Russian interference in the dispute and that she will proceed to settle her differences with her little neighbor by herself.[2]

It was against this backdrop of mutual distrust and hatred that the events of the summer of 1914 were played out.

THE ASSASSINATION OF FRANCIS FERDINAND: A "BLANK CHECK"? The assassination of the Austrian Archduke Francis Ferdinand and his wife, Sophia, on June 28, 1914, was carried out by a Bosnian activist who worked for the Black Hand, a Serbian terrorist organization dedicated to the creation of a pan-Slavic kingdom. Although the Austrian government did not know whether the Serbian government had been directly involved in the archduke's assassination, it saw an opportunity to "render Serbia innocuous once and for all by a display of force," as the Austrian foreign minister put it. Fearful of Russian intervention on Serbia's behalf, Austrian leaders sought the backing of their German allies. Emperor William II and his chancellor responded with the infamous "blank check," their assurance that Austria-Hungary could rely on Germany's "full support," even if "matters went to the length of a war between Austria-Hungary and Russia." Much historical debate has focused on this "blank check" extended to the Austrians. Did the Germans realize that an Austrian-Serbian war could lead to a wider war? If so, did they actually want

The Outbreak of War: Summer 1914

Militarism, nationalism, and the desire to stifle internal dissent may all have played a role in the coming of World War I, but the decisions made by European leaders in the summer of 1914 directly precipitated the conflict. It was another crisis in the Balkans that forced this predicament on European statesmen.

As we have seen, states in southeastern Europe had struggled to free themselves from Ottoman rule in the course of the nineteenth and early twentieth centuries. But the rivalry between Austria-Hungary and Russia for domination of these new states created serious tensions in the region. By 1914, Serbia, supported by Russia, was determined to create a large, independent Slavic state in the Balkans, while Austria-Hungary, which had its own one? Historians are still divided on the answers to these questions.

DECLARATIONS OF WAR Strengthened by German support, Austrian leaders issued an ultimatum to Serbia on July 23 in which they made such extreme demands that Serbia had little choice but to reject some of them in order to preserve its sovereignty. Austria then declared war on Serbia on July 28. Although the Austrians had hoped to keep the war limited to Serbia and Austria in order to ensure their success in the Balkans, Russia was determined to support Serbia's cause. Thus, on July 28, Tsar Nicholas II ordered partial mobilization of the Russian army against Austria. The Russian General Staff informed the tsar that their mobilization plans were based on a war against both Germany and Austria simultaneously. They could not execute partial mobilization without creating chaos in the army. Consequently, the Russian government ordered full mobilization of the Russian army on July 29, knowing that the Germans would consider this an act of war against them. Germany quickly responded with an ultimatum that the Russians must halt their mobilization within twelve hours. When the Russians ignored it, Germany declared war on Russia on August 1.

At this stage of the conflict, German war plans determined whether France would become involved in the war. Under the guidance of General Alfred von Schlieffen (AHL-fret fun SHLEE-fun), chief of staff from 1891 to 1905, the German General Staff had devised a military plan based on the assumption of a two-front war with France and Russia because the two powers had formed a military alliance in 1894. The Schlieffen Plan called for a minimal troop deployment against Russia while most of the German army would make a rapid invasion of France before Russia could become effective in the east or before the British could cross the English Channel to help France. This meant invading France by advancing through neutral Belgium, with its level coastal plain on which the army could move faster than on the rougher terrain to the southeast. After the planned quick defeat of the French, the German army expected to redeploy to the east against Russia. Under the Schlieffen Plan, Germany could not mobilize its troops solely against Russia and therefore declared war on France on August 3 after issuing an ultimatum to Belgium on August 2 demanding the right of German troops to pass through Belgian territory. On August 4, Great Britain declared war on Germany, officially over this violation of Belgian neutrality but in fact over the British desire to maintain world power. As one British diplomat argued, if Germany and Austria were to win the war, "what would be the position of a friendless England?" By August 4, all the great powers of Europe were at war.

The Great War

Q FOCUS QUESTIONS: Why did the course of World War I turn out to be so different from what the belligerents had expected? How did World War I affect the belligerents' governmental and political institutions, economic affairs, and social life?

Before 1914, many political leaders had become convinced that war involved so many political and economic risks that it was not worth fighting. Others had believed that "rational" diplomats could control any situation and prevent the outbreak of war. At the beginning of August 1914, both of these prewar illusions were shattered, but the new illusions that replaced them soon proved to be equally foolish.

1914–1915: Illusions and Stalemate

Europeans went to war in 1914 with great enthusiasm (see the box on p. 600). Government propaganda had been successful in stirring up national antagonisms before the war. Now, in August 1914, the urgent pleas of governments for defense against aggressors found many receptive ears in every belligerent nation. A new set of illusions also fed the enthusiasm for war. In August 1914, almost everyone believed that the war would be over in a few weeks. People were reminded that the major battles in European wars since 1815 had ended in a matter of weeks. Both the soldiers who exuberantly boarded the trains for the war front in August 1914 and the jubilant citizens who bombarded them with flowers when they departed believed that the warriors would be home by Christmas.

German hopes for a quick end to the war rested on a military gamble. The Schlieffen Plan had called for the

The Schlieffen Plan

The Excitement of War

POLITICS & GOVERNMENT

The incredible outpouring of patriotic enthusiasm that greeted the declaration of war at the beginning of August 1914 demonstrated the power that nationalistic feeling had attained at the beginning of the twentieth century. Many Europeans seemingly believed that the war had given them a higher purpose, a renewed dedication to the greatness of their nations. These selections are taken from three sources: the autobiography of Stefan Zweig (SHTE-fahn TSVYK), an Austrian writer; the memoirs of Robert Graves, a British writer; and a letter by a German soldier, Walter Limmer, to his parents.

Stefan Zweig, *The World of Yesterday*

The next morning I was in Austria. In every station placards had been put up announcing general mobilization. The trains were filled with fresh recruits, banners were flying, music sounded, and in Vienna I found the entire city in a tumult. . . . There were parades in the street, flags, ribbons, and music burst forth everywhere, young recruits were marching triumphantly, their faces lighting up at the cheering. . . .

And to be truthful, I must acknowledge that there was a majestic, rapturous, and even seductive something in this first outbreak of the people from which one could escape only with difficulty. And in spite of all my hatred and aversion for war, I should not like to have missed the memory of those days. As never before, thousands and hundreds of thousands felt what they should have felt in peace time, that they belonged together. A city of two million, a country of nearly fifty million, in that hour felt that they were participating in world history, in a moment which would never recur, and that each one was called upon to cast his infinitesimal self into the glowing mass, there to be purified of all selfishness. All differences of class, rank, and language were flooded over at that moment by the rushing feeling of fraternity. . . .

What did the great mass know of war in 1914, after nearly half a century of peace? They did not know war, they had hardly given it a thought. It had become legendary, and distance had made it seem romantic and heroic. They still saw it in the perspective of their school readers and of paintings in museums; brilliant cavalry attacks in glittering uniforms, the fatal shot always straight through the heart, the entire campaign a resounding march of victory—"We'll be home at Christmas," the recruits shouted laughingly to their mothers in August of 1914. . . . A rapid excursion into the romantic, a wild, manly adventure—that is how the war of 1914 was painted in the imagination of the simple man, and the younger people were honestly afraid that they might miss this most wonderful and exciting experience of their lives; that is why they hurried and thronged to the colors, and that is why they shouted and sang in the trains that carried them to the slaughter; wildly and feverishly the red wave of blood coursed through the veins of the entire nation.

Robert Graves, *Goodbye to All That*

I had just finished with Charterhouse and gone up to Harlech, when England declared war on Germany. A day or two later I decided to enlist. In the first place, though the papers predicted only a very short war—over by Christmas at the outside—I hoped that it might last long enough to delay my going to Oxford in October, which I dreaded. Nor did I work out the possibilities of getting actively engaged in the fighting, expecting garrison service at home, while the regular forces were away. In the second place, I was outraged to read of the Germans' cynical violation of Belgian neutrality. Though I discounted perhaps twenty percent of the atrocity details as wartime exaggeration, that was not, of course, sufficient.

Walter Limmer, Letter to His Parents

In any case I mean to go into this business. . . . That is the simple duty of every one of us. And this feeling is universal among the soldiers, especially since the night when England's declaration of war was announced in the barracks. We none of us got to sleep till three o'clock in the morning, we were so full of excitement, fury, and enthusiasm. It is a joy to go to the Front with such comrades. We are bound to be victorious! Nothing else is possible in the face of such determination to win.

Q *What do these excerpts reveal about the motivations of people to join and support World War I? Do the passages reveal anything about the power of nationalism in Europe in the early twentieth century?*

Source: From *The World of Yesterday* by Stefan Zweig, translated by Helmut Ripperger. Translation copyright 1943 by the Viking. Press, Inc.

German army to proceed through Belgium into northern France with a vast circling movement that would sweep around Paris and surround most of the French army. But the German advance was halted only 20 miles from Paris at the First Battle of the Marne (September 6–10). The war quickly turned into a stalemate as neither the Germans nor the French could dislodge each other from the trenches they had begun to dig for shelter (see Map 23.2).

In contrast to the Western Front, the war in the east was marked by much more mobility, although the cost in lives was equally enormous. At the beginning of the war, the Russian army moved into eastern Germany but was decisively defeated at the Battles of Tannenberg on August 30 and the Masurian Lakes on September 15. The Russians were no longer a threat to German territory.

The Austrians, Germany's allies, fared less well initially. They had been defeated by the Russians in Galicia (guh-LISH-ee-uh) and thrown out of Serbia as well. To make matters worse, the Italians betrayed the Germans and Austrians and entered the war on the Allied side by attacking Austria in May 1915. (France, Great Britain, and Russia were called the Allied Powers, or Allies.) By this time, the Germans had come to the aid of the Austrians. A German-Austrian army routed the Russian army in

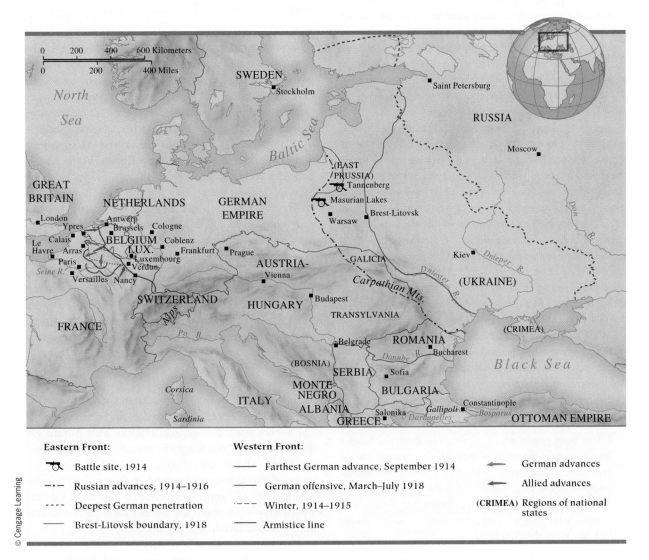

Eastern Front:

🔫 Battle site, 1914

–·– Russian advances, 1914–1916

- - - - Deepest German penetration

—— Brest-Litovsk boundary, 1918

Western Front:

—— Farthest German advance, September 1914

—— German offensive, March–July 1918

- - - - Winter, 1914–1915

—— Armistice line

⬅ German advances

⬅ Allied advances

(CRIMEA) Regions of national states

© Cengage Learning

MAP 23.2 World War I, 1914–1918. This map shows how greatly the Western and Eastern Fronts of World War I differed. After initial German gains in the west, the war became bogged down in trench warfare, with little change in the battle lines between 1914 and 1918. The Eastern Front was marked by considerable mobility, with battle lines shifting by hundreds of miles.

Q *How do you explain the difference in the two fronts?*

Galicia and pushed the Russians back 300 miles into their own territory. Russian casualties stood at 2.5 million killed, captured, or wounded; the Russians had almost been knocked out of the war. Buoyed by their success, the Germans and Austrians, joined by the Bulgarians in September 1915, attacked and eliminated Serbia from the war.

1916–1917: The Great Slaughter

The successes in the east enabled the Germans to move back to the offensive in the west. The early trenches dug in 1914, stretching from the English Channel to the frontiers of Switzerland, had by now become elaborate systems of defense. Both lines of trenches were protected by barbed-wire entanglements 3 to 5 feet high and 30 yards wide, concrete machine-gun nests, and mortar batteries, supported farther back by heavy artillery. Troops lived in holes in the ground, separated from each other by a "no-man's land."

The unexpected development of **trench warfare** on the Western Front baffled military leaders, who had been trained to fight wars of movement and maneuver. Periodically, the high command on either side would order an offensive that would begin with an artillery barrage to flatten the enemy's barbed wire and leave the enemy in a state of shock. After "softening up" the enemy in this fashion, a mass of soldiers would climb out of their trenches with fixed bayonets and hope to work their way toward the enemy trenches. The attacks rarely worked, as the machine gun put hordes of men advancing unprotected across open fields at a severe disadvantage. In 1916 and 1917, millions of young men were sacrificed in the search for the elusive breakthrough. In ten months at Verdun (ver-DUHN) in 1916, 700,000 men lost their lives over a few miles of terrain.

Warfare in the trenches of the Western Front produced unimaginable horrors (see the box on p. 603). Battlefields were hellish landscapes of barbed wire, shell holes, mud, and injured and dying men. The introduction of poison gas in 1915 produced new forms of injuries. As one British writer described them:

> I wish those people who write so glibly about this being a holy war could see a case of mustard gas . . . could see the poor things burnt and blistered all over with great mustard-coloured suppurating blisters with blind eyes all sticky . . . and stuck together, and always fighting for breath, with voices a mere whisper, saying that their throats are closing and they know they will choke.[3]

Soldiers in the trenches also lived with the persistent presence of death. Since combat went on for months, soldiers had to carry on in the midst of countless bodies of dead men or the remains of men dismembered by artillery barrages. Many soldiers remembered the stench of decomposing bodies and the swarms of rats that grew fat in the trenches.

The Widening of the War

As another response to the stalemate on the Western Front, both sides looked for new allies who might provide a winning advantage. The Ottoman Empire had already come into the war on Germany's side in August 1914. Russia, Great Britain, and France declared war on the Ottoman Empire in November. Although the Allies attempted to open a Balkan front by landing forces at Gallipoli (gah-LIP-poh-lee), southwest of Constantinople, in April 1915, the entry of Bulgaria into the war on the side of the Central Powers (as Germany, Austria-Hungary, and the Ottoman Empire were called) and a disastrous campaign at Gallipoli caused them to withdraw.

A GLOBAL CONFLICT Because the major European powers controlled colonial empires in other parts of the world, the war in Europe soon became a world conflict (see the comparative illustration on p. 604). In the Middle East, the British officer T. E. Lawrence (1888–1935), who came to be known as Lawrence of Arabia, incited Arab princes to revolt against their Ottoman overlords in 1917. In 1918, British forces from Egypt and Mesopotamia destroyed the rest of the Ottoman Empire in the Middle East. For their Middle East campaigns, the British mobilized forces from India, Australia, and New Zealand.

The Allies also took advantage of Germany's preoccupation in Europe and lack of naval strength to seize German colonies in Africa. The first British shots of World War I were actually fired in Africa when British African troops moved into the German colony of Togoland near the end of August 1914. But in East Africa, the German commander, Colonel Paul von Lettow-Vorbeck (POWL fun LEH-toh-FOR-bek), managed to keep his African troops fighting one campaign after another for four years; he did not surrender until two weeks after the armistice ended the war in Europe.

In the battles in Africa, Allied governments drew mainly on African soldiers, but some states, especially France, also recruited African troops to fight in Europe. The French drafted more than 170,000 West African soldiers, many of whom fought in the trenches on the Western Front. African troops were also used as occupation forces in the German Rhineland at the end of the war. About 80,000 Africans were killed or injured in Europe, where they were often at a distinct disadvantage due to the unfamiliar terrain and climate.

Hundreds of thousands of Africans were also used for labor, especially for carrying supplies and building roads and bridges. In East Africa, both sides drafted Africans as carriers for their armies. More than 100,000 of these workers died from disease and starvation resulting from neglect.

The immediate impact of World War I in Africa was the extension of colonial rule since Germany's African

The Reality of War: Trench Warfare

POLITICS & GOVERNMENT

The romantic illusions about the excitement and adventure of war that filled the minds of so many young men as they marched off to battle quickly disintegrated after a short time in the trenches on the Western Front. This description of trench warfare is taken from the most famous novel that emerged from World War I, Erich Maria Remarque's *All Quiet on the Western Front,* published in 1929. Remarque had fought in the trenches in France.

Erich Maria Remarque, *All Quiet on the Western Front*

We wake up in the middle of the night. The earth booms. Heavy fire is falling on us. We crouch into corners. We distinguish shells of every calibre.

Each man lays hold of his things and looks again every minute to reassure himself that they are still there. The dugout heaves, the night roars and flashes. We look at each other in the momentary flashes of light, and with pale faces and pressed lips shake our heads.

Every man is aware of the heavy shells tearing down the parapet, rooting up the embankment and demolishing the upper layers of concrete. . . . Already by morning a few of the recruits are green and vomiting. They are too inexperienced. . . .

The bombardment does not diminish. It is falling in the rear too. As far as one can see it spouts fountains of mud and iron. A wide belt is being raked.

The attack does not come, but the bombardment continues. Slowly we become mute. Hardly a man speaks. We cannot make ourselves understood.

Our trench is almost gone. At many places it is only eighteen inches high; it is broken by holes, and craters, and mountains of earth. A shell lands square in front of our post. At once it is dark. We are buried and must dig ourselves out. . . .

Towards morning, while it is still dark, there is some excitement. Through the entrance rushes in a swarm of fleeing rats that try to storm the walls. Torches light up the confusion. Everyone yells and curses and slaughters. The madness and despair of many hours unloads itself in this outburst. Faces are distorted, arms strike out, the beasts scream; we just stop in time to avoid attacking one another. . . .

Suddenly it howls and flashes terrifically, the dugout cracks in all its joints under a direct hit, fortunately only a light one that the concrete blocks are able to withstand.

It rings metallically; the walls reel; rifles, helmets, earth, mud, and dust fly everywhere. Sulfur fumes pour in. . . . The recruit starts to rave again and two others follow suit. One jumps up and rushes out, we have trouble with the other two. I start after the one who escapes and wonder whether to shoot him in the leg—then it shrieks again; I fling myself down and when I stand up the wall of the trench is plastered with smoking splinters, lumps of flesh, and bits of uniform. I scramble back.

The first recruit seems actually to have gone insane. He butts his head against the wall like a goat. We must try tonight to take him to the rear. Meanwhile we bind him, but so that in case of attack he can be released.

Suddenly the nearer explosions cease. The shelling continues but it has lifted and falls behind us; our trench is free. We seize the hand grenades, pitch them out in front of the dugout, and jump after them. The bombardment has stopped and a heavy barrage now falls behind us. The attack has come.

No one would believe that in this howling waste there could still be men; but steel helmets now appear on all sides out of the trench, and fifty yards from us a machine gun is already in position and barking.

The wire entanglements are torn to pieces. Yet they offer some obstacle. We see the storm troops coming. Our artillery opens fire. Machine guns rattle, rifles crack. The charge works its way across. Haie and Kropp begin with the hand grenades. They throw as fast as they can; others pass them, the handles with the strings already pulled. Haie throws seventy-five yards, Kropp sixty; it has been measured; the distance is important. The enemy as they run cannot do much before they are within forty yards.

We recognize the distorted faces, the smooth helmets: they are French. They have already suffered heavily when they reach the remnants of the barbed-wire entanglements. A whole line has gone down before our machine guns; then we have a lot of stoppages and they come nearer.

I see one of them, his face upturned, fall into a wire cradle. His body collapses, his hands remain suspended as though he were praying. Then his body drops clean away and only his hands with the stumps of his arms, shot off, now hang in the wire.

What is causing the "madness and despair" Remarque describes in the trenches? Why does the recruit in this scene apparently go insane?

POLITICS & GOVERNMENT

Soldiers from around the World. Although World War I began in Europe, it soon became a global conflict fought in different areas of the world and with soldiers from all parts of the globe. France, especially, recruited troops from its African colonies to fight in Europe. The photo at the top shows French African troops fighting in the trenches on the Western Front. About 80,000 Africans were killed or injured in Europe. The photo at the bottom shows a group of German soldiers in their machine-gun nest on the Western Front.

Q *What do these photographs reveal about the nature of World War I and the role of African troops in the conflict?*

© Bettmann/CORBIS

© General Photographic Agency/Getty Images

colonies were simply transferred to the winning powers, especially the British and the French. But the war also had unintended consequences for the Europeans. African soldiers who had gone to war for the Allies, especially those who left Africa and fought in Europe, became politically aware and began to advocate political and social equality. As one African who had fought for the French said, "We were not fighting for the French, we were fighting for ourselves [to become] French citizens."[4] Moreover, educated African elites, who had aided their colonial overlords in enlisting local peoples to fight, did so in the belief that they would be rewarded with citizenship and new political possibilities after the war. When their hopes were frustrated, they soon became involved in anticolonial movements (see Chapter 24).

In East Asia and the Pacific, Japan joined the Allies on August 23, 1914, primarily to seize control of German territories in Asia. As one Japanese statesman declared, the war in Europe was "divine aid . . . for the development of the destiny of Japan."[5] The Japanese took possession of German territories in China, as well as the German-occupied islands in the Pacific. New Zealand and Australia quickly joined the Japanese in conquering the German-held parts of New Guinea.

ENTRY OF THE UNITED STATES Most important to the Allied cause was the entry of the United States into the war. American involvement grew out of the naval conflict between Germany and Great Britain. Britain used its superior naval power to maximum effect by setting up a naval blockade of Germany. Germany retaliated by imposing a counterblockade enforced by the use of unrestricted submarine warfare. Strong American protests over the German sinking of passenger liners, especially the British ship *Lusitania* on May 7, 1915, when more than a hundred Americans lost their lives, forced the

German government to suspend unrestricted submarine warfare in September 1915.

In January 1917, however, eager to break the deadlock in the war, the Germans decided on another military gamble by returning to unrestricted submarine warfare. German naval officers convinced Emperor William II that the use of unrestricted submarine warfare could starve the British into submission within five months, certainly before the Americans could act. The return to unrestricted submarine warfare brought the United States into the war on April 6, 1917. Although U.S. troops did not arrive in Europe in large numbers until the following year, the entry of the United States into the war gave the Allied Powers a psychological boost when they needed it.

The year 1917 had not been a good year for them. Allied offensives on the Western Front were disastrously defeated. The Italian armies were smashed in October, and in November, the Bolshevik Revolution in Russia (see "The Russian Revolution" later in this chapter) led to Russia's withdrawal from the war and left Germany free to concentrate entirely on the Western Front. The cause of the Central Powers looked favorable, although war weariness in the Ottoman Empire, Bulgaria, Austria-Hungary, and Germany was beginning to take its toll. The home front was rapidly becoming a cause for as much concern as the war front.

The Home Front: The Impact of Total War

The prolongation of World War I made it a **total war** that affected the lives of all citizens, however remote they might be from the battlefields. The need to organize masses of men and matériel for years of combat (Germany alone had 5.5 million men in active units in 1916) led to increased centralization of government powers, economic regimentation, and manipulation of public opinion to keep the war effort going.

POLITICAL CENTRALIZATION AND ECONOMIC REGIMENTATION Because the war was expected to be short, little thought had been given to long-term wartime needs. Governments had to respond quickly, however, when the war machines failed to achieve their knockout blows and made ever greater demands for men and matériel. To meet these needs, governments expanded their powers. Countries drafted tens of millions of young men for that elusive breakthrough to victory.

Throughout Europe, wartime governments expanded their powers over their economies. Free market capitalistic systems were temporarily shelved as governments experimented with price, wage, and rent controls; rationed food supplies and materials; and nationalized transportation systems and industries. Under total war

mobilization, the distinction between soldiers at war and civilians at home was narrowed. In the view of political leaders, all citizens constituted a national army.

CONTROL OF PUBLIC OPINION As the Great War dragged on and casualties mounted, the patriotic enthusiasm that had marked the early days of the conflict waned. By 1916, there were numerous signs that civilian morale was beginning to crack under the pressure of total war. Governments took strenuous measures to fight the growing opposition to the war. Even parliamentary regimes resorted to an expansion of police powers to stifle internal dissent. The British Parliament, for example, passed the Defence of the Realm Act (DORA), which allowed the public authorities to arrest dissenters and charge them as traitors. Newspapers were censored, and sometimes their publication was even suspended.

Wartime governments also made active use of propaganda to arouse enthusiasm for the war. At first, public

British Recruiting Poster. As the conflict persisted month after month, governments resorted to active propaganda campaigns to generate enthusiasm for the war. In this British recruiting poster, the government tried to pressure men into volunteering for military service. By 1916, the British were forced to adopt compulsory military service.

Women in the Factories

FAMILY & SOCIETY

During World War I, women were called on to assume new job responsibilities, including factory work. In this selection, Naomi Loughnan, a young, upper-middle-class woman, describes the experiences in a munitions plant that considerably broadened her perspective on life.

Naomi Loughnan, "Munition Work"

We little thought when we first put on our overalls and caps and enlisted in the Munition Army how much more inspiring our life was to be than we had dared to hope. Though we munition workers sacrifice our ease, we gain a life worth living. Our long days are filled with interest, and with the zest of doing work for our country in the grand cause of Freedom. As we handle the weapons of war we are learning great lessons of life. In the busy, noisy workshops we come face to face with every kind of class, and each one of these classes has something to learn from the others. . . .

Engineering mankind is possessed of the unshakable opinion that no woman can have the mechanical sense. If one of us asks humbly why such and such an alteration is not made to prevent this or that drawback to a machine, she is told, with a superior smile, that a man has worked her machine before her for years, and that therefore if there were any improvement possible it would have been made. As long as we do exactly what we are told and do not attempt to use our brains, we give entire satisfaction, and are treated as nice, good children. Any swerving from the easy path prepared for us by our males arouses the most scathing contempt in their manly bosoms. . . . Women have, however, proved that their

entry into the munition world has increased the output. Employers who forget things personal in their patriotic desire for large results are enthusiastic over the success of women in the shops. But their workmen have to be handled with the utmost tenderness and caution lest they should actually imagine it was being suggested that women could do their work equally well, given equal conditions of training—at least where muscle is not the driving force. . . .

The coming of the mixed classes of women into the factory is slowly but surely having an educative effect upon the men. "Language" is almost unconsciously becoming subdued. There are fiery exceptions, who make our hair stand up on end under our close-fitting caps, but a sharp rebuke or a look of horror will often straighten out the most savage. . . . It is grievous to hear the girls also swearing and using disgusting language. Shoulder to shoulder with the children of the slums, the upper classes are having their eyes opened at last to the awful conditions among which their sisters have dwelt. Foul language, immorality, and many other evils are but the natural outcome of overcrowding and bitter poverty. . . . Sometimes disgust will overcome us, but we are learning with painful clarity that the fault is not theirs whose actions disgust us, but must be placed to the discredit of those other classes who have allowed the continued existence of conditions which generate the things from which we shrink appalled.

 What did Naomi Loughnan learn about men and lower-class women while working in the munitions factory? What did she learn about herself?

Source: From "Munition Work" by Naomi Loughnan in Gilbert Stone, ed., *Women War Workers* (London: George Harrap and Company, 1971), pp. 25, 35, 38.

officials needed to do little to achieve this goal. The British and French, for example, exaggerated German atrocities in Belgium and found that their citizens were only too willing to believe these accounts. But as the war dragged on and morale sagged, governments were forced to devise new techniques for stimulating declining enthusiasm.

WOMEN IN THE WAR EFFORT World War I also created new roles for women. With so many men off

fighting at the front, women were called on to assume jobs and responsibilities that had not been open to them before, including jobs that had been considered beyond the "capacity of women." These included such occupations as chimney sweeps, truck drivers, farm laborers, and factory workers in heavy industry (see the box above). In Germany, 38 percent of the workers in the Krupp (KROOP) armaments works in 1918 were women. Nevertheless, despite the noticeable increase in women's wages that resulted from government regulations, women working at industrial jobs were still being paid less than men at the end of the war.

Even worse, women's place in the workforce was far from secure. Both men and women seemed to assume that many of the new jobs for women were only temporary, an expectation quite evident in the British poem "War Girls," written in 1916:

> There's the girl who clips your ticket for the train,
> And the girl who speeds the lift from floor to floor,
> There's the girl who does a milk-round in the rain,
> And the girl who calls for orders at your door.
> Strong, sensible, and fit,
> They're out to show their grit,
> And tackle jobs with energy and knack.
> No longer caged and penned up,
> They're going to keep their end up
> Till the khaki soldier boys come marching back.[6]

At the end of the war, governments moved quickly to remove women from the jobs they had encouraged them to take earlier, and wages for women who remained employed were lowered.

Nevertheless, in some countries, the role played by women in the wartime economies did have a positive impact on the women's movement for social and political emancipation. The most obvious gain was the right to vote, granted to women in Britain in January 1918 and in Germany and Austria immediately after the war. Contemporary media, however, tended to focus on the more noticeable yet in some ways more superficial social emancipation of upper- and middle-class women. In ever-larger numbers, these young women took jobs, had their own apartments, and showed their new independence by smoking in public, wearing shorter dresses, and adopting radical new hairstyles.

Crisis in Russia and the End of the War

Q **FOCUS QUESTION:** What were the causes of the Russian Revolution of 1917, and why did the Bolsheviks prevail in the civil war and gain control of Russia?

By 1917, total war was creating serious domestic turmoil in all of the European belligerent states. Only one, however, experienced the kind of complete collapse that others were predicting might happen throughout Europe. Out of Russia's collapse came the Russian Revolution.

The Russian Revolution

Tsar Nicholas II was an autocratic ruler who relied on the army and the bureaucracy to uphold his regime. But World War I magnified Russia's problems and severely challenged the tsarist government. Russian industry was unable to produce the weapons needed for the army. Ill-led and ill-armed, Russian armies suffered incredible losses. Between 1914 and 1916, 2 million soldiers were killed, and another 4 to 6 million were wounded or captured.

In the meantime, Tsar Nicholas II was increasingly insulated from events by his German-born wife, Alexandra, a well-educated woman who had fallen under the sway of Rasputin (rass-PYOO-tin), a Siberian peasant whom the tsarina regarded as a holy man because he alone seemed able to stop the bleeding of her hemophiliac son, Alexis. Rasputin's influence made him a power behind the throne, and he did not hesitate to interfere in government affairs. As the leadership at the top experienced a series of military and economic disasters, the middle class, aristocrats, peasants, soldiers, and workers grew more and more disenchanted with the tsarist regime. Even conservative aristocrats who supported the monarchy felt the need to do something to reverse the deteriorating situation. For a start, they assassinated Rasputin in December 1916. By then it was too late to save the monarchy, and its fall came quickly at the beginning of March 1917.

THE MARCH REVOLUTION In early 1917, a series of strikes led by working-class women broke out in the capital city of Petrograd (formerly Saint Petersburg). A few weeks earlier, the government had introduced bread rationing in the capital city after the price of bread had skyrocketed. Many of the women who stood in the lines waiting for bread were also factory workers who had put in twelve-hour days. The Russian government soon became aware of the volatile situation in the capital. One police report stated: "Mothers of families, exhausted by endless standing in line at stores, distraught over their half-starving and sick children, are today perhaps closer to revolution than [the liberal opposition leaders] and of course they are a great deal more dangerous because they are the combustible material for which only a single spark is needed to burst into flame."[7] On March 8, a day celebrated since 1910 as International Women's Day, about ten thousand Petrograd women marched in parts of the city demanding "peace and bread." Soon the women were joined by other workers, and together they called for a general strike that succeeded in shutting down all the factories in the city on March 10. Nicholas ordered his troops to disperse the crowds by shooting them if necessary, but large numbers of the soldiers soon joined the demonstrators. The Duma (DOO-muh), or legislative body, which the tsar had tried to dissolve, met anyway and on March 12 declared that it was assuming governmental responsibility. It established a provisional government on March 15; the tsar abdicated the same day.

The Provisional Government, which came to be led in July by Alexander Kerensky (kuh-REN-skee), decided to carry on the war to preserve Russia's honor—a major blunder because it satisfied neither the workers nor the peasants, who above all wanted an end to the war. The Provisional Government also faced another authority, the **soviets**, or councils of workers' and soldiers' deputies. The Petrograd soviet had been formed in March 1917; at the same time, soviets sprang up spontaneously in army units, factory towns, and rural areas. The soviets represented the more radical interests of the lower classes and were largely composed of socialists of various kinds. One group—the Bolsheviks (BOHL-shuh-viks)—came to play a crucial role.

LENIN AND THE BOLSHEVIK REVOLUTION The Bolsheviks were a small faction of Russian Social Democrats who had come under the leadership of Vladimir Ulianov (VLAD-ih-meer ool-YA-nuf), known to the world as Lenin (LEH-nin) (1870–1924). Under Lenin's direction, the Bolsheviks became a party dedicated to violent revolution. He believed that only a revolution could destroy the capitalist system and that a "vanguard" of activists must form a small party of well-disciplined professional revolutionaries to accomplish this task. Between 1900 and 1917, Lenin spent most of his time in exile in Switzerland. When the Provisional Government was set up in March 1917, he believed that an opportunity for the Bolsheviks to seize power had come. Just weeks later, with the connivance of the German High Command, which hoped to create disorder in Russia, Lenin was shipped to Russia in a "sealed train" by way of Finland.

Lenin believed that the Bolsheviks must work to gain control of the soviets of soldiers, workers, and peasants and then use them to overthrow the Provisional Government. At the same time, the Bolsheviks sought mass support through promises geared to the needs of the people: an end to the war, redistribution of all land to the peasants, the transfer of factories and industries from capitalists to committees of workers, and the relegation of government power from the Provisional Government to the soviets. Three simple slogans summed up the Bolshevik program: "Peace, Land, Bread," "Worker Control of Production," and "All Power to the Soviets."

By the end of October, the Bolsheviks had achieved a slight majority in the Petrograd and Moscow soviets. The number of party members had also grown from 50,000 to 240,000. With Leon Trotsky (TRAHT-skee) (1877–1940), a fervid revolutionary, as chairman of the Petrograd soviet, Lenin and the Bolsheviks were in a position to seize power in the name of the soviets. During the night of November 6, pro-soviet and pro-Bolshevik forces took control of Petrograd. The Provisional Government quickly collapsed, with little bloodshed. The following night, the All-Russian Congress of Soviets, representing local soviets from all over the country, affirmed the transfer of power. At the second session, on the night of November 8, Lenin announced the new Soviet government, the Council of People's Commissars, with himself as its head.

But the Bolsheviks, soon renamed the Communists, still had a long way to go. For one thing, Lenin had promised peace, and that, he realized, was not an easy task because of the humiliating losses of Russian territory that it would entail. There was no real choice, however. On March 3, 1918, Lenin signed the Treaty of Brest-Litovsk (BREST-li-TUFFSK) with Germany and gave up eastern Poland, Ukraine, and the Baltic provinces. He had promised peace to the Russian people, but real peace did not come, for the country soon sank into civil war.

CIVIL WAR There was great opposition to the new Communist regime, not only from groups loyal to the tsar but also from bourgeois and aristocratic liberals and anti-Leninist socialists. In addition, thousands of Allied troops were eventually sent to different parts of Russia in the hope of bringing Russia back into the war.

Between 1918 and 1921, the Communist (Red) Army was forced to fight on many fronts. The first serious threat to the Communists came from Siberia, where White (anti-Communist) forces attacked westward and advanced almost to the Volga River. Attacks also came from the Ukrainians in the southwest and from the Baltic regions. In mid-1919, White forces swept through Ukraine and advanced almost to Moscow before being pushed back. By 1920, the major White forces had been defeated, and Ukraine had been retaken. The next year, the Communist regime regained control over the independent nationalist governments in the Caucasus: Georgia, Russian Armenia, and Azerbaijan (az-ur-by-JAHN).

How had Lenin and the Bolsheviks triumphed over what seemed at one time to be overwhelming forces? For one thing, the Red Army became a well-disciplined fighting force, largely due to the organizational genius of Leon Trotsky. As commissar of war, Trotsky reinstated the draft and insisted on rigid discipline; soldiers who deserted or refused to obey orders were summarily executed.

The disunity of the anti-Communist forces seriously weakened their efforts. Political differences created distrust among the Whites and prevented them from cooperating effectively with each other. It was difficult

Lenin and Trotsky. Vladimir Lenin and Leon Trotsky were important figures in the Bolsheviks' successful seizure of power in Russia. On the left, Lenin is seen addressing a rally in Moscow in 1917. On the right, Trotsky, who became commissar of war in the new regime, is shown haranguing his troops.

enough to achieve military cooperation; political differences made it virtually impossible. The lack of a common goal on the part of the Whites was in sharp contrast to the Communists' single-minded sense of purpose.

The Communists also succeeded in translating their revolutionary faith into practical instruments of power. A policy of **war communism**, for example, was used to ensure regular supplies for the Red Army. War communism included the nationalization of banks and most industries, the forcible requisition of grain from peasants, and the centralization of state power under Bolshevik control. Another Bolshevik instrument was "revolutionary terror." A new Red secret police, known as the Cheka (CHEK-uh), instituted the Red Terror, aimed at nothing less than the destruction of all who opposed the new regime.

Finally, the intervention of foreign armies enabled the Communists to appeal to the powerful force of Russian patriotism. Appalled by the takeover of power in Russia by the radical Communists, the Allied Powers intervened. At one point, more than 100,000 foreign troops—mostly Japanese, British, American, and French—were stationed on Russian soil. This intervention by the Allies enabled the Communist government to appeal to patriotic Russians to fight the attempts of foreigners to control their country.

By 1921, the Communists were in control of Russia. In the course of the civil war, the Communist regime had also transformed Russia into a bureaucratically centralized state dominated by a single party. It was also a state that was largely hostile to the Allied Powers that had sought to assist the Communists' enemies in the civil war.

The Last Year of the War

For Germany, the withdrawal of the Russians in March 1918 offered renewed hope for a favorable end to the war. The victory over Russia persuaded Erich von Ludendorff (LOO-dun-dorf) (1865–1937), who guided German military operations, and most German leaders to make one final military gamble—a grand offensive in the west to break the military stalemate. The German attack was launched in March and lasted into July, but an Allied counterattack, supported by the arrival of 140,000 fresh American troops, defeated the Germans at the Second Battle of the Marne on July 18. Ludendorff's gamble had failed.

On September 29, 1918, General Ludendorff informed German leaders that the war was lost and insisted that the government sue for peace at once. When German officials discovered, however, that the Allies were unwilling to make peace with the autocratic imperial

	1914
Battle of Tannenberg	August 26–30
First Battle of the Marne	September 6–10
Battle of Masurian Lakes	September 15
	1915
Battle of Gallipoli begins	April 25
Italy declares war on Austria-Hungary	May 23
	1916
Battle of Verdun	February 21–December 18
	1917
United States enters the war	April 6
	1918
Last German offensive	March 21–July 18
Second Battle of the Marne	July 18
Allied counteroffensive	July 18–November 10
Armistice between Allies and Germany	November 11

government, reforms were instituted to create a liberal government. Meanwhile, popular demonstrations broke out throughout Germany. William II capitulated to public pressure and abdicated on November 9, and the Socialists under Friedrich Ebert (FREED-rikh AY-bert) (1871–1925) announced the establishment of a republic. Two days later, on November 11, 1918, the new German government agreed to an armistice. The war was over.

THE CASUALTIES OF THE WAR   World War I devastated European civilization. Between 8 and 9 million soldiers died on the battlefields; another 22 million were wounded. Many of those who survived the war died later from war injuries or lived on without arms or legs or with other forms of mutilation. The birthrate in many European countries declined noticeably as a result of the death or maiming of so many young men. World War I also created a lost generation of war veterans who had become accustomed to violence and who would later band together in support of Mussolini and Hitler in their bids for power.

Nor did the killing affect only soldiers. Untold numbers of civilians died from war injuries or starvation. In 1915, using the excuse of a rebellion by the Armenian minority and their supposed collaboration with the Russians, the Turkish government began systematically to kill Armenian men and expel women and children. Within seven months, 600,000 Armenians had been killed, and 500,000 had been deported. Of the latter,

400,000 died while marching through the deserts and swamps of Syria and Mesopotamia. By September 1915, an estimated one million Armenians were dead, the victims of genocide.

The Peace Settlement

In January 1919, the delegations of twenty-seven victorious Allied nations gathered in Paris to conclude a final settlement of the Great War. Over a period of years, the reasons for fighting World War I had been transformed from selfish national interests to idealistic principles.

No one expressed these principles better than U.S. President Woodrow Wilson (1856–1924). Wilson's proposals for a truly just and lasting peace included "open covenants of peace, openly arrived at" instead of secret diplomacy; the reduction of national armaments to a "point consistent with domestic safety"; and the self-determination of people so that "all well-defined national aspirations shall be accorded the utmost satisfaction." As the spokesman for a new world order based on democracy and international cooperation, Wilson was enthusiastically cheered by many Europeans when he arrived in Europe for the peace conference, held at the palace of Versailles. Wilson's rhetoric on self-determination also inspired peoples in the colonial world, in Africa, Asia, and the Middle East, and was influential in developing anticolonial nationalist movements in these areas (see Chapter 24).

Wilson soon found, however, that more practical motives guided other states at the Paris Peace Conference. The secret treaties and agreements that had been made before the war could not be totally ignored, even if they did conflict with the principle of self-determination enunciated by Wilson. National interests also complicated the deliberations of the Paris Peace Conference. David Lloyd George (1863–1945), prime minister of Great Britain, had won a decisive electoral victory in December 1918 on a platform of making the Germans pay for this dreadful war.

France's approach to peace was primarily determined by considerations of national security. To Georges Clemenceau (ZHORZH kluh-mahn-SOH) (1841–1929), the feisty premier of France who had led his country to victory, the French people had borne the brunt of German aggression. They deserved revenge and security against future German aggression (see the box on p. 611).

The most important decisions at the Paris Peace Conference were made by Wilson, Clemenceau, and Lloyd George. In the end, only compromise made it possible to achieve a peace settlement. Wilson's wish that the creation of an international peacekeeping organization be the

OPPOSING ✕ VIEWPOINTS

Three Voices of Peacemaking

POLITICS & GOVERNMENT

When the Allied powers met in Paris in January 1919, it soon became apparent that the victors had different opinions on the kind of peace they expected. The first selection is an excerpt from a speech by Woodrow Wilson in which the American president presented his idealistic goals for a peace based on justice and reconciliation.

The French leader Georges Clemenceau had a vision of peacemaking quite different from Wilson's. The French sought revenge and security. In this selection from his book *Grandeur and Misery of Victory*, Clemenceau revealed his fundamental dislike and distrust of Germany.

A third voice of peacemaking was heard in Paris in 1919, although not at the peace conference. W. E. B. Du Bois (doo-BOYZ), an African American writer and activist, had organized the Pan-African Congress to meet in Paris during the sessions of the Paris Peace Conference. The goal of the Pan-African Congress was to present a series of resolutions that promoted the cause of Africans and people of African descent. As can be seen in the selection presented here, the resolutions did not call for immediate independence for African nations.

Woodrow Wilson, Speech, May 26, 1917

We are fighting for the liberty, the self-government, and the undictated development of all peoples, and every feature of the settlement that concludes this war must be conceived and executed for that purpose. Wrongs must first be righted and then adequate safeguards must be created to prevent their being committed again. . . .

No people must be forced under sovereignty under which it does not wish to live. No territory must change hands except for the purpose of securing those who inhabit it a fair chance of life and liberty. No indemnities must be insisted on except those that constitute payment for manifest wrongs done. No readjustments of power must be made except such as will tend to secure the future peace of the world and the future welfare and happiness of its peoples.

And then the free peoples of the world must draw together in some common covenant, some genuine and practical cooperation that will in effect combine their force to secure peace and justice in the dealings of nations with one another.

Georges Clemenceau, *Grandeur and Misery of Victory*

War and peace, with their strong contrasts, alternate against a common background. For the catastrophe of 1914 the Germans are responsible. Only a professional liar would deny this. . . .

What after all is this war, prepared, undertaken, and waged by the German people, who flung aside every scruple of conscience to let it loose, hoping for a peace of enslavement under the yoke of a militarism, destructive of all human dignity? It is simply the continuance, the recrudescence, of those never-ending acts of violence by which the first savage tribes carried out their depredations with all the resources of barbarism. . . .

I have sometimes penetrated into the sacred cave of the Germanic cult, which is, as every one knows, the *Bierhaus* [beer hall]. A great aisle of massive humanity where there accumulate, amid the fumes of tobacco and beer, the popular rumblings of a nationalism upheld by the sonorous brasses blaring to the heavens the supreme voice of Germany, *Deutschland über alles! Germany above everything!* Men, women, and children, all petrified in reverence before the divine stoneware pot, brows furrowed with irrepressible power, eyes lost in a dream of infinity, mouths twisted by the intensity of willpower, drink in long draughts the celestial hope of vague expectations.

Pan-African Congress

Resolved

That the Allied and Associated Powers establish a code of law for the international protection of the natives of Africa. . . .

The Negroes of the world demand that hereafter the natives of Africa and the peoples of African descent be governed according to the following principles:

1. The Land: the land and its natural resources shall be held in trust for the natives and at all times they shall have effective ownership of as much land as they can profitably develop. . . .

(Continued)

3. Labor: slavery and corporal punishment shall be abolished and forced labor except in punishment for crime. . . .

5. The State: the natives of Africa must have the right to participate in the government as fast as their development permits, in conformity with the principle that the government exists for the natives, and not the natives for the government.

 How did the peacemaking aims of Wilson and Clemenceau differ? How did their different views affect the deliberations of the Paris Peace Conference and the nature of the final peace settlement? How and why did the views of the Pan-African Congress differ from those of Wilson and Clemenceau?

Sources: Woodrow Wilson, Speech, May 26, 1917. Excerpts from *The Public Papers of Woodrow Wilson: War and Peace*, edited by Ray Stannard Baker. Copyright 1925, 1953 by Edith Bolling Wilson. Georges Clemenceau, *Grandeur and Misery of Victory*. From Georges Clemenceau, *Grandeur and Misery of Victory* (New York: Harcourt, 1930), pp. 105, 107, 280. Pan-African Congress. Excerpts from Resolution from the Pan-African Congress, Paris, 1919.

first order of business was granted, and already on January 25, 1919, the conference adopted the principle of the League of Nations. In return, Wilson agreed to make compromises on territorial arrangements to guarantee the establishment of the League, believing that a functioning League could later rectify bad arrangements.

THE TREATY OF VERSAILLES

The final peace settlement consisted of five separate treaties with the defeated nations—Germany, Austria, Hungary, Bulgaria, and Turkey. The Treaty of Versailles with Germany, signed on June 28, 1919, was by far the most important one. The Germans considered it a harsh peace and were particularly unhappy with Article 231, the so-called **War Guilt Clause**, which declared Germany (and Austria) responsible for starting the war and ordered Germany to pay **reparations** for all the damage to which the Allied governments and their people were subjected as a result of the war.

The military and territorial provisions of the treaty also rankled Germans. Germany had to reduce its army to 100,000 men, cut back its navy, and eliminate its air force. German territorial losses included the return of Alsace and Lorraine to France and sections of Prussia to the new Polish state (see Map 23.3). German land west and as far as 30 miles east of the Rhine was established as a demilitarized zone and stripped of all armaments or fortifications to serve as a barrier to any future German military moves westward against France. Outraged by the "dictated peace," the new German government complained but accepted the treaty.

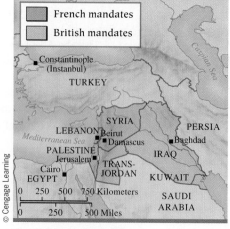

French mandates

British mandates

Constantinople (Instanbul)

TURKEY

SYRIA

LEBANON Beirut

Mediterranean Sea Damascus

PALESTINE

Jerusalem

Cairo

EGYPT

TRANS-JORDAN

PERSIA

Baghdad

IRAQ

KUWAIT

SAUDI ARABIA

Caspian Sea

0   250 500 750 Kilometers

0   250   500 Miles

© Cengage Learning

The Middle East in 1919

THE OTHER PEACE TREATIES

The separate peace treaties made with the other Central Powers extensively redrew the map of eastern Europe. Many of these changes merely ratified what the war had already accomplished. Both the German and Russian Empires lost considerable territory in eastern Europe, and the Austro-Hungarian Empire disappeared altogether. New nation-states emerged from the lands of these three empires: Finland, Latvia, Estonia, Lithuania, Poland, Czechoslovakia, Austria, and Hungary. Territorial rearrangements were also made in the Balkans. Serbia formed the nucleus of a new southern Slavic state, called Yugoslavia, which combined Serbs, Croats, and Slovenes under a single monarch.

Although the Paris Peace Conference was supposedly guided by the principle of self-determination, the mixtures of peoples in eastern Europe made it impossible to draw boundaries along neat ethnic lines. As a result of compromises, virtually every eastern European state was left with a minorities problem that could lead to future conflicts. Germans in Poland; Hungarians, Poles, and Germans in Czechoslovakia; Hungarians in Romania; and the combination of Serbs, Croats, Slovenes, Macedonians, and Albanians in Yugoslavia all became sources of later conflict.

Yet another centuries-old empire, the Ottoman Empire, was dismembered by the peace settlement after the war. To gain Arab support against the Ottoman Turks during the war, the Western Allies had promised to recognize the independence of Arab states in the Middle Eastern lands of the Ottoman Empire. But the imperialist habits of Western nations died hard. After the war, France was given control of

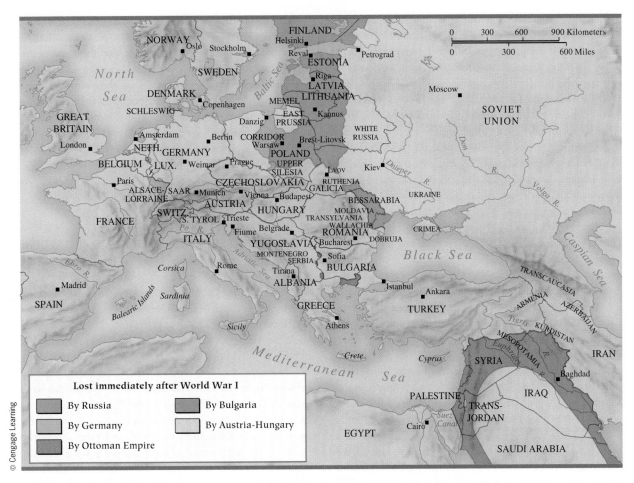

Lost immediately after World War I

- By Russia
- By Germany
- By Ottoman Empire
- By Bulgaria
- By Austria-Hungary

MAP 23.3 Territorial Changes in Europe and the Middle East After World War I. The victorious Allies met in Paris to determine the shape and nature of postwar Europe. At the urging of U.S. President Woodrow Wilson, many nationalist aspirations of former imperial subjects were realized with the creation of several new countries from the prewar territory of Austria-Hungary, Germany, Russia, and the Ottoman Empire.

 What new countries emerged in Europe and the Middle East?

Lebanon and Syria, while Britain received Iraq and Palestine (including Trans-Jordan). Officially, both acquisitions were called **mandates**, a system whereby a nation officially administered a territory on behalf of the League of Nations. The system of mandates could not hide the fact that the principle of national self-determination at the Paris Peace Conference was largely for Europeans.

An Uncertain Peace

Q **FOCUS QUESTION:** What problems did Europe and the United States face in the 1920s?

Four years of devastating war had left many Europeans with a profound sense of despair and disillusionment. The Great War indicated to many people that something was dreadfully wrong with Western values. In *The Decline of the West*, the German writer Oswald Spengler (1880–1936) reflected this disillusionment when he emphasized the decadence of Western civilization and posited its collapse.

The Search for Security

The peace settlement at the end of World War I had tried to fulfill the nineteenth-century dream of nationalism by creating new boundaries and new states. From its inception, however, this peace settlement had left nations unhappy and eager to revise it.

U.S. President Woodrow Wilson had recognized that the peace treaties contained unwise provisions that could serve as new causes for conflicts, and he had placed many of his hopes for the future in the League of Nations. The League, however, was not particularly effective in maintaining the peace. The failure of the United States to join the League in a backlash of isolationist sentiment undermined its effectiveness from the beginning. Moreover, the League could use only economic sanctions to halt aggression.

France's search for security between 1919 and 1924 was founded primarily on a strict enforcement of the Treaty of Versailles. This tough policy toward Germany began with the issue of reparations, the payments that the Germans were supposed to make to compensate for war damage. In April 1921, the Allied Reparations Commission settled on a sum of 132 billion marks ($33 billion) for German reparations, payable in annual installments of 2.5 billion (gold) marks. The new German republic made its first payment in 1921, but by the following year, facing financial problems, the German government announced that it was unable to pay more. Outraged, the French government sent troops to occupy the Ruhr valley, Germany's chief industrial and mining center. If the Germans would not pay reparations, the French would collect reparations in kind by operating and using the Ruhr mines and factories.

Both Germany and France suffered from the French occupation of the Ruhr. The German government adopted a policy of passive resistance to French occupation that was largely financed by printing more paper money. This only intensified the inflationary pressures that had already begun in Germany by the end of the war. The German mark became worthless, and economic disaster fueled political upheavals. All the nations, including France, were happy to cooperate with the American suggestion for a new conference of experts to reassess the reparations problem.

In August 1924, an international commission produced a new plan for reparations. The Dawes Plan, named after the American banker who chaired the commission, reduced the reparations and stabilized Germany's payments on the basis of its ability to pay. The Dawes Plan also granted an initial $200 million loan for German recovery, which opened the door to heavy American investments in Europe that helped create a new era of European prosperity between 1924 and 1929.

With prosperity came a new age of European diplomacy. A spirit of cooperation was fostered by the foreign ministers of Germany and France, Gustav Stresemann (GOOS-tahf SHTRAY-zuh-mahn) and Aristide Briand (ah-ruh-STEED bree-AHNH), who concluded the Treaty of Locarno (loh-KAHR-noh) in 1925. This guaranteed Germany's new western borders with France and Belgium. Although Germany's new eastern borders with Poland were conspicuously absent from the agreement, the Locarno pact was viewed by many as the beginning of a new era of European peace.

The spirit of Locarno was based on little real substance, however. Germany lacked the military power to alter its western borders even if it wanted to. And the issue of disarmament soon proved that even the spirit of Locarno could not bring nations to cut back on their weapons. Germany, of course, had been disarmed with the expectation that other states would do likewise. Numerous disarmament conferences, however, failed to achieve anything substantial as states were unwilling to trust their security to anyone but their own military forces.

The Great Depression

Almost as devastating as the two world wars in the first half of the twentieth century was the economic collapse that ravaged the world in the 1930s. Two events set the stage for the Great Depression: a downturn in domestic economic activities and an international financial crisis created by the collapse of the American stock market in 1929.

Already in the mid-1920s, prices for agricultural goods were beginning to decline rapidly due to overproduction of basic commodities, such as wheat. In addition to domestic economic troubles, much of the European prosperity between 1924 and 1929 had been built on American bank loans to Germany. The crash of the U.S. stock market in October 1929 led panicky American investors to withdraw many of their funds from Germany and other European markets. The withdrawal of funds seriously weakened the banks of Germany and other central European states. By 1931, trade was slowing down, industrialists were cutting back production, and unemployment was increasing as the ripple effects of international bank failures had a devastating impact on domestic economies.

Economic depression was by no means a new phenomenon in European history, but the depth of the economic downturn after 1929 fully justifies the Great Depression label. During 1932, the worst year of the depression, one British worker in four was unemployed; in Germany, 6 million people, or 40 percent of the labor force, were out of work. Unemployed and homeless people filled the streets of cities throughout the advanced industrial world.

Governments seemed powerless to deal with the crisis. The classic liberal remedy for depression was a deflationary policy of balanced budgets, which involved cutting costs by lowering wages and raising tariffs to exclude other countries' goods from home markets, but this policy only served to worsen the economic crisis and cause even greater mass discontent. This in turn led to serious political repercussions. Increased government activity in the economy was one reaction. Another effect was a renewed interest in Marxist doctrines. Hadn't Marx predicted that capitalism would destroy itself through overproduction? Communism took on new popularity,

The Great Depression: Bread Lines in Paris. The Great Depression devastated the European economy and had serious political repercussions. Because of its more balanced economy, France did not feel the effects of the depression as quickly as other European countries. By 1931, however, even France was experiencing lines of unemployed people at free-food centers.

people back to work constructing highways and public buildings, even if governments had to go into debt to pay for these public works, a concept known as **deficit spending**.

After the defeat of Germany, France had become the strongest power on the European continent, but between 1921 and 1926, no French government seemed capable of solving the country's financial problems. Like other European countries, though, France did experience a period of relative prosperity between 1926 and 1929.

Because it had a more balanced economy than other nations, France did not begin to feel the full effects of the Great Depression until 1932. Then economic instability soon had political repercussions. During a nineteen-month period in 1932 and 1933, six different cabinets were formed as France faced political chaos. Finally, in June 1936, a coalition of leftist parties—Communists, Socialists, and Radicals—formed a new government, the Popular Front, but its policies failed to solve the problems of the depression. By 1938, the French were experiencing a serious decline of confidence in their political system.

especially with workers and intellectuals. Finally, the Great Depression increased the attractiveness of simplistic dictatorial solutions, especially from a new movement known as fascism. Everywhere, democracy seemed on the defensive in the 1930s (see Chapter 25).

The Democratic States

After World War I, Great Britain went through a period of serious economic difficulties. During the war, Britain had lost many of the markets for its industrial products, especially to the United States and Japan. The postwar decline of such staple industries as coal, steel, and textiles led to a rise in unemployment, which reached the 2 million mark in 1921. But Britain soon rebounded and from 1925 to 1929 experienced an era of renewed prosperity.

By 1929, however, Britain faced the growing effects of the Great Depression. A national government (a coalition of Liberals and Conservatives) claimed credit for bringing Britain out of the worst stages of the depression, primarily by using the traditional policies of balanced budgets and protective tariffs. British politicians had largely ignored the new ideas of a Cambridge economist, John Maynard Keynes (KAYNZ) (1883–1946), who published his *General Theory of Employment, Interest and Money* in 1936. He condemned the traditional view that in a free economy, depressions should be left to work themselves out. Keynes argued that unemployment stemmed not from overproduction but from a decline in demand and maintained that demand could be increased by putting

After the imperial Germany of William II had come to an end in 1918 with Germany's defeat in World War I, a German democratic state known as the Weimar (VY-mar) Republic was established. From its beginnings, the Weimar Republic was plagued by a series of problems. The republic had no truly outstanding political leaders and faced serious economic difficulties. In 1922 and 1923, Germany experienced runaway inflation; widows, orphans, the retired elderly, army officers, teachers, civil servants, and others who lived on fixed incomes all watched their monthly stipends become worthless and their lifetime savings disappear. Their economic losses increasingly pushed the middle class to the rightist parties that were hostile to the republic. To make matters worse, after a period of prosperity from 1924 to 1929, Germany faced the Great Depression. Unemployment increased to 3 million in March 1930 and 4.4 million by December of the same year. The depression paved the way for the rise of extremist parties.

After Germany, no Western nation was more affected by the Great Depression than the United States. By 1932, U.S. industrial production fell to 50 percent of what it had been in 1929. By 1933, there were 15 million unemployed.

Under these circumstances, the Democrat Franklin Delano Roosevelt (1882–1945) was able to win a landslide electoral victory in 1932. He and his advisers pursued a policy of active government intervention in the economy that came to be known as the New Deal. Economic intervention included a stepped-up program of public works, such as the Works Progress Administration (WPA), which was established in 1935 and employed between 2 and 3 million people who worked at building bridges, roads, post offices, and airports. In 1935, the Social Security Act created a system of old-age pensions and unemployment insurance.

The New Deal provided some social reform measures, but it did not solve the unemployment problems of the Great Depression. In May 1937, during what was considered a period of full recovery, American unemployment still stood at 7 million.

Socialism in Soviet Russia

The civil war in Russia had taken an enormous toll of life. Lenin had pursued a policy of war communism, but once the war was over, peasants began to sabotage the program by hoarding food. Added to this problem was drought, which caused a great famine between 1920 and 1922 that claimed as many as 5 million lives. Industrial collapse paralleled the agricultural disaster. By 1921, industrial output was only 20 percent of its 1913 levels. Russia was exhausted. A peasant banner proclaimed, "Down with Lenin and horseflesh, Bring back the Tsar and pork." As Leon Trotsky said, "The country, and the government with it, were at the very edge of the abyss."[8]

In March 1921, Lenin pulled Russia back from the abyss by adopting his **New Economic Policy** (NEP), a modified version of the old capitalist system. Peasants were now allowed to sell their produce openly. Retail stores and small industries that employed fewer than twenty employees could now operate under private ownership, although heavy industry, banking, and mines remained in the hands of the government.

In 1922, Lenin and the Communists formally created a new state called the Union of Soviet Socialist Republics, known as the USSR by its initials or the Soviet Union by its shortened form. Already by that year, a revived market and a good harvest had brought the famine to an end; Soviet agricultural production climbed to 75 percent of its prewar level.

Lenin's death in 1924 inaugurated a struggle for power among the seven members of the Politburo (POL-it-byoor-oh), the institution that had become the leading organ of the party. The Politburo was severely divided over the future direction of the country. The Left, led by Leon Trotsky, wanted to end the NEP, launch Russia on the path of rapid industrialization, and spread the revolution abroad.

Another group in the Politburo, called the Right, rejected the cause of world revolution and wanted instead to concentrate on constructing a socialist state. This group also favored a continuation of Lenin's NEP.

These ideological divisions were underscored by an intense personal rivalry between Leon Trotsky and Joseph Stalin (1879–1953). In 1924, Trotsky held the post of commissar of war and was the leading spokesman for the Left in the Politburo. Stalin was content to hold the dull bureaucratic job of party general secretary while other Politburo members held party positions that enabled them to display their brilliant oratorical abilities. Stalin was skillful at avoiding allegiance to either the Left or Right factions in the Politburo. He was also a good organizer (his fellow Bolsheviks called him "Comrade Index-Card") and used his post as party general secretary to gain complete control of the Communist Party. Trotsky was expelled from the party in 1927. By 1929, Stalin had succeeded in eliminating the Bolsheviks of the revolutionary era from the Politburo and establishing a dictatorship.

In Pursuit of a New Reality: Cultural and Intellectual Trends

Q **FOCUS QUESTION:** How did the cultural and intellectual trends of the post–World War I years reflect the crises of the time as well as the lingering effects of the war?

The enormous suffering and the deaths of almost 10 million people during the Great War had shaken society to its foundations. As they tried to rebuild their lives, Europeans wondered what had gone wrong with Western civilization. The Great Depression only added to the desolation left behind by the war.

Political and economic uncertainties were paralleled by social innovations. The Great War had served to break down many traditional middle-class attitudes, especially toward sexuality. In the 1920s, women's physical appearance changed dramatically. Short skirts, short hair, the use of cosmetics that were once thought to be the preserve of prostitutes, and the new practice of suntanning gave women a new image. This change in physical appearance, which stressed more exposure of a woman's body, was also accompanied by frank discussions of sexual matters. In 1926, the Dutch physician Theodor van de Velde (TAY-oh-dor vahn duh VEL-duh) published *Ideal Marriage: Its Physiology and Technique*, which became an international best-seller. Van de Velde described female and male anatomy, discussed birth control techniques, and glorified sexual pleasure in marriage.

COMPARATIVE ESSAY

A Revolution in the Arts

ART & IDEAS

The period between 1880 and 1930 witnessed a revolution in the arts throughout Western civilization. Fueled in part by developments in physics and psychology, artists and writers rebelled against the traditional belief that the task of art was to represent "reality" and experimented with innovative new techniques in order to approach reality from a totally fresh perspective.

From Impressionism and Expressionism to Cubism, abstract art, Dadaism, and Surrealism, painters seemed intoxicated with the belief that their canvases would help reveal the radically changing world. Especially after the cataclysm of World War I, which shattered the image of a rational society, artists sought an absolute freedom of expression, confident that art could redefine humanity in the midst of chaos. Other arts soon followed their lead: James Joyce turned prose on its head by focusing on his characters' innermost thoughts, and Arnold Schönberg (AR-nawlt SHURN-bayrk) created atonal music by using a scale composed of twelve notes independent of any tonal key.

This revolutionary spirit had already been exemplified by Pablo Picasso's *Les Demoiselles d'Avignon*, painted in 1907 (see the illustration on p. 540). Picasso used geometrical designs to create a new reality and appropriated non-Western cultural resources, including African masks, in the desire to revitalize Western art.

Another example of the revolutionary approach to art was the decision by the French artist Marcel Duchamp (mar-SEL duh-SHAHN) to enter a porcelain urinal in a 1917 art exhibit held in New York City. By signing it and giving it the title *Fountain*, Duchamp proclaimed that he had transformed the urinal into a work of art. His "ready-mades" (as such art would henceforth be labeled) declared that art was whatever the artist proclaimed as art. The Dadaist Kurt Schwitters (KOORT SCHVIT-urz) brought together postage stamps, old handbills, streetcar tickets, newspaper scraps, and pieces of cardboard to form his works of art.

Such intentionally irreverent acts demystified the nearly sacred reverence that had traditionally been attached to works of art. Essentially, Duchamp and others claimed

© 2012 Artists Rights Society (ARS), New York/VG Bild-Kunst, Bonn//Digital Image bpk, Berlin/Kupferstichkabinett (Jörg P. Anders)/Art Resource, NY

Kurt Schwitters, *Der Harz*. Kurt Schwitters became identified with the Dada movement when he began to create his collages. He wrote in 1928, "Fundamentally I cannot understand why one is not able to use in a picture, exactly in the same way as commercially made color . . . all the old junk which piles up in closets or the rubbish heaps."

that anything under the sun could be selected as a work of art because the mental choice itself equaled the act of artistic creation. Therefore, art need not be a manual construct; it need only be a mental conceptualization. This liberating concept opened the floodgates of the art world, allowing the artists of the new century to swim in this free-flowing, exploratory torrent.

How was the revolution in the arts between 1880 and 1930 related to the political, economic, and social developments of the same period?

Nightmares and New Visions

Uncertainty also pervaded the cultural and intellectual achievements of the postwar years. Artistic trends were largely a working out of the implications of prewar developments. Abstract painting, for example, became ever more popular (see the comparative essay "A Revolution in the Arts" above). In addition, prewar fascination with the absurd and the unconscious content of the mind seemed even more appropriate after the nightmare landscapes of World War I battlefronts. This gave rise to both the Dada movement and Surrealism.

Dadaism (DAH-duh-iz-um) attempted to enshrine the purposelessness of life; revolted by the insanity of life, the Dadaists tried to give it expression by creating "anti-art." The 1918 Berlin Dada Manifesto maintained that "Dada is the international expression of our times, the great rebellion of artistic movements." Many Dadaists assembled pieces of junk (wire, string, rags, scraps of newspaper, nails, washers) into collages, believing that they were transforming the refuse of their culture into art. In the hands of Hannah Höch (HURKH) (1889–1978), Dada became an instrument to comment on women's roles in the new mass culture.

Perhaps more important as an artistic movement was **Surrealism**, which sought a reality beyond the material, sensible world and found it in the world of the unconscious through the portrayal of fantasies, dreams, or nightmares. The Spaniard Salvador Dalí (sahl-vah-DOR dah-LEE) (1904–1989) became the high priest of Surrealism and in his mature phase became a master of representational Surrealism. Dalí portrayed recognizable objects entirely divorced from their normal context. By placing objects into unrecognizable relationships, Dalí created a disturbing world in which the irrational had become tangible.

Probing the Unconscious

The interest in the unconscious, evident in Surrealism, was also apparent in the development of new literary techniques that emerged in the 1920s. One of its most apparent manifestations was the "stream of consciousness" technique in which the writer presented an interior monologue or a report of the innermost thoughts of each character. One example of this genre was written by the Irish exile James Joyce (1882–1941). His *Ulysses*, published in 1922, told the story of one day in the life of ordinary people in Dublin by following the flow of their inner dialogue.

The German writer Hermann Hesse (hayr-MAHN HESS-uh) (1877–1962) dealt with the unconscious in a different fashion. His novels reflected the influence of new psychological theories and Eastern religions and focused on, among other things, the spiritual loneliness of modern human beings in a mechanized urban society. Hesse's novels made a large impact on German youth in the 1920s. He won the Nobel Prize for Literature in 1946.

For much of the Western world, the best way to find (or escape) reality was through mass entertainment. The 1930s represented the heyday of the Hollywood studio system, which in the single year of 1937 turned out nearly six hundred feature films. Supplementing the movies were cheap paperback books and radio, which brought sports, soap operas, and popular music to the masses.

The increased size of audiences and the ability of radio and cinema, unlike the printed word, to provide an immediate mass experience added new dimensions to mass culture. Favorite film actors and actresses became stars, whose lives then became subject to public adoration and scrutiny. Sensuous actresses such as Marlene Dietrich, whose appearance in the early sound film *The Blue Angel* catapulted her to fame, projected new images of women's sexuality.

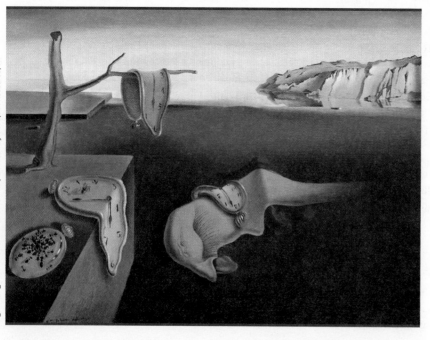

Salvador Dalí, *The Persistence of Memory*. Surrealism was an important artistic movement in the 1920s. Influenced by the theories of Freudian psychology, Surrealists sought to reveal the world of the unconscious, or the "greater reality" that they believed existed beyond the world of physical appearances. As is evident in this painting, Salvador Dalí sought to portray the world of dreams by painting recognizable objects in unrecognizable relationships.

CHAPTER SUMMARY

The assassination of Archduke Francis Ferdinand of Austria-Hungary in the summer of 1914 in the Bosnian capital of Sarajevo led within six weeks to a major war among the major powers of Europe. The Germans drove the Russians back in the east, but in the west a stalemate developed, with trenches defended by barbed wire and machine guns extending from the Swiss border to the English Channel. After German submarine attacks, the United States entered the war in 1917, but even from the beginning of the war, battles also took place in the African colonies of the European belligerents as well as in the East, making this a truly global war.

Unprepared for war, Russia soon faltered and collapsed, resulting in a revolution against the tsar. But the new provisional government in Russia also soon failed, enabling the revolutionary Bolsheviks of V. I. Lenin to seize power. Lenin established a dictatorship and made a costly peace with Germany. After American troops entered the war, the German government collapsed, leading to an armistice on November 11, 1918.

World War I was the defining event of the twentieth century. The incredible destruction and the deaths of almost 10 million people undermined the whole idea of progress. World War I was also a total war that required a mobilization of resources and populations and increased the centralization of government power. Civil liberties, such as freedom of the press, speech, and assembly, were circumscribed in the name of national security. Governments' need to plan the distribution of goods restricted economic freedom. World War I made the practice of strong central authority a way of life.

Finally, World War I ended the age of European hegemony over world affairs. In 1917, the Russian Revolution had laid the foundation for the creation of a new Eurasian power, the Soviet Union, and the United States had entered the war. The waning of the European age was not immediately evident to all, however, for it was clouded by American isolationism and the withdrawal of the Soviets from world affairs while they nurtured the growth of their own socialist system. These developments, though temporary, created a political vacuum in Europe that all too soon would be filled by the revival of German power.

Although World War I had destroyed the liberal optimism of the prewar era, many people in the 1920s still hoped that the progress of Western civilization could somehow be restored. These hopes proved  largely unfounded. France, feeling vulnerable to another invasion, sought to weaken Germany. European recovery, largely the result of American loans and investments, ended with the onset of the Great Depression at the end of the 1920s. Democratic states, such as Great Britain, France, and the United States, spent much of the 1930s trying to recover from the depression. In the Soviet Union, Lenin's New Economic Policy helped to stabilize the economy, but on his death a struggle for power ensued that ended with the establishment of a dictatorship under Joseph Stalin.

CHAPTER TIMELINE

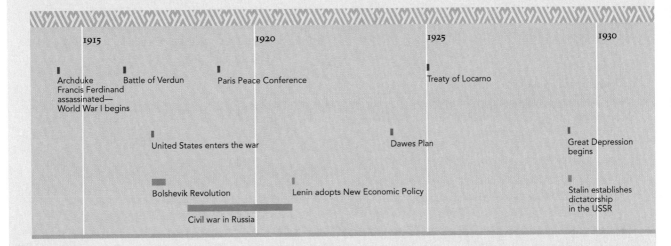

1915	1920	1925	1930

Archduke Francis Ferdinand assassinated— World War I begins

Battle of Verdun

Paris Peace Conference

Treaty of Locarno

United States enters the war

Dawes Plan

Great Depression begins

Bolshevik Revolution

Lenin adopts New Economic Policy

Stalin establishes dictatorship in the USSR

Civil war in Russia

CHAPTER REVIEW

Upon Reflection

Q What nation, if any, was the most responsible for causing World War I? Why?

Q How did Lenin and the Bolsheviks manage to seize and hold power despite their small numbers?

Q What were the causes of the Great Depression, and how did European states respond to it?

Key Terms

conscription (p. 597)
militarism (p. 597)
trench warfare (p. 602)
total war (p. 605)
soviets (p. 608)
war communism (p. 609)
War Guilt Clause (p. 612)
reparations (p. 612)
mandates (p. 613)
deficit spending (p. 615)
New Economic Policy (p. 616)
Dadaism (p. 618)
Surrealism (p. 618)

Suggested Reading

GENERAL WORKS ON TWENTIETH-CENTURY EUROPE A number of general works on European history in the twentieth century provide a context for under-

standing both World War I and the Russian Revolution. Especially valuable is N. Ferguson, *The War of the World: Twentieth-Century Conflict and the Descent of the West* (New York, 2006). See also R. Paxton, *Europe in the Twentieth Century,* 4th ed. (New York, 2004).

CAUSES OF WORLD WAR I The historical literature on the causes of World War I is vast. Good starting points are the works by J. Joll and G. Martel, *The Origins of the First World War,* 3rd ed. (London, 2006), and A. Mombauer, *The Origins of the First World War: Controversies and Consensus* (London, 2002). On the events leading to war, see D. Fromkin, *Europe's Last Summer: Who Started the Great War in 1914?* (New York, 2004).

WORLD WAR I The best brief account of World War I is H. Strachan, *The First World War* (New York, 2004). On the global nature of World War I, see M. S. Neiberg, *Fighting the Great War: A Global History* (Cambridge, Mass., 2005), and William S. Storey, *The First World War: A Concise Global History* (New York, 2010). On the role of women in World War I, see S. Grayzel, *Women and the First World War* (London, 2002). On the Paris Peace Conference, see M. MacMillan, *Paris, 1919: Six Months That Changed the World* (New York, 2002).

THE RUSSIAN REVOLUTION A good introduction to the Russian Revolution can be found in R. A. Wade, *The Russian Revolution, 1917,* 2nd ed. (Cambridge, 2005), and S. Fitzpatrick, *The Russian Revolution, 1917–1932,* 2nd ed. (New York, 2001). On Lenin, see R. Service, *Lenin: A Biography* (Cambridge, Mass., 2000).

THE 1920s For a general introduction to the post–World War I period, see M. Kitchen, *Europe Between the Wars,* 2nd ed. (London, 2006). On European security issues after the Peace of Paris, see S. Marks, *The Illusion of Peace: Europe's International Relations, 1918–1933,* 2nd ed. (New York, 2003). On the Great Depression, see C. P. Kindleberger, *The World in Depression, 1929–1939,* rev. ed. (Berkeley, Calif., 1986).

CHAPTER

24

Nationalism, Revolution, and Dictatorship: Asia, the Middle East, and Latin America from 1919 to 1939

Nguyen the Patriot at Tours

CHAPTER OUTLINE AND FOCUS QUESTIONS

The Rise of Nationalism

Q What were the various stages in the rise of nationalist movements in Asia and the Middle East, and what problems did they face?

Revolution in China

Q What problems did China encounter between the two world wars, and what solutions did the Nationalists and the Communists propose to solve them?

Japan Between the Wars

Q How did Japan address the problems of nation building in the first decades of the twentieth century, and why did democratic institutions not take hold more effectively?

Nationalism and Dictatorship in Latin America

Q What problems did the nations of Latin America face in the interwar years? To what degree were they a consequence of foreign influence?

CRITICAL THINKING

Q How did the societies discussed in this chapter deal with the political, economic, and social challenges that they faced after World War I, and how did these challenges differ from one region to another?

ON CHRISTMAS DAY IN 1920, a young Asian man in an ill-fitting rented suit stood up nervously to address the several hundred delegates of the French Socialist Party (FSP) who had gathered in the French city of Tours (TOOR). The speaker called himself Nguyen Ai Quoc (nuh-WEN EYE QUOHK), or Nguyen the Patriot, and was a Vietnamese subject of the French colony of Indochina.

The delegates had assembled to decide whether the FSP would follow the path of violent revolution recommended by the new Bolshevik regime in Soviet Russia. Among those voting in favor of the proposal was Nguyen Ai Quoc, who had decided that only the path of Karl Marx and Lenin could lead to national independence for his compatriots. Later he would become the founder of the Vietnamese Communist Party and become known to the world by the pseudonym Ho Chi Minh (HOH CHEE MIN).

The meeting in Tours was held at a time when resistance to colonial rule was on the rise, and the decision that Nguyen Ai Quoc faced of whether to opt for violent revolution was one that would be faced by colonial peoples throughout the world. As Europeans devastated their own civilization on the battlefields of Europe, the subject peoples of their vast colonial empires were quick to recognize the opportunity to shake free of foreign domination. In those areas, movements for national independence began to take shape. Some were inspired by the nationalist and liberal movements of the West, while others looked to the new Marxist model provided by the victory of the Communists in Soviet Russia, who soon worked to spread their revolutionary vision to African and Asian societies. In the Middle East, World War I ended the rule of the Ottoman Empire and led to the creation of new states, many of which were placed under Western domination.

The societies of Latin America were no longer under direct colonial rule and thus, for the most part, did not face the same types of challenges as their counterparts in Asia and Africa. Nevertheless, in some cases the economies of the Latin American countries were virtually controlled by foreign interests. A similar situation prevailed in China and Japan, which had managed with some difficulty to retain a degree of political independence, despite severe pressure from the West. But the political flux and economic disruption that characterized much of the world during the two decades following World War I had affected Latin America, China, and Japan as well, leading many in these regions to heed the siren call of fascist dictatorship or social revolution. For all the peoples of Asia, the Middle East, and Latin America, the end of the Great War had not created a world safe for democracy, as Woodrow Wilson had hoped, but an age of great peril and uncertainty.

The Rise of Nationalism

Q FOCUS QUESTION: What were the various stages in the rise of nationalist movements in Asia and the Middle East, and what problems did they face?

Although the West had emerged from World War I relatively intact, its political and social foundations and its self-confidence had been severely undermined. Within Europe, doubts about the viability of Western civilization were widespread, especially among the intellectual elite. These doubts were quick to reach perceptive observers in Asia and Africa and contributed to a rising tide of unrest against Western political domination throughout the colonial and semicolonial world. That unrest took various forms but was most evident in increasing worker activism, rural protests, and a rising national fervor among anticolonialist intellectuals. In areas of Asia, Africa, and Latin America where independent states had successfully resisted the Western onslaught, the discontent fostered by the war and later by the Great Depression led to a loss of confidence in democratic institutions and the rise of political dictatorships.

Modern Nationalism

The first stage of resistance to the West in Asia and Africa (see Chapters 21 and 22) had resulted in humiliation and failure and must have confirmed many Westerners' conviction that colonial peoples lacked the strength and the know-how to create modern states and govern their own destinies. In fact, the process was just beginning. The next phase—the rise of modern nationalism—began to take shape at the beginning of the twentieth century and was the product of the convergence of several factors. The most vocal source of anticolonialist sentiment was a new urban middle class of westernized intellectuals. In many cases, these merchants, petty functionaries, clerks, students, and professionals had been educated in Western-style schools. A few had spent time in the West. Many spoke Western languages, wore Western clothes, and worked in occupations connected with the colonial regime. Some even wrote in the languages of their colonial masters.

The results were paradoxical. On the one hand, this "new class" admired Western culture and sometimes harbored a deep sense of contempt for traditional ways. On the other hand, many strongly resented the foreigners and their arrogant contempt for colonial peoples. Though eager to introduce Western ideas and institutions into their own society, these intellectuals were dismayed at the gap between ideal and reality, theory and practice, in colonial policy. Although Western political thought exalted democracy, equality, and individual freedom, democratic institutions were primitive or nonexistent in the colonies.

Equality in economic opportunity and social life was also noticeably lacking. Normally, the middle classes did not suffer in the same manner as impoverished peasants or menial workers, but they, too, had complaints. They were usually relegated to low-level jobs in the government or business and paid less than Europeans in similar positions. The superiority of the Europeans was expressed in a variety of ways, including "whites only" clubs and the use of the familiar form of the language (normally used by adults to children) when addressing the locals.

Under these conditions, many of the new urban educated class were very ambivalent toward their colonial masters and the civilization that they represented. Out of this mixture of hope and resentment emerged the first stirrings of modern nationalism in Asia and Africa. During the first quarter of the century, in colonial and semi-colonial societies from the Suez Canal to the Pacific Ocean, educated native peoples began to organize political parties and movements seeking reforms or the end of foreign rule and the restoration of independence.

RELIGION AND NATIONALISM   At first, many of the leaders of these movements did not focus as much on nationhood as on the defense of indigenous religious beliefs or economic interests. In Burma, the first expression of modern nationalism came from students at the University of Rangoon, who protested against official persecution of the Buddhist religion and British lack of respect for local religious traditions (such as failing to remove footware when entering a Buddhist temple). The protesters adopted the name Thakin (TAHK-in), a polite term in the Burmese language meaning "lord" or "master," thus emphasizing their demand for the right to rule themselves. Only in the 1930s did the Thakins begin to focus specifically on national independence.

In the Dutch East Indies, Sarekat (SAR-eh-kaht) Islam (Islamic Association) began as a self-help society among Muslim merchants to fight against domination of the local economy by Chinese interests. Eventually, activist elements realized that the problem was not the Chinese merchants but the colonial presence, and in the 1920s, Sarekat Islam was transformed into the Nationalist Party of Indonesia (PNI), which focused on national independence. Like the Thakins in Burma, this party would lead the country to independence after World War II.

THE NATIONALIST QUANDARY: INDEPENDENCE OR MODERNIZATION?   Building a new nation, however, requires more than a shared sense of grievances against the foreign invader. A host of other issues also had to be resolved. Soon patriots throughout the colonial world were debating such questions as whether independence or modernization should be their primary objective. The answer depended in part on how the colonial regime was perceived. If it was viewed as a source of needed reforms, a gradualist approach made sense. But if it was seen primarily as an impediment to change, the first priority, for many, was to bring it to an end. The vast majority of patriotic individuals were convinced that to survive, their societies must adopt much of the Western way of life; yet many were equally determined that the local culture would not, and should not, become a carbon copy of the West. What was the national identity, after all, if it did not incorporate some traditional elements?

Another reason for using traditional values was to provide ideological symbols that the common people could understand and would rally around. Though aware that they needed to enlist the mass of the population in the struggle, most urban intellectuals had difficulty communicating with the rural populations who did not understand such unfamiliar concepts as democracy and nationhood. As the Indonesian intellectual Sutan Sjahrir (SOO-tan syah-REER) lamented, many westernized intellectuals had more in common with their colonial rulers than with the people in the villages (see the box on p. 624). As one French colonial official remarked in some surprise to a French-educated Vietnamese reformist, "Why, Monsieur, you are more French than I am!"

Gandhi and the Indian National Congress

Nowhere in the colonial world were these issues debated more vigorously than in India. Before the Sepoy Rebellion (see Chapter 21), Indian consciousness had focused mainly on the question of religious identity. But in the latter half of the nineteenth century, a stronger sense of national consciousness began to arise, provoked by the conservative policies and racial arrogance of the British colonial authorities.

The first Indian nationalists were almost invariably upper class and educated. Many were from urban areas such as Bombay (now Mumbai), Madras (now Chennai), and Calcutta (now Kolkata). At first, many tended to prefer reform to revolution and believed that India needed modernization before taking on the problems of independence. Such reformists did have some effect. In the 1880s, the government allowed a measure of self-government, but all too often, such efforts were sabotaged by local British officials.

The slow pace of reform convinced many Indian nationalists that relying on British benevolence was futile. In 1885, a small group of Indians, with some British participation, met in Bombay to form the Indian National Congress (INC). They hoped to speak for all India, but most were high-class English-trained Hindus. Like their reformist predecessors, members of the INC did not demand immediate independence and accepted the need for reforms to end traditional abuses like child marriage and *sati*. At the same time, they called for an Indian share in the governing process and more spending on economic development and less on military campaigns along the frontier. The British responded with a few concessions, but change was glacially slow.

The INC also had difficulty reconciling religious differences within its ranks. Its stated goal was self-determination for all Indians regardless of class or religion, but many of its leaders were Hindu and inevitably reflected Hindu concerns. In the first decade of the twentieth

The Dilemma of the Intellectual

ART & IDEAS

Sutan Sjahrir (1909–1966) was a prominent leader of the Indonesian nationalist movement who briefly served as prime minister of the Republic of Indonesia in the 1950s. Like many Western-educated Asian intellectuals, he was tortured by the realization that by education and outlook he was closer to his colonial masters—in his case, the Dutch—than to his own people. He wrote the following passage in a letter to his wife in 1935 and later included it in his book *Out of Exile*.

Sutan Sjahrir, *Out of Exile*

Am I perhaps estranged from my people? . . . Why are the things that contain beauty for them and arouse their gentler emotions only senseless and displeasing for me? In reality, the spiritual gap between my people and me is certainly no greater than that between an intellectual in Holland . . . and the undeveloped people of Holland. . . . The difference is rather . . . that the intellectual in Holland does not feel this gap because there is a portion—even a fairly large portion—of his own people on approximately the same intellectual level as himself. . . .

This is what we lack here. Not only is the number of intellectuals in this country smaller in proportion to the total population—in fact, very much smaller—but in addition, the few who are here do not constitute any single entity in spiritual outlook, or in any spiritual life or single culture whatsoever. . . . It is for them so much more difficult than for the intellectuals in Holland. In Holland they build—both consciously and unconsciously—on what is already there. . . . Even if

they oppose it, they do so as a method of application or as a starting point.

In our country this is not the case. Here there has been no spiritual or cultural life, and no intellectual progress for centuries. There are the much-praised Eastern art forms but what are these except bare rudiments from a feudal culture that cannot possibly provide a dynamic fulcrum for people of the twentieth century? . . . Our spiritual needs are needs of the twentieth century; our problems and our views are of the twentieth century. . . .

We intellectuals here are much closer to Europe or America than we are to the Borobudur or Mahabharata or to the primitive Islamic culture of Java and Sumatra. . . .

So, it seems, the problem stands in principle. It is seldom put forth by us in this light, and instead most of us search unconsciously for a synthesis that will leave us internally tranquil. We want to have both Western science and Eastern philosophy, the Eastern "spirit," in the culture. But what is this Eastern spirit? It is, they say, the sense of the higher, of spirituality, of the eternal and religious, as opposed to the materialism of the West. I have heard this countless times, but it has never convinced me.

Q Why did Sutan Sjahrir feel estranged from his native culture? What was his answer to the challenges faced by his country in coming to terms with the modern world?

Source: From *The World of Southeast Asia: Selected Historical Readings*, Harry J. Benda and John A. Larkin, eds. Copyright © 1967 by Harper & Row, Publishers.

century, the separate Muslim League was created to represent the interests of the millions of Muslims in Indian society.

NONVIOLENT RESISTANCE In 1915, a young Hindu lawyer returned from South Africa to become active in the INC. He transformed the movement and galvanized India's struggle for independence and identity. Mohandas Gandhi (moh-HAHN-dus GAHN-dee) was born in

1869 in Gujarat (goo-juh-RAHT), in western India, the son of a government minister. After studying law in London, in 1893 he went to South Africa to work in a law firm serving Indian émigrés working as laborers there. He soon became aware of the racial prejudice and exploitation experienced by Indians living in the territory and tried to organize them to protect their interests.

On his return to India, Gandhi became active in the independence movement, setting up a movement based on nonviolent resistance—the Hindi term was *satyagraha* (SUHT-yuh-grah-hah), meaning "hold fast to the truth"—to try to force the British to improve the lot of the poor and grant independence to India. His goals were to convert the British to his views while simultaneously strengthening the unity and sense of self-respect of his compatriots. When the British attempted to suppress dissent, he called on his followers to refuse to obey British regulations. He began to manufacture his own clothes, dressing in a simple *dhoti* (DOH-tee) made of coarse homespun cotton, and adopted the spinning wheel as a symbol of Indian resistance to imports of British textiles.

© Cengage Learning

British India Between the Wars

Gandhi, now increasingly known as Mahatma (mah-HAHT-muh), India's "Great Soul," organized mass protests to achieve his aims, but in 1919, they got out of hand and led to violence and British reprisals. British troops killed hundreds of unarmed protesters in the city of Amritsar (am-RIT-sur) in northwestern India. Gandhi was horrified at the violence and briefly retreated from active politics. Nevertheless, he was arrested for his role in the protests and spent several years in prison.

Gandhi combined his anticolonial activities with an appeal to the spiritual instincts of all Indians. Though he had been born and raised a Hindu, his universalist approach to the idea of God transcended individual religion, although it was shaped by historical Hindu themes. In a speech in 1931, he described God as "an indefinable mysterious power that pervades everything . . . , an unseen power which makes itself felt and yet defies all proof."[1]

While Gandhi was in prison, the political situation continued to evolve. In 1921, the British passed the Government of India Act, transforming the heretofore advisory Legislative Council into a bicameral parliament, two-thirds of whose members would be elected. Similar bodies were created at the provincial level. In a stroke, 5 million Indians were enfranchised. But such reforms were no longer enough for many members of the INC, who wanted to push aggressively for full independence. The British exacerbated the situation by increasing the salt tax and prohibiting the Indian people from manufacturing or harvesting their own salt. Gandhi, now released from prison, returned to his earlier policy of **civil disobedience** by joining several dozen supporters in a 240-mile walk to the sea, where he picked up a lump of salt and urged Indians to ignore the law (see the Film & History feature on p. 626). Gandhi and many other members of the INC were arrested.

Organizations to promote women's rights in India had been established shortly after 1900, and Indian women now played an active role in the movement. Women accounted for about 20,000, or nearly 10 percent, of all those arrested for taking part in demonstrations during the interwar period. Women marched, picketed foreign shops, and promoted the spinning and wearing of homemade cloth. By the 1930s, women's associations were also actively promoting social reforms, including women's education, the introduction of birth control devices, the abolition of child marriage, and universal suffrage. In 1929, the Sarda Act raised the minimum age of marriage to fourteen.

NEW LEADERS AND NEW PROBLEMS In the 1930s, a new figure entered the movement in the person of Jawaharlal Nehru (juh-WAH-hur-lahl NAY-roo) (1889–1964), son of an earlier INC leader. Educated in the law in Great Britain and a *brahmin* by birth, Nehru personified the new Anglo-Indian politician: secular, rational, upper class, and intellectual. In fact, he appeared to be everything that Gandhi was not. With his emergence, the independence movement embarked on two paths, religious and secular, Indian and Western, traditional and modern. The dual character of the INC leadership may well have strengthened the movement by bringing together the two primary impulses behind the desire for independence: elite nationalism and the primal force of Indian traditionalism. But it portended trouble for the nation's new leadership in defining India's future path. In the meantime, Muslim discontent with Hindu dominance over the INC was increasing. In 1940, the Muslim League called for the creation of a separate Muslim state of Pakistan ("land of the pure") in the northwest. As strife between Hindus and Muslims increased, many Indians came to realize with sorrow (and some British colonialists with satisfaction) that British rule was all that stood between peace and civil war.

The Nationalist Revolt in the Middle East

In the Middle East, as in Europe, World War I hastened the collapse of old empires. The Ottoman Empire, which had dominated the eastern Mediterranean since the seizure of Constantinople in 1453, had been growing

FILM & HISTORY

Gandhi (1982)

To many of his contemporaries, Mohandas Gandhi was the conscience of India. Son of a senior Indian official from Gujarat and trained as a lawyer at University College in London, Gandhi first encountered racial discrimination when he provided legal assistance to Indian laborers living under the apartheid regime in South Africa. On his return to India, he rapidly emerged as a fierce critic of British colonial rule. His message of *satyagraha*—embodying the idea of steadfast but nonviolent resistance to the injustice and inhumanity inherent in the colonial enterprise—inspired his compatriots in their long struggle for national independence. It also earned the admiration and praise of sympathetic observers around the world. His death by assassination at the hands of a Hindu fanatic in 1948 shocked the world.

Time, however, has somewhat dimmed his message. Gandhi's vision of a future India was symbolized by the spinning wheel—he rejected the industrial age and material pursuits in favor of the simple life of the traditional Indian village. Since independence, however, India has followed the path of national wealth and power laid out by Jawaharlal Nehru, Gandhi's friend and colleague. Gandhi's appeal for religious tolerance and mutual respect at home rapidly gave way to a bloody conflict between Hindus and Muslims that has not yet been eradicated. His vision of world peace and brotherly love has been similarly ignored, first during the Cold War and more recently by the "clash of civilizations" between Western countries and the forces of militant Islam.

It was partly in an effort to revive Gandhi's message that the British filmmaker Richard Attenborough directed the film *Gandhi* (1982). Epic in length and scope, the film presents a faithful rendition of the life of its subject, from his introduction to apartheid in South Africa to his tragic death after World War II. Actor Ben Kingsley, son of an Indian father and an English mother, plays the title role with intensity and conviction. The film was widely praised and earned eight Academy Awards. Kingsley received an Oscar in the Best Actor category.

© Columbia Pictures/Courtesy The Everett Collection, Inc.

Jawaharlal Nehru (Roshan Seth), Mahatma Gandhi (Ben Kingsley), and Muhammad Ali Jinnah (Alyque Padamsee) confer before the partition of India into Hindu and Muslim states.

---

weaker since the end of the eighteenth century, troubled by government corruption, the declining effectiveness of the sultans, and the loss of considerable territory in the Balkans and southwestern Russia. In North Africa, Ottoman authority, tenuous at best, had disintegrated in the nineteenth century, enabling the French to seize Algeria and Tunisia and the British to establish a protectorate over the Nile River valley.

DECLINE OF THE OTTOMAN EMPIRE Reformist elements in Istanbul had tried from time to time to resist the trend, but military defeats continued: Greece declared its independence, and Ottoman power declined steadily in the Middle East. A rising sense of nationality among Serbs, Armenians, and other minority peoples threatened the stability and cohesion of the empire. In the 1870s, a new generation of reformers seized power in Istanbul and pushed through a constitution creating a legislative assembly representing all peoples in the state. But the sultan they placed on the throne suspended the new charter and attempted to rule by traditional authoritarian means.

By the end of the century, the defunct 1876 constitution had become a symbol of change for reformist elements, now grouped together under the name **Young Turks**. They found support in the army and administration and among Turks living in exile. In 1908, the Young Turks forced the sultan to restore the constitution, and he was removed from power the following year.

But the Young Turks had appeared at a moment of crisis for the empire. Internal rebellions, combined with Austrian annexations of Ottoman territories in the Balkans, undermined support for the new government and provoked the army to step in. With most minorities from the old empire now removed from Istanbul's authority, many ethnic Turks began to embrace a new concept of a Turkish state based on those of Turkish nationality.

The final blow to the old empire came in World War I, when the Ottoman government allied with Germany in the hope of driving the British from Egypt and restoring Ottoman rule over the Nile valley. In response, the British declared an official protectorate over Egypt and, aided by the efforts of the dashing if eccentric British adventurer T. E. Lawrence (popularly known as Lawrence of Arabia), sought to undermine Ottoman rule in the Arabian peninsula by encouraging Arab nationalists there. In 1916, the local governor of Mecca declared Arabia independent from Ottoman rule, while British troops, advancing from Egypt, seized Palestine (see the map on p. 631). In October 1918, having suffered more than 300,000 casualties during the war, the Ottoman Empire negotiated an armistice with the Allied Powers.

Mustafa Kemal Atatürk. The war hero Mustafa Kemal took the initiative in creating the republic of Turkey. As president, Atatürk ("Father Turk") worked hard to transform Turkey into a modern secular state by restructuring the economy, adopting Western dress, and breaking the powerful hold of Islamic traditions. He is now reviled by Muslim fundamentalists for his opposition to an Islamic state. In this photograph, Atatürk, at the left in civilian clothes, hosts the shah of Persia during his visit to Turkey in 1934.

MUSTAFA KEMAL AND THE MODERNIZATION OF TURKEY During the next years, the tottering empire began to fall apart as the British and the French made plans to divide up Ottoman territories in the Middle East and the Greeks won Allied approval to seize the western parts of the Anatolian peninsula for their dream of re-creating the substance of the old Byzantine Empire. The impending collapse energized key elements in Turkey under the leadership of a war hero, Colonel Mustafa Kemal (moos-tah-FAH kuh-MAHL) (1881–1938), who had successfully defended the Dardanelles against the British during World War I. Now he resigned from the army and convoked a national congress that called for the creation of an elected government and the preservation of the empire's remaining territories in a new republic of Turkey. Establishing his capital at Ankara (AN-kuh-ruh), Kemal drove the Greeks from the Anatolian peninsula and persuaded the British to agree to a new treaty. In 1923, the last Ottoman sultan fled the country, which was now declared a Turkish republic. The Ottoman Empire had come to an end.

During the next few years, President Mustafa Kemal, now popularly known as Atatürk (ah-tah-TIRK), or "Father Turk," attempted to transform Turkey into a modern secular republic. The trappings of a democratic

system were put in place, centered on an elected Grand National Assembly, but the president was relatively intolerant of opposition and harshly suppressed critics. Turkish nationalism was emphasized, and the Turkish language, now written in the Roman alphabet, was shorn of many of its Arabic elements. Popular education was emphasized, old aristocratic titles like *pasha* and *bey* were abolished, and all Turkish citizens were given family names in the European style.

Atatürk also took steps to modernize the economy. overseeing the establishment of a light industrial sector producing textiles, glass, paper, and cement and instituting a five-year plan on the Soviet model to provide for state direction over the economy. Atatürk was no admirer of Soviet communism, however, and the Turkish economy can be better described as a form of state capitalism. He also established training institutions and model farms in an effort to modernize the agricultural sector, but such reforms had little effect on the predominantly conservative peasantry.

Perhaps the most significant aspect of Atatürk's reform program was his attempt to break the power of the Islamic clerics and transform Turkey into a secular state. The caliphate was formally abolished in 1924 (see the box on p. 628), and *Shari'a* (Islamic law) was replaced

OPPOSING ✕ VIEWPOINTS

Islam in the Modern World: Two Views

POLITICS & GOVERNMENT

As part of his plan to transform Turkey into a modern society, Mustafa Kemal Atatürk sought to eliminate what he considered to be outdated practices imposed by traditional beliefs. The first selection is from a speech in which he proposed an end to the caliphate, which had been in the hands of Ottoman sultans since the formation of the empire. But not all Muslims wished to move toward a more secular society. Mohammed Iqbal (ik-BAHL), a well-known Muslim poet in colonial India, was a prominent advocate of the creation of a separate state for Muslims in South Asia. The second selection is from an address he presented to the All-India Muslim League, explaining the rationale for his proposal.

Atatürk, Speech to the Assembly (October 1924)

The sovereign entitled Caliph was to maintain justice among the three hundred million Muslims on the terrestrial globe, to safeguard the rights of these peoples, to prevent any event that could encroach upon order and security, and confront every attack which the Muslims would be called upon to encounter from the side of other nations. It was to be part of his attributes to preserve by all means the welfare and spiritual development of Islam. . . .

If the Caliph and Caliphate, as they maintained, were to be invested with a dignity embracing the whole of Islam, ought they not to have realized in all justice that a crushing burden would be imposed on Turkey, on her existence; her entire resources and all her forces would be placed at the disposal of the Caliph? . . .

For centuries our nation was guided under the influence of these erroneous ideas. But what has been the result of it? Everywhere they have lost millions of men. "Do you know," I asked, "how many sons of Anatolia have perished in the scorching deserts of the Yemen? Do you know the losses we have suffered in holding Syria and Egypt and in maintaining our position in Africa? And do you see what has come out of it? Do you know?

"Those who favor the idea of placing the means at the disposal of the Caliph to brave the whole world and the power to administer the affairs of the whole of Islam must not appeal to the population of Anatolia alone but to the great Muslim agglomerations which are eight or ten times as rich in men.

"New Turkey, the people of New Turkey, have no reason to think of anything else but their own existence and their own welfare. She has nothing more to give away to others."

Mohammed Iqbal, Speech to the All-India Muslim League (1930)

It cannot be denied that Islam, regarded as an ethical ideal plus a certain kind of polity—by which expression I mean a social structure regulated by a legal system and animated by a specific ethical ideal—has been the chief formative factor in the life history of the Muslims of India. It has furnished those basic emotions and loyalties which gradually unify scattered individuals and groups and finally transform them into a well-defined people. Indeed it is no exaggeration to say that India is perhaps the only country in the world where Islam, as a people-building force, has worked at its best. In India, as elsewhere, the structure of Islam as a society is almost entirely due to the working of Islam as a culture inspired by a specific ethical ideal. What I mean to say is that Muslim society, with its remarkable homogeneity and inner unity, has grown to be what it is under the pressure of the laws and institutions associated with the culture of Islam.

Communalism in its higher aspect, then, is indispensable to the formation of a harmonious whole in a country like India. The units of Indian society are not territorial as in European countries. India is a continent of human groups belonging to different religions. Their behavior is not at all determined by a common race consciousness. Even the Hindus do not form a homogeneous group. The principle of European democracy cannot be applied to India without recognizing the fact of communal groups. The Muslim demand for the creation of a Muslim India within India is, therefore, perfectly justified. . . .

I therefore demand the formation of a consolidated Muslim State in the best interests of India and Islam. For India it means security and peace resulting from an

(Continued)

internal balance of power; for Islam an opportunity to rid itself of the stamp that Arabian imperialism was forced to give it, to mobilize its law, its education, its culture, and to bring them into closer contact with its own original spirit and with the spirit of modern times.

Q Why did Mustafa Kemal believe that the caliphate no longer met the needs of the Turkish people? Why did Mohammed Iqbal believe that a separate state for Muslims in India would be required? How did he attempt to persuade non-Muslims that this would be to their benefit as well?

Sources: Atatürk, Speech to the Assembly (October 1924). From *Ataturk's Speech to the Assembly*, pp. 432–433. A speech delivered by Ghazi Mustafa Kemal, President of the Turkish Republic, October 1927. Mohammed Iqbal, Speech to the All-India Muslim League (1930). Excerpt from *The Sources of Indian Tradition*, pp. 218–222 by Stephen Hay, ed. Copyright © 1988 by Columbia University Press, New York. Reprinted with permission of the publisher.

by a revised version of the Swiss law code. The fez (the brimless cap worn by Turkish Muslims) was abolished as a form of headdress, and women were discouraged from wearing the traditional Islamic veil. Women received the right to vote in 1934 and were legally equal to men in all aspects of marriage and inheritance. Education and the professions were now open to citizens of both genders, and some women even began to participate in politics. All citizens were given the right to convert to another religion at will.

The legacy of Mustafa Kemal Atatürk was enormous. Although not all of his reforms were widely accepted in practice, especially by devout Muslims, most of the changes he introduced were retained after his death in 1938. In virtually every respect, the Turkish republic was the product of his determined efforts to create a modern Turkish nation.

MODERNIZATION IN IRAN   In the meantime, a similar process was under way in Persia. Under the Qajar (kuh-JAHR) dynasty (1794–1925), the country had not been very successful in resisting Russian advances in the Caucasus or resolving its domestic problems. To secure themselves from foreign influence, the Qajars moved the capital from Tabriz to Tehran (teh-RAHN), in a mountainous area south of the Caspian Sea. During the mid-nineteenth century, one modernizing shah attempted to introduce political and economic reforms but faced resistance from tribal and religious—predominantly Shi'ite—forces. Increasingly, the dynasty turned to Russia and Great Britain to protect itself from its own people.

Eventually, the growing foreign presence led to the rise of a Persian nationalist movement. Supported by Shi'ite religious leaders, opposition to the regime rose steadily among both peasants and merchants in the cities, and in 1906, popular pressure forced the shah to grant a constitution on the Western model.

As in the Ottoman Empire and Manchu China, however, the modernizers had moved too soon, before their

power base was secure. With the support of the Russians and the British, the shah regained control, while the two foreign powers began to divide the country into separate spheres of influence. One reason for the foreign interest in Persia was the discovery of oil reserves there in 1908. Over the next years, oil exports increased rapidly, with the bulk of the profits going to British investors.

In 1921, Reza Khan (ree-ZAH KAHN) (1878–1944), an officer in the Persian army, seized power in Tehran. He had intended to establish a republic, but resistance from traditional forces impeded his efforts. In 1925, the new Pahlavi (PAH-luh-vee), dynasty with Reza Khan as shah, replaced the now defunct Qajar dynasty. During

Iran Under the Pahlavi Dynasty

the next few years, Reza Khan attempted to follow the example of Atatürk in Turkey, introducing reforms to strengthen the central government, modernize the civilian and military bureaucracy, and establish a modern economic infrastructure. In 1935, he officially changed the name of the nation to Iran.

Unlike Atatürk, Reza Khan did not attempt to destroy the power of Islamic beliefs, but he did encourage the establishment of a Western-style educational system and forbade women to wear the veil in public. Women continued to be exploited, however; the carpets produced by their intensive labor were a major export—second only to oil—in the interwar period. To strengthen Iranian nationalism and reduce the power of Islam, Reza Khan attempted to popularize the symbols and beliefs of pre-Islamic times. Like his Qajar predecessors, however, he was hindered by strong foreign influence. When the

Soviet Union and Great Britain decided to send troops into the country during World War II, he resigned in protest and died three years later.

NATION BUILDING IN IRAQ Another consequence of the collapse of the Ottoman Empire was the emergence of a new political entity along the Tigris and Euphrates Rivers, once the heartland of ancient empires. Lacking defensible borders and sharply divided along ethnic and religious lines—a Shi'ite majority in rural areas, a vocal Sunni minority in the cities, and a largely Kurdish population in the northern mountains—the region had been under Ottoman rule since the seventeenth century. During World War I, British forces occupied the area from Baghdad southward to the Persian Gulf to protect the oil-producing regions in neighboring Iran from a German takeover.

Although the British claimed to have arrived as liberators, in 1920 the League of Nations placed the country under British control as the mandate of Iraq. Civil unrest and growing anti-Western sentiment rapidly dispelled any plans for the emergence of an independent government, and in 1921, after the suppression of resistance forces, the country was placed under the titular authority of King Faisal (FY-suhl) of Syria, a descendant of the Prophet Muhammad. Faisal relied for support primarily on the politically more sophisticated urban Sunni population, although they represented less than a quarter of the population. The discovery of oil near Kirkuk (kir-KOOK) in 1927 increased the value of the area to the British, who granted formal independence to Iraq in 1932, although British advisers retained a strong influence over the fragile government.

THE RISE OF ARAB NATIONALISM As we have seen, the Arab uprising during World War I helped bring about the demise of the Ottoman Empire. There had been resistance to Ottoman rule in the Arabian peninsula since the eighteenth century, when the devoutly Muslim Wahhabi (wuh-HAH-bee) sect attempted to drive out outside influences and cleanse Islam of corrupt practices that had developed in past centuries. The revolt was eventually suppressed, but Wahhabi influence persisted.

CHRONOLOGY	The Middle East Between the Wars
Balfour Declaration on Palestine	1917
Reza Khan seizes power in Persia	1921
End of Ottoman Empire and establishment of a republic in Turkey	1923
Rule of Mustafa Kemal Atatürk in Turkey	1923–1938
Beginning of Pahlavi dynasty in Iran	1925
Establishment of kingdom of Saudi Arabia	1932

World War I offered an opportunity for the Arabs to throw off the shackles of Ottoman rule—but what would replace them? The Arabs were not a nation but an idea, a loose collection of peoples who often did not see eye to eye on matters that affected their community. Disagreement over what constitutes an Arab has plagued generations of political leaders who have sought unsuccessfully to knit together the disparate peoples of the region into a single Arab nation.

When the Arab leaders in Mecca declared their independence from Ottoman rule in 1916, they had hoped for British support, but they were to be sorely disappointed. At the close of the war, the British and French created a number of mandates in the area under the supervision of the League of Nations (see Chapter 23). Iraq was assigned to the British; Syria and Lebanon (the two areas were separated so that Christian peoples in Lebanon could be placed under Christian administration) were given to the French.

In the early 1920s, Ibn Saud (IB-un sah-OOD) (1880–1953), a Wahhabi leader and descendant of the family that had led the eighteenth-century revolt, united Arab tribes in the northern part of the Arabian peninsula and drove out the remnants of Ottoman rule. Devout and gifted, Ibn Saud won broad support among Arab tribal peoples and established the kingdom of Saudi Arabia throughout much of the peninsula in 1932.

At first, the new kingdom, consisting essentially of the vast desert wastes of central Arabia, was desperately poor and depended on the income from Muslim pilgrims visiting the holy sites in Mecca and Medina. But during the 1930s, American companies began to explore for oil, and in 1938, Standard Oil made a successful strike at Dhahran (dah-RAHN), on the Persian Gulf. Soon an Arabian-American oil conglomerate, popularly called Aramco, was established, and the isolated kingdom was suddenly inundated by Western oilmen and untold wealth.

THE ISSUE OF PALESTINE The land of Palestine—once the home of the Jews but now inhabited primarily by Muslim Arabs—was made a separate mandate and immediately became a thorny problem for the British. In 1897, the Austrian-born journalist Theodor Herzl (TAY-oh-dor HAYRT-sul) (1860–1904) had convened an international conference in Switzerland that led to the creation of the World Zionist Organization (WZO). Its aim was to create a homeland in Palestine for the Jewish people, who had long been dispersed throughout Europe, North Africa, and the Middle East.

Over the next decade, Jewish immigration into Palestine, then under Ottoman rule, increased with WZO support. By the outbreak of World War I, about 85,000 Jews lived in Palestine, representing about 15 percent of the total population. In 1917, responding to appeals from the

British chemist Chaim Weizmann (KY-im VYTS-mahn), British Foreign Secretary Lord Arthur Balfour (BAL-foor) issued a declaration saying Palestine was to be a national home for the Jews. The Balfour Declaration, which was later confirmed by the League of Nations, was ambiguous on the legal status of the territory and promised that the rights of non-Jewish peoples currently living in the area would not be undermined. But Arab nationalists were incensed. How could a national home for the Jewish people be established in a territory where the majority of the population was Muslim?

After World War I, more Jewish settlers began to arrive in Palestine in response to the promises made in the Balfour Declaration. As tensions between the new arrivals and existing Muslim residents began to escalate, the British tried to restrict Jewish immigration into the territory while Arab voices rejected the concept of a separate state. In a bid to relieve Arab sensitivities, Great Britain created the separate emirate of Trans-Jordan out of the eastern portion of Palestine. After World War II, it would become the independent kingdom of Jordan. The stage was set for the conflicts that would take place in the region after World War II.

THE BRITISH IN EGYPT Great Britain had maintained a loose protectorate over Egypt since the mid-nineteenth century, although the area remained nominally under Ottoman rule. London formalized its protectorate in 1914 to protect the Suez Canal and the Nile valley from possible seizure by the Central Powers. After the war, however, nationalist elements became restive and formed the Wafd (WAHFT) Party, a secular organization dedicated to the creation of an independent Egypt based on the principles of representative government. The Wafd received the support of many middle-class Egyptians who, like Atatürk in Turkey, hoped to meld Islamic practices with the secular tradition of the modern West. This modernist form of Islam did not have broad appeal outside the cosmopolitan centers, however, and in 1928 the Muslim cleric Hasan al-Bana (hah-SAHN al-BAN-ah) organized the Muslim Brotherhood, which demanded strict adherence to the teachings of the Prophet, as set forth in the Qur'an. The Brotherhood rejected Western ways and sought to create a new Egypt based firmly on the precepts of *Shari'a*. By the 1930s, the organization had as many as a million members.

French mandates
British mandates

Constantinople (Istanbul)
TURKEY
SYRIA
LEBANON Beirut
Mediterranean Sea Damascus
PALESTINE
Jerusalem
Cairo TRANS-JORDAN
EGYPT
PERSIA
Baghdad
IRAQ
KUWAIT
SAUDI ARABIA
Caspian Sea

0 250 500 750 Kilometers
0 250 500 Miles

© Cengage Learning

The Middle East After World War I

Nationalism and Revolution

Before the Russian Revolution, to most intellectuals in Asia and Africa, "westernization" referred to the capitalist democratic civilization of western Europe and the United States, not the doctrine of social revolution developed by Karl Marx. Until 1917, Marxism was regarded as a utopian idea rather than a concrete system of government. Moreover, Marxism appeared to have little relevance to conditions in Asia and Africa. Marxist doctrine, after all, declared that a communist society would arise only from the ashes of an advanced capitalism that had already passed through an industrial revolution. From the perspective of Marxist historical analysis, most societies in Asia and Africa were still at the feudal stage of development; they lacked the economic conditions and political awareness to achieve a socialist revolution that would bring the working class to power. Finally, the Marxist view of nationalism and religion had little appeal in the non-Western world. Marx believed that nationhood and religion were false ideas that diverted the oppressed masses from the critical issues of class struggle. Instead, Marx stressed an "internationalist" outlook based on class consciousness and the eventual creation of a classless society with no artificial divisions based on culture, nation, or religion.

LENIN AND THE EAST The situation began to change after the Russian Revolution. Lenin's Bolsheviks had demonstrated that a revolutionary party espousing Marxist principles could overturn a corrupt, outdated system and launch a new experiment dedicated to ending human inequality and achieving a paradise on earth. In 1920, Lenin proposed a new revolutionary strategy designed to relate Marxist doctrine and practice to non-Western societies. His reasons were not entirely altruistic. Soviet Russia, surrounded by capitalist powers, desperately needed allies in its struggle to survive in a hostile world. To Lenin, the anticolonial movements emerging in North Africa, Asia, and the Middle East after World War I were natural allies of the beleaguered new regime in Moscow. Lenin was convinced that only the ability of the imperialist powers to find markets, raw materials, and sources of capital investment in the non-Western world kept capitalism alive. If the tentacles of capitalist influence in Asia and Africa could be severed, imperialism would weaken and collapse.

Establishing such an alliance was not easy, however. Most nationalist leaders in colonial countries belonged to the urban middle class, and many abhorred the idea of a comprehensive revolution to create a totally egalitarian society. In addition, many still adhered to traditional religious beliefs and were opposed to the atheistic principles of classic Marxism.

Since it was unrealistic to expect bourgeois nationalist support for social revolution, Lenin sought a compromise that would enable Communist parties to be organized among the working classes in the preindustrial societies of Asia and Africa. These parties would then forge informal alliances with existing middle-class parties to struggle against the traditional ruling class and Western imperialism. Such an alliance, of course, could not be permanent because many bourgeois nationalists in Asia and Africa would reject an egalitarian, classless society. Once the imperialists had been overthrown, therefore, the Communist parties would turn against their erstwhile nationalist partners to seize power on their own and carry out the socialist revolution.

Lenin's strategy became a major element in Soviet foreign policy in the 1920s. Soviet agents fanned out across the world to carry Marxism beyond the boundaries of industrial Europe. The primary instrument of this effort was the **Communist International**, or **Comintern** for short. Formed in 1919 at Lenin's prodding, the Comintern was a worldwide organization of Communist parties dedicated to world revolution. At its headquarters in Moscow, agents from around the world were trained in the precepts of world communism and then sent back to their countries to form Marxist parties and promote social revolution. By the end of the 1920s, almost every colonial or semicolonial society in Asia had a party based on Marxist principles. The Soviets had less success in the Middle East, where Marxism appealed mainly to minorities such as Jews and Armenians in the cities, and in black Africa, where Soviet strategists in any case felt that conditions were not sufficiently advanced for the creation of Communist organizations.

THE APPEAL OF COMMUNISM According to Marxist doctrine, Communist parties should be made up of urban factory workers alienated from capitalist society by inhuman working conditions. In practice, many of the leaders even in European Communist parties tended to be urban intellectuals or members of the lower middle class. That phenomenon was even more true in the non-Western world, where most early Marxists were rootless intellectuals. Some were probably drawn to the movement for patriotic reasons and saw Marxist doctrine as a new, more effective means of modernizing their societies and removing the colonial exploiters (see the box on p. 633). Others were attracted by the utopian dream of a classless society. For those who had lost their faith in traditional religion, communism often served as a new secular ideology that replaced the lost truth of traditional faiths.

Of course, the new doctrine's appeal was not the same in all non-Western societies. In Confucian societies such as China and Vietnam, where traditional belief systems had been badly discredited by their failure to counter the Western challenge, communism had an immediate impact and rapidly became a major factor in the anticolonial movement. In Buddhist and Muslim societies, where traditional religion remained strong and became a cohesive factor in the resistance movement, communism had less success. To maximize their appeal and minimize potential conflict with traditional ideas, Communist parties frequently attempted to adapt Marxist doctrine to indigenous values and institutions. In the Middle East, for example, the Ba'ath (BAHTH) Party in Syria adopted a hybrid socialism combining Marxism with Arab nationalism. In Africa, radical intellectuals talked vaguely of a uniquely "African road to socialism."

The parties' success in establishing alliances with nationalist parties while building support among the working classes also varied from place to place. In some instances, the Communists were briefly able to work with the bourgeois parties. The most famous example was the alliance between the Chinese Communist Party and Sun Yat-sen's Nationalist Party (discussed in the next section). In 1928, however, the Comintern, reacting to Chiang Kai-shek's betrayal of the alliance, gave up these efforts and declared that Communist parties should focus on recruiting the most revolutionary elements in society—notably, the urban intellectuals and the working class. Harassed by colonial authorities and saddled with directions from Moscow that often had little relevance to local conditions, Communist parties in most colonial societies had little success in the 1930s and failed to build a secure base of support among the mass of the population.

Revolution in China

Q **FOCUS QUESTION:** What problems did China encounter between the two world wars, and what solutions did the Nationalists and the Communists propose to solve them?

Overall, revolutionary Marxism had its greatest impact in China, where a group of young radicals founded the Chinese Communist Party (CCP) in 1921. The rise of the CCP was a consequence of the failed revolution of 1911. When political forces are too weak or too divided to consolidate their power during a period of instability, the military usually steps in to fill the vacuum. In China, Sun Yat-sen (SOON yaht-SEN) and his colleagues had accepted General Yuan Shikai (yoo-AHN shee-KY) as president of the new Chinese republic in 1911 because they lacked the

The Path of Liberation

POLITICS & GOVERNMENT

In 1919, the Vietnamese revolutionary Ho Chi Minh (1890–1969) was living in exile in France, where he first became acquainted with the revolutionary experiment in Bolshevik Russia. Later he became a leader of the Vietnamese Communist movement. In the following passage, written in 1960, he reminisces about his reasons for becoming a Communist. The Second International, mentioned in the excerpt, was created in 1889 by moderate socialists who pursued their goal by parliamentary means. Lenin created the Third International, or Comintern, in 1919 to promote violent revolution.

Ho Chi Minh, "The Path Which Led Me to Leninism"

After World War I, I made my living in Paris, now as a retoucher at a photographer's, now as a painter of "Chinese antiquities" (made in France!). I would distribute leaflets denouncing the crimes committed by the French colonialists in Vietnam.

At that time, I supported the October Revolution [in Russia] only instinctively, not yet grasping all its historic importance. I loved and admired Lenin because he was a great patriot who liberated his compatriots; until then, I had read none of his books.

The reason for my joining the French Socialist Party was that these "ladies and gentlemen"—as I called my comrades at that moment—had shown their sympathy toward me, toward the struggle of the oppressed peoples. But I understood neither what was a party, a trade union, nor what was Socialism nor Communism.

Heated discussions were then taking place in the branches of the Socialist Party, about the question whether the Socialist Party should remain in the Second International, should a Second-and-a-Half International be founded, or should the Socialist Party join Lenin's Third International? I attended the meetings regularly, twice or three times a week, and attentively listened to the discussion. First, I could not understand thoroughly. Why were the discussions so heated? Either with the Second, Second-and-a-Half, or Third International, the revolution could be waged. What was the use of arguing then? As for the First International, what had become of it?

What I wanted most to know—and this precisely was not debated in the meetings—was: which International sides with the peoples of colonial countries?

I raised this question—the most important in my opinion—in a meeting. Some comrades answered: It is the Third, not the Second International. And a comrade gave me Lenin's "Thesis on the national and colonial questions," published by *l'Humanité*, to read.

There were political terms difficult to understand in this thesis. But by dint of reading it again and again, finally I could grasp the main part of it. What emotion, enthusiasm, clearsightedness, and confidence it instilled in me! I was overjoyed to tears. Though sitting alone in my room, I shouted aloud as if addressing large crowds: "Dear martyrs, compatriots! This is what we need, this is the path to our liberation!"

After that, I had entire confidence in Lenin, in the Third International.

Q *Why did Ho Chi Minh believe that the Third International was the key to the liberation of the colonial peoples? What were the essential elements of Lenin's strategy for bringing that about?*

Source: From *Vietnam: History, Documents, and Opinions on a Major World Crisis*, Marvin Gentleman, ed. (New York: Fawcett Publications, 1965), pp. 30–32.

military force to compete with his control over the army. But some had misgivings about Yuan's intentions. As one remarked in a letter to a friend, "We don't know whether he will be a George Washington or a Napoleon."

As it turned out, he was neither. Showing little comprehension of the new ideas sweeping into China from the West, Yuan ruled in a traditional manner, reviving Confucian rituals and institutions and eventually trying to found a new imperial dynasty. Yuan's dictatorial inclinations rapidly led to clashes with Sun's party, now renamed the Guomindang (gwoh-min-DAHNG) (Kuomintang), or Nationalist Party. When Yuan dissolved the new parliament, the Nationalists launched a rebellion. When it failed, Sun Yat-sen fled to Japan.

Yuan was strong enough to brush off the challenge from the revolutionary forces but not to turn back the clock of history. He died in 1916 and was succeeded by one of his military subordinates. For the next several years, China slipped into semianarchy as the power of the central government disintegrated and military warlords seized power in the provinces.

Mr. Science and Mr. Democracy: The New Culture Movement

In the meantime, discontent with existing conditions continued to rise. The most vocal protests came from radical intellectuals, who were now convinced that political change could not take place until the Chinese people were more familiar with trends in the outside world. Braving the displeasure of Yuan and his successors, intellectuals at Peking University launched the **New Culture Movement**, aimed at abolishing the remnants of the old system and introducing Western values and institutions. Through their classrooms and newly established progressive magazines and newspapers, the intellectuals introduced a host of new ideas, from the philosophy of Friedrich Nietzsche (FREED-rikh NEE-chuh) to the feminist plays of Henrik Ibsen. Soon educated Chinese youths were chanting "Down with Confucius and sons" and talking of a new era dominated by "Mr. Sai" (Mr. Science) and "Mr. De" (Mr. Democracy). No one was a greater defender of free thought and speech than the chancellor of Peking University, Cai Yuanpei (TSY yoo-wahn-PAY) (Ts'ai Yüan-p'ei): "Regardless of what school of thought a person may adhere to, so long as that person's ideas are justified and conform to reason and have not been passed by through the process of natural selection, although there may be controversy, such ideas have a right to be presented."[2] Not surprisingly, such views were not appreciated by conservative army officers, one of whom threatened to lob artillery shells into the university to destroy the poisonous new ideas.

Soon, however, the intellectuals' discontent was joined by a growing protest against Japan's efforts to expand its influence on the mainland. Early in the twentieth century, Japan had taken advantage of the Qing's decline to extend its domination over Manchuria and Korea (see Chapter 22). In 1915, the Japanese government insisted that Yuan Shikai accept twenty-one demands that would have given Japan a virtual protectorate over the Chinese government and economy. Yuan was able to fend off the most far-reaching demands by arousing popular outrage in China, but at the Paris Peace Conference four years later, Japan received Germany's sphere of influence in Shandong (SHAHN-doong) Province as a reward for its support of the Allied cause in World War I. On hearing that the Chinese government had accepted the decision, on May 4, 1919, patriotic students demonstrated in Beijing and other major cities. Although this May Fourth Movement did not lead to the restoration of Shandong to Chinese rule, it did alert the politically literate population to the threat to national survival and the incompetence of the warlord government.

The Nationalist-Communist Alliance

By 1920, central authority had almost ceased to exist in China. Two competing political forces now began to emerge from the chaos: Sun Yat-sen's Nationalist Party and the CCP. Following Lenin's strategy, Comintern agents advised the CCP to link up with the more experienced Nationalists. Sun Yat-sen needed the expertise and diplomatic support that Soviet Russia could provide because his anti-imperialist rhetoric had alienated many Western powers. In 1923, the two parties formed an alliance to oppose the warlords and drive the imperialist powers out of China.

For three years, the two parties submerged their mutual suspicions and mobilized a revolutionary army to march north and seize control over China. The so-called Northern Expedition began in the summer of 1926 (see Map 24.1). By the following spring, revolutionary forces were in control of all Chinese territory south of the Yangtze River, including the major river ports of Wuhan (WOO-HAHN) and Shanghai (SHANG-hy). But tensions between the two parties now surfaced. Sun Yat-sen had died in 1925 and was succeeded as head of the Nationalist Party by his military subordinate, Chiang Kai-shek (ZHANG ky-SHEK) (see the comparative illustration on p. 636). Chiang feigned support for the alliance with the Communists but actually planned to destroy them. In April 1927, he struck against the Communists in Shanghai, killing thousands. After the massacre, most of the Communist leaders went into hiding in the city, attempting to revive the movement in its traditional base among the urban working class. Some party members, however, led by the young Communist organizer Mao Zedong (mow zee-DOONG ["ow" as in "how"]) (Mao Tse-tung), fled to the hilly areas south of the Yangtze River.

Unlike most CCP leaders, Mao was convinced that the Chinese revolution must be based not on workers in the big cities but on the impoverished peasants in the countryside. The son of a prosperous farmer, Mao served as an agitator in villages in his native province of Hunan (HOO-NAHN) during the Northern Expedition in 1926. At that time, he wrote a report to the party leadership suggesting that the CCP support peasant demands for a

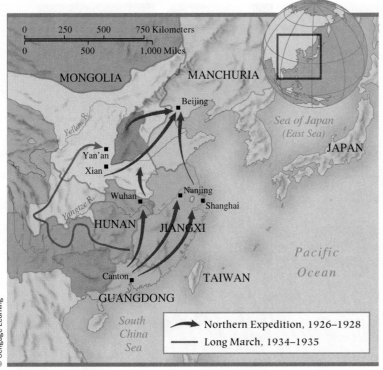

MAP 24.1 **The Northern Expedition and the Long March.** This map shows the routes taken by the combined Nationalist-Communist forces during the Northern Expedition of 1926–1928. The blue arrow indicates the route taken by Communist units during the Long March led by Mao Zedong.

Q *Where did Mao establish his new headquarters?*

land revolution (see the box on p. 637). But his superiors refused, fearing that such radical policies would destroy the alliance with the Nationalists.

The Nanjing Republic

In 1928, Chiang Kai-shek founded a new Chinese republic at Nanjing, and over the next three years, he sought to reunify China by a combination of military operations and inducements to various northern warlords to join his movement. He also attempted to put an end to the Communists, rooting them out of their urban base in Shanghai and their rural redoubt in the hills of Jiangxi (JAHNG-shee) (Kiangsi) Province. In 1931, he succeeded in forcing most party leaders to flee Shanghai for Mao's base in southern China. Three years later, Chiang's troops surrounded the Communist base in Jiangxi, causing Mao's People's Liberation Army (PLA) to embark on the famous Long March, an arduous journey of thousands of miles on foot to the provincial town of Yan'an (yuh-NAHN) (Yenan) in northern China (see Map 24.1).

Meanwhile, Chiang was trying to build a new nation. When the Nanjing Republic was established in 1928, Chiang publicly declared his commitment to Sun Yat-sen's Three People's Principles. In 1918, Sun had written about the all-important second stage of "political tutelage":

China . . . needs a republican government just as a boy needs school. As a schoolboy must have good teachers and helpful friends, so the Chinese people, being for the first time under republican rule, must have a farsighted revolutionary government for their training. This calls for the period of political tutelage, which is a necessary transitional stage from monarchy to republicanism. Without this, disorder will be unavoidable.[3]

In keeping with Sun's program, Chiang announced a period of political indoctrination to prepare the Chinese people for constitutional government. In the meantime, the Nationalists would use their power to carry out a land reform program and modernize the industrial sector.

But it would take more than paper plans to create a new China. There were faint signs of an impending industrial revolution in the major urban centers, but most people in the countryside, drained by warlord exactions and civil strife, were still grindingly poor and overwhelmingly illiterate. A westernized urban middle class had begun to emerge and formed the natural constituency of the Nanjing government. But this new westernized elite, preoccupied with individual advancement and material accumulation, had few links with the peasants or the rickshaw drivers "running in this world of suffering," in the words of a Chinese poet. Some critics dismissed Chiang and his chief followers as "banana Chinese"—yellow on the outside, white on the inside.

THE BEST OF EAST AND WEST Aware of the difficulty of introducing exotic foreign ideas into a culturally conservative society, Chiang attempted to synthesize modern Western ideas with traditional Confucian values of hard work, obedience, and moral integrity. Through the New Life Movement, sponsored by his Wellesley-educated wife, Mei-ling Soong (may-LING SOONG), Chiang sought to propagate traditional Confucian social ethics such as propriety and righteousness, while rejecting what he considered the excessive individualism and material greed of Western capitalism.

AP Images/Max Desfor

Private Collection//© Archives Charmet/The Bridgeman Art Library

COMPARATIVE ILLUSTRATION

POLITICS & GOVERNMENT

Masters and Disciples. When the founders of nationalist movements passed leadership over to their successors, the result was often a change in the movement's strategy and tactics. When Jawaharlal Nehru (left photo, on the left) replaced Mahatma Gandhi (wearing a simple Indian *dhoti* rather than the Western dress favored by his colleagues) as leader of the Indian National Congress, the movement adopted a more secular posture. In China, Chiang Kai-shek (right photo, standing) took Sun Yat-sen's Nationalist Party in a more conservative direction after Sun's death in 1925.

Q *How do these four leaders compare in terms of their roles in furthering political change in their respective countries?*

Unfortunately for Chiang, Confucian ideas—at least in their institutional form—had been widely discredited by the failure of the traditional system to solve China's problems. With only a tenuous hold over the provinces, a growing Japanese threat in the north, and a world suffering from the Great Depression, Chiang made little progress. By repressing all opposition and censoring free expression, he alienated many intellectuals and moderates. A land reform program was enacted in 1930 but had little effect.

Chiang's government also made little progress in promoting industrial development. During the decade of precarious peace following the Northern Expedition, industrial growth averaged only about 1 percent annually. Much of the national wealth was in the hands of senior officials and close subordinates of the ruling elite. Military expenses consumed half the budget, and distressingly little was devoted to social and economic development.

The new government, then, had little success in dealing with China's deep-seated economic and social problems. The deadly combination of internal disintegration and foreign pressure now began to coincide with the virtual collapse of the global economic order during the Great Depression and the rise of militant political forces in Japan determined to extend Japanese influence and power in an unstable Asia. These forces and the turmoil they unleashed will be examined in the next chapter.

"Down with Confucius and Sons": Economic, Social, and Cultural Change in Republican China

The transformation of the old order that had begun at the end of the Qing era continued during the early Chinese republic. The industrial sector continued to grow, albeit slowly. Although about 75 percent of all industrial goods were still manually produced in the early 1930s, mechanization was beginning to replace manual labor in a number of traditional industries, notably in the manufacture of textile goods. Traditional Chinese exports, such as silk and tea, were hard-hit by the Great Depression, however, and manufacturing declined during the 1930s. In the countryside, farmers were often victimized by the

A Call for Revolt

POLITICS & GOVERNMENT

In the fall of 1926, Nationalist and Communist forces moved north on their Northern Expedition to defeat the warlords. The young Communist Mao Zedong accompanied revolutionary troops to his home province of Hunan, where he submitted a report to the CCP Central Committee calling for a massive peasant revolt. The report shows his confidence that peasants could play an active role in the Chinese revolution despite the skepticism of many of his colleagues.

Mao Zedong, "The Peasant Movement in Hunan"

During my recent visit to Hunan I made a firsthand investigation of conditions. . . . In a very short time, . . . several hundred million peasants will rise like a mighty storm, . . . a force so swift and violent that no power, however great, will be able to hold it back. . . . They will sweep all the imperialists, warlords, corrupt officials, local tyrants, and evil gentry into their graves. Every revolutionary party and every revolutionary comrade will be put to the test, to be accepted or rejected as they decide. There are three alternatives. To march at their head and lead them? To trail behind them, gesticulating and criticizing? Or to stand in their way and oppose them? Every Chinese is free to choose, but events will force you to make the choice quickly.

The main targets of attack by the peasants are the local tyrants, the evil gentry and the lawless landlords, but in passing they also hit out against patriarchal ideas and institutions, against the corrupt officials in the cities and against bad practices and customs in the rural areas.

. . . As a result, the privileges which the feudal landlords enjoyed for thousands of years are being shattered to pieces. . . . With the collapse of the power of the landlords, the peasant associations have now become the sole organs of authority, and the popular slogan "All power to the peasant associations" has become a reality.

The peasants' revolt disturbed the gentry's sweet dreams. When the news from the countryside reached the cities, it caused immediate uproar among the gentry. . . . From the middle social strata upwards to the Kuomintang right-wingers, there was not a single person who did not sum up the whole business in the phrase, "It's terrible!" . . . Even quite progressive people said, "Though terrible, it is inevitable in a revolution." In short, nobody could altogether deny the word "terrible." But . . . the fact is that the great peasant masses have risen to fulfill their historic mission. . . . What the peasants are doing is absolutely right; what they are doing is fine! "It's fine!" is the theory of the peasants and of all other revolutionaries. Every revolutionary comrade should know that the national revolution requires a great change in the countryside. The Revolution of 1911 did not bring about this change, hence its failure. This change is now taking place, and it is an important factor for the completion of the revolution. Every revolutionary comrade must support it, or he will be taking the stand of counterrevolution.

Q *Why did Mao Zedong believe that the peasants could help bring about a social revolution in China? How does his vision compare with the reality of the Bolshevik Revolution in Russia?*

Source: From *Selected Works of Mao Tse-Tung* (London: Lawrence and Wishart, Ltd., 1954), Vol. 1, pp. 21–23.

---

endemic conflict and the high taxes imposed by local warlords.

SOCIAL CHANGES Social changes followed shifts in the economy and the political culture. By 1915, the assault on the old system and values by educated youth was intense. The main focus of the attack was the Confucian concept of the family—in particular, filial piety and the subordination of women. Young people insisted on the right to choose their own mates and their own

careers. Women began to demand rights and opportunities equal to those enjoyed by men (see the comparative essay "Out of the Doll's House" on p. 639). More broadly, progressives called for an end to the concept of duty to the community and praised the Western individualist ethos. The popular short story writer Lu Xun (loo SHUN) (Lu Hsun) criticized the Confucian concept of family as a "man-eating" system that degraded humanity. In a famous short story titled "Diary of a Madman," the protagonist remarks:

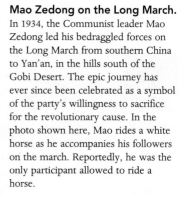

Mao Zedong on the Long March. In 1934, the Communist leader Mao Zedong led his bedraggled forces on the Long March from southern China to Yan'an, in the hills south of the Gobi Desert. The epic journey has ever since been celebrated as a symbol of the party's willingness to sacrifice for the revolutionary cause. In the photo shown here, Mao rides a white horse as he accompanies his followers on the march. Reportedly, he was the only participant allowed to ride a horse.

© Rene Burri/Magnum Photos

I remember when I was four or five years old, sitting in the cool of the hall, my brother told me that if a man's parents were ill, he should cut off a piece of his flesh and boil it for them if he wanted to be considered a good son. I have only just realized that I have been living all these years in a place where for four thousand years they have been eating human flesh.[4]

Such criticisms did have some beneficial results. During the early republic, the tyranny of the old family system began to decline, at least in urban areas, under the impact of economic changes and the urgings of the New Culture intellectuals. Women began to escape their cloistered existence and seek education and employment. Free choice in marriage became commonplace among affluent families in the cities, where the teenage children of westernized elites aped the clothing, social habits, and even the musical tastes of their contemporaries in Europe and the United States.

But, as a rule, the new individualism and women's rights did not penetrate to the textile factories, where more than a million women worked in conditions resembling slave labor, or to the villages, where traditional attitudes and customs still held sway. Arranged marriages continued to be the rule rather than the exception, and concubinage remained common. According to a survey taken in the 1930s, well over two-thirds of the marriages even among urban couples had been arranged by their parents (see the box on p. 640).

A NEW CULTURE Nowhere was the struggle between traditional and modern more visible than in the area of culture. Beginning in the New Culture era, radical reformists criticized traditional culture as the symbol and instrument of feudal oppression. During the 1920s and 1930s, Western literature and art became highly popular, especially among the urban middle class. Traditional culture continued to prevail among more conservative elements, however, and some intellectuals argued for a new art that would synthesize the best of Chinese and foreign culture. But the most creative artists were interested in imitating foreign trends, while traditionalists were more concerned with preservation.

Literature in particular was influenced by foreign ideas. Although most Chinese novels written after World War I dealt with Chinese subjects, they reflected the Western tendency toward social realism and often dealt with the new westernized middle class, as in *Midnight* by Mao Dun (mow DOON ["ow" as in "how"]), which describes the changing mores of Shanghai's urban elites. Another favorite theme was the disintegration of the traditional Confucian family—Ba Jin's novel *Family* is an example. Most of China's modern authors displayed a clear contempt for the past.

CHRONOLOGY	Revolution in China
May Fourth demonstrations	1919
Formation of Chinese Communist Party	1921
Death of Sun Yat-sen	1925
Northern Expedition	1926–1928
Establishment of Nanjing Republic	1928
Long March	1934–1935

Out of the Doll's House

FAMILY & SOCIETY

In Henrik Ibsen's play *A Doll's House* (1879), Nora Helmer informs her husband, Torvald, that she will no longer accept his control over her life and announces her intention to leave home to start her life anew (see the box on p. 531). When the outraged Torvald cites her sacred duties as wife and mother, Nora replies that she has other duties just as sacred, those to herself. "I can no longer be satisfied with what most people say," she declares. "I must think things out for myself."

To Ibsen's contemporaries, such remarks were revolutionary. In nineteenth-century Europe, the traditional characterization of the sexes, based on gender-defined social roles, had been elevated to a universal law. As the family wage earners, men went off to work, while women stayed home to care for home and family. Women were advised to accept their lot and play their role as effectively and gracefully as possible. In other parts of the world, women generally had even fewer rights. Often, as in traditional China, they were viewed as sex objects.

The ideal, however, did not always match the reality. With the advent of the Industrial Revolution, many women, especially those in the lower classes, were driven by the need for supplemental income to seek employment outside the home. Some women, inspired by the ideals of human dignity and freedom expressed during the Enlightenment and the French Revolution, began to protest against a tradition of female inferiority that had long kept them in a "doll's house" of male domination and to claim equal rights before the law.

© Marc Charmet/CCI/The Art Archive at Art Resource, NY

The Chinese "Doll's House." A woman in traditional China binding her feet.

The movement to liberate women first gained ground in English-speaking countries such as Great Britain and the United States, but it gradually spread to the European continent and then to colonies in Africa and Asia. By the early twentieth century, women's liberation movements were under way in parts of North Africa, the Middle East, and East Asia, calling for access to education, equal treatment before the law, and the right to vote. In China, a small minority of educated women began to agitate for equal rights with men.

Progress, however, was often agonizingly slow, especially in societies where traditional values had not been undermined by the Industrial Revolution. Colonialism had also been a double-edged sword, as the sexist bias of European officials combined with indigenous traditions of male superiority to marginalize women even further. As men moved to the cities to exploit opportunities provided by the colonial administration, women were left to cope with their traditional responsibilities in the villages, often without the safety net of male support that had sustained them during the precolonial era. With the advent of nationalist movements, the drive for women's rights in many colonial societies was subordinated to the goal of national independence. In some instances, too, women's liberation movements were led by educated elites who failed to take note of the concerns of working-class women.

Q *To what extent, if at all, did women benefit from the policies applied by the Europeans in their colonies?*

An Arranged Marriage

FAMILY & SOCIETY

Under Western influence, Chinese social customs changed dramatically for many urban elites in the interwar years. A vocal women's movement campaigned aggressively for universal suffrage and an end to sexual discrimination. Some progressives called for free choice in marriage and divorce and even for free love. By the 1930s, the government had taken some steps to free women from patriarchal marriage constraints. But life was generally unaffected in the villages, where traditional patterns held sway. This often created severe tensions between older and younger generations, as this passage from a novel by the popular twentieth-century writer Ba Jin (BAH JIN) shows.

Ba Jin, *Family*

Brought up with loving care, after studying with a private tutor for a number of years, Chueh-hsin entered middle school. One of the school's best students, he graduated four years later at the top of his class. He was very interested in physics and chemistry and hoped to study abroad, in Germany. . . .

In his fourth year at middle school, he lost his mother. . . . Chueh-hsin was aware of his loss, for he knew full well that nothing could replace the love of a mother. But her death left no irreparable wound in his heart; he was able to console himself with rosy dreams of his future. Moreover, he had someone who understood him and could comfort him—his pretty cousin Mei, "mei" for "plum blossom."

But then, one day, his dreams were shattered, cruelly and bitterly shattered. The evening he returned home carrying his diploma, the plaudits of his teachers and friends still ringing in his ears, his father called him into his room and said:

"Now that you've graduated, I want to arrange your marriage. Your grandfather is looking forward to having a great-grandson, and I, too, would like to be able to hold a grandson in my arms. You're old enough to be married; I won't feel easy until I fulfill my obligation to find you a wife. Although I didn't accumulate much money in my years away from home as an official, still I've put by enough for us to get along on. My health isn't what it used to be; I'm thinking of spending my time at home and having you help me run the household affairs. All the more reason you'll be needing a wife. I've already arranged a match with the Li family. The thirteenth of next month is a good day. We'll announce the engagement then. You can be married within the year. . . ."

Chueh-hsin did not utter a word of protest, nor did such a thought ever occur to him. He merely nodded to indicate his compliance with his father's wishes. But after he returned to his own room, and shut the door, he threw himself down on his bed, covered his head with the quilt and wept. He wept for his broken dreams.

He was deeply in love with Mei, but now his father had chosen another, a girl he had never seen, and said that he must marry within the year. What's more, his hopes of continuing his studies had burst like a bubble. It was a terrible shock to Chueh-hsin. His future was finished, his beautiful dreams shattered.

He cried his disappointment and bitterness. But the door was closed and Chueh-hsin's head was beneath the bedding. No one knew. He did not fight back, he never thought of resisting. He only bemoaned his fate. But he accepted it. He complied with his father's will without a trace of resentment. But in his heart he wept for himself, wept for the girl he adored—Mei, his "plum blossom."

 Why does Chueh-hsin comply with the wishes of his father in the matter of his marriage? Why were arranged marriages so prevalent in traditional China?

Japan Between the Wars

Q FOCUS QUESTION: How did Japan address the problems of nation building in the first decades of the twentieth century, and why did democratic institutions not take hold more effectively?

During the first two decades of the twentieth century, Japan made remarkable progress toward the creation of an advanced society on the Western model. The political system based on the Meiji Constitution of 1890 began to evolve along Western pluralistic lines, and a multiparty system took shape. The economic and social reforms launched during the Meiji era led to increasing prosperity and the development of a modern industrial and commercial sector.

Experiment in Democracy

During the first quarter of the twentieth century, Japanese political parties expanded their popular following and became increasingly competitive. Individual pressure groups began to appear, along with an independent press and a bill of rights. The influence of the old ruling oligarchy, the *genro*, had not yet been significantly challenged,

however, nor had that of its ideological foundation, the *kokutai* (koh-kuh-TY).

These fragile democratic institutions were able to survive throughout the 1920s, often called the era of **Taisho** (TY-SHOH) **democracy**, from the reign title of the emperor. During this period, the military budget was reduced, and a suffrage bill enacted in 1925 granted the vote to all Japanese males. Although women were still disenfranchised, many women were active in the labor movement and in campaigning for social reforms.

But the era was also marked by growing social turmoil, and two opposing forces within the system were gearing up to challenge the prevailing wisdom. On the left, a Marxist labor movement began to take shape in the early 1920s. On the right, ultranationalist groups called for a rejection of Western models of development and a more militant approach to realizing national objectives.

This cultural conflict between old and new, indigenous and foreign, was reflected in literature. Japanese self-confidence had been restored after the victories over China and Russia and launched an age of cultural creativity in the early twentieth century. Fascination with Western literature gave birth to a striking new genre called the "I novel." Defying traditional Japanese reticence, some

Geishas, Old and New. The geisha (GAY-shuh) ("accomplished person") was a symbol of old Japan. Dressed in traditional costumes, her body movements highly stylized, she served not only as an entertainer and an ornament but also as a beautiful purveyor of elite Japanese culture. That image was dramatically transformed in a new Japan that had been inundated by the influence of the modern West. In the photo on the left, geishas in early-twentieth-century Tokyo mimic Western fashions and dance positions. In the photo on the right, three young Japanese women in traditional costumes stroll in contemporary Kyoto.

authors reveled in self-exposure with confessions of their innermost thoughts. Others found release in the "proletarian literature" movement of the early 1920s. Inspired by Soviet literary examples, these authors wanted literature to serve socialist goals and improve the lives of the working class. Finally, some Japanese writers blended Western psychology with Japanese sensibility in exquisite novels reeking with nostalgia for the old Japan. One well-known example is *Some Prefer Nettles* (1929) by Junichiro Tanizaki (jun-ih-CHEE-roh tan-ih-ZAH-kee), which delicately juxtaposed the positive aspects of both traditional and modern Japan. By the 1930s, however, military censorship increasingly inhibited free literary expression.

A *Zaibatsu* Economy

Japan also continued to make impressive progress in economic development. Spurred by rising domestic demand and continued government investment in the economy, the production of raw materials tripled between 1900 and 1930, and industrial production increased more than twelvefold. Much of the increase went into exports, and Western manufacturers began to complain about competition from the Japanese.

As often happens, rapid industrialization was accompanied by some hardship and rising social tensions. In the Meiji model, various manufacturing processes were concentrated in a single enterprise, the *zaibatsu* (zy-BAHT-soo), or financial clique. Some of these firms were existing companies that had the capital and the foresight to move into new areas. Others were formed by enterprising samurai, who used their status and managerial experience to good account in a new environment. Whatever their origins, these firms, often with official encouragement, developed into large conglomerates that controlled major segments of the Japanese economy. By 1937, the four largest *zaibatsu*—Mitsui (MIT-swee), Mitsubishi (mit-soo-BEE-shee), Sumitomo (soo-mee-TOH-moh), and Yasuda (yah-SOO-duh)—controlled 21 percent of the banking industry, 26 percent of mining, 35 percent of shipbuilding, 38 percent of commercial shipping, and more than 60 percent of paper manufacturing and insurance.

This concentration of power and wealth in a few industrial combines created problems in Japanese society. In the first place, it resulted in the emergence of a dual economy: on the one hand, a modern industry characterized by up-to-date methods and massive government subsidies, and on the other, a traditional manufacturing sector characterized by conservative methods and small-scale production techniques.

Concentration of wealth also led to growing economic inequalities. As we have seen, economic growth had been achieved at the expense of the peasants, many of whom fled to the cities to escape rural poverty. That labor surplus benefited the industrial sector, but the urban proletariat was still poorly paid and ill-housed. A rapid increase in population (the total population of the Japanese islands increased from an estimated 43 million in 1900 to 73 million in 1940) led to food shortages and

The Great Tokyo Earthquake. On September 1, 1923, a massive earthquake struck the central Japanese island of Honshu, causing more than 130,000 deaths and virtually demolishing the capital city of Tokyo. Though the quake was a national tragedy, it also came to symbolize the ingenuity of the Japanese people, who rapidly reconstructed the city in a new and more modern style. That unity of national purpose would be demonstrated again a quarter of a century later in Japan's swift recovery from the devastation of World War II.

© Topical Press Agency/Getty Images

rising unemployment. In the meantime, those left on the farm continued to suffer. As late as the beginning of World War II, an estimated one-half of all Japanese farmers were tenants.

Shidehara Diplomacy

A final problem for Japanese leaders in the post-Meiji era was the familiar dilemma of finding sources of raw materials and foreign markets for the nation's manufactured goods. Until World War I, Japan had dealt with the problem by seizing territories such as Taiwan, Korea, and southern Manchuria and transforming them into colonies or protectorates. That policy had begun to arouse the concern and, in some cases, the hostility of the Western nations. China was also becoming apprehensive; as we have seen, Japanese demands for Shandong Province at the Paris Peace Conference in 1919 aroused massive protests in China.

The United States was especially concerned about Japanese aggressiveness. Although the United States had been less active than some European states in pursuing colonies in the Pacific, it had a strong interest in keeping the area open for U.S. commercial activities. In 1922, in Washington, D.C., the United States convened a major conference of nations with interests in the Pacific to discuss problems of regional security. The Washington Conference led to agreements on several issues, but the major accomplishment was a nine-power treaty recognizing the territorial integrity of China and the Open Door. The other participants induced Japan to accept these provisions by accepting its special position in Manchuria.

During the remainder of the 1920s, Japan attempted to play by the rules laid down at the Washington Conference. Known as Shidehara (shee-deh-HAH-rah) diplomacy, after the foreign minister (and later prime minister) who attempted to carry it out, this policy sought to achieve Japanese interests in Asia through diplomatic and economic means. But this approach came under severe pressure as Japanese industrialists began to move into new areas, such as chemicals, mining, and the manufacturing of appliances and automobiles. Because such industries needed resources not found in abundance locally, the Japanese government came under increasing pressure to find new sources abroad.

THE RISE OF MILITANT NATIONALISM In the early 1930s, with the onset of the Great Depression and growing tensions in the international arena, nationalist forces rose to dominance in the Japanese government. The changes that occurred in the 1930s, which we shall discuss in Chapter 25, were not in the constitution or the institutional structure, which remained essentially intact, but in the composition and attitudes of the ruling group. Party leaders during the 1920s had attempted to realize Tokyo's aspirations within the existing global political and economic framework. The military officers and ultra-nationalist politicians who dominated the government in the 1930s were convinced that the diplomacy of the 1920s had failed and advocated a more aggressive approach to protecting national interests in a brutal and competitive world.

TAISHO DEMOCRACY: AN ABERRATION? The dramatic shift in Japanese political culture that occurred in the early 1930s has caused some historians to question the breadth and depth of the trend toward democratic practices in the 1920s. Was Taisho democracy merely a fragile attempt at comparative liberalization in a framework dominated by the Meiji vision of empire and *kokutai*? Or was the militant nationalism of the 1930s an aberration brought on by the Great Depression, which caused the inexorable emergence of democracy in Japan to stall?

Clearly, there is some truth in both contentions. A process of democratization was taking place in Japan during the first decades of the twentieth century, but without shaking the essential core of the Meiji concept of the state. When the "liberal" approach of the 1920s failed to solve the problems of the day, the shallow roots of democracy in Japan were exposed, and the shift toward a more aggressive approach became inevitable.

Still, the course of Japanese history after World War II (see Chapter 30) suggests that the emergence of multiparty democracy in the 1920s was not an aberration but a natural consequence of evolutionary trends in Japanese society. The seeds of democracy nurtured during the Taisho era were nipped in the bud by the cataclysmic effects of the Great Depression, but in the more conducive climate after World War II, a democratic system—suitably adjusted to Japanese soil—reached full flower.

Nationalism and Dictatorship in Latin America

Q FOCUS QUESTIONS: What problems did the nations of Latin America face in the interwar years? To what degree were they a consequence of foreign influence?

Although the nations of Latin America played little role in World War I, that conflict nevertheless exerted an impact on the region, especially on its economy. By the end of the 1920s, the region was also strongly influenced by another event of global proportions—the Great Depression.

A Changing Economy

At the beginning of the twentieth century, virtually all of Latin America, except the three Guianas, British Honduras, and some of the Caribbean islands, had achieved independence (see Map 24.2). The economy of the region was based largely on the export of foodstuffs and raw materials. Some countries relied on exports of only one or two products. Argentina, for example, exported primarily beef and wheat; Chile, nitrates and copper; Brazil and the Caribbean nations, sugar; and the Central American states, bananas. A few reaped large profits from these exports, but for the majority of the population, the returns were meager.

THE ROLE OF THE YANKEE DOLLAR   World War I led to a decline in European investment in Latin America and a rise in the U.S. role in the local economies. By the late 1920s, the United States had replaced Great Britain as the foremost source of investment in Latin America. Unlike the British, however, U.S. investors put their funds directly into production enterprises, causing large segments of the area's export industries to fall into American hands. A number of Central American states, for example, were popularly labeled "banana republics" because of the power and influence of the U.S.-owned United Fruit Company. American firms also dominated the copper mining industry in Chile and Peru and the oil industry in Mexico, Peru, and Bolivia.

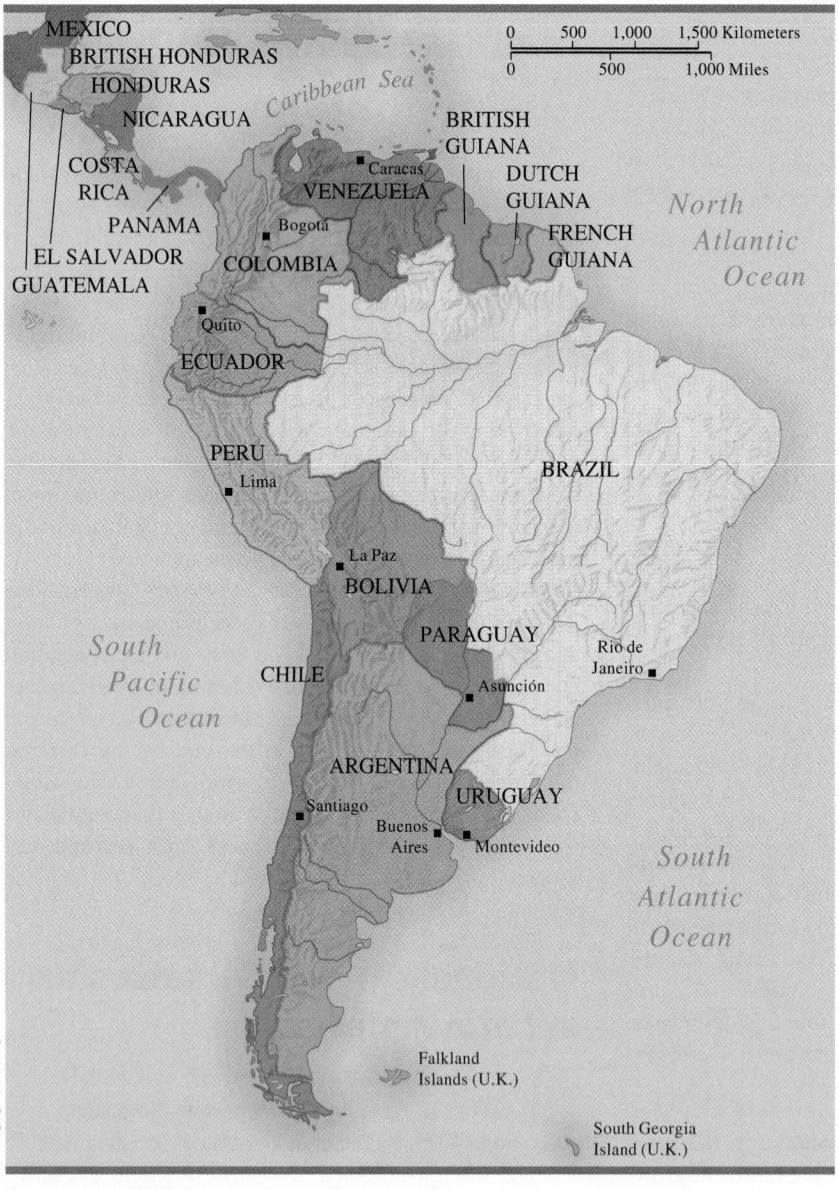

The Effects of Dependency

During the late nineteenth century, most governments in Latin America had been increasingly dominated by landed or military elites, who controlled the mass of the population—mostly impoverished peasants—by the blatant use of military force. This trend toward authoritarianism increased during the 1930s as domestic instability caused by the effects of the Great Depression led to the creation of dictatorships throughout the region. This trend was especially evident in Argentina and Brazil and to a lesser degree in Mexico—three countries that together possessed more than half of the land and wealth of Latin America.

MAP 24.2 Latin America in the First Half of the Twentieth Century. Shown here are the boundaries dividing the countries of Latin America after the independence movements of the nineteenth century.

Q *Which areas remained under European rule?*

ARGENTINA The political domination of Argentina by an elite minority often had disastrous effects. The Argentine government, controlled by landowners who had benefited from the export of beef and wheat, was slow to recognize the importance of establishing a local industrial base. In 1916, Hipólito Irigoyen (ee-POH-lee-toh ee-ree-GOH-yen) (1852–1933), head of the Radical Party, was elected president on a program to improve conditions for the middle and lower classes. Little was achieved, however, as the party became increasingly corrupt and drew closer to the large landowners. In 1930, the army overthrew Irigoyen's government and reestablished the power of the landed class. But their efforts to return to the previous export economy and suppress the growing influence of the labor unions failed.

BRAZIL Brazil followed a similar path. In 1889, the army replaced the Brazilian monarchy with a republic, but it was controlled by landed elites, many of whom derived their wealth from vast rubber and coffee plantations. Exports of Brazilian rubber dominated the world market until just before World War I. When it proved easier to produce rubber in Southeast Asia, however, Brazilian exports suddenly collapsed, leaving the economy of the Amazon River basin in ruins.

The coffee industry also suffered problems. In 1900, three-quarters of the world's coffee was grown in Brazil. As in Argentina, the ruling oligarchy ignored the importance of establishing an urban industrial base. When the Great Depression ravaged profits from coffee exports, a wealthy rancher, Getúlio Vargas (zhi-TOO-lyoo VAHR-guhs) (1883–1954), seized power and ruled the country as president from 1930 to 1945. At first, Vargas sought to appease workers by instituting an eight-hour workday and a minimum wage, but influenced by the apparent success of fascist regimes in Europe, he ruled by increasingly autocratic means and relied on a police force that used torture to silence his opponents. His industrial policy was relatively enlightened, however, and by the end of World War II, Brazil had become Latin America's major industrial power. In 1945, the army, fearing that Vargas might prolong his power illegally after calling for new elections, forced him to resign.

MEXICO After the dictator Porfirio Díaz (por-FEER-yoh DEE-ahs) was ousted from power in 1910 (see Chapter 20), Mexico entered a state of turbulence that lasted for years. The ineffective leaders who followed Díaz were unable to solve the country's economic problems or bring an end to the civil strife. In southern Mexico, the landless peasants responded eagerly to Emiliano Zapata (ee-mee-LYAH-noh zup-PAH-tuh) (1879–1919), when he called for agrarian reform and began to seize the haciendas of wealthy landholders.

Hipólito Irigoyen becomes president of Argentina	1916
Argentinian military overthrows Irigoyen	1930
Rule of Getúlio Vargas in Brazil	1930–1945
Beginning of Good Neighbor policy	1933
Presidency of Lázaro Cárdenas in Mexico	1934–1940

For the next several years, Zapata and rebel leader Pancho Villa (pahn-CHOH VEE-uh) (1878–1923), who operated in the northern state of Chihuahua (chih-WAH-wah), became an important political force by calling for measures to redress the grievances of the poor. But neither fully grasped the challenges facing the country, and power eventually gravitated to a more moderate group of reformists around the Constitutionalist Party. They were intent on breaking the power of the great landed families and U.S. corporations, but without engaging in radical land reform or the nationalization of property. After a bloody conflict that cost the lives of thousands, the moderates consolidated power, and in 1917, they promulgated a new constitution that established a strong presidency, initiated land reform, established limits on foreign investment, and set an agenda for social welfare programs.

In 1920, the Constitutionalist Party leader Alvaro Obregón (AHL-vah-roh oh-bree-GAHN) assumed the presidency and began to carry out his reform program. But real change did not take place until the presidency of General Lázaro Cárdenas (LAH-zah-roh KAHR-day-nahss) (1895–1970) in 1934. Cárdenas ordered the redistribution of 44 million acres of land controlled by landed elites and seized control of the oil industry, which had hitherto been dominated by major U.S. oil companies. In 1933, in a bid to improve relations with Latin American countries, U.S. President Franklin D. Roosevelt had announced the **Good Neighbor policy**, which renounced the use of U.S. military force in the region. Now Roosevelt refused to intervene, and eventually Mexico agreed to compensate U.S. oil companies for their lost property. It then set up PEMEX, a governmental organization, to run the oil industry.

Latin American Culture

The first half of the twentieth century witnessed a dramatic increase in literary activity in Latin America. Much of it reflected the region's ambivalent relationship with Europe and the United States. Many authors, while experimenting with imported modernist styles, also used native themes and social issues to express Latin America's unique identity. In *The Underdogs* (1915), for example,

Struggle for the Banner. Like Diego Rivera, David Alfaro Siqueiros (dah-VEED al-FAHR-oh see-KAY-rohss) (1896–1974) decorated public buildings with large murals that celebrated the Mexican Revolution and the workers' and peasants' struggle for freedom. Beginning in the 1930s, Siqueiros expressed sympathy for the exploited and downtrodden peoples of Mexico in dramatic frescoes such as this one. He painted similar murals in Uruguay, Argentina, and Brazil and was once expelled from the United States, where his political art and views were considered too radical.

Mariano Azuela (mahr-YAHN-oh ah-SWAY-luh) (1873–1952) presented a sympathetic but not uncritical portrait of the Mexican Revolution.

Some writers extolled the region's vast virgin lands and the diversity of its peoples. In *Don Segundo Sombra* (1926), Ricardo Guiraldes (ree-KAHR-doh gwee-RAHL-dess) (1886–1927) celebrated the life of the gaucho (cowboy), defining Argentina's hope and strength as the enlightened management of its fertile earth. In *Dona Barbara* (1929), Romulo Gallegos (ROH-moo-loh gay-YAY-gohs) (1884–1969) wrote in a similar vein about his native Venezuela. Other authors pursued the theme of solitude and detachment, reflecting the region's physical separation from the rest of the world.

Latin American artists followed their literary counterparts in joining the Modernist movement in Europe, yet they too were eager to celebrate the emergence of a new regional and national essence. In Mexico, where the government provided financial support for painting murals on public buildings, the artist Diego Rivera (DYAY-goh rih-VAIR-uh) (1886–1957) began to produce a monumental style of mural art that served two purposes: to illustrate the national past by portraying Aztec legends and folk customs and to popularize a political message in favor of realizing the social goals of the Mexican Revolution. His wife, Frida Kahlo (FREE-duh KAH-loh) (1907–1954), incorporated Surrealist whimsy in her own paintings, many of which were portraits of herself and her family.

CHAPTER SUMMARY

The turmoil brought about by World War I not only resulted in the destruction of several major Western empires and a redrawing of the map of Europe but also opened the door to political and social upheavals elsewhere in the world. In the Middle East, the decline and fall of the Ottoman Empire led to the creation of the secular republic of Turkey. The state of Saudi Arabia emerged in the Arabian peninsula, and Palestine became a source of tension between newly arrived Jewish immigrants and longtime Muslim residents.

Other parts of Asia and Africa also witnessed the rise of movements for national independence. In many cases, these movements were spearheaded by local leaders who had been educated in Europe or the United States. In India, Mahatma Gandhi and his campaign of civil disobedience played a crucial role in his country's bid to be free of British rule. Communist movements also began to emerge in Asian societies as radical elements sought new methods of bringing about the overthrow of Western imperialism. Japan continued to follow its own path to modernization, which, although successful from an economic perspective, took a menacing turn during the 1930s.

Between 1919 and 1939, China experienced a dramatic struggle to establish a modern nation. Two dynamic political organizations—the Nationalists and the Communists—competed for legitimacy as the rightful heirs of the old order. At first, they formed an alliance in an effort to defeat their common adversaries, but cooperation ultimately turned to conflict. The Nationalists under Chiang Kai-shek emerged supreme, but Chiang found it difficult to control the remnants of the warlord regime in China, while the Great Depression undermined his efforts to build an industrial nation.

During the interwar years, the nations of Latin America faced severe economic problems because of their dependence on exports. Increasing U.S. investments in Latin America contributed to growing hostility toward the powerful neighbor to the north. The Great Depression forced the region to begin developing new industries, but it also led to the rise of authoritarian governments, some of them modeled after the fascist regimes of Italy and Germany.

By demolishing the remnants of their old civilization on the battlefields of World War I, Europeans had inadvertently encouraged the subject peoples of their vast colonial empires to begin their own movements for national independence. The process was by no means completed in the two decades following the Treaty of Versailles, but the bonds of imperial rule had been severely strained. Once Europeans began to weaken themselves in the even more destructive conflict of World War II, the hopes of African and Asian peoples for national independence and freedom could at last be realized. It is to that devastating world conflict that we must now turn.

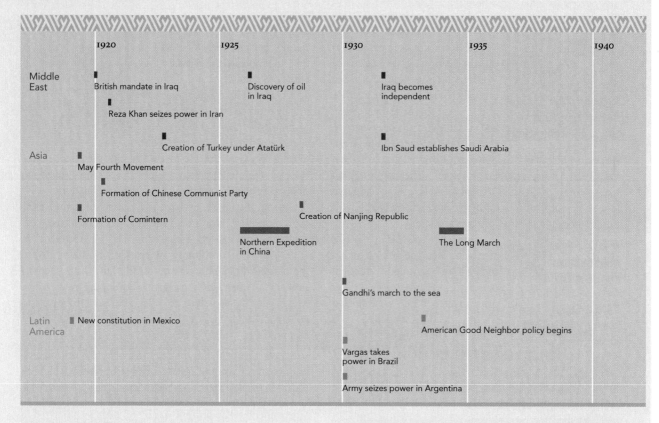

Timeline labels:

1920   1925   1930   1935   1940

Middle East
- British mandate in Iraq
- Reza Khan seizes power in Iran
- Discovery of oil in Iraq
- Iraq becomes independent

Asia
- Creation of Turkey under Atatürk
- Ibn Saud establishes Saudi Arabia
- May Fourth Movement
- Formation of Chinese Communist Party
- Formation of Comintern
- Creation of Nanjing Republic
- Northern Expedition in China
- The Long March
- Gandhi's march to the sea

Latin America
- New constitution in Mexico
- American Good Neighbor policy begins
- Vargas takes power in Brazil
- Army seizes power in Argentina

CHAPTER REVIEW

Upon Reflection

Q In what ways did Japan's political system and social structure in the interwar years combine modern and traditional elements? How successful was the attempt to create a modern political system while retaining indigenous traditions of civil obedience and loyalty to the emperor?

Q During the early twentieth century did conditions for women change for the better or for the worse in the countries discussed in this chapter? Why?

Q Communist parties were established in many Asian societies in the years immediately following the Bolshevik Revolution. How successful were these parties in winning popular support and achieving their goals?

Key Terms

satyagraha (p. 625)
civil disobedience (p. 625)
Young Turks (p. 627)
Communist International (Comintern) (p. 632)

New Culture Movement (p. 634)
Taisho democracy (p. 641)
zaibatsu (p. 642)
Good Neighbor policy (p. 645)

Suggested Reading

NATIONALISM The most up-to-date survey of modern nationalism is **E. Gellner,** *Nations and Nationalism,* 2nd ed. (Ithaca, N.Y., 2009), but it has little to say about the non-Western world. For a provocative study of the roots of nationalism in Asia, see **B. Anderson,** *Imagined Communities: Reflections on the Origins and Spread of Nationalism* (London, 1983).

INDIA There have been a number of studies of Mahatma Gandhi and his ideas. See, for example, **S. Wolpert,** *Gandhi's Passion: The Life and Legacy of Mahatma Gandhi* (Oxford, 1999), and **D. Dalton,** *Mahatma Gandhi: Nonviolent Power in Action* (New York, 1995). For a study of Nehru, see **J. M. Brown,** *Nehru* (New York, 2000).

MIDDLE EAST For a general survey of events in the Middle East in the interwar era, see **E. Bogle,** *The*

Modern Middle East: From Imperialism to Freedom (Upper Saddle River, N.J., 1996). For more specialized studies, see **I. Gershoni et al.,** *Egypt, Islam, and the Arabs: The Search for Egyptian Nationhood* (Oxford, 1993), and **W. Laqueur,** *A History of Zionism: From the French Revolution to the Establishment of the State of Israel* (New York, 1996). The role of Atatürk is examined in **A. Mango,** *Atatürk: The Biography of the Founder of Modern Turkey* (New York, 2000). The Palestinian issue is dealt with in **B. Morris,** *Righteous Victims: The Palestinian Conflict, 1880–2000* (New York, 2001). On the founding of Iraq, see **S. Mackey,** *The Reckoning: Iraq and the Legacy of Saddam Hussein* (New York, 2002). For a penetrating account of the fall of the Ottoman Empire and its consequences for the postwar era, see **D. Fromkin,** *A Peace to End All Peace: The Fall of the Ottoman Empire and the Creation of the Modern Middle East* (New York, 2001).

CHINA AND JAPAN On the early Chinese republic, a good study is **J. Fitzgerald,** *Awakening China: Politics, Culture, and Class in the Nationalist Revolution* (Stanford, Calif., 1996). The rise of the Chinese Communist Party is charted in **A. Dirlik,** *The Origins of Chinese Communism* (Oxford, 1989). Also see **J. Taylor,** *The Generalissimo: Chiang Kai-shek and the Struggle for Modern China* (Cambridge, Mass., 2009). On Japan, see **J. McLain,** *Japan: A Modern History* (New York, 2001).

LATIN AMERICA For an overview of Latin American history during the interwar period, see **J. Chasteen,** *Born in Blood and Fire: A Concise History of Latin America,* 2nd ed. (New York, 2005). For documents, see **J. Wood** and **J. Chasteen, eds.,** *Problems in Latin American History: Sources and Interpretations,* 3rd ed. (New York, 2009).

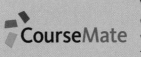

Visit the CourseMate website at www.cengagebrain.com for additional study tools and review materials for this chapter.

The Crisis Deepens: World War II

Adolf Hitler salutes military leaders and soldiers during a military rally.

CHAPTER OUTLINE AND FOCUS QUESTIONS

Retreat from Democracy: Dictatorial Regimes

Q What are the characteristics of totalitarian states, and to what degree were these characteristics present in Fascist Italy, Nazi Germany, and Stalinist Russia? To what extent was Japan a totalitarian state?

The Path to War

Q What were the underlying causes of World War II, and what specific steps taken by Nazi Germany and Japan led to war?

World War II

Q What were the main events of World War II in Europe and Asia?

The New Order

Q What was the nature of the new orders that Germany and Japan attempted to establish in the territories they occupied?

The Home Front

Q What were conditions like on the home front for the major belligerents in World War II?

Aftermath of the War

Q What were the costs of World War II? How did World War II affect the European nations' colonial empires? How did the Allies' visions of the postwar differ, and how did these differences contribute to the emergence of the Cold War?

CRITICAL THINKING

Q What was the relationship between World War I and World War II, and how did the ways in which the wars were fought differ?

ON FEBRUARY 3, 1933, three days after he had been appointed chancellor of Germany, Adolf Hitler met secretly with Germany's leading generals. He revealed to them his desire to remove the "cancer of democracy," create a new authoritarian leadership, and forge a new domestic unity. All Germans would need to realize that "only a struggle can save us and that everything else must be subordinated to this idea." Since Germany's living space was too small for its people, Hitler said, Germany must rearm and prepare for "the conquest of new living space in the east and its ruthless Germanization." Even before he had consolidated his power, Adolf Hitler had a clear vision of his goals, and their implementation meant another war.

World War II in Europe was clearly Hitler's war. Although other countries may have helped make the war possible by not resisting Hitler earlier, it was Nazi Germany's actions that made World War II inevitable.

But World War II was more than just Hitler's war. It was in fact two separate and parallel conflicts, one provoked by the ambitions of Germany in Europe and the other by the ambitions of Japan in Asia. Around the same time that Hitler was consolidating his power in the early 1930s, the United States and major European nations raised the tariffs they imposed on Japanese imports in a desperate effort to protect local businesses and jobs. In response, militant groups in Tokyo began to argue that Japan must obtain by violent action what it could not secure by peaceful means. By 1941, when the United States became embroiled in both wars, the two had merged into a single global conflict.

Although World War I had been described as a total war, World War II was even more so and was fought on a scale unheard of in history. Almost everyone in the warring countries was involved in one way or another: as soldiers; as workers in wartime industries; as ordinary citizens subject to invading armies, military occupation, or bombing raids; as refugees; or as victims of mass extermination. The world had never witnessed such widespread human-induced death and destruction.

Retreat from Democracy: Dictatorial Regimes

Q FOCUS QUESTIONS: What are the characteristics of totalitarian states, and to what degree were these characteristics present in Fascist Italy, Nazi Germany, and Stalinist Russia? To what extent was Japan a totalitarian state?

The rise of dictatorial regimes in the 1930s had a great deal to do with the coming of World War II. By 1939, only two major states in Europe, France and Great Britain, remained democratic. Italy and Germany had succumbed to the political movement called **fascism**, and Soviet Russia under Stalin moved toward repressive totalitarianism. A host of other European states and Latin American countries adopted authoritarian structures of various kinds, while a militarist regime in Japan moved that country down the path to war.

The dictatorial regimes between the wars assumed both old and new forms. Dictatorship was not new, but the modern **totalitarian state** was. The totalitarian regimes, best exemplified by Stalinist Russia and Nazi Germany, greatly extended the functions and power of the central state. The new "total states" expected the active loyalty and commitment of citizens to the regime's

goal, whether it be war, a socialist society, or a thousand-year Reich (RYKH) (empire). They used modern mass propaganda techniques and high-speed communications to conquer the minds and hearts of their subjects. The total state sought to control not only the economic, political, and social aspects of life but the intellectual and cultural aspects as well.

The modern totalitarian state was to be led by a single leader and a single party. It ruthlessly rejected the liberal ideal of limited government power and constitutional guarantees of individual freedoms. Indeed, individual freedom was to be subordinated to the collective will of the masses, organized and determined for them by the leader or leaders. Modern technology also gave total states unprecedented police controls to enforce their wishes on their subjects.

The Birth of Fascism

In the early 1920s, Benito Mussolini (buh-NEE-toh moos-suh-LEE-nee) (1883–1945) bestowed on Italy the first successful fascist movement in Europe. In 1919, Mussolini, a veteran of World War I, had established a new political group, the *Fascio di Combattimento* (FASH-ee-oh dee com-bat-ee-MEN-toh) (League of Combat), which won support from middle-class industrialists fearful of working-class agitation and large landowners who objected to strikes by farmers. The movement gained momentum as Mussolini's nationalist rhetoric and the middle-class fear of socialism, Communist revolution, and disorder made the Fascists seem more and more attractive. On October 29, 1922, after Mussolini and the Fascists threatened to march on Rome if they were not given power, King Victor Emmanuel (1900–1946) capitulated and made Mussolini prime minister of Italy.

By 1926, Mussolini had established the institutional framework for a Fascist dictatorship. The prime minister was made "head of government" with the power to legislate by decree. A law empowered the police to arrest and confine anybody for both nonpolitical and political crimes without pressing charges. The government was given the power to dissolve political and cultural associations. In 1926, all anti-Fascist parties were outlawed, and a secret police force was established. By the end of the year, Mussolini ruled Italy as *Il Duce* (eel DOO-chay), the leader.

Mussolini conceived of the Fascist state as totalitarian: "Fascism is totalitarian, and the Fascist State, the synthesis and unity of all values, interprets, develops and gives strength to the whole life of the people."[1] Mussolini did try to create a police state, but it was not very effective. Likewise, the Italian Fascists' attempt to exercise control over all forms of mass media, including newspapers, radio, and cinema, so that they could use propaganda as an instrument to integrate the masses into the state, was rarely effective. Most commonly, Fascist propaganda was disseminated through simple slogans, such as "Mussolini is always right," plastered on walls all over Italy.

The Fascists portrayed the family as the pillar of the state and women as the basic foundation of the family. "Woman into the home" became the Fascist slogan. Women were to be homemakers and baby producers, "their natural and fundamental mission in life," according to Mussolini, for population growth was viewed as an indicator of national strength. Employment outside the home might distract women from conception: "It forms an independence and consequent physical and moral habits contrary to child bearing."[2]

Despite the instruments of repression, the use of propaganda, and the creation of numerous Fascist organizations, Mussolini never achieved the degree of totalitarian control attained in Hitler's Germany or Stalin's Soviet Union. Mussolini and the Fascist Party never completely destroyed the old power structure, and they were soon overshadowed by a much more powerful fascist movement to the north.

Hitler and Nazi Germany

In 1923, a small rightist party led by an obscure Austrian rabble-rouser named Adolf Hitler (1889–1945) attempted to seize power in southern Germany in the notorious Beer Hall Putsch. Although the effort failed, the attempted putsch brought Hitler and the Nazis to national prominence.

HITLER'S RISE TO POWER, 1919–1933 At the end of World War I, after four years of service on the Western Front, Hitler went to Munich and decided to enter politics. In 1919, he joined the obscure German Workers' Party, one of a number of right-wing extreme nationalist parties in Munich. By the summer of 1921, Hitler had assumed control of the party, which he renamed the National Socialist German Workers' Party (NSDAP), or Nazi Party for short. In two years, membership reached 55,000, including 15,000 in the party militia known as the SA, the *Sturmabteilung* (SHTOORM-ap-ty-loonk) (Storm Troops).

Overconfident, Hitler staged an armed uprising against the government in Munich in November 1923. The so-called Beer Hall Putsch was quickly crushed, and Hitler was sentenced to prison. During his brief stay in jail, he wrote *Mein Kampf* (myn KAHMPF) (*My Struggle*), an autobiographical account of his movement and its underlying ideology. Extreme German nationalism, virulent anti-Semitism, and anticommunism are linked together by a social Darwinian theory of struggle that stresses the right of superior nations to *Lebensraum*

(LAY-benz-rown) (living space) through expansion and the right of superior individuals to secure authoritarian leadership over the masses.

During his imprisonment, Hitler also came to the realization that the Nazis would have to come to power by constitutional means, not by overthrowing the Weimar (VY-mar) Republic. After his release from prison, Hitler reorganized the Nazi Party and competed for votes with the other political parties. By 1929, the Nazis had a national party organization.

Three years later, the Nazi Party had 800,000 members and had become the largest party in the Reichstag (RYKHSS-tahk). Germany's economic difficulties were a crucial factor in the Nazis' rise to power. Unemployment rose dramatically, from 4 million in 1931 to 6 million by the winter of 1932. Claiming to stand above all differences, Hitler promised that he would create a new Germany free of class differences and party infighting. His appeal to national pride, national honor, and traditional militarism struck receptive chords in his listeners. After attending one of Hitler's rallies, a schoolteacher in Hamburg said: "When the speech was over, there was roaring enthusiasm and applause. . . . Then he went—How many look up to him with touching faith as their savior, their deliverer from unbearable distress."[3]

Increasingly, the right-wing elites of Germany—the industrial magnates, landed aristocrats, military establishment, and higher bureaucrats—came to see Hitler as the man who had the mass support to establish a right-wing, authoritarian regime that would save Germany and their privileged positions from a Communist takeover. Under pressure, since the Nazi Party had the largest share of seats in the Reichstag, President Paul von Hindenburg agreed to allow Hitler to become chancellor (on January 30, 1933) and form a new government.

Within two months, Hitler had laid the foundations for the Nazis' complete control over Germany. The crowning step in Hitler's "legal seizure" of power came on March 23, when the Reichstag, by a two-thirds vote, passed the Enabling Act, which empowered the government to dispense with constitutional forms for four years while it issued laws to deal with the country's problems.

With their new source of power, the Nazis acted quickly to bring all institutions under Nazi control. The civil service was purged of Jews and democratic elements, concentration camps were established for opponents of the new regime, trade unions were dissolved, and all political parties except the Nazis were abolished. By the end of the summer of 1933, Hitler and the Nazis had established the foundations for a totalitarian state. When Hindenburg died on August 2, 1934, the office of Reich president was abolished, and Hitler became *der Führer* ((FYOOR-ur) (the leader)—sole ruler of Germany.

THE NAZI STATE, 1933–1939 Having smashed the parliamentary state, Hitler now felt the real task was at hand: to develop the "total state." Hitler's goal was the development of an Aryan racial state that would dominate Europe and possibly the world for generations to come. Hitler stated:

> We must develop organizations in which an individual's entire life can take place. Then every activity and every need of every individual will be regulated by the collectivity represented by the party. There is no longer any arbitrary will, there are no longer any free realms in which the individual belongs to himself. . . . The time of personal happiness is over.[4]

The Nazis pursued the realization of this totalitarian ideal in a variety of ways.

Mass demonstrations and spectacles were employed to integrate the German nation into a collective fellowship and to mobilize it as an instrument for Hitler's policies. These mass demonstrations, especially the party rallies that were held in Nuremberg every September, combined the symbolism of a religious service with the merriment of a popular amusement and usually evoked mass enthusiasm and excitement.

Despite the symbolism and Hitler's goal of establishing an all-powerful government that would maintain absolute control and order, in actuality, Nazi Germany was the scene of almost constant personal and institutional conflict, which resulted in administrative chaos. Struggle characterized relationships within the party, within the state, and between party and state. Hitler, of course, remained the ultimate decision maker and absolute ruler.

In the economic sphere, Hitler and the Nazis also worked to establish control. Although the regime used public works projects and "pump-priming" grants to private construction firms to foster employment and end the depression, there is little doubt that rearmament contributed far more to solving the unemployment problem. Unemployment, which had stood at 6 million in 1932, dropped to 2.6 million in 1934 and less than 500,000 in 1937. This was an important factor in convincing many Germans to accept the new regime, despite its excesses.

For Germans who needed coercion, the Nazi total state had its instruments of terror. Especially important were the *Schutzstaffel* (SHOOTS-shtah-fuhn) (guard squadrons), known simply as the SS. The SS, under the direction of Heinrich Himmler (1900–1945), came to control all of the regular and secret police forces. Himmler and the SS functioned on the basis of two principles: terror and ideology. Terror included the instruments of repression and murder: secret police, criminal police, concentration camps, and later execution squads and death camps for the extermination of the Jews. For Himmler, the primary goal of the SS was to further the Aryan "master race."

The creation of the Nazi total state also had an impact on women. Women played a crucial role in the Aryan racial state as bearers of the children who would bring about the triumph of the Aryan race. To the Nazis, the differences between men and women were natural: men were destined to be warriors and political leaders; women were to be wives and mothers.

The Nazi total state was intended to be an Aryan racial state. From its beginning, the Nazi Party reflected the strong anti-Semitic beliefs of Adolf Hitler. Once in power, the Nazis translated anti-Semitic ideas into anti-Semitic policies. In September 1935, at the annual party rally in Nuremberg, the Nazis announced new racial laws,

The Nazi Mass Spectacle. Hitler and the Nazis made clever use of mass spectacles to rally the German people behind the Nazi regime. These mass demonstrations evoked intense enthusiasm, as is evident in this photograph of Hitler arriving at the Bückeberg (BOOK-uh-bayrk) near Hamelin for the Harvest Festival in 1937. Almost one million people were present for the celebration.

© Hugo Jaeger/Time Life Pictures//Getty Images

which excluded German Jews from German citizenship and forbade marriages and extramarital relations between Jews and German citizens.

A more violent phase of anti-Jewish activity took place in 1938 and 1939, initiated on November 9–10, 1938, by the infamous *Kristallnacht* (kri-STAHL-nahkht), or night of shattered glass. The assassination of a secretary in the German embassy in Paris became the excuse for a Nazi-led rampage against the Jews in which synagogues were burned, 7,000 Jewish businesses were destroyed, and at least one hundred Jews were killed. Jews were barred from all public buildings and prohibited from owning or working in any retail store.

The Stalinist Era in the Soviet Union

Joseph Stalin made a significant shift in economic policy in 1928 when he launched his first five-year plan. Its real goal was nothing less than the transformation of the agrarian Soviet Union into an industrial country virtually overnight. Instead of consumer goods, the first five-year plan emphasized maximum production of capital goods and armaments and succeeded in quadrupling the production of heavy machinery and doubling oil production. Between 1928 and 1937, during the first two five-year plans, steel production increased from 4 million to 18 million tons per year.

Rapid industrialization was accompanied by an equally rapid collectivization of agriculture. Its goal was to eliminate private farms and push people onto collective farms. Strong resistance to Stalin's plans from peasants who hoarded crops and killed livestock only caused him to step up the program. By 1934, Russia's 26 million family farms had been collectivized into 250,000 units, though at a tremendous cost, since the hoarding of food and the slaughter of livestock produced widespread famine. Perhaps 10 million peasants died in the artificially created famines of 1932 and 1933. The only concession Stalin made to the peasants was to allow each collective farm worker to have one tiny, privately owned garden plot.

To achieve his goals, Stalin strengthened the party bureaucracy under his control. Anyone who resisted was sent into forced labor camps in Siberia. Stalin's desire for sole control of decision making also led to purges of the Old Bolsheviks. Between 1936 and 1938, the most prominent Old Bolsheviks were put on trial and condemned to death. During this same time, Stalin undertook a purge of army officers, diplomats, union officials, party members, intellectuals, and numerous ordinary citizens. Estimates are that 8 million Russians were arrested; millions died in Siberian forced labor camps. This gave Stalin the distinction of being one of the greatest mass murderers in human history.

The Stalinist era also reversed much of the permissive social legislation of the early 1920s. Advocating complete equality of rights for women, the Communists had made divorce and abortion easy to obtain while also encouraging women to work outside the home and to set their own moral standards. After Stalin came to power, the family was praised as a miniature collective in which parents were responsible for inculcating values of duty, discipline, and hard work. Abortion was outlawed, and divorced fathers who failed to support their children were fined heavily.

The Rise of Militarism in Japan

The rise of militarism in Japan resulted not from a seizure of power by a new political party but from the growing influence of militant forces at the top of the political hierarchy. In the early 1930s, confrontations with China in Manchuria, combined with the onset of the Great Depression, brought an end to the fragile stability of the immediate postwar years.

The depression had a disastrous effect on Japan, as many European countries, along with the United States, raised stiff tariff walls against cheap Japanese imports in order to protect their struggling domestic industries. The ensuing economic slowdown imposed a heavy burden on the fragile democracy in Japan. Although civilian cabinets tried desperately to cope with the economic challenges presented by the world depression, the political parties were no longer able to stem the growing influence of militant nationalist elements. Extremist patriotic organizations began to terrorize Japanese society by assassinating businessmen and public figures identified with the policy of conciliation toward the outside world. Some argued that Western-style political institutions should be replaced by a new system that would return to traditional Japanese values and imperial authority. Their message of "Asia for the Asians" became increasingly popular as the Great Depression convinced many Japanese that capitalism was unsuitable for Japan.

During the mid-1930s, the influence of the military and extreme nationalists over the government steadily increased. National elections continued to take place, but cabinets were dominated by the military or advocates of Japanese expansionism. In February 1936, junior army officers led a coup, briefly occupying the Diet building and other key government installations in Tokyo and assassinating several members of the cabinet. The ringleaders were quickly tried and convicted of treason, but under conditions that further strengthened the influence of the military.

The Path to War

 FOCUS QUESTION: What were the underlying causes of World War II, and what specific steps taken by Nazi Germany and Japan led to war?

Only twenty years after the "war to end war," the world plunged back into the nightmare. The efforts at collective security in the 1920s proved meaningless in view of the growth of Nazi Germany and the rise of militant Japan.

The Path to War in Europe

World War II in Europe had its beginnings in the ideas of Adolf Hitler, who believed that only so-called Aryans were capable of building a great civilization. To Hitler, Germany needed more land to support a larger population and be a great power. Already in the 1920s, in the second volume of *Mein Kampf*, Hitler had indicated that a National Socialist regime would find this land to the east—in Russia.

On March 9, 1935, in defiance of the Treaty of Versailles, Hitler announced the creation of an air force and one week later the introduction of a military draft that would expand Germany's army from 100,000 to 550,000 troops. Hitler's unilateral repudiation of the Versailles treaty brought a swift reaction as France, Great Britain, and Italy condemned Germany's action and warned against future aggressive steps. But nothing concrete was done.

Meanwhile, Hitler gained new allies. In October 1935, Benito Mussolini had committed Fascist Italy to imperial expansion by invading Ethiopia. Mussolini welcomed Hitler's support and began to draw closer to the German dictator. In October 1936, Hitler and Mussolini concluded an agreement that recognized their common interests, and one month later, Mussolini referred publicly to the new Rome-Berlin Axis. Also in November, Germany and Japan (the rising military power in the Far East) concluded the Anti-Comintern Pact and agreed to maintain a common front against communism.

By 1937, Germany was once more a "world power," as Hitler proclaimed. Hitler was convinced that neither the French nor the British would provide much opposition to his plans and decided in 1938 to move to achieve one of his longtime goals: union with Austria. By threatening Austria with invasion, Hitler coerced the Austrian chancellor into putting Austrian Nazis in charge of the government. The new government promptly invited German troops to enter Austria and assist in maintaining law and order. One day later, on March 13, 1938, after his triumphal return to his native land, Hitler formally annexed Austria to Germany.

Hitler's next objective was the destruction of Czechoslovakia, and he believed that France and Britain would not use force to defend that nation. He was right again. On September 15, 1938, Hitler demanded the cession of the Sudetenland (soo-DAY-tun-land) (an area in northwestern Czechoslovakia inhabited largely by ethnic Germans) to Germany and expressed his willingness to risk "world war" if he was refused. Instead of objecting, the British, French, Germans, and Italians—at a hastily arranged conference at Munich—reached an agreement that met all of Hitler's demands (see the box on p. 656). German troops were allowed to occupy the Sudetenland. Increasingly, Hitler was convinced of his own infallibility, and he had by no means been satisfied at Munich. In March 1939, Hitler occupied all the Czech lands (Bohemia and Moravia), while the Slovaks, with Hitler's encouragement, declared their independence of the Czechs and became a puppet state (Slovakia) of Nazi Germany. On the evening of March 15, 1939, Hitler triumphantly declared in Prague that he would be known as the greatest German of them all.

At last, the Western states reacted to Hitler's threat. When Hitler began to demand the return of Danzig (which had been made a free city by the Treaty of Versailles to serve as a seaport for Poland) to Germany, Britain offered to protect Poland in the event of war. At the same time, both France and Britain realized that only the Soviet Union was powerful enough to help contain Nazi aggression and began political and military negotiations with Stalin and the Soviets.

Meanwhile, Hitler pressed on. To preclude an alliance between the West and the Soviet Union, which would open the danger of a two-front war, Hitler negotiated his own nonaggression pact with Stalin and shocked the world with its announcement on August 23, 1939. The treaty with the Soviet Union gave Hitler the freedom to attack Poland. He told his generals: "Now Poland is in the position in which I wanted her. . . . I am only afraid that at the last moment some swine or other will yet submit to me a plan for mediation."[5] He need not have worried. On September 1, German forces invaded Poland; two days later, Britain and France declared war on Germany. Europe was again at war.

The Path to War in Asia

During the mid-1920s, Japan had maintained a strong military and economic presence in Manchuria, an area in northeastern China controlled by a Chinese warlord. Then, in September 1931, Japanese military officers stationed in the area launched a coup to bring about a complete Japanese takeover of the region. Despite worldwide protests from the League of Nations, which eventually

OPPOSING ✕ VIEWPOINTS

The Munich Conference

POLITICS & GOVERNMENT

At the Munich Conference, the leaders of France and Great Britain capitulated to Hitler's demands on Czechoslovakia. Although the British prime minister, Neville Chamberlain, defended his actions at Munich as necessary for peace, another British statesman, Winston Churchill, characterized the settlement at Munich as "a disaster of the first magnitude."

Winston Churchill, Speech to the House of Commons, October 5, 1938

I will begin by saying what everybody would like to ignore or forget but which must nevertheless be stated, namely, that we have sustained a total and unmitigated defeat, and that France has suffered even more than we have. . . . The utmost my right honorable Friend the Prime Minister . . . has been able to gain for Czechoslovakia and in the matters which were in dispute has been that the German dictator, instead of snatching his victuals from the table, has been content to have them served to him course by course. . . . And I will say this, that I believe the Czechs, left to themselves and told they were going to get no help from the Western Powers, would have been able to make better terms than they have got. . . .

We are in the presence of a disaster of the first magnitude which has befallen Great Britain and France. Do not let us blind ourselves to that. . . .

And do not suppose that this is the end. This is only the beginning of the reckoning. This is only the first sip, the first foretaste of a bitter cup which will be proffered to us year by year unless by a supreme recovery of moral health and martial vigor, we arise again and take our stand for freedom as in the olden time.

Neville Chamberlain, Speech to the House of Commons, October 6, 1938

That is my answer to those who say that we should have told Germany weeks ago that, if her army crossed the border of Czechoslovakia, we should be at war with her. We had no treaty obligations and no legal obligations to Czechoslovakia. When we were convinced, as we became convinced, that nothing any longer would keep the Sudetenland within the Czechoslovakian State, we urged the Czech Government as strongly as we could to agree to the cession of territory, and to agree promptly. . . . It was a hard decision for anyone who loved his country to take, but to accuse us of having by that advice betrayed the Czechoslovakian State is simply preposterous. What we did was to save her from annihilation and give her a chance of new life as a new State, which involves the loss of territory and fortifications, but may perhaps enable her to enjoy in the future and develop a national existence under a neutrality and security comparable to that which we see in Switzerland today. Therefore, I think the Government deserve the approval of this House for their conduct of affairs in this recent crisis which has saved Czechoslovakia from destruction and Europe from Armageddon.

Q *What were the opposing views of Churchill and Chamberlain on the Munich Conference? Why did they disagree so much? With whom do you agree? Why?*

Sources: Winston Churchill, Speech to the House of Commons, October 5, 1938. From *Parliamentary Debates, House of Commons* (London: His Majesty's Stationery Office, 1938), vol. 339, pp. 361–369. Neville Chamberlain, Speech to the House of Commons, October 6, 1938. From Neville Chamberlain, *In Search of Peace* (New York: Putnam, 1939), pp. 215, 217.

condemned the seizure, Japan steadily strengthened its control over Manchuria, renaming it Manchukuo (man-CHOO-kwoh), and then began to expand into northern China.

For the moment, Chiang Kai-shek attempted to avoid a direct confrontation with Japan so that he could deal with the Communists, whom he he considered the greater threat. When clashes between Chinese and Japanese troops broke out, he sought to appease the Japanese by granting them the authority to administer areas in North China. But as the Japanese moved steadily southward, popular protests in Chinese cities against Japanese aggression intensified. In December 1936, Chiang ended his military efforts against the Communists in Yan'an and

A Japanese Victory in China. After consolidating their authority over Manchuria, the Japanese began to expand into northern China. Direct hostilities between Japanese and Chinese forces began in 1937. This photograph shows victorious Japanese forces riding under the arched Chungshan Gate in Nanjing in January 1938 after they had conquered the Chinese capital city. By 1939, Japan had conquered most of eastern China.

formed a new united front against the Japanese. When Chinese and Japanese forces clashed at the Marco Polo Bridge, south of Beijing, in July 1937, China refused to apologize, and hostilities spread.

Japan had not planned to declare war on China, but neither side would compromise, and the 1937 incident eventually turned into a major conflict. The Japanese advanced up the Yangtze River valley and seized the Chinese capital of Nanjing in December, but Chiang Kai-shek refused to capitulate and moved his government upriver to Hankou (HAHN-kow). When the Japanese seized that city, he retreated to Chongqing (chung-CHING), in remote Sichuan (suh-CHWAHN) province, and kept his capital there for the remainder of the war.

Japanese strategists had hoped to force Chiang to join a Japanese-dominated New Order in East Asia, comprising Japan, Manchuria, and China. This was part of a larger Japanese plan to seize Soviet Siberia, with its rich resources, and create a new "Monroe Doctrine for Asia," under which Japan would guide its Asian neighbors on the path to development and prosperity (see the box on p. 658). After all, who better to instruct Asian societies on modernization than the one Asian country that had already achieved it?

During the late 1930s, Japan began to cooperate with Nazi Germany on the assumption that the two countries would ultimately launch a joint attack on the Soviet Union and divide up its resources between them. But when Germany surprised the world by signing a nonaggression pact with the Soviets in August 1939, Japanese strategists were compelled to reevaluate their long-term objectives. The Japanese were not strong enough to defeat the Soviet Union alone and so began to shift their eyes southward, to the vast resources of Southeast Asia—the oil of the Dutch East Indies, the rubber and tin of Malaya, and the rice of Burma and Indochina.

A move southward, of course, would risk war with the European colonial powers and the United States. Japan's attack on China in the summer of 1937 had already aroused strong criticism abroad, particularly from the United States. When Japan demanded the right to occupy airfields and exploit economic resources in French Indochina in the summer of 1940, the United States warned the Japanese that it would cut off the sale of oil and scrap iron unless Japan withdrew from the area and returned to its borders of 1931.

The Japanese viewed the American threat of retaliation as an obstacle to their long-term objectives. Japan badly needed oil and scrap iron from the United States. Should they be cut off, Japan would have to find them elsewhere. The Japanese were thus caught in a vise. To obtain guaranteed access to natural resources that were necessary to fuel the Japanese military machine, Japan must risk being cut off from its current source of raw materials that would be needed in the event of a conflict. After much debate, Japan decided to launch a surprise attack on American and European colonies in Southeast Asia in the hope of a quick victory that would evict the United States from the region.

World War II

Q FOCUS QUESTION: What were the main events of World War II in Europe and Asia?

Unleashing an early form of **blitzkrieg** (BLITZ-kreeg), or "lightning war," Hitler stunned Europe with the speed and efficiency of the German attack. Armored columns

Japan's Justification for Expansion

Advocates of Japanese expansion justified their proposals by claiming both economic necessity and moral imperatives. Note the familiar combination of motives in this passage written by an extremist military leader in the late 1930s.

Hashimoto Kingoro on the Need for Emigration and Expansion

We have already said that there are only three ways left to Japan to escape from the pressure of surplus population. We are like a great crowd of people packed into a small and narrow room, and there are only three doors through which we might escape, namely emigration, advance into world markets, and expansion of territory. The first door, emigration, has been barred to us by the anti-Japanese immigration policies of other countries. The second door, advance into world markets, is being pushed shut by tariff barriers and the abrogation of commercial treaties. What should Japan do when two of the three doors have been closed against her?

It is quite natural that Japan should rush upon the last remaining door.

It may sound dangerous when we speak of territorial expansion, but the territorial expansion of which we speak does not in any sense of the word involve the occupation of the possessions of other countries, the planting of the Japanese flag thereon, and the declaration of their annexation to Japan. It is just that since the Powers have suppressed the circulation of Japanese materials and merchandise abroad, we are looking for some place overseas where Japanese capital, Japanese skills and Japanese labor can have free play, free from the oppression of the white race.

We would be satisfied with just this much. What moral right do the world powers who have themselves closed to us the two doors of emigration and advance into world markets have to criticize Japan's attempt to rush out of the third and last door?

If they do not approve of this, they should open the doors which they have closed against us and permit the free movement overseas of Japanese emigrants and merchandise. . . .

At the time of the Manchurian incident, the entire world joined in criticism of Japan. They said that Japan was an untrustworthy nation. They said that she had recklessly brought cannon and machine guns into Manchuria, which was the territory of another country, flown airplanes over it, and finally occupied it. But the military action taken by Japan was not in the least a selfish one. Moreover, we do not recall ever having taken so much as an inch of territory belonging to another nation. The result of this incident was the establishment of the splendid new nation of Manchuria. The Powers are still discussing whether or not to recognize this new nation, but regardless of whether or not other nations recognize her, the Manchurian empire has already been established, and now, seven years after its creation, the empire is further consolidating its foundations with the aid of its friend, Japan.

And if it is still protested that our actions in Manchuria were excessively violent, we may wish to ask the white race just which country it was that sent warships and troops to India, South Africa, and Australia and slaughtered innocent natives, bound their hands and feet with iron chains, lashed their backs with iron whips, proclaimed these territories as their own, and still continues to hold them to this very day.

Q *What arguments did Hashimoto Kingoro make in favor of Japanese territorial expansion? What was his reaction to the condemnation of Japan by Western nations?*

Source: From *Sources of Japanese Tradition* by William Theodore de Bary. Copyright © 1958 by Columbia University Press.

or panzer divisions (a *panzer division* was a strike force of about three hundred tanks and accompanying forces and supplies) supported by airplanes broke quickly through Polish lines and encircled the bewildered Polish troops. Conventional infantry units then moved in to hold the newly conquered territory. Within four weeks, Poland had surrendered. On September 28, 1939, Germany and the Soviet Union officially divided Poland between them.

Europe at War

After a winter of waiting, Hitler resumed the war on April 9, 1940, with another blitzkrieg against Denmark and Norway (see Map 25.1). One month later, on May 10, the Germans launched their attack on the Netherlands, Belgium, and France. The main assault through Luxembourg and the Ardennes forest was completely unexpected by the French and British forces. German panzer divisions broke through the weak French defensive positions there and raced across northern France, splitting the Allied armies and trapping French troops and the entire British army on the beaches of Dunkirk. Only by heroic efforts did the British achieve a gigantic evacuation of 330,000 Allied troops. The French capitulated on June 22. German armies occupied about three-fifths of France while the French hero of World War I, Marshal Henri Petain (AHN-ree pay-TAHN), established an authoritarian regime—known as Vichy (VISH-ee) France—over the remainder. Germany was now in control of western and central Europe, but Britain still had not been defeated.

As Hitler realized, an amphibious invasion of Britain would be possible only if Germany gained control of the

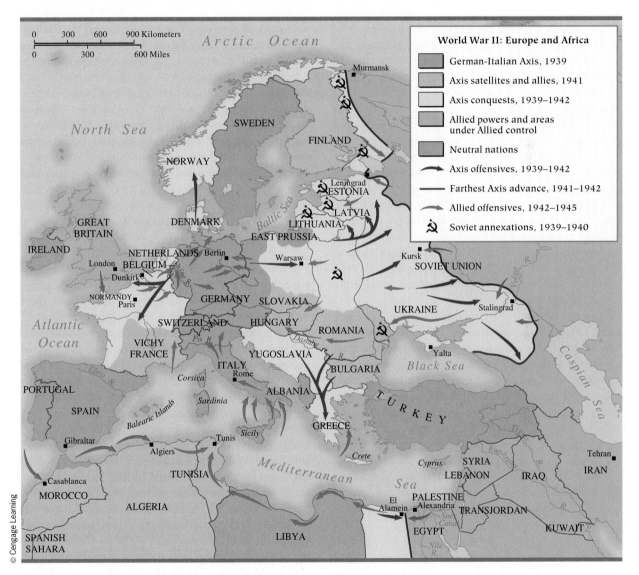

MAP 25.1 World War II in Europe and North Africa. With its fast and effective military, Germany quickly overwhelmed much of western Europe. Hitler overestimated his country's capabilities, however, and underestimated those of his opponents. By late 1942, his invasion of the Soviet Union was failing, and the United States had become a major factor in the war. The Allies successfully invaded Italy in 1943 and France in 1944.

Q *Which countries were neutral, and how did geography help make their neutrality an option?*

air. At the beginning of August 1940, the German air force, or Luftwaffe (LOOFT-vahf-uh), launched a major offensive against British air and naval bases, harbors, communication centers, and war industries. The British fought back doggedly, supported by an effective radar system that gave them early warning of German attacks. Nevertheless, the British air force suffered critical losses by the end of August and was probably saved by a change in Hitler's strategy. In September, in retaliation for a British attack on Berlin, Hitler ordered a shift from military targets to massive bombing of British cities to break British morale. The British rebuilt their air strength quickly and were soon inflicting major losses on Luftwaffe bombers. By the end of September, Germany had lost the Battle of Britain, and the invasion of Britain had to be postponed.

Although he had no desire for a two-front war, Hitler became convinced that Britain was remaining in the war only because it expected Soviet support. If the Soviet Union were smashed, Britain's last hope would be eliminated. Although the invasion of the Soviet Union was scheduled for spring 1941, the attack was delayed because of problems in the Balkans. Hitler had already obtained the political cooperation of Hungary, Bulgaria, and Romania, but Mussolini's disastrous invasion of Greece in October 1940 exposed Hitler's southern flank to British air bases in Greece. To secure his Balkan flank, German troops seized both Yugoslavia and Greece in April. Feeling reassured, Hitler turned to the east and invaded the Soviet Union on June 22, 1941.

The massive attack stretched out along a 1,800-mile front. German troops advanced rapidly, capturing 2 million Soviet soldiers. By November, one German army group had swept through Ukraine, while a second was besieging Leningrad; a third approached within 25 miles of Moscow, the Soviet capital. An early winter and unexpected Soviet resistance, however, brought a halt to the German advance. For the first time in the war, German armies had been stopped. A Soviet counterattack in December 1941 came as an ominous ending to the year for the Germans. By that time, another of Hitler's decisions—the declaration of war on the United States—turned another European conflict into a global war.

Japan at War

On December 7, 1941, Japanese carrier-based aircraft attacked the U.S. naval base at Pearl Harbor in the Hawaiian Islands. The same day, other units launched assaults on the Philippines and began advancing toward the British colony of Malaya (see Map 25.2). Shortly thereafter, Japanese forces invaded the Dutch East Indies and occupied a number of islands in the Pacific Ocean.

By the spring of 1942, almost all of Southeast Asia and much of the western Pacific had fallen into Japanese hands. Japan declared the establishment of the Greater East Asia Co-Prosperity Sphere, encompassing the entire region under Japanese tutelage, and announced its intention to liberate the colonial areas of Southeast Asia from Western colonial rule. For the moment, however, Japan needed the resources of the region for its war machine and placed the countries under its own rule on a wartime basis.

Japanese leaders had hoped that their lightning strike at American bases would destroy the U.S. Pacific fleet and persuade President Franklin D. Roosevelt to accept Japanese domination of the Pacific. But the Japanese had miscalculated. The attack on Pearl Harbor galvanized American opinion and won broad support for Roosevelt's war policy. The United States now joined with European nations and Nationalist China in a combined effort to defeat Japan and end its hegemony in the Pacific. Believing that American involvement in the Pacific would render the United States ineffective in the European theater of war, Hitler declared war on the United States four days after Pearl Harbor.

The Turning Point of the War, 1942–1943

The entry of the United States into the war created a coalition (the Grand Alliance) that ultimately defeated the Axis Powers (Germany, Italy, and Japan). To overcome mutual suspicions, the three major Allies, Britain, the United States, and the Soviet Union, agreed to stress military operations while ignoring political differences. At the beginning of 1943, the Allies also agreed to fight until the Axis Powers surrendered unconditionally, a decision that had the effect of cementing the Grand Alliance by making it nearly impossible for Hitler to divide his foes.

As 1942 began, however, defeat was far from Hitler's mind. As Japanese forces advanced into the Pacific after crippling the American naval fleet at Pearl Harbor, Hitler continued the war in Europe against Britain and the Soviet Union. Until the fall of 1942, it appeared that the Germans might still prevail on the battlefield. Reinforcements in North Africa enabled the Afrika Korps under General Erwin Rommel (RAHM-ul) to break through the British defenses in Egypt and advance toward Alexandria. In the spring of 1942, a renewed German offensive in the Soviet Union led to the capture of the entire Crimea. But by the fall of 1942, the war had turned against the Germans.

In North Africa, British forces had stopped Rommel's troops at El Alamein (ell ah-lah-MAYN) in the summer of 1942 and then forced them back across the desert. In

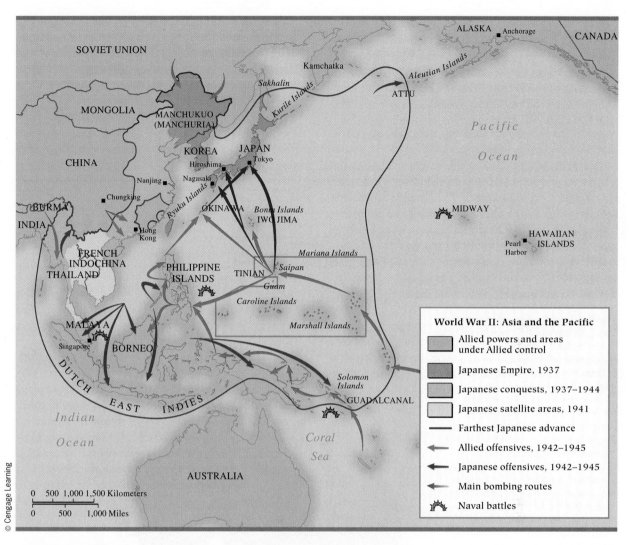

MAP 25.2 **World War II in Asia and the Pacific.** In 1937, Japan invaded northern China, beginning its effort to create a "Great East Asia Co-Prosperity Sphere." Further Japanese expansion caused the United States to end iron and oil sales to Japan. Deciding that war with the United States was inevitable, Japan engineered a surprise attack on Pearl Harbor.

Q *Why was control of the islands in the western Pacific of great importance both to the Japanese and to the Allies?*

November 1942, British and American forces invaded French North Africa and forced the German and Italian troops to surrender in May 1943. On the Eastern Front, the turning point of the war occurred at Stalingrad. After the capture of the Crimea, Hitler decided that Stalingrad, a major industrial center on the Volga, should be taken next. Between November 1942 and February 1943, German troops were stopped, then encircled, and finally forced to surrender on February 2, 1943 (see the box on p. 663). The entire German Sixth Army of 300,000 men was lost. By February 1943, German forces in the Soviet Union were back to their positions of June 1942.

The tide of battle in the Far East also turned dramatically in 1942. In the Battle of the Coral Sea on May 7–8, 1942, American naval forces stopped the Japanese advance and temporarily relieved Australia of the threat of invasion. On June 4, at the Battle of Midway Island, American carrier planes destroyed all four of the attacking Japanese aircraft carriers and established American naval superiority in the Pacific. The victory came at a high cost; about two-fifths of the American planes were shot down in the encounter. By the fall of 1942, Allied forces were beginning to gather for offensive operations in three areas: from bases in north Burma and India into the

The Battle of Stalingrad. The Battle of Stalingrad was a major turning point on the Eastern Front. Shown in the first photograph is a German infantry platoon in the ruins of a tractor factory they had captured in the northern part of Stalingrad. This victory took place on October 15, 1942, at a time when Hitler still believed he was winning the battle for Stalingrad. That belief was soon dashed as a Soviet counteroffensive in November led to a total defeat for the Germans. The second photograph shows thousands of captured soldiers being marched across frozen Soviet soil to prison camps. The soldiers in white fur hats are Romanian. Fewer than 6,000 captured soldiers survived to go home; the remainder—almost 85,000 prisoners—died in captivity.

rest of Burma; in the Solomon Islands and on New Guinea, with forces under the direction of American general Douglas MacArthur moving toward the Philippines; and across the Pacific where combined U.S. Army, Marine, and Navy forces would mount attacks against Japanese held islands. After a series of bitter engagements in the waters of the Solomon Islands from August to November 1942, Japanese fortunes began to fade.

The Last Years of the War

By the beginning of 1943, the tide of battle had turned against Germany, Italy, and Japan. After the Axis forces had surrendered in Tunisia on May 13, 1943, the Allies crossed the Mediterranean and carried the war to Italy. After taking Sicily, Allied troops began the invasion of mainland Italy in September. In the meantime, after the ouster and arrest of Benito Mussolini, a new Italian government offered to surrender to Allied forces. But Mussolini was liberated by the Germans in a daring raid and then set up as the head of a puppet German state in northern Italy while German troops moved in and occupied much of Italy. The new defensive lines established by the Germans in the hills south of Rome were so effective that the Allied advance up the Italian peninsula was a painstaking affair accompanied by heavy casualties. Rome did not fall to the Allies until June 4, 1944. By that time, the Italian war had assumed a secondary role anyway as the Allies prepared to open their long-awaited "second front" in western Europe.

Under the direction of the American general Dwight D. Eisenhower (1890–1969), the Allies landed five assault

A German Soldier at Stalingrad

POLITICS & GOVERNMENT

The Soviet victory at Stalingrad was a major turning point in World War II. This excerpt comes from the diary of a German soldier who fought and died in the Battle of Stalingrad. His dreams of victory and a return home with medals were soon dashed by the realities of Soviet resistance.

Diary of a German Soldier

Today, after we'd had a bath, the company commander told us that if our future operations are as successful, we'll soon reach the Volga, take Stalingrad, and then the war will inevitably soon be over. Perhaps we'll be home by Christmas.

July 29. The company commander says the Russian troops are completely broken, and cannot hold out any longer. To reach the Volga and take Stalingrad is not so difficult for us. The Führer knows where the Russians' weak point is. Victory is not far away. . . .

August 10. The Führer's orders were read out to us. He expects victory of us. We are all convinced that they can't stop us.

August 12. This morning outstanding soldiers were presented with decorations. Will I really go back to Elsa without a decoration? I believe that for Stalingrad the Führer will decorate even me. . . .

September 4. We are being sent northward along the front toward Stalingrad. We marched all night and by dawn had reached Voroponovo Station. We can already see the smoking town. It's a happy thought that the end of the war is getting nearer. That's what everyone is saying. . . .

September 8. Two days of nonstop fighting. The Russians are defending themselves with insane stubbornness. Our regiment has lost many men. . . .

September 16. Our battalion, plus tanks, is attacking the [grain storage] elevator, from which smoke is pouring—the grain in it is burning; the Russians seem to have set light to it themselves. Barbarism. The battalion is suffering heavy losses. . . .

Source: From Vasili Chuikov, *The Battle of Stalingrad* (Grafton Books).

October 10. The Russians are so close to us that our planes cannot bomb them. We are preparing for a decisive attack. The Führer has ordered the whole of Stalingrad to be taken as rapidly as possible. . . .

October 22. Our regiment has failed to break into the factory. We have lost many men; every time you move you have to jump over bodies. . . .

November 10. A letter from Elsa today. Everyone expects us home for Christmas. In Germany everyone believes we already hold Stalingrad. How wrong they are. If they could only see what Stalingrad has done to our army. . . .

November 21. The Russians have gone over to the offensive along the whole front. Fierce fighting is going on. So, there it is—the Volga, victory, and soon home to our families! We shall obviously be seeing them next in the other world.

November 29. We are encircled. It was announced this morning that the Führer has said: "The army can trust me to do everything necessary to ensure supplies and rapidly break the encirclement."

December 3. We are on hunger rations and waiting for the rescue that the Führer promised. . . .

December 14. Everybody is racked with hunger. Frozen potatoes are the best meal, but to get them out of the ice-covered ground under fire from Russian bullets is not so easy. . . .

December 26. The horses have already been eaten. I would eat a cat; they say its meat is also tasty. The soldiers look like corpses or lunatics, looking for something to put in their mouths. They no longer take cover from Russian shells; they haven't the strength to walk, run away, and hide. A curse on this war!

Q *What did this soldier believe about the Führer? Why? What was the source of his information? Why is the battle for Stalingrad considered a major turning point in World War II?*

---

divisions on the beaches of Normandy on June 6, 1944, in history's greatest naval invasion. An initially indecisive German response enabled the Allied forces to establish a beachhead. Within three months, they had landed 2 million men and a half-million vehicles that pushed inland and broke through German defensive lines.

After the breakout, Allied troops moved south and east and liberated Paris by the end of August. By March

1945, they had crossed the Rhine River and advanced farther into Germany. At the end of April 1945, Allied armies in northern Germany moved toward the Elbe River, where they finally linked up with the Soviets. The Soviets had come a long way since the Battle of Stalingrad in 1943. In the summer of 1943, they soundly defeated German forces at the Battle of Kursk (KOORSK) (July 5–12), the greatest tank battle of World War II. Soviet forces then began a relentless advance westward. The Soviets had reoccupied Ukraine by the end of 1943 and lifted the siege of Leningrad and moved into the Baltic states by the beginning of 1944. Advancing along a northern front, Soviet troops occupied Warsaw in January 1945 and entered Berlin in April. Meanwhile, Soviet troops along a southern front swept through Hungary, Romania, and Bulgaria.

In January 1945, Hitler had moved into a bunker 55 feet under Berlin to direct the final stages of the war. In his final political testament, Hitler, consistent to the end in his rabid anti-Semitism, blamed the Jews for the war. Hitler committed suicide on April 30, two days after Mussolini had been shot by partisan Italian forces. On May 7, German commanders surrendered. The war in Europe was over.

DEFEAT OF JAPAN   The war in Asia continued. Beginning in 1943, American forces had gone on the offensive and proceeded, slowly at times, across the Pacific. The Americans took an increasing toll of enemy resources, especially at sea and in the air. As Allied military power drew inexorably closer to the main Japanese islands in the first months of 1945 (see the Film & History feature on p. 665), President Harry Truman, who had succeeded to the presidency on the death of Franklin Roosevelt in April, had an excruciatingly difficult decision to make. Should he use atomic weapons (at the time, only two bombs had been developed, and their effectiveness had not been demonstrated) to bring the war to an end without the necessity of an Allied invasion of the Japanese homeland? As the world knows, Truman answered that question in the affirmative. The first bomb was dropped on the city of Hiroshima (hee-roh-SHEE-muh) on August 6. Three days later, a second bomb was dropped on Nagasaki (nah-gah-SAH-kee). Japan surrendered unconditionally on August 14. World War II was finally over.

The New Order

 FOCUS QUESTION: What was the nature of the new orders that Germany and Japan attempted to establish in the territories they occupied?

The initial victories of the Germans and the Japanese had given them the opportunity to create new orders in Europe and Asia. Both followed policies of ruthless domination of their subject peoples.

The New Order in Europe

In 1942, the Nazi empire stretched across continental Europe from the English Channel in the west to the outskirts of Moscow in the east. Nazi-occupied Europe was largely organized in one of two ways. Some areas, such as western Poland, were directly annexed by Nazi Germany and made into German provinces. The rest of occupied Europe was administered by German military or civilian officials in combination with different degrees of indirect control from collaborationist regimes.

Because the conquered lands in the east contained the living space for German expansion and were populated in Nazi eyes by racially inferior Slavic peoples, Nazi administration there was considerably more ruthless than in the west. Soon after the conquest of Poland, Heinrich Himmler, a strong believer in Nazi racial ideology and the leader of the SS, was put in charge of German resettlement plans in the east. Himmler's task was to evacuate the inferior Slavic peoples and replace them with Germans, a policy first applied to the new German provinces

CHRONOLOGY	The Course of World War II
Germany and the Soviet Union divide Poland	September 28, 1939
Blitzkrieg against Denmark and Norway	April 1940
Blitzkrieg against Belgium, Netherlands, and France	May 1940
France surrenders	June 22, 1940
Battle of Britain	Fall 1940
Nazi seizure of Yugoslavia and Greece	April 1941
Germany invades the Soviet Union	June 22, 1941
Japanese attack on Pearl Harbor	December 7, 1941
Battle of the Coral Sea	May 7–8, 1942
Battle of Midway Island	June 4, 1942
Allied invasion of North Africa	November 1942
German surrender at Stalingrad	February 2, 1943
Axis forces surrender in North Africa	May 1943
Battle of Kursk	July 5–12, 1943
Allied invasion of mainland Italy	September 1943
Allied invasion of France	June 6, 1944
Hitler commits suicide	April 30, 1945
Germany surrenders	May 7, 1945
Atomic bomb dropped on Hiroshima	August 6, 1945
Japan surrenders	August 14, 1945

FILM & HISTORY

Letters from Iwo Jima (2006)

In February 1945, U.S. forces launched an attack on Iwo Jima, a 5-mile-long volcanic island, located about 650 miles southeast of Tokyo. With its three airstrips, Iwo Jima was an important element in the ring of defenses protecting Japan, and the Allies intended to use it as an air base from which to bomb the main Japanese islands.

The Battle of Iwo Jima is the subject of two films directed by Clint Eastwood and released in 2006: *Flag of Our Fathers* presented the battle from the American viewpoint, and *Letters from Iwo Jima* presented the Japanese perspective. The second film won numerous awards, including a nomination for Best Picture.

Letters from Iwo Jima is a realistic portrayal of the Japanese defense of the island. The plot focuses on two characters: the fictional Private Saigo (Kazunari Ninomiya), an ordinary soldier whose desire is to return home to his wife and daughter, and Lieutenant General Tadamichi Kuribayashi (Ken Watanabe), the actual commander of the Japanese forces on Iwo Jima. Kuribayashi is accurately portrayed as a man who shared the hardships of his men and had gained firsthand experience of the United States while spending three years there as a military attaché. Kuribayashi was largely responsible for the Japanese strategy of letting the U.S. Marines land on the beaches of Iwo Jima before attacking them with flanking fire from forces that were well protected in pillboxes and the miles of caves that permeated the island. The strategy proved very effective. The Japanese force of 22,000 men took a devastating toll on the Americans: out of the landing force of 110,000 men, 6,800 were killed and more than 17,000 were wounded. The assault that the U.S. military had expected to last only fourteen days dragged on instead for thirty-six.

Warner Bros. (Merie W. Wallace)/The Kobal Collection at Art Resource, NY

General Tadamichi Kuribayashi (Ken Watanabe) prepares for the U.S. invasion of Iwo Jima.

The film also realistically portrays the code of *bushido* that motivated the Japanese forces. Based on an ideal of loyalty and service, the code emphasized the obligation to honor and defend emperor, country, and family, and to sacrifice one's life if one failed in this sacred mission. Before committing suicide, Captain Tanida (Takumi Bando) says to his men, "Men, we are honorable soldiers of the emperor. Don't ever forget that. The only way left for us is to die with honor." But the film also presents another, more human view of the Japanese soldiers that differs from the stereotype found in many American movies about World War II. For the most part, the Japanese and American soldiers are portrayed as being much the same: as men who were willing to kill and die, but who would prefer to simply go home and be with their families.

---

created from the lands of western Poland. One million Poles were uprooted and dumped in southern Poland. Hundreds of thousands of ethnic Germans (descendants of Germans who had migrated years earlier from Germany to different parts of southern and eastern Europe) were encouraged to colonize designated areas in Poland. By 1942, 2 million ethnic Germans had been settled in Poland.

Labor shortages in Germany led to a policy of ruthless mobilization of foreign labor for Germany. In 1942, a special office was created to recruit labor for German farms and industries. By the summer of 1944, 7 million foreign workers were laboring in Germany, constituting 20 percent of the labor force. At the same time, another 7 million workers were supplying forced labor in their own countries on farms, in industries, and even in military camps. The brutality of Germany's recruitment policies often led more and more people to resist the Nazi occupation forces.

The Holocaust

No aspect of the Nazi new order was more terrifying than the deliberate attempt to exterminate the Jews of Europe. Racial struggle was a key element in Hitler's ideology and meant to him a clearly defined conflict of opposites: the Aryans, creators of human cultural development, against the Jews, parasites who were trying to destroy the Aryans. Himmler and the SS organization closely shared Hitler's racial ideology. The SS was given responsibility for what the Nazis called their **Final Solution** to the "Jewish problem"—the annihilation of the Jewish people. After the defeat of Poland, the SS ordered the *Einsatzgruppen* (YN-zahtz-groop-un), or special strike forces, to round up all Polish Jews and concentrate them in ghettos established in a number of Polish cities.

In June 1941, the *Einsatzgruppen* were given new responsibilities as mobile killing units. These SS death squads followed the regular army's advance into Russia. Their job was to round up Jews in their villages and execute and bury them in mass graves, often giant pits dug by the victims themselves before they were shot. Such constant killing produced morale problems among the SS executioners. During a visit to Minsk in the Soviet Union, Himmler tried to build morale by pointing out that he "would not like it if Germans did such a thing gladly. But their conscience was in no way impaired, for they were soldiers who had to carry out every order unconditionally. He alone had responsibility before God and Hitler for everything that was happening."[6]

Although it has been estimated that as many as a million Jews were killed by the *Einsatzgruppen*, this approach to solving the Jewish problem was soon perceived as inadequate. So the Nazis opted for the systematic annihilation of the European Jewish population in death camps. Jews from countries occupied by Germany (or sympathetic to Germany) were rounded up, packed like cattle into freight trains, and shipped to Poland, where six extermination centers were built for this purpose. The largest and most famous was Auschwitz-Birkenau (OW-shvitz-BEER-kuh-now). Medical technicians chose Zyklon B (the commercial name for hydrogen cyanide) as the most effective gas for quickly killing large numbers of people in gas chambers designed to look like shower rooms to facilitate the cooperation of the victims.

The death camps were up and running by the spring of 1942; by the summer, Jews were also being shipped from France, Belgium, and the Netherlands. Even as the Allies were making significant advances in 1944, Jews were being shipped from Greece and Hungary. A harrowing experience awaited the Jews when they arrived at one of the six death camps. Rudolf Höss (HESS), commandant at Auschwitz-Birkenau, described it:

We had two SS doctors on duty at Auschwitz to examine the incoming transports of prisoners. The prisoners would be marched by one of the doctors who would make spot decisions as they walked by. Those who were fit for work were sent into the camp. Others were sent immediately to the extermination plants. Children of tender years were invariably exterminated since by reason of their youth they were unable to work. . . . At Auschwitz we endeavored to fool the victims into thinking that they were to go through a delousing process. Of course, frequently they realized our true intentions and we sometimes had riots and difficulties due to that fact.[7]

About 30 percent of the arrivals at Auschwitz were sent to a labor camp; the remainder went to the gas chambers (see the box on p. 667). After they had been gassed, the bodies were burned in specially built crematoria. The victims' goods and even their bodies were used for economic gain. Women's hair was cut off, collected, and used to stuff mattresses or make cloth. Altogether, the Germans killed between 5 and 6 million Jews, more than 3 million of them in the death camps. About 90 percent of the Jewish populations of Poland, the Baltic countries, and Germany were exterminated. Overall, the Holocaust was responsible for the death of nearly two of every three Jews in Europe.

The Nazis were also responsible for another Holocaust, the death by shooting, starvation, or overwork of at least another 9 to 10 million people. Because the Nazis also considered the Gypsies of Europe (like the Jews) a race containing alien blood, they were systematically rounded up for extermination. About 40 percent of Europe's one million Gypsies were killed in the death camps. The leading elements of the "subhuman" Slavic peoples—the clergy, intelligentsia, civil leaders, judges, and lawyers—were arrested and deliberately killed. Probably an additional 4 million Poles, Ukrainians, and Byelorussians lost their lives as slave laborers for Nazi Germany, and 3 to 4 million Soviet prisoners of war were killed in captivity. The Nazis also singled out homosexuals for persecution, and thousands lost their lives in concentration camps.

The New Order in Asia

Once the takeover was completed, Japanese war policy in the occupied areas in Asia became essentially defensive, as Japan hoped to use its new possessions to meet its burgeoning needs for raw materials, such as tin, oil, and rubber, and also as an outlet for Japanese manufactured goods. To provide an organizational structure for the arrangement, Japanese leaders set up the Great East Asia Co-Prosperity Sphere, a self-sufficient economic community designed to provide mutual benefits to the occupied areas and the home country.

The Holocaust: The Camp Commandant and the Camp Victims

POLITICS & GOVERNMENT

The systematic annihilation of millions of men, women, and children in extermination camps makes the Holocaust one of the most horrifying events in history. The first document is taken from an account by Rudolf Höss, commandant of the extermination camp at Auschwitz-Birkenau. In the second document, a French doctor explains what happened at one of the crematoria described by Hoss.

Commandant Höss Describes the Equipment

The two large crematoria, Nos. I and II, were built during the winter of 1942–43. . . . Each . . . could cremate c. 2,000 corpses within twenty-four hours. . . . Crematoria I and II both had underground undressing and gassing rooms which could be completely ventilated. The corpses were brought up to the ovens on the floor above by lift. The gas chambers could hold c. 3,000 people.

The firm of Topf had calculated that the two smaller crematoria, III and IV, would each be able to cremate 1,500 corpses within twenty-four hours. However, owing to the wartime shortage of materials, the builders were obliged to economize, and so the undressing rooms and gassing rooms were built above ground and the ovens were of a less solid construction. But it soon became apparent that the flimsy construction of these two four-retort ovens was not up to the demands made on it. No. III ceased operating altogether after a short time and later was no longer used. No. IV had to be repeatedly shut down since after a short period in operation of 4–6 weeks, the ovens and chimneys had burnt out. The

victims of the gassing were mainly burnt in pits behind crematorium IV.

The largest number of people gassed and cremated within twenty-four hours was somewhat over 9,000.

A French Doctor Describes the Victims

It is mid-day, when a long line of women, children, and old people enter the yard. The senior official in charge . . . climbs on a bench to tell them that they are going to have a bath and that afterward they will get a drink of hot coffee. They all undress in the yard. . . . The doors are opened and an indescribable jostling begins. The first people to enter the gas chamber begin to draw back. They sense the death which awaits them. The SS men put an end to this pushing and shoving with blows from their rifle butts beating the heads of the horrified women who are desperately hugging their children. The massive oak double doors are shut. For two endless minutes one can hear banging on the walls and screams which are no longer human. And then—not a sound. Five minutes later the doors are opened. The corpses, squashed together and distorted, fall out like a waterfall. . . . The bodies, which are still warm, pass through the hands of the hairdresser, who cuts their hair, and the dentist, who pulls out their gold teeth. . . . One more transport has just been processed through No. IV crematorium.

Q What "equipment" does Höss describe? What process does the French doctor describe? Is there any sympathy for the victims in either account? Why or why not? How could such a horrifying process have been allowed to occur?

Sources: Commandant Höss Describes the Equipment. From *Commandant of Auschwitz: The Autobiography of Rudolph Hoss*, Cleveland World Publishing Company. A French Doctor Describes the Victims. From *Nazism: A History in Documents and Eyewitness Accounts*, Vol. II by J. Noakes and G. Pridham. Copyright © 1988 by Department of History and Archaeology, University of Exeter.

The Japanese conquest of Southeast Asia had been accomplished under the slogan "Asia for the Asians." Japanese officials in the occupied territories quickly promised that independent governments would be established under Japanese tutelage. Such governments were eventually established in Burma, the Dutch East Indies, Vietnam, and the Philippines.

In fact, however, real power rested with the Japanese military authorities in each territory, and the local Japanese military command was directly subordinated to the army general staff in Tokyo. The economic resources of the colonies were exploited for the benefit of the Japanese war machine, while natives were recruited to serve in local military units or conscripted to work on public works projects. In some cases, the people living in the occupied areas were subjected to severe hardships. In Indochina, for example, forced requisitions of rice by the local Japanese authorities for shipment abroad created a food shortage that caused the starvation of more than a million Vietnamese in 1944 and 1945.

At first, many Southeast Asian nationalists took Japanese promises at face value and agreed to cooperate with their new masters. But as the exploitative nature of Japanese occupation policies became clear, sentiment turned against the new order. Japanese officials sometimes unwittingly provoked such attitudes by their arrogance and contempt for local customs.

Like German soldiers in occupied Europe, Japanese military forces often had little respect for the lives of their subject peoples. In their conquest of Nanjing, China, in 1937, Japanese soldiers had devoted several days to killing, raping, and looting. Almost 800,000 Koreans were sent overseas, most of them as forced laborers, to Japan. Tens of thousands of women from Korea and the Philippines were forced to be "comfort women" (prostitutes) for Japanese troops. The Japanese also made extensive use of both prisoners of war and local peoples as laborers on construction projects for the war effort. In building the Burma-Thailand railway in 1943, for example, the Japanese used 61,000 Australian, British, and Dutch prisoners of war and almost 300,000 workers from Burma, Malaya, Thailand, and the Dutch East Indies. By the time the railway was completed, 12,000 Allied prisoners of war and 90,000 local workers had died from the inadequate diet and appalling work conditions in an unhealthy climate.

The Home Front

Q FOCUS QUESTION: What were conditions like on the home front for the major belligerents in World War II?

World War II was even more of a total war than World War I. Fighting was much more widespread and covered most of the world. The number of civilians killed was also far higher.

Mobilizing the People: Three Examples

The initial defeats of the Soviet Union led to drastic emergency mobilization measures that affected the civilian population. Leningrad, for example, experienced nine hundred days of siege, during which its inhabitants became so desperate for food that they ate dogs, cats, and mice. As the German army made its rapid advance into Soviet territory, the factories in the western part of the Soviet Union were dismantled and shipped to the interior—to the Urals, western Siberia, and the Volga region. Machines were set down on the bare earth, and walls went up around them as workers began their work.

Stalin called the widespread military and industrial mobilization of the nation a "battle of machines," and the Soviets won, producing 78,000 tanks and 98,000 artillery pieces. In 1943, fully 55 percent of Soviet national income went for war matériel, compared to 15 percent in 1940 (see the comparative essay "Paths to Modernization" on p. 669).

Soviet women played a major role in the war effort. Women and girls were enlisted for work in industries, mines, and railroads. Overall the number of women working in industry increased almost 60 percent. Soviet women were also expected to dig antitank ditches and work as air raid wardens. In addition, the Soviet Union was the only country in World War II to use women as combatants. Soviet women functioned as snipers and as crews in bomber squadrons.

In August 1914, Germans had enthusiastically cheered their soldiers marching off to war; in September 1939, the streets were quiet. Many Germans were apathetic or, even worse for the Nazi regime, had a foreboding of disaster. Hitler was very aware of the importance of the home front. He believed that the collapse of the home front in World War I had caused Germany's defeat. To avoid a repetition of that experience, he adopted economic policies that may indeed have cost Germany the war.

To maintain the morale of the home front during the first two years of the war, Hitler refused to cut production of consumer goods or increase the production of armaments. After German defeats on the Russian front and the American entry into the war, however, the situation changed. Early in 1942, Hitler finally ordered a massive increase in armaments production and the size of the army. Hitler's architect, Albert Speer (AHL-bert SHPAYR), was made minister for armaments and munitions in 1942. By eliminating waste and rationalizing procedures, Speer was able to triple the production of armaments between 1942 and 1943, despite the intense Allied air raids. Speer's urgent plea for a total mobilization of resources for the war effort went unheeded, however. Hitler, fearful of civilian morale problems that would undermine the home front, refused any dramatic cuts in the production of consumer goods. A total mobilization of the economy was not implemented until 1944, but by that time, it was too late.

The war caused a reversal in Nazi attitudes toward women. Nazi resistance to female employment declined as the war progressed and more and more men were called up for military service. Nazi magazines now proclaimed, "We see the woman as the eternal mother of

COMPARATIVE ESSAY

Paths to Modernization

POLITICS & GOVERNMENT

To the casual observer, the most important feature of the first half of the twentieth century was the rise of a virulent form of competitive nationalism that began in Europe and ultimately descended into the cauldron of two destructive world wars. Behind the scenes, however, another competition was taking place over the most effective path to modernization.

The traditional approach, in which modernization was fostered by an independent urban merchant class, had been adopted by Great Britain, France, and the United States and led to the emergence of democratic societies on the capitalist model. In the second approach, adopted in the late nineteenth century by imperial Germany and Meiji Japan, modernization was carried out by traditional elites in the absence of a strong independent bourgeois class. Both Germany and Japan relied on strong government intervention to promote the growth of national wealth and power, and in both nations, modernization led ultimately to the formation of fascist and militarist regimes during the depression years of the early 1930s.

The third approach, selected by Vladimir Lenin after the Bolshevik Revolution in 1917, was designed to carry out an industrial revolution without going through an intermediate capitalist stage. Guided by the Communist Party in the almost total absence of an urban middle class, an advanced industrial society would be created by destroying the concept of private property. Although Lenin's plans called for the eventual "withering away of the state," the party adopted totalitarian methods to eliminate enemies of the revolution and carry out the changes needed to create a future classless utopia.

How did these various approaches contribute to the crises that afflicted the world during the first half of the twentieth century? The democratic-capitalist approach proved to be a considerable success in an economic sense, leading to advanced economies that could produce manufactured goods at a rate never seen before. Societies just beginning to undergo their own industrial revolutions tried to imitate the success of the capitalist nations by carrying out their own "revolutions from above," as in Germany and Japan. But the Great Depression and competition over resources and markets

© Bettmann/CORBIS

The Path to Modernization. One aspect of the Soviet effort to create an advanced industrial society was the collectivization of agriculture, which included the rapid mechanization of food production. In this photograph, peasants are watching a new tractor at work.

soon led to an intense rivalry between the established capitalist states and their ambitious late arrivals, a rivalry that ultimately erupted into global conflict.

In the first decade of the twentieth century, imperial Russia appeared ready to launch its own bid to join the ranks of the industrialized nations. But that effort was derailed by its entry into World War I, and before that conflict had come to an end, the Bolsheviks were in power. Isolated from the capitalist marketplace by mutual consent, the Soviet Union was able to avoid being dragged into the Great Depression but, despite Stalin's efforts, was unsuccessful in staying out of the "battle of imperialists" that followed at the end of the 1930s. As World War II came to an end, the stage was set for a battle of the victors—the United States and the Soviet Union—over political and ideological supremacy.

Q *What were the three major paths to modernization in the first half of the twentieth century, and why did they lead to conflict?*

our people, but also as the working and fighting comrade of the man."[8] But the number of women working in industry, agriculture, commerce, and domestic service increased only slightly. In September 1944, 14.9 million women were employed, compared with 14.6 million in May 1939. Many women, especially those of the middle class, resisted regular employment, particularly in factories.

Wartime Japan was a highly mobilized society. To guarantee its control over all national resources, the government set up a planning board to control prices, wages, the utilization of labor, and the allocation of resources. Traditional habits of obedience and hierarchy, buttressed by the concept of imperial divinity, were emphasized to encourage citizens to sacrifice their resources, and sometimes their lives, for the national cause. The system culminated in the final years of the war, when young Japanese were encouraged to volunteer en masse to serve as pilots in the suicide missions—known as *kamikaze* (kah-mi-KAH-zee), or "divine wind"—against U.S. battleships.

Women's rights too were to be sacrificed to the greater national cause. Already by 1937, Japanese women were being exhorted to fulfill their patriotic duty by bearing more children and by espousing the slogans of the Greater Japanese Women's Association. Japan was extremely reluctant to mobilize women on behalf of the war effort, however. General Hideki Tojo (hee-DEK-ee TOH-joh), prime minister from 1941 to 1944, opposed female employment, arguing that "the weakening of the family system would be the weakening of the nation. . . . We are able to do our duties only because we have wives and mothers at home."[9] Female employment increased during the war, but only in areas where women traditionally worked, such as the textile industry and farming. Instead of using women to meet labor shortages, the Japanese government brought in Korean and Chinese laborers.

The Frontline Civilians: The Bombing of Cities

Bombing was used in World War II against nonhuman military targets, against enemy troops, and against civilian populations. The bombing of civilians made World War II as devastating for noncombatants as it was for frontline soldiers. A small number of bombing raids in the last year of World War I had given rise to the argument that public outcry over the bombing of civilian populations would be an effective way to coerce governments into making peace. Consequently, European air forces began to develop long-range bombers in the 1930s.

The first sustained use of civilian bombing failed to support the theory. Beginning in early September 1940, the German Luftwaffe subjected London and many other British cities and towns to nightly air raids, making the Blitz (as the British called the German air raids) a national experience. Londoners took the first heavy blows but kept up their morale, setting the standard for the rest of the British population (see the comparative illustration on p. 671).

The British failed to learn from their own experience, however. Prime Minister Winston Churchill and his advisers believed that destroying German communities would break civilian morale and bring victory. Major bombing raids began in 1942. On May 31, 1942, Cologne became the first German city to be subjected to an attack by a thousand bombers. Bombing raids added an element of terror to circumstances already made difficult by growing shortages of food, clothing, and fuel. Germans especially feared incendiary bombs, which ignited firestorms that swept destructive paths through the cities. The ferocious bombing of Dresden from February 13 to 15, 1945, created a firestorm that may have killed as many as 35,000 inhabitants and refugees.

Germany suffered enormously from the Allied bombing raids. Millions of buildings were destroyed, and possibly half a million civilians died from the raids. Nevertheless, it is highly unlikely that Allied bombing sapped the morale of the German people. Instead Germans, whether pro-Nazi or anti-Nazi, fought on stubbornly, often driven simply by a desire to live. Nor did the bombing destroy Germany's industrial capacity. The Allied strategic bombing survey revealed that the production of war matériel actually increased between 1942 and 1944.

In Japan, the bombing of civilians reached a horrendous new level with the use of the first atomic bomb. Attacks on Japanese cities by the new American B-29 Superfortresses, the biggest bombers of the war, had begun on November 24, 1944. By the summer of 1945, many of Japan's industries had been destroyed, along with one-fourth of its dwellings. After the Japanese government decreed the mobilization of all people between the ages of thirteen and sixty into the so-called People's Volunteer Corps, President Truman and his advisers decided that Japanese fanaticism might mean a million American casualties, and Truman decided to drop the newly developed atomic bomb on Hiroshima and Nagasaki. The destruction was incredible. Of 76,000 buildings near the hypocenter of the explosion in Hiroshima, 70,000 were flattened, and 140,000 of the city's 400,000 inhabitants had died by the end of 1945. Over the next five years, another 50,000 perished from the effects of radiation. The dropping of the atomic bomb on Hiroshima on August 6, 1945, announced the dawn of the nuclear age.

COMPARATIVE ILLUSTRATION

FAMILY & SOCIETY

The Bombing of Civilians—East and West. World War II was the most destructive war in world history, not only for frontline soldiers but for civilians at home as well. The most devastating bombing of civilians came near the end of World War II when the United States dropped atomic bombs on the Japanese cities of Hiroshima and Nagasaki. At the left is a view of Hiroshima after the bombing that shows the incredible devastation produced by the atomic bomb. The picture at the right shows a street in Clydebank, near Glasgow in Scotland, the day after the city was bombed by the Germans in March 1941. Only 7 of the city's 12,000 houses were left undamaged; 35,000 of the 47,000 inhabitants became homeless overnight.

Q *What was the rationale for bombing civilian populations? Did such bombing achieve its goal?*

Aftermath of the War

Q FOCUS QUESTIONS: What were the costs of World War II? How did World War II affect the European nations' colonial empires? How did the Allies' visions of the postwar differ, and how did these differences contribute to the emergence of the Cold War?

World War II was the most destructive war in history. Much had been at stake. Nazi Germany followed a worldview based on racial extermination and the enslavement of millions in order to create an Aryan racial empire. The Japanese, fueled by extreme nationalist ideals, also pursued dreams of empire in Asia that led to mass murder and untold devastation. Fighting the Axis Powers in World War II required the mobilization of millions of ordinary men and women in the Allied countries who struggled to preserve a different way of life. As Winston Churchill once put it, "War is horrible, but slavery is worse."

The Costs of World War II

The costs of World War II were enormous. At least 21 million soldiers died. Civilian deaths were even greater and are now estimated at around 40 million, of whom more than 28 million were Russian and Chinese. The Soviet Union experienced the greatest losses: 10 million soldiers and 19 million civilians. In 1945, millions of people around the world faced starvation: in Europe, 100 million people depended on food relief of some kind.

Millions of people had also been uprooted by the war and became "displaced persons." Europe alone may have had 30 million displaced persons, many of whom found it hard to return home. In Asia, millions of Japanese were returned from the former Japanese empire to Japan, while thousands of Korean forced laborers returned to Korea.

Devastation was everywhere. Most areas of Europe had been damaged or demolished. China was in shambles after eight years of conflict, the Philippines had suffered heavy damage, and large sections of the major cities in Japan had been destroyed in air raids. The total monetary cost of the war has been estimated at $4 trillion. The economies of most belligerents, with the exception of the United States, were left drained and on the brink of disaster.

World War II and the European Colonies: Decolonization

As we saw in Chapter 24, movements for independence had begun in earnest in Africa and Asia in the years between World War I and World War II. After World War II, these movements grew even louder. The ongoing subjugation of peoples by colonial powers seemed at odds with the goals the Allies had pursued in overthrowing the repressive regimes of Germany, Italy, and Japan. Then, too, indigenous peoples everywhere took up the call for national self-determination and expressed their determination to fight for independence.

The ending of the European powers' colonial empires did not come easy, however. In 1941, Churchill had said, "I have not become His Majesty's Chief Minister in order to preside over the liquidation of the British Empire." Britain and France in particular seemed reluctant to let go of their colonies, but for a variety of reasons both eventually gave in the obvious—the days of empire were over.

During the war, the Japanese had already humiliated the Western states by overrunning their colonial empires. In addition, colonial soldiers who had fought on behalf of the Allies (India, for example, had contributed large numbers of troops to the British Indian Army) were well aware that Allied war aims included the principle of self-determination for the peoples of the world. Equally important to the process of **decolonization**, the power of the European states had been destroyed by the exhaustive struggles of World War II. The greatest empire builder, Great Britain, no longer had the energy or the wealth to maintain its empire. Given this combination of circumstances, a rush of decolonization swept the world after the war.

The Allied War Conferences

The total victory of the Allies in World War II was not followed by a real peace but by the emergence of a new conflict known as the **Cold War**, which dominated world politics until the end of the 1980s. The Cold War grew out of military, political, and ideological differences, especially between the Soviet Union and the United States, that became apparent at the Allied war conferences held in the last years of the war.

Stalin, Roosevelt, and Churchill, the leaders of the Big Three of the Grand Alliance, met at Tehran, the capital of Iran, in November 1943 to decide the future course of the war. Stalin and Roosevelt argued successfully for an American-British invasion of the Continent through France, which they scheduled for the spring of 1944. This meant that Soviet and British-American forces would meet in defeated Germany along a north-south dividing line and that Soviet forces would most likely liberate eastern Europe. The Allies also agreed to a partition of postwar Germany.

By the time of the conference at Yalta in southern Russia in February 1945, the defeat of Germany was a foregone conclusion. The Western powers now faced the reality of 11 million Red Army soldiers taking possession of eastern and central Europe. Stalin, deeply suspicious of the Western powers, desired a buffer to protect the Soviet Union from possible future Western aggression. At the same time, however, Stalin was eager to obtain economically important resources and strategic military positions. Roosevelt by this time was moving toward the idea of self-determination for Europe. The Grand Alliance approved a declaration on liberated Europe. This was a pledge to assist liberated European nations in the creation of "democratic institutions of their own choice." Liberated countries were to hold free elections to determine their political systems.

At Yalta, Roosevelt sought Russian military help against Japan. The atomic bomb was not yet assured, and American military planners feared the possibility of heavy losses in amphibious assaults on the Japanese home islands. Roosevelt therefore agreed to Stalin's price for military assistance against Japan: possession of Sakhalin and the Kurile Islands, as well as two warm-water ports and railroad rights in Manchuria.

The creation of the United Nations was a major American concern at Yalta. Roosevelt hoped to ensure the participation of the Big Three powers in a postwar international organization before difficult issues divided them into hostile camps. After a number of compromises, both Churchill and Stalin accepted Roosevelt's plans for a United Nations organization and set the first meeting for San Francisco in April 1945.

The issues of Germany and eastern Europe were treated less decisively. The Big Three reaffirmed that Germany must surrender unconditionally and created four occupation zones (see Map 25.3). A compromise was also worked out in regard to Poland. Stalin agreed to free elections in the future to determine a new government. But the issue of free elections in eastern Europe caused a serious rift between the Soviets and the Americans. In principle, eastern European governments were to be freely elected, but they were also supposed to be pro-Soviet. This attempt to reconcile two irreconcilable goals was doomed to failure, as soon became evident at the next conference of the Big Three.

The Potsdam conference of July 1945 began under a cloud of mistrust. Roosevelt had died on April 12 and

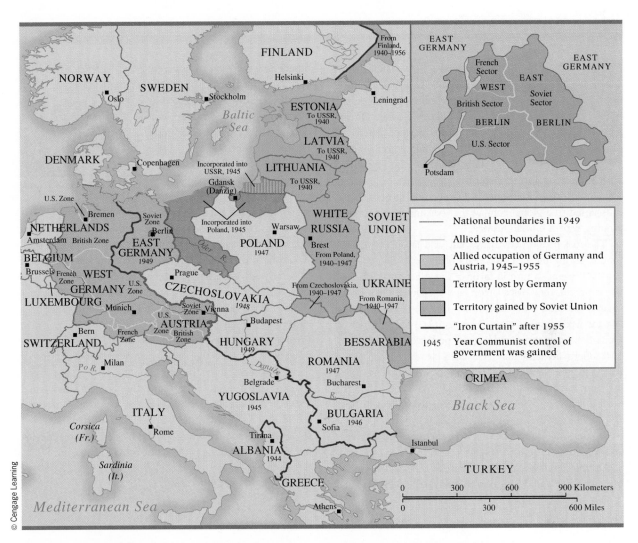

MAP 25.3 Territorial Changes in Europe After World War II. In the last months of World War II, the Red Army occupied much of eastern Europe. Stalin sought pro-Soviet satellite states in the region as a buffer against future invasions from western Europe, whereas Britain and the United States wanted democratically elected governments. Soviet military control of the territory settled the question.

Q *Which country gained the greatest territory at the expense of Germany?*

had been succeeded as president by Harry Truman. At Potsdam, Truman demanded free elections throughout eastern Europe. Stalin responded, "A freely elected government in any of these East European countries would be anti-Soviet, and that we cannot allow."[10] After a bitterly fought and devastating war, Stalin sought absolute military security. To him, it could be gained only by the presence of Communist states in eastern Europe. Free elections might result in governments hostile to the Soviets. By the middle of 1945, only an invasion by Western forces could undo developments in eastern Europe, and few people favored such a policy.

As the war slowly receded into the past, the reality of conflicting ideologies had reappeared. Many in the West

interpreted Soviet policy as part of a worldwide Communist conspiracy. The Soviets viewed Western, especially American, policy as nothing less than global capitalist expansionism or, in Leninist terms, economic imperialism. In March 1946, in a speech to an American audience, former British prime minister Winston Churchill declared that "an iron curtain" had "descended across the continent," dividing Germany and Europe into two hostile camps. Stalin branded Churchill's speech a "call to war with the Soviet Union." Only months after the world's most devastating conflict had ended, the world seemed once again to be bitterly divided in the Cold War.

CHAPTER SUMMARY

Between 1933 and 1939, Europeans watched as Adolf Hitler rebuilt Germany into a great military power. During that same period, Japan fell under the influence of military leaders who conspired with right-wing forces to push a program of expansion. The ambitions of Germany in Europe and those of Japan in Asia led to a global conflict that became the most devastating war in human history.

The Axis nations, Germany, Italy, and Japan, proved victorious during the first two years of the war. By 1942, the war had begun to turn in favor of the Allies, an alliance of Great Britain, the Soviet Union, and the United States. The Japanese advance was ended at the naval battles of the Coral Sea and Midway in 1942. In February 1943, the Soviets won the Battle of Stalingrad and began a push westward. By mid-1943, Germany and Italy had been driven out of North Africa; in June 1944, Rome fell to the Allies, and an Allied invasion force landed in Normandy in France. After the Soviets linked up with British and American forces in April 1945, Hitler committed suicide, and the war in Europe came to an end. After atomic bombs were dropped on Hiroshima and Nagasaki in August 1945, the war in Asia also ended.

During its domination of Europe, the Nazi empire brought death and destruction to many, especially Jews and

others that the Nazis considered racially inferior. The Japanese New Order in Asia, while claiming to promote "Asia for the Asians" also brought exploitation, severe hardship, and often death for the peoples under Japanese control. All sides bombed civilian populations, making the war as devastating for civilians as for frontline soldiers.

If Hitler had been successful, the Nazi New Order, built on authoritarianism, racial extermination, and the brutal oppression of peoples, would have meant a triumph of barbarism and the end of freedom and equality, which, however imperfectly realized, had become important ideals in Western civilization.

The Nazis lost, but only after tremendous sacrifices and costs. Much of European civilization lay in ruins. Europeans now watched helplessly as the two new superpowers created by the two world wars took control of their destinies. Even before the last battles had been fought, the United States and the Soviet Union had arrived at different visions of the postwar European world. No sooner had the war ended than their differences gave rise to a new and potentially even more devastating conflict known as the Cold War.

CHAPTER TIMELINE

	1925	1930	1935	1940	1945
Europe	Mussolini creates Fascist dictatorship in Italy	Stalin's first five-year plan begins	Hitler and Nazis come to power in Germany — *Kristallnacht*	Fall of France — The Holocaust	German defeat at Stalingrad — Conferences at Yalta and Potsdam
Japan		Japanese takeover of Manchuria		Japanese attack on Pearl Harbor — The Great East Asia Co-Prosperity Sphere	Atomic bomb dropped on Hiroshima

Upon Reflection

Q How do you account for the early successes of the Germans from 1939 to 1941?

Q How did the Nazis and the Japanese attempt to establish new orders in Europe and Asia after their military victories, and what were the results of their efforts?

Q How did the attempt to arrive at a peace settlement after World War II lead to the beginnings of a new conflict known as the Cold War?

Key Terms

fascism (p. 651)
totalitarian state (p. 651)
blitzkrieg (p. 657)
Final Solution (p. 666)
Einsatzgruppen (p. 666)
decolonization (p. 672)
Cold War (p. 672)

Suggested Reading

THE DICTATORIAL REGIMES The best biography of Mussolini is **R. J. B. Bosworth,** *Mussolini* (London, 2002). A brief but sound survey of Nazi Germany is **J. J. Spielvogel** and **D. Redles,** *Hitler and Nazi Germany: A History,* 6th ed. (Upper Saddle River, N.J., 2010). The best biography of Hitler is **I. Kershaw,** *Hitler, 1889–1936: Hubris* (New York, 1999), and *Hitler: Nemesis* (New York, 2000). On the Nazis in power, see **R. J. Evans,** *The Third Reich in Power, 1933–1939* (New York, 2005). The collectivization of agriculture in the Soviet Union is examined in **S. Fitzpatrick,** *Stalin's Peasants: Resistance and Survival in the Russian Village After Collectivization* (New York, 1995). On Stalin himself, see **R. Service,** *Stalin: A Biography* (Cambridge, Mass., 2006).

THE PATH TO WAR On the causes of World War II, see **A. J. Crozier,** *Causes of the Second World War* (Oxford, 1997). On the origins of the war in the Pacific, see **A. Iriye,** *The Origins of the Second World War in Asia and the Pacific* (London, 1987).

WORLD WAR II The best general work on World War II is **G. Weinberg,** *A World at Arms: A Global History of World War II,* 2nd ed. (Cambridge, 2005). A good military history of World War II can be found in **W. Murray** and **A. R. Millett,** *A War to Be Won: Fighting the Second World War* (Cambridge, Mass., 2000).

THE HOLOCAUST Excellent studies of the Holocaust include **S. Friedander,** *The Years of Extermination: Nazi Germany and the Jews, 1939–1945* (New York, 2007), and **L. Yahil,** *The Holocaust* (New York, 1990). For a brief study, see **D. Dwork** and **R. J. van Pelt,** *Holocaust: A History* (New York, 2002).

THE HOME FRONT On the home front in Germany, see **M. Kitchen,** *Nazi Germany at War* (New York, 1995). The Soviet Union during the war is examined in **M. Harrison,** *Soviet Planning in Peace and War, 1938–1945* (Cambridge, 1985). The Japanese home front is examined in **T. R. H. Havens,** *The Valley of Darkness: The Japanese People and World War Two* (New York, 1978). On the Allied bombing campaign against Germany, see **R. Hansen,** *Fire and Fury: The Allied Bombing of Germany, 1942–1945* (London, 2008).

Visit the CourseMate website at www.cengagebrain.com for additional study tools and review materials for this chapter.

PART V

Toward a Global Civilization?
The World Since 1945

AS WORLD WAR II came to an end, the survivors of that bloody struggle could afford to face the future with a cautious optimism. There was reason to hope that the bitter rivalry that had marked relations among the Western powers would finally be put to an end and that the wartime alliance of the United States, Great Britain, and the Soviet Union could be maintained into the postwar era.

More than sixty years later, these hopes have been only partly realized. In the decades following the war, the Western capitalist nations managed to recover from the economic depression that had led into World War II. The bloody conflicts that had erupted among European nations during the first half of the twentieth century ended, and Germany and Japan were fully reintegrated into the world community.

At the same time, the prospects for a stable, peaceful world and an end to balance-of-power politics were hampered by the emergence of a grueling and sometimes tense ideological struggle between the socialist and capitalist camps, a competition headed by the only remaining great powers, the Soviet Union and the United States.

In the shadow of this rivalry, the Western European states made a remarkable economic recovery and reached untold levels of prosperity. In Eastern Europe, Soviet domination, both political and economic, seemed so complete that many people doubted it could ever be undone. But communism had never put down deep roots in Eastern Europe, and in the late 1980s, when Soviet leader Mikhail Gorbachev indicated that his government would no longer intervene militarily to keep the Eastern European states in line, they were quick to embrace their freedom and adopt new economic structures based on Western models.

The peoples of Africa and Asia had their own reasons for optimism as World War II came to a close. In the Atlantic Charter, Franklin Roosevelt and Winston Churchill had set forth a joint declaration of their peace aims calling for the self-determination of all peoples.

As it turned out, some colonial powers were reluctant to divest themselves of their colonies. Still, World War II had severely undermined the stability of the colonial order, and by the end of the 1940s, most colonies in Asia had received their independence. Africa followed a decade or two later.

Broadly speaking, the leaders of these newly liberated countries set forth three goals at the outset of independence. They wanted to throw off the shackles of Western economic domination and ensure material prosperity for all of their citizens. They wanted to introduce new political institutions that would enhance the right of self-determination of their peoples. And they wanted to develop a sense of common nationhood within the population and establish secure territorial boundaries. Most opted to follow a capitalist or a moderately socialist path toward economic development. In a few cases—most notably in China and Vietnam—revolutionary leaders opted for the communist mode of development.

Regardless of the path chosen, to many the results were often disappointing. Much of Africa and Asia remained economically dependent on the advanced industrial nations. Some societies faced severe problems of urban and rural poverty. Others were rent by bitter internal conflicts.

What had happened to tarnish the bright dream of economic affluence? During the late 1950s and early 1960s, the dominant school of thought among scholars and

government officials in the United States was modernization theory, which took the view that the problems faced by the newly independent countries were a consequence of the difficult transition from a traditional to a modern society. Modernization theorists were convinced that agrarian countries were destined to follow the West and create modern industrial societies but that they would need both time and substantial amounts of economic and technological assistance from the West to do so.

Eventually, modernization theory came under attack from a new generation of scholars, who argued that the responsibility for continued economic underdevelopment in the postcolonial world lay not with the countries themselves but with their continued domination by the former colonial powers. In this view, known as dependency theory, the countries of Asia, Africa, and Latin America were the victims of the international marketplace, in which high prices were charged for the manufactured goods of the West while low prices were paid to the preindustrial countries for their raw material exports. Efforts by such countries to build up their industrial sectors and move into the stage of self-sustaining growth were hampered by foreign control of many of their resources via European- and American-owned corporations. To end this "neocolonial" relationship, the dependency theory advocates argued, developing societies should reduce their economic ties with the West and institute a policy of economic self-reliance, thereby taking control over their own destinies.

Leaders of African and Asian countries also encountered problems creating new political cultures responsive to the needs of their citizens. At first, most accepted the concept of democracy as the defining theme of that culture. Within a decade, however, democratic systems throughout the developing world were replaced by military dictatorships or one-party governments that redefined the concept of democracy to fit their own preferences. It was clear that the difficulties in building democratic political institutions in developing societies had been underestimated.

The establishment of a common national identity has in some ways been the most daunting of all the challenges facing the new nations of Asia and Africa. Many of these new states were a composite of various ethnic, religious, and linguistic groups that found it difficult to agree on common symbols of nationalism or national values. The process of establishing an official language and delineating territorial boundaries left over from the colonial era created difficulties in many countries. Internal conflicts spawned by deep-rooted historical and ethnic hatreds have proliferated throughout the world, causing vast numbers of people to move across state boundaries in migrations as large as any since the great migrations of the thirteenth and fourteenth centuries.

The introduction of Western cultural values and customs has also had a destabilizing effect in many areas. Though welcomed by some groups, such ideas are firmly resisted by others. Where Western influence has the effect of undermining traditional customs and religious beliefs, it often provokes violent hostility and sparks tension and even conflict within individual societies. Much of the anger recently directed at the United States in Muslim countries has undoubtedly been generated by such feelings.

Nonetheless, social and political attitudes are changing rapidly in many Asian and African countries as new economic circumstances have led to a more secular worldview, a decline in traditional hierarchical relations, and a more open attitude toward sexual practices. In part, these changes are a consequence of the influence of Western music, movies, and television. But they are also a product of the growth of an affluent middle class in many societies of Asia and Africa.

Today, we live not only in a world economy but in a world society, where a revolution in the Middle East can cause a rise in the price of oil in the United States and a change in social behavior in Malaysia and Indonesia, where the collapse of an empire in Asia can send shock waves as far as Hanoi and Havana, and where a terrorist attack in New York City or London can disrupt financial markets around the world. ◆

Churchill, Roosevelt, and Stalin at Yalta

Imperial War Museum, London//© The Art Archive at Art Resource, NY

East and West in the Grip of the Cold War

CHAPTER OUTLINE
AND FOCUS QUESTIONS

The Collapse of the Grand Alliance

Q Why were the United States and the Soviet Union suspicious of each other after World War II, and what events between 1945 and 1949 heightened the tensions between the two nations?

Cold War in Asia

Q How and why did Mao Zedong and the Communists come to power in China, and what were the Cold War implications of their triumph?

From Confrontation to Coexistence

Q What events led to the era of coexistence in the 1960s, and to what degree did each side contribute to the reduction in international tensions?

An Era of Equivalence

Q Why did the Cold War briefly flare up again in the 1980s, and why did it come to a definitive end at the end of the decade?

CRITICAL THINKING

Q How have historians answered the question of whether the United States or the Soviet Union bears the primary responsibility for the Cold War, and what evidence can be presented on each side of the issue?

"OUR MEETING HERE in the Crimea has reaffirmed our common determination to maintain and strengthen in the peace to come that unity of purpose and of action which has made victory possible and certain for the United Nations in this war. We believe that this is a sacred obligation which our Governments owe to our peoples and to all the peoples of the world."[1]

With these ringing words, drafted at the Yalta Conference in February 1945, U.S. President Franklin D. Roosevelt, Soviet leader Joseph Stalin, and British Prime Minister Winston Churchill affirmed their common hope that the Grand Alliance that had been victorious in World War II could be sustained into the postwar era. Only through continuing and growing cooperation and understanding among the three Allies, the statement asserted, could a secure and lasting peace be realized that, in the words of the Atlantic Charter, would "afford assurance that all the men in all the lands may live out their lives in freedom from fear and want."

Roosevelt hoped that the decisions reached at Yalta would provide the basis for a stable peace in the postwar era. Allied occupation forces—American, British, and French in the west and Soviet in the east—were to bring about the end of Axis administration and to organize the free election of democratic governments throughout Europe. To foster mutual trust and an end to the suspicions that had marked relations between the capitalist world and the Soviet Union prior to the war, Roosevelt tried to reassure Stalin that Moscow's legitimate territorial aspirations and genuine security needs would be adequately met in a durable peace settlement.

It was not to be. Within months after the German surrender, the mutual trust among the Allies—if it had ever truly existed—rapidly disintegrated, and the dream of a stable peace was replaced by the specter of a potential nuclear holocaust. The United Nations, envisioned by its founders as a mechanism for adjudicating international disputes, became mired in partisan bickering. As the Cold War between Moscow and Washington intensified, Europe was divided into two armed camps, while the two superpowers, glaring at each other across a deep ideological divide, held the survival of the entire world in their hands. 📖

The Collapse of the Grand Alliance

Q **FOCUS QUESTION:** Why were the United States and the Soviet Union suspicious of each other after World War II, and what events between 1945 and 1949 heightened the tensions between the two nations?

The problems started in Europe. At the end of the war, Soviet military forces occupied all of Eastern Europe and the Balkans (except Greece, Albania, and Yugoslavia), while U.S. and other Allied forces secured the western part of the Continent. Roosevelt had assumed that free elections, administered promptly by "democratic and peace-loving forces," would lead to democratic governments responsive to the local population. But it soon became clear that the Soviet Union interpreted the Yalta agreement differently. When Soviet occupation authorities began forming a new Polish government, Stalin refused to accept the Polish government-in-exile—headquartered in London during the war and composed mostly of landed aristocrats who harbored a deep distrust of the Soviet Union—and instead set up a government composed of Communists who had spent the war in Moscow. Roosevelt complained to Stalin but eventually agreed to a compromise whereby two members of the

London government were included in the new Communist regime. A week later, Roosevelt was dead of a cerebral hemorrhage, emboldening Stalin to do much as he pleased.

Soviet Domination of Eastern Europe

Similar developments took place in all of the states occupied by Soviet troops. Coalitions of all political parties (except fascist or right-wing parties) were formed to run the government, but within a year or two, the Communist Party in each coalition had assumed the lion's share of power. It was then a short step to the establishment of one-party Communist governments. Between 1945 and 1947, Communist governments became firmly entrenched in East Germany, Bulgaria, Romania, Poland, and Hungary. In Czechoslovakia, with its strong tradition of democratic institutions, the Communists did not achieve their goals until 1948. After the Czech elections of 1946, the Communist Party shared control of the government with the non-Communist parties. When the latter appeared likely to win new elections early in 1948, the Communists seized control of the government on February 25. All other parties were dissolved, and the Communist leader Klement Gottwald (KLEM-ent GUT-vald) (1896–1953) became the new president of Czechoslovakia.

Yugoslavia was a notable exception to the pattern of Soviet dominance in Eastern Europe. The Communist Party there had led resistance to the Nazis during the war and easily assumed power when the war ended. Josip Broz (yaw-SEEP BRAWZ), known as Tito (TEE-toh) (1892–1980), the leader of the Communist resistance movement, appeared to be a loyal Stalinist. After the war, however, he moved to establish an independent Communist state. Stalin hoped to take control of Yugoslavia, but Tito refused to capitulate to Stalin's demands and gained the support of the people (and some sympathy in the West) by portraying the struggle as one of Yugoslav national freedom. In 1958, the Yugoslav party congress asserted that Yugoslav Communists did not see themselves as deviating from communism, only from Stalinism. They considered their more decentralized system, in which workers managed themselves and local communes exercised some political power, closer to the Marxist-Leninist ideal.

To Stalin (who had once boasted, "I will shake my little finger, and there will be no more Tito"), the creation of pliant pro-Soviet regimes throughout Eastern Europe to serve as a buffer zone against the capitalist West may simply have represented his interpretation of the Yalta peace agreement and a reward for sacrifices suffered during the war. If the Soviet leader had any intention of promoting future Communist revolutions in Western Europe—and there is some indication that he did—such developments would have to await the appearance of a new capitalist crisis a decade or more into the future. As Stalin undoubtedly recalled, Lenin had always maintained that revolutions come in waves.

Descent of the Iron Curtain

To the United States, however, the Soviet takeover of Eastern Europe represented an ominous development that threatened Roosevelt's vision of a durable peace. Public suspicion of Soviet intentions grew rapidly, especially among the millions of Americans who still had relatives living in Eastern Europe. Winston Churchill was quick to put such fears into words. In a highly publicized speech at Westminster College in Fulton, Missouri, in March 1946, the former British prime minister declared that an "iron curtain" had "descended across the Continent," dividing Germany and Europe itself into two hostile camps. Stalin responded by branding Churchill's speech a "call to war with the Soviet Union." But he need not have worried. Although public opinion in the United States placed increasing pressure on Roosevelt's successor, Harry Truman (1884–1972), to devise an effective strategy to counter Soviet advances abroad, the American people were in no mood for another war.

The first threat of a U.S.-Soviet confrontation took place in the Middle East. During World War II, British and Soviet troops had been stationed in Iran to prevent Axis occupation of the rich oil fields in that country. Both nations had promised to withdraw their forces after the war, but at the end of 1945, there were ominous signs that Moscow might attempt to use its troops as a bargaining chip to annex Iran's northern territories—known as Azerbaijan (az-ur-by-JAHN)—into the Soviet Union. When the government of Iran, with strong U.S. support, threatened to take the issue to the United Nations, the Soviets backed down and removed their forces from that country in the spring of 1946.

The Truman Doctrine

A civil war in Greece created another potential arena for confrontation between the superpowers and an opportunity for the Truman administration to take a stand. Communist guerrilla forces supported by Tito's Yugoslavia had taken up arms against the pro-Western government in Athens. Great Britain had initially assumed primary responsibility for promoting postwar reconstruction in the eastern Mediterranean, but in 1947, continuing

Eastern Europe in 1948

economic problems caused the British to withdraw from the active role they had been playing in both Greece and Turkey. President Truman, alarmed by British weakness and the possibility of Soviet expansion into the eastern Mediterranean, responded with the **Truman Doctrine**, which said in essence that the United States would provide financial aid to countries that claimed they were threatened by Communist expansion (see the box on p. 683). If the Soviets were not stopped in Greece, the Truman argument ran, then the United States would have to face the spread of communism throughout the free world. As Dean Acheson, the U.S. secretary of state, explained, "Like apples in a barrel infected by disease, the corruption of Greece would infect Iran and all the East . . . likewise Africa . . . Italy . . . France. . . . Not since Rome and Carthage has there been such a polarization of power on this earth."[2]

The somewhat apocalyptic tone of Acheson's statement was intentional. Not only were the American people in no mood for foreign adventures, but the administration's Republican opponents in Congress were in an isolationist frame of mind. Only the prospect of a dire threat from abroad, the president's advisers argued, could persuade the nation to take action. The tactic worked, and Congress voted to provide the aid Truman had requested.

The U.S. suspicion that Moscow was actively supporting the insurgent movement in Greece turned out to be unfounded, however. Stalin was apparently unhappy with Tito's role in the conflict, not only because he suspected that the latter was attempting to create his own sphere of influence in the Balkans but also because it risked provoking a direct confrontation between the United States and the Soviet Union. But the Truman Doctrine had its intended effect in the United States, as public concern about the future intentions of the Soviets rose to new heights.

The Marshall Plan

The proclamation of the Truman Doctrine was followed in June 1947 by the European Recovery Program, better known as the **Marshall Plan**, which provided $13 billion in U.S. assistance for the economic recovery of war-torn Europe. Underlying the program was the belief that Communist aggression fed off economic turmoil. General George C. Marshall had noted in a speech at Harvard University, "Our policy is not directed against any

The Truman Doctrine

POLITICS & GOVERNMENT

In 1947, the battle lines in the Cold War had been clearly drawn. This excerpt is taken from a speech by President Harry Truman to the U.S. Congress in which he justified his request for aid to Greece and Turkey. Truman expressed the urgent need to contain the expansion of communism. Compare this statement with that of Soviet leader Leonid Brezhnev cited on p. 701.

Truman's Speech to Congress, March 12, 1947

The gravity of the situation which confronts the world today necessitates my appearance before a joint session of the Congress. The foreign policy and the national security of this country are involved.

One aspect of the present situation, which I wish to present to you at this time for your consideration and decision, concerns Greece and Turkey.

The United States has received from the Greek Government an urgent appeal for financial and economic assistance. Preliminary reports from the American Economic Mission now in Greece and reports from the American Ambassador in Greece corroborate the statement of the Greek Government that assistance is imperative if Greece is to survive as a free nation.

I do not believe that the American people and the Congress wish to turn a deaf ear to the appeal of the Greek Government.

Greece is not a rich country. Lack of sufficient natural resources has always forced the Greek people to work hard to make both ends meet. Since 1940, this industrious and peace loving country has suffered invasion, four years of cruel enemy occupation, and bitter internal strife. . . .

The peoples of a number of countries of the world have recently had totalitarian regimes forced upon them against their will. The Government of the United States has made frequent protests against coercion and intimidation, in violation of the Yalta agreement, in Poland, Rumania, and Bulgaria. I must also state that in a number of other countries there have been similar developments.

At the present moment in world history nearly every nation must choose between alternative ways of life. The choice is too often not a free one.

One way of life is based upon the will of the majority, and is distinguished by free institutions, representative government, free elections, guarantees of individual liberty, freedom of speech and religion, and freedom from political oppression.

The second way of life is based upon the will of a minority forcibly imposed upon the majority. It relies upon terror and oppression, a controlled press and radio; fixed elections, and the suppression of personal freedoms.

I believe that it must be the policy of the United States to support free peoples who are resisting attempted subjugation by armed minorities or by outside pressures.

I believe that we must assist free peoples to work out their own destinies in their own way.

I believe that our help should be primarily through economic and financial aid which is essential to economic stability and orderly political processes.

The world is not static, and the status quo is not sacred. But we cannot allow changes in the status quo in violation of the Charter of the United Nations by such methods as coercion, or by such subterfuges as political infiltration. In helping free and independent nations to maintain their freedom, the United States will be giving effect to the principles of the Charter of the United Nations.

It is necessary only to glance at a map to realize that the survival and integrity of the Greek nation are of grave importance in a much wider situation. If Greece should fall under the control of an armed minority, the effect upon its neighbor, Turkey, would be immediate and serious. Confusion and disorder might well spread throughout the entire Middle East.

Moreover, the disappearance of Greece as an independent state would have a profound effect upon those countries in Europe whose peoples are struggling against great difficulties to maintain their freedoms and their independence while they repair the damages of war.

It would be an unspeakable tragedy if these countries, which have struggled so long against overwhelming odds, should lose that victory for which they sacrificed so much. Collapse of free institutions and loss of independence would be disastrous not only for them but for the world. Discouragement and possibly failure would quickly be the lot of neighboring peoples striving to maintain their freedom and independence.

Should we fail to aid Greece and Turkey in this fateful hour, the effect will be far reaching to the West as well as to the East.

We must take immediate and resolute action. . . .

(Continued)

(Continued)

The assistance that I am recommending for Greece and Turkey amounts to little more than 1 tenth of 1 per cent of this investment. It is only common sense that we should safeguard this investment and make sure that it was not in vain.

The seeds of totalitarian regimes are nurtured by misery and want. They spread and grow in the evil soil of poverty and strife. They reach their full growth when the hope of a people for a better life has died. We must keep that hope alive.

The free peoples of the world look to us for support in maintaining their freedoms.

If we falter in our leadership, we may endanger the peace of the world—and we shall surely endanger the welfare of our own nation.

Great responsibilities have been placed upon us by the swift movement of events.

I am confident that the Congress will face these responsibilities squarely.

How did President Truman defend his request for aid to Greece and Turkey? What role did this decision play in intensifying the Cold War?

Source: U.S. Congress, *Congressional Record*, 80th Congress, 1st Session (Washington, D.C.: U.S. Government Printing Office, 1947), Vol. 93, p. 1981.

country or doctrine but against hunger, poverty, desperation, and chaos."[3]

From the Soviet perspective, the Marshall Plan was capitalist imperialism, a thinly veiled attempt to buy the support of the smaller European countries "in return for the relinquishing . . . of their economic and later also their political independence."[4] A Soviet spokesperson described the United States as the "main force in the imperialist camp," whose ultimate goal was "the strengthening of imperialism, preparation for a new imperialist war, a struggle against socialism and democracy, and the support of reactionary and antidemocratic, profascist regimes and movements." Although the Marshall Plan was open to the Soviet Union and its Eastern European satellite states, Soviet leaders viewed the offer as a devious capitalist ploy and refused to participate. Under heavy pressure from Moscow, Eastern European governments did so as well. The Soviets were in no position to compete financially with the United States, however, and could do little to counter the Marshall Plan except tighten their control in Eastern Europe.

Europe Divided

By 1947, the split in Europe between East and West had become a fact of life. At the end of World War II, the United States had favored a quick end to its commitments in Europe. But American fears of Soviet aims caused the United States to play an increasingly important role in European affairs. In an article in *Foreign Affairs* in July 1947, George Kennan, a well-known U.S. diplomat with much knowledge of Soviet affairs,

advocated a policy of **containment** against further aggressive Soviet moves. Kennan favored the "adroit and vigilant application of counter-force at a series of constantly shifting geographical and political points, corresponding to the shifts and maneuvers of Soviet policy." When the Soviets blockaded Berlin in 1948, containment of the Soviet Union became formal U.S. policy.

THE BERLIN BLOCKADE The fate of Germany had become a source of heated contention between East and West. Aside from **denazification** (dee-naht-sih-fuh-KAY-shun) and the partitioning of Germany (and Berlin) into four occupied zones, the Allied powers had agreed on little with regard to the conquered nation. The Soviet Union, hardest hit by the war, took reparations from Germany by pillaging German industry. The technology-starved Soviets dismantled and removed to Russia 380 factories from the western zones of Berlin before transferring their control to the Western powers. By the summer of 1946, two hundred chemical, paper, and textile factories in the East German zone had likewise been shipped to the Soviet Union. At the same time, the German

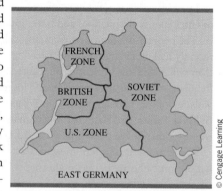

Berlin at the Start of the Cold War

A City Divided. In 1948, U.S. planes airlifted supplies into Berlin to break the blockade that Soviet troops had imposed to isolate the city. Shown here is "Checkpoint Charlie," located at the boundary between the U.S. and Soviet zones of Berlin, just as Soviet roadblocks are about to be removed. The banner at the entrance to the Soviet sector reads, ironically, "The sector of freedom greets the fighters for freedom and right of the Western sectors."

Communist Party was reestablished, under the control of Walter Ulbricht (VAHL-tuh OOL-brikkt) (1893–1973), and was soon in charge of the political reconstruction of the Soviet zone in eastern Germany.

Although the foreign ministers of the four occupying powers kept meeting in an attempt to arrive at a final peace treaty with Germany, they moved further and further apart. At the same time, the British, French, and Americans gradually began to merge their zones economically and by February 1948 were making plans for unification of these sectors and the formation of a national government. In an effort to secure all of Berlin and to halt the creation of a West German government, the Soviet Union imposed a blockade of West Berlin that prevented all traffic from entering the city's western zones through Soviet-controlled territory in East Germany.

The Western powers faced a dilemma. Direct military confrontation seemed dangerous, and no one wished to risk World War III. Therefore, an attempt to break through the blockade with tanks and trucks was ruled out. The solution was to deliver supplies for the city's inhabitants by plane. At its peak, the Berlin Airlift flew 13,000 tons of supplies daily into Berlin. The Soviets, also not wanting war, did not interfere and finally lifted the blockade in May 1949. The blockade of Berlin had severely increased tensions between the United States and the Soviet Union and brought the separation of Germany into two states. The Federal Republic of Germany was formally created from the three Western zones in September 1949, and a month later, the separate German Democratic Republic (GDR) was established in East Germany. Berlin remained a divided city and the source of much contention between East and West.

NATO AND THE WARSAW PACT The search for security in the new world of the Cold War also led to the formation of military alliances. The North Atlantic Treaty Organization (NATO) was formed in April 1949 when Belgium, Denmark, France, Great Britain, Iceland, Italy, Luxembourg, the Netherlands, Norway, and Portugal signed a treaty with the United States and Canada. All the powers agreed to provide mutual assistance if any one of them was attacked. A few years later, Greece, Turkey, and West Germany joined NATO.

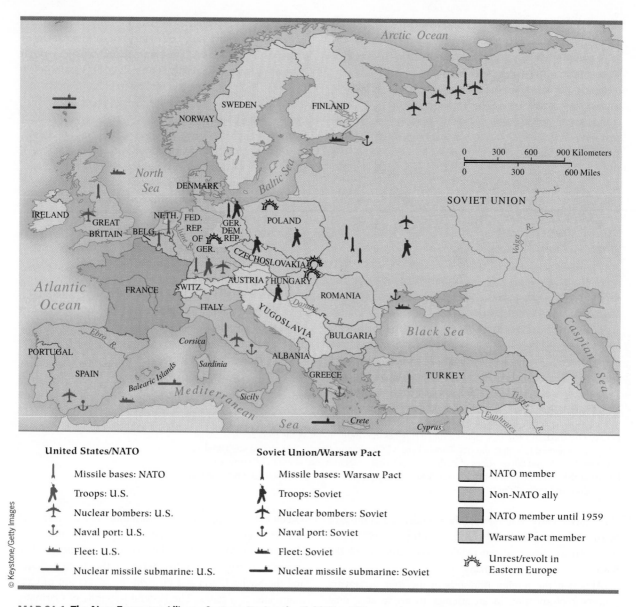

MAP 26.1 **The New European Alliance Systems During the Cold War.** This map shows postwar Europe as it was divided during the Cold War into two contending power blocs, the NATO alliance and the Warsaw Pact. Major military and naval bases are indicated by symbols on the map.

Q *Where on the map was the "iron curtain"?*

The Eastern European states soon followed suit. In 1949, they formed the Council for Mutual Economic Assistance (COMECON) for economic cooperation. Then, in 1955, Albania, Bulgaria, Czechoslovakia, East Germany, Hungary, Poland, Romania, and the Soviet Union organized a formal military alliance, the Warsaw Pact. Once again, Europe was tragically divided into hostile alliance systems (see Map 26.1).

WHO STARTED THE COLD WAR? There has been considerable historical debate over who bears responsibility

for starting the Cold War. In the 1950s, most scholars in the West assumed that the bulk of the blame must fall on the shoulders of Stalin, whose determination to impose Soviet rule on Eastern Europe snuffed out hopes for freedom and self-determination there and aroused justifiable fears of Communist expansion in the West. During the next decade, however, revisionist historians—influenced in part by their hostility to aggressive U.S. policies in Southeast Asia—began to argue that the fault lay primarily in Washington, where Truman and his anti-Communist advisers abandoned the precepts of Yalta and sought to encircle the Soviet Union with a tier of pliant U.S. client states. More recently, many historians have adopted a more nuanced view, noting that both the United States and the Soviet Union took some unwise steps that contributed to rising tensions at the end of World War II.

In fact, both nations were working within a framework conditioned by the past. The rivalry between the two superpowers ultimately stemmed from their different historical perspectives and their irreconcilable political ambitions. Intense competition for political and military supremacy had long been a regular feature of Western civilization.

The United States and the Soviet Union were the heirs of that European tradition of power politics, and it should come as no surprise that two such different systems would seek to extend their way of life to the rest of the world. Because of its need to secure its western border, the Soviet Union was not prepared to give up the advantages it had gained in Eastern Europe from Germany's defeat. But neither were Western leaders prepared to accept without protest the establishment of a system of Soviet satellites that not only threatened the security of Western Europe but also deeply offended Western sensibilities because of its blatant disregard of the Western concept of human rights.

This does not necessarily mean that both sides bear equal responsibility for starting the Cold War. Some revisionist historians have claimed that the U.S. doctrine of containment was a provocative action that aroused Stalin's suspicions and drove him into a position of hostility toward the West. This charge lacks credibility. Although the Soviets were understandably concerned that the United States might use its monopoly of nuclear weapons to attempt to intimidate them, information now available from the Soviet archives and other sources makes it increasingly clear that Stalin's suspicions of the West were rooted in his Marxist-Leninist worldview and long predated Washington's enunciation of the doctrine of containment. As his foreign minister, Vyacheslav Molotov, once remarked, Soviet policy was inherently aggressive and would be triggered whenever the opportunity offered. Although Stalin apparently had no master plan to advance Soviet power into Western Europe, he was probably prepared to make every effort to do so once the next revolutionary wave arrived. Western leaders were fully justified in reacting to this possibility by strengthening their own lines of defense.

On the other hand, a case can be made that in deciding to respond to the Soviet challenge in a primarily military manner, Western leaders overreacted and virtually guaranteed that the Cold War would be transformed into an arms race that could conceivably result in a new and uniquely destructive war. George Kennan, the original architect of the doctrine of containment, had initially proposed a primarily political approach and eventually disavowed the means by which the containment strategy was carried out.

Cold War in Asia

Q FOCUS QUESTION: How and why did Mao Zedong and the Communists come to power in China, and what were the Cold War implications of their triumph?

The Cold War was somewhat slower to make its appearance in Asia. At Yalta, Stalin formally agreed to enter the Pacific War against Japan three months after the close of the conflict with Germany. As a reward for Soviet participation in the struggle against Japan, Roosevelt promised that Moscow would be granted "preeminent interests" in Manchuria (reminiscent of the interests possessed by imperial Russia prior to its defeat by Japan in 1904–1905) and be allowed to establish a Soviet naval base at Port Arthur. In return, Stalin promised to sign a treaty of alliance with the Republic of China, thus implicitly committing the Soviet Union not to aid the Chinese Communists in a possible future civil war. Although many observers would later question Stalin's sincerity in making such a commitment to the vocally anti-Communist Chiang Kai-shek, in Moscow the decision probably had a logic of its own. Stalin had no particular liking for the independent-minded Mao Zedong and indeed did not anticipate a Communist victory in any civil war in China. Only an agreement with Chiang could provide the Soviet Union with a strategically vital economic and political presence in northern China.

The Truman administration was equally reluctant to get embroiled in a confrontation with Moscow over the unfolding events in East Asia. Suspicion of Chiang Kai-shek ran high in Washington, and as we shall see, many key U.S. policymakers hoped to avoid a deeper involvement in China by brokering a compromise agreement between Chiang and his Communist rival, Mao.

Despite these commitments, the Allied agreements soon broke down, and East Asia was sucked into the vortex of the Cold War by the end of the 1940s. The root of the problem lay in the underlying weakness of Chiang's regime, which threatened to create a political vacuum in East Asia that both Moscow and Washington would be tempted to fill.

The Chinese Civil War

As World War II came to an end in the Pacific, relations between the government of Chiang Kai-shek in China and its powerful U.S. ally had become frayed. Although Roosevelt had hoped that republican China would be the keystone of his plan for peace and stability in Asia after the war, U.S. officials became disillusioned with the corruption of Chiang's government and his unwillingness to risk his forces against the Japanese (he hoped to save them for use against the Communists after the war in the Pacific ended), and China was no longer the object of Washington's close attention as the war came to a close. Nevertheless, U.S. military and economic aid to China had been substantial, and at the war's end, the new Truman administration still hoped that it could rely on Chiang to support U.S. postwar goals in the region.

While Chiang Kai-shek wrestled with Japanese aggression and problems of national development, the Communists were building up their strength in northern China. To enlarge their political base, they carried out a "mass line" policy (a term in Communist jargon that meant responding to the needs of the mass of the population), reducing land rents and confiscating the lands of wealthy landlords. By the end of World War II, 20 to 30 million Chinese were living under the administration of the

Communists, and their People's Liberation Army (PLA) included nearly one million troops.

As the war came to an end, world attention began to focus on the prospects for renewed civil strife in China. Members of a U.S. liaison team stationed in Yan'an (yuh-NAHN) were impressed by the performance of the Communists, and some recommended that the United States should support them or at least remain neutral in a possible conflict between Communists and Nationalists for control of China. The Truman administration, though skeptical of Chiang's ability to forge a strong and prosperous country, was increasingly concerned about the spread of communism in Europe and tried to find a peaceful solution through the formation of a coalition government of all parties in China.

THE COMMUNIST TRIUMPH The effort failed. By 1946, full-scale war between the Nationalist government, now reinstalled in Nanjing, and the Communists resumed. Initially, most of the fighting took place in Manchuria, where newly arrived Communist units began to surround Nationalist forces occupying the major cities.

Now Chiang Kai-shek's errors came home to roost. In the countryside, millions of peasants, attracted to the Communists by promises of land and social justice, flocked to serve in Mao Zedong's PLA. In the cities, middle-class Chinese, normally hostile to communism, were alienated by Chiang's brutal suppression of all dissent and his government's inability to slow the ruinous rate of inflation or solve the economic problems it caused. By the end of 1947, almost all of Manchuria was under Communist control.

The Truman administration reacted to the spread of Communist power in China with acute discomfort. Washington had no desire to see a Communist government on the mainland, but it had little confidence in Chiang Kai-shek's ability to realize Roosevelt's dream of a strong, united, and prosperous China. In December 1945, President Truman sent General George C. Marshall to China in a last-ditch effort to bring about a peaceful settlement, but anti-Communist elements in the Republic of China resisted U.S. pressure to create a coalition government with the Chinese Communist Party (CCP). During the next two years, the United States gave limited military support to Chiang's regime but refused to commit U.S. power to guarantee its survival. The administration's hands-off policy deeply angered many

Mao Zedong and Chiang Kai-shek Exchange a Toast. After World War II, the United States sent General George C. Marshall to China in an effort to prevent civil war between Chiang Kai-shek's government and Mao Zedong's Communists. Marshall's initial success was symbolized by this toast between Mao (at the left) and Chiang. But suspicion ran too deep, and soon conflict ensued, leading to a Communist victory in 1949. Chiang's government retreated to the island of Taiwan.

© Jack Wilkes/Time Life Pictures//Getty Images

members of Congress, who charged that the White House was "soft on communism" and called for increased military assistance to the Nationalist government.

With morale dropping in the cities, Chiang's troops began to defect to the Communists. Sometimes whole divisions, officers as well as ordinary soldiers, changed sides. By 1948, the PLA was advancing south out of Manchuria and had encircled Beijing. Communist troops took the old imperial capital, crossed the Yangtze the following spring, and occupied the commercial hub of Shanghai (see Map 26.2). During the next few months, Chiang's government and 2 million of his followers fled to Taiwan, which the Japanese had returned to Chinese control after World War II.

With the Communist victory in China, Asia became a major theater of the Cold War and an integral element in American politics. In a white paper issued by the State Department in the fall of 1949, the Truman administration placed most of the blame for the debacle on Chiang Kai-shek's regime (see the box on p. 688). Republicans in Congress, however, disagreed, arguing that Roosevelt had betrayed Chiang Kai-shek at Yalta by granting privileges in Manchuria to the Soviet Union. In their view, Soviet troops had hindered the dispatch of Nationalist forces to the area and provided the PLA with weapons to use against their rivals.

In later years, sources in Moscow and Beijing made clear that in actuality the Soviet Union gave little assistance to the CCP in its postwar struggle against the Nanjing regime. In fact, Stalin—likely concerned at the prospect of a military confrontation with the United States—advised Mao against undertaking the effort. Although Communist forces undoubtedly received some assistance from Soviet occupation troops in Manchuria, their victory ultimately stemmed from conditions inside China. Nevertheless, the White House responded to its critics. During the spring of 1950, under pressure from Congress and public opinion to define U.S. interests in Asia, the Truman administration adopted a new national security policy that implied that the United States would take whatever steps were necessary to stem the further expansion of communism in the region. Containment had come to East Asia.

The New China

Communist leaders in China, from their new capital of Beijing, probably hoped that their accession to power in 1949 would bring about an era of peace in the region and permit their new government to concentrate on domestic goals. But the desire for peace was tempered by their determination to erase a century of humiliation at the hands of imperialist powers and to restore the traditional outer frontiers of the empire. In addition to recovering territories that had been part of the Manchu Empire, such as Manchuria, Taiwan, and Tibet, the Chinese leaders also hoped to restore Chinese influence in former tributary areas such as Korea and Vietnam.

It soon became clear that these two goals were not always compatible. Negotiations between Mao and Stalin, held in Moscow in January 1950, led to Soviet recognition of Chinese sovereignty over Manchuria and Xinjiang (SHIN-jyahng)—the desolate lands north of Tibet that were known as Chinese Turkestan because many of the peoples in the area were of Turkic origin—although the Soviets retained a measure of economic influence in both areas. Chinese troops occupied Tibet in 1950 and brought it under Chinese administration for the first time in more than a century. But in Korea and Taiwan, China's efforts to re-create the imperial buffer zone provoked new conflicts with foreign powers.

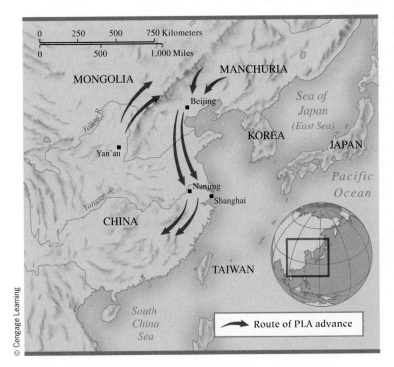

© Cengage Learning

MAP 26.2 The Chinese Civil War. After the close of the Pacific War in 1945, the Nationalist Chinese government and the Chinese Communists fought a bitter civil war that ended with a victory by the latter in 1949. The path of the Communist advance is shown on the map.

Q Where did Chiang Kai-shek's government retreat to after its defeat?

Who Lost China?

POLITICS & GOVERNMENT

In 1949, with China about to fall under the control of the Communists, President Truman instructed the State Department to prepare a "white paper" report explaining why the U.S. policy of seeking to avoid a Communist victory in China had failed. The authors of the paper concluded that responsibility lay at the door of Nationalist Chinese leader Chiang Kai-shek and that there was nothing the United States could have done to alter the result. Most China observers today would accept that assessment, but it did little at the time to deflect criticism of the administration for selling out the interests of our ally in China.

U.S. State Department White Paper on China, 1949

When peace came the United States was confronted with three possible alternatives in China: (1) it could have pulled out lock, stock, and barrel; (2) it could have intervened militarily on a major scale to assist the Nationalists to destroy the Communists; (3) it could, while assisting the Nationalists to assert their authority over as much of China as possible, endeavor to avoid a civil war by working for a compromise between the two sides.

The first alternative would, and I believe American public opinion at the time so felt, have represented an abandonment of our international responsibilities and of our traditional policy of friendship for China before we had made a determined effort to be of assistance. The second alternative policy, while it may look attractive theoretically, in retrospect, was wholly impracticable. The Nationalists had been unable to destroy the Communists during the ten years before the war. Now after the war the Nationalists were . . . weakened, demoralized, and unpopular. They had quickly dissipated their popular support and prestige in the areas liberated from the Japanese by the conduct of their civil and military officials.

The Communists on the other hand were much stronger than they had ever been and were in control of most of North China. Because of the ineffectiveness of the Nationalist forces, which was later to be tragically demonstrated, the Communists probably could have been dislodged only by American arms. It is obvious that the American people would not have sanctioned such a colossal commitment of our armies in 1945 or later. We therefore came to the third alternative policy whereunder we faced the facts of the situation and attempted to assist in working out a modus vivendi which would avert civil war but nevertheless preserve and even increase the influence of the National Government. . . .

The distrust of the leaders of both the Nationalist and Communist Parties for each other proved too deep-seated to permit final agreement, notwithstanding temporary truces and apparently promising negotiations. The Nationalists, furthermore, embarked in 1946 on an overambitious military campaign in the face of warnings by General Marshall that it not only would fail but would plunge China into economic chaos and eventually destroy the National Government. . . .

The unfortunate but inescapable fact is that the ominous result of the civil war in China was beyond the control of the government of the United States. Nothing that this country did or could have done within the reasonable limits of its capabilities could have changed that result; nothing that was left undone by this country has contributed to it. It was the product of internal Chinese forces, forces which this country tried to influence but could not. A decision was arrived at within China, if only a decision by default.

Q *How did the authors of the white paper explain the Communist victory in China? According to this argument, what actions might have prevented it?*

Source: From *United States Relations with China* (Washington, D.C., Dept. of State, 1949), pp. iii–xvi.

The problem of Taiwan was a consequence of the Cold War. As the civil war in China came to an end, the Truman administration appeared determined to avoid entanglement in China's internal affairs and indicated that it would not seek to prevent a Communist takeover of the island, now occupied by Chiang Kai-shek's Republic of China. But as tensions between the United States and the new Chinese government escalated during the winter of 1949–1950, influential figures in the United States began to argue that Taiwan was crucial to U.S. defense strategy in the Pacific.

A Pledge of Eternal Friendship. After the Communist victory in the Chinese civil war, Chairman Mao Zedong traveled to Moscow, where in 1950 he negotiated a treaty of friendship and cooperation with the Soviet Union. The poster shown here trumpets the results of the meeting: "Long live and strengthen the unbreakable friendship and cooperation of the Soviet and Chinese peoples!" The two leaders, however, did not get along. Mao reportedly complained to colleagues that obtaining assistance from Stalin was "like taking meat from a tiger's mouth."

The Korean War

The outbreak of war in Korea also helped bring the Cold War to East Asia. After the Sino-Japanese War in 1894–1895, Korea, long a Chinese tributary, had fallen increasingly under the rival influences of Japan and Russia. After the Japanese defeated the Russians in 1905, Korea became an integral part of the Japanese Empire and remained so until 1945. The removal of Korea from Japanese control had been one of the stated objectives of the Allies in World War II, and on the eve of the Japanese surrender in August 1945, the Soviet Union and the United States agreed to divide the country into two separate occupation zones at the 38th parallel. They originally planned to hold national elections after the restoration of peace to reunify Korea under an independent government. But as U.S.-Soviet relations deteriorated, two separate governments emerged in Korea, a Communist one in the north and an anti-Communist one in the south.

Tensions between the two governments ran high along the dividing line, and on June 25, 1950, with the apparent approval of Stalin, North Korean troops invaded the south.

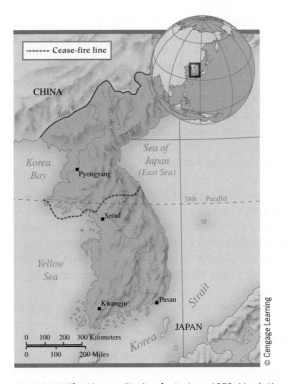

MAP 26.3 The Korean Peninsula. In June 1950, North Korean forces crossed the 38th parallel in a sudden invasion of the south. Shown here is the cease-fire line that brought an end to the war in 1953.

Q *What is the significance of the Yalu River?*

The Truman administration immediately ordered U.S. naval and air forces to support South Korea, and the United Nations Security Council (with the Soviet delegate absent to protest the UN's refusal to assign China's seat to the new government in Beijing) passed a resolution calling on member nations to jointly resist the invasion, in line with the security provisions of the United Nations Charter. By September, UN forces under the command of U.S. General Douglas MacArthur marched northward across the 38th parallel with the aim of unifying Korea under a single, non-Communist government.

President Truman worried that by approaching the Chinese border at the Yalu (YAH-loo) River, the UN troops could trigger Chinese intervention, but MacArthur assured him that China would not respond. In November, however, Chinese "volunteer" forces intervened in force on the side of North Korea and drove the UN troops southward in disarray. A static defense line was eventually established near the original dividing line at the 38th parallel (see Map 26.3), although the war continued.

To many Americans, the Chinese intervention in Korea was clear evidence that China intended to promote communism throughout Asia, and recent evidence suggests that Mao was convinced that a revolutionary wave was on the rise in Asia. In fact, however, China's decision to enter the war was probably motivated in large part by the fear that hostile U.S. forces might be stationed on the Chinese frontier and perhaps even launch an attack across the border. MacArthur intensified such fears by calling publicly for air attacks on Manchurian cities in preparation for an attack on Communist China.

In any case, the outbreak of the Korean War was particularly unfortunate for China. Immediately after the invasion, President Truman dispatched the U.S. Seventh Fleet to the Taiwan Strait to prevent a possible Chinese invasion of Taiwan. Even more unfortunate, the invasion hardened Western attitudes against the new Chinese government and led to China's isolation from the major capitalist powers for two decades. The United States continued to regard the Nationalist government in Taiwan as the only legal representative of the Chinese people and to support its retention of China's seat on the UN Security Council. As a result, China was cut off from all forms of economic and technological assistance and was forced to rely almost entirely on the Soviet Union, with which it had signed a pact of friendship and cooperation in early 1950.

Conflict in Indochina

During the mid-1950s, China sought to build contacts with the nonsocialist world. A cease-fire agreement brought the Korean War to an end in July 1953, and China signaled its desire to live in peaceful coexistence with other independent countries in the region. But a relatively minor conflict now began to intensify on China's southern flank, in French Indochina. The struggle had begun after World War II, when the Indochinese Communist Party led by Ho Chi Minh (HOH CHEE MIN) (1890–1969), at the head of a multiparty nationalist alliance called the Vietminh (vee-et-MIN) Front, seized power in northern and central Vietnam. After abortive negotiations between Ho's government and the returning French, war broke out in December 1946. French forces occupied the cities and the densely populated lowlands, while the Vietminh took refuge in the mountains.

For three years, the Vietminh waged a "people's war" of national liberation from colonial rule, gradually increasing in size and effectiveness. At the time, however, the conflict in Indochina attracted relatively little attention from world leaders, who viewed the events there as only one aspect of the transition to independence of colonial territories in postwar Asia. The Truman administration was uneasy about Ho's long-standing credentials as a Soviet agent but was equally reluctant to anger anticolonialist elements in the region by intervening on behalf of the French. Moscow had even less interest in the issue. Stalin—still hoping to see the Communist Party come to power in Paris—ignored Ho's request for recognition of his movement as the legitimate representative of the national interests of the Vietnamese people.

But what had begun as an anticolonial struggle by the Vietminh Front against the French became entangled in the Cold War after the CCP came to power in China. In early 1950, Beijing began to provide military assistance to the Vietminh to burnish its revolutionary credentials and protect its own borders from hostile forces. The Truman administration, increasingly concerned that a revolutionary "Red tide" was sweeping through the region, decided to provide financial and technical assistance to the French while pressuring them to prepare for an eventual transition to independent non-Communist governments in Vietnam, Laos, and Cambodia.

© AFP/Getty Images

Ho Chi Minh Plans an Attack on the French. Unlike many of the peoples of Southeast Asia, the Vietnamese had to fight for their independence after World War II. That fight was led by the talented Communist leader Ho Chi Minh. In this 1950 photograph taken at his secret base in the mountains of North Vietnam, Ho plans an attack on French positions. He changed the location of his headquarters on several occasions to evade capture by French forces.

Despite growing U.S. involvement in the war, Vietminh forces continued to gain strength, and in the spring of 1954, with Chinese assistance, they besieged a French military outpost at Dien Bien Phu (DEE-en bee-en FOO), not far from the border of Laos. The French sent reinforcements, and the decisive battle of the conflict was under way.

With casualties mounting and the French public tired of fighting the "dirty war" in Indochina, the French had agreed to hold peace talks with the Vietminh in May of 1954. On the day before the peace conference convened in Geneva, Switzerland, Vietminh forces overran the French bastion at Dien Bien Phu. The humiliating defeat weakened French resolve to maintain a presence in Indochina. In July, the two sides agreed to a settlement. Vietnam was temporarily divided into a Communist northern half, known as the Democratic Republic of Vietnam (DRV), and a non-Communist southern half based in Saigon (sy-GAHN) (now Ho Chi Minh City) that eventually came to be known as the Republic of Vietnam. A demilitarized zone separated the two at the 17th parallel. Elections were to be held in two years to create a unified government. Cambodia and Laos were both declared independent under neutral governments. French forces were withdrawn from all three countries.

Indochina After 1954

China had played an active role in bringing about the settlement and clearly hoped that it would reduce tensions in the area, but subsequent efforts to improve relations between China and the United States foundered on the issue of Taiwan. In the fall of 1954, the United States signed a mutual security treaty with the Republic of China guaranteeing U.S. military support in case of an invasion of Taiwan. When Beijing demanded U.S. withdrawal from Taiwan as the price for improved relations, diplomatic talks between the two countries collapsed.

From Confrontation to Coexistence

Q FOCUS QUESTION: What events led to the era of coexistence in the 1960s, and to what degree did each side contribute to the reduction in international tensions?

The decade of the 1950s opened with the world teetering on the edge of a nuclear holocaust. The Soviet Union had detonated its first nuclear device in 1949, and the two blocs—capitalist and socialist—viewed each other across an ideological divide that grew increasingly bitter with each passing year. Yet as the decade drew to a close, a measure of sanity crept into the Cold War, and the leaders of the major world powers began to seek ways to coexist in a peaceful and stable world (see Map 26.4).

The first clear sign of change occurred after Stalin's death in early 1953. His successor, Georgy Malenkov (gyee-OR-gyee muh-LEN-kawf) (1902–1988), openly hoped to improve relations with the Western powers in order to reduce defense expenditures and shift government spending to growing consumer needs. Nikita Khrushchev (nuh-KEE-tuh KHROOSH-chawf) (1894–1971), who replaced Malenkov in 1955, continued his predecessor's efforts to reduce tensions with the West and improve the living standards of the Soviet people.

In an adroit public relations touch, in 1956 Khrushchev promoted an appeal for a policy of **peaceful coexistence** with the West. In 1955, he had surprisingly agreed to negotiate an end to the postwar occupation of Austria by the victorious allies and allow the creation of a neutral country with strong cultural and economic ties with the West. He also called for a reduction in defense expenditures and reduced the size of the Soviet armed forces.

Ferment in Eastern Europe

At first, Western leaders were suspicious of Khrushchev's motives, especially in light of events that were taking place in Eastern Europe. The key to security along the western frontier of the Soviet Union was the string of Eastern European satellite states that had been assembled in the aftermath of World War II (see Map 26.1 on p. 684). Once Communist domination had been assured, a series of "little Stalins" put into power by Moscow instituted Soviet-type five-year plans that emphasized heavy industry rather than consumer goods, the collectivization of agriculture, and the nationalization of industry. They also appropriated the political tactics that Stalin had perfected in the Soviet Union, eliminating all non-Communist parties and establishing the classical institutions of

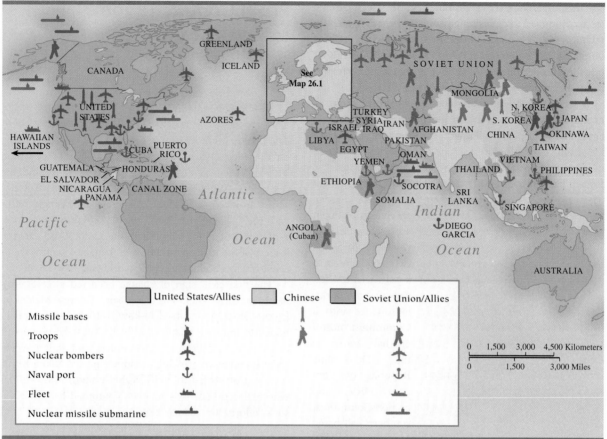

MAP 26.4 **The Global Cold War.** This map shows the location of the major military bases and missile sites maintained by the three contending power blocs at the height of the Cold War.

Q *Which continents were the most heavily armed? Why?*

repression—the secret police and military forces. Dissidents were tracked down and thrown into prison, and "national Communists" who resisted total subservience to the Soviet Union were charged with treason in mass show trials and executed.

Despite these repressive efforts, discontent became increasingly evident in several Eastern European countries. Hungary, Poland, and Romania harbored bitter memories of past Russian domination and suspected that Stalin, under the guise of proletarian internationalism, was seeking to revive the empire of the tsars. For the vast majority of peoples in Eastern Europe, the imposition of so-called people's democracies (a term invented by Moscow to refer to societies in the early stage of socialist transition) resulted in economic hardship and severe threats to the most basic political liberties. The first indications of unrest appeared in East Berlin, where popular riots broke out against Communist rule in 1953. The riots eventually subsided, but the virus had spread to neighboring countries.

In Poland, public demonstrations against an increase in food prices in 1956 escalated into widespread protests against the regime's economic policies, restrictions on the freedom of Catholics to practice their religion, and the continued presence of Soviet troops (as called for by the Warsaw Pact) on Polish soil. In a desperate effort to defuse the unrest, the party leader stepped down and was replaced by Wladyslaw Gomulka (vlah-DIS-lahf goh-MOOL-kuh) (1905–1982), a popular figure who had previously been demoted for his "nationalist" tendencies. When Gomulka took steps to ease the crisis, Khrushchev flew to Warsaw to warn him against adopting policies that could undermine the political dominance of the party and weaken security links with the Soviet Union. After a tense confrontation, Poland agreed to remain in the Warsaw Pact and to maintain the sanctity of party rule; in return, Gomulka was authorized to adopt domestic reforms, such as easing restrictions on religious practice and ending the policy of forced collectivization in rural areas.

THE HUNGARIAN REVOLUTION The developments in Poland sent shock waves throughout the region. The impact was strongest in neighboring Hungary, where the methods of the local "little Stalin," Mátyás Rákosi (MAH-tyash RAH-koh-see) (1892–1971), were so brutal that he had been summoned to Moscow for a lecture. In late October 1956, student-led popular riots broke out in the capital of Budapest and soon spread to other towns and villages throughout the country. Rákosi was forced to resign and was replaced by Imre Nagy (IM-ray NAHJ) (1896–1958), a national Communist who attempted to satisfy popular demands without arousing the anger of Moscow. Unlike Gomulka, however, Nagy was unable to contain the zeal of leading members of the protest movement, who sought major political reforms and the withdrawal of Hungary from the Warsaw Pact. On November 1, Nagy promised free elections, which, given the mood of the country, would probably have brought an end to Communist rule. After a brief moment of uncertainty, Moscow decided on firm action. Soviet troops, recently withdrawn at Nagy's request, returned to Budapest and installed a new government under the more pliant party leader János Kádár (YAH-nush KAH-dahr) (1912–1989). While Kádár rescinded many of Nagy's measures, Nagy sought refuge in the Yugoslav embassy. A few weeks later, he left the embassy under the promise of safety but was quickly arrested, convicted of treason, and executed (see the box on p. 694).

DIFFERENT ROADS TO SOCIALISM The dramatic events in Poland and Hungary graphically demonstrated the vulnerability of the Soviet satellite system in Eastern Europe, and many observers throughout the world anticipated that the United States would intervene on behalf of the freedom fighters in Hungary. After all, the Eisenhower administration had promised that it would "roll back" communism, and radio broadcasts by the U.S.-sponsored Radio Liberty and Radio Free Europe had encouraged the peoples of Eastern Europe to rise up against Soviet domination. In reality, Washington was well aware that U.S. intervention could lead to nuclear war and limited itself to protests against Soviet brutality in crushing the uprising.

The year of discontent was not without consequences, however. Soviet leaders now recognized that Moscow could maintain control over its satellites in Eastern Europe only by granting them the leeway to adopt domestic policies appropriate to local conditions. Khrushchev had already embarked on this path in 1955 when he assured Tito that there were "different roads to socialism." Some Eastern European Communist leaders now took Khrushchev at his word and adopted reform programs to make socialism more palatable to their subject populations. Even Kádár, derisively labeled the "butcher of Budapest," managed to preserve many of Nagy's reforms to allow a measure of capitalist incentive and freedom of expression in Hungary.

CRISIS OVER BERLIN But in the late 1950s, a new crisis erupted over the status of Berlin. The Soviet Union had launched its first intercontinental ballistic missile (ICBM) in August 1957, arousing U.S. fears of a missile gap between the United States and the Soviet Union. Khrushchev attempted to take advantage of the U.S. frenzy over missiles to solve the problem of West Berlin, which had remained a "Western island" of prosperity inside the relatively poverty-stricken state of East Germany. Many East Germans sought to escape to West Germany by fleeing through West Berlin, a serious blot on the credibility of the GDR and a potential source of instability in East-West relations. In November 1958, Khrushchev announced that unless the West removed its forces from West Berlin within six months, he would turn over control of the access routes to the East Germans. Unwilling to accept an ultimatum that would have abandoned West Berlin to the Communists, U.S. President Dwight D. Eisenhower and the West stood firm, and Khrushchev eventually backed down.

Despite such periodic crises in East-West relations, there were tantalizing signs that an era of true peaceful coexistence between the two power blocs could be achieved. In the late 1950s, the United States and the Soviet Union initiated a cultural exchange program. While Leningrad's Kirov Ballet appeared at theaters in the United States, Benny Goodman and the film *West Side Story* played in Moscow. In 1958, Khrushchev visited the United States and had a brief but friendly encounter with President Eisenhower at the presidential retreat in northern Maryland.

Rivalry in the Third World

Yet Khrushchev could rarely avoid the temptation to gain an advantage over the United States in the competition for influence throughout the world, a posture that exacerbated the unstable relationship between the two global superpowers. Unlike Stalin, who had exhibited a profound distrust of all political figures who did not slavishly follow his lead, Khrushchev viewed the dismantling of colonial regimes in Asia, Africa, and Latin America as a potential advantage for the Soviet Union. When neutralist leaders like Nehru in India, Tito in Yugoslavia, and Sukarno (soo-KAHR-noh) in Indonesia founded the **Nonaligned Movement** in 1955 to provide an alternative to the two major power blocs, Khrushchev took every opportunity to promote Soviet interests in the Third

Soviet Repression in Eastern Europe: Hungary, 1956

INTERACTION & EXCHANGE

Developments in Poland in 1956 inspired the Communist leaders of Hungary to begin to extricate their country from Soviet control. But there were limits to Khrushchev's tolerance, and he sent Soviet troops to crush Hungary's movement for independence. The first selection is a statement by the Soviet government justifying its use of troops, while the second is the brief and tragic final statement from Imre Nagy, the Hungarian leader.

Statement of the Soviet Government, October 30, 1956

The Soviet Government regards it as indispensable to make a statement in connection with the events in Hungary.

The course of the events has shown that the working people of Hungary, who have achieved great progress on the basis of their people's democratic order, correctly raise the question of the necessity of eliminating serious shortcomings in the field of economic building, the further raising of the material well-being of the population, and the struggle against bureaucratic excesses in the state apparatus.

However, this just and progressive movement of the working people was soon joined by forces of black reaction and counterrevolution, which are trying to take advantage of the discontent of part of the working people to undermine the foundations of the people's democratic order in Hungary and to restore the old landlord and capitalist order.

The Soviet Government and all the Soviet people deeply regret that the development of events in Hungary has led to bloodshed. On the request of the Hungarian People's Government the Soviet Government consented to the entry into Budapest of the Soviet Army units to assist the Hungarian People's Army and the Hungarian authorities to establish order in the town.

The Last Message of Imre Nagy, November 4, 1956

This fight is the fight for freedom by the Hungarian people against the Russian intervention, and it is possible that I shall only be able to stay at my post for one or two hours. The whole world will see how the Russian armed forces, contrary to all treaties and conventions, are crushing the resistance of the Hungarian people. They will also see how they are kidnapping the Prime Minister of a country which is a Member of the United Nations, taking him from the capital, and therefore it cannot be doubted at all that this is the most brutal form of intervention. I should like in these last moments to ask the leaders of the revolution, if they can, to leave the country. I ask that all that I have said in my broadcast, and what we have agreed on with the revolutionary leaders during meetings in Parliament, should be put in a memorandum, and the leaders should turn to all the peoples of the world for help and explain that today it is Hungary and tomorrow, or the day after tomorrow, it will be the turn of other countries because the imperialism of Moscow does not know borders, and is only trying to play for time.

Q *How did the United States and its allies respond to the events in Hungary? Why did the United States decide not to intervene in support of the dissident forces?*

Source: From *Department of State Bulletin*, Nov. 12, 1956, pp. 746–747.

World (as the nonaligned countries of Asia, Africa, and Latin America were now popularly called). Khrushchev openly sought alliances with strategically important neutralist countries like India, Indonesia, and Egypt, while Washington's ability to influence events at the United Nations began to wane.

In January 1961, just as John F. Kennedy (1917–1963) assumed the U.S. presidency, Khrushchev unnerved the new president at an informal summit meeting in Vienna by declaring that the Soviet Union would provide active support to national liberation movements throughout the world. There were rising fears in Washington of Soviet meddling in such sensitive trouble spots as Southeast Asia, where insurgent activities in Indochina continued to simmer; in Central Africa, where the pro-Soviet tendencies of radical leader Patrice Lumumba (puh-TREES

The Kitchen Debate. During the late 1950s, the United States and the Soviet Union sought to defuse Cold War tensions by encouraging cultural exchanges between the two countries. On one occasion, U.S. Vice President Richard M. Nixon visited Moscow in conjunction with the arrival of an exhibit to introduce U.S. culture and society to the Soviet people. Here Nixon lectures Soviet Communist Party chief Nikita Khrushchev on the technology of the U.S. kitchen. On the other side of Nixon, at the far right, is future Soviet president Leonid Brezhnev.

AP Images

loo-MOOM-buh) (1925–1961) aroused deep suspicion in Washington; and in the Caribbean, where a little-known Cuban revolutionary named Fidel Castro threatened to transform his country into an advanced base for Soviet expansion in the Americas.

The Cuban Missile Crisis and the Move Toward Détente

In 1959, a left-wing revolutionary named Fidel Castro (fee-DELL KASS-troh) (b. 1927) overthrew the Cuban dictator Fulgencio Batista (full-JEN-see-oh bah-TEES-tuh) and established a Soviet-supported totalitarian regime. As tensions increased between the new government in Havana and the United States, the Eisenhower administration broke relations with Cuba and drafted plans to overthrow Castro, who reacted by drawing closer to Moscow.

Soon after taking office in early 1961, Kennedy approved a plan to support an invasion of Cuba by anti-Castro exiles. But the attempted landing at the Bay of Pigs in southern Cuba was an utter failure. At Castro's invitation, the Soviet Union then began to station nuclear missiles in Cuba, within striking distance of the American mainland. (Khrushchev was quick to point out that the United States had placed nuclear weapons in Turkey within easy range of the Soviet Union.) When U.S. intelligence discovered that a Soviet fleet carrying more missiles was heading to Cuba, Kennedy decided to dispatch U.S. warships into the Atlantic to prevent the fleet from reaching its destination.

This approach to the problem was risky but had the benefit of delaying confrontation and giving the two sides

time to find a peaceful solution. After a tense standoff during which the two countries came frighteningly close to a direct nuclear confrontation (the Soviet missiles already in Cuba were launch-ready), Khrushchev finally sent a conciliatory letter to Kennedy agreeing to turn back the fleet if Kennedy pledged not to invade Cuba. In a secret concession not revealed until many years later, the president also promised to dismantle U.S. missiles in Turkey. To the world, however (and to an angry Castro), it appeared that Kennedy had bested Khrushchev. "We were eyeball to eyeball," noted U.S. Secretary of State Dean Rusk, "and they blinked" (see the Film & History feature on p. 696).

The ghastly realization that the world might have faced annihilation in a matter of days had a profound effect on both sides. A communication hotline between Moscow and Washington was installed in 1963 to expedite rapid communication between the two superpowers in time of crisis. In the same year, the two powers agreed to ban nuclear tests in the atmosphere, a step that served to lessen the tensions between the two nations.

The Sino-Soviet Dispute

Nikita Khrushchev had launched his slogan of peaceful coexistence as a means of improving relations with the capitalist powers; ironically, one result of the campaign was to undermine Moscow's ties with its close ally China. During Stalin's lifetime, Beijing had accepted the Soviet Union as the acknowledged leader of the socialist camp. After Stalin's death, however, relations began to deteriorate. Part of the reason may have been Mao Zedong's contention that he, as the most experienced

The Missiles of October (1973)

Never has the world been closer to nuclear holocaust than in October 1962, when U.S. and Soviet leaders found themselves in direct confrontation over Nikita Khrushchev's decision to introduce Soviet missiles into Cuba, just 90 miles from the U.S. coast. When President John F. Kennedy announced that U.S. warships would intercept Soviet freighters destined for Cuban ports, the two countries teetered on the verge of war. Only after protracted and delicate negotiations was the threat defused. The confrontation sobered leaders on both sides and led to the signing of the first nuclear test ban treaty, as well as the opening of a hotline between Moscow and Washington.

The Missiles of October, a made-for-TV film produced in 1973, is a tense political drama that is all the more riveting because it is based on fact. Although less well known than the more recent *Thirteen Days* (2000), it is in many ways more persuasive, and the acting is demonstrably superior. The film stars William Devane as

Courtesy The Everett Collection, Inc.

John Kennedy (William Devane, seated) and Robert Kennedy (Martin Sheen) confer with advisers.

John F. Kennedy and Martin Sheen as his younger brother, Robert. Based in part on Robert Kennedy's book *Thirteen Days* (New York, 1969), the film traces the tense discussions that took place in the White House as the president's key advisers debated how to respond to the Soviet challenge. President Kennedy remains cool as he reins in his more bellicose advisers to bring about a compromise that successfully avoids a nuclear confrontation with Moscow.

Because the film is based on the recollections of Robert Kennedy, it presents a favorable portrait of his brother's handling of the crisis, as might be expected, and the somewhat triumphalist attitude at the end is perhaps a bit exaggerated. But Khrushchev's colleagues in the Kremlin and his Cuban ally, Fidel Castro, viewed the U.S.-Soviet agreement as a humiliation for Moscow that nevertheless set the two superpowers on the road to a more durable and peaceful relationship. It was one Cold War story that had a happy ending.

Marxist leader, should now be acknowledged as the most authoritative voice within the socialist community. But another determining factor was that just as Soviet policies were moving toward moderation, China's were becoming more radical.

Several other issues were involved, including territorial disputes along the Sino-Soviet border and China's unhappiness with limited Soviet economic assistance. But the key sources of disagreement involved ideology and the Cold War. Chinese leaders were convinced that the successes of the Soviet space program confirmed that the socialists were now technologically superior to the capitalists (the East Wind, trumpeted the Chinese official press, had triumphed over the West Wind), and they urged Khrushchev to go on the offensive to promote world

revolution. Specifically, China wanted Soviet assistance in retaking Taiwan from Chiang Kai-shek. But Khrushchev was trying to improve relations with the West and rejected Chinese demands for support against Taiwan.

By the end of the 1950s, the Soviet Union had begun to remove its advisers from China, and in 1961, the dispute broke into the open. Increasingly isolated, China voiced its hostility to what Mao described as the "urban industrialized countries" (which included the Soviet Union) and portrayed itself as the leader of the "rural underdeveloped countries" of Asia, Africa, and Latin America in a global struggle against imperialist oppression. In effect, China had applied Mao Zedong's concept of people's war in an international framework (see the box on p. 697).

OPPOSING ✕ VIEWPOINTS

Peaceful Coexistence or People's War?

INTERACTION & EXCHANGE

The Soviet leader Vladimir Lenin had contended that war between the socialist and imperialist camps was inevitable because the imperialists would never give up without a fight. That assumption had probably guided Joseph Stalin, who told colleagues shortly after World War II that a new war would break out in fifteen to twenty years. But Stalin's successor, Nikita Khrushchev, feared that a new world conflict could result in a nuclear holocaust and contended that the two sides must learn to coexist, although peaceful competition would continue. In this speech given in Beijing in 1959, Khrushchev attempted to persuade the Chinese to accept his views. But Chinese leaders argued that the "imperialist nature" of the United States would never change and countered that the crucial area of competition was in the Third World, where "people's wars" would bring down the structure of imperialism. That argument was presented in 1966 by Marshal Lin Biao (LIN BYOW) of China, at that time one of Mao Zedong's closest allies.

Khrushchev's Speech to the Chinese, 1959

Comrades! Socialism brings to the people peace—that greatest blessing. The greater the strength of the camp of socialism grows, the greater will be its possibilities for successfully defending the cause of peace on this earth. The forces of socialism are already so great that real possibilities are being created for excluding war as a means of solving international disputes. . . .

When I spoke with President Eisenhower—and I have just returned from the United States of America—I got the impression that the President of the U.S.A.—and not a few people support him—understands the need to relax international tension. . . .

There is only one way of preserving peace—that is the road of peaceful coexistence of states with different social systems. The question stands thus: either peaceful coexistence or war with its catastrophic consequences. Now, with the present relation of forces between socialism and capitalism being in favor of socialism, he who would continue the "cold war" is moving towards his own destruction. . . .

It is not at all because capitalism is still strong that the socialist countries speak out against war, and for peaceful coexistence. No, we have no need of war at all. If the people do not want it, even such a noble and progressive system as socialism cannot be imposed by force of arms. The socialist countries therefore, while carrying through a consistently peace-loving policy, concentrate their efforts on peaceful construction; they fire the hearts of men by the force of their example in building socialism, and thus lead them to follow in their footsteps. The question of when this or that country will take the path to socialism is decided by its own people. This, for us, is the holy of holies.

Lin Biao, "Long Live the Victory of People's War"

Many countries and peoples in Asia, Africa, and Latin America are now being subjected to aggression and enslavement on a serious scale by the imperialists headed by the United States and their lackeys. . . . As in China, the peasant question is extremely important in these regions. The peasants constitute the main force of the national-democratic revolution against the imperialists and their lackeys. In committing aggression against these countries, the imperialists usually begin by seizing the big cities and the main lines of communication. But they are unable to bring the vast countryside completely under their control. . . . The countryside, and the countryside alone, can provide the revolutionary basis from which the revolutionaries can go forward to final victory. Precisely for this reason, Mao Tse-tung's theory of establishing revolutionary base areas in the rural districts and encircling the cities from the countryside is attracting more and more attention among the people in these regions.

Taking the entire globe, if North America and Western Europe can be called "the cities of the world," then Asia, Africa, and Latin America constitute "the rural areas of the world." Since World War II, the proletarian revolutionary movement has for various reasons been temporarily held back in the North American and West European capitalist countries, while the people's revolutionary movement in Asia, Africa, and Latin America has been growing vigorously. In a sense, the contemporary world revolution also presents a picture of the encirclement of cities by the rural areas. In the final analysis, the whole cause of world revolution hinges on

(Continued)

(Opposing Viewpoints Continued)

the revolutionary struggles of the Asian, African, and Latin American peoples, who make up the overwhelming majority of the world's population. The socialist countries should regard it as their internationalist duty to support the people's revolutionary struggles in Asia, Africa, and Latin America. . . .

Ours is the epoch in which world capitalism and imperialism are heading for their doom and communism is marching to victory. Comrade Mao Tse-tung's theory of people's war is not only a product of the Chinese revolution, but has also the characteristic of our epoch.

The new experience gained in the people's revolutionary struggles in various countries since World War II has provided continuous evidence that Mao Tse-tung's thought is a common asset of the revolutionary people of the whole world.

 Why did Nikita Khrushchev feel that the conflict between the socialist and capitalist camps that Lenin had predicted was no longer inevitable? How did Lin Biao respond?

Sources: Khrushchev's Speech to the Chinese, 1959. From G. F. Hudson et al., eds. *The Sino-Soviet Dispute* (New York: Frederick Praeger, 1961), pp. 61–63, cited in *Peking Review*, No. 40, 1959. Lin Biao, "Long Live the Victory of People's War." From *Nationalism and Communism*, Norman Grabner, ed. Copyright © 1977 by D. C. Heath and Company.

The Second Indochina War

China's radicalism was intensified in the early 1960s by the renewed outbreak of war in Indochina. The Eisenhower administration had opposed the peace settlement at Geneva in 1954, which divided Vietnam temporarily into two separate regroupment zones, specifically because the provision for future national elections opened up the possibility that the entire country would come under Communist rule. But Eisenhower had been unwilling to send U.S. military forces to continue the conflict without the full support of the British and the French, who preferred to seek a negotiated settlement. In the end, Washington promised not to break the provisions of the agreement but refused to commit itself to the results.

During the next several months, the United States began to provide aid to the new government in South Vietnam. Under the leadership of the anti-Communist politician Ngo Dinh Diem (NGHOH din DEE-em), the government began to root out dissidents. With the tacit approval of the United States, Diem refused to hold the national elections called for by the Geneva Accords. It was widely anticipated, even in Washington, that the Communists would win such elections. In 1959, Ho Chi Minh, despairing of the peaceful unification of the country under Communist rule, decided to return to a policy of revolutionary war in the south.

Late the following year, a political organization that was designed to win the support of a wide spectrum of the population was founded in an isolated part of South Vietnam. Known as the National Liberation Front (NLF), it was under the secret but firm leadership of high-ranking Communists in North Vietnam (the Democratic Republic of Vietnam).

By 1963, South Vietnam was on the verge of collapse. Diem's autocratic methods and inattention to severe economic inequality had alienated much of the population,

and revolutionary forces, popularly known as the Viet Cong (Vietnamese Communists) and supported by the Communist government in North Vietnam, expanded their influence throughout much of the country. In the fall of 1963, with the approval of the Kennedy administration, senior military officers overthrew the Diem regime. But factionalism kept the new military leadership from reinvigorating the struggle against the insurgent forces, and the situation in South Vietnam grew worse. By early 1965, the Viet Cong, their ranks now swelled by military units infiltrating from North Vietnam, were on the verge of seizing control of the entire country. In March, President Lyndon Johnson decided to send U.S. combat troops to South Vietnam to prevent the total defeat of the anti-Communist government in Saigon. Over the next three years, U.S. troop levels steadily increased as the White House counted on U.S. firepower to persuade Ho Chi Minh to abandon his quest to unify Vietnam under Communist leadership (see the comparative illustration on p. 699).

THE ROLE OF CHINA Chinese leaders observed the gradual escalation of the conflict in South Vietnam with mixed feelings. They were undoubtedly pleased to have a firm Communist ally—one that had in many ways followed the path of Mao Zedong—just beyond their southern frontier. Yet they were concerned that bloodshed in South Vietnam might enmesh China in a new conflict with the United States. Nor did they welcome the specter of a powerful and ambitious united Vietnam, which might wish to extend its influence throughout mainland Southeast Asia, an area that Beijing considered its own backyard.

Chinese leaders therefore tiptoed delicately through the minefield of the Indochina conflict. As the war escalated in 1964 and 1965, Beijing publicly announced that the Chinese people fully supported their comrades seeking

POLITICS & GOVERNMENT

War in the Rice Paddies.
The first stage of the Vietnam War consisted primarily of guerrilla conflict, as Viet Cong insurgents relied on guerrilla tactics in their effort to bring down the U.S.-supported government in Saigon. In 1965, however, President Lyndon Johnson ordered U.S. combat troops into South Vietnam (top photo) in a desperate bid to prevent a Communist victory in that beleaguered country. The Communist government in North Vietnam responded in kind, sending its own regular forces down the Ho Chi Minh Trail to confront U.S. troops on the battlefield. In the photo on the bottom, North Vietnamese troops storm the U.S. Marine base at Khe Sanh (KAY SAHN), near the demilitarized zone, in 1968, the most violent year of the war. Although U.S. military commanders believed that helicopters would be a key factor in defeating the insurgent forces in Vietnam, this conflict was one instance when technological superiority did not produce a victory on the battlefield.

Q *How do you think helicopters were used to assist U.S. operations in South Vietnam? Why didn't their use result in a U.S. victory?*

AP Images

© Three Lions/Getty Images

national liberation but privately assured Washington that China would not directly enter the conflict unless U.S. forces threatened its southern border. Beijing also refused to cooperate fully with Moscow in shipping Soviet goods to North Vietnam through Chinese territory.

Despite its dismay at the lack of full support from China, the Communist government in North Vietnam responded to U.S. escalation by infiltrating more of its own regular troops into the South, and by 1968, the war had reached a stalemate. The Communists were not strong enough to overthrow the government in Saigon, whose weakness was shielded by the presence of half a million U.S. troops, but President Johnson was reluctant to engage in all-out war on North Vietnam for fear of provoking a global nuclear conflict. In the fall, after the Communist-led Tet offensive undermined claims of progress in Washington and aroused intense antiwar protests in the United States, peace negotiations began in Paris.

QUEST FOR PEACE Richard Nixon came into the White House in 1969 on a pledge to bring an honorable end to the Vietnam War. With U.S. public opinion sharply divided on the issue, he began to withdraw U.S. troops while continuing to hold peace talks in Paris. But the centerpiece of his strategy was to improve relations with China and thus undercut Chinese support for the North Vietnamese war effort. During the 1960s, relations between Moscow and Beijing had reached a point of extreme tension, and thousands of troops were stationed on both sides of their long common frontier. To intimidate their Communist rivals, Soviet sources hinted that they might launch a preemptive strike to destroy Chinese nuclear facilities in Xinjiang. Sensing an opportunity to split the two onetime allies, Nixon sent his emissary, Henry Kissinger, on a secret trip to China. Responding to assurances that the United States was determined to withdraw from Indochina and hoped to improve relations with the mainland regime, Chinese leaders invited President Nixon to visit China in early 1972. Nixon accepted, and the two sides agreed to set aside their differences over Taiwan to pursue a better mutual relationship.

THE FALL OF SAIGON Incensed at the apparent betrayal by their close allies, North Vietnamese leaders decided to seek a peaceful settlement of the war. In January 1973, a peace treaty was signed in Paris calling for the removal of all U.S. forces from South Vietnam. In return, the Communists agreed to halt military operations and to engage in negotiations to resolve their differences with the Saigon regime. But negotiations between north and south over the political settlement soon broke down, and in early 1975, the Communists resumed the offensive. At the end of April, under a massive assault by North Vietnamese military forces, the South Vietnamese government surrendered. A year later, the country was unified under Communist rule.

The Communist victory in Vietnam was a severe humiliation for the United States, but its strategic impact was limited because of the new relationship with China. During the next decade, Sino-American relations continued to improve. In 1979, diplomatic ties were established between the two countries under an arrangement whereby the United States renounced its mutual security treaty with the Republic of China in return for a pledge from China to seek reunification with Taiwan by peaceful means. By the end of the 1970s, China and the United States had forged a "strategic relationship" in which they would cooperate against the common threat of Soviet hegemony in Asia.

Why had the United States failed to achieve its objective of preventing a Communist victory in Vietnam? One leading member of the Johnson administration later commented that Washington had underestimated the determination of its adversary in Hanoi and overestimated the patience of the American people. Deeper reflection suggests, however, that another factor was equally important: the United States had overestimated the ability of its client state in South Vietnam to defend itself against a disciplined adversary. In subsequent years, it became a crucial lesson to the Americans on the perils of nation building.

An Era of Equivalence

Q FOCUS QUESTION: Why did the Cold War briefly flare up again in the 1980s, and why did it come to a definitive end at the end of the decade?

When the Johnson administration sent U.S. combat troops to South Vietnam in 1965, Washington's main concern was with Beijing, not Moscow. By the mid-1960s, U.S. officials viewed the Soviet Union as an essentially conservative power, more concerned with protecting its vast empire than with expanding its borders. In fact, U.S. policy makers periodically sought Soviet assistance in seeking a peaceful settlement of the Vietnam War. As long as Khrushchev was in power, they found a receptive ear in Moscow. Khrushchev was firmly dedicated to promoting peaceful coexistence (at least on his terms) and sternly advised the North Vietnamese against a resumption of revolutionary war in South Vietnam.

After October 1964, when Khrushchev was replaced by a new leadership headed by party chief Leonid Brezhnev (lee-oh-NYEET BREZH-neff) (1906–1982) and Prime Minister Alexei Kosygin (uh-LEK-say kuh-SEE-gun) (1904–1980), Soviet attitudes about Vietnam became more ambivalent. On the one hand, the new Soviet leaders had no desire to see the Vietnam conflict poison relations between the great powers. On the other hand, Moscow was eager to demonstrate its support for the North Vietnamese to deflect Chinese charges that the Soviet Union had betrayed the interests of the oppressed peoples of the world. As a result, Soviet officials publicly voiced sympathy for the U.S. predicament in Vietnam but put no pressure on their allies to bring an end to the war. Indeed, the Soviet Union became Hanoi's main supplier of advanced military equipment in the final years of the war.

The Brezhnev Doctrine

In the meantime, new Cold War tensions were brewing in Eastern Europe, where discontent with Stalinist policies began to emerge in Czechoslovakia. The latter had not shared in the thaw of the mid-1950s and remained under the rule of the hard-liner Antonín Novotný (AHN-toh-nyeen NOH-vaht-nee) (1904–1975), who had been installed in power by Stalin himself. By the late 1960s, however, Novotný's policies had led to widespread popular alienation, and in 1968, with the support of intellectuals and reformist party members, Alexander Dubček (DOOB-check) (1921–1992) was elected first secretary of the Communist Party. He immediately attempted to create what was popularly called "socialism with a human face," relaxing restrictions on freedom of speech and the press and the right to travel abroad. Economic reforms were announced, and party control over all aspects of society was reduced. A period of euphoria erupted that came to be known as the "Prague Spring."

It proved to be short-lived. Encouraged by Dubček's actions, some Czechs called for more far-reaching reforms, including neutrality and withdrawal from the Soviet bloc. To forestall the spread of this "spring fever," the Soviet Red Army, supported by troops from other

The Brezhnev Doctrine

POLITICS & GOVERNMENT

In the summer of 1968, when the new Communist Party leaders in Czechoslovakia were seriously considering proposals for reforming the totalitarian system there, the Warsaw Pact nations met under the leadership of Soviet party chief Leonid Brezhnev to assess the threat to the socialist camp. Soon afterward, military forces of several Soviet bloc nations entered Czechoslovakia and imposed a new government subservient to Moscow. The move was justified by the spirit of "proletarian internationalism" and was widely viewed as a warning to China and other socialist states not to stray too far from Marxist-Leninist orthodoxy, as interpreted by the Soviet Union. But Moscow's actions also raised tensions in the Cold War.

A Letter to the Central Committee of the Communist Party of Czechoslovakia

Dear comrades!

On behalf of the Central Committees of the Communist and Workers' Parties of Bulgaria, Hungary, the German Democratic Republic, Poland, and the Soviet Union, we address ourselves to you with this letter, prompted by a feeling of sincere friendship based on the principles of Marxism-Leninism and proletarian internationalism and by the concern of our common affairs for strengthening the positions of socialism and the security of the socialist community of nations.

The development of events in your country evokes in us deep anxiety. It is our firm conviction that the offensive of the reactionary forces, backed by imperialists, against your Party and the foundations of the social system in the Czechoslovak Socialist Republic, threatens to push your country off the road of socialism and that consequently it jeopardizes the interests of the entire socialist system. . . .

We neither had nor have any intention of interfering in such affairs as are strictly the internal business of your Party and your state, nor of violating the principles of respect, independence, and equality in the relations among the Communist Parties and socialist countries. . . .

At the same time we cannot agree to have hostile forces push your country from the road of socialism and create a threat of severing Czechoslovakia from the socialist community. . . . This is the common cause of our countries, which have joined in the Warsaw Treaty to ensure independence, peace, and security in Europe, and to set up an insurmountable barrier against the intrigues of the imperialist forces, against aggression and revenge. . . . We shall never agree to have imperialism, using peaceful or nonpeaceful methods, making a gap from the inside or from the outside in the socialist system, and changing in imperialism's favor the correlation of forces in Europe. . . .

That is why we believe that a decisive rebuff of the anti-Communist forces, and decisive efforts for the preservation of the socialist system in Czechoslovakia are not only your task but ours as well. . . .

We express the conviction that the Communist Party of Czechoslovakia, conscious of its responsibility, will take the necessary steps to block the path of reaction. In this struggle you can count on the solidarity and all-round assistance of the fraternal socialist countries.

Warsaw, July 15, 1968.

Q *How did Leonid Brezhnev justify the Soviet decision to invade Czechoslovakia? To what degree do you find his arguments persuasive?*

Source: From *Moscow News*, Supplement to No, 30 (917), 1968, pp. 3–6.

Warsaw Pact states, invaded Czechoslovakia in August 1968 and crushed the reform movement. Gustav Husák (goo-STAHV HOO-sahk) (1913–1991), a committed Stalinist, replaced Dubček and restored the old order, while Moscow attempted to justify its action by issuing the so-called **Brezhnev Doctrine** (see the box above).

In East Germany as well, Stalinist policies continued to hold sway. The ruling Communist government in East Germany, led by Walter Ulbricht, had consolidated its position in the early 1950s and became a faithful Soviet satellite. Industry was nationalized and agriculture collectivized. After the 1953 workers' revolt was crushed by Soviet tanks, a steady flight of East Germans to West Germany ensued, primarily through the city of Berlin. This exodus of mostly skilled laborers ("Soon only party chief Ulbricht will be left," remarked one Soviet observer sardonically) created economic problems and in 1961 led the East German government to erect a wall separating

East Berlin from West Berlin, as well as even more fearsome barriers along the entire border with West Germany. After building the Berlin Wall, East Germany succeeded in developing the strongest economy among the Soviet Union's Eastern European satellites. In 1971, Ulbricht was succeeded by Erich Honecker (AY-reekh HON-nek-uh) (1912–1994), a party hard-liner. Propaganda increased, and the use of the Stasi (SHTAH-see), the secret police, became a hallmark of Honecker's virtual dictatorship. Honecker ruled unchallenged for the next eighteen years.

An Era of Détente

Still, under Brezhnev and Kosygin, the Soviet Union continued to pursue peaceful coexistence with the West and adopted a generally cautious posture in foreign affairs. By the early 1970s, a new age in Soviet-American relations had emerged, often referred to as **détente** (day-TAHNT), a French term meaning a reduction of tensions between the two sides. One symbol of détente was the Anti-Ballistic Missile (ABM) Treaty, often called SALT I (for Strategic Arms Limitation Talks), signed in 1972, in which the two nations agreed to limit the size of their ABM systems.

Washington's objective in pursuing the treaty was to make it unlikely that either superpower could win a nuclear exchange by launching a preemptive strike against the other. U.S. officials believed that a policy of "equivalence," in which the two sides had roughly equal power, was the best way to avoid a nuclear confrontation. Détente was pursued in other ways as well. When President Nixon took office in 1969, he sought to increase trade and cultural contacts with the Soviet Union. His purpose was to set up a series of "linkages" in U.S.-Soviet relations that would persuade Moscow of the economic and social benefits of maintaining good relations with the West.

A symbol of that new relationship was the Helsinki Accords. Signed in 1975 by the United States, Canada, and all European nations on both sides of the iron curtain, these accords recognized all borders in Europe that had been established since the end of World War II, thereby formally acknowledging for the first time the Soviet sphere of influence in Eastern Europe. The Helsinki Accords also committed the signatories to recognize and protect the human rights of their citizens, a clear effort by the Western states to improve the performance of the Soviet Union and its allies in that arena.

Renewed Tensions in the Third World

Protection of human rights became one of the major foreign policy goals of the next U.S. president, Jimmy Carter (b. 1924). Ironically, just at the point when U.S. involvement in Vietnam came to an end and relations with China began to improve, U.S.-Soviet relations began to sour, for several reasons. Some Americans had become increasingly concerned about aggressive new tendencies in Soviet foreign policy. The first indication came in Africa. Soviet influence was on the rise in Somalia, across the Red Sea from South Yemen, and later in neighboring Ethiopia. In Angola, once a colony of Portugal, an insurgent movement supported by Cuban troops came to power. In 1979, Soviet troops were sent across the border into Afghanistan to protect a newly installed Marxist regime facing internal resistance from fundamentalist Muslims. Some observers suspected that the ultimate objective of the Soviet advance into hitherto neutral Afghanistan was to extend Soviet power into the oil fields of the Persian Gulf. To deter such a possibility, the White House promulgated the Carter Doctrine, which stated that the United States would use its military power, if necessary, to safeguard Western access to the oil reserves in the Middle East. In fact, sources in Moscow later disclosed that the Soviet advance had little to do with the oil of the Persian Gulf but was an effort to increase Soviet influence in a region increasingly beset by Islamic fervor. Soviet officials feared that Islamic activism could spread to the Muslim populations in the Soviet republics in Central Asia and were confident that the United States was too distracted by the so-called **Vietnam syndrome** (the public fear of U.S. involvement in another Vietnam-type conflict) to respond.

Another reason for the growing suspicion of the Soviet Union in the United States was that some U.S. defense analysts began to charge that the Soviet Union had rejected the policy of equivalence and was seeking strategic superiority in nuclear weapons. Accordingly,

CHRONOLOGY	The Cold War to 1980	
Truman Doctrine		1947
Formation of NATO		1949
Soviet Union explodes first nuclear device		1949
Communists come to power in China		1949
Nationalist government retreats to Taiwan		1949
Korean War		1950–1953
Geneva Conference ends Indochina War		1954
Warsaw Pact created		1955
Khrushchev calls for peaceful coexistence		1956
Sino-Soviet dispute breaks into the open		1961
Cuban Missile Crisis		1962
SALT I treaty signed		1972
Nixon's visit to China		1972
Fall of South Vietnam		1975
Soviet invasion of Afghanistan		1979

they argued for a substantial increase in U.S. defense spending. Such charges, combined with evidence of Soviet efforts in Africa and the Middle East and reports of the persecution of Jews and dissidents in the Soviet Union, helped undermine public support for détente in the United States. These changing attitudes were reflected in the failure of the Carter administration to obtain congressional approval of a new arms limitation agreement (SALT II), signed with the Soviet Union in 1979.

Countering the Evil Empire

The early years of the administration of President Ronald Reagan (1911–2004) witnessed a return to the harsh rhetoric, if not all of the harsh practices, of the Cold War. President Reagan's anti-Communist credentials were well known. In a speech given shortly after his election in 1980, he referred to the Soviet Union as an "evil empire" and frequently voiced his suspicion of Soviet motives in foreign affairs. In an effort to eliminate perceived Soviet advantages in strategic weaponry, the White House began a military buildup that stimulated a renewed arms race. In 1982, the Reagan administration introduced the nuclear-tipped cruise missile, whose ability to fly at low altitudes made it difficult to detect by enemy radar. Reagan also became an ardent exponent of the Strategic Defense Initiative (SDI), nicknamed **Star Wars**. The intent behind this proposed defense system was not only to create a space shield that could destroy incoming missiles but also to force Moscow into an arms race that it could not hope to win.

The Reagan administration also adopted a more activist, if not confrontational, stance in the Third World. That attitude was most directly demonstrated in Central America, where the revolutionary Sandinista (san-duh-NEES-tuh) regime had been established in Nicaragua after the overthrow of the Somoza dictatorship in 1979. Charging that the Sandinista regime was supporting a guerrilla insurgency movement in nearby El Salvador, the Reagan administration began to provide material aid to the government in El Salvador while simultaneously supporting an anti-Communist guerrilla movement (the **Contras**) in Nicaragua. Though the administration insisted that it was countering the spread of communism in the Western Hemisphere, its Central American

Northern Central America

policy aroused considerable controversy in Congress, where some members charged that growing U.S. involvement could lead to a repeat of the nation's bitter experience in Vietnam.

The Reagan administration also took the offensive in other areas. By providing military support to the anti-Soviet insurgents in Afghanistan, the White House helped maintain a Vietnam-like war in Afghanistan that entangled the Soviet Union in its own quagmire. Like the Vietnam War, the conflict in Afghanistan resulted in heavy casualties and demonstrated that the influence of a superpower was limited in the face of strong nationalist, guerrilla-type opposition.

Toward a New World Order

In 1985, Mikhail Gorbachev (meek-HAYL GOR-buh-chawf) (b. 1931) was elected secretary of the Communist Party of the Soviet Union. During Brezhnev's last years and the brief tenures of his two successors (see Chapter 27), the Soviet Union had entered an era of serious economic decline, and the dynamic new party chief was well aware that drastic changes would be needed to rekindle the dreams that had inspired the Bolshevik Revolution. During the next few years, he launched a program of restructuring, or *perestroika* (per-uh-STROI-kuh), to revitalize the Soviet system. As part of that program, he set out to improve relations with the United States and the rest of the capitalist world. When he met with President Reagan in Reykjavik (RAY-kyuh-vik), the capital of Iceland, the two leaders agreed to set aside their ideological differences.

Gorbachev's desperate effort to rescue the Soviet Union from collapse was too little and too late. In 1989, popular demonstrations against Communist rule broke out across Eastern Europe. The contagion soon spread eastward, and in 1991 the Soviet Union, so long an apparently permanent fixture on the global scene, suddenly disintegrated. In its place arose fifteen new nations. That same year, the string of Soviet satellites in Eastern Europe broke loose from Moscow's grip and declared their independence from Communist rule. The Cold War was over (see Chapter 27).

The end of the Cold War lulled many observers into the seductive vision of a new world order that would be characterized by peaceful cooperation and increasing prosperity. Sadly, such hopes have not been realized (see the comparative essay "Global Village or Clash of Civilizations?" on p. 704). A bitter civil war in the Balkans in the mid-1990s graphically demonstrated that old fault lines of national and ethnic hostility still divided the post–Cold War world. Elsewhere, bloody ethnic and religious disputes broke out in Africa and the Middle East. Then, on September 11, 2001, the world entered a dangerous new era when terrorists attacked the nerve centers of U.S. power in New York City and Washington, D.C.,

Global Village or Clash of Civilizations?

INTERACTION & EXCHANGE

As the Cold War came to an end in 1991, policymakers, scholars, and political pundits began to forecast the emergence of a "new world order." One hypothesis, put forth by the political philosopher Francis Fukuyama, was that the decline of communism signaled that the industrial capitalist democracies of the West had triumphed in the world of ideas and were now poised to remake the rest of the world in their own image.

Not everyone agreed with this optimistic view of the world situation. In *The Clash of Civilizations and the Remaking of the World Order*, the historian Samuel P. Huntington suggested that the post–Cold War era, far from marking the triumph of Western ideals, would be characterized by increased global fragmentation and a "clash of civilizations" based on ethnic, cultural, or religious differences. According to Huntington, the twenty-first century would be dominated by disputatious cultural blocs in East Asia, Western Europe and the United States, Eurasia, and the Middle East. The dream of a universal order—a global village—dominated by Western values, he concluded, is a fantasy.

Recent events have lent some support to Huntington's hypothesis. The collapse of the Soviet Union led to the emergence of an atmosphere of conflict and tension all along the perimeter of the old Soviet empire. More recently, the terrorist attack on the United States in September 2001 set the advanced nations of the West and much of the Muslim world on a collision course. As for the new economic order—now enshrined as official policy in Western capitals—public anger at the impact of globalization has reached disturbing levels in many countries, leading to a growing demand for self-protection and group identity in an impersonal and rapidly changing world.

Are we then headed toward multiple power blocs divided by religion and culture as Huntington predicted? His thesis is indeed a useful corrective to the complacent tendency of many observers to view Western civilization as the zenith of human achievement. By dividing the world into competing cultural blocs, however, Huntington has underestimated the centrifugal forces at

© William J. Duiker

Ronald McDonald in Indonesia. This giant statue welcomes young Indonesians to a McDonald's restaurant in Jakarta, the capital city. McDonald's food chain symbolizes the globalization of today's world civilization.

work in the various regions of the world. As the industrial and technological revolutions spread across the face of the earth, their impact is measurably stronger in some societies than in others, thereby intensifying historical rivalries in a given region while establishing links between individual societies and counterparts in other parts of the world. In recent years, for example, Japan has had more in common with the United States than with its traditional neighbors, China and Korea.

The most likely scenario for the next few decades, then, is more complex than either the global village hypothesis or its rival, the clash of civilizations. The twenty-first century will be characterized by simultaneous trends toward globalization and fragmentation as the thrust of technology and information transforms societies and gives rise to counterreactions among societies seeking to preserve a group identity and sense of meaning and purpose in a confusing world.

Q *How has the recent global economic recession affected the issues discussed in this essay?*

inaugurating a new round of tension between the West and the forces of militant Islam. These events will be discussed in greater detail in the chapters that follow.

In the meantime, other issues beyond the headlines clamor for attention. Environmental problems and the threat of global warming, the growing gap between rich and poor nations, and tensions caused by migrations of peoples all present a growing threat to political stability and the pursuit of happiness. The recent financial crisis, which has severely undermined the overall health of the global economy, is an additional impediment. As the twenty-first century progresses, the task of guaranteeing the survival of the human race appears to be just as challenging, and even more complex, than it was during the Cold War.

CHAPTER SUMMARY

At the end of World War II, a new conflict arose as the two superpowers, the United States and the Soviet Union, began to compete for political domination. This ideological division soon spread throughout the world as the United States fought in Korea and Vietnam to prevent the spread of communism, promoted by the new Maoist government in China, while the Soviet Union used its influence to prop up pro-Soviet regimes in Asia, Africa, and Latin America.

What had begun, then, as a confrontation across the great divide of the "iron curtain" in Europe eventually took on global significance, much as the major European powers had jostled for position and advantage in Africa and eastern Asia prior to World War I. As a result, both Moscow and Washington became entangled in areas that in themselves had little importance in terms of real national security interests.

As the twentieth century wore on, however, there were tantalizing signs of a thaw in the Cold War. In 1979, China and the United States established mutual diplomatic relations, a consequence of Beijing's decision to focus on domestic reform and stop supporting wars of national liberation in Asia. Six years later, the ascent of Mikhail Gorbachev to leadership in the Soviet Union, which culminated in the dissolution of the Soviet Union in 1991, brought an end to almost half a century of bitter rivalry between the world's two superpowers.

The Cold War thus ended without the horrific vision of a mushroom cloud. Unlike the earlier rivalries that had resulted in two world wars, this time the antagonists had gradually come to realize that the struggle for supremacy could be carried out in the political and economic arena rather than on the battlefield. And in the final analysis, it was not military superiority, but political, economic, and cultural factors that brought about the triumph of Western civilization over the Marxist vision of a classless utopia. The world's policymakers could now shift their focus to other problems of mutual concern.

CHAPTER TIMELINE

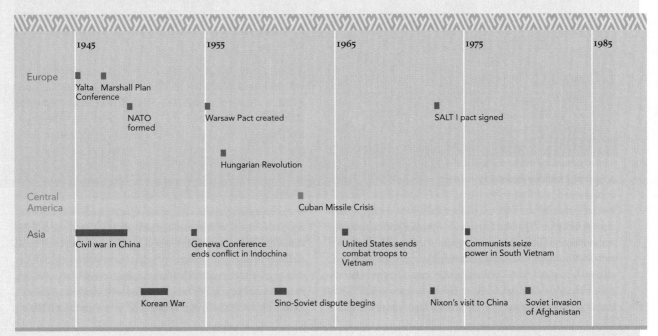

CHAPTER REVIEW

Upon Reflection

Q This chapter has described the outbreak of the Cold War as virtually inevitable, given the ambitions of the two superpowers and their ideological differences. Do you agree? How might the Cold War have been avoided?

Q What disagreements brought about an end to the Sino-Soviet alliance in 1961? Which factors appear to have been most important?

Q How did the wars in Korea and Vietnam relate to the Cold War and affect its course?

Key Terms

Truman Doctrine (p. 680)
Marshall Plan (p. 680)
containment (p. 682)
denazification (p. 682)
peaceful coexistence (p. 691)
Nonaligned Movement (p. 693)
Brezhnev Doctrine (p. 701)
détente (p. 702)
Vietnam syndrome (p. 702)
Star Wars (p. 703)
Contras (p. 703)

Suggested Reading

COLD WAR Literature on the Cold War is abundant. Revisionist studies have emphasized U.S. responsibility for the Cold War, especially its global aspects. See, for example, **W. La Feber, *America, Russia, and the Cold War, 1945–1966,*** 8th ed. (New York, 2002). For a highly competent retrospective analysis of the Cold War era, see **J. L. Gaddis, *We Now Know: Rethinking Cold War History*** (Oxford, 1997). Also see his more general work ***The Cold War: A New History*** (New York, 2005). For the perspective of a veteran journalist, see **M. Frankel, *High Noon in the Cold War: Kennedy, Khrushchev, and the Cuban Missile Crisis*** (New York, 2004).

A number of studies of the early stages of the Cold War are based on documents unavailable until the late 1980s or early 1990s. See, for example, **O. A. Westad, *Cold War and Revolution: Soviet-American Rivalry and the Origins of the Chinese Civil War*** (New York, 1993), and **Chen Jian, *China's Road to the Korean War: The Making of the Sino-American Confrontation*** (New York, 1994). **S. Goncharov, J. W. Lewis,** and **Xue Litai, *Uncertain Partners: Stalin, Mao, and the Korean War*** (Stanford, Calif., 1993), provides a fascinating view of the war from several perspectives. For a perspective that places much of the blame for the Korean War on the United States, see **B. Cumings, *The Korean War: A History*** (New York, 2010).

CHINA There are several informative surveys of Chinese foreign policy since the Communist rise to power. A particularly insightful account is **Chen Jian, *Mao's China and the Cold War*** (Chapel Hill, N.C., 2001). On Chinese policy in Korea, see **Shu Guang Zhang, *Mao's Military Romanticism: China and the Korean War*** (Lawrence, Kans., 2001), and **Xiaobing Li et al., *Mao's Generals Remember Korea*** (Lawrence, Kans., 2001). On Sino-Vietnamese relations, see **Ang Cheng Guan, *Vietnamese Communists' Relations with China and the Second Indochina Conflict*** (Jefferson, N.C., 1997).

THE COLD WAR ENDS Two recent works that deal with the end of the Cold War are the gripping account by **M. E. Sarotte, *1989: The Struggle to Create Post–Cold War Europe*** (Princeton, N.J., 2009), and **V. Sebestyen, *Revolution 1989: The Fall of the Soviet Empire*** (New York, 2008).

CourseMate

Visit the CourseMate website at **www.cengagebrain.com** for additional study tools and review materials for this chapter.

Brave New World:
Communism on Trial

Shopping in Moscow

© William J. Duiker

CHAPTER OUTLINE
AND FOCUS QUESTIONS

The Postwar Soviet Union

Q How did Nikita Khrushchev change the system that the Soviet dictator Joseph Stalin had put in place before his death in 1953? To what degree did his successors adopt Khrushchev's policies?

The Disintegration of the Soviet Empire

Q What were the key components of *perestroika*, which Mikhail Gorbachev espoused during the 1980s? Why did it fail?

The East Is Red: China Under Communism

Q What were Mao Zedong's chief goals for China, and what policies did he institute to try to achieve them?

"Serve the People": Chinese Society Under Communism

Q What significant political, economic, and social changes have taken place in China since the death of Mao Zedong?

CRITICAL THINKING

Q Why has communism survived in China when it failed to survive in Eastern Europe and Russia? Are Chinese leaders justified in claiming that without party leadership, the country would fall into chaos?

ACCORDING TO KARL MARX, capitalism is a system that involves the exploitation of man by man; under socialism, it is the other way around. That wry joke was typical of popular humor in post–World War II Moscow, where the dreams of a future utopia had faded in the grim reality of life in the Soviet Union.

For the average Soviet citizen after World War II, few images better symbolized the shortcomings of the Soviet system than a long line of people queuing up outside an official state store selling consumer goods. Because the command economy was so inefficient, items of daily use were chronically in such short supply that when a particular item became available, people often lined up immediately to buy several for themselves and their friends. Sometimes, when people saw a line forming, they would automatically join the queue without even knowing what item was available for purchase!

Despite the evident weaknesses of the centralized Soviet economy, the Communist monopoly on power seemed secure, as did Moscow's hold over its client states in Eastern Europe. In fact, for three decades after the end of World War II, the Soviet empire appeared to be a permanent feature of the international landscape. But by the early 1980s, it was clear that there were cracks in the Kremlin wall. The Soviet economy was stagnant, the minority nationalities were restive, and Eastern European leaders were increasingly emboldened to test the waters of the global capitalist marketplace. In the United States, the newly elected president, Ronald Reagan, boldly predicted the imminent collapse of the "evil empire."

Within a period of less than three years (1989–1991), the Soviet Union ceased to exist as a nation. Russia and other former Soviet republics declared their separate independence, Communist regimes in Eastern Europe were toppled, and the long-standing division of postwar Europe came to an end. Although Communist parties survived the demise of the system and have showed signs of renewed vigor in some countries in the region, their monopoly is gone, and they must now compete with other parties for power.

The fate of communism in China has been quite different. Despite some turbulence, communism has survived in China, even as that nation takes giant strides toward becoming an economic superpower. Yet, as China's leaders struggle to bring the nation into the modern age, many of the essential principles of Marxist-Leninist dogma have been tacitly abandoned.

The Postwar Soviet Union

Q FOCUS QUESTIONS: How did Nikita Khrushchev change the system that the Soviet dictator Joseph Stalin had put in place before his death in 1953? To what degree did his successors adopt Khrushchev's policies?

At the end of World War II, the Soviet Union was one of the world's two superpowers, and its leader, Joseph Stalin, was in a position of strength. He and his Soviet colleagues were now in control of a vast empire that included Eastern Europe, much of the Balkans, and new territory gained from Japan in East Asia.

From Stalin to Khrushchev

At the same time, World War II had devastated the Soviet Union. Nearly 30 million citizens lost their lives, and cities such as Kiev (KEE-yev), Kharkov (KHAR-kawf), and Leningrad had suffered enormous physical destruction. As the lands that had been occupied by the German forces were liberated, the Soviet government turned its attention to restoring their economic

structures. Nevertheless, in 1945, agricultural production was only 60 percent and steel output only 50 percent of prewar levels. The Soviet people faced incredibly difficult conditions: ill-housed and poorly clothed, they worked longer hours and ate less they than before the war.

STALINISM IN ACTION In the immediate postwar years, the Soviet Union removed goods and materials from occupied Germany and extorted valuable raw materials from its satellite states in Eastern Europe (see Map 27.1). More important, however, to create a new industrial base, Stalin returned to the method he had used in the 1930s—the extraction of development capital from Soviet labor. Working hard for little pay and for precious few consumer goods, Soviet laborers were expected to produce goods for export with little in return for themselves. The incoming capital from abroad could then be used to purchase machinery and Western technology. The loss of millions of men in the war meant that much of this tremendous workload fell upon Soviet women, who performed almost 40 percent of the heavy manual labor.

The pace of economic recovery in the years immediately after the war was impressive. By 1947, industrial production had returned to 1939 levels. New power plants, canals, and giant factories were built, and industrial enterprises and oil fields were established in Siberia and Soviet Central Asia.

Although Stalin's economic strategy was successful in promoting growth in heavy industry, primarily for the benefit of the military, consumer goods remained scarce as long-suffering Soviet citizens were still being asked to suffer for a better tomorrow. Heavy industry grew at a rate three times that of personal consumption. Moreover, the housing shortage was acute, with living conditions especially difficult in the overcrowded cities.

When World War II ended in 1945, Stalin had been in power for more than fifteen years. Political terror enforced by several hundred thousand secret police ensured that he would remain in power. By the late 1940s, an estimated 9 million Soviet citizens were in Siberian concentration camps.

Increasingly distrustful of potential competitors, Stalin exercised sole authority and pitted his subordinates against each other. His morbid suspicions extended to even his closest colleagues, causing them to become completely cowed. As he remarked mockingly on one occasion, "When I die, the imperialists will strangle all of you like a litter of kittens."[1]

THE RISE AND FALL OF KHRUSHCHEV Stalin died—presumably of natural causes—in 1953 and, after some bitter infighting within the party leadership, was

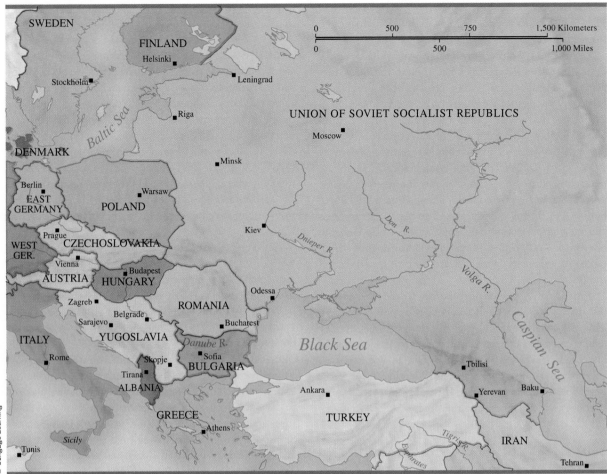

MAP 27.1 Eastern Europe Under Soviet Rule. After World War II, the boundaries of Eastern Europe were redrawn as a result of Allied agreements reached at the Tehran and Yalta conferences. This map shows the new boundaries that were established throughout the region, placing Soviet power at the center of Europe.

Q *How had the boundaries changed from the prewar era?*

succeeded by Georgy Malenkov, a veteran administrator and ambitious member of the Politburo (POL-it-byoor-oh), the party's governing body. But Malenkov's reform goals did not necessarily appeal to key groups, including the army, the Communist Party, the managerial elite, and the security services (now known as the Committee on Government Security, or KGB). In 1953, Malenkov was removed from his position as party leader, and by 1955 power had shifted to his rival, the new party general secretary, Nikita Khrushchev.

Once in power, Khrushchev moved vigorously to boost the performance of the Soviet economy and revitalize Soviet society. In an attempt to release the national economy from the stranglehold of the central bureaucracy, he abolished dozens of government ministries and split up the party and government apparatus. Khrushchev

also attempted to rejuvenate the stagnant agricultural sector. He attempted to spur production by increasing profit incentives and opened "virgin lands" in Soviet Kazakhstan (ka-zak-STAN *or* kuh-zahk-STAHN) to bring thousands of acres of new land under cultivation.

An innovator by nature, Khrushchev had to overcome the inherently conservative instincts of the Soviet bureaucracy, as well as those of the mass of the Soviet population. His plan to remove the "dead hand" of the state, however laudable in intent, alienated much of the Soviet official class, and his effort to split the party angered those who saw it as the central force in the Soviet system. Khrushchev's agricultural schemes inspired similar opposition. His effort to persuade Russians to eat more corn (an idea he had apparently picked up during a visit to the United States) earned him the mocking nickname

"Cornman." The industrial growth rate, which had soared in the early 1950s, now declined dramatically, from 13 percent in 1953 to 7.5 percent in 1964.

Khrushchev was probably best known for his policy of **de-Stalinization**. Khrushchev had risen in the party hierarchy as a Stalin protégé, but he had been deeply disturbed by his mentor's excesses and, once in a position of authority, moved to excise the Stalinist legacy from Soviet society The campaign began at the Twentieth National Congress of the Communist Party in February 1956, when Khrushchev gave a long speech in private criticizing some of Stalin's major shortcomings. The speech had apparently not been intended for public distribution, but it was quickly leaked to the Western press and created a sensation throughout the world (see the box on p. 711). Under Khrushchev's instructions, thousands of prisoners were released from concentration camps.

Khrushchev's personality, however, did not endear him to higher Soviet officials, who frowned at his tendency to crack jokes and play the clown. Foreign policy failures further damaged Khrushchev's reputation among his colleagues (see Chapter 26). While he was away on vacation in 1964, a special meeting of the Soviet Politburo voted him out of office (because of "deteriorating health") and forced him into retirement.

The Brezhnev Years (1964–1982)

The ouster of Nikita Khrushchev in October 1964 vividly demonstrated the challenges that would be encountered by any leader sufficiently bold to try to reform the Soviet system. Leonid Brezhnev (1906–1982), the new party chief, was undoubtedly aware of these realities of Soviet politics, and his long tenure in power was marked, above all, by the desire to avoid changes that might provoke instability, either at home or abroad. Brezhnev was himself a product of the Soviet system. He had entered the ranks of the party leadership under Stalin, and although he was not a particularly avid believer in party ideology, he was no partisan of reform.

Still, Brezhnev sought stability in the domestic arena. He and his prime minister, Alexei Kosygin (1904–1980), undertook what might be described as a program of "de-Khrushchevization," returning the responsibility for long-term planning to the central ministries and reuniting the Communist Party apparatus. Despite some cautious attempts to stimulate the stagnant agricultural sector, there was no effort to revise the basic system of collective farms. In the industrial sector, the regime launched a series of reforms designed to give factory managers (themselves employees of the state) more responsibility for setting prices, wages, and production quotas. These

"Kosygin reforms" had little effect, however, because they were stubbornly resisted by the bureaucracy.

A CONTROLLED SOCIETY Brezhnev also initiated a significant retreat from Khrushchev's policy of de-Stalinization. Criticism of the "Great Leader" had angered conservatives both within the party hierarchy and among the public at large, many of whom still revered Stalin as a hero and a defender of Russia against Nazi Germany. Early in Brezhnev's reign, Stalin's reputation began to revive. Although his alleged shortcomings were not totally ignored, he was now described in the official press as "an outstanding party leader" who had been primarily responsible for the successes achieved by the Soviet Union.

The regime also adopted a more restrictive policy toward dissidents in Soviet society. Critics of the Soviet system, such as the physicist Andrei Sakharov (ahn-DRAY SAH-kuh-rawf) (1921–1989), were harassed and arrested or, like the famous writer Alexander Solzhenitsyn (sohl-zhuh-NEET-sin) (1918–2008), forced to leave the country. Free expression was also restricted. The media were controlled by the state and presented only what the state wanted people to hear. The government made strenuous efforts to prevent the Soviet people from being exposed to harmful foreign ideas, especially modern art, literature, and contemporary Western rock music. When the Summer Olympic Games were held in Moscow in 1980, Soviet newspapers advised citizens to keep their children indoors to prevent them from being polluted with "bourgeois" ideas passed on by foreign visitors.

For citizens of Western democracies, such a political atmosphere would seem highly oppressive, but for the Russian people, an emphasis on law and order was an accepted aspect of everyday life inherited from the tsarist period. It was firmly enshrined in the Soviet constitution, which subordinated individual freedom to the interests of the state (see the box on p. 712). Conformity was the rule in virtually every corner of Soviet society, from the educational system (characterized at all levels by rote memorization and political indoctrination) to child rearing (it was forbidden, for example, to be left-handed) and even to yearly vacations (most workers took their vacations at resorts run by their employer, where the daily schedule of activities was highly regimented). Young Americans studying in the Soviet Union reported that their Soviet friends were often shocked to hear U.S. citizens criticizing the U.S. president.

A STAGNANT ECONOMY Soviet leaders also failed to achieve their objective of revitalizing the national economy. Whereas growth rates during the early Khrushchev era had been impressive (prompting Khrushchev during

Khrushchev Denounces Stalin

POLITICS & GOVERNMENT

Three years after Stalin's death, the new Soviet premier, Nikita Khrushchev, addressed the Twentieth Congress of the Communist Party and denounced the former Soviet dictator for his crimes. This denunciation was the beginning of a policy of de-Stalinization.

Khrushchev Addresses the Twentieth Party Congress, February 1956

Comrades, . . . quite a lot has been said about the cult of the individual and about its harmful consequences. . . . The cult of the person of Stalin . . . became at a certain specific stage the source of a whole series of exceedingly serious and grave perversions of Party principles, of Party democracy, of revolutionary legality.

Stalin absolutely did not tolerate collegiality in leadership and in work and . . . practiced brutal violence, not only toward everything which opposed him, but also toward that which seemed to his capricious and despotic character, contrary to his concepts.

Stalin abandoned the method of ideological struggle for that of administrative violence, mass repressions and terror. . . . Arbitrary behavior by one person encouraged and permitted arbitrariness in others. Mass arrests and deportations of many thousands of people, execution without trial and without normal investigation created conditions of insecurity, fear, and even desperation.

Stalin showed in a whole series of cases his intolerance, his brutality, and his abuse of power. . . . He often chose the path of repression and annihilation, not only against actual enemies, but also against individuals who had not committed any crimes against the Party and the Soviet government. . . .

Many Party, Soviet, and economic activists who were branded in 1937–8 as "enemies" were actually never enemies, spies, wreckers, and so on, but were always honest communists; they were only so stigmatized, and often, no longer able to bear barbaric tortures, they charged themselves (at the order of the investigative judges-falsifiers) with all kinds of grave and unlikely crimes.

This was the result of the abuse of power by Stalin, who began to use mass terror against the Party cadres. . . . Stalin put the Party and the NKVD [the Soviet police agency] up to the use of mass terror when the exploiting classes had been liquidated in our country and when there were no serious reasons for the use of extraordinary mass terror. The terror was directed . . . against the honest workers of the Party and the Soviet state. . . .

Stalin was a very distrustful man, sickly, suspicious. . . . Everywhere and in everything he saw "enemies," "two-facers," and "spies." Possessing unlimited power, he indulged in great willfulness and choked a person morally and physically. A situation was created where one could not express one's own will. When Stalin said that one or another would be arrested, it was necessary to accept on faith that he was an "enemy of the people." What proofs were offered? The confession of the arrested. . . . How is it possible that a person confesses to crimes that he had not committed? Only in one way— because of application of physical methods of pressuring him, tortures, bringing him to a state of unconsciousness, deprivation of his judgment, taking away of his human dignity.

> **Q** What were the key charges that Khrushchev made against Stalin? Can it be said that Khrushchev corrected these problems?

Source: From *Congressional Record*, 84th Congress, 2nd Session, Vol. 102, Part 7, pp. 9389–9402 (June 4, 1956).

---

a reception at the Kremlin in the 1950s to chortle to an American guest, "We will bury you," referring to the United States), under Brezhnev industrial growth declined to an annual rate of less than 4 percent in the early 1970s and less than 3 percent in the period from 1975 to 1980. Successes in the agricultural sector were equally meager.

One of the primary problems with the Soviet economy was the absence of incentives. Salary structures offered little reward for hard labor and extraordinary achievement. Pay differentials operated in a much narrower range than in most Western societies, and there was little danger of being dismissed. According to the Soviet constitution, every Soviet citizen was guaranteed an opportunity to work.

The Rights and Duties of Soviet Citizens

POLITICS & GOVERNMENT

In the Soviet Union, and in other countries modeled on the Soviet system, the national constitution was viewed not as a timeless document, but as a reflection of conditions at the time it was framed. As Soviet society advanced from a state of "raw communism" to a fully socialist society, new constitutions were drafted to reflect the changes taking place in society as a whole. The first two constitutions of the Soviet Union, promulgated in 1924 and 1936, declared that the state was a "dictatorship of the proletariat" guided by the Communist Party, the vanguard organization of the working class in the Soviet Union. But the so-called Brezhnev constitution of 1977 described the Soviet Union as a "state of all the people," composed of workers, farmers, and "socialist intellectuals," although it confirmed the role of the Communist Party as the "leading force" in society. The provisions from the 1977 constitution presented here illustrate some of the freedoms and obligations of Soviet citizens. Especially noteworthy are Articles 39 and 62, which suggest that the interests and prestige of the state took precedence over individual liberties.

The Soviet Constitution of 1977

Chapter 1: The Political System

Article 6. The leading and guiding force of the Soviet society and the nucleus of its political system, of all state organizations and public organizations, is the Communist Party of the Soviet Union. The CPSU exists for the people and serves the people.

The Communist Party, armed with Marxism-Leninism, determines the general perspectives of the development of society and the course of the home and foreign policy of the USSR, directs the great constructive work of the Soviet people, and imparts a planned, systematic, and theoretically substantiated character to their struggle for the victory of communism.

Chapter 6: Equality of Citizens' Rights

Article 35. Women and men have equal rights in the USSR. Exercise of these rights is ensured by according women equal access with men to education and vocational and professional training, equal opportunities in employment, remuneration and promotion, and in social and political, and cultural activity, and by the special labor and health protection measures for women; by providing conditions enabling mothers to work; by legal protection, and material and moral support for mothers and children, including paid leaves and other benefits for expectant mothers and mothers, and gradual reduction of working time for mothers with small children.

Chapter 7: The Basic Rights, Freedoms, and Duties of Citizens of the USSR

Article 39. Citizens of the USSR enjoy in full the social, economic, political, and personal rights and freedoms proclaimed and guaranteed by the Constitution of the USSR and by Soviet laws. The socialist system ensures enlargement of the rights and freedoms of citizens and continuous improvement of their living standards as social, economic, and cultural development programs are fulfilled. Enjoyment by citizens of their rights and freedoms must not be to the detriment of the interests of society or the state, or infringe the rights of other citizens.

Article 62. Citizens of the USSR are obliged to safeguard the interests of the Soviet state, and to enhance its power and prestige. Defense of the Socialist Motherland is the sacred duty of every citizen of the USSR. Betrayal of the Motherland is the gravest of crimes against the people.

Q *Which of these provisions would seem out of place if they were to appear in the U.S. Constitution?*

Source: Excerpts from *The Soviet Constitution of 1977*. Novosti Press Agency Publishing House. Moscow, 1985.

There were, of course, some exceptions to the general rule. Athletic achievement was highly prized, and a gymnast of Olympic stature would receive great rewards in the form of prestige and lifestyle. Senior officials did not receive high salaries but were provided with countless perquisites, such as access to foreign goods, official automobiles with a chauffeur, and entry into prestigious institutions of higher learning for their children.

AN AGING LEADERSHIP Brezhnev died in November 1982 and was succeeded by Yuri Andropov (YOOR-ee ahn-DRAHP-awf) (1914–1984), a party veteran and head of the Soviet secret services. During his brief tenure as party chief, Andropov was a vocal advocate of reform, but when he died after only a few months in office, little had been done to change the system. He was succeeded, in turn, by a mediocre party stalwart, the elderly Konstantin Chernenko (kuhn-stuhn-TEEN chirn-YEN-koh) (1911–1985). With the Soviet system in crisis, Moscow seemed stuck in a time warp.

Cultural Expression in the Soviet Bloc

In his occasional musings about the future Communist utopia, Karl Marx had predicted that a new, classless society would replace the exploitative and hierarchical systems of feudalism and capitalism. In their free time, workers would produce a new, advanced culture, proletarian in character and egalitarian in content.

The reality in the post–World War II Soviet Union and Eastern Europe was somewhat different. Under Stalin, a series of government decrees made all forms of literary and scientific expression dependent on the state. All Soviet culture was expected to follow the party line. Historians, philosophers, and social scientists all grew accustomed to quoting Marx, Lenin, and, above all, Stalin as their chief

authorities. Novels and plays, too, were supposed to portray Communist heroes and their efforts to create a better society. No criticism of existing social conditions was permitted. Some areas of intellectual activity were virtually abolished; the science of genetics disappeared, and few movies were made during Stalin's final years.

Stalin's death brought a modest respite from cultural repression. Writers and artists banned during the Stalin years were again allowed to publish. Still, Soviet authorities, including Khrushchev, were reluctant to allow cultural freedom to move far beyond official Soviet ideology.

These restrictions, however, did not prevent the emergence of some significant Soviet literature, although authors paid a heavy price if they alienated the Soviet authorities. Boris Pasternak (buh-REESS PASS-tur-nak) (1890–1960), who began his literary career as a poet, won the Nobel Prize in 1958 mainly for his celebrated novel *Doctor Zhivago*, written between 1945 and 1956 and published in Italy in 1957. But the Soviet government condemned Pasternak's anti-Soviet tendencies, banned the novel, and would not allow him to accept the prize. The author had alienated the authorities by describing a society scarred by the excesses of Bolshevik revolutionary zeal.

Alexander Solzhenitsyn created an even greater furor than Pasternak. Solzhenitsyn had spent eight years in forced labor camps for criticizing Stalin, and his *One Day in the Life of Ivan Denisovich*, one of the works that won him the Nobel Prize in 1970, was an account of life in those camps. Khrushchev allowed the book's publication as part of his de-Stalinization campaign. Solzhenitsyn then wrote *The Gulag Archipelago*, a detailed indictment of the whole system of Soviet oppression. Soviet authorities expelled Solzhenitsyn from the Soviet Union in 1973.

In the Eastern European satellites, cultural freedom varied considerably from country to country. In Poland, intellectuals had access to Western publications as well as greater freedom to travel to the West. Hungarian and Yugoslav Communists, too, tolerated a certain level of intellectual activity that was not liked but at least was not prohibited. Elsewhere, intellectuals were forced to conform to the regime's demands. After the Soviet invasion of Czechoslovakia in 1968, Czech Communists pursued a policy of strict cultural control.

© William J. Duiker

Stalinist Heroic: An Example of Socialist Realism. Under Stalin and his successors, art was assigned the task of indoctrinating the Soviet population on the public virtues, such as hard work, loyalty to the state, and patriotism. Grandiose statuary erected to commemorate the heroic efforts of the Red Army during World War II appeared in every Soviet city. Here is an example in Minsk, today the capital of Belarus.

Social Changes

According to Marxist doctrine, state control of industry and the elimination of private property were supposed to lead to a classless society. Although that ideal was never achieved, it did have important social consequences. The desire to create a classless society, for example, led to noticeable changes in education. In some countries, laws mandated quota systems based on class. As education became crucial for obtaining new jobs in the Communist system, enrollments rose in both secondary schools and universities.

The new managers of society, regardless of their class background, realized the importance of higher education and used their power to gain special privileges for their children. By 1971, 60 percent of the children of white-collar workers attended a university, but only 36 percent of the children of blue-collar families did so, although these families constituted 60 percent of the population.

Ideals of equality also did not include women. Men dominated the leadership positions of the Communist parties. Women did have greater opportunities in the workforce and even in the professions, however. In the Soviet Union, women comprised 51 percent of the labor force in 1980; by the mid-1980s, they constituted 50 percent of the engineers, 80 percent of the doctors, and 75 percent of the teachers and teachers' aides. But many of these were low-paying jobs; most female doctors, for example, worked in primary care and were paid less than skilled machinists. The chief administrators in hospitals and schools were still men.

Moreover, although women made up nearly half of the workforce, they were never freed from their traditional roles in the home. Most women had to work what came to be known as the "double shift." After working eight hours in their jobs, they came home to do the housework and care for the children. They might also spend two hours a day in long lines at a number of stores waiting to buy food and clothes. Because of the housing shortage, several families would share a kitchen, making even meal preparation a complicated task.

Nearly three-quarters of a century after the Bolshevik Revolution, then, the Marxist dream of an advanced, egalitarian society was as far away as ever. Although in some respects, conditions in the socialist camp were a distinct improvement over those before World War II, many problems and inequities were as intransigent as ever.

The Disintegration of the Soviet Empire

Q FOCUS QUESTIONS: What were the key components of *perestroika,* which Mikhail Gorbachev espoused during the 1980s? Why did it fail?

On the death of Konstantin Chernenko in 1985, party leaders selected the talented and vigorous Soviet official Mikhail Gorbachev to succeed him. The new Soviet leader had shown early signs of promise. Born into a peasant family in 1931, Gorbachev combined farmwork with school and received the Order of the Red Banner for his agricultural efforts. This award and his good school record enabled him to study law at the University of Moscow. After receiving his law degree in 1955, he returned to his native southern Russia, where he eventually became first secretary of the Communist Party in the city of Stavropol (STAH-vruh-puhl *or* stav-ROH-puhl). In 1978, he was made a member of the party's Central Committee in Moscow. Two years later, he became a full member of the ruling Politburo and secretary of the Central Committee.

During the early 1980s, Gorbachev began to realize the immensity of Soviet problems and the crucial need for massive reform to transform the system. During a visit to Canada in 1983, he discovered to his astonishment that Canadian farmers worked hard on their own initiative. "We'll never have this for fifty years," he reportedly remarked.[2] On his return to Moscow, he set in motion a series of committees to evaluate the situation and recommend measures to improve the system.

The Gorbachev Era

With his election as party general secretary in 1985, Gorbachev seemed intent on taking earlier reforms to their logical conclusions. The cornerstone of his program was *perestroika* (per-uh-STROI-kuh), or "restructuring." At first, it meant only a reordering of economic policy, as Gorbachev called for the beginning of a market economy with limited free enterprise and some private property (see the comparative illustration on p. 715). But Gorbachev soon perceived that in the Soviet system, the economic sphere was intimately tied to the social and political spheres. Any efforts to reform the economy without political or social reform would be doomed to failure. One of the most important instruments of *perestroika* was *glasnost* (GLAHZ-nohst), or "openness." Soviet citizens and officials were encouraged to openly discuss the strengths and weaknesses of the Soviet Union. The arts also benefited from the new policy as previously banned works were now published and motion pictures were allowed to depict negative aspects of Soviet life. Music based on Western styles, such as jazz and rock, could now be performed openly. Religious activities, long banned by the authorities, were once again tolerated.

Political reforms were equally revolutionary. In June 1987, the principle of two-candidate elections was introduced; previously, voters had been presented with only one candidate. At the Communist Party conference in 1988, Gorbachev called for the creation of a new Soviet

COMPARATIVE ILLUSTRATION

POLITICS & GOVERNMENT

Sideline Industries: Creeping Capitalism in a Socialist Paradise. In the late 1980s, Communist leaders in both the Soviet Union and China began to encourage their citizens to engage in private commercial activities as a means of reviving moribund economies. In the photo on the left, a Soviet farmworker displays fruits and vegetables for sale on a street corner in Odessa, a seaport on the Black Sea. On the right, a Chinese woman sells her dumplings to passersby in Shandong province. As her smile suggests, the Chinese took up the challenge of entrepreneurship with much greater success and enthusiasm than their Soviet counterparts did.

Q *Why did Chinese citizens adopt capitalist reforms in the countryside more enthusiastically than their Soviet counterparts?*

parliament, the Congress of People's Deputies, whose members were to be chosen in competitive elections. It convened in 1989, the first such meeting in the nation since 1918. Early in 1990, Gorbachev legalized the formation of other political parties and struck out Article 6 of the Soviet constitution, which guaranteed the "leading role" of the Communist Party. Hitherto, the position of first secretary of the party was the most important post in the Soviet Union, but as the Communist Party became less closely associated with the state, the powers of this office diminished. Gorbachev attempted to consolidate his power by creating a new state presidency, and in March 1990, he became the Soviet Union's first president.

THE BEGINNING OF THE END One of Gorbachev's most serious problems stemmed from the character of the Soviet Union. The Union of Soviet Socialist Republics was a truly multiethnic country, containing 92 nationalities and 112 recognized languages. Previously, the iron hand of the Communist Party, centered in Moscow, had kept a lid on the centuries-old ethnic tensions that had

periodically erupted throughout the history of the region. As Gorbachev released this iron grip, ethnic groups throughout the Soviet Union began to call for sovereignty of the republics and independence from Russian-based rule centered in Moscow. Such movements sprang up first in Georgia in late 1988 and then in Latvia (LAT-vee-uh), Estonia (ES-toh-nee-uh), Moldova (mohl-DOH-vuh), Uzbekistan (ooz-BEK-ih-stan), Azerbaijan (az-ur-by-JAHN), and Lithuania (lih-thuh-WAY-nee-uh).

In December 1989, the Communist Party of Lithuania declared itself independent of the Communist Party of the Soviet Union. Despite pleas from Gorbachev, who supported self-determination but not secession, other Soviet republics eventually followed suit. Ukraine voted for independence on December 1, 1991. A week later, the leaders of Russia, Ukraine, and Belarus (bell-uh-ROOSS) announced that the Soviet Union had "ceased to exist" and would be replaced by a "commonwealth of independent states." Gorbachev resigned on December 25, 1991, and turned over his responsibilities as commander in chief to Boris Yeltsin (YELT-sun) (1931–2007), the president of Russia. By the end of 1991, one of the largest empires in world history had come to an end, and a new era had begun in its lands (see Chapter 28).

Eastern Europe: From Satellites to Sovereign Nations

The disintegration of the Soviet Union had an immediate impact on its neighbors to the west. First to respond, as in 1956, was Poland, where popular protests at high food prices had erupted in the early 1980s, leading to the rise of an independent labor movement called Solidarity. Led by Lech Walesa (LEK vah-WENT-sah) (b. 1943), Solidarity rapidly became an influential force for change and a threat to the government's monopoly of power. In 1988, the Communist government bowed to the inevitable and permitted free national elections to take place, resulting in the election of Walesa as president of Poland in December 1990. When Moscow took no action to reverse the verdict in Warsaw, Poland entered the post-Communist era.

In Hungary, as in Poland, the process of transition had begun many years previously. After crushing the Hungarian revolution of 1956, the Communist government of János Kádár had tried to assuage popular opinion by enacting a series of far-reaching economic reforms (labeled "communism with a capitalist face-lift"). But as the 1980s progressed, the economy sagged, and in 1989, the regime permitted the formation of opposition political parties, leading eventually to the formation of a non-Communist coalition government in elections held in March 1990.

The transition in Czechoslovakia was more abrupt. After Soviet troops crushed the Prague Spring in 1968, hard-line Communists under Gustav Husák followed a policy of massive repression to maintain their power. In 1977, dissident intellectuals formed an organization called Charter 77 as a vehicle for protest against violations of human rights. Dissident activities increased during the 1980s, and when massive demonstrations broke out in several major cities in 1989, President Husák's government, lacking any real popular support, collapsed. At the end of December, he was replaced by Václav Havel (VAHT-slahf HAH-vul) (1936–2011), a dissident playwright who had been a leading figure in Charter 77.

But the most dramatic events took place in East Germany, where a persistent economic slump and the ongoing oppressiveness of the regime of Erich Honecker led to a flight of refugees and mass demonstrations against the regime in the summer and fall of 1989. Capitulating to popular pressure, the Communist government opened its entire border with the West. The Berlin Wall, the most tangible symbol of the Cold War, became the site of a massive celebration, and most of it was dismantled by joyful Germans from both sides of the border. In March 1990, free elections led to the formation of a non-Communist government that rapidly carried out a program of political and economic reunification with West Germany (see Chapter 28).

Why Did the Soviet Union Collapse?

What caused the sudden disintegration of the Soviet system? It is popular in some quarters in the United States to argue that the ambitious defense policies adopted by the Reagan administration forced Moscow into an arms race that it could not afford and that ultimately led to the collapse of the Soviet economy. This contention has some superficial plausibility as Soviet leaders did indeed react to Reagan's "Star Wars" program by increasing their own defense expenditures, which put a strain on the Soviet budget.

Most knowledgeable observers, however, believe that the fall of the Soviet Union was primarily a consequence of conditions inherent in the system, several of which have been pointed out in this chapter. For years, if not decades, leaders in the Kremlin had disguised or ignored the massive inefficiencies in the Soviet economy. In the 1980s, time began to run out. The perceptive Mikhail Gorbachev tried to stem the decline by instituting radical reforms, but by then it was too late.

An additional factor should also be considered. One of the most vulnerable aspects of the Soviet Union was its multiethnic character, with only a little more than half of the total population composed of ethnic Russians. Many of the minority nationalities were becoming increasingly restive and were demanding more autonomy or even independence for their regions. By the end of the 1980s, such demands brought about the final collapse of the system. The Soviet empire died at least partly from imperial overreach.

The East Is Red: China Under Communism

FOCUS QUESTION: What were Mao Zedong's chief goals for China, and what policies did he institute to try to achieve them?

"A revolution is not a dinner party, or writing an essay, or painting a picture, or doing embroidery; it cannot be so refined, so leisurely and gentle, so temperate and kind, courteous, restrained, and magnanimous. A revolution is an insurrection, an act of violence by which one class overthrows another."[3] With these words—written in 1926, at a time when the Communists, in cooperation with Chiang Kai-shek's Nationalist Party, were embarked on their Northern Expedition to defeat the warlords and reunify China—the young revolutionary Mao Zedong warned his colleagues that the road to victory in the struggle to build a Communist society would be arduous and would inevitably involve acts of violence against the class enemy.

In the fall of 1949, China was at peace for the first time in twelve years. The newly victorious Communist Party, under the leadership of its chairman, Mao Zedong, turned its attention to consolidating its power base and healing the wounds of war. Its long-term goal was to construct a socialist society, but its leaders realized that popular support for the revolution was based on the party's platform of honest government, land reform, social justice, and peace rather than on the utopian goal of a classless society. Accordingly, the new regime temporarily set aside Mao Zedong's stirring exhortation of 1926 and adopted a moderate program of political and economic recovery known as New Democracy.

New Democracy

With **New Democracy**—patterned roughly after Lenin's New Economic Policy in Soviet Russia in the 1920s (see Chapter 23)—the new Chinese leadership tacitly recognized that time and extensive indoctrination would be needed to convince the Chinese people of the superiority of socialism. In the meantime, the party would rely on capitalist profit incentives to spur productivity. Manufacturing and commercial firms were permitted to remain under private ownership, although with stringent government regulations. To win the support of the poorer peasants, who made up the majority of the population, a land redistribution program was adopted, but the collectivization of agriculture was postponed.

In a number of key respects, New Democracy was a success. About two-thirds of the peasant households in the country received land and thus had reason to be grateful to the new regime (see the box on p. 718). Spurred by official tolerance for capitalist activities and the end of internal conflict, the national economy began to rebound, although agricultural production still lagged behind both official targets and the growing population, which was increasing at an annual rate of more than 2 percent.

The Transition to Socialism

In 1953, party leaders launched the nation's first five-year plan (patterned after similar Soviet plans), which called for substantial increases in industrial output. Lenin had believed that mechanization would induce Russian peasants to join collective farms, which, because of their greater size and efficiency, could better afford to purchase expensive farm machinery. But the difficulty of providing tractors and reapers for millions of rural villages eventually convinced Mao that it would take years, if not decades, for China's infant industrial base to meet the needs of a modernizing agricultural sector. He therefore decided to begin collectivization immediately, in the hope that collective farms would increase food production and release land, labor, and capital for the industrial sector. Accordingly, beginning in 1955, virtually all private farmland was collectivized (although peasant families were allowed to retain small private plots), and most businesses and industries were nationalized.

Collectivization was achieved without provoking the massive peasant unrest that had taken place in the Soviet Union during the 1930s, but the hoped-for production increases did not materialize. In 1958, at Mao's insistent urging, party leaders approved a more radical program known as the **Great Leap Forward**. Existing rural collectives, normally the size of a traditional village, were combined into vast "people's communes," each containing more than 30,000 people. These communes were to be responsible for all administrative and economic tasks at the local level. The party's official slogan promised "Hard work for a few years, happiness for a thousand."[4]

The communes were a disaster. Administrative bottlenecks, bad weather, and peasant resistance to the new system (which, among other things, attempted to eliminate work incentives and destroy the traditional family as the basic unit of Chinese society) combined to drive food production downward, and over the next few years, as many as 15 million people may have died of starvation. In 1960, the experiment was essentially abandoned. Although the commune structure was retained, ownership and management were returned to the collective level. Mao was severely criticized by some of his more pragmatic colleagues.

Land Reform in Action

FAMILY & SOCIETY

One of the great achievements of the new Communist regime in China was the land reform program, which resulted in the distribution of farmland to almost two-thirds of the rural population. The program consequently won the gratitude of millions of Chinese. But it also had a dark side as local land reform tribunals routinely convicted "wicked landlords" of crimes against the people and then put them to death. The following passage, written by a foreign observer, describes the process in one village.

Revolution in a Chinese Village

T'ien-ming [a Party cadre] called all the active young cadres and the militiamen of Long Bow [village] together and announced to them the policy of the county government, which was to confront all enemy collaborators and their backers at public meetings, expose their crimes, and turn them over to the county authorities for punishment. He proposed that they start with Kuo Te-yu, the puppet village head. Having moved the group to anger with a description of Te-yu's crimes, T'ien-ming reviewed the painful life led by the poor peasants during the occupation and recalled how hard they had all worked and how as soon as they harvested all the grain the puppet officials, backed by army bayonets, took what they wanted, turned over huge quantities to the Japanese devils, forced the peasants to haul it away, and flogged those who refused.

As the silent crowd contracted toward the spot where the accused man stood, T'ien-ming stepped forward. . . . "This is our chance. Remember how we were oppressed. The traitors seized our property. They beat us and kicked us. . . .

"Let us speak out the bitter memories. Let us see that the blood debt is repaid. . . ."

He paused for a moment. The peasants were listening to every word but gave no sign as to how they felt. . . .

"Come now, who has evidence against this man?"

Again there was silence.

Kuei-ts'ai, the new vice-chairman of the village, found it intolerable. He jumped up [and] struck Kuo Te-yu on the jaw with the back of his hand. "Tell the meeting how much you stole," he demanded.

The blow jarred the ragged crowd. It was as if an electric spark had tensed every muscle. Not in living memory had any peasant ever struck an official. . . .

The people in the square waited fascinated as if watching a play. They did not realize that in order for the plot to unfold they themselves had to mount the stage and speak out what was on their minds.

That evening T'ien-ming and Kuei-ts'ai called together the small groups of poor peasants from various parts of the village and sought to learn what it was that was really holding them back. They soon found the root of the trouble was fear of the old established political forces, and their military backers. The old reluctance to move against the power of the gentry, the fear of ultimate defeat and terrible reprisal that had been seared into the consciousness of so many generations, lay like a cloud over the peasants' minds and hearts.

Emboldened by T'ien-ming's words, other peasants began to speak out. They recalled what Te-yu had done to them personally. Several vowed to speak up and accuse him the next morning. After the meeting broke up, the passage of time worked its own leaven. In many a hovel and tumbledown house talk continued well past midnight. Some people were so excited they did not sleep at all. . . .

On the following day the meeting was livelier by far. It began with a sharp argument as to who would make the first accusation, and T'ien-ming found it difficult to keep order. Before Te-yu had a chance to reply to any questions, a crowd of young men, among whom were several militiamen, surged forward ready to beat him.

Q *What was the Communist Party's purpose in carrying out land reform in China? How did the tactics employed here support that strategy?*

Source: From Richard Solomon, *Mao's Revolution and the Chinese Political Culture*, pages 198–199. Copyright © 1971 Center for Chinese Studies, University of Michigan.

The Great Proletarian Cultural Revolution

But Mao was not yet ready to abandon either his power or his dream of a totally egalitarian society. In 1966, he returned to the attack, mobilizing discontented youth and disgruntled party members into revolutionary units soon to be known as Red Guards, who were urged to take to the streets to cleanse Chinese society—from local schools and factories to government ministries in Beijing—of impure elements who (in Mao's mind, at least) were guilty of "taking the capitalist road." Supported by his wife, Jiang Qing (jahng CHING), and other radical party figures, Mao launched China on a new forced march toward communism.

The so-called **Great Proletarian Cultural Revolution** lasted for ten years, from 1966 to 1976. Some Western observers interpreted it as a simple power struggle between Mao Zedong and some of his key rivals such as Liu Shaoqi (lyoo show-CHEE ["ow" as in "how"]) (Liu Shao-ch'i), Mao's designated successor, and Deng Xiaoping (DUHNG show-PING ["ow" as in "how"]) (Teng Hsiao-p'ing), the party's general secretary. Both were removed from their positions, and Liu later died, allegedly of torture, in a Chinese prison. But real policy disagreements were involved. Mao and his supporters feared that capitalist values and the remnants of "feudalist" Confucian ideas would undermine ideological fervor and betray the revolutionary cause. He was convinced that only an atmosphere of "**uninterrupted revolution**" could enable the Chinese to overcome the lethargy of the past and achieve the final stage of utopian communism.

Mao's opponents argued for a more pragmatic strategy that gave priority to nation building over the ultimate Communist goal of spiritual transformation (Deng Xiaoping reportedly once remarked, "Black cat, white cat, what does it matter so long as it catches the mice?"). But with Mao's supporters now in power, the party carried out vast economic and educational reforms that virtually eliminated any remaining profit incentives, established a new school system that emphasized "Mao Zedong thought," and stressed practical education at the elementary level at the expense of specialized training in

AP Images

Punishing China's Enemies During the Cultural Revolution. The Cultural Revolution, which began in 1966, was a massive effort by Mao Zedong and his radical supporters to eliminate rival elements within the Chinese Communist Party and the government. Accused of being "capitalist roaders," such individuals were subjected to public criticism and removed from their positions. Some were imprisoned or executed. Here Red Guards parade a victim wearing a dunce cap through the streets of Beijing.

OPPOSING ⚔ VIEWPOINTS

Students Appeal for Democracy

POLITICS & GOVERNMENT

In the spring of 1989, thousands of students gathered in Tiananmen Square in downtown Beijing to provide moral support to their many compatriots who had gone on a hunger strike in an effort to compel the Chinese government to reduce the level of official corruption and enact democratic reforms, opening the political process to the Chinese people. The first selection is from an editorial published on April 26 by the official newspaper *People's Daily*. Fearing that the student demonstrations would get out of hand, as had happened during the Cultural Revolution, the editorial condemned the protests for being contrary to the Communist Party. The second selection is from a statement by Zhao Ziyang, the party general secretary, who argued that many of the students' demands were justified. On May 17, student leaders distributed flyers explaining the goals of the movement to participants and passersby, including the author of this chapter. The third selection is from one of these flyers.

People's Daily Editorial, April 26, 1989

This is a well-planned plot . . . to confuse the people and throw the country into turmoil. . . . Its real aim is to reject the Chinese Communist Party and the socialist system at the most fundamental level. . . . This is a most serious political struggle that concerns the whole Party and nation.

Statement by Party General Secretary Zhao Ziyang Before Party Colleagues, May 4, 1989

Let me tell you how I see all this. I think the student movement has two important characteristics. First, the students' slogans call for things like supporting the Constitution, promoting democracy, and fighting corruption. These demands all echo positions of the Party and the government. Second, a great many people from all parts of society are out there joining the demonstrations and backing the students. . . . This has grown into a nationwide protest. I think the best way to bring the thing to a quick end is to focus on the mainstream views of the majority.

"Why Do We Have to Undergo a Hunger Strike?"

By 2:00 P.M. today, the hunger strike carried out by the petition group in Tiananmen Square has been under way for 96 hours. By this morning, more than 600 participants have fainted. When these democracy fighters were lifted into the ambulances, no one who was present was not moved to tears.

Our petition group now undergoing the hunger strike demands that at a minimum the government agree to the following two points:

1. To engage on a sincere and equal basis in a dialogue with the "higher education dialogue group." In addition, to broadcast the actual dialogue in its entirety. We absolutely refuse to agree to a partial broadcast, to empty gestures, or to fabrications that dupe the people.
2. To evaluate in a fair and realistic way the patriotic democratic movement. Discard the label of "troublemaking" and redress the reputation of the patriotic democratic movement.

It is our view that the request for a dialogue between the people's government and the people is not an unreasonable one. Our party always follows the principle of seeking truths from actual facts. It is therefore only natural that the evaluation of this patriotic democratic movement should be done in accordance with the principle of seeking truths from actual facts.

Our classmates who are going through the hunger strike are the good sons and daughters of the people! One by one, they have fallen. In the meantime, our "public servants" are completely unmoved. Please, let us ask where your conscience is.

Q *What were the key demands of the protesters in Tiananmen Square? Why were they rejected by the Chinese government?*

Sources: *People's Daily* Editorial, April 26, 1989. From *People's Daily Editorial*, April 26, 1989. Statement by Party General Secretary Zhao Ziyang before Party colleagues, May 4, 1989. "Why Do We Have to Undergo a Hunger Strike?" Original flyer in possession of author.

been a tacit recognition that Marxist exhortations were no longer an effective means of enforcing social discipline, the party sought to make use of Confucianism. Ceremonies celebrating the birth of Confucius now received official sanction, and the virtues promoted by the Master, such as righteousness, propriety, and filial piety, were widely cited as an antidote to the tide of antisocial behavior. As a further indication of its willingness to employ traditional themes to further its national interest, the Chinese government has begun to sponsor the establishment of Confucian centers in countries around the world to promote its view that Confucian humanism is destined to replace traditional religious faiths in coming decades.

In effect, Chinese leaders have tacitly conceded that Marxism is increasingly irrelevant to today's China, which responds much more forcefully to the siren call of nationalism. In a striking departure from the precepts of Marxist internationalism, official sources in Beijing cite Confucian tradition to support their assertion that China is unique and will not follow the path of "peaceful evolution" (to use their term) toward a future democratic capitalist society.

That attitude is also reflected in foreign policy, as China is playing an increasingly active role in the region. To some of its neighbors, including Japan, India, and Russia, China's new posture is disquieting and raises suspicions that China is once again preparing to flex its muscle as it did in the imperial era. The first example of this new attitude took place as early as 1979, when Chinese forces briefly invaded Vietnam as punishment for the Vietnamese occupation of neighboring Cambodia. More recently, China has aroused concern in the region by claiming sole ownership over the Spratly (sprat-LEE) Islands in the South China Sea and over the Diaoyu (DYOW-you) Islands (also claimed by Japan, which calls them the Senkakus) near Taiwan (see Map 27.2).

To Chinese leaders, however, such actions represent legitimate efforts to resume China's rightful role in the affairs of the region. After a century of humiliation at the hands of the Western powers and neighboring Japan, the nation, in Mao's famous words of 1949, "has stood up" and no one will be permitted to humiliate it again. For the moment, at least, a fervent patriotism seems to be on the rise in China, actively promoted by the party as a means of holding the country together. The decision by the International Olympic Committee to award the 2008 Summer Games to Beijing led to widespread celebration throughout the country. The event served to symbolize China's emergence as a major national power on the world stage.

Pumping up the spirit of patriotism, however, is not the

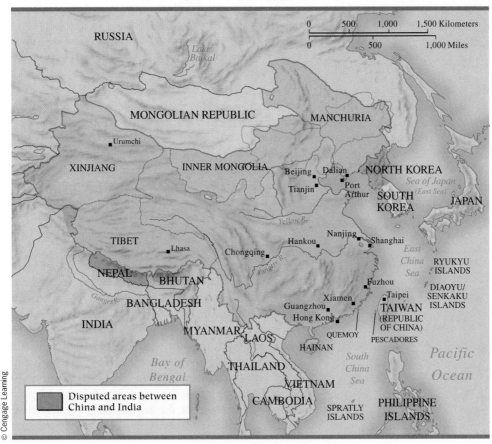

© Cengage Learning

MAP 27.2 **The People's Republic of China.** This map shows China's current boundaries. Major regions are indicated in capital letters.

Q *In which regions are there movements against Chinese rule?*

The Potala Palace in Tibet. Tibet was a distant and reluctant appendage of the Chinese Empire during the Qing dynasty. Since the rise to power of the Communist Party in 1949, the regime in Beijing has consistently sought to integrate the region into the People's Republic of China. Resistance to Chinese rule, however, has been widespread. In recent years, the Dalai Lama, the leading religious figure in Tibetan Buddhism, has attempted without success to persuade Chinese leaders to allow a measure of autonomy for the Tibetan people. In 2008, massive riots by frustrated Tibetans took place in the capital city of Lhasa (LAH-suh) just before the opening of the Olympic Games in Beijing. The Potala Palace, symbol of Tibetan identity, was constructed in the seventeenth century in Lhasa and serves today as the foremost symbol of the national and cultural aspirations of the Tibetan people.

Falun Gong (FAH-loon GONG) religious movement, which the government has attempted to eliminate as a potentially serious threat to its authority, is an additional indication that with the disintegration of the old Maoist utopia, the Chinese people will need more than a pallid version of Marxism-Leninism or a revived Confucianism to fill the gap.

New leaders installed in 2002 and 2003 appeared aware of the magnitude of the problem. Hu Jintao (HOO jin-TOW ["ow" as in "how"]) (b. 1943), who replaced Jiang Zemin as CCP general secretary and head of state, called for further reforms to open up Chinese society and bridge the yawning gap between rich and poor. In recent years, the government has shown a growing tolerance for the public exchange of ideas, which has surfaced with the proliferation of bookstores, avant-garde theater, experimental art exhibits, and the Internet. In 2005, an estimated 27 percent of all Chinese citizens possessed a cellphone, and the number has increased dramatically since then. Today, despite the government's efforts to restrict access to certain websites, more people are "surfing the Net" in China than in any other country except the United States. The Internet is wildly popular with those under thirty, who use it for online games, downloading videos and music, and instant messaging. The challenges, however, continue to be daunting. At the CCP's Seventeenth National Congress, held in October 2007, President Hu emphasized the importance of adopting a "scientific view of development," a vague concept calling for social harmony, improved material prosperity, and a reduction in the growing income gap between rich and poor in Chinese society. But he insisted that the Communist Party must remain the sole political force in charge of carrying out the revolution. Ever fearful of chaos, party leaders are convinced that only a firm hand at the tiller can keep the ship of state from crashing onto the rocks.

solution to all problems. Unrest is growing among China's national minorities: in Xinjiang (SHIN-jyahng), where restless Muslim peoples are observing with curiosity the emergence of independent Islamic states in Central Asia, and in Tibet, where the official policy of quelling separatist sentiment has led to the violent suppression of Tibetan culture and an influx of thousands of ethnic Chinese immigrants. In the meantime, the

CHRONOLOGY	China Under Communist Rule
New Democracy	1949–1955
Era of collectivization	1955–1958
Great Leap Forward	1958–1960
Great Proletarian Cultural Revolution	1966–1976
Death of Mao Zedong	1976
Era of Deng Xiaoping	1978–1997
Tiananmen Square incident	1989
Presidency of Jiang Zemin	1993–2002
Hu Jintao becomes president	2002
Olympic Games held in Beijing	2008

"Serve the People": Chinese Society Under Communism

 FOCUS QUESTION: What significant political, economic, and social changes have taken place in China since the death of Mao Zedong?

When the Communist Party came to power in 1949, Chinese leaders made it clear that their policies would differ from the Soviet model in one key respect. Whereas the Bolsheviks had relied almost exclusively on the use of force to achieve their objectives, the CCP carried out reforms aimed at winning support from the mass of the population. This "mass line" policy, as it was called, worked fairly well until the late 1950s, when Mao and his radical allies adopted policies such as the Great Leap Forward that began to alienate much of the population. Ideological purity was valued over expertise in building an advanced and prosperous society.

Economics in Command

When he came to power in the late 1970s, Deng Xiaoping recognized the need to restore credibility to a system on the verge of breakdown and hoped that rapid economic growth would satisfy the Chinese people and prevent them from demanding political reforms. The post-Mao leaders clearly emphasized economic performance over ideological purity. To stimulate the stagnant industrial sector, they reduced bureaucratic controls over state industries and allowed local managers to have more say over prices, salaries, and quality control. Productivity was encouraged by permitting bonuses for extra effort, a policy that had been discouraged during the Cultural Revolution. The regime also tolerated the emergence of a small private sector. The unemployed were encouraged to set up restaurants or small shops on their own initiative (see the comparative illustration on p. 715).

Finally, the regime opened up the country to foreign investment and technology. Special economic zones were established in urban centers near the coast (ironically, many were located in the old nineteenth-century treaty ports), where lucrative concessions were offered to encourage foreign firms to build factories. The tourist industry was encouraged, and students were sent abroad to study.

The new leaders especially stressed educational reform. The system adopted during the Cultural Revolution, emphasizing practical education and ideology at the expense of higher education and modern science, was rapidly abandoned (Mao's Little Red Book was even withdrawn from circulation), and a new system based generally on the Western model was instituted. Admission to higher education was based on success in merit examinations, and courses in science and mathematics received high priority.

AGRICULTURAL REFORM   No economic reform program could succeed unless it included the countryside. Three decades of socialism had done little to increase food production or to lay the basis for a modern agricultural sector. China, with a population numbering one billion, could still barely feed itself. Peasants had little incentive to work and few opportunities to increase production through mechanization, the use of fertilizer, or better irrigation.

Under Deng Xiaoping, agricultural policy made a rapid about-face. Under the new **rural responsibility system**, collectives leased land to peasant families, who paid rent to the collective. Anything produced on the land above that payment could be sold on the private market or consumed. To soak up excess labor in the villages, the government encouraged the formation of so-called sideline industries, a modern equivalent of the traditional cottage industries in pre-modern China. Peasants raised fish, made consumer goods, and even assembled furniture and appliances for sale to their newly affluent compatriots.

The reform program had a striking effect on rural production. Grain production increased rapidly, and farm income doubled during the 1980s. Yet it also created problems. Income at the village level became more unequal as some enterprising farmers (known locally as "ten-thousand-dollar households") earned profits several times those realized by their less fortunate or less industrious neighbors. When some farmers discovered that they could earn more by growing cash crops they devoted less land to rice and other grain crops, thereby threatening the supply of China's most crucial staple. Finally, the agricultural policy threatened to undermine the government's population control program, which party leaders viewed as crucial to the success of the Four Modernizations.

Since a misguided period in the mid-1950s when Mao Zedong had argued that more labor would result in higher productivity, China had been attempting to limit its population growth. By 1970, the government had launched a stringent family planning program—including education, incentives, and penalties for noncompliance—to persuade the Chinese people to limit themselves to one child per family. The program has had some success, and population growth was reduced drastically in the early 1980s. The rural responsibility system, however, undermined the program because it encouraged farm families to pay the penalties for having additional children in the belief that their labor would increase family income and provide the parents with a form of social security for their old age. Today, China's population has surpassed 1.3 billion.

EVALUATING THE FOUR MODERNIZATIONS Still, the overall effects of the modernization program were impressive. The standard of living improved for the majority of the population. Whereas a decade earlier, the average Chinese had struggled to earn enough to buy a bicycle, by the late 1980s, many were beginning to purchase refrigerators and color television sets. Yet the rapid growth of the economy created its own problems: inflationary pressures, increased corruption, and—most dangerous of all for the regime—rising expectations. Young people in particular resented restrictions on employment (many are still required to accept the jobs that are offered to them by the government or school officials) and opportunities to study abroad. Disillusionment ran high, especially in the cities, where lavish living by officials and rising prices for goods aroused widespread alienation and cynicism. Such conditions undoubtedly contributed to the unrest that erupted during the spring of 1989.

During the 1990s, industrial growth rates continued to be high as domestic capital became increasingly available. The government finally recognized the need to close down inefficient state enterprises, and by the end of the decade, the private sector accounted for more than 10 percent of gross domestic product. A stock market opened, and with the country's entrance into the World Trade Organization (WTO) in 2001, China's prowess in the international marketplace improved dramatically. Today, China has the second-largest economy in the world and is the largest exporter of goods. Even the global economic crisis that struck the world in the fall of 2008 has not derailed the Chinese juggernaut, which quickly recovered from the drop in demand for Chinese goods in countries suffering from the economic downturn.

As a result of these developments, China now possesses a large and increasingly affluent middle class and a burgeoning domestic market for consumer goods. More than 80 percent of all urban Chinese now own a color television set, a refrigerator, and a washing machine. For the more affluent, a private automobile is increasingly a possibility, and in 2010, more vehicles were sold in China than in the United States.

But as Chinese leaders have discovered, rapid economic change never comes without cost. The closing of state-run factories led to the dismissal of millions of workers each year, and the private sector, although growing at more than 20 percent annually, initially struggled to absorb them. Poor working conditions and low salaries in Chinese factories have resulted in periodic outbreaks of labor unrest. Demographic conditions, however, are changing. The reduction in birthrates since the 1980s is creating a labor shortage, which is putting upward pressure on workers' salaries. As a result, China is facing inflation in the marketplace and increased competition from exports produced by factories located in lower-wage countries in South and Southeast Asia.

Discontent has also been increasing in the countryside, where farmers earn only about half as much as their urban counterparts. China's entry into the WTO was greeted with great optimism but has been of little benefit to farmers facing the challenges of cheap foreign imports. Taxes and local corruption add to their complaints. In desperation, millions of rural Chinese have left for the big cities, where many of them are unable to find steady employment and live in squalid conditions in crowded tenements or in the sprawling suburbs. Millions of others remain on their farms and attempt to augment their income by producing for the market or, despite the risk of stringent penalties, by increasing the size of their families. A land reform law passed in 2008 authorizes farmers to lease or transfer land use rights, although in principle all land in rural areas belongs to the local government.

Another factor hindering China's economic advance is the impact on the environment. With the rising population, fertile land is in increasingly short supply (China's population has doubled since 1950, but only two-thirds as much irrigable land is available). Soil erosion is a major problem, especially in the north, where the desert is encroaching on farmlands. Water is also a problem. An ambitious plan to transport water by canals from the Yangtze River to the more arid northern provinces has run into a number of roadblocks. Another massive project to construct dams on the Yangtze River has sparked protests from environmentalists, as well as from local peoples forced to migrate from the area. Air pollution is ten times the level in the United States. To add to the challenge, more than 700,000 new cars and trucks appear on the country's roads each year. To reduce congestion on roadways, China is constructing a network for high-speed bullet trains that will connect all the major regions in the country.

Social Problems

At the root of Marxist-Leninist ideology is the idea of building a new citizen free from the prejudices, ignorance, and superstition of the "feudal" era and the capitalist desire for self-gratification. This new citizen would be characterized not only by a sense of racial and sexual equality but also by the selfless desire to contribute his or her utmost for the good of all.

WOMEN AND THE FAMILY From the very start, the Chinese Communist government intended to bring an

The Three Gorges Dam. The damming of the Yangtze River over the past two decades is one of the most massive and ambitious construction projects in human history. Designed to increase the amount of farmland in the Yangtze River valley and enable precious water resources to be redistributed to drought-prone regions of the country, the project has also caused considerable environmental damage throughout the Yangtze River valley and displaced several million Chinese from their ancestral homes. Shown here is the famous Three Gorges Dam at Yichang (EE-CHAHNG).

end to the Confucian legacy in modern China. Women were given the vote and encouraged to become active in the political process. At the local level, an increasing number of women became active in the CCP and in collective organizations. In 1950, a new marriage law guaranteed women equal rights with men. Most important, perhaps, it permitted women for the first time to initiate divorce proceedings against their husbands. Within a year, nearly one million divorces had been granted.

At first, the new government moved carefully on family issues to avoid unnecessarily alienating its supporters in the countryside. When collective farms were established in the mid-1950s, payment for hours worked in the form of ration coupons was made not to the individual but to the family head, thus maintaining the traditionally dominant position of the patriarch. When people's communes were established in the late 1950s, however, payments went to the individual.

During the Great Leap Forward, children were encouraged to report to the authorities any comments by their parents that criticized the system. Such practices continued during the Cultural Revolution, when children were expected to tell on their parents, students on their teachers, and employees on their superiors. Some have suggested that Mao encouraged such practices to bring an end to the traditional "politics of dependency." According to this theory, historically the famous "five relationships" forced individuals to swallow their anger and accept the hierarchical norms established by Confucian ethics (known in Chinese as "to eat bitterness"). By encouraging oppressed elements—the young, the female, and the poor—to voice their bitterness, Mao hoped to break the tradition of dependency. Such denunciations had been issued against landlords in the land reform tribunals of the late 1940s and early 1950s. Later, during the Cultural Revolution, they were applied to other authority figures.

LIFESTYLE CHANGES The post-Mao era brought a decisive shift away from revolutionary utopianism and back toward the pragmatic approach to nation building. For most people, this meant improved living conditions and a qualified return to family traditions. Young people whose parents had given them patriotic names such as Build the Country, Protect Mao Zedong, and Assist Korea began to choose more elegant and cosmopolitan names for their own children. Some names, such as Surplus Grain or Bring a Younger Brother, expressed hope for the future.

The new attitudes were also reflected in physical appearance. For a generation after the civil war, clothing had been restricted to the traditional baggy "Mao suit" in olive drab or dark blue, but by the 1980s, young people craved such fashionable Western items as designer jeans and trendy sneakers. Cosmetic surgery to create a more buxom figure or a more Western facial look became increasingly common among affluent young women in the cities. Many had the epicanthic fold over their eyelids removed or their noses enlarged—a curious decision in view of the tradition of referring derogatorily to foreigners as "big noses" (see the comparative essay "Family and Society in an Era of Change" on p. 729).

Religious practices and beliefs have also changed. As the government has become more tolerant, some Chinese have begun to return to the traditional Buddhist faith or to folk religions, and Buddhist and Taoist temples are crowded with worshipers. Despite official efforts to suppress its more evangelical forms, Christianity has become popular as well; like the "rice Christians" (persons who supposedly converted for economic reasons) of the past, many now view it as a symbol of success.

As with all social changes, China's reintegration into the outside world has had a price. Arranged marriages, nepotism, and mistreatment of females (for example, under the one-child rule, parents reportedly killed female infants to regain the possibility of having a son) have come back, although such behavior likely survived under the cloak of revolutionary purity for a generation (see the box on p. 730). Materialistic attitudes are prevalent among young people, along with a corresponding cynicism about politics and the CCP. Expensive weddings are now increasingly common, and bribery and favoritism are all too frequent. Crime of all types, including an apparently growing incidence of prostitution and sex crimes against women, appears to be on the rise. To discourage sexual abuse, the government now seeks to provide free legal services for women living in rural areas.

There is also a price to pay for the trend toward privatization. Under the Maoist system, the elderly and the sick were provided with retirement benefits and health care by the state or by the collective organizations. Under current conditions, with the latter no longer playing such a social role and more workers operating in the private sector, the safety net has been removed. The government recently attempted to fill the gap by enacting a social security law, but because of lack of funds, eligibility is limited primarily to individuals in the urban sector of the economy. Those living in the countryside—who still represent 60 percent of the population—are essentially unprotected, prompting legislation in 2010 to provide modest pensions and medical insurance to the poorest members of Chinese society. Yet much more needs to be done. As the population ages, the lack of a retirement system represents a potential time bomb.

China's Changing Culture

During the first half of the twentieth century, Chinese culture was strongly influenced by currents from the West (see Chapter 24). The rise to power of the

Communists in 1949 added a new dimension to the debate over the future of culture in China. The new leaders rejected the Western attitude of "art for art's sake" and, like their Soviet counterparts, viewed culture as an important instrument of indoctrination. The standard would no longer be aesthetic quality or the personal preference of the artist but "art for life's sake," whereby culture would serve the interests of socialism.

CULTURE IN A REVOLUTIONARY ERA At first, the new emphasis on socialist realism did not entirely extinguish traditional culture. Mao and his colleagues tolerated—and even encouraged—efforts by artists to synthesize traditional ideas with socialist concepts. During the Cultural Revolution, however, all forms of traditional culture came to be viewed as reactionary. Socialist realism became the only acceptable standard. All forms of traditional expression were forbidden, and the deification of Mao and his central role in building a Communist paradise became virtually the only acceptable form of artistic expression.

Characteristic of the shifting cultural climate in China was the experience of author Ding Ling (DING LING). Born in 1904 and educated in a school for women set up by leftist intellectuals during the hectic years after the May Fourth Movement, she became involved in party activities in the early 1930s and settled in Yan'an, where she wrote her most famous novel, *The Sun Shines over the Sangan River,* which described the CCP's land reform program in favorable terms. It was awarded the Stalin Prize three years later.

During the early 1950s, Ding Ling was one of the most prominent literary lights of the new China, but in the more ideological climate at the end of the decade, she was attacked for her individualism and her previous criticism of the party. Although temporarily rehabilitated, she was sentenced to hard labor on a commune during the Cultural Revolution and was not released until the late 1970s after the death of Mao. Crippled and in poor health, she died in 1981. Ding Ling's fate mirrored the fate of thousands of progressive Chinese intellectuals who were not able to satisfy the constantly changing demands of a repressive regime.

ART AND MUSIC After Mao's death, Chinese culture was finally released from the shackles of socialist realism. In painting, where for a decade the only acceptable standard for excellence was praise for the party and its policies, the new permissiveness led to a revival of interest in both traditional and Western forms. Although some painters continued to blend Eastern and Western styles, others imitated trends from abroad, experimenting with a wide range of previously prohibited art styles, including Cubism and abstract painting.

In the late 1980s, two avant-garde art exhibits shocked the Chinese public and provoked the wrath of the party.

COMPARATIVE ESSAY

Family and Society in an Era of Change

FAMILY & SOCIETY

One of the paradoxes of the modern world is that at a time of political stability and economic prosperity for many people in the advanced capitalist societies, public cynicism about the system is increasingly widespread. Alienation and drug use are at dangerously high levels, and the crime rate in most areas remains much higher than in the immediate postwar era.

Although various reasons have been advanced to explain this paradox, many observers contend that the decline of the traditional family system is responsible for many contemporary social problems. There has been a steady rise in the percentage of illegitimate births and single-parent families in countries throughout the Western world. In the United States, approximately half of all marriages end in divorce. In many European countries, the birthrate has dropped to alarming levels.

Observers point to several factors as an explanation for these conditions: the growing emphasis on an individualistic lifestyle devoted to instant gratification; the rise of the feminist movement, which has not only freed women from the servitude imposed on their predecessors, but has also relieved them of full-time responsibility for the care of the next generation; and the increasing mobility of contemporary life, which disrupts traditional family ties and creates a sense of rootlessness.

These trends are not unique to Western civilization. Even in East Asia, where the Confucian tradition of family solidarity has been endlessly touted as a major factor in the region's economic success, the incidence of divorce and illegitimate births is on the rise, as is the percentage of women in the workforce. Older citizens frequently complain that the Asian youth of today are too materialistic and steeped in the individualistic values of the West.

In societies less exposed to the individualist lifestyle portrayed in Western culture, traditional attitudes about the family continue to hold sway. In the Middle East, governmental and religious figures seek to prevent the Western media from undermining accepted mores. Success is sometimes elusive, however, as the situation in Iran demonstrates. Despite the zealous guardians of Islamic morality, many young Iranians are clamoring for the individual freedoms that have been denied to them since the Islamic Revolution (see Chapter 29).

© William J. Duiker

China's "Little Emperors." To curtail population growth, Chinese leaders launched a massive family planning program that restricted urban families to a single child. Under these circumstances, in conformity with tradition, sons are especially prized, and some Chinese complain that many parents overindulge their children, turning them into spoiled "little emperors."

To what degree and in what ways are young people in China becoming more like their counterparts in the West?

An exhibition of nude paintings, the first ever held in China, attracted many viewers but reportedly offended the modesty of many Chinese. The other exhibit, which presented various schools of modern and postmodern art, resulted in some expressions of public hostility. After a Communist critic lambasted the works as promiscuous and ideologically reactionary, the government declared that henceforth it would regulate all art exhibits. Since the 1990s, some Chinese artists, such as the world-famous Ai Weiwei (I WAY-WAY) (b. 1957), have aggressively challenged the government's authority. In response, the government razed Ai's art studio in Shanghai in 2011. He was subsequently taken into custody on charges related to tax evasion. Nonetheless, Chinese contemporary art has expanded exponentially and commands exorbitant prices on the world market.

Like the fine arts, Western classical music was suppressed during the Cultural Revolution. Significant changes have occurred in the post-Mao era, however, as the government has encouraged interest in classical

Love and Marriage in China

FAMILY & SOCIETY

"What men can do, women can also do." So said Chairman Mao as he "liberated" and masculinized Chinese women to work alongside men. Women's individuality and sexuality were sacrificed for the collective good of his new socialist society. Marriage, which had traditionally been arranged by families for financial gain, was now dictated by duty to the state. The Western concept of romantic love did not enter into a Chinese marriage, as this interview of a schoolteacher by the reporter Zhang Xinxin (JANG SHEEN-SHEEN) in the mid-1980s illustrates. According to recent surveys, the same is true today.

Zhang Xinxin, *Chinese Lives*

My husband and I never did any courting—honestly! We registered our marriage a week after we'd met. He was just out of the forces and a worker in a building outfit. They'd been given a foreign-aid assignment in Zambia, and he was selected. He wanted to get his private life fixed up before he went, and someone introduced us. Seeing how he looked really honest, I accepted him.

No, you can't say I didn't know anything about him. The person who introduced us told me he was a Party member who'd been an organization commissar. Any comrade who's good enough to be an organization cadre is politically reliable. Nothing special about our standing of living—it's what we've earned. He's still a worker, but we live all right, don't we?

He went off with the army as soon as we'd registered our marriage and been given the wedding certificates. He was away three years. We didn't have the wedding itself before he went because we hadn't got a room yet.

Those three years were a test for us. The main problem was that my family was against it. They thought I was still only a kid and I'd picked the wrong man. What did they have against him? His family was too poor. Of course I won in the end—we'd registered and got our wedding certificates. We were legally married whether we had the family ceremony or not.

We had our wedding after he came back in the winter of 1973. His leaders and mine all came to congratulate us and give us presents. The usual presents those days were busts of Chairman Mao. I was twenty-six and he was twenty-nine. We've never had a row.

I never really wanted to take the college entrance exams. Then in 1978 the school leadership got us all to put our names forward. They said they weren't going to hold us back: the more of us who passed, the better it would be for the school. So I put my name forward, crammed for six weeks, and passed. I already had two kids then. . . .

I reckoned the chance for study was too good to miss. And my husband was looking after the kids all by himself. I usually only came back once a fortnight. So I couldn't let him down.

My instructors urged me to take the exams for graduate school, but I didn't. I was already thirty-four, so what was the point of more study? There was another reason too. I didn't want an even wider gap between us: he hadn't even finished junior middle school when he joined the army.

It's bad if the gap's too wide. For example, there's a definite difference in our tastes in music and art, I have to admit that. But what really matters? Now we've set up this family we have to preserve it. Besides, look at all the sacrifices he had to make to see me through college. Men comrades all like a game of cards and that, but he was stuck with looking after the kids. He still doesn't get any time for himself—it's all work for him.

We've got a duty to each other. Our differences? The less said about them the better. We've always treated each other with the greatest respect.

Of course some people have made suggestions, but my advice to him is to respect himself and respect me. I'm not going to be like those men who ditch their wives when they go up in the world.

I'm the head of our school now. With this change in my status I've got to show even more responsibility for the family. Besides, I know how much he's done to get me where I am today. I've also got some duties in the municipal Women's Federation and Political Consultative Conference. No, I'm not being modest. I haven't done anything worth talking about, only my duty.

We've got to do a lot more educating people. There have been two cases of divorce in our school this year.

Q *Do you think the marriage described here is successful? Why or why not? What do you think this woman feels about her marriage?*

Source: From *Chinese Lives: An Oral History of Contemporary China*, by Zhang Xinxin and Sang Ye, copyright © 1987 by W.J.F. Jenner and Delia Davin.

music by opening conservatories and building concert halls. China today is producing legions of musicians, who are filling orchestras in Western countries.

LITERATURE   The limits of freedom of expression were most apparent in literature. During the early 1980s, party leaders encouraged Chinese writers to express their views on the mistakes of the past, and a new "literature of the wounded" began to describe the brutal and arbitrary character of the Cultural Revolution.

One of the most prominent writers was Bai Hua (by HWA) (b. 1930), whose film script *Bitter Love* described the life of a young Chinese painter who joined the revolutionary movement during the 1940s but whose work was condemned as counterrevolutionary during the Cultural Revolution. In describing the excesses of the Cultural Revolution, Bai Hua was only responding to Deng Xiaoping's appeal for intellectuals to speak out, but he was soon criticized for failing to point out the essentially beneficial role of the CCP in recent Chinese history. The film was withdrawn from circulation in 1981, and Bai Hua was compelled to recant his errors and to state that the great ideas of Mao Zedong on art and literature were "still of universal guiding significance today."[5] As the attack on Bai Hua illustrates, many party leaders remained suspicious of "decadent" bourgeois culture. The official press periodically warned that China should adopt only the "positive" aspects of Western culture (notably, its technology and its work ethic) and not the "negative" elements such as drug use, pornography, and hedonism.

Conservatives were especially incensed by the tendency of many writers to dwell on the shortcomings of the socialist system. One such writer is Mo Yan (muh YAHN) (b. 1956), whose novels *The Garlic Ballads* (1988) and *Life and Death Are Wearing Me Out* (2008), expose the rampant corruption of contemporary Chinese society, the roots of which he attributes to one-party rule. Yu Hua (yoo HWA) (b. 1960), another outstanding novelist, uses narratives marked by exaggerated and grotesque humor to criticize the cruelty of the Communist regime in *To Live* (2003).

Today, Chinese culture has been dramatically transformed by the nation's adoption of a market economy and the spread of the Internet. A new mass literature explores the aspirations and frustrations of a generation obsessed with material consumption and the right of individual expression. Lost in the din are the voices of China's rural poor.

Confucius and Marx: The Tenacity of Tradition

Why has communism survived in China, albeit in a substantially altered form, when it failed in Eastern Europe and the Soviet Union? One of the primary factors is probably cultural. Although the doctrine of Marxism-Leninism originated in Europe, many of its main precepts, such as the primacy of the community over the individual and the denial of the concept of private property, run counter to trends in Western civilization. This inherent conflict is especially evident in the societies of central Europe, which were strongly influenced by Enlightenment philosophy and the Industrial Revolution. These forces were weaker farther to the east, although they had begun to penetrate tsarist Russia by the end of the nineteenth century.

In contrast, Marxism-Leninism found a more receptive climate in China and other countries in the region influenced by Confucian tradition. In its political culture, the Communist system exhibits many of the same characteristics as traditional Confucianism—a single truth, an elite governing class, and an emphasis on obedience to the community and its governing representatives. Although a significant and influential minority of the Chinese population—primarily urban and educated—finds the idea of personal freedom against the power of the state appealing, such concepts have little meaning in rural villages, where the interests of the community have always been emphasized over the desires of the individual. It is no accident that Chinese leaders now seek to reintroduce the precepts of State Confucianism to bolster a fading belief in the existence of a future Communist paradise.

Party leaders today are banking on the hope that China can be governed as it has always been—by an elite class of highly trained professionals dedicated to pursing a predefined objective. In fact, however, real changes are taking place in China today. Although the youthful protesters in Tiananmen Square were comparable in some respects to the reformist elements of the early republic, the China of today is fundamentally different from that of the early twentieth century. Literacy rates and the standard of living are far higher, the pressures of outside powers are less threatening, and China has entered its own industrial and technological revolution. Many Chinese depend more on independent talk radio and the Internet for news and views than on the official media. Whereas Sun Yat-sen, Chiang Kai-shek, and even Mao Zedong broke their lances on the rocks of centuries of tradition, poverty, and ignorance, the present leaders rule a country much more aware of the world and China's place in it. Although the shift in popular expectations may be gradual, China today is embarked on a journey to a future for which the past no longer provides a roadmap.

CHAPTER SUMMARY

For four decades after the end of World War II, the two major Communist powers appeared to have become permanent features on the international landscape. Suddenly, though, in the late 1980s, the Soviet Union entered a period of internal crisis that shook the foundations of Soviet society. In 1991, the system collapsed, to be replaced by a series of independent states based primarily on ethnic and cultural differences that had existed long before the Bolshevik Revolution. China went through an even longer era of instability, beginning with the Cultural Revolution in 1966, but it managed to survive under a hybrid system that combines features of a Leninist command economy with capitalist practices adapted from the modern West.

Why were the outcomes so different? Although the cultural differences we have described were undoubtedly an important factor, the role of human action should not be ignored. Whereas Mikhail Gorbachev introduced the idea of *glasnost* to permit the emergence of a more pluralistic political system in the Soviet Union, Chinese leaders crushed the protest movement in the spring of 1989 and reasserted the authority of the Communist Party. Deng Xiaoping's gamble paid off, and today the party stands at the height of its power.

CHAPTER TIMELINE

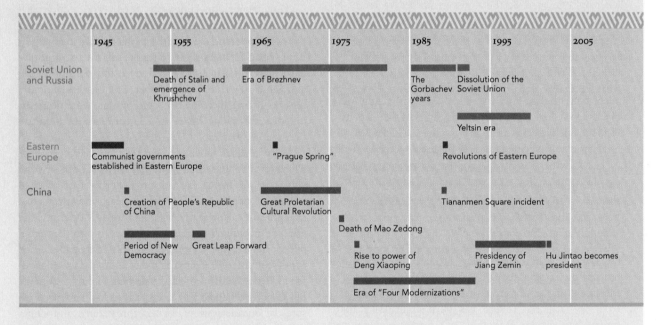

CHAPTER REVIEW

Upon Reflection

Q How have six decades of Communist rule affected the concept of the family in China? How does the current state of the family in China compare with the family in other parts of the world?

Q What strategies were used by the leaders of the Soviet Union and the People's Republic of China as they sought to build Communist societies in their countries? In what ways were the strategies different, and in what ways were they similar? To what degree were they successful?

Q How has the current generation of leadership in China made use of traditional values to solidify Communist control over the country? To what degree has this approach contradicted the theories of Karl Marx?

Key Terms

de-Stalinization (p. 710)
perestroika (p. 714)
glasnost (p. 714)
New Democracy (p. 717)
Great Leap Forward (p. 717)
Great Proletarian Cultural Revolution (p. 719)
uninterrupted revolution (p. 719)
Four Modernizations (p. 720)
rural responsibility system (p. 725)

Suggested Reading

RUSSIA AND THE SOVIET UNION For a general view of modern Russia, see **M. Malia**, *Russia Under Western Eyes* (Cambridge, Mass., 1999), and **M. T. Poe**, *The Russian Moment in World History* (Princeton, N.J., 2003). On the Khrushchev years, see **W. Taubman**, *Khrushchev: The Man and His Era* (New York, 2004). For an inquiry into the reasons for the Soviet collapse, see **R. Conquest**, *Reflections on a Ravaged Century* (New York, 1999), and **R. Strayer**, *Why Did the Soviet Union Collapse? Understanding Historical Change* (New York, 1998).

CHINA UNDER MAO ZEDONG A number of useful surveys deal with China after World War II. The most comprehensive treatment of the Communist period is **M. Meisner**, *Mao's China and After: A History of the People's Republic* (New York, 1999). Also see **R. Macfarquhar**, ed., *The Politics of China: The Eras of Mao and Deng* (Cambridge, 1997). A recent critical biography of China's "Great Helmsman" is **J. Chang** and **J. Halliday**, *Mao: The Unknown Story* (New York, 2005).

POST-MAO CHINA The 1989 demonstrations and their aftermath are described in an eyewitness account by **L. Feigon**, *China Rising: The Meaning of Tiananmen* (Chicago, 1990). Documentary materials relating to the events of 1989 are chronicled in **A. J. Nathan** and **P. Link**, eds., *The Tiananmen Papers* (New York, 2001). Subsequent events are analyzed in **J. Fewsmith**, *China Since Tiananmen: The Politics of Transition* (Cambridge, 2001). On China's challenge from the process of democratization, see **J. Gittings**, *The Changing Face of China: From Mao to Market* (Oxford, 2005). Also see **T. Saich**, *Governance and Politics in China* (New York, 2002). China's evolving role in the world is traced in **S. Shirk**, *China: Fragile Superpower* (Oxford, 2007).

CHINESE LITERATURE AND ART For a comprehensive introduction to twentieth-century Chinese literature, consult **E. Widmer** and **D. Der-Wei Wang**, eds., *From May Fourth to June Fourth: Fiction and Film in Twentieth-Century China* (Cambridge, Mass., 1993), and **J. Lau** and **H. Goldblatt**, *The Columbia Anthology of Modern Chinese Literature* (New York, 1995). For the most comprehensive analysis of twentieth-century Chinese art, consult **M. Sullivan**, *Arts and Artists of Twentieth-Century China* (Berkeley, Calif., 1996).

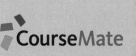

CourseMate

Visit the CourseMate website at www.cengagebrain.com for additional study tools and review materials for this chapter.

Children play amid the ruins of Warsaw, Poland, at the end of World War II.

© Bettmann (Reginald Kenny)/CORBIS

Europe and the Western Hemisphere Since 1945

CHAPTER OUTLINE AND FOCUS QUESTIONS

Recovery and Renewal in Europe

Q What problems have the nations of Western Europe faced since 1945, and what steps have they taken to try to solve these problems? What problems have Eastern European nations faced since 1989?

Emergence of the Superpower: The United States

Q What political, social, and economic changes has the United States experienced since 1945?

The Development of Canada

Q What political, social, and economic developments has Canada experienced since 1945?

Latin America Since 1945

Q What problems have the nations of Latin America faced since 1945, and what role has Marxist ideology played in their efforts to solve these problems?

Society and Culture in the Western World

Q What major social, cultural, and intellectual developments have occurred in Western Europe and North America since 1945?

CRITICAL THINKING

Q What are the similarities and differences between the major political, economic, and social developments in the first half of the twentieth century and those in the second half of the century?

THE END OF WORLD WAR II in Europe had been met with great joy. A visitor in Moscow reported, "I looked out of the window [at 2 A.M.], almost everywhere there were lights in the windows—people were staying awake. Everyone embraced everyone else, someone sobbed aloud." But after the celebrations, Europeans awoke to a devastating realization: their civilization was in ruins. Almost 40 million people (soldiers and civilians) had been killed over the last six years. Air raids and artillery bombardments had reduced many of the cities of Europe to heaps of rubble. The Polish capital of Warsaw had been almost completely obliterated. An American general described Berlin: "Wherever we looked, we saw desolation. It was like a city of the dead. Suffering and shock were visible in every face. Dead bodies still remained in canals and lakes and were being dug out from under bomb debris." Millions of Europeans faced starvation as grain harvests were only half their 1939 levels. Millions were also homeless.

Yet by 1970, Western Europe had not only recovered from the effects of World War II but also experienced an economic resurgence that seemed nothing less than miraculous. Economic growth continued so long that the first postwar recession, in 1973, came as a shock. It was short-lived, however, and economic growth resumed. With this economic expansion came the creation of the welfare state—a prominent social development in postwar Europe. After the collapse of Communist governments in the revolutions of 1989, a number of Eastern European states sought to create market economies and join the military and economic unions first formed by Western European states.

The most significant factor after 1945 was the emergence of the United States as the world's richest and most powerful nation. American prosperity reached new heights in the first two decades after World War II, but the nation has nevertheless faced a series of social and economic problems—including racial division and staggering budget deficits—in the postwar era.

To the south of the United States, Latin America had its own unique heritage. Although some Latin Americans in the nineteenth century had looked to the United States as a model for their own development, in the twentieth century, many strongly criticized U.S. military and economic domination of Central and South America. At the same time, many Latin American countries struggled with economic and political instability.

Toward the end of the century, as the West adjusted from Cold War to post–Cold War realities, other changes were also shaping the Western outlook. The demographic face of European countries changed as massive numbers of immigrants created more ethnically diverse populations. New artistic and intellectual currents, the continued advance of science and technology, the effort to come to grips with environmental problems, and the women's liberation movement—all spoke of a vibrant, ever-changing world. At the same time, a devastating terrorist attack in the United States in 2001 made the Western world vividly aware of its vulnerability to international terrorism. 🕮

Recovery and Renewal in Europe

Q FOCUS QUESTIONS: What problems have the nations of Western Europe faced since 1945, and what steps have they taken to try to solve these problems? What problems have Eastern European nations faced since 1989?

All the nations of Europe faced similar problems at the end of World War II. First and foremost, they needed to rebuild their shattered economies. Remarkably, within a few years, an incredible economic revival brought renewed growth to Western Europe.

Western Europe: The Triumph of Democracy

With the economic aid of the Marshall Plan, the countries of Western Europe recovered relatively rapidly from the devastation of World War II. Between the early 1950s and late 1970s, industrial production surpassed all previous records, and Western Europe experienced virtually full employment.

FRANCE: FROM DE GAULLE TO NEW UNCERTAINTIES The history of France for nearly a quarter century after the war was dominated by one man—Charles de Gaulle (SHAHRL duh GOHL) (1890–1970). Initially, he had withdrawn from politics, but in 1958, frightened by the bitter divisions caused by the Algerian crisis (see Chapter 29), the leaders of the Fourth Republic offered to let de Gaulle take over the government and revise the constitution.

De Gaulle's constitution for the Fifth Republic greatly enhanced the office of the president, who now had the power to choose the prime minister, dissolve parliament, and supervise defense and foreign policy. As the new president, de Gaulle sought to return France to the status of a great power. With that goal in mind, he invested heavily in the nuclear arms race. France exploded its first nuclear bomb in 1960. Nevertheless, de Gaulle did not really achieve his ambitious goals; in truth, France was too small for such global ambitions.

Under de Gaulle, France became a major industrial producer and exporter, particularly in automobiles and armaments. But the expansion of traditional industries, such as coal, steel, and railroads, which had all been nationalized, led to large government deficits. The cost of living increased faster than in the rest of Europe. Growing dissatisfaction led to a series of student protests in May 1968, followed by a general strike by the labor unions. Although he restored order, de Gaulle resigned from office in April 1969 and died the next year.

The worsening of France's economic situation in the 1970s brought a shift to the left politically. By 1981, the Socialists had become the dominant party in the National Assembly, and the Socialist leader, François Mitterrand (frahnh-SWAH MEE-tayr-rahnh) (1916–1995), was elected president. Mitterrand passed a number of measures to aid workers: an increased minimum wage, expanded social benefits, a fifth week of paid vacation, and a thirty-nine-hour workweek. The Socialists also enacted some more radical reforms, nationalizing the major banks, the space and electronics industries, and important insurance firms.

The Socialist policies largely failed, however, and within three years, the Mitterrand government returned some of the economy to private enterprise. But France's economic decline continued, and in 1993, a coalition of conservative parties won 80 percent of the seats. The move to the right was strengthened when the conservative mayor of Paris, Jacques Chirac (ZHAHK shee-RAK) (b. 1932), was elected president in May 1995 and reelected in 2002. Resentment against foreign-born residents led to calls for restrictions on immigration. Chirac himself pursued a plan of sending illegal immigrants back to their home countries.

In the fall of 2005, however, antiforeign sentiment provoked a backlash, as young Muslims in the crowded suburbs of Paris rioted against dismal living conditions and the lack of employment opportunities. Tensions between the Muslim community and the remainder of the French population became a chronic source of unrest that Nicolas Sarkozy (nee-kohl-AH sar-koh-ZEE) (b. 1955), elected as president in 2007, promised to address, but without much success. In 2009, unemployment among those under twenty-five was almost 22 percent, but in the predominantly Muslim suburbs, youth joblessness exceeded 50 percent. In May 2012, Sarkozy lost his bid for a second term to the Socialist candidate, François Hollande (frahnh-SWAH oh-LAWND) (b. 1954), who promised to cancel tax cuts for the rich and raise the tax rate on those earning one million euros to 75 percent.

FROM WEST GERMANY TO GERMANY As noted in Chapter 26, the three western zones of Germany were unified as the Federal Republic of Germany in 1949. Konrad Adenauer (AD-uh-now-ur) (1876–1967), the leader of the Christian Democratic Union, served as chancellor from 1949 to 1963 and became the Federal Republic's "founding hero."

Adenauer's chancellorship is largely associated with the remarkable resurrection of the West German economy. Although West Germany had only 52 percent of the territory of prewar Germany, by 1955 the West German gross domestic product exceeded that of prewar Germany. Unemployment fell from 8 percent in 1950 to 0.4 percent in 1965.

After the Adenauer era, German voters moved politically from the center-right of the Christian Democrats to the center-left; in 1969, the Social Democrats became the leading party. The first Social Democratic chancellor was Willy Brandt (VIL-ee BRAHNT) (1913–1992). In 1971, Brandt negotiated a treaty with East Germany that led to greater cultural, personal, and economic contacts between West and East Germany. In 1972, he received the Nobel Peace Prize for this "opening toward the east"—known as *Ostpolitik* (OHST-poh-lee-teek).

In 1982, the Christian Democrat Helmut Kohl (HEL-moot KOHL) (b. 1930) formed a new center-right government. Kohl benefited from an economic boom in the mid-1980s and the 1989 revolution in East Germany, which led in 1990 to the reunification of the two Germanies, making the new restored Germany, with its 79 million people, the leading power in Europe. Soon, however, the realization set in that the revitalization of eastern Germany would cost far more than anticipated, and Kohl's government faced the politically unpopular prospect of raising taxes substantially. Moreover, the virtual collapse of the economy in eastern Germany led to extremely high unemployment. In 1998, voters responded by returning the Social Democrats to power with the election of Gerhard Schröder (GAYR-hahrt SHRUR-dur) (b. 1944). But Schröder failed to cure Germany's economic woes, and as a result of elections in 2005, Angela Merkel (AHNG-uh-luh MERK-uhl) (b. 1954), leader of the Christian Democrats, became Germany's first female chancellor. Merkel pursued health care reform and new energy policies at home while taking a leading role in the affairs of the European Union (EU). Elected to a second term in 2009, she led the EU effort that resulted in a bailout of Greece's deteriorating economy and a restructuring of its debt in 2012.

THE DECLINE OF GREAT BRITAIN The end of World War II left Britain with massive economic problems. In elections held immediately after the war, the Labour Party overwhelmingly defeated Winston Churchill's Conservatives. Labour's promise of far-reaching social welfare measures was quite appealing in a country with a tremendous shortage of consumer goods and housing. The new Labour government under Clement Attlee (1883–1967) proceeded to turn Britain into a modern **welfare state**.

The process began with the nationalization of the Bank of England, the coal and steel industries, public transportation, and public utilities, such as electricity and gas. In 1946, the new government established a comprehensive social security program and nationalized medical insurance. A health act established a system of socialized medicine that forced doctors and dentists to work with state hospitals, although private practice could be maintained. The British welfare state became the model for most European nations.

Continuing economic problems, however, brought the Conservatives back into power from 1951 to 1964. Although they favored private enterprise, the Conservatives accepted the welfare state. By now the British economy had recovered from the war, but its slow growth reflected a long-term economic decline. At the same time, Britain's ability to play the role of a world power had declined substantially. Between 1964 and 1979, Conservatives and Labour alternated in power, but neither party was able to deal with the ailing economy.

In 1979, the Conservatives returned to power under Margaret Thatcher (b. 1925), who became the first woman prime minister in British history (see the box on p. 738). The "Iron Lady," as she was called, broke the power of the labor unions, but she was not able to eliminate the basic components of the welfare state. Her economic policy, termed "Thatcherism," improved the economic situation, but at a price. The south of England, for example, prospered, but the old industrial areas of the Midlands and north declined and were beset by high unemployment, poverty and sporadic violence.

Thatcher dominated British politics in the 1980s. But in 1990, Labour's fortunes revived when Thatcher's government attempted to replace local property taxes with a flat-rate tax payable by every adult. Critics argued that this was effectively a poll tax that would allow the rich to pay the same rate as the poor. In 1990, Thatcher resigned, and later, in new elections in 1997, the Labour Party won a landslide victory. The new prime minister, Tony Blair (b. 1953), was a moderate whose youthful energy instilled new vigor on the political scene. Blair was one of the leaders in forming an international coalition against terrorism after the terrorist attack on the United States in 2001. Four

Margaret Thatcher. Great Britain's first female prime minister, Margaret Thatcher was a strong leader who dominated British politics in the 1980s. This picture of Thatcher was taken during a meeting with French president François Mitterrand in 1986.

years later, however, his support of the U.S. war in Iraq, when a majority of Britons opposed it, caused his popularity to plummet. In the summer of 2007, he stepped down and allowed the new Labour Party leader Gordon Brown (b. 1951) to become prime minister.

In 2010, in the wake of climbing unemployment and a global financial crisis, the Labour Party's thirteen-year rule ended when the Conservative Party candidate David Cameron (b. 1966) became prime minister on the basis of a coalition with the Liberal Democrats. Cameron promised to reduce the government debt by cutting government waste and social services and overhauling the health care system.

Eastern Europe After Communism

The fall of Communist governments in Eastern Europe during the revolutions of 1989 brought an end to a postwar European order that had been imposed on unwilling peoples by the victorious forces of the Soviet Union (see Chapter 26). In 1989 and 1990, new governments throughout Eastern Europe worked diligently to scrap the old system and introduce the democratic procedures and market systems they believed would revitalize their scarred lands. But this process proved to be neither simple nor easy. Nevertheless, by 2000, many of these states, especially Poland and the Czech Republic, were making a successful transition to free markets and democracy. In 1997, Poland, the Czech Republic, and Hungary joined the North Atlantic Treaty Organization (NATO).

In some states, the shift to non-Communist rule was complicated by old problems, especially ethnic issues. Although Czechs and Slovaks agreed to a peaceful division of Czechoslovakia into the Czech Republic and Slovakia, the situation was quite different in Yugoslavia.

THE DISINTEGRATION OF YUGOSLAVIA From its creation in 1919, Yugoslavia had been an artificial entity. Strong leaders—especially the dictatorial Marshal Tito after World War II—had managed to hold together the six disparate republics and two autonomous provinces that made up the country. After Tito's death in 1980, no strong leader emerged, and eventually Yugoslavia was caught up in the reform movements sweeping through Eastern Europe.

After negotiations among the six republics failed, Slovenia and Croatia declared their independence in June 1991. This action was opposed by Slobodan Milošević (sluh-BOH-dahn mih-LOH-suh-vich) (1941–2006), the leader of Serbia, who insisted that the republics adjust their borders to accommodate their Serb minorities who did not want to live outside the boundaries of Serbia. Serbian forces attacked both new states and, although

Margaret Thatcher: Entering a Man's World

POLITICS & GOVERNMENT

In 1979, Margaret Thatcher became the first woman to serve as Britain's prime minister and went on to be its longest-serving prime minister as well. In this excerpt from her autobiography, Thatcher describes how she was interviewed by Conservative Party officials when they first considered her as a possible candidate for Parliament from Dartford. Thatcher ran for Parliament for the first time in 1950; she lost but increased the Conservative vote total in the district by 50 percent over the previous election.

Margaret Thatcher, *The Path to Power*

And they did [consider her]. I was invited to have lunch with John Miller and his wife, Phee, and the Dartford Woman's Chairman, Mrs. Fletcher, on the Saturday on Llandudno Pier. Presumably, and in spite of any reservations about the suitability of a woman candidate for their seat, they liked what they saw. I certainly got on well with them. . . . After lunch we walked back along the pier to the Conference Hall in good time for a place to hear Winston Churchill give the Party Leader's speech. . . . Foreign affairs naturally dominated his speech—it was the time of the Berlin blockade and the Western airlift—and his message was somber, telling us that only American nuclear weapons stood between Europe and communist tyranny and warning of "what seems a remorselessly approaching third world war."

I did not hear from Dartford until December, when I was asked to attend an interview. . . . With a large number of other hopefuls I turned up on the evening of Thursday 30 December for my first Selection Committee. Very few outside the political arena know just how nerve-racking such occasions are. The interviewee who is not nervous and tense is very likely to perform badly: for, as any chemist will tell you, the adrenaline needs to flow if one is to perform at one's best. I was lucky in that at Dartford there were some friendly faces around the table, and it has to be said that on such occasions there are advantages as well as disadvantages to being a young woman making her way in the political world.

I found myself short-listed, and was asked to go to Dartford itself for a further interview. Finally, I was invited . . . to address the Association's Executive Committee of about fifty people. As one of five would-be candidates, I had to give a fifteen-minute speech and answer questions for a further ten minutes.

It was the questions which were more likely to cause me trouble. There was a good deal of suspicion of woman candidates, particularly in what was regarded as a tough industrial seat like Dartford. This was quite definitely a man's world into which not just angels feared to tread. There was, of course, little hope of winning it for the Conservatives, though this is never a point that the prospective candidate even in a Labour seat as safe as Ebbw Vale would be advised to make. The Labour majority was an all but unscalable 20,000. But perhaps this unspoken fact turned to my favour. Why not take the risk of adopting the young Margaret Roberts? There was not much to lose, and some good publicity for the Party to gain.

The most reliable sign that a political occasion has gone well is that you have enjoyed it. I enjoyed that evening at Dartford, and the outcome justified my confidence. I was selected.

Q *In this account, is Margaret Thatcher's being a woman more important to her or to others? Why would this disparity exist?*

Source: Pages 62–65 from THE PATH TO POWER by Margaret Thatcher. Copyright © 1995 by Margaret Thatcher. Reprinted by permission of HarperCollins Publishers and HarperCollins Publishers Ltd.

unsuccessful against Slovenia, captured one-third of Croatia's territory.

International recognition of independent Slovenia and Croatia in 1992 and of Macedonia and Bosnia and Herzegovina soon thereafter did not deter the Serbs, who now turned on Bosnia. By mid-1993, Serbian forces had acquired 70 percent of Bosnian territory. The Serbian policy of **ethnic cleansing**—killing or forcibly removing Bosnian Muslims from their lands—revived memories of Nazi atrocities in World War II. In the town of Srebrenica (sreb-bruh-NEET-suh), almost eight thousand men and boys were killed in a Serbian massacre. This account by a

Muslim survivor from the town is eerily reminiscent of the activities of the Nazi *Einsatzgruppen* (see Chapter 25):

> When the truck stopped, they told us to get off in groups of five. We immediately heard shooting next to the trucks. . . . About ten Serbs with automatic rifles told us to lie down on the ground face first. As we were getting down, they started to shoot, and I fell into a pile of corpses. I felt hot liquid running down my face. I realized that I was only grazed. As they continued to shoot more groups, I kept on squeezing myself in between dead bodies.[1]

As the fighting spread, European nations and the United States began to intervene to stop the bloodshed, and in 1995, a fragile cease-fire agreement was reached. An international peacekeeping force was stationed in the area to prevent further hostilities.

Peace in Bosnia, however, did not bring peace to Yugoslavia. A new war erupted in 1999 over Kosovo (KAWSS-suh-voh), an autonomous province within the Serbian republic. Kosovo's inhabitants were mainly ethnic Albanians, but the province was also home to a Serbian minority. In 1994, groups of ethnic Albanians had founded the Kosovo Liberation Army (KLA) and begun a campaign against Serbian rule in Kosovo. When Serb forces began to massacre ethnic Albanians in an effort to crush the KLA, the United States and its NATO allies mounted a bombing campaign that forced Milošević to stop. In the elections of 2000, Milošević himself was ousted from power, and he was later put on trial by an international tribunal for war crimes against humanity

CHRONOLOGY Western Europe

Welfare state emerges in Great Britain	1946
Konrad Adenauer becomes chancellor of West Germany	1949
Charles de Gaulle reassumes power in France	1958
Student protests in France	1968
Willy Brandt becomes chancellor of West Germany	1969
Margaret Thatcher becomes prime minister of Great Britain	1979
François Mitterrand becomes president of France	1981
Helmut Kohl becomes chancellor of West Germany	1982
Reunification of Germany	1990
Conservative victory in France	1993
Election of Chirac	1995
Labour Party victory in Great Britain	1997
Social Democratic victory in Germany	1998
Angela Merkel becomes chancellor of Germany	2005
Nicolas Sarkozy becomes president of France	2007
David Cameron becomes prime minister of Great Britain	2010
Socialist victory in France	2012

for his ethnic cleansing policies. He died in prison in 2006 before his trial could be completed.

Peacekeeping forces still remain in Bosnia and Kosovo to maintain the uneasy peace. In 2004, Yugoslavia itself ceased to exist when the new national government

The War in Bosnia. By mid-1993, irregular Serb forces had overrun much of Bosnia and Herzegovina amid scenes of untold suffering. This photograph shows a woman running past the bodies of victims of a mortar attack on Sarajevo on August 21, 1992. Three mortar rounds landed, killing at least three people.

AP Images/Rikard Larma

officially renamed the truncated country Serbia and Montenegro. Two years later, Montenegrins voted in favor of independence. Thus, by 2006, all six republics cobbled together to form Yugoslavia in 1918 were once again independent nations. In 2008, Kosovo unilaterally proclaimed its independence from Serbia and was recognized by most other nations as the seventh sovereign state to emerge from the former Yugoslavia.

The New Russia

Soon after the disintegration of the Soviet Union in 1991, a new era began in Russia with the presidency of Boris Yeltsin. A new constitution created a two-chamber parliament and established a strong presidency. During the mid-1990s, Yeltsin was able to maintain a precarious grip on power while seeking to implement reforms that would lead to a pluralistic political system and a market economy. But the new post-Communist Russia remained as fragile as ever. Burgeoning economic inequality and rampant corruption shook the confidence of the Russian people in the superiority of the capitalist system over the Communist one. A nagging war in the Caucasus—where the people of Chechnya (CHECH-nee-uh) sought national independence from Russia—drained the government budget and exposed the decrepit state of the once vaunted Red Army. Yeltsin was reelected in 1996, but his precarious health raised serious questions about his ability to govern.

THE PUTIN ERA At the end of 1999, Yeltsin suddenly resigned and was replaced by Vladimir Putin (VLAD-ih-meer POO-tin) (b. 1952), a former member of the KGB. Putin vowed to bring an end to the rampant corruption and to strengthen the role of the central government. He also vowed to bring the breakaway state of Chechnya back under Russian authority and to assume a more assertive role in international affairs. The new president took advantage of growing public anger at Western plans to expand the NATO alliance into Eastern Europe to restore Russia's position as an influential force in the world.

Putin attempted to deal with Russia's chronic problems by centralizing his control over the system and by silencing critics—notably in the Russian media. Although these moves were criticized in the West, many Russians sympathized with Putin's attempts to restore a sense of pride and discipline. Putin's popularity among the Russian people was also strengthened by Russia's growing prosperity in the first years of the century. Putin made significant economic reforms while rising oil prices boosted the Russian economy, which grew dramatically until the 2008–2009 global economic crisis.

In 2008, Dmitry Medvedev (di-MEE-tree mehd-VYEH-dehf) (b. 1965) became president of Russia when Putin could not run for reelection under Russia's constitution. Instead, Putin became prime minister, and the two men shared power. In 2011, Putin's plans to run again for president sparked protests, but he was elected to a third term in March 2012.

The Unification of Europe

As we saw in Chapter 26, the divisions created by the Cold War led the nations of Western Europe to seek military security by forming NATO in 1949. The destructiveness of two world wars, however, caused many thoughtful Europeans to look for some additional form of unity.

In 1957, France, West Germany, the Benelux countries (Belgium, the Netherlands, and Luxembourg), and Italy signed the Treaty of Rome, which created the European Economic Community (EEC). The EEC eliminated customs barriers for the six member nations and created a large free-trade area protected by a common external tariff. All the member nations benefited economically. In 1973, Great Britain, Ireland, and Denmark joined what now was called the European Community (EC). Greece joined in 1981, followed by Spain and Portugal in 1986. In 1995, Austria, Finland, and Sweden also became members.

THE EUROPEAN UNION In the 1980s and 1990s, the EC moved toward even greater economic integration. The Treaty on European Union, which went into effect on January 1, 1994, turned the European Community into the European Union, a true economic and monetary union. By 2000, it contained 370 million people and constituted the world's largest single trading entity, transacting one-fourth of the world's commerce. One of its goals was achieved in 1999 with the introduction of a common currency, the euro. On January 1, 2002, the euro officially replaced twelve national currencies. By 2012, the euro had been adopted by seventeen countries and was serving approximately 327 million people.

A major crisis for the euro began in 2010, however, when Greece's burgeoning public debt threatened to cause the bankruptcy of that country as well as financial difficulties for many European banks. Other EU members, led by Germany, put together a financial rescue plan, but subsequently other nations, including Ireland, Portugal, and Spain, also faced serious financial problems.

In another step toward integration, the EU has established a common agricultural policy, which provides subsidies to farmers to enable them to compete on the world market. The end of national passports has given millions of Europeans greater flexibility in travel. The EU has been less successful in setting common foreign policy goals, primarily because individual nations still see foreign policy as a national priority and are reluctant to give up this power to a single overriding institution. In 2009, however, the EU ratified the Lisbon Treaty, which

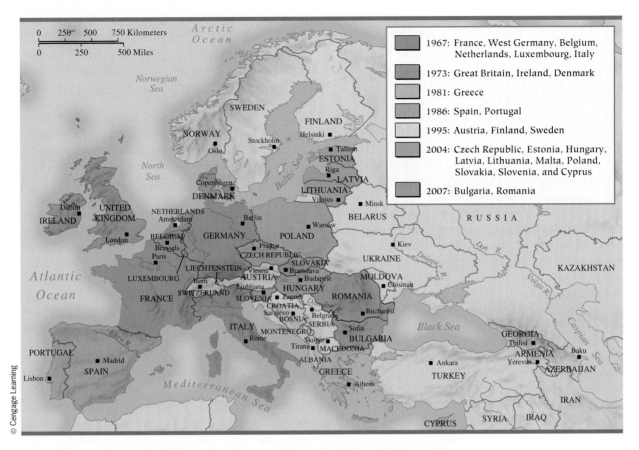

MAP 28.1 European Union, 2007. Beginning in 1957 as the European Economic Community, or Common Market, the union of European states seeking to integrate their economies has gradually grown from six members to twenty-seven. By 2002, the European Union had achieved two major goals—the creation of a single internal market and a common currency—although it has been less successful at achieving common political and foreign policy goals.

Q *What additional nations do you think will eventually join the European Union?*

Map legend:
- 1967: France, West Germany, Belgium, Netherlands, Luxembourg, Italy
- 1973: Great Britain, Ireland, Denmark
- 1981: Greece
- 1986: Spain, Portugal
- 1995: Austria, Finland, Sweden
- 2004: Czech Republic, Estonia, Hungary, Latvia, Lithuania, Malta, Poland, Slovakia, Slovenia, and Cyprus
- 2007: Bulgaria, Romania

created a full-time presidential post and a new voting system that reflects each country's population size. It also provided more power for the European Parliament in an effort to promote the EU's foreign policy goals.

TOWARD A UNITED EUROPE At the beginning of the twenty-first century, the EU established a new goal: to incorporate into the union the states of eastern and southeastern Europe, including the nations that had recently emerged from Communist rule. Many of these states were considerably poorer than the current members, which raised the possibility that adding these nations might weaken the EU itself. To lessen that danger, the EU required applicants to demonstrate their commitment both to market capitalism and to democracy, including respect for minorities and human rights. In 2004, the EU took the plunge and added ten new members: Cyprus, the Czech Republic, Estonia, Hungary, Latvia, Lithuania, Malta, Poland, Slovakia, and Slovenia, thereby enlarging the

population of the EU to 455 million people. In 2007, the EU expanded again as Bulgaria and Romania joined the union (see Map 28.1).

Emergence of the Superpower: The United States

Q FOCUS QUESTION: What political, social, and economic changes has the United States experienced since 1945?

At the end of World War II, the United States emerged as one of the world's two superpowers. As its Cold War confrontation with the Soviet Union intensified, the United States directed much of its energy toward combating the spread of communism. With the collapse of the Soviet Union at the beginning of the 1990s, the

United States became the world's foremost military power.

American Politics and Society Through the Vietnam Era

Franklin Roosevelt's New Deal of the 1930s initiated a basic transformation of American society that included a dramatic increase in the role and power of the federal government, the rise of organized labor as a significant force in the economy and politics, a commitment to the welfare state, a grudging acceptance of ethnic minorities, and a willingness to experiment with deficit spending as a means of stimulating the economy. These trends were bolstered by the election of three Democratic presidents—Harry Truman in 1948, John F. Kennedy in 1960, and Lyndon B. Johnson in 1964. Even the election of a Republican, Dwight D. Eisenhower, in 1952 and 1956 did not significantly alter the fundamental direction of American politics.

The economic boom after World War II fueled confidence in the American way of life. A shortage of consumer goods during the war left Americans with both surplus income and the desire to purchase these goods after the war. Then, too, the growing influence of organized labor enabled more and more workers to get the wage increases that spurred the growth of the domestic market. Between 1945 and 1973, real wages grew an average of 3 percent a year, the most prolonged advance in U.S. history.

Starting in the 1960s, however, problems that had been glossed over earlier came to the fore. The decade began on a youthful and optimistic note when John F. Kennedy (1917–1963), at age forty-three, became the youngest elected president in U.S. history and the first born in the twentieth century. His administration, cut short by an assassin's bullet on November 22, 1963, focused primarily on foreign affairs. Kennedy's successor, Lyndon B. Johnson (1908–1973), who won a new term as president in a landslide in 1964, used his mandate to expand the welfare state that had begun under the New Deal. Johnson's programs included health care for the elderly and the War on Poverty, to be fought with food stamps and the Job Corps.

Johnson's other domestic passion was achieving equal rights for black Americans. In August 1963, the eloquent Reverend Martin Luther King Jr. (1929–1968) led the March on Washington for Jobs and Freedom to dramatize blacks' desire for freedom. This march and King's impassioned plea for racial equality had an electrifying effect on the American people. At President Johnson's initiative, Congress enacted the Civil Rights Act of 1964, which created the machinery to end segregation and discrimination in the workplace and all public accommodations. The Voting Rights Act of 1965 eliminated obstacles to black participation in elections in southern states. But laws alone could not guarantee the Great Society that Johnson envisioned, and soon the administration faced bitter social unrest.

In the North and the West, blacks had had voting rights for many years, but local patterns of segregation resulted in considerably higher unemployment rates for blacks (and Hispanics) than for whites and left blacks segregated in huge urban ghettos. In the summer of 1965, race riots erupted in the Watts district of Los Angeles that led to thirty-four deaths and the destruction of more than a thousand buildings. After King was assassinated in 1968, riots erupted in more than one hundred cities, including Washington, D.C., the nation's capital. The riots led to a "white backlash" and a severe racial division of America.

Antiwar protests also divided the American people after President Johnson committed U.S. troops to a costly war in Vietnam (see Chapter 26). The killing of four student protesters at Kent State University in 1970 by the Ohio National Guard shocked both activists and ordinary Americans, and thereafter the antiwar movement began to subside. But the combination of antiwar demonstrations and riots in the cities caused many people to call for "law and order," an appeal used by Richard Nixon (1913–1994), the Republican presidential candidate in 1968. Nixon's election started a shift to the right in American politics.

The Shift Rightward After 1973

Nixon eventually ended American involvement in Vietnam by gradually withdrawing U.S. troops. Politically, he pursued a "southern strategy," calculating that "law and order" issues would appeal to southern whites. The Republican strategy, however, also won support among white Democrats in northern cities, where court-mandated busing to achieve racial integration had provoked a white backlash.

As president, Nixon was paranoid about conspiracies and resorted to subversive methods of gaining political intelligence on his opponents. Nixon's zeal led to the Watergate scandal—a botched attempt to bug the Democratic National Headquarters and the ensuing coverup. Although Nixon repeatedly denied involvement in the affair, secret tapes he made of his own conversations in the White House revealed otherwise. On August 9, 1974, Nixon resigned in disgrace, an act that saved him from almost certain impeachment and conviction.

After Watergate, American politics focused on economic issues. Gerald Ford (1913–2006) became president when Nixon resigned, only to lose in the 1976 election to Jimmy Carter (b. 1924). By 1980, the Carter administration faced two devastating problems. High inflation and a decline in average earnings were causing a perceptible drop in Americans' living standards. At the same time, a crisis abroad had erupted when fifty-three Americans were taken hostage by the Iranian government of Ayatollah Khomeini and held for nearly fifteen months (see Chapter 29). Carter's inability to gain the release of the hostages led to perceptions at home that he was a weak president. In the election of 1980, he suffered an overwhelming loss to Ronald Reagan (1911–2004), the chief exponent of right-wing Republican policies.

The Reagan Revolution, as it has been called, sent U.S. policy in new directions. Reagan cut back on the welfare state by decreasing spending on food stamps, school lunch programs, and job programs. At the same time, he fostered the largest peacetime military buildup in American history. Total federal spending rose from $631 billion in 1981 to more than $1 trillion by 1986. The administration's spending policies produced record government deficits, which loomed as an obstacle to long-term growth. In the 1970s, the total national debt was $420 billion; under Reagan it reached three times that level.

The inability of Reagan's successor, George H. W. Bush (b. 1924), to deal with the deficit problem, coupled with an economic downturn, led to the election of a Democrat, Bill Clinton (b. 1946), in 1992. The new president was a southerner who claimed to be a new Democrat—one who favored a number of the Republican policies of the 1980s. This was a clear indication that the Democratic victory had not ended the rightward drift in American politics.

Clinton's political fortunes were aided considerably by a lengthy economic revival. A steady reduction in the government's budget deficit strengthened confidence in the national economy. Much of Clinton's second term, however, was overshadowed by charges of misconduct stemming from the president's affair with a White House intern. After a bitter partisan struggle, the U.S. Senate acquitted the president on two articles of impeachment brought by the House of Representatives. But Clinton's problems helped the Republican candidate, George W Bush (b. 1946), to win the presidential election in 2000.

The first four years of Bush's administration were largely occupied with the war on terrorism and the U.S.-led war on Iraq (see Chapter 29). The Department of Homeland Security was established after the 2001 terrorist assaults to help protect the country from future terrorist acts. At the same time, Bush pushed tax cuts through Congress that favored the wealthy and helped produce record deficits reminiscent of the Reagan years. Environmentalists were disturbed by the administration's efforts to weaken environmental laws and regulations to benefit American corporations. During his second term, Bush's popularity plummeted as discontent grew over the Iraq War, financial corruption in the Republican Party, and the administration's poor handling of relief efforts after Hurricane Katrina devastated New Orleans in 2005.

The many failures of the Bush administration led to the lowest approval ratings for a modern president and opened the door for a dramatic change in American politics. The new and often inspiring voice of Barack Obama (b. 1961) who called for "change we can believe in" and ending the war in Iraq led to an overwhelming Democratic victory in the 2008 elections. The Democrats were aided by the financial crisis that began in the fall of 2008. In 2009, Obama moved quickly to deal with the economic recession that some called the worst since the Great Depression. At the same time, Obama emphasized the need to deal with the health care crisis, climate change, the decline in the educational system, and failed economic policies. The Obama administration succeeded in passing a health care reform bill and the Dodd-Frank Act on financial regulation, as well as establishing the Consumer Financial Protection Bureau.

The Development of Canada

Q FOCUS QUESTION: What political, social, and economic developments has Canada experienced since 1945?

For twenty-five years after World War II, Canada experienced extraordinary economic prosperity as it set out on a new path of development, including the electronic, aircraft, nuclear, and chemical engineering industries. Much of the Canadian growth, however, was financed by capital from the United States, which resulted in American ownership of Canadian businesses. While many Canadians welcomed the economic growth, others feared American economic domination of Canada.

After 1945, the Liberal Party continued to dominate Canadian politics. Under Lester Pearson (1897–1972), the Liberals created Canada's welfare state by enacting a national social security system (the Canada Pension Plan) and a national health insurance program. The most prominent Liberal government, however, was that of Pierre Trudeau (PYAYR troo-DOH) (1919–2000), who came to power in 1968.

Trudeau's government pushed a vigorous program of industrialization, but inflation and Trudeau's efforts to impose the will of the federal government on the powerful provincial governments alienated voters and weakened his government. Economic recession in the early 1980s brought Brian Mulroney (b. 1939), leader of the

Progressive Conservative Party, to power in 1984. Mulroney's government sought to privatize many of Canada's state-run corporations and negotiated a free-trade agreement with the United States. Bitterly resented by many Canadians, the agreement cost Mulroney's government much of its popularity. In 1993, the Conservatives were overwhelmingly defeated, and the Liberal leader, Jean Chrétien (ZHAHNH kray-TEN) (b. 1934), became prime minister. Chrétien's conservative fiscal policies, combined with strong economic growth, enabled his government to have a budgetary surplus by the late 1990s and led to another Liberal victory in the elections of 1997. Charges of widespread financial corruption in the government, however, led to a Conservative victory early in 2006, and Stephen Harper (b. 1959) became the new prime minister. Harper's government collapsed in March 2011, but elections held in May resulted in Harper remaining as prime minister.

Latin America Since 1945

Q FOCUS QUESTION: What problems have the nations of Latin America faced since 1945, and what role has Marxist ideology played in their efforts to solve these problems?

The Great Depression of the 1930s had led to political instability in many Latin American countries that resulted in military coups and militaristic regimes (see Chapter 24). But the depression also provided the impetus for Latin America to move from a traditional to a modern economic structure. Since the nineteenth century, Latin Americans had exported raw materials, especially minerals and foodstuffs, while buying the manufactured goods of the industrialized countries in Europe and the United States. As a result of the depression, however, exports were cut in half, and the revenues available to buy manufactured goods declined. This encouraged many Latin American countries to develop industries to produce goods that were formerly imported. Due to a shortage of capital in the private sector, governments often invested in the new industries, thus leading, for example, to government-run steel industries in Chile and Brazil and oil industries in Argentina and Mexico.

South America

By the 1960s, however, Latin American countries were still dependent on the United States, Europe, and now Japan for the advanced technology needed for modern industries. Because of the great poverty in many Latin American countries, domestic markets were limited in size, and many countries failed to find markets abroad for their products. These failures led to instability and a new reliance on military regimes, especially to curb the power of the new industrial middle class and working classes, which had emerged as a result of industrialization. In the 1960s, repressive military regimes in Chile, Brazil, and Argentina abolished political parties and often returned to export-import economies financed by foreigners.

In the 1970s, Latin American regimes grew even more dependent on borrowing from abroad to maintain their failing economies. Between 1970 and 1982, debt to foreigners, mostly U.S. and European banks, increased from $27 billion to $315.3 billion. By 1982, several governments announced that they could no longer pay interest on their debts, and their economies began to crumble.

The debt crisis of the 1980s was accompanied by a move toward democracy. Many people realized that military power without popular consent was incapable of providing a strong state. By the 1980s and early 1990s, democratic regimes were in place everywhere except Cuba, some of the Central American states, Chile, and Paraguay. At the end of the twentieth century and beginning of the twenty-first, a noticeable political trend in Latin America has been the election of left-wing governments, evident in the election of Hugo Chávez (OO-goh CHAH-vez) (b. 1954) in Venezuela in 1998; Luiz Inácio Lula de Silva (LWEES ee-NAH-syoh LOO-luh duh SEEL-vuh) (b. 1945) in Brazil in 2002, followed by Dilma Rousseff (DIL-muh ROO-seff) (b. 1947) in 2010; Michelle Bachelet (mih-SHELL BAHSH-uh-let) (b. 1951) in Chile in 2006, followed by Sebastián Piñera (say-bahs-TYAHN peen-YAIR-uh) (b. 1949) in 2010, a center-right candidate who promised to uphold the Socialists' social and economic policies; and Daniel Ortega (dah-NYEL awr-TAY-guh) (b. 1945) in Nicaragua in 2007.

The United States has also played an important role in Latin America since 1945. Since the

1920s, the United States had been the foremost investor in Latin America. As a result, American companies had gained control of large segments of important Latin American industries including the copper and oil industries. This control by American investors reinforced a growing nationalist sentiment in Latin America against the United States as a neo-imperialist power.

But the United States also tried to pursue a new relationship with Latin America. In 1948, the nations of the Western Hemisphere formed the Organization of American States (OAS), which was intended to eliminate unilateral interference by one state in the internal or external affairs of any other state. But as the Cold War intensified, American policy makers grew anxious about the possibility of Communist regimes arising in Central America and the Caribbean and returned to a policy of unilateral action when they believed that Soviet agents were attempting to establish Communist governments. Especially after the success of Castro in Cuba (see the next section), the desire of the United States to prevent "another Cuba" largely determined American policy toward Latin America. Until the end of the Cold War in the early 1990s, the United States provided massive military aid to anti-Communist regimes, regardless of their nature.

The Threat of Marxist Revolutions: The Example of Cuba

A dictatorship, headed by Fulgencio Batista (1901–1973) and closely tied economically to American investors, had ruled Cuba since 1934. In the 1950s, Batista's government came under attack by a strong opposition movement, led by Fidel Castro. Castro maintained that only armed force could overthrow Batista, but when their initial assaults on Batista's regime met with little success, Castro's forces turned to guerrilla warfare (see the box on p. 746). Batista's regime responded with such brutality that he alienated his own supporters. The dictator fled in December 1958, and Castro's revolutionaries seized Havana on January 1, 1959.

Relations between Cuba and the United States quickly deteriorated early in 1960 when the Soviet Union agreed to buy Cuban sugar and provide $100 million in credits. In October 1960, the United States imposed a trade embargo on Cuba, which drove Castro closer to the Soviet Union. On January 3, 1961, the United States broke diplomatic relations with Cuba. The new American president, John F. Kennedy, supported a coup attempt against Castro's government, but the landing of 1,400 Cuban exiles with assistance from the Central Intelligence Agency (CIA) at the Bay of Pigs in Cuba on April 17, 1961, was a total military disaster. The Soviets now made an even greater commitment to Cuban independence by installing nuclear missiles in the country, an act that led to a showdown with the United States (see Chapter 26). As its part of the bargain to defuse the missile crisis, the United States agreed not to invade Cuba.

In Cuba, Castro's socialist revolution proceeded, with mixed results. The Cuban people obtained some social gains, especially in health care and education. The regime provided free medical services for all citizens, and the population's health improved noticeably. Illiteracy was wiped out by developing new schools and establishing teacher-training institutes that tripled the number of teachers within ten years.

Eschewing rapid industrialization, Castro encouraged agricultural diversification. But the Cuban economy continued to rely on the production of sugar. Economic problems forced the regime to depend on Soviet subsidies and the purchase of Cuban sugar by Soviet bloc countries. After the collapse of these Communist regimes in 1989, Cuba lost their support. Although economic conditions continued to decline, Fidel Castro remained in power until illness forced him to resign the presidency in 2008, when his brother, Raul Castro (b. 1931), succeeded him.

Nationalism and the Military: The Example of Argentina

The military became the power brokers of many twentieth-century Latin American nations. Fearful of the forces unleashed by industrialization, the military intervened in Argentine politics in 1930 and propped up the cattle and wheat oligarchy that had controlled the reins of power since the beginning of the century. In June 1943, a group of restless army officers overthrew the civilian oligarchy. One member of the new regime, Juan Perón (WAHN puh-ROHN) (1895–1974), used his position as labor secretary to curry favor with the workers. But as Perón grew more popular, other army officers grew fearful of his power and arrested him. An uprising by workers forced the officers to back down, and in 1946, Perón was elected president.

To please his chief supporters—labor and the urban middle class—Perón pursued a policy of increased industrialization. At the same time, he sought to free Argentina from foreign investors. The government bought the railways; took over the banking, insurance, shipping, and communications industries; and regulated imports and exports. But Perón's regime was also authoritarian. His wife, Eva Perón, founded women's organizations to support the government while Perón organized fascist gangs, modeled after Hitler's Brown Shirts, who used violence to intimidate his opponents. But growing corruption in Perón's government and the alienation of more and more people by the regime's excesses encouraged the military

Castro's Revolutionary Ideals

POLITICS & GOVERNMENT

On July 26, 1953, Fidel Castro and a small group of supporters launched an ill-fated attack on the Moncada Barracks in Santiago de Cuba. Castro was arrested and put on trial. This excerpt is taken from the speech he presented in his defense, in which he discussed the goals of the revolutionaries.

Fidel Castro, "History Will Absolve Me"

I stated that the second consideration on which we based our chances for success was one of social order because we were assured of the people's support. When we speak of the people we do not mean the comfortable ones, the conservative elements of the nation, who welcome any regime of oppression, any dictatorship, and despotism, prostrating themselves before the master of the moment until they grind their foreheads into the ground. When we speak of struggle, the people means the vast unredeemed masses, to whom all make promises and whom all deceive; we mean the people who yearn for a better, more dignified, and more just nation. . . .

In the brief of this cause there must be recorded the five revolutionary laws that would have been proclaimed immediately after the capture of the Moncada barracks. . . .

The First Revolutionary Law would have returned power to the people and proclaimed the Constitution of 1940 the supreme Law of the land, until such time as the people should decide to modify or change it. . . .

The Second Revolutionary Law would have granted property, not mortgageable and not transferable, to all planters, subplanters, lessees, partners, and squatters who hold parcels of five or less *caballerias* [about 33 acres] of land, and the state would indemnify the former owners on the basis of the rental which they would have received for these parcels over a period of ten years.

The Third Revolutionary Law would have granted workers and employees the right to share 30 percent of the profits of all the large industrial, mercantile, and mining enterprises, including the sugar mills. . . .

The Fourth Revolutionary Law would have granted all planters the right to share 55 percent of the sugar production and a minimum quota of forty thousand *arrobas* [25 pounds] for all small planters who have been established for three or more years.

The Fifth Revolutionary Law would have ordered the confiscation of all holdings and ill-gotten gains of those who had committed frauds during previous regimes, as well as the holdings and ill-gotten gains of all their legatees and heirs.

Q *What did Fidel Castro intend to accomplish by his revolution in Cuba? On whose behalf did he fight this revolution?*

Source: Excerpt from *Latin American Civilization* by Benjamin Keen, ed. (Boston: Houghton Mifflin, 1974), pp. 369–373.

---

to overthrow him in September 1955. Perón went into exile in Spain.

Overwhelmed by problems, however, the military leaders allowed Perón to return from exile. Reelected president in September 1973, Perón died one year later. In 1976, the military installed a new regime and used the occasion to kill more than six thousand leftists. But economic problems persisted, and the regime tried to divert people's attention by invading the Falkland Islands in April 1982. Great Britain, which had controlled the islands since the nineteenth century, decisively defeated the Argentine forces. The loss discredited the military

and opened the door to civilian rule. In 1983, Raúl Alfonsín (rah-OOL al-fahn-SEEN) (1927–2009) was elected president and tried to reestablish democratic practices. In elections in 1989, the Perónist Carlos Saúl Menem (KAHR-lohs sah-OOL MEN-em) (b. 1930) won. This peaceful transfer of power gave hope that Argentina was moving on a democratic path. Despite problems of foreign debt and inflation, Argentina has witnessed economic growth since 2003, first under the government of President Nestor Kirchner (NAY-stor KEERCH-nehr) (b. 1950) and then under his wife, Cristina Fernández de Kirchner (kris-TEE-nuh fehr-NAHN-des day

Juan and Eva Perón. Elected president of Argentina in 1946, Juan Perón soon established an authoritarian regime that nationalized some of Argentina's basic industries and organized fascist gangs to overwhelm its opponents. He is shown here with his wife, Eva, during the inauguration ceremonies initiating his second term as president in 1952.

dependent on oil revenues. When world oil prices dropped in the mid-1980s, Mexico was no longer able to make payments on its $80 billion of foreign debt. The debt crisis and rising unemployment increased dissatisfaction with the government, as was evident in the 1988 election, when the PRI's candidate, Carlos Salinas (KAHR-lohs sah-LEE-nahs) (b. 1948), won by only a 50.3 percent majority instead of the expected landslide. Growing dissatisfaction with the government's economic policies finally led to the unthinkable: in 2000, Vicente Fox (vee-SEN-tay FOKS) (b. 1942) defeated the PRI candidate for the presidency. Despite high hopes, Fox's administration failed to deal with police corruption and bureaucratic inefficiency in the government. His successor, Felipe Calderón (feh-LEE-pay kahl-duh-ROHN) (b. 1963), made immigration reform a priority, with little success. In 2012, the PRI returned to power when its candidate, Enrique Peña Nieto (en-REE-kay PAYN-yah nee-EH-toh) (b. 1966), was elected to the presidency.

KEERCH-nehr) (b. 1953), who in 2007 became the first elected female president of Argentina.

The Mexican Way

During the 1950s and 1960s, Mexico's ruling party—the Institutional Revolutionary Party, or PRI—focused on a balanced program of industrial policy. Fifteen years of steady economic growth combined with low inflation and real gains in wages made those years seem a golden age in Mexico's economic development. But at the end of the 1960s, students began to protest the one-party system. On October 2, 1968, police opened fire on a demonstration of university students in Mexico City, killing hundreds of the students. Leaders of the PRI became concerned about the need to change the system.

During the 1970s, the next two presidents, Luis Echeverría (loo-EES eh-cheh-vahr-REE-uh) (b. 1922) and José López Portillo (hoh-SAY LOH-pehz pohr-TEE-yoh) (1920–2004), introduced reforms. Rules for registering political parties were eased, making their growth more likely, and greater freedom of debate in the press and at universities was allowed. But economic problems continued. In the late 1970s, vast new reserves of oil were discovered, making the government even more

Society and Culture in the Western World

Q FOCUS QUESTION: What major social, cultural, and intellectual developments have occurred in Western Europe and North America since 1945?

Socially, culturally, and intellectually, the Western world since 1945 has been marked by much diversity.

The Emergence of a New Society

During the postwar era, such products of new technologies as computers, television, jet planes, contraceptive devices, and new surgical techniques dramatically altered the nature of human life. The rapid changes in postwar society were fueled by scientific advances and economic growth. Called a *technocratic society* by some observers and the **consumer society** by others, postwar Western society was marked by a fluid social structure and new movements for change.

Especially noticeable in European society after 1945 were the changes in the middle class. Such traditional middle-class groups as businesspeople and professionals in law and medicine were greatly augmented by increasing numbers of white-collar supervisory and administrative personnel employed by large companies and government agencies.

Changes also occurred among the traditional lower classes. Especially notable was the shift of people from rural to urban areas. The number of people in agriculture declined drastically. But the size of the industrial working class did not expand. In West Germany, industrial workers made up 48 percent of the labor force throughout the 1950s and 1960s. Thereafter, the number of industrial workers began to dwindle as the number of white-collar service employees increased. At the same time, a substantial increase in real wages enabled the working classes to aspire to the consumption patterns of the middle class. Buying on the installment plan became widespread in the 1950s and enabled workers to purchase televisions, home appliances, and automobiles.

Rising incomes, combined with shorter working hours, also increased the market for mass leisure activities. Between 1900 and 1980, the workweek fell from sixty hours to around forty hours, and the number of paid holidays increased. All aspects of popular culture—music, sports, media—became commercialized and offered opportunities for leisure activities.

Social change was also evident in educational patterns. Before World War II, higher education had largely remained the preserve of the wealthier classes. After the war, European states began to foster greater equality of opportunity in higher education by eliminating fees, and universities experienced an influx of students from the middle and lower classes. Enrollments grew dramatically. In France, 4.5 percent of young people went to a university in 1950; by 1965, the figure had increased to 14.5 percent.

But there were problems. Overcrowded classrooms, professors who paid little attention to students, administrators who acted in an authoritarian fashion, and an education that many deemed irrelevant to the modern age led to an outburst of student revolts in the late 1960s. In part, these were an extension of the anti-Vietnam War protests in American universities in the mid-1960s. Perhaps the most famous student revolt occurred in France in 1968. It erupted at the University of Nanterre outside Paris but soon spread to the Sorbonne, the main campus of the University of Paris. French students demanded a greater voice in the university's administration, occupied buildings, and then expanded their protests by inviting workers to join them. Half of France's workforce went on strike. After the Gaullist government instituted a hefty wage hike, the workers returned to work, and the police repressed the remaining student protesters.

There were several reasons for the student radicalism. Some students were genuinely motivated by the desire to reform the university. Others were protesting the Vietnam War, which they viewed as a product of Western imperialism. They also attacked the materialism of Western society and expressed concern about becoming cogs in a large, impersonal bureaucratic machine. For many students, the calls for democratic decision making in the universities reflected their deeper concerns about the direction of Western society.

The Permissive Society

Some critics referred to the new society of postwar Europe as the **permissive society**. Sweden took the lead in the so-called sexual revolution of the 1960s, and the rest of Europe and the United States soon followed. Sex education in the schools and the decriminalization of homosexuality were but two aspects of Sweden's liberal approach. The introduction of the birth control pill, which was widely available by the mid-1960s, gave people more freedom. Meanwhile, sexually explicit movies, plays, and books broke new ground in the treatment of once-hidden subjects.

The new standards were evident in the breakdown of the traditional family. Divorce rates increased dramatically, especially in the 1960s, while premarital and extramarital sexual experiences also rose substantially. A survey in the Netherlands in 1968 revealed that 78 percent of men and 86 percent of women had engaged in extramarital sex.

The 1960s also saw the emergence of the drug culture. Marijuana, though illegal, was widely used by university students. For young people more interested in higher levels of consciousness, Timothy Leary, who had done research at Harvard on the psychedelic (perception-altering) effects of lysergic acid diethylamide (LSD), became the high priest of hallucinogenic experiences.

New attitudes toward sex and the use of drugs were only two manifestations of a growing youth movement that questioned authority and fostered rebellion against the older generation. Spurred on by opposition to the Vietnam War and a growing political consciousness, the youth rebellion became a youth protest movement by the second half of the 1960s (see the box on p. 750).

Women in the Postwar World

Despite their enormous contributions to the war effort, women were removed from the workforce at the end of World War II so that there would be jobs for the soldiers returning home. After the horrors of war, people seemed willing for a while to return to traditional family practices. Female participation in the workforce declined, and birthrates rose, creating a "baby boom." This increase in the birthrate did not last, however, and the size of

© Henry Diltz/CORBIS

The "Love-In." In the 1960s, outdoor public festivals for young people combined music, drugs, and sex. Flamboyant dress, face painting, free-form dancing, and drugs were vital ingredients in creating an atmosphere dedicated to "love and peace." Shown here are "hippies" dancing around a decorated bus at a "love-in" during 1967's Summer of Love.

traditionally female jobs. Many women also still faced the double burden of earning income on the one hand and raising a family and maintaining the household on the other. Such inequalities led increasing numbers of women to rebel.

THE FEMINIST MOVEMENT: THE QUEST FOR LIBERATION The participation of women in World Wars I and II helped them achieve one of the major aims of the nineteenth-century feminist movement—the right to vote. After World War I, many governments acknowledged the contributions of women to the war effort by granting them suffrage. Sweden, Great Britain, Germany, Poland, Hungary, Austria, and Czechoslovakia did so in 1918, followed by the United States in 1920. Women in France and Italy did not obtain the right to vote until 1945. After World War II, little was heard of feminist concerns, but by the 1960s, women began to assert their rights again and speak as feminists. Along with the student upheavals of the late 1960s came renewed interest in feminism, or the **women's liberation movement**, as it was now called.

Of great importance to the emergence of the women's liberation movement was the work of Simone de Beauvoir (see-MUHN duh boh-VWAR) (1908–1986), who supported herself as a teacher and later as a writer. De Beauvoir believed that she lived a "liberated" life for a twentieth-century European woman, but she still came to perceive that as a woman, she faced limits that men did not. In her highly influential work *The Second Sex* (1949), she argued that as a result of male-dominated societies, women had been defined by their differences from men and consequently received second-class status: "What particularly signalizes the situation of woman is that she—a free autonomous being like all human creatures—nevertheless finds herself in a world where men compel her to assume the status of the Other."[2]

TRANSFORMATION IN WOMEN'S LIVES To ensure natural replacement of a country's population, women need to produce an average of 2.1 children each. Many

families began to decline by the mid-1960s. Largely responsible for this decline was the widespread practice of birth control. The condom, invented in the nineteenth century, was already in wide use, but the development of birth control pills in the 1960s provided a convenient and reliable means of birth control that quickly spread to all Western countries.

The trend toward smaller families contributed to changes in women's employment in both Europe and the United States, primarily because women now needed to devote far fewer years to rearing children. That led to a large increase in the number of married women in the workforce. At the beginning of the twentieth century, even working-class wives tended to stay at home if they could afford to do so. In the postwar period, this was no longer the case. In the United States, for example, in 1900, married women made up about 15 percent of the female labor force; by 1970, their number had increased to 62 percent.

But the increased number of women in the workforce did not change some old patterns. Working-class women in particular still earned less than men for equal work. In the 1960s, women earned only 60 percent of men's wages in Britain, 50 percent in France, and 63 percent in West Germany. In addition, women still tended to enter

"The Times They Are a-Changin'": The Music of Youthful Protest

ART & IDEAS

In the 1960s, the lyrics of rock music reflected the rebellious mood of many young people. Bob Dylan (b. 1941), a vastly influential performer and recording artist, expressed the feelings of the younger generation. His song "The Times They Are a-Changin'," released in 1964, has been called an "anthem for the protest movement."

Bob Dylan, "The Times They Are a-Changin'"

Come gather 'round people
Wherever you roam
And admit that the waters
Around you have grown
And accept it that soon
You'll be drenched to the bone
If your time to you
Is worth savin'
Then you better start swimmin'
Or you'll sink like a stone
For the times they are a-changin' . . .

Come senators, congressmen
Please heed the call
Don't stand in the doorway
Don't block up the hall
For he that gets hurt
Will be he who has stalled
There's a battle outside
And it is ragin'

It'll soon shake your windows
And rattle your walls
For the times they are a-changin'

Come mothers and fathers
Throughout the land
And don't criticize
What you can't understand
Your sons and your daughters
Are beyond your command
Your old road
Is rapidly agin'
Please get out of the new one
If you can't lend your hand
For the times they are a-changin'

The line it is drawn
The curse it is cast
The slow one now
Will later be fast
As the present now
Will later be past
The order is
Rapidly fadin'
And the first one now
Will later be last
For the times they are a-changin'

 What caused the student campus revolts of the 1960s? What and whom does Dylan identify as the problem in this song?

European countries fall far short of this mark; their populations stopped growing in the 1960s, and the trend has continued ever since. By the 1990s, in the nations of the European Union, the average number of children per mother was 1.4. At 1.31 in 2009, Spain's rate was among the lowest in the world.

At the same time, the number of women in the workforce has continued to rise. In Britain, for example, women accounted for 32 percent of the labor force in 1970 but 44 percent in 1990. Moreover, women have entered new employment areas. Greater access to universities and professional schools has enabled women to take jobs in law, medicine, government, business, and education. In the Soviet Union, for example, about 70 percent of doctors and teachers were women. Nevertheless, women still often are paid less than men for comparable work and receive fewer promotions to management positions.

Feminists in the women's liberation movement came to believe that women themselves must transform the fundamental conditions of their lives. In the 1960s and 1970s, hundreds of thousands of European women gained a measure of control over their own bodies by working to repeal laws that outlawed contraception and abortion. Even in Catholic countries, where the church opposed abortion, legislation allowing contraception and abortion was passed in the 1970s and 1980s.

As more women have become activists, they have also become involved in new issues. Some women have tried to affect the political environment by allying with the anti-nuclear movement. In 1981, a group of women protested American nuclear missiles in Britain by chaining themselves to the fence of a U.S. military base. Thousands more joined in creating a peace camp around the military compound. Enthusiasm ran high; one participant said, "I'll never forget that feeling; it'll live with me for ever. . . . As we walked round, and we clasped hands. . . . It was for women; it was for peace; it was for the world."[3]

Women in the West have also reached out to work with women from the rest of the world in changing the conditions of their lives. Between 1975 and 1995, the United Nations held a series of conferences on women's issues. These meetings made clear the differences between women from Western and non-Western countries. Whereas women from Western countries spoke about political, economic, cultural, and sexual rights, women from developing countries in Latin America, Africa, and Asia focused on bringing an end to the violence, hunger, and disease that haunt their lives.

The Growth of Terrorism

Acts of terror by individuals and groups opposed to governments have become a frightening aspect of modern Western society. During the late 1970s and early 1980s, small bands of terrorists used assassination, indiscriminate killing of civilians, the taking of hostages, and the hijacking of airplanes to draw attention to their demands or to destabilize governments in the hope of achieving their political goals.

Motivations for terrorist acts varied considerably. Left- and right-wing terrorist groups flourished in the late 1970s and early 1980s, but terrorist acts also stemmed from militant nationalists who wished to create separatist states. Most prominent was the Irish Republican Army (IRA), which resorted to vicious attacks against the ruling government and innocent civilians in Northern Ireland.

Although left- and right-wing terrorist activities declined in Europe in the 1980s, international terrorism continued. Angered by the loss of their territory to Israel, some militant Palestinians responded with terrorist attacks against Israel's supporters. Palestinian terrorists mounted attacks on both Europeans and American tourists in Europe, including attacks on vacationers at airports in Rome and Vienna in 1985. State-sponsored terrorism was often an integral part of international terrorism. Militant governments, especially in Iran, Libya, and Syria, assisted terrorist organizations that carried out attacks on Europeans and Americans. On December 21, 1988, Pan American flight 103 from Frankfurt to New York exploded over Lockerbie, Scotland, killing all 259 passengers and crew members. The bomb responsible for the explosion had been planted by two Libyan terrorists.

TERRORIST ATTACK ON THE UNITED STATES   One of the most destructive acts of terrorism occurred on September 11, 2001, in the United States. Terrorists hijacked four commercial jet airplanes after takeoff from Boston, Newark, and Washington, D.C. The hijackers flew two of the airplanes into the towers of the World Trade Center in New York City, causing these buildings, as well as several surrounding buildings, to collapse. A third hijacked plane slammed into the Pentagon near Washington, D.C. The fourth plane, apparently headed for Washington, crashed in an isolated area of Pennsylvania. In total, more than three thousand people were killed.

These coordinated acts of terror were carried out by hijackers connected to the international terrorist organization known as al-Qaeda, run by Osama bin Laden (1957–2011). A native of Saudi Arabia of Yemeni extraction, bin Laden used an inherited fortune to set up terrorist training camps in Afghanistan, under the protection of that nation's militant fundamentalist Islamic rulers known as the Taliban.

U.S. president George W. Bush vowed to wage a war on terrorism and worked to create a coalition of nations to assist in ridding the world of al-Qaeda and other terrorist groups. Within weeks of the attack on America, U.S. and NATO air forces began bombing Taliban-controlled command centers and al-Qaeda hiding places in Afghanistan. On the ground, Afghan forces, assisted by U.S. special forces, pushed the Taliban out and gained control of the country by the end of 2001. A democratic multiethnic government was installed but continues to face problems from revived Taliban activity (see Chapter 29).

Guest Workers and Immigrants

As the economies of the Western European countries revived in the 1950s and 1960s, a severe labor shortage forced them to rely on foreign workers. Thousands of Turks and eastern and southern Europeans relocated to Germany, North Africans to France, and people from the Caribbean, India, and Pakistan to Great Britain. Overall, there were probably 15 million **guest workers** in Europe in the 1980s.

Although these workers were recruited for economic reasons, their presence has created social and political problems for their host countries. Not only has the influx of foreigners strained the social services of European countries, but high concentrations of guest workers, many of them nonwhite, in certain areas have led to tensions with the local native populations who oppose making their countries ethnically diverse. By 1998, English was not the first language of one-third of inner-city children in London. Foreign workers constitute almost one-fifth of the population in the German cities of Frankfurt, Munich, and Stuttgart. Antiforeign sentiment has increased with growing unemployment.

Even nations that have traditionally been open to immigrants are changing their policies. In the Netherlands, 19 percent of the people have a foreign background, representing almost 180 nationalities. In 2004, however, the Dutch government passed tough new immigration laws that required newcomers to pass a Dutch language and culture test before being admitted to the country. Sometimes these policies have been aimed at religious practices. In France, the growing number of Muslims has led to restrictions on the display of Islamic symbols. In 2004, France enacted a law prohibiting female students from wearing a headscarf (*hijib*) to school. Small religious symbols, such as small crosses or medallions, were not included. Critics argue that this law will exacerbate ethnic and religious tensions in France, while supporters maintain that it upholds the French tradition of secularism and equality for women (see the box on p. 753).

The Environment and the Green Movements

Environmentalism first became an important item on the European political agenda in the 1970s. By that time, serious ecological problems had become all too apparent. Air pollution, created by emissions from road vehicles, power plants, and industrial factories, was causing respiratory illnesses and having corrosive effects on buildings and monuments. Many rivers, lakes, and seas had become so polluted that they posed serious health risks. In 1986, a disastrous accident at the Soviet nuclear power plant at Chernobyl, Ukraine, made Europeans even more aware of potential environmental hazards. The opening of Eastern Europe after the revolutions of 1989 revealed the environmental destruction caused by unfettered industrial pollution in that region.

Growing ecological awareness gave rise to Green movements and Green parties throughout Europe beginning in the 1970s. Most visible was the Green Party in Germany, which was officially organized in 1979 and had elected forty-two delegates to the West German parliament by 1987. Green parties also competed successfully in Sweden, Austria, and Switzerland. As support for the Green movement grew, the major political parties began to advocate new environmental regulations, and 1987 was touted as the "year of the environment." By the 1990s, European governments were taking steps to safeguard the environment and clean up the worse sources of pollution.

By the early twenty-first century, European cities began to recognize the need for urban sustainability. Many cities have enacted laws that limit new construction, increase the quantity and quality of green spaces within the city, and foster the construction and use of public transportation systems, including rail, metro, bus, and bicycle (see the comparative illustration on p. 755).

Western Culture Since 1945

Intellectually and culturally, the Western world since World War II has been notable for innovation as well as diversity. Especially since 1970, new directions have led some observers to speak of a "Postmodern" cultural world.

POSTWAR LITERATURE A significant trend in postwar literature was the Theater of the Absurd. Its most famous proponent was the Irishman Samuel Beckett (1906–1990), who lived in France. In Beckett's *Waiting for Godot* (1952), the action on the stage is transparently unrealistic. Two men wait for someone, with whom they may or may not have an appointment. During the course of the play, nothing seems to be happening. The audience is never told if the action in front of them is real or imagined. Suspense is maintained not by having the audience wonder "What is going to happen next?" but simply "What is happening now?"

The Theater of the Absurd reflected its time. The postwar era was one of disillusionment with fixed ideological beliefs in politics and religion. The same disillusionment that underscored the bleak worldview of absurdist drama also inspired the **existentialism** of writers Albert Camus (ahl-BAYR ka-MOO) (1913–1960) and Jean-Paul Sartre (ZHAHNH-POHL SAR-truh) (1905–1980), with its sense of the world's meaninglessness. The beginning point of the existentialism of Sartre and Camus was the absence of God in the universe. Although the death of God was tragic, it also meant that humans had no preordained destiny and were utterly alone in the universe with no future and no hope. As Camus expressed it:

> A world that can be explained even with bad reasons is a familiar world. But, on the other hand, in a universe suddenly divested of illusions and lights, man feels an alien, a stranger. His exile is without remedy since he is deprived of

Islam and the West: Secularism in France

FAMILY & SOCIETY

The ban on headscarves in French schools was preceded by a debate on the secular state in France. While recognizing the right to religious expression, French law dictates that religious expression must remain in the private sphere and cannot enter the public realm. Before the law banning headscarves was enacted, President Jacques Chirac set up a commission to interview school, religious, and political leaders on whether headscarves should be allowed in schools. The commission decided in favor of prohibiting all conspicuous religious symbols in schools. The first selection is taken from a speech by Chirac, who favored the ban. The second selection is taken from interviews with French Muslim women. Many of these women questioned how the law protects their individual rights and freedom of religious expression.

French President Jacques Chirac on Secularism in French Society

The debate on the principle of secularism goes to the very heart of our values. It concerns our national cohesion, our ability to live together, our ability to unite on what is essential. . . . Many young people of immigrant origin, whose first language is French, and who are in most cases of French nationality, succeed and feel at ease in society which is theirs. This kind of success must also be made possible by breaking the wall of silence and indifference which surrounds the reality of discrimination today. I know about the feeling of being misunderstood, of helplessness, sometimes even of revolt, among young French people of immigrant origin whose job applications are rejected because of the way their names sound, and who are too often confronted with discrimination in the fields of access to housing. . . . All of France's children, whatever their history, whatever their origin, whatever their beliefs, are the daughters and sons of the republic. They have to be recognized as such, in law but above all in reality. By ensuring respect for this requirement, by reforming our integration policy, by our ability to bring equal opportunities to life, we shall bring national cohestion to life again. We shall also do so by bringing to life the principle of secularism, which is a pillar of our constitution. . . . Secularism guarantees freedom of conscience. It protects the freedom to believe or not to believe. . . . We also need to reaffirm

secularism in schools, because schools must be preserved absolutely. . . .

There is of course no question of turning schools into a place of uniformity, of anonymity, where religious life or belonging would be banned. . . . Until recently, as a result of a reasonable custom which was respected spontaneously, nobody ever doubted that pupils, who are naturally free to live their faith, should nevertheless not arrive in schools . . . in religious clothes. It is not a question of inventing new rules or of shifting the boundaries of secularism. It is a question of expressing, with respect but clearly and firmly, a rule which has been part of our customs and practices for a very long time. . . . I have examined the arguments put forward by . . . political parties, by religious authorities, by major representatives of major currents of thought. In all conscience, it is my view that the wearing of clothes or of symbols which conspicuously demonstrate religious affiliations must be banned in state schools.

North African Women in France Respond to the Headscarf Ban

Labiba (Thirty-Five-Year-Old Algerian)

I don't feel that they should interfere in the private life of people in the respect that we're in a secular country; France shouldn't take a position toward one religion to the detriment of another. . . . I think that in a secular school, we should all be secular, otherwise we need to have religious school and then everyone is free to wear what he wants.

Nour (Thirty-Four-Year-Old Algerian)

Honestly, you know the secular school, it doesn't miss celebrating Easter, and when they celebrate Easter, it doesn't bother me. My daughter comes home with painted Easter eggs and everything; it's pretty; it's cute. There are classes that are over 80 percent [Muslim] in the suburbs, and they celebrate Easter, they celebrate Christmas, you see? And that's not a problem for the secular school. And I don't find that fair.

I find that when it's Ramadan, they should talk about Ramadan. Honestly, me, it wouldn't be a problem. On the contrary, someone who comes into class . . . with a veil, that would pose a question actually, that we could

(Continued)

discuss in class, to know why this person wears the veil. So why punish them, amputate them from that part of their culture without discussing it? Why is it so upsetting to have someone in class who wears a veil, when we could make it a subject of discussion on all religions? Getting stuck on the veil hides the question. They make such a big deal out of it, the poor girls, they take them out of school. . . . In the end we turn them into people who have problems in their identities, in their culture and everything. . . . For a country that is home to so many cultures, there's no excuse.

Isma (Thirty-Six-Year-Old Algerian)

The girls who veil in France, especially in the high school and junior high students, it's first of all a question of

identity, because these girls are born in France to foreign parents. . . . At a given time an adolescent wants to affirm himself, so he thinks, I'd say, he thinks that it's by his clothes that he shows that he comes from somewhere, that he's from someone. So then, I think you should let them do it, and afterwards, by themselves, people come back to who they really are.

 What were the perspectives of the French president and the French Muslim women who were interviewed? How do they differ? Do you think there might be a way to reconcile the opposing positions? Why or why not?

Source: French President Jacques Chirac on Secularism in French Society. North African Women in France Respond to the Headscarf Ban. Caitlin Killian, *Gender and Society* Vol. 17, No. 4, pp. 567–590, copyright 2003 by SAGE Publications. Reprinted by permission of SAGE Publications.

the memory of a lost home or the hope of a promised land. This divorce between man and his life, the actor and his setting, is properly the feeling of absurdity.[4]

According to Camus, then, the world was absurd and without meaning; humans, too, are without meaning and purpose. Reduced to despair and depression, humans have but one source of hope—themselves.

POSTMODERNISM The term *Postmodern* covers a variety of intellectual and artistic styles and ways of thinking that have been prominent since the 1970s. In the broadest sense, **Postmodernism** rejects the modern Western belief in an objective truth and instead focuses on the relative nature of reality and knowledge.

While existentialists wrestled with notions of meaning and existence, a group of French philosophers in the 1960s attempted to understand how meaning and knowledge operate through the study of language and signs. **Poststructuralism,** or **deconstruction**, formulated by Jacques Derrida (ZHAHK DEH-ree-duh) (1930–2004), holds that culture is created and can therefore be analyzed in a variety of ways, according to the manner in which people create their own meaning. Hence, there is no fixed truth or universal meaning.

Michel Foucault (mih-SHELL foo-KOH) (1926–1984) drew on Derrida to explore relationships of power. Believing that "power is exercised, rather than possessed," Foucault argued that the diffusion of power and oppression marks all relationships. For example, any act of teaching

entails components of assertion and submission, as the student adopts the ideas of the person in power. Therefore, all norms are culturally produced and entail some degree of power struggle.

Postmodernism was also evident in literature. An example is the work of Milan Kundera (MEE-lahn koon-DAYR-uh) (b. 1929). Kundera blended fantasy with realism, using fantasy to examine moral issues while remaining optimistic about the human condition. In his novel *The Unbearable Lightness of Being* (1984), Kundera does not despair because of the political repression in his native Czechoslovakia that he so aptly describes but allows his characters to use love as a way to a better life. The human spirit can be lessened but not destroyed.

Trends in Art

After the war, the United States dominated the art world, much as it did the world of popular culture. New York City replaced Paris as the artistic center of the West. The Guggenheim Museum, the Museum of Modern Art, and the Whitney Museum of Modern Art, together with New York's numerous art galleries, promoted modern art and helped determine artistic tastes throughout much of the world. One of the styles that became synonymous with the emergence of the New York art scene was **Abstract Expressionism**.

Dubbed "action painting" by one critic, Abstract Expressionism was energetic and spontaneous, qualities evident in the enormous canvases of Jackson Pollock (1912–1956). In

COMPARATIVE ILLUSTRATION

EARTH & ENVIRONMENT

Green Urbanism. One of the ways that many cities are combating carbon dioxide emissions and promoting urban sustainability is by encouraging the use of bicycles. In Beijing (shown on the left), almost 4 million cyclists use the bicycle as their main form of transportation. In Paris, a public bicycle program, called the *Velib*, short for "free bike," began in 2007, with 10,000 bicycles and 700 rental stations. Today, the program has 17,000 bikes and approximately 1,200 rental stations where visitors and citizens can rent a bike by the hour, as shown on the right.

Q *How do you account for the success of the Velib program?*

such works as *Lavender Mist* (1950), paint seems to explode, enveloping the viewer with emotion and movement. Pollock's swirling forms and seemingly chaotic patterns broke all conventions of form and structure. Inspired by Native American sand painters, Pollock painted with the canvas on the floor. He explained, "On the floor I am more at ease. I feel nearer, more a part of the painting, since this way I can walk around it, work from four sides and be literally in the painting. When I am in the painting, I am not aware of what I am doing. There is pure harmony."

Postmodernism's eclectic commingling of past tradition with Modernist innovation was especially evident in architecture. Robert Venturi argued that architects should look for inspiration as much to the Las Vegas Srip as to the historical styles of the past. The work of Charles Moore (1929–1993) provides an example. His *Piazza d'ltalia* (1976–1980) in New Orleans is an outdoor plaza that combines Classical Roman columns with stainless steel and neon lights. This blending of modern-day materials with historical references distinguished the Postmodern architecture of the late 1970s and 1980s from the Modernist glass box.

Throughout the 1980s and 1990s, the art and music industries increasingly adopted the techniques of marketing and advertising. With large sums of money invested in painters and musicians, pressure mounted to achieve critical and commercial success. Negotiating the distinction between art and popular culture was essential since many equated merit with sales or economic value.

In the art world, Neo-Expressionism reached its zenith in the mid-1980s. Neo-Expressionist artists like Anselm Kiefer (AN-selm KEEF-uhr) (b. 1945) became increasingly popular. Born in Germany the year the war ended, Kiefer combines aspects of Abstract Expressionism, collage, and German Expressionism to create stark and haunting works. His *Departure from Egypt* (1984) is a meditation on Jewish history and its descent into the horrors of Nazism. Kiefer hoped that a portrayal of Germany's atrocities could free Germans from their past and bring some good out of evil.

The World of Science and Technology

Many of the scientific and technological achievements since World War II have revolutionized people's lives. During World War II, university scientists were recruited

Jackson Pollock at Work. After World War II, Abstract Expressionism moved to the center of the artistic mainstream. One of its best-known practitioners was Jackson Pollock, who achieved his ideal of total abstraction in his drip paintings. He is shown here at work at his Long Island studio. Pollock found it easier to cover his large canvases with exploding patterns of color when he put them on the floor.

to work for their governments and develop new weapons and practical instruments of war. British physicists played a crucial role in developing an improved radar system that helped defeat the German air force in the Battle of Britain in 1940. German scientists created self-propelled rockets as well as jet airplanes to keep Hitler's hopes alive for a miraculous turnaround in the war. The computer, too, was a wartime creation. The British mathematician Alan Turing designed a primitive computer to assist British intelligence in breaking the secret codes of German ciphering machines. The most famous product of wartime scientific research was the atomic bomb, created by a team of American and European scientists under the guidance of the physicist J. Robert Oppenheimer. Though created for destructive purposes, many wartime developments such as computers and nuclear energy were soon adapted for peacetime uses.

The postwar alliance of science and technology led to an accelerated rate of change that became a fact of life in Western society (see the comparative essay "From the Industrial Age to the Technological Age" on p. 757). One product of this alliance—the computer—may prove to be the most revolutionary of all the technological inventions of the twentieth century. Early computers were large and hot and took up considerable space. The transistor and then the silicon chip revolutionized computer design. With the invention of the microprocessor in 1971, the road was open for the development of the personal computer. By the 1990s, the personal computer had become a fixture in businesses, schools, and homes.

Despite the marvels produced by science and technology, some people have come to question the assumption that the ability to manipulate the environment that scientific knowledge provides is always beneficial. They maintain that some technological advances have far-reaching side effects that are damaging to the environment. Chemical fertilizers, for example, once touted for producing larger crops, have wreaked havoc with the ecological balance of streams, rivers, and woodlands.

The Explosion of Popular Culture

Since 1900, and especially since World War II, popular culture has played an important role in helping Western people define themselves. It also reflects the economic system that supports it, for this system manufactures, distributes, and sells the images that people consume as popular culture. Thus, modern popular culture is inextricably tied to the mass consumer society in which it has emerged.

The United States has been the most influential force in shaping popular culture in the West and, to a lesser degree, the entire world. Through movies, music, advertising, and television, the United States has spread its particular form of consumerism and the American dream to millions around the world. In 1923, the *New York Morning Post* noted that "the film is to America what the flag was once to Britain. By its means Uncle Sam may hope some day . . . to Americanize the world."[5] That day has already come.

Motion pictures were the primary vehicle for the diffusion of American popular culture in the years immediately following World War I and continued to find ever wider markets as the century rolled on. Television, developed in the 1930s, did not become readily available until the late 1940s, but by 1954, there were 32 million sets in the United States as television became the centerpiece of middle-class life. In the 1960s, as television spread around the world, American networks unloaded their products on Europe and the Third World at extraordinarily low prices.

The United States has also dominated popular music since the end of World War II. Jazz, blues, rhythm and blues, rap, and rock and roll have been by far the most popular music forms in the Western world—and much of the non-Western world—during this time. All of them

COMPARATIVE ESSAY

From the Industrial Age to the Technological Age

SCIENCE & TECHNOLOGY

As many observers have noted, the world economy is in transition to a "postindustrial age" that is both increasingly global and technology-intensive. Since World War II, an array of technological changes—especially in transportation, communications, medicine, and agriculture—have transformed the world. These changes have also raised new questions and concerns. Some scientists worry that genetic engineering might accidentally result in new strains of deadly bacteria. Some doctors warn that the overuse of antibiotics has created supergerms that are resistant to antibiotic treatment. Technological advances have also led to more deadly methods of destruction, including nuclear weapons.

The advent of the postindustrial world, which the futurologist Alvin Toffler has dubbed the Third Wave (the first two being the Agricultural and Industrial Revolutions), has led to difficulties for many people. They include blue-collar workers, whose jobs have disappeared as factories have moved abroad to use lower-cost labor; the poor and uneducated, who lack the technical skills to handle complex tasks; and even members of the middle class,

who have lost their jobs as employers outsource jobs to compete in the global marketplace.

It is now increasingly clear that the Technological Revolution, like the Industrial Revolution that preceded it, will entail enormous consequences. The success of advanced capitalist states in the postwar era has been built on a consensus on the importance of two propositions: (1) the need for high levels of government investment in education, communications, and transportation and (2) the desirability of maintaining open markets for the free exchange of goods.

Today, these assumptions are increasingly under attack as citizens refuse to vote for the tax increases required to support education and oppose the formation of trading alliances to promote the free movement of goods and labor across national borders. The breakdown of the public consensus raises serious questions about whether the coming challenges of the Third Wave can be successfully met without a rise in political and social tension.

© Adastra/Getty Images

The Technological Age. A communication satellite is seen orbiting above the earth.

 What is implied by the term Third Wave, and what challenges does the Third Wave present to humanity?

originated in the United States, and all are rooted in African American musical innovations. These forms later spread to the rest of the world, inspiring local artists, who then transformed the music in their own ways.

The introduction of the video music channel MTV in the early 1980s radically changed the music scene by making image as important as sound in the selling of records. Artists like Michael Jackson and Madonna became superstars by treating the music video as an art form. Rather than merely a recorded performance, many videos were short films with elaborate staging and special effects set to music.

In the postwar years, sports have become a major product of both popular culture and the leisure industry. Satellite television and various electronic breakthroughs have helped make sports a global phenomenon. Olympic Games can now be broadcast around the globe from anywhere in the world. In 2010, approximately 715 million people, or one out of every ten people in the world, watched the World Cup championship match. Sports have become a cheap form of entertainment, as fans do not have to leave their homes to enjoy athletic competitions. Many sports now receive the bulk of their yearly revenue from television contracts.

CHAPTER SUMMARY

Western Europe reinvented itself in the 1950s and 1960s as a remarkable economic recovery fostered a new optimism. Western European states embraced political democracy, and with the development of the European Community, many of them began to move toward economic unity. A new European society also emerged after World War II. White-collar workers increased in number, and installment plan buying helped create a consumer society. The welfare state provided both pensions and health care. Birth control led to smaller families, and more women joined the workforce.

Although many people were optimistic about a "new world order" after the collapse of communism, uncertainties still prevailed. Germany was successfully reunited, and the European Union adopted a common currency in the euro. Yugoslavia, however, disintegrated into warring states that eventually all became independent, and ethnic groups that had once been forced to live under distinct national banners began rebelling to form autonomous states. Although some were successful, others were brutally repressed.

In the Western Hemisphere, the United States and Canada built prosperous economies and relatively stable

communities in the 1950s, but there, too, new problems, including ethnic, racial, and linguistic differences, along with economic difficulties, dampened the optimism of earlier decades. Although some Latin American nations shared in the economic growth of the 1950s and 1960s, it was not accompanied by political stability. Not until the 1980s did democratic governments begin with consistency to replace oppressive military regimes.

While the "new world order" was fitfully developing, other challenges emerged. The arrival of many foreigners, especially in Western Europe, not only strained the social services of European countries but also led to anti-foreign sentiment. Environmental abuses led to growing threats not only to Europeans but also to all humans. Terrorism, especially that perpetrated by some parts of the Muslim world, emerged as a threat to many Western states. Since the end of World War II, terrorism seems to have replaced communism as the number one enemy of the West. At the beginning of the twenty-first century, a major realization has been the recognition that the problems afflicting the Western world have become global problems.

CHAPTER TIMELINE

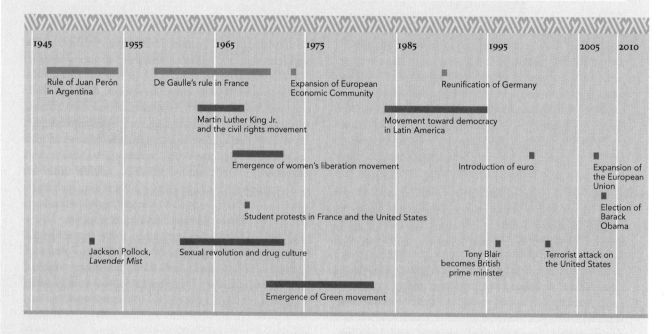

Upon Reflection

Q What were the major successes and failures of the Western European democracies between 1945 and 2010?

Q What directions did Eastern European nations take after they became free from Soviet control? Why did they react as they did?

Q What role did popular culture play in the Western world after 1945?

Key Terms

welfare state (p. 736)
ethnic cleansing (p. 738)
consumer society (p. 747)
permissive society (p. 748)
women's liberation movement (p. 749)
guest workers (p. 751)
existentialism (p. 752)
Postmodernism (p. 754)
Poststructuralism, or deconstruction (p. 754)
Abstract Expressionism (p. 754)

Suggested Reading

EUROPE SINCE 1945 For a well-written survey on Europe since 1945, see **T. Judt,** *Postwar: A History of Europe Since 1945* (New York, 2005). See also **W. I. Hitchcock,** *The Struggle for Europe: The Turbulent History of a Divided Continent, 1945–2002* (New York, 2002). On the building of common institutions in Western Europe, see **S. Henig,** *The Uniting of Europe: From Discord to Concord* (London, 1997). On Eastern Europe, see **P. Kenney,** *The Burden of Freedom: Eastern Europe Since 1989* (London, 2006).

THE UNITED STATES AND CANADA For a general survey of U.S. history since 1945, see **W. H. Chafe,** *Unfinished Journey: America Since World War II* (Oxford, 2006). More detailed accounts can be found in two volumes by **J. T. Patterson** in the Oxford History of the United States series: *Grand Expectations: The United States, 1945–1974* (Oxford, 1997) and *Restless Giant: The United States from Watergate to Bush v. Gore* (Oxford, 2005). Information on Canada can be found in **C. Brown, ed.,** *The Illustrated History of Canada,* 4th ed. (Toronto, 2003).

LATIN AMERICA For general surveys of Latin American history, see **M. C. Eakin,** *The History of Latin America: Collision of Cultures* (New York, 2007), and **E. Bradford Burns** and **J. A. Charlip,** *Latin America: An Interpretive History,* 8th ed. (Upper Saddle River, N.J., 2007). The twentieth century is the focus of **T. E. Skidmore** and **P. H. Smith,** *Modem Latin America,* 6th ed. (Oxford, 2004).

SOCIETY IN THE WESTERN WORLD On the turbulent 1960s, see **A. Marwick,** *The Sixties: Social and Cultural Transformation in Britain, France, Italy, and the United States* (Oxford, 1999). On the sexual revolution of the 1960s, see **D. Allyn,** *Make Love, Not War: The Sexual Revolution—An Unfettered History* (New York, 2000).

The changing role of women is examined in **R. Rosen,** *The World Split Open: How the Modern Women's Movement Changed America* (New York, 2001). On terrorism, see **C. E. Simonsen** and **J. R. Spendlove,** *Terrorism Today: The Past, the Players, the Future,* 3rd ed. (Upper Saddle River, N.J., 2006). The problems of guest workers and immigrants are examined in **W. Laqueur,** *The Last Days of Europe: Epitaph for an Old Continent* (New York, 2007).

WESTERN CULTURE SINCE 1945 For a general view of postwar thought and culture, see **J. A. Winders,** *European Culture Since 1848: From Modern to Postmodern and Beyond,* rev. ed. (New York, 2001). On Postmodernism, see **C. Butler,** *Postmodernism: A Very Short Introduction* (Oxford, 2002). On the arts, see **A. Marwick,** *Arts in the West Since 1945* (Oxford, 2002).

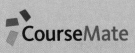

Visit the CourseMate website at www.cengagebrain.com for additional study tools and review materials for this chapter.

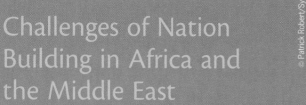
Challenges of Nation
Building in Africa and
the Middle East

© Patrick Robert/Sygma/CORBIS

Answering the call of the muezzin

CHAPTER OUTLINE AND FOCUS QUESTIONS

Uhuru: The Struggle for Independence in Africa

Q What role did nationalist movements play in the transition to independence in Africa, and how did such movements differ from their counterparts elsewhere?

The Era of Independence

Q How have dreams clashed with realities in the independent nations of Africa, and how have African governments sought to meet these challenges?

Continuity and Change in Modern African Societies

Q How did the rise of independent states affect the lives and the role of women in African societies? How does that role compare with the role played by women in other parts of the contemporary world?

Crescent of Conflict

Q What problems have the nations of the Middle East faced since the end of World War II, and to what degree have they managed to resolve those problems?

Society and Culture in the Contemporary Middle East

Q How have religious issues affected economic, social, and cultural conditions in the Middle East in recent decades?

CRITICAL THINKING

Q What factors can be advanced to explain the chronic instability and internal conflict that have characterized conditions in Africa and the Middle East since World War II?

BY THE END OF World War II, many societies in Asia and Africa had endured more than half a century of colonial rule. Although Europeans complacently assumed that colonialism was a necessary step in the process of introducing civilization to "backward" peoples around the globe, many of their colonial subjects disagreed. Some even argued that the Western drive for political hegemony and economic profit, far from being a panacea for the world's ills, was a plague that threatened ultimately to destroy human civilization.

One of the aspects of Western civilization that some thoughtful Asians and Africans rejected was the concept of the nation-state as the natural unit of communal identity in the modern world. In their view, nationalism was at the root of many of the evils of the twentieth century and should be abandoned as a model for development in the postwar period. In Africa, some intellectuals pointed to the traditional village community as a unique symbol of the humanistic and spiritual qualities of the people; they felt that the village might serve as a common bond that would knit all the peoples of the continent into a cohesive African community. The nation-state was similarly repudiated by some observers in the Middle East, where many Muslims viewed Western materialist culture as a threat to the fundamental principles of Islam. To fend off the new threat from their old adversary, some leaders dreamed of resurrecting the concept of a global caliphate (see Chapter 7) to unify all Muslim peoples and allow them to pursue their common destiny throughout the Islamic world.

Time has not been kind to such dreams of transnational solidarity and cooperation in the postwar world. Although the peoples of Africa and the Middle East were gradually liberated from the formal trappings of European authority, most political elites in both regions adopted the model of the nation-state with enthusiasm. The results have been mixed, and sometimes costly. Political inexperience and continued European economic domination have frustrated efforts to achieve political stability. At the same time, arbitrary boundaries imposed by the colonial powers, in combination with ethnic and religious divisions, have led to bitter conflicts that undermine attempts to realize the dream of solidarity and cooperation. Today, these two regions, although blessed with enormous potential, are among the most volatile and conflict-ridden areas in the world.

Uhuru: The Struggle for Independence in Africa

Q **FOCUS QUESTION:** What role did nationalist movements play in the transition to independence in Africa, and how did such movements differ from their counterparts elsewhere?

In the three decades following the end of World War II, the peoples of Africa were gradually liberated from the formal trappings of European colonialism.

The Colonial Legacy

As in Asia, colonial rule had a mixed impact on the societies and peoples of Africa (see Chapter 21). The Western presence brought a number of short-term and long-term benefits to Africa, such as improved transportation and communication facilities, and in a few areas laid the foundation for a modern industrial and commercial sector. Improved sanitation and medical care increased life expectancy. Yet the benefits of colonialism were distributed very unequally, and the vast majority of Africans found their lives little improved, if at all. Most Africans continued to be subsistence farmers growing food for their own consumption. Only South Africa and French-held Algeria developed modern industrial sectors, extensive railroad networks, and modern communications systems. In both countries, European settlers were numerous, most investment capital for industrial ventures was European, and whites constituted almost the entire professional and managerial class. Members of the indigenous population were generally restricted to unskilled or semiskilled jobs at wages less than one-fifth those enjoyed by Europeans.

The Rise of Nationalism

Political organizations for African rights did not arise until after World War I, and then only in a few areas, such as British-ruled Kenya and the Gold Coast. After World War II, following the example of independence movements elsewhere, groups organized political parties with independence as their objective. In the Gold Coast, Kwame Nkrumah (KWAH-may en-KROO-muh) (1909–1972) led the Convention People's Party, the first formal political party in black Africa. In the late 1940s, Jomo Kenyatta (JOH-moh ken-YAHT-uh) (1894–1978) founded the Kenya African National Union (KANU), which focused on economic issues but had an implied political agenda as well.

For the most part, these political activities were basically nonviolent and were led by Western-educated African intellectuals. Their constituents were primarily urban professionals, merchants, and members of labor unions. But the demand for independence was not entirely restricted to the cities. In Kenya, for example, the widely publicized Mau Mau (MOW MOW ["ow" as in "how"]) movement among the Kikuyu (ki-KOO-yoo) people used guerrilla tactics as an essential element of its program to achieve *uhuru* (oo-HOO-roo) (Swahili for "freedom") from the British. Although most of the violence was directed against other Africans, the specter of a nationwide revolt alarmed the European population and convinced the British government in 1959 to promise eventual independence.

In areas such as South Africa and Algeria, where the political system was dominated by European settlers, the transition to independence was equally complicated. In South Africa, political activity by local Africans began with the formation of the African National Congress (ANC) in 1912. Initially, the ANC was dominated by

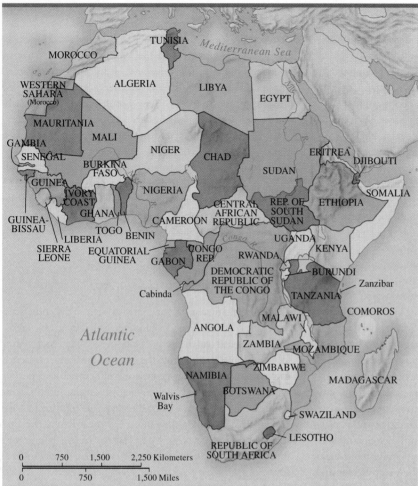

MAP 29.1 Modern Africa. This map shows the independent states in Africa today.

Q *Why was unity so difficult to achieve in African regions?*

Ahmad Ben Bella (AH-muhd ben BELL-uh) (1918–2004) in 1962. The armed struggle in Algeria hastened the transition to statehood in its neighbors as well. Tunisia won its independence in 1956 after some urban agitation and rural unrest but retained close ties with Paris. The French attempted to suppress the nationalist movement in Morocco by sending Sultan Muhammad V into exile, but the effort failed; in 1956, he returned as the ruler of the independent state of Morocco.

Most black African nations achieved their independence in the late 1950s and 1960s, beginning with the Gold Coast, now renamed Ghana, in 1957 (see Map 29.1). It was soon followed by Nigeria; the Belgian Congo, renamed Zaire (zah-EER) and then the Democratic Republic of the Congo; Kenya; Tanganyika (tang-an-YEE-kuh), later joined with Zanzibar (ZAN-zi-bar) and renamed Tanzania (tan-zuh-NEE-uh); and several other countries. Most of the French colonies agreed to accept independence within the framework of de Gaulle's French Community. By the late 1960s, only parts of southern Africa and the Portuguese possessions of Mozambique and Angola remained under European rule.

Western-oriented intellectuals and had limited mass support. Its goal was to achieve economic and political reforms, including full equality for educated Africans, within the framework of the existing system. But the ANC's efforts met with little success, while conservative white parties managed to stiffen the segregation laws and impose a policy of full legal segregation, called **apartheid** (uh-PAHRT-hyt), in 1948. In response, the ANC became increasingly radicalized, and by the 1950s, the prospects for a violent confrontation were growing.

In Algeria, resistance to French rule by Berbers and Arabs in rural areas had never ceased. After World War II, urban agitation intensified, leading to a widespread rebellion in the mid-1950s. At first, the French government tried to maintain its authority in Algeria. But when Charles de Gaulle became president in 1958, he reversed French policy, and Algeria became independent under President

The Era of Independence

Q FOCUS QUESTION: How have dreams clashed with realities in the independent nations of Africa, and how have African governments sought to meet these challenges?

The newly independent African states faced intimidating challenges. Although Western political institutions, values, and technology had been introduced, at least in the cities, the exposure to European civilization had been superficial at best for most Africans and tragic for many. At the outset of independence, most African societies were still primarily agrarian and traditional, and their modern sectors depended mainly on imports from the West.

The Destiny of Africa: Unity or Diversity?

Like their counterparts in South and Southeast Asia, most African leaders came from the urban middle class. They had studied in either Europe or the United States and spoke and read European languages. Although most were profoundly critical of colonial policies, they appeared to accept the relevance of the Western model to Africa and gave at least lip service to Western democratic values.

Their views on economics were somewhat more diverse. Some, like Jomo Kenyatta of Kenya and General Mobutu Sese Seko (moh-BOO-too SES-ay SEK-oh) (1930–1997) of Zaire, were advocates of Western-style capitalism. Others, like Julius Nyerere (ny-REHR-ee) (1922–1999) of Tanzania, Kwame Nkrumah of Ghana, and Sekou Touré (say-KOO too-RAY) (1922–1984) of Guinea, preferred an "African form of socialism," which bore slight resemblance to the Marxist-Leninist socialism practiced in the Soviet Union. According to its advocates, it was descended from traditional communal practices in precolonial Africa.

At first, most of the new African leaders accepted the national boundaries established during the colonial era. But as we have seen, these boundaries were artificial creations of the colonial powers. Virtually all of the new states included widely diverse ethnic, linguistic, and territorial groups. Zaire, for example, was composed of more than two hundred territorial groups speaking seventy-five different languages. Such conditions posed a severe challenge to the task of forming cohesive nation-states.

A number of leaders—including Nkrumah of Ghana, Touré of Guinea, and Nyerere of Tanganyika—were enticed by **pan-Africanism**, the concept of a continental unity that transcended national boundaries. Nkrumah in particular hoped that a pan-African union could be established that would unite all of the new countries of the continent in a broader community. His dream was not widely shared by other African political figures, however, who eventually settled on a more innocuous concept of regional cooperation on key issues. The concrete manifestation of this idea was the Organization of African Unity (OAU), founded in Addis Ababa (AH-diss AH-bah-buh) in 1963.

Dream and Reality: Political and Economic Conditions in Independent Africa

The program of the OAU called for an Africa based on freedom, equality, justice, and dignity and on the unity, solidarity, prosperity, and territorial integrity of African states. It did not take long for reality to set in. Vast disparities in education and wealth made it hard to establish material prosperity in much of Africa. Expectations that independence would lead to stable political structures based on "one person, one vote" were soon disappointed as the initial phase of pluralistic governments gave way to a series of military regimes and one-party states. Between 1957 and 1982, more than seventy leaders of African countries were overthrown by violence, and the pace has not abated in recent years.

THE PROBLEM OF NEOCOLONIALISM Part of the problem could be (and was) ascribed to the lingering effects of colonialism. Most new countries in Africa were dependent on the export of a single crop or natural resource. When prices fluctuated or dropped, these countries were at the mercy of the vagaries of the international market. In several cases, the resources were still controlled by foreigners, leading to the charge that colonialism had been succeeded by **neocolonialism**, in which Western domination was maintained primarily by economic rather than by political or military means. To make matters worse, most African states had to import technology and manufactured goods from the West, and the prices of those goods rose more rapidly than those of the export products.

The new states contributed to their own problems. Scarce national resources were squandered on military equipment or expensive consumer goods rather than used to create the infrastructure needed to provide the foundation for an industrial economy. Corruption, a painful reality throughout the modern world, became almost a way of life in Africa as bribery became necessary to obtain even the most basic services (see the box on p. 764).

AFRICA IN THE COLD WAR Many of the problems encountered by the new nations of Africa were also ascribed to the fact that independence did not bring an end to Western interference in Africa's political affairs. Many African leaders were angered when Western powers led by the United States conspired to overthrow the left-leaning politician Patrice Lumumba (put-TREES loo-MOOM-buh) (1925–1961) in the Congo in the early 1960s. Lumumba, who had been educated in the Soviet Union, aroused fears in Washington that he might promote Soviet influence in Central Africa (see Chapter 26). Eventually, he was assassinated under mysterious circumstances.

The episode was a major factor influencing African leaders to form the OAU as a means of reducing Western influence on the continent, but the strategy achieved few results. Although many African leaders agreed to adopt a neutral stance in the Cold War, competition between Moscow and Washington throughout the region was fierce, often undermining the efforts of fragile

Stealing the Nation's Riches

After 1965, African novelists transferred their anger from the foreign oppressor to their own national leaders, deploring their greed, corruption, and inhumanity. One of the most pessimistic expressions of this betrayal of newly independent Africa is found in *The Beautiful Ones Are Not Yet Born*, a novel published by the Ghanaian author Ayi Kwei Armah (AY-yee KWAY AR-mah) in 1968. The author decried the government of Kwame Nkrumah and was unimpressed with the rumors of a military coup, which, he predicted, would simply replace the regime with a new despot and his entourage of "fat men." Ghana today has made significant progress in reducing the level of corruption.

Ayi Kwei Armah, *The Beautiful Ones Are Not Yet Born*

The net had been made in the special Ghanaian way that allowed the really big corrupt people to pass through it. A net to catch only the small, dispensable fellows, trying in their anguished blindness to leap and to attain the gleam and the comfort the only way these things could be done. And the big ones floated free, like all the slogans. End bribery and corruption. Build Socialism. Equality. Shit. A man would just have to make up his mind that there was never going to be anything but despair, and there would be no way of escaping it. . . .

In the life of the nation itself, maybe nothing really new would happen. New men would take into their hands the power to steal the nation's riches and to use it for their own satisfaction. That, of course, was to be expected. New people would use the country's power to get rid of men and women who talked a language that did not flatter them. There would be nothing different in that. That would only be a continuation of the Ghanaian way of life. But here was the real change. The individual man of power now shivering, his head filled with the fear of the vengeance of those he had wronged. For him everything was going to change. And for those like him who had grown greasy and fat singing the praises of their chief, for those who had been getting themselves ready for the enjoyment of hoped-for favors, there would be long days of pain ahead. The flatterers with their new white Mercedes cars would have to find ways of burying old words. For those who had come directly against the old power, there would be much happiness. But for the nation itself there would only be a change of embezzlers and a change of the hunters and the hunted. A pitiful shrinking of the world from those days Teacher still looked back to, when the single mind was filled with the hopes of a whole people. A pitiful shrinking, to days when all the powerful could think of was to use the power of a whole people to fill their own paunches. Endless days, same days, stretching into the future with no end anywhere in sight.

 According to Ayi Kwei Armah, who was to blame for conditions in his country? Could the OAU have dealt with situations such as this? Why or why not?

Source: From *The Beautiful Ones Are Not Yet Born* by Ayi Kwei Armah (Heinemann, 1989).

---

governments to build stable new nations. To make matters worse, African states had difficulty achieving a united position on many issues, and their disagreements left the region vulnerable to external influence and conflict. Border disputes festered in many areas of the continent, and in some cases—as with Morocco and a rebel movement in Western Sahara and between Kenya and Uganda—flared into outright war. In Central Africa, the ambition of Libyan president Muammar Qaddafi (moo-AHM-ahr guh-DAH-fee) (1942–2011) to create a greater Muslim nation in the Sahara led to conflict with neighboring Chad.

THE POPULATION BOMB Finally, rapid population growth crippled efforts to create modern economies. By the 1980s, annual population growth averaged nearly 3 percent throughout Africa, the highest rate of any continent. Drought conditions and the inexorable spread of the Sahara (usually known as *desertification*, caused partly by overcultivation of the land) led to widespread hunger and starvation, first in West African countries such as Niger and Mali and then in Ethiopia, Somalia, and Sudan.

Predictions are that the population of Africa will increase by at least 200 million over the next ten years, but that estimate does not take into account the prevalence of AIDS, which has reached epidemic proportions in Africa. According to a United Nations study, at least 5 percent of the entire population of sub-Saharan Africa is infected with the virus, including a high percentage of the urban middle class. More than 65 percent of the AIDS cases reported around the world are on the continent of Africa. Some observers estimate that without measures to curtail the effects of the disease, it will have a significant impact on several African countries by reducing population growth.

Poverty is widespread in Africa, particularly among the three-quarters of the population still living off the land. Urban areas have grown tremendously, but as in much of Asia, most are surrounded by massive squatter settlements of rural peoples who have fled to the cities in search of a better life. The expansion of the cities has overwhelmed fragile transportation and sanitation systems and led to rising pollution and perpetual traffic jams, while millions are forced to live without running water and electricity. Meanwhile, the fortunate few (all too often government officials on the take) live the high life and emulate the consumerism of the West (in a particularly expressive phrase, the rich in many East African countries are known as *wabenzi*, or "Mercedes-Benz people").

The Search for Solutions

While the problems of nation building described here have to one degree or another afflicted all of the emerging states of Africa, each has sought to deal with the challenge in its own way, sometimes with strikingly different consequences. Some African countries have made dramatic improvements in the past two decades, but others have encountered increasing difficulties. Despite all its shared problems, Africa today remains one of the most diverse regions of the globe.

TANZANIA: AN AFRICAN ROUTE TO SOCIALISM Concern over the dangers of economic inequality inspired a number of African leaders to restrict foreign investment and nationalize the major industries and utilities while promoting democratic ideals and values. Julius Nyerere of Tanzania was the most consistent, promoting the ideals of socialism and self-reliance through his Arusha (uh-ROO-shuh) Declaration of 1967, which set forth the principles for building a socialist society in Africa. Nyerere did not seek to establish a Leninist-style dictatorship of the proletariat in Tanzania, but neither was he a proponent of a multiparty democracy, which in his view would be divisive under the conditions prevailing in Africa:

> Where there is one party—provided it is identified with the nation as a whole—the foundations of democracy can be firmer, and the people can have more opportunity to exercise a real choice, than when you have two or more parties.

To import the Western parliamentary system into Africa, he argued, could lead to violence, since the opposition parties would be viewed as traitors by the majority of the population.[1]

Taking advantage of his powerful political influence, Nyerere placed limitations on income and established village collectives to avoid the corrosive effects of economic inequality and government corruption. Sympathetic foreign countries provided considerable economic aid to assist the experiment, and many observers noted that levels of corruption, political instability, and ethnic strife were lower in Tanzania than in many other African countries. Nyerere's vision was not shared by all of his compatriots, however. Political elements on the island of Zanzibar, citing the stagnation brought by two decades of socialism, agitated for autonomy or even total separation from the mainland. Tanzania also has poor soil, inadequate rainfall, and limited resources, all of which have contributed to its slow growth and continuing rural and urban poverty.

In 1985, Nyerere voluntarily retired from the presidency. In his farewell speech, he confessed that he had failed to achieve many of his ambitious goals to create a socialist society in Africa. But Nyerere insisted that many of his policies had succeeded in improving social and economic conditions, and he argued that the only real solution was to consolidate the multitude of small countries in the region into a larger East African Federation. Today, a quarter of a century later, Nyerere's Party of the Revolution continues to rule the country. The current president, Jakaya Kikwete (jah-KAH-yah kee-KWEH-tee) (b. 1950), was reelected in 2010 by a comfortable margin, although there were charges of electoral fraud.

KENYA: THE PERILS OF CAPITALISM The countries that opted for capitalism faced their own dilemmas. Neighboring Kenya, blessed with better soil in the highlands, a local tradition of aggressive commerce, and a residue of European settlers, welcomed foreign investment and profit incentives. The results have been mixed. Kenya has a strong current of indigenous African capitalism and a substantial middle class, mostly based in the capital, Nairobi (ny-ROH-bee). But landlessness, unemployment, and income inequities are high, even by African standards. The rate of population growth—about 2.5 percent annually—is one of the highest in the world. Almost 80 percent of the population remains rural, and 50 percent of the people live below the poverty line.

Kenya's problems have been exacerbated by chronic disputes between disparate ethnic groups and simmering tensions between farmers and pastoralists. For many years, the country maintained a fragile political stability under the dictatorial rule of President Daniel arap Moi (uh-RHAP moh-YEE) (b. 1924), one of the most authoritarian of African leaders. Plagued by charges of corruption, Moi finally agreed to retire in 2002, but under his successor, Mwai Kibaki (MWY kih-BAH-kee) (b. 1931), the twin problems of political instability and widespread poverty continue to afflict the country. When presidential elections held in 2008 led to a victory for Kibaki's party, opposition elements—angered by the government's perceived favoritism toward Kibaki's Kikuyu constituents—launched numerous protests, and violent riots occurred throughout the country. A fragile truce was eventually put in place, but popular anger at current conditions smolders just beneath the surface.

SOUTH AFRICA: AN END TO APARTHEID Perhaps Africa's greatest success story is South Africa. Under strong international pressure, the white government—which had long maintained a policy of racial segregation (apartheid) and restricted black sovereignty to a series of small "Bantustans" in relatively infertile areas of the country—finally accepted the inevitability of African involvement in the political process and the national economy. In 1990, the government of President Frederik W. de Klerk (b. 1936) released African National Congress leader Nelson Mandela (man-DELL-uh) (b. 1918) from prison, where he had been held since 1964. In 1993, the two leaders agreed to hold democratic national elections the following spring. In the meantime, ANC representatives agreed to take part in a transitional coalition government with de Klerk's National Party. Those elections resulted in a substantial majority for the ANC, and Mandela became president. In May 1996, a new constitution was approved, calling for a multiracial state.

In 1999, a major step toward political stability was taken when Mandela stepped down from the presidency, to be replaced by his long-time disciple Thabo Mbeki (TAH-boh uhm-BAY-kee) (b. 1942). The new president faced a number of intimidating problems, including rising unemployment, widespread lawlessness, chronic corruption, and an ominous flight of capital and professional personnel from the country. Mbeki's conservative economic policies earned the support of some white voters and the country's new black elite but were criticized by labor unions, which contended that the benefits of the new black leadership were not seeping down to the poor. The government's promises to carry out an extensive land reform program—aimed at providing farmland to the nation's 40 million black farmers—were not fulfilled, provoking some squatters to seize unused private lands near Johannesburg. In 2008, disgruntled ANC members forced Mbeki out of office. A year later, his onetime vice president and rival Jacob Zuma (ZOO-muh) (b. 1942) was elected president.

South Africa remains the wealthiest and most industrialized state in Africa and the best hope that a multiracial society can succeed on the continent. The country's black elite now number nearly one-quarter of its wealthiest households, compared with only 9 percent in 1991 (see the comparative illustration on p. 767).

NIGERIA: A NATION DIVIDED If the situation in South Africa provides grounds for modest optimism, the situation in Nigeria provides reason for serious concern. Africa's largest country in terms of population and one of its wealthiest because of substantial oil reserves, Nigeria was for many years in the grip of military strongmen. During his rule, General Sani Abacha (SAH-nee ah-BAH-chuh) (1943–1998) ruthlessly suppressed all opposition and in late 1995 ordered the execution of a writer despite widespread protests from human rights groups abroad. Ken Saro-Wiwa (SAH-roh WEE-wah) (1941–1995) had criticized environmental damage caused by foreign interests in southern Nigeria. When Abacha died in 1998 under mysterious circumstances, national elections led to the creation of a civilian government under Olusegun Obasanjo (ohl-OO-seh-goon oh-buh-SAHN-joh) (b. 1937).

Civilian leadership has not been a panacea for Nigeria's problems, however. Although Obasanjo promised reforms to bring an end to the corruption and favoritism that had long plagued Nigerian politics, the results were disappointing (the state power company—known as NEPA—was so inefficient that Nigerians joked that the initials stood for "never expect power again"). When presidential elections in 2007 led to the election of Umaru Yar'Adua (oo-MAHR-oo YAHR-ah-doo-uh) (b. 1951–2010), an obscure member of Obasanjo's ruling political party, opposition forces and neutral observers complained that the vote had been seriously flawed. After Yar'Adua died from an illness in 2010, he was succeeded by his vice president, Goodluck Jonathan (b. 1957), who was elected president in his own right in 2011.

One of the most critical problems facing the Nigerian government in recent years has its roots in religious disputes. In early 2000, riots between Christians and Muslims broke out in several northern cities as a result of the decision by Muslim provincial officials to apply *Shari'a* throughout their jurisdictions. The violence temporarily abated as local officials managed to craft compromise policies that limited the application of some of the harsher aspects of Muslim law, but periodic clashes between Christians and Muslims continue to threaten the fragile unity of Africa's most populous country.

TENSIONS IN THE DESERT The religious tensions that erupted in Nigeria have spilled over into neighboring states on the border of the Sahara. In the neighboring

© William J. Duiker

© William J. Duiker

COMPARATIVE ILLUSTRATION

FAMILY & SOCIETY

New Housing for the Poor.
Under apartheid, much of the black population in South Africa was confined to so-called townships, squalid slums located along the fringes of the country's major cities. The top photo shows a crowded township on the edge of Cape Town, one of the most modern cities on the continent of Africa. Today, the government is actively building new communities that provide better housing, running water, and electricity for their residents. The photo on the bottom shows a new township on the outskirts of the city of New London. The township has many modern facilities and even a new shopping mall with consumer goods for local residents.

Q *How do the social and economic policies adopted by the current South African government compare with those practiced by the previous ruling class operating under the rule of apartheid?*

state of Mali, a radical Islamic group has seized power in the northern part of the country, applying strict punishments on local residents for alleged infractions against *Shari'a* law and destroying Muslim shrines in the historic city of Timbuktu.

A similar rift has been at the root of the lengthy civil war that has been raging in Sudan. Conflict between Muslim pastoralists—supported by the central government in Khartoum—and predominantly Christian black farmers in the southern part of the country raged for years until the government finally agreed to permit a plebiscite in the south under the sponsorship of the United Nations to determine whether the local population there wished to secede from the country. In elections held in early 2011, voters overwhelmingly

supported independence as the new nation of the Republic of South Sudan, but clashes along the disputed border continue to provoke tensions.

The dispute between Muslims and Christians throughout the southern Sahara is a contemporary African variant of the traditional tensions that have existed between farmers and pastoralists throughout recorded history. Muslim cattle herders, migrating southward to escape the increasing desiccation of the grasslands south of the Sahara, compete for precious land with primarily Christian farmers. As a result of the religious revival now under way throughout the continent, the confrontation often leads to outbreaks of violence with strong religious and ethnic overtones (see the comparative essay "Religion and Society" on p. 769).

CENTRAL AFRICA: CAULDRON OF CONFLICT The most tragic situation is in the Central African states of Rwanda and Burundi, where a chronic conflict between the minority Tutsis and the Hutu majority has led to a bitter civil war, with thousands of refugees fleeing to the neighboring Congo. The nomadic Tutsis, supported by the colonial Belgian government, had long dominated the sedentary Hutu population. It was the attempt of the Hutus to bring an end to Tutsi domination that initiated the most recent conflicts, marked by massacres on both sides. In the meantime, the presence of large numbers of foreign troops and refugees intensified centrifugal forces inside Zaire, where General Mobutu Sese Seko had long ruled with an iron hand. In 1997, military forces led by Mobutu's longtime opponent Laurent-Désiré Kabila (loh-RAHN-DAY-zee-ray kah-BEE-luh) (1939–2001) managed to topple the general's corrupt government. Once in power, Kabila renamed the country the Democratic Republic of the Congo and promised a return to democratic practices. The new government systematically suppressed political dissent, however, and in January 2001, Kabila was assassinated. He was succeeded by his son, Joseph Kabila (b. 1971). Peace talks to end the conflict began that fall, but the fighting has continued. In elections held in the fall of 2011, Kabila was returned to office after a campaign marked by widespread violence.

Africa: A Continent in Flux

The brief survey of events in some of the more important African countries provided here illustrates the enormous difficulty that historians of Africa face in drawing any general conclusions about the pace and scope of change that has taken place in the continent in recent decades. Progress in some areas has been countered by growing problems elsewhere, and signs of hope in one region contrast with feelings of despair in another.

The shifting fortunes experienced throughout the continent are most prominently illustrated in the political arena. Over the past two decades, the collapse of one-party regimes has led to the emergence of fragile democracies in several countries. In other instances, however, democratic governments erupted in civil war or were replaced by authoritarian leaders. One prominent example of the latter is the Ivory Coast, long considered one of West Africa's most stable and prosperous countries. After the death of President Félix Houphouet-Boigny (fay-LEEKS oo-FWAY-

Morning in Timbuktu. The boundary between pastoral and agricultural peoples—the steppe and the sown—has been one of the crucial fault lines in human history. Nowhere is this more true today than in West Africa, where Muslim herders compete with Christian farmers for precious land and water resources. The dispute is at the root of the ethnic and religious conflicts that are now erupting throughout the region. In this photo, a pastoral family greets the new day just outside the historic city of Timbuktu, in the state of Mali.

© Ruth Petzold

COMPARATIVE ESSAY

Religion and Society

RELIGION & PHILOSOPHY

The nineteenth and twentieth centuries witnessed a steady trend toward secularization as people increasingly turned from religion to science for explanations of natural phenomena and for answers to the challenges of everyday life.

In recent years, however, the trend has reversed as religious faith in all its guises appears to be reviving in much of the world. Although the percentage of people regularly attending religious services or professing firm religious convictions has been dropping steadily in many countries, the intensity of religious belief appears to be growing among the faithful. This phenomenon has been widely publicized in the United States, where the evangelical movement has become a significant force in politics and an influential factor in defining many social issues. But it has also occurred in Latin America, where a drop in membership in the Roman Catholic Church has been offset by significant increases in the popularity of evangelical Protestant sects. In the Muslim world, the influence of traditional Islam has been steadily rising, not only in the Middle East but also in non-Arab countries such as Malaysia and Indonesia (see Chapter 30). In Africa, as we observe in this chapter, the appeal of both Christianity and Islam appears to be on the rise. Even in Russia and China, where half a century of Communist government sought to eradicate religion as the "opiate of the people," the popularity of religion is growing.

A major reason for the popularity of religion in contemporary life is the desire to counter the widespread sense of malaise brought on by the absence of any sense of meaning and purpose in life—a purpose that religious faith provides. For many evangelical Christians in the United States, for example,

the adoption of a Christian lifestyle is seen as a necessary prerequisite for resolving problems of crime, drugs, and social alienation. It is likely that a similar phenomenon is present with other religions and in other parts of the world. Religious faith also provides a sense of community at a time when village and family ties are declining in many countries.

Historical evidence suggests, however, that although religious fervor may enhance the sense of community and commitment among believers, it can have a highly divisive impact on society as a whole, as the examples of Northern Ireland, Yugoslavia, Africa, and the Middle East vividly attest. Even if less dramatically, as in the United States and Latin America, religion divides as well as unites, and it will be a continuing task for religious leaders of all faiths to promote tolerance for peoples of other persuasions.

Another challenge for contemporary religion is to find ways to coexist with expanding scientific knowledge. Influential figures in the evangelical movement in the United States, for example, not only support a conservative social agenda but are also suspicious of the role of technology and science in the contemporary world. Similar views are often expressed by significant factions in other world religions. Although fear of the impact of science on contemporary life is widespread, efforts to turn the clock back to a mythical golden age are not likely to succeed in the face of powerful forces for change set in motion by advances in scientific knowledge.

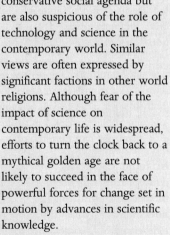

Carrying Food to the Temple. Bali is the only island in Indonesia where the local population adheres to the Hindu faith. Here worshipers carry food to the local temple to be blessed before being consumed.

 What are some of the reasons for the growing intensity of religious faith in many parts of the world today?

© William J. Duiker

---

bwah-NYEE) in 1993, long-simmering resentment between Christians in the south and newly arrived Muslim immigrants in the north erupted into open conflict. National elections held in 2010 led to sporadic violence

and a standoff between opposition forces and the sitting president, who was forced to resign the following year. By contrast, in Liberia, a bitter civil war recently gave way to the emergence of a stable democratic government under Ellen Johnson-Sirleaf (b. 1938), one of the continent's first female presidents.

The economic picture in Africa has also been mixed. Most African states are still poor and their populations illiterate. Moreover, African concerns continue to carry little weight in the international community. A recent agreement by the World Trade Organization (WTO) on the need to reduce agricultural subsidies in the advanced nations has been widely ignored. Some observers argue that external assistance cannot succeed unless the nations of Africa adopt measures to bring about good government and sound economic policies.

Despite the African continent's chronic economic problems, however, there are signs of hope. The overall rate of economic growth for the region as a whole is twice what it was during the 1980s and 1990s. African countries were also less affected by the recent economic downturn than was much of the rest of the world. Although poverty, AIDs, and a lack of education and infrastructure are still major impediments in much of the region, rising commodity prices—most notably, an increase in oil revenues—are enabling many countries to make additional investments and reduce their national debt.

THE AFRICAN UNION: A GLIMMER OF HOPE   A significant part of the problem is that Africans must find better ways to cooperate with one another and to protect and promote their own interests. A first step in that direction was taken in 1991, when the OAU agreed to establish the African Economic Community (AEC). In 2001, the OAU was replaced by the **African Union**, which is intended to provide greater political and economic integration throughout the continent on the pattern of the European Union (see Chapter 28). The new organization has already sought to mediate several of the conflicts in the region. As Africa evolves, it is useful to remember that economic and political change is often an agonizingly slow and painful process. Introduced to industrialization and concepts of Western democracy only a century ago, African societies are still groping for ways to graft Western political institutions and economic practices onto a structure still significantly influenced by traditional values and attitudes.

Continuity and Change in Modern African Societies

Q FOCUS QUESTIONS: How did the rise of independent states affect the lives and the role of women in African societies? How does that role compare with the role played by women in other parts of the contemporary world?

In general, the impact of the West has been greater on urban and educated Africans and more limited on their rural and illiterate compatriots. After all, the colonial presence was first and most firmly established in the cities. Many cities, including Dakar, Lagos, Johannesburg, Cape Town, Brazzaville, and Nairobi, are direct products of the colonial experience. Most African cities today look like their counterparts elsewhere in the world. They have high-rise buildings, blocks of residential apartments, wide boulevards, neon lights, movie theaters, and traffic jams.

Education

Europeans introduced modern Western education into Africa in the nineteenth century. At first, the schools concentrated on vocational training, with some instruction in European languages and Western civilization. Eventually, pressure from Africans led to the introduction of professional training, and the first institutes of higher learning were established in the early twentieth century.

With independence, African countries established their own state-run schools. The emphasis was on the primary level, but high schools and universities were established in major cities. The basic objectives have been to introduce vocational training and improve literacy rates. Unfortunately, both funding and trained teachers are scarce in most countries, and few rural areas have schools. As a result, illiteracy remains high, estimated at about 70 percent of the population across the continent. There has been a perceptible shift toward education in the vernacular languages. In West Africa, only about one in four adults is conversant in a Western language.

Urban and Rural Life

The cities are where the African elites live and work. Affluent Africans, like their contemporaries in other developing countries, have been strongly attracted to the glittering material aspects of Western culture. They live in Western-style homes or apartments and eat Western foods stored in Western refrigerators, and those who can afford it drive Western cars. It has been said, not wholly in praise, that there are more Mercedes-Benz automobiles in Nigeria than in Germany, where they are manufactured.

Outside the major cities, where about three-quarters of the continent's inhabitants live, Western influence has had less impact. Millions of people throughout Africa live much as their ancestors did, in thatch huts without modern plumbing and electricity; they farm or hunt by traditional methods, practice time-honored family rituals, and believe in the traditional deities. Even here, however, change is taking place. Slavery has been eliminated, for the most part, although there have been persistent reports of raids by slave traders on defenseless villages in the southern Sudan. Economic need, though, has

Learning the ABCs in Niger. Educating the young is one of the most crucial problems for many African societies today. Few governments are able to allocate the funds necessary to meet the challenge, so religious organizations—Muslim or Christian—often take up the slack. In this photo, students at a madrasa—a Muslim school designed to teach the Qur'an—are learning how to read Arabic, the language of Islam's holy scripture. Madrasas are one of the most prominent forms of schooling in Muslim societies in West Africa today.

brought about massive migrations as some leave to work on plantations, others move to the cities, and still others flee abroad or to refugee camps to escape starvation. Migration itself is a wrenching experience, disrupting familiar family and village ties and enforcing new social relationships.

African Women

As noted in Chapter 21, one of the consequences of colonialism in Africa was a change in the relationship between men and women. Some of these changes could be described as beneficial, but others were not. Women were often introduced to Western education and given legal rights denied to them in the precolonial era. But they also became a labor source and were sometime recruited or compelled to work on construction projects.

Independence has had a significant impact on gender roles in African society. Almost without exception, the new governments established the principle of sexual equality and permitted women to vote and run for political office. Yet as elsewhere, women continue to operate at a disability in a world dominated by males. Politics remains a male preserve, and although a few professions, such as teaching, child care, and clerical work, are dominated by women, most African women are employed in menial positions such as agricultural labor, factory work, and retail trade or as domestics. Education is open to all at the elementary level, but women comprise less than 20 percent of students at the upper levels in most African societies today.

URBAN WOMEN Not surprisingly, women have made the greatest strides in the cities. Most urban women, like men, now marry on the basis of personal choice, although a significant minority are still willing to accept their parents' choice. After marriage, African women appear to occupy a more equal position than their counterparts in most Asian countries. Each marriage partner tends to maintain a separate income, and women often have the right to possess property separate from their husbands. While many wives still defer to their husbands in the traditional manner, others are like the woman in Abioseh Nicol's story "A Truly Married Woman," who, after years of living as a common law wife with her husband, is finally able to provide the price and finalize the marriage. After the wedding, she declares, "For twelve years I have got up every morning at five to make tea for you and breakfast. Now I am a truly married woman [and] you must treat me with a little more respect. You are now my husband and not a lover. Get up and make yourself a cup of tea."[2]

WOMEN IN RURAL AREAS In rural areas, where traditional attitudes continue to exert a strong influence, individuals may still be subordinated to communalism. In some societies, female genital mutilation, the traditional rite of passage for a young girl's transit to womanhood, is still widely practiced. Polygamy is also not uncommon, and arranged marriages are still the rule rather than the exception. The dichotomy between rural and urban values can lead to acute tensions. Many African villagers regard the cities as the fount of evil, decadence, and corruption. Women in particular have suffered from the tension between the pull of the city and the village. As men are drawn to the cities in search of employment and excitement, their wives and girlfriends are left behind, both literally and figuratively, in the village.

African Culture

Inevitably, the tension between traditional and modern, indigenous and foreign, and individual and communal

Salt of the Earth. During the precolonial era, many West African societies were forced to import salt from Mediterranean countries in exchange for tropical products and gold. Today, the people of Senegal satisfy their domestic needs by mining salt deposits contained in lakes like this one in the interior of the country. These lakes are the remnants of vast seas that covered the region of the Sahara in prehistoric times. Note that women are doing much of the heavy labor while men hold the managerial positions.

that has permeated contemporary African society has spilled over into culture. In general, in the visual arts and music, utility and ritual have given way to pleasure and decoration. In the process, Africans have been affected to a certain extent by foreign influences but have retained their distinctive characteristics. Wood carving, metalwork, painting, and sculpture, for example, have preserved their traditional forms but are now increasingly adapted to serve the tourist industry and the export market.

LITERATURE Since independence, no area of African culture has been so strongly affected by political and social events as literature. Angry at the negative portrayal of Africa in Western literature, African authors initially wrote primarily for a European audience as a means of establishing black dignity and purpose. Many glorified the emotional and communal aspects of the traditional African experience (see the box on p. 773). The Nigerian Chinua Achebe (CHIN-wah ah-CHAY-bay) (b. 1930) is considered the first major African novelist to write in the English language. In his writings, he attempted to interpret African history from an African perspective and to forge a new sense of African identity. In his trailblazing novel *Things Fall Apart* (1958), he recounted the story of a Nigerian who refused to submit to the new British order

and eventually committed suicide. Criticizing his contemporaries who accepted foreign rule, the protagonist lamented that the white man "has put a knife on the things that held us together and we have fallen apart."

In recent decades, the African novel has taken a dramatic turn, shifting its focus from the brutality of the foreign oppressor to the shortcomings of the the continent's indigenous leaders. Having reaped the benefits of independence, African politicians are portrayed as mimicking and even outdoing the injustices committed by their colonial predecessors. A prominent example of this genre is the work of the Kenyan Ngugi Wa Thiong'o (GOO-gee wah tee-AHNG-goh) (b. 1938). His first novel, *A Grain of Wheat*, takes place on the eve of *uhuru*, or independence. Although it mocks the racism, snobbishness, and superficiality of local British society, its chief interest lies in its unsentimental and even unflattering portrayal of ordinary Kenyans in their daily struggle for survival.

Many of Ngugi's contemporaries have followed his lead and focused their frustration on the failure of the continent's new leadership to carry out the goals of independence (see the box on p. 764). One of the most outstanding is the Nigerian Wole Soyinka (woh-LAY soh-YEENK-kuh) (b. 1934). His novel *The Interpreters* (1965) lambasted the corruption and hypocrisy of Nigerian

OPPOSING ✕ VIEWPOINTS

Africa: Dark Continent or Radiant Land?

INTERACTION & EXCHANGE

Colonialism camouflaged its economic objectives under the cloak of a "civilizing mission," which in Africa was aimed at illuminating the so-called Dark Continent with Europe's brilliant civilization. In 1899, the Polish-born English author Joseph Conrad (1857–1924) fictionalized his harrowing journey up the Congo River in the novella *Heart of Darkness*. Conrad's protagonist, Marlow, travels upriver to locate a Belgian trader who has mysteriously disappeared. The novella describes Marlow's gradual recognition of the egregious excesses of colonial rule, as well as his realization that such evil lurks in everyone's heart. The story concludes with a cry: "The horror! The horror!" Voicing views that reflected his Victorian perspective, Conrad described an Africa that was incomprehensible, sensual, and primitive.

Over the years, Conrad's work has provoked much debate. Author Chinua Achebe, for one, lambasted *Heart of Darkness* as a radical diatribe. Since independence, many African writers have been prompted to counter Conrad's portrayal by reaffirming the dignity and purpose of the African people. One of the first to do so was the Guinean author Camara Laye (1928–1980), who in 1954 composed a brilliant novel, *The Radiance of the King*, which can be viewed as the mirror image of Conrad's *Heart of Darkness*. In Laye's work, Clarence, another European protagonist, undertakes a journey into the impenetrable heart of Africa. This time, however, he is enlightened by the process, thereby obtaining self-knowledge and ultimately salvation.

Joseph Conrad, *Heart of Darkness*

We penetrated deeper and deeper into the heart of darkness. It was very quiet there. At night sometimes the roll of drums behind the curtain of trees would run up the river and remain sustained faintly, as if hovering in the air high over our heads, till the first break of day.

Whether it meant war, peace, or prayer we could not tell. . . . But suddenly, as we struggled round a bend, there would be a glimpse of rush walls, of peaked grass-roofs, a burst of yells, a whirl of black limbs, a mass of hands clapping, of feet stamping, of bodies swaying, of eyes rolling, under the droop of heavy and motionless foliage. The steamer toiled along slowly on the edge of a black and incomprehensible frenzy. The prehistoric man was cursing us, praying to us, welcoming us—who could tell? We were cut off from the comprehension of our surroundings; we glided past like phantoms, wondering and secretly appalled, as sane men would be before an enthusiastic outbreak in a madhouse.

Camara Laye, *The Radiance of the King*

At that very moment the king turned his head, turned it imperceptibly, and his glance fell upon Clarence. . . .

"Yes, no one is as base as I, as naked as I," he thought. "And you, lord, you are willing to rest your eyes upon me!" Or was it because of his very nakedness? . . . "Because of your very nakedness!" the look seemed to say. "That terrifying void that is within you and which opens to receive me; your hunger which calls to my hunger; your very baseness which did not exist until I gave it leave; and the great shame you feel. . . ."

When he had come before the king, when he stood in the great radiance of the king, still ravaged by the tongue of fire, but alive still, and living only through the touch of that fire, Clarence fell upon his knees, for it seemed to him that he was finally at the end of his seeking, and at the end of all seekings.

Q Compare the depictions of the continent of Africa in these two passages. Is Laye making a response to Conrad? If so, what is it?

Sources: Joseph Conrad, *Heart of Darkness*. From *Heart of Darkness* by Joseph Conrad. Penguin Books, 1991. Camara Laye, *The Radiance of the King*. From *The Radiance of the King* by Camara Laye, translated from the French by James Kirkup. New York: Vintage, 1989.

politics. Succeeding novels and plays have continued that tradition, resulting in a Nobel Prize for Literature in 1986.

A number of Africa's most prominent writers today are women. Traditionally, African women were valued for their talents as storytellers, but writing was strongly discouraged by both traditional and colonial authorities on the grounds that women should occupy themselves with their domestic obligations. In recent years, however, a number of women have emerged as prominent writers of African fiction. One example is Ama Ata Aidoo (b. 1942) of Ghana, who has focused on the identity of today's African women and the changing relations between men and women in society. In her novel *Changes: A Love Story* (1991), she chronicles the lives of three women, none presented as a victim but all caught up in the struggle for survival and happiness.

What Is the Future of Africa?

Nowhere in the developing world is the dilemma of continuity and change more agonizing than in Africa. Mesmerized by the spectacle of Western affluence yet repulsed by the bloody trail from slavery to World War II and the atomic bombs over Hiroshima and Nagasaki, African intellectuals have been torn between the dual images of Western materialism and African uniqueness. For the average African, of course, such intellectual dilemmas pale before the daily challenge of survival. But the fundamental gap between traditional and modern is perhaps wider in Africa than anywhere else in the world and may well be harder to bridge.

What is the future of Africa? It seems almost foolhardy to seek an answer to such a question, given the degree of ethnic, linguistic, and cultural diversity that exists throughout the vast continent. Not surprisingly, visions of the future are equally diverse. Some Africans still yearn for the dreams embodied in the program of the OAU. Novelist Ngugi Wa Thiong'o calls for "an internationalization of all the democratic and social struggles for human equality, justice, peace, and progress."[3] Others have discarded the democratic ideal and turned their attention to systems based on the subordination of the individual to the community as the guiding principle of national development. Like all peoples, Africans must ultimately find their own solutions within the context of their own traditions, not by seeking to imitate the example of others.

Crescent of Conflict

 FOCUS QUESTION: What problems have the nations of the Middle East faced since the end of World War II, and to what degree have they managed to resolve those problems?

"We Muslims are of one family even though we live under different governments and in various regions."[4] So said Ayatollah Ruholla Khomeini (ah-yah-TUL-uh roo-HUL-uh khoh-MAY-nee), the Islamic religious figure and leader of the 1979 revolution that overthrew the shah in Iran. The ayatollah's remark was dismissed by some as just a pious wish by a religious mystic. In fact, however,

it illustrates a crucial aspect of the political dynamics in the region.

If the concept of cultural uniqueness represents an alternative to the system of nation-states in Africa, the desire for Muslim unity has played a similar role in the Middle East. In both regions, a yearning for a sense of community beyond national borders tugs at the emotions and intellect of their inhabitants.

A dramatic example of the powerful force of pan-Islamic sentiment took place on September 11, 2001, when Muslim militants hijacked four U.S. airliners and turned them into missiles aimed at the center of world capitalism. The headquarters of the terrorist network that carried out the attack—known as al-Qaeda and led by Osama bin Laden (see Chapter 28)—was located in Afghanistan, but the militants themselves came from several different Muslim states. Although moderate Muslims throughout the world condemned the attack, it was clear that bin Laden and his cohorts had tapped into a wellspring of hostility and resentment directed at much of the Western world.

What were the sources of Muslim anger? In a speech released on videotape shortly after the attack, bin Laden declared that the attacks were a response to the "humiliation and disgrace" that have afflicted the Islamic world for more than eighty years, a period dating back to the end of World War I. For the Middle East, the period between the two world wars was an era of transition. With the fall of the Ottoman and Persian Empires, new modernizing regimes emerged in Turkey and Iran, and a more traditionalist but fiercely independent government was established in Saudi Arabia. Elsewhere, however, European influence was on the ascendant; the British and French had mandates in Syria, Lebanon, Jordan, and Palestine, and British influence persisted in Iraq, in southern Arabia, and throughout the Nile valley.

During World War II, the Middle East became the cockpit of European rivalries, as it had been during World War I. The region was more significant to the warring powers than previously because of the growing importance of oil and the Suez Canal''s position as a vital sea route.

The Question of Palestine

The end of World War II led to the emergence of a number of independent states in the Middle East. Jordan, Lebanon, and Syria, all European mandates before the war, became independent. Egypt, Iran, and Iraq, though still under a degree of Western influence, became increasingly autonomous. Sympathy for the idea of Arab unity led to the formation of the Arab League in 1945, but different points of view among its members prevented it from achieving anything of substance.

The one issue on which all Muslim states in the area could agree was the question of Palestine. As tensions between Jews and Arabs in that mandate intensified during the 1930s, the British attempted to limit Jewish immigration into the area and firmly rejected proposals for independence, despite the promise made in the 1917 Balfour Declaration (see Chapter 24).

After World War II ended, the situation drifted rapidly toward crisis, as thousands of Jewish refugees, many of them from displaced persons camps in Europe, sought to migrate to Palestine despite British efforts to prevent their arrival. As violence between Muslims and Jews intensified in the fall of 1947, the issue was taken up in the United Nations General Assembly. After an intense debate, the assembly voted to approve the partition of Palestine into two separate states, one for the Jews and one for the Arabs. The city of Jerusalem was to be placed under international control. A UN commission was established to iron out the details and determine the future boundaries.

During the next several months, growing hostility between Jewish and Arab forces—the latter increasingly supported by neighboring Muslim states—caused the British to announce that they would withdraw their own peacekeeping forces by May 15, 1948. Shortly after the stroke of midnight, as the British mandate formally came to a close, the Zionist leader David Ben-Gurion (ben-GOOR-ee-uhn) (1886–1973) announced the independence of the state of Israel. Later that same day, the new state was formally recognized by the United States, while military forces from several neighboring Muslim states—all of which had vigorously opposed the formation of a Jewish state in the region—entered Israeli territory but were beaten back. Thousands of Arab residents of the new state fled. Internal dissonance among the Arabs, combined with the strength of Jewish resistance groups, contributed to the failure of the invasion, but the bitterness between the two sides did not subside. The Muslim states refused to recognize the new state of Israel, which became a member of the United Nations, legitimizing it in the eyes of the rest of the world. The stage for future conflict was set.

The exodus of thousands of Palestinian refugees into neighboring Muslim states had repercussions that are still felt today. Jordan, which had become an independent kingdom under its Hashemite (HASH-uh-myt) ruler, was flooded by the arrival of a million urban Palestinians, overwhelming its own half million people, most of whom were Bedouins. To the north, the state of Lebanon had been created to provide the local Christian community with a country of their own, but the arrival of the Palestinian refugees upset the delicate balance between Christians and Muslims. Moreover, the creation of Lebanon had angered the Syrians, who had lost that land as well as other territories to Turkey as a result of European decisions before and after the war.

Nasser and Pan-Arabism

The dispute over Palestine placed Egypt in an uncomfortable position. Technically, Egypt was not an Arab state. King Farouk (fuh-ROOK) (1920–1965), who had acceded to power in 1936, had frequently declared support for the Arab cause, but the Egyptian people were not Bedouins and shared little of the culture of the peoples across the Red Sea. In 1952, King Farouk, whose corrupt habits had severely eroded his early popularity, was overthrown by a military coup engineered by young military officers who abolished the monarchy and established a republic.

In 1954, one of those officers, Colonel Gamal Abdul Nasser (guh-MAHL AB-dool NAH-sur) (1918–1970), seized power in his own right and immediately instituted a land reform program. He also adopted a policy of neutrality in foreign affairs and expressed sympathy for the Arab cause. The British presence had rankled many Egyptians for years, for even after granting Egypt independence, Britain had retained control over the Suez Canal to protect its route to the Indian Ocean. In 1956, Nasser suddenly nationalized the Suez Canal Company, which had been under British and French administration. Seeing a threat to their route to the Indian Ocean, the British and the French launched a joint attack on Egypt to protect their investment. They were joined by Israel, whose leaders had grown exasperated at sporadic Arab commando raids on Israeli territory and now decided to strike back. But the Eisenhower administration in the United States, concerned that the attack smacked of a revival of colonialism, supported Nasser and brought about the withdrawal of foreign forces from Egypt and of Israeli troops from the Sinai peninsula.

THE UNITED ARAB REPUBLIC Nasser now turned to **pan-Arabism**. In 1958, Egypt united with Syria as the United Arab Republic (UAR). The union had been proposed by the Ba'ath (BAHTH) Party, which advocated the unity of all Arab states in a new socialist society. Nasser was named president of the new state.

Egypt and Syria hoped that the union would eventually include all Arab states, but other Arab leaders, including young King Hussein (1935–1999) of Jordan and the kings of Iraq and Saudi Arabia, were suspicious. The latter two in particular feared pan-Arabism on the reasonable assumption that they would be asked to share their vast oil revenues with the poorer states of the Middle East. Indeed, in Nasser's view, through Arab unity, this wealth could be used to improve the standard of living in the area.

In the end, Nasser's plans brought an end to the UAR. When the government announced the nationalization of a large number of industries and utilities in 1961, a military coup overthrew the Ba'ath leaders in Damascus, and the new authorities declared that Syria would end its relationship with Egypt.

The breakup of the UAR did not end the dream of pan-Arabism. During the mid-1960s, Egypt took the lead in promoting Arab unity against Israel. At a meeting of Arab leaders held in Jerusalem in 1964, the Palestine Liberation Organization (PLO) was set up under Egyptian sponsorship to represent the interests of the Palestinians. According to the charter of the PLO, only the Palestinian people (and thus not Jewish immigrants from abroad) had the right to form a state in the old British mandate. A guerrilla movement called al-Fatah (al-FAH-tuh), led by the dissident PLO figure Yasir Arafat (yah-SEER ah-ruh-FAHT) (1929–2004), began to launch terrorist attacks on Israeli territory.

The Arab-Israeli Dispute

Growing Arab hostility was a constant threat to the security of Israel, whose leaders dedicated themselves to creating a Jewish homeland. The government attempted to build a democratic and modern state that would be a magnet for Jews throughout the world and a symbol of Jewish achievement.

Ensuring the survival of the tiny state surrounded by antagonistic Arab neighbors was a considerable challenge, made more difficult by divisions within the Israeli population. Some were immigrants from Europe, while others came from other states in the Middle East. Some were secular and even socialist in their views, while others were politically and religiously conservative. The state was also home to Christians as well as Muslim Palestinians who had not fled to other countries. To balance these diverse interests, Israel established a parliament, called the Knesset (kuh-NESS-it), on the European model, with proportional representation based on the number of votes each party received in the general election. The parties were so numerous that none ever received a majority of votes, and all governments had to be formed from a coalition of several parties. As a result, moderate secular leaders such as longtime prime minister David Ben-Gurion had to cater to more marginal parties composed of conservative religious groups.

THE SIX-DAY WAR In the spring of 1967, Nasser attempted to improve his standing in the Arab world by imposing a blockade against Israeli commerce through the Gulf of Aqaba. Concerned that it might be isolated, and lacking firm support from Western powers (which had originally guaranteed Israel the freedom to use the Gulf of Aqaba), in June 1967, Israel suddenly launched air strikes against Egypt and several of its Arab neighbors. Israeli armies then broke the blockade at the head of the Gulf of Aqaba and occupied the Sinai peninsula. Other Israeli forces attacked Jordanian territory on the West Bank of the Jordan River (Jordan's King Hussein had recently signed an alliance with Egypt and placed his army under Egyptian command), occupied the whole of Jerusalem,

and seized Syrian military positions in the Golan Heights, along the Israeli-Syrian border (see Map 29.2). Israel's brief, six-day war had tripled the size of its territory but aroused even more bitter hostility among the Arabs; one million Palestinians were added inside its borders, most of them on the West Bank of the Jordan River.

During the next few years, the focus of the Arab-Israeli dispute shifted as Arab states demanded the return of the territories lost in the 1967 war. Nasser died in 1970 and was succeeded by his vice president, ex-general Anwar al-Sadat (ahn-WAHR al-sah-DAHT) (1918–1981). Sadat attempted to renew Arab unity through a new confrontation with Israel. In 1973, on Yom Kippur (the Jewish Day of Atonement), an Israeli national holiday, Egyptian forces suddenly launched an air and artillery attack on Israeli positions in the Sinai just east of the Suez Canal. Syrian armies attacked Israeli positions in the Golan Heights. After early Arab successes, the Israelis managed to recoup some of their losses on both fronts. As a superpower confrontation between the United States and the Soviet Union loomed, a cease-fire was finally reached.

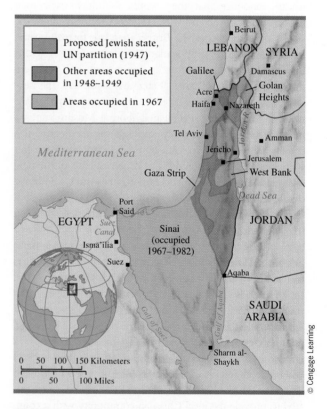

MAP 29.2 **Israel and Its Neighbors.** This map shows the evolution of the state of Israel since its founding in 1948. Areas occupied by Israel after the Six-Day War in 1967 are indicated in green.

Q *What is the significance of the West Bank?*

THE CAMP DAVID AGREEMENT After his election as U.S. president in 1976, Jimmy Carter began to press for a compromise peace based on Israel's return of territories occupied during the 1967 war and Arab recognition of the state of Israel. In September 1978, Sadat and Israeli prime minister Menachem Begin (muh-NAH-kuhm BAY-gin) (1913–1992) met with Carter at Camp David, the presidential retreat in Maryland. In the first treaty signed with a Muslim state, Israel agreed to withdraw from the Sinai but not from other occupied territories unless other Muslim countries recognized Israel. The promise of the Camp David agreement however, was not fulfilled. One reason was the assassination of Sadat by Islamic militants in October 1981. But there were deeper causes, including the continued unwillingness of many Arab governments to recognize Israel and the Israeli government's encouragement of Jewish settlements on the occupied West Bank.

THE PLO AND THE *INTIFADA* During the 1980s, the militancy of the Palestinians increased, leading to rising unrest, popularly labeled the *intifada* (in-tuh-FAH-duh) (uprising), among PLO supporters living inside Israel. In response, U.S.-sponsored peace talks opened between Israel and a number of its neighbors, but progress was slow. Terrorist attacks by Palestinian militants resulted in heavy casualties and shook the confidence of many Jewish citizens that their security needs had been adequately protected. At the same time, Jewish residents of the West Bank resisted the extension of Palestinian authority in the area.

In 1999, a new Labour government under Prime Minister Ehud Barak (EH-hud bah-RAHK) (b. 1942) sought to revitalize the peace process. Negotiations resumed with the PLO and also got under way with Syria over a peace settlement in Lebanon and the possible return of

the Golan Heights. But the talks broke down over the future of the city of Jerusalem, leading to massive riots by Palestinians and a dramatic increase in bloodshed on both sides. The death of Yasi Arafat in 2004 and his replacement by Palestinian moderate Mahmoud Abbas (mah-MOOD ah-BAHS) (b. 1935), as well as the withdrawal of Israeli settlers from Gaza in 2005, raised modest hopes for progress in peace talks, but a year later, radical Muslim forces operating in southern Lebanon launched massive attacks on Israeli cities. In response, Israeli troops crossed the border in an effort to wipe out the source of the assault. Two years later, militants in the Gaza Strip launched their own rocket attacks on sites in southern Israel. The latter responded forcefully, thereby raising the specter of a wider conflict. As attitudes hardened, national elections in early 2009 led to the return to office of former Israeli prime minister Benjamin Netanyahu (net-ahn-YAH-hoo) (b. 1949) and a virtual stalemate in the peace process.

© William J. Duiker

The Temple Mount at Jerusalem. The Temple Mount is one of the most sacred sites in the city of Jerusalem. Originally, it was the site of a temple built during the reign of Solomon, king of the Israelites, about 1000 B.C.E. The Western Wall of the temple is shown in the foreground. Beyond the wall is the Dome of the Rock complex, built on the place from which Muslims believe that Muhammad ascended to heaven. Sacred to both religions, the Temple Mount is now a major bone of contention between Muslims and Jews and a prime obstacle to a final settlement of the Arab-Israeli dispute.

Revolution in Iran

In the late 1970s, another trouble spot arose in Iran, one of the key oil-exporting countries in the region. Under the leadership of Shah Mohammad Reza Pahlavi (ree-ZAH PAH-luh-vee) (1919–1980), who had taken over from his father in 1941, Iran had become one of the richest countries in the Middle East. During the 1950s and 1960s, Iran became a prime U.S. ally in the Middle East.

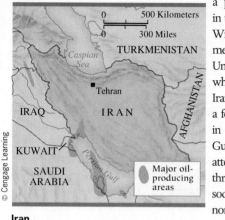

Iran

With encouragement from the United States, which hoped that Iran could become a force for stability in the Persian Gulf, the shah attempted to carry through a series of social and economic reforms to transform the country into the most advanced in the region. Per capita income increased dramatically, literacy rates improved, a modern communications infrastructure took shape, and an affluent middle class emerged in the capital of Tehran (teh-RAHN).

Under the surface, however, trouble was brewing. Despite an ambitious land reform program, many peasants were still landless, unemployment among intellectuals was dangerously high, and the urban middle class was squeezed by high inflation. Some of the unrest took the form of religious discontent as millions of devout Muslims looked with distaste at a new Iranian civilization based on greed, sexual license, and material accumulation.

THE FALL OF THE SHAH Leading the opposition was Ayatollah Ruholla Khomeini (1900–1989), an austere Shi'-ite cleric who had been exiled to Iraq and then to France because of his outspoken opposition to the shah's regime. From Paris, Khomeini continued his attacks in print, on television, and in radio broadcasts. By the late 1970s, large numbers of Iranians began to respond to Khomeini's diatribes against the "satanic regime," and demonstrations by his supporters were repressed with ferocity by the police. But workers' strikes grew in intensity. In 1979, the government collapsed and was replaced by a hastily formed Islamic republic. The new government, dominated by Shi'ite clergy under the guidance of Ayatollah Khomeini, immediately began to introduce traditional Islamic law (see the Film & History feature on p. 779). A new reign of terror ensued as supporters of the shah were rounded up and executed.

Though much of the outside world focused on the U.S. embassy in Tehran, where militants held a number of foreign hostages, the Iranian Revolution involved much more. In the eyes of the ayatollah and his followers, the United States was "the great Satan," the powerful protector of Israel, and the enemy of Muslim peoples everywhere. Furthermore, it was responsible for the corruption of Iranian society under the shah. With economic conditions in Iran rapidly deteriorating, the Islamic revolutionary government finally agreed to free the hostages in return for the release of Iranian assets in the United States.

During the late 1990s, the intensity of the Iranian Revolution moderated slightly as a new president, the moderate cleric Mohammad Khatami (KHAH-tah-mee) (b. 1941), displayed a modest tolerance for loosening clerical control over freedom of expression and social activities. But rising public criticism of rampant official corruption and a high rate of inflation sparked a new wave of government repression; newspapers were censored, the universities were purged of disloyal or "un-Islamic" elements, and religious militants raided private homes in search of blasphemous activities.

In 2004, presidential elections brought a new leader, Mahmoud Ahmadinejad (mah-MOOD ah-mah-dee-nee-ZHAHD) (b. 1956), to power in Tehran. He immediately inflamed the situation by calling publicly for the destruction of the state of Israel, while his government aroused unease throughout the world by indicating its determination to develop a nuclear energy program, ostensibly for peaceful purposes. Iran has also provided support for **Hezbollah** (hes-bah-LAH or HEZ-bull-lah), a militant Shi'ite organization based in Lebanon, and other terrorist groups in the region. Despite worsening conditions at home that eroded the government's popularity, Ahmadinejad was reelected in June 2009, although opponents claimed that numerous irregularities had occurred during the elections.

Crisis in the Persian Gulf

Although much of the Iranians' anger was directed against the United States during the early phases of the revolution, Iran had equally hated enemies closer to home. To the north, the immense power of the Soviet Union, driven by atheistic communism, was viewed as a modern version of the Russian threat of previous centuries. To the west was a militant and hostile Iraq, now under the leadership of the ambitious Saddam Hussein (suh-DAHM hoo-SAYN) (1937–2006). Iraq had just passed through a turbulent period. The monarchy had been overthrown by a military coup in 1958, but conflicts within the ruling military junta led to chronic instability, and in 1979 Colonel Saddam Hussein, a prominent member of the local Ba'athist Party, seized power on his own.

Persepolis (2007)

The Iranian author Marjane Satrapi (b. 1969) has re-created *Persepolis*, her autobiographical graphic novel, as an enthralling animated film of the same name. Using simple black-and-white animation, the movie recounts key stages in the turbulent history of modern Iran as seen through the eyes of a spirited young girl, also named Marjane. The dialogue is in French with English subtitles (a version dubbed in English is also available), and the voices of the characters are rendered beautifully by Danielle Darrieux, Catherine Deneuve, Chiara Mastroianni, and other European film stars.

In the film, Marjane is the daughter of middle-class left-wing intellectuals who abhor the dictatorship of the shah and actively participate in his overthrow in 1979. After the revolution, however, the severity of the ayatollah's Islamic rule arouses their secularist and democratic impulses. Encouraged by her loving grandmother, who reinforces her modernist and feminist instincts, Marjane resents having to wear a head scarf and the educational restrictions imposed by the puritanical new Islamic regime, but to little avail. Emotionally exhausted and fearful of political retribution from the authorities, her family finally sends her to study in Vienna.

Study abroad, however, is not a solution to Marjane's problems. She is distressed by the nihilism and emotional shallowness of her new Austrian school friends, who seem oblivious to the contrast between their privileged lives and her own experience of living under a tyrannical regime. Disillusioned by the loneliness of exile and several failed love affairs, she descends into a deep depression and then decides to return to Tehran. When she discovers that her family is still suffering from political persecution, however, she decides to leave the country permanently and settles in Paris.

Observing the events, first through the eyes of a child and then through the perceptions of an innocent schoolgirl, the viewer of the film is forced to fill in the blanks, as Marjane initially cannot comprehend the meaning of the adult conversations swirling around her. As Marjane passes through adolescence into adulthood, the folly of human intransigence and superstition becomes painfully clear, both to her and to the audience. Although animated films have long been a cinematic staple, thanks in part to Walt Disney, both the novel and the film *Persepolis* demonstrate how graphic design can depict a momentous event in history with clarity and compassion.

THE VISION OF SADDAM HUSSEIN Saddam Hussein was a fervent believer in the Ba'athist vision of a single Arab state in the Middle East and soon began to persecute non-Arab elements in Iraq, including Persians and Kurds. He then turned his sights to territorial expansion to the east.

Iraq and Iran had long had an uneasy relationship, fueled by religious differences (Iranian Islam is predominantly Shi'ite, while the ruling caste in Iraq was Sunni) and a perennial dispute over borderlands adjacent to the Persian Gulf, the vital waterway for the export of oil from both countries. Like several of its neighbors, Iraq had long dreamed of unifying the Arabs but had been hindered by internal factions and suspicion among its neighbors.

During the mid-1970s, Iran gave some support to a Kurdish rebellion in the mountains of Iraq. In 1975, the government of the shah agreed to stop aiding the rebels in return for territorial concessions at the head of the Gulf. Five years later, however, the Kurdish revolt had been suppressed.

Saddam Hussein now saw his opportunity; accusing Iran of violating the territorial agreement, he launched an attack on his neighbor in 1980. The war was a bloody one and lasted for nearly ten years. Poison gas was used against civilians, and children were employed to clear minefields. Finally, with both sides virtually exhausted, a cease-fire was arranged in the fall of 1988.

The bitter conflict with Iran had not slaked Saddam Hussein's appetite for territorial expansion. In early August 1990, Iraqi military forces suddenly moved across the border and occupied the small neighboring country of Kuwait at the head of the Gulf. The immediate pretext was the claim that Kuwait was pumping oil from fields inside Iraqi territory. Baghdad was also angry over the Kuwaiti government's demand for repayment of loans it had made to Iraq during the war with Iran. But the underlying reason was Iraq's contention that Kuwait was legally a part of Iraq. Kuwait had been part of the Ottoman Empire until the beginning of the twentieth century, when the local prince had agreed to place his patrimony under British protection. When Iraq became independent in 1932, it claimed the area on the grounds that the state of Kuwait had been created by British imperialism, but opposition from major Western powers and other countries in the region, which feared the consequences of a "greater Iraq," prevented an Iraqi takeover.

OPERATION DESERT STORM The Iraqi invasion of Kuwait in 1990 sparked an international outcry, and the United States assembled a multinational coalition that, under the name Operation Desert Storm, liberated the country and destroyed a substantial part of Iraq's armed forces. President George H. W. Bush had promised the American people that U.S. troops would not fight with one hand tied behind their backs (a clear reference to the Vietnam War), but the allied forces did not occupy Baghdad at the end of the war out of fear that doing so would cause a breakup of the country, an eventuality that would operate to the benefit of Iran. The allies hoped instead that Saddam's regime would be ousted by an internal revolt. In the meantime, harsh economic sanctions were imposed on the Iraqi government as the condition for peace. The anticipated overthrow of Saddam Hussein did not materialize, however, and his tireless efforts to evade the conditions of the cease-fire continued to bedevil the next U.S. president, Bill Clinton, and his successor, George W Bush.

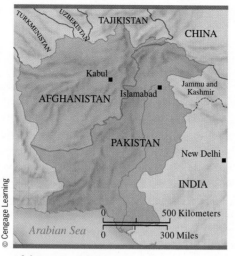

Afghanistan and Pakistan

Conflicts in Afghanistan and Iraq

The terrorist attacks launched against U.S. cities in September 2001 added a new dimension to the Middle Eastern equation. After the failure of the Soviet Union to quell the rebellion in Afghanistan during the 1980s, a fundamentalist Muslim group known as the Taliban, supported covertly by the United States, seized power in Kabul and ruled the country with a fanaticism reminiscent of the Cultural Revolution in China. Backed by conservative religious forces in Pakistan, the Taliban provided a base of operations for Osama bin Laden's al-Qaeda terrorist network. After the attacks of September 11, a coalition of forces led by the United States overthrew the Taliban and attempted to build a new and moderate government in Afghanistan. But the country's history of bitter internecine warfare among tribal groups presented a severe challenge to those efforts, and Taliban forces have managed to regroup and continue to operate in the mountainous region adjacent to the Pakistani border. The terrorist threat from al-Qaeda, however, was dealt a major blow in May 2011, when Osama bin Laden was killed by U.S. special operations forces during a raid on his hideout in northern Pakistan.

After moving against the Taliban at the end of 2001, the administration of George W. Bush, charging that Iraqi dictator Saddam Hussein had not only provided support to bin Laden's terrorist organization but also stockpiled weapons of mass destruction for use against his enemies, threatened to invade Iraq and remove him from power. It was the president's hope that the overthrow of the Iraqi dictator would promote the spread of democracy throughout the region. The plan, widely debated in the media and opposed by many of the United States' traditional allies, disquieted Arab leaders and fanned anti-American sentiment throughout the Muslim world. Nevertheless, in March 2003, U.S.-led forces attacked Iraq and overthrew Saddam Hussein's regime. In the months that followed, occupation forces sought to restore stability to the country while setting out plans on which to build a democratic society. But although Saddam Hussein was captured by U.S. troops and later executed, armed resistance by militant Muslim elements continued.

When the Obama administration came into office in 2009, it focused its efforts on training an Iraqi military

CHRONOLOGY	The Modern Middle East
King Farouk overthrown in Egypt	1952
Egypt nationalizes the Suez Canal	1956
Formation of the United Arab Republic	1958
Iranian Revolution	1979
Iran-Iraq War begins	1980
Iraqi invasion of Kuwait	1990
Persian Gulf War (Operation Desert Storm)	1991
Al-Qaeda terrorist attack on the United States	2001
U.S.-led forces invade Iraq	2003
Ahmadinejad elected president of Iran	2005
Popular riots in the Middle East	2011–2012
Overthrow of Egyptian President Hosni Mubarak	2011

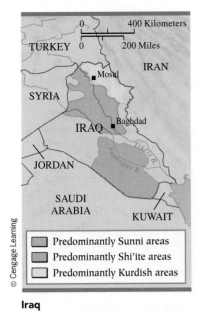

Iraq

Predominantly Sunni areas
Predominantly Shi'ite areas
Predominantly Kurdish areas

© Cengage Learning

force capable of defeating the remaining insurgents. In the meantime, a fragile government has been formed in Baghdad, the embryo of a possible pro-Western state that could serve as an emblem of democracy in the Middle East. Squabbling among Sunni, Shi'ite, and Kurdish elements within the country, however, continued as the last U.S. combat troops were removed in the fall of 2011.

Revolution in the Middle East

In the early months of 2011, popular protests against current conditions broke out in several countries in the Middle East. Beginning in Tunisia, the riots spread rapidly to Egypt—where they brought about the abrupt resignation of long-time president Hosni Mubarak (HAHS-nee moo-BAH-rahk) (b. 1929)—and then to other countries in the region, including Syria, Libya, and Yemen, where political leaders sought to quell the unrest, often by violent means. In Libya, the brutal regime of dictator Muammar Qaddafi was overthrown by a popular revolt with the assistance of NATO air strikes. The uprisings aroused hopes around the world that the seeds of democracy had been planted in a region long dominated by autocratic governments, but also provoked widespread concern that unstable conditions could lead to further violence and a rise in international terrorism. In the months following the outbreak of unrest, the prognosis for the future of the region was still unclear.

Society and Culture in the Contemporary Middle East

Q FOCUS QUESTION: How have religious issues affected economic, social, and cultural conditions in the Middle East in recent decades?

In the Middle East today, all aspects of society and culture—from political and economic issues to literature, art, and the role of the family—are intertwined with questions of religious faith.

Varieties of Government: The Politics of Islam

To many seasoned observers, the strategy applied by President George W. Bush in Iraq appeared unrealistic, since democratic values are not deeply rooted in the culture of the Middle East. In many countries, feudal rulers remain securely in power. The kings of Saudi Arabia, for example, continue to govern by traditional precepts and, citing the distinctive character of Muslim society, have been reluctant to establish representative political institutions.

To be sure, there have been variations in government throughout the region. In some societies, traditional authority has been replaced by charismatic one-party rule or military dictatorships. Nasser's Egypt was a single-party state where the leader won political power by the force of his presence or personality. The regimes of Ayatollah Khomeini in Iran, Muammar Qaddafi in Libya, and Saddam Hussein in Iraq could also trace much of their power to the personal appeal of the leader.

Other states have seen the emergence of modernizing bureaucratic regimes. Examples include the governments of Syria, Yemen, Turkey, and Egypt, where Anwar al-Sadat and his successor, Hosni Mubarak, focused on performance. Most of these regimes have remained highly autocratic in character, however, except in Turkey, where free elections and the sharing of power have become more prevalent in recent years.

A few Arab nations, such as Bahrain, Kuwait, and Jordan, have engaged in limited forms of democratic experimentation. Most of the region's recent leaders, however, have maintained that Western-style democracy is not appropriate for their societies. Bashar al Assad (bah-SHAHR al-ah-SAHD) (b. 1965), the president of Syria, once remarked that he would tolerate only "positive criticism" of his policies. President Mubarak of Egypt often insisted to foreign critics that only authoritarian rule could prevent the spread of Islamic radicalism throughout his country. Most world leaders have accepted the logic of these contentions, provoking some critics to charge that Western governments coddle Middle Eastern dictatorships as a means of maintaining stability in the region and preserving their access to the vast oil reserves located on the Arabian peninsula (see the box on p. 782).

The sudden outbreak of popular unrest that has erupted from North Africa to the Arabian peninsula since the spring of 2011 raises questions about the potential for democratic changes to emerge in the countries throughout the region. Are democratic institutions and the principles of human freedom truly antithetical to the culture of the Middle East and the principles of Islam? As we await the consequences of the current wave of popular unrest, the fate of the region hangs in the balance.

Islam and Democracy

RELIGION & PHILOSOPHY

One of George W. Bush's key objectives in launching the invasion of Iraq in 2003 was to promote the emergence of democratic states throughout the Middle East. According to U.S. officials, one of the ultimate causes of the formation of terrorist movements in Muslim societies is the prevalence in such countries of dictatorial governments that do not serve the interests of their citizens. According to the Pakistani author of this editorial, the problem lies as much with the actions of Western countries as it does with political attitudes in the Muslim world.

M. J. Akbar, "Linking Islam to Dictatorship"

Let us examine a central canard, that Islam and democracy are incompatible. This is an absurdity. There is nothing Islamic or un-Islamic about democracy. Democracy is the outcome of a political process, not a religious process.

It is glibly suggested that "every" Muslim country is a dictatorship, but the four largest Muslim populations of the world—in Indonesia, India, Bangladesh, and Turkey—vote to change governments. Pakistan could easily have been on this list.

Voting does not make these Muslims less or more religious. There are dictators among Muslims just as there are dictators among Christians, Buddhists, and Hindus (check out Nepal). . . . Christian Latin America has seen ugly forms of dictatorship, as has Christian Africa.

What is unique to the Muslim world is not the absence of democracy but the fact that in 1918, after the defeat of the Ottoman Empire, every single Muslim in the world lived under foreign subjugation.

Every single one, from Indonesia to Morocco via Turkey. The Turks threw out their invaders within a few years under the great leadership of Kemal Atatürk, but the transition to self-rule in other Muslim countries was slow, uncertain, and full of traps planted by the world's preeminent powers.

The West, in the shape of Britain, France, or America, was never interested in democracy when a helpful dictator or king would serve. When people got a chance to express their wish, it was only logical that they would ask for popular rule. It was the street that brought Mossadegh to power in Iran and drove the shah of Iran to tearful exile in Rome. Who brought the shah of Iran and autocracy back to Iran? The CIA.

If Iranian democracy had been permitted a chance in 1953, there would have been no uprising led by Ayatollah Khomeini in 1979. In other countries, where the struggle for independence was long and brutal, as in Algeria and Indonesia, the militias who had fought the war institutionalized army authority. In other instances, civilian heroes confused their own well-being with national health. They became regressive dictators. Once again, there was nothing Islamic about it.

Muslim countries will become democracies, too, because it is the finest form of modern governance. But it will be a process interrupted by bloody experience as the street wrenches power from usurpers.

Democracy has happened in Turkey. It has happened in Bangladesh. It is happening in Indonesia. It almost happened in Pakistan, and the opportunity will return. Democracy takes time in the most encouraging environments.

Democracy has become the latest rationale for the occupation of Iraq. . . . Granted, democracy is always preferable to tyranny no matter how it comes. But Iraqis are not dupes. They will take democracy and place it at the service of nationalism. A decade ago, America was careless about the definition of victory. Today it is careless about the definition of democracy.

There is uncertainty and apprehension across the Muslim nations: uncertainty about where they stand, and apprehension about both American power and the repugnant use of terrorism that in turn invites the exercise of American power. There is also anger that a legitimate cause like that of Palestine can get buried in the debris of confusion. Muslims do not see Palestinians as terrorists.

Q *How does the author of this editorial answer the charge that democracy and Islam are incompatible? To what degree, in his view, is the West responsible for the problems of the Middle East?*

Source: From M.J. Akbar, "Linking Islam to Dictatorship," in *World Press Review*, May 2004.

The Economics of the Middle East: Oil and Sand

Few areas exhibit a greater disparity of individual and national wealth than the Middle East. While millions live in abject poverty, a fortunate few rank among the wealthiest people in the world. The primary reason for this disparity is oil. Unfortunately for most of the peoples of the region, oil reserves are distributed unevenly and all too often are located in areas where the population density is low (see the spot map on p. 778). Egypt and Turkey, with more than 75 million inhabitants apiece, have almost no oil reserves. The combined population of oil-rich Kuwait, the United Arab Emirates, and Saudi Arabia is about 35 million people. This disparity in wealth inspired Nasser's quest for Arab unity but has also posed a major obstacle to that unity.

ECONOMICS AND ISLAM   Not surprisingly, considering their different resources and political systems, the states of the Middle East have adopted diverse approaches to the problem of developing strong and stable economies. Some, like Nasser in Egypt and the leaders of the Ba'ath Party in Syria, briefly attempted to create a form of Arab socialism, favoring a high level of government involvement in the economy to relieve the inequities of the free enterprise system. Others turned to the Western capitalist model to maximize growth while using taxes or massive development projects to build a modern infrastructure, redistribute wealth, and maintain political stability and economic opportunity for all (see the comparative illustration on p. 784). Rapid population growth, widespread corruption, and the absence of adequate educational and technological skills, however, have all acted as a drag on economic growth throughout the region. Unfortunately, the Qur'an provides little guidance to Muslims searching for the proper road to economic prosperity.

AGRICULTURAL POLICIES   Although the amount of arable land is relatively small, most countries in the Middle East rely on farming to supply food for their growing populations. Much of the fertile land was once owned by wealthy absentee landlords, but land reform programs in several countries have attempted to alleviate this problem.

The most comprehensive and probably the most successful land reform program was instituted in Egypt, where Nasser and his successors managed to reassign nearly a quarter of all cultivable lands by limiting the amount a single individual could hold. Similar programs in Iran, Iraq, Libya, and Syria generally had less effect. After the 1979 revolution in Iran, many farmers forcibly seized lands from the landlords, raising questions of ownership that the revolutionary government has tried to resolve with only minimal success

Agricultural productivity throughout the region has been plagued by a lack of water. With populations growing at more than 2 percent annually on average in the Middle East (more than 3 percent in some countries), several governments have tried to increase the amount of water available for irrigation. Many attempts have been sabotaged by government ineptitude, political disagreements, and territorial conflicts, however. For example, disputes between Israel and its neighbors over water rights and between Iraq and its neighbors over the exploitation of the Tigris and Euphrates Rivers have caused serious tensions in recent years. Today, the dearth of water in the region is reaching crisis proportions.

The Islamic Revival

In recent years, developments in the Middle East have often been described in terms of a resurgence of traditional values and customs in response to Western influence.

MODERNIST ISLAM   Initially, many Muslim intellectuals responded to Western influence by trying to create a "modernized" set of Islamic beliefs and practices that would not clash with the demands of the twentieth century. This process took place to some degree in most Islamic societies, but it was especially prevalent in Turkey, Egypt, and Iran. Mustafa Kemal Atatürk embraced the strategy when he attempted to secularize the Islamic religion in the new Turkish republic. The Turkish model was followed by Shah Reza Khan and his son Mohammad Reza Pahlavi in Iran and then by Nasser in postwar Egypt, all of whom attempted to honor Islamic values while asserting the primacy of other issues such as political and economic development. Religion, in effect, had become the handmaiden of political power, national identity, and economic prosperity.

These secularizing trends were particularly noticeable among the political, intellectual, and economic elites in urban areas. They had less influence in the countryside, among the poor, and among devout elements within the clergy. Many of the clerics believed that Western influence in the cities had given birth to political and economic corruption, sexual promiscuity, hedonism, individualism, and the prevalence of alcohol, pornography, and drugs. Although such practices had long existed in the Middle East, they were now far more visible and socially acceptable.

RETURN TO TRADITION   Reaction among conservatives against the modernist movement was quick to emerge in several countries and reached its zenith in the late 1970s with the return of the Ayatollah Khomeini to Iran. It is not surprising that Iran took the lead in light of its long tradition of ideological purity within the Shi'ite

COMPARATIVE ILLUSTRATION

POLITICS & GOVERNMENT

Wealth and Poverty in the Middle East. Although many of the countries in the Middle East are relatively poor by world standards, a favored few have amassed great wealth as a result of their fortunate geographic location. Such is the case with the United Arab Emirates, a small country situated strategically on the eastern edge of the Arabian peninsula and located directly over some of the most abundant oil reserves in the world. The modern city of Dubai (top photo), resplendent in its opulence, serves today as a playground for the rich and a vivid symbol of the wealth that has flowed into the region because of the world's thirst for energy. At the opposite extreme is Yemen, on the southern edge of the Arabian peninsula. Lacking valuable resources, the people of Yemen live by traditional pursuits, as shown in the photo at the bottom.

Q *Which are the wealthiest states in the region? Which are the poorest?*

sect as well as the uncompromisingly secular character of the shah's reforms in the postwar era. In Iran today, traditional Islamic beliefs are all-pervasive and extend into education, clothing styles, social practices, and the legal system. In recent years, for example, Iranian women have been heavily fined or even flogged for violating the Islamic dress code.

The cultural and social effects of the Iranian Revolution soon began to spread. In Algeria, the political influence of fundamentalist Islamic groups enabled them to win a stunning victory in the national elections in 1992. When the military stepped in to cancel the second round of elections and crack down on the militants, the latter responded with a campaign of terrorism against moderates that claimed thousands of lives.

A similar trend emerged in Egypt, where militant groups such as the Muslim Brotherhood, formed in 1928 as a means of promoting personal piety, engaged in terrorism, including the assassination of President Anwar al-Sadat and attacks on foreign tourists, who are considered carriers of corrupt Western influence. In recent years, the Brotherhood has adopted a more moderate public stance and received broad support in elections held after the overthrow of the Mubarak regime.

Even in Turkey, generally considered the most secular of Islamic societies, a Muslim political group took power in a coalition government formed in 1996. The new government adopted a pro-Arab stance in foreign affairs and threatened to reduce the country's economic and political ties to Europe. Worried moderates voiced their concern that the secular legacy of Kemal Atatürk was being eroded, and eventually the government resigned under heavy pressure from the military. But a new Islamist organization, known as the Justice and Development Party (the AK Party), won elections held in 2007 and has signaled its intention to guarantee the rights of devout Muslims to display their faith publicly. In elections held in June 2011, the AK Party won a clear victory with about 50 percent of the vote.

Throughout the Middle East, even individuals who do not support efforts to return to pure Islamic principles have adjusted their behavior and beliefs in subtle ways. In Egypt, for example, the authorities encourage television programs devoted to religion in preference to comedies and adventure shows imported from the West, and alcohol is discouraged or at least consumed more discreetly.

Women in the Middle East

Nowhere have the fault lines between tradition and modernity in Muslim societies in the Middle East been so sharp as in the ongoing debate over the role of women. At the beginning of the twentieth century, women's place in Middle Eastern society had changed little since the death of the prophet Muhammad. Women were secluded in their homes and had few legal, political, or social rights.

During the first decades of the twentieth century, advocates of modernist views began to contend that Islamic doctrine was not inherently opposed to women's rights. To modernists, Islamic traditions such as female seclusion, wearing the veil, and polygamy were actually pre-Islamic folk traditions that had been tolerated in the early Islamic era and continued to be practiced in later centuries. Such views had a considerable impact on a number of Middle Eastern societies, including Turkey and Iran. As we have seen, greater rights for women were a crucial element in the social revolution promoted by Kemal Atatürk in Turkey. In Iran, Shah Reza Khan and his son granted female suffrage and encouraged the education of women. In Egypt, a vocal feminist movement arose in educated women's circles in Cairo as early as the 1920s.

The same is true in Israel, where, except in Orthodox religious communities, women have achieved substantial equality with men and are active in politics, the professions, and even the armed forces. Golda Meir (may-EER) (1898–1978), prime minister of Israel from 1969 to 1974, became an international symbol of the ability of women to be world leaders.

In recent years, a more traditional view of women's role has tended to prevail in many Middle Eastern countries. Attacks by religious conservatives on the growing role of women contributed to the emotions underlying the Iranian Revolution of 1979. Iranian women were instructed to wear the veil and to dress modestly in public.

The most conservative nation by far remains Saudi Arabia, where following Wahhabi tradition, women are not only segregated and expected to wear the veil in public but also restricted in education and forbidden to drive automobiles (see the box on p. 786). Still, women's rights have been extended in a few countries. In 1999, women obtained the right to vote in Kuwait, and they have been granted an equal right with their husbands to seek a divorce in Egypt. Even in Iran, women have many freedoms that they lacked before the twentieth century; for example, they can receive military training, vote, practice birth control, and publish fiction. Most important, today nearly 60 percent of university entrants in Iran are women.

Literature and Art

As in other areas of Asia and Africa, the encounter with the West in the nineteenth and twentieth centuries stimulated a cultural renaissance in the Middle East. Muslim authors translated Western works into Arabic and Persian and began to experiment with new literary forms.

LITERATURE Iran has produced one of the most prominent national literatures in the contemporary Middle East. Since World War II, Iranian literature has been hampered somewhat by political considerations, since it has been expected to serve first the Pahlavi monarchy and then the Islamic republic. Nevertheless, Iranian writers are among the most prolific in the region and often write in prose, which has finally been accepted as the equal of poetry.

Despite the male-oriented character of Iranian society, many of the new writers have been women. Since the revolution, the veil and the *chador* (CHUH-der or CHAH-der), an all-enveloping cloak, have become the central metaphor in Iranian women's writing. Those who favor the veil and *chador* praise them as the last bastion of defense against Western cultural imperialism. Behind the veil, the Islamic woman can breathe freely, unpolluted by foreign exploitation and moral corruption. Other Iranian women, however, consider the *chador* a "mobile prison" or an oppressive anachronism from the Dark Ages. As one writer, Sousan Azadi, expressed it, "As I pulled the *chador* over me, I felt a heaviness descending over me. I was hidden and in hiding. There was nothing visible left of Sousan Azadi."[5] Whether or not they accept the veil and *chador*, women writers are a vital part of contemporary Iranian literature and are addressing all aspects of social issues.

Keeping the Camel out of the Tent

FAMILY & SOCIETY

"Almighty God created sexual desire in ten parts; then he gave nine parts to women and one to men." So pronounced Ali, Muhammad's son-in-law, as he explained why women are held morally responsible as the instigators of sexual intercourse. Consequently, over the centuries, Islamic women have been secluded, veiled, and in many cases genitally mutilated in order to safeguard male virtue. Women are forbidden to look directly at, speak to, or touch a man prior to marriage. Even today, they are often sequestered at home or limited to strictly segregated areas away from all male contact. Women normally pray at home or in an enclosed antechamber of the mosque so that their physical presence will not disturb men's spiritual concentration.

Especially limiting today are the laws governing women's behavior in Saudi Arabia. Schooling for girls has never been compulsory because fathers believe that "educating women is like allowing the nose of the camel into the tent; eventually the beast will edge in and take up all the room inside." The country did not establish its first girls' school until 1956. The following description of Saudi women is from *Nine Parts Desire: The Hidden World of Islamic Women* by the journalist Geraldine Brooks.

Geraldine Brooks, *Nine Parts Desire*

Women were first admitted to university in Saudi Arabia in 1962, and all women's colleges remain strictly segregated. Lecture rooms come equipped with closed-circuit TVs and telephones, so women students can listen to a male professor and question him by phone, without having to contaminate themselves by being seen by him. When the first dozen women graduated from university in 1973, they were devastated to find that their names hadn't been printed on the commencement program. The old tradition, that it dishonors women to mention

them, was depriving them of recognition they believed they'd earned. The women and their families protested, so a separate program was printed and a segregated graduation ceremony was held for the students' female relatives. . . .

But while the opening of women's universities widened access to higher learning for women, it also made the educational experience much shallower. Before 1962, many progressive Saudi families had sent their daughters abroad for education. They had returned to the kingdom not only with a degree but with experience of the outside world. . . . Now a whole generation of Saudi women have completed their education entirely within the country. . . .

Lack of opportunity for education abroad means that Saudi women are trapped in the confines of an education system that still lags men's. Subjects such as geology and petroleum engineering—tickets to influential jobs in Saudi Arabia's oil economy—remain closed to women. . . . Few women's colleges have their own libraries, and libraries shared with men's schools are either entirely off limits to women or open to them only one day per week. . . .

But women and men sit for the same degree examinations. Professors quietly acknowledge the women's scores routinely outstrip the men's. "It's no surprise," said one woman professor. "Look at their lives. The boys have their cars, they can spend the evenings cruising the streets with their friends, sitting in cafés, buying black-market alcohol and drinking all night. What do the girls have? Four walls and their books. For them, education is everything."

 According to Geraldine Brooks, do women in Saudi Arabia have an opportunity to receive an education? To what degree do they take advantage of it?

Source: From *Nine Parts Desire: The Hidden World of Islamic Women*, by Geraldine Brooks (Doubleday, 1996).

Like Iran, Egypt in the twentieth century experienced a flowering of literature accelerated by the establishment of the Egyptian republic in the early 1950s. The most illustrious contemporary Egyptian writer was Naguib

Mahfouz (nah-GEEB mah-FOOZ) (1911–2006), who won the Nobel Prize for Literature in 1988. His *Cairo Trilogy* (1952) chronicles three generations of a merchant family in Cairo during the tumultuous years between the world wars. Mahfouz was particularly adept at blending panoramic historical events with the intimate lives of ordinary human beings. Unlike many other modern writers, his message was essentially optimistic and reflected his hope that religion and science can work together for the overall betterment of humankind.

ART Like literature, the art of the modern Middle East has been profoundly influenced by its exposure to Western culture. At first, artists tended to imitate Western models, but later they began to experiment with national styles, returning to earlier forms for inspiration. Some emulated the writers in returning to the village to depict peasants and shepherds, but others followed international trends and attempted to express the alienation and disillusionment that characterize so much of modern life.

CHAPTER SUMMARY

The Middle East is one of the most unstable regions in the world today. In part, this turbulence is due to the continued interference of outsiders attracted by the massive oil reserves under the parched wastes of the Arabian peninsula and in the vicinity of the Persian Gulf. Oil is indeed both a blessing and a curse to the peoples of the region. The similarities with Africa are striking, as governments in both regions struggle to achieve regional cooperation among themselves while fending off the influence of powerful foreign states or multinational corporations.

Some would argue, however, that anger at Western meddling in the Middle East began generations or even centuries earlier. According to the historian Bernard Lewis, the roots of Muslim resentment emerged centuries ago, when Arab hegemony in the region was replaced by European domination. That sense of humiliation culminated in the early twentieth century, when much of the Middle East was occupied by Western colonial regimes. Today, the world is reaping the harvest of that long-cultivated bitterness, as recruits flock to terrorist movements like al-Qaeda in response to the call to eliminate all Western influence in the Arab world.

Another factor contributing to the volatility of the Middle East is the tug-of-war between the sense of ethnic identity in the form of nationalism and the intense longing to be part of a broader Islamic community, a dream that dates back to the time of the prophet Muhammad. Sometimes, the motive for  seeking Arab unity may simply be self-aggrandizement—two such examples are Nasser and Saddam Hussein. But there are undoubtedly others who view restoration of the caliphate as a means of reversing the stain of moral decline that they see taking place throughout the region. Muslims, of course, are not alone in believing that a purer form of religious faith is the best antidote for such social evils as hedonism, sexual license, and political corruption. But it is hard to deny that the issue has been pursued with more anger and passion in the Middle East than in almost any other part of the world. The current wave of popular protest has been focused primarily on internal political and economic concerns in each country. But whatever the outcome, the role of Islam in society will be one of the foremost issues that will face new leaders in the region. The consequences of this struggle cannot yet be foreseen.

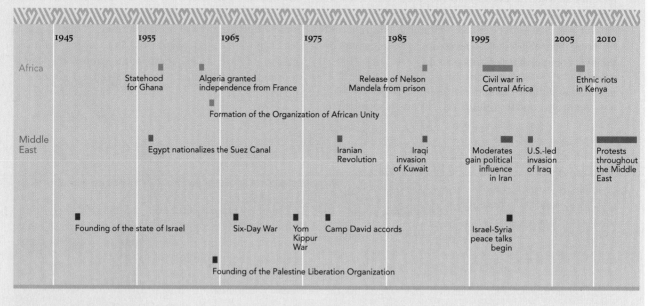

Upon Reflection

Q What are some of the key reasons advanced to explain why democratic institutions have been slow to take root in the Middle East?

Q Why do tensions between farmers and pastoral peoples appear to be on the rise in Africa today? In what parts of the continent is the problem most serious?

Q What are the main sources of discord in the Middle East today? How do they contribute to the popularity of radical terrorist organizations in the region?

Key Terms

uhuru (p. 761)
apartheid (p. 762)
pan-Africanism (p. 763)
neocolonialism (p. 763)
African Union (p. 770)
pan-Arabism (p. 775)
intifada (p. 777)
Hezbollah (p. 778)

Suggested Reading

AFRICA: GENERAL For general surveys of contemporary African history, see **P. Nugent,** *Africa Since Independence* (New York, 2004); **M. Meredith,** *The Fate of Africa* (New York, 2005); and **H. French,** *A Continent for the Taking: The Tragedy and Hope of Africa* (New York, 2004).

AFRICAN LITERATURE AND ART For a survey of African literature, see **A. Kalu, ed.,** *The Rienner Anthropology of African Literatures* (London, 2007); **M. J. Hay,** *African Novels in the Classroom* (Boulder, Colo., 2000); and **M. J. Daymond et al., eds.,** *Women Writing Africa: The Southern Region* (New York, 2003). On art, see **S. L. Kasfir,** *Contemporary African Art* (London, 1999).

WOMEN IN AFRICA For interesting analyses of women's issues in the Africa of this time frame, see **M. Kevane,** *Women and Development in Africa: How Gender Works* (Boulder, Colo., 2004).

RECENT EVENTS IN AFRICA For contrasting views on the reasons for Africa's current difficulties, see **J. Marah,** *The African People in the Global Village: An Introduction to Pan-African Studies* (Lanham, Md., 1998), and **G. Ayittey,** *Africa in Chaos* (New York, 1998).

THE MIDDLE EAST A good general survey of the modern Middle East is **A. Goldschmidt Jr.,** *A Concise History of the Middle East* (Boulder, Colo., 2005).

ISRAEL AND PALESTINE On Israel and the Palestinian question, see **D. Ross,** *The Missing Peace: The Inside Story of the Fight for Middle East Peace* (New York, 2004). On Jerusalem, see **B. Wasserstein,** *Divided Jerusalem: The Struggle for the Holy City* (New Haven, Conn., 2000).

IRAN AND IRAQ On the Iranian Revolution, see **S. Bakash**, *The Reign of the Ayatollahs* (New York, 1984). Iran's role in Middle Eastern politics and diplomacy is analyzed in **T. Parsi**, *Treacherous Alliance: The Secret Dealings of Israel, Iran, and the United States* (New Haven, Conn., 2007). The Iran-Iraq War is discussed in **S. C. Pelletiere**, *The Iran-Iraq War: Chaos in a Vacuum* (New York, 1992). The issue of oil is examined in **D. Yergin et al.**, *The Prize: The Epic Quest for Oil, Money, and Power* (New York, 1993).

For historical perspective on the invasion of Iraq, see **J. Kendell**, *Iraq's Unruly Century* (New York, 2003). **R. Khalidi**, *Resurrecting Empire: Western Footprints and America's Perilous Path in the Middle East* (Boston, 2003), is a critical look at U.S. policy in the region.

For expert analysis on the current situation in the region, see **B. Lewis**, *What Went Wrong? Western Impact and Middle Eastern Response* (Oxford, 2001), and **P. L. Bergen**, *Holy War, Inc.: Inside the Secret World of Osama bin Laden* (New York, 2001). Also see **M. Afkhami** and **E. Friedl**, *In the Eye of the Storm: Women in Post-Revolutionary Iran* (Syracuse, N.Y., 1994).

MIDDLE EASTERN LITERATURE For a scholarly but accessible overview of Arabic literature, see **M. M. Badawi**, *A Short History of Modern Arab Literature* (Oxford, 1993).

CourseMate Visit the CourseMate website at www.cengagebrain.com for additional study tools and review materials for this chapter.

Toward the Pacific Century?

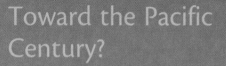

The Petronas Towers in Kuala Lumpur, Malaysia

CHAPTER OUTLINE
AND FOCUS QUESTIONS

South Asia

Q How did Gandhi's and Nehru's goals for India differ, and what role did each leader's views play in shaping modern India?

Southeast Asia

Q What kinds of problems have the nations of Southeast Asia faced since 1945, and how have they attempted to solve these problems?

Japan: Asian Giant

Q How did the Allied occupation after World War II change Japan's political and economic institutions, and what remained unchanged?

The Little Tigers

Q What factors have contributed to the economic success achieved by the Little Tigers? To what degree have they applied the Japanese model in forging their developmental strategies?

CRITICAL THINKING

Q What differences and similarities do you see in the performances of the nations of South, Southeast, and East Asia since World War II? What do you think accounts for the differences?

FIRST-TIME VISITORS to the Malaysian capital of Kuala Lumpur (KWAH-luh loom-POOR) are astonished to observe a pair of twin towers thrusting up above the surrounding buildings into the clouds. The Petronas Towers rise 1,483 feet from ground level; they were the world's tallest buildings at the time of their completion in 1998. (They have since been surpassed by Taipei 101, in Taiwan; the Shanghai World Financial Center; and Burj Khalifa, in Dubai.)

Beyond their status as an architectural achievement, the Petronas Towers announced the emergence of Southeast Asia as a major player on the international scene. It is no accident that the foundations were laid on the site of the Selangor Cricket Club, symbol of British colonial hegemony in Southeast Asia. "These towers," commented one local official, "will do wonders for Asia's self-esteem and confidence, which I think is very important, and which I think at this moment are at the point of takeoff."[1]

The sky-piercing towers in Kuala Lumpur and Taipei (TY-PAY) are not alone in signaling Asia's new prominence on the world stage in the century now unfolding. Several other cities in the region, including Hong Kong, Singapore, Tokyo, and Shanghai, have become major capitals of finance and monuments of economic prowess, rivaling the traditional centers of New York, London, Berlin, and Paris.

That the nations of the Pacific Rim would become a driving force in global development was all but unimaginable after World War II, when the Communist triumph in China ushered in an era of intense competition between the capitalist and socialist camps. Bitter conflicts in Korea and Vietnam were visible manifestations of a region in turmoil. Yet today, many of the nations of eastern Asia have become models of successful nation building, characterized by economic prosperity and political stability. They have heralded the opening of what has been called the "Pacific Century." ✍

South Asia

Q FOCUS QUESTION: How did Gandhi's and Nehru's goals for India differ, and what role did each leader's views play in shaping modern India?

In 1947, nearly two centuries of British colonial rule came to an end when two new independent nations, India and Pakistan, came into being.

The End of the British Raj

During the 1930s, the nationalist movement in India was severely shaken by factional disagreements between Hindus and Muslims. The outbreak of World War II subdued these sectarian clashes, but they erupted again after the war ended in 1945. Battles between Hindus and Muslims broke out in several cities, and Muhammad Ali Jinnah (muh-HAM-ad ah-LEE JIN-uh) (1876–1948), leader of the Muslim League, demanded the creation of a separate state for each. Meanwhile, the Labour Party, which had long been critical of the British colonial legacy on both moral and economic grounds, had come to power in Britain, and the new prime minister, Clement Attlee, announced that power would be transferred to "responsible Indian hands" by June 1948.

But the imminence of independence did not dampen communal strife. As riots escalated, the British reluctantly accepted the inevitability of partition and declared that on August 15, 1947, two independent nations— Hindu India and Muslim Pakistan—would be established. Pakistan would be divided between the main area of Muslim habitation in the Indus River valley in the west and a separate territory in east Bengal 2,000 miles to the east. Although Mahatma Gandhi warned that partition would provoke "an orgy of blood,"[2] he was increasingly regarded as a figure of the past, and his views were ignored.

The British instructed the rulers in the princely states to choose which state they would join by August 15, but problems arose in predominantly Hindu Hyderabad (HY-der-uh-bahd), where the nawab (viceroy) was a Muslim, and mountainous Kashmir (KAZH-meer), where a Hindu prince ruled over a Muslim population. After independence was declared, the flight of millions of Hindus and Muslims across the borders led to violence and the deaths of more than a million people. One of the casualties was Gandhi, who was assassinated on January 30, 1948, as he was going to morning prayer. The assassin, a Hindu militant, was apparently motivated by Gandhi's opposition to a Hindu India.

Independent India

With independence, the Indian National Congress, now renamed the Congress Party, moved from opposition to the responsibility of power under Jawaharlal Nehru (juh-WAH-hur-lahl NAY-roo), the new prime minister. The prospect must have been intimidating. The vast majority of India's 400 million people were poor and illiterate. The new nation encompassed a significant number of ethnic groups and fourteen major languages. Although Congress Party leaders spoke bravely of building a new nation, Indian society still bore the scars of past wars and divisions.

The government's first problem was to resolve disputes left over from the transition period. The rulers of Hyderabad and Kashmir had both followed their own preferences rather than the wishes of their subject populations. Nehru was determined to include both states within India. In 1948, Indian troops invaded Hyderabad and annexed the area. India was also able to seize most of Kashmir, but at the cost of creating an intractable problem that has poisoned relations with Pakistan to the present day.

AN EXPERIMENT IN DEMOCRATIC SOCIALISM Under Nehru's leadership, India adopted a political system on the British model, with a figurehead president and a parliamentary form of government. A number of political parties operated legally, but the Congress Party, with its enormous prestige and charismatic leadership, was dominant at both the central and the local levels.

Nehru had been influenced by British socialism and patterned his economic policy roughly after the program of the British Labour Party. The state took over ownership of the major industries and resources, transportation, and utilities, while private enterprise was permitted at the local and retail levels. Farmland remained in private hands, but rural cooperatives were officially encouraged.

OPPOSING ✕ VIEWPOINTS

Two Visions for India

POLITICS & GOVERNMENT

Although Jawaharlal Nehru and Mohandas Gandhi agreed on their desire for an independent India, their visions of the future of their homeland were dramatically different. Nehru favored industrialization to build material prosperity, whereas Gandhi praised the simple virtues of manual labor. The first excerpt is from a speech by Nehru; the second is from a letter written by Gandhi to Nehru.

Nehru's Socialist Creed

I am convinced that the only key to the solution of the world's problems and of India's problems lies in socialism, and when I use this word I do so not in a vague humanitarian way but in the scientific economic sense. . . . I see no way of ending the poverty, the vast unemployment, the degradation and the subjection of the Indian people except through socialism. That involves vast and revolutionary changes in our political and social structure, the ending of vested interests in land and industry, as well as the feudal and autocratic Indian states system. That means the ending of private property, except in a restricted sense, and the replacement of the present profit system by a higher ideal of cooperative service. . . . In short, it means a new civilization, radically different from the present capitalist order. Some glimpse we can have of this new civilization in the territories of the U.S.S.R. Much has happened there which has pained me greatly and with which I disagree, but I look upon that great and fascinating unfolding of a new order and a new civilization as the most promising feature of our dismal age.

A Letter to Jawaharlal Nehru

I believe that if India, and through India the world, is to achieve real freedom, then sooner or later we shall have to go and live in the villages—in huts, not in palaces. Millions of people can never live in cities and palaces in comfort and peace. Nor can they do so by killing one another, that is, by resorting to violence and untruth. . . . We can have the vision of . . . truth and nonviolence only in the simplicity of the villages. That simplicity resides in the spinning wheel and what is implied by the spinning wheel. . . .

You will not be able to understand me if you think that I am talking about the villages of today. My ideal village still exists only in my imagination. . . . In this village of my dreams the villager will not be dull—he will be all awareness. He will not live like an animal in filth and darkness. Men and women will live in freedom, prepared to face the whole world. There will be no plague, no cholera, and no smallpox. Nobody will be allowed to be idle or to wallow in luxury. Everyone will have to do body labor. Granting all this, I can still envisage a number of things that will have to be organized on a large scale. Perhaps there will even be railways and also post and telegraph offices. I do not know what things there will be or will not be. Nor am I bothered about it. If I can make sure of the essential thing, other things will follow in due course. But if I give up the essential thing, I give up everything.

 What are the key differences between these two views on the future of India? Why do you think Nehru's proposals triumphed over Gandhi's?

Sources: Nehru's Socialist Creed. From *Sources of Indian Tradition* by William Theodore De Bary. Copyright © 1988 by Columbia University Press, New York. A Letter to Jawaharlal Nehru. Excerpt from Gandhi "Letter to Jawaharlal Nehru" pp. 328–331 from *Gandhi In India: In His Own Words*, Martin Green, ed. Copyright © 1987 by Navajivan Trust. Lebanon, NH: University Press of New England.

In other respects, Nehru was a devotee of Western materialism. He was convinced that to succeed, India must industrialize. In advocating industrialization, Nehru departed sharply from Gandhi, who believed that materialism was morally corrupting and that only simplicity and nonviolence (as represented by the traditional Indian village and the symbolic spinning wheel) could save India, and the world itself, from self-destruction (see the box above).

The primary themes of Nehru's foreign policy were anticolonialism and antiracism. Under his guidance, India took a neutral stance in the Cold War and sought to provide leadership to all newly independent nations in Asia, Africa, and Latin America. India's neutrality put it at odds with the United States, which during the 1950s was trying to mobilize all nations against what it viewed as the menace of international communism.

Relations with Pakistan continued to be troubled. India refused to consider Pakistan's claim to Kashmir, even though the majority of the population there were Muslims. Tension between the two countries persisted, erupting into war in 1965. In 1971, when riots against the Pakistani government broke out in East Pakistan, India intervened on the side of East Pakistan, which declared its independence as the new nation of Bangladesh (see Map 30.1).

THE POST-NEHRU ERA   Nehru's death in 1964 aroused concern that Indian democracy was dependent on the Nehru mystique. When his successor, a Congress Party veteran, died in 1966, party leaders selected Nehru's daughter, Indira Gandhi (in-DEER-uh GAHN-dee) (no relation to Mahatma Gandhi), as the new prime minister. Gandhi (1917–1984) was inexperienced in politics, but she quickly showed the steely determination of her father.

Like Nehru, Gandhi embraced democratic socialism and a policy of neutrality in foreign affairs, but she was more activist in promoting her objectives than her father. To combat rural poverty, she nationalized banks, provided loans to peasants on easy terms, built low-cost housing, distributed land to the landless, and introduced electoral reforms to enfranchise the poor.

Gandhi was especially worried by India's growing population and, in an effort to curb the growth rate, adopted a policy of forced sterilization. This policy proved unpopular, however, and, along with growing official corruption and Gandhi's authoritarian tactics, led to her defeat in the general election of 1975, the first time the Congress Party had failed to win a majority at the national level.

A minority government of procapitalist parties was formed, but within two years, Gandhi was back in power. She now faced a new challenge, however, in the rise of religious strife. The most dangerous situation was in the Punjab (pun-PAHB), where militant Sikhs (SEEKS or SEE-ikhz) were demanding autonomy or even independence from India. Gandhi did not shrink from a confrontation and attacked Sikh rebels hiding in their Golden Temple in the city of Amritsar (uhm-RIT-ser). The incident aroused widespread anger among the Sikh community, and in 1984, Sikh members of Gandhi's personal bodyguard assassinated her.

By now, Congress Party politicians were convinced that the party could not remain in power without a member of the Nehru family at the helm. Gandhi's son Rajiv Gandhi (rah-JEEV GAHN-dee) (1944–1991), a commercial airline pilot with little interest in politics, was persuaded to replace his mother as prime minister. Rajiv lacked the strong ideological and political convictions of his mother and grandfather and allowed a greater role for private enterprise. But his government was criticized for cronyism, inefficiency, and corruption.

Rajiv Gandhi also sought to play a role in regional affairs, mediating a dispute between the government in Sri Lanka and Tamil rebels (known as the Elam Tigers) who were ethnically related to the majority population in southern India. The decision cost him his life: while campaigning for reelection in 1991, he was assassinated by a member of the Tiger organization. India faced the future without a member of the Nehru family as prime minister.

During the early 1990s, the Congress Party remained the leading party, but the powerful hold it once had on the Indian electorate was gone. New parties, such as the militantly Hindu Bharatiya Janata (BAR-ruh-tee-uh JAH-nuh-tuh) Party (BJP), actively vied with the Congress Party for control of the central and state governments. Growing political instability at the center was accompanied by rising tensions between Hindus and Muslims.

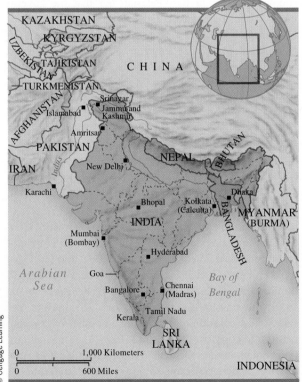

© Cengage Learning

MAP 30.1 Modern South Asia. This map shows the boundaries of all the states in contemporary South Asia.

Q *Which of the countries on this map have a Muslim majority?*

India and Pakistan become independent	1947
Assassination of Mahatma Gandhi	1948
Death of Jawaharlal Nehru	1964
Indo-Pakistani War	1965
Indira Gandhi elected prime minister	1966
Bangladesh declares its independence	1971
Assassination of Indira Gandhi	1984
Assassination of Rajiv Gandhi	1991
Destruction of mosque at Ayodhya	1992
Benazir Bhutto removed from power in Pakistan	1997
Military coup overthrows civilian government in Pakistan	1999
U.S.-led forces oust Taliban in Afghanistan	2001
Congress Party returns to power in India	2004
Assassination of Benazir Bhutto	2007
Massive floods in the Indus River valley	2010
Osama bin Laden killed in Pakistan	2011

When a coalition government formed under Congress leadership collapsed, the BJP, under Prime Minister A. B. Vajpayee (VAHJ-py-ee) (b. 1924), ascended to power and played on Hindu sensibilities to build its political base. The new government based its success on an aggressive program of privatization in the industrial and commercial sectors and made a major effort to promote the nation's small but growing technological base. But BJP leaders had underestimated the discontent of India's less affluent citizens, and in the spring of 2004, a stunning defeat in national elections forced the Vajpayee government to resign. The Congress Party returned to power at the head of a coalition government based on a commitment to maintain economic growth while carrying out reforms in rural areas, including public works projects and hot lunch programs for all primary school children. The Congress Party remained in power after national elections held in the spring of 2009, but serious problems, including pervasive official corruption and sectarian strife between Hindus and Muslims, continue to bedevil the government.

The Land of the Pure: Pakistan Since Independence

When Pakistan achieved independence in August 1947, it was, unlike its neighbor India, in all respects a new nation, based on religious conviction rather than historical or ethnic tradition. The unique state consisted of two separate territories 2,000 miles apart. West Pakistan, including the Indus River basin and the West Punjab,

was perennially short of water and was populated by dry crop farmers and peoples of the steppe. East Pakistan was made up of the marshy deltas of the Ganges and Brahmaputra Rivers. Densely populated with rice farmers, it was the home of the artistic and intellectual Bengalis (ben-GAH-leez).

The peoples of West Pakistan were especially diverse and included, among others, Pushtuns, Baluchis (buh-LOO-cheez), and Punjabis (pun-JAHB-eez). The Pushtuns are organized on a tribal basis and have kinship ties with the majority population across the border in neighboring Afghanistan. Many are nomadic and cross the border on a regular basis with their flocks. The Baluchis straddle the border with Iran, while the region of Punjab was divided between Pakistan and India at the moment of independence.

Even though the new state was an essentially Muslim society, its first years were marked by intense internal conflicts over religious, linguistic, and regional issues. Muhammad Ali Jinnah's vision of a democratic state that would assure freedom of religion and equal treatment for all was opposed by those who advocated a state based on Islamic principles.

Even more dangerous was the division between east and west. Many in East Pakistan felt that the government, based in the west, ignored their needs. In 1952, riots erupted in East Pakistan over the government's decision to adopt Urdu, a language derived from Hindi and used by Muslims in northern India, as the national language of the entire country. Most East Pakistanis spoke Bengali, an unrelated language. Tensions persisted, and in March 1971, East Pakistan declared its independence as the new nation of Bangladesh. Pakistani troops attempted to restore the central government's authority in the capital of Dhaka (DAK-uh or DAH-kuh), but rebel forces supported by India went on the offensive, and the government bowed to the inevitable and recognized independent Bangladesh.

The breakup of the union between East and West Pakistan undermined the fragile authority of the military regime that had ruled Pakistan since 1958 and led to its replacement by a civilian government under Zulfikar Ali Bhutto (ZOOL-fee-kahr ah-LEE BOO-toh) (1928–1979). But now religious tensions came to the fore, despite a new constitution that made a number of key concessions to conservative Muslims. In 1977, a new military government under General Zia Ul Ha'q (ZEE-ah ool HAHK) (1924–1988) came to power with a commitment to make Pakistan a truly Islamic state. Islamic law became the basis for social behavior as well as for the legal system. Laws governing the consumption of alcohol and the role of women were tightened in accordance with strict Muslim beliefs. But after Zia was killed in a plane crash, Pakistanis elected Benazir Bhutto (ben-uh-ZEER BOO-toh) (1953–2007), the daughter of Zulfikar Ali Bhutto and a supporter of secularism who had been educated in the United States. She too was removed from power by a military regime, in 1990, on charges of incompetence and corruption. Reelected in 1993, she attempted to crack down on opposition forces but was removed once again in 1997 amid renewed charges of official corruption. Her successor soon came under fire for the same reason and in 1999 was ousted by a military coup led by General Pervez Musharraf (pur-VEZ moo-SHAHR-uf) (b. 1943), who promised to restore political stability and honest government.

In September 2001, Pakistan became the focus of international attention when a coalition of forces arrived in neighboring Afghanistan to overthrow the Taliban regime and destroy the al-Qaeda terrorist network. Despite considerable support for the Taliban among the local population, President Musharraf pledged his help in bringing terrorists to justice. He also promised to return his country to the secular principles espoused by Muhammad Ali Jinnah. His situation was complicated by renewed tensions with India over Kashmir and a series of violent clashes between Muslims and Hindus in India. In 2003, however, relations began to improve as both sides promised to seek a peaceful solution to the Kashmir dispute.

By then, however, problems had begun to escalate on the domestic front. As Musharraf sought to fend off challenges from radical Muslim groups—some of them allied with Taliban forces in Afghanistan—secular opposition figures criticized the authoritarian nature of his regime. When Benazir Bhutto returned from exile to present herself as a candidate in presidential elections to be held early in 2008, she was assassinated, leading to widespread suspicions of official involvement. In September 2008, amid growing political turmoil, Benazir Bhutto's widower, Asif Ali Zardari (AH-seef ah-LEE zahr-DAR-ree) (b. 1955), was elected president of Pakistan.

The new civilian government, which is composed of an uneasy coalition of several political parties, faces a number of challenges in coping with the multitude of problems affecting the country today. Half of the entire population of 150 million live in poverty, and illiteracy is widespread. Massive flooding of the Indus River in 2010 killed nearly 2,000 people and left millions homeless.

In a nation where much of the rural population still professes loyalty to traditional tribal leaders, the sense of nationalism remains fragile, while military elites, who have long played a central role in Pakistani politics, continue to press their own agenda. The internal divisions within the country's ruling class became painfully apparent when the al-Qaeda leader Osama bin Laden was killed in a U.S. raid on his compound in the spring of 2011. The terrorist leader had been living secretly in Pakistan, in a villa in the military town of Abbottabad, within two hours' drive from the national capital of Islamabad. Many observers suspected that elements within Pakistan's military were aware of his presence, and the U.S. raid further exacerbated relations with its reputed ally.

Poverty and Pluralism in South Asia

The leaders of the new states that emerged in South Asia after World War II faced a number of problems. The peoples of South Asia were still overwhelmingly poor and illiterate, while the sectarian, ethnic, and cultural divisions that had plagued Indian society for centuries had not dissipated.

THE POLITICS OF COMMUNALISM   Perhaps the most sincere effort to create democratic institutions was in India, where the new constitution called for social justice, liberty, equality of status and opportunity, and fraternity. All citizens were guaranteed protection from discrimination based on religious belief, race, caste, gender, or place of birth.

In theory, then, India became a full-fledged democracy on the British parliamentary model. In actuality, a number of distinctive characteristics made the system less than fully democratic in the Western sense but may also have enabled it to survive. As we have seen, India became in essence a one-party state. By leading the independence movement, the Congress Party had amassed massive public support, which enabled it to retain its preeminent position in Indian politics for three decades. After Nehru's death in 1964, however, problems emerged that had been disguised by his adept maneuvering. Part of the problem was the familiar one of a party too long in power. Party officials became complacent and all too easily fell prey to the temptations of corruption and pork-barrel politics.

Another problem was **communalism**. Beneath the surface unity of the new republic lay age-old ethnic, linguistic, and religious divisions. Because of India's vast size and complex history, no national language had ever emerged. Hindi was the most prevalent, but it was the native language of less than one-third of the population. During the colonial period, English had served as the official language of government, but it was spoken only by the educated elite and represented an affront to national pride. Eventually, India recognized fourteen official tongues, making the parliament sometimes sound like the Tower of Babel.

Divisiveness increased after Nehru's death, and under his successors, official corruption grew. Only the lack of appeal of its rivals and the Nehru family charisma carried on by his daughter Indira Gandhi kept the Congress Party in power. But she was unable to prevent the progressive disintegration of the party's power base at the state level, where regional or ideological parties won the allegiance of voters by exploiting ethnic or social revolutionary themes.

During the 1980s, religious tensions began to intensify. As we have seen, Gandhi's uncompromising approach to Sikh separatism led to her assassination in 1984. Under her son, Rajiv Gandhi, Hindu militants at Ayodhya (ah-YOHD-yuh), in northern India, demanded the destruction of a mosque built on the traditional site of King Rama's birthplace, where a Hindu temple had previously existed. In 1992, Hindu demonstrators destroyed the mosque and erected a temporary temple at the site, provoking clashes between Hindus and Muslims throughout the country. In protest, rioters in neighboring Pakistan destroyed a number of Hindu shrines in that country. In 2010, an Indian court ordered that the land that had contained the mosque be divided between the Hindu and Muslim plaintiffs.

In the early years of the new century, communal divisions intensified as militant Hindu groups demanded a state that would cater to the Hindu majority, now numbering more than 700 million people. In the eastern state of Orissa, pitched battles have broken out between Hindus and Christians over efforts by the latter to win converts to their faith. Manmohan Singh (MUHN-moh-hahn SING) (b. 1932), India's prime minister since 2004, has lamented what he calls an assault on India's "composite culture."[3]

THE ECONOMY   Nehru's answer to the social and economic inequality that had long afflicted the subcontinent was socialism. He instituted a series of five-year plans, which led to the creation of a relatively large and reasonably efficient state-run industrial sector, centered on steel, vehicles, and textiles. Industrial production almost tripled between 1950 and 1965, and per capita income rose by 50 percent between 1950 and 1980, although it was still less than $300 (in U.S. dollars). By the 1970s, however, industrial growth had slowed. The lack of modern infrastructure was a problem, as was the rising price of oil, most of which had to be imported.

India's major economic weakness, however, was in agriculture. At independence, mechanization was almost unknown, fertilizer was rarely used, and most farms were small and uneconomical because of the Hindu tradition of dividing the land equally among all male children. As a result, the vast majority of the Indian people lived in conditions of abject poverty. Landless laborers outnumbered landowners by almost two to one. The government attempted to relieve the problem by redistributing land to the poor, limiting the size of landholdings, and encouraging farmers to form voluntary cooperatives. But all three programs ran into widespread opposition.

Another problem was overpopulation. Even before independence, the country had had difficulty supporting its people. In the 1950s and 1960s, the population grew by more than 2 percent annually, twice the nineteenth-century rate. Beginning in the 1960s, the Indian government sought to curb population growth. Indira Gandhi instituted a program combining monetary rewards and compulsory sterilization. Popular resistance undermined the program, however, and the goals were scaled back in the 1970s. Nevertheless, as a result of media popularization and better government programs, the trend today, even in poor rural villages, is toward smaller families. The average number of children a woman bears has declined from six in 1950 to three today. Still, India is on target to become the world's most populous nation, surpassing China by the year 2025.

After the death of Indira Gandhi in 1984, her son Rajiv proved more receptive to foreign investment and a greater role for the private sector in the economy. India began to export more manufactured goods, including computer software. The pace of change has accelerated under Rajiv Gandhi's successors, who have continued to transfer state-run industries to private hands. These policies have stimulated the growth of a prosperous new middle class, now estimated at more than 100 million. Consumerism has soared, and sales of television sets, DVD players, cell phones, and even automobiles have increased dramatically. Equally important, Western imports are being replaced by new products manufactured in India with Indian brand names, while large multinational corporations, such as the retail giant Walmart, have encountered difficulties in breaking into the Indian market (see the box on p. 797).

One consequence of India's entrance into the industrial age has been the emergence of a small but vibrant technological sector that provides many important services to the world's advanced nations. The city of Bengaluru (BEHNG-uh-luh-roo) (Bangalore) in South India has become an important technological center, benefiting from low wages and the presence of skilled labor with proficiency in the English language. It has also become a symbol of the "outsourcing" of jobs from the United States and Europe, a practice that has led to an increase in middle-class unemployment throughout the Western world.

As in the industrialized countries of the West, economic growth in India has been accompanied by environmental damage. Water and air pollution has led to illness

Say No to McDonald's and KFC!

INTERACTION & EXCHANGE

One of the consequences of Rajiv Gandhi's decision to deregulate the Indian economy has been an increase in the presence of foreign corporations, including U.S. fast-food restaurant chains. Their arrival set off a storm of protest in India: from environmentalists concerned that raising grain for chickens is an inefficient use of land, from religious activists angry at the killing of animals for food, and from nationalists anxious to protect the domestic market from foreign competition. Fast-food restaurants now represent a growing niche in Indian society, but most cater to local tastes, avoiding beef products and offering many vegetarian dishes, such as the Veg Pizza McPuff. This piece, which appeared in the *Hindustan Times*, was written by Maneka Gandhi, a daughter-in-law of Indira Gandhi and a onetime minister of the environment who has emerged as a prominent rival of Congress Party president Sonia Gandhi.

Why India Doesn't Need Fast Food

India's decision to allow Pepsi Foods Ltd. to open 60 restaurants in India—30 each of Pizza Hut and Kentucky Fried Chicken—marks the first entry of multinational, meat-based junk-food chains into India. If this is allowed to happen, at least a dozen other similar chains will very quickly arrive, including the infamous McDonald's.

The implications of allowing junk-food chains into India are quite stark. As the name denotes, the foods served at Kentucky Fried Chicken (KFC) are chicken-based and fried. This is the worst combination possible for the body and can create a host of health problems, including obesity, high cholesterol, heart ailments, and many kinds of cancer. Pizza Hut products are a combination of white flour, cheese, and meat—again, a combination likely to cause disease. . . .

Then there is the issue of the environmental impact of junk-food chains. Modern meat production involves misuse of crops, water, energy, and grazing areas. In addition, animal agriculture produces surprisingly large amounts of air and water pollution.

KFC and Pizza Hut insist that their chickens be fed corn and soybeans. Consider the diversion of grain for this purpose. As the outlets of KFC and Pizza Hut increase in number, the poultry industry will buy up more and more corn to feed the chickens, which means that the corn will quickly disappear from the villages, and its increased price will place it out of reach for the common man. Turning corn into junk chicken is like turning gold into mud. . . .

It is already shameful that, in a country plagued by famine and flood, we divert 37 percent of our arable land to growing animal fodder. Were all of that grain to be consumed directly by humans, it would nourish five times as many people as it does after being converted into meat, milk, and eggs. . . .

Of course, it is not just the KFC and Pizza Hut chains of Pepsi Foods Ltd. that will cause all of this damage. Once we open India up by allowing these chains, dozens more will be eagerly waiting to come in. Each city in America has an average of 5,000 junk-food restaurants. Is that what we want for India?

Q *Why does the author of this article oppose the introduction of fast-food restaurants in India? Do you think her complaints apply in the United States as well?*

Source: From *World Press Review* (September 1995), p. 47.

---

and death for many people, and an environmental movement has emerged. Some critics, reflecting the traditional anti-imperialist attitude of Indian intellectuals, blame Western capitalist corporations for the problem, as in the highly publicized case of leakage from a foreign-owned chemical plant at Bhopal (boh-PAHL). Much of the problem, however, comes from state-owned factories erected with Soviet aid. And not all the environmental damage can be ascribed to industrialization. The Ganges River is so polluted by human overuse that it is risky for Hindu believers to bathe in it (see the comparative essay "One World, One Environment" on p. 798).

Moreover, many Indians have not benefited from the new prosperity. Nearly one-third of the population lives below the national poverty line. Millions continue to live in urban slums, such as the famous "City of Joy" in Kolkata (Calcutta), and most farm families remain desperately poor. Despite the socialist rhetoric of India's

COMPARATIVE ESSAY

One World, One Environment

EARTH & ENVIRONMENT

A crucial factor affecting the evolution of society and the global economy in the early twenty-first century is the growing concern over the impact of industrialization on the earth's environment. Humans have always caused some harm to their natural surroundings, but never before has the danger of significant ecological damage been so extensive. The effects of chemicals introduced into the atmosphere or into rivers, lakes, and oceans are increasingly threatening the health and well-being of all living species.

For many years, environmental concern was focused on the developed countries of the West, where industrial effluents, automobile emissions, and the use of artificial fertilizers and insecticides led to urban smog, extensive damage to crops and wildlife, and a major reduction of the ozone layer in the upper atmosphere. In recent years, the problem has spread. China's headlong rush to industrialization has resulted in major ecological damage in that country. Industrial smog has created almost unlivable conditions in many cities in Asia, while hillsides denuded of their forests have led to severe erosion that has destroyed farmlands. Destruction of the rain forest is a growing problem in many parts of the world, notably in Brazil and Indonesia. With the forest cover across the earth rapidly disappearing, there is less plant life to perform the crucial process of reducing carbon dioxide levels in the atmosphere.

One positive note is that environmental concerns have taken on a truly global character. While the causes of global warming have not yet been definitively proved, though the release of carbon dioxide and other gases into

Destruction of the Environment. This stunted tree has been killed by acid rain, a combination of sulfuric and nitric acids mixed with moisture in the air. Entire forests of trees killed by acid rain are becoming common sights in Canada, the United States, and northern Europe.

© Judyth Platt/Ecoscene/CORBIS

the atmosphere as a result of industrialization apparently plays a part, it has become a source of sufficient concern to be the subject of an international conference in Kyoto, Japan, in December 1997. If, as many scientists predict, worldwide temperatures continue to increase, the rise in sea levels could pose a significant threat to low-lying islands and coastal areas throughout the world, while climatic change could lead to severe droughts or excessive rainfall in cultivated areas.

It is one thing to recognize a problem, however, and another to solve it. So far, cooperative efforts among nations to alleviate environmental problems have all too often been hindered by economic forces or by political, ethnic, and religious disputes. The 1997 conference on global warming, for example, was marked by bitter disagreement over the degree to which developing countries should share the burden of cleaning up the environment. Few nations have been willing to take unilateral action that might pose an obstacle to economic development plans or lead to a rise in unemployment. In 2001, President George W. Bush refused to sign the Kyoto Agreement on the grounds that it discriminated against advanced Western countries. Subsequent conferences on global warming, including the 2009 conference in Copenhagen, Denmark, and the 2011 conference in Durban, South Africa, also have yielded few concrete results, despite a more active role by the United States.

 What are the major reasons why progress in cleaning up the environment has been so difficult to achieve?

leaders, the inequality of wealth in India is as pronounced as it is in capitalist nations in the West. Indeed, India has been described as two nations: an educated urban India of 100 million people surrounded by more than nine times that many impoverished peasants in the countryside (see the comparative illustration on p. 799).

Such problems are even more serious in neighboring Pakistan and Bangladesh. The overwhelming majority of

Two Indias. Contemporary India is a study in contrasts. In the photo at the top, middle-class students learn to use a computer, a symbol of their country's recent drive to join the global technological marketplace. Yet India today remains primarily a nation of villages. In the photo below, women in colorful saris fill their pails with water at the village well. As in many developing countries, the scarcity of water is one of India's most crucial problems.

Q *Do such stark contrasts between wealth and poverty define conditions in all other countries in Asia?*

© Indranil Mukherjee/AFP/Getty Images

© William J. Duiker

Pakistan's citizens are poor, and at least half are illiterate. The recent flooding along the Indus River has had a devastating effect on people living in the region and was described by a United Nations official as the worst humanitarian crisis in the sixty-five years of the UN's existence. Prospects for the future are not bright, for Pakistan lacks a modern technological sector to serve as a magnet for the emergence of a modern middle class.

CASTE, CLASS, AND GENDER The Indian constitution of 1950 guaranteed equal treatment and opportunity for all, regardless of caste, and prohibited discrimination based on untouchability. In recent years, the government has enacted a number of laws guaranteeing access to education and employment to all Indians, regardless of caste affiliation, and a number of individuals of low caste have attained high positions in Indian society. Nevertheless, prejudice is hard to eliminate, and the problem persists, particularly in rural villages, where *harijans* (HAR-ih-jans), now called *dalits* (DAH-lits), still perform menial tasks and are often denied fundamental rights.

Gender equality has also been difficult to establish. After independence, India's leaders also sought to equalize treatment of the sexes. The constitution expressly

Young Hindu Bride in Gold Bangles.
Awaiting the marriage ceremony, a young bride sits with her female relatives at the Meenakshi Hindu temple, one of the largest in southern India. Although child marriage is illegal, Indian girls are still married at a young age. With the marital union arranged by the parents, this young bride may not have met her groom. Bedecked in gold jewelry and rich silks—part of her dowry—she nervously waits the priest's blessing before she moves to her husband's home. There she will begin a life of servitude to her in-laws' family.

© William J. Duiker

forbade discrimination based on gender and called for equal pay for equal work. Laws prohibited child marriage, *sati*, and the payment of a dowry by the bride's family. Women were encouraged to attend school and enter the labor market.

Such laws, along with the dynamics of economic and social change, have had a major impact on the lives of many Indian women. Middle-class women in urban areas are much more likely to seek employment outside the home, and many hold managerial and professional positions. Some Indian women, however, choose to play a dual role—a modern one in their work and in the marketplace and a more submissive, traditional one at home.

Like other aspects of life, the role of women has changed much less in rural areas. In the early 1960s, many villagers still practiced the institution of *purdah*. Female children are still much less likely to receive an education. The overall literacy rate in India today is about 60 percent, but it is less than 50 percent among women. Laws relating to dowry, child marriage, and inheritance are routinely ignored in the countryside. There have been a few highly publicized cases of *sati*, although undoubtedly more women die of mistreatment at the hands of their husband or of other members of his family.

South Asian Literature Since Independence

Recent decades have witnessed a prodigious outpouring of literature in India. Because of the vast quantity of works published (India is currently the third-largest publisher of English-language books in the world), only a few of the most prominent fiction writers can be mentioned here. Anita Desai (dess-SY) (b. 1937) was one of the first prominent female writers to emerge from contemporary India. Her writing focuses on the struggle of Indian women to achieve a degree of independence. In her first novel, *Cry, the Peacock*, the heroine finally seeks liberation by murdering her husband, preferring freedom at any cost to remaining a captive of traditional society.

The most controversial writer from India today is Salman Rushdie (b. 1947). In *Midnight's Children* (1980), he linked his protagonist, born on the night of independence, to the history of modern India, its achievements, and its frustrations. Rushdie's later novels have tackled such problems as religious intolerance, political tyranny, social injustice, and greed and corruption. His attack on Islamic fundamentalism in *The Satanic Verses* (1988) won plaudits from literary critics but provoked widespread criticism among Muslims, including a death sentence by Iran's Ayatollah Khomeini.

What Is the Future of India?

Indian society looks increasingly Western in form, if not in content. As in a number of other Asian and African societies, the distinction between traditional and modern, or indigenous and westernized, sometimes seems to be a simple dichotomy between rural and urban. The major cities appear modern and westernized, but the villages have changed little since precolonial days.

Yet traditional practices appear to be more resilient in India than in many other societies, and the result is often a synthesis rather than a clash between conflicting institutions and values. Clothing styles in the streets where the *sari* and *dhoti* continue to be popular, religious practices in the temples, and social relationships in the home all testify to the importance of tradition in India.

One disadvantage of the eclectic approach, which seeks to blend the old and the new rather than choosing one over the other, is that sometimes contrasting traditions cannot be reconciled. In his book *India: A Wounded Civilization*, V. S. Naipaul (NY-pahl) (b. 1932), a Trinidadian of Indian descent who received the Nobel Prize for Literature in 2001, charged that Mahatma Gandhi's glorification of poverty and the simple Indian village was an obstacle to efforts to overcome the poverty, ignorance, and degradation of India's past and build a prosperous modern society. Gandhi's vision of a spiritual India, Naipaul complained, was a balm for defeatism and an excuse for failure.

Yet the appeal of Gandhi's philosophy remains a major part of the country's heritage. As historian Martha Nussbaum points out in *The Clash Within: Democracy, Religious Violence, and India's Future*, much of India's rural population continues to hold traditional beliefs, such as the concept of *karma* and inherent caste distinctions, that are incompatible with the capitalist work ethic and the democratic belief in equality before the law. Yet these beliefs provide a measure of identity and solace often lacking in other societies where such traditional spiritual underpinnings have eroded.

India, like Pakistan, also faces a number of other serious challenges. As a democratic and pluralistic society, India is unable to launch major programs without popular consent and thus cannot move as quickly or often as effectively as an authoritarian system like China's. At the same time, India's institutions provide a mechanism to prevent the emergence of a despotic government elite interested only in its own survival. Nevertheless, whether India will be able to meet its challenges remains an open question.

Southeast Asia

Q FOCUS QUESTION: What kinds of problems have the nations of Southeast Asia faced since 1945, and how have they attempted to solve these problems?

As we have seen (see Chapter 25), Japanese wartime occupation had a great impact on attitudes among the peoples of Southeast Asia. It demonstrated the vulnerability of colonial rule in the region and showed that an Asian power could defeat Europeans. The Allied governments themselves also contributed—sometimes unwittingly—to rising aspirations for independence by promising self-determination for all peoples at the end of the war.

Some followed through on their promise. In July 1946, the United States granted total independence to the Philippines. The Americans maintained a military presence on the islands, however, and U.S. citizens retained economic and commercial interests in the new country.

The British, too, were willing to bring an end to a century of imperialism in the region. In 1948, the Union of Burma received its independence. Malaya's turn came in 1957, after a Communist guerrilla movement had been suppressed.

The French and the Dutch, however, both regarded their colonies in the region as economic necessities as well as symbols of national grandeur and refused to turn them over to nationalist movements at the end of the war. The Dutch attempted to suppress a rebellion in the East Indies led by Sukarno (soo-KAHR-noh) (1901–1970), leader of the Indonesian Nationalist Party. But the United States, which feared a Communist victory there, pressured the Dutch to grant independence to Sukarno and his non-Communist forces, and in 1950, the Dutch finally agreed to recognize the new Republic of Indonesia.

The situation was somewhat different in Vietnam, where the Communists seized power throughout most of the country. After the French refused to recognize the new government and reimposed their rule, war broke out in December 1946. At the time, it was only an anticolonial war, but it would soon become much more (see Chapter 26).

In the Shadow of the Cold War

Many of the leaders of the newly independent states in Southeast Asia (see Map 30.2 on p. 802) admired Western political institutions and hoped to adapt them to their own countries. New constitutions were patterned on Western democratic models, and multiparty political systems quickly sprang into operation.

THE SEARCH FOR A NEW POLITICAL CULTURE   By the 1960s, most of these budding experiments in pluralist democracy had been abandoned or were under serious threat. Some had been replaced by military or one-party autocratic regimes. In Burma, a moderate government based on the British parliamentary system and dedicated to Buddhism and nonviolent Marxism had given way to a military dictatorship. In Thailand, too, the military now ruled. In the Philippines, President Ferdinand Marcos (MAHR-kohs) (1917–1989) discarded democratic restraints and established his own centralized control. In South Vietnam, under pressure from Communist-led insurgents, Ngo Dinh Diem and his successors paid lip

MAP 30.2 **Modern Southeast Asia.** Shown here are the countries that comprise contemporary Southeast Asia. The names of major islands are indicated in italic type.

Q *Which of the countries in Southeast Asia have democratic governments?*

service to the Western democratic model but ruled by authoritarian means. The North, under the rule of Ho Chi Minh and his colleagues, became a Communist dictatorship.

One problem faced by most of these states was that independence had not brought material prosperity or ended economic inequality and the domination of the local economies by foreign interests. Most economies in the region were still characterized by tiny industrial sectors; they lacked technology, educational resources, and capital investment.

The presence of widespread ethnic, linguistic, cultural, and economic differences also made the transition to Western-style democracy difficult. In Malaya, for example, the majority Malays—most of whom were farmers— feared economic and political domination by the local

Chinese minority, who were much more experienced in industry and commerce. In 1961, the Federation of Malaya, whose ruling party was dominated by Malays, integrated former British possessions on the island of Borneo into the new Union of Malaysia in a move to increase the non-Chinese proportion of the country's population.

The most prominent example of a failed experiment in democracy was in Indonesia. In 1950, the new leaders drew up a constitution creating a parliamentary system under a titular presidency. Sukarno was elected the first president. A spellbinding orator, Sukarno played a major role in creating a sense of national identity among the disparate peoples of the Indonesian archipelago (see the box on p. 803).

But Sukarno grew exasperated at the incessant maneuvering among devout Muslims, Communists, and the

The Golden Throat of President Sukarno

POLITICS & GOVERNMENT

President Sukarno of Indonesia was a spellbinding speaker and a charismatic leader of his nation's struggle for independence. These two selections are from speeches in which Sukarno promoted two of his favorite projects: Indonesian nationalism and "guided democracy." The force that would guide Indonesia, of course, was to be Sukarno himself.

Sukarno on Indonesian Greatness

What was Indonesia in 1945? What was our nation then? It was only two things, only two things. A flag and a song. That is all. (Pause, finger held up as afterthought.) But no, I have omitted the main ingredient. I have missed the most important thing of all. I have left out the burning fire of freedom and independence in the breast and heart of every Indonesian. That is the most important thing—this is the vital chord—the spirit of our people, the spirit and determination to be free. This was our nation in 1945—the spirit of our people!

And what are we today? We are a great nation. We are bigger than Poland. We are bigger than Turkey. We have more people than Australia, than Canada, we are bigger in area and have more people than Japan. In population now we are the fifth-largest country in the world. In area, we are even bigger than the United States of America. The American Ambassador, who is here with us, admits this. Of course, he points out that we have a lot of water in between our thousands of islands. But I say to him—America has a lot of mountains and deserts, too!

Sukarno on Guided Democracy

Indonesia's democracy is not liberal democracy. Indonesian democracy is not the democracy of the world of Montaigne or Voltaire. Indonesia's democracy is not à la America, Indonesia's democracy is not the Soviet—NO! Indonesia's democracy is the democracy which is implanted in the breasts of the Indonesian people, and it is that which I have tried to dig up again, and have put forward as an offering to you. . . . If you, especially the undergraduates, are still clinging to and being borne along the democracy made in England, or democracy made in France, or democracy made in America, or democracy made in Russia, you will become a nation of copyists!

Q *What are Sukarno's criticisms of Western democracy? Can you think of other instances in Asia or Africa where new leaders sought to adapt Western institutions to local realities?*

Source: From Howard Jones, *Indonesia: The Possible Dream* (New York: Harcourt Brace Jovanovich, Hoover Institute, 1971), pp. 223, 237.

---

army, and in the late 1950s he dissolved the constitution and attempted to rule on his own through what he called guided democracy. As he described it, **guided democracy** was closer to Indonesian traditions and superior to the Western variety. Highly suspicious of the West, Sukarno nationalized foreign-owned enterprises and sought economic aid from China and the Soviet Union while relying for domestic support on the Indonesian Communist Party.

The army and many devout Muslims resented Sukarno's increasing reliance on the Communists, and Muslims were further upset by his refusal to consider a state based on Islamic principles. In 1965, military officers launched a coup d'état that provoked a mass popular uprising, which resulted in the slaughter of several hundred thousand suspected Communists, many of whom were overseas Chinese, long distrusted by the Muslim majority (see the Film & History feature on p. 804). In 1967, a military government under General Suharto (soo-HAHR-toh) (1921–2008) was installed.

The new government made no pretensions of reverting to democratic rule, but it did restore good relations with the West and sought foreign investment to repair the country's ravaged economy. But it also found it difficult to placate Muslim demands for an Islamic state.

On the Road to Political Reform

With the end of the Vietnam War and the gradual rapprochement between China and the United States in the late 1970s, the ferment and uncertainty that had marked the first three decades of independence in Southeast Asia

The Year of Living Dangerously (1982)

President Sukarno of Indonesia was one of the most prominent figures in Southeast Asia in the first two decades after World War II. A key figure in the nationalist movement while the country was under Dutch colonial rule, he was elected president of the new republic when it was granted formal independence in 1950. The charismatic Sukarno initially won broad popular support for his efforts to end colonial dependency and improve living conditions for the impoverished local population. But the government's economic achievements failed to match his fiery oratory, and when political unrest began to spread through Indonesian society in the early 1960s, Sukarno dismantled the parliamentary system that had been installed at independence and began to crack down on dissidents.

These conditions provide the setting for the Australian film *The Year of Living Dangerously* (1982). Based on a novel of the same name by Christian Koch, the movie takes place in the summer of 1965, when popular unrest against the dictatorial government had reached a crescendo and the country appeared about to descend into civil war. The newly arrived Australian reporter Guy Hamilton (Mel Gibson) is befriended by a diminutive Chinese-Indonesian journalist named Billy Kwan, effectively played by Linda Hunt, who won an Academy Award for her performance. Kwan, who has become increasingly disenchanted with Sukarno's failure to live up his promises, introduces Hamilton to the seamy underside of Indonesian society, as well as to radical elements connected to the Communist Party who are planning a coup to seize power in Jakarta.

The movie reaches a climax as Hamilton—a quintessentially ambitious reporter out to get a scoop on the big story—inadvertently becomes involved in the Communist plot and arouses the suspicions of

Photographer Billy Kwan (Linda Hunt) and reporter Guy Hamilton (Mel Gibson) film a political protest.

government authorities. As Indonesia appears ready to descend into chaos, Hamilton finally recognizes the danger and manages to board the last plane from Jakarta. Others are not so fortunate, as Sukarno's security police crack down forcefully on critics of his regime.

The Year of Living Dangerously (the title comes from a remark made by Sukarno during his presidential address in August 1964) is an important if underrated film that dramatically portrays a crucial incident in a volatile region caught in the throes of the Cold War. The beautiful scenery (the movie was shot in the Philippines because the story was banned in Indonesia) and a haunting film score help create a mood of tension spreading through a tropical paradise.

gradually gave way to an era of greater political stability and material prosperity. In the Philippines, the dictatorial Marcos regime was overthrown by a massive public uprising in 1986 and replaced by a democratically elected government under President Corazon Aquino (KOR-uh-zahn ah-KEE-noh) (1933–2009), the widow of a popular politician assassinated a few years earlier. Aquino was unable to resolve many of the country's chronic economic and social difficulties, however, and political stability remains elusive. At the same time, Muslims on the southern island of Mindanao (min-duh-NAH-oh) have mounted a terrorist campaign in an effort to obtain autonomy or independence.

In other nations, the trends have been modestly favorable. Malaysia is a practicing democracy, although tensions persist between Malays and Chinese as well as between secular and orthodox Muslims who seek to create an Islamic state. In neighboring Thailand, the military has found it expedient to hold national elections for civilian governments, but the danger of a military takeover is never far beneath the surface. In the fall of 2008, massive protests against the existing government threatened to throw Thai society into a state of paralysis. Burma, now renamed Myanmar, continues to be ruled by a military junta, although the governement has recently shown tantalizing signs of willingness to moderate its policies to open doors to the outside world.

INDONESIA AFTER SUHARTO   For years, a major exception to the trend toward political pluralism in the region was Indonesia, where Suharto ruled without restraints. But in 1997, protests against widespread official corruption and demands by Muslims for a larger role for Islam in Indonesian society led to violent street riots and calls for Suharto's resignation. Forced to step down in the spring of 1998, Suharto was replaced by his deputy B. J. Habibie (hab-BEEB-ee) (b. 1936), who called for the establishment of a national assembly to select a new government based on popular aspirations.

The new government faced internal challenges from dissident elements seeking autonomy or separation from the republic, as well as from religious forces seeking to transform the country into an Islamic state. Under pressure from the international community, Indonesia agreed to grant independence to the onetime Portuguese colony of East Timor, where the majority of the people are Roman Catholics. But violence provoked by pro-Indonesian militia units forced many refugees to flee the country. Religious tensions also erupted between Muslims and Christians elsewhere in the archipelago, and Muslim rebels in western Sumatra demanded a new state based on strict adherence to fundamentalist Islam. In the meantime, a terrorist attack directed at tourists on the island of Bali aroused fears that the Muslim nation had become a haven for terrorist elements throughout the region.

In direct presidential elections held in 2004, General Susilo Yudhyono (soo-SEE-loh yood-heh-YOH-noh) (b. 1949) defeated Megawati Sukarnoputri (meg-uh-WAH-tee soo-kahr-noh-POO-tree) (b. 1947), the incumbent president and Sukarno's daughter. The new chief executive promised a new era of political stability, honest government, and economic reform while ceding more authority to the country's thirty-three provinces. Pressure from traditional Muslims to abandon the nation's secular tradition and move toward the creation of an Islamic state continues, but the level of religious and ethnic tension has declined somewhat. In elections held in 2009, Yudhyono won a second term in office, while popular support for Islamic parties dropped from 38 percent to 26 percent. That the country was able to hold democratic elections in the midst of such tensions holds some promise for the future.

THE VIETNAMESE EXCEPTION   As always, Vietnam is a special case. After achieving victory over South Vietnam with the fall of Saigon in the spring of 1975 (see Chapter 26), the Communist government in Hanoi pursued the rapid reunification of the two zones under Communist Party rule and laid plans to carry out a socialist transformation throughout the country, now renamed the Socialist Republic of Vietnam. The result was an economic disaster, and in 1986, party leaders followed the example of Mikhail Gorbachev in the Soviet Union and introduced their own version of *perestroika* in Vietnam (see Chapter 27). The trend in recent years has been toward a mixed capitalist-socialist economy along Chinese lines and a greater popular role in the governing process. Elections for the unicameral parliament are more open than in the past. The government remains suspicious of Western-style democracy, however, and represses any opposition to the Communist Party's guiding role over the state.

FINANCIAL CRISIS AND RECOVERY   The trend toward more representative systems of government in the region has been due in part to increasing prosperity and the growth of an affluent and educated middle class. Although Indonesia, Burma, and the three Indochinese states are still overwhelmingly agrarian, Malaysia and Thailand have been undergoing relatively rapid economic development.

In the late summer of 1997, however, these economic gains were threatened and popular faith in the ultimate benefits of globalization was shaken as a financial crisis swept through the region. The crisis was triggered by a number of problems, including growing budget deficits caused by excessive government expenditures on ambitious development projects, irresponsible lending and investment practices by financial institutions, and an overvaluation of local currencies relative to the U.S. dollar. An underlying problem was the prevalence of backroom deals between politicians and business leaders that temporarily enriched both groups at the cost of eventual economic dislocation.

As local currencies plummeted in value, the International Monetary Fund agreed to provide assistance, but only on the condition that the governments concerned permit greater transparency in their economic systems and allow market forces to operate more freely, even at the price of bankruptcies and the loss of jobs. By the early 2000s, there were signs that the economies in the region had weathered the crisis and were beginning to recover. The massive tsunami that struck the region in

December 2004 was another setback to economic growth, as well as a human tragedy of enormous proportions, but as the decade wore on, progress resumed, and today the nations of Southeast Asia, with a few exceptions, are among the fastest growing in the world.

Regional Conflict and Cooperation: The Rise of ASEAN

Southeast Asian states have also been hampered by serious tensions among themselves. Some of these tensions were a consequence of historical rivalries and territorial disputes that had been submerged during the long era of colonial rule. Cambodia, for example, has bickered with both of its neighbors, Thailand and Vietnam, over mutual frontiers drawn up originally by the French for their own convenience.

After the fall of Saigon and the reunification of Vietnam under Communist rule in 1975, the lingering border dispute between Cambodia and Vietnam erupted again. In April 1975, a brutal revolutionary regime under the leadership of the Khmer Rouge (KMAIR ROOZH) dictator Pol Pot (POHL PAHT) (c. 1928–1998) came to power in Cambodia and proceeded to carry out the massacre of more than one million Cambodians. Then, claiming that vast territories in the Mekong delta had been seized from Cambodia by the Vietnamese in previous centuries, the Khmer Rouge regime launched attacks across the common border. In response, Vietnamese forces invaded Cambodia in December 1978 and installed a pro-Hanoi regime in Phnom Penh (puh-NAHM PEN). Fearful of Vietnam's increasing power in the region, China launched a brief attack on Vietnam to demonstrate its displeasure.

The outbreak of war among the erstwhile Communist allies aroused the concern of other countries in the neighborhood. In 1967, several non-Communist countries had

© William J. Duiker

Holocaust in Cambodia. When the Khmer Rouge seized power in Cambodia in April 1975, they immediately emptied the capital of Phnom Penh and systematically began to eliminate opposition elements throughout the country. Thousands were tortured in the infamous Tuol Sleng prison and then marched out to the countryside, where they were massacred. Their bodies were thrown into massive pits. The succeeding government disinterred the remains, which are now displayed at an outdoor museum on the site. Today, a measure of political and economic stability has begun to return to the country. In 2010, the commandant of the prison, Comrade Duch, was convicted of war crimes and crimes against humanity.

established the Association of Southeast Asian Nations, or **ASEAN**. Composed of Indonesia, Malaysia, Thailand, Singapore, and the Philippines, ASEAN at first concentrated on cooperative social and economic endeavors, but after the end of the Vietnam War, it cooperated with other states in an effort to force the Vietnamese to withdraw from Cambodia. In 1991, the Vietnamese finally withdrew, and a new government was formed in Phnom Penh.

The growth of ASEAN from a weak collection of diverse states into a stronger organization whose members cooperate militarily and politically has helped provide the nations of Southeast Asia with a more cohesive voice to represent their interests on the world stage. The admission of Vietnam into ASEAN in 1996 provided both Hanoi and its neighbors with greater leverage in dealing with China—their powerful neighbor to the north, whose claims of ownership over islands in the South China Sea have aroused widespread concern among its neighbors to the south.

Daily Life: Town and Country in Contemporary Southeast Asia

The urban-rural dichotomy observed in India also is found in Southeast Asia, where the cities resemble those in the West while the countryside often appears little changed from precolonial days. In cities such as Bangkok, Manila, and Jakarta, broad boulevards lined with skyscrapers alternate with muddy lanes passing through neighborhoods packed with wooden shacks topped by thatch or rusty tin roofs. Nevertheless, in recent decades, millions of Southeast Asians have fled to these urban slums. Although most available jobs are menial, the pay is better than in the villages.

TRADITIONAL CUSTOMS, MODERN VALUES The urban migrants change not only their physical surroundings but their attitudes and values as well. Sometimes the move leads to a decline in traditional beliefs. Nevertheless, Buddhist, Muslim, and Confucian beliefs remain strong, even in cosmopolitan cities such as Bangkok, Jakarta, and Singapore. This preference for the traditional also shows up in lifestyle. Native dress—or an eclectic blend of Asian and Western dress—is still common. Traditional music, art, theater, and dance remain popular, although Western rock music has become fashionable among the young, and Indonesian filmmakers complain that Western films are beginning to dominate the market.

CHANGING ROLES FOR WOMEN One of the most significant changes that has taken place in Southeast Asia in recent decades is in the role of women in society. In general, women in the region have historically faced fewer restrictions on their activities and enjoyed a higher status than women elsewhere in Asia. Nevertheless, they were not the equal of men in every respect. With independence, Southeast Asian women gained new rights. Virtually all of the constitutions adopted by the newly independent states granted women full legal and political rights, including the right to work. Today, women have increased opportunities for education and have entered careers previously reserved for men. Women have become more active in politics, and some have served as heads of state.

Yet women are not truly equal to men in any country in Southeast Asia. In Vietnam, women are legally equal to men, yet until recently no women had served in the Communist Party's ruling politburo. In Thailand, Malaysia, and Indonesia, women rarely hold senior positions in government service or in the boardrooms of major corporations.

A Region in Flux

Today, the Western image of a Southeast Asia mired in the Vietnam conflict and the tensions of the Cold War has become a memory. In ASEAN, the states in the region have created the framework for a regional organization that can serve their common political, economic, technological, and security interests. A few members of ASEAN are already on the road to advanced development.

To be sure, there are continuing signs of trouble. The financial crisis of the late 1990s aroused serious political unrest in Indonesia, and the region's economies, though recovering, still bear the scars of the crisis. Radical Islamic terrorist groups have established a presence in the region. Although there are tantalizing signs of change in Myanmar, the country remains mired in a state of chronic underdevelopment. The three states of Indochina remain potentially unstable and have not yet been fully integrated into the region as a whole. All things considered, however, the situation is more promising today than would have seemed possible a generation ago. Unlike the situation in Africa and the Middle East, the nations of Southeast Asia have put aside the bitter legacy of the colonial era to embrace the wave of globalization that has been sweeping the world in the post–World War II era.

Japan: Asian Giant

Q **FOCUS QUESTION:** How did the Allied occupation after World War II change Japan's political and economic institutions, and what remained unchanged?

In August 1945, Japan was in ruins, its cities destroyed, its vast Asian empire in ashes, its land occupied by a foreign army. Half a century later, Japan had emerged as the second-greatest industrial power in the world, democratic in form and content and a source of stability throughout the region. Japan's achievement spawned a number of Asian imitators.

The Transformation of Modern Japan

For five years after the end of the war in the Pacific, Japan was governed by an Allied administration under the command of U.S. General Douglas MacArthur. As commander of the occupation administration, MacArthur was responsible for demilitarizing Japanese society, destroying the Japanese war machine, trying Japanese civilian and military officials charged with war crimes, and laying the foundations of postwar Japanese society.

One of the sturdy pillars of Japanese militarism had been the giant business cartels, known as *zaibatsu* (see Chapter 24). Allied policy was designed to break up the *zaibatsu* into smaller units in the belief that corporate concentration not only hindered competition but was inherently undemocratic and conducive to political authoritarianism. Occupation planners also intended to promote the formation of independent labor unions in order to lessen the power of the state over the economy and provide a mouthpiece for downtrodden Japanese workers. Economic inequality in rural areas was to be reduced by a comprehensive land reform program that would turn the land over to those who farmed it. Finally, the educational system was to be remodeled along American lines so that it would turn out independent individuals rather than automatons subject to manipulation by the state.

The Allied program was an ambitious and even audacious plan to remake Japanese society and has been justly praised for its clear-sighted vision and altruistic motives. Parts of the program, such as the constitution, the land reforms, and the educational system, succeeded brilliantly. But as other concerns began to intervene, changes or compromises were made that were not always successful. In particular, with the rise of Cold War sentiment in the United States in the late 1940s, the goal of decentralizing the Japanese economy gave way to the desire to make Japan a key partner in the effort to defend East Asia against international communism. Convinced of the need to promote economic recovery in Japan, U.S. policy makers began to show more tolerance for the *zaibatsu*. Concerned about growing radicalism within the new labor movement, U.S. occupation authorities placed less emphasis on the independence of the labor unions.

The Cold War also affected U.S. foreign relations with Japan. On September 8, 1951, the United States and other former belligerent nations signed a peace treaty restoring

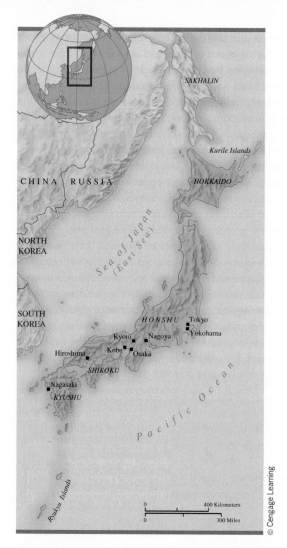

MAP 30.3 Modern Japan. Shown here are the four main islands that comprise the contemporary state of Japan.

Q *Which island is the largest?*

Japanese independence. In turn, Japan renounced any claim to such former colonies or territories as Taiwan, Korea, and southern Sakhalin and the Kurile Islands (see Map 30.3). On the same day, Japan and the United States signed a defensive alliance and agreed that the latter could maintain military bases on the Japanese islands. Japan was now formally independent but in a new dependency relationship with the United States. A provision in the new constitution renounced war as an instrument of national policy and prohibited the raising of an army.

POLITICS AND GOVERNMENT The Allied occupation administrators started with the conviction that Japanese expansionism was directly linked to the institutional and ideological foundations of the Meiji Constitution. Accordingly, they set out to change Japanese politics into something closer to the pluralistic model used in most Western nations. Yet a number of characteristics of the postwar Japanese political system reflected the tenacity of the traditional political culture. Although Japan had a multiparty system with two major parties, the Liberal Democrats and the Socialists, in practice there was a "government party" and a permanent opposition—the Liberal Democrats were not voted out of office for thirty years.

That tradition changed suddenly in 1993, when the ruling Liberal Democrats, shaken by persistent reports of corruption and cronyism between politicians and business interests, failed to win a majority of seats in parliamentary elections. The new coalition government, however, quickly split into feuding factions, and in 1995, the Liberal Democrats returned to power. Successive prime ministers proved unable to carry out promised reforms, and in 2001, Junichiro Koizumi (joo-nee-CHAY-roh koh-ee-ZOO-mee) (b. 1942), a former minister of health and welfare, was elected prime minister. His personal charisma raised expectations that he might be able to bring about significant changes, but bureaucratic resistance to reform and chronic factionalism within the Liberal Democratic Party thwarted his efforts. In 2009, three years after he left office, the Liberal Democrats were once again voted out of power. But subsequent governments have been criticized for the ineptitude of their recovery efforts after the massive earthquake and tsunami that struck the main island of Honshu in 2011.

JAPAN, INCORPORATED   One of the problems plaguing the current system has been the centralizing tendencies that it inherited from the Meiji period. The government is organized on a unitary rather than a federal basis; the local administrative units, called prefectures, have few of the powers of states in the United States. Moreover, the central government plays an active and sometimes intrusive role in various aspects of the economy, mediating management-labor disputes, establishing price and wage policies, and subsidizing vital industries and enterprises producing goods for export. This government intervention in the economy has traditionally been widely accepted and is often cited as a key reason for the efficiency of Japanese industry and the emergence of the country as an industrial giant.

In recent years, though, the tradition of active government involvement in the economy has increasingly come under fire. Japanese businesses, which previously sought government protection from imports, now argue that deregulation is needed to enable Japanese firms to innovate in order to keep up with the competition. Such reforms, however, have been resisted by powerful government ministries in Tokyo, which are accustomed to playing an active role in national affairs.

A third problem is that the Liberal Democratic Party has long been divided into factions that seek to protect their own interests and often resist changes that might benefit society as a whole. This tradition of factionalism has tended to insulate political figures from popular scrutiny and encouraged susceptibility to secret dealing and official corruption. A number of senior politicians, including two recent prime ministers, have been forced to resign because of serious questions about improper financial dealings with business associates. Concern over political corruption was undoubtedly a major factor in the defeats suffered by the Liberal Democrats in 1993 and 2009, and the issue continues to plague the political scene.

ATONING FOR THE PAST   Lingering social problems also need to be addressed. Minorities such as the *eta*, now known as the **Burakumin** (BOOR-uh-koo-min), and Korean residents in Japan continue to be subjected to legal and social discrimination. For years, official sources were reluctant to divulge growing evidence that thousands of Korean women were conscripted to serve as prostitutes (euphemistically called "comfort women") for Japanese soldiers during the war, and many Koreans living in Japan contend that such prejudicial attitudes continue to exist. Representatives of the "comfort women" have demanded both financial compensation and a formal letter of apology from the Japanese government for the treatment they received during the Pacific War. Negotiations over the issue have been under way for several years.

Japan's behavior during World War II has been an especially sensitive issue. During the early 1990s, critics at home and abroad charged that textbooks printed under the guidance of the Ministry of Education did not adequately discuss the atrocities committed by the Japanese armed forces during World War II. Other Asian governments were particularly incensed at Tokyo's failure to accept responsibility for such behavior and demanded a formal apology. The government expressed remorse, but only in the context of the aggressive actions of all colonial powers during the imperialist era.

The Economy

Nowhere are the changes in postwar Japan so visible as in the economic sector, where Japan developed into a major industrial and technological power in the space of a century, surpassing such advanced Western societies as Germany, France, and Great Britain. Although this "Japanese miracle" has often been described as beginning after the war as a result of the Allied reforms, rapid economic growth in fact began much earlier, with the Meiji reforms, which helped transform Japan from an autocratic society based on semifeudal institutions into an advanced capitalist democracy.

OCCUPATION REFORMS   As noted earlier, the officials of the Allied occupation identified the Meiji economic system with centralized power and the rise of Japanese militarism. But with the rise of Cold War tensions, the policy of breaking up the *zaibatsu* was scaled back. Looser ties between companies were still allowed, and a new type of informal relationship, sometimes called the **keiretsu** (key-RET-soo), or "interlocking arrangement," began to take shape. Through such arrangements among suppliers, wholesalers, retailers, and financial institutions, the *zaibatsu* system was reconstituted under a new name.

The occupation administration had more success with its program to reform the agricultural system. Half of the population still lived on farms, and half of all farmers were still tenants. Under the land reform program, all lands owned by absentee landlords and all cultivated landholdings over an established maximum were sold on easy credit terms to the tenants. The program created a strong class of yeoman farmers, and tenants declined to about 10 percent of the rural population.

THE "JAPANESE MIRACLE"?   During the next fifty years, Japan re-created the stunning results of the Meiji era. In 1950, the Japanese gross domestic product was about one-third that of Great Britain or France. Thirty years later, it was larger than both put together and well over half that of the United States. Japan is one of the greatest exporting nations in the world, and its per capita income equals or surpasses that of most advanced Western states.

In the last decades, however, the Japanese economy has run into serious difficulties, raising the question of whether the Japanese model is as appealing as many observers earlier declared. A rise in the value of the yen hurt exports and burst the bubble of investment by Japanese banks that had taken place under the umbrella of government protection. Lacking a domestic market equivalent in size to the United States, in the 1990s the Japanese economy slipped into a recession that has not yet entirely abated. Economic conditions worsened in 2008 and 2009 as Japanese exports declined significantly as a consequence of the global economic downturn.

These economic difficulties have placed heavy pressure on some of the vaunted features of the Japanese economy. The tradition of lifetime employment created a bloated white-collar workforce and has made downsizing difficult. Today, job security is on the decline as increasing numbers of workers are being laid off. A disproportionate burden has fallen on women, who lack seniority and continue to suffer from various forms of discrimination in the workplace.

A final change is that slowly but inexorably, the Japanese market is beginning to open up to international competition. Foreign automakers are winning a growing share of the domestic market, and the government—concerned at the prospect of food shortages—has committed itself to facilitating the importation of rice from abroad. Greater exposure to foreign competition may improve the performance of Japanese manufacturers. In recent years, Japanese consumers have become increasingly critical of the quality of some domestic products, causing one cabinet minister to complain about "sloppiness and complacency" among Japanese firms (even the Japanese automaker Toyota, whose vehicles consistently rank high in quality tests, has been faced with quality problems in its bestselling fleet of motor vehicles). The massive earthquake and tsunami that struck the coast of Japan in 2011 added to the nation's difficulties when they exposed the failure of the government to maintain proper safeguards for its nuclear plants in the vicinity. The costs of rebuilding after the disaster have posed a major challenge to Japanese leaders, who already face a crisis of confidence from their constituents.

A Society in Transition

During the occupation, Allied planners set out to change social characteristics that they believed had contributed to Japanese aggressiveness before and during World War II. The new educational system removed all references to filial piety, patriotism, and loyalty to the emperor while emphasizing the individualistic values of Western civilization. The new constitution and a revised civil code eliminated remaining legal restrictions on women's rights to obtain a divorce, hold a job, or change their domicile. Women were guaranteed the right to vote and were encouraged to enter politics.

Such efforts to remake Japanese behavior through legislation have had mixed success. During the past sixty years, Japan has unquestionably become a more individualistic and egalitarian society. At the same time, many of the distinctive characteristics of traditional Japanese society have persisted to the present day, although in somewhat altered form. The emphasis on loyalty to the group and community relationships, for example, is reflected in the strength of corporate loyalties in postwar Japan.

Emphasis on the work ethic also remains strong. The tradition of hard work is taught at a young age. The Japanese school year runs for 240 days a year, compared with 180 days in the United States, and work assignments outside class tend to be more extensive. The results are

Growing Up in Japan

FAMILY & SOCIETY

Japanese schoolchildren grow up in a much more regimented environment than U.S. children experience. Most Japanese schoolchildren, for example, wear black-and-white uniforms to school. These regulations are examples of rules adopted by middle school systems in various parts of Japan. The Ministry of Education in Tokyo concluded that these regulations were excessive, but they are probably typical.

School Regulations, Japanese Style

1. Boys' hair should not touch the eyebrows, the ears, or the top of the collar.
2. No one should have a permanent wave, or dye his or her hair. Girls should not wear ribbons or accessories in their hair. Hair dryers should not be used.
3. School uniform skirts should be _____ centimeters above the ground, no more and no less (differs by school and region).
4. Keep your uniform clean and pressed at all times. Girls' middy blouses should have two buttons on the back collar. Boys' pant cuffs should be of the prescribed width. No more than 12 eyelets should be on shoes. The number of buttons on a shirt and tucks in a shirt are also prescribed.
5. Wear your school badge at all times. It should be positioned exactly.
6. Going to school in the morning, wear your book bag strap on the right shoulder; in the afternoon on the way home, wear it on the left shoulder. Your book case thickness, filled and unfilled, is also prescribed.
7. Girls should wear only regulation white underpants of 100% cotton.
8. When you raise your hand to be called on, your arm should extend forward and up at the angle prescribed in your handbook.
9. Your own route to and from school is marked in your student rule handbook; carefully observe which side of each street you are to use on the way to and from school.
10. After school you are to go directly home, unless your parent has written a note permitting you to go to another location. Permission will not be granted by the school unless this other location is a suitable one. You must not go to coffee shops. You must be home by _____ o'clock.
11. It is not permitted to drive or ride a motorcycle, or to have a license to drive one.
12. Before and after school, no matter where you are, you represent our school, so you should behave in ways we can all be proud of.

Q *What is the apparent purpose of these regulations? Why does Japan appear to place more restrictions on students' behavior than most Western countries do?*

Source: From *The Material Child: Coming of Age in Japan and America* (New York: Free Press, 1993).

---

impressive: Japanese schoolchildren consistently earn higher scores on achievement tests than children in other advanced countries. At the same time, this devotion to success has often been accompanied by bullying by teachers and an emphasis on conformity (see the box above).

By all accounts, however, independent thinking is on the increase in Japan. In some cases, it leads to antisocial behavior, such as crime or membership in a teenage gang. Usually, it is expressed in more indirect ways, such as the recent fashion among young people of dyeing their hair brown (known in Japanese as "tea hair"). Because the practice is banned in many schools and generally frowned on by the older generation (one police chief dumped a pitcher of beer on a student with brown hair whom he noticed in a bar), many young Japanese dye their hair as a gesture of independence. When seeking employment or getting married, however, they often return their hair to its natural color.

WOMEN IN JAPANESE SOCIETY One of the most tenacious legacies of the past in Japanese society is sexual inequality. Although women are now legally protected against discrimination in employment, very few have reached senior levels in business, education, or politics.

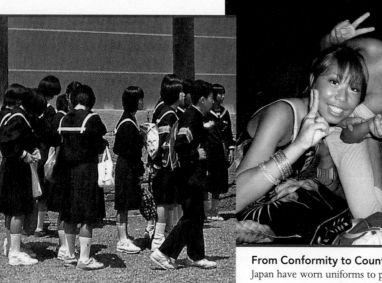

© William J. Duiker

© Barry Cronin/Getty Images

From Conformity to Counterculture. Traditionally, schoolchildren in Japan have worn uniforms to promote conformity with the country's communitarian social mores. In the photo on the left, young students dressed in identical uniforms are on a field trip to Kyoto's Nijo Castle, built in 1603 by Tokugawa Ieyasu. Recently, however, a youth counterculture has emerged in Japan. On the right, fashion-conscious teenagers with "tea hair"—heirs of Japan's long era of affluence—revel in their expensive hip-hop outfits, platform shoes, and layered dresses. Such fashion choices symbolize the growing revolt against conformity in contemporary Japan.

Women now comprise nearly 50 percent of the workforce, but most are in retail or service occupations. Less than 10 percent of managerial workers in Japan are women, compared with nearly half in the United States. There is a feminist movement in Japan, but it has none of the vigor and mass support of its counterpart in the United States.

THE DEMOGRAPHIC CRISIS Many of Japan's current dilemmas stem from its growing demographic problems. Today, Japan has the highest proportion of people older than sixty-five of any industrialized country—almost 23 percent of the country's total population. By the year 2024, an estimated one-third of the Japanese population will be over the age of sixty-five, and the median age will be fifty, ten years older than the median in the United States. This demographic profile is due both to declining fertility and a low level of immigration. Immigrants make up only 1 percent of the total population of Japan. Together, the aging population and the absence of immigrants are creating the prospect of a dramatic labor shortage in coming years. Nevertheless, prejudice against foreigners persists in Japan, and the government remains reluctant to ease restrictions against immigrants from other countries in the region.

Japan's aging population has many implications for the future. Traditionally, it was the responsibility of the eldest child in a Japanese family to care for aging parents, but that system is beginning to break down because of limited housing space and the growing tendency of working-age women to seek jobs in the marketplace. The proportion of Japanese older than sixty-five years of age who live with their children has dropped from 80 percent in 1970 to about 50 percent today. At the same time, public and private pension plans are under increasing financial pressure, partly because of the low birthrate and the graying population.

RELIGION AND CULTURE As in the West, increasing urbanization has led to a decline in the practice of organized religion in Japan, although evangelical sects have proliferated in recent years. The largest and best-known sect is Soka Gakkai (SOH-kuh GAK-ky), a lay Buddhist organization that has attracted millions of followers and formed its own political party, the Komeito (koh-MAY-toh). Zen Buddhism retains its popularity, and some businesspeople seek to use Zen techniques to learn how to focus their willpower as a means of outwitting a competitor. Many Japanese also follow Shinto, no longer identified with reverence for the emperor and the state.

Western literature, art, and music have also had a major impact on Japanese society. After World War II, many of the writers who had been active before the war resurfaced, but now their writing reflected demoralization. Many were attracted to existentialism, and some turned to hedonism and nihilism. For these disillusioned authors, defeat was compounded by fear of the Americanization of postwar Japan. One of the best examples of this attitude was the novelist Yukio Mishima (yoo-KEE-oh mi-SHEE-muh) (1925–1970), who led a crusade to stem the tide of what he described as America's "universal and uniform 'Coca-Colonization'" of the world in general and Japan in particular.[4] Mishima's ritual suicide in 1970 was the subject of widespread speculation and transformed him into a cult figure.

One of Japan's most serious-minded contemporary authors is Kenzaburo Oe (ken-zuh-BOO-roh OH-ay) (b. 1935). His work, rewarded with a Nobel Prize for Literature in 1994, focuses on Japan's ongoing quest for modern identity and purpose. His characters reflect the spiritual anguish precipitated by the collapse of the imperial Japanese tradition and the subsequent adoption of Western culture—a trend that Oe contends has culminated in unabashed materialism, cultural decline, and a moral void. Yet unlike Mishima, Oe does not wish to reinstill the imperial traditions of the past but rather seeks to regain spiritual meaning by retrieving the sense of communality and innocence found in rural Japan.

Since the 1970s, increasing affluence and a high literacy rate have contributed to a massive quantity of publications, ranging from popular potboilers to first-rate fiction. Much of this new literature deals with the common concerns of all affluent industrialized nations, including the effects of urbanization, advanced technology, and mass consumption. A wildly popular genre is the "art-manga," or graphic novel. Some members of the youth counterculture have used manga to rebel against Japan's rigid educational and conformist pressures.

Other aspects of Japanese culture have also been influenced by Western ideas, although without the intense preoccupation with synthesis that is evident in literature. Western music is very popular in Japan, and scores of Japanese classical musicians have succeeded in the West. Even rap music has gained a foothold among Japanese youth, although without the association with sex, drugs, and violence that it has in the United States. Although some of the lyrics betray an attitude of modest revolt against the uptight world of Japanese society, most lack any such connotations.

The Japanese Difference

Whether the unique character of modern Japan will endure is unclear. Confidence in the Japanese "economic miracle" has been shaken by the long recession, and there are indications of a growing tendency toward hedonism and individualism among Japanese youth. Older Japanese frequently complain that the younger generation lacks their sense of loyalty and willingness to sacrifice. There are also signs that the concept of loyalty to one's employer may be beginning to erode among Japanese youth. Some observers have predicted that with increasing affluence Japan will become more like the industrialized societies in the West. Although Japan is unlikely to evolve into a photocopy of the United States, the vaunted image of millions of dedicated "salarymen" heading off to work with their briefcases and their pin-striped suits may no longer be an accurate portrayal of reality in contemporary Japan.

The Little Tigers

Q **FOCUS QUESTIONS:** What factors have contributed to the economic success achieved by the Little Tigers? To what degree have they applied the Japanese model in forging their developmental strategies?

The success of postwar Japan in meeting the challenge from the capitalist West soon caught the eye of other Asian nations. By the 1980s, several smaller states in the region—known collectively as the "Little Tigers"—had successively followed the Japanese example.

South Korea: A Peninsula Divided

In 1953, the Korean peninsula was exhausted from three years of bitter fraternal war, a conflict that took the lives of an estimated 4 million Koreans on both sides of the 38th parallel. Although a cease-fire was signed in July 1953, it was a fragile peace that left two heavily armed and mutually hostile countries facing each other suspiciously.

North of the truce line was the People's Republic of Korea (PRK), a police state under the dictatorial rule of the Communist leader Kim Il-Sung (KIM ILL SOONG) (1912–1994). To the south was the Republic of Korea, under the equally

The Korean Peninsula Since 1953

autocratic President Syngman Rhee (SING-muhn REE) (1875–1965), a fierce anti-Communist who had led the resistance to the northern invasion. After several years of harsh rule in the Republic of Korea, marked by government corruption, fraudulent elections, and police brutality, demonstrations broke out in the capital city of Seoul in the spring of 1960 and forced Rhee into retirement.

In 1961, a coup d'état in South Korea placed General Chung Hee Park (1917–1979) in power. The new regime promulgated a new constitution, and in 1963, Park was elected president of a civilian government. He set out to foster recovery of the economy from decades of foreign occupation and civil war. Because the private sector had been relatively weak under Japanese rule, the government played an active role in the process by instituting a series of five-year plans that targeted specific industries for development, promoted exports, and funded infrastructure development.

The program was a solid success. Benefiting from the Confucian principles of thrift, respect for education, and hard work, as well as from Japanese capital and technology, Korea gradually emerged as a major industrial power in East Asia. The largest corporations—including Samsung, Daewoo, and Hyundai—were transformed into massive conglomerates called *chaebol* (jay-BOHL *or* je-BUHL), the Korean equivalent of the *zaibatsu* of prewar Japan. Korean businesses began to compete actively with the Japanese for export markets in Asia and throughout the world.

But like many other countries in the region, South Korea was slow to develop democratic principles. Although his government functioned with the trappings of democracy, Park continued to rule by autocratic means and suppressed all forms of dissidence. In 1979, Park was assassinated. But after a brief interregnum of democratic rule, in 1980 a new military government under General Chun Doo Hwan (JUN DOH HWAHN) (b. 1931) seized power. The new regime was as authoritarian as its predecessors, but after student riots in 1987, by the end of the decade opposition to autocratic rule had spread to much of the urban population.

National elections were finally held in 1989, and South Korea reverted to civilian rule. Successive presidents sought to rein in corruption while cracking down on the *chaebols* and initiating contacts with the Communist regime in the PRK on possible steps toward eventual reunification of the peninsula. After the Asian financial crisis in 1997, economic conditions temporarily worsened, but they have since recovered, and the country is increasingly competitive in world markets today. Symbolic of South Korea's growing self-confidence is the nation's current president, Lee Myung-bak (LEE MYUNG-BAHK) (b. 1941), elected in 2007. An ex-mayor of Seoul, he is noted for his rigorous efforts to beautify the city and improve the quality of life of his compatriots, including the installation of a new five-day workweek. His most serious challenge, however, is to protect the national economy, which is heavily dependent on exports, from the ravages of the recent economic crisis.

In the meantime, relations with North Korea, now on the verge of becoming a nuclear power, remain tense. Multinational efforts to persuade the regime to suspend its nuclear program continue, although North Korea claimed to have successfully conducted a nuclear test in 2009. To add to the uncertainty, the regime faced a succession crisis, when Kim Jong-Il (1941–2011), the son and successor of founder Kim Il-Sung, died suddenly in 2011 and was replaced by his inexperienced son.

Taiwan: The Other China

After retreating to Taiwan following the defeat by the Communists, Chiang Kai-shek's government, which continued to refer to itself as the Republic of China (ROC), contended that it remained the legitimate representative of the Chinese people and would eventually return in triumph to the mainland.

In the relatively secure environment provided by a security treaty with the United States, signed in 1954, the ROC was able to concentrate on economic growth without worrying about a Communist invasion. The government moved rapidly to create a solid agricultural base. A land reform program led to the reduction of rents, and landholdings over 3 acres were purchased by the government and resold to the tenants at reasonable prices. At the same time, local manufacturing and commerce were strongly encouraged. By the 1970s, Taiwan had become one of the most dynamic industrial economies in East Asia.

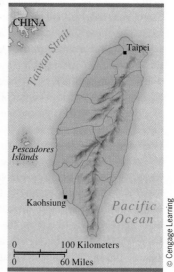

Modern Taiwan

In contrast to the Communist regime in the People's Republic of China (PRC), the ROC actively maintained Chinese tradition, promoting respect for Confucius and the ethical principles of the past, such as hard work, frugality, and filial piety. The overall standard of living increased substantially, health and sanitation improved, literacy rates were quite high, and an active family planning program reduced the rate of population growth.

After the death of Chiang Kai-shek in 1975, the ROC slowly began to move toward a more representative form of government, including elections and legal opposition parties. A national election in 1992 resulted in a bare majority for the Nationalists over strong opposition from the Democratic Progressive Party (DPP). But political liberalization had its dangers; some members of the DPP began to agitate for an independent Republic of Taiwan, a possibility that aroused concern within the Nationalist government in Taipei and frenzied hostility in the PRC. The election of DPP leader Chen Shui-bian (CHUHN SHWAY-BEE-ahn) (b. 1950) as ROC president in March 2000 angered Beijing, which threatened to invade Taiwan should the island continue to delay unification with the mainland. The return to power of the Nationalist Party in 2008 has at least for the time being eased relations with mainland China. As a result, economic and cultural contacts between Taiwan and the mainland are steadily increasing.

Singapore and Hong Kong: The Littlest Tigers

The smallest but by no means the least successful of the Little Tigers are Singapore and Hong Kong. Both contain large populations densely packed into small territories.

The Republic of Singapore

Singapore, once a British colony and briefly a part of the state of Malaysia, is now an independent nation. Hong Kong was a British colony until it was returned to PRC control in 1997. In recent years, both have emerged as industrial powerhouses, with standards of living well above those of their neighbors.

The success of Singapore must be ascribed in good measure to the will and energy of its political leaders. When it became independent in August 1965, Singapore's longtime position as an entrepôt for trade between the Indian Ocean and the South China Sea was on the wane.

Within a decade, Singapore's role and reputation had dramatically changed. Under the leadership of Prime Minister Lee Kuan-yew (LEE kwahn-YOO) (b. 1923), the government cultivated an attractive business climate while engaging in public works projects to feed, house, and educate its 2 million citizens. The major components of success have been shipbuilding, oil refineries, tourism, electronics, and finance—the city-state has become the banking hub of the entire region.

As in the other Little Tigers, an authoritarian political system has guaranteed a stable environment for economic growth. Until his retirement in 1990, Lee Kuan-yew and his People's Action Party dominated Singapore politics, and opposition elements were intimidated into silence or arrested. The prime minister openly declared that the Western model of pluralist democracy was not appropriate for Singapore. Confucian values of thrift, hard work, and obedience to authority were promoted as the ideology of the state.

But economic success has begun to undermine the authoritarian foundations of the system as a more sophisticated citizenry voices aspirations for more political freedoms and an end to

The Taiwan Democracy Memorial in Taipei. While the Chinese government on the mainland attempted to destroy all vestiges of traditional culture, the Republic of China on Taiwan sought to preserve the cultural heritage as a link between past and present. This policy was graphically displayed in the mausoleum for Chiang Kai-shek that was erected in downtown Taipei. The mausoleum, with its massive entrance gate, was designed not only to glorify the nation's deceased president but also to recall the grandeur of old China. In 2007, the mausoleum was renamed the Taiwan Democracy Memorial Hall in a bid by the government to downplay the island's historical ties to the mainland.

Unlike the other societies discussed in this chapter, Hong Kong has relied on an unbridled free market system rather than active state intervention in the economy. At the same time, by allocating substantial funds for transportation, sanitation, education, and public housing, the government has created favorable conditions for economic development.

When Britain's ninety-nine-year lease on the New Territories, the foodbasket of the colony, expired on July 1, 1997, Hong Kong returned to mainland authority. Although the Chinese promised the British that for fifty years, the people of Hong Kong would live under a capitalist system and be essentially self-governing, recent statements by Chinese leaders have raised questions about the degree of autonomy Hong Kong will continue to receive under Chinese rule.

Explaining the East Asian Miracle

What explains the striking ability of Japan and the four Little Tigers to transform themselves into export-oriented societies capable of competing with the advanced nations of Europe and the Western Hemisphere? Some analysts point to the traditional character traits of Confucian societies, such as thrift, a work ethic, respect for education, and obedience to authority. In a recent poll of Asian executives, more than 80 percent expressed the belief that Asian values differ from those of the West, and most add that these values have contributed significantly to the region's recent success. Others place more emphasis on deliberate steps taken by government and economic leaders to meet the political, economic, and social challenges their societies face.

There seems no reason to doubt that cultural factors connected to East Asian social traditions have contributed to the economic success of these societies. Certainly, habits such as frugality, industriousness, and subordination of individual desires have all played a role in their governments' ability to concentrate on the collective interest. As this and preceding chapters have shown, however, without active encouragement by political elites, such traditions cannot be effectively harnessed for the good of society as a whole. The creative talents of the Chinese people, for example, were not efficiently utilized under Mao Zedong during the frenetic years of the Cultural Revolution. Only when Deng Xiaoping and other pragmatists took charge and began to place a high priority on economic development were the stunning advances of recent decades achieved. By the same token, political elites elsewhere in East Asia were aware of traditional values and willing to use them for national purposes. In effect, the rapid rise of East Asia in the postwar era was no miracle, but a fortuitous combination of favorable cultural factors and deliberate human action.

government paternalism. In 2004, Lee Hsien-luong (LEE HAZ-ee-en-LAHNG) (b. 1952), the son of Lee Kuan-yew, became prime minister. Under his leadership, the government has relaxed its restrictions on freedom of speech and assembly, and elections held in 2011 resulted in growing support for members of opposition parties.

The future of Hong Kong is not so clear-cut. As in Singapore, sensible government policies and the hard work of its people have enabled Hong Kong to thrive.

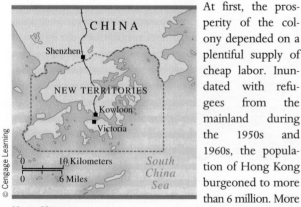

Hong Kong

At first, the prosperity of the colony depended on a plentiful supply of cheap labor. Inundated with refugees from the mainland during the 1950s and 1960s, the population of Hong Kong burgeoned to more than 6 million. More recently, Hong Kong has benefited from increased tourism, manufacturing, and the growing economic prosperity of neighboring Guangdong province, the most prosperous region of the PRC.

The Hong Kong Skyline. Hong Kong reverted to Chinese sovereignty in 1997 after a century of British rule. To commemorate the occasion, the imposing Conference Center, shown here in the foreground, was built on reclaimed shore land in the Hong Kong harbor.

On the Margins of Asia: Postwar Australia and New Zealand

Technically, Australia and New Zealand are not part of Asia, and throughout their short history, both countries have identified culturally and politically with the West rather than with their Asian neighbors. Their political institutions and values are derived from Europe, and their economies resemble those of the advanced countries of the world rather than the preindustrial societies of much of Southeast Asia. Both are currently members of the British Commonwealth and of the U.S.-led ANZUS (Australia, New Zealand, and the United States) alliance.

Yet trends in recent years have been drawing both states, especially Australia, closer to Asia. In the first place, immigration from East and Southeast Asia has increased rapidly. More than one-half of current immigrants into Australia come from East Asia, and about 7 percent of the population of about 18 million people is now of Asian descent. In New Zealand, residents of Asian descent represent only about 3 percent of the population of 3.5 million, but about 12 percent of the population are Maoris, Polynesian peoples who settled on the islands about a thousand years ago. Second, trade relations with Asia are increasing rapidly. About 60 percent of Australia's export markets today are in East Asia, and the region is the source of about one-half of its imports. Asian trade with New Zealand is also on the increase. Concern about China's rising strength in the region is cause for concern, however, and was undoubtedly a factor in the agreement reached in 2011 to station 2,500 U.S. troops in Australia.

CHAPTER SUMMARY

In the years following the end of World War II, the peoples of Asia emerged from a century of imperial rule to face the challenge of building stable and prosperous independent states. Initially, progress was slow, as new political leaders were forced to deal with the legacy of colonialism and internal disagreements over their visions for the future. By the end of the century, however, most nations in the area were beginning to lay the foundations for the creation of advanced industrial societies. Today, major Asian states like China,

Japan, and India have become major competitors of the advanced Western nations in the international marketplace.

To some observers, these economic achievements have come at a high price, in the form of political authoritarianism and a lack of attention to human rights. Rapid economic development has also exacted an environmental price. Industrial pollution in China and India and the destruction of the forest cover in Southeast Asia increasingly threaten the fragile ecosystem and create friction among nations in the region. Unless they learn to cooperate effectively to deal with the challenge in future years, it will ultimately undermine the dramatic economic and social progress that has taken place.

Still, a look at the historical record suggests that, for the most part, the nations of southern and eastern Asia have made dramatic progress in coping with the multiple challenges of independence. Political pluralism is often a by-product of economic growth, while a rising standard of living should enable the peoples of the region to meet the social and environmental challenges that lie ahead.

CHAPTER TIMELINE

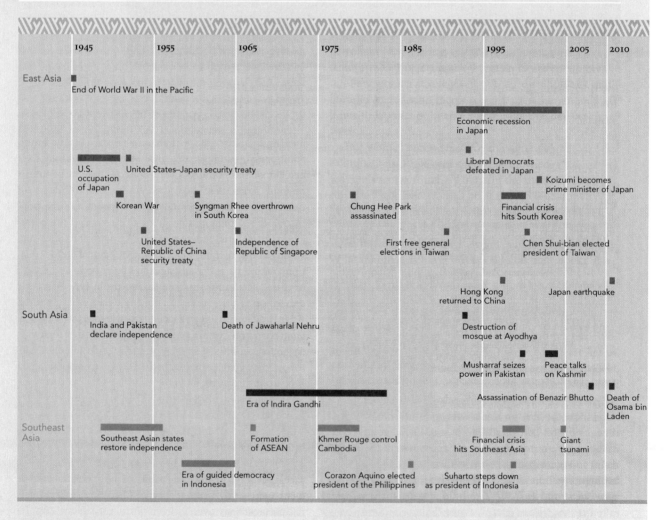

CHAPTER REVIEW

Upon Reflection

Q What kinds of environmental problems are currently being faced by the nations of southern and eastern Asia? How have the region's political leaders sought to deal with the problems?

Q How has independence affected the role of women in southern and eastern Asia? What factors are involved?

Q How have the nations in the region dealt with the challenge of integrating their ethnic and religious minorities into their political systems?

Key Terms

communalism (p. 795)
dalits (p. 799)
guided democracy (p. 803)
ASEAN (p. 807)
Burakumin (p. 809)
keiretsu (p. 810)
chaebol (p. 814)

Suggested Reading

THE INDIAN SUBCONTINENT SINCE 1945 For a survey of postwar Indian history, see S. Tharoor, *India: From Midnight to the Millennium* (New York, 1997). On India's founding father, see J. Brown, *Nehru: A Political Life* (New Haven, Conn., 2003). The life and career of Indira Gandhi have been well chronicled. See K. Frank, *Indira: The Life of Indira Nehru Gandhi* (New York, 2000). On Pakistan, see O. B. Jones, *Pakistan: Eye of the Storm* (New Haven, Conn., 2002). Also of interest is C. Baxter, *Bangladesh: From a Nation to a State* (Boulder, Colo., 1997).

SOUTHEAST ASIA SINCE 1945 There are a number of standard surveys of the history of modern Southeast Asia. One is N. Tarling, *Southeast Asia: A Modern History* (Oxford, 2002). For a more scholarly approach, see N.

Tarling, ed., *The Cambridge History of Southeast Asia*, vol. 4 (Cambridge, 1999).

T. Friend, *Indonesian Destinies* (Cambridge, Mass., 2003), is a fine introduction to Indonesian society and culture. The rise of terrorism in the region is discussed in Z. Abuza, *Militant Islam in Southeast Asia: Crucible of Terror* (Boulder, Colo., 2003). For an overview of women's issues in contemporary South and Southeast Asia, consult B. Ramusack and S. Sievers, *Women in Asia* (Bloomington, Ind., 1999).

JAPAN SINCE 1945 For a balanced treatment of all issues relating to postwar Japan, see J. McLain, *Japan: A Modern History* (New York, 2001). I. Buruma, *Inventing Japan* (New York, 2002), offers a more journalistic approach that raises questions about the future of democracy in Japan.

THE LITTLE TIGERS On the four Little Tigers and their economic development, see D. Oberdorfer, *The Two Koreas: A Contemporary History* (Indianapolis, 1997); Lee Kuan Yew, *From Third World to First: The Singapore Story, 1965–2000* (New York, 2000); and K. Rafferty, *City on the Rocks: Hong Kong's Uncertain Future* (London, 1991). Also see M. Rubinstein, *Taiwan: A New History* (New York, 2001).

CourseMate

Visit the CourseMate website at **www.cengagebrain.com** for additional study tools and review materials for this chapter.

EPILOGUE: A GLOBAL CIVILIZATION

ON A VISIT TO NUREMBERG, Germany, with his family in 2000, Jackson Spielvogel, one of the authors of this textbook, was startled to find that the main railroad station, where he had once arrived as a Fulbright student, was now adorned with McDonald's Golden Arches. McDonald's was the brainstorm of two brothers who opened a cheap burger restaurant in California in 1940. When they expanded their operations to Arizona, they began to use two yellow arches to make their building visible from blocks away. After Ray Kroc, an enterprising businessman, bought the burgeoning business, McDonald's arches rapidly spread all over the United States. And they didn't stop there. The fast-food industry, which now relied on computers for the automated processing of its food, found an international market. McDonald's spread to Japan in 1971 and to Russia and China in 1990; by 1995, more than half of all McDonald's restaurants were located outside the United States. By 2000, McDonald's was serving 50 million people a day.

McDonald's is but one of numerous U.S. companies that use the latest technology and actively seek global markets. Indeed, sociologists have coined the term *McDonaldization* to refer to "the process whereby the principles of the fast-food restaurant are coming to dominate more and more sectors of American society as well as the rest of the world."[1] Multinational corporations like McDonald's have brought about a worldwide homogenization of societies and made us aware of the political, economic, and social interdependence of the world's nations and the global nature of our contemporary problems. An important part of this global awareness is the technological dimension. New technology has made possible levels of world communication that simply did not exist before. At the same time that Osama bin Laden and al-Qaeda were denouncing the forces of modernization, they were spreading their message through the use of recently developed telecommunication systems. The Technological Revolution has tied peoples and nations closely together and contributed to **globalization**, the term that is frequently used to describe the process by which peoples and nations have become more interdependent.

The Global Economy

Especially since the 1970s, the world has developed a **global economy** in which the production, distribution, and sale of goods are accomplished on a worldwide scale. Several international institutions have contributed to the

McDonald's in India. McDonald's has become an important symbol of U.S. cultural influence throughout the world. Seen here is an Indian street child sipping a McDonald's soft drink at a McDonald's outside the Victoria Terminus Station in Mumbai.

rise of the global economy. Soon after the end of World War II, the United States and other nations established the World Bank and the International Monetary Fund (IMF) as a means of expanding global markets and avoiding economic crises such as the Great Depression of the 1930s. The World Bank comprises five international organizations, largely controlled by developed countries, which provide grants, loans, and advice for economic development to developing countries. The IMF oversees the global financial system by supervising exchange rates and offering financial and technical assistance to developing nations. Today, 188 countries are members of the IMF. Critics have argued, however, that both the World Bank and the IMF sometimes push non-Western nations to adopt inappropriate Western economic practices that only aggravate the poverty and debt of developing nations.

Another reflection of the new global economic order is the **multinational** or **transnational corporation** (a company that has divisions in more than two countries). Prominent examples of multinational corporations include Siemens, Coca-Cola, ExxonMobil, Mitsubishi, and Sony. These companies are among the two hundred largest multinational corporations, which are responsible for more than half of the world's industrial production. In 2000, some 71 percent of these corporations were headquartered in just three countries—the United States, Japan, and Germany. These supercorporations have come to dominate much of the world's investment capital, technology, and markets. A recent comparison of corporate sales and national gross domestic product disclosed that only forty-nine of the world's hundred largest economic entities are nations; the remaining fifty-one are corporations. For this reason, some observers believe that economic globalization is more appropriately labeled "corporate globalization."

Another important component of economic globalization is free trade. In 1947, talks led to the creation of the General Agreement on Tariffs and Trade (GATT), a global trade organization that was replaced in 1995 by the World Trade Organization (WTO). With more than 150 member nations, the WTO arranges trade agreements and settles trade disputes. The WTO's goal is to open up world markets and maximize global production, but many critics charge that the WTO has ignored environmental and health concerns, harmed small and developing countries, and contributed to the growing gap between rich and poor nations.

While production, capital, and trade have increased as a result of globalization, the steps taken to increase trade have also led to an interconnected world of finance. The extent to which the financial markets are now globalized was evident in 2008 when a collapse of the largely unregulated financial markets in the United States quickly led to a worldwide recession. Manufacturing plunged, unemployment rose, and banks faltered as countries around the world faced new and daunting economic challenges. The IMF estimated that global output would fall by 1.3 percent in 2009, the first decline in sixty years. Although there were some signs of recovery by May of 2010, most economists believed that the worst global slump since the Great Depression of the 1930s was far from over.

Global Culture and the Digital Age

Since the invention of the microprocessor in 1971, the capabilities of computers have expanded by leaps and bounds, resulting in today's digital age. Beginning in the 1980s, companies like Apple and Microsoft competed to create more powerful computers and software. By the 1990s, the booming technology industry had made Microsoft founder Bill Gates the richest man in the world. Much of this success was due to several innovations that made computers indispensable for communication, information, and entertainment.

Global Communication

The advent of electronic mail, or e-mail, transformed communication in the mid-1990s. At the same time, the Internet, especially its World Wide Web, was becoming an information exchange for people around the world. As web capabilities have increased, new forms of communication have emerged including Twitter, Facebook, and YouTube, now used for international news broadcasts and for President Obama's weekly radio addresses.

Advances in telecommunications led first to cellular or mobile phones and later to smartphones. Though cellular phones existed in the 1970s and 1980s, it was not until the digital components of these devices were reduced in size in the 1990s that cellphones became truly portable. The ubiquity of cellphones and their ability to transfer data electronically have made text messaging a global form of communication. Text and instant messaging have revolutionized written language, as shorthand script has replaced complete sentences for relaying brief messages. Worldwide the number of people with access to a mobile phone increased from 12.4 million in 1990 to almost 4.6 billion in 2009. In 2012, more than a billion people worldwide were using smartphones.

A number of the innovations that have enhanced consumers' ability to share music, watch movies, and search the web were introduced by Apple, Inc., and subsequently imitated by other companies. The iPod, a portable digital music player, has revolutionized the music industry, as downloading music electronically from the Internet has largely replaced the purchasing of physical recordings. The iPhone enables users to connect to the Internet from their phone, allowing information to be instantly updated for various telecommunication sites, such as Twitter and Facebook. The iPad, a handheld tablet computer, is challenging computer sales worldwide, as almost 7.5 million iPads were sold in the first six months.

Reality in the Digital Age

Advances in communication and information during the digital age have led many people to suggest that world cultures are becoming increasingly interdependent and homogenized. Many contemporary artists have questioned the effects of the computer age on identity and material reality. According to some, the era of virtual reality has displaced cultural uniqueness and bodily presence.

THE BODY AND IDENTITY IN CONTEMPORARY ART By focusing on bodily experience and cultural norms, contemporary artists have attempted to restore what has been lost in the digital age. Kiki Smith (b. 1954), an American artist born in Germany, creates sculptures of the human body that often focus on anatomical processes. These works, commonly made of wax or plaster, question the politics surrounding the body, including AIDS and domestic abuse, while reconnecting to bodily experiences.

Contemporary artists also continue to explore the interaction between the Western and non-Western world, particularly the **multiculturalism** generated by global migrations. For example, the art of Yinka Shonibare (YEEN-kuh SHOH-nih-bar-eh) (b. 1962), who was born in London, raised in Nigeria, and now resides in England, investigates the notion of hybrid identity as he creates clothing and life-size figures that fuse European designs with African traditions.

Globalization and the Environmental Crisis

As many people take a global perspective in the twenty-first century, they are realizing that everywhere on the planet, human beings are interdependent in terms of the air they breathe, the water they drink, the food they consume, and the climate that affects their lives. At the same time, however, human activities are creating environmental challenges that threaten the very foundation of human existence on earth.

One problem is population growth. As of September 2012, the world population was estimated at more than 7 billion people, only twenty-four years after passing the 5 billion mark. At its current rate of growth, the world population could reach 12.8 billion by 2050, according to the United Nations' long-range population projections. The result has been an increased demand for food and other resources that has put great pressure on the earth's ecosystems. At the same time, the failure to grow enough food for more and more people, a problem exacerbated by drought conditions developing on several continents, has created a severe problem, as an estimated 1 billion people worldwide today suffer from hunger. Every year, more than 8 million people die of hunger, many of them young children.

Another problem is the pattern of consumption as the wealthy nations of the Northern Hemisphere consume vast quantities of the planet's natural resources. The United States, for example, which has 6 percent of the world's people, consumes 30 to 40 percent of its resources. The spread of these consumption patterns to other parts of the world raises serious questions about the ability of the planet to sustain itself and its population. As a result of the growing Chinese economy, for example, more automobiles are now sold annually in China than in the United States.

Yet another threat to the environment is **global climate change**, which has the potential to create a worldwide crisis. Virtually all of the world's scientists agree that the **greenhouse effect**, the warming of the earth because of the buildup of carbon dioxide in the atmosphere, is contributing to devastating droughts and storms, the melting of the polar ice caps, and rising sea levels that could inundate coastal regions in the second half of the twenty-first century. Also alarming is the potential loss of biodiversity. Seven out of ten biologists believe the planet is now experiencing an alarming extinction of both plant and animal species.

The Social Challenges of Globalization

Since 1945, tens of millions of people have migrated from one part of the world to another. These migrations have occurred for many reasons. Persecution for political reasons caused many people from Pakistan, Bangladesh, Sri Lanka, and eastern Europe to seek refuge in western European countries, while brutal civil wars in Asia, Africa, the Middle East, and Europe led millions of refugees to seek safety in neighboring countries. Most people who have migrated, however, have done so to find jobs. Latin Americans seeking a better life have migrated to the United States, while guest workers from Turkey, southern and eastern Europe, North Africa, India, and Pakistan have migrated to more prosperous western European countries. In 2005, nearly 200 million people, about 3 percent of the world's population, lived outside the country where they were born.

The migration of millions of people has also provoked a social backlash in many countries. Foreign workers often become scapegoats when countries face economic problems. Political parties in France and Norway, for example, have called for the removal of blacks, Muslims, and Arabs in order to protect the ethnic or cultural purity of their nations, while in Asian countries, there is animosity against other Asian ethnic groups.

Another challenge of globalization is the wide gap between rich and poor nations. The rich nations, or **developed nations**, are located mainly in the Northern Hemisphere. They include the United States, Canada, Germany, and Japan, which have well-organized industrial and agricultural systems, advanced technologies, and effective educational systems. The poor nations, or **developing nations**, include many nations in Africa,

Asia, and Latin America, which often have primarily agricultural economies with little technology. A serious problem in many developing nations is explosive population growth, which has led to severe food shortages often caused by poor soil but also by economic factors. Growing crops for export to developed countries, for example, may lead to enormous profits for large landowners but leaves many small farmers with little land on which to grow food.

Civil wars have also created food shortages. War not only disrupts normal farming operations, but warring groups try to limit access to food to weaken or kill their enemies. In Sudan, 1.3 million people starved when combatants of a civil war in the 1980s prevented food from reaching them. As unrest continued during the early 2000s in Sudan's Darfur region, families were forced to leave their farms. As a result, an estimated 70,000 people had starved by mid-2004.

Global Movements and New Hopes

As people have become aware that the problems humans face are not just national or regional but global in scope, they have responded to this challenge in different ways. One approach has been to develop grassroots social movements, including ones devoted to environmental concerns, women's and men's liberation, human potential, appropriate technology, and nonviolence. "Think globally, act locally" is frequently the slogan of these grassroots groups. Related to the emergence of these social movements is the growth of **nongovernmental organizations (NGOs)**. According to one analyst, NGOs are an important instrument in the cultivation of global perspectives: "Since NGOs by definition are identified with interests that transcend national boundaries, we expect all NGOs to define problems in global terms, to take account of human interests and needs as they are found in all parts of the planet."[2] NGOs are often represented at the United Nations and include professional, business, and cooperative organizations; foundations; religious, peace, and disarmament groups; youth and women's organizations; environmental and human rights groups; and research institutes. The number of international NGOs has increased from 176 in 1910 to 40,000 in 2007.

And yet hopes for global approaches to global problems have also been hindered by political, ethnic, and religious differences. Pollution of the Rhine River by factories along its banks provokes angry disputes among European nations, and the United States and Canada have argued about the effects of acid rain on Canadian forests. While droughts in Russia and China wreak havoc on the world's grain supply, floods in Pakistan challenge the stability of Asia. The collapse of the Soviet Union and its satellite system seemed to provide an enormous boost to the potential for international cooperation on global issues, but it has had almost the opposite effect. The bloody conflict in the former Yugoslavia indicates the dangers inherent in the rise of nationalist sentiment among various ethnic and religious groups in eastern Europe. The widening gap between wealthy nations and poor, developing nations threatens global economic stability. Many conflicts begin with regional issues and then develop into international concerns. International terrorist groups seek to wreak havoc around the world.

Thus, even as the world becomes more global in culture and interdependent in its mutual relations, centrifugal forces are still at work attempting to redefine the political, cultural, and ethnic ways in which the world is divided. Such efforts are often disruptive and can sometimes work against measures to enhance our human destiny. But they also represent an integral part of human character and human history and cannot be suppressed in the relentless drive to create a world society.

There are already initial signs that as the common dangers posed by environmental damage, overpopulation, and scarcity of resources become even more apparent, societies around the world will find ample reason to turn their attention from cultural differences to the demands of global interdependence. The greatest challenge of the twenty-first century may be to reconcile the drive for individual and group identity with the common needs of the human community.

Suggested Reading

Useful books on different facets of the new global civilization include **M. B. Steger, *Globalization: A Very Short Introduction*** (New York, 2003); **J. H. Mittelman, *The Globalization Syndrome*** (Princeton, N.J., 2000); **M. Waters, *Globalization*,** 2nd ed. (London, 2001); **P. O'Meara et al., eds., *Globalization and the Challenges of the New Century*** (Bloomington, Ind., 2000); and **H. French, *Vanishing Borders*** (New York, 2000). For a comprehensive examination of the digital age, see **M. Castells, *The Information Age*,** 3 vols. (Oxford, 1996–1998).

GLOSSARY

abbess the head of a convent or monastery for women.

abbot the head of a monastery.

absolutism a form of government where the sovereign power or ultimate authority rested in the hands of a monarch who claimed to rule by divine right and was therefore responsible only to God.

Abstract Expressionism a post–World War II artistic movement that broke with all conventions of form and structure in favor of total abstraction.

abstract painting an artistic movement that developed early in the twentieth century in which artists focused on color to avoid any references to visual reality

African Union the organization that replaced the Organization of African Unity in 2001; designed to bring about increased political and economic integration of African states.

Agricultural (Neolithic) Revolution *see* Neolithic Revolution.

agricultural revolution the application of new agricultural techniques that allowed for a large increase in productivity in the eighteenth century.

Amerindians earliest inhabitants of North and South America. Original theories suggested migration from Siberia across the Bering Land Bridge; more recent evidence suggests migration also occurred by sea from regions of the South Pacific to South America.

Analects the body of writing containing conversations between Confucius and his disciples that preserves his worldly wisdom and pragmatic philosophies.

ANC the African National Congress. Founded in 1912, it was the beginning of political activity by South African blacks. Banned by politically dominant European whites in 1960, it was not officially "unbanned" until 1990. It is now the official majority party of the South African government.

anti-Semitism hostility toward or discrimination against Jews.

apartheid the system of racial segregation practiced in the Republic of South Africa until the 1990s, which involved political, legal, and economic discrimination against nonwhites.

appeasement the policy, followed by the European nations in the 1930s, of accepting Hitler's annexation of Austria and Czechoslovakia in the belief that meeting his demands would assure peace and stability.

Aramaic a Semitic language dominant in the Middle East in the first century B.C.E.; still in use in small regions of the Middle East and southern Asia.

aristocracy a class of hereditary nobility in medieval Europe; a warrior class who shared a distinctive lifestyle based on the institution of knighthood, although there were social divisions within the group based on extremes of wealth.

Arthasastra an early Indian political treatise that sets forth many fundamental aspects of the relationship of rulers and their subjects. It has been compared to Machiavelli's *The Prince* and has provided principles upon which many aspects of social organization have developed in the region.

Aryans Indo-European-speaking nomads who entered India from the Central Asian steppes between 1500 and 1000 B.C.E. and greatly affected Indian society, notably by establishing the caste system. The term was later adopted by German Nazis to describe their racial ideal.

asceticism a lifestyle involving the denial of worldly pleasures. Predominantly associated with Hindu, Buddhist, or Christian religions, adherents perceive their practices as a path to greater spitiuality.

ASEAN the Association for the Southeast Asian Nations formed in 1967 to promote the prosperity and political stability of its member nations. Currently, Brunei, Cambodia, Indonesia, Laos, Malaysia, Myanmar, the Philippines, Singapore, Thailand, and Vietnam are members. Other countries in the region participate as "observer" members.

assimilation the concept, originating in France, that the colonial peoples should be assimilated into the parent French culture.

association the concept, developed by French colonial officials, that the colonial peoples should be permitted to retain their precolonial cultural traditions.

Atman in Brahmanism, the individual soul.

Ausgleich the "Compromise" of 1867 that created the dual monarchy of Austria-Hungary. Austria and Hungary each had its own capital, constitution, and legislative assembly, but were united under one monarch.

authoritarian state a state that has a dictatorial government and some other trappings of a totalitarian state, but does not demand that the masses be actively involved in the regime's goals as totalitarian states do.

bakufu the centralized government set up in Japan in the twelfth century. *See also* shogunate system.

Banners originally established in 1639 by the Qing dynasty, the Eight Banners were administrative divisions into which all Manchu families were placed. Banners quickly evolved into the basis of Manchu military organization with each required to raise and support a prescribed number of troops.

Bao-jia **system** the Chinese practice, reportedly originated by the Qin dynasty in the third century B.C.E., of organizing families into groups of five or ten to exercise mutual control and surveillance and reduce loyalty to the family.

bard in Africa, a professional storyteller.

Baroque a style that dominated Western painting, sculpture, architecture, and music from about 1580 to 1730, generally characterized by elaborate ornamentation and dramatic effects. Important practitioners included Bernini, Rubens, Handel, and Bach.

Bedouins nomadic tribes originally from northern Arabia, who became important traders after the domestication of the camel during the first millennium B.C.E. Early converts to Islam, their values and practices deeply affected the religion of Islam.

Berbers an ethnic group indigenous to western North Africa.

bey a provincial governor in the Ottoman Empire.

bhakti in Hinduism, devotion as a means of religious observance open to all persons regardless of class.

Black Death the outbreak of plague (mostly bubonic) in the mid-fourteenth century that killed from 25 to 50 percent of Europe's population.

blitzkrieg "lightning war." A war conducted with great speed and force, as in Germany's advance at the beginning of World War II.

bodhi wisdom in India. Sometimes described as complete awareness of the true nature of the universe.

bodhisattvas in some schools of Buddhism, individuals who have achieved enlightenment but, because of their great compassion, have chosen to renounce Nirvana and to remain on earth in spirit form to help all human beings achieve release from reincarnation.

Boers the Afrikaans-speaking descendants of Dutch settlers in southern Africa who left the Cape Colony in the nineteenth century to settle in the Orange Free State and Transvaal; defeated by the British in the Boer War (1899–1902) and ultimately incorporated into the Union of South Africa.

Bolsheviks a small faction of the Russian Social Democratic Party who were led by Lenin and dedicated to violent revolution; seized power in Russia in 1917 and were subsequently renamed the Communists.

bonsai the cultivation of stunted trees and shrubs to create exquisite nature scenes in miniature; originated in China in the first millenium B.C.E. and imported to Japan between 700 and 900 C.E.

Brahman the Hindu word roughly equivalent to God; the Divine basis of all being; regarded as the source and sum of the cosmos.

Brahmanism the early religious beliefs of the Aryan people in India, which eventually gave rise to Hinduism.

brahmin a member of the Hindu priestly caste or class; literally "one who has realized or attempts to realize Brahman." Traditionally, duties of a *brahmin* include studying Hindu religious scriptures and transmitting them to others orally. The priests of Hindu temples are *brahmin*.

Brezhnev Doctrine the doctrine, enunciated by Leonid Brezhnev, that the Soviet Union had a right to intervene if socialism was threatened in another socialist state; used to justify the use of Soviet troops in Czechoslovakia in 1968.

Buddhism a religion and philosophy based on the teachings of Siddhartha Gautama in about 500 B.C.E. Principally practiced in China, India, and other parts of Asia, Buddhism has 360 million followers and is considered a major world releigion.

Burakumin a Japanese minority similar to *dalits* (untouchables) in Indian culture. Past and current discrimination has resulted in lower educational attainment and socioeconomic status for members of this group. Movements with objectives ranging from "liberation" to integration have tried over the years to change this situation.

Bushido the code of conduct observed by samurai warriors; comparable to the European concept of chivalry.

caliph the secular leader of the Islamic community.

calpulli in Aztec society, a kinship group, often of a thousand or more, which served as an intermediary with the central government, providing taxes and conscript labor to the state.

caravels mobile sailing ships with both lateen and square sails that began to be constructed in Europe in the sixteenth century.

caste system a system of rigid social hierarchcy in which all members of that society are assigned by birth to specific "ranks," and inherit specific roles and privileges.

Catholic Reformation a movement for the reform of the Catholic Church in the sixteenth century.

caudillos strong leaders in nineteenth-century Latin America, who were usually supported by the landed elites and ruled chiefly by military force, though some were popular; they included both modernizers and destructive dictators.

censorate one of the three primary Chinese ministries, originally established in the Qin dynasty, whose inspectors surveyed the efficiency of officials throughout the system.

centuriate assembly the chief popular assembly of the Roman Republic. It passed laws and elected the chief magistrates.

chaebol a South Korean business structure similar to the Japanese *keiretsu*.

Chan Buddhism a Chinese sect (Zen in Japanese) influenced by Daoist ideas, which called for mind training and a strict regimen as a means of seeking enlightenment.

chinampas in Mesoamerica, artificial islands crisscrossed by canals that provided water for crops and easy transportation to local markets.

chonmin in Korea, the lowest class in society consisting of slaves and workers in certain undesirable occupations such as butchers; literally, "base people."

Christian (northern) humanism an intellectual movement in northern Europe in the late fifteenth and early sixteenth centuries that combined the interest in the classics of the Italian Renaissance with an interest in the sources of early Christianity, including the New Testament and the writings of the church fathers.

chu nom an adaptation of Chinese written characters to provide a writing system for spoken Vietnamese; in use by the ninth century C.E.

civil disobedience the tactic of using illegal but nonviolent means of protest; designed by the Indian nationalist leader Mohandas Gandhi to resist British colonial rule.

civilization a complex culture in which large numbers of humans share a variety of common elements, including cities; religion; political, military, and social structures; writing; and significant artistic and intellectual activity.

civil service examination an elaborate Chinese system of selecting bureaucrats on merit, first introduced in 165 C.E., developed by the Tang dynasty in the seventh century C.E. and refined under the Song dynasty; later adopted in Vietnam and with less success in Japan and Korea. It contributed to efficient government, upward mobility, and cultural uniformity.

class struggle the basis of the Marxist analysis of history, which says that the owners of the means of production have always oppressed the workers and predicts an inevitable revolution. *See also* Marxism.

Cold War the ideological conflict between the Soviet Union and the United States after World War II.

Columbian Exchange the exchange of animals, plants, and culture, but also communicable diseases and human populations including slaves, between the Western and Eastern Hemispheres that occurred after Columbus's voyages to the Americas.

commercial capitalism beginning in the Middle Ages, an economic system in which people invested in trade and goods in order to make profits.

common law law common to the entire kingdom of England; imposed by the king's courts beginning in the twelfth century to replace the customary law used in county and feudal courts that varied from place to place.

communalism in South Asia, the tendency of people to band together in mutually antagonistic social subgroups; elsewhere used to describe unifying trends in the larger community.

Communist International (Comintern) a worldwide organization of Communist parties, founded by Lenin in 1919, dedicated to the advancement of world revolution; also known as the Third International.

Confucianism a system of thought based on the teachings of Confucius (551–479 B.C.E.) that developed into the ruling ideology of the Chinese state. *See also* Neo-Confucianism.

conquistadors "conquerors." Leaders in the Spanish conquests in the Americas, especially Mexico and Peru, in the sixteenth century.

conscription a military draft.

conservatism an ideology based on tradition and social stability that favored the maintenance of established institutions, organized religion, and obedience to authority and resisted change, especially abrupt change.

consuls the chief executive officers of the Roman Republic. Two were chosen annually to administer the government and lead the army in battle.

consumer society a term applied to Western society after World War II as the working classes adopted the consumption patterns of the middle class and installment plans, credit cards, and easy credit made consumer goods such as appliances and automobiles widely available.

containment a policy adopted by the United States in the Cold War. It called for the use of any means, but hopefully short of all-out war, to limit Soviet expansion.

Continental System Napoleon's effort to bar British goods from the Continent in the hope of weakening Britain's economy and destroying its capacity to wage war.

Contras in Nicaragua in the 1980s, an anti-Sandinista guerrilla movement supported by the U.S. Reagan administration.

Coptic a form of Christianity, originally Egyptian, that has thrived in Ethiopia since the fourth century C.E.

cottage industry a system of textile manufacturing in which spinners and weavers worked at home in their cottages using raw materials supplied to them by capitalist entrepreneurs.

council of the plebs in the Roman Republic, a council only for the plebeians. After 287 B.C.E., its resolutions were binding on all Romans.

creoles in Latin America, American-born descendants of Europeans.

Crusade in the Middle Ages, a military campaign in defense of Christendom.

Cubism an artistic style developed at the beginning of the twentieth century, especially by Pablo Picasso, that used geometric designs to re-create reality in the viewer's mind.

cuneiform "wedge-shaped." A system of writing developed by the Sumerians that consisted of wedge-shaped impressions made by a reed stylus on clay tablets.

Dadaism an artistic movement in the 1920s and 1930s by artists who were revolted by the senseless slaughter of World War I and used their "anti-art" to express contempt for the Western tradition.

daimyo prominent Japanese families who provided allegiance to the local shogun in exchange for protection; similar to vassals in Europe.

dalits commonly referred to as untouchables; the lowest level of Indian society, technically outside the caste system and considered less than human; named *harijans* ("children of God") by Gandhi, they remain the object of discrimination despite affirmative action programs.

Dao a Chinese philosophical concept, literally "the Way," central to both Confucianism and Daoism, that describes the behavior proper to each member of society; somewhat similar to the Indian concept of *dharma*.

Daoism a Chinese philosophy traditionally ascribed to the perhaps legendary Lao Tzu, which holds that acceptance and spontaneity are the keys to harmonious interaction with the universal order; an alternative to Confucianism.

decolonization the process of becoming free of colonial status and achieving statehood; occurred in most of the world's colonies between 1947 and 1962.

deficit spending the concept, developed by John Maynard Keynes in the 1930s, that in times of economic depression governments should stimulate demand by hiring people to do public works, such as building highways, even if this increases the public debt.

deism belief in God as the creator of the universe who, after setting it in motion, ceased to have any direct involvement in it and allowed it to run according to its own natural laws.

demesne the part of a manor retained under the direct control of the lord and worked by the serfs as part of their labor services.

denazification after World War II, the Allied policy of rooting out any traces of Nazism in German society by bringing prominent Nazis to trial for war crimes and purging any known Nazis from political office.

de-Stalinization the policy of denouncing and undoing the most repressive aspects of Stalin's regime; begun by Nikita Khrushchev in 1956.

détente the relaxation of tension between the Soviet Union and the United States that occurred in the 1970s.

devshirme in the Ottoman Empire, a system (literally, "collection") of training talented children to be administrators or members of the sultan's harem; originally meritocratic, by the seventeenth century, it degenerated into a hereditary caste.

dharma in Hinduism and Buddhism, the law that governs the universe, and specifically human behavior.

dictator in the Roman Republic, an official granted unlimited power to run the state for a short period of time, usually six months, during an emergency.

diffusion hypothesis the hypothesis that the Yellow River valley was the ancient heartland of Chinese civilization and that technological and cultural achievements radiated from there to other parts of East Asia. Recent discoveries of other early agricultural communities in China have led to some modification of the hypothesis to allow for other centers of civilization.

diocese the area under the jurisdiction of a Christian bishop; based originally on Roman administrative districts.

direct rule a concept devised by European colonial governments to rule their colonial subjects without the participation of local authorities. It was most often applied in colonial societies in Africa.

divination the practice of seeking to foretell future events by interpreting divine signs, which could appear in various forms, such as in entrails of animals, in patterns in smoke, or in dreams.

divine-right monarchy a monarchy based on the belief that monarchs receive their power directly from God and are responsible to no one except God.

dyarchy during the Qing dynasty in China, a system in which all important national and provincial admininstrative positions were shared equally by Chinese and Manchus, which helped to consolidate both Manchu rule and their assimilation.

economic imperialism the process in which banks and corporations from developed nations invest in underdeveloped regions and establish a major presence there in the hope of making high profits; not necessarily the same as colonial expansion in that businesses invest where they can make a profit, which may not be in their own nation's colonies.

Einsatzgruppen in Nazi Germany, special strike forces in the SS that played an important role in rounding up and killing Jews.

El Niño periodic changes in water temperature at the surface of the Pacific Ocean, which can lead to major environmental changes and may have led to the collapse of the Moche civilization in what is now Peru.

emir "commander" in Arabic; a title used by Muslim rulers in southern Spain and elsewhere.

encomienda a grant from the Spanish monarch to colonial conquistadors.

encomienda system the system by which Spain first governed its American colonies. Holders of an *encomienda* were supposed to protect the Indians as well as using them as laborers and collecting tribute but in practice exploited them.

enlightened absolutism an absolute monarchy where the ruler follows the principles of the Enlightenment by introducing reforms for the improvement of society, allowing freedom of speech and the press, permitting religious toleration, expanding education, and ruling in accordance with the laws.

Enlightenment an eighteenth-century intellectual movement, led by the philosophes, that stressed the application of reason and the scientific method to all aspects of life.

Epicureanism a philosophy founded by Epicurus in the fourth century B.C.E. that taught that happiness (freedom from emotional turmoil) could be achieved through the pursuit of pleasure (intellectual rather than sensual pleasure).

eta in feudal Japan, a class of hereditary slaves who were responsible for what were considered degrading occupations, such as curing leather and burying the dead.

ethnic cleansing the policy of killing or forcibly removing people of another ethnic group; used by the Serbs against Bosnian Muslims in the 1990s.

Eucharist a Christian sacrament in which consecrated bread and wine are consumed in celebration of Jesus's Last Supper; also called the Lord's Supper or communion.

eunuch a man whose testicles have been removed; a standard feature of the Chinese imperial system, the Ottoman Empire, and the Mughal dynasty, among others.

existentialism a philosophical movement that arose after World War II that emphasized the meaninglessness of life, born of the desperation caused by two world wars.

fascism an ideology or movement that exalts the nation above the individual and calls for a centralized government with a dictatorial leader, economic and social regimentation, and forcible suppression of opposition; in particular, the ideology of Mussolini's Fascist regime in Italy.

feminism the belief in the social, political, and economic equality of the sexes; also, organized activity to advance women's rights.

fief a landed estate granted to a vassal in exchange for military services.

filial piety in traditional China, in particular, a hierarchical system in which every family member has his or her place, subordinate to a patriarch who has in turn reciprocal responsibilities.

Final Solution the physical extermination of the Jewish people by the Nazis during World War II.

Five Pillars of Islam the core requirements of the Muslim faith: belief in Allah and his Prophet Muhammad; prescribed prayers; observation of Ramadan; pilgrimage to Mecca; and giving alms to the poor.

five relationships in traditional China, the hierarchical interpersonal associations considered crucial to social order, within the family, between friends, and with the king.

foot binding an extremely painful process, common in China throughout the second millenium C.E., that compressed girls' feet to half their natural size, representing submissiveness and self-discipline, which were considered necessary attributes for an ideal wife.

Four Modernizations the slogan for radical reforms of Chinese industry, agriculture, technology, and national defense, instituted by Deng Xiaoping after his accession to power in the late 1970s.

genin landless laborers in feudal Japan, who were effectively slaves.

genro the ruling clique of aristocrats in Meiji Japan.

geocentric theory the idea that the earth is at the center of the universe and that the sun and other celestial objects revolve around the earth.

glasnost "openness." Mikhail Gorbachev's policy of encouraging Soviet citizens to openly discuss the strengths and weaknesses of the Soviet Union.

good emperors the five emperors who ruled from 96 to 180 (Nerva, Trajan, Hadrian, Antoninus Pius, and Marcus Aurelius), a period of peace and prosperity for the Roman Empire.

Good Neighbor policy a policy adopted by the administration of President Franklin D. Roosevelt to practice restraint in U.S. relations with Latin American nations.

Gothic a term used to describe the art and especially the architecture of Europe in the twelfth, thirteenth, and fourteenth centuries.

Gothic literature a form of literature used by Romantics to emphasize the bizarre and unusual, especially evident in horror stories.

Grand Council the top of the government hierarchy in the Song dynasty in China.

grand vizier the chief executive in the Ottoman Empire, under the sultan.

Great Leap Forward a short-lived, radical experiment in China, started in 1958, which created vast rural communes and attempted to replace the family as the fundamental social unit.

Great Proletarian Cultural Revolution an attempt to destroy all vestiges of tradition in China, in order to create a totally egalitarian society. Launched by Mao Zedong in 1966, it devolved into virtual anarchy and lasted only until Mao's death in 1976.

Great Schism the crisis in the late medieval church when there were first two and then three popes; ended by the Council of Constance (1414–1418).

guest workers foreign workers working temporarily in European countries.

guided democracy the name given by President Sukarno of Indonesia in the late 1950s to his style of government, which theoretically operated by consensus.

guild an association of people with common interests and concerns, especially people working in the same craft. In medieval Europe, guilds came to control much of the production process and to restrict entry into various trades.

guru teacher, especially in the Hindu, Buddhist and Sikh religious traditions, where it is an important honorific.

Hadith a collection of the sayings of the Prophet Muhammad, used to supplement the revelations contained in the Qur'an.

harem the private domain of a ruler such as the sultan in the Ottoman Empire or the caliph of Baghdad, generally large and mostly inhabited by the extended family.

Hegira the flight of Muhammad from Mecca to Medina in 622, which marks the first date on the official calendar of Islam.

heliocentric theory the idea that the sun (not the earth) is at the center of the universe.

Hellenistic literally, "to imitate the Greeks"; the era after the death of Alexander the Great when Greek culture spread into the Near East and blended with the culture of that region.

helots serfs in ancient Sparta, who were permanently bound to the land that they worked for their Spartan masters.

heresy the holding of religious doctrines different from the official teachings of the church.

Hezbollah a militant Shi'ite organization and political party based in modern Lebanon.

hieroglyphics a highly pictorial system of writing most often associated with ancient Egypt. Also used (with different "pictographs") by other ancient peoples such as the Maya.

high colonialism the more formal phase of European colonial policy in Africa after World War I when the colonial administrative network was extended to outlying areas and more emphasis was placed on improving social services and fostering economic development, especially the exploitation of natural resources, to enable the colonies to achieve self-sufficiency.

high culture the literary and artistic culture of the educated and wealthy ruling classes.

Hinayana the scornful name for Theravada Buddhism ("lesser vehicle") used by devotees of Mahayana Buddhism.

Hinduism the main religion in India. It emphasizes reincarnation, based on the results of the previous life, and the desirability of escaping this cycle. Its various forms feature both asceticism and the pleasures of ordinary life, and encompass a multitude of gods as different manifestations of one ultimate reality.

Holocaust the mass slaughter of European Jews by the Nazis during World War II.

Hopewell culture a Native American society that flourished from about 200 B.C.E. to 400 C.E., noted for large burial mounds and extensive manufacturing. Largely based in Ohio, its traders ranged as far as the Gulf of Mexico.

hoplites heavily armed infantry soldiers used in ancient Greece in a phalanx formation.

Hundred Schools schools of philosophy in China around the third century B.C.E. that engaged in a wide-ranging debate over the nature of human beings, society, and the universe; included Legalism and Daoism, as well as Confucianism.

hydraulic society a society organized around a large irrigation system to control the allocation of water.

iconoclasm an eighth-century Byzantine movement against the use of icons (pictures of sacred figures), which was condemned as idolatry.

imam an Islamic religious leader. Some traditions say there is only one per generation; others use the term more broadly.

imperialism the policy of extending one nation's power either by conquest or by establishing direct or indirect economic or cultural authority over another. Generally driven by economic self-interest, it can also be motivated by a sincere (if often misguided) sense of moral obligation.

Impressionism an artistic movement that originated in France in the 1870s. Impressionists sought to capture their impressions of the changing effects of light on objects in nature.

indirect rule a colonial policy of foreign rule in cooperation with local political elites. Though implemented in much of India and Malaya and in parts of Africa, it was not feasible where resistance was strong.

individualism emphasis on and interest in the unique traits of each person.

indulgence the remission of part or all of the temporal punishment in purgatory due to sin; granted for charitable contributions and other good deeds. Indulgences became a regular practice of the Christian church in the High Middle Ages, and their abuse was instrumental in sparking Luther's reform movement in the sixteenth century.

infanticide the practice of killing infants.

inflation a sustained rise in the price level.

informal empire the growing presence of Europeans in Africa during the first decades of the nineteenth century. During this period, most African states were nonetheless still able to maintain their independence.

interdict in the Catholic Church, a censure by which a region or country is deprived of receiving the sacraments.

intervention, principle of the idea, after the Congress of Vienna, that the great powers of Europe had the right to send armies into countries experiencing revolution to restore legitimate monarchs to their thrones.

intifada the "uprising" of Palestinians living under Israeli control, especially in the 1980s and 1990s.

Islam the religion derived from the revelations of Muhammad, the Prophet of Allah; literally, "submission" (to the will of Allah); also, the culture and civilization based on the faith.

Jainism an Indian religion, founded in the fifth century B.C.E. that stresses extreme simplicity.

Janissaries an elite core of eight thousand troops personally loyal to the sultan of the Ottoman Empire.

jati a kinship group, the basic social organization of traditional Indian society, to some extent specialized by occupation.

jihad in Islam, "striving in the way of the Lord." The term is ambiguous and has been subject to varying interpretations, from the practice of conducting raids against local neighbors to the conduct of "holy war" against unbelievers.

joint-stock company a company or association that raises capital by selling shares to individuals who receive dividends on their investment while a board of directors runs the company.

Jomon the earliest known Neolithic inhabitants of Japan, named for the cord pattern of their pottery.

justification by faith the primary doctrine of the Protestant Reformation; taught that humans are saved not through good works, but by the grace of God, bestowed freely through the sacrifice of Jesus.

Kabuki a form of Japanese theater that developed in the seventeenth century C.E. Originally disreputable, it became a highly stylized art form.

kami spirits worshiped in early Japan that resided in trees, rivers and streams. *See also* Shinto.

karma a fundamental concept in Hindu (and later Buddhist, Jain, and Sikh) philosophy, that rebirth in a future life is determined by actions in this or other lives. The word refers to the entire process, to the individual's actions, and also to the cumulative result of those actions, for instance, a store of good or bad *karma*.

keiretsu a type of powerful industrial or financial conglomerate that emerged in post–World War II Japan following the abolition of the *zaibatsu*.

khanates Mongol kingdoms, in particular the subdivisions of Genghis Khan's empire ruled by his heirs.

kokutai the core ideology of the Japanese state, particularly during the Meiji Restoration, stressing the uniqueness of the Japanese system and the supreme authority of the emperor.

kowtow the ritual of prostration and touching the forehead to the ground, demanded of all foreign ambassadors to the Chinese court as a symbol of submission.

kshatriya originally, the warrior class of Aryan society in India; ranked below (sometimes equal to) *brahmins*; in modern times, often government workers or soldiers.

laissez-faire "to let alone." An economic doctrine that holds that an economy is best served when the government does not interfere but allows the economy to self-regulate according to the forces of supply and demand.

latifundia large landed estates in the Roman Empire (singular: *latifundium*).

lay investiture the practice in which a layperson chose a bishop and invested him with the symbols of both his temporal office and his spiritual office; led to the Investiture Controversy, which was ended by compromise in the Concordat of Worms in 1122.

Legalism a Chinese philosophy that argued that human beings were by nature evil and would follow the correct path only if coerced by harsh laws and stiff punishments. Adopted as official ideology by the Qin dynasty, it was later rejected but remained influential.

legitimacy, principle of the idea that after the Napoleonic wars peace could best be reestablished in Europe by restoring legitimate monarchs who would preserve traditional institutions; guided Metternich at the Congress of Vienna.

liberal arts the seven areas of study that formed the basis of education in medieval and early modern Europe. Following Boethius and other late Roman authors, they consisted of grammar, rhetoric, and dialectic or logic (the *trivium*) and arithmetic, geometry, astronomy, and music (the *quadrivium*).

liberalism an ideology based on the belief that people should be as free from restraint as possible. Economic liberalism is the idea that the government should not interfere in the workings of the economy. Political liberalism is the idea that there should be restraints on the exercise of power so that people can enjoy basic civil rights in a constitutional state with a representative assembly.

limited (constitutional) monarchy a system of government in which the monarch is limited by a representative assembly and by the duty to rule in accordance with the laws of the land.

lineage group the descendants of a common ancestor; relatives, often as opposed to immediate family.

Longshan a Neolithic society from near the Yellow River in China, sometimes identified by its black pottery.

maharaja originally, a king in the Aryan society of early India (a great raja); later used more generally to denote an important ruler.

Mahayana a school of Buddhism that promotes the idea of universal salvation through the intercession of bodhisattvas; predominant in north Asia.

majlis a council of elders among the Bedouins of the Roman era.

Malayo-Polynesian a family of languages whose speakers originated on Taiwan or in southeastern China and spread from there to the Malay peninsula, the Indonesian archipelago, and many islands of the South Pacific.

mandate of Heaven the justification for the rule of the Zhou dynasty in China. The king was charged to maintain order as a representative of Heaven, which was viewed as an impersonal law of nature.

mandates a system established after World War I whereby a nation officially administered a territory (mandate) on behalf of the League of Nations. Thus, France administered Lebanon and Syria as mandates, and Britain administered Iraq and Palestine.

manor an agricultural estate operated by a lord and worked by peasants who performed labor services and paid various rents and fees to the lord in exchange for protection and sustenance.

mansa in the West African state of Mali, a chieftain who served as both religious and administrative leader and was responsible for forwarding tax revenues from the village to higher levels of government.

Marshall Plan the European Recovery Program, under which the United States provided financial aid to European countries to help them rebuild after World War II.

Marxism the political, economic, and social theories of Karl Marx, which included the idea that history is the story of class struggle and that ultimately the proletariat will overthrow the bourgeoisie and establish a dictatorship en route to a classless society.

mass education a state-run educational system, usually free and compulsory, that aims to ensure that all children in society have at least a basic education.

mass leisure forms of leisure that appeal to large numbers of people in a society including the working classes; emerged at the end of the nineteenth century to provide workers with amusements after work and on weekends; used during the twentieth century by totalitarian states to control their populations.

mass politics a political order characterized by mass political parties and universal male and (eventually) female suffrage.

mass society a society in which the concerns of the majority—the lower classes—play a prominent role; characterized by extension of voting rights, an improved standard of living for the lower classes, and mass education.

matrilinear passing through the female line, for example, from a father to his sister's son rather than his own, as practiced in some African societies; not necessarily, or even usually, combined with matriarchy, in which women rule.

megaliths large stones, widely used in Europe from around 4000 to 1500 B.C.E. to create monuments, including sophisticated astronomical observatories.

Meiji Restoration the period during the late nineteenth and early twentieth centuries in which fundamental economic and cultural changes occurred in Japan, tranforming it from a feudal and agrarian society to an industrial and technological society.

mercantilism an economic theory that held that a nation's prosperity depended on its supply of gold and silver and that the total volume of trade is unchangeable; therefore, advocated that the government play an active role in the economy by encouraging exports and discouraging imports, especially through the use of tariffs.

Mesoamerica the region stretching roughly from modern central Mexico to Honduras, in which the Olmec, Mayan, Aztec and other civilizations developed.

Mesolithic Age the period from 10,000 to 7000 B.C.E., characterized by a gradual transition from a food-gathering/hunting economy to a food-producing economy.

mestizos the offspring of intermarriage between Europeans, originally Spaniards, and native American Indians.

Middle Passage the journey of slaves from Africa to the Americas as the middle leg of the triangular trade.

Middle Path a central concept of Buddhism, which advocates avoiding extremes of both materialism and asceticism; also known as the Eightfold Way.

mihrab the niche in a mosque's wall that indicates the direction of Mecca, usually containing an ornately decorated panel representing Allah.

militarism a policy of aggressive military preparedness; in particular, the large armies based on mass conscription and complex, inflexible plans for mobilization that most European nations had before World War I.

millet an administrative unit in the Ottoman Empire used to organize religious groups.

ministerial responsibility a tenet of nineteenth-century liberalism that held that ministers of the monarch should be responsible to the legislative assembly rather than to the monarch.

Modernism the new artistic and literary styles that emerged in the decades before 1914 as artists rebelled against traditional efforts to portray reality as accurately as possible (leading to Impressionism and Cubism) and writers explored new forms.

monasticism a movement that began in early Christianity whose purpose was to create communities of men or women who practiced a communal life dedicated to God as a moral example to the world around them.

monk a man who chooses to live a communal life divorced from the world in order to dedicate himself totally to the will of God.

monotheistic/monotheism having only one god; the doctrine or belief that there is only one god.

muezzin the man who calls Muslims to prayer at the appointed times; nowadays often a tape-recorded message played over loudspeakers.

mulattoes the offspring of Africans and Europeans, particularly in Latin America.

mutual deterrence the belief that nuclear war could best be prevented if both the United States and the Soviet Union had sufficient nuclear weapons so that even if one nation launched a preemptive first strike, the other could respond and devastate the attacker.

mystery religions religions that involve initiation into secret rites that promise intense emotional involvement with spiritual forces and a greater chance of individual immortality.

nationalism a sense of national consciousness based on awareness of being part of a community—a "nation"—that has common institutions, traditions, language, and customs and that becomes the focus of the individual's primary political loyalty.

nationalization the process of converting a business or industry from private ownership to government control and ownership.

nation in arms the people's army raised by universal mobilization to repel the foreign enemies of the French Revolution.

nation-state a form of political organization in which a relatively homogeneous people inhabits a sovereign state, as opposed to a state containing people of several nationalities.

NATO the North Atlantic Treaty Organization; a military alliance formed in 1949 in which the signatories (Belgium, Canada, Denmark, France, Great Britain, Iceland, Italy, Luxembourg, the Netherlands, Norway, Portugal, and the United States) agreed to provide mutual assistance if any one of them was attacked; later expanded to include other nations, including former members of the Warsaw Pact—Poland, the Czech Republic, and Hungary.

natural law a body of laws or specific principles held to be derived from nature and binding upon all human society even in the absence of positive laws.

natural rights certain inalienable rights to which all people are entitled; include the right to life, liberty, and property, freedom of speech and religion, and equality before the law.

natural selection Darwin's idea that organisms that are most adaptable to their environment survive and pass on the variations that enabled them to survive, while other, less adaptable organisms become extinct; "survival of the fittest."

Nazi New Order the Nazis' plan for their conquered territories; included the extermination of Jews and others considered inferior, ruthless exploitation of resources, German colonization in the east, and the use of Poles, Russians, and Ukrainians as slave labor.

neocolonialism the use of economic rather than political or military means to maintain Western domination of developing nations.

Neo-Confucianism the dominant ideology of China during the second millennium C.E. It combined the metaphysical speculations of Buddhism and Daoism with the pragmatic Confucian approach to society, maintaining that the world is real, not illusory, and that fulfillment comes from participation, not withdrawal. It encouraged an intellectual environment that valued continuity over change and tradition over innovation.

Neolithic Revolution the shift from hunting animals and gathering plants for sustenance to producing food by systematic agriculture that occurred gradually between 10,000 and 4000 B.C.E. (the Neolithic or "New Stone" Age).

New Culture Movement a protest launched at Peking University after the failure of the 1911 revolution, aimed at abolishing the remnants of the old system and introducing Western values and institutions into China.

New Deal the reform program implemented by President Franklin Roosevelt in the 1930s, which included large public works projects and the introduction of Social Security.

New Democracy the initial program of the Chinese Communist government, from 1949 to 1955, focusing on honest government, land reform, social justice, and peace rather than on the utopian goal of a classless society.

New Economic Policy a modified version of the old capitalist system introduced in the Soviet Union by Lenin in 1921 to revive the economy after the ravages of the civil war and war communism.

new imperialism the revival of imperialism after 1880 in which European nations established colonies throughout much of Asia and Africa.

new monarchies the governments of France, England, and Spain at the end of the fifteenth century, where the rulers were successful in reestablishing or extending centralized royal authority, suppressing the nobility, controlling the church, and insisting upon the loyalty of all peoples living in their territories.

Nirvana in Buddhist thought, enlightenment, the ultimate transcendence from the illusion of the material world; release from the wheel of life.

Nok culture in northern Nigeria, one of the most active early ironworking societies in Africa, artifacts from which date back as far as 500 B.C.E.

Nonaligned Movement an organization of neutralist nations established in the 1950s to provide a counterpoise between the socialist bloc, headed by the Soviet Union, and the capitalist nations led by the United States. Chief sponsors of the movement were Jawaharlal Nehru of India, Gamal Abdul Nasser of Egypt, and Sukarno of Indonesia.

noncentralized societies societies characterized by autonomous villages organized by clans and ruled by a local chieftain or clan head; typical of the southern half of the African continent before the eleventh century C.E.

nuclear family a family group consisting only of father, mother, and children.

nun a woman who withdraws from the world and joins a religious community; the female equivalent of a monk.

old regime/old order the political and social system of France in the eighteenth century before the Revolution.

oligarchy rule by a few.

Open Door notes a series of letters sent in 1899 by U.S. Secretary of State John Hay to Great Britain, France, Germany, Italy, Japan, and Russia, calling for equal economic access to the China market for all states and for the maintenance of the territorial and administrative integrity of the Chinese Empire.

691; emperors in, 375; Europeans and, 377; France and, 550, 690–91, 698; government of, 805; imperialism of, 457; Japan and, 667, 668; U.S. and, 690–91, 698–700; after World War II, 690–91, 698–700. *See also* Indochina; South Vietnam
Vietnam syndrome, 702
Vietnam War, 698–700
Villa, Pancho, 645
Villages: in Africa, 761; in Japan, 451. *See also* Cities and towns
Vindication of the Rights of Woman (Wollstonecraft), 466
Vizier, 413, 415
Voltaire (François-Marie Arouet), 465
Voting and voting rights: in England, 508; in France, 503; in Japan, 641; in Latin America, 523; in U.S., 525, 742, 749; for women, 530, 607, 749, 785
Voyages: of Columbus, 361, 362; European, 358, 360, 362; of Zhenghe, 355, 434

Wabenzi, in Africa, 765
Wafd Party (Egypt), 631
Wahhabi movement, 630, 785
Walesa, Lech, 716
Wallachia, 506
Walled cities, 409
Wallerstein, Immanuel, 352
Wang Tao (Wang T'ao), on reform, 575
Wang Xiji (China), 587
War communism, in Russia, 609, 616
War crimes: in Cambodia, 806
"War Girls" (poem), 607
War Guilt Clause (Versailles Treaty), 612
War on Poverty, 742
Warriors: in Japan, 450. *See also* Samurai
Wars and warfare: in 17th century, 397; 1870–1914, 512–514; changes in, 409, 409, 473, 489; French, 398; in French Revolution, 480–81; global, 473; military revolution and, 396; Mughal India and, 427; naval, 358, 359. *See also* Military; specific battles and wars
Warsaw, 734
Warsaw Pact, 684, 692, 701
Wars of religion: in France, 392
Washington, George, 471
Washington Conference (1922), 643
Water: in African cities, 765; in China, 726; in Middle East, 783; as power source, 491
Watergate scandal, 742
Waterloo, battle at, 485
Water pollution, 796–97
Watt, James, 491
Watteau, Antoine, 467, 467
Watts riots, 742
Wealth and wealthy: from Americas, 364; in China, 636; in Europe, 528; in India, 798; in Japan, 642, 813; in Latin America, 523; in Middle East, 783, 784; in South Africa, 766; in U.S., 526; value of trade and, 395
Weapons, 352, 560, 564; 17th century warfare and, 396; in Africa, 372; in China, 580; in Japan, 448; of mass destruction, 489, 780; Portuguese and, 361; siege weapons and, 409; Turks and, 408. *See also* Atomic bomb; Firearms; Gunpowder; specific weapons

Weaving, 468, 492
Weimar Republic, 615, 652
Weizmann, Chaim, 631
Welfare: in Canada, 743; in England, 736; in U.S., 742, 743
Welfare state, 511
West, the. *See* Western world
West Africa: Europeans and, 372, 554–55, 558, 559–60; France and, 558, 602; imperialism in, 563, 581; Islam in, 356–57; slavery and, 369; states of, 768, 768–70
West Bank, 776, 777
West Berlin. *See* Berlin
Western Asia, 410
Western Europe: democracy in, 511, 735–37; NATO in, 683, 684. *See also* Western world
Western Front: in World War I, 601, 602
Western Hemisphere: colonial empires in, 469–71, 489; decline of slave trade in, 554; relationships in, 745; trade and, 468, 469; world involvement by, 352. *See also* Americas; New World
Westernization: in Asia and Africa, 631, 800; in Japan, 812–813
Western world (the West): Africa and, 374–75, 770; China and, 439–43, 576–77; colonialism by, 543, 543–44, 760–61; colonial resistance to, 563–64, 566–67, 622–623; cultural life in, 532–539; East Asia and, 434, 587; emergence of, 352; expansion by, 489; industrialization in, 488–89; Islam, democracy, and, 782; Japanese culture and, 586, 641; peaceful coexistence with Soviets, 691, 695, 697, 701; Russia and, 400; Scientific Revolution in, 462–63; society in, 729; trade and, 468, 469; after World War II, 734–58. *See also* Europe
West Germany, 716, 736. *See also* Berlin; Germany
West India Company. *See* Dutch West India Company
West Indies, 370, 469–70, 481
West Pakistan, 794
Westphalia, Peace of, 395
West Punjab, 794
Wet rice. *See* Rice
Whigs. *See* Liberal Party, in England
Whistler, James, 591
White-collar workers, 500, 528
White Lotus Rebellion (China), 438
White Man's Burden, The (Kipling), 547
White people: in South Africa, 561, 766
Whites (Russian civil war), 608–9
White supremacy: in U.S., 525
"Why India Doesn't Need Fast Food," 797
Widows: in China, 444
William I (Germany), 507, 508
William II (Germany), 512, 514, 598, 605, 610, 615
William IV (England), 509
William of Nassau (prince of Orange), 392
William of Orange: in England, 402
Willis, John Christopher, 581
Wilson, Richard, 470
Wilson, Woodrow, 526, 610–12, 613, 622
Winkelmann, Maria, 466
Witchcraft hysteria, 393–95, 394
Witte, Sergei, 499

Wittenberg, Luther at, 385, 386
Wollstonecraft, Mary, 466
Woman in Her Social and Domestic Character (Sanford), 531
Women: in 1920s, 616, 618; in Africa, 562, 770, 771; as African writers, 773–74; in America colonies, 364; in China, 444, 582, 582, 637–38, 639, 727, 730; as comfort women, 668, 809; in Enlightenment, 465–66; in factories, 493, 606; in fascist Italy, 652; foot binding and, 582, 582; in France, 477, 478–79, 752, 753–54; as Impressionist painters, 538–39, 539; in India, 428–29, 625, 799–800; industrialization and, 497, 531–32, 668; in Iran, 596, 629, 741, 748, 748, 779, 784, 785; Islamic, 784, 785, 786; in Japan, 451, 586–88, 641, 641, 670, 810, 811–12; in Latin America, 364, 536; in mass society, 528–30; in middle classes, 529, 531–32; in Middle East, 784, 785; in modern world, 729; Muslim, 752, 753–54; in Nazi Germany, 653, 668–69; in Ottoman harem, 412–413; Protestant, 389; Protestant Reformation and, 389; in Russian Revolution, 607; Safavid, 416; in Southeast Asia, 379, 807; in Soviet Union, 654, 668, 708, 712, 714; voting rights for, 530, 607; witchcraft accusations against, 393–95; as workers, 497, 500, 749; World War I and, 530, 606–7; World War II and, 652, 653, 654, 668–69, 670; after World War II, 748–51. *See also* Gender
Women of Algiers (Delacroix), 534, 535
Women's liberation, 749, 751
Women's rights movements, 466, 529–30, 588, 607, 639
Women's Social and Political Union (England), 530
Woodblock printing, 384, 453, 454–55, 455
Wordsworth, William, 532
Workers: in African colonies, 559; in France, 748; in industrial factories, 492, 493, 497; in Japan, 586; in Third Estate, 384; in West, 748; women as, 497, 500, 586–88, 606–7, 749. *See also* Labor; Working classes
Work ethic: in Japan, 810–11
Working classes: in England, 508–9; housing reforms for, 528; industrial, 491, 495–97, 748; in Latin America, 523, 744; organizing of, 500–501; urban, 495, 528; women in, 529, 749
Works Progress Administration (WPA), 616
World Bank, 820–21
World Cup, 757
World-machine (Newton), 463, 465
World markets, 494
World of Yesterday, The (Zweig), 600
World power: U.S. as, 526–27
World Trade Center, destruction of, 751
World Trade Organization (WTO), 726, 770, 821
World War I, 580, 596, 596–97, 601; in 1918, 609–10; culture and intellectual thought after, 616–18; events before, 597–99; as global conflict, 602–604; home front in, 605–7; Latin America after, 643–46; mandates after, 612, 612–613, 630; Ottoman Empire and, 627; outbreak of,

World War I (*continued*)
598–99; peace settlement after, 610–13; public opinion in, 600, 605–6; Russia and, 607–9; Schlieffen Plan in, 599–601; territorial changes after, 613; trench warfare in, 596, 601, 602, 603, *604*; U.S. in, 604–5, 609; Versailles Treaty after, 612; women and, 530, 606–7

World War II, 489; Africa after, 761–62; Asia and, 655–56, 660, 661–62, 666–68; costs of, 671–72; dictatorships before, 652–54; in Europe, 659, 662–664; Europe after, 734–35, 735–41; events leading to, 665–67; home front in, 668, 670; Japanese behavior in, 809; last years of, 662–664; Middle East after, 631, 774–81; in North Africa, 659, 660–61; in Pacific region, 660, 661–62; prisoners of war in, 662, *662*, 666, 668; turning point of, 660–61, 662; women in, 668–69, 670. *See also* Fascism; Japan; Nazi Germany

World Wide Web, 821
World Zionist Organization (WZO), 630
Worms: Luther in, 382
Wright, Orville and Wilbur, 498
Writers. *See* Literature
Wrought iron, 492

Xavier, Francis, 389–90, 447
Xianyang, China, 687
Xinjiang, China, 439

Yalta Conference, 672, 678, 679, 685, 687, 709
Yalu River region, 455, 689
Yam crops, *442*
Yan'an, China, 635, 686
Yangban (aristocracy, Korea), 455
Yangon. *See* Rangoon (Yangon), Burma
Yangtze River region (China), 440, 572, 726–27, *727*
Yar' Adua, Umaru, 766
Yathrib. *See* Medina
Year of Living Dangerously, The (film), 804
Yeltsin, Boris, 715–16, 740
Yemen, 781
Yeoman farmers: in Japan, 810
Yi dynasty (Korea), 455–56, 457, 588
Yi Song Gye (Korea), 455
Yi Sunshin (Korea), 457
Yom Kippur War (1973–1974), 776
Yongle (China), 436, *438*, 440, 445
Yorktown, battle at, 471
Young Girl by a Window (Morisot), *539*
Young Italy movement, 506
Young people: in China, 637; in Japan, 586, 811, *812*, 813
Young Turks, 626–27
Young Victoria, The (film), 509
YouTube, 821
Yuan Shikai (Yuan Shih-k'ai), 579, 632–633, 634
Yudhyono, Susilo (Indonesia), 805
Yugoslavia, 612, 660, 679, 737; former, 823
Yu Hua, 731

Zaibatsu (Japan), 642–643, 808, 810, 814
Zaire, 762, 763, 768. *See also* Democratic Republic of the Congo
Zambezi River region, 560, 562
Zambia. *See* Northern Rhodesia (Zambia)
Zamindars (Mughal officials), 421, 426, 429, 548, 563
Zand dynasty (Persia), 417
Zanzibar, 556, 558, 762, 765
Zapata, Emiliano, 524, *524*, 645
Zardari, Asif Ali, 795
Zemsky Sobor (Russian assembly), 400
Zen (Chan) Buddhism, 812
Zhang Xinxin, 730
Zhang Zhidong (Chang Chih-tung), 575
Zhao Ziyang, 720, 722
Zhenghe (China): voyages of, 355, 434
Zhu Yuanzhang (China), 434, 436
Zia Ul Ha'q (Pakistan), 794–95
Zimbabwe, 369. *See also* Great Zimbabwe
Zionism, 537, 630
Zones of occupation: in Germany and Berlin, 682–683
Zulus, 557, *558*, 563
Zuma, Jacob, 766
Zürich: Protestantism in, 386–88
Zweig, Stefan, 600
Zwingli, Ulrich, and Zwinglianism, 386–88
Zyklon B, 666